S0-AYW-215

ANCESTRY'S RED BOOK

American State, County & Town Sources

Edited by Alice Eichholz, Ph.D., C.G.

Maps by William Dollarhide

P.O. Box 476
Salt Lake City, UT 84110

Library of Congress Cataloging-in-Publication Data

Ancestry's Red Book : American state, county & town sources / edited by Alice Eichholz ; maps by William Dollarhide. — Rev. ed.
p. cm.
Includes bibliographical references and index.
ISBN 0-916489-47-7
1. United States—Genealogy—Handbooks, manuals, etc.
I. Eichholz, Alice, 1942- .
CS49.A55 1991
929' . 1'072073—dc20 91-30311
CIP

Managing Editor, Robert J. Welsh
Design and Production, Robb Barr and Robert Passaro

Published 1989. Revised Edition 1992
10 9 8 7 6 5 4 3 2 1

Printed in the United States of America

for Cady,

who dances rings

around her

ancestors

Misprints, Errors, and Changes

Ancestry has made every effort to ensure that the many thousands of statements of fact in this book are as accurate and up to date as possible; hundreds of experts, professionals, and a wide array of sources were consulted over the course of the book's compilation. But, as is inevitable in a work of this magnitude and scope, inaccuracies and changes are likely to develop.

It is our customers, however, who are the real experts, and we need and welcome your feedback. If at any time while you are using this book you discover a factual error or inaccurate statement, please bring it to our attention. We will make verifiable corrections in future printings and editions of the work, thereby assuring the most scrupulous and exact book possible. This is Ancestry's ongoing commitment to our individual customers and the genealogical and historical community at large. Please send your suggestions and corrections to the Editorial Department, Ancestry, P.O. Box 476, Salt Lake City, Utah 84110.

Thank you,
John C. Sittner, Publisher

TABLE OF CONTENTS

ACKNOWLEDGMENTS

In a book of this size and scope, a cooperative effort is essential. That effort for this revised edition has included assistance from a host of professional genealogical researchers and all the state archivists and their staffs, not all of whose names can be included here. Each of the following people have generously shared their expertise and information concerning available resources: Desmond Walls Allen; Robert C. Anderson, C.G., F.A.S.G.; Ellie Arguimbau; Janet Nixon Baccus; Bette M. Barker; Debra Basham; Ruth Ellen Bauer; Karen Baumann; Michael Beard; Gary Behan; Carol Willsey Bell, C.G.; Le Roy Barnett; M. Gary Bettis; Jeanne Bigger; Lloyd Bockstruck; Nancy Bounds; Jean Brainard; Donaly E. Brice; Barbara J. Brown, C.G.R.S.; Mickey Brown; Arden Brugger; Earl Brunner; John F. Burns; Jerry W. Carlton; Sharon Carnahan; Timothy Cary; Martha Clark; Ruth Clark; David J. Coles; Peter Stebbins Craig; Frances James Dallett, F.A.S.G.; John Daly; Donn Devine, C.G.I.; Jim Donahue; Arlene H. Eakle, Ph.D.; Conley Edwards; Marcia J. Eisenberg; Terry Ellis; Kathleen C. Eustis; John L. Ferguson; Jane Fletcher Fiske; Jeanette Fiskum; James Folts; Patricia Galloway, Ph.D.; Laura Glum; Randy L. Gross; Greg Gubler, Ph.D.; Mary H. Hall; James H. Hansen; Dwight Harris; Bruce Hasse; Marcia J. Hartshorn; James S. Henderson; Gordon O. Hendrickson; Lawrence E. Hibpsham; Elbert R. Hilliard; Kathleen W. Hinckley, C.G.R.S., C.G.L.; Le Roy Hinckley; Roseann Hogan; Sue E. Holbert; Elizabeth P. Jacox; Jeffery O. Johnson; Mark H. Jones, Ph.D., C.A.; Roger D. Joslyn, C.G., F.A.S.G.; Jane J. Kelsey; Thomas J. Kemp; Terry Ketelsen; John M. Kinney; Jeffery Kintop; Nancy Kepley; Joseph R. Klett; Thomas W. Kremm; Ann Smith Lainhart; Donald J. Lemieux, Ph.D.; Frank Levstik, Ph.D.; Connie Lenzen, C.G.R.S.; Charles H. Lesser; Bonnie J. Linck; Anne Lipscomb; Patricia M. Luebbert; Sandra Hargreaves Luebking; Harry Macy, Jr.; Zoe Magden; Louis H. Manarin, Ph.D.; Joanne Mattern; Sid McAlpin; C. Russell McCabe; Linda S. McCleary; Tom McFarland; Carol McGinnis; Pat Melville; Frank C. Mevers; Harold L. Miller; Phil Miller; Anita Cheek Milner, J.D.; Alden Monroe; Cynthia E. Monroe; Norman Monroe; James Moore; Karl R. Moore; Steven W. Nyers; Gerald G. Newborg; Karl J. Niederer; Thomas W. Nielsen; Joseph Oldenburg; Marcia O'Neil; Elaine Owens; Nancy Parker; George Parkinson; Andrea I. Paul; Becki Peterson; Judith M. Plummer; Jeanne Pramaggiore; Jim Prichard; Benjamin Primer, Ph.D.; Samuel Proctor; Dorothy Provine; Al Ragensberg; Joy Reisinger, C.G.R.S.; Gordon L. Remington; Mary Fallon Richards; Vera Richardson; Richard Roberts; Richard C. Roberts; Donna Valley Russell, C.G., F.A.S.G.; George Ely Russell, C.G., F.A.S.G.; Rhea Sahlor; Donald Sanborn, Ph.D.; Melinde L. Sanborn; D. Greg Sanford; William K. Schoeffler; Antoinette J. Segraves; Ruth Wilder Sherman, C.G., F.A.S.G.; Phyllis Silva; Timothy A. Slavin; Pat Smith (White Buffalo Woman); Howard Snedden; Kip Sperry, A.G., C.G., F.A.S.G.; Jonathan R. Stayer; Marsha Stewart; Bill Summers; Loretto Dennis Szucs; Neil D. Thompson, Ph.D., C.G., F.A.S.G.; William Thorndale, C.G.; John H. Thweatt; Lois Ware Thurston, C.G.; Delores Vyzralek; Justin E. Walsh, Ph.D.; Jon Walstrom; Jo Waterhouse; William Welge; Albert H. Whitaker, Jr.; Susun M. Wilkinson; Curt B. Witcher; Theodore Wohlson; Evelyn Young.

Maps were prepared by William Dollarhide with drafting assistance from Robert Lindquist and Linda Lawless. Robb Barr and Bob Passaro engineered the design, formatting, and the production of the book. Editorial work was assisted by Erika Butler, Linda Cunningham, Ann Marie Dunton, Donna Kaynor, Suzanne LeBaron, Sherry Slaughter, Marjorie Spencer. Technical support was provided by Norwich University and the publications staff at Ancestry, Inc.

Robert C. Anderson, C.G., F.A.S.G., took a fitting proprietary role as a welcomed, essential second reader, offering extensive comments and suggestions on every aspect of the book. Roger D. Joslyn, C.G., F.A.S.G., remained a constant, appropriately critical colleague throughout the entire process.

With the assistance and input of so many people and institutions, the authors, editors, and publisher sincerely hope they have presented all of the information provided coherently and accurately. The intent has been to produce a resource guide that assists in improving both the quality of family history research and the growth of interest in family history among a broader audience. We are grateful for the efforts of everyone involved in that process.

How to Use This Book

Alice Eichholz, Ph.D., C.G.

Today, with the increased awareness of the necessity for preserving local records and with the use of computer technology for retrieving, organizing, and indexing records, much can be discovered regarding the specifics of a family's past—no matter what the locality.

Designed to help recover the multigenerational facts of your ancestry, this book is an expansive guide to the most useful resources in each of the fifty United States and the District of Columbia. Conducting research at a distance from the places one's ancestors lived can be quite a challenge. There still is no substitute for on-site research because not *everything* is, or probably ever will be, on microfilm, in print, or available through interlibrary loan. But this book's format assists the research process by describing some original, printed, and microfilmed sources for every state and the District of Columbia.

The book is arranged alphabetically by state. Within this chapter and each state's chapter, topics are organized to conform with one methodology of research. While research in different locations may require different strategies, the format of this book was designed to provide a consistent and detailed guide within limited space for each state. Excellent guides for modifying research strategy in a specific state are included in the listing of Background Sources for each state.

Every state's chapter begins with a brief historical background discussion. Records used in genealogical research come out of a historical context. Knowledge about the history, settlement patterns, and context in which the records were kept helps the research process. Additional sources for augmenting each state's brief overview are also listed under Background Sources for that state.

Vital Records

Procuring vital records is a step too often skipped for the generations within recent or living memory. Collecting *all* vital records available for every generation is essential because small details on any one of the records may provide important clues. The process of gathering all available vital records for each generation of an entire family encourages consideration of collateral lines in problem solving.

Every state has a division charged with the responsibility of maintaining and dispersing information from its vital record holdings. This section for each state indicates the availability of birth, death, marriage, and divorce records and the agencies responsible for maintaining them.

Updated information about the cost of copies of vital records can be found in *Where to Write for Vital Records* (Hyattsville, Md.: U.S. Department of Health and Human Services, 1990), Document #017-022-001109-3, available from the Superintendent of Documents, Government Printing Office, Washington, D.C. 20402, for a small fee—phone orders, (202) 783-3238. A complete collection of vital records application forms for all states can be found in Thomas K. Kemp, *International Vital Records Handbook* (Baltimore, Md.: Genealogical Publishing Co., 1990).

One major index to birth and marriage records in all states, although far from comprehensive, is the International Genealogical Index (IGI), amended regularly by the Genealogical Society of Utah and accessible through its Family History Library (FHL) and branch centers (see page 9). The IGI, arranged alphabetically by state and therein by surname, includes *some*, but not all, primary and secondary sources for birth and marriage records. It provides a reference for each entry, making it possible to verify the information with the original source. Since the material in the IGI comes from either a program of extracting primary source material in state vital records, or from information submitted by members of the LDS church, it is essential to verify the source and accuracy.

There are many sources for birth, death, and marriage events that are not in a state's vital records office. Cemeteries, church records, newspapers, military records, immigration and naturalization records, as well as family records in letters and Bibles, are all places where evidence of vital events might be found. Suggestions for locating these alternate sources are described in later sections of each chapter.

Once vital records have been researched, and especially if none are available for the location and time period required, a good procedure would be to try to locate ancestors using census records.

Census Records

There are numerous ways to determine the location in which to concentrate research for an ancestor. One of the most popular and productive is the census. In the United States, the federal census has been taken every ten years since 1790. Federal population schedules (through the 1920 census) still exist and are available to the general public at the National Archives (see pages 8–9). Microfilm copies are distributed by the National Archives to various agencies as described later. The 1920 federal census will become available after March 1992. Only fragments of the 1890 population schedules remain since they were badly damaged by fire in 1921. Some states have incomplete or no schedules for other years because of the loss of census records.

Each census offers slightly different information depending on what Congress was interested in enumerating for that decade. The earlier federal census schedules name only the head of household in each locality and number of males and females in different age categories. The order of households is sometimes alphabetical but more often the result of door-to-door visits by the census takers. Later census returns include the name of every member of the household and get progressively more detailed, including such information as relationship to the head of household, the address (and consequently neighbors), month and year of birth, location of parents' births, number of years married, date of immigration, occupation, and value of personal and real estate.

Available federal census schedules—population, mortality, agriculture and industry, slave, veterans—are listed first in each state's Census Records section. It is appropriate to start with the most recent census for the area and work backwards in time to develop a census history for a family.

In this age of electronic indexing, the majority of federal census records have been indexed by name of head of household. Most of the population schedules have been indexed by Accelerated Indexing Systems International, Inc. (AISI), 42 North Highway 89, North Salt Lake, Utah 84054, phone (800) 368-2474. They can supply a catalog of their publications for purchase. Published indexes exist for nearly all federal censuses from 1790 through 1860. Those AISI indexes available for each state are in the list of "Indexed" population schedules under Federal listings. A microfiche version of AISI indexes is available at branch libraries of the FHL (see Archives, Libraries, and Societies).

Precision Indexing, P. O. Box 303, Bountiful, Utah 84011, phone (800) 657-9442, publishes a wide variety of microform, printed, and looseleaf-bound indexes. Individual county-wide and statewide indexes of some federal population schedules are available as well as computer searches using their database.

Other printed indexes, when they exist, are described in the narrative portion following the federal listings. Most states hold microfilm copies of their own federal census records in various repositories. The narrative in this section indicates places in the state where they are available either on microfilm or in original form.

Although all indexes are subject to error (some estimate as much as 30 percent), they can be one way of determining the presence of an ancestor in a particular location. Tracing a family through the census provides a history of migration and indicates the locations in which research should be centered.

Soundex is an index coding system for surnames that was used by the WPA in the preparation of 3-by-5 index cards, eventually microfilmed. Using the Soundex makes locating a particular person on the full census return easier. Available for the 1880, 1900, 1920, and some 1910 census records, the Soundex coding system drops all vowels and a few consonants in a surname and produces a number code to be used in locating families with similarly sounding surnames in any given state. Such an index is particularly useful given the wide variations in spelling of many surnames.

The Soundex for 1880 was used only for households in which there was a child under age ten. Census records for a few states in the 1910 census have what is called Miracode, which uses the same coding system as Soundex, but Miracode cards reference the full census returns with a number given in order of visitation by the census taker instead of the page and line number reference on the Soundex cards.

There are several other ways to see a census record. First, in addition to the full set of schedules and indexes at the National Archives, a full set of federal census microfilms and some or most of the AISI indexes are deposited in each regional center of the archives (see pages 8–9). If those centers are not nearby, there are several "interlibrary loan" programs that make census microfilms available.

A local library or an individual (with access to a microfilm machine) can borrow the necessary microfilm reels through interlibrary loan from: National Archives Census Microfilm Rental Program, P.O. Box 30, Annapolis Junction, Maryland 20701, phone (301) 604-3699. The program uses the National Archives numbering system to identify the reels of either Soundex or censuses. Guides for ordering films are also available from the above address. A nominal fee is charged for the loan of the reels.

Microfilms can also be borrowed for personal use from the American Genealogical Lending Library, P.O. Box 244, Dept. 101, Bountiful, Utah 84010, phone (801) 298-5358. There is an annual membership fee and a per-reel charge for rental, but membership includes loan access to over 100,000 other microfilm, microfiche, and in-print research materials.

All of the federal census records that have been microfilmed are also available for a small fee through the Family History Library (FHL) and its centers throughout the world (see Archives, Libraries, and Societies).

Census information is to be used as a *guide* to the facts about a family and is not always accurate. When using census records for research keep the following in mind:

- Census information forwarded to the federal government was hand-copied and consequently subject to human error; microfilm copies reproduce the same errors. Some original copies of specific censuses are extant in some state repositories. If they are known to exist, the discussion in the state's chapter will so specify.
- Some handwriting is difficult to read. Try to compare the way the writer patterned letters in other names that are easier to read.
- The type of information on each census varies. For example, the 1840 census specified Revolutionary War veterans receiving a pension; the 1870 census, which was taken after blacks were granted citizenship, is the first one that lists all blacks by name; and the 1900 census reports number of children born to a woman and number still living.
- County lines changed very quickly during the nineteenth century. You will want to refer to William Thorndale and William Dollarhide, *Map Guide to the U.S. Federal Censuses, 1790–1920* (Baltimore, Md.: Genealogical Publishing Co., 1987), to determine how the county lines changed between ten-year periods. In some cases ward maps of municipalities may be necessary to pinpoint a location in metropolitan areas.

Along with the population schedules, supplemental federal schedules were taken with 1850–80 census returns. Not all exist for each state, but where they are known to exist, they are listed. These include:

Mortality Schedules. Names, dates, and causes of death for those who died in the twelve-month period preceding the 1850, 1860, 1870, and 1880 census enumerations are listed in this schedule.

Industry Schedules. Goods and services provided and quantities furnished by listed businesses were added in separate volumes to the 1850, 1860, 1870, and 1880 federal enumerations. The 1880 schedules are labeled "Manufactures."

Agriculture Schedules. Acreage farmed with different commodities and extent and type of animal husbandry listed by farmer's name are among those items listed in this separate schedule for 1850, 1860, 1870, and 1880.

Union Veterans and Widows of Union Veterans of the Civil War (hereafter Union Veterans schedules). Those who qualified, including pensioners, widows, and minors, and were receiving pensions in 1890, were enumerated in a separate schedule. Returns for Alabama to Kansas appear to have been lost before 1943.

Slave schedules. While free blacks are named and slaves are counted (not named) in federal returns beginning in 1790, separate Slave Schedules were generated for slave-owning states in 1850 and 1860. They tally the number of males and females in specific age groupings listed by slave owner's name.

Many mortality and Union veterans schedules have been indexed and published while other supplemental schedules—slave, industry, and agriculture—have been microfilmed. The census section under each state indicates what federal supplemental schedules have survived and where they can be found.

In addition to federal censuses, some states conducted their own enumerations at various times, including territorial or colonial censuses before statehood. Following the narrative on federal censuses, these are outlined for each state. An attempt has been made to include *only* those that are enumerations by name and not those that are statistical without names.

Once a family is located in the census records, the next step is to determine *everything* that locality has to offer in providing clues or direct proof of ancestors.

Background Sources

Targeting an area for research requires an awareness of three groups of background sources. Readings in local history and guides to appropriate methodology and resources are the first two and they are covered in Background Sources for each state. Maps are covered in the following section. There is a wide variety of helpful resources. Individual contributors have included their reference material, used to develop their chapters, and their personal suggestions based on their professional experience.

Three references should be used to augment these individual discussions:

Filby, P. William. *A Bibliography of American County Histories.* Baltimore, Md.: Genealogical Publishing Co., 1985. Contained here are bibliographic surveys of printed county histories for every state.

Kaminkow, Marion J. *United States Local Histories in the Library of Congress—A Bibliography.* 5 vols. Baltimore, Md.: Magna Carta, 1975. With supplement dated 1986, this resource lists the large number of local histories available in the Library of Congress. Although they cannot be obtained on interlibrary loan through this library, other local or regional libraries may allow some volumes of their accessions to circulate.

Schreiner-Yantis, Nettie. *Genealogical and Local History Books in Print.* 4th ed. Springfield, Va.: Genealogical Books in Print, 1985. This four-volume work is a handy reference to a large number of books and microforms in print organized by state and county and therein by topic. The name of the publisher and the price of publication are included in each listing.

Two libraries with extensive genealogical collections, the National Genealogical Society Library in Arlington, Virginia, and the New England Historic Genealogical Society in Boston (see page 9 for both), offer book-loan services by mail for their members. The FHL's huge research facility in Salt Lake City has microfilmed or microfiched nearly all printed material in its collection, which can be ordered for viewing at any of its local branch center libraries.

Maps

The third group of materials used in targeting an area for research is maps, an often overlooked research tool. People often lived on political boundaries, across state lines or rivers and travelled the path of least geographic resistance. Therefore, maps can provide important clues for where to look next when an ancestor disappears from a locality. This section provides ideas for obtaining good maps for genealogical research purposes. Maps without present-day political boundaries can be helpful in understanding migration trails and the geographic features that may have influenced settlements. When political divisions became established, maps help determine what jurisdictions to consider in looking for genealogical evidence such as land, probate, and court records.

County atlases, detailing roads, physical features, and often structures or owners' names, are found in abundance throughout the country. Political boundaries (wards, school districts, townships, etc.) are often standard in many atlases, aiding considerably in pinpointing the location of people in the context of their surroundings. Plat maps indicate how specific counties and towns were divided and identified, providing a visual reference to use with descriptions of land in deeds and divisions of estates. Many state highway departments print present-day maps with more helpful and detailed information than standard road maps.

For several states, the maps suggested are the Sanborn Fire Insurance maps, which were extensively used to map structures in towns in the late nineteenth century and early twentieth century. One way of locating these maps is through the Library of Congress publication *Fire Insurance Maps in the Library of Congress: Plans of North American Cities and Towns Produced by the Sanborn Map Company* (Washington, D.C.: Library of Congress, 1981).

U.S. Geological Survey (USGS) maps are another often suggested source. They exist for all states, illustrating geographical features of an area including the location of structures and cemeteries. Local USGS maps are often available in stationery and office supply stores or at sporting outfitters for hiking, fishing, and hunting. An index to identify the map sections needed for an area is available from the U.S. Geological Survey Office, Reston, Virginia 22092, phone (703) 648-6892, but all map sales are handled through the USGS Map Sales, Box 25286, Denver, Colorado 80225.

Once vital records and census histories have been collected on ancestral lines, and an understanding of the area from background sources and maps has been achieved, it is time to turn to the genealogical source materials available in the county, town, or parish records. While the order of topics discussed is consistent throughout the book, beginning with this next topic, a research strategy may need to be specially tailored depending on a specific problem or location. For example, in some situations, using probate records is more productive first because of their specificity in indicating family relationships, but by far, more people owned land than appear in probate records and consequently using land records may prove more successful.

Land Records

The Land Records section of each state's chapter focuses on what types of land records are available, and whether they are indexed, abstracted, published, or on microfilm. This section indicates the officials or repositories in charge of the original records.

The following is a very brief discussion of general types of land records. For excellent, comprehensive discussions of the history and use of land records in the United States, see William Thorndale, "Land and Tax Records," in *The Source: A Guidebook of American Genealogy,* edited by Arlene Eakle and Johni Cerny (Salt Lake City, Utah: Ancestry, 1984), pages 217–53; Val D. Greenwood, *The Researcher's Guide to American Genealogy* (2d ed. Baltimore, Md.: Genealogical Publishing Co., 1990), pages 321–44; and E. K. Kirkham, *The Land Records of America and Their Genealogical Value* (Salt Lake City, Utah: Deseret, 1964).

As Greenwood points out, land records begin when the government claiming the land (be it crown, colonial, territorial, and, later, federal or state) conveys it to private individuals for, among other reasons, political favors, a fee, military service, or homesteading. These first-grant records are generally kept by the government that issued them.

After the Revolution, land or property was transferred to private individuals either by the federal government in Public-domain (federal-land) states or by the state in state-land states. Public-domain states include Alabama, Alaska, Arizona, Arkansas, California, Colorado, Florida, Idaho, Illinois, Indiana, Iowa, Kansas, Louisiana, Michigan, Minnesota, Mississippi, Missouri, Montana, Nebraska, Nevada, New Mexico, North Dakota, Ohio, Oklahoma, Oregon, South Dakota, Utah, Washington, Wisconsin, and Wyoming.

Federal land was divided into townships emanating from one or more principal meridians and a base line (rectangular survey). Thorndale's discussion (cited above) includes illustrations of the rectangular survey system of identifying land in addition to a comprehensive explanation of the types of records generated. See also James Truslow Adams and Roy V. Coleman, *Atlas of American History* (New York: Charles Scribner's Sons, 1943), plate number 87.

Essential references for dealing with federal land are:

McMullin, Phillip W., ed. *Grassroots of America: A Computerized Index to the American State Papers: Land Grants and Claims, 1789–1837.* Salt Lake City, Utah: Gendex Corp., 1972. This indexes *American State Papers, Public Lands* (Washington, S.C.: Gales and Seaton, 1832–61).

Smith, Clifford Neal. *Federal Land Series.* 4 vols. (vol 4 in 2 pts.) Chicago: American Library Association, 1972–86.

Yoshpe, Harry P., and Philip P. Brower. *Preliminary Inventory of Land-Entry Papers of the General Land Office.* No. 22. Washington, D.C.: National Archives and Records Service, 1949.

Land records for public-domain states east of the Mississippi River and those on the west bank of the river are served by the Bureau of Land Management, Eastern States Land Office, 350 South Pickett Street, Alexandria, Virginia 22304. Western public-domain states are served by General Land Offices within each state or an adjacent state, but copies of tractbooks for western states are also in the National Archives. Both sets—those held by the Eastern States Land Office and those by the National Archives—are available on microfilm at those locations. The National Archives holdings on land records is outlined in National Archives Records Service, *Guide to Genealogical Research in the National Archives* (rev. Washington, D.C.: National Archives Trust Fund Board, 1985), chapter 15.

Regional centers of the National Archives (see Archives, Libraries, and Societies) often have copies of microfilms dealing with transactions in that region. In some cases the claims for donation or homestead land have been abstracted and published.

State-land states include: Connecticut, Delaware, Georgia, Hawaii, Kentucky, Maine, Maryland, Massachusetts, New Hampshire, New Jersey, New York, North Carolina, Pennsylvania, Rhode Island, South Carolina, Tennessee, Texas, Vermont, Virginia, and West Virginia. Legal descriptions for land in these states do not use the rectangular survey, but several other means of surveying—metes and bounds, or range and lot numbers among them. In addition to Thorndale, cited above, for an explanation of metes and bounds and mapping terms see, Julian G. Hoffman and B. Ransom McBride, "Mapping," in Helen F. M. Leary and Maurice R. Stirewalt, *North Carolina Research: Genealogy and Local History* (Raleigh, N.C.: North Carolina Genealogical Society, 1980).

Once land has been conveyed by the government, a second group of land records documents transactions between individuals. Each state's discussion indicates where government conveyances and individual conveyances are found. In the large majority of states, the county exercises jurisdiction over land transactions. But in others, deeds were recorded with towns, parishes, and judicial districts. Each state's section clarifies this. States may have used different terms in deeds to describe the property, and those differences are reported in this section.

Probate Records

Depending on the state, various courts or districts were responsible for recording the disposition of property after the death of its owner, whether by will (testate) or without one (intestate). Probate records might show not only dispositions of estates but also guardianships, adoptions, name changes, and other functions that they served as well. This section will provide an understanding of peculiarities in probate for that state, the title and location of the governmental agency responsible in the area, and an understanding of the changing boundaries of jurisdiction.

While probate records produce some of the most definitive information for genealogical research, not everyone had the disposition of his or her property documented in probate records. When an estate is probated, there are usually two kinds of materials generated by the proceedings. The clerk enters specific documents in the probate record book or volume. However, many of the original "loose" papers pertaining to the proceedings are not entered into the probate book. Some are only kept in an estate file or packet, separate from the record books. Included in estate files might be the original will with the signatures of the testator and witnesses, creditors and legatee receipts for payments from the estate, and petitions from guardians. Availability of both probate record books and packet files or "loose" papers is reported in this section when they are applicable for a state.

Understanding probate terminology is an important aspect of using probate material. A testate estate is any estate with a valid will; in general, valid wills conform to current estate law, name one or more executors, and are properly witnessed. An intestate estate is an estate without a valid will; a technically invalid will may be used as a guide to property division in an intestate estate. Executors conduct testate estates, and administrators are appointed by the probate court for intestate estates.

Common law rules of descent still generally apply today, although each state (and colony) modified them by their own laws. Two important principles during the colonial period were primogeniture and the right of dower. Primogeniture, although only applied in certain colonies, was a procedure by which an estate was given to the eldest son, by right of birth. The right of dower provided a woman a portion of her deceased husband's real estate for the remainder of her natural life; the dower was generally one-third. Widows also had a dower right to their late husbands' personal property; once again, the dower was generally one-third, but there was sometimes an equal division with all of the surviving children. Most states provide somewhat differently for widows today. One place the legal process of probate is discussed is Val D. Greenwood, ed., *The Researcher's Guide to American Genealogy* (2d ed. Baltimore, Md.: Genealogical Publishing Co., 1990), pages 255–320.

Court Records

Court systems and the records they produce are outlined next for each of the states. Although naturalization and divorce records are matters for courts as well, they may be discussed in other sections. In this section the concentration is on civil and criminal court records. Although each of the state's County (or Town or Parish) Resources section indicates the first dates when *some* court proceedings are extant in that location, the exact court from which those records emanate is not necessarily indicated.

The value of civil and criminal cases found in court records is in the portrait they paint of the lives involved. Civil cases regarding debt are historically the most common concerns coming before a local court. Inability to pay a debt may have provided a reason for leaving an area as well. But there are numerous other types of disputes gracing the pages of court records.

Criminal court records, or at least the results of them, are often detailed in the pages of newspapers if not through the court records themselves. The proceedings are likely to be much more detailed than civil court cases and allow a glimpse of the strains of life experienced by our ancestors.

Nearly all states have too large an array of court records to be discussed in total here. Instead, referring to the discussion in this section will provide a background understanding with which to guide your research. For a more comprehensive discussion of records generated by court proceedings see:

Eakle, Arlene. "American Court Records," in Eakle, Arlene and Johni Cerny, eds. *The Source: A Guidebook of American Genealogy*. Salt Lake City, Utah: Ancestry, 1984, pages 150–215.

Tax Records

Taxes serve a variety of purposes in genealogical research. Tax records can indicate age (or at least majority), wealth, and presence in an area, even for those who were not landowners.

There are numerous examples of interesting tax lists and the information they convey. Few are published. Most exist in original form in a state or local repository. This section discusses availability of those tax records.

Cemetery Records

Cemetery records usually refer to information collected from grave markers. Inscriptions on gravestones and the location of a grave in relation to those of others in the same cemetery provide good evidence for genealogical research. The major problem with using cemetery records is trying to locate the cemetery in which a person was buried.

If the cemetery records for a targeted area have not been transcribed and published, which is likely to be the case, then on-site work is the solution. More and more local historical groups have been transcribing gravestones found in their local cemeteries, so the task is becoming less overwhelming. For years, local and state chapters of the National Society of the Daughters of the American Revolution (DAR) have been traipsing through cemeteries, making yearly contributions to this source material. They combine cemetery records with family, Bible, and church records in local areas to document vital events and family relationships. Three typescript copies are made for each volume produced. One copy stays with the chapter, and one is deposited in one of the state's repositories. Some states have not identified a single repository to be the recipient of the volumes, and they are spread out among several sites. The third copy is held by the DAR Library in Washington, D. C. Many volumes have been microfilmed and are additionally available through the FHL.

A source that might be helpful in locating cemeteries in a particular state is J. D. Stemmons and E. D. Stemmons, *The Cemetery Record Compendium* (Logan, Utah: Everton Publishers, 1979).

Church Records

Church records of baptisms, marriages, and burials can be a valuable major source of vital record documentation. In addition, membership lists can indicate migration by noting movement from one church to another. Minutes of meetings may describe values held and community concerns—providing a richer understanding of the tensions and relationships in a community. Each state's section will next outline what church records are known to be available in published volumes and what guides and sources exist for locating the original records.

The national headquarters for a particular denomination may be able to supply the information regarding availability of records. The search for church records will encourage your best detective work.

For an excellent discussion on church records, see Richard W. Dougherty, "Church Records in the United States," in Arlene Eakle and Johni Cerny, eds., *The Source: A Guidebook of American Genealogy* (Salt Lake City, Utah: Ancestry, 1984), pages 130–48.

Military Records

War has been a frequent occurrence in United States history, and with it comes a monumental number of records. Besides chronicles of campaigns in various forms, both service records and pension records play a role in discovering ancestors.

There are military records for all the wars, although the most popularly used for genealogical purposes are undoubtedly those of the Revolutionary War (including Loyalists), War of 1812, and Civil War, principally because they can provide the most genealogical information for the most people through pension records.

Surviving records of military service during the colonial period are often in print. Service records for most states in the three principal wars of genealogical research interest listed above may also be found in print. Those that are available are outlined in each state's section.

The National Archives has *extensive* holdings, not all in microform, of both military service and pension records beginning with the Revolutionary War. Microfilm holdings are described in their publication, *Military Service Records: A Select Catalog of National Archives Microfilm Publications* (Washington, D.C.: National Archives and Records Service, 1985), many of which are also available through the FHL, American Genealogical Lending Library (see Census Records), or the regional centers of the National Archives.

In addition, the National Genealogical Society, *Index of Revolutionary War Pension Applications in the National Archives* (Washington, D.C.: National Genealogical Society, 1976); and Virgil D. White, comp., *Index to War of 1812 Pension Files*, 3 vols. (Waynesboro, Tenn.: National Historical Publishing Co., 1989), are two examples of printed indexes covering all states.

An excellent discussion of military records is Johni Cerny "Military Records," in Arlene Eakle and Johni Cerny, eds., *The Source: A Guidebook of American Genealogy* (Salt Lake City, Utah: Ancestry, 1984), pages 254–98.

Periodicals, Newspapers, and Manuscript Collections

Periodicals

Every year the list of genealogical and historical periodicals grows. There are clearly hundreds that are distributed to subscribers that often do not make it to a local library for research purposes. They vary even more as to their quality. Any one of them might include records of value that have been transcribed or show useful methodology.

The major currently published periodicals of high professional quality that cover more than one state or region are *The American Genealogist* (*TAG;* see Rhode Island—Periodicals); *National Genealogical Society Quarterly* (*NGSQ;* see Societies with Libraries, page 9, and District of Columbia—Periodicals); *The New England Historical and Genealogical Register* (*The Register;* see Societies with Libraries, page 9, and Massachusetts—Periodicals); the *New York Genealogical and Biographical Record* (*The Record;* see New York—Periodicals); and the *Detroit Society for Genealogical Research Magazine* (see Michigan—Periodicals). These focus principally on publishing well-documented, compiled, multigenerational accounts of individuals and families in addition to illustrating use of resources and methodology. All have individual indexes, but many are also indexed in combined indexes (see below).

Most states have periodicals as well, either published by state or local historical or genealogical societies. Each state's section will outline a few. In some states many local genealogical societies publish periodicals. In fact, their number is too extensive to report each here. Local state libraries and genealogical organizations, the Federation of Genealogical Societies (see pages 9–10), and the yearly issue of the *Genealogical Helper* (published by Everton Publishers) devoted to that purpose can direct a researcher to those periodicals that are currently being published.

There are combined periodical indexes as well. Each periodical generally indexes its own issues annually, but some indexes are available for several periodicals. Donald Lines Jacobus, *Index to Genealogical Periodicals* (reprint, Baltimore, Md.: Genealogical Publishing Co., 1963–65), indexes those prominent in the first part of the twentieth century. The annually published *Genealogical Periodical Annual Index* (Bowie, Md.: Heritage Books, 1974–present) indexes 277 periodicals currently being published. *PERiodical Source Index* (*PERSI*), produced by the Allen County Public Library (see Indiana—Periodicals), covers over 2,000 periodicals and is divided into five sections: U.S. places; Canadian places; Foreign places; Research methodology; and Families (including queries).

Newspapers

Death (including cause) and marriage (occasionally with parents of couple indicated) notices might appear in a newspaper, although birth notices rarely do before the twentieth century. Obituaries for non-prominent persons begin to appear more regularly at the end of the nineteenth century. However, extensive social notices (including travels and visitors), court decisions, accidents, military engagements and those serving in them, weather conditions and events, business events, letters unclaimed at the post office, and ships' arrivals give a more detailed description of the press' perception of life in the community of readers.

Since the vast majority of older newspapers are on microfilm, it is possible to borrow many on interlibrary loan through a local library. Titles and dates of publication are listed for some newspapers in this section for each state, although most major libraries have the *Union List* (see below) or know how to request microfilmed newspapers through interlibrary loan. The following sources can help in locating specific newspapers:

Brigham, Clarence Saunders. *History and Bibliography of American Newspapers, 1690–1820.* 2 vols. 1947. Reprint. Westport, Conn.: Greenwood Press, 1976.

Gregory, Winifred, ed. *American Newspapers 1821–1936: A Union List of Files Available in the United States and Canada.* New York: H.W. Wilson Co., 1937. This continues the work of Brigham.

Library of Congress. Catalog Publication Division. *Newspapers in Microforms: United States, 1948–1972.* Washington, D.C.: Library of Congress, 1984.

Manuscripts

The extent of any library's manuscript collection may vary considerably. Manuscripts of note are included for each state in this section. However, there are thousands more available.

The Library of Congress publishes a *National Union Catalog of Manuscript Collections,* which is continuously updated. Each repository is listed with details about the holdings of its manuscript collection including diaries and personal papers. "Finding Manuscript Collections: NUCMC, NIDS, and RLIN," by Mary McCampbell Bell, Clifford Dwyer, and William Abbot Henderson, in *National Genealogical Society Quarterly* 77 (September 1989): 208–18, can be helpful in learning how to locate specific manuscript material.

A source for diaries is Laura Arksey, Nancy Pries, and Marcia Reed, *An Annotated Bibliography of Published American Diaries and Journals,* 2 vols. (Detroit, Mich.: Gale Research, 1983–87).

Archives, Libraries, and Societies

This section indicates the major genealogically significant repositories and organizations for each state. Those that have collections or memberships that are national in scope are included here.

Archives

National Archives and Records Administration
Eighth and Pennsylvania Avenues
Washington, DC 20408

The National Archives (NARA) has extensive holdings, often referred to throughout the book. The indispensable *Guide to Genealogical Research in the National Archives* (Rev., Washington, D.C.: National Archives and Records Service, 1985) indicates some of the extent of the records for genealogical research. Additional guides for each of the groups of materials are also available for purchase from the National Archives.

Regional centers of the National Archives have been established throughout the United States. These centers hold duplicate microfilms of the major holdings in Washington, D.C., making the records considerably more accessible. The regional centers also have considerable original source material that is endemic only to that region, such as naturalizations, court records, and land records. In addition to individual published guides available at each regional center, *The Archives: A Guide to the National Archives Field Branches,* compiled by Loretto Dennis Szucs and Sandra Hargreaves Luebking (Salt Lake City, Utah: Ancestry, 1988), is an important reference to the records in each of the centers.

National Archives-New England Region
380 Trapelo Road
Waltham, MA 02154

Serves Connecticut, Maine, Massachusetts, New Hampshire, Rhode Island, and Vermont.

National Archives-Northeast Region
Building 22, Military Ocean Terminal
Bayonne, NJ 07002

Although presently at the above address, a new location in New York City is anticipated. Serves New York, New Jersey, Puerto Rico, and U.S. Virgin Islands.

National Archives-Mid Atlantic Region
9th and Market Streets, Room 1350
Philadelphia, PA 19107

Serves Pennsylvania, Delaware, Maryland, Virginia, and West Virginia.

National Archives-Southeast Region
1557 St. Joseph Avenue
East Point, GA 30344

Serves Alabama, Georgia, Florida, Kentucky, Mississippi, North Carolina, South Carolina, and Tennessee.

National Archives-Great Lakes Region
7358 South Pulaski Road
Chicago, IL 60629

Serves Illinois, Indiana, Michigan, Minnesota, Ohio, and Wisconsin.

National Archives-Central Plains Region
2312 East Bannister Road
Kansas City, MO 64131

Serves Iowa, Kansas, Missouri, and Nebraska.

National Archives-Southwest Region
501 West Felix Street, P.O. Box 6216
Fort Worth, TX 76115

Serves Arkansas, Louisiana, Oklahoma, Texas, and New Mexico.

National Archives-Rocky Mountain Region
Building 48, Denver Federal Center
Denver, CO 80225

Serves Colorado, Montana, North Dakota, South Dakota, Utah, and Wyoming.

National Archives-Pacific Sierra Region
1000 Commodore Drive
San Bruno, CA 94066
Serves northern California, Hawaii, Nevada (except Clark County), American Samoa, and the Pacific Ocean area.

National Archives-Pacific Southwest Region
24000 Avilla Road, P.O. Box 6719
Laguna Niguel, CA 92677
Serves southern California, Arizona, and Nevada (Clark County).

National Archives-Pacific Northwest Region
6125 Sand Point Way N.E.
Seattle, WA 98115
Serves Idaho, Oregon, and Washington.

National Archives-Alaska Region
Federal Office Building
654 West Third Avenue, Room 012
Anchorage, AK 99501
Serves Alaska.

National Archives Suitland Reference Branch
Washington National Records Center
4205 Suitland Road
Suitland, MD 20746
Mailing address:
National Archives
Civil Archives Division
Washington, DC 20409
This branch holds records for the District of Columbia and U.S. government field offices.

Libraries

Bibliographic information for every book cataloged in numerous libraries is being entered into a national on-line computer database called the On-line Computer Library Center (OCLC). This makes it possible to determine what printed material is available at various locations in the country and whether it is accessible by interlibrary loan.

Family History Library of the Church of Jesus Christ of Latter-day Saints (The Mormons)
35 North West Temple
Salt Lake City, UT 84150
The FHL has the largest international collection of family history research materials. Although physically located at the above address and open for research to the general public, all of the FHL's materials that are on microfilm can be borrowed through any of the local Family History Centers, most of which are attached to local meetinghouses of the church. There is usually a waiting period for receiving films, but the cost is nominal. For a listing of all currently operating FHL centers, write to the above address.

For a comprehensive guide to the collection, see Johni Cerny and Wendy Elliott, eds., *The Library: A Guide to the LDS Family History Library* (Salt Lake City, Utah: Ancestry, 1988).

Library of Congress and Annex
1st-2nd Streets, S.E.
Washington, DC 20504
The Library of Congress has extensive holdings on local and family history. James C. Neagles, *The Library of Congress: A Guide to Genealogical and Historical Research* (Salt Lake City, Utah: Ancestry, 1990), provides an explanation of the library's resources and how they can be used.

Societies with Libraries

National Genealogical Society
4527 Seventeenth Street North
Arlington, VA 22207
A membership society with an excellent library of books, magazines, pamphlets, and manuscripts open to the public. Publishes *National Genealogical Society Quarterly,* offers an extensive educational program, computer interest group, and annual national conferences covering research methods and sources.

National Society, Daughters of the American Revolution Library
1776 D Street, N.W.
Washington, DC 20006
A membership society with an extensive library including original source material and collection of family and cemetery records gathered by local chapters. The library is open to the general public for a small fee.

New England Historic Genealogical Society
101 Newbury Street
Boston, MA 02116
Not limited to research material on New England, the collection here is described in the Massachusetts chapter.

Other Libraries

The Newberry Library in Chicago (see Illinois), the New York Public Library in New York City (see New York), the Allen County Public Library in Fort Wayne (see Indiana), and the State Historical Society of Wisconsin (see Wisconsin) all have extensive collections not limited to the state in which they are located, and include printed and microform materials from many regions of the country.

Societies

Federation of Genealogical Societies
P.O. Box 3385
Salt Lake City, UT 84110-3385
This federation of a large number of state and local genealogical societies is an excellent source for locating genealogical and historical societies not covered in each state's section but which are simply too numerous to present an exhaustive listing here. FGS produces the quarterly

FGS *Forum,* which is distributed free to all members of genealogical societies belonging to the FGS who request it. FGS sponsors annual national conferences where attendees can learn about research sources and methodology.

A current list of some genealogical and historical societies is included in Mary K. Meyer, ed., *Meyer's Directory of Genealogical Societies in the USA and Canada,* 8th ed. (Mt. Airy, Md.: the author, 1990). In addition there are many libraries, public and private, throughout the country that have significant collections of genealogical material. Some of these are listed in *Directory of American Libraries with Genealogy or Local History Collections,* compiled by P. William Filby (Wilmington, Del.: Scholarly Resources, 1988). Elizabeth Petty Bentley's *The Genealogist's Address Book* (Baltimore, Md.: Genealogical Publishing Co., 1991) lists current addresses, phone numbers, and hours of operation of many libraries, societies, and archives of interest to genealogists.

Special Focus Categories

This section for each state discusses topics which, for that state, require a special emphasis. Although not every state includes discussion of all categories, Black American research, Native American research, immigration and naturalization, and research on particular ethnic groups are the most commonly discussed. Some resources for these categories that apply to all states are described below.

Immigration

We are, with the exception of Native American residents, all descendants of immigrants—some not by choice. Nearly all of twentieth-century immigration records from ships' arrivals on the eastern and southern coasts of the United States have been indexed or Soundexed (as with census records) and can be viewed on microfilm in collections at the National Archives. Their publication, *Immigrant and Passenger Arrivals: A Select Catalog of National Archives Microfilm Publications,* lists these records.

Federal records before the twentieth century are on microfilm but not completely indexed. When indexes do not exist, the passenger lists may still exist, but the port of entry, name of ship, and date of arrival need to be known. Even when aided by the 1900 census information as to year of immigration (if accurately given), it still means searching through several reels of microfilm.

Before 1820, information may be found in numerous places. The most comprehensive index to all immigrant arrivals is published in the multivolume set edited initially by P. William Filby and Mary K. Meyer and updated annually by Filby and others: *Passenger and Immigration Lists Index* (Detroit, Mich.: Gale Research, 1981–87) lists over 1,275,000 names in both the original volumes and the annual supplements. The original and secondary source material used in the compilation will still need to be located to verify accuracy.

Naturalization

A naturalization might have been initiated in nearly any court in any state. The immigrant first went to court to declare the intent to become a citizen. A court record was then initiated. Next, the person reappeared in a court, though not necessarily the same one, once the requirements of citizenship had been met. Finally, the court would award citizenship. At all three stops, records were produced. Locating the correct court is not always easy. Many naturalization records (mostly federal) are now held by the regional centers of the National Archives (see pages 8–9). After 1906 the naturalization process was carried out in U.S. district courts, with records generally available through the appropriate court for each state. For an excellent discussion of the process and the records it created, see John J. Newman, *American Naturalization Processes and Procedures, 1790–1985* (Indianapolis, Ind.: Indiana Historical Society, 1985). For some states, naturalization is discussed under Court Records.

Black American

Research on families with African-American ancestry generally follows the same techniques as those with European-American ancestry. Records chronicling the lives of Americans of African descent exist in abundance in the Western world and Africa. All the record sources discussed here (vital, land, probate, court, etc.) include evidence for research on black families, particularly free blacks, although not always specifically identifying an individual with any ethnic or racial description.

The historical past of those with African ancestry is likely to include ancestors who were slaves as well as free, black as well as white. The institution of slavery generated a voluminous number of documents about slaves. Unfortunately, most of them have not been published or microfilmed and remain difficult to locate for genealogical purposes. The major exceptions to this are the enumerations of free blacks and slaves on the federal census (see Census Records) and other record groups, such as the Freedman's Bureau records, held by the National Archives. Debra L. Newman, *Black History: A Guide to Civilian Records in the National Archives* (Washington, D.C.: National Archives, 1984), catalogs and describes the vast extent of those holdings.

During the 1930s, the WPA collected oral histories from many elderly ex-slaves. A superb collection, it has been reproduced in a multivolume set, organized by state. See the multivolume series, George P. Rawick, ed., *The American Slave: A Composite Autobiography,* (Westport, Conn.: Greenwood Publishing Co., 1972).

James M. Rose and Alice Eichholz, *Black Genesis* (Detroit, Mich.: Gale Research Co., 1978), although limited, is the most comprehensive guide to the use of the extensive genealogical records involving blacks. Other sources include Charles L. Blockson, with Ron Fry, *Black Genealogy*

(Englewood Cliffs, N.J.: Prentice-Hall, 1977); and Johni Cerny, "Black Ancestral Research," in Arlene Eakle and Johni Cerny, eds., *The Source: A Guidebook of American Genealogy* (Salt Lake City, Utah: Ancestry, 1984), pages 579–95.

The Afro-American Historical and Genealogical Society, P.O. Box 73086, Washington, D.C. 20056, and the African-American Family History Association, P.O. Box 115268, Atlanta, Georgia 30310, publish a journal and a newsletter, respectively, focused on researching families with African ancestry.

David T. Thackery and Dee Woodhor, *Case Studies in Afro-American Genealogy* (Chicago: Newberry Library, 1989), presents four case studies using different methodological approaches as examples for guiding research in other cases.

Native American

Research in Native American ancestry produces another challenge and, unlike research for black Americans, such research relies heavily on federal records and not the county or state material used for research with other groups.

Many sources for Native Americans are not indexed, and some require a knowledge of Native American beliefs and customs. In addition to the sources listed under the states where Native American research requires a special focus, Native American records are cited in the National Archives and Records Service, *American Indians: A Select Catalog of National Archives Microfilm Publications* (Washington, D.C.: National Archives and Records Service, 1984).

Edward E. Hill, *Preliminary Inventory of the Records of the Bureau of Indian Affairs*, 2 vols. (Washington, D.C.: National Archives and Records Service, 1965), explains the administrative structure of the Bureau of Indian Affairs (BIA) and helps locate appropriate records for genealogical purposes. Like his *Guide to Records in the National Archives of the United States Relating to American Indians* (Washington, D.C.: National Archives and Records Service, 1981), Hill's inventory is an essential reference.

Other important sources include *The Source: A Guidebook of American Genealogy* (Salt Lake City, Utah: Ancestry, 1984), which has George J. Nixon's chapter on Native American research regarding the Five Civilized Tribes, citing Creek and Seminole census records, emigration lists, annuity payrolls, and miscellaneous rolls; and Stewart Rafert, "American-Indian Genealogical Research in the Midwest: Resources and Perspectives," in *National Genealogical Society Quarterly* 76 (September 1988): 212–24. E. Kay Kirkham's two-volume *Our Native Americans and Their Records of Genealogical Value* (Logan, Utah: Everton Publishers, 1980–84) lists a number of helpful resources.

Federal and State Indian Reservations and Indian Trust Areas (Washington, D.C.: U. S. Department of Commerce, Government Printing Office, stock number 0311-00076) will provide addresses of reservations and other useful resources.

County Resources

Finally, each state's chapter outlines, in chart form, the county (town or parish) resources that can be found either on microfilm or in the local holding agencies. Accompanying each state's chart is a map detailing the political divisions and some geographic features. Addresses are given for those agencies, with the date that the county or town was formed, parent counties, other names, and (where possible or available) the first year that primary sources remain extant in that location. Beginning dates for vital records, land, probate, and court records held in the counties, towns, or parishes are included. Inquires to these counties should be addressed to the county courthouse or town clerk's office at that address, and more specifically if the individual chapter or chart so indicates. The column labeled "Map" gives coordinates that correspond to the state map giving the location of the county or town within that state.

Information for this part of each state's section was gathered in a number of ways. State archives, county officials, the FHL, and local repository catalogs were all used. Not all sources agree. There were numerous discrepancies. An annotated edition would have produced a volume three times this size. The listing of beginning dates for primary sources is a *guide* only and not to be considered a definitive work of every extant record in every location. A question mark (?) indicates that records exist, but the starting date is uncertain. Dashes (—) indicate that there are no known records in that category. Many states are thoroughly organized with centralized records. However, many states are not. Several have not had many of their records microfilmed, and others are in progress. What is given in the county chart here is the best information that could be gathered.

Sources for county formation used in this section, in addition to the personal knowledge of the contributors and sources listed under each state, included:

Thorndale, William, and William Dollarhide. *Map Guide to the U.S. Federal Censuses 1790–1920.* Baltimore, Md.: Genealogical Publishing Co., 1987.

Long, John H., ed. *Historical Atlas and Chronology of County Boundaries, 1788–1980.* 5 vols. Boston: G.K. Hall, 1984.

Abbreviations

The following abbreviations are used throughout the text:

AISI: Accelerated Indexing Systems International of Bountiful, Utah.

BLM: Bureau of Land Management (see GLO).

DAR: Daughters of the American Revolution.

FHL: Family History Library in Salt Lake City, Utah.

GLO: General Land Office (became the BLM in 1946).

IGI: International Genealogical Index.

M### (also T###): A capital *T* or *M* followed by a number is the reference for a National Archives microfilm.

NARA: National Archives and Records Administration.

OCLC: On-line Computer Library Center.

USGS: United States Geological Survey.

WPA: Works Progress Administration (also Work Projects Administration).

Conclusion

The challenge in genealogical research is the complexity and depth of the problem. It is somewhat like piecing together a multilayered jigsaw puzzle. One's own resistance to finding out about the past can impede progress, but this resistance can be overcome.

Somehow we feel that others must have known more than we do, and consequently, all that has been found is all that can be found. People who have spent years researching a family line will often tell stories about how they "happened" upon information. It probably was just as much skill as accident. We all are capable of acquiring some of that skill. It is like trying to understand your car. Maybe you never will be a mechanic who is expert in fixing a car or an engineer who can design one, but everyone can be capable of having a meaningful discussion about one.

Genealogical research is like that. Even if you never become a professional, you can acquire many skills in order to construct a good research strategy, solve many problems, and have a good working relationship with any professional with whom you consult in problem solving.

There are numerous guides to help overcome the concern about not knowing enough. Among the most valuable are the following:

Cerny, Johni, and Arlene Eakle. *Ancestry's Guide to Research: Case Studies in American Genealogy.* Salt Lake City, Utah: Ancestry, 1985.

Eakle, Arlene and Johni Cerny, eds. *The Source: A Guidebook of American Genealogy.* Salt Lake City, Utah: Ancestry, 1984.

Greenwood, Val D. *The Researcher's Guide to American Genealogy.* 2d ed. Baltimore, Md.: Genealogical Publishing Co., 1990.

Jacobus, Donald Lines. *Genealogy as Pastime and Profession.* Baltimore, Md.: Genealogical Publishing Co., 1978.

Stratton, Eugene A. *Applied Genealogy.* Salt Lake City, Utah: Ancestry, 1988.

Stevenson, Noel. *Genealogical Evidence: A Guide to Standards of Proof Relating to Pedigrees, Ancestry, Heirship and Family History.* Rev. ed. Laguna Hills, Calif.: Aegean Park Press, 1989.

The process of research requires documentation of sources. A standard format used for documenting family relationships is presented in:

Lackey, Richard S. *Cite Your Sources: A Manual for Documenting Family Histories and Genealogical Records.* New Orleans, La.: Polyanthos, 1980.

Another type of resistance has to do with concern about what will be discovered—those "skeletons in the closet." We all have them. We all descend from a very diverse group of people. No one has a "perfect" ancestry any more than "perfect" parents. Each of our ancestors probably did the best that he or she could, frequently under extremely difficult circumstances. We all have divorces, illegitimacies, felons, adulterers, dissenters, persecutors, rich, poor, Democrats, Republicans, religious zealots and dissenters, and people from diverse ethnic or racial groups in our backgrounds. We all have ancestors who perished in or survived unfavorable odds—slavery, crossing the ocean, leaving the "known" and journeying into the "unknown," loss of income, childbirth, successive deaths, disease, plagues, droughts, disasters. We are all both ordinary and special.

One of the most pleasurable rewards of genealogy is sharing and celebrating what you have done and learned with others—whether it is at a national or local conference, with a professional, or with other family members. Searching for roots can establish a clear understanding of the past in order to provide tethers as we approach an even more rapid-paced future.

ALABAMA

Mary Bess Paluzzi

Alabama shares the rich cultural history of the Southeastern region. From 1519, when the first Spanish explorer, Alonso Alvarez de Pineda, navigated Mobile Bay, the state was claimed explored, and settled by the Spanish, French, and British.

The first permanent European settlers in Alabama were French. The LeMoyne brothers, Pierre LeMoyne, Sieur d'-Iberville, and Jean Baptiste LeMoyne, Sieur de Bienville, sailed into Mobile Bay in 1699. By 1711, Fort Louis (on the present site of Mobile) had been settled as the capital of the French colony known as Louisiana.

With the Treaty of Paris in 1763, the French ceded most of Louisiana to Great Britain. When Spain declared war on Great Britain in 1779, the American Revolution came to Alabama. In 1780, Bernardo Galvez captured Mobile from the British. The Treaty of Paris in 1783 ceded to Spain the British holdings in the Mobile region.

In 1795, the Treaty of San Lorenzo more specifically stated that all Alabama lands below the 31st parallel belonged to Spain, and lands above the 31st parallel belonged to the United States and in turn to the Native Americans living there. At the same time the Ellicott Line was being surveyed, "squatters" (those having no legal claim to the lands they settled) began to move into Alabama forcing the various tribes off their lands. Washington, the first Alabama county, was created in 1800 from Mississippi Territory. The area below the 31st parallel was added to Mississippi Territory in 1812. Later counties were created as more white settlers moved into ceded native lands until Alabama Territory was created on 3 March 1817. Alabama became a state 14 December 1819 and, in 1835, the last native lands were ceded.

During the early years of statehood the most significant genealogical event was the opening of lands formerly held by Native Americans to white settlers between 1802 and 1835. Mary Elizabeth Young, *Redskins, Ruffleshirts and Rednecks: Indian Allotments in Alabama and Mississippi, 1830–1860* (Norman, Okla.: University of Oklahoma Press, 1961), details these developments. By 1840 all but a few scattered tribes had been moved west beyond the Mississippi River.

Alabama suffered economic and agricultural problems in the 1840s and 1850s. The financial panic and depression which swept across the United States in 1837 resulted in banking problems that caused many Alabamians to lose their savings. Crops were ruined by drought, and several epidemics of yellow fever brought added suffering.

Economic rivalry between the industrial North and the agricultural South raised conflicts concerning states' rights and slavery. The unresolved conflict deepened until, on 11 January 1861, Alabama seceded from the Union and joined the Confederate States of America.

When compared with other Confederate states, Alabama, with the exception of the Mobile area, experienced relatively little military action. However, the conflict devastated the economic, political, and social life of the state. Though the state was readmitted to the Union on 25 June 1868, the devastation continued through the Reconstruction period. The deepening poverty experienced resulted in mass migration. In the 1860s and 1870s, 10 to 15 percent of the entire white population of Alabama migrated, with a third of these migrants going to Texas.

Railroads were completed across the state in the 1870s, leading to the industry of mining of Alabama's rich mineral deposits of coal, iron ore, and limestone. By 1880, steel, iron, lumber, and textile industries were rapidly expanding.

Alabama's industry and commerce grew with the United States' entry into World War I. Agricultural production increased, and a significant growth in Mobile's shipbuilding industry led to increased foreign trade. During the Great Depression, Alabamians suffered new financial hardships. The Tennessee Valley Authority, established in 1933 by the federal government, developed dams and power plants on the Tennessee River for inexpensive electricity, boosting Alabama's industrial growth.

World War II led to expansion of the state's agricultural and industrial production, and installation of several military training sites, including Redstone Arsenal in Huntsville—which launched the United States into the space age. During the 1950s and 1960s, agriculture and industry became more diversified, requiring fewer agricultural workers who were forced to seek employment in urban areas outside the state. Alabama faced serious racial questions during the time period. The Montgomery Bus Boycott in 1955–56, the Birmingham demonstrations in 1963, and the Selma March in 1965 attracted much media attention. With the passage of the U.S. Voting Rights Act in August 1965, blacks played an increasing role in local and state politics and commerce.

Vital Records

Prior to 1881 a limited amount of information concerning births and deaths of a few individuals is available indirectly from probate court records. Such records include adoptions, guardianships and apprenticeships, recorded wills, and the various records maintained in the settlement and division of an estate. These records seldom provide more information than establishing race, sex, and parentage of the adoptee, ward, apprentice, or legatee (heir).

An act of 1881 provided that all births and deaths were to be registered with a county health officer. It became mandatory for every physician, midwife, or birth attendee to report to the county health officer all births, specifying the name of parents, the date of the birth, and the sex and race of the child. It also became mandatory to report all deaths specifying the name, age, sex, race, date, place, and cause of death. Later legislation required that these registrations be made within the first five days after the birth or death and required that the county health officer's registry books be deposited with the county probate judge. Unfortunately, few such records are actually found today in the county courthouses.

The date for the beginning of mandatory state-level registration of births and deaths in Alabama is 1 January 1908. The state, however, did not achieve 90 percent completeness of birth registration until 1927 and of death registration until 1925.

All original birth and death records are now filed with the Alabama Department of Public Health. A fee of $5 is charged for a record search and one certified copy of a certificate. A $2 charge is made for each additional copy requested at the same time. A fee of $8 is required to amend an omission or to amend information that was incorrectly given. Allow six to eight weeks for each request. Certified copies of birth and death certificates may be requested from the Division of Vital Statistics, Alabama Department of Public Health, State Office Building, Montgomery, Alabama 36130.

A marriage license has been required since the territorial period. Between 1805 and 1850, marriage licenses were issued by the clerk of the county orphans' court in which the bride resided. After 1850 the orphans' court was superseded by the probate court, which is still charged with the issuance of marriage licenses.

To enter into a marriage contract a man had to be at least seventeen years of age and a woman had to be at least fourteen years of age. If the man was under twenty-one or the woman under eighteen and as yet unmarried, the consent of the parent or guardian of the minor was required before a license could be issued. The marriage of these licensed parties could then be solemnized by a territorial, state, or county judge, an ordained minister, or a justice of the peace. The officiant was then required to file a marriage certificate with the probate judge of the county in which the marriage took place.

Before 1900 a marriage certificate indicated the names of the bride, groom, bondsmen, and officiant along with the license bond and marriage date. Early twentieth-century records may also include the names of parents, physical descriptions, ages and occupations of the parties, the number of previous marriages for each, and the blood relationship, if any, between the parties.

A certified copy of a marriage certificate may be obtained from the probate judge of the county in which the certificate was filed and recorded. The standard fee is $5 for each certificate requested, and six to eight weeks should be allowed for response to a request.

Though divorce decrees were tried in county chancery court until 1865, the state legislature had the exclusive right to finalize all divorce decrees. These early decrees are thus a part of the legislative record and are published in the *Senate and House Journals*. An index to legislative divorce decrees was published in the *Alabama Genealogical Society, Inc., Magazine* 13–14 (1979–80).

After 1865 the county chancery court was authorized to issue final divorce decrees. In 1917 the chancery court was merged with the circuit court of the county. Thus, divorce records from 1819 are maintained among the equity records of the circuit court of the county in which the suit was filed. Though not required by law, several county clerks maintained divorce records separate from other equity files. A certified copy of a divorce certificate may be obtained from the circuit court clerk in the county in which the divorce suit was tried. A standard fee of $5 is requested, and six to eight weeks should be allowed for response to a request.

In 1942, the Alabama Historical Records Survey Project prepared a preliminary edition of a *Guide to Public Vital Statistics in Alabama.* About 77 percent of all county vital statistics records were surveyed between 1937 and 1942. No update or revision has been compiled.

Census Records

Federal

Population Schedules.

- Indexed—1820 (part), 1830, 1840, 1850, 1860, 1870, 1890 (fragment)
- Soundex—1880, 1900, 1910, 1920

Industry and Agriculture Schedules.

- 1850, 1860, 1870, 1880

Mortality Schedules.

- 1850, 1860, 1870, 1880

Slave Schedules.

- 1850, 1860

The first federal census was taken in 1820. Records exist for only eight of the thirty enumerated counties. These counties include Baldwin, Conecuh, Dallas, Franklin, Limestone, St. Clair, Shelby, and Wilcox. The *Alabama Historical Quarterly* 6 (Fall 1944) abstracts these enumerations.

The only extant records for Alabama of the almost destroyed 1890 census are portions of Perryville (Beat No. 11) and Severe (Beat No. 8) of Perry County.

Territorial and State

Alabama's census records are scant when compared with other states of the same age. Elizabeth Shown Mills cites twelve groups of census or census substitute materials for 1706 through 1816–19, all with enumerations compiled before statehood, in her essay "Alabama" in *Genealogical Research: Methods and Sources*, Vol. 2, rev. ed. (Washington, D.C.: American Society of Genealogists, 1983). Sources for locating the census and substitutes are cited as well. She reasons that Alabama's "sparse population and the administrative neglect which the region often suffered has limited the numbers of extant subsequent enumerations" (page 224).

State censuses were taken sporadically, and sizable but not complete collections exist for 1855 and 1866. The originals are housed in the Alabama Department of Archives and History. Microfilmed copies may be purchased from them (see Archives, Libraries, and Societies for address). Part of the 1820 state census, Lawrence County, still exists and is also housed at the state archives. It has been published as *1820 State Census of Lawrence County, Alabama* (Huntsville, Ala.: Tennessee Valley Genealogical Society, 1977).

Enumerations of native Alabama inhabitants were made before cession of their lands. Other significant sources for Alabama's Native Americans are cited in National Archives and Records Service, *American Indians: A Select Catalog of National Archives Microfilm Publications* (Washington, D.C.: NARA, 1984) (see page 11). The enumerations include these works:

Crumpton, Barbara J. *1884 Hester Roll of the Eastern Cherokee.* Duncan, Okla.: Creative Copies, 1986 (NARA M685, reel 12).

Felldin, Jeanne Roby, and Charlotte Magee Tucker. *1832 Census of Creek Indians Taken By Parsons and Abbott (With an Added Full Names Index of "White" Names).* Tomball, Tex.: Genealogical Publications, 1978 (NARA T275, 1 reel).

———. *Index to the Cherokee Indians East of the Mississippi River.* Tomball, Tex.: Genealogical Publications, 1978 (Henderson Roll, 1835, NARA T496, 1 reel).

Jordan, Jerry Wright. *Cherokee By Blood: Records of Eastern Cherokee Ancestry in the U.S. Court of Claims, 1906–1910.* Bowie, Md.: Heritage Books, 1987–present (Guion Miller Roll, NARA M685, 12 reels).

Siler, David W. *The Eastern Cherokees: A Census of the Cherokee Nation in North Carolina, Tennessee, Alabama and Georgia in 1851.* Cottonport, La.: Polyanthos, 1972.

U.S. Congress. *American State Papers. Documents of the Congress of the United States in Relation to Public Land . . .* Vol. 7. Washington, D.C.: Gales and Seaton, 1860 (Armstrong Roll of Choctaws, 1831).

In 1907 a census was taken of Alabama's Confederate veterans. County tax assessors canvassed all persons who were receiving a pension for Confederate service. Information enumerated includes name, place of residence, date and place of birth, enlistment and discharge or parole, rank, and name of military unit. Originals are housed in the Alabama Department of Archives and History and are now available from them on microfilm. The *Alabama Genealogical Society, Inc., Magazine* from 1958 through 1982 published Alabama Confederate pensioners lists from several counties.

Another census was taken in 1921 of Confederate pensioners in Alabama. This census was taken by mail with each pensioner being asked to complete and return the form to the state. The original forms may be examined at the Alabama Department of Archives and History.

Background Sources

Several different bibliographic works cite published local historical and genealogical titles. Elizabeth Shown Mills's bibliographic essay in *Genealogical Research: Methods and Sources* (see Census Records) presents an excellent introduction to genealogical research in Alabama. In particular, her selective bibliography cites the essential scholarly studies on Alabama history as well as the previously mentioned citations to colonial and territorial enumerations.

Marilyn Davis Barefield's *Researching in Alabama: A Genealogical Guide* (Easley, S.C.: Southern Historical Press, 1988) is a useful instructional tool that includes brief descriptions of the holdings of the state's major genealogical libraries, statements on the formation of counties, and essays on Alabama land office records and military records. The guide contains an excellent series of maps illustrating the development of the state, extensive bibliographies of published genealogical and historical works for each county, and unpublished WPA manuscripts. No periodical sources are cited.

The WPA project, "Index to Alabama Biography: An Index to Biographical Sketches of Individual Alabamians in State, Local, and to Some Extent National Collections" (Birmingham, Ala.: WPA Project sponsored by the Birmingham Public Library, 1956), will assist the researcher looking for prominent persons in Alabama in the late nineteenth and early twentieth centuries. The project indexed over 100 biographical and historical titles. Some of the titles included follow:

DuBose, Joel C. *Notable Men of Alabama.* 2 vols. Atlanta, Ga.: Southern Historical Association, 1904.

Memorial Record of Alabama. 2 vols. Madison, Wis.: Brant & Fuller, 1893.

Moore, Albert Burton. *History of Alabama and Her People.* 3 vols. Chicago, Ill.: American Historical Society, 1927.

Owen, Thomas McAdory. *History of Alabama and Dictionary of Alabama Biography.* 4 vols. Chicago, Ill.: S. J. Clark, 1921.

Saunders, James Edwards. *Early Settlers of Alabama.* New Orleans, La.: L. Graham & Sons, 1899.

The index is available in the Tutwiler Collection of the Birmingham Public Library (see Archives, Libraries, and Societies).

Maps

To date about 95 percent of Alabama has been mapped in cooperation with the U.S. Geological Survey and the Geological Survey of Alabama (see page 4). These topographic quadrangle maps show selected man-made and natural features as well as the shape and elevation of features. Features include state, county, and municipal boundary lines; townships, ranges, roads, railroads, and buildings; and mountains, valleys, streams, and rivers. The earliest survey maps for Alabama are dated from 1901.

The Alabama Highway Department has prepared a series of county road maps. These maps contain more detailed information about man-made features than the geological survey maps. In addition to roads and boundaries, these maps locate rural communities, churches, and cemeteries. The maps are available for a nominal fee from the Alabama Highway Department, Bureau of Planning and Programming, Montgomery, Alabama 36130.

Another important series of maps for incorporated municipalities is the Sanborn Fire Insurance maps (see page 4). These maps, dating from 1884 to 1950, include 110 Alabama communities. The maps indicate street names, property boundaries, building use, and in some cases property owners. Originals are available in the Library of Congress and in the University of Alabama Library (see Archives, Libraries, and Societies). They were microfilmed (twelve reels) in 1982 by Chadwyck-Healy of Alexandria, Virginia.

Sara Elizabeth Mason's bibliography, *A List of Nineteenth Century Maps of the State of Alabama* (Birmingham, Ala.: Birmingham Public Library, 1973), is very helpful in identifying and locating early Alabama maps. The list includes the holdings of the library of the Alabama Department of Archives and History, Auburn University in Auburn, the University of Alabama, Samford University, Mobile Public Library, and Birmingham Public Library (see Archives, Libraries, and Societies). Descriptive annotations as well as detailed physical descriptions add to the usefulness of the list.

The Rucker Agee Map Collection, a privately acquired donation found at the Birmingham Public Library, is an incomparable collection of maps documenting the cartographic history of the southeast and in particular Alabama.

Land Records

Public-Domain State

Colonial settlers acquired title to Alabama lands from the French, the Spanish, the British, and the Native Americans. Original copies of these grants from the first three groups may be found, respectively, in the Archives Nationales in Paris, the Archivo General de Indias in Seville, and the Public Record Office in London. When land title was transferred from Great Britain to the United States in 1783, following the American Revolution, preemptive landowners were required to file proof of their land title with the U.S. GLO. Abstracts of the files are found in the *American States Papers: Documents, Legislative and Executive of the Congress, Class VIII, Public Lands* (Washington, D.C.: Gales and Seaton, 1832–61). These volumes are indexed in *C.I.S. U.S. Serial Set Index, Part I, American States Papers and the 15th–34th Congresses, 1789–1857* (Washington, D.C.: Congressional Information Services, 1977).

Title to previously ungranted lands was vested in the federal government, and titles were conveyed to individuals either by sale or by bounty-land warrant. The Land Act of 1800, as amended in 1803, simplified the claiming of land titles by authorizing local public land offices to survey and auction lands within their charge. Sales were sanctioned through thirteen land offices including St. Stephens (established December 1806, transferred to Mobile 1867); Huntsville (established at Nashville in March 1807, transferred to Huntsville 1811, transferred to Montgomery May 1866); Cahaba (established at Milledgeville, Georgia, August 1817, transferred to Cahaba October 1818, transferred to Grenville 1856); Tuscaloosa (established May 1820, transferred to Montgomery 1832); Sparta-Conecuh

Courthouse (established May 1820, transferred to Montgomery 1854); Montgomery (established July 1832, closed 1927); Mardisville-Montevallo (established July 1832, transferred to Lebanon 1842); Demopolis (established March 1833, transferred to Montgomery March 1866); Lebanon (established April 1842, transferred to Centre 1858); Elba (established April 1854, transferred to Montgomery April 1867); Greenville (established 1856, transferred to Montgomery 1866); Centre (established 1858, transferred to Huntsville 1866); and Mobile (established 1867, transferred to Montgomery June 1879).

When the land offices were closed, their original records were sent to the Washington, D.C., office. Photocopies of the original records may be requested by legal description (subdivision, section, township, range, survey meridian, and state of the land) from the National Archives Suitland Reference Branch (see page 9). Photocopies of the presidential patents are available by legal description from the U.S. BLM, Eastern States Office, 350 South Pickett Street, Alexandria, Virginia 22304. Duplicate copies of some of these records are located in the Alabama Department of Archives and History, the office of the Alabama Secretary of State, and the University of Alabama library's special collections. Plat maps and field notes for these original land grants are also available at these repositories. The Southern Historical Press has published Marilyn Davis Hahn Barefield's abstracts of several of the land offices' records including those of Centre, Demopolis, Elba, Huntsville, Lebanon, Mardisville, Sparta, St. Stephens, and Tuscaloosa; Southern University Press has published her abstracts from the Cahaba Land Office. Other abstracts for north Alabama counties are being privately published by Margaret M. Cowart of Huntsville; her abstracts are for Colbert, Franklin, Jackson, Limestone, Madison, and Morgan counties.

Tract books indicating the original sale of property from the federal government, or the state of Alabama in case of a sixteenth section, are housed in the county probate judge's office. The books, arranged by legal description, include the name of the purchaser, the amount of acres purchased, the price, date of purchase, certificate number, and whether or not the land was obtained under a military act. These records do not include lands cut away to form new counties or subsequent sales of original tracts.

All subsequent title transactions following the original title transfer from the federal government are recorded in the probate judge's records of the county in which the property lies. These records include conveyance records, which detail the transfer of property either by sale or donation.

In some counties, mortgages were recorded in the same volumes as outright conveyance of real property, while in others liens and deeds of trust are recorded separately as "Mortgages."

Probate Records

The office of the probate judge is the county office where the most significant genealogical records are created and maintained in Alabama. A variety of records are housed in this office.

These records may be labeled wills, estates, inventories, administrations or guardian's bonds, and orphan's court records. Within each category there may or may not be separate volumes labeled "record" or "minutes." The "record" volumes contain relatively full accounts of probate proceedings, while the "minutes" volumes normally contain only brief abstracts of the proceedings. Early adoption records and records for the binding-out of poor orphans are recorded here. Until the 1900s adoption records were not filed separately. Record books and files created especially for adoption proceedings are now closed to the public by law. Sometimes bastardy cases and naturalization records are here. In all cases these records are merely copies of the original and contain only such data as the clerk thought legally important. More significant than the clerk's ledger, the "loose papers" contain the documents submitted to prove a will, such as the petition to probate, which listed all heirs of the deceased. Generally, these files are not housed in the record room. The researcher should request these files from the probate clerk. The office of the probate judge in Alabama also recorded other documents intermittently in probate, deed, or commissioner's court records. Particularly useful are proofs of freedom filed by free blacks or natives (often with white deponents), indenture papers, contracts for hiring military substitutes during the Civil War, and lists of slaves brought into the state or loaned to the Confederacy.

Court Records

The records of the office of the court clerk or the circuit court records are the most poorly organized and most frequently missing court records. In smaller counties both chancery and circuit court records are maintained by the same clerk. In larger counties the records may be separated. The state administrative office of the court oversees the maintenance of the circuit court records.

The state-level office of the supreme court clerk has authority over the records of the state supreme court. After five years these records are moved to the state's archives.

Alabama Digest, 1820 to Date . . . (St. Paul, Minn.: West Publishing Co., 1950–present) indexes the decisions and opinions of the Alabama Supreme Court, court of criminal appeals, and court of civil appeals as well as the federal courts from the district level to the supreme court. The final volume is a defendant-plaintiff name index to cases cited.

Tax Records

County tax records are housed in the office of the tax assessor. These records are usually arranged by legal description and are not indexed. There are few counties with tax records before 1860. The National Archives has a microfilm publication titled *Internal Revenue Assessment Lists for Alabama, 1865–1866* (NARA M754, 6 reels).

Cemetery Records

No statewide systematic or comprehensive inventory of cemeteries or bibliography of published transcriptions have been compiled. Scattered volumes have been published by various patriotic, historical, and genealogical societies. Many individual cemetery transcriptions have been published in periodicals.

Church Records

The Baptists (Southern Convention) form the largest denomination in Alabama. The first Baptist church was founded 2 October 1808 on Flint River near Huntsville. The Baptists are the only denomination having some form of centralized state and congregational historic records. Their records are housed in the Samford University Library, Birmingham, Alabama. Included are not only microfilmed minutes of defunct and active congregations, but also the personal papers of many churchmen and a run of the denomination's state newspaper, the *Alabama Baptist* (1835–present).

The state's oldest denomination, Roman Catholic, has records dating from the coming of Iberville's colony near Mobile in 1699. Most parish records are maintained by the local parish.

The first ordained Episcopal minister in the state was licensed in 1764 to minister to British settlers. The WPA Historical Records Survey in 1939 compiled a volume surveying the records of the Protestant Episcopal church in Alabama. The inventory contains a brief history of each parish, a statement on extant parish records, and an index by location and by parish names. Parish records are maintained by the parish. Unfortunately, the survey did not inventory any other denominational records. A copy of Alabama Historical Records Survey, *Inventory of the Church Archives of Alabama, Protestant Episcopal Church* (Birmingham, Ala.: Historical Records Survey Project, 1939), is at the Birmingham Public Library.

In 1803 Lorenzo Dow, who claimed to be a Methodist, did his first preaching in Alabama. Methodist missionaries were sent by the South Carolina Conference into the Tombigbee area in 1809. Today, some Methodist records for north Alabama churches are housed at Birmingham Southern College, and south Alabama church records are housed at Huntingdon College, Montgomery. Birmingham Southern College has a run of the state denominational newspaper, the *Christian Advocate* (1880–present).

The first Presbyterian church was organized in 1818 at Huntsville. Historical records for active Presbyterian churches are usually maintained by the local congregation. Some records of defunct churches are held by Samford University and the Alabama Department of Archives and History.

Military Records

Since Bernardo de Gálvez, the Spanish governor of Louisiana, captured Mobile from the British in 1780, Alabamians have seen military service in all wars of the United States. Military records are found at both the state and federal levels.

The most voluminous and readily available military records for Alabama are those of the National Archives (see page 7).

Roster of Revolutionary Soldiers and Patriots Alabama (Montgomery, Ala.: Alabama Society DAR, 1979) lists those soldiers who lived and died in Alabama as well as some who died in other states. Data from scattered published and unpublished sources was edited and compiled. The volume includes a statement on the soldier's military service; a brief biographical sketch including the names of his parents, wife, and children; and bibliographic citations to sources.

The Alabama Department of Archives and History has made their military service surname files available on microfilm. These files include a series for Revolutionary War veterans residing in Alabama; service in the Indian Wars of 1812, 1813, and 1814; territorial service in 1818; the Indian War of 1836; the Mexican War in 1846; and the Spanish-American War in 1898. The series contains a card for each soldier indicating name, military unit, rank, and the source of the information. Most of the sources cited are unofficial as there are limited records for state military service.

The state of Alabama paid its Confederate veterans a pension. The files contain the usual military pension application information: name, rank, unit, dates of service, places of enlistment and discharge, if wounded, and qualifications for pension. If the widow was making the application, she stated when and where she was born, her father's name, date and place of his death, and the date and place of her marriage. To qualify, a pensioner's annual income could not exceed $300 and his real property could not be valued at more than $400. The original files are housed in the Alabama Department of Archives and History. The applications have been microfilmed by the Genealogical Society of Utah and are available on loan through the FHL.

No comprehensive list of Alabama's Confederate or Union soldiers has been compiled. C. E. Dornbusch's *Regimental Publications and Personal Narratives of the Civil War: A Checklist*, 4 vols. (New York, N.Y.: New York

Public Library, 1961–88), cites published accounts of Alabama regiments. Clement Aslem Evans' *Confederate Military History,* 17 vols., extended (1899; reprint, Wilmington, N.C.: Broadfoot, 1987) includes a separate volume on Alabama, which gives a brief history of each regiment, some biographical sketches, and unit citations found in the U.S. War Department, *Official Records of the Union and Confederate Armies in the War of the Rebellion,* 128 vols. (Washington, D.C.: Government Printing Office, 1901; reprint, Gettysburg, Pa.: National Historical Society, 1971). See also U.S. War Department, *Official Records of the Union and Confederate Navies in the War of the Rebellion,* 31 vols. (Washington, D.C.: Government Printing Office, 1894–1927).

The Alabama Department of Archives and History also has scattered records of local militia units from the Civil War. Most of these files are correspondence between the governor and the county probate judge concerning militia rosters.

Periodicals, Newspapers, and Manuscript Collections

Periodicals

Because of the limited amount of published materials on most Alabama counties, periodical literature is essential. There are more than thirty-five periodicals published in Alabama by local and state historical and genealogical organizations. The *Genealogical Periodical Annual Index* and the *Periodical Source Index, 1847–1985* (see page 7) survey some of these publications as well as articles on Alabama from periodicals done outside the state.

The following are useful genealogical and historical publications:

Alabama Genealogical Quarterly, Vols. 1– (1979–present).

Alabama Genealogical Register (1959–69).

Alabama Genealogical Society, Inc. Magazine (1967–present). Publication of the Alabama Genealogical Society, 800 Lakeshore Drive, Birmingham, Alabama 35229.

Alabama Historical Quarterly, Vol. 1–44 (1930–82). Publication of Alabama Department of Archives and History.

Alabama Review (1942–present). Publication of Alabama Historical Association.

Central Alabama Genealogical Society Quarterly (1976–present). Publication of the Central Alabama Genealogical Society, P.O. Box 125, Selma, Alabama 36701.

Deep South Genealogical Quarterly (1963–present). Publication of Mobile Genealogical Society, P.O. Box 6224, Mobile, Alabama 36606.

Natchez Trace Traveler (1981–present). Publication of the Natchez Trace Genealogical Society, P.O. Box 420, Florence, Alabama 35631.

Pea River Trails (1975–present). Publication of the Pea River Historical Society, P.O. Box 628, Enterprise, Alabama 36330.

Pioneer Trails (1959–present). Publication of the Birmingham Genealogical Society, P.O. Box 2432, Birmingham, Alabama 35201.

Settlers of Northeast Alabama (1962–present). Publication of the Northeast Alabama Genealogical Society, P.O. Box 674, Gadsden, Alabama 35902.

Tap Roots (1963–present). Publication of the Genealogical Society of East Alabama, P.O. Drawer 1351, Auburn, Alabama 36831-1351.

Valley Leaves (1966–present). Publication of the Tennessee Valley Genealogical Society, P.O. Box 1568, Huntsville, Alabama 35807-0568.

Newspapers

The earliest newspapers in the state were located in the Tombigbee-Mobile area and included the *Mobile Sentinel,* Fort Stoddert, 1811; *Mobile Gazette,* Mobile, 1812; *Halcyon,* St. Stephens, 1815; and *Blakeley Sun* and *Alabama Advertiser,* Blakeley, 1819. Early newspapers from the Tennessee Valley included the *Madison Gazette,* Huntsville, 1812; *Florence Gazette,* Florence, 1820; and *Tuscumbia Advertiser,* Tuscumbia, 1821. Other pre-statehood papers included the *Cahawba Press* and *Alabama Intelligencer,* Cahawba, 1819; *Alabama Courier,* Claiborne, 1819; and *Tuscaloosa Republican,* Tuscaloosa, 1819.

Alabama law requires that all county newspapers that carry legal notices be maintained by that county's probate judge. Few of the county collections are complete.

The Alabama Department of Archives and History has participated in a National Endowment for the Humanities project to preserve old newspapers. A statewide inventory of all repositories was followed by a project to microfilm newspapers of historic significance. A national union list is available for the project, which indexes newspapers by name, place of publication, language, and date of publication. Each entry indicates which issues of the newspaper are extant and the repository which houses those issues. Larger libraries and archives should have the publication *United States Newspaper Project National Union List, Microfilm: June 1987,* 2d ed. (Dublin, Ohio, 1987).

Through the Alabama Newspaper Project, the Alabama Department of Archives and History has microfilmed newspapers from every county in the state. These papers are available for purchase or through interlibrary loan from the department.

Manuscripts

There are several important genealogical manuscript collections that should be considered. The *National Union*

Catalog of Manuscript Collections (see page 8) is the first source to check for major collections in Alabama, although many minor collections will not be cited. The Alabama Department of Archives and History is the official repository for records of all state agencies and for the personal papers of many important public figures. Of significance to the genealogist, one collection housed by the University of Alabama's archives is that of Pauline Jones Gandrud, a professional genealogical researcher for over forty-five years. Gandrud compiled 245 volumes of abstracted records from forty Alabama counties. These have been published under the title *Alabama Records* and are available from Southern Historical Press (1980–). The university also maintains various pre-statehood records for Madison County.

Samford University, in addition to housing the Alabama Baptist Historical Society records, also houses the Albert E. Casey Collection. The Casey materials represent one of the largest accumulations of research materials on Ireland in the country. A bibliography of the materials is available from the Samford University Library for $10. The Bledsoe-Kelly Collection, gathered by Maude McLure Kelly, contains abstracted local and state records as well as church, family, and correspondence files.

Archives, Libraries, and Societies

Alabama Department of Archives and History
624 Washington Street
Montgomery, AL 36130

Military and state census records are housed at this repository in addition to some copies of county materials on microfilm. In the future, the latest statewide microfilming project will add considerably to this collection. For the present, the library provides family histories and papers, the state's most inclusive collection of Alabama newspapers and books, and a card index to the part of their collection that is cataloged.

Alabama Historical Association
P.O. Box 2877
Tuscaloosa, AL 35486

Founded in 1947, the membership is composed of both lay and professional historians.

Birmingham Public Library
2100 Park Place
Birmingham, AL 35203

The Tutwiler Collection located here is the state's most comprehensive genealogical collection. Included are extensive microfilm holdings of U.S. Bureau of Indian Affairs records for Alabama, state and U.S. census records, military service and pension records, and Jefferson county newspapers. The nineteenth-century Alabama county records are being acquired from the Genealogical Society of Utah as they are microfilmed.

University of Alabama Library
Special Collections
P.O. Box 870266
Tuscaloosa, AL 35487-0266

The special collections of the Amelia Gayle Gorgas Library include published and unpublished records documenting the history of the state. Of particular importance is the comprehensive manuscript collection which contains business and personal papers. The map holdings cover the Sanborn insurance maps (see page 4) and copies of many original surveyor's plat maps and field notes.

Mobile Public Library
701 Government Street
Mobile, AL 36602

The genealogical department is the starting place for research in the state's colonial Gulf Coast history. The collection has holdings of Mobile newspapers, scattered original records relating to the Panton, Leslie and Company of Pensacola, and the WPA transcripts of pre-statehood land records.

Samford University Library
800 Lakeshore Drive
Birmingham, AL 35229

The Samford University Institute of Genealogy and Historical Research was begun in 1965. The institute is cosponsored by the Samford University Library and History Department and the National Board for Certification of Genealogists. The training format includes courses in beginning and intermediate research as well as advanced research in southern states. In recent years, the program has expanded to include a course for research in the British Isles held at Samford's London Study Center.

Alabama Genealogical Society
800 Lakeshore Drive
Birmingham, AL 35229

There are numerous other genealogical and historical societies scattered across Alabama. The names and addresses of several active organizations are listed with their periodicals. A few other active groups include these:

Birmingham Historical Society
1 Sloss Quarter
Birmingham, AL 35203

Historic Chattahoochee Commission
P.O. Box 33
Eufaula, AL 36027

Tennessee Valley Historical Society
P.O. Box 149
Sheffield, AL 35660

Tuscaloosa Genealogical Society
1439 49th Avenue
East Tuscaloosa, AL 35404

Special Focus Categories

Immigration

Mobile served as a port of entry and is included in the National Archives microfilm of *Copies of Lists of Passengers arriving at Miscellaneous Ports on the Atlantic and Gulf Coasts and at Ports on the Great Lakes, 1820–1873* (NARA Microfilm Publication M575). An index is available entitled *Index to Passenger Lists of Vessels Arriving at Ports in Alabama, Florida, Georgia, and South Carolina, 1890–1924* (T517).

Black American

Several distinct sources for researching black families in Alabama are available. As previously stated, separate slave censuses were taken in 1850 and 1860 in addition to enumerations of slaves on earlier censuses. The records of the Bureau of Refugees, Freedmen, and Abandoned Lands (see page 10) detail this bureau's work to ease the problems faced by black freedmen after the Civil War. Two microfilmed series are available from the National Archives: *Records of the Assistant Commissioner for the State of Alabama, 1867–70* (M809, 23 reels) and *Records of the Superintendent of Education for the State of Alabama, 1865–70* (M810, 8 reels).

A publication entitled Alabama Center for Higher Education, Collection and Evaluation Materials about Black Americans Program, *Catalogue of the Records of Black Organizations in Alabama* (Birmingham, Ala.: Alabama Center for Higher Education, 1979), should be particularly helpful to researchers seeking access to records of black business, religious, civic, political, social, and educational organizations. Entries for 239 different organizations indicate briefly when the organization was founded, what records are available, and whom to contact for access to the records.

See also the brief discussion of free blacks in Probate Records.

Native American

Census records have already been cited as resources. A sizeable group of materials on native inhabitants who occupied Alabama's land has been microfilmed through the National Archives (see page 11). Topics included are documents relating to the negotiation of ratified and unratified treaties (T494); Cherokee Indian Agency in Tennessee (M208), which concerns Alabama residents; and trading house rolls for the Creek and Choctaw (M4 and T500 respectively).

County Resources

For genealogists doing research in Alabama there is no effective substitute for an on-site search of county courthouse records. County level records have not yet been centralized. A comprehensive statewide microfilming project by the Genealogical Society of Utah is scheduled for completion in 1991. These microfilmed records will be available for purchase from the society. No single county's records have been significantly abstracted or transcribed, making a courthouse visit essential. County records vary widely from county to county in both quality and quantity. Some have been carefully preserved while others have been much abused and neglected. Some records have simply disappeared. Other scattered records are now preserved by the Alabama Department of Archives and History, the University of Alabama Library, and the Samford University Library.

Ten Alabama counties have had significant destruction of records by fire. These "burned" counties and counties that have had less destructive fires are indicated on the chart. However, not all records were lost.

Between 1935 and 1945 the Historical Records Survey conducted a preliminary inventory of fifteen county archives; see Alabama Historical Records Survey, *Inventory of the County Archives of Alabama* (Birmingham, Ala.: Alabama Historical Records Survey, 1838–1942). Each county's volume contains a historical sketch of the county followed by a description and history of each county office as well as an inventory of each office's records. The counties that were surveyed include Clay, Colbert, Conecuh, Cullman, Greene, Hale, Lauderdale, Lowndes, Madison, Marengo, Sumter, Talladega, Wilcox, and Winston. Unfortunately, the inventory has never been updated, revised, or expanded to include counties not originally surveyed. The University of Alabama Library's special collections department also has inventories of the DeKalb and Cherokee county courthouse holdings compiled in 1979.

In the chart that follows, former names of counties are indicated. Court records are at the district court at the county seat, and no survey has been completed for all counties. Land and probate records are in the probate judge's office at the county seat. Until the microfilming project is completed, exact dates for existing records are questionable, and different records will be available at different repositories. Specific, accurate information must be obtained individually from a courthouse visit. Three counties have two county seats.

Drawn by William Dollarhide

Map	County Address	Date Formed Parent County/ies	Birth Marriage Death	Land Probate Court
F4	Autauga Fourth and Court Streets Prattville 36067 **Earlier marriages located in legal files in courthouse storage room.*	1818 Montgomery	— 1832* —	1820 1824 ?
	Baker	1868 (renamed Chilton, 1874)		
K2	Baldwin Courthouse Square Bay Minette 36507	1809 Washington	1884 1810 1884	1809 1811 ?
H7	Barbour/Clayton Division Court Square Clayton 36016 *and* Barbour/Eufaula Division Broad Street Eufaula 36027	1832 Creek cession/Pike	1881 1838 1881	1832 1833 ?
	Benton	1832 (renamed Calhoun, 1858)		
E4	Bibb Centreville 35042	1818 (as Cahawba) Monroe	1900 1820 1900	1818 1830 ?
	Blaine	1868 (renamed Etowah)		
B5	Blount 220 Second Avenue Oneonta 35212	1818 Creek cession	— 1820 —	1818 1829 ?
G6	Bullock P.O. Box 472 Union Springs 36089	1866 Barbour/Macon/Montgomery/Pike	— 1867 —	1867 1867 ?
H4	Butler Commerce Street Greenville 36037 *Record loss, 1853.*	1819 Conecuh/Monroe	1894 1853 1894	1853 1853 ?
	Cahawba	1818 (renamed Bibb, 1820)		
C6	Calhoun P.O. Box 610, 25 W. 11th Anniston 36201 *Record loss, 1861 and 1865.*	1832 (as Benton; renamed, 1858) Creek cession	1919 1834 1919	1832 1891 ?
E7	Chambers Court Square Lafayette 36862	1832 Creek cession	— 1853 —	1833 1833 ?
B7	Cherokee Main Street Centre 35960 *Record loss, 1882.*	1836 Cherokee cession	1899 1882 —	1882 1882 ?
E4	Chilton P.O. Box 557, Second Avenue N. Clanton 35045	1868 (as Baker; renamed, 1874) Autauga/Bibb/Perry/Shelby	1908–19 1870 1908–19	1868 1887 ?
G1	Choctaw 117 S. Mulberry Butler 36904 *Record loss, 1863 and 1871.*	1847 Sumter/Washington	1881–93 1871 1881–93	1873 1873 ?

Map	County Address	Date Formed Parent County/ies	Birth Marriage Death	Land Probate Court
H2	Clarke 117 Court Street Grove Hill 36451	1812 Washington	1908 1814 1908	1812 1813 ?
D6	Clay Courthouse Square Ashland 36251 *Record loss, 1875.*	1866 Randolph/Talladega	1920 1872 1920	1875 1876 1876
C7	Cleburne 406 Vickery Street Heflin 36264	1866 Calhoun/Randolph/Talladega	— — —	1867 1867 ?
J6	Coffee/Elba Division 230 Court Street Elba 36232 *Record loss, 1877.* *and* Coffee/Enterprise Division N. Edward Street Enterprise 36330	1841 Dale	1908 1866 1920 1907 1907 1907	1887 1902 ?
A2	Colbert 201 N. Main Tuscumbia 35674	1867 (reorganized, 1869) Franklin	1881 1867 1881	1867 1867 1867
J4	Conecuh Court Square Evergreen 35401 *Record loss, 1868, 1875, 1885, 1895.*	1818 Monroe	1881 1866 1881	1866 1870 1881
E5	Coosa P.O. Box 218 Rockford 35136 *Record loss, 1900.*	1832 Creek cession	1878 1834 1920	1832 1834 ?
	Cotaco	1818 (renamed Morgan, 1821)		
J5	Covington 1 Court Square Andalusia 36420 *Record loss, 1895.*	1821 Henry	1889 1895 1909	1896 1896 ?
H5	Crenshaw Glenwood Avenue Luverne 36049 **Deeds 1868–72 in the Alabama Archives; record loss, 1898.*	1865 Butler/Coffee/Pike/Covington/Lowndes	— 1882 —	1876* 1886 ?
B4	Cullman 500 Second Avenue S.W. Cullman 35055	1877 Blount/Walker/Winston	1877 1877 1887	1877 1877 ?
H7	Dale P.O. Box 246 Ozark 36360 *Record loss, 1895.*	1824 Covington/Henry/Barbour/Pike	1919 1884 1920	1895 1895 ?
F4	Dallas 105 Lauderdale Street Selma 36701	1818 Montgomery	1922 1818 1922	1818 1821 ?
A6	De Kalb 300 Grand Avenue S. Fort Payne 35967	1836 Cherokee cession	1885 1836 1885	1836 1850 ?

Map	County Address	Date Formed Parent County/ies	Birth Marriage Death	Land Probate Court
F5	Elmore P.O. Box 280 Wetumpka 36092	1866 Autauga/Coosa/Montgomery/ Tallapoosa	1884 1867 1927	1867 1867 ?
J3	Escambia Belleville Avenue Brewton 36426 *Record loss, 1868.*	1868 Baldwin/Conecuh	1909 1879 1909	1868 1868 ?
B6	Etowah 800 Forrest Avenue Gadsden 35901	1868 (as Blaine) Blount/Calhoun/Dekalb/ Marshall/Saint Clair/Cherokee	1894 1867 1898	1867 1867 ?
C2	Fayette 113 Temple Avenue Fayette 35555 *Record loss, 1866 and 1916.*	1824 Marion/Pickens/Tuscaloosa	1884 1866 1899	1824 1851 ?
A2	Franklin 410 Jackson Street Russellville 35653 *Record loss, 1890.*	1818 Cherokee and Chickasaw cession	1916 1916 1890–1930	1818 ? ?
J6	Geneva P.O. Box 430 Geneva 36340 *Record loss, 1898.*	1868 Coffee/Dale/Henry	1937 1898 1937	1868 1898 ?
E2	Greene Main and Prairie Eutaw 35462 *Record loss, 1868.*	1819 Marengo/Tuscaloosa	1912 1823 1909	1821 1820 1867
E2	Hale 1001 Main Street Greensboro 36744	1867 Greene/Marengo/Perry/Tuscaloosa	1881 1867 1881	1867 1867 1865
	Hancock	1850 (renamed Winston, 1858)		
H7	Henry P.O. Box 457 Abbeville 36310	1819 Conecuh	1931 1823 1930	1819 1822 ?
J7	Houston 100 N. Oates Street Dothan 36301	1903 Dale/Geneva/Henry	1908 1903 1908	1903 1903 ?
A6	Jackson Courthouse Square Scottsboro 35768 *Record loss, 1864, 1920.*	1819 Cherokee cession	— 1851 —	1819 1866 ?
C4	Jefferson 716 N. 21st Street Birmingham 35203 *Record loss, 1870. Two county seats after 1916.* *and* 1801 Third Avenue N. Bessemer 35020	1819 Blount	1881 1823* 1881	1819 1819 ?
	Jones	1867 (renamed Sanford, 1868; renamed Lamar, 1877)		

Map	County Address	Date Formed Parent County/ies	Birth Marriage Death	Land Probate Court
C2	Lamar Pond Street Vernon 35592	1867 (as Jones; renamed Sanford, 1868; renamed Lamar, 1877) Fayette/Marion	— 1867 —	1867 1867 ?
A3	Lauderdale P.O. Box 1059 S. Court Street Florence 35630	1818 Cherokee and Chickasaw cession	1880 1820 1890	1818 1818 1858
A3	Lawrence Moulton 35650	1818 Cherokee and Chickasaw cession	— 1818 —	1818 1818 ?
F7	Lee 215 Ninth Street Opelika 36801	1866 Chambers/Macon/Russell/Tallapoosa	1916 1867 1916	1867 1867 ?
A4	Limestone Courthouse Square Athens 35611 *Record loss, 1862.*	1818 Cherokee and Chickasaw cession	1881 1832 1881	1818 1818 ?
G4	Lowndes Hayneville 36040	1830 Butler/Dallas/Montgomery	1881 1830 1881	1830 1830 1830
F6	Macon Commodore Circle Tuskegee 36083	1832 Creek cession	1928 1834 1928	1837 1834 ?
A5	Madison Huntsville 35801	1808 Cherokee and Chickasaw cession	1881 1809 1881	1810 1818 1820
G2	Marengo 101 E. Coats Avenue Linden 36748 *Record loss, 1848, 1965.*	1818 Choctaw cession	1881 1819 1906	1820 1818 1917
B2	Marion Military Street Hamilton 35570 *Record loss, 1887.*	1818 Tuscaloosa	1902 1887 1902	1887 1887 ?
A5	Marshall Box 540, Ringold Street Guntersville	1836 Blount/Jackson/Cherokee cession	— 1836 —	1836 1843 ?
K2	Mobile 109 Government Street Mobile 36602 *Record loss, 1823, 1840, 1872.*	1812 Mississippi Territory	1871 1813 1820	1812 1814 ?
H3	Monroe P.O. Box 8 Monroeville 36460 *Record loss, 1832.*	1815 Creek cession	1881 1833 1908	1833 1833 ?
G5	Montgomery 251 S. Lawrence Street Montgomery 36104	1816 Monroe	1908 1817 1908	1816 1819 ?

Map	County Address	Date Formed Parent County/ies	Birth Marriage Death	Land Probate Court
A4	Morgan 302 Lee Street N.E. Decatur 35601	1818 (as Cotaco; renamed, 1821) Cherokee cession	1983 1821 1893	1818 1818 ?
F3	Perry P.O. Box 478 Marion 36756	1819 Montgomery	1908 1820 1908	1819 1823 ?
D2	Pickens Box 460, 100 Phoenix Avenue Carrollton 35447 *Record loss, 1864 and 1876.*	1820 Tuscaloosa	1903 1876 1903	1876 1876 ?
H6	Pike Church Street Troy 36081 *Record loss, 1830.*	1821 Henry/Montgomery	1881 1833 1881	1830 1830 ?
D7	Randolph Main Street Wedowee 36278 *Record loss, 1896.*	1832 Creek cession	1886 1896 1886	1897 1897 ?
F7	Russell 14th Street Phenix City **Also births, marriages, and death for Seale—1913, 1934, 1913 respectively.*	1832 Creek cession	1934* 1928* 1934*	1832 1837 ?
C5	St. Clair Sixth Avenue Ashville 35953 *and* Cogswell Avenue Pell City 35125 *Births, marriages, and deaths for Pell City—1916, 1903, 1896 respectively.*	1818 Shelby	1893 1819 —	1818 1819 ?
	Sanford	1867 (as Jones; renamed Sanford, 1868; renamed Lamar, 1877)		
D5	Shelby Main Street Columbiana 35051	1818 Montgomery	— — —	1819 1819 ?
F2	Sumter Box 70 Lafayette Street Livingston 35470 *Record loss, 1901.*	1832 Choctaw cession	1888 1833 1881	1825 1828 1876
D5	Talladega Court Square Talladega 35160	1832 Creek cession	1897 1834 1897	1833 1833 1833
E6	Tallapoosa Dadeville 36853	1832 Creek cession	— 1834 —	1832 1838 ?
D3	Tuscaloosa 714 Greensboro Avenue Tuscaloosa 35401	1818 Choctaw cession	1880 1823 1880	1823 1821 ?
C3	Walker 19th Street Jasper 35501 *Record loss, 1865, 1877, 1886, 1932.*	1823–77 Marion/Tuscaloosa	1929 1877 1890	1877 1877 ?

Map	County Address	Date Formed Parent County/ies	Birth Marriage Death	Land Probate Court
J1	Washington P.O. Box 146 Chatom 36518	1800 Mississippi Territory	1908 1826 1908	1786 1820 ?
G3	Wilcox P.O. Box 488 Camden 36726	1819 Monroe/Dallas	1905 1820 1905	1820 1820 ?
B3	Winston Box 147 Double Springs 35553 **Also Haleyville 1920.*	1850 (as Hancock; renamed, 1858) Walker	1889 1891 1912*	1891 1891 1892

ALASKA

Dwight A. Radford

Vitus Bering, a Dane in the service of Russia, made the first European sighting of the Alaskan coast in 1741. It was not until the end of the eighteenth century, however, that the Russians gained control of the area.

The Russian-American Company was chartered in 1799 for twenty years, to monopolize Russian activities in North America. The company did little but develop the fur trading along the coast and among the island chains. Russians explored the Yukon and Kuskokwim region to a limited extent. Although Russian settlements were founded, their populations were small and scattered.

The Crimean War had depleted the Russian treasury, and their American colony's expenses were mounting. It was decided that the sale of Russian America would replenish the treasury and unload an indefensible and unprofitable colony, since the fur industry had collapsed. The Russians knew of the existence of gold in the colony, and they thought that the United States might eventually annex the area just as they did California. Russia preferred that the United States gain control of the region rather than Great Britain, Russia's principal foe. Thus, Alaska would provide a buffer between Russian Siberia and British North America.

Many Americans and Russians did not welcome the American purchase of Alaska from Russia which, in 1867, was bought for $7,200,000. The United States was not totally unaware of the economic potential of Alaska. American trading ships and whalers knew Alaskan waters well, and the Western Union Telegraph Company had made a survey from Canada to the Bering Strait.

The Alaska Gold Rush was not a single strike; rather, it was a combination of strikes. Gold was mined at Stewart River, Forty Mile, Circle, Nome, Valdez, Fairbanks, and Dawson. Gold was found and mined in the neighboring Yukon Territory, Canada, by Americans. The Alaskan Gold Rush of 1897–98 brought some 50,000 persons into the region before it began to subside in 1920. At that time, the population of Alaska dropped from 64,000 to 55,000.

Nome was founded in 1899, and Fairbanks was founded in 1902 by gold miners. Anchorage was founded in 1915 as the headquarters of the Alaska Railroad, and Alaska became a U.S. territory in 1912.

In 1943, 140,000 U.S. military personnel were stationed in Alaska. Many remained after the close of World War II. However, a substantial increase in the settlement of Alaska did not begin until after the war. Alaska became a state on 3 January 1959. Although Alaska is America's largest state geographically, its permanent population was estimated at only 516,324 in February 1984.

A summary of the governmental jurisdictions of Alaska is as follows: Russian American Company (1799–1861); Russian Imperial Administration (1861–67); U.S. War Department (1867–77); U.S. Treasury Department Administration for Customs (1868–77); U.S. Treasury Department Administration (1877–84); U.S. District status (1884–1912); U.S. Territorial status (1912–59); and statehood (1959–present).

Vital Records

Alaska began recording births, deaths, and marriages in 1913. Copies of certificates can be obtained by writing the Department of Health and Social Services, Bureau of Vital Statistics, P.O. Box H-O2G, Juneau, Alaska 99811-0675. The department does not accept personal checks from individuals, thus money orders should be used and made payable to the Bureau of Vital Statistics.

The Bureau of Vital Statistics has assembled an extensive collection of Alaska church records in order to create delayed birth certificates for people who did not have an official record at their birth. The bureau borrows the original church registers, microfilms them, and returns them to the congregation of origin. The Bureau of Vital Statistics will conduct searches of these "delayed" birth records, but requests will be denied if the information is needed for genealogical purposes. For a listing of some of the church records collected and microfilmed by the Bureau of Vital Statistics, see Church Records.

Alaska has divorce records beginning in 1950 that can be obtained from the Bureau of Vital Statistics. Earlier divorce records are at the clerk of superior court in the judicial district where the divorce was granted. This includes Juneau and Ketchikan (First District), Nome (Second District), Anchorage (Third District), and Fairbanks (Fourth District).

Census Records

Federal

Population Schedules.

- Soundex—1900, 1920
- Unindexed—1910

Although Alaska was purchased in 1867, the U.S. government did not record an 1870 census. The U.S. censuses for 1880 and 1890 for accessible villages have not survived.

In the absence of Alaskan counties, the census takers created enumeration areas for 1880 to 1900 and used judicial divisions for 1910. The Act of 1912, which made Alaska a territory, prohibited the creation of counties without the approval of Congress, therefore, no counties were ever created. The 1910 federal census was enumerated in four judicial divisions.

Alaska censuses were enumerated for Sitka in 1870, 1879, 1880, and 1881; the Aleutian Islands (villages of Belkovsky, Nicholayevsk, and Protossoff which is also called Morzovog) in 1878; St. Paul and St. George Islands in 1904, 1905, 1906–07, 1914, and 1917; Cape Smyth, Point Barrow in 1885; and the Pribiloff Islands in 1890–95. Early Alaskan censuses are indexed in several different publications as well as the volume entitled *Alaska Census Records, 1870–1907*, by Ronald Vern Jackson (Bountiful, Utah: Accelerated Indexing Systems, 1976).

Background Sources

Balcom, Mary G. *Ghost Towns of Alaska.* Chicago, Ill.: Adams Press, 1965. A short guide to the ghost towns of Alaska and other sites such as mines, canneries, hatcheries, military forts, and cemeteries.

Frederick, Robert A. "Caches of Alaskana: Library and Archival Sources of Alaskan History." *Alaska Review* 2 (Fall and Winter 1966–67). This excellent reference provides a bibliography of Alaskan newspapers, manuscript collections, maps, and photograph collections not only in Alaska libraries and archives but nationwide.

Gibson, James R. *Imperial Russia In Frontier America: The Changing Geography of Supply of Russian America, 1784–1867.* New York, N.Y.: Oxford University Press, 1976. This volume covers topics such as the Russian occupation of Alaska, overseas transport (from Siberia and Russia), agriculture, and foreign trade. A well written volume with numerous graphs, drawings, and a bibliography at the end of each chapter.

Lada-Mocarski, Valerian. *Bibliography of Books on Alaska Published Before 1868.* New Haven, Conn., and London, England: Yale University Press, 1969. Twenty-five percent of the works listed in this bibliography are written in Russian. Topics listed include the settlement of Alaska, religious books, geographical atlases, and single maps.

Orth, Donald J. *Dictionary of Alaska Place Names.* Washington, D.C.: Government Printing Office, 1971. This book is an alphabetical list of the geographic names that are or have been places and features of Alaska.

Ulibarri, George S. *Documenting Alaskan History: Guide to Federal Archives Relating to Alaska.* Fairbanks, Alaska: University of Alaska Press, 1982. This guide is an aid to locating federal records in the National Archives and Records Administration.

Maps

The United States Geological Survey publishes a catalog of topographical maps that cover the entire state of Alaska (see page 4). Ask for the publications entitled "Alaska Catalog of Topographical and other Published Maps" and "Alaska Index to Topographic and Map Coverage." The catalog lists the over-the-counter dealers of USGS maps in Alaska. Residents of Alaska may order Alaska maps from the Alaska Distribution Section, U.S. Geological Survey, New Federal Building, Box 12, 101 Twelfth Avenue, Fairbanks, Alaska 99701.

Many libraries maintain reference files of the published maps of the U.S. Geological Survey. In Alaska, maps are deposited in the libraries of the Alaska Division of Geological and Geophysical Surveys in Anchorage; Alaska Division of Geological and Geophysical Surveys in College; University of Alaska in Fairbanks; Alaska Department of Fish and Game and Alaska Division of Geological and Geophysical Surveys, both in Juneau; the Alaska Division of Geological and Geophysical Surveys and the public library in

Ketchikan; and Matanuska-Susitna Community College in Palmer.

The National Archives-Alaska Region (see page 9) has a large collection of Alaskan maps indexed in the "Guide to Cartographic Records in the National Archives" (Special List #13). They include railroad maps, federal lands, various historical maps, mining areas, judicial district maps, mineral claims, steamship routes, early Eskimo and Russian settlements, and topographical maps. One map of special interest in conducting native research is an 1875 map showing the distribution of native tribes in Alaska and the adjoining territories. The Massachusetts Historical Society in Boston (see Massachusetts–Archives, Libraries, and Societies) has an unusual collection of Alaska historical maps dating from 1865 to 1888 that should not be overlooked.

Land Records

Public-Domain State

The First Organic Act of 1884 extended the laws of Oregon to Alaska only "so far as [they] may be applicable." Alaska became public domain, and unclaimed land was surveyed by the federal government and sold. Land offices were established at Sitka in 1885, Juneau in 1902, and Nome in 1907.

A person could obtain a title to a tract of public land only after it had been surveyed. After an individual obtained a certificate of title, a patent was issued. These are in patent books in the BLM in Washington, D.C. (see page 5).

Records for the Land offices of Juneau, Nome, and Sitka include cash entries, homestead final certificates, canceled homestead entries, and canceled Indian allotments. The BLM in Washington, D.C., has these records as well as an index to the cash entry files for Alaska.

Patents, tract books, and township plats are on file at the BLM, Anchorage Federal Office Building, 701 C Street, Anchorage, Alaska 99513.

The National Archives-Alaska Region (see page 9) has records of the surveyor general of the territory of Alaska. These records generally include correspondence and applications from settlers for land or mineral surveys (Fairbanks, Copper River, and Seward meridians). Copies of the tract books, township plats, and other records of the GLO (forerunner to the BLM) can be found here.

Land records outside the BLM are available at the Division of Lands, Department of Natural Resources, Anchorage, Alaska 99501. The Alaska State Archives (see Archives, Libraries, and Societies) has descriptions and maps of mining claims. The Alaska Department of Natural Resources, Division of Geological and Geophysical Survey, Fairbanks, Alaska 99701, has a large collection of mining claims. The majority of this collection dates after 1953, although earlier records are also on file.

Land transferred by sale or grant to private ownership could be sold again, inherited, or lost. These records are filed at the office of the district recorder in each judicial district (see District Resources), which is similar to a county recorder in other states. Some land records are also available in the territorial era district court records.

Probate Records

Probate records in Alaska were kept by the district courts prior to statehood in 1959. These records are available at the Alaska State Archives. After 1959, Alaska created the superior court, which has probate jurisdiction (see Court Records).

Court Records

Alaska court records are one of the best sources of genealogical information in the Alaska State Archives. These records relate to ethnic groups, particularly the naturalization records.

From the Alaska purchase in 1867 until 1884, there was no formal government in Alaska. An act of Congress in 1884 provided for a government at Sitka and conferred district status on Alaska. An act of 1912 designated Alaska a U.S. territory. Its capital was established at Juneau.

Prior to 1959 when Alaska became a state, the U.S. District Court of the Territory of Alaska administered its judicial affairs. The U.S. commissioner's courts administered the justices of the peace.

The pre-1959 district courts were district-wide courts and had jurisdiction over civil and criminal affairs. Federal judges were appointed as early as 1884. The whole of Alaska Territory at that time had only one district, which was administered by a judge in Sitka until 1903. Prior to 1884 cases were tried in a district court of either California, Oregon, or Washington. The general laws of Oregon were made applicable to the territory, and appeals were to be taken to the circuit court in Oregon.

In 1903 three judicial divisions were established with judges in Juneau, Saint Michaels, and Eagle City. A fourth district was created in 1909, and the four seats were placed in Juneau, Nome, Valdez, and Fairbanks. The Valdez district seat was moved to Anchorage in 1948. These districts, for all practical purposes, can be compared to counties in other American states.

District 1 (Juneau) covers the southeastern Alexander Archipelago including the cities of Juneau, Ketchikan, Sitka, and Wrangell.

District 2 (Nome) covers the northern portion of Alaska including the cities of Barrow and Nome.

District 3 (Valdez and later Anchorage) covers the southern portion of Alaska including the Aleutian Islands and the cities of Anchorage and Kodiak.

District 4 (Fairbanks) covers the central portion of Alaska including Bethel, Fairbanks, and Toksook Bay.

Since statehood, district court records, which are similar to the circuit and district courts of other states, have been limited to minor civil and criminal matters. The post-1959 district court duties include the issuing of marriage licenses, arrest warrants, misdemeanor cases, and acting as the temporary custodian of a deceased person's property.

The Alaska State Archives has the territorial court records in Record Groups 505–09, which include Record Group (RG) 505, District of Alaska (1884–1900); RG 506, First Judicial District (1900–60); RG 507, Second Judicial District (1900–60); RG 508, Third Judicial District (1900–60); and RG 509, Fourth Judicial District (1900–60). Many of these records are also on file at the National Archives-Alaska Region. An inventory of Alaskan Territorial Court Records is available through the State Archives in the booklet entitled *Record Group Inventory: District and Territorial Court System* (Juneau, Alaska: Alaska State Archives, Department of Administration, 1987).

Alaskan territorial courts were endowed with authorities commonly assumed by county governments and school districts in other portions of the United States. Thus, Alaskan territorial district court records are a valuable tool for studying Alaskan frontier life.

The post-1959 Alaska state court system was extended to include the supreme court, superior court, and the magistrates court. The supreme court is a statewide appellate court that issues injunctions and other writs. The superior court is also a statewide court with jurisdiction over all civil and criminal matters, including probate and juvenile matters, as well as appeals from the magistrate court. Magistrate courts are district-wide courts with jurisdiction over misdemeanors and violations of municipal ordinances. Alaska has one supreme court in Juneau, four superior courts, four district courts, and sixty-two magistrate courts.

Tax Records

The Department of Taxation was an agency of the Territory of Alaska, and the Department of Revenue was an agency of the State of Alaska. When Alaska became a state, the Department of Revenue absorbed many of the functions of the territorial agencies.

The Alaska State Archives has published both the Record Group Inventory as well as Series Inventories and Container Lists, which cover the Department of Revenue records including territorial records. The State Archives also has records created by the following territorial agencies that had revenue or taxation functions:

RG 103 Territorial Department of Taxation, 1949–52 (unarranged).

RG 105 Office of the Territorial Treasurer, 1913–57 (Series Inventories and Container Lists).

RG 106 Territorial Department of Audit, Series 102, Fox Brand Program, 1923–43 (Series Inventory and Container Lists).

RG 321 Territorial Banking Board, 1914–58 (unpublished Series Inventories and Container Lists).

Cemetery Records

There is no major statewide collection or inventory of cemetery records for Alaska. One major cemetery that has been indexed is the Sitka National Cemetery. This cemetery is one of the smallest national cemeteries with over 500 graves of military personnel and their families and dates from 1867. A listing of the burials in the Sitka National Cemetery was published in the *Illinois State Genealogical Society Quarterly* 7 (Spring 1975): 17–19. Additional information on the cemetery can be obtained by writing the Superintendent, Sitka National Cemetery, P.O. Box 152, Sitka, Alaska 99835. Another valuable research tool for the Sitka area is Thayne I. Andersen, *Sitka, Alaska Death and Burial Register to 1986* (Fairbanks, Alaska: the author, 1987).

Church Records

Alaska is home to many different faiths. Because of the lack of early Alaska vital records, church records should not be overlooked as a major record source. Prior to the twentieth century the Russian Orthodox Church was the largest religious organization in Alaska. Other large denominations include the Episcopal, Methodist, Moravian, Presbyterian, Roman Catholic, and the Church of Jesus Christ of Latter-day Saints (Mormons).

Many church registers have been collected by the Alaska Bureau of Vital Statistics and used to compile delayed birth certificates. Some of the registers collected and microfilmed by the Bureau of Vital Statistics are Juneau Catholic church records, Nulato Catholic church records, Anvik Episcopal church records, Fort Yukon Episcopal church records, Quaker records from Douglas and Kotzebue Friends, Lutheran church records, Kake Presbyterian baptismal records, Mekoryuk Mission Convent baptismal records, and the Kodiak baptismal newsletter. For additional details see David A. Hales, "Uncle Joe Went North! Or How to Find Your Illustrious, Illusive Alaskan Ancestors," *Genealogy Digest* (June 1983). Write to the original congregation to obtain a record of birth or baptism.

The Russian Orthodox Church, Diocese of Alaska, gave their record archives to the Library of Congress in 1927. These valuable records were in turn translated from Russian, indexed, and microfilmed. This vast collection of 401 reels of microfilm is inventoried in *Inventory: The Alaskan Russian Church Archives* (Washington, D.C.: Manuscript Division, Library of Congress, 1984).

Microfilm copies of the Russian Orthodox Church Archives are available at the National Archives-Pacific Northwest Region; the University of Alaska, Rasmuson Library, Fairbanks; the Alaska State Library, Juneau; University of Alaska Library in Anchorage (see Archives, Libraries, and Societies); and the FHL.

An index of early Russian Orthodox parish registers is found in John Dorosh, *Index to Baptisms, Marriages and Deaths in the Archives of the Russian Orthodox Greek Catholic Church in Alaska, 1816–1886* (Washington, D.C.: Library of Congress, 1973).

The Roman Catholic Church officially arrived in the Alaska territory in 1902 through efforts of the Sisters of Providence. They were responsible for establishing hospitals in Anchorage, Fairbanks, and Nome. The Sisters of Providence Archives is located at 4800 37th Avenue, S.W., Seattle, Washington 90126. This archives houses the hospital records of Providence Hospital of Anchorage (1938–present), St. Joseph Hospital in Fairbanks (1910–68), and Holy Cross Hospital in Nome (1902–14).

There is no central repository for Alaskan Catholic parish registers, and most are still in the custody of the local parish. There are three dioceses in Alaska: Diocese of Juneau, 416 Fifth Street, Juneau, Alaska 99801; Catholic Diocese of Fairbanks, 1316 Peger Road, Fairbanks, Alaska 99701; and the Archdiocese of Anchorage, 1026 West 4th Avenue, Room 203, Anchorage, Alaska 99501.

Moravian church records have mainly been deposited in Bethel, Alaska. Contact Alaska Moravian Church, P.O. Box 545, Bethel, Alaska 99559. The records for the Moravian church at Aleknagik and Dillingham are at the Dillingham Moravian Church, P.O. Box 203, Dillingham, Alaska 99576. Recent church records are held by the pastor in charge of a district within the church.

Presbyterian ministers arrived in Alaska during the 1870s. Mission work was conducted at Fort Wrangell and Sitka. The Presbyterian church records through 1965 are deposited at the Presbyterian Historical Society, 425 Lombard Street, Philadelphia, Pennsylvania 19147.

The Alaska Friends church is largely Native American. Alaska Quaker records are included in the "Alaska Quaker Documents Collection" on file at the Alaska and Polar Regions Collection at the University of Alaska, Fairbanks. See also:

Roberts, Arthur O. *Tomorrow is Growing Old: Stories of the Quakers in Alaska.* Newberg, Oreg.: Barclay Press, 1978.

Military Records

United States servicemen have been in Alaska since 1867. At that time Alaska was placed under the jurisdiction of the War Department. Most of the resident soldiers were from the lower forty-eight states. For information on the Sitka National Cemetery, see Cemetery Records.

The National Archives-Alaska Region has U.S. Military Post returns for Ft. Davis, Dyea, Ft. Egbert, Ft. Gibbon, Ft. Kodiak, Ft. Liscum, Ft. St. Michael, Sitka, Skagway, Ft. Tongass, Valdez, Ft. Wm. H. Seward, Ft. Wrangell, Circle City, Council City, Dutch Harbor, New Archangel, Camp Rampart, St. Paul Island, and Treadwell. These post returns are part of NARA microfilm M617. Post returns generally show the units that were stationed at a particular post, officers present and absent, record of events, and official communications.

Periodicals, Newspapers, and Manuscript Collections

Periodicals

Several periodicals of historical and genealogical value concerning Alaska have been published. These include the *Alaska Journal,* published quarterly by the Alaska Northwest Publishing Company, which contains many articles on Alaska culture and history; and the semi-annual *Alaska History,* the official journal of the Alaska Historical Society (see Archives, Libraries, and Societies). The society also publishes a quarterly entitled *Alaska History News.* Two reference aids for genealogical research include David A. Hales, "Genealogical Sources in Alaska," *The Sourdough* (newsletter of the Alaska Library Association) (October 1983): 17–23; and India Spartz, "Alaska Historical Library: A List of Genealogical Sources," an unpublished reference aid compiled by the Alaska Historical Library.

Newspapers

Alaska has several publications which are valuable in researching Alaskan newspapers. An index to vital records which have been extracted from various Fairbanks newspapers is *Index of Births, Deaths, Marriages and Divorces in Fairbanks, Alaska Newspapers, 1903–1930* (Anchorage, Alaska: Alaska Historical Commission Studies in History, 1986). The index was compiled by members of the Fairbanks Genealogical Society who utilized the following newspapers: *Fairbanks News; Fairbanks Evening News; Fairbanks Daily News;* and the *Fairbanks Daily News Miner.*

The Alaskan, a newspaper published in Sitka, has been indexed in Robert N. DeArmond, *Subject Index to* The Alaskan, *1885–1907, A Sitka Newspaper* (Juneau, Alaska: Alaska Division of State Libraries, 1974).

An index to the *Anchorage Daily Times* obituaries was compiled from 1915 to 1980, and an index to the newspapers in Petersburg is on file at the Rasmuson Library in Fairbanks.

A valuable source that can be utilized in identifying the existence of Alaskan newspapers is William R. Galbraith, *The Alaskan Newspaper Tree* (Fairbanks, Alaska: Elmer Rasmuson Library, 1975). This research tool is useful for historians studying Alaska. The bibliography lists newspapers concerning Alaska available at the Rasmuson Library, University of Alaska at Fairbanks, as well as elsewhere.

Several newspapers were published by the Alaskan native population, some of which are on file at the Oregon Historical Society in Portland (see Oregon—Archives, Libraries, and Societies). For additional information on these newspapers, see Daniel F. Littlefield, Jr., and James W. Parins, *American Indian and Alaska Native Newspapers and Periodicals, 1826–1924* (Westport, Conn.: Greenwood Press, 1984).

Manuscripts

The microfilm collection of the Russian Orthodox Church Archives provides historical materials as well as the church's parish registers. These Alaska diocesan records are divided into eight basic series (see Church Records). Because of the lack of early Alaska record sources, this is a major collection.

Although the Russians left Alaska in 1867, they had a small consulate in Nome. Their records are filed with the Seattle Russian Consulate (for additional details on these records see Hawaii—Periodicals, Newspapers, and Manuscript Collections).

The Alaska and Polar Regions Department of the Rasmuson Library, University of Alaska, Fairbanks, is a major repository in Alaska. The library attempts to collect at least one copy of everything ever printed on Alaska.

Manuscript collections outside of Alaska include the Governor Brady Collection at Yale University, New Haven, Connecticut. This collection consists of the early records of the unofficial town government of Sitka. The Yale library also has most of the early maps showing the exploration of the Alaskan coast. The Library of Congress (see page 8) has the Russian-American Company Papers (1786–1830), which relate to the exploration and colonization of Alaska (MS 63-410).

Sheldon Jackson was the U.S. General Agent for education in Alaska. His papers, known as the Sheldon Jackson Collection, mainly consist of correspondence and cover the period from 1885 to 1907. This collection provides historical accounts of education in Alaska and its teachers and is deposited at the Presbyterian Historical Society in Philadelphia with microfilm copies at the FHL.

Archives, Libraries, and Societies

Alaska Historical Society
524 West 4th Avenue, Suite 208
Anchorage, AK 99501

Alaska State Archives and Record Management Services
141 Willoughby Avenue
Juneau, AK 99801-1720

Consortium Archives
University of Alaska Anchorage
4101 University Drive
Anchorage, AK 99508

E. E. Rasmuson Library
Rare Books, Archives and Manuscripts
University of Alaska, Fairbanks
Fairbanks, AK 99701

Genealogical Society of Southeastern Alaska
P.O. Box 6313
Ketchikan, AK 99901

Alaska State Library - Historical Library
P.O. Box G
Juneau, AK 99811

University of Alaska, Anchorage
Library System
Archives and Manuscripts Department
3211 Providence Drive
Anchorage, AK 99508

Special Focus Categories

Immigration

Alaska had six major ports of immigration: Anchorage, Juneau, Ketchikan, Kodiak, Nome, and Sitka. No passenger arrival records have currently been located. The 1898 gold rush to the Yukon, along with the impending Yukon-Alaska boundary disputes, prompted the Canadian government to send two divisions of the Mounted Police to the Yukon. These divisions headquartered at Dawson and Whitehorse maintained registrations of persons and boats entering and leaving the Yukon at various ports. Many of those registered came to Alaska. These records are held at the Public Archives of Canada in Ottawa, Ontario, and the Glenbow-Alberta Institute of Archives, Calgary, Alberta.

Many people who came during the Alaska Gold Rush in 1898 were never heard from again. Often families were left behind with no knowledge of a husband's or father's whereabouts. One valuable source for locating missing immigrants to Alaska is the Pioneers' Home. Many of these people lived and died in the various Alaska Pioneers' Homes, the Sitka Home being the oldest institution. Other Homes were located in Anchorage, Fairbanks, Juneau, Ketchikan, Palmer, and Sitka. The Alaska Pioneers' Homes are state agencies and thus transfer permanent records to the state archives. Many of these records are currently on file at the state archives. A listing of the residents as well as the deaths at the Sitka Home up to 1 October 1920 has been published in Joe H. Ashby, "Alaska's Greatest Institution, The Pioneers' Home," *Illinois State Genealogical Society Quarterly* 13 (Winter 1981): 221–24.

One historical migration from the lower forty-eight took place in 1935. This migration, known as the Matanuska colony, was a government sponsored relocation of 200 farming families from Michigan, Minnesota, and Wisconsin to the Matanuska Valley near Anchorage. Orlando W. Miller, *The Frontier In Alaska and the Matanuska Colony* (New Haven, Conn., and London, England: Yale University Press, 1975), provides an excellent account of this colonization experiment. The National Archives-Alaska Region has many documents relating to the Matanuska colony.

Naturalization

Residents of Alaska became U.S. citizens when the area was purchased from Russia in 1867. Naturalization and citizenship records for those arriving after that time were filed in the judicial districts. These are also on file at the Alaska State Archives and the FHL, and they include old territorial records of Fairbanks, Juneau, and Nome that have been transferred to the superior court. The National Archives-Alaska Region has many citizenship records for Alaska. These include declaration of intention (1900–29) and special court orders (1914–32) for Juneau; declaration of intention (1901–17) for Skagway; petition case files (1910–14) for Fairbanks; and petition case files (1910–20) for Iditarod.

Native Alaskan

There are three separate groups of native Alaskans who make up the population. These three tribes are the Athabascan, the Tlingit, and the Haida. The Athabascan tribal area originally covered most of the Alaskan interior, the Tlingit tribe occupied the southeastern and some coastal areas of Alaska, and the Haida tribe was largely confined to the island of Prince of Wales in southeastern Alaska. The major groups of Alaskan Native Americans and their numerous offshoots now number about 22,000 persons.

The native population also consists of those inappropriately called "Eskimos." These groups differ in origin from what could be called the Indians. The Eskimos call themselves Inuit (or Inupiat) and Yupik, which means people, and number about 50,000. About 8,000 Inuits are Aleuts. The Dawes Act (1924) extended United States Citizenship to all Native Americans, including Alaska Natives. The Russian Orthodox church is the predominant religion of the Aleuts, and many other Inuits still practice native religions. A valued collection of Barrow "Eskimo" genealogy is *Genealogical Records of Barrow Eskimo Families,* compiled by Edna MacLean (Barrow, Alaska: Naval Arctic Research Laboratory, 1971), which is on microfiche at the Rasmuson Library (see Archives, Libraries, and Societies) and the FHL. Many Native Alaskan records are available, including the Juneau Area Agency records (1905–64), at the National Archives-Alaska Region and on microfilm at the FHL. These records include such things as student case files, welfare case files, and individual accounts. Juneau Agency School records (1927–52) include school censuses, applications, village histories, age lists of village children, and village censuses.

Another valuable collection that should be examined when conducting Native Alaskan research is the Oregon Province Archives of the Society of Jesus Alaska Mission Collection. This massive collection of records covers twenty-four Jesuit mission stations in Alaska between 1886 and 1955. The mission records typically generated by these Jesuit missions include diaries, censuses, and church records for the native population.

Mission stations included in this massive collection are Akularak, Andreafsky, Bethel District, Chaniliut, Dillingham, Douglas, Eagle, Fairbanks, Holy Cross, Hooper Bay, Juneau, Kashunuk, Ketchikan, King Island and Little Diomede, Kokrines, Kotzebue, Mountain Village, Nome, Nulato, Pilgrim Springs, Pilot Station, St. Michael, Southeast Alaska (Cordova, Seward, Sitka, Skagway, Valdez, and Wrangell), and Tanana.

This collection is on file at the Oregon Province Archives, Crosby Library, Gonzaga University, in Spokane, Washington, with microfilm copies available. For a guide to the microfilm version of these collections, refer to Robert C. Carriker, Jennifer Ann Boharski, Eleanor R. Carriker, and Clifford A. Carroll, *Guide to the Microfilm Edition of the Oregon Province Archives of the Society of Jesus Alaska Mission Collection* (Spokane, Wash.: Gonzaga University, 1980).

A valuable book in the study of native Alaskans is June Helms, *The Indians of the Subarctic: A Critical Bibliography* (Bloomington, Ind.: Indiana University Press, n.d.). This bibliography provides many sources concerning culture, individual tribes, and historical and contemporary issues.

In researching Native Alaskan dispersals, the following major sources should not be overlooked: Indian Agency records of British Columbia, the Yukon, and Washington State; the Chemawa Indian School (see Oregon—Native American Records); and early Catholic parish records of Washington State.

The search for Native dispersals should also stretch as far east as Manitoba, Canada. A Manitoba source that should not be overlooked is D. N. Sprague and R. P. Frye, *The Genealogy of the First Metis Nation: The Development and Dispersal of the Red River Settlement, 1820–1900* (Winnipeg, Manitoba: Pemmican Publications, 1983).

District Resources

Alaska does not have counties; instead there are fourteen divisions called municipalities and boroughs, and another thirteen Alaska Native Claims Settlement Act Corporations (ANCSA). These twenty-seven entities were created after statehood. Many of the original district records are deposited at the State Archives or the National Archives-Alaska Region (see page 9).

Municipalities and Boroughs

Aleutians East Borough
Second Class Borough
P.O. Box 349
Sand Point, AK 99661
Incorporation Date: 1987

Municipality of Anchorage
Unified Home Rule Municipality
P.O. Box 196650
Anchorage, AK 99519-6650
Incorporation Date: 1975

Bristol Bay Borough
Second Class Borough
P.O. Box 189
Naknek, AK 99633
Incorporation Date: 1962

Fairbanks North Star Borough
Second Class Borough
P.O. Box 1267
Fairbanks, AK 99707
Incorporation Date: 1964

Haines Borough
Third Class Borough
P.O. Box 1209
Haines, AK 99827
Incorporation Date: 1968

City and Borough of Juneau
Unified Home Rule Borough
155 S. Seward Street
Juneau, AK 99801
Incorporation Date: 1970

Kenai Peninsula Borough
Second Class Borough
144 N. Binkley Street
Soldotna, AK 99669
Incorporation Date: 1964

Ketchikan Gateway Borough
Second Class Borough
344 Front Street
Ketchikan, AK 99901
Incorporation Date: 1963

Kodiak Island Borough
Second Class Borough
710 Mill Bay Road
Kodiak, AK 99615
Incorporation Date: 1963

Lake and Peninsula Borough
Home Rule Borough
P.O. Box 10041
Dillingham, AK 99576
Incorporation Date: 1989

Matanuska-Susitna Borough
Second Class Borough
P.O. Box 1638
Palmer, AK 99645
Incorporation Date: 1964

North Slope Borough
Home Rule Borough
P.O. Box 69
Barrow, AK 99723
Incorporation Date: 1972

Northwest Arctic Borough
First Class Borough
P.O. Box 1110
Kotzebue, AK 99752
Incorporation Date: 1986

City and Borough of Sitka
Unified Home Rule Municipality
304 Lake Street
Sitka, AK 99835
Incorporation Date: 1971

Alaska Native Claims Settlement Act Corporations

ANCSA Regional Corporations
Ahtna, Inc.
P.O. Box 649
Glennallen, AK 99588

Aleut Corporation
One Aleut Plaza, Suite 300
400 Old Seward Highway
Anchorage, AK 99503

Arctic Slope Regional Corporation
P.O. Box 129
Barrow, AK 99723

Bering Straits Native Corporation
P.O. Box 1008
Nome, AK 99762

Bristol Bay Native Corporation
P.O. Box 100220
Anchorage, AK 99510

Calista Corporation
516 Denall Street
Anchorage, AK 99501

Chugach Alaska Corporation
3000 A Street, Suite 400
Anchorage, AK 99503

Cook Inlet Region, Inc.
P.O. Box 93330
Anchorage, AK 99509

Doyon, Ltd.
201 First Avenue
Fairbanks, AK 99701

Koniag, Inc.
4300 B Street, Suite 407
Anchorage, AK 99503

NANA Corporation
P.O. Box 49
Kotzebue, AK 99752

Sealaska Corporation
One Sealaska Plaza, Suite 400
Juneau, AK 99801

Thirteenth Regional Corporation
First Place Plaza, Suite 200
12503 S.E. Mill Plain Road
Vancouver, WA 98684

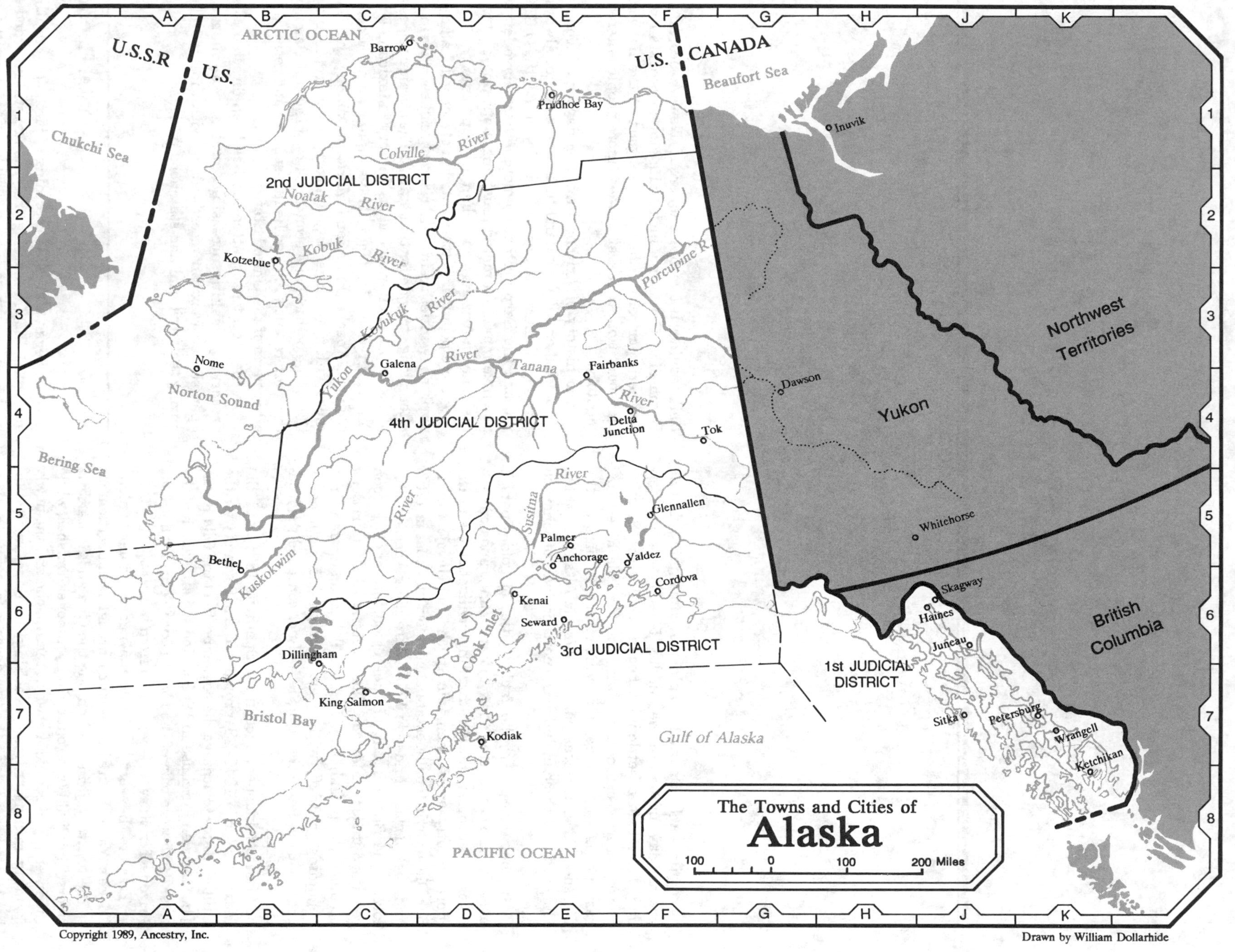
The Towns and Cities of
Alaska
100 0 100 200 Miles
U.S.S.R
U.S.
CANADA
Chukchi Sea
ARCTIC OCEAN
Beaufort Sea
Bering Sea
Norton Sound
Bristol Bay
Gulf of Alaska
PACIFIC OCEAN
Northwest Territories
Yukon
British Columbia
1st JUDICIAL DISTRICT
2nd JUDICIAL DISTRICT
3rd JUDICIAL DISTRICT
4th JUDICIAL DISTRICT
Barrow
Prudhoe Bay
Kotzebue
Nome
Galena
Bethel
Dillingham
King Salmon
Kodiak
Kenai
Seward
Palmer
Anchorage
Valdez
Cordova
Glennallen
Fairbanks
Delta Junction
Tok
Inuvik
Dawson
Whitehorse
Skagway
Haines
Juneau
Sitka
Petersburg
Wrangell
Ketchikan
Colville River
Noatak River
Kobuk River
Koyukuk River
Yukon River
Tanana River
Porcupine R.
Susitna River
Kuskokwim
Cook Inlet
Drawn by William Dollarhide

ARIZONA

Nell Sachse Woodard

While early Spanish explorers came into what is present-day Arizona in the middle 1500s, it was considerably later before settlement began. Under the Spanish crown, an area extending south from the Gila River (corresponding to that portion which became part of the Gadsden Purchase) was part of Primeria Alta (land of the Upper Pima), which included the northern part of Sonora in Mexico.

In their search for the fabled cities of gold, Spanish expeditions encountered the Hopi and Zuni, sandstone villages of centuries-old, cliff-dwelling civilizations, and the more recently arrived nomadic Apache and Navajo. Governor Diego Ortiz Parilla established a fort at Tubac in 1753, and Tucson was founded in 1775. Marauding Apaches later forced the Spanish out of the region, although Tucson remained under a Mexican flag until the 1840s. Garrisons occupied the presidios at Tucson, Tubac, and Santa Cruz beginning in 1826, with their surrounding settlements precarious because the Apache had not conceded the frontier to Mexico.

Mexico's independence from Spain in 1821, and the Mexican War in 1846–48, provided the opportunity for the United States to acquire the region north of the Gila River. The Gadsden Purchase in 1853 added the area south of the river. Both were part of the New Mexico Territory until the Arizona Territory was separated from it in 1863.

Treks to the west for California's gold, primarily along Cooke's Wagon Route in the south, brought some settlement to the territory, principally along the Gila and Santa Cruz rivers. The Civil War produced only minor skirmishes, while the intensity of conflict between the Apache and the newly forming mining, cattle, ranching, and trading establishments heated up in the two decades following the war. Railroad lines between Albuquerque, New Mexico, and San Bernardino, California, included a stop at Flagstaff in the northern part of the territory. As part of the network of transportation from east to west, more people entered the territory.

The history of Arizona's frontier days has been often chronicled on television and in the movies, not always accurately. Tombstone, Cochise and Geronimo, the O.K. Corral, and the Earp brothers, among others, have left their indelible marks on many, providing a striking contrast to life today in Arizona's suburban developments.

A more populous settlement, and statehood, had to wait until the twentieth century. Arizona became a state in 1912, after a long struggle for that status. The ethnic composition of its population reflects its history. Mexican, Native American (Navajo, Hopi, Havasupai, Yuma, Cocopah, Mohave, Apache, Pima, and Maricopa, among them), and those with frontier heritage all comprise a prominent portion of the political and economic life of the state, alongside the more recently arrived health-seekers and retirees from other parts of the United States.

In the recent past, attention has been directed toward preserving, making accessible, and microfilming early Spanish and Mexican records along with those developed during the territorial and statehood periods.

Vital Records

Arizona began statewide recording of births and deaths in July 1909, though marriage records are still recorded only in the county superior court clerk's office where the marriage occurred. The Office of Vital Records, Arizona Department of Health Services, P.O. Box 3887, Phoenix, Arizona 85030-3887, will supply either a short or certified form of birth or death records for a fee. They are not open for public inspection, and the request must be notarized, indicating relationship to the person in the certificate.

Requests for marriage records and any birth or death records that might exist previous to 1909 should be addressed to the clerk of the superior court in the appropriate county seat (see County Resources). The Department of Library, Archives, and Public Records (see Archives, Libraries, and Societies—Arizona State Archives) has territorial records of marriage licenses in their manuscript collection.

Divorces may be found in civil court records in the county, although responsibility for divorce records in Arizona has varied. Originally part of the Territorial Legislature (1863), it moved to the district courts (see Court Records) during the 1870s. The specific court with the responsibility for divorce records within the superior court has changed over time.

Census Records

Federal

Population Schedules.

- Indexed—1860 (Arizona County only), 1870
- Soundex—1880, 1900, 1920
- Unindexed—1910

Mortality Schedules.

- 1870 (Mohave through Yuma counties only), 1880 (index available)

The federal 1860 census contains only that portion of the present state below the Gila River (as Arizona County) that was enumerated as part of the New Mexico Territory. People who resided in Pah-Ute County in 1870 were enumerated as part of Pah-Ute County, Nevada, and possibly part of Washington County, Utah.

Territorial and State

Both the 1864 and 1866 territorial censuses are available as well. Original and duplicates of the 1864 territorial census, in addition to being on microfilm, are housed in the Arizona State Archives, which also holds microfilm copies of the 1882 state census available for Cochise, Gila, Graham, Maricopa, Mohave, Pima Yavapai, and Yuma counties. Also at the archives are the "great registers" of voters, a substitute for state census records. The following counties are represented: Apache, 1884–1910; Cochise, 1882–1910; Coconino, 1894–1910; Gila, 1882–1910; Graham, 1882–1911; Maricopa, 1876–1938; Mohave, 1866–82; Navajo, 1895–1932; Pima 1876–1913; Pinal, 1894–1911; Santa Cruz, 1902–35; Yuma, 1882–1910; and Yavapai, 1882–1906.

Background Sources

Bancroft, Hubert Howe. *History of Arizona and New Mexico 1530–1888.* San Francisco, Calif.: History Publishing Co., 1889.

Beers, Henry Putney. *Spanish and Mexican Records of the American Southwest: A Bibliographical Guide to Archive and Manuscript Sources.* Tucson, Ariz.: University of Arizona Press, 1979.

Faulk, Odie B. *Arizona: A Short History.* Norman, Okla.: University of Oklahoma Press, 1970.

Powell, Lawrence Clark. *Arizona: A Bicentennial History.* New York, N.Y.: W. W. Norton and Co.; and Nashville, Tenn.: American Association for State and Local History, 1976.

Wagoner, Jay J. *Early Arizona: Prehistory to Civil War.* Tucson, Ariz.: University of Arizona Press, 1975.

———. *Arizona Territory, 1863–1912: A Political History.* Tucson, Ariz.: University of Arizona Press, 1970.

Maps

All of the Sanborn maps of Arizona are on microfilm and are not available for interlibrary loan. They can be photocopied for a small fee from the Department of Library, Archives, and Public Records, Research Division. County and city maps in various sizes may be purchased from the Arizona Department of Transportation, Highways Division, 206 S. 17th Avenue, Phoenix, Arizona 85007. First order the general Highway Map Brochure for the latest listings offered.

Map collections are also found at Arizona State University, Tempe, Arizona 85287, and the University of Arizona at Tucson, Arizona 85721. The Arizona Historical Society (see Archives, Libraries, and Societies) lists several thousand maps from the Spanish era to the present.

See also:

Granger, Byrd H. *Will C. Barnes' Arizona Place Names.* Tucson, Ariz.: University of Arizona Press, 1960.

Walker, Henry P. and Don Bufkin. *Historical Atlas of Arizona.* Norman, Okla.: University of Oklahoma Press, 1986.

Land Records

Public-Domain State

On 24 February 1863 Arizona became a territory. From 1850 until that date it was part of New Mexico Territory. In 1866, what was then Pah-Ute County was ceded to Nevada. Until long after its early explorers came in the 1500s, the state had very little settlement, and then only in the area of Tucson.

The wars with Native Americans did not end until 1886 and were a continuing impediment to frontier expansion. For lands granted to the United States in 1848 and for private land claims, write to the National Archives-Southwest Region. In the late 1800s, by the time U.S. authorities authenticated private land claims. Fraudulent claims were relatively frequent. In 1960 these private land registers were transferred to the National Archives-Southwest Region. The Pima County Recorder's Office at Tucson should be researched for Gadsden Purchase land records, which also include mission claims.

Arizona is a public-domain land state, meaning that land could be acquired directly from the federal government. While admitted as a territory in 1863, it was not until 1870 that the U.S. Federal District Land Office was first opened in Prescott. Later, another opened in Phoenix. Many of these early land claims were for mining enterprises. Patents, copies of tract books, and plat maps are at the BLM Arizona State Office, 201 N. Central, Phoenix, Arizona 85004. When searching for early land records in Arizona, one needs to include the U.S. Land Office entries at the National Archives-Southwest Region (see page 8), which has mining and homestead surveys, land claims, grazing service records, and rights-of-way claims and settlements for Gila, Salt River, and Navajo Meridians or the National Archives-Rocky Mountain Region (see page 8), which has state office and district land tract books and registers. The National Archives (see page 8) has land entry case files. When inquiring, indicate the person's name, state of Arizona, and whether it was before 1908. Arizona records prior to 1908 have been alphabetically indexed.

The county recorder for each county has jurisdiction over land records within their respective counties. Before good use can be made of land records in Arizona, the researcher must bear in mind how ownership was originally acquired. Since Arizona entered the jurisdiction of the United States as part of the New Mexico Territory, where pueblos had already been established, most of the previous claims were recognized by the federal government. In examining land records, it will be normal to find Spanish phrases such as "leagues" and "varas," as units of measurement for surveys.

Probate Records

Probate records, generated by the legal aspects surrounding a person's death, adoption, or guardianship, are valuable sources in Arizona for solving numerous problems relating to individuals, families, and family relationships. Probate records are located in the offices of the clerk of the superior court.

If a person died testate, meaning that a proper last will and testament has been prepared, the estate is settled in the county of residence or where property was held. Intestates are filed in the same way. If minor heirs are involved, additional records would be forthcoming, and, depending on the ages of these minors, their names might appear in court records for as long as they remained minors. Note that in the records indicated for probate in the County Resources, two counties list adoptions as well. Counties not indicating such records should also be checked. A search should include a careful examination of all indexes and files involving all of the pertinent court records in order to uncover all of the information in these materials.

Court Records

Arizona's judicial system is similar to that of other states in the southwest. Courts start close to their people and by steps progress to more complicated and further removed cases and jurisdiction. The justice of the peace hears civil and small claims, while municipal courts hear town and city violations. Each county has a clerk of the superior court who maintains the court calendar and records. The superior courts hear both civil and criminal cases of their own, including divorces, as well as appeals from justices of the peace and municipal (or city magistrate or police) courts in their counties. The supreme court functions statewide and hears extraordinary writs and appeals from the court of appeals, which sits at Phoenix and Tucson, and also hears both writs and appeals from the county superior courts.

Tax Records

The Arizona State Archives has county tax, license, and assessment rolls for many counties. Some are for a single year, and others are for consecutive years. For specifics on lists available refer to the archive's printed *Guide*, cited under its listing in Archives, Libraries, and Societies.

Cemetery Records

Three volumes of books published by the Arizona State Genealogical Society on cemeteries in the state are located at the Department of Library, Archives, and Public Records, Research Division. The archives also holds more than three hundred sheets of microfiche alphabetically listing people who lived in the state thirty years or more prior to their death. It is derived from an index to obituaries which appeared mainly in Phoenix newspapers, but covered deaths from all over the state from 1865–1986.

There is also an organized group which is actively preserving some of Phoenix's old cemeteries and making accurate records for posterity. They may be reached at the following address: Pioneers' Cemetery Association, Inc., P.O. Box 63342, Phoenix, Arizona 85082-3342.

Church Records

Spanish efforts to begin missions in Primeria Alta (Arizona) were not successful until well into the 1800s. The Jesuits fell out of favor and were followed by the Franciscans, who fared no better. In 1833 the missions yielded to the Mexican Act of Secularization and succumbed to decay. Only a tiny fraction of vital and historical records are extant. Numerous suggestions for research during the Spanish and Mexican periods are given in chapter 34 of Beers, *Spanish and Mexican Records of the American Southwest* (see Background Sources). For records of modern times, consult either the churches in question or the public library in the location where ancestors were residing. The Arizona Historical Society has a cross-referenced catalog on church records in their card catalog.

Military Records

The Arizona Historical Society (see Archives, Libraries, and Societies) has a good collection of government records, including the records of each of the frontier military posts in Arizona, and quartermaster records relating to supply, construction, and equipment of Arizona military posts. The collection has been microfilmed and cross-referenced in their card catalog. They will consult the catalog and supply copies of their materials for a small fee.

State military records are housed at the Arizona State Adjutant General's Office, 5636 East McDowell Road, Phoenix, Arizona 85008.

There is one reel of microfilm of the Union Army Volunteers of the Civil War. It is listed as M532 in the National Archives catalog. Also there is one reel for Confederate service (M318). The index is M375.

Periodicals, Newspapers, and Manuscript Collections

Periodicals

Arizona Highways and *Journal of Arizona History* are located in numerous libraries around the country. Two genealogical publications are the *Copper State Bulletin*, the current publication of the Arizona State Genealogical Society, and *The Genealogical and Historical Magazine of the Arizona Temple District*, published 1924–49.

Newspapers

The Arizona Historical Society has newspapers on microfilm for Arizona and surrounding states. The Department of Library, Archives, and Public Records, Research Division, has a catalog listing newspapers on microfilm available for interlibrary loan. Loans are for a two week period, and there is no charge for the loan.

A cooperative effort is underway between the Arizona Historical Society and the libraries in Arizona to microfilm holdings of newspapers in various libraries. For the present, the publication by Estelle Lutrell, *Newspapers and Periodicals of Arizona* (Tucson, Ariz.: University of Arizona Press, 1949), serves as a guide to available newspapers. The following newspapers, with place of publication and date of first issue, may be available at the Arizona Historical Society; the University of Arizona at Tucson, Special Collections; or the Department of Library, Archives, and Public Records:

Weekly Arizonan, also called *(Tucson) Arizonian*, Tucson, 1859.

The Arizona Miner, Prescott, 1864.

Citizen, Tucson, 1870.

The Yuma Daily Sun, Yuma, 1872

The Arizona Daily Star, Tucson, 1877.

Arizona Silver Belt, Globe, 1878.

Arizona Business Gazette, Phoenix, 1880.

The Courier, Prescott, 1882.

Florence Reminder & Blade-Tribune, Florence, 1882.

Mohave Daily Miner, Kingman, 1882.

Daily News Tribune, Tempe, 1887.

White Mountain Independent, Show Low, 1888.

The Wickenburg Sun, Wickenburg, 1888.

The Copper Era, Clifton, 1889.

Williams-Grand Canyon News, Williams, 1889.

The Arizona Republic, Phoenix, 1890.

Mesa Tribune, Mesa, 1890.

San Pedro Valley New-Sun, Benson, 1892.

Mail, Winslow, 1894.

Review, Bisbee, 1898.

Manuscripts

The most extensive collection of manuscript materials are at the Arizona State Archives and the Arizona State Historical Society.

In the recent past, much attention has been directed toward preserving, making accessible, and microfilming early Spanish and Mexican records. Manuscript collections of much of the material can be found at both repositories.

Archives, Libraries, and Societies

Arizona State Archives
Department of Library, Archives and Public Records
State Capitol
1700 W. Washington Street
Phoenix, AZ 85007

A *Guide to Public Records in the Arizona State Archives* is available. Researchers are encouraged to call or write before using the archives to make sure the material they want can be made available from off-site storage. The state genealogy librarian, Linda McCleary, has compiled a catalog and supplements called "Cassette Tapes Available at the Department of Library, Archives and Public Records Genealogy Library." These list tapes collected from various conferences held throughout the nation by the National Genealogical Society Conferences from 1985 to the present. The tapes may be ordered through interlibrary loan. The catalogs should be obtained before ordering so that exact titles may be requested.

Arizona Historical Society
949 E. Second Street
Tucson, AZ 85719

The society holds a fine collection of 60,000 books and pamphlets, letters, diaries, maps, and newspapers on microfilm. The holdings date from the earliest Spanish colonial period to the present. Their photographic department boasts 250,000 separate items. Each item is cross-referenced in the card catalog.

Arizona State Genealogical Society
P.O. Box 42075
Tucson, AZ 86733

Special Focus Categories

Native American

Among the native tribes of Arizona are the Hopi, Navajo, Apache, Havasupais, Hualapi, Yavapai, Pima, and Papago. For help in locating Native American history and records, contact the Arizona Archaeological and Historical Society, Arizona State Museum, University of Arizona, Tucson, Arizona 85721; Arizona Commission of Indian Affairs, 1645 W. Jefferson, Suite 201, Phoenix, Arizona 85007, or Inter-Tribal Council of Arizona, 124 W. Thomas Road, Suite 201, Phoenix, Arizona 85013. It should be noted that Native American records can also be located at National Archives-Southwest Region (see page 8). No tribal census records have been located other than those included in the Arizona federal census.

County Resources

Four original counties were created in September 1864: Yavapai being the first of the four, followed by Mohave, Yuma, and Pima. In some cases, cities other than the current county seat served as county seats, although the cities have no record collections. These cities are indicated in parentheses below the county and address. Historically they should be considered for migration reasons. Dates given for land, probate, and court holdings are those reported by the counties themselves. Occasionally there may be earlier records interspersed with later ones. Earlier dates for some of these materials are catalogued by the Arizona State Archives. The county recorder's office at the county seat's address should be contacted for land records. Marriages, divorces, probate, and court records are at the county superior court clerk's office.

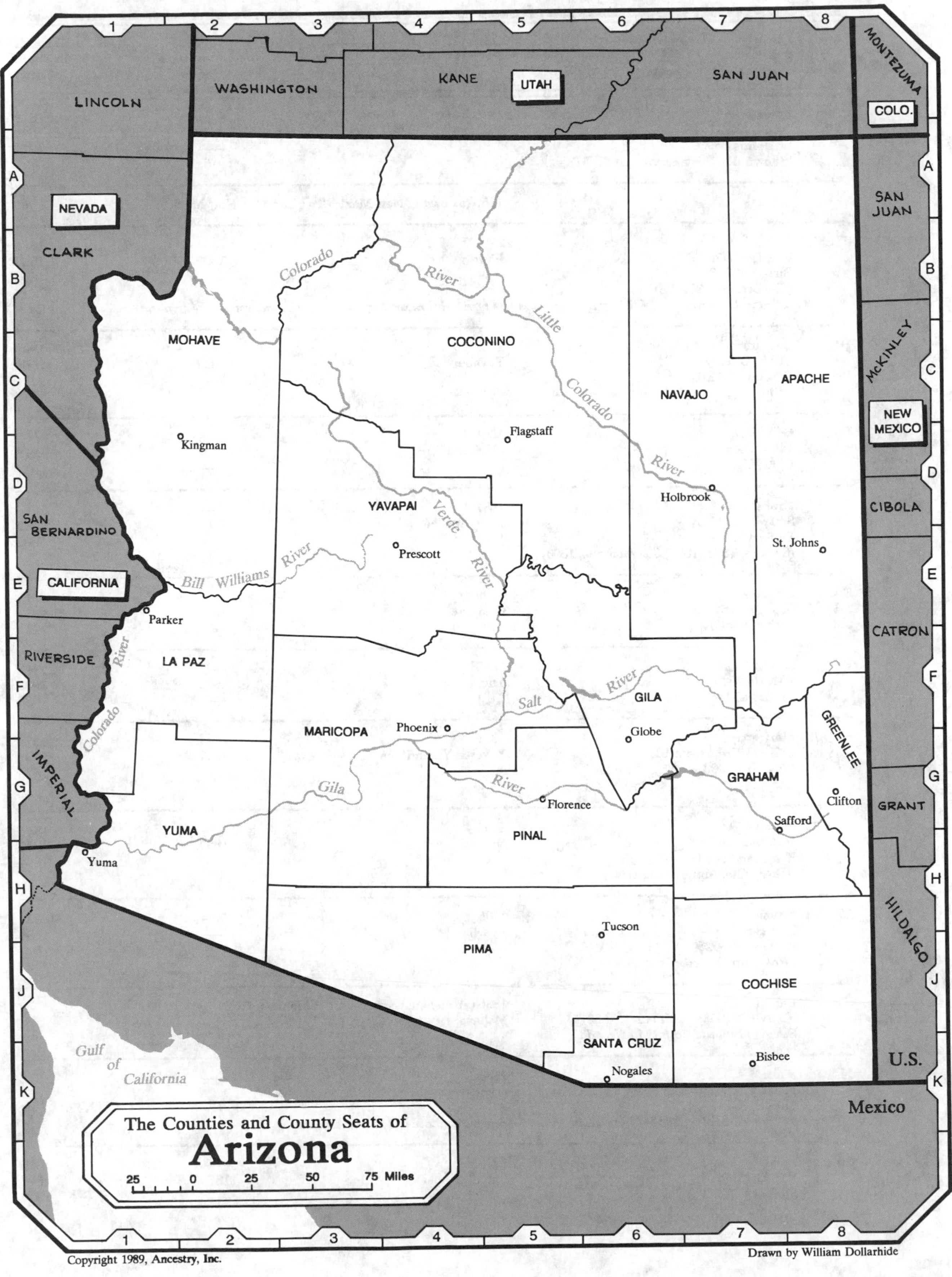

Drawn by William Dollarhide

Map	County Address (former county seats)	Date Formed Parent County/ies	Birth Marriage Death	Land Probate Court
C8	Apache P.O. Box 425 St. Johns 85936 (Snowflake, Springerville, 1880–81)	1879 Yavapai	— 1879 —	1879 1879 1879
	Arizona	1859 (as part of New Mexico Territory; see New Mexico)		
J7	Cochise P.O. Box 184 Bisbee 85603 (Tombstone, 1881–88) *Arizona Department of Library and Archives has territorial records of marriage licenses and some criminal cases.*	1881 Pima	— 1890 —	1881 1890 1890
B4	Coconino 219 E. Cherry Flagstaff 86001 **Adoptions included.*	1891 Yavapai	— 1892 —	1891 1900* 1891
F6	Gila 1400 E. Ash Globe 85501	1881 Maricopa/Pinal	— 1882 —	1881 1912 1912
G7	Graham 800 Main Street Safford 85546 (Safford, 1881–1883; Solomonville, 1883)	1881 Pima/Apache	— 1881 —	1881 1889 1882
G8	Greenlee P.O. Box 1625 Clifton 85533	1909 Graham	— 1911 —	1911 1911 1911
F1	La Paz P.O. Box 940 Parker 85344	1983 Yuma	— 1983 —	1983 1983 1983
F4	Maricopa 111 S. Third, Room 103 Phoenix 85003 **Adoptions.*	1871 Yavapai/Yuma/Pima	— 1877 —	1871 1933* 1878
C2	Mohave P.O. Box 70 Kingman 86401 (Hardyville, Mineral Park)	1864 original	— 1887 —	1864 1871 1874
C7	Navajo P.O. Box 668 Holbrook 86025 **Holds earlier records.*	1895 Apache	— — —	1893* 1895 1895
	Pah-ute (Callville, 1865; St. Thomas, 1866) *See also Pah-ute County in Nevada.*	1865 (abolished; became part of Mohave, 1871) Mohave		
J5	Pima 115 N. Church, Room 101 Tucson 85701 *Territorial capital 1867–77, including all of Gadsden Purchase of 1854 in Arizona.*	1864 original	— ? —	1912 ? ?
G5	Pinal P.O. Box 848 Florence 85232	1875 Pima/Yavapai	— 1875 —	1875 1875 1876

Map	County Address (former county seats)	Date Formed Parent County/ies	Birth Marriage Death	Land Probate Court
K6	Santa Cruz Court Street and Morley Avenue Nogales 85621	1899 Pima	— 1899 —	1899 1899 1912
D3	Yavapai Courthouse Prescott 86301 **Some early birth and marriage records exist in the county recorder's office.*	1864 original	* 1870 *	1864 1865 1870
G1	Yuma 168 S. Second Avenue Yuma 85364 *The town of Yuma was originally called Arizona City.*	1864 original	— 1864? —	1864 1864 1864?

Arkansas

Wendy L. Elliott, C.G., C.G.L.

Geographically located north of Louisiana and flanked on the east by the Mississippi River's west bank, the development of the state of Arkansas spanned three centuries. Long before frontiersmen from the newly formed United States crossed the Blue Ridge Mountains and attempted settlement along the Ohio and Mississippi rivers, Spanish and French explorers came upon the native peoples living in what is now Arkansas. Hernando de Soto's Spanish expedition crossed the Mississippi River to Arkansas in 1541, spending several months in the area.

French explorers traveled through today's Arkansas during the seventeenth century. A small French expedition of two canoes from Canada voyaged down the Mississippi River to Arkansas in 1673, led by Jacques Marquette, a Catholic priest, and Louis Joliet, a fur trader. LaSalle's expedition followed nearly ten years later, claiming the land for France. In 1686, Henri de Tonti founded Arkansas Post, the first settlement in the lower Mississippi River Valley. It served as a trading post, a way-station for Mississippi River travel, and the home of a Jesuit mission for a few years. The French later established several settlements south of the Arkansas Post in 1699, including Natchez and Orleans.

Prior to France's decisive defeat by Britain in the Seven Years War (or French and Indian War), in 1762 France ceded New Orleans and land west of the Mississippi River, which eventually became the Louisiana Purchase, to Spain. The Spanish began governing the area in 1766, but their authority was not firmly established for several years. Arkansas was in an area supervised by a lieutenant governor at St. Louis. Arkansas Post remained the center of administration for this District of Arkansas, a huge, undefined region, including all of present-day Arkansas and Oklahoma.

Settlers from the British colonies, preoccupied with severing their ties from the Crown, had not yet broken through the Blue Ridge mountains to the east. Once independence was won, however, the land formerly held by native Americans became "fair game" for grants to those who had served their new country well in battle.

Land grants to Americans, the majority from Kentucky and Tennessee, began to increase in number by about 1792, with settlers making their homes along the rivers of eastern and southern Arkansas. Early settlements cropped up at Big Prairie, near the mouth of the St. Francis River, and present-day Helena, but inhabitants were few.

Following the Louisiana Purchase in 1803, Arkansas settlements officially came under United States jurisdiction as part of Louisiana Territory. In June 1812, Arkansas became part of Missouri Territory as a result of Louisiana's admittance to the union.

The northern quarter of Arkansas was established as part of the New Madrid District in Louisiana Territory. Directly to the south and running to the Arkansas River, an area shaped like a mirror image of Virginia formed the District of Arkansas. Both districts became counties when Missouri Territory was created. The remaining half of Arkansas, located on the southern side of the Arkansas River, was claimed by native Americans.

The Osage and Quapaw had resided in the area from a much earlier time, while the Cherokee and Choctaw received land grants from the federal government for land in Arkansas, having been forced out of their homelands in the east. Delaware, Shawnee, Caddo, and other native tribes made Arkansas their home. The Quapaw claimed the land south of the Arkansas River for approximately 100 miles and indefinitely to the west. The Osage had claimed a large region north of the Arkansas River, and in 1808 ceded land which became part of the District of Arkansas, then still part of Louisiana Territory. Treaties with the Osage chiefs were made again in 1816, 1818, and 1825, resulting in the loss of their Arkansas land and their removal to today's Oklahoma.

Two million acres, situated between the Arkansas and St. Francis rivers, were offered as bounty land for military service in the War of 1812. Each veteran was given a warrant for 160 acres, allocated by a lottery process.

An 1818 conference between the Osage and Cherokee met with Major William Lovely, Cherokee agent in Missouri Territory, resulting in the Osage ceding lands they had held in the northeastern section of present-day Oklahoma and a northwestern portion of today's Arkansas, at the time still part of Missouri Territory.

Arkansas Territory was organized from Missouri Territory in 1819 with a little over 14,000 inhabitants, exclusive of native peoples. Included was what is now Oklahoma except for the panhandle strip. Arkansas Post was designated as the capital. Lands formerly belonging to the Cherokee nation were organized as Crawford County. Little Rock became the capital in 1821. As the territory continued to develop between 1819 and 1836, more cession agreements between native tribes in Arkansas and the United States government opened the land to further settlement and eventual statehood.

Arkansas became the twenty-fifth state in 1836. Following the Panic of 1837, many people moved into Arkansas from southern and eastern states. Men from Arkansas served in the U.S. Army during the Mexican War, some receiving bounty lands prior to 1855. The Gold Rush in California attracted people from Arkansas, most beginning the trek from Fort Smith.

During the Civil War, Arkansas men served in both the Union and Confederate armies, although the greater majority served for the Confederate cause. In May 1861, after Arkansas seceded from the United States, the Provisional Congress of the Confederate States of America divided Arkansas into eastern and western districts, with governmental seats at Little Rock and Van Buren, respectively. Federal forces occupied Van Buren in late 1862 and took control of Little Rock on 10 September 1863, forcing the state government to relocate to Washington in Hempstead County during the occupation. By late 1863, Confederates were forced into southwestern Arkansas, leaving most of Arkansas under Union control with subsequent raiding and plundering by Union troops.

One of the many campaigns and skirmishes fought on Arkansas soil was at Pea Ridge in Benton County in 1862. Among later ones were those at Fort Smith, Little Rock, and Prairie Grove. Pine Bluff was the site of a victory for Arkansas troops.

During the strife some families moved, and others sent their sons to Texas to avoid the difficulties. Some families from northwestern Arkansas migrated north into Missouri and Illinois to avoid the conflict. After the close of the war, Arkansas tried to attract European immigrants. Some settled on the rich land located between the Arkansas and White rivers. The development of railroads in the last quarter of the nineteenth century encouraged more foreign-born immigration. Immigration continued into the twentieth century, but the population remained predominantly rural, with an economy reliant on cotton, until after World War II. Black Americans, many whose ancestry has been part of Arkansas history from the territorial period, make up about one-fifth of the population.

Vital Records

Statewide registration of births and deaths in Arkansas did not begin until February 1914. Compliance was not complete for approximately three decades. The Division of Vital Records, Arkansas Department of Health, 4815 West Markham Street, Little Rock, Arkansas 72201, has records from that date. Some local vital records for Little Rock and Fort Smith are maintained by the Arkansas History Commission (see Archives, Libraries, and Societies). When requesting copies, include a statement of purpose and relationship. Delayed birth certificates are also available.

Statewide registration of marriage did not begin until 1917, but, once counties were organized, most of them began recording marriages. The Division of Vital Records maintains marriage records only since 1917. Earlier records must be obtained from the respective county clerk where the license was issued, which is frequently the county of the bride's residence. Many early marriage records include names of bride and groom, ages, and residence. Later records contain more information.

Full certified copies of divorce records may be obtained from the circuit or chancery clerk in the respective county in which the divorce was granted. Records of divorces granted beginning in 1923 are also available from the Division of Vital Records.

Census Records

Federal

Population Schedules.

- Indexed—1830, 1840, 1850, 1860, 1870
- Soundex—1880, 1900, 1910 (Miracode), 1920

Industry and Agriculture Schedules.

- 1850, 1860, 1870, 1880

Mortality Schedules.

- 1850, 1860, 1870, 1880

Slave Schedules.

- 1850, 1860

The Arkansas History Commission has an excellent collection of compiled and/or published federal censuses and census indexes for most of the state's counties in addition to microfilm copies of all federal censuses for the state. The original agriculture, industry, and mortality schedules are maintained by the Special Collections Library of the University of Arkansas (see Archives, Libraries, and Societies). Microfilm copies of the agriculture, industry, mortality, and slave schedules are housed at the Arkansas History Commission. Originals of the slave schedules are at the National Archives. Arkansas mortality schedules have been indexed and published for 1850–80 in Bobbi Jones McLane, *Mortality Schedules for Arkansas,* 4 vols. (Hot Springs, Ark.: Arkansas Ancestors, 1968–75).

The Arkansas Genealogical Society (see Archives, Libraries, and Societies) is currently sponsoring a statewide program to reconstruct the missing 1890 federal census with compilations of tax and other local records for that period. Of the seventy-five counties in Arkansas, sixty-six have a completed replacement of the 1890 federal census. Only Grant, Chicot, Drew, Hot Spring, Franklin, Poinsett, Sharp, Woodruff, and a portion of Lee counties remain to be finished. The Arkansas Genealogical Society should be contacted for the current status of the project.

Recent publications as a result of this project include Margaret Hubbard, *Prairie County, Arkansas 1890 Census Reconstruction: A Sesquicentennial Project* (Hot Springs, Ark.: the author, 1987). This compilation includes both northern and southern districts of the county and was compiled from tax assessment records. Additionally, the 1893 tax assessment rolls for the southern district are included in this volume. Some reconstructions of the 1890 census have been published by others, such as Billie W. New's *Bradley County, Arkansas, 1890* (Jacksonville, Ark.: the author, 1988).

A source developed from 1850 federal population census information was originally published in 1958–60 in *Genealogical Newsletter* (Washington, D.C.: Waldenmaier, 1956–60). Inez Waldenmaier, *Arkansas Travelers* (Washington, D.C.: the author, n.d.), contains the names of each man in every Arkansas county in 1850 who was sixty years old or older.

Territorial and State

A collection of French and Spanish records that lists early Europeans in Arkansas between 1686–1804 is Morris S. Arnold and Dorothy Jones Core, comps. and eds., *Arkansas Colonials* (Gillett, Ark.: Grand Prairie Historical Society, 1986).

Federal territorial census records for 1810 included those settlements in the Arkansas District of Hopefield (West Memphis), St. Francis, and settlements along the Arkansas River, but these enumerations were lost. The 1820 federal territorial census included Miller County, which was organized that year by the Arkansas territorial government but actually was partially in Texas under Spanish control. This census was also lost.

Arkansas Territory sheriffs were to enumerate the citizens biennially beginning in 1823. Although these censuses were recorded in 1823, 1825, and 1827, only the 1823 schedule for Arkansas County remains of the three early enumerations. The 1829 sheriff's census includes the name of the head of household, but only fragments remain. Those counties for which complete returns are available are Arkansas, Chicot, Clark, Conway, Crawford, Crittenden, Independence, Lawrence, Miller (old), St. Francis, and Washington. None are available for Pope or Sevier counties, and only the total number of inhabitants were submitted by the sheriffs of Hempstead, Izard, Lafayette, Phillips, and Pulaski counties. The extant 1823 and 1829 records have been published as Ronald Vern Jackson and Gary Ronald Teeples, eds., *Arkansas Sheriff's Censuses: 1823 & 1829* (Salt Lake City, Utah: Accelerated Indexing Systems, n.d.).

Background Sources

Excellent, comprehensive discussions of Arkansas history are available and were used in developing the material in this chapter. John L. Ferguson and J. H. Atkinson, *Historic Arkansas* (Little Rock, Ark.: Arkansas History Commission, 1966), and John Gould Fletcher, *Arkansas* (Chapel Hill, N.C.: University of North Carolina Press, 1947), are two excellent single-volume treatments of all periods of Arkansas history.

Several regionally based volumes of biographical and historical information on Arkansas and its people were published by Goodspeed Publishing Company in the late 1880s. These volumes, reprinted in 1978 by Southern Historical Press, are divided into the following regions: East, West, Northeast, Northwest (which included the Ozark region), and South. The counties of Baxter, Boone, Cleburne, Marion, Newton, Searcy, Stone, and Van Buren in the Ozark region of the state are only briefly covered in the Northwest volume.

Many histories have been published for Arkansas counties. Copies of these are in the Arkansas History Commission, which maintains two alphabetical card files—one biographical and the other on subject/place—abstracted from primary sources and published volumes. These cards note names, dates, places, and sources in various works pertaining to Arkansas and its people.

Among numerous works helpful in developing an understanding of Arkansas are the following:

Carter, Clarence Edwin, comp. and ed. *The Territorial Papers of the United States: The Territory of Arkansas, 1819–1825.* Vol. 19. Washington, D.C.: Government Printing Office, 1953.

———. *The Territorial Papers of the United States: The Territory of Arkansas, 1825–1829.* Vol. 20. Washington, D.C.: Government Printing Office, 1953.

———. *The Territorial Papers of the United States: The Territory of Arkansas, 1829–1836.* Vol. 21. Washington, D.C.: Government Printing Office, 1953.

Dillard, Tom W., and Michael B. Dougan, comps. *Arkansas History: A Selected Research Bibliography.* Little

Rock, Ark.: Rose Publishers, 1979. A valuable list of publications pertaining to the state.

Hallum, John. *Biographical and Pictorial History of Arkansas.* 1887. Reprint. Easley, S.C.: Southern Historical Press, n.d. Early history of the state and its pioneers.

Hempstead, Fay. *Historical Review of Arkansas.* 1911. Reprint. Easley, S.C.: Southern Historical Press, 1977.

Herndon, Dallas Tabor. *Centennial History of Arkansas.* 3 vols. 1922. Reprint. Easley, S.C.: Southern Historical Press, 1977. Vol. 1 is general history; vols. 2 and 3 are biographical sketches.

———. *Annals of Arkansas* .... 4 vols. Hopkinsville, Ark.: Historical Records Association, 1947. A continuation of the above three volumes by Herndon.

Shinn, Josiah Hazen. *Pioneers and Makers of Arkansas.* 1908. Reprint. Baltimore, Md.: Genealogical Publishing Co., 1967. Basic reference for Arkansas researchers.

Thomas, David Yancey, ed. *Arkansas and Its People, A History, 1541–1930.* 4 vols. New York, N.Y.: American Historical Society, 1930. A detailed historical work with biographical information.

Writers' Program, WPA, Arkansas. *Arkansas: A Guide to the State.* New York, N.Y.: n.pub., 1941. Contains historical data and an excellent bibliography.

Maps

The Arkansas State Highway Commission, in cooperation with the U.S. Department of Agriculture, prepared a complete set of Arkansas county maps entitled *General Highway and Transportation Maps of Counties of Arkansas,* (N.p., n.d.). These detailed maps show such landmarks as roads, cemeteries, towns, railroads, watercourses, dwellings, farms, churches, schools, businesses, factory or industrial plants, and sawmills for each county in the state. Copies of this softbound compilation, no longer available for purchase, are available for research at the Arkansas History Commission, which also houses a fine collection of maps pertaining to Arkansas.

Copies of individual county maps and reproductions of old Arkansas maps may be obtained from the Arkansas State Highway and Transportation Department, Map Sales, P.O. Box 2261, Little Rock, Arkansas 72203. A large collection of maps, atlases, and gazetteers for Arkansas and other states is maintained by the University of Arkansas at Fayetteville.

Other helpful map sources include:

Arkansas Encyclopedia. 4 vols. Little Rock, Ark.: Arkansas Industrial Development Commission, 1968. An industrial history and economic atlas.

Baker, Russell Pierce. *From Memdag to Norsk: A Historical Directory of Arkansas Post Offices 1832–1971.* Hot Springs, Ark.: Arkansas Genealogical Society, 1988.

———. *Township Atlas of Arkansas.* Hot Springs, Ark.: Arkansas Genealogical Society, 1985. Data taken from federal census, "Civil Appointment" in the secretary of state's office, and county court records. Includes township location, date of formation and changes in name, and area covered.

Land Records

Public-Domain State

When Missouri Territory, encompassing the present state of Arkansas, was established in 1812, the United States government agreed to acknowledge private land previously granted by Spain and Mexico. Two grants were also awarded to previous French claims.

The largest percentage of Spanish and Mexican grants were located in the present-day counties of Arkansas and Desha. Preemption rights were acknowledged in 1814, and private land claims were heard by land commissions. Spanish control of land was loose, and many officials and landowners failed to comply with regulations, resulting in continuous claim problems, some extending for forty years after statehood. At times, no surveys were conducted for these grants. Frequently forgeries were made of the governor's signature on land grants, resulting in a high percentage of fraudulent claims. Early Spanish land claims and the original tract book are available at the National Archives and the FHL (see *Territorial Papers* references in Background Sources).

A French measurement term used in some Spanish grants is "arpents"; one arpent is a little more than four-fifths of an acre. Most early land grants to heads of household were for parcels of 800 arpents, or approximately sixty-eight acres. An additional parcel of fifty arpents or about forty-two acres was awarded for each child.

Between 1803 and 1836, Native Americans were forced to cede their lands in Arkansas and move west. As the federal government acquired land, it was made available for settlement. Territorial land transactions began in 1803 for the Arkansas District (part of Louisiana Territory until 1812 when the district became part of Missouri Territory) and in 1819, when it became Arkansas Territory. *First Settlers of the Missouri Territory,* 2 vols. (Nacogdoches, Tex.: Ericson Books, 1983), lists early land grants in Arkansas. Originally negotiated by William Lovely as cession land, Lovely Purchase Donation Claims generated from the private sale of land for the present-day area of northwest Arkansas are grouped and microfilmed along with disputed Spanish land claims and the original tract book.

Bounty land for War of 1812 service was distributed by lottery. See Katherine Christensen, *Arkansas Military Bounty Grants (War of 1812)* (Hot Springs, Ark.: Arkansas Ancestors, 1971).

The rectangular survey system (see pages 4–5) of land measurement was incorporated in 1815 with one principal meridian located at the eastern border of present-day Monroe and at the western border of Lee and Phillips counties. The first land office was established in 1818 with the GLO ordering a survey of sixty townships. The first survey was finished in 1819, but no land was actually sold until 1821. Land offices opened at Arkansas Post and Davidsonville in 1820 were soon moved to Little Rock and Batesville, respectively.

In 1832 Congress divided the territory into four land districts. Two additional land offices were then opened at Fayetteville and Washington. Increased demand for land led to additional offices at Helena and Clarksville before 1840, followed by Champagnole before 1850 and Huntsville in the next decade. New land offices appeared by 1870 at Camden, Dardanelle, and Harrison. But, between 1880 and 1900 the only land offices open in all of Arkansas were those located in Camden, Dardanelle, Harrison, and Little Rock. The latter remained open until 1933.

The original case files, claims, applications, and records for initial acquisition of Arkansas' public-domain land are in the National Archives (see page 8). Land patents granted for successful claims are housed at the BLM, Eastern States Land Office (see page 5). Copies of tract books, plat maps, and field notes of land offices are kept at the Arkansas State Land Commissioner's Office, State Capitol, Little Rock, Arkansas 72206. These records are organized by legal description or claim number only, and there is no comprehensive index yet. Microfilm copies of the tract books are in the Arkansas History Commission.

In 1862 Congress passed the Homestead Act; Arkansas was included since it was a federal-land state. Original and entry case files and application papers for homestead land are in the National Archives. The Arkansas History Commission has some homestead records, although not case files, generated by the state.

After the initial acquisition, all subsequent land transfers are recorded at the county seat through the county clerk's office.

Probate Records

Generally, probate court records in Arkansas are generated by the chancery court and maintained by the county clerk. Wills and records created from probate proceedings for both testate and intestate estates are among the most valuable county records. Bound volumes of probate records include the recorded will, appointments of administrators, court orders for the inventory of an estate, the inventory, estate sale records, guardianship appointments and accounts, administrator/executor accounts, list of heirs, and final accounts.

Probate records and/or wills for the period prior to 1920 for most of the counties in Arkansas are available on microfilm through the FHL and the Arkansas History Commission. Volumes of published wills or probate records are available for some Arkansas counties.

Most county clerks also maintain bundles of loose probate records. These packets contain documents, not always in the record books themselves, filed in probate court in connection with estate settlements, guardianships, and insanity cases. Some are arranged in chronological order. Others are organized in semi-alphabetical order regardless of date. Original Pulaski County loose probate packets are at the Arkansas History Commission. In a few cases, other county probate packets have been microfilmed and are available there as well. Desmond Walls Allen, Henryetta Walls Vanaman, and Connie Olds Trent, *Guide to Faulkner County, Arkansas, Loose Probate Packets 1873–1917* (Conway, Ark.: Arkansas Research, 1987), was compiled in an attempt to save information from loose probate packets before the records deteriorate.

Corinne Cox Stevenson and Mrs. Edward Lynn Westbrooke, *Index to Wills and Administrations of Arkansas from the Earliest to 1900* (Jonesboro, Ark.: Vowels Printing Co., 1986), is arranged by county, with alphabetical lists within each county, but not statewide.

Court Records

Courts with countywide jurisdiction are circuit, chancery, county, and justice of peace. Jurisdiction varies from county to county, but generally circuit courts hear criminal, naturalization, and major civil cases. Chancery courts have jurisdiction over equity, divorce, probate, and adoption cases. County courts have jurisdiction over juvenile, tax, and claim cases, as well as county financial matters. Justice of peace courts hear preliminary criminal and minor contract cases. These records are generally available from the time of the county's organization except in those counties where records were destroyed by fire or other causes. Courts of common pleas existed during the territorial period, but no records remain. The county clerk's office maintains records for all courts functioning in the county. Because jurisdiction varies, check each county for its procedures.

The state supreme court has appellate jurisdiction from lower courts, and its records can be valuable for those counties with record losses. This particular group of records was indexed in Joan Thurman Taunton's *Abstracts of Arkansas Reports: January 1837 through January 1861* (Hot Springs, Ark.: Arkansas Genealogical Society, 1988). Jack Damon Ruple, *Genealogists Guide to Arkansas Courthouse Research* (N.p., 1989), is also useful.

Tax Records

Tax records are available at the respective county courthouses and in the Arkansas History Commission. Nearly 600 tax books, original or microfilmed, for Arkansas counties are included in the collection at the Commission. Legislation was enacted in Arkansas which required that copies of early county tax records be sent to the state auditor in Little Rock. Where county records were lost, the state auditor's copies are especially valuable. A complete list of these extant early tax records is included in Russell Pierce Baker, *Guide to Microfilmed County Records at the Arkansas History Commission* (Conway, Ark.: Professional Genealogists of Arkansas, 1989).

Personal property tax records have been published for a few counties. Tax lists, along with other sources, are being used to reconstruct the lost 1890 federal population census (see Census Records).

Cemetery Records

Local county genealogical and historical organizations have copied, cataloged, and published records of local cemeteries. Most of these are in the collection at the Arkansas History Commission; many are in the DAR Library (see page 6). Most of those in the DAR collection have been microfilmed by the FHL.

The Arkansas Family Historian, a publication of the Arkansas Genealogical Society (see Periodicals), publishes transcriptions of gravestones from cemeteries as do many local and regional periodicals. No statewide index to cemetery records exists, but notable publications include the following:

Andreas, Leonardo, comp. *Graveyards in Arkansas.* Salt Lake City, Utah: filmed by the Genealogical Society of Utah, 1974.

Cemetery Records of Arkansas. 8 vols. Salt Lake City, Utah: Genealogical Society of Utah, 1957.

Daughters of the American Revolution, Prudence Hall Chapter. *Index to Sources for Arkansas Cemetery Inscriptions.* North Little Rock, Ark.: Daughters of the American Revolution, ca. 1976. An excellent guide to compiled cemetery records for the state.

Church Records

Some church records for Arkansas churches are available at the Arkansas History Commission. These include published church histories, church records, newspapers, and manuscript collections.

The following are repositories for Arkansas church records:

Baptist. Arkansas Baptist State Convention Collection, Ouachita Baptist University, Riley Library, 410 Ouachita, Arkadelphia, Arkansas 71923.

Episcopal. The Bishop's Office, 509 Scott Street, Little Rock, Arkansas 72201.

Lutheran. Missouri Synod of the Lutheran Church, 3558 South Jefferson Street, St. Louis, Missouri 63103.

Methodist. North Arkansas Conference Depository, Hendrix College, Olin C. Bailey Library, Washington and Front Streets, Conway, Arkansas 72032; and Little Rock Conference Depository, Methodist Headquarters Building, 1723 Broadway, Little Rock, Arkansas 72204

Presbyterian. Arkansas College Library, Batesville, Arkansas 72501.

Roman Catholic. Chancery Office, St. John's Seminary, North Tyler and I Streets, Little Rock, Arkansas 72201.

Other helpful sources include the following:

WPA. *A Directory of Churches and Religious Organizations in the State of Arkansas.* Little Rock, Ark.: Historical Records Survey, 1942.

———. *Guide to Vital Statistics Records in Arkansas.* Vol. 2, Church Archives. Little Rock, Ark.: Historical Records Survey, 1942.

Military Records

The Arkansas History Commission maintains the finest collection of records pertaining to Arkansas military men and service. Included are microfilmed indexes to many of the National Archives compiled service records, such as those for the Revolutionary War, War of 1812, and various Indian Wars. The Commission also has compiled service records for Arkansas men for the Mexican War, Civil War (both Union and Confederate), and Spanish-American War; returns from United States Military Posts, 1800–1916, including reports, rosters, and related papers; Confederate States Army Casualties: Lists and Narrative Reports, 1861–65; Register of Confederate Soldiers, Sailors, and Citizens Who Died in Federal Prisons and Military Hospitals in the North, 1861–65; and Registers of Confederate Prisoners Held in the Military Prison at Little Rock, Arkansas, 1863–65. The commission's pamphlet, "Historical and Genealogical Source Materials," available upon request with a self addressed stamped envelope, describes these holdings.

In addition, the commission has the state's Confederate veteran or widow's pension applications and indexes to Confederate pension records for Arkansas, Oklahoma, Tennessee, and Texas. In 1911 the Public Acts of Arkansas, Number 353, provided that an enumeration of Confederate veterans residing in the state be made by each county's tax assessor. Records are available for forty-four of the counties, but there are no extant records for thirty-one counties. There are 1,751 questionnaires that usually include the following information: full name of veteran; his address; date and place of birth; date, state, and county of enlistment; full name and place of birth of veteran's parents, grandparents; maiden name of wife, with date and place of marriage; names of her parents; and full list of children with spouses. These applications are published in Bobbie Jones McLane and Capitola Glazner's *Arkansas 1911 Census of Confederate Veterans,* 3 vols. (N.p., 1977–81). *An Index to the Three Volumes: Arkansas 1911 Census of Confederate Veterans* (Hot Springs, Ark.: Arkansas Ancestors, 1899), compiled by Bobbie Jones McLane, is an every-name index and is available from the publisher at 222 McMahan Drive, Hot Springs, Arkansas 71913. The Arkansas History Commission has the actual 1911 Confederate veterans census for Arkansas and copies of *Confederate Veteran* magazine for the period 1893 through 1932.

Confederate veteran or widow pension applications, not just those for veterans living in 1911, contain valuable information such as name, rank, unit, length of time of service, veteran's wife's name, widow's birth date, veteran's death date, veteran or widow's residence at time of application, and the amount of the approved pension. Frances Ingmire, *Arkansas Confederate Veterans and Widows Pension Applications* (St. Louis, Mo.: the author, 1985), serves as an alphabetically arranged guide to soldier's and widow's pension applications, listing name, unit, residence, and date of application.

Several indexes to military records have been compiled by Desmond Walls Allen and are available from the publisher, Arkansas Research, P.O. Box 303, Conway, Arkansas 72032-0303. They include *Arkansas' Mexican War Soldiers* (1988); *Index to Arkansas Confederate Soldiers* (3 vols., 1990); *Arkansas' Damned Yankees: An Index to Union Soldiers in Arkansas Regiments* (1987); *Arkansas Union Soldiers Pension Application Index* (1987); and *Arkansas' Spanish American War Soldiers* (1988).

In addition to Christensen's volume on military bounty grants (see Land Records) for the War of 1812, the following are helpful printed sources for military related data:

Payne, Dorothy. *Arkansas Pensioners, 1818–1900: Records of Some Arkansas Residents Who Applied to the Federal Government for Benefits . . . .* Easley, S.C.: Southern Historical Press, 1985.

Pompey, Sherman Lee. *Muster Lists of the Arkansas Confederate Troops . . . .* Independence, Calif.: Historical and Genealogical Publishing Co., 1965. A guide to names of men who served under the Confederate flag.

War of 1812 Pensioners Living in Arkansas During the 1880's: Abstracted from the Executive Documents. Cullman, Ala.: Gregath Co., 1980.

Watkins, Raymond Wesley. *Confederate Burials in Arkansas Cemeteries.* Little Rock, Ark.: n.pub., 1981. Typescript available at the Arkansas History Commission.

Periodicals, Newspapers, and Manuscript Collections

Periodicals

The Arkansas Genealogical Society's publication *Arkansas Family Historian* serves the entire state. *The Arkansas Historical Quarterly,* published for over fifty years by the Arkansas Historical Association, University of Arkansas, Fayetteville, Arkansas 72701, contains relevant background information for both genealogists and historians. Many other county and regional genealogical and/or historical societies publish periodicals which contain valuable records pertaining to the region or locality they serve. Often these publications carry articles concerning records that are not available elsewhere. The Arkansas History Commission maintains copies of most of the state's published periodicals.

Newspapers

Two important early newspapers were the *Arkansas Advocate* and the *Arkansas Gazette.* Abstracts of articles and data from both newspapers have been published. These volumes are available at the Arkansas History Commission. A valuable source is the *Union List of Arkansas Newspapers, 1819–1942: Partial Inventory of Arkansas Newspaper Files Available in Offices of Publishers, Libraries, and Private Collections in Arkansas* which was prepared by the Historical Records Survey, Division of Community Service Programs, WPA (Little Rock, Ark.: Historical Records Survey, 1942). Although current publications are not included, it is an excellent guide to those newspapers published during the territorial period through the beginning of World War I.

The Arkansas History Commission maintains files of approximately 700 Arkansas newspapers published at about 200 different places for the period 1819 to date. It also has an index to the *Arkansas Gazette* for 1819 through 1881 and 1964 through 1983. See also:

Allsopp, Fred W. *History of the Arkansas Press for a Hundred Years and More.* 1922. Reprint. Easley, S.C.: Southern Historical Press, 1978.

Several recent compilations by James Logan Morgan, published by Morgan Books in Newport, Arkansas, cover vital records abstracts from Arkansas newspapers. One example is:

Morgan, James Logan. *Arkansas Newspaper Abstracts: 1819–1845.* Vol 1. *Obituaries and Biographical Notes from Arkansas Newspapers.* Newport, Ark.: Morgan Books, 1981.

Manuscripts

Copies of the DAR (see page 9) collection of vital records, which includes family records, marriages, and Bible records for Arkansas, are available at the Downtown Branch, Central Arkansas Library System, 700 South Louisiana, Little Rock, and on microfilm both at the Arkansas History Commission and through the FHL.

The Arkansas History Commission in Little Rock has a card index to its extensive manuscript collection. A second major source of manuscript material is located at the Special Collections Library, University of Arkansas at Fayetteville.

Archives, Libraries, and Societies

Arkansas History Commission
One Capitol Mall
Little Rock, AR 72201

Indubitably the finest in Arkansas and one of the oldest state agencies, this excellent repository maintains territorial, state, and county records for each county and region. It is the state's official repository for legislative records, acts of Arkansas, senate and house journals, journals of constitutional conventions, various special studies and reports, all from 1819 to date. It is a public research facility that makes an extensive array of material available. Research materials are not limited to those examples described in the various sections of this chapter.

The commission maintains selected copies of records for seventy-five counties from 1797 to 1920, including records of marriage, estates, deeds, county courts, inventories, and some indexes. A valuable guide to the collection is available (see County Resources).

Arkansas Genealogical Society
P.O. Box 908
Hot Springs, AR 71902

Publishes *Arkansas Family Historian.*

Downtown Branch
Central Arkansas Library System
700 South Louisiana
Little Rock, AR 72203

This branch holds an extensive genealogy section.

Orphan Train Heritage Society of America
Route 4, Box 565
Springdale, AR 72764

An organization with a national focus, its publication is *The Orphan Train Heritage Society of America Newsletter.*

Professional Genealogists of Arkansas, Inc.
P.O. Box 1807
Conway, AR 72032

As a statewide society of professionals, it publishes *PGA Newsletter.*

Southwest Arkansas Regional Archives
Old Washington Historic State Park
Washington, AR 71862

A few records for counties in this region are located here.

University of Arkansas
Special Collections Library
Fayetteville, AR 72701

Maps, manuscripts, and census records can be found here.

There are approximately forty county genealogical/historical societies in Arkansas. An excellent guide to these, along with information concerning statewide sources, courthouse addresses, funeral homes, libraries, Chambers of Commerce, and newspapers, is *Genealogists' Arkansas Address Book* (Conway, Ark.: Professional Genealogists of Arkansas, 1989).

Special Focus Categories

Naturalization

Naturalization records for Arkansas are maintained by the federal district courts in Little Rock, Helena, Batesville, Fort Smith, and Texarkana. Naturalization records for 1809 to 1906 were indexed in 1942 by the WPA. Some World War I soldiers from throughout the midwest who were stationed at Camp Pike during the war were naturalized in Pulaski County Circuit Court. See Desmond Walls Allen, *1918 Camp Pike, Arkansas, Index to Soldiers' Naturalizations* (Conway, Ark.: Arkansas Research, 1988).

Native American

The Arkansas History Commission maintains an excellent collection of Native American records. Included in the collection are agency records, correspondence, and census of Creek Indians, 1832; census of Cherokees east of the Mississippi, 1835 and index; Cherokee census, 1890; Old Settler Cherokee census roll, 1895; index to payment roll, Old Settler Cherokees, 1896; compilation of Choctaw Nation records, 1896; Choctaw Nation census index for 1896 and final rolls of citizens and freedmen of the Cherokee, Choctaw, and Chickasaw tribes, and the Creek and Seminole tribes in Indian Territory, 1906; enrollment cards for the Five Civilized Tribes (in Oklahoma), 1896–1914; and the U.S. census Indian Territory, 1900. Other references include:

Baker, Jack D. *Cherokee Emigration Rolls, 1817–1835.* Oklahoma City, Okla.: Baker Publishing, 1977. Transcription of records maintained by the Bureau of Indian Affairs.

Foreman, Grant. *Indian Removal: The Emigration of the Five Civilized Tribes of Indians.* Norman, Okla.: University of Oklahoma Press, 1986. A history of the Trail of Tears.

Black American

A few black slaves were in Arkansas before the Louisiana Purchase; however, after statehood, many black slaves moved into Arkansas with migrating white families coming from Alabama, Mississippi, and Tennessee. Their lives were primarily tied to the delta region in the southeastern part of the state where a plantation economy existed. In addition to copies of the slave enumerations associated with the federal census (see page 3) located at the Arkansas History Commission, Freedmen's Bureau records (see page 10) in the National Archives are a valuable source for research on black families in Arkansas.

County Resources

Arkansas county vital, land, and probate records are held by the county clerk, with some counties having two courthouses. This is indicated by "and" followed by a second address. Either one might have been used for recording purposes. Some county clerks also maintain court records, but most are at the office of the clerk of the circuit court.

Dates given are for the first known records in the category in that county; these dates do not imply that all records are extant from that date. For data concerning county record losses, creation dates, boundary changes, and additional information, see Russell Pierce Baker, *Guide to the Microfilmed County Records at the Arkansas History Commission* (Conway, Ark.: Professional Genealogists of Arkansas, 1989), and James Logan Morgan, *A Survey of the County Records of Arkansas* (Newport, Ark.: Arkansas Records Association, 1972). Both were used in compiling the chart which follows.

Although 1914 was the date of initial registration of births and deaths, compliance was extremely limited; therefore, only a small percentage of actual births and deaths were recorded during the first decades after the law was enacted. For that reason, beginning dates of births and deaths are not given in the chart.

Parent counties are those defined here as those in session laws. Later boundary changes between counties also occurred, but these are not included. See the Baker and Morgan sources cited above for this information.

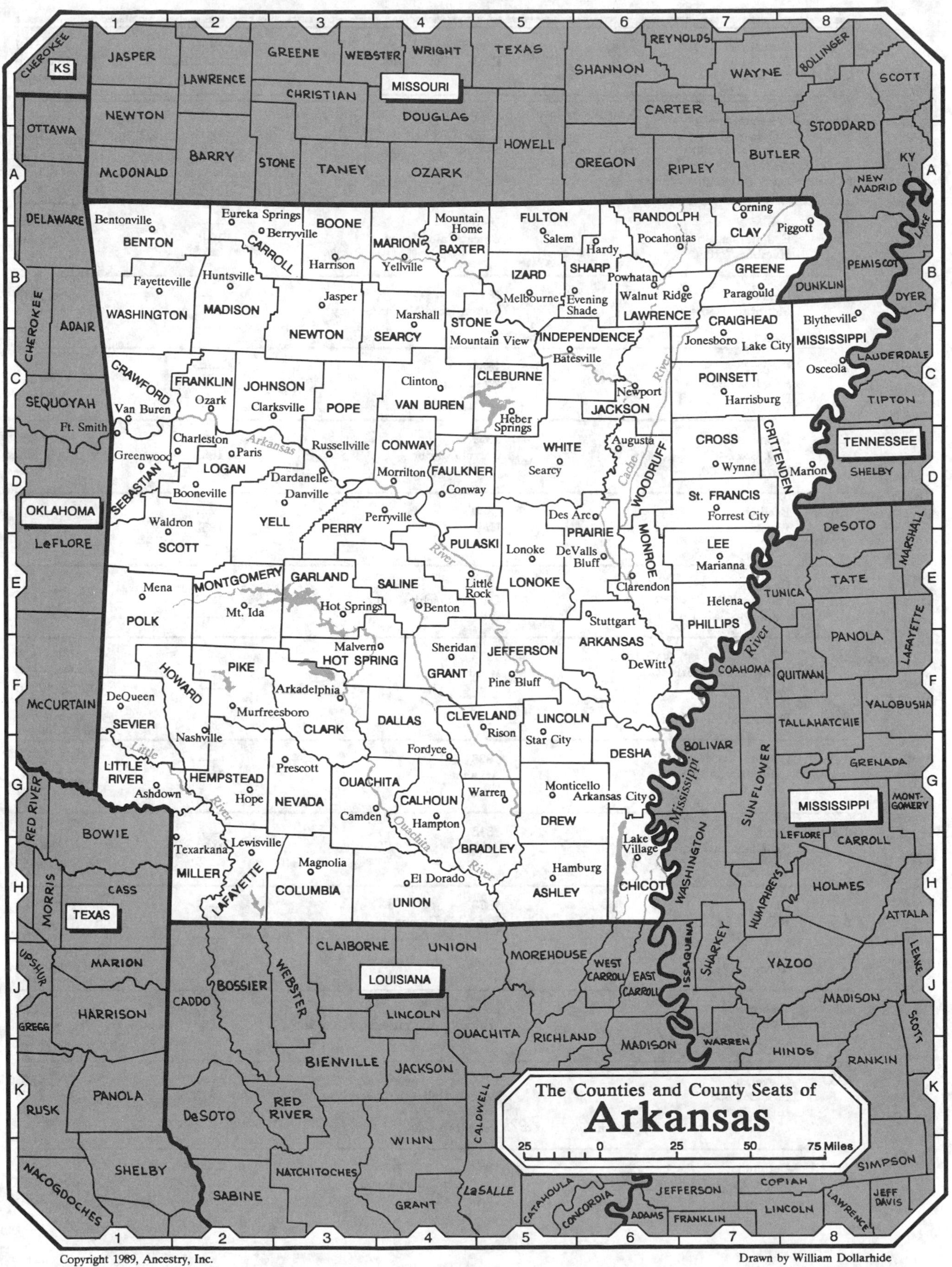

Drawn by William Dollarhide

Map	County Address	Date Formed Parent County/ies	Birth Marriage Death	Land Probate Court
F6	Arkansas P.O. Box 719 Stuttgart 72160 *and* De Witt 72042	1813 original	— 1839 —	1808 1819 1819
H5	Ashley E. Jefferson Street Hamburg 71646	1848 Chicot/Union/Drew	— 1848 —	1849 1849 1849
B4	Baxter Mountain Home 72653	1873 Fulton/Izard/Marion/Searcy	— 1873 —	1876 1874 1874
B1	Benton P.O. Box 699 Bentonville 72712	1836 Washington	— 1861 —	1837 1866 1837
B3	Boone P.O. Box 846 Harrison 72602	1869 Carroll/Marion	— 1869 —	1869 1869 1869
G5	Bradley Warren 71671	1840 Union	— 1853 —	1841 1841 1841
G4	Calhoun P.O. Box 626 Hampton 71744	1850 Dallas/Ouachita/Union	— 1851 —	1851 1851 1851
B2	Carroll 210 W. Church Street Berryville 72616 *and* Eureka Springs 72632	1833 Izard	— 1870 —	1870 1870 1870
H6	Chicot Lake Village 71653	1823 Arkansas	— 1840	1823 1839 1824
F3	Clark Arkadelphia 71923	1818 Arkansas	— 1821 —	1819 1840 1838
B7	Clay P.O. Box 306 Piggott 72454 *and* Corning 72422	1873 Randolph/Greene	— 1881 —	1881 1881 1881
C5	Cleburne Courthouse Square Heber Springs 72543	1883 White/Van Buren/Independence	— 1883 —	1883 1883 1883
G5	Cleveland P.O. Box 368 Rison 71665 *Created as Dorsey County; name changed to Cleveland in 1888.*	1873 (as Dorsey; renamed, 1885) Bradley/Dallas/Jefferson/Lincoln	— 1873 —	1836 1873 1873
H3	Columbia Magnolia 71753	1852 Layfayette/Hempstead/ Ouachita/Union	— 1853 —	1853 1853 1853

Map	County Address	Date Formed Parent County/ies	Birth Marriage Death	Land Probate Court
D4	Conway Morrilton 72110	1825 Pulaski	— 1851 —	1825 1837 1842
C7	Craighead Jonesboro 72956 *and* Lake City 72437	1859 Mississippi/Greene/Poinsett	— 1878 —	1878 1878 1878
C1	Crawford Van Buren 72956	1820 Pulaski	— 1877 —	1851 1877 1877
D8	Crittenden Marion 72364	1825 Phillips	— 1837 —	1826 1839 1826
D7	Cross 705 E. Union Street Wynne 72396	1862 Crittenden/Poinsett/ St. Francis	1863 1863 —	1863 1865 1865
F4	Dallas Fordyce 71742	1845 Clark/Bradley	— 1845 —	1843 1845 1845
G6	Desha P.O. Box 188 Arkansas City 71630	1838 Arkansas	— 1852 —	1839 1852 1840
	Dorsey	1873 (renamed Cleveland, 1885)		
G5	Drew 210 S. Main Monticello 71655	1846 Arkansas/Bradley	— 1847 —	1847 1847 1847
D4	Faulkner Conway 72032	1873 Pulaski/Conway	— 1873 —	1873 1873 1873
C2	Franklin Ozark 72949 *and* Charleston 72933	1837 Crawford	— 1850 —	1837 1840 1852
B5	Fulton P.O. Box 278 Salem 72576	1842 Izard	— 1887 —	1870 1870 1870
E3	Garland 501 Ouachita Avenue Hot Springs 71901	1873 Montgomery/Hot Spring/Saline	— 1874 —	1873 1877 1874
F4	Grant P.O. Box 364 Sheridan 72150	1869 Jefferson/Hot Spring/Saline	— 1877 —	1877 1877 1877
B7	Greene P.O. Box 364 Paragould 72451	1833 Lawrence	— 1876 —	1858 1876 1871
G2	Hempstead Hope 71801	1818 Arkansas	— 1820 —	1816 1826 1819

Map	County Address	Date Formed Parent County/ies	Birth Marriage Death	Land Probate Court
F3	Hot Spring Third and Locust Malvern 72104	1829 Clark	— 1825 —	1831 1839 1843
F2	Howard 421 N. Main Street Nashville 71852	1873 Pike/Hempstead/Polk/Sevier	— 1873 —	1873 1873 1873
C6	Independence 1982 E. Main Street Batesville 72501	1820 Arkansas/Lawrence	— 1826 —	1820 1839 1821
B5	Izard Melbourne 72556	1825 Independence/Fulton	— 1889 —	1889 1889 1889
C6	Jackson P.O. Box 641 Newport 72112	1829 Independence	— 1846 —	1831 1845 1830
F5	Jefferson P.O. Box 6317 Pine Bluff 71611	1829 Arkansas/Pulaski	— 1830 —	1830 1829 1837
C3	Johnson P.O. Box 278 Clarksville 72830	1833 Pope	— 1855 —	1836 1844 1841
H2	Lafayette P.O. Box 754 Lewisville 71845	1827 Hempstead	— 1828 —	1828 1828 1828
B6	Lawrence P.O. Box 553 Walnut Ridge 72476	1815 New Madrid, Mo.	— 1821 —	1815 1817 1816
E7	Lee 15 E. Chestnut Marianna 72360	1873 Phillips/Monroe/ Crittenden/Saint Francis	— 1873 —	1873 1873 1873
F5	Lincoln Star City 71667	1871 Arkansas/Bradley/ Desha/Drew/Jefferson	— 1871 —	1871 1871 1871
G1	Little River Ashdown 71822	1867 Hempstead/Sevier	— 1880 —	1867 1869 1868
D2	Logan Booneville 72927 *and* Paris 72855 *Created as Sarber County in 1871; name changed to Logan in 1875.*	1875 Franklin/Scott/ Yell/Johnson	— 1877 —	1878 1873 1877
E5	Lonoke Lonoke 72086	1873 Pulaski/Prairie	— 1873 —	1873 1873 1873
	Lovely	1827 (abolished, 1828) Crawford/Lovely Purchase		
B2	Madison P.O. Box 37 Huntsville 72740	1836 Washington/Carroll	— 1896 —	1843 1860 1866

Map	County Address	Date Formed Parent County/ies	Birth Marriage Death	Land Probate Court
B4	Marion Yellville 72687	1835 Izard	— 1876 —	1859 1886
	Miller (old)	1820 (abolished, 1838; see also Texas) Hempstead		
	In 1828 a boundary change left old Miller County entirely in Texas. In 1838, it was abolished to create Red River County, Texas. Extant records at Arkansas History Commission include probate (1830-38); circuit court (1830-35); and tax records (1832,1837).			
H2	Miller (present) 4 Laurel Street Texarkana 75502	1874 Lafayette	— 1875 —	1874 1874 1874
C8	Mississippi Blytheville 72315 *and* Osceola 72370	1833 Crittenden	— 1867 —	1844 1865 1865
E6	Monroe 123 Madison Street Clarendon 72029	1829 Phillips/Arkansas	— 1850 —	1829 1829 1830
E2	Montgomery Mount Ida 71957	1842 Hot Spring	— 1845 —	1845 1845 1845
G3	Nevada Prescott 71857	1871 Hempstead/Columbia/Ouachita	— 1871 —	1871 1871 1871
	New Madrid	(now in Missouri)		
B3	Newton P.O. Box 435 Jasper 72641	1842 Carroll	— 1867 —	1866 1866 1866
G3	Ouachita Camden 71701	1842 Union	— 1878 —	1869 1876 1875
D4	Perry P.O. Box 358 Perryville 72126	1840 Conway	— 1881 —	1882 1882 1874
E7	Phillips Helena 72342	1820 Arkansas	— 1831 —	1820 1821 1820
F2	Pike Murfreesboro 71958	1833 Clark/Hempstead	— 1895 —	1895 1895
C7	Poinsett Harrisburg 72432	1838 Greene/St. Francis	— 1873 —	1873 1873 1871
E1	Polk 507 Church Street Mena 71953	1844 Sevier	— 1881 —	1881 1876 1876
C3	Pope Russellville 72801	1829 Crawford	— 1830 —	1828 1844 1836

Map	County Address	Date Formed Parent County/ies	Birth Marriage Death	Land Probate Court
E6	Prairie P.O. Box 278 Des Arc 72040 *and* De Vallf Bluff 72041	1846 Pulaski	— 1854 —	1851 1852 1854
E4	Pulaski 405 W. Markham Little Rock 72201	1818 Arkansas	— 1839 —	1819 1847 1839
B6	Randolph 201 Marr Street Pocahontas 72455	1835 Lawrence	— 1837 —	1837 1836 1836
D7	St. Francis 313 S. Izard Street Forrest City 72335	1827 Phillips	— 1875 —	1860 1865 1872
E4	Saline Benton 72015	1835 Pulaski	— 1836 —	1836 1836 1836
	Sarber	(see Logan)		
E1	Scott Waldron 72958	1833 Crawford/Pope	— 1882 —	1882 1882 1882
B4	Searcy Marshall 72650	1838 Marion	— 1880 —	1848 1859 1867
D1	Sebastian Fort Smith 72901 *and* Greenwood 72936	1851 Scott/Polk/Crawford	— 1865 —	1861 1851 *1851*
F1	Sevier De Queen 71832	1828 Hempstead/Miller (old)	— 1839 —	1830 1839 1830
B6	Sharp Ash Flat 72513	1868 Lawrence	— 1880 —	1880 1880 1871
C5	Stone P.O. Box 437 Mountain View 72560	1873 Izard/Independence/ Searcy/Van Buren	— 1873 —	1873 1873 1873
H4	Union El Dorado 71730	1829 Hempstead/Clark	— 1847 —	1830 1839 1830
C4	Van Buren P.O. Box 80 Clinton 72031	1833 Independence/Conway/Izard	— 1865 —	1855 1859 1859
B1	Washington 2 N. College Street Fayetteville 72701	1828 Crawford/Lovely	— 1845 —	1834 1833 1835
	Whashita	(alternate spelling of Ouachita)		

Map	County Address	Date Formed Parent County/ies	Birth Marriage Death	Land Probate Court
D5	White 300 N. Spruce Searcy 72143	1835 Pulaski/Jackson/Independence	— 1836 —	1837 1848 1836
D6	Woodruff 500 N. Third Augusta 72006	1862 Jackson/St. Francis	— 1864 —	1851 1865 1865
D3	Yell Danville 72833 *and* Dardanelle 72834	1840 Pope/Scott	— 1841 —	1849 1858 1865

CALIFORNIA

Thelma Berkey Walsmith and Nell Sachse Woodard

In 1769 a small group of military men and missionaries, sent by the Spanish crown, arrived at what was to become San Diego. Alta (Upper) California, as it was known during the Spanish and Mexican eras, had been inhabited at that time by various indigenous tribes. It was Spain's goal to conquer the natives and settle the area. They built missions a day's journey apart on El Camino Real (the King's Highway) in fertile valleys beside permanent streams. Inhabitants raised crops and livestock. Several missions were destroyed when a severe earthquake struck in 1812. However, construction continued until the Mexican government secularized the mission holdings in 1833 and the land passed into private ownership. Citizens of Spain and Mexico occupied the coastal area between San Diego and San Francisco Bay.

The first considerable gold discovery in California was made thirty-five miles north of Los Angeles in 1842 by a Mexican rancher named Francisco Lopez. This was followed by a larger discovery at Sutter's Mill in Coloma in 1848. California is not only known for its yellow ore. California's reputation as the "Golden State" came from the early sea otter and cattle-hide trade, the black gold of oil, the fruit growing industry in southern California, and the large development of agriculture statewide beginning in the nineteenth century.

In 1800 the Russian American Fur Company of Alaska loaned twenty Aleut natives to a New England ship captain to engage in the illegal but highly successful hunting of sea otters off the California coast. The Russians followed and built Fort Ross about eighty miles north of San Francisco Bay. Some of their descendants are living in the area today.

On 31 July 1846, over 200 Mormons from New York landed in San Francisco after sailing around Cape Horn. These Mormons decided to stay on the Coast and worked in lumber camps on the Marin Peninsula across the Golden Gate from San Francisco.

Following the discovery of gold and the Mexican War in 1848, the United States acquired all of the southwestern Mexican possessions. A large number of immigrants, including a substantial influx of Italians, began arriving in California after the declaration of statehood on 9 September 1850. The acquisition of the southwestern lands resulted in many land claims, and much litigation was required both in the courts and in the regulatory agencies before these cases were adjudicated. Not until March 1851 did Congress send land commissioners west to review all grant titles.

The Central Railroad (later Southern Pacific), after its completion in May 1869, brought thousands of new migrants and goods westward. Numerous towns grew up along the transcontinental route. Thousands of Chinese migrated to California, providing cheap labor in the mines as well as on the railroads. Mormons migrating to the West added more to the population.

The most severe earthquake in California's recorded history occurred on 18 April 1906. The city of San Francisco was almost totally destroyed by the quake, and the subsequent fire caused the loss of much of the city as well as many important records.

The depression of the 1920s and drought of the 1930s were followed, with the advent of World War II, by an ever-growing demand for labor and military and naval personnel. Since 1945 the growth of the state has been phenomenal. The census bureau counted more than twenty-three million residents in 1980, increasing about three million since the 1970 enumeration. While early settlers may have been drawn to California for fishing, hunting otters, raising livestock, searching for gold, and engaging in grain agriculture, in this century many have been attracted to the "Golden State" because of the rapidly expanding markets for cotton, fruit, nuts, and vegetables, and the entertainment, aerospace and technological (computer) industries.

Vital Records

Vital records in California have been kept by the state registrar of vital statistics since 1 July 1905. Earlier vital records are entered in the county where the event took place. Pre-1905 records in the counties may be quite slim. In Sacramento County, for example, only three births were entered for the period 1858–74, and only forty-three deaths for 1858–64. Marriages, on the other hand, seem to have been recorded more regularly. Some court-ordered delayed birth certificates have been registered by the state registrar. For all vital records, write to the Office of the State Registrar of Vital Statistics, Department of Health Services, 304 "S" Street, Sacramento, California 94814. There is no statewide index that includes the pre-1905 records held by counties. Service is only by mail. In-person access is no longer available.

The California Room at the California State Library in Sacramento (see Archives, Libraries, and Societies) has a hardbound index to deaths 1905–39 and marriages 1949–59. Photocopying of this index is not permitted and only on-site examination is allowed. Also at the California State Library, and in other libraries as well, are microfiche indexes to deaths 1940–88 and marriages 1960–85. Microfiche indexes can be purchased from the Department of Health Services. Unlike the book indexes of deaths for 1905–39, the fiche indexes do not include the age at death, but they do show the decedent's Social Security number.

There is also an index to births 1956–88 at the Vital Statistics Office, which can be examined by appointment. It shows the name of the person, the date and county of birth, and the mother's maiden name.

Divorce records are available in the office of the clerk of the superior court in the county in which the proceedings were conducted.

Throughout the mission system of the Catholic church, many vital records were entered in parish church books and are available either from the Catholic church archives, libraries, or museums (see Church Records).

Census Records

Federal

Population Schedules.

- Indexed—1850, 1860, 1870
- Soundex—1880, 1900, 1910 (Miracode), 1920

Industry and Agriculture Schedules.

- 1850, 1860, 1870, 1880

Mortality Schedules.

- 1850, 1860, 1870, 1880

The California State Library is a repository for the microfilm of the original censuses. The California State Archives (see Archives, Libraries, and Societies) holds the original state copies for the federal 1860 and 1880 population schedules. In addition to the AISI index for 1850, Alan P. Bowman's *Index to the 1850 Census of the State of California* (Baltimore, Md.: Genealogical Publishing Co., 1972) has no statewide index but is arranged by county and then each name is presented alphabetically, with age and place of birth.

Missing from the 1850 federal census are the population schedules for Contra Costa, San Francisco, and Santa Clara counties, making the 1852 state census (see below) even more useful.

Mission and State

There were censuses taken for the following missions: San Carlos (1796), San Luis Obispo (1797, 1798), San Antonio (1798), and Soledad (1798). They are all in original form at the California State Archives. They have been reprinted in *Historical Society of Southern California Quarterly*, volumes 41–43.

The California Constitution of 1849 provided for a census of the state population in the years 1852 and 1855 and each succeeding ten years thereafter. The census of 1852, similar to the 1850 federal census, but using an additional column showing the prior residence of each person, was the only one actually taken. The original returns for 1852 are in the California State Archives. The California State Library, which will answer requests by mail, has a typed copy that is available for public use. There is an index available. Microfilms of the DAR transcriptions of the 1852 census are available in many libraries including the FHL. The constitution was altered in 1879 to provide for the use of the federal census in the matter of apportioning the state for legislative representation.

A few cities and towns have special censuses for California through the twentieth century. The California State Archives has a listing of its holdings in this category.

Background Sources

A standard and superior source for understanding California history is Hubert Howe Bancroft's seven-volume *The History of California: 1542–1880* (San Francisco, Calif.: A. L. Bancroft and Co., 1884–90). These volumes came out irregularly and have been reprinted many times. They are available in a facsimile edition from the California Historical Society (see Archives, Libraries, and Societies). The companion *California Pioneer Register and Index, 1542–1848, Including Inhabitants of California, 1769–1800 and*

List of Pioneers, Extracted from Hubert Howe Bancroft's History of California (1884–90; reprint, Baltimore, Md.: Genealogical Publishing Co., 1964), readily available in libraries, provides a handy reference.

Other helpful sources in providing research perspective on California and its people are:

Cleland, Robert Glass. *The Cattle on a Thousand Hills: Southern California 1850–1870.* San Marino, Calif.: Huntington Library, 1951.

———. *From Wilderness to Empire: A History of California, 1542–1900.* New York, N.Y.: Alfred A. Knopf, 1944.

———. *A History of California; The American Period.* 1922. Reprint. Westport, Conn.: Greenwood Press, 1975.

Dillon, Richard H. *Fool's Gold: The Decline and Fall of Captain John Sutter of California.* Santa Cruz, Calif.: Western Tanager, 1981. Good for history of the time during which Sutter lived.

Gilmore, N. Ray, and Gladys Gilmore. *Readings in California History.* New York, N.Y.: Thomas Y. Crowell Co., 1966.

Hawthorne, Hildegarde. *California's Missions: Their Romance and Beauty.* New York, N.Y.: D. Appleton-Century Co., 1942.

Hutchinson, C. Alan. *Frontier Settlement in Mexican California: the Hijar-Padres Colony & Its Origins, 1769–1835.* New Haven, Conn.: Yale University Press, 1969.

Ogle, Sandra K. "Genealogical Research in California" *National Genealogical Society Quarterly* 76 (Sept. 1988): 194–211.

Parker, J. Carlyle. *Index to Biographees in 19th Century California County Histories.* Detroit, Mich.: Gale Research, 1979. An excellent cross index to a large number of California's county histories.

Rocq, Margaret Miller, ed. *California Local History: A Bibliography and Union List of Library Holdings.* 2d ed. Palo Alto, Calif.: Stanford University Press, 1970, and *Supplement to the Second Edition. 1961–70,* 1970.

Ryskamp, George R. *Tracing Your Hispanic Heritage.* Riverside, Calif.: Hispanic Family History Research, 1984. Text augmented by helpful appendices and a good glossary.

Stein, Walter J. *California and the Dust Bowl Migrations: Contributions in American History.* No. 21. Westport, Conn.: Greenwood Press, 1973.

Maps

Warren A. Beck's *Historical Atlas of California* (Oklahoma Press, 1974), available in many libraries, provides a basic map reference at different points in California's history. Other useful references in maps and guides to California place-names and published atlases are the following:

Durrenberger, Robert W. *Patterns on the Land: Geographical, Historical, and Political Maps of California.* Palo Alto, Calif.: National Press Books, 1965.

Gudde, Irwin G. *California Place Names: The Origin and Etymology of Current Geographical Names.* 3d ed. Berkeley, Calif.: University of California Press, 1969.

Gudde, Irwin G. *California Gold Camps: A Geographical and Historical Dictionary of Camps, Towns, and Localities Where Gold was Found and Mined . . .* (Berkeley, Calif.: University of California Press, 1975).

Sanborn maps are available for California (see page 4). Most libraries in California have both political and geographic maps for the state. Particularly noteworthy is the collection at the Map Center, 2440 Bancroft Way, Berkeley, California 94704.

Land Records

Public-Domain State

The earliest land records relate to the Spanish (1769–1822) and Mexican (1822–48) eras and are mostly in Spanish. During the Spanish period, California was divided into four districts for purposes of administration: San Diego in 1769, Monterey in 1770, San Francisco in 1776, and finally the district of Santa Barbara in 1782. The bulk of the records surviving are in the county recorders' offices. The most notable collection of this period is undoubtedly the recorder's collection (1781–1850) in Monterey County, but it covers a multitude of proceedings as Monterey was the seat of government for all of Alta California. Santa Cruz has a similar set of documents (1797–1845), and the San Jose clerk's archives hold various records from 1792.

For the period of Mexican jurisdiction, there are two major collections, one in Los Angeles and one in San Francisco, with the larger group of land records in San Francisco.

Under both the Spanish and Mexican regimes, land in California was allocated first to pueblos for the use of its towns and its inhabitants, second to presidios for use of the military in defending the citizenry and in keeping the peace, and third to the Catholic missions for the purpose of extending the church's theology to the native population.

Almost as soon as the last of the edifices in the chain of missions was completed in 1833, the Mexican government secularized all mission lands (about one-sixth of Alta California) and allowed these lands to be bought for private use. By 1846 some 500 ranches were parcelled out, generating numerous records and documents.

Spain had begun the practice of allowing concessions of private ranchos when, in 1784, Governor Pedro Fages bestowed ranchos upon three of his *soldados de cuero* (leather jacket troops) that he had led into California in 1769. These ranchos were San Rafael, San Pedro, and Los Nietos. By 1851, when the U.S. Board of Land Commissioners and the courts of record began hearing land claims cases, there were over 900 private land claims of named ranchos and an additional twenty-six unnamed grants. From 1851 through 1856, the Commission heard 813 cases in which title to over twelve million acres was decided. Of these, the board approved 520 claims and refused to recognize 273. Only a fraction of these decisions were overturned by the courts. Since the land commission met in San Francisco, a great hardship was created for the southern California claimants.

Records pertaining to Spanish and Mexican land claims were bound into seven volumes by the U.S. Surveyor General's Office, a part of the Department of the Interior. For details write to the U.S. Geological Survey Office, 119 National Center, Reston, Virginia 22092. The records of the BLM (Record Group 49), Private Land Claims No. 183, are located in the National Archives in Washington D.C.

Robert Cowan writes in *Ranchos of California: A List of Spanish Concessions, 1775–1822 and Mexican Grants, 1822–1846* (Los Angeles, Calif.: Historical Society of Southern California, 1977) that there were 3,500 people in Alta California, and by the end of the Mexican administration in 1846 the population had increased to almost 7,000. The Alta California records for the period of the Mexican-American war, 1846–48, may be found in the archives in Los Angeles, Monterey, San Francisco, and Sonoma counties.

During the Spanish and Mexican occupations, a government agent called the *alcalde* was the equivalent of our present-day mayor, only with greatly enhanced powers and singular jurisdictions (singular in that he performed many functions not commonly associated with that office today). Several counties have preserved their *alcaldes'* records for the period between 1848 and 1850 when California statehood became official. Counties with such records include Contra Costa, El Dorado, Marin, Monterey, Napa, Sacramento, San Francisco, San Luis Obispo, Santa Clara, Santa Cruz, Sonoma, Sutter, and Yuba.

California is a public-domain land state (see pages 4–5), consequently, land acquired by the U.S. Government in 1848 was disposed of by means of patents. The first of ten land offices opened at Los Angeles and Benicia in 1853. Patents and copies of tract books and maps are located at the BLM California State Office, 2800 College Way, Sacramento, California 95825. Both the National Archives-Pacific Sierra and Pacific Southwest regions (see page 9) hold land office records for their respective regions.

Land records for sales between private individuals throughout the state begin with the formation of the county, with the possible exception of those counties where there have been unusual circumstances, such as the San Francisco earthquake and fire of 1906. Contact the county recorder for the county in which the land is situated. In some instances the parent county must be searched also.

The county recorder is usually in charge of the document, book notation, index, etc., except where the records are so old that they have been placed in an archive within the county or in the state archives in Sacramento. Ultimately, the county board of supervisors is responsible for the records and repositories. In order to chart the ownership of land in California, the records are executed with a "chain of title." This record begins with the oldest entry of the land down to the most recent.

A compilation of indexes to real property owners was begun in the 1980s. In the alphabetical lists (for 1 July 1984, 1988, and 1989, available at the California State Library), one can find the name and mailing address of all property owners. Because the state no longer allows open access to all driver's license applications, and because city and county directories are not available for all locations, the Property Owners Index is quite useful for tracing living persons.

Land Definitions

The following definitions will be useful for anyone conducting research in California.

Haciendas: Not widely used in California, it is the Mexican equivalent of "rancho."

Ranchos: Land grants made by the government. The first one made in California was for 140 varas near Carmel. Of some 800 ranchos that were in existence when the U.S. government took possession of California, just over 500 were later confirmed by American courts.

Pueblos: Towns for civilian settlers, a tract four square leagues or 17,500 acres.

Presidios: Land granted for the use of the military to carry out its duties to defend the province against foreign invasion and to keep civil order. Title was actually passed in fee simple. Presidios were established in Santa Barbara, Monterey, San Diego, and San Francisco.

Missions: Land set aside for the use of the church in its work with the Indians native to the area. Title was not passed to the mission, nor to an individual. After the Act of Secularization, the missions were broken up and the lands were mostly granted to those making a petition to the government.

Districts: There were originally four districts set up for the administration of each province of Alta California, as mentioned earlier. Later, Los Angeles was added to the list. Each district had a presidio and a mission, although there might have been more than one mission in each.

Probate Records

The court that has jurisdiction over an estate is the superior court in the county in which the person resided at the time of his or her death. When a probate case is opened, the clerk of the court keeps a journal for that particular numbered file and maintains that file when the case is closed. Files can be searched at the office of the clerk of the superior court in which the probate occurred. Check for the file and then request the entire journal. The "Petition for Final Distribution" is ordered when all of the legal requirements have been met and the estate is to be distributed to the heirs. This is an important instrument to the researcher as it may give insights into the relationships of the heirs to the decedent. If the estate is contested, if there are minor heirs, or if other nonroutine proceedings occur, all of these will generate additional materials to be researched.

When researching in San Francisco County, it is important to remember that many of the records were destroyed in the 1906 earthquake and fire. Some local and county genealogical societies in the state have published indexes to early probate records.

Court Records

The California court system has four levels of jurisdiction: the municipal court, which largely took the place of the earlier justice of the peace court at the local level; the superior court, a countywide court that handles both civil and criminal cases and cases involving minors; the six district courts of appeal, which review all cases coming from the superior courts except those involving the death penalty; and the state supreme court, which takes extraordinary writs, all appeals in death penalty cases, and may review all other appeals.

Each of these courts has a clerk of the court, and correspondence regarding a case should be directed to the clerk of the particular court having jurisdiction over the litigation. If there is doubt as to the proper court from which to seek information, the State Attorney General's Office, 1515 "K" Street, Sacramento, California 95814, will be able to provide the information.

Some early court records from at least Humboldt, Marin, Mendocino, Nevada, Sonoma, and Sutter counties have been sent to the California State Archives. Besides court minutes and judgements, these records include tax lists, wills, deeds, estate inventories, and marriage bonds.

Tax Records

The U.S. Internal Revenue Service Assessment List for California, 1862–66, is available on thirty-three microfilm reels at the California State Library in Sacramento. The lists include names, location and description of business, and tax rate for individuals taxed.

Similar to tax records in their yearly listing of residents are the "Great Registers" of California, which are miscellaneous county voting registers that exist from the mid-nineteenth century. The registers were compiled and printed about every two years. Before 1900 they show name, address, and age (but the age may remain the same after a man's first entry). From about the mid-1800s, physical descriptions are included, but after the 1898 register only the name, address, party affiliation, and sometimes occupation are listed.

Before 1892 the lists are countywide, but usually alphabetical only by first letter or surname. They are particularly valuable for foreign-born voters, as the date and court of naturalization are listed. Copies of the "Great Registers" (1866–1944) are at the California State Library, which also has alphabetical card file abstracts for some of the earlier registers for San Francisco. Records from 1946 are with the individual county registrars of voters.

Cemetery Records

Printed secondary sources of transcribed cemeteries exist for most California counties. The California State Society of the DAR has collected hundreds of such records. Transcripts are housed both at the national DAR and with some local chapters and libraries. They are also available on microfilm through the FHL and the Sutro Library in San Francisco (see Archives, Libraries, and Societies). A complete set of the DAR records (over 180 volumes) is also in the California Room of the California State Library. Included in this collection are census, newspaper, cemetery, court, Bible, and family records.

Several cemeteries, previously located in San Francisco, were "moved" out of the city in the 1930s to South San Francisco and Coloma, for example.

Church Records

There are no centralized repositories dealing with church records in California. Scattered records can be found in genealogical publications, the DAR compilations (see page 6), and on microfilm. Three timely, comprehensive articles about church records can be found in the Summer, Fall, and Winter 1990 issues of *Southern California Historical Quarterly*, published by the Historical Society of Southern California, 200 East Avenue 43, Los Angeles, California 90031. Entitled "Archival Sources for the History of Religion in California," Part 1 is subtitled "Catholic Sources" and was compiled by Monsignor Francis J. Weber; Part 2, "Jewish Religious Sources," is by William M. Kramer and Norton B. Stern; and Part 3, "Protestant Sources," is by Eldon G. Ernst.

The Spanish missions have played a central role in California's religious history. Father Junipero Serra, a Franciscan, raised the standard to his sovereign on 2 June 1769 and began the trek that led him the length of the state of California. He founded a string of missions that led the state in the settlement of the vast uncharted land and the conversion of its natives. About a third of the total missions built were founded by Father Serra.

Microfiche of an alphabetical list of some vital records from the missions is available at the FHL in addition to the microfilm entries below:

- Mission San Diego de Alcala—San Diego
- Mission Luis Rey de Francia—Oceanside
- Mission San Juan Capistrano—San Juan Capistrano
- Mission San Gabriel Arcangel—San Gabriel
- Mission San Fernando Rey de España—San Fernando Valley
- Mission San Buenaventura—Ventura
- Mission Santa Barbara—Santa Barbara [records (1776–1912) can be located at the Santa Barbara Heritage Library (see Archives, Libraries, and Societies) and are available on microfilm at the FHL]
- Mission Santa Ines—in the town of Solvang
- Mission La Purisima Concepción—Lompoc
- Mission San Luis Obispo de Tolosa—San Luis Obispo (microfilm is available at the FHL for 1772–1906)
- Mission San Miguel Arcangel—nine miles north of Paso Robles
- Mission San Antonio de Padua—three miles southwest of King City
- Mission Nuestra Señora de la Soledad—three miles south of Soledad
- Mission San Carlos Borromeo de Carmelo—south of Carmel
- Mission San Juan Bautista—San Juan Bautista
- Mission Santa Cruz—Santa Cruz (microfilm of the original records of baptism and correspondence, 1791–1814, is available from Library Microfilms, Palo Alto, California)
- Mission Santa Clara de Asis—Santa Clara (microfilm is available at the FHL for 1777–1855)
- Mission San Jose de Guadalupe—Fremont
- Mission San Francisco de Asis—also known as Dolores, in San Francisco
- Mission San Rafael Arcangel—San Rafael
- Mission San Francisco Solano de Sonoma—Sonoma State Park

Military Records

The California State Archives has become the state's official repository for service records of Californians from the Indian Wars through the World Wars, including National Guard records. Some of these are on microfilm at the National Archives and are also available through the FHL.

Richard H. Orton, ed., *Records of California Men in the War of Rebellion, 1861–1867* (Sacramento, Calif.: State Printing Office, 1890), and J. Carlyle Parker, comp., *A Personal Name Index to Orton's. . .*, Vol. 5 of Gale Genealogy and Local History Series (Detroit, Mich.: Gale Research, 1978), provide printed sources for those serving in the Civil War. The National Archives' seven-reel microfilm index to compiled service records for California's Union Army Volunteers is available for research at the California State Library and through the FHL.

The California State Library also has the National Archives' seventeen-reel microfilm series of the California War History Committee's "World War I Records of California Service Men." The information in this collection is believed to have been submitted voluntarily and therefore does not cover all California veterans, but includes birth date, parents, service records, and sometimes material such as educational background and newspaper clippings.

The Bancroft Library at the University of California at Berkeley has an extensive collection of source material for military records. Included are the Wyles Collection of the Civil War, University of California at Santa Barbara; Herbert E. Bolton's *Anza's Californian Expedition,* Vol. 4 (Berkeley, Calif.: University of California Press, 1930.); "List of Militia Men for Southern California, 1809"; "Monterey Padron del Presidio anode 1808"; "Monterey, 1804: Lista para Complimiento de Yglasia," in the *Provincial State Papers; Benecia Military, XXIV;* and "Monterey Presidio of 1782."

Periodicals, Newspapers, and Manuscript Collections

Periodicals

Nearly every local genealogical society in the state has a form of publication, although no statewide guide exists that includes all of them. Many contain how-to articles (pertaining to California research), query columns, and book reviews. The Sutro Branch of the California State Library has a large collection of California periodicals.

California Historical Society's *Index to California Historical Society Quarterly* (1922–61; 1962–75), available from Channing Books in Marion, Massachusetts, cross-indexes fifty-four volumes of the periodical. The California Genealogical Society publishes a newsletter six times a year.

Newspapers

Among the older newspapers in the state are the *San Diego Union* (1868), the *San Francisco Chronicle* (1865), and the *Los Angeles Times* (1881). The most extensive collection of California newspapers is in the California Room of the State Library in Sacramento. Some have been microfilmed and are available on interlibrary loan.

Besides the California Information File index in the California Room, which covers some newspaper items, there is also an index of about 922,000 cards with over 1,800,000 citations of San Francisco newspaper items from 1904 to the present. A published index to the *San Francisco Call* covers that newspaper back to 1894.

The Sutro Branch of the California State Library has California newspapers beginning in 1846 on microfilm and available on interlibrary loan. Their newspaper index contains approximately 3 million entries from 1850 to the present. Many other California libraries have access to microfilm editions of newspapers on interlibrary loan.

Manuscripts

Probably the largest manuscript collection in the state is at the Bancroft Library, University of California at Berkeley. The library's collection on the West is strong and includes many diaries, collections of personal papers, and letters. A guide to the manuscript collection is available.

The California State Library also has one of the largest manuscript collections. See Thomas H. Fante, comp., *Catalogued Manuscripts and Diaries of the California Section* (Sacramento, Calif.: California State Library, 1981).

For a statewide guide, see *Directory of Archival and Manuscript Repositories in California* (Redlands, Calif.: Beacon Printery, 1975).

For material on the Spanish and Mexican periods, see:

Beers, Henry Putney. *Spanish and Mexican Records of the American Southwest: A Bibliographical Guide to Archive and Manuscript Sources.* Tucson, Ariz.: University of Arizona Press, 1979.

Archives, Libraries, and Societies

California State Library
914 Capitol Mall
Sacramento, CA 95814

Microfilms of the federal censuses are housed here as well as a number of statewide research materials described above.

Some of the important collections include the following:

The California Information File is about 640,000 index cards covering 1.2 million items in such things as newspapers, manuscripts, periodicals, and county histories. Microfilmed county histories are available on interlibrary loan.

Pioneer Record File has biographical material on Californians who emigrated before 1860—information submitted by the actual pioneers or by their descendants.

Biographical files cover California artists, authors, actors, and musicians, along with material on California political leaders that may be of interest.

There is a large collection of city, county (from 1850s), and telephone directories (from 1897). See also Nathan C. Parker's *Personal Name Index to the 1856 City Directories of California,* Vol. 10 of Gale Genealogy and Local History Series (Detroit, Mich.: Gale Research, 1980).

The California State Library is the parent organization of the Sutro Library (see guidebook and address below) with a fine collection of its own.

Sutro Library
California State Library (Sutro Branch)
480 Winston Drive
San Francisco, CA 94132

This library is a branch of the California State Library but differs from the main library in Sacramento in its holdings. The focus in Sutro is on genealogical research outside of California, although the collection includes many California materials (census, local newspapers, periodicals). *Local History and Genealogy Resources of the California State Library and Its Sutro Branch* (Sacramento, Calif.: California State Library Foundation, 1983) helps distinguish between the holdings of these two important research facilities in the state. The Sutro collection is available to the public either at the library or through interlibrary loan. Both the Genealogy Catalog and Local History Catalog (the index to the bulk of the library's holdings) can be obtained on microfiche and are supplemented on a regular basis by the publication of additional titles as they arrive.

California State Archives,
Office of Secretary of State
1020 O Street, Room 130
Sacramento, CA 95814

The collections in the California State Archives are indicated in various sections in this chapter. A published guide to the archives holdings is available.

Besides those census, military, court, and land records available at the state archives, legislative and Department of Education records (names of teachers, by county, 1863–1920) located here may be of genealogical use. The archives also has indexes to inmates of Folsom and San Quentin prisons through 1940.

There are many genealogical and historical societies and institutions catering to people with various research problems. Only a few are listed below. Since many California residents active in local history and genealogy may themselves be recent migrants to the state, local organizations' focus may be on research problems in other locations rather than within California.

California State Genealogical Alliance
19765 Grand Avenue
Lake Elsinore, CA 92330

One way to access many local and county genealogical and historical societies is through the Alliance, which publishes its own newsletter.

California Genealogical Society
300 Branan Street, Suite 409
San Francisco, CA 94107

California Heritage Council
680 Beach Street, #351
San Francisco, CA 94109

California Society of Colonial Pioneers
456 McAlister Street
San Francisco, CA 94102
Collection: 1783 to 1918

Chinese Historical Society
17 Adler Place
San Francisco, CA 94133
Collection: 1865 to the present

Presidio Army Museum
Corner Lincoln and Funston Streets
San Francisco, CA 94129-5502
Collection: nineteenth century

University of California and California State University Libraries

There are excellent special collections at universities throughout the state including the Bancroft collection at the University of California at Berkeley, the Wyles collection of Civil War materials at the University of California at Santa Barbara, the Mandeville collection at the University of California at San Diego, the Western Association of Map Libraries at University of California at Santa Cruz, and the California State Library at Chico and Turlock.

California Public Libraries

In California, within the entire library system, there is an interlibrary loan program that can be called upon for many printed materials. The reference librarian at the local library, for a small fee, can request assistance in locating a particular book through this system.

The Los Angeles Public Library, History and Genealogy Department, 433 South Spring Street (location), 630 West Fifth Street (mailing address), Los Angeles, California 90071, has been reopened to the public and is rebuilding its excellent collection for genealogical research.

The Glendale Branch (1130 East Wilson Avenue, Glendale, California 91206) of the FHL has a large collection of printed and microfilm source material in addition to access to the extensive collection available by mail service from the Salt Lake City collection.

Special Focus Categories

Immigration

The California State Library has microfilms of San Francisco ships' passenger lists for 1893–1953, plus additional immigrants and crew lists covering 1954–57. The twenty-eight-reel index to these records for 1893–1934 and thirty-two reels listing Chinese passengers arriving at San Francisco 1882–1914 are also at the state library in Sacramento. Many immigrants in this period were from China and Japan, but a good number were from Europe, Australia, and elsewhere. Louis J. Rasmussen's *San Francisco Ship Passenger Lists (1850–1984)*, 4 vols. (Coloma, Calif.: San Francisco Historic Records, 1965–70; Vol. 1. 1965; reprint, Baltimore, Md.: Genealogical Publishing Co., 1978), covers a time period of sea travel, while his *Railway Passenger Lists of Overland Trains to San Francisco and the West*, 2 vols. (Coloma, Calif.: San Francisco Historic Records, 1966), starts with 1870.

Naturalization

As with other states, prior to 1906 a person might have filed for naturalization in any court in the state; for this time period, there are no guides for locating a naturalization in the state other than those which were entered at federal district court. Many of those have been gathered and are located at either of the National Archives regional branches: Pacific Sierra at San Bruno or Pacific Southwest at Laguna Niguel (see page 9).

Ethnic Groups

California's Native American population was unique in that there were many small tribes living a pastoral life when the Spaniards, founding missions and presidios, arrived. The missions fell into decay, and the natives dispersed after the Mexican revolution. By the time of the first census in 1850, California's nonnative population had swelled to 92,600. Of this population, 70,000 were Americans living mostly in northern California.

Migrants, from every ethnic group in the country, continued to arrive at roughly the rate of 300,000 annually until 1900. Many were farmers from the southern tier of the United States including Texas, Missouri, Arkansas, and Oklahoma. The population increased at an even higher rate for the next four decades.

The Golden Promised Land, as California has been thought of, has not always been a paradise for minority groups. Chinese, Japanese, Hindus, and other Asians from many eastern lands came to work on the railroad projects and were subject to the prejudices of the resident population. The Okies, from the drought-stricken dust bowl, tried to find work in southern California and the San Joaquin Valley in the 1930s. The demand for workers rose abruptly in World War II bringing many black Americans, Mexicans, and more recently Latin Americans and Southeast Asians. The public records of California include all ethnic groups, and most libraries can be helpful in focusing research on any particular group. In addition to Ryskamp's resource guide (see Background Sources) and Beers's guide (see Manuscripts), the following are sources or contain background information for some California ethnic groups:

Beasely, Delilah Leontium. *The Negro Trail Blazers of California.* New York, N.Y.: Negro University Press, 1969.

Burchell, R. A. *The San Francisco Irish, 1848–1880.* Berkeley, Calif.: University of California Press, 1980.

Goode, Kenneth G. *California's Black Pioneers: A Brief Historical Survey.* Santa Barbara, Calif.: McNally & Loftin, 1974.

Nicosia, Francesco M. *Italian Pioneers of California.* Italian American Chamber of Commerce of the Pacific Coast, 1960.

Northrop, Marie E. *Spanish-Mexican Families of Early California: 1769–1850.* Vol. 1. Burbank, Calif.: Southern California Genealogical Society, 1986. *Spanish-Mexican Families of Early California: 1769–1850.* Vol. 2. Burbank, Calif.: Southern California Genealogical Society, 1984.

For research on Native Americans in California, contact the American Indian Council of Central California, P.O. Box 3341, Bakersfield, California 93385, or the California Native American Heritage Commission, 915 Capitol Mall, Sacramento, California 95814. Also, Albert L. Hurtado, *Indian Survival on the California Frontier* (New Haven, Conn.: Yale University Press, 1988), may be helpful.

Gold Rush

For anyone seeking an ancestor who left for the California gold fields in 1848–50, it would be wise to examine the emigrant companies from Massachusetts and the available lists of Argonauts. Northern California pioneers were called Argonauts in reference to those in ancient Greek mythology who sailed with Jason on the ship *Argo.* Octavius Thorndike Howe's *Argonauts of '49: History and Adventures of the Emigrant Companies from Massachusetts, 1849–1850* (Cambridge, Mass.: Harvard University Press, 1923) includes a list of the mining companies going from Massachusetts to California in 1849. The list gives the name of the company, the ship's name, the ship's master, and the date of sailing. It catalogs 124 sailings and the number of persons in the company.

In 1890 Charles Warren Haskins published his personal memoirs, *The Argonauts of California. Being the Reminiscences of Scenes and Incidents that Occurred in California in Early Mining Days; by a Pioneer* (New York, N.Y.: Fords, Howard & Hulbert, 1890). In his narrative, Haskins included the names of people who arrived in California from both land and sea routes. Original sources are not indicated for entries because many sources which might have been used were lost in the San Francisco earthquake and fire. J. Carlyle Parker's preface in the Society of California Pioneers' *Index to the Argonauts of California* (New Orleans, La.: Polyanthos Press, 1975) is a discussion of the problems with Argonaut lists and has an index.

Libera Martina Spinazze developed index cards for the names in Haskins's *The Argonauts,* which were deposited in the California State Library and, in time, the Sequoia Chapter, DAR, acquired four incomplete copies of these files. The Spinazze files were finally completed and bound into four sets, copies of which were given by the DAR to the DAR Library in Washington, D.C., the Bancroft Library at the University of California at Berkeley, the California Historical Society, the California State Library in Sacramento, and the Los Angeles Public Library.

The 1852 census, the card catalog, and manuscript and published material in the California State Library are other useful sources regarding the gold rush era. The Bancroft collection of diaries at the University of California, Berkeley, is also useful. The San Joaquin Genealogical Society published five volumes of probate records, newspapers, and vital records, covering the period of 1850–66 for their county in *Gold Rush Days,* which is available from Western Reserve Historical Society, 10825 East Boulevard, Cleveland, Ohio 44106.

County Resources

The following is a listing of the extant vital, land, probate, and court records for each county. Some counties encompass land settled in the eighteenth century; their records predate county formation. Land transactions and vital records recorded in the county are at the county recorder's office. The county clerk generally has probate books and files from the county's superior court, civil court records, and naturalizations. Divorces may be in either place, depending on how filed.

The California State Archives has microfilm of selected county records, 1850–1919, reproduced by the Utah State Genealogical Society and available through the FHL.

In addition to surveying county officials, the following references were used to compile county chart information:

Coy, Owen C. *California County Boundaries: A Study of the Division of the State into Counties and the Subsequent Changes in Their Boundaries.* Berkeley, Calif.: California Historical Survey Commission, 1923.

———. *Guide to the County Archives of California.* Sacramento, Calif.: California State Printing Office, 1919.

 Drawn by William Dollarhide

Map	County Address	Date Formed Parent County/ies	Birth Marriage Death	Land Probate Court
D6	Alameda 1221 Oak Street Oakland 94612	1853 Contra Costa/Santa Clara	1873 1854 1905*	1853 1880 1853
	**Some death records are available from 1876; search will be performed by the clerk for a fee.*			
D4	Alpine P.O. Box 158 Markleeville 96120	1853 El Dorado/Amador/ Calaveras/Tuolumne	1894 1894 1894	1894 1900 1900
C8	Amador 108 Court Street Jackson 95642	1854 Calaveras/El Dorado	1854 1864 1873	1854 1854 1854
	Branciforte	1850 (renamed Santa Cruz, 1850) original		
C2	Butte 25 County Center Drive Oroville 95965	1850 original	1859 1851 1859	1850 1851 1851
C8	Calaveras 891 Mountain Ranch Road San Andreas 95249	1850 original	1877 1862 1859	1852 1866 1866
A6	Colusa 546 Jay Street Colusa 95932	1850 original	1873 1853 1889	1853 1853 1853
	Attached to Butte County for administration until it was organized in 1851.			
D6	Contra Costa 651 Pine Street Martinez 94553	1850 original	1906 1906 1906	1848 1850 1850
A1	Del Norte County Courthouse Crescent City 95531	1857 Klamath	1873 1853 1873	1873 1848 1848
	No explanation is given for the discrepancy between date of formation and first land records.			
B8	El Dorado 360 Fair Lane Placerville 95667	1850 original	1910 1910 1909	1848 1849* 1920*
	**A fire in 1920 destroyed most courthouse records. For probate records prior to 1951, write County Museum, 100 Placerville Drive, Placerville 95667; for probate after 1951, write to Judicial Section, 495 Main Street, Placerville 95667.*			
G3	Fresno 110 Van Ness Avenue Fresno 93721	1856 Merced/Mariposa	1873 1855 1873	1855 1860 1860
C2	Glenn P.O. Box 391 Willows 95988	1891 Colusa	1887 1891 1905	1891 1891 1926
A1	Humboldt 825 Fifth Street Eureka 95501	1853 Trinity	1876 1864 1873	1864 1886 1886
K8	Imperial 940 Main Street El Centro 92243	1907 San Diego	1900 1900 1900	1900 1900 1900
G6	Inyo 168 N. Edwards Street Independence 93526	1866 Tulare	1905 1875 1905	1866 1866 1866

Map	County Address	Date Formed Parent County/ies	Birth Marriage Death	Land Probate Court
H5	Kern 1415 Truxton Avenue Bakersfield 93301	1866 Tulare/Los Angeles	1850 1850 1850	1850 1866 1866
G4	Kings 1400 W. Lacy Boulevard Hanford 93230	1893 Tulare	1893 1893 1893	1893 1893 1893
	Klamath	1851 (abolished 1874; parts annexed to Humboldt and Siskiyou) Trinity		
C1	Lake 255 N. Forbes Street Lakeport 95453	1861 Napa	1867 1867 1867	1867 1867 1867
A3	Lassen S. Lassen Street Susanville 96130 **Marriage records are incomplete for 1864 through 1925.*	1864 Plumas/Shasta	1870 1864* 1870	1870 1864 1864
J5	Los Angeles 500 W. Temple Street, Room 383 Los Angeles 90012 **Alcalde records from 1781. See Land Records.*	1850 original	1866 1856 1877	1856* 1850 1850
F4	Madera Government Center Madera 93637	1893 Fresno	1893 1893 1893	1893 1893 1893
D1	Marin Civic Center, Room 190 San Raphael 94903	1850 original	1863 1856 1863	1848 1910 1910
E4	Mariposa Courthouse Mariposa 95338	1850 original	1850 1850 1850	1850 1850 1850
C1	Mendocino Courthouse Ukiah 95482	1850 original	1850 1850 1850	1850 1872 1858
F3	Merced 2222 M Street Merced 95340	1855 Mariposa	1873 1870 1890	1855 1855 1855
A4	Modoc Courthouse Alturas 96101	1874 Siskiyou	1874 1874 1874	1874 1874 1874
E5	Mono P.O. Box 537 Bridgeport 93517	1861 Calaveras/Fresno	1873 1873 1881	1864 1864 1864
G2	Monterey 240 Church Street Salinas 93901 **Alcalde records from 1781. See Land Records.* ***Many birth, death, and marriage records are incomplete.*	1850 original	1870** 1870** 1870**	1850* 1850 1850
C6	Napa P.O. Box 880 Napa 94559	1850 original	1873 1850 1873	1848 1850 1850

Map	County Address	Date Formed Parent County/ies	Birth Marriage Death	Land Probate Court
A8	Nevada County Courthouse Nevada City 95959	1851 Yuba	1873 1856 1851	1856 1880 1880
K5	Orange 10 Civic Center Plaza, 3rd Floor Santa Ana 92701	1889 Los Angeles	1889 1889 1889	1889 1889 1889
B8	Placer 175 Fulweiler Avenue, Room 206 Auburn 95603	1851 Yuba/Sutter	closed 1850 1908	1850 1851 1851
B3	Plumas P.O. Box 207 Quincy 95971	1854 Butte	1873 1873 1873	1854 1860 1860
K7	Riverside 4080 Lemon Street Riverside 92501	1893 San Diego/San Bernardino	1893 1893 1893	1893 1893 1893
C7	Sacramento 700 H Street Sacramento 95814	1850 original	1858 1850 1858	1848 1880 1880
F2	San Benito Courthouse, Room 206 Hollister 95023 **Although the county office was required to begin filing vital statistics in 1905, some records exist prior to that date..*	1874 Monterey	1905* 1905* 1905*	1874 1874 1874
J7	San Bernardino 385 N. Arrowhead Avenue San Bernardino 92415-0110	1853 Los Angeles	1873 1854 1873	1854 1856 1856
K6	San Diego 220 W. Broadway San Diego 92101	1850 original	1881 1856 1898	1769 1855 1855
F1	San Francisco 400 Van Ness Avenue San Francisco 94102 *Extensive record loss caused by the 1906 earthquake.*	1850 original	1906 1906 1906	1906 1906 1906
D7	San Joaquin 222 E. Weber Avenue, Room 704 Stockton 95292	1850 original	1850 1850 1850	1850 1851 1851
H3	San Luis Obispo County Government Center San Luis Obispo 93408	1850 original	1873 1850 1850	1848 1854 1854
E1	San Mateo 401 Marshall Street Redwood City 94063	1856 San Francisco/Santa Cruz	1866 1856 1865	1856 1880 1866
J3	Santa Barbara 105 E. Anapamu Street Santa Barbara 93101 **Alcade records included from 1782. See Land Records.*	1850 original	1873 1850 1888	1850* 1850 1850
F2	Santa Clara 70 W. Hedding Street San Jose 95110	1850 original	closed 1859 closed	1848 1859 1859

Map	County Address	Date Formed Parent County/ies	Birth Marriage Death	Land Probate Court
F2	Santa Cruz 701 Ocean Street Santa Cruz 95060 **Alcalde records included from 1779. See Land Records.*	1850 (as Branciforte; renamed, 1850) original	1850 1850 1850	1850* 1850 1850
A2	Shasta 1500 Court Street Redding 96009 *For the first year of organization, Trinity County was attached to Shasta.*	1850 original	1873 1852 1873	1852 1880 1880
C3	Sierra P.O. Box D Downieville 95936	1852 Yuba	1857 1853 1873	1852 1852 1852
A2	Siskiyou 311 Fourth Street Yreka 96097	1852 Shasta/Klamath	1850 1852 1873	1852 1852 1852
C6	Solano Hall of Justice Fairfield 94533 *No explanation is given for the late date for deeds.*	1850 original	1880 1880 1880	1880 1850 1850
D1	Sonoma 575 Administration Drive Santa Rosa 95401	1850 original	1871 1847 1873	1847 1850 1850
E3, D7	Stanislaus 111 H Street Modesto 95354	1854 Tuolumne/San Joaquin	1873 1854 1873	1854 1854 1854
B7	Sutter 463 Second Street Yuba City 95991	1850 original	1873 1850 1873	1848 1850 1850
B2	Tehama P.O. Box 250 Red Bluff 96080	1856 Colusa/Butte/Shasta	1889 1856 1889	1856 1856 1856
B1	Trinity Courthouse, Main Street Weaverville 96093 *For the first year of organization, Trinity County was attached to Shasta County.*	1850 original	1873 1850 1873	1850 1890 1890
G4	Tulare County Civic Center Visalia 93291	1852 Mariposa	1852 1852 1873	1852 1854 1857
E4	Tuolumne 2 S. Green Street Sonora 95370	1850 original	1859 1852 1859	1850 1852 1852
J4	Ventura 800 S. Victoria Avenue Ventura 93009 **Alcalde records from 1782; county land records begin 1871.*	1872 Santa Barbara	1873 1873 1873	1871* 1873 1873
B6	Yolo 625 Court Street Woodland 95695	1850 original	1879 1895 1879	1850 1879 1879
A7	Yuba 215 Fifth Street *Marysville 95901*	1850 original	1850 1850 *1850*	1848 1850 *1850*

COLORADO

Marsha Hoffman Rising, C.G., C.G.L.

Colorado fell under several governmental jurisdictions during its developmental history, being for a time part of the territories of Spain, Missouri, Mexico, Utah, United States, New Mexico, unorganized Native American land, and finally Nebraska and Kansas. Records, however, exist only for the domains of Utah, New Mexico, Kansas, and Nebraska territories. The territory of Colorado, with its seventeen counties, was formed in 1861. Sixteen years later, on 1 August 1876, it was admitted as the thirty-eighth state in the Union.

The San Luis Valley was the site of the first permanent white settlement in what became Colorado, with the town of San Luis being founded in 1851. One year later, Fort Massachusetts, later replaced by Fort Garland, was erected on the Ute Creek to protect travelers on the Santa Fe Trail. At that time most pioneers were not settling in Colorado but rather moving through to California and Oregon.

Mining accounted for the first extensive settlement around what is now Denver. Reports of gold began in the spring of 1858 and brought many newcomers to the area. Later that year the "Pike's Peak or Bust" gold rush began, and in 1859 a "Second Stampede" brought additional thousands searching for gold, including both settlers and speculators. Two censuses, taken one year apart, indicate that the population of Colorado was beginning to shift from speculator to settler. The 1860 territorial census of Colorado counted 32,654 white males and 1,577 white females, but by May 1861 the census of Territorial Governor William Gilpin counted 20,798 males and 4,484 females. Clearly, the type of people coming to Colorado was beginning to change.

Early native tribes in Colorado included the Ute, the Apache, and "the wandering tribes" of Cheyenne, Arapaho, and Sioux. On 18 February 1861 the Cheyenne and Arapaho negotiated a treaty at Fort Wise, Colorado, in which they ceded all lands in the Pike's Peak region to the United States. A treaty with the Ute followed in 1864, ceding all Ute land east of the Continental Divide. By 1881 the Ute had finished moving from the western part of the state into Utah, and large sections of Colorado became open for settlement.

During the Civil War, many Northerners living in Colorado returned to their prior residences to help fight for the Union cause, but other settlers remained in their new domicile. Colorado participated in a major battle in the Civil War that occurred in March 1862 when Governor Gilpin organized one of three Colorado companies to stop the Confederate attempt to block the western supply of gold to the eastern states. Forces clashed at Glorieta Pass, New Mexico, and the Confederate forces retreated.

After the Civil War, the population of Colorado began to expand primarily through the development of railroads. The first "Iron Horse" arrived in Denver on 24 June 1870. The researcher with early Colorado ancestors should watch for migration during the 1870s and follow the growth of the railroads. A promotional organization, the Colorado Board of Immigration, was created in 1872, and the population of Colorado tripled between 1870–75. Unfortunately, this decade also brought grasshoppers and economic depression—forcing many settlers to return to the east. Throughout the difficult times, mining and agriculture remained the two important industries.

Migration to Colorado came from a block of states extending from New York and Pennsylvania on the east to Kansas and Nebraska on the west. In 1860 Ohio had the greatest number of immigrants to Colorado, followed by Illinois, New York, Missouri, and Indiana. The population explosion after the Civil War brought native-born Americans primarily from the states of Missouri, Kansas, Nebraska, and Iowa. The population of Colorado also included a large number of foreign-born immigrants such as Czechs, Slovaks, Irish, Germans, Russians, Canadians, Swedish, Scots, Italians, and Chinese. By 1880, one-fifth of the population of Colorado was foreign-born. In the 1890s Germans arrived, an ethnic group which predominates in eastern Colorado today.

Vital Records

A law enacted in 1875 provided for registration of births and deaths, but compliance was sporadic. Some early vital records may be located in the county courthouses or the county health departments, but the location is not consistent. The *Guide to Vital Statistics of Colorado*, prepared by Colorado Historical Records Survey, Division of Community Service Programs of the WPA is out of date but remains the only comprehensive state guide. Volume one of the publication describes the records held by public archives, and volume two discusses those held in church archives. This guide is located in the Colorado Historical Society Library (see Archives, Libraries, and Societies) as well as other major libraries and repositories.

Statewide registration of births began in 1910 and deaths in 1900. Although the county health departments existed in one form or another from 1900, Colorado did not join the national death registration system until 1906, and birth registration was even later, beginning in 1928. Birth and death records are available from the Vital Records Section, Colorado Department of Health, 4210 East 11th Avenue, Denver, Colorado 80220. Some county health departments do have incomplete birth records from earlier dates that are not available at the state level.

There are restrictions as to who may gain access to these records, with death records more available than birth. A list of persons eligible to apply for the records is printed on the back of the application form. Some relatives of a deceased individual who are pursuing genealogical research may be issued a death certificate.

The county clerk maintains marriage records, and the clerk of the district court holds divorce records. A statewide list of marriages and divorces indexed by name of the groom exists for the years 1900–39 (with a few prior entries) and is located at the Colorado State Archives and Denver Public Library Genealogy Department (see Archives, Libraries, and Societies), along with many early marriage records. Both agencies have a microfiche Marriage Index (by bride and groom) for 1975–present and a Divorce Index for the same time period. The Colorado Historical Society has a small card catalog index for early vital records (births, deaths, marriages) that appeared in Colorado newspapers for the years 1860–1940.

The Colorado Genealogical Society publication *Marriages of Arapahoe County, Colorado 1859–1901* (Denver, Colo.: the society, 1986) includes marriages from the territory that later evolved into the counties of Adams, Arapahoe, Denver, Clear Creek, Jefferson, Elbert, Lincoln, Washington, and the others located in east central Colorado. The certificates themselves are located at the Colorado State Archives.

Census Records

Federal

Population Schedules.

- Indexed—1860 (as various territories, see below), 1870
- Soundex—1880, 1900, 1920
- Unindexed—1910

Mortality Schedules.

- 1870, 1880

Industry and Agriculture Schedules.

- 1870, 1880

The Colorado Historical Society has microfilmed copies of the Colorado decennial census with indexes for 1860, 1870, and 1880. The Colorado Historical Society does not currently own the Soundex to the 1900 census, although one is located at the National Archives-Rocky Mountain Region in Denver and the Denver Public Library, Genealogy Department. An "index" that can be used for the 1910 Colorado census is the Denver street guide. A location guide to the Boulder County 1910 federal census has been published in the *Boulder Genealogical Society Quarterly* 11 (November 1986): 151–54. Otherwise, no index exists. The Denver Public Library holds microfilmed copies of the 1860 Kansas territorial census (which includes parts of Colorado), the 1870, and the 1880 population census. The Colorado State Archives has the 1860 censuses on microfilm for Utah, New Mexico, Nebraska, and Kansas that cover the present geographic boundaries of Colorado. No survey of available *state* copies of the federal censuses exists; however, Clear Creek County holds theirs for 1880, and there may be others.

Microfilmed copies of the 1870 and 1880 mortality schedules are located at the National Archives-Rocky Mountain Region (see page 8) and the Denver Public Library. A printed index has been compiled. The original schedules are housed with the Daughters of the American Revolution in Washington, D.C. (see page 9).

Territorial and State

The first census of those who lived in what would become Colorado was taken in 1860 as part of several territorial censuses. Arapahoe County, which covered the central eastern section, was included in the Kansas territorial census for that year. The areas of Boulder City, Boulder Creek Settlement, Gold Hill Settlement, Miraville City, and the Platte River Settlement were enumerated with Nebraska Territory. Denver City was partly enumerated with Nebraska and partly with the Kansas territorial census. The southeast portion of Colorado was enumerated in parts of Taos and Mora counties of New Mexico Territory. Leadville, although a booming mining town at the time and located in what is now Lake County, was in Utah Territory and not enumerated.

Colorado Territory was organized in 1861, and voters residing in the territory were listed at that time. The original poll books (which list only males) remain in the Colorado State Archives and have been microfilmed. An index by the Colorado Genealogical Society (see Archives, Libraries, and Societies) is currently in progress.

An 1866 enumeration was taken, but the only extant returns are for the northeastern section, which included the counties of Logan, Morgan, Phillips, Sedgwick, Weld, and parts of Washington and Yuma. Heads of household with number of males over and under twenty-one and females over and under eighteen are included in a document available at the Colorado State Archives.

The microfilmed copy of the 1885 special federal census, encompassing population, agricultural, manufacturing, and mortality returns, is located at the Colorado State Archives, the National Archives-Rocky Mountain Region in Denver, Colorado Historical Society, and the Denver Public Library. Some counties have abridged copies that arranged names of residents alphabetically, making them seem to be indexes. However, researchers should be aware this "index" does not refer the reader to the page number of the original census, and it is an incomplete extraction with only partial data from the census. For complete information, the researcher will need to use the original and not the county copy. These microfilms are available on interlibrary loan. The Colorado Council of Genealogical Societies (see Archives, Libraries, and Societies) is currently preparing a statewide index from the originals.

Background Sources

Abbott, Carl, Stephen J. Leonard, and David McComb. *Colorado: History of the Centennial State.* Boulder, Colo.: Colorado Associated University Press, 1982.

Atheran, Robert G. *The Coloradans.* Albuquerque, N.Mex.: University of New Mexico Press, 1976.

Baker, James H., and LeRoy R. Hafen. *History of Colorado.* 3 vols. Denver, Colo.: Linderman Co., 1927. Two of these volumes are biographies.

Colorado Genealogical Society, comp. *Colorado Families: A Territorial Heritage.* Denver, Colo.: Colorado Genealogical Society, 1981. These family pedigrees and histories of families in Colorado by or before 1876 include maps and an every-name index.

Gannett, Henry. *A Gazetteer of Colorado.* Washington, D.C.: Government Printing Office, 1906. Helps in locating Colorado towns, villages, and sites.

Hafen, LeRoy R. *Colorado and Its People: A Narrative and Topical History of the Centennial State.* 4 vols. New York, N.Y.: Lewis Historical Publishing Co., 1948.

Hinckley, Kathleen W. "Genealogical Research in Colorado." *National Genealogical Society Quarterly* 77 (June 1989): 107–27. Provides a current survey of resources in the state.

Joy, Carol M., and Terry Ann Mood, comps. *Colorado Local History: A Directory.* Denver, Colo.: Colorado Historical Society, 1986. Contains descriptions of over 100 smaller repository collections.

Ubbelohde, Carl, Maxine Benson, and Duane A. Smith. *A Colorado History.* 6th ed. Boulder, Colo.: Pruett Publishing Co., 1988.

Wynar, Bohdan S., and Roberta J. Depp, eds. *Colorado Bibliography.* Littleton, Colo.: Libraries Unlimited for the National Society of Colonial Dames of America in the State of Colorado, 1980.

The Colorado Historical Society has a card index of some names that have been extracted from Colorado published histories. The staff will check the index by mail for specific names.

References for early Colorado records include these:

Blodgett, Ralph E. "Colorado Territorial Board of Immigration." *Colorado Magazine* 46 (Summer 1969): 345–56.

Noel, Thomas J., ed. *The W.P.A. Guide to 1930's Colorado.* 1941. Reprint. Lawrence, Kans.: University of Kansas Press, 1987.

Maps

Colorado Geological Survey Maps are available from the National Archives-Rocky Mountain Region. The Western History Collection at the Denver Public Library has an extensive map collection of over 2,000 maps that include explorations, surveys, railroad maps, trails, mining expeditions, and land grants. Included in their collection is a reference by George R. Eichler called *Colorado Place Names* (Boulder, Colo.: Johnson Publishing, 1980).

Good map collections are also located at Norlin Library of the University of Colorado, Boulder, 80224; Colorado State Archives; and the Colorado School of Mines' Arthur Lakes Library in Golden.

Guide to the Colorado Ghost Towns and Mining Camps (4th ed. rev., Athens, Ohio: Shallow Press, 1974), compiled by Perry Eberhart, discusses an important aspect of Colorado's political geography.

Land Records

Public-Domain State

Records of the Spanish and Mexican land grants are located in the Western History Collection at the Denver Public Library, 1357 Broadway, Denver, Colorado 80203.

Once the area fell under U.S. jurisdiction, land was first transferred from the federal government to individuals. The Homestead Act of 1862 provided for the disposal of most of Colorado's land.

Land offices existed in Central City, Del Norte, Denver, Durango, Glenwood Springs, Gunnison, Hugo, Lamar, Leadville, Montrose, Pueblo, and Sterling. While some early land records of Denver were lost to floods, others have survived. The Homestead Tract Books and Register of Homestead Entries are found at the National Archives-Rocky Mountain Region in Denver (see page 8). The patent case files are located at the BLM, 2850 Youngfield Street, Lakewood, Colorado 80215. The researcher must know the legal description of the land of interest.

Once granted, transactions of land are recorded at the county level in deed books. These land records, including mortgages and land plats, are the responsibility of the county clerk and recorder's office.

Probate Records

The county court, created by the 1876 state constitution, retains jurisdiction of all matters of probate. Researchers can expect to find indexes to probate records, case files of probate records, administration of estates including record of wills, testamentary and administration matters, appraisements, inventories, sales records, and guardianships. These records are held at the county level, although some early records have been deposited with the Colorado State Archives.

Court Records

The district court holds original jurisdiction in all equity cases, divorce proceedings, naturalizations granted by the county court, coroners' inquests, civil cases, criminal cases, adoptions, and paternity suits.

Tax Records

Tax records in Colorado may be found in a variety of locations. Some are located in the treasurer's office at the county level, while others have been moved to libraries, historical societies, or the state archives. Others have been lost or, with permission of the state of Colorado, destroyed. A few dating to the 1870s or earlier have survived. The researcher may wish to check for an extant WPA Historical Records Survey (see County Resources) for the county of interest. Otherwise, a search on an individual basis will be required.

Cemetery Records

Kay R. Merrill, ed., *The Colorado Cemetery Directory* (Colorado Council of Genealogical Societies, 1985), attempts to identify, locate, and publish information from every known cemetery in the state of Colorado. The book is divided by county and then by alphabetical name of the cemetery. Location, type of cemetery, history, status, and whether published records exist are included in this comprehensive publication.

The Colorado National Guard maintains an incomplete military graves registration that covers military burials from 1862–1949. This index is located at the Colorado State Archives and is restricted, but information from it can be accessed through the archives. If a copy of the original record or cause of death is desired, the researcher will need authorization from the Office of the Adjutant General, Colorado Department of Military Affairs, Administration, 6848 S. Revere Parkway, Englewood, Colorado 80112.

There are two national cemeteries in Colorado: Fort Logan National Cemetery, 3698 S. Sheridan Boulevard, Denver, Colorado 80235, and Fort Lyon National Cemetery, VA Medical Center, Fort Lyon, Colorado 81038.

Church Records

Guide to Vital Statistics Records in Colorado-Church Records, published under the auspices of the WPA, is housed at the Colorado Historical Society. It is also available at the FHL and several other major repositories. The best collection of Roman Catholic records for northern Colorado is located in the Archdiocese of Denver, 200 Josephine Street, Denver, Colorado 80206, and for the southern section at the Archdiocese of Pueblo, Chancery Office, 1426 Grand Avenue, Pueblo, Colorado 81003. These records may be used by genealogical researchers.

A few Colorado church records have been microfilmed and are available for loan through the FHL. A more detailed discussion of church records can be found in Hinckley's article "Genealogical Research in Colorado" (see Background Sources).

Military Records

The Division of State Archives and Public Records holds the National Guard muster rolls from 1861–1919 and the Colorado National Guard service records from 1861–1945. The Adjutant General (see Cemetery Records for address) has a microfilmed copy of the "Index to Compiled Service Records of the Union Army for Colorado."

The researcher may also wish to search Sherman Lee Pompey's *Confederate Soldiers Buried in Colorado* (Independence, Calif.: Historical and Genealogical Publishing Co., 1965) and John H. Nankivel's *History of the Military*

Organizations of the State of Colorado 1860–1935 (Denver, Colo.: W. H. Kistler Stationery Co., ca. 1935).

Soldiers' discharge papers for post World War II and later conflicts are located at the county level in the clerk and recorder's office.

Periodicals, Newspapers, and Manuscript Collections

Periodicals

The Colorado Magazine, published by the Colorado Historical Society since 1923, and called *Heritage* after 1979, contains excellent background material for understanding Colorado family history in the context of local history.

The Colorado Genealogical Society has published *The Colorado Genealogist* since 1939. The subject index for volumes 1–42 was compiled in 1982 by Kay R. Merrill and is very helpful in locating published county records. Every-name indexes to the journal are also available.

Other periodicals include: quarterlies from the Boulder Genealogical Society, P.O. Box 3246, Boulder, Colorado 80307; Genealogical Society of Weld County, P.O. Box 278, Greeley, Colorado 80631; Southeastern Colorado Genealogical Society, P.O. Box 4086, Pueblo Colorado 81003; and *The Foothills Inquirer* published by the Foothills Genealogical Society, P.O. Box 15382, Lakewood, Colorado 80215.

Newspapers

One of the first serious indications of settlement is the formation of a newspaper, and the first issue of *The Rocky Mountain News* was printed on 23 April 1859. The most extensive newspaper collections are housed at the Colorado Historical Society, the Denver Public Library, and Norlin Library of the University of Colorado, Boulder, 80309. There is an unpublished card index to *The Rocky Mountain News* 1865–85 at the Western History Collection at the Denver Public Library. This library also holds an obituary file for *The Denver Post* and *The Rocky Mountain News* beginning in 1939 and includes a few earlier records. These will be searched by library staff for a fee. Microfilm of the newspaper collection at the Colorado Historical Society is available for purchase. The most recent price was $22 per reel.

Two helpful aids to the researcher are Donald E. Oehlerts, comp., *Guide to Colorado Newspapers 1859–1963* (Denver, Colo.: Bibliographic Center for Research, 1964), and Walter R. Griffin and Jay L. Rasmussen, "A Comprehensive Guide to the Location of Published and Unpublished Newspaper Indexes in Colorado Repositories," *The Colorado Magazine* 72 (Fall 1972): 328–39.

Manuscripts

The Western History Collection at the Denver Public Library has a good variety of diaries, journals, letters, membership lists of organizations, and other unpublished sources. It has diaries of Central City and Black Hawk covering years 1859, 1860, and 1861. Other records include the Spanish land grants, Mexican land grants, and mining manuscripts. A helpful resource is the *Catalog of the Western History Department*, Denver Public Library, 7 vols. (Boston, Mass.: G.K. Hall, 1970).

The Colorado Portrait and Biographical Index, developed by Henrietta Bromwell, is housed at the Colorado Historical Society Library and Western History Department at Denver. It is a pre-1900, four-volume index to the biographical works of Colorado, with a two-volume appendix. The developer attempted to include all names mentioned in published works including some magazines and newspapers.

The Dawson Scrapbooks, with an unpublished index, is an eighty-volume collection of names and biographies housed at the Colorado Historical Society.

The 1876 Colorado Business Directory and Denver city directories (beginning 1873) are located at the Colorado Historical Society and the Denver Public Library.

Archives, Libraries, and Societies

Division of State Archives and Public Records (Colorado State Archives)
1313 Sherman Street
Denver, CO 80203

Much of its holdings have been described in various sections above. Additionally, the Colorado State Archives holds the House and Senate journals for the territorial period. It also retains the session laws enacted in Jefferson Territory (1859) and Colorado Territory (1861–76). All out-of-state requests are charged a search fee of $5 per name, payable in advance. This fee is then applied to the copies of information up to three pages. Additional pages are fifty cents per page. There is an additional fee of $3 if certified copies are needed.

Colorado Historical Society
The Stephen H. Hart Library
Colorado Heritage Center
1300 Broadway
Denver, CO 80203

There is an admission fee to the state museum but no fee to use the library, which has extensive holdings described above. No material is circulated.

Denver Public Library
Social Sciences and Genealogy Department
1357 Broadway
Denver, CO 80203

In addition to being a good collection of genealogical research materials and a microfilm collection of census records, the Western History Collection in the library is an extra source for local history and manuscripts.

Colorado Genealogical Society
P.O. Box 9218
Denver, CO 80209

Colorado Council of Genealogical Societies
P.O. Box 24379
Denver, CO 80224
The council can provide a list of all genealogical societies in the state if a self-addressed stamped envelope is included in the request.

County Resources

The WPA published a number of county inventories for Colorado. They have been reprinted and placed on microfiche by the Colorado Genealogical Society. The unpublished manuscripts for these have been deposited at the Colorado State Archives. A survey was *not*, however, completed for every county. With the exceptions listed in the chart below, it is presumed county records exist from the date of county formation, but this has not been verified for all counties. The individual researcher will need to check the specific county of interest. Many of Colorado's early county records have been deposited at the Colorado State Archives.

In the chart below, vital records created before state recording began (see Vital Records) are located at the clerk and recorder's office in the county seat along with land records, unless otherwise noted. Probate records are at the clerk of the county court, and court records at the district court.

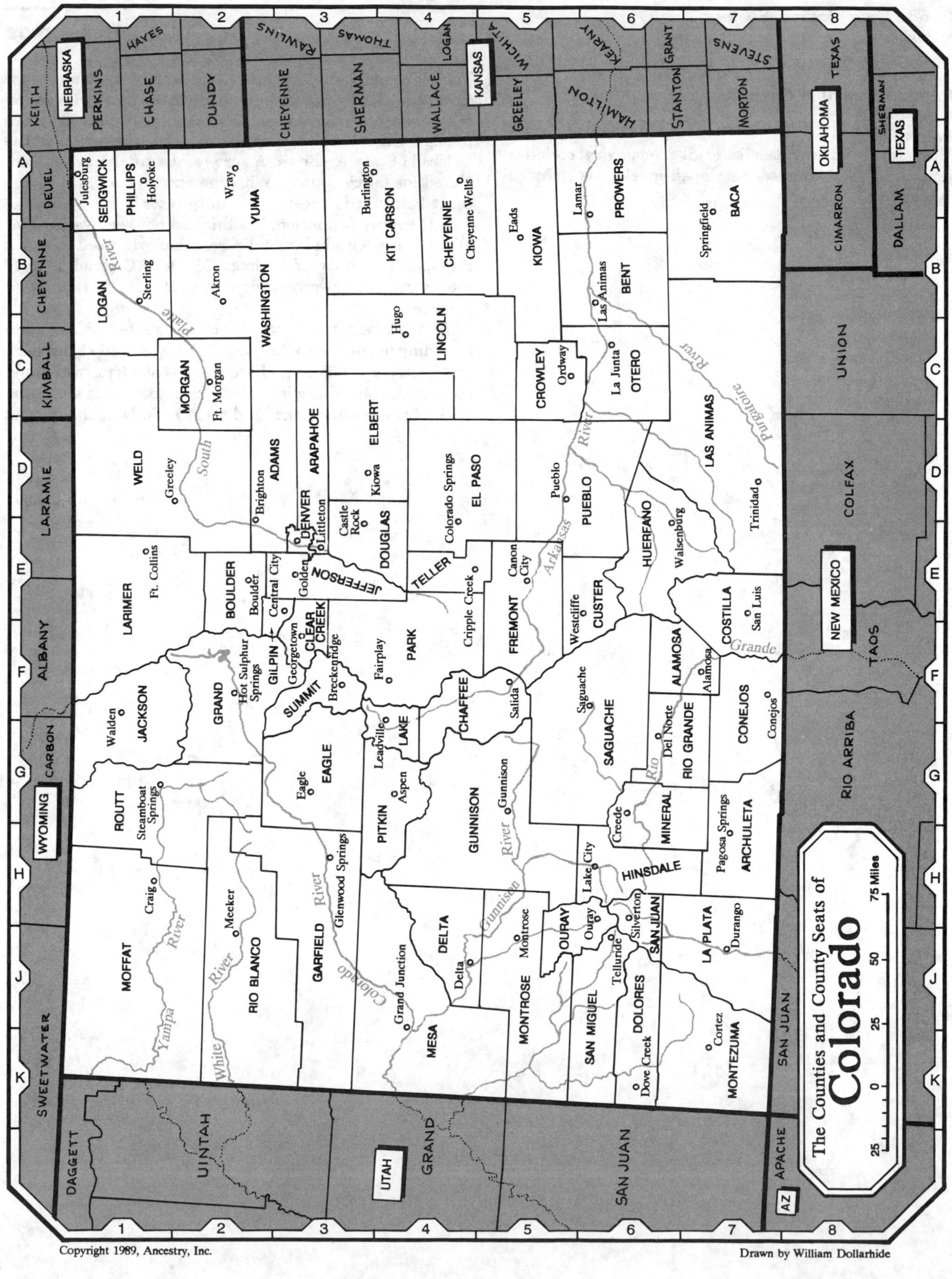

Drawn by William Dollarhide

Map	County Address	Date Formed Parent County/ies	Birth Marriage Death	Land Probate Court
G3	Adams Brighton 80601	1901 Arapahoe	1902–06 1902 1902–08	1902 1902 1902
	Part of Denver County; annexed, 1909.			
E7	Alamosa Alamosa 81101	1913 Costilla/Conejos	— 1913 1913*	1913 1913 1913
	**At Lorton and Miracle Mortuaries in Alamosa.*			
G3	Arapahoe Littleton 80120	1861 original	1872–1902* 1860–1903* 1887–1902*	1861 1902** 1902**
	**At Colorado Department of Health, Vital Records Section.* ***Most records for Denver prior to 1902 have been deposited with the Colorado State Archives. Early land records, surveys, post offices, and territorial government papers are extant for Arapahoe County, and some are located in both the Colorado and Kansas historical societies. However, typical county records such as probate or county court minutes do not exist for the early territorial period of the county before state formation.*			
C7	Archuleta Pagosa Springs 81147	1885 Conejos	1892–1907 1886 1900–07	1886 1886 1886
K7	Baca Springfield 81073	1889 Las Animas	— 1889 —	1889 1889 1889
J6	Bent Las Animas 81054	1870 Greenwood	— 1888 —	1874? 1874? 1874?
F2	Boulder Boulder 80301	1861 original	1880–1909* 1864 1880–1903*	1864 1864 1864
	**City Hall in Boulder. Estate files from 1862 are housed at the Colorado State Archives.*			
	Carbonate	1861 (renamed Lake, 1879)		
E4	Chaffee Salida 81201	1861 (as Lake; renamed, 1879) original	1884–1907 1866 1884–1907	1879? 1879? 1879?
K4	Cheyenne	1889 Bent/Elbert	1893–1907 1889 1893–1904	1889? 1889? 1889?
E3	Clear Creek Georgetown 80444	1861 original	1905–07* 1864* 1902–07*	1859 1861 1861
	**County Archives in Georgetown.*			
E7	Conejos Conejos 81129	1861 (as Guadalupe; renamed, 1869) original	1877–1907 1871 1877–1907	1871 1875 1877
	Some loss of records occurred by fire.			
F7	Costilla San Luis 81152	1861 original	— 1863 1902–07*	1861 1876 1876
	**Alamosa County, Lorton and Miracle Mortuary.*			
H5	Crowley Ordway 81063	1911 Bent/Otero	— 1911 —	1911 1911 1911

Map	County Address	Date Formed Parent County/ies	Birth Marriage Death	Land Probate Court
F6	Custer Westcliffe 81252	1877 Fremont	1905–07 1877* 1902–07	1877 1877 1877
	**Some earlier in Fremont County miscellaneous file.*			
B4	Delta Delta 81416	1883 Gunnison	1895–1909 1883 1895–1909	1883 1883 1883
F3	Denver Denver 80202	1901 Arapahoe	1872–1907 1860 1887–1907	1902 1865–1959* 1902
	In 1911, Denver City and Denver County merged. Births and Deaths, 1964–present, are at Vital Statistics Room, Denver General Hospital. **Many early Denver records have been deposited at the Colorado State Archives.*			
B6	Dolores Dove Creek 81324	1881 Ouray	1894 1881 1894–1907	1881 1881 1881
F3	Douglas Castle Rock 80104	1861 original	1894–1908 1864 1894	1863 1861? 1861?
	Original county seat was at Franktown. Counthouse burned in 1978 with minimal loss of records.			
D3	Eagle Eagle 81631	1883 Summit	1894–1901 1879 1894–1901	1883 1883 1883
G3	Elbert Kiowa 80117	1874 Douglas	1894–1907 1874* 1876–96	1874 1874 1874
G4	El Paso Colorado Springs 80902	1861 original	1890–1906* 1861 1893–1907*	1861 1861? 1861?
	**City Health Department.*			
E5	Fremont Canon City 81212	1861 original	1884–1907 1865 1884–1907	1862 1874 1868
B3	Garfield Glenwood Springs 81601	1883 Summit	1893–1909 1884 1883–89*	1883 1883 1883
	**Rio Blanco County marriages 1883–89.*			
E22	Gilpin Central City 80427	1861 original	— 1865 —	1861? 1861? 1861?
E2	Grand Hot Sulphur Springs 80451	1874 Summit	1895–1908 1881 1894–1907	1874? 1874? 1874?
	Greenwood	1870 (abolished 1874; parts annexed to Elbert and Bent)		
	Guadalupe	1861 (renamed Conejos, 1869) original		
C4	Gunnison Gunnison 81230	1877 Lake	1895–1908 1877 1894–97	1877? 1877? 1877?

Map	County Address	Date Formed Parent County/ies	Birth Marriage Death	Land Probate Court
C6	Hinsdale Lake City 81235	1874 Conejos	1899–1907 1876 1899–1907	1874 1876 1876
F6	Huerfano Walsenburg 81089 **Courthouse basement.*	1861 original	— 1875 1902–06*	1861? 1861? 1861?
D1	Jackson Walden 80480	1909 Grand	— 1909 —	1909? 1909? 1909?
F3	Jefferson Golden 80401 *A small part was annexed to Park, 1903.*	1861 original	1893–1906 1874–76; 1881 1893–1906	1861? 1861? 1861?
J5	Kiowa Eads 81036	1889 Cheyenne/Bent	— 1889 —	1889? 1889? 1889?
K3	Kit Carson Burlington 80807 **Courthouse basement; other deaths (1876–1907) at clerk and recorder's office.*	1889 Elbert	1893–1907* 1889 1892–1907*	1889? 1889? 1889?
	Lake (old)	1861 (renamed Chaffee, 1879) original		
E4	Lake (present) Leadville 80461 **City clerk, Leadville.*	1861 (as Carbonate; renamed, 1879) original	1891–1906* 1869 1881–1903*	1861? 1861? 1861?
B7	La Plata Durango 81301 **Vital statistics registrar, City Hall, Durango; also clerk and recorder's office 1900–12; early marriages in San Juan County clerk and recorder's office.*	1874 Conejos/Lake	1895–1918* 1880* 1895–1918	1874? 1874? 1874?
F1	Larimer Fort Collins 80521	1861 original	1902–08 1862 1902–08	1862 1862 1862
G7	Las Animas Trinidad 81082 **Also, city of Trinidad 1893–1907.*	1866 Huerfano	1893–96* 1868 1893–1904	1866? 1866? 1866?
J4	Lincoln Hugo 80821 **Courthouse basement.*	1889 Elbert	1889–1920* 1887 1889–1907*	1889? 1889? 1889?
J1	Logan Sterling 80751	1887 Weld	— 1887 —	1866 1887 1887
B4	Mesa Grand Junction 81501 **Courthouse storage.*	1883 Gunnison	1893–1909* 1883 1893–1901*	1883? 1883? 1883?

Map	County Address	Date Formed Parent County/ies	Birth Marriage Death	Land Probate Court
D6	Mineral Creede 81130	1892 Hinsdale	1896–1909 1891 1896–1907	1893? 1893? 1893?
B1	Moffat Craig 81625	1911 Routt	— 1911 —	1911? 1911? 1911?
A7	Montezuma Cortez 81321	1889 La Plata	— 1889 —	1889? 1889? 1889?
B5	Montrose Montrose 81401 **Courthouse basement vault, births 1900–07.*	1883 Gunnison	1900–07* 1883 1883–1907*	1883? 1883? 1883?
H2	Morgan Fort Morgan 80701 **Vital statistics registrar, Fort Morgan births.*	1889 Weld	1894–1908* 1889 1894–1908*	1873 1889 1889
H6	Otero La Junta 81050 **Vital statistics registrar, La Junta.*	1889 Bent	1889* 1889 1887–1907	1889? 1889? 1889?
C5	Ouray Ouray 81427 **Vital statistics registrar, Ouray; also clerk and recorder's office deaths 1880–1907.*	1877 (as Uncompahgre; renamed, 1883) Hinsdale/San Juan	1880–1907* 1881 1894*	1877? 1877? 1873
E4	Park Fairplay 80440 *A small part of Jefferson was annexed, 1903*	1861 original	1892–1908 1876 1899–1907	1861? 1861? 1861?
K1	Phillips Holyoke 80734	1889 Logan	1903–05 1889 1902–05	1889? 1889? 1889?
D4	Pitkin Aspen 81611	1881 Gunnison	1890–1907 1881 1890–1907	1881? 1881? 1881?
K6	Prowers Lamar 81052	1889 Bent	1891–1907 1889 1891–1907	1889 1889 1889
G6	Pueblo Pueblo 81003 *Pueblo City-County Health Department, 1511 Central Mail, Pueblo 81003, has early vital records not found at Colorado Department of Health.*	1861 original	1887–1901 1860 1887–1907	1861 1861 1861
B2	Rio Blanco Meeker 81641 ** Also 1905–07.*	1889 Summit	1889–1907 1883 1892–1903*	1889 1889 1889
D6	Rio Grande Del Norte 81132	1874 Conejos/Costilla	1898–1907 1874 1902–07	1874? 1874? 1874?

Map	County Address	Date Formed Parent County/ies	Birth Marriage Death	Land Probate Court
D1	Routt Steamboat Springs 80477	1877 Grand	1903–08 1877 1903–08	1877? 1877? 1877?
D6	Saguache Saguache 81149	1866 Costilla	1894–1908 1869 1872–1907	1866? 1866? 1866?
C6	San Juan Silverton 81433 **City clerk, Silverton.*	1876 La Plata	1901–07* 1871 1902–07*	1876 1876? 1876?
B6	San Miguel Telluride 81435 **Vital statistics registrar, Telluride.*	1883 Ouray	1900–07* 1883 1907–20*	1883? 1883? 1883?
K1	Sedgwick Julesburg 80737	1889 Logan	1897–1906 1889 1897–1906	1889? 1889? 1889?
E3	Summit Breckenridge 80424	1861 original	1892–96 1862 1892–1905	1861? 1861? 1861?
F4	Teller Cripple Creek 80813 **Incomplete. County death records are separate and extant from those kept by the city of Cripple Creek, which were lost by fire.*	1899 El Paso	1904 1899 1902–08*	1899? 1899? 1899?
	Uncompahgre	1877 (renamed Ouray, 1883)		
J2	Washington Akron 80720 **Vital statistics registrar.*	1887 Weld/Arapahoe	1894–1911* 1887 1894–1907*	1872 1887 1887
G1	Weld Greeley 80631	1861 original	1872–1909 1864 1872–1908	1865 1861? 1861?
K2	Yuma Wray 80758	1889 Washington/Arapahoe	1893–1907 1889 1893–1907	1889? 1889? 1889?

CONNECTICUT

Alice Eichholz, Ph.D., C.G.

The first colonies that would become Connecticut developed along the shores of Long Island Sound and the banks of the Housatonic and Connecticut rivers. Influenced by Rev. Thomas Hooker's principle of authority growing out of the free expression of its people, the utopian experiment of Connecticut Colony began between 1633–35. It produced little class distinction, a change from the heavy-handed authoritarian expectations of the Massachusetts colonies. The Congregational church was not only thoroughly integrated into town life, but interpretation of its theology seemed to create less social stratification.

Similar to Rhode Island in its political organization, Connecticut differed from the new settlements in Rhode Island and Providence Plantations in that if possessed a rich agricultural terrain. The first settlements along the Connecticut River near Windsor coexisted with Native American villages and a Dutch trading post near what is now Hartford. Settlers from Massachusetts reached these settlements primarily by foot. Concurrently, John Winthrop, Jr., sailed a group from England to establish Saybrook along the coast. By 1638, with other settlements already harvesting their crops and increasing their number of clapboard houses, New Haven Colony, under the theological leadership of John Davenport, entrenched itself along the coast and began building the more elaborate houses they had become accustomed to in England.

New Haven Colony merged with Connecticut Colony in 1662, while new settlements moved farther north on the Connecticut River to settle western Massachusetts towns; one group founded Newark, New Jersey. More and more of the rich agricultural land was purchased from the Native Americans. From intitial settlement through the middle of the eighteenth century Connecticut's, as well as the rest of New England's, relationship with the original inhabitants continued to deteriorate and culminated in the French and Indian wars.

Connecticut's homogeneous population and community-centered form of government existed away from the mainstream of royal imperial affairs and remained focused on the town and its people. With voices of the impending Revolution espousing the principles of freedom of expression, Connecticut began to move away from a solely town focus and look out toward the broader community of colonies opposing Royal authority. Connecticut people fought on both sides of the conflict, with many Loyalists migrating north and east to Canada, including what are now the eastern provinces.

By the end of the Revolution family farms were unable to support the large number of young people in the area. The population boom made it necessary for more and more descendants of original settlers to leave for the north, west, and south to provide for themselves and their families. Cheaper, available land elsewhere provided much of the motivation. Farms gave way to the newly burgeoning Industrial Revolution, and new ethnic groups—Italians, Poles, French-Canadians in the nineteenth century; Blacks, Puerto Ricans, and Asians in the twentieth—wended their way along the Long Island Sound's shoreline of Connecticut's growing metropolitan areas.

Today Connecticut enjoys the distinction of being the New England state with the most centrally located resources for genealogical research. Its 169 towns still function without county government, and the size and shape of Connecticut's terrain affords easy, fairly quick access to its centrally located capital of Hartford.

Vital Records

Marriages were recorded in Connecticut as early as 1640. Registration of births, marriages, and deaths had become the town clerk's responsibility by 1650. Since a fine was assessed for not recording an event, some industrious town clerks have excellent, fairly complete records; however, others do not. Following the Revolution to the mid-nineteenth century, the recording is not as thorough, but by 1870, when the State Board of Health was established, recording in all towns improved.

Recording of vital events is the town clerk's responsibility. After 1 July 1897, copies were sent to the State Department of Health, Vital Records Unit, 150 Washington Street, Hartford, Connecticut 06106.

The Lucius Barnes Barbour Collection is well known to the Connecticut researcher. It is housed in the Connecticut State Library (see Archives, Libraries, and Societies), but microfilm copies of it are widely available. Begun after establishment of the State Department of Health, Barbour's project was to abstract and collect all town vital records up to the mid-1800s. There are two formats to the material. The first is a statewide paper slip alphabetical index containing a complete abstract of each vital record taken from the books in each town. The card file holding this index takes up an entire wall at the Connecticut State Library. The second format is the group of separately bound volumes of abstracts of vital records for most towns, prepared from the slips.

A recent microfilming project of Connecticut town records between 1850 and 1897 makes access to vital records after the Barbour collection cut-off (ca. 1850) and before statewide recording easier. The microfilms, held by the Connecticut State Library and the FHL, are of original records and are *not* indexed statewide as is the Barbour collection. After 1 July 1897 the records at the Vital Records Unit are indexed statewide. Consequently, no statewide index exists between 1850–97, making it necessary to know the town in which the event occurred to locate a record for those years.

Since not all vital events were recorded in the town office, church and cemetery records need to be consulted as well as other genealogical alternatives to official records.

Divorces are presently granted by the superior court, although this was not always the case. Most of the early records for Connecticut divorces are at the Connecticut State Library, including the packets of original documents and the superior court records books. Recently, Grace L. Knox and Barbara Ferris have published through Heritage Books a two-volume index to Connecticut divorce packets. Volume one covers New London, Tolland, and Windham counties; volume two covers Litchfield and Hartford counties. Recent divorce packets remain in the court. For details on changes of jurisdiction for divorces in Connecticut see Henry S. Cohn's "Connecticut's Divorce Mechanism, 1636–1969," *The American Journal of Legal History* 14 (January 1970): 35–54, which is summarized in an information leaflet on divorce records available from the Connecticut State Library.

Census Records

Federal

Population Schedules.

- Indexed—1790, 1800, 1810, 1820, 1830, 1840, 1850, 1860
- Soundex—1880, 1900, 1920
- Unindexed—1870, 1910

Industry and Agriculture Schedules.

- 1850, 1860, 1870, 1880

Mortality Schedules.

- 1850, 1860, 1870, 1880 (not indexed)

Connecticut has a complete set of federal census records. Either originals or microfilm copies and all available book indexes to the above are at the Connecticut State Library. A special index from 1790 to 1850 at the Connecticut State Library is from a duplicate set of census schedules housed in the state archives. It is not collated in the same way as the "official" set at the National Archives and consequently cannot be used for locating a particular individual on the federal set of returns. However, the Connecticut version of the index includes *all* names in the 1850 census and not just heads of households.

Colonial

A number of inventories and enumerations of population or census substitutes exist (with and without names). The most complete compilation is Jay Mack Holbrook's *Connecticut 1670 Census* (Oxford, Mass.: Holbrook Research Institute, 1977), which combines a number of sources (tax, land, church, freeman, probate) in an attempt to count the heads of household by name for the entire colony in the time period 1667–73. As with all such compilations, it is particularly important to check the original sources the compiler used.

The 1669/1670 Grain Inventory for Hartford, Wethersfield, and Windsor inventories heads of household, by name and number of family members, as well as bushels of wheat and corn held by the family. Published in volume 21 of *Collections of the Connecticut Historical Society* (Hartford, Conn.: the society, 1924), pages 190–99, the inventory is not a complete listing of inhabitants for that year but provides an interesting perspective on the settlements.

Enumerations exist for 1756, 1762, and 1774 but they do not list names, only numbers of people in town in the categories of race, sex, and age groups. Details on the first and last can be found in volume 14 of *Public Records of the Colony of Connecticut, 1636–1776* (see Court Records). The 1762 returns are published in Christopher P. Bickford's "The Lost Connecticut Census of 1762 Found," *Connecticut Historical Society Bulletin* 44 (April 1979): 33–43.

State

No state population censuses were taken for Connecticut, but a unique census was taken by the state in the twentieth century. The Military Census of 1917 listed all males between at least twenty and thirty years of age, although most towns reported those sixteen through sixty. Given along with the name and age were place of birth and number of dependents, ability to perform certain tasks, and occupation. Both the originally completed sheets and the index cards have been microfilmed in a separate series and are available at the Connecticut State Library and the FHL. The microfilm for the index cards is arranged by town and then alphabetically by surname. The form number on index cards is needed to locate the original sheets on microfilm (Record Group 29).

Background Sources

Connecticut's wealth and centralization of genealogical sources is matched by its compilations of genealogies, guidebooks, place-name directories, and local historical materials.

Perhaps the grandparent of genealogical compilations for an entire community is Donald Lines Jacobus, *Families of Ancient New Haven* (1922–32; reprint, 9 vols. in 3, Baltimore, Md.: Genealogical Publishing Co., 1981), which follows the families who settled in New Haven County towns before 1800. It comprises the families in the towns of New Haven, East Haven, North Haven, Hamden, Bethany, Woodbridge, and West Haven and incorporates vital, church, cemetery, probate, court, and town records.

Similar compilations were done by others for Guilford, Hartford, Milford, and Wallingford. *The New England Historical and Genealogical Register* has included a succession of articles on Connecticut families that has been reprinted in three volumes as *Genealogies of Connecticut Families* (Baltimore, Md.: Genealogical Publishing Co., 1983).

A comprehensive bibliography to local history can be found in Roger Parks, ed., *Connecticut: A Bibliography of its History* (Hanover, N.H.: University Press of New England, 1986).

Although not limited to Connecticut people only, Fremont Rider's *American Genealogical-Biographical Index* (Middletown, Conn.: Godfrey Memorial Library, 1952–present) has its roots in this state. Updated in alphabetical volumes, this unusual set indexes many census records, genealogies, tax lists, and other sources to provide the researcher with an indication of where to locate information for different surnames at different times and places. In the days before indexing became the norm for genealogical work, this publication provided one of the first comprehensive indexes not specifically focused on periodicals.

Other publications useful in Connecticut research are:

Abbe, Elizabeth, "Connecticut Genealogical Research: Sources and Suggestions," *The New England Historical and Genealogical Register* 134 (January 1980): 3–26.

Bushman, Richard L. *From Puritan to Yankee: Character and the Social Order in Connecticut, 1690–1765.* Cambridge, Mass.: Harvard University Press, 1967. This excellent study encourages a broad overview of understanding the individual in relationship to the community. Studying the psychological and economic underpinnings of a community increases awareness of the motivation of ancestors.

Hughes, Arthur H., and Morse S. Allen. *Connecticut Place Names.* Hartford, Conn.: Connecticut Historical Society, 1976. This excellent place-name directory lists rivers, topographical features, names of Native American origin, towns and sections of towns, and geological points. It has an excellent cross-index. This is important because early churches, post offices, and industrial sections often had different names than those of the incorporated town in which they were located.

Kemp, Thomas Jay. *Connecticut Researcher's Handbook.* Detroit, Mich.: Gale Research Co., 1981. This guidebook provides a solid bibliography by subject and a town-by-town description of resources available.

Secretary of State. *Connecticut State Register and Manual.* Hartford, Conn.: Secretary of State, annually. Known as the Blue Book, this reference guide to state and town information with addresses, phone numbers, and hours of operation is essential in pursuing records in person in town offices.

Sperry, Kip. *Connecticut Sources for Family Historians and Genealogists.* Logan, Utah: Everton Publishers, 1980. The itemization of resources indicates availability on the local level, including an excellent listing and description of the archives available at the Connecticut State Library. Those materials on microfilm through the FHL are indicated as well.

Maps

Essential companions to place-name directories in Connecticut are the fine series of Beers Atlases produced in the 1860–70s detailing structures, property owners, places of business, schools, cemeteries, and churches in each town. Bound in folio-sized books by county, these excellent resources can be found in many Connecticut libraries, in addition to the Connecticut State Library. The earlier, 1852 Clark's County Maps are equally available at the same locations.

Present-day street maps by county are readily available in most large stationery stores.

Land Records

State-Land State

England had what it considered legal right to the land in Connecticut, like the rest of New England. It was not until 1662, nearly thirty years after British subjects established the settlements of Connecticut, that a royal charter affirmed the settlements' legal right to land. New Haven Colony and Connecticut Colony formed a united commonwealth of Connecticut as a result of the charter. Previous to 1662, land was generally recognized by settlers as belonging to Native Americans and, consequently, acquired or purchased from them.

The Fundamental Orders of Connecticut, adopted in 1639, provided for the recording of land transactions in town records. The Connecticut General Assembly (originally the Connecticut General Court) had first jurisdiction over the colony and established town proprietors to dispose of land in their control. Land was divided and sold in lots; registration of deed transactions remains the responsibility of the town clerk.

While few land records in Connecticut have been published, the exception is volume 14 of *Collections of The Connecticut Historical Society* (Hartford, Conn.: the Society, 1912), which includes all the Hartford land records from 1639 to the 1680s. A supplement, although only an index, is the *General Index of the Land Records of the Town of Hartford, 1639–1879* (Hartford, Conn.: Connecticut Historical Society, 1873–83).

Deed books are generally indexed individually. Town clerks usually have comprehensive indexes to grantors and grantees. Formerly microfilmed only to 1850, the deed books to 1900 have now been microfilmed and can be consulted either in the central location at the Connecticut State Library or through the FHL and its branches. There is no statewide index to all deeds, however.

Probate Records

Connecticut can boast centralization of many research sources and clear jurisdiction on land and vital records. Finding the correct probate jurisdiction for a particular time period is more complicated. For the 169 towns, there are about 130 probate districts. Jurisdictional lines have changed considerably over the three centuries, but their function has been consistent in probating wills, distributing estates, and appointing guardians.

Before 1698 probate jurisdiction was succesively held by the general court (general assembly) or the secretary of the colony, the particular courts, and then the county courts. When the probate courts were created in 1698, the probate jurisdiction paralleled that of the county, but by 1719 the four original probate districts started to divide. Each present probate district has a genealogy of its own. Space restrictions in the Town Resources section below necessitate an abbreviated lineage indicating only one parent probate district. *A Checklist of Probate Records in the Connecticut State Library* delineates the lines of descent for each present district. This publication, originally done in 1970, is even now out-dated, but the Connecticut State Library is working on a new revised edition that may be published in the near future. Kemp's research guide (see Background Sources) also indicates which probate district a town belonged to at different times.

As with all probate records, not only the court record books themselves (clerk's transcripts of probate proceedings), but the estate papers or files (original wills, receipts, affidavits, etc.) also contain essential genealogical information. The record books remain in the probate clerk's office with microfilm copies to about 1915 in the Connecticut State Library and the FHL. The exception is New Haven, whose original record books are at the Connecticut State Library instead of the probate clerk's office. Many of the district estate papers or files to 1900 (some later) have been deposited in the Connecticut State Library. Packets of these original documents have been microfilmed to 1880 and are available on microfilm at both the Connecticut State Library and the FHL. Photocopies of original files are no longer permitted because of their fragile condition. There is a statewide index of these probate packets at the Connecticut State Library.

A printed source for one district is Charles W. Manwaring, *A Digest of the Early Connecticut Probate Records,* 3 vols. (Hartford, Conn.: R. S. Peck & Co., 1904–06), which covers the Hartford Probate District records from 1635–1750.

Court Records

With court records, the researcher finds Connecticut's centralization welcome again, with many held at the Connecticut State Library. Despite this centralization, the array of courts whose records might include such things as debts, apprenticeships, warrants, and misdemeanors, presents a somewhat complicated research challenge.

Justices of the peace represented the law closest to the people; the justices having been originally appointed by the general assembly. What remain of many of these records through the nineteenth century are at the Connecticut State Library.

Before the creation of counties in 1666, the particular court was a court of first instance. "Records of the Particular Court of Connecticut, 1639–1663," *Collections of The Connecticut Historical Society,* Vol. 22 (Hartford, Conn.: the Society, 1928), conveys most of these proceedings. Original court records are in the Connecticut State Library.

In the next phase, between 1665–1711, the court of assistants became the trial court, and county courts were added. All criminal activities were the purview of the court of assistants, as well as appeals from lower courts regarding disputes, including divorces. In 1711, the court of assistants was succeeded by the superior court, which remains part of Connecticut's judicial system today. Records of the court of assistants (1665-1771) are generally available at the Connecticut State Library.

Superior court districts are defined by county designation. In the Town Resources section, the county is listed; however, in trying to determine jurisdiction for earlier records, listings of parent counties will be helpful. Records through the nineteenth century of superior courts operating in each county are generally available at the Connecticut State Library.

Those matters not in the realm the superior court were heard by the county courts (initially called prerogative or common pleas court). The county court, begun in 1666, was abolished in 1855, and its functions were divided between justice courts and superior courts. Most of the county court records, to its abolition date, are at the Connecticut State Library.

Courts of common pleas were authorized in the late nineteenth century to assume work that could not be handled by either the justice or superior courts. In 1961 the court system reorganized, abolishing justice courts, creating district courts, and retaining the county superior court and the statewide supreme court.

Two publications contain court records for the seventeenth century. The first three volumes of J. Hammond Trumbull, *The Public Records of the Colony of Connecticut* (Hartford, Conn.: State Printers, 1850–59), cover the years 1636–89 for the older colony. The equivalent records for New Haven are in Charles J. Hoadly, *Records of the Colony . . . of New Haven,* 2 vols. (Hartford, Conn.: State Printers, 1857–58). Volume 1 covers the years 1638–49, while volume 2 covers the years 1653–64.

Tax Records

Taxes were levied for personal property and land through most of Connecticut's history. The town assessor (or lister) made annual lists or rates of all taxables. This generated a considerable number of tax lists over time. The Connecticut State Library has a list of various tax records still at the town clerk's offices. The Connecticut Historical Society and the genealogical collections throughout the state have some records. See Frederick Robertson Jones, *History of Taxation in Connecticut, 1636–1776* (Baltimore, Md.: Johns Hopkins Press, 1896).

A highly valuable tax record for Connecticut is the U.S. Direct Tax for 1798. The records are extant for nearly half of the towns with some also having rate lists for 1813, 1814, 1815, and 1816. The original booklets indicate rate based on land, dwellings, and personal property, the latter of which is usually itemized. Later years indicate out-of-state owners. The records have not been microfilmed as a group, but the originals can be researched at the Connecticut Historical Society.

Cemetery Records

Centralization is the norm for Connecticut's cemetery records. The Connecticut State Library holds the Hale Collection containing over one million gravestone inscriptions. The project to collect these began in 1916 by Charles R. Hale but was continued by an act of the General Assembly and the WPA through the 1930s. While clearly many stones had been lost or destroyed by that time, over 2,000 cemeteries were located statewide and included in the collection. Each town's inscriptions are bound in separate volumes, but an alphabetical index for the entire state is available. Both have been microfilmed and are available through the FHL.

Cemeteries might have been church, family, town, or private ones. Only twentieth-century death records have place of burial indicated, but most administrators operating cemeteries in the state have records of their own, and many historical societies in the state have collections of town cemeteries not included in the Hale Collection. The DAR's volumes of Bible, cemetery, and family records are deposited at the Connecticut State Library and the DAR Library in Washington, D.C.

Town clerks usually keep "Burial Books," generally beginning in the late nineteenth century, which indicate place of burial in that town for those who died outside of town.

Church Records

Early Connecticut settlers established the Congregational church as the tax-supported state church until 1818 when the state constitution was accepted abolishing the connection between church and state. Sometimes, if one parish was getting too large, a second parish was formed that became a precursor to a new town, with the permission of the general assembly. Other denominations followed eventually, particularly the Baptists from Rhode Island on the eastern border with Connecticut, Episcopalians and Quakers. Information in Connecticut's church records has often been found to be more informative, complete, or accurate than the town vital records.

Among the printed sources of Connecticut church records is Frederick W. Bailey's *Early Connecticut Marriages as Found on Ancient Church Records Prior to 1800* (1896–1906; reprint, 7 vols. in 1, Baltimore, Md.: Genealogical Publishing Co., 1982), which covers mainly Congregational and Episcopal records.

Approximately one-quarter of those records housed at the Connecticut State Library have been indexed in a format similar to that of the Barbour (see Vital Records) and Hale (see Cemetery Records) collections with individual index slips and bound compilations of individual churches. This Church Record Index File is statewide, goes beyond 1850, but does not include all church records. Even in a town with more than one Congregational church, generally only the first is included in this index. Notably, many church records in incorporated cities have not been indexed.

As with other record categories discussed above, guides are available. *A Guide to Vital Statistics in the Church Records of Connecticut,* prepared by the Connecticut Historical Records Survey (New Haven, Conn.: Historical

Records Survey, 1942), assists in locating what categories of records remain in each town and for each time period. It was incomplete when it was taken and has not been updated. Many town churches have deposited their older records for safekeeping with the Connecticut State Library.

A List of Church Records in the Connecticut State Library (available at the cost of photocopy and postage), the library's Manuscripts and Archives catalogs, and the Church Records Survey conducted by the WPA (State Archives Record Group 33) are additional sources that can be used to locate church records not in the Church Records Index.

As a supplement to vital records, indications of migration are found in listings of church membership, which frequently include dates of admission to the local church or dismissal to a new church.

Military Records

Connecticut's military records, starting with the Pequot War, have been published and are widely available. In addition to the sources available at the National Archives (see page 7) and archival sources at the Connecticut State Library, the following can be consulted:

Shepard, James. *Connecticut Soldiers in the Pequot War of 1637.* Meriden, Conn.: Journal Publishing Co., 1913.

Collections of the Connecticut Historical Society. *Rolls of Connecticut Men in the French and Indian War, 1755–1762.* Vol. IX and X. Hartford, Conn.: Connecticut Historical Society, 1903–05.

Connecticut Adjutant-General. *Record of Service of Connecticut Men in the War of the Revolution, War of 1812, Mexican War.* Hartford, Conn.: Connecticut General Assembly, 1889. Transcripts of original papers with a cross index to all records. Connecticut provided large numbers in the ranks of patriots and the largest number of black soldiers from all the colonies (see Black Americans).

Many Connecticut men were Loyalists, although a comprehensive listing of them is not available. Many sought refuge in Canada. See Angus Baxter, *In Search of Your Canadian Roots* (Baltimore, Md.: Genealogical Publishing Co., 1989), for a discussion of United Empire Loyalists.

Connecticut Adjutant-General. *Record of Service of Connecticut Men in the Army and Navy of the United States During the War of Rebellion.* Hartford, Conn.: Case, Lockwood and Brainard Co., 1889.

The Connecticut Historical Society has a large collection of military documents and manuscripts. The Connecticut State Library maintains a card file on veteran's deaths with place of burial.

Periodicals, Newspapers, and Manuscript Collections

Periodicals

New Haven Genealogical Magazine (formerly *The Families of Ancient New Haven* and now *The American Genealogist*) was begun by Donald Lines Jacobus and still sets a standard for its depth and documentation (see page 7).

Connecticut Nutmegger (1968–present) is a current publication of the Connecticut Society of Genealogists (see Archives, Libraries, and Societies).

Newspapers

The *Connecticut Courant* served not only Connecticut but the burgeoning frontier to its north, in Massachusetts and Vermont, and its west in New York. It is an important early source for marriages and deaths. Births are rarely in its pages. Reports from the frontier are quite common including land advertisements, letters from former residents, and social items. It is widely available on microfilm, and an index (1764–1820) by Doris Cook is available at the Connecticut Historical Society.

Donald Gustafson, *A Preliminary Checklist of Connecticut Newspapers, 1755–1975,* 2 vols. (Hartford, Conn.: Connecticut State Library, 1978), indicates what is extant and where it is available. A statewide Hale Index (1750 to ca. 1870), at the Connecticut State Library and available on microfilm, surveyed more than ninety of the newspapers for marriages and deaths. A large collection of newspapers themselves are on microfilm to the present.

Between 1910 and 1967, the *Hartford Times* ran a genealogical query column, similar to that of the *Boston Evening Transcript* (see Massachusetts—Newspapers), which has been indexed and microfilmed by the Godfrey Memorial Library in Middletown and distributed to many major research libraries.

Manuscripts

As with all record categories, the manuscript collections in Connecticut are excellent. The major repositories —Connecticut State Library, Connecticut Historical Society, Greenwich Library, Ferguson Library in Stamford, and Otis Library in Norwich—all have extensive collections. Family papers abound in these collections, but other items such as school records, church records, and original copies of wills and deeds can sometimes be found. There are no every-name indexes, but the collections are well cataloged.

Archives, Libraries, and Societies

Connecticut State Library
History and Genealogy Unit
231 Capitol Avenue
Hartford 06106

This major research repository is composed of two parts: the State Archives and the History and Genealogy Unit. The unit provides the researcher in person and mail access to the archival material, genealogical indexes, and published materials described in various sections above. The staff is not available for research, however. Guides to their original source materials are available at the cost of photocopying and postage. They are extremely helpful in focusing research.

Connecticut Historical Society
1 Elizabeth Street
Hartford 06105

This is a major genealogical reference library with excellent holdings in family genealogies, town histories, census records, and a book loan program for members.

Connecticut Society of Genealogists
P.O. Box 435
Glastonbury 06033

Their publication, *Connecticut Nutmegger,* is available by subscription or with membership. The society meets often during the year with an educational program for genealogists.

Connecticut Ancestry Society
P.O. Box 249
Stamford 06904

Formerly called the Stamford Genealogical Society, it has a publication called *Connecticut Ancestry,* previously *Bulletin of the Stamford Genealogical Society* (1971) and holds monthly meetings.

Special Focus Categories

Immigration

Connecticut's immigration lists are included in the NARA microfilm publication, M575, *Copies of Lists of Passengers Arriving at Miscellaneous Ports on the Atlantic and Gulf Coasts 1820–1873* (see page 10, for earlier sources).

Naturalization

As with other states, naturalizations might have been granted in any Connecticut court up to the twentieth century. Some are still in the county courthouses, but all that were held at the Connecticut State Library were transferred to the National Archives-New England Region (see page 8) in 1984 and are being microfilmed with a copy of the film to be returned for research at the state library. Those filed and granted after 1906 are in the federal district court for Bridgeport, Hartford, or New Haven.

Black American

From colonial times, blacks have been a major ethnic group in Connecticut, providing a large number of Revolutionary soldiers.

White, David Oliver. *Connecticut's Black Soldiers, 1775–1783.* Connecticut Bicentennial Series, no. 4. Chester, Conn.: Pequot Press, 1973.

Rose, James M., and Barbara W. Brown. *Black Roots in Southeastern Connecticut, 1650–1900.* Detroit, Mich.: Gale Research Co., 1980.

Rose, James M. *Tapestry: A Living History of the Black Family in Southeastern Connecticut.* New London, Conn.: New London Historical Society, 1979.

Weed, Ralph Foster. *Slavery in Connecticut.* New Haven, Conn.: Yale University Press, 1935.

Native American

See Massachusetts—Special Focus Categories for sources on historical background.

County Resources

Counties were abolished officially in 1959, their purpose had been chiefly to define county court districts. For genealogical research purposes counties become necessary when using the federal census returns, since they are all cataloged by county. Connecticut's original four counties had become eight counties by the time of the first federal census in 1790. Although some towns on county borders crossed county jurisdictions for different census enumerations, the most accurate indication of these changes can be found in William Thorndale and William Dollarhide, *Map Guide to the U.S. Federal Censuses, 1790–1920* (Baltimore, Md.: Genealogical Publishing Co., 1987). It should be consulted when using census records. Each town's present county is given in the Town Resources section.

Map	County	Date Formed	Parent County/ies
B6	Fairfield	1666	original
E2	Hartford	1666	original
B2	Litchfield	1751	Fairfield/Hartford
F5	Middlesex	1785	Hartford/New Haven
D5	New Haven	1666	original
J5	New London	1666	original
G2	Tolland	1785	Windham
J2	Windham	1726	New London

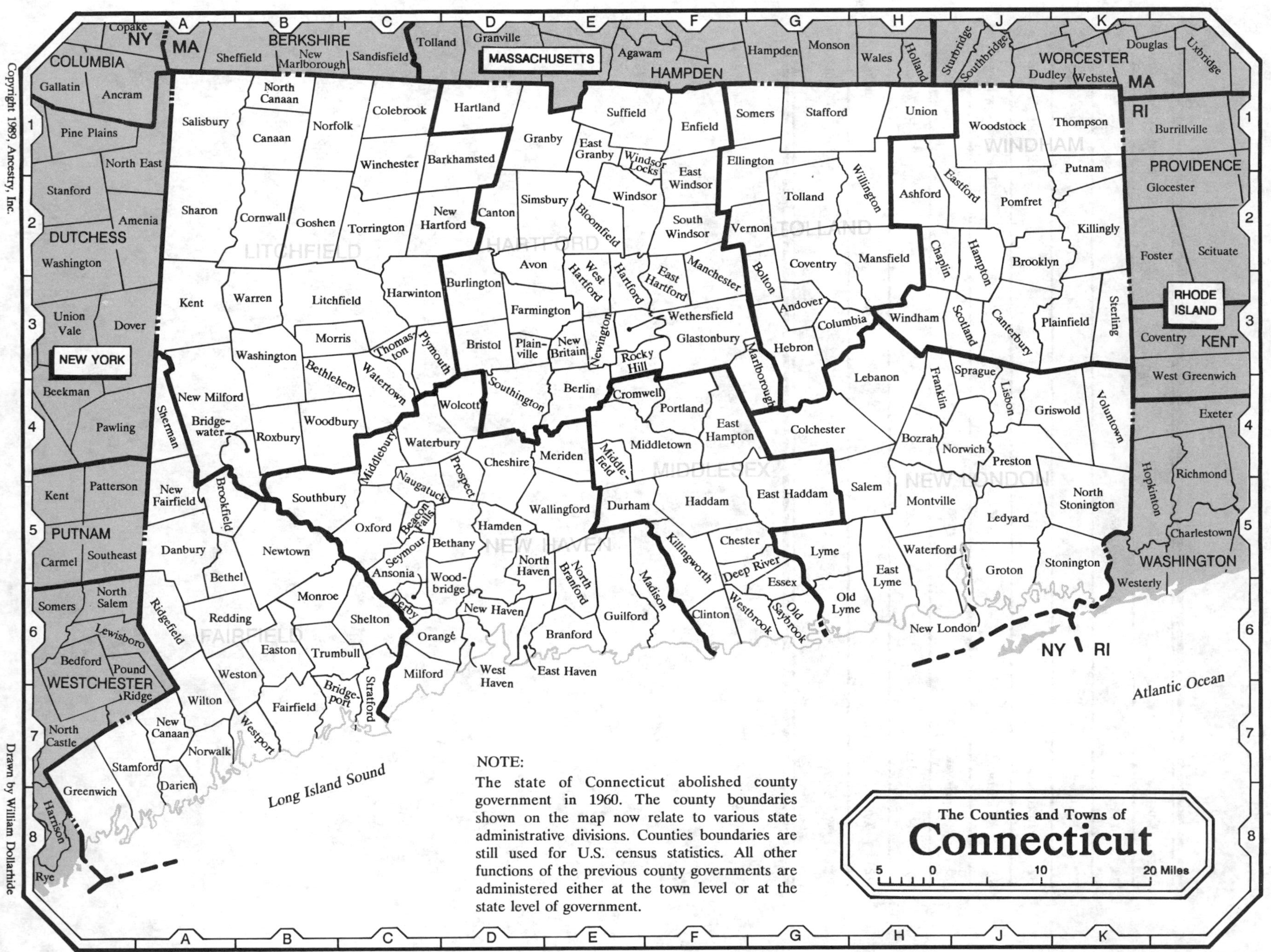

Drawn by William Dollarhide

Town Resources

In the list of town offices that follows, the first column indicates the address supplied by the secretary of state for the town clerk's office where town meeting, vital records, and land records are found. If the address specifies "city" or "municipal," the official in charge of the records is the city or municipal clerk. The second column indicates the date the town was incorporated and the parent town or towns; dashes (——) indicate that the town was not original but was formed from unorganized land rather than another town. Some seventeenth-century towns were settled or organized a year or two before incorporation. The third column lists the most recent county, which can be used for census identification (see County Resources) and superior court records. The final column indicates the present probate district, the date the town became part of that district, and the previous chronological parent district or districts. For earlier probate divisions see Probate Records section above. If a town was formed *after* its probate district, only that district is listed.

All deeds, vital records, and probate records for all Connecticut towns are available to 1900 on microfilm at the Connecticut State Library or through the FHL. Town meeting records, with their rich material describing various aspects of town life, are not automatically included in the microfilms and may need to be searched in the town office itself.

Information on the Town Resources is partially based on a chart produced by Ann P. Barry, "Connecticut Towns and Their Establishment" distributed by the Connecticut State Library. Additional sources included informational publications printed by the History and Genealogy Unit of the library and Marcia Wiswall Lindberg, *Genealogist's Handbook for New England,* 2d ed. (Boston, Mass.: New England Historic Genealogical Society, 1985).

Map	Town Address	Date Formed Parent Towns	County	Probate Parent
G3	Andover School Road Andover 06232	1848 Coventry/Hebron	Tolland	Andover 1851 Hebron
C6	Ansonia City Hall 253 Main Street Ansonia 06401	1889 Derby	New Haven	Derby
H2	Ashford Route 44, Box 38 Ashford 06278	1714 ——	Windham	Ashford 1830 Pomfret
D3	Avon 60 W. Main Street Avon 06001	1830 Farmington	Hartford	Avon 1844 Farmington
D2	Barkhamsted Route 318, Box 185 Pleasant Valley 06063	1779 ——	Litchfield	Barkhamsted 1834 New Hartford
C5	Beacon Falls 10 Maple Avenue Beacon Falls 06403	1871 Bethany/Oxford/Seymour/Naugatuck	New Haven	Naugatuck
E4	Berlin P.O. Box 1 Kensington 06037	1785 Farmington/Middletown/Wethersfield	Hartford	Berlin 1824 Hartford/ Middletown/ Farmington
D5	Bethany 40 Peck Road Bethany 06525	1832 Woodbridge	New Haven	Bethany 1854 New Haven
A5	Bethel P.O. Box 3, Library Place Bethel 06801	1855 Danbury	Fairfield	Bethel 1859 Danbury
B4	Bethlehem RR 1, Box 53 Bethlehem 06751	1787 Woodbury	Litchfield	Woodbury

Map	Town Address	Date Formed Parent Towns	County	Probate Parent
E2	Bloomfield 800 Bloomfield Avenue P.O. Box 337 Bloomfield 06002	1835 Windsor/Farmington/Simsbury	Hartford	Hartford
G3	Bolton 222 Bolton Center Road Bolton 06040	1720 ——	Tolland	Andover 1851 Hebron
H4	Bozrah Fitchville 06334	1786 Norwich	New London	Bozrah 1843 Norwich
E6	Branford Box 150, 1019 Main Street Branford 06405	1685 New Haven	New Haven	Branford 1850 Guilford
B7	Bridgeport City Hall 45 Lyon Terrace Bridgeport 06604	1821 Stratford/Fairfield	Fairfield	Bridgeport 1840 Stratford
B5	Bridgewater Main Street, P.O. Box 216 Bridgewater 06752	1856 New Milford	Litchfield	New Milford
D3	Bristol City Hall 111 N. Main Street Bristol 06010	1785 Farmington	Hartford	Bristol 1830 Farmington
A5	Brookfield Poncono Road, Box 106 Brookfield Ctr. 06805	1788 Danbury/New Milford/Newton	Fairfield	Brookfield 1850 Newton
J2	Brooklyn P.O. Box 356 Brooklyn 06234	1786 Pomfret/Canterbury	Windham	Brooklyn 1833 Pomfret/ Plainfield
D3	Burlington 200 Spielman Highway Burlington 06013	1806 Bristol	Hartford	Burlington 1834 Farmington
B1	Canaan P.O. Box 155 Main Street Falls Village 06031	1739 ——	Litchfield	Canaan 1846 Sharon
J3	Canterbury Route 14, P.O. Box 27 Canterbury 06331	1703 Plainfield	Windham	Canterbury 1835 Plainfield
D2	Canton P.O. Box 168 4 Market Street Collinsville 06022	1806 Simsbury	Hartford	Canton 1841 Simsbury
H2	Chaplin Route 198 Chaplin 06235	1822 Windham/Hampton/Mansfield	Windham	Chaplin 1850 Windham
D4	Cheshire 84 S. Main Street Cheshire 06410	1780 Wallingford	New Haven	Cheshire 1829 Wallingford

Map	Town Address	Date Formed Parent Towns	County	Probate Parent
F5	Chester 65 Main Street Chester 06412	1836 Saybrook	Middlesex	Saybrook
F6	Clinton 54 E. Main Street P.O. Box 174 Clinton 06413	1838 Killingworth	Middlesex	Clinton 1862 Killingworth
G4	Colchester 40 Norwich Avenue Colchester 06415	1698 —	New London	Colchester 1832 East Haddam
C1	Colebrook Route 183, Box 5 Colebrook Ctr. 06021	1779 —	Litchfield	Winchester 1838 Norfolk
G3	Columbia Yeomans Hall Route 87, Box 165 Columbia 06237	1804 Lebanon	Tolland	Andover 1851 Hebron
B2	Cornwall Pine St., Box 97 Cornwall 06753	1740 —	Litchfield	Cornwall 1847 Litchfield
G2	Coventry 1712 Main Street P.O. Box 185 Coventry 06238	1712 —	Tolland	Coventry 1849 Hebron
E4	Cromwell 5 West Street Cromwell 06416	1851 Middletown	Middlesex	Middletown
A5	Danbury City Hall 155 Deer Hill Avenue Danbury 06810	1687 —	Fairfield	Danbury 1744 Fairfield
A8	Darien 2 Renshaw Road Darien 06820	1820 Stamford	Fairfield	Darien 1921 Stamford
F5	Deep River Main Street Deep River 06417	1635 (as Saybrook; renamed, 1947)	Middlesex	Deep River 1949 Saybrook
C6	Derby City Hall 35 Fifth Street Derby 06418	1675 —	New Haven	Derby 1858 New Haven
E5	Durham Town House Road P.O. Drawer H Durham 06422	1708 —	Middlesex	Middletown 1752 Hartford/Guilford/ East Haddam
E1	East Granby 9 Center Street East Granby 06026	1858 Granby/Windsor Locks	Hartford	East Granby 1865 Granby
G5	East Haddam Goodspeed Plaza, Box K East Haddam 06423	1734 Haddam	Middlesex	East Haddam 1741 Hartford

Map	Town Address	Date Formed Parent Towns	County	Probate Parent
F4	East Hampton 20 E. High Street East Hampton 06424	1767 (as Chatham; renamed, 1915) Middletown	Middlesex	East Hampton 1824 Middletown
E3	East Hartford 740 Main Street East Hartford 06108	1783 Hartford	Hartford	East Hartford 1887 Hartford
D6	East Haven 250 Main Street East Haven 06512	1785 New Haven	New Haven	East Haven 1955 New Haven
H5	East Lyme Town Hall, Box 519 108 Pennsylvania Avenue Niantic 06357	1839 Lyme/Waterford	New London	East Lyme
F2	East Windsor 11 Rye Street, Box 213 Broad Brook 06016	1768 Windsor	Hartford	East Windsor 1782 Hartford/ Stafford
J2	Eastford Town Office Building Westford Road, P.O. Box 296 Eastford 06242	1847 Ashford	Windham	Eastford 1849 Ashford
B5	Easton 225 Center Road Easton 06612	1845 Weston	Fairfield	Trumbull 1959 Bridgeport
F2	Ellington 55 Main Street, Box 236 Ellington 06029	1786 East Windsor	Tolland	Ellington 1826 East Windsor/ Stafford
F1	Enfield 820 Enfield Street Enfield 06082	1683 (part of Massachusetts until 1749) ——	Hartford	Enfield 1831 East Windsor
G6	Essex 29 West Avenue Essex 06426 *Name of town was Old Saybrook from 1852–54, when a new town of Old Saybrook was separated from this one. The town created in 1852 changed its name to Essex. The probate district was named Old Saybrook until 1859. A new probate district called Old Saybrook was created and the old one changed its name to Essex.*	1852 Saybrook	Middlesex	Essex 1853 Saybrook
B7	Fairfield 611 Old Post Road Fairfield 06430	1639 original	Fairfield	Fairfield 1666 original
D3	Farmington 1 Monteith Drive Farmington 06034	1645 original	Hartford	Farmington 1769 Hartford
H4	Franklin Town Hall, RFD 1 Meeting House Hill Road North Franklin 06254	1786 Norwich	New London	Norwich
F3	Glastonbury 2155 Main Street Glastonbury 06033	1690 Wethersfield	Hartford	Glastonbury 1975 Hartford
B2	Goshen North Street, Box 175 Goshen 06756	1739	Litchfield	Torrington 1847 Litchfield

Map	Town Address	Date Formed Parent Towns	County	Probate Parent
D1	Granby 15 N. Granby Road Granby 06035	1786 Simsbury	Hartford	Granby 1807 Simsbury/ Hartford
A8	Greenwich 101 Field Point Road P.O. Box 1249 Greenwich 06830	1665 Stamford (part of New Amsterdam, 1642–56)	Fairfield	Greenwich 1853 Stamford
J4	Griswold School Street Jewett City 06351	1815 Preston	New London	Griswold 1979 Norwich
J6	Groton 45 Fort Hill Road Groton 06340	1705 New London	New London	Groton 1839 Stonington
E6	Guilford 31 Park Street Guilford 06437	1643	New Haven	Guilford 1719 New Haven/ New London
F5	Haddam P.O. Box 87 Main Street, Route 9A Haddam 06438	1668	Middlesex	Haddam 1830 Middletown/ Chatham
D5	Hamden Memorial Town Hall 2372 Whitney Avenue Hamden 06518	1786 New Haven	New Haven	Hamden 1945 New Haven
J3	Hampton Old Route 6, Box 143 Hampton 06247	1786 Windham/Pomfret/Brooklyn/ Canterbury/Mansfield	Windham	Hampton 1836 Windham
E3	Hartford Municipal Building 550 Main Street Hartford 06103	1635	Hartford	Hartford 1666 original
D1	Hartland South Road East Hartland 06027	1761 —	Hartford	Hartland 1836 Granby
C3	Harwinton Harwinton Consolidated School Harwinton 06791	1737	Litchfield	Harwinton 1835 Litchfield
G3	Hebron P.O. Box 156 Hebron 06248	1708 —	Tolland	Hebron 1789 Windham/ East Windsor/ East Haddam
	Huntington	1789 (renamed Shelton, 1919)		
A3	Kent RD Box 44, S. Main Street Kent 06757	1739 —	Litchfield	Kent 1831 New Milford
K2	Killingly 172 Main Street Danielson 06239	1708 —	Windham	Killingly 1830 Pomfret/ Plainfield

Map	Town Address	Date Formed Parent Towns	County	Probate Parent
F5	Killingworth 323 Route 81 Killingworth 06417	1667 ——	Middlesex	Killingworth 1834 Saybrook
H4	Lebanon Route 207, P.O. Box 28 Lebanon 06249	1700 ——	New London	Lebanon 1826 Windham
J5	Ledyard 741 Colonel Ledyard Highway Ledyard 06339	1836 Groton	New London	Ledyard 1837 Stonington
J4	Lisbon RFD 2 Corner Route 138 and 169 Lisbon 06351	1786 Norwich	New London	Norwich
B3	Litchfield West Street Litchfield 06759	1719 ——	Litchfield	Litchfield 1742 Hartford/Woodbury New Haven
G5	Lyme Route 156, RR 2 Old Lyme 06371	1667 Saybrook	New London	Lyme 1869 Old Lyme
E6	Madison 8 Meeting House Lane Madison 06443	1826 Guilford	New Haven	Madison 1834 Guilford
F3	Manchester 41 Center Street Manchester 06040	1823 East Hartford	Hartford	Manchester 1850 East Hartford
H3	Mansfield 4 S. Eagleville Road Storrs 06268	1702 Windham	Tolland	Mansfield 1831 Windham
F4	Marlborough P.O. Box 29 N. Main Street Marlborough 06447	1803 Colchester/Glastonbury/Hebron	Hartford	Marlborough 1846 Colchester
E4	Meriden City Hall, Room 124 142 E. Main Street Meriden 06450	1806 Wallingford	New Haven	Meriden 1836 Wallingford
C4	Middlebury 1212 Whittemore Road Middlebury 06762	1807 Waterbury/Woodbury/Southbury	New Haven	Waterbury
E4	Middlefield Town Admistration Building 383 Jackson Hill Road Middlefield 06455	1866 Middletown	Middlesex	Middletown
F4	Middletown Municipal Building Box 1300 Dekoven Drive and Connecticut Street Middletown 06457	1651 ——	Middlesex	Middletown 1752 Hartford/Guilford/ East Haddam
C6	Milford City Hall River Street Milford 06460	1639 ——	New Haven	Milford 1832 New Haven

Map	Town Address	Date Formed Parent Towns	County	Probate Parent
B6	Monroe 7 Fan Hill Road Monroe 06468	1823 Huntington	Fairfield	Trumbull 1959 Bridgeport
H5	Montville 310 Norwich-New London Road Uncasville 06382	1786 New London	New London	Montville 1851 New London
B3	Morris Morris Community Hall P.O. Box 66 Morris 06763	1859 Litchfield	Litchfield	Litchfield
C5	Naugatuck 229 Church Street Naugatuck 06770	1844 Waterbury/Bethany/Oxford	New Haven	Naugatuck 1863 Waterbury
E3	New Britain City Hall 27 W. Main Street New Britain 06051	1850 Berlin	Hartford	Berlin
A7	New Canaan 77 Main Street New Canaan 06840	1801 Norwalk/Stamford	Fairfield	New Canaan 1937 Norwalk
A5	New Fairfield Route 39, P.O. Box 8896 New Fairfield 06812	1740 —	Fairfield	New Fairfield 1975 Danbury
D2	New Hartford Main Street, Box 316 New Hartford 06057	1738 —	Litchfield	New Hartford 1825 Simsbury
D6	New Haven Hall of Records 200 Orange Street, Room 204 New Haven 06510	1638	New Haven	New Haven 1666 original
H6	New London 181 Captain's Walk New London 06320	1648 —	New London	New London 1666 original
A4	New Milford P.O. Box 360 New Milford 06776	1712 —	Litchfield	New Milford 1787 Woodbury/Sharon/ Danbury
E3	Newington 131 Cedar Street Newington 06111	1871 Wethersfield	Hartford	Newington 1975 Hartford
B5	Newtown 45 Main Street Newtown 06470	1711 —	Fairfield	Newtown 1820 Danbury
B1	Norfolk Greenwoods Road P.O. Box 552 Norfolk 06058	1758 —	Litchfield	Norfolk 1779 Simsbury/Litchfield
E6	North Branford 1599 Foxon Road North Branford 06471	1831 Branford	New Haven	North Branford 1937 Guilford/Wallingford

Map	Town Address	Date Formed Parent Towns	County	Probate Parent
B1	North Canaan Pease Street, Box 338 Canaan 06018	1858 Canaan	Litchfield	Canaan
D5	North Haven 18 Church Street North Haven 06473	1786 New Haven	New Haven	North Haven 1955 New Haven
K5	North Stonington Main Street, Box 91 North Stonington 06359	1807 Stonington	New London	N. Stonington 1835 Stonington
A7	Norwalk P.O. Box 5152 125 East Avenue Norwalk 06854	1651 —	Fairfield	Norwalk 1802 Fairfield/Stamford
J4	Norwich City Hall, Room. 214 100 Broadway Norwich 06360	1662 —	New London	Norwich 1748 New London
G6	Old Lyme P.O. Box 338 52 Lyme Street Old Lyme 06371	1855 (as South Lyme; renamed, 1857) Lyme	New London	Old Lyme
G6	Old Saybrook P.O. Box 618 302 Main Street Old Saybrook 06475	1854 (see Essex for explanation of the town's formation) Old Saybrook (now named Essex)	Middlesex	Old Saybrook 1859 Essex
C6	Orange 617 Orange Center Road Orange 06477	1822 Milford/New Haven	New Haven	Orange 1975 New Haven
C5	Oxford 486 Oxford Road Oxford 06483	1798 Derby/Southbury	New Haven	Oxford 1846 New Haven
J3	Plainfield P.O. Box 133 8 Community Avenue Plainfield 06374	1699 —	Windham	Plainfield 1747 Windham
D3	Plainville Municipal Center P.O. Box 250, 1 Central Square Plainville 06062	1869 Farmington	Hartford	Plainville 1909 Farmington
C3	Plymouth 19 E. Main Street Terryville 06786	1795 Watertown	Litchfield	Plymouth 1833 Waterbury
J2	Pomfret RFD 1 (Route 44) Box 180 Pomfret Center 06259	1713 —	Windham	Pomfret 1752 Windham/Plainfield
F4	Portland P.O. Box 71, 265 Main Street Portland 06480	1841 Chatham	Middlesex	Portland 1913 Chatham

Map	Town Address	Date Formed Parent Towns	County	Probate Parent
J4	Preston RFD 1, Route 2 Norwich 06360	1687 ——	New London	Norwich 1748 New London
D5	Prospect 36 Center Street Prospect 06712	1827 Cheshire/Waterbury	New Haven	Cheshire 1829 Wallingford
K2	Putnam 126 Church Street Putnam 06260	1855 Thompson/Pomfret/Killingly	Windham	Putnam 1856 Thompson
A6	Redding Route 107, P.O. Box 28 Redding Center 06875	1767 Fairfield	Fairfield	Redding 1839 Danbury
D7	Ridgefield 400 Main Street Ridgefield 06877	1709 ——	Fairfield	Ridgefield 1841 Danbury
E3	Rocky Hill P.O. Box 657 699 Old Main Street Rocky Hill 06067	1843 Wethersfield	Hartford	Newington 1975 Hartford
B4	Roxbury Box 365, Church Street Roxbury 06783	1796 Woodbury	Litchfield	Roxbury 1842 Woodbury
H5	Salem RFD 3, Route 85 Salem 06415	1819 Colchester/Lyme/Montville	New London	Salem 1841 Colchester/ New London
A1	Salisbury Main Street Salisbury 06068	1741 ——	Litchfield	Salisbury 1847 Sharon
	Saybrook	1635 (renamed Deep River, 1947)		
J3	Scotland P.O. Box 122, Route 97 Scotland 06264	1857 Windham	Windham	Windham 1719 Hartford/ New London
C5	Seymour 1 First Street Seymour 06483	1850 Derby	New Haven	Derby 1858 New Haven
A2	Sharon Main Street, P.O. Box 224 Sharon 06069	1739 ——	Litchfield	Sharon 1755 Litchfield
C6	Shelton P.O. Box 364 54 Hill Street Shelton 06484 *Both the town and probate district of Shelton were called Huntington until 1919.*	1789 (as Huntington; renamed, 1919) Stratford	Fairfield	Shelton 1889 Bridgeport
A4	Sherman Mallory Town Hall Route 39, Box 39 Sherman 06784	1802 New Fairfield	Fairfield	Sherman 1846 New Milford

Map	Town Address	Date Formed Parent Towns	County	Probate Parent
E2	Simsbury P.O. Box 495 760 Hopmeadow Street Simsbury 06070	1670 —	Hartford	Simsbury 1769 Hartford
G1	Somers P.O. Box 203, 600 Main Street Somers 06071	1734 Enfield (part of Massachusetts until 1749)	Tolland	Somers 1834 Ellington
	South Lyme	1855 (renamed Old Lyme, 1857)		
F2	South Windsor 1540 Sullivan Avenue South Windsor 06074	1845 East Windsor	Hartford	East Windsor
B5	Southbury 501 Main Street S. Southbury 06488	1787 Woodbury	New Haven	Southbury 1967 Woodbury
D4	Southington 75 Main Street Southington 06489	1779 Farmington	Hartford	Southington 1825 Farmington
J4	Sprague P.O. Box 162 1 Main Street Baltic 06330	1861 Lisbon/Franklin	New London	Norwich
G1	Stafford Warren Memorial Town Hall P.O. Box 11 Stafford Springs 06076	1719 —	Tolland	Stafford 1759 Hartford/ Pomfret
A7	Stamford Government Center P.O. Box 891 Stamford 06904	1641 —	Fairfield	Stamford 1728 Fairfield
K3	Sterling Route 14A, Box 157 Oneco 06373	1794 Voluntown	Windham	Sterling 1852 Plainfield
K5	Stonington P.O. Box 352, Elm Street Stonington 06378 *Was originally part of Rhode Island from 1649 and was called Mistic.*	1662 —	New London	Stonington 1766 New London
C7	Stratford 2725 Main Street Room 101 Stratford 06497	1639 —	Fairfield	Stratford 1782 Fairfield
E1	Suffield P.O. Box 238 Mountain Road Suffield 06078	1674 — (part of Massachusetts until 1749)	Hartford	Suffield 1821 Hartford/Granby
C3	Thomaston 158 Main Street Thomaston 06787	1875 Plymouth	Litchfield	Thomaston 1882 Litchfield
K1	Thompson Route 12, P.O. Box 160 North Grosvenor Dale 0625	1785 Killingly	Windham	Thompson 1832 Pomfret

Map	Town Address	Date Formed Parent Towns	County	Probate Parent
G2	Tolland Hicks Memorial Municipal Offices 21 Tolland Green Tolland 06084	1715 —	Tolland	Tolland 1830 Stafford
C2	Torrington Municipal Building 140 Main Street Torrington 06790	1740 —	Litchfield	Torrington 1847 Litchfield
B6	Trumbull 5866 Main Street Trumbull 06611	1797 Stratford	Fairfield	Trumbull 1959 Bridgeport
H1	Union 606 Buckley Highway Union 06076	1734 —	Tolland	Stafford 1759 Hartford/Pomfret
G2	Vernon Memorial Building P.O. Box 245, 14 Park Place Rockville 06066	1808 Bolton	Tolland	Ellington 1826 East Windsor/ Stafford
K4	Voluntown P.O. Box 96, Main Street Voluntown 06384	1721 —	New London	Norwich 1830 Plainfield
E5	Wallingford 45 S. Main Street P.O. Box 427 Wallingford 06492	1670 New Haven	New Haven	Wallingford 1776 New Haven/ Guilford
B3	Warren Box 25, Sackett Hill Road Warren 06754	1786 Kent	Litchfield	Litchfield
D4	Washington Bryan Memorial Town Hall Washington 06794	1779 Woodbury/Litchfield/Kent/New Milford	Litchfield	Washington 1832 Litchfield/Woodbury
D5	Waterbury City Hall 235 Grand Street Waterbury 06702	1686 —	New Haven	Waterbury 1779 Woodbury
H5	Waterford Hall of Records 15 Rope Perry Road Waterford 06385	1801 New London	New London	New London
C4	Watertown 37 Deforest Street Watertown 06795	1780 Waterbury	Litchfield	Watertown 1834 Waterbury
E3	West Hartford 50 S. Main Street West Hartford 06107	1854 Hartford	Hartford	Hartford
D6	West Haven City Hall 355 Main Street West Haven 06516	1921 Orange	New Haven	West Haven 1941 New Haven

Map	Town Address	Date Formed Parent Towns	County	Probate Parent
G6	Westbrook Hall of Records 1163 Boston Post Road Box G Westbrook 06498	1840 Saybrook	Middlesex	Westbrook 1854 Old Saybrook
A6	Weston P.O. Box 1007 56 Norfield Road Weston 06883	1787 Fairfield	Fairfield	Westport 1835 Weston/Fairfield/ Norwalk
B7	Westport P.O. Box 549 110 Myrtle Avenue Westport 06881	1835 Fairfield/Norwalk/Weston	Fairfield	Westport 1835 Fairfield/Norwalk/ Weston
E3	Wethersfield 505 Silas Deane Highway Wethersfield 06109	1634 —	Hartford	Newington 1975 Hartford
H1	Willington P.O. Box 94 Old Farms Road West Willington 06279	1727 —	Tolland	Tolland 1830 Stafford
A7	Wilton 238 Danbury Road Wilton 06897	1802 Norwalk	Fairfield	Norwalk 1802 Fairfield/ Stamford
C2	Winchester 338 Main Street Winsted 06098	1771 —	Litchfield	Winchester 1838 Norfolk
H3	Windham P.O. Box 94 979 Main Street Willimantic 06226	1692 —	Windham	Windham 1719 Hartford/ New London
E2	Windsor P.O. Box 472 Windsor 06095	1633 —	Hartford	Windsor 1855 Hartford
E1	Windsor Locks 50 Church Street P.O. Box L Windsor Locks 06096	1854 Windsor	Hartford	Windsor Locks 1961 Hartford
D4	Wolcott 10 Kenea Avenue Wolcott 06716	1796 Waterbury/Southington	New Haven	Waterbury 1779 Woodbury
D6	Woodbridge 11 Meetinghouse Lane Woodbridge 06525	1784 New Haven/Milford	New Haven	New Haven
B4	Woodbury P.O. Box 369 275 Main Street Woodbury 06798	1673 —	Litchfield	Woodbury 1719 Hartford/Fairfield/ New Haven
J1	Woodstock P.O. Box 123 Route 169 *Woodstock 06281*	1690 — (called New Roxbury at first as *a part of Massachusetts until 1749)*	Windham	Woodstock 1831 Pomfret

DELAWARE

Roger D. Joslyn, C.G., F.A.S.G.

For such a small state (only Rhode Island is smaller), Delaware has an involved history. Henry Hudson discovered Delaware Bay in 1609, but the first attempted settlement there was in 1631 by the Dutch, who were driven out by native Americans. From 1638 to 1655 Delaware was controlled by the Swedes as part of New Sweden. The Dutch regained control for the next nine years, during which time some Finns settled, as did more Dutch and some Mennonites. When New Netherland was taken over by the English, Delaware fell under the suzerainty of the Duke of York from 1664 to 1682, with the Dutch regaining control briefly in 1673–74. By deeds executed in 1682, Delaware became the "Three Lower Counties" of Pennsylvania under a proprietary system. William Penn introduced the English tradition of "hundreds" as subdivisions of counties, and Delaware is the only place where the term is still used today, mostly as a geographical description in wills, deeds, and assessment records. Delaware remained a part of Pennsylvania until the Revolutionary War but had its own assembly from 1704.

While many English came directly to Delaware, most of them, including English Quakers, migrated from Pennsylvania and Maryland. For a long time there was a dispute between Delaware and Maryland over who controlled the areas of western Kent and western and southern Sussex counties. Consequently, very few Delaware records exist for this area before 1775.

Delaware experienced no major battles during the Revolutionary War, but the British did come through on their way to Philadelphia. It has been estimated that about half the population was Loyalist, although there was not as great an exodus from the colony as there had been from New York and New Jersey. After the war, many soldiers headed south to Georgia, where they took advantage of attractive land grants.

The Dutch had imported some slaves to the area from Africa, but Maryland planters were responsible for bringing the largest number of blacks to Delaware. Mostly through manumission, the number of slaves had decreased substantially by the time of the Civil War. After the American Revolution, some French arrived from the West Indies and others came directly from France, including the famous du Pont family. The mid-nineteenth century saw the immigration of large numbers of Irish Catholics and Germans, and in the latter part of the 1800s Jews, Poles, and Italians arrived, with smaller numbers of eastern Europeans and Scandinavians. Most of these people settled in the Wilmington area.

Calling itself the "First State," Delaware was the first of the thirteen colonies to ratify the Constitution on 7 December 1787. From that time the state's development has been characterized as stable, conservative, and placid, except during the Civil War. Economically, Delaware was allied with the North, especially with its river trade and the coming of the railroads; but there was also strong sympathy with the South, particularly after the war.

Delaware was originally created as part of Pennsylvania and has long been associated with that state, mostly because it shares the commerce and transportation of the Delaware River. This has also caused major growth in the northern part of the state, with much industry developing in and around Wilmington. By the early twentieth century, over half the population and wealth of the state were concentrated in the north, where it remains today. Until recently, the southern part of the state has been more agriculturally oriented. Delaware is one of the most densely populated states.

Vital Records

State copies of vital records for Delaware are available from the Bureau of Vital Statistics, Division of Public Health, Department of Health and Social Services, State Health Building, P.O. Box 637, Dover, Delaware 19901-0637. The bureau holds birth records from 1920 and marriages and deaths from 1930. The current fee is $5 for each record requested. Records and indexes in the Bureau of Vital Statistics, since 1913, are restricted, and copies are available only to those with "a direct interest" or a need to establish personal or property rights.

Earlier records at the Delaware State Archives (see Archives, Libraries, and Societies) include those formerly at the Bureau of Vital Statistics, covering births and deaths for 1861 to 1863; 1881 to 1919 for births; 1881 to 1929 for deaths; and 1847 to 1929 for marriages. Copies of these records are also $5 each.

After 1881 the City of Wilmington had a registrar of vital statistics, with fairly complete records. Elsewhere, recording of vital events was the responsibility of the county recorders of deeds, and recording practices were quite poor until the creation of the bureau in 1913. Recorders of deeds' records of a very few births and deaths for 1861–63 and for 1881–1913, and marriages for 1847–1913, are at the state archives. Also at the state archives are county clerks of the peace marriage bonds from 1744 (more complete after 1793) to 1913 when bonds were no longer required.

For the period 1680 to the present, the state archives also has cards that index births, baptisms, marriages, and deaths from a variety of sources, such as marriage bonds, church and Bible records, and newspaper notices. There is a supplementary index for some deaths for 1888–1910. Some Kent County vital records for the late 1600s were recorded in deed books and published in *Publications of The Genealogical Society of Pennsylvania* 7 (1920): 158–62 and reprinted in *The Maryland and Delaware Genealogist* 10 (1969) and 11 (1970). Some Kent and Sussex County vital records for the late 1600s to the 1750s were published in the *Delaware Genealogical Society Journal* 1 (1982): 92–96. A private doctor's records of births for Sussex County, 1835–69, were published in volumes 6–8 of *The Maryland and Delaware Genealogist* (1965–67). Also, "New Castle County . . . Court Records . . . of Illegitimate Births" was published in *The Pennsylvania Genealogical Magazine* 33 (1984): 353–58.

For the period up to 1975, divorces should be sought in the county superior courts, of which the prothonotary is the clerk. Some of these records are at the state archives, but permission to see them must first be obtained from the court. After 1975 the records are in the county family court where the divorce was granted. The earliest divorces in Delaware, to 1773, were a matter for the governor and council. The legislature had jurisdiction until 1897, and the superior court had concurrent jurisdiction from 1832.

Legislative divorces are indexed as private acts in the published *Laws of Delaware*, 2–20 (1777–1897). Since 1913 courts have been required to register divorces and annulments with the state registrar.

Census Records

Federal

Population Schedules.

- Indexed—1800, 1810, 1820, 1830, 1840, 1850, 1860, 1870
- Soundex—1880, 1900, 1920
- Unindexed—1910

Industry and Agriculture Schedules.

- 1850, 1860, 1870, 1880

Mortality Schedules.

- 1850, 1860, 1870, 1880 (all published)

Slave Schedules.

- 1850, 1860 (both published)

From the second federal census of 1800, the records are complete for Delaware and are widely available (see pages 2–3). Published indexes through 1870 are also available, with two each for 1850 and 1870 and three for 1860.

The first census for 1790 was lost or destroyed. The claim that it was found in the Cornell University Library is unfounded, but a reconstruction from tax and assessment records was compiled by former State Archivist Leon de Valinger, Jr., and published by the National Genealogical Society as *Reconstructed 1790 Census of Delaware*, NGS Special Publication No. 10, 2d printing (Washington, D.C.: NGS, 1962).

The original mortality schedules, which are at the Delaware State Archives, have been published, as have the 1850 and 1860 slave schedules. Other non-population schedules for 1850–80 are at the state archives, as are the original state copies of the federal population censuses for these years.

Colonial

Some earlier Delaware "censuses" have been published from tax records. These include Harold B. Hancock, ed., *The Reconstructed Delaware State Census of 1782* (Wilmington, Del.: Delaware Genealogical Society, 1983), and Ronald Vern Jackson, *Early Delaware Census Records 1665–1697* (Bountiful, Utah: Accelerated Indexing Systems, 1977), compiled from tax and other lists. A 1688 census for Kent County was published in volume 37 of *The Pennsylvania Genealogical Magazine* in 1991, which corrects the incomplete "Kent County Census" in *Delaware Genealogical Journal* 3 (1986): 49–51.

Background Sources

The earliest state history is *Original Settlements on the Delaware,* by Benjamin Ferris (1846; reprint with index, Wilmington, Del.: Delaware Genealogical Society, 1987), but J. Thomas Scharf's *History of Delaware 1609–1888,* 2 vols. (1888; reprint, Washington, N.Y.: Kennikat Press, 1972, and Westminster, Md.: Family Line Publications, 1990), indexed by Gladys M. Coghlan and Dale Fields, 3 vols. (Wilmington, Del.: Historical Society of Delaware, 1976), is the standard for the state. It has errors but is useful for its many lists of names from tax records, petitions, road lists, and other records. Henry C. Conrad's *History of the State of Delaware,* 3 vols. (Wilmington, Del.: the author, 1908), is also helpful for pinpointing individuals through its state and county civil lists.

More modern works are Carol E. Hoffecker, comp., *Readings in Delaware History* (Newark, Del.: University of Delaware Press, 1973), and John A. Munroe, *A History of Delaware,* 2d ed. (Newark, Del.: University of Delaware Press, 1984).

H. Clay Reed, ed., *Delaware: History of the First State,* 3 vols. (New York, N.Y.: Lewis Historical Publishing Co., 1947), is also good, but volume 3 is a "mug book." The term mug book refers to those printed sources which present pictures and biographies of those who subscribed to the publication. Similar works, which must be used with care, are Wilson Lloyd Bevan, ed., *History of Delaware Past and Present,* 4 vols. (New York, N.Y.: Lewis Historical Publishing Co., 1929), with mug books for the last two volumes; *Biographical and Genealogical History of the State of Delaware,* 2 vols. (Chambersburg, Pa.: J. M. Runk & Co., 1899); and James M. McCarter and B. F. Jackson, *Historical and Biographical Encyclopedia of Delaware* (Wilmington, Del.: Aldine Publishing and Engraving Co., 1882).

There are many useful histories with a narrower focus, particularly concerning the Dutch, English, and Swedes. Clinton A. Weslager has written four works: *Dutch Explorers, Traders and Settlers in the Delaware Valley 1609–1664* (Philadelphia, Pa.: University of Pennsylvania Press, 1961); *The English on the Delaware 1610–1682* (New Brunswick, N.J.: Rutgers University Press, 1967); *The Swedes and Dutch at New Castle;* and *New Sweden on the Delaware 1638–1655,* the latter two published by Middle Atlantic Press, 1987 and 1988, respectively. Weslager also abstracted Dutch notarial records relating to the colony on the Delaware, 1656–76, published in *Delaware History* 20 (1982):1–26, 73–97.

Amandus Johnson's *The Swedish Settlements on the Delaware 1638–1664,* 2 vols. (1911; reprint, Baltimore, Md.: Genealogical Publishing Co., 1969), is the standard work on the subject, but Israel Acrelius's *A History of New Sweden* (1874; reprint, New York, N.Y.: Arno Press, 1972) is also one of the basics, as is Rev. Jehu Curtis Clay's *Annals of the Swedes on the Delaware,* 4th ed. (Chicago, Ill.: John Ericsson Memorial Committee, 1938), although the earlier editions are better. Two excellent, newer works are Stellan Dahlgren and Hans Norman, *The Rise and Fall of New Sweden* (Stockholm, Sweden: Alurqvist and Wiksell, 1988), and Alf Åberg, *The People of New Sweden* (Stockholm, Sweden: Naturochkultur, 1988). These histories should be used with *New York Historical Manuscripts: Dutch Volumes XVIII–XIX Delaware Papers (Dutch Period) . . . 1648–1664* and *New York Historical Manuscripts: Dutch Volumes XX–XXI Delaware Papers (English Period) . . . 1664–1682,* both edited by Charles T. Gehring (Baltimore, Md.: Genealogical Publishing Co., 1981, 1977). Unfortunately, Evert Alexander Louhi's *The Delaware Finns* (New York, N.Y.: Humanity Press, 1925) is far too imaginative to be considered accurate.

For a later period see Charles H. B. Turner, comp., *Rodney's Diary and Other Delaware Records* (Philadelphia, Pa.: Allen, Lane & Scott, 1911), which includes records for 1813–29 from public and private sources of Delaware as well as Maryland, Pennsylvania, New Jersey, and New York. Bruce A. Bendler's *Colonial Delaware Assemblymen 1682–1776* (Westminster, Md.: Family Line Publications, 1989) is a biographical dictionary covering over 300 Delaware officials, but see the review essay of this work in *The Pennsylvania Genealogical Magazine* 36 (1990): 251–56, and the *Pennsylvania Magazine of History and Biography* 115 (1991): 262–64.

Guides

For a fine, general background of history and genealogical sources, consult the chapter on Delaware by Milton Rubincam, F.A.S.G., in *Genealogical Research: Methods and Sources,* Vol. 1, rev. ed., ed. by Milton Rubincam (Washington, D.C.: American Society of Genealogists, 1980), pages 261–70. More up-to-date is *Delaware Genealogical Research Guide* (Wilmington, Del.: Delaware Genealogical Society, 1989).

Delaware Place Names, by L. W. Heck and others, Geological Survey Bulletin No. 1245 (Washington, D.C.: Government Printing Office, 1966), is very good and should be supplemented with Henry Gannett's *A Gazetteer of Maryland and Delaware,* 2 vols. (1904; reprint in one vol., Baltimore, Md.: Genealogical Publishing Co., 1976).

Henry Clay and Marion B. Reed, *A Bibliography of Delaware Through 1960* (Newark, Del.: University of Delaware Press, 1966), lists biographies and family histories and is supplemented by *Bibliography of Delaware 1960–1974* (Newark, Del.: University of Delaware Press, 1976) and by updates in *Delaware History,* beginning in volume 17.

Maps

Although somewhat dated, another good collection of maps is the *Atlas of the State of Delaware* by Daniel G. Beers (1868; reprint, Georgetown, Del.: Sussex Prints, 1978). For quick reference, maps of Delaware hundreds are on the inside back cover of the *Delaware Genealogical Society Journal* and in Hancock's *The Reconstructed Delaware State Census of 1782* (see Census Records). One of the best collections of Delaware maps is at the Delaware State Archives.

Land Records

State-Land State

From 1680 the original deed and mortgage volumes, microfilms of them, or both, are at the Delaware State Archives, with corresponding indexes. Kent County holdings at the archives extend to 1970; New Castle to 1962; and Sussex to 1968. The state archives also has a card index of original land patents, warrants, and surveys, arranged by county, as well as a list of some of the Maryland grants now located in Delaware. Information on related Maryland land should also be sought in the published *Archives of Maryland.* Warrants and surveys made during the proprietorship of the Penn family, 1682–1776 are at the state archives; those for 1759–61 are included in *Warrants and Surveys of the Province of Pennsylvania including the Three Lower Counties 1759* (see Pennsylvania—Land Records). Some land purchases are chronicled in the *Pennsylvania Archives,* 2d Series, vols. 7 and 19. Other published land records are *Original Land Titles in Delaware Commonly Known as The Duke of York Records . . . 1646–1679* (1899; reprint, Westminster, Md.: Family Line Publications, 1989) and A. R. Dunlap "Dutch and Swedish Land Records Relating to Delaware: Some New Documents and A Checklist," *Delaware History* 6 (1954): 25–52. The state archives acquired microfilm of official grants of land in present-day Delaware from New York and Pennsylvania sources, and these are listed in Edward E. Heite, *Delaware's Fugitive Records* (Dover, Del.: Delaware Division of Historical and Cultural Affairs, 1980).

In addition to county taxes, colonial Delaware landowners had to pay annual quitrents to the proprietor. The quitrents for 1665–71 (during the period Delaware was controlled by New York) were published in B. Fernow, ed., *Documents Relative to the History of Dutch and Swedish Settlements on the Delaware River,* Vol. 12 of *Documents Relative to the Colonial History of New York* (Albany, N.Y.: Argus Co., 1877), pages 490–92. This volume contains other lists of Delaware residents during the 1670s. Some quitrent information is also found in private proprietors' records such as the Logan Papers at the Historical Society of Pennsylvania in Philadelphia.

In each of Delaware's three counties, the recorder of deeds has the primary land records, with deeds and mortgages kept separately. Only the most recent deeds are in the counties, however. Most have been transferred to the archives (see above).

Probate Records

The early probate records for Delaware, from 1676 into the twentieth century, are at the Delaware State Archives, either in their original form of books and files, or on microfilm, or both. From the early 1700s, there are orphans' court records with very useful partitions of land of intestates and consolidated card file indexes by county covering estates to 1850. Earlier probate information should be sought in records of Maryland, Pennsylvania, and New York. It should also be pointed out that many early wills pertaining to Delaware residents, while proved, were never recorded. Later records are filed with the appropriate county register of wills. Calendars have been published for the wills of all three counties: *Calendar of Kent County Delaware Probate Records 1680–1800* and *Calendar of Sussex County Delaware Probate Records 1680–1800,* both compiled by state archivist Leon de Valinger, Jr. (Dover, Del.: Public Archives Commission, 1944, 1964), and *A Calendar of Delaware Wills New Castle County 1682–1800,* by the Historic Research Committee of the Delaware Society of the Colonial Dames of America (1911; reprint, Baltimore, Md.: Genealogical Publishing Co., 1977, and Baltimore, Md.: Clearfield Co., 1989). The former two include the volume and page numbers not only for the county record volumes but also for those volumes at the state archives into which the early original documents were mounted. The latter work on New Castle County does not include intestate records.

Court Records

Many of the early court records of Delaware have been published, such as *Records of the Court of New Castle on Delaware 1676–1681,* with a second volume for the years 1681–1699, *Land and Probate Abstract Only* (Lancaster and Meadville, Pa.: Colonial Society of Pennsylvania, 1904, 1935). Another example is *Court Records of Kent County, Delaware 1680–1705,* edited by Leon de Valinger, Jr. (Washington, D.C.: American Historical Association, 1959), and recently published is Craig W. Horle's *Sussex County Court Records 1677–1710* (Philadelphia, Pa.: University of Pennsylvania Press, 1991). *The Inventory of the County Archives of Delaware: No. 1, New Castle County,* by the Delaware Historical Records Survey (Dover, Del.: Public Archives Commission, 1941), while dated and published for only one county, still provides good detail about the court system and records. Charles H. B. Turner's *Some Records of Sussex County Delaware* (1909; reprint, Bowie, Md.: Heritage Books, 1989) includes not only court, but civil, ecclesiastical, vestry, Bible, and other records.

The Delaware State Archives has state and county level court records back to the colonial period covering civil and criminal records, naturalizations, and indentures. Some earlier records are in Maryland, New York, and Pennsylvania. At the county level, the court of common pleas and superior court handle civil and criminal matters, depending on the offense. Cases involving equity and trust estates are heard in the chancery court. The office of the county prothonotary has custody of divorces until 1975, civil and criminal court records, and naturalizations, although the latter are now in the state archives. Land records are with the recorder of deeds, and estate matters are handled by the register of wills and orphans' court. The orphans' court was consolidated in 1975 with the court of chancery to handle estate disputes and other partitions, with records kept by the register in chancery in each county.

Tax Records

Early tax or assessment lists for the three Delaware counties are found at the Delaware State Archives and start in 1726 for Kent, 1738 for New Castle, and 1769 for Sussex. Some earlier records are at the Historical Society of Pennsylvania in Philadelphia: 1693 for all three counties and an incomplete list for 1696 for New Castle County. For the former, see "Provincial Tax List of the Three Lower Counties 1693" in *The Pennsylvania Genealogical Magazine* 37 (1991): 1–32. It has sometimes been stated that the 1798 U.S. direct tax records for Delaware are at the Historical Society of Delaware. They are not extant, however, and were perhaps destroyed in a fire in Philadelphia. Some tax records have been published as "censuses" (see Census Records). An 1861 national tax and its corresponding refund records of 1901 are at the state archives. Internal Revenue assessments for Delaware, 1862–66, are on microfilm at the National Archives-Mid Atlantic Region (see page 8). Modern tax information should be sought in the county courthouses.

Cemetery Records

The largest central file of grave marker transcriptions and abstracts is in the Tatnell Tombstone Collection at the Delaware State Archives, compiled by the Historical Records Survey. Also at the state archives is the Hudson Collection of Sussex County tombstones, which is more thorough than the Tatnell. For Kent County see also Raymond Walter Dill and others, *Souls in Heaven, Names in Stone: Kent County, Delaware Cemetery Records*, 2 vols. (Baltimore, Md.: Gateway Press, 1989). Some cemetery records are at the Historical Society of Delaware (see Archives, Libraries, and Societies), and some have been printed in the *Delaware Genealogical Society Journal* and in other publications.

Church Records

The *Directory of Churches and Religious Organizations in Delaware*, compiled and published by the Public Archives Commission of the State of Delaware (Dover, Del., 1942), while somewhat dated, is good for determining what records existed at that time. It is supplemented by Elizabeth Waterston's *Churches in Delaware During the Revolution* (Wilmington, Del.: Historical Society of Delaware, 1925), which also lists records available. Frank P. Zebley's *The Churches of Delaware* (Wilmington, Del.: the author, 1947), while it does not discuss their records, identifies almost 900 existing and defunct churches in the state.

The records of one of the oldest and most noted churches were published as *The Records of Holy Trinity (Old Swedes) Church, Wilmington, Del., From 1697 to 1773, with Abstracts of English Records from 1773–1810*, with a supplemental *Catalogue and Errata*, translated and edited by Horace Burr, in Papers of the Historical Society of Delaware, 9 and 9-A (Wilmington, Del.: Historical Society of Delaware, 1890, 1919). Because of the erroneous translations, this work should be used with material by Courtland B. Springer and Ruth L. Springer in *Delaware History*, vols. 5 and 6 (1954, 1957); the *Delaware Genealogical Society Journal;* and in manuscript at the Historical Society of Delaware. Other major publications of church records include *Records of the Welsh Tract Baptist Meeting, Pencader Hundred, New Castle County, Delaware, 1701 to 1828*, Papers of the Historical Society of Delaware, 42 (Wilmington, Del.: Historical Society of Delaware, 1904); *Friends in Wilmington 1738–1938* (N.p., n.d.), which includes marriages, burials, and genealogies; and Christopher M. Agnew, ed., *God with Us: A Continuing Presence* (New Castle, Del.: Immanuel Church, 1986), with an alphabetical list of baptisms, marriages, and burials, 1714–1985, of New Castle's historic Immanuel Church (Episcopal). Some Delaware church records have been printed in the *Delaware Genealogical Society Journal, Delaware History,* and in other publications. Original and WPA-transcribed records of many Delaware churches are at the state archives and some are at the Historical Society of Delaware. At the historical society, the Kelso Collection contains a large amount of nineteenth- and twentieth-century Methodist records, mostly from rural circuits and charges, for Delaware and Maryland's eastern shore. An index to this valuable collection is in progress. Some Quaker records are at the state archives and the Historical Society of Delaware; others are at the Friends Historical Library in Swarthmore, Pennsylvania.

A project has been approved by the Catholic Diocese of Wilmington (which includes Delaware and the nine eastern shore counties of Maryland) to place microfilms of its baptismal records to 1910 and first communion, confirmation, marriage, and burial records to 1955 at the state archives and historical societies in the two states.

Military Records

The *Delaware Archives*, 5 vols. (1911–16; reprint, New York, N.Y.: A.M.S. Press, 1974), contains military rolls, pensions, and other records from colonial soldiers of 1744 through militia lists of 1815. Material for an unfinished sixth volume at the Delaware State Archives covers nonmilitary records of the Revolutionary War era. Background information on the early period is well covered in *Colonial Military Organization in Delaware, 1638–1776*, by Leon de Valinger, Jr. (Wilmington, Del.: Delaware Tercentenary Commission, 1938). William Gustavus Whiteley compiled *The Revolutionary Soldiers of Delaware*, Papers of the Historical Society of Delaware, 14 (Wilmington, Del.: Historical

Society of Delaware, 1896). Christopher L. Ward, *The Delaware Continentals 1776–1783* (Wilmington, Del.: Historical Society of Delaware, 1941), should be read for proper historical background, and Harold Bell Hancock, *The Delaware Loyalists* (1940; reprint, Boston, Mass.: Gregg, 1973), should be consulted for information about those on the other side of the conflict. Scharf included a list of Delaware Civil War soldiers in an appendix in Volume 1 of his *History of Delaware* (see Background Sources). The National Archives-Mid Atlantic Region (see page 8) has a microfilm index of names of Delaware Civil War soldiers. Lists of Confederate prisoners at Fort Delaware are in the state archives, as are several card indexes of those called or who volunteered for federal service in the Civil War, the Spanish-American War, and the Mexican Border Campaign, 1916–17. The archives also has a card file of World War I service medical applications, giving service information and often date of death and place of burial. *Delaware's Role in World War II, 1940–1946*, by William H. Conner and Leon de Valinger, Jr. (Dover, Del.: Public Archives Commission, 1955), does not list all military personnel, although thousands of names are mentioned. De Valinger's collection of World War II photographs, letters, and lists of deceased soldiers should also be consulted at the state archives. Much military material is also found at the Historical Society of Delaware.

Periodicals, Newspapers, and Manuscript Collections

Periodicals

Delaware History has been published by the Historical Society of Delaware semi-annually since 1946; volumes 1–7 were reprinted in 1968 by Kraus Reprint of Millwood, N.Y. The society has also published papers in sixty-seven volumes from 1879 to 1922 and in three volumes in a new series from 1927 to 1940.

The *Delaware Genealogical Society Journal* has published, since 1980, the usual fare of source record material, including Bible records, births of blacks, orphans' court indexes (for Sussex County), and Maryland records. For *The Maryland and Delaware Genealogist*, see Maryland—Periodicals.

Two short-lived periodicals with useful source record material are *Delaware Historical and Genealogical Recall* (1933; reprint, Wilmington, Del.: Delaware Genealogical Society, 1984) and *Del-Gen-Data Bank*, edited by Mary Fallon Richards (Wilmington, Del.: the editor, 1986).

Newspapers

For a good list of Delaware papers, see *Union List of Newspapers in Microform* (Newark, Del.: Delaware University Press, 1964). The Historical Society of Delaware has an extensive collection of early northern Delaware newspapers, but papers in the adjoining states of Maryland, Pennsylvania, and New Jersey should also be consulted. Southern Delaware newspapers are at the Delaware State Archives. F. Edward Wright, *Delaware Newspaper Abstracts, 1786–95* (Silver Springs, Md.: Family Line Publications, 1984), covers two Wilmington papers.

Manuscripts

By far the largest single collection of private, unpublished genealogical material on Delaware families is that of the Rev. Joseph Brown Turner at the Delaware State Archives, compiled over a forty-year period and arranged by family name. Reverend Turner's interest in families of the Del-Mar-Va peninsula extended to the origins of some in the British Isles. The papers of Harold B. Hancock, also at the state archives, likewise contain English material on Delaware families. The collections of the Rev. Charles Henry Black Turner (mostly southern Delaware) and Matilda Spicer Hart are at the Historical Society of Pennsylvania in Philadelphia (see Pennsylvania).

The Delaware Historical Records Survey, *Inventory of the County Archives of Delaware No. 1 New Castle County* (Dover, Del.: Public Archives Commission, 1941), which was published for only one county, is very useful for its historical background and for identifying records.

H. Clay Reed, "Manuscript Books in the Historical Society of Delaware," *Delaware History* 11 (1965): 65–82, is a finding aid to part of that society's collection.

Archives, Libraries, and Societies

Delaware State Archives
Hall of Records
Dover, DE 19901

The Delaware State Archives is the central repository for noncurrent state as well as county and municipal records. It also has a large collection of private records, including family Bible records and papers, church and cemetery records, and federal censuses. Its holdings are enhanced by maps, still and motion pictures, and sound recordings. Microfilms of early New York and Pennsylvania material pertaining to what is now Delaware have also been acquired. The *Preliminary Inventory of the Holdings of the Delaware State Archives*, compiled by Joanne Mattern (Dover, Del.: Delaware State Archives, 1978), will be replaced with a new guide, probably in 1992.

The Historical Society of Delaware
505 Market Street
Wilmington, DE 19801

Founded in 1864, the Historical Society of Delaware has much manuscript material including church, military, and family Bible records; transcribed grave marker inscriptions; business and medical records; diaries and journals; and microfilms (with published indexes) of Delaware censuses and many state archives records. The society has a name file to items in newspapers and books, and the Delaware DAR's collection of Bible records. See Dale Fields, "Genealogical Source Material in the Historical Society of Delaware," *The Pennsylvania Genealogical Magazine* 28 (1973): 86–93. Some of the society's material has been published in their journal, *Delaware History*. For a small fee, a search of basic materials can be requested by mail.

Delaware Genealogical Society
505 Market Street Mall
Wilmington, DE 19801

While it does not maintain a library, the Delaware Genealogical Society publishes the very useful *Delaware Genealogical Society Journal* and books of Delaware interest.

Special Focus Categories

Immigration

Ship passenger arrival lists for Wilmington, 1820–49, are on microfilm at the National Archives-Mid Atlantic Region (see page 9). See also Carl Boyer, ed., *Ship Passenger Lists: Pennsylvania and Delaware, 1641–1825* (Newhall, Calif.: the author, 1980). Priscilla Thompson's *Arriving in Delaware: The Italian-American Experience* (Wilmington, Del.: History Store, 1989) provides a study of one immigrant group, from about 1870.

Naturalization

A card index at the Delaware State Archives to a few naturalizations for 1788–1905 actually gives brief abstracts of the records. Federal court naturalizations for 1845–1910 are at the National Archives-Mid Atlantic Region, and county records originally with the prothonotary are now at the state archives. Naturalizations for New Castle County, 1826–58, were published in *The Maryland and Delaware Genealogist* 18 (1977): 2–4 and 19 (1978): 1.

Native American

Information about Delaware's Native Americans is found in at least six works. Frank Gouldsmith Speck wrote *The Nanticoke and Conoy Indians* (Wilmington, Del.: Historical Society of Delaware, 1927). The other five, by Clinton A. Weslager, are entitled *Delaware's Forgotten Folk: The Story of the Moors and Nanticokes* (Washington, D.C.: Library of Congress, 1970); *Delaware Indians: A History* (New Brunswick, N.J.: Rutgers University Press, 1972); *The Delaware Indian Westward Migration* (Wallingford. Pa.: Middle Atlantic Press, 1978); *Red Men on the Brandywine* (1953; reprint, Wilmington, Del.: Delmar News Agency, 1976); and *The Delaware: A Critical Bibliography* (Bloomington, Ind.: Indiana University Press, 1978).

Black American

Chapters 29 and 30 of Reed's *History* (see Background Sources) provide an overview on Delaware blacks, and articles of interest have been published in *Delaware History*. See also two articles by Mary Fallon Richards, "Black Birth Records, New Castle County, Delaware, 1810–1853," *National Genealogical Society Quarterly* 67 (1979): 264–66, listing the name of the black child and its date of birth, names of parents (mostly mother) and master or mistress, and date of registration; and "Licenses to Import and Export Slaves," *Delaware Genealogical Society Journal* 1 (1980–81): 8–12, 30–37.

Special Interest

John Martin Hammond's *Colonial Mansions of Maryland and Delaware* (Philadelphia, Pa.: J. B. Lippincott Co., 1914) offers an interesting, illustrated source for this aspect of family history research.

County Resources

Delaware has only three counties, the smallest number of any state. Most earlier records and many into the twentieth century have been transferred to the Delaware State Archives, although some counties have microfilms of transferred material. Records of land conveyance are found in the county recorder of deeds' offices. Estates are in the office of the register of wills where files are maintained from 1925. The first column below indicates the map coordinate. The second column gives the name of the county and the mailing address of the recorder of deeds. The third column shows the date the county was created and from what county or district. The earliest date of recording of a county deed is listed in the fourth column. The fifth column shows the date the first estate was recorded, followed by the year the orphans' court records begin, and then the mailing address of the register of wills, if different from that of the recorder. The prothonotary is the clerk with custody of such records as divorces (to 1975), and civil and criminal court matters. For births, marriages, and deaths recorded by the counties, see Vital Records.

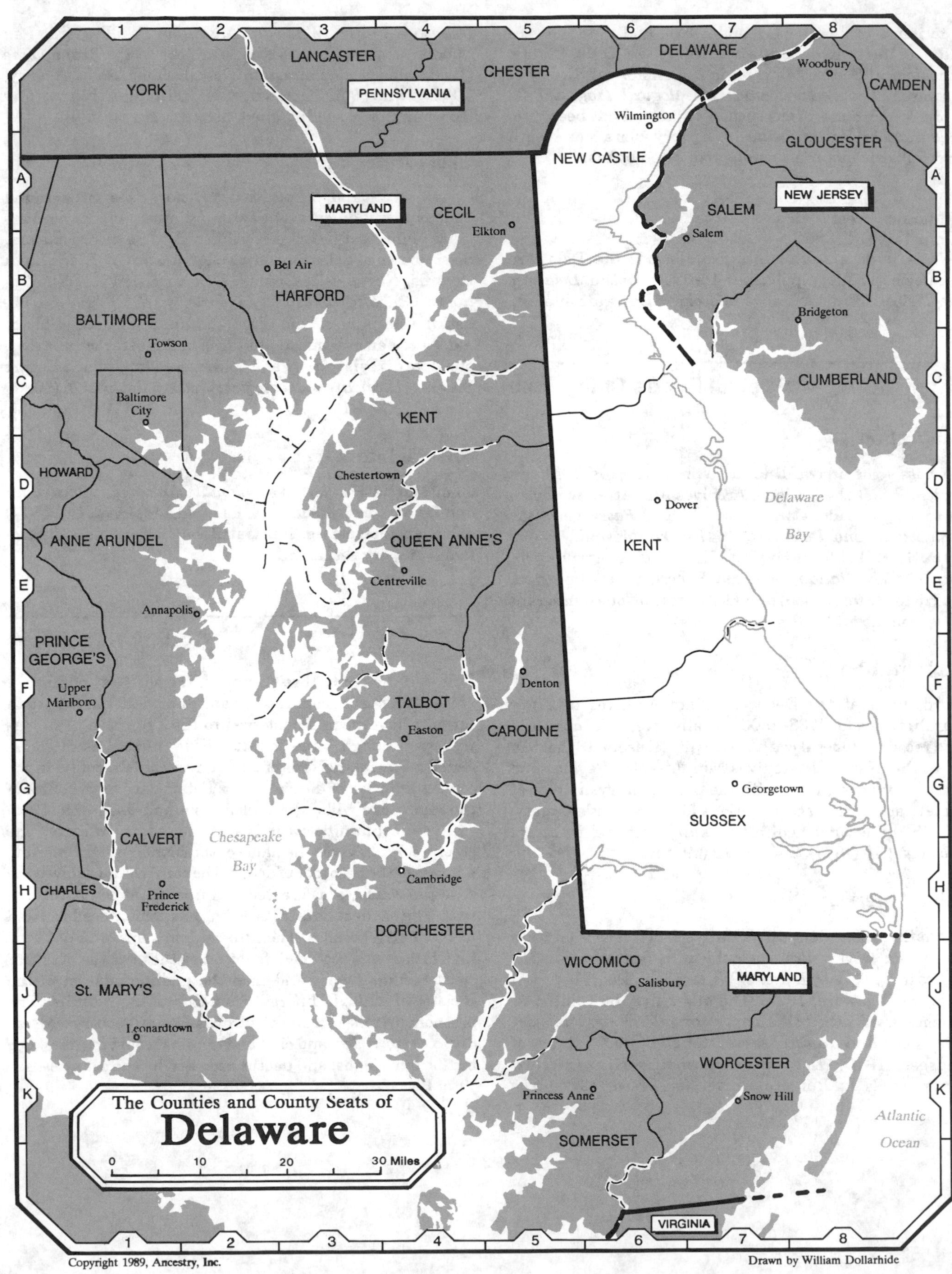

Drawn by William Dollarhide

Map	County Recorder of Deeds	Date Formed Parent County	Deeds	Orphans' Court Register of Wills
	Deale	1670 (as Whorekill; renamed Deale, 1680; renamed Sussex, 1682)		
E6	Kent 414 Federal Street Dover 19901-3605	1680 (as St. Jones; renamed, 1682) Whorekill	1680	1681/1766
A6	New Castle 800 French Street Wilmington 19801-3590	1664 (named New Amstel, 1672–73) original	1676	1682/1742 11th and King Streets Wilmington 19801
	St. Jones	1680 (renamed Kent, 1682)		
G7	Sussex Courthouse P. O. Box 505 Georgetown 19947-0505	1670 (as Whorekill; renamed Deale, 1680; renamed Sussex, 1682) New Castle	1693	1683/1728 P.O. Box 111 Georgetown 19947-0111
	Whorekill (Horekill)	1670 (renamed Deale, 1680; renamed Sussex, 1682)		

DISTRICT OF COLUMBIA

Johni Cerny

Congress created the District of Columbia as the seat of the federal government on 16 July 1790. On 9 September 1791 George Washington appointed three commissioners to lay out the city, although the federal government did not relocate to the District of Columbia until 1801. The area chosen as the seat of government was carved from Fairfax County, Virginia (created in 1742) and from part of Prince George's (created 1695) and Montgomery (created 1776) counties, Maryland. The area taken from Virginia was returned to that state in 1846.

By 1800 the District's population was about 14,000, but the federal government was still operating in Philadelphia. In the interim before the government relocated, residents of the District used record-keeping services in Fairfax County, Virginia, and Montgomery County, Maryland, until local government offices were established. By 1820 the population had grown to about 33,000 as more government jobs were made available and retail businesses grew to accommodate the populace. Those moving into the area came mainly from surrounding states, but some merchants arrived from Europe. Blacks have always been a major element of the District's population; however, their number increased dramatically during the Civil War and Reconstruction era. Nearly 20 percent of the total population in 1860 were free blacks and slightly more than 4 percent were slaves.

Tracing families in the District of Columbia requires a complete understanding of the record periods and jurisdictions and the tenacity to track them down in one of the many repositories.

Records for those living in the area created for the District of Columbia before 1801 would have to be sought either in Maryland's or Virginia's records. When the portion of Virginia originally taken to create the District of Columbia was returned in 1846, the pre-1846 records were returned as well.

Vital Records

Birth records from the year 1874 (and some beginning in 1872) and death records from 1855 may be obtained for a fee by writing the Department of Human Services, Vital Records Section, Room 3007, 425 I Street, N.W., Washington, D.C. 20001. While the public may not examine vital records in person, District of Columbia law states that when 100 years have elapsed after the date of birth or fifty years after the date of death, those documents become public records and anyone may obtain a copy upon submitting a proper application. Those who can prove a relationship to a person of record can obtain a copy of that individual's record for research purposes. Death records do not exist for the Civil War years, 1861–65.

District of Columbia marriage records date from December 1811 and continue to the present. Indexes are available through 1921. After that records are only filed chronologically. When fifty years have elapsed after the date of the marriage, a record becomes public and anyone may obtain a copy upon application. Copies of records may be obtained from the Clerk of the Superior Court of the District of Columbia, Marriage License Bureau, 500 Indiana Avenue, N.W, Washington, D.C. 20001.

Divorce records in the nation's capital date from 1803. Early proceedings between 1803 and 1848 are logged in the divorce docket, consist of four volumes, and are located at the Washington National Records Center in Suitland, Maryland (see page 9). Obtain full divorce records from 1803 to September 1956 from the Clerk of the U. S. District Court, Constitution Avenue and John Marshall Place, N.W., Washington, D.C. 20001. Records dated from September 1956 are available from the Clerk of the Superior Court, Family Division, 500 Indiana Avenue, N.W., Washington, D.C. 20001.

Census Records

Federal

Population Schedules.

- Indexed—1800, 1820, 1830, 1840, 1850, 1860, 1870, 1890 (fragment)
- Soundex—1880, 1900, 1920
- Unindexed—1910

Industry and Agriculture.

- 1850, 1860, 1870, 1880

Mortality Schedules.

- 1850, 1860, 1870, 1880

Union Veterans.

- 1890

Slave Schedules.

- 1850, 1860

When the first federal census was taken in 1790, residents of the nation's capital were enumerated in two separate states. Those living north of the Potomac River were enumerated with Prince George's and Montgomery counties in Maryland. Those south of the river were listed with Virginians; however, Virginia's census has been destroyed.

No federal returns exist for 1810. All of the population schedules are available at the National Archives (see page 8) in the Microfilm Reading Room. Supplemental schedules are at the Washington National Records Center in Suitland, Maryland (see page 9).

Background Sources

The following volumes, with comprehensive bibliographies, provide excellent background on social and cultural history:

Bryan, Wilhelmus Borgart. *A History of the National Capital.* 2 vols. New York, N.Y.: Macmillan Co., 1914–16.

Green, Constance McLaughlin. *Washington, Capital City, 1800–1950. 2 vols.* Princeton, N.J.: Princeton University Press, 1962.

The following are excellent references to District of Columbia research and records:

A Guide to Genealogical Research in the Nation's Capitol. 7th ed. N.p.: Annandale Stake, Church of Jesus Christ of Latter-day Saints, 1989.

Angevine, Erma Miller. "Genealogical Research on Families of the District of Columbia." *National Genealogical Society Quarterly* 78 (March 1990): 15–32.

Cook, Eleanor M. V. *Guide to the Records of Your District of Columbia Ancestors.* Silver Spring, Md.: Family Line Publications, 1987.

Provine, Dorothy S. *Preliminary Inventory of the Records of the Government of the District of Columbia.* Record Group 351. Washington, D.C.: National Archives and Records Service, 1976.

Maps

The largest collections of District of Columbia maps are found at the National Archives and the Library of Congress. Joseph Martin, *A New and Comprehensive Gazetteer of Virginia and the District of Columbia* (Charlottesville, Va.: the author, 1835), is available at the Library of Congress, the FHL in Salt Lake City, and the University of Virginia Library in Charlottesville. See also the National Geographic Society (U.S.) Cartographic Division, *Round About the Nation's Capital* (Washington, D.C.: National Geographic Society, 1956). The FHL has a series of Washington, D.C., ward maps dating from 1829 to 1868. Some Maryland and Virginia gazetteers, maps, and atlases include sections for the District of Columbia.

Sanborn Fire Insurance Maps for Washington, D.C., 1888–1950, are housed at the Library of Congress and microfilm copies are available at the District of Columbia Archives (see Archives, Libraries, and Societies). Real estate atlases and plat maps dating from 1887 to the present may be found at the Washingtoniana Division of the Martin Luther King, Jr., Memorial Library, 900 F Street, N.W., Washington, D.C. 20036. The Historical Society of Washington, D.C. (see Archives, Libraries, and Societies), has a collection of maps and atlases. Both the Washingtoniana Division and the Historical Society have a complete set of local city directories dating from 1822.

Land Records

Federal District

District of Columbia land transactions that took place prior to 1792 are found among records for Maryland or Virginia.

Microfilm copies of Alexandria County, Virginia deeds from 1783 to 1865 are also available at the FHL, along with Maryland Circuit Court deeds for Prince George's County from 1696 to 1884 and Montgomery County from 1777 to 1863.

Bessie Wilmarth Gahn, *Original Patentees of Land at Washington Prior to 1700* (1836; reprint, Baltimore, Md.: Genealogical Publishing Co., 1969), lists the earlier land owners a century before the District of Columbia was created.

Deeds (or an index to them) from 1792 to the present are located at the Recorder of Deeds, 515 D Street, N.W., Washington, D.C. 20001. Earliest deeds (1792–1869) are at the National Archives, but a search of the index at the recorder's office will be helpful first. Those for the period 1792 to 1886 and accompanying index volumes have been microfilmed and are available through the FHL. Of interest to those tracing slave ancestors is the presence of manumission records among the deeds.

Probate Records

Probate Records for the District of Columbia (see Court Records) include proceedings, indexes to wills and administration of estates case files, transcripts of wills, administration case dockets, accounts, inventories and sales of estates, guardianship records, and apprenticeships.

Original wills from 1801 to the present and related probate records may be obtained by writing to the Register of Wills, Room 5006, 500 Indiana Avenue, N.W., Washington, D.C. 20001.

Transcripts of wills dated 1810 to 1888, accompanying name indexes, and related probate case records for 1801 to 1878 are located in Record Group 21, National Archives and Records Administration, General Archives Division (NNFG), Washington National Records Center, Suitland, Maryland 20409. See Homer A. Walker's *Historical Court Records of Washington, D.C.: Death Records, 1801–78* (Washington, D.C.: the author, n.d.) for a name index to the Administrative Case Files, Old Series, 1801–78, that are also in the General Archives Division. Also useful are Mrs. Alexander H. Bell, *Abstracts of Wills in the District of Columbia, 1776–1815,* 2 vols. (Washington, D.C., 1945–46); Daughters of the American Revolution, E Pluribus Unum Chapter, *Transcripts of Probate Records, 1799–1837* (Salt Lake City, Utah: Genealogical Society of Utah, 1972); and *Record, Abstract of Wills,* 4 vols., 1828–37 (Washington, D.C.: Municipal Court, n.d.).

Court Records

Prior to 1801, land ceded by Maryland, which later became the district's Washington County, was under Prince George's and Montgomery county jurisdiction. The land originally belonging to Virginia consisted of Fairfax County and later Alexandria County. People living in those areas came under those counties' jurisdiction until the district was created.

The District of Columbia's court system began in 1801 with the creation of the U.S. Circuit Court and the U.S. District Court of Potomac and the District of Columbia. A criminal court was added in 1838.

The U.S. Circuit Court had jurisdiction in civil and criminal matters, took over the functions previously performed by the Virginia and Maryland county courts, and had appellate jurisdiction over the orphans' courts in the District counties of Washington and Alexandria. This court's records, dating 1801 to 1863, pertaining to law, appellate, and criminal cases (to 1838) include docket books, case papers, bonds to secure release of debtors, and grand jury lists. Chancery or equity functions of this court include divorce and other dockets, case files, and divorce records. Other records dealing with bankruptcy, manumissions and emancipations, fugitive slave case records, habeas corpus papers, and marriage licenses for 1837 to 1862 were also created here.

The U.S. District Court of the District of Potomac and the District of Columbia's records for the pre-1863 period consist of minutes, the docket of admiralty cases, admiralty case files, and title pages of copyright works. This court's records are housed in Record Group 21 at the Washington National Records Center, Suitland, Maryland (see page 9). Circuit court minutes for 1801–63 are also on microfilm (NARA M1021).

The U.S. Criminal Court for the District of Columbia was established in 1838, and it replaced the circuit and district courts' jurisdiction over criminal cases. Records produced by this court between 1838 and 1963 include dockets, minutes, proceedings, and case papers.

The U.S. Supreme Court of the District of Columbia was established in 1863 to replace all the circuit, district, and criminal courts of the District of Columbia. In 1936 its name was changed to the District Court of the United States for the District of Columbia. Records created by this court include minutes, dockets, and case papers in equity cases including adoptions, criminal, and bankruptcy, to name a few.

Records of naturalizations in the courts of the District of Columbia include indexes, naturalization records, copies of declarations of intention, and military naturalization records.

Tax Records

Assessment records for the District of Columbia from about 1814 to 1940 are in Record Group 351, Records of the Government of the District of Columbia, National Archives and Records Administration, Washington, D.C. 20408. Some lists are housed in the Washingtoniana Division of the Martin Luther King, Jr., Memorial Library. Some lists cover Georgetown and Washington County.

Tax books for the District of Columbia date back to 1880. Earlier records for the city of Washington cover 1824 to 1879. See NARA microfilm publication M605 for microfilm copies of *Records of the City of Georgetown (D.C.), 1800–79.*

Typed copies of Georgetown real property assessments for 1783, 1793, and 1798 are at the Peabody Room of the

Georgetown Regional Library, Wisconsin Avenue and R Street, N.W., Washington D.C. The Maryland Historical Society in Baltimore (see Maryland—Archives, Libraries, and Societies) has the original District of Columbia U.S. District Tax of 1798. Microfilm copies of it are available at the Georgetown Regional Library of the District of Columbia Archives (see Archives, Libraries, and Societies) and at the Maryland Archives in Annapolis.

Cemetery Records

The DAR has the best collection of tombstone inscriptions for the area, including the original registers of burials in the District of Columbia cemeteries. The six-volume set covers 1847 to 1938 and is at the DAR Library in Washington, D.C. Other publications include a series compiled and published by the Columbian Harmony Society. The following are representative: Paul E. Sluby, Sr., and Stanton L. Wormley, Sr., *Civil War Cemeteries of the District of Columbia Metropolitan Area; Register of Burials of the Joseph F. Birch Funeral Home* (4 vols., covers the period 1847 to 1938; *Mt. Zion Cemetery Washington, D.C.: A Brief History and Interments;* and *Selected Small Cemeteries of Washington, D.C.*

Church Records

Early religious denominations in the District of Columbia included Episcopalians (Episcopal Church Historian, Washington Cathedral, Mount Saint Alban, Washington, D.C. 20016); Roman Catholics (Archdiocese of Washington, P.O. Box 29260, Washington, D.C. 20017); Baptists (American Baptist Historical Society, 1106 South Goodman Street, Rochester, New York 14620); and Methodists (Commission on Archives and History, United Methodist Church, P.O. Box 127, Madison, New Jersey 07940) (see also Maryland and Virginia—Church Records).

There is a WPA inventory for Episcopal records: *Inventory of Church Archives in the District of Columbia: The Protestant Episcopal Church, Diocese of Washington,* Vol. 1—District of Columbia, Montgomery, Prince George's, Charles, St. Mary's counties, Maryland (Washington, D.C.: Historical Records Survey, 1940); and Vol. 2—Washington Cathedral (Washington, D.C.: Historical Records Survey, n.d.).

Military Records

Military records for those living in the District of Columbia are included in the NARA microfilm publications (see page 7). The District of Columbia maintained its own militia. See Frederick P. Todd, "Militia and Volunteers of the District of Columbia, 1783–1820," *Records of the Columbia Historical Society* 50 (1948): 387–88, published by the society, 1307 New Hampshire Avenue, N.W., Washington, D.C.

Periodicals, Newspapers, and Manuscript Collections

Periodicals

Washington History, formerly the *Records of the Columbia Historical Society,* which started publication in 1897 and changed titles in 1989, is the journal of the local historical society. See also page 7 for periodicals published in the District of Columbia area but of national scope.

Newspapers

The Library of Congress Newspaper Division has the largest holdings of local newspapers in the area. Most early District of Columbia newspapers are on microfilm at the Martin Luther King, Jr., Memorial Library, including the *Daily National Intelligencer,* which began publication in 1800.

Manuscripts

See page 8.

Archives, Libraries, and Societies

Washington National Records Center
4505 Suitland Road
Suitland, MD
Mailing address for District of Columbia records:
General Branch, Civil Archives Division
National Archives and Records Administration
Washington, DC 20409

District of Columbia Archives
1300 Naylor Court, N.W.
Washington, DC 20001-4255

Historical Society of Washington, D.C.
1307 New Hampshire Avenue, N.W.
Washington, DC 20036
Publishes *Washington History.*

District of Columbia Public Library
Martin Luther King, Jr., Memorial Library
Washingtoniana Division
901 G Street, N.W.
Washington, DC 20001

Maryland State Archives
361 Rowe Street
Annapolis, MD 21401

The National Archives (see page 8) and the following organizations are located in the District of Columbia area. They are of national significance, however, in their holdings for researchers (see page 9 for further details).

Library of Congress and Annex
1st and 2nd Streets, S.E.
Washington, DC 20504

National Genealogical Society
4527 Seventeenth Street North
Arlington, VA 22207

National Society, Daughters of the American Revolution Library
1776 D Street, N.W.
Washington, DC 20006

Special Focus Categories

Immigration

Most immigrants to the District of Columbia arrived at ports in Maryland and Pennsylvania See Maryland—Immigration and Pennsylvania—Immigration.

Black American

Large numbers of freedmen and their families began settling in the District of Columbia before the Civil War, and they were joined by thousands of others after the war ended. Most records in the district consist of census schedules, military records, and Freedmen's Bureau and related records compiled by the federal government.

Until about 1821, slave manumissions usually were recorded in deed books. After that time, many appear in the Freedom Registration Books that are Record Group 21 in the General Archives Division of the National Archives.

See also Letitia Woods Brown, *Free Negroes in the District of Columbia, 1790–1846,* The Urban Life in America Series (New York, N.Y.: Oxford University Press, 1972), and Paul E. Sluby, Sr., and Stanton L. Wormley, Sr., *Blacks in the Marriage Records of the District of Columbia, December 23, 1811–June 16, 1870.* 2 vols. (Washington, D.C.: Columbian Harmony Society, n.d.).

County Resources

Only one courthouse exists for the District of Columbia since it encompasses a single county. Land records are at the recorder of deeds; probate records are at the register of wills; and court records before 1863 are at Washington National Records Center. Later court records are in the appropriate court's office.

County Address	Date Formed Parent County/ies	Birth Marriage Death	Land Probate Court
District of Columbia 500 Indiana Avenue N.W. Washington, DC 20001	1790 Montgomery, Md./Prince George's, Md./ Alexandria, Va.	1874* 1811* 1874*	1792 1801 1801

* *See Vital Records above for location of records.*

FLORIDA

Brian E. Michaels

"No man would immigrate into Florida—no, not from Hell itself," declared the Honorable John Randolph of Roanoke in the United States House of Representatives. The newly annexed territory was, he declared, nothing more than "a land of swamps, of quagmires, of frogs and alligators and mosquitoes."

Nonetheless, Florida's 1980 census count of 9.7 million was to make it the nation's seventh-most-populous state, and by 1987 it ranked fourth. Because native Floridians perpetually seem to be scarce (fewer than a third of the state's current inhabitants were born there), there is a persistent myth that few Americans outside the state today could have had Florida ancestors. Many of the settlers who flooded the state from Georgia and the Carolinas before and especially after 1821, however, eventually fled the swamps, alligators, and mosquitoes to return home or to migrate further west. Numerous "brick walls" in Southern genealogy have toppled when a missing ancestor or family suddenly turned up in Florida, either permanently or en route to Alabama, Mississippi, Louisiana, Texas, or gold-rush California.

Many are surprised to learn that numerous living Americans can document their ancestry a full ten generations in Florida. Nearly two thousand Florida pioneer lineages (those pre-dating statehood in 1845) have been identified and documented in the past decade alone.

The early history of Florida falls neatly into the following periods: 1513, discovery; 1565–1763, first Spanish colonial period; 1763–83, British colonial period; 1784–1821, second Spanish period; 1821–45, U.S. territorial period; and 1845, statehood as the twenty-seventh state.

The Spanish colonial presence began with the landing of Juan Ponce de Leon at Eastertide of 1513, ninety-four years before Jamestown, and Spanish Florida ultimately embraced all of the present state and much of the Gulf Coast including Alabama, Mississippi, and Louisiana.

In 1564 French Huguenots settled Fort Caroline on the St. Johns River near present-day Jacksonville. The Spanish reacted immediately, establishing St. Augustine as the first permanent European settlement in America and immediately destroying Fort Caroline. After further hostilities, France abandoned her designs on peninsular Florida. Elizabethan England, however, was not so easily intimidated.

Spain was to spend much of the seventeenth century attempting to dissuade the English by scattering colonists across Florida, and by the 1680s San Marcos de Apalache (now St. Marks) on the Gulf coast had grown to noteworthy proportions. In the final third of the century, pressure from the French to the west and the English and their Native American allies to the north prompted Spain to fortify St. Augustine and to re-establish a former settlement at Pensacola in 1698. In 1702 and 1703 there were numerous British raids. Seventeen years later the French took and briefly held Pensacola before relinquishing the town, joining with Spain against England and finally retiring further westward along the Gulf Coast.

Following an indecisive treaty in 1748 and a decade of peace with Spain, England was again at war with France. By 1761 Spain, fearful that a French defeat could damage its own colonial interests, finally took sides with France, but it was too late. The Treaty of Paris, ending the Seven Years' War in 1763, saw Spain cede Florida to England in exchange for the captured city of Havana.

British East Florida reached from the Atlantic to the Apalachicola River; British West Florida ran from the Apalachicola to the Mississippi. In 1765 England sent Surveyor General William Gerard de Brahm and Royal Botanist John Bartram to the new possession and offered bounties, land grants, and other inducements to settlers. Thus East and West Florida remained loyal to Britain during the American Revolution, and St. Augustine became crowded with Tory refugees from Georgia and the Carolinas.

In 1781 Spain captured Pensacola from Britain, which two years later exchanged both Floridas for the Bahama Islands. Between 1785 and 1821, there were sporadic Spanish-American border disputes until the Pinckney Treaty of 1795 at last fixed the 31st parallel as the northern boundary of West Florida and gave the United States undisputed control of an area that now comprises nearly a third of Alabama and Mississippi.

Spain supported the British in the War of 1812 but never declared war on the United States. Nonetheless, Andrew Jackson seized and then abandoned Spanish Pensacola in 1814 and helped to convince Spain of the folly of trying to hold an overseas colony contiguous to a large and unfriendly nation already coveting its lands. Under the terms of the Adams-Onis Treaty, which took effect in 1821, Spain gave up East and West Florida in exchange for American settlement of U. S. citizens' claims against Spain.

In 1821 Congress provided for a territorial governor, territorial courts, and a thirteen-member legislative council. The first two counties were established on 21 July 1821. By its first territorial census in 1830, three years before skeptical John Randolph of Roanoke died, Florida boasted 34,730 inhabitants. By statehood fifteen years later, its population had surpassed 66,500, and by 1990 Florida's "swamps and quagmires" were inhabited by more than thirteen million Americans.

The massacre of Army Major Francis Langhorne Dade and two companies of soldiers in December of 1835 marked the opening hostilities of the Second Seminole War, which would end seven years later after an expenditure of more than twenty million dollars and the loss of 1,500 soldiers. By 1858, 3,824 Native Americans and blacks were relocated to Arkansas; Native American and white civilian casualties and property losses cannot accurately be calculated.

Florida, first among the Atlantic coast colonies settled but last admitted to the Union, attained statehood on 3 March 1845. By then her people had lived under the flags of four sovereign nations: Spain, France, Great Britain, and the United States. Since attaining United States territorial status in 1821, Floridians had been "free." Under statehood, at long last they were "equal."

Vital Records

The Bureau of Vital Statistics of the State Department of Health and Rehabilitative Services, P.O. Box 210, Jacksonville, Florida 32231, has custody of birth and death records filed from January 1917 to date. Scattered birth records from 1865 through 1916 are also held by the bureau, and some city health departments have some additional scattered records (e.g., Jacksonville, 1893–1913; Pensacola, 1897–1916).

Death records begin about 1877, but the first state law mandating registration of deaths was passed in 1899, and records before 1917 are spotty. It is always wise to check with city health departments. Some years ago, for example, the St. Augustine Health Department deposited a number of "death certificates and burial permits" written on scraps of paper, prescription blanks, etc., for the late 1870s and early 1880s with its local historical society library.

Applications for central-registry birth and death records must be submitted on standard forms available from the bureau at the above address. Under a statutory revision effective in 1987, "all birth records . . . shall be considered confidential documents . . . ." Birth certificates, computer certifications, and birth cards are available only to the registrant (if of the legal age of eighteen) or to his or her parent, guardian, or other legal representative. Death records are still issued to anyone paying the required fee, but the cause-of-death section of the original certificate is deemed confidential and will not be supplied.

If the bureau cannot supply a record, it is sometimes productive to have a search made at the local health department as some early Florida records simply did not get to Jacksonville. It is also wise to scan the periodical and genealogical society literature for items such as the West Florida Genealogical Society's 460-page *Early Pensacola Vital Records, Volume 1: 1891–1899* (Pensacola, Fla.: West Florida Genealogical Society, 1987).

Florida adoption records are confidential. The original papers are filed with the clerk of the circuit court in the county where the adoption took place. Medical background on the birth family is given to the adoptive family at adoption. It can be obtained by the adoptee at age eighteen from the Family and Children Services Program, Florida Department of Health and Rehabilitative Services, 1323 Winewood Boulevard, Tallahassee, Florida 32301, which also has a file on each adoption. Since October of 1980 it has been possible, when both the adoptee and the birth parent desire it and have submitted waivers of confidentiality, for a reunion to be arranged. Initial contact by searching adoptees should be with the department. Unsettling to many genealogists is the state's practice of sealing original birth certificates in the case of step-parent adoptions and issuing "amended" certificates showing the step-parent as the parent. Adoptions are governed by Chapter 63, *Florida Statutes*, which are amended yearly. They and the latest legislative session updates should be consulted at the outset of the search.

The Bureau of Vital Statistics has custody of marriage, divorce, and annulment records filed after 6 June 1927. For records prior to that date, and there are thousands of them, query the clerk of courts in the county where the license or decree was issued. Numerous divorces and resulting name changes are to be found in William A. Wolfe and Janet B. Wolfe, *Names and Abstracts from the Acts of the Legislative Council of the Territory of Florida, 1822–1845* (Pass-A-Grille Beach, Fla.: the authors, 1985), available from the Florida State Genealogical Society, P.O. Box 10249, Tallahassee, Florida 32302. Copies of marriage license applications are available only from the clerk of courts in the county courthouse. Standard request forms for copies of state-held records are necessary and available as indicated above.

Census Records

Federal

Population Schedules.

- Indexed—1830, 1840, 1850, 1860, 1870
- Soundex—1880, 1900, 1910 (miracode), 1920

Industry and Agriculture Schedules

- 1850, 1860, 1870, 1880

Mortality Schedules.

- 1850, 1860, 1870, 1880

Slave Schedules.

- 1850, 1860

The Southern Genealogist's Exchange Society has published statewide indexes to the 1830 and 1840 territorial censuses and the 1850 federal census of the new state of Florida. That same organization also transcribed the entire 1850 federal census (the first one to list names of all residents of a household) into small and inexpensive paperbound volumes of great usefulness. Accelerated Indexing Systems (see page 2) and others have produced microfiche and paper indexes to the 1860 and 1870 censuses. The West Florida Genealogical Society has published an eighty-page *Every-Name Index to the 1870 U.S. Census of Escambia County, Florida.* All Florida federal population schedules are available on microfilm at the Florida State Archives.

Spanish

The Spanish took a number of censuses during their periods of colonial control (1565–1763 and 1784–1821). Most have been published, though some may be hard to find. "The 1783 Spanish Census of Florida" was published in four consecutive issues of the *Georgia Genealogical Magazine*, beginning with no. 39 (Winter, 1971). William S. Coker and G. Douglas Inglis's *The Spanish Censuses of Pensacola, 1784–1820: A Genealogical Guide to Spanish Pensacola* (Pensacola, Fla.: Perdido Bay Press, 1980) reproduces ten valuable censuses and population lists, one or another taken roughly every four years. Joseph B. Lockey's important article "The 1786 St. Augustine Census," *Florida Historical Quarterly* 18 (July 1939): 11–31, has been complemented by Philip D. Rasico in "The Minorcan Population of St. Augustine in the Spanish Census of 1786" *Florida Historical Quarterly* 65 (October 1987): 160–84. "Religious Censuses of Pensacola,1796–1801" are discussed by William S. Coker in the *Florida Historical Quarterly* 61 (July 1982): 54–63. "The 1814 East Florida Spanish Census" appeared in the *Jacksonville Genealogical Society Quarterly* 4 (December 1976): 197–218. Record Group 599 ("Spanish Archives") of the Florida State Archives contains 175 reels of "The East Florida Papers," along with "Miscellaneous Land Records (1804–1849)"; "Memorials and Concessions" (1786–1821) to British subjects who stayed, swore allegiance to Spain, and cultivated their lands during the second Spanish period after the departure of the English in 1783; and "Memorials" (petitions) for city lots in St. Augustine (1764–1821) and Fernandina (1808–21). Most of these documents are in Spanish, but on occasion they can richly repay careful research. Regarding these records, see *Guide to the Records of the Florida State Archives* (Tallahassee, Fla.: Florida Department of State, 1988). For further understanding of the Spanish period generally, see chapters 2–6 of Paul S. George's *A Guide to the History of Florida* (Westport, Conn.: Greenwood Press, 1989).

State

The State of Florida conducted its own censuses in 1845, 1855, and every ten years from 1875 through 1945. Unfortunately, very few enumeration schedules have survived. A Leon County fragment appeared in Dorothy Dodd, "The Florida Census of 1825," *Florida Historical Quarterly* 22 (1943): 34–40. Brian E. Michaels, "Marion County in the 1855 State Census," appeared in *The Florida Armchair Researcher* 1 (1984); 3: 24–36 and 4: 30–41. The 1895 enumeration for Nassau County has been published by the Jacksonville Genealogical Society, 4589 Amherst Street, Jacksonville, Florida 32205.

In the holdings of the Florida State Archives (see Archives, Libraries, and Societies) are some fragmentary census returns of families with school-age children. One for Franklin County dates from 1855, and another for Franklin from 1866 has been published: see "Franklin County Children Ages 5–18 in 1866," *The Florida Armchair Researcher* 1 (Spring 1984): 7–8. The archives has census returns for 1867 from Hernando, Madison, Orange, and Santa Rosa counties. The 1875 Alachua County census also survives at the state archives.

Fortunately, Florida accepted partial funding from the federal government for a census taken as of 1 June 1885. There were schedules for population, agriculture, manufactures, and mortality. They are arranged alphabetically by name of county and thereunder numerically by type of schedule. Arrangement within the schedules is by enumeration district, precinct, or city. Thirty-five of the thirty-nine counties of the state in 1885 are included on the thirteen reels of National Archives Microfilm Publication M845 (the schedules for Alachua, Clay, Columbia, and Nassau appear to have been lost). *The Putnam County Genealogical Society Quarterly Journal* (P.O. Box 2354, Palatka, Florida 32178) has published a series of fully indexed transcriptions of the 1885 Putnam County population schedules, and several similar projects are reported to be in progress, so a query to local genealogical or historical societies might yield good things. AISI published an index to heads of households.

The Florida State Archives has the original schedules of the state censuses of 1935 and 1945, accessible alphabetically by county and thereunder by numbered election precincts. The schedules give name, address (and whether inside or outside city limits), age, sex, race, relation to family, place of birth, degree of education, and occupation. There is no index to these records; a personal visit is required.

Background Sources

The best modern history of Florida, with an excellent bibliography, is Charlton Tebeau, *A History of Florida* (Coral Gables, Fla.: University of Miami Press, 1971). A brief and popular but authoritative treatment is Rembert W. Patrick, *Florida Under Five Flags*, 3d ed. (Gainesville, Fla.: University of Florida Press, 1960). One of the most useful recent publications on the Sunshine State is *A Guide to the History of Florida*, edited by Paul S. George (Westport, Conn.: Greenwood Press, 1989). An indispensable source for articles, references, and book reviews is the *Florida Historical Quarterly (FHQ)*. Back numbers are available on microfilm and their usefulness is further enhanced by the *Florida Historical Quarterly Index, Volumes I–XXXV* (1908–56 with hiatus), edited by Julien C. Yonge and F. W. Hoskins (Gainesville, Fla.: Florida Historical Society), and Karen Lee Singh, *Florida Historical Quarterly Volume Indexes, XXXVI–LIII* (1957–75) (Tampa, Fla.: Florida Historical Society, 1976). Dated but not yet superseded and still useful is Michael H. Harris, *Florida History: A Bibliography* (Metuchen, N.J.: Scarecrow Press, 1972).

The Florida Room of the State Library, R. A. Gray Building, Tallahassee, Florida 32301, maintains a current and much more exhaustive bibliography of county histories, some of which may be acquired by interlibrary loan at public libraries within the state.

Maps

Noteworthy collections of Florida maps are held by the Florida Historical Society Library at the University of South Florida Library, Tampa, Florida 33620; the P. K. Yonge Library of Florida History and the Map Collection, University of Florida Libraries, Gainesville, Florida 32611; the Robert Manning Strozier Library, Florida State University, Tallahassee, Florida 32306; Special Collections, University of Miami, Coral Gables, Florida 33124; and the John C. Pace Library, University of West Florida, Pensacola, Florida 32514.

The National Topographic Map Series of the U.S. Geological Survey (see page 4) includes several series of very useful maps at various scales. Also extremely useful is the Florida Department of Transportation's county highway map series at a scale of one inch to one-half mile. Maps that show property ownership and boundaries are usually obtainable at the county property appraiser's office. Sanborn and other fire insurance maps should not be overlooked for urban areas (see page 4), and the Map Department, University of Florida Libraries (address above) has an excellent set of Sanborn original duplicate copies transferred from the Library of Congress. The Florida and Genealogy Collection at the Miami-Dade Public Library (see Archives, Libraries, and Societies) also has a microfilm collection of Sanborn maps of south Florida's major cities.

Land Records

Public-Domain State

Spanish Land Grants. The Florida State Archives holds a vast body of records created about 1820–22 for the use of the federal government in affirming or denying earlier Spanish grants of land. In many cases, these are the only surviving references to some of the pre-territorial residents of the area. The indexed documents are filed by claimant, and the amount of information they contain varies greatly, but the affidavits often tell when an individual arrived in Florida and how many were in his family, including names and ages. The acreage granted often depended on the number of "heads" in the family.

The original fragile records, largely in Spanish, are extant, but the WPA made a five-volume transcript, *Spanish Land Grants in Florida* (Tallahassee, Fla.: Florida State Library Board, 1940), which includes confirmed and unconfirmed Spanish Grants, British Grants, and Private Land Claims and is available at the Florida State Archives and in a number of libraries, as well as in an inexpensive microfiche edition from the archives.

Armed Occupation Act Records. In 1842, during the Second Seminole War, the federal government granted lands south of the line (a line running east and west about three miles north of Palatka) dividing rectangular survey Townships Nine and Ten South to individuals who agreed to claim, populate, and hold—by force of arms, if necessary—some of the undeveloped lands of eastern Florida. More than 1,000 persons responded, cleared the minimum five acres of their 160-acre grant, and lived on the property for the required five years. The records give the date an individual arrived in the territory, marital status, location of the grant holding, and the like. A strict alphabetical index compiled by Nora S. Michaels was published in *The Florida Armchair Researcher* 1 (Spring 1984): 9–21, and a copy is held by the custodians of the records, most of which are now in the Florida State Archives.

Division of State Lands Records. The Land Ordinance of 1785 decreed the use of a land-survey system known as the rectangular system of survey (see pages 4–5). Florida was the first state, and remains the only state on the Eastern Seaboard, to be surveyed in orderly squares rather than under the old English system of "metes and bounds" utilized in the thirteen original "state-land" states. The original surveyors' field notes and plats have been transferred to the state archives, along with the original tract books and records of all grants of land from the state to the initial grantee, whether by purchase or otherwise. A fascinating and valuable resource, the notes and other files depict for the careful researcher the topography, settlements, and even the houses of the early territorial period and beyond.

Homestead Files. The homestead applications filed by Florida settlers, 1881–1905, have been transferred to the Florida State Archives. Information contained includes name of applicant, place of residence at time of application, tract description, and number of acres granted. There is a surname index. Other homestead records included in Record Group 598 include tax receipts required to prove that claimants were paying taxes on their claims, unindexed miscellaneous and legal records concerning homesteads, and correspondence of the State Land Office, 1858–1913.

A number of Florida land records, including the "Florida Donation Entry Files" and "Private Land Claims" are held by the National Archives, and a number of them can be found indexed in *Florida Land: Records of the Tallahassee and Newnansville General Land Office[s], 1825–1892* (Bowie, Md.: Heritage Books, 1989). This useful volume compiled by Alvie L. Davidson lists lands transferred from the federal government by grant and sale during the territorial period and much of the nineteenth century. The sources used by the compiler may have been misleading in one respect, however. While the book's cover and front matter indicate that the listing includes those claiming land under the Armed Occupation Act of 1842 (see above), such does not appear to be the case. A search for fifty of the names listed in the index to those records revealed that none of them was included in *Florida Land.* This in no way affects the usefulness of the volume concerning the other lands granted through the two federal land offices named, but it should in no case be relied upon in a search for Armed Occupation Act settlers.

Subsequent Land Transactions. Deeds after the first grants are recorded generally through the clerk of the courts in the county seat.

Probate Records

Florida probate records include the wills, intestate administrations, bonds, inventories and appraisements, guardianships, and property divisions familiar in most states. The records formerly held by probate courts have been transferred to the counties' clerks of courts and are readily accessible in most jurisdictions. The searcher who relies upon the recorded documents and fails to examine the bundled paper packets, however, may miss valuable clues. The Florida volumes of *The Territorial Papers of the United States* (see Special Focus Categories) and land records may also contain lineage information.

Court Records

Article Five of the present Constitution of Florida has simplified locating and using the recorded instruments of the state: all judicial power is now vested in a supreme court, district courts of appeal, circuit courts, and county courts. No other courts may be established by the state, any political subdivision, or any municipality. Under a 1973 reorganization of the judicial system, the clerk of courts in each county was made custodian of all records of all predecessor courts, whether justice of the peace, city, county, probate, civil, or criminal.

Tax Records

Early tax rolls, especially between census years, can be a gold mine for the fortunate researcher. Most existing rolls can be found in the counties of origin, but the Florida State Archives also has some bound volumes sent to the state comptroller during the period 1829–81. Normal information includes the taxpayer's name, land ownership, number of white males above taxable age (twenty-one), slaves, horses, wagons, and other taxable items of personal property such as jewelry, watches, musical instruments, and carriages. Many of the counties' records in the series are incomplete, but there are some in the Florida State Archives that the originating counties no longer have. This valuable resource is not indexed. It must be searched in the county, at the Florida State Archives, or both.

Cemetery Records

Cemetery records are held by most Florida libraries and archives. One important compiled source is the WPA *Register of Deceased Veterans Buried in Florida,* which covers fifty-one of the sixty-seven counties (St. Augustine, Fla.: Veterans' Graves Registration Project, 1940–41). Access to the massive amount of cemetery information scattered throughout the state is being facilitated by a continuing cemetery location project of the Florida State Genealogical Society. The information will be published, but queries on locations and published surveys may in the meantime be directed to Cemetery Survey Chairman,

Florida State Genealogical Society (see Archives, Libraries, and Societies). It is important to note that this is a directory of cemeteries and published records, not of personal names.

Church Records

As in most former frontier societies, early Florida church records are hit-and-miss, but they can be valuable when located. The Roman Catholic faith accompanied the earliest Spanish settlers to Florida; an excellent account is Michael V. Gannon, *The Cross in the Sand: The Early Catholic Church in Florida, 1513–1870* (Gainesville, Fla.: University of Florida Press, 1965). By 1822 the Baptists, Methodists, Episcopalians, and Presbyterians were also active in the new territory. A good brief account is W. T. Cash, "Social Life in Florida in 1845," reprinted in Brian E. Michaels, *Florida Voters in their First Statewide Election: May 26, 1845* (Tallahassee, Fla.: Florida State Genealogical Society, 1987), pages 5–8. By 1845 the Baptists had split into the Missionary and Primitive varieties (probably totaling more than 5,000 Florida members), and all of the above groups had become more or less well organized. For information on early Baptists and an excellent bibliography, see Edward Earl Joiner, *A History of Florida Baptists* (Jacksonville, Fla.: Convention Press, 1972). Methodists had two churches in Fernandina as early as 1822 (under the South Carolina Conference) and more than 10,000 members by statehood.

The newest account of Methodists in Florida is Robert Mickler Temple, Jr., *Florida Flame: A History of the Florida Conference of the United Methodist Church* (Nashville, Tenn.: Parthenon Press, 1987). Unfortunately, this well-documented volume relies on chapter endnotes and has no comprehensive bibliography. By 1845 the Episcopalians had parishes at Apalachicola, Jacksonville, Key West, Pensacola, and Tallahassee in addition to others in several smaller towns. See Joseph D. Cushman, *A Goodly Heritage: The Episcopal Church in Florida, 1821–1892* (Gainesville, Fla.: University of Florida Press, 1965), which contains a bibliography. In 1840 Florida Presbyterian churches were divided among the Florida, Georgia, and Alabama Presbyteries (see James R. Bullock, *Heritage and Hope: A Story of Presbyterians in Florida [Orlando, Fla.: Synod of Florida, Presbyterian Church, 1987]*). An incomplete but voluminous list of Florida churches in existence fifty years ago is the WPA volume *Preliminary List of Religious Bodies in Florida* (Jacksonville, Fla.: Historical Records Survey, 1939). A microfiche edition is available from the Florida State Archives, and the original survey forms from which the volume was compiled are now in the state library's Florida Room. Church records are also to be had in the holdings of most libraries and archival depositories throughout the state, but denominational representatives should be consulted for specific repositories peculiar to their particular churches.

Saint Augustine's Roman Catholic Cathedral Parish records beginning in 1594 are maintained by the parish's archivist at the records center, St. Augustine Catholic Diocese, 11625 St. Augustine Road, Jacksonville, Florida 32223. It includes marriages, baptisms, and burials.

Military Records

The Florida Department of Military Affairs, Historical Services Division, State Arsenal, P. O. Box 1008, St. Augustine, Florida 32045, has produced an ongoing series of approximately one hundred "Special Archives Publications" distributed to an extremely limited number of depositories in Florida and elsewhere. Rich in transcriptions from newly discovered original records that are being transferred to the Florida State Archives, these softbound fascicles are of great usefulness. Selected volumes will be noted in the discussions below, but researchers are encouraged to query the director of the historical services division at the above address regarding a list of pertinent titles.

The Revolutionary War. Because Florida remained loyal to the Crown during the Revolution, Jessie R. Fritot's *Pension Records of Soldiers of the Revolution Who Removed to Florida* (Jacksonville, Fla.: Jacksonville Chapter, Daughters of the American Revolution, 1946) remains among the few genealogically valuable references to later Floridians who had served during that conflict. An early treatment of the period and the massive influx of Tories to St. Augustine and its environs is Wilbur H. Siebert's *Loyalists in East Florida, 1774–85*, 2 vols. (1929; reprint, Boston, Mass.: Gregg, 1973). See also J. Leitch Wright, *Florida in the American Revolution* (Gainesville, Fla.: University Presses of Florida, 1975).

Indian Wars. In 1903 the Florida Board of State Institutions published an unindexed and somewhat flawed volume entitled *Soldiers of Florida in the Seminole Indian, Civil, and Spanish-American Wars* (1903; reprint, Macclenny, Fla.: Richard J. Ferry, 1983). The P. K. Yonge Library (see Archives, Libraries, and Societies) has a WPA index to the Civil War section, and the state library has another by Dorothy Dodd. The volume's chief usefulness is as a lead to original source materials.

The Florida State Archives holds a reference copy of the sixty-three-reel National Archives microfilm number M1086, *Compiled Service Records of Volunteers Who Served in Organizations from the State of Florida During the Florida Indian Wars, 1835–1858.* There is no state index, but participants are included in the master *Index to Compiled Service Records of Volunteer Soldiers Who Served During Indian Wars and Disturbances, 1815–1858* (M629, forty-two reels).

The Mexican War. Florida had recently been through the Second Seminole War and had been a state just over a year when "Polk's War" with Mexico began. Yet the five-company quota assigned to Florida was quickly filled. Very little attention has thus far been paid to the new state's part in the Mexican War, but one excellent account, including rosters of the five companies, is "Florida's Part in the War with Mexico," *Florida Historical Quarterly* 20 (1942): 235–59, by T. Frederick Davis. The Florida State Archives has recently acquired film copies of original muster rolls of the various Florida companies in the War with Mexico, and some Florida libraries will have *Compiled Muster Rolls and Service Abstracts, Florida Militia Volunteers, War with Mexico, 1846–1848,* Special Archives Publication No. 9 (St. Augustine, Fla.: Florida Department of Military Affairs). There is also a microfilmed alphabetical master index (National Archives film M616) to compiled Mexican War service records that can prove helpful.

Civil War. Florida seceded from the Union on 10 January 1861, remained an independent nation until 22 April of that year, and ended the Civil War with the only Confederate capital east of the Mississippi not captured and occupied by federal forces. More than 16,000 Floridians served in the Civil War (15,000 Confederate and 1,290 Union). On Florida in the Civil War, see William Watson Davis, *The Civil War and Reconstruction in Florida* (1913; reprint, Gainesville, Fla.: University of Florida Press, 1964), and Jerrell H. Shofner, *Nor Is It Over Yet: Florida in the Era of Reconstruction, 1863–1877* (Gainesville, Fla.: University Presses of Florida, 1974).

The Florida State Archives has reference copies of the National Archives microfilm *Consolidated Index to Compiled Service Records of Confederate Soldiers* (M253) as well as the *Compiled Service Records of Confederate Soldiers Who Served in Organizations from the State of Florida* (M251; index, M225) and the index and files of *Compiled Service Records of Volunteer Union Soldiers Who Served in Organizations from the State of Florida* (M225 and M400).

Several volumes of the special publications of the Florida Department of Military Affairs (discussed at the beginning of Military Records) pertain to Union and Confederate soldiers from Florida, and more are planned. Query the Historical Services Division for more information and/or new publications.

Florida granted pensions to Confederate veterans and their widows under laws passed in 1885, 1887, and 1889. In 1915 a peak total of 5,134 veterans and widows were on the rolls. The Florida State Archives has a collection of some 12,775 approved and rejected pension applications. The files are indexed by both veterans' and widows' names. Available from the archives is a microfiche *Computer-Based Register and Index to the Florida State Board of Pensions' Confederate Service Pension Applications, 1885–1954.* Inquirers, in person or by mail, may order copies of the files, which generally include original and supplemental applications, full name, date and place of birth, service unit, wounds received, date and place of enlistment and discharge, county of residence when applying, and length of residence in the state. Widows' records add maiden name, date and place of marriage, and date and place of the veteran's death. The archives' central reference unit will report whether a pension is on file and quote costs for copies (typically for four to ten pages).

The Spanish-American War. Most of the Florida volunteers in the infantry units of what John Hay called a "splendid little war" moved smartly about the state, into and out of training camps and guard detachments, but never left it. Several hundred of them are listed, with capsule unit histories, in *Soldiers of Florida* (see Indian Wars above). The section is unindexed but can serve to alert researchers to further resources. A thirteen-reel National Archives and Records Administration microfilm publication (M1087), *Compiled Service Records of Volunteer Soldiers Who Served in the Florida Infantry During the War with Spain,* is generally more reliable; access to the records is facilitated by a 126-reel index (M871). Florida Department of Military Affairs Special Publication No. 3 is *Mobilization Lists, Florida State Troops and Naval Militia, Spanish-American War, 1898–1899.*

Militia. Florida has had a militia since its earliest territorial days. When voters lined up to register for the young state's first election in 1845, every able-bodied man over twenty and under forty-five was enrolled in the militia before being allowed to vote; only age or infirmity excused the prospective voter from his military obligation.

Home guard (state militia) units were under state command during the Civil War, and their personnel and other records were never provided to Confederate officials. Most of the records that survived the war were placed in the State Arsenal, which has recently transferred them and other treasures to the Florida State Archives. Including records as early as the 1820s, as well as muster rolls from the Second Seminole, Mexican, and Civil Wars, this new accession constitutes a major source for Florida researchers. Later records include documents of the Florida Militia, Florida State Troops, and Florida National Guard covering the period 1870–1917. World War I induction lists and a card roster of Floridians who served 1917–19 add to the value of this record group (RG 197). See Robert Hawk, *Florida's Army: Militia/State Troops/National Guard, 1565–1985* (Englewood, Fla.: Pineapple Press, 1986).

Important and newly discovered lists of territorial militia officers and men for the period 1826–30 have appeared in the fall 1987 and winter 1989 issues of *The Florida Genealogist.*

As in so many other areas, there are some militia rolls and related files that never reached the state archives. They can sometimes be found, often to the amazement of their custodians, in the miscellaneous courthouse files and county commission minutes of the older counties. Again, personal search is the only way to find them.

Periodicals, Newspapers, and Manuscript Collections

Periodicals

The Florida Genealogist, published by the Florida State Genealogical Society, P.O. Box 10249, Tallahassee, Florida 32302, is the only genealogical periodical of statewide coverage. A number of local societies publish useful periodicals, and a current list of genealogical societies in the state is available from the Florida State Genealogical Society at the address above.

The Southern Genealogist's Exchange Quarterly, issues published 1957–81, are available at most large libraries with collections on the South.

Newspapers

Newspaper collections are found in the state library and most large libraries, but local societies and libraries in the area of geographical interest should also be queried. The St. Augustine Historical Society Library (see Archives, Libraries, and Societies) and most university libraries have collections of varying coverage, but the most comprehensive collection is located at the P. K. Yonge Library of Florida History in Gainesville (see Archives, Libraries, and Societies), whose *Catalog*, 4 vols. (Boston, Mass.: G. K. Hall, 1977), lists newspapers as early as the *St. Augustine-East Florida Herald* of 1823.

Manuscripts

Manuscript collections are found in university and historical libraries throughout the South and in several large public collections as well as those of the state's larger historical societies and the Florida State Archives, whose *Guide* contains more than fifty pages of manuscript descriptions. The *National Union Catalog of Manuscript Collections* (see page 8) lists numerous Florida holdings but is not intended to be exhaustive. Specific and narrowly focused queries to individual collections can also be productive.

Archives, Libraries, and Societies

Florida State Archives and the State Library of Florida
Division of Library and Information Services
500 South Bronough Street
Tallahassee, FL 32399

The archives is the state's official repository for public records. It holds excellent collections, already described, reaching beyond this mandate. The state library maintains printed and secondary source material for the state, such as city directories, histories, biographies, and church surveys as well as manuscripts.

P. K. Yonge Library of Florida History
University of Florida
Gainesville, FL 32611

Largest collection of Spanish colonial documents in the United States and largest microfilm collection of Florida newspapers. See *Catalog of the P. K. Yonge Library of Florida History*, 4 vols. (Boston, Mass.: G. K. Hall, 1977).

John C. Pace Library
University of West Florida
Pensacola, FL 32514

A Guide to the Manuscripts and Special Collections of the John C. Pace Library describes the extent of this valuable research material, particularly the Panton, Leslie, and Company Papers (1783–1821), a significant block of material on British and Spanish West Florida trade with Native Americans.

Other libraries with significant genealogical collections include the following:

Miami-Dade Public Library
101 West Flagler Street
Miami, FL 33130

Its genealogy collection contains microfilm copies of all federal population censuses.

Polk County Historical and Genealogical Library
Old Courthouse Building
Main and Broadway
Bartow, FL 33830

Especially strong in Florida and the southeast.

Orlando Public Library
101 East Central Boulevard
Orlando, FL 32801

Records depository for the Florida Daughters of the American Revolution.

Haydon Burns Public Library
122 North Ocean Street
Jacksonville, FL 32202

Excellent holdings on Jacksonville and northern Florida.

The Florida State Genealogical Society
P.O. Box 10249
Tallahassee, FL 32302

St. Augustine Historical Society
271 Charlotte Street
St. Augustine, FL 32084

Especially strong in early St. Augustine and Spanish Florida.

Pensacola Historical Society
405 South Adams Street
Pensacola, FL 32501

Strong on West Florida and has a large photographic collection.

Special Focus Categories

Immigration

Florida immigration records, as such, are rare. Most of the early settlers came overland from the neighboring states to the north but below the Mason-Dixon Line, and the majority of them were from Georgia. However, see Frank M. Hawes, "New Englanders in the Florida Census of 1850," *New*

England Historical and Genealogical Register 76 (1922): 44–54. There were some seaports through which immigrants came into the territory and state, but most of the recorded activity was as late as the turn of this century. There are copies and transcripts of customs passenger lists for Key West (1837–52, 1857–68), for St. Augustine (1821–22, 1822–24, 1827, 1875), and St. Johns (1865) on National Archives microfilm M575, for which the 188 reels of M334 are an alphabetical index (Key West, reel 4; St. Augustine and St. Johns, reel 16).

National Archives microfilm publication T940 is forty-one reels of *Passenger Lists of Vessels Arriving at Key West, 1898–1945,* and T517 comprises a twenty-six-reel *Index to Passenger Lists of Vessels Arriving at Miscellaneous Ports in Alabama, Florida, Georgia, and South Carolina, 1890–1924.* Fortunately, the latter is arranged alphabetically by name of the passenger rather than by the port. A number of post-1899 Florida lists are noticed in Table 8 of the National Archives' *Guide to Genealogical Research in the National Archives* (Washington, D.C., 1985).

Naturalization

The National Archives-Southeast Region (see page 8) has naturalization petitions and records from the U.S. district courts at Key West (1867–1948) and Miami (1913–48). Naturalizations prior to 1907 can be found in the files of some circuit courts, such as in Escambia (1821–1903), Hillsborough (1899–present), and Putnam (1853–1906) counties. They often are not indexed separately. Dated but potentially still useful is the WPA volume *Naturalization Records in Florida* (Tallahassee, 1940).

Black American

Voluminous records of various aspects of black life in Florida have been surveyed for *The Black Experience: A Guide to Afro-American Resources in the Florida State Archives* (Tallahassee, Fla.: Florida State Archives, 1988). Compiled by Delbra D. McGriff, former curator of the archives' genealogy collection, this invaluable new resource gives record groups and series titles, coverage dates, and descriptions for a vast array of primary sources for research on the blacks of Florida. The work is available from the state archives.

The archives' public record and manuscript holdings include slave books; black church membership lists; the governors' administrative correspondence; Black Teacher Association papers; and the papers of Judge Joseph Lee, a prominent black Republican of Duval County. Black marriage records, deeds documenting black ownership of land, and probate files containing wills and appraisement inventories including lists of slaves are interspersed throughout the archives' county records microfilm collection. A few counties (Gadsden, Leon, and Gulf) provide indexes for "Negro" or "Colored" marriages, but there are no separate indexes for black deeds or probates. Chancery case files, marks and brands, mortgages, guardianships, and court-order books can also be useful to the researcher of black genealogy.

The state library's Florida Collection has clipping files on prominent Florida blacks, a card file on black legislators, black newspapers, the 1850 and 1860 slave schedules, the microfilmed papers of Mary McLeod Bethune (founder of Bethune-Cookman College in Daytona Beach), and the 646-piece J. G. Gavin family papers of Wakulla County. Other manuscript sources (e.g., the John T. Bryan and the George A. Dekle papers) include bills of sale for slaves. There are a number of printed sources in the Florida Collection, and the periodical literature and the records in the National Archives (see pages 8–9) should not be overlooked. See, for example, "An Evaluation of the Freedmen's Bureau in Florida," *Florida Historical Quarterly* 41 (1963): 223–38, and "Florida Black Codes," *Florida Historical Quarterly* 47 (1969): 365–79.

Federal census records, 1870–1910, are very useful for black research, as are the 1935 and 1945 Florida state censuses mentioned above. The 1868 Florida voter records list each registrant's name, race, length of residence in the county and state, nativity (by state), naturalization (where, when, how), and the date of registration. Another useful source for some families is the Spanish land grants compilation mentioned above; files occasionally include lists of slaves by name and age, with designations such as "Negra," "Negro," and "Mulatto."

Some of the state's ubiquitous black midwives were eventually licensed by the state. The Florida State Archives has midwifery files, 1924–75 (Record Group 894, Series 904), which contain a few applications for licensing of black midwives under the state midwifery program.

Florida Agricultural and Mechanical University, the state's historically black university, maintains a Black Archives Research Center and Museum on its Tallahassee campus (P. O. Box 809, Tallahassee, Florida 32307). The Black Archives, History and Research Foundation of South Florida, Inc. (5400 Northwest 22nd Avenue, Miami, Florida 33142), constitutes another resource for researchers into black history and genealogy. Chapters entitled "Black Floridians" and "Black Archives Research Center and Museum of Florida A & M University" in George's, *A Guide to the History of Florida* (see Background Sources) are indispensable for this field of research. Research into black genealogy is not easy in Florida, but neither is it without surprisingly substantial resources.

Native American

In 1980 Florida boasted 24,714 Native Americans representing thirty-four different tribes. Today's true "Florida Indians," however, constitute three separate but historically related groups: the Seminole, the Miccosukee, and the Creek tribes.

The Seminoles originally comprised the Yemassee (who fled the Carolinas in the second decade of the eighteenth century), the Oconee, and the Creeks. Thousands of them were transported during the mid-1800s to Oklahoma where they formed one of the "Five Civilized Tribes." Many still live on federal and state reservations in or near the Everglades. The Seminoles have three substantial reservations: Big Cypress, Brighton, and Hollywood, with a total population of approximately 3,350.

The Miccosukee have a reservation at Forty-Mile-Bend on the Tamiami Trail (population 275) and a large uninhabited state reservation. Today, Miccosukees and Seminoles are scattered through large cities and small towns, and strong family bonds have enabled them to adapt to the modern world without losing their cultural identity.

The Florida Creeks, descendants of the Poarch Band of Creeks in Alabama, the Apalachicola River Creeks of Calhoun County, and others who resisted removal to the West, reside primarily in the northwest part of the state between the Apalachicola River and the Florida-Alabama line. Escambia County, Blountstown in Calhoun County, and Bruce in Walton County are their three centers of major activity. Most of the early Creeks survived by living in small isolated groups apart from whites, but that has changed in more modern times.

An extremely valuable resource is John K. Mahon's article, "The Seminole and Miccosukee Indians of Florida," in George's *A Guide to the History of Florida* (see Background Sources).

Perhaps the most common starting place for Native American research on the Florida tribes is the 213-reel microfilm publication T529, *Final Rolls of the Five Civilized Tribes in Indian Territory Choctaw, Chickasaw, Cherokee, Creek, Seminole.* A full set of these films is at the Valparaiso Community Library in Okaloosa County.

Individual research into Florida Native American ancestry can be successful, but it can also be a difficult and frustrating experience.

Other Ethnic Groups

Florida is a melting pot of people from different backgrounds. First among the various groups were the Native Americans, who today constitute a small fraction of one percent of the Florida populace. Blacks constituted half of the state's population during the mid-1800s, but by 1980 were only 14 percent. Heavy immigration to southern Florida by Jewish northeasterners of European heritage in the 1920s boosted today's Jewish percentage to about 5 percent. Large Hispanic migration, except for areas such as St. Augustine, Tampa, and Pensacola, generally occurred in this century and has been heaviest in the past three decades.

Among the earliest still-traceable foreign colonies are the Minorcans, who came from the Greek, Spanish, and Italian isles with Dr. Andrew Turnbull to settle his ill-fated New Smyrna plantation on the coast south of St. Augustine in 1768. Jane Quinn, *Minorcans in Florida: Their History and Heritage* (St. Augustine, Fla.: Mission Press, 1975), tells the fascinating story of this fabled group. Nixon Smiley has compiled a brief overview of the dozen or so overseas groups who have followed the Minorcans. On the Jews, the researcher should see Samuel Proctor, "Pioneer Jewish Settlement in Florida, 1765–1900" in *Proceedings of the Conference on the Writing of Regional History in the South* (New York, 1956), pages 81–115. On nineteenth-century English settlers, Scandinavians, the Conchs of Key West, the Greeks at Tarpon Springs, Slovaks, Czechs, Poles, Japanese, Russians, Cubans, Mexicans, Hungarians, Vietnamese, and Haitians, see "Foreign Colonies Since 1768 and Still Today" in *The Florida Handbook, 1979–1980* (Tallahassee, Fla.: Peninsula Publishing, 1979), pages 305–08. It is necessary to note, however, that most of these groups arrived only in the early 1900s, and that some of the transplantations were not successful.

Territorial Records

Volumes 22–26 of *The Territorial Papers of the United States* (Washington, D.C.: Government Printing Office, 1956–65) list the names of thousands of Florida residents between 1821 and 1845 in hundreds of letters, reports, and petitions ("memorials") of the territorial period. Information varies, but the wide coverage and excellent index make the volumes essential to a full understanding of the people and their era. Most large libraries in the United States have these, as do college and university collections.

Not all territorial papers are included in the above volumes, however. The *Territorial Papers of the United States Senate, 1789–1873: Florida 1806–1845* (National Archives and Records Administration M200, reels 9–11); *State Department Territorial Papers, Florida, 1777–1824* (M116, 11 reels); and *Territorial Papers of the United States: The Territory of Florida, 1821–1845* (M721, reels 14–16) are also potential sources, but many of the territorial papers generated have never been filmed.

An excellent finding-aid to the existing territorial legislative council session laws is *Names and Abstracts from the Acts of the Legislative Council of the Territory of Florida, 1822–1845* (Pass-A-Grille Beach, Fla.: William A. and Janet B. Wolfe, 1985).

Early Election Records

The Florida State Archives has 2,000 folders of important early election records. Voter rolls have an advantage over deeds; if an individual *voted* in a jurisdiction, he *lived* there. Land records can be misleading on absentee owners, but election records were sworn documents requiring proof of residence, usually six months in the county, two years in the state. The files are arranged by year, and thereunder by county, but they must be used in person; there is no index in existence or planned. These voter rolls and returns list the names of candidates, clerks, and inspectors in local, state, congressional, referendum, and militia elections from 1824. Until 1865 each voter's name and precinct of residence is listed. A discussion and county-by-county availability listing (1824–1926) by Donald Draper Campbell appeared in *The Florida Genealogist* 8 (Spring 1985): 76–82. Not all such records have reached the state archives, however, and many courthouse clerks are unaware that some remain in their custody—they may have to be cajoled into locating and producing them or allowing the researcher to do so.

Among the most useful records for those tracing ancestors at the time of statehood are the returns of the first statewide election, held on 26 May 1845, in Brian E. Michaels, *Florida Voters in Their First Statewide Election.* (Tallahassee, Fla.: Florida State Genealogical Society, 1987), which is available from the society.

Another voter record of genealogical significance is the 1868 Florida voter registration, which required an oath of allegiance to the U.S. government. It was also the first voter enrollment open to blacks. While it is neither indexed nor complete for all counties, this important re-registration for the post-war constitutional convention election includes name, qualifying date, race, length of residence, nativity by state, and naturalization. The rolls are arranged by county and thereunder by the date of individual registration. These records compiled in the turbulent times of Reconstruction help to determine in many cases that an individual survived the Civil War (though absence of a particular individual is not proof of the contrary). They can also aid in backtracking immigrants from other states.

The Florida Pioneer Papers

Proof of lineal descent from an individual, male or female, who settled in Florida before 3 March 1845 entitles one to recognition by the Florida State Genealogical Society as a "Florida Pioneer Descendant." Since 1977 nearly 2,000 Florida Pioneer lineages have been documented. Lists of pioneers, biographical sketches, and pedigree charts have been published in most issues of *The Florida Genealogist,* and a fully indexed set of the original papers has been placed in the Florida State Archives, where it is available for research in person or by mail.

County Resources

Among the records useful to the genealogist and usually held by the county courthouses are original marriage and divorce records. Probate court records include wills, administrations, bonds, inventories and appraisements, and guardianships. Land grants, homesteads, deeds, mortgages, and similar or related records are found in earlier individual books, but for a number of years in most jurisdictions such records have been combined into "Official Record" books. Recorded plat books, civil and criminal court dockets (case schedules), minutes, order books, naturalizations, incorporations, incompetencies, soldier and sailor discharge records, Confederate oaths of allegiance, delayed birth certificates, and marks and brands are all generally useful as well.

Deed, probate, tax, and marriage records are available for most Florida counties. Other miscellaneous records are available for particular counties. They may include delayed birth certificates, birth and death records, family history, naturalization record indexes, court records, foreign judgments, homesteads, marks and brands, burial permits, cemetery records, and lists of registered voters.

Tax assessment lists and tax rolls, poll tax records (on free white males of twenty-one and up) are helpful, as are listings of local lawyers, physicians, and dentists. Official minutes of county commissions, road and bridge trustees, and other taxing authorities may also be of interest.

In the majority of counties, the original records are retained in the office of the clerk of courts located in the county seat, although a list of "County Records on Microfilm at the State Archives" appeared in *The Florida Genealogist* 11, no. 2 (Winter 1988): 41–44.

Queries and requests for information from Florida counties should be addressed to the "Clerk of Courts, ______ County Courthouse," at the address given in the chart below. Names in parentheses are former names of the county.

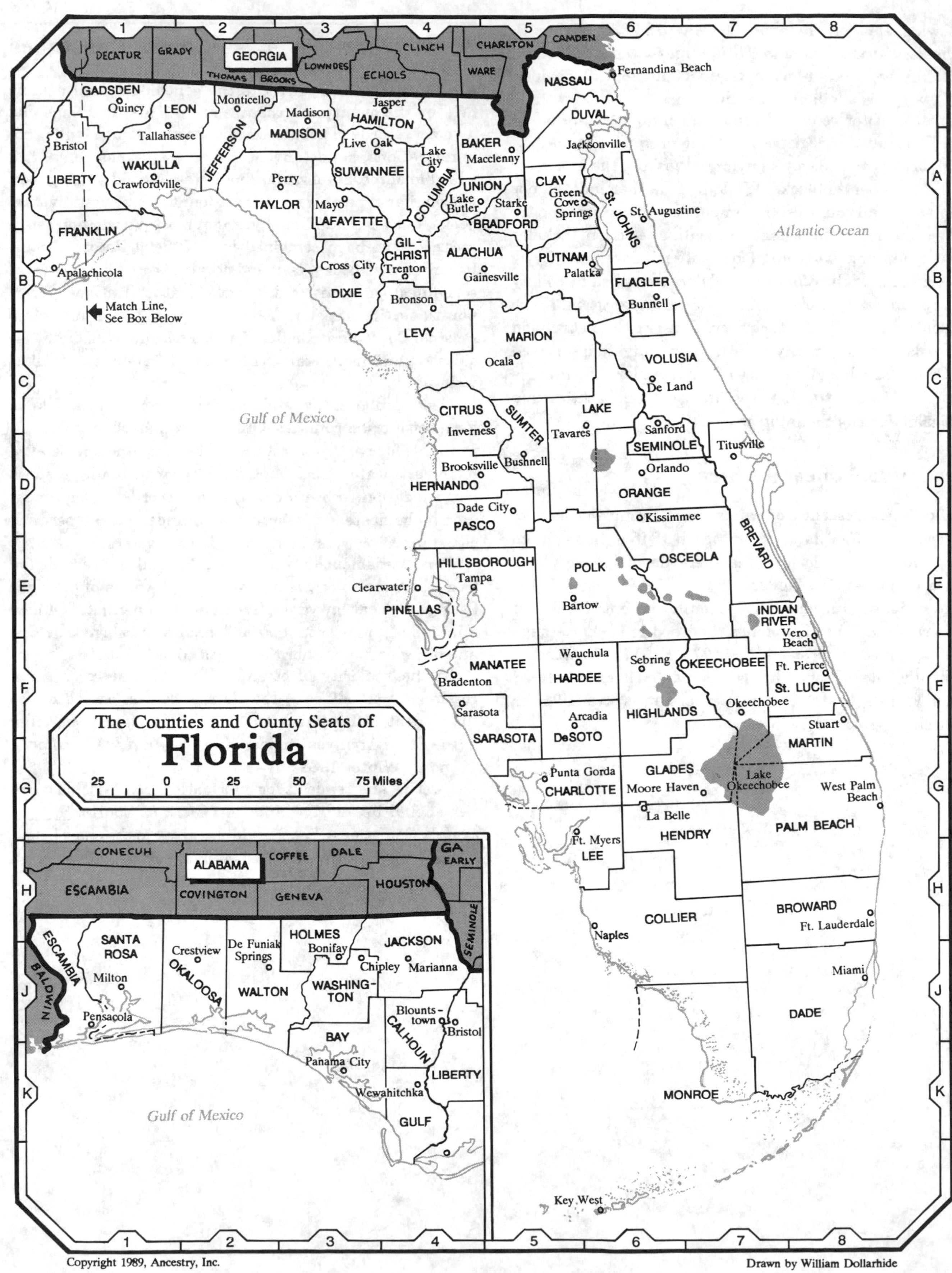

Drawn by William Dollarhide

Map	County Address	Date Formed Parent County/ies	Birth Marriage Death	Land Probate Court
B4	Alachua P.O. Box 600 Gainesville 32602	1824 St. Johns	— 1837 —	1826 1840 1850
A5	Baker 339 E. Macclenny Avenue Macclenny 32063	1861 New River	— 1877 —	1877 1877 1880
K3	Bay P.O. Box 2269 Panama City 32402 *Washington County land records transferred.*	1913 Calhoun/Washington	— 1913 —	1885 1913 1913
	Benton	(see Hernando)		
A5	Bradford P.O. Drawer B Starke 32091	1858 (as New River; renamed, 1861) Columbia	— 1875 —	1875 1868 1875
D7	Brevard P.O. Box H Titusville 32780	1844 (as St. Lucie; renamed, 1855) Mosquito	— 1868 —	1871 1877 1879
H7	Broward 515 S.E. Second Street Ft. Lauderdale 33301	1915 Dade/Palm Beach	1906 1915 1917	1915 1917 1915
J4	Calhoun 425 E. Central Avenue Blountstown 32424	1838 Franklin	1880 1862 —	1862 1877 1877
G5	Charlotte P.O. Box 1687 Punta Gorda 33951	1921 DeSoto	— 1921 —	1921 1921 1921
C4	Citrus 110 N. Apopka Avenue Inverness 32650	1887 Hernando	— 1887 —	1887 1887 1887
A5	Clay P.O. Box 698 Green Cove Springs 32043	1858 Duval	— 1872 —	1871 1859 1859
H6	Collier P.O. Box 413020 Naples 33941	1923 Lee	— 1923 —	1923 1923 1923
A4	Columbia P.O. Box 1965 Lake City 32056	1832 Alachua	— 1876 —	1871 1868 1895
J8	Dade 73 W. Flagler, Room 242 Miami 33130	1836 Monroe	— 1840 —	1844 1869 1888
F5	DeSoto P.O. Box 591 Arcadia 33821	1887 Manatee	— 1887 —	1887 1887 1887
B3	Dixie P.O. Box 1206 Cross City 32628	1921 Lafayette	— 1924 —	1921 1871 1921

Map	County Address	Date Formed Parent County/ies	Birth Marriage Death	Land Probate Court
A6	Duval Jacksonville 32202	1822 St. Johns	— 1822 —	1901 1905 1901
J1	Escambia 190 Governmental Center Pensacola 32501	1821 original	1891 1821 1919	1821 1821 1821
	Fayette	1832 (abolished, 1834; territory annexed to Jackson)		
B6	Flagler P.O. Box 787 Bunnell 32110	1917 St. Johns/Volusia	— 1917 —	1917 1917 1917
B1	Franklin P.O. Box 340 Apalachicola 32320	1832 Jackson	— 1887 —	1874 1832 1832
A1	Gadsden P.O. Box 1649 Quincy 32351	1823 Jackson	— 1849 —	1849 1837 1849
B4	Gilchrist P.O. Box 37 Trenton 32693	1925 Alachua	— 1926 —	1926 1926 1926
G6	Glades P.O. Box 10 Moore Haven 33471	1921 DeSoto	— 1921 —	1921 1921 1921
K4	Gulf 1000 Fifth Street Port St. Joe 32456	1925 Calhoun	— 1925 —	1925 1925 1925
A3	Hamilton P.O. Box 312 Jasper 32052	1827 Jefferson	— 1824 —	1836 1830 1881
F5	Hardee P.O. Drawer 1749 Wauchula 33873	1921 DeSoto	— 1921 —	1921 1921 1921
H6	Hendry P.O. Box 1760 LaBelle 33935	1923 Lee	— 1923 —	1923 1923 1923
D4	Hernando P.O. Box 1660 Brooksville 44298	1843 (as Benton; renamed, 1850) Alachua	— 1900 —	1878 1900 1877
F6	Highlands P.O. Box 1827 Sebring 33871	1921 DeSoto	— 1921 —	1921 1921 1921
E4	Hillsborough P.O. Box 1110 Tampa 33601	1834 Alachua	1875 1846 1900	1837 1845 1846
J3	Holmes 201 N. Oklahoma Street Bonifay 32425	1848 Jackson/Walton	— 1902 —	1900 1902 1900

Map	County Address	Date Formed Parent County/ies	Birth Marriage Death	Land Probate Court
E7	Indian River P.O. Box 1028 Vero Beach 32961	1925 St. Lucie	— 1925 —	1925 1925 1925
J4	Jackson P.O. Drawer 510 Marianna 32446	1822 Escambia	— 1848 —	1848 1848 1848
A2	Jefferson Monticello 32344	1827 Leon	— 1827 —	1827 1900 1900
A3	Lafayette P.O. Box 88 Mayo 32066	1826 Madison	— 1857 —	1873 1838 ?
D5	Lake 315 W. Main Street Tavares 32778	1887 Orange/Sumter	— 1887 —	1887 1887 1887
H5	Lee P.O. Box 2469 Ft. Myers 33902	1887 Monroe	— ? —	? ? ?
A2	Leon P.O. Box 726 Tallahassee 32302	1824 Gadsden/Duval	— 1825 —	1825 1824 1825
C4	Levy P.O. Drawer 610 Bronson 32621	1845 Alachua/Hillsborough	— 1854 —	1850 1847 1850
A1, K4	Liberty P.O. Box 399 Bristol 32321	1855 Gadsden	— 1857 —	1857 1859 1884
A3	Madison P.O. Box 237 Madison 32340	1827 Jefferson	— 1831 —	1831 1846 1838
F5	Manatee P.O. Box 1000 Bradenton 34206	1855 Hillsborough	1901 1856 1915	1843 1857 1858
C5	Marion P.O. Box 1030 Ocala 32678	1844 Alachua/Mosquito	— 1844 —	1844 1846 1849
G8	Martin P.O. Drawer 779 Stuart 33495	1925 Palm Beach/St. Lucie	— 1925 —	1925 1925 1925
K7	Monroe 500 Whitehead Street Key West 33040	1823 St. Johns	— 1826 —	1826 1888 1826
	Mosquito	(see Orange)		
A5	Nassau P.O. Box 456 Fernandina Beach 32034	1824 Duval	— 1867 —	1840 1873 1873
	New River	(see Bradford)		

Map	County Address	Date Formed Parent County/ies	Birth Marriage Death	Land Probate Court
J2	Okaloosa County Courthouse Annex Shalimar 32579	1915 Santa Rosa/Walton	— 1915 —	1915 1915 1915
F7	Okeechobee 304 N.W. Second Street Okeechobee 33472	1917 Osceola/Palm Beach/ St. Lucie	1915 1925 1915	1887 1917 1917
D6	Orange 150 N. Orange Avenue Orlando 32801	1824 (as Mosquito; renamed, 1845) St. Johns	— 1869 —	1847 1871 1847
E6	Osceola 12 S. Vernon Avenue Kissimmee 34741	1887 Brevard/Orange	— 1887 —	1887 1887 1887
G7	Palm Beach P.O. Drawer H West Palm Beach 33402	1909 Dade	— 1909 —	1909 1909 1909
D4	Pasco 705 E. Live Oak Avenue Dade City 33525	1887 Hernando	— 1887 —	1876 1882 1887
E4	Pinellas 315 Court Street Clearwater 34616	1911 Hillsborough	— 1911 —	1911 1911 1911
E5	Polk P.O. Box 9000 Bartow 33830	1861 Brevard/Hillsborough	1892 1862 —	1862 1861 1867
B5	Putnam P.O. Box 758 Palatka 32178	1849 Alachua/Marion/St. Johns	— 1849 —	1849 1849 1849
A6	St. Johns P.O. Drawer 300 St. Augustine 32085	1821 original	— 1823 —	1821 1844 1821
	St. Lucie (old)	1844 (changed to Brevard, 1855)		
F8	St. Lucie (present) 2300 Virginia Avenue Ft. Pierce 33482	1905 Brevard	— 1905 —	1905 1905 1905
J1	Santa Rosa P.O. Box 472 Milton 32572	1842 Escambia	— 1869 —	1869 1878 1869
G5	Sarasota P.O. Box 3079 Sarasota 34230	1921 Manatee	— 1921 —	1921 1921 1921
D6	Seminole North Park Avenue Sanford 32771	1913 Orange	— 1913 —	1913 1913 1913
D5	Sumter 209 N. Florida Street Bushnell 33513	1853 Marion	— 1853 —	1854 1856 1853

Map	County Address	Date Formed Parent County/ies	Birth Marriage Death	Land Probate Court
A3	Suwannee Live Oak 32060	1858 Columbia	— 1859 —	1859 1860 1859
A2	Taylor P.O. Box 620 Perry 32347	1856 Madison	— 1857 —	1857 1870 1857
A4	Union Lake Butler 32054	1921 Bradford	— 1921 —	1921 1921 1921
C6	Volusia P.O. Box 43 DeLand 32721	1854 Orange	— 1856 —	1869 1855 1855
A1	Wakulla P.O. Box 337 Crawfordville 32327	1843 Wakulla	— 1892 —	1843 1892 1843
J2	Walton P.O. Box 1260 DeFuniak Springs 32433	1824 Escambia/Jackson	— 1885 —	1886 1882 1886
J3	Washington P.O. Box 647 Chipley 32428	1825 Jackson/Walton	— 1877 —	1880 1880 1890

GEORGIA

Johni Cerny and Robert S. Davis, Jr.

Georgia was founded in 1733 to give new lives to deserving non-Roman Catholics in the New World. Despite involvements of Georgia's founder, James Oglethorpe, with debtors prisons, no debtors and no criminals were allowed to be sent to Georgia. The myth that Georgia was a debtors' colony or a type of Botany Bay seems impossible to lay to rest with the truth.

Trustees of the colony sent about 5,000 persons from Great Britain to Georgia, and information about those colonists is published in E. Merton Coulter and Albert B. Saye, *A List of the Early Settlers of Georgia* (Athens, Ga.: University of Georgia Press, 1949). Each colonist received fifty acres of land, while those who paid their own passage might have received up to 500 acres.

The Salzburgers, central European Protestants, became the first non-British group to settle in Georgia beginning in 1734. They established themselves at Ebenezer in what is now Effingham County. After Georgia became a royal province in 1753, settlers began to move in from Virginia and the Carolinas in large numbers. Other immigrants included Piedmontese from Italy, Scots-Highlanders, Swiss, and Portuguese Jews.

When the Revolutionary War began, Georgia consisted of twelve parishes (these did not function as governments, however) and a large area of ceded lands which the Cherokee and Creek Indians had turned over to the colony in 1773. Georgia's first constitution, dated 1777, provided for the creation of Wilkes, Richmond, Burke, Effingham, Chatham, Liberty, Glynn, and Camden counties. In 1784 Washington and Franklin counties were organized. By 1820 Georgia established fifty counties, mostly from the area that comprised the original ten counties.

The Civil War left Georgia devastated with enormous strains upon the state's few factories and fragile railroad system. Factories and foundries of Atlanta, Griswaldville, Rome, and Roswell were completely destroyed. Millions of dollars in capital was lost by the emancipation of slaves. The soil was worn out and farm animals were gone.

The end of the war did not bring immediate recovery. Federal direct taxes added to the burden. Thousands of people, black and white, were displaced or missed in the 1870 federal census. Economic and social pressures led to racial conflict.

The decades following the war brought Georgia its last wave of nineteenth-century migration. North Carolinians came south to take advantage of the pine forests for turpentine and naval stores. Lumber, marble, granite, coal, and kaoline became major businesses, but cotton remained "king" through much of the twentieth century.

Atlanta recovered almost immediately after the Civil War as a transportation center. Today, it is still the hub of the South, with interstate roads, interstate railways, and air travel. The growth of Atlanta has been explosive, producing two distinct parts of Georgia—Atlanta and its suburbs as a modern, industrial, urban complex with many people born outside the state; and the rest of the state, which remains rural with declining population and wealth.

Vital Records

Georgia attempted to require registration of births, marriages, and deaths on a county level in 1875, but the law was repealed in 1876. Some vital records for fourteen Georgia counties for 1875 have been microfilmed and are available at the Georgia Department of Archives and History (see Archives, Libraries, and Societies).

In 1919 Georgia law required the registration of all births and deaths in the state. As in many other states, Georgia's county governments were slow to respond to the new law and most did not comply until 1928. See Georgia Historical Records Survey, *Guide to Public Vital Statistics in Georgia* (Atlanta, Ga.: the author, 1941) for the records kept by individual counties. A few major cities required birth and death registration early:

- Atlanta—births, 1896; deaths, 1887. Fulton County Health Department, 99 Butler Street, S.E., Atlanta, GA 30303.
- Savannah—births, 1890; deaths, 1803. Chatham County Health Department, P.O. Box 14257, Savannah, GA 31406. Early death records have been published by the Georgia Historical Society.
- Macon—births, 1891; deaths, 1882. Bibb County Health Department, 770 Hemlock Street, Macon, GA 31298.
- Columbus—births, 1869; deaths, 1890. Muscogee County Health Department, 1958 Eighth Avenue, Columbus, GA 31901.
- Gainesville—births, 1865; deaths, 1909. Available on microfilm at the Georgia Department of Archives and History.

Birth and death records in Georgia can be requested from the Georgia Department of Human Resources, Vital Records Unit, Room 217-H, Health Building, 47 Trinity Avenue, S.W., Atlanta, Georgia 30334. If your request is urgent, call and charge certificates to a Visa or MasterCard. There is an additional fee for this service.

Like in most other states, marriage records in Georgia are created at the county level. Some Georgia counties kept early marriage bonds before 1805; however, Georgia law did not require marriage licenses to be recorded until 1805. Officials were careless in adhering to the law and some marriages were consequently not recorded. Some records were also lost in various courthouse fires. All recorded Georgia marriages to 1900 are available on microfilm at the Georgia Department of Archives and History and the FHL. The former also has some loose, original county marriage records. Heritage Papers' periodical *Georgia Genealogist* contains published marriages to 1810. Mary B. Warren's *Georgia Marriages 1811 Through 1820* (Danielsville, Ga.: Heritage Papers, 1988) continued publishing the marriages.

From 1793 to 1832, divorces in Georgia were subject to legislative approval after being approved by the county superior court. The divorce files continue to be in the custody of the county superior courts. Divorces, name changes, and decrees of *feme sole* granted by the Georgia legislature are abstracted in Robert S. Davis, Jr., *The Georgia Black Book II* (Easley, S.C.: Southern Historical Press, 1987).

Census Records

Federal

Population Schedules.

- Indexed—1820, 1830, 1840, 1850, 1860, 1870, 1890 (fragment)
- Soundex—1880, 1900, 1910, 1920

Industry and Agriculture Schedules.

- Industry—1820, 1880
- Agriculture—1850, 1860, 1870, 1880

Mortality Schedules.

- 1850, 1860, 1870, 1880

Slave Schedules.

- 1850, 1860

Unfortunately, the 1820 census is the earliest enumeration of Georgia's population to have survived, making it necessary to substitute other lists for the missing censuses. The 1820 census of Georgia is also lost for Franklin, Rabun, and Twiggs counties; for many other counties, names were often omitted or unreadable. Land lottery, military and tax lists, and other records, discussed under other headings, are available as census substitutes and supplements for the 1820 and earlier censuses.

The R. J. Taylor, Jr., Foundation in Atlanta has selected and indexed some tax digests for the years 1789–1819. Tax records no longer exist for every county, and others were omitted from the foundation's publications, which makes the title misleading. See *An Index to Georgia Tax Digests* (see Tax Records); Ruth Blair, *Some Early Tax Digests of Georgia* (1926; reprint, Easley, S.C.: Southern Historical Press, 1971); Virginia S. Wood and Ralph V. Wood, *The 1805 Land Lottery of Georgia* (Cambridge, Mass.: Greenwood Press, 1964), which lists nearly every Georgia head of household in 1802–03, making it the best substitute for the 1800 federal census of Georgia.

Both the Georgia Department of Archives and History and the FHL have a complete set of Georgia census records and mortality schedules.

State

Georgia conducted state censuses for various years from 1787 to 1866. Only a relatively few of these returns survive, and they are only lists of heads of households with some minor statistical information. The returns prior to 1852 have been published in various sources. Later census returns, when they survive, are almost all on microfilm at the Georgia Department of Archives and History. For what survives of Georgia state and federal census records see Robert S. Davis, *Research in Georgia* (cited under Background Sources), pages 27–41, 44, 147–68.

Background Sources

Georgia records and research are discussed in detail in Robert S. Davis, Jr., *Research in Georgia* (Easley, S.C.: Southern Historical Press, 1980), and Ted O. Brooke and Robert S. Davis, Jr. *Georgia Genealogical Workbook* (Atlanta, Ga.: Georgia Genealogical Society, 1987). James E. Dorsey's *Georgia Genealogy and Local History* (Spartanburg, S.C.: Reprint Co., 1983) offers articles and abstracts of Georgia records. It was updated annually in the *Georgia Historical Quarterly* until 1989 when the *Georgia Genealogical Society Quarterly* began publishing the updates.

Sources for the state's history include:

Coleman, Kenneth, ed. *A History of Georgia.* 2d ed. Athens, Ga.: University of Georgia Press, 1991.

Coulter, E. Merton. *Georgia: A Short History.* Chapell Hill, N.C.: University of North Carolina Press, 1964.

Maps

Early Georgia maps are crucial for tracing colonial families. See Marion R. Hemperley, *Map of Colonial Georgia, 1773–1777* (Atlanta, Ga.: Georgia Surveyor General Department, 1979), which shows parish boundaries before 1777, and his *Georgia Early Roads and Trails Circa 1730–1850* (Atlanta, Ga.: Georgia Surveyor General Department, 1979), which shows migration trails in the state. The Georgia Department of Archives and History also has maps of Georgia for sale showing the land lottery and the militia districts.

For changes in Georgia county boundaries, see William Thorndale and William Dollarhide, *Map Guide to the U.S. Federal Censuses, 1790–1920* (Baltimore, Md.: Genealogical Publishing Co., 1987), and Pat Bryant and Ingrid Shields, *Georgia Counties: Their Changing Boundaries* (Atlanta, Ga.: Georgia Surveyor General Department, 1983).

The largest collection of historical Georgia maps includes some 30,000 items, with many county maps and large, detailed state maps. The Georgia Surveyor General Department, Floor 2V of the Georgia Department of Archives and History, has the collection and will make copies for a fee. Modern maps of Georgia counties and some cities can be ordered for a fee from Map Room, Georgia Department of Transportation, 2 Capitol Square, Atlanta, Georgia 30334.

Land Records

State-Land State

Land and property records, combined with tax digests, can be important keys to successful research in Georgia. Surviving colonial and state land grant records of Georgia, including loose, original records not available on microfilm, are in the Georgia Surveyor General Department, Floor 2V, Georgia Department of Archives and History. See also Marion R. Hemperley, *The Georgia Surveyor General Department* (Atlanta, Ga.: Georgia Surveyor General Department, 1982), and Pat Bryant, *Entry of Claims for Georgia Landholders, 1733–1755* (Atlanta, Ga.: State Printing Office, 1975). The latter is a book of titles given to Georgians in 1755 for their lands under the trustees between 1733 and 1755.

The most complete record of colonial Georgia land grants between 1758 and 1776 is Mary B. Warren, *Georgia Land Owners' Memorials, 1758–1776* (Danielsville, Ga.: Heritage Papers, 1988). The most extensive information on colonial Georgia land grantees is in Allen D. Candler, *The Colonial Records of the State of Georgia,* 39 vols. (Atlanta, Ga.: various printers, 1906–40).

The first effective legislation, dated 17 February 1783, concerning land grants after Georgia became a state provided for headrights and bounty-land grants. The law allowed each head of household 200 acres free as his own headright and fifty additional acres for each member of his family and each slave at a cost of from one to four shillings per acre. Grants were limited to 1,000 acres, and the grantee was responsible for paying survey and grant fees. Those who had received grants under colonial jurisdiction were entitled to the lands they occupied when the law went into effect.

The 1783 act also provided for establishing a land court in each county. A land grant applicant would appear before five justices to swear under oath concerning the size of his family and the number of slaves he owned to obtain a warrant of survey. Once the county surveyor completed his layout of the applicant's land, a copy of the plat of survey was forwarded to the surveyor general, and the original was filed in the county. The applicant was then required to live on the land for a year and cultivate 3 percent of the total acreage. After meeting those requirements, the applicant could apply to the governor's office for his grant and pay all fees. At that point the grant would be issued and recorded. Headright grants were made in Bryan, Bullock, Burke, Camden, Chatham, Clarke, Columbia, Effingham, Elbert, Emanuel, Franklin, Glascock, Glynn, Greene, Hancock, Hart, Jackson, Jefferson, Johnson, Laurens, Liberty, Lincoln, Madison, McDuffie, McIntosh, Montgomery, Oconee, Oglethorpe, Richmond, Screven, Taliaferro, Tattnall, Warren, Washington, and Wilkes counties.

Bounty-land grants were made to soldiers who served in the Georgia military, civilian residents of 1781–82, and Georgia citizens who went to other states during the Revolution to continue the war. Most of the surviving Georgia Revolutionary War bounty certificates (except for civilian residents) are abstracted (see Hemperley, *Military Certificates,* cited in Military Records).

A second act of 25 February 1784 created new counties and designated some of the area as bounty lands for Georgia veterans who had served in the Continental Line or Navy. Most of the area that later became Greene County was reserved for bounty-land grants. See Silas Emmett Lucas, Jr., *Index to the Headright and Bounty Grants of Georgia, 1756–1909* (Vidalia, Ga.: Georgia Genealogical Reprints, 1970). The Georgia Department of Archives and History and the FHL have microfilm copies of original land grants.

Only Georgia has the distinction of distributing lands by lottery. Lands given to Georgia citizens by lotteries from 1805 to 1833 are in the present western and northern three-quarters of Georgia. Lotteries took place in 1805, 1807, 1820, 1821, 1827, and two in 1832. All Georgia citizens were eligible to qualify for a lottery, although the 1820, 1827, and 1832 lotteries also gave special consideration to war veterans. Published lottery books are excellent sources for pinpointing where a Georgia family lived when a lottery was held. For more information on the Georgia land lotteries, consult the following works:

Davis, Robert. *The 1830 Land Lottery of Georgia and Other Missing Names of Winners in the Georgia Land Lotteries.* Greenville, S.C.: Southern Historical Press, 1991.

Davis, Robert S., and Silas E. Lucas. *The Georgia Land Lottery Papers, 1805–1914.* Easley, S.C.: Southern Historical Press, 1979.

Houstun, Martha Lou. *Reprint of Official Register of the Land Lottery of Georgia, 1827.* Baltimore, Md.: Genealogical Publishing Co., 1967.

Lucas, Silas E. *The 1807 Land Lottery of Georgia.* Easley, S.C.: Southern Historical Press, 1973.

———. *The 1821 Land Lottery of Georgia.* Easley, S.C.: Southern Historical Press, 1986.

———. *The 1832 Gold Lottery of Georgia: Containing a List of the Fortunate Drawers in Said Lottery.* Easley, S.C.: Southern Historical Press, 1986.

Smith, James F. *The Cherokee Land Lottery . . . 1838.* Reprint. Vidalia, Ga.: Georgia Genealogical Reprints, 1968.

Wood, Virginia S. and Ralph V. Wood. *1805 Land Lottery of Georgia.* Cambridge, Mass.: Greenwood Press, 1964.

Where Georgians sold lots won in the lotteries, researchers will find that deeds may be valuable sources of genealogical information. Those deeds should have been recorded in the counties where the land was located, but in some cases references may be found in the counties where the owner resided. Land transaction between private individuals are recorded with the clerk of superior court in the appropriate county.

Most surviving pre-1900 county land records, including deeds and land court minutes, are on microfilm at the Georgia Department of Archives and History and the FHL. Many of the mortgage and county plat books are not included in the FHL's microfilm collection.

Probate Records

In Georgia, estate records are produced by courts with jurisdiction at the county level beginning in 1777 and with the creation of the county ordinary courts. Prior to that date, most estate matters were handled at the colonial capitol in Savannah. See *Index to Probate Records of Colonial Georgia, 1733–1778* (Atlanta, Ga.: R. J. Taylor, Jr. Foundation, 1983) and Ted O. Brooke, *In the Name of God, Amen, Georgia Wills 1733–1860: An Index to Testator Wills* (Atlanta, Ga.: Pilgrim Press, 1976) for published probate indexes. Most all of Georgia's colonial estate, colonial deed, mortgage, and deed of gift records survive at the Georgia Department of Archives and History.

County ordinary courts kept probate records from 1777–98 and began keeping them again in 1852. County inferior courts were responsible for probate matters from 1798–1852. Almost all pre-1900 county probate records are on microfilm at the Georgia Department of Archives and History and the FHL. The Archives also has many loose, original Georgia county records. After 1900, probate records are in the county's ordinary court.

Court Records

Unfortunately, no colonial Georgia court records survive. Georgia's state constitution provided for two county level courts to be created in 1777. Superior courts were established at the county level to hear cases dealing with divorce, civil and criminal charges, naturalization, military discharges, homesteads, prisons, and slaves. Simultaneously, courts of ordinary were created to hear and record cases involving probate matters. It also dealt with indentures, paupers, licenses, voting, and marriage. Each court kept minutes, which are useful in genealogical research.

Inferior courts were created in 1798 and were responsible for probate matters (until 1852), civil matters, and misdemeanor type civil and criminal cases. Georgia's state supreme court began in 1846, and the case files and records of this court are in the Georgia Department of Archives and History. The decisions of that court are published annually in the *Georgia Reports.* With the exception of only the most recent records, the federal district and circuit court records for Georgia are at the National Archives-Southeast Region in East Point, Georgia (see page 8).

Georgia's state prison and asylum records are housed at the Georgia Department of Archives and History. These records are open to researchers when over seventy-five years have passed from the date of their creation. The earliest Georgia prison and asylum records are used in Robert S. Davis, Jr.'s two volume, *Georgia Black Book* (Easley, S.C.: Southern Historical Press, 1982).

The FHL has a broad collection of court records from each of Georgia's courts at the county level, as well as the U.S. Circuit Court, District of Georgia.

Tax Records

None of Georgia's colonial tax records have survived. Surviving Georgia tax records begin on a county basis in the late 1780s. By 1783 Georgia tax laws provided for taxing land according to its quality and quantity, and male polls were white males over twenty-one. Other taxes were imposed on town lots, slaves, and free persons of color, buildings and improvements, merchandise, lawyers, and doctors. The poll tax on all adult males made Georgia tax digests good census substitutes and supplements.

R. J. Taylor, Jr., Foundation, *An Index to Georgia Tax Digests, 1789–1817,* 5 vols. (Spartanburg, S.C.: Reprint Co., 1986), is a select index to Georgia tax digests for that period. The Georgia Department of Archives and History has other tax digests for 1789–1817 which are not included in the above publication. A complete set of originals for the years 1872 to the present is at the Georgia Department of Archives and History. Some earlier digests are on microfilm at the Georgia Archives and the FHL.

Federal direct tax records for Georgia and the southeastern United States for 1865–73 are at the National Archives-Southeast Region (see page 8). The years 1865–66 are on microfilm.

Cemetery Records

The Daughters of the American Revolution (DAR) and others have compiled and published volumes of cemetery records, but no statewide collection has been prepared to date. DAR publications include Bible, court, and probate records in addition to cemetery inscriptions. Consult holdings of the Georgia Department of Archives and History, Daughters of the American Revolution Library (see page 6), and the FHL for major collections of published tombstone inscriptions. Other public and private libraries may have smaller collections.

A statewide bibliography of Georgia cemetery records through 1985 is Ted O. Brooke, *Georgia Cemetery Directory and Bibliography* (Marietta, Ga.: the author, 1985).

Church Records

Few of Georgia's major religious groups maintained records rich in genealogical information. However, their historical records provide a deeper understanding of religious life in earlier times and document someone's residence when they are listed on membership rolls.

Georgia's major religious denominations include the Baptists: Georgia Baptist Historical Collection, Eugene W. Stetson Memorial Library, Mercer University, Macon, Georgia 31207; Methodists: United Methodist Museum, P.O. Box 408, St. Simons Island, Georgia 31522; and Roman Catholics: Savannah and Diocesan Archives, 302 East Liberty Street, P.O. Box 8789, Savannah, Georgia 31402. Other early denominations present in Georgia in fewer numbers include Lutherans, Presbyterians, Episcopalians, and Congregationalists. While their respective repositories house historical records, the Georgia Department of Archives and History has a good collection of church records on microfilm. Surviving records of Georgia's Wrightsborough Quaker community (located in present-day McDuffie County) for 1767 to 1805 are in the Friends Historical Collection, Guilford College Library, Guilford, North Carolina, and have been published verbatim in Robert S. Davis, Jr., *Quaker Records in Georgia* (Augusta, Ga.: Augusta Genealogical Society, 1986). Consult the holdings of other major genealogical libraries with southern collections for additional sources, including the FHL.

Military Records

Georgia was founded to serve as a bulwark against the Spanish and French in the lands beyond the Carolinas, and as such, its men were called into service frequently during the colonial period. Unfortunately, few informative records remain to tell who was involved in what conflict. Murtie June Clark, *Colonial Soldiers of the South, 1732–1774* (Baltimore, Md.: Genealogical Publishing Co., 1983), lists soldiers who served prior to the Revolutionary War.

Revolutionary War. Georgia's total population in 1776 numbered less than 20,000 people, of whom perhaps 3,500 men were eligible for military service when the Revolution began. Many of Georgia's soldiers were recruited from the Carolinas and Virginia; many were neutral or fought for the king. Some of the original service records for the Revolutionary War were destroyed. It is doubtful that a comprehensive list of Georgia veterans of this war exists. Georgia Revolutionary War rolls at the National Archives are published with other records in Robert S. Davis, Jr., *Georgia Citizens and Soldiers of the Revolution* (Easley, S.C.: Southern Historical Press, 1979). See also Allen D. Candler, *The Revolutionary Records of the State of Georgia,* 3 vols. (Atlanta, Ga.: State Printer, 1906). Louise F. Hays, comp., *Georgia Military Affairs, 1775–1842,* 9 vols. (N.p., 1940), includes indexed, unpublished typescripts from the Georgia Department of Archives and History which cover a much broader period than the Revolution. This collection is an excellent people finder and census substitute and supplement.

Bounty-land warrants were issued to soldiers who served in the Georgia military, civilian residents of 1781–82, and Georgia citizens who went to other states during the Revolution to continue the war. After the war, soldiers who served in the Continental Line and others applied for a warrant and, when approved, received a certificate to be exchanged for a warrant. The land to be issued was in Georgia. See Marion R. Hemperley, *Military Certificates of Georgia, 1776–1800* (Atlanta, Ga.: Georgia Surveyor General Department, 1983). The original records are in the Georgia Surveyor General Department.

Indian Wars, 1784–1811 and 1815–38; Mexican War, 1845–48. Georgia supplied thousands of soldiers for various federal campaigns. The genealogically significant bounty and pension files are in the National Archives (see page 7).

War of 1812. Information included in service records for the War of 1812 is similar to that in the same records of soldiers in the colonial wars and Revolutionary War. See also Judy Kratovil, *An Index to War of 1812 Service Records for Volunteer Soldiers of Georgia* (Atlanta, Ga.: the author, 1986). The National Archives records from which Kratovil's book is taken represents roughly one-fifth of the males of military age in Georgia during the War of 1812.

Civil War. While the original Georgia pension records for Confederate veterans are at the Georgia Department of Archives and History, microfilm copies are at the FHL. See also Lillian Henderson, *Roster of the Confederate Soldiers of Georgia, 1861–1865,* 7 vols. (Hapeville, Ga.: Longino & Porter, 1960–64), which does not include Georgia's cavalry, artillery, legions, militia, state troops, and confederate non-state units. Georgians also served in the Union Army.

The Georgia Department of Archives and History has extensive state records relating to the Civil War including militia rolls, salt lists, veterans censuses, to name only a few sources. The most valuable to researchers is an "Alphabetical Index" to Georgia Confederate records on microfilm at the Georgia Archives.

Later Wars. Some military records for Georgia after the Civil War are in the Georgia Department of Archives and History as original records or as microfilm copies. Included are rosters of the Spanish American War, the Philippine Insurrection, and the Poncho Villa Campaign. The state archives also has on microfilm many county copies of service records for World War I, World War II, the Korean War, and the Vietnam War. The National Archives-Southeast Branch (see page 8) has World War I draft registration records. Service records and photographs of Georgians who died in World War I were published in Bert E. Boss, *Georgia Memorial Book* (Macon, Ga.: Georgia Memorial Association, 1921).

Periodicals, Newspapers, and Manuscript Collections

Periodicals

Two historical periodicals include *Georgia Historical Quarterly,* published by the Georgia Historical Society, and *Atlanta History: A Journal of Georgia and the South,* published by the Atlanta Historical Society.

A host of periodicals regarding Georgia genealogy is currently being published, including *Georgia Genealogical Society Quarterly* (Atlanta, Ga.: Georgia Genealogical Society, 1964–present) and *Georgia Genealogical Magazine* (Easley, S.C.: Silas E. Lucas, Jr., 1961–present). The Georgia Department of Archives and History and the FHL have copies of these periodicals and others.

Newspapers

The Georgia Department of Archives and History and the University of Georgia in Athens have the largest newspaper collections. Other university, public, and genealogical libraries have smaller collections, including the FHL. Consult holdings for titles.

The *Georgia Newspaper Project* of the University of Georgia Libraries has to date microfilmed over 8,000 reels of Georgia newspapers. This collection is not available on interlibrary loan, but copies can be purchased. The Georgia Historical Society in Savannah and the University of Georgia Libraries in Athens have every-name indexes to the Savannah newspapers from 1763 to 1845. The Georgia Department of Archives and History has this index to 1830 and parts of it for 1835–45. Indexes have also been published for early Augusta and Milledgeville newspapers. Many other Georgia newspapers have published and indexed abstracts to marriage and death notices. A statewide reference is Mary B. Warren, *Marriages and Deaths from Extant Georgia Newspapers,* 2 vols. (Danielsville, Ga.: Heritage Papers, 1968 and 1972), covering 1763 to 1829.

Manuscripts

Georgia has more than 100 manuscript repositories, many of which have excellent local sources. See Sally Flocks, *Directory of Georgia's Historical Organizations and Resources* (N.p., 1987), for addresses and other information.

The Hargrett Rare Book and Manuscripts Library of the University of Georgia Libraries in Athens and the Georgia Historical Society in Savannah, have Georgia's most extensive manuscript collections.

Leon S. Hollingsworth's genealogical card file was microfilmed by the R. J. Taylor, Jr., Foundation in 1978. Recently refilmed, the 45,000 three-by-five cards in this collection reference people from thousands of original source records in Georgia. Notations include an abstract of the information and citation of the original source. The collection is both a name file and place-name index, but it does not include Hollingsworth's client research files. The collection is available at the FHL and for purchase from Reprint Co., Box 4501, Spartanburg, South Carolina 29304. Hollingsworth's research files are only available for use by researchers at the Georgia Department of Archives and History. The Hargrett Rare Book and Manuscripts Library has the similar, but much earlier, James A. LeConte Genealogical Collection on microfilm.

Archives, Libraries, and Societies

Georgia Department of Archives and History
330 Capitol Avenue, S.E.
Atlanta, GA 30334

Official repository for permanent records created as a function of state government, the archives operates a Central Research Room which makes its holdings available to the public. It is extremely limited and specific mail requests are answered by mail.

Georgia Genealogical Society
P.O. Box 38066
Atlanta, GA 30334

The society publishes *Georgia Genealogical Society Quarterly.*

Georgia Historical Society and Library
501 Whittaker Street
Savannah, GA 31499

The oldest collection of private manuscripts is a feature of its library.

Atlanta Historical Society
3101 Andrews Drive, N.W.
Atlanta, GA 30366

The society maintains a library on Atlanta history and publishes a periodical entitled *Atlanta History* (see Periodicals). The historian of the society has a personal interest in the history of whites in the city and consequently maintains files on all white Atlanta census, cemetery, and obituary records through 1920. Mail requests are answered.

Atlanta Public Library
1 Margaret Mitchell Square
Atlanta, GA 30303

Included in its card catalog are references to biographical sketches of prominent black Americans.

Georgia Salzburger Society
P.O. Box 916
Rincon, GA 31326

The society publishes *Georgia Salzburger Society Newsletter.*

Georgia has many county and regional genealogical societies and libraries. (See Davis and Brooke, *Georgia Genealogical Workbook,* cited in Background Sources).

Special Focus Categories

Immigration

Savannah, Georgia, served as one of the nation's southern immigration ports. Passenger lists of immigrants arriving at Savannah are available (however, they are sketchy during early years) on federal microfilm M575, *Passengers Arriving at Miscellaneous Ports on the Atlantic and Gulf Coasts,* at the National Archives and the FHL.

Georgia governors issued passports of good character for families passing through the Indian lands for the West prior to 1820. These passports are abstracted in Dorothy Williams Potter, *Passports of Southeastern Pioneers, 1770–1823* (Baltimore, Md.: Gateway Press, 1982). See also Marion R. Hemperley "Savannah Federal Naturalization Oaths, 1790–1860." *Georgia Historical Quarterly* 51 (1967), 454–87.

The Federal Writers' Project produced in 1940 *Drums and Shadows: Surviving Studies Among the Georgia Coastal Negroes* (Westport, Conn.: Greenwood Press, 1973), which covers the social history of a specific group of blacks in Georgia's history.

Native American

The majority of Georgia's Native American population consisted of Cherokees and Creeks, both of whom were removed from the area to the west onto land that would become the Indian and Oklahoma territories before Oklahoma statehood. Some remaining Creeks removed themselves to land in Alabama. While the history of Georgia's native population differs from that of North Carolina, the records in which they are documented are similar. See Native Americans section under North Carolina for a complete discussion of available records and their whereabouts. Early federal records of Cherokees are more extensive for Georgia than any other eastern state. These records are in the National Archives in Washington, D.C. The Georgia Department of Archives and History has indexed unpublished typescripts of state records concerning the Creeks and Cherokees, including information on their white relations.

See Robert S. Davis, Jr., *A Guide to Native American (Indian) Research Sources at the Georgia Department of Archives and History* (Jasper, Ga.: the author, 1985).

Black American

The Georgia Department of Archives and History has lists of free persons of color, marriages, slave lists, imported slave lists, apprenticeship bonds, trial dockets, lists of slave owners, cemetery records, church records, bills of sale, deeds transferring slaves, plantation records, and other miscellaneous records. Not every Georgia county created nor preserved each type of record listed above. In fact, the number of local records attesting to a specific slave is minuscule when compared to those available for free persons.

Also consult collections at Atlanta University and Emory University, both in Atlanta; the Georgia Historical Society and Savannah State College, both in Savannah; and the University of Georgia in Athens.

The National Archives has federal census schedules, military records, Freedmen's Bureau, and related records (see page 10). The FHL has some federal records pertaining to former slaves. Each of the guidebooks noted in Background Sources discusses federal records as they pertain to black research.

County Resources

Counties were not formed in Georgia until 1777, covering at that time only a portion of Georgia's present jurisdiction. Eventually, as Native American land was acquired, new counties were created. Land records were then generally recorded with the clerk of the superior court in each county. Probate records were generally recorded with the clerk of the ordinary court, as were marriages. Most civil court cases were handled completely by the superior court.

The Georgia Department of Archives and History has nearly all of the state's pre-1900, bound, county records on microfilm and has several collections of loose, original records.

The Counties and County Seats of
Georgia
25 0 25 50 75 Miles
TENNESSEE
NORTH CAROLINA
SOUTH CAROLINA
ALABAMA
FLORIDA
Atlantic Ocean
Gulf of Mexico
MARION
HAMILTON
BRADLEY
McMINN
MONROE
POLK
GRAHAM
CHEROKEE
CLAY
MACON
JACKSON
TRANSYLVANIA
HENDERSON
RUTHERFORD
CLEVELAND
GASTON
MECKLENBURG
UNION
PICKENS
OCONEE
GREENVILLE
SPARTANBURG
YORK
CHESTER
LANCASTER
LAURENS
ANDERSON
FAIRFIELD
KERSHAW
ABBEVILLE
GREENWOOD
NEWBERRY
RICHLAND
SALUDA
LEXINGTON
McCORMICK
EDGEFIELD
CALHOUN
AIKEN
ORANGEBURG
BARNWELL
BAMBERG
ALLENDALE
COLLETON
HAMPTON
JASPER
DeKALB
CHEROKEE
CALHOUN
CLEBURNE
CLAY
RANDOLPH
TALLAPOOSA
CHAMBERS
LEE
MACON
RUSSELL
BULLOCK
BARBOUR
DALE
HENRY
HOUSTON
GENEVA
HOLMES
WASHINGTON
JACKSON
BAY
CALHOUN
LIBERTY
GADSDEN
LEON
JEFFERSON
MADISON
HAMILTON
SUWANNEE
COLUMBIA
BAKER
NASSAU
DUVAL
UNION
BRADFORD
CLAY
ST. JOHNS
TAYLOR
LAFAYETTE
DIXIE
GILCHRIST
ALACHUA
PUTNAM
DADE
Trenton
CATOOSA
Ringgold
WALKER
LaFayette
WHITFIELD
Dalton
MURRAY
Chatsworth
FANNIN
GILMER
Ellijay
Blue Ridge
Blairsville
UNION
TOWNS
Hiawassee
Clayton
RABUN
HABERSHAM
WHITE
Clarkesville
Toccoa
STEPHENS
LUMPKIN
Dahlonega
Cleveland
CHATTOOGA
Summerville
Calhoun
GORDON
Jasper
PICKENS
Dawsonville
DAWSON
HALL
BANKS
Homer
FRANKLIN
Carnesville
HART
Hartwell
FLOYD
Rome
BARTOW
Cartersville
CHEROKEE
Canton
FORSYTH
Cumming
Gainesville
JACKSON
Jefferson
Danielsville
MADISON
ELBERT
Elberton
Cedartown
POLK
PAULDING
Dallas
Marietta
COBB
GWINNETT
Lawrenceville
BARROW
Winder
Athens
CLARKE
Watkinsville
OCONEE
OGLETHORPE
Lexington
WILKES
Washington
LINCOLN
Lincolnton
HARALSON
Buchanan
Douglasville
DOUGLAS
Atlanta
FULTON
DeKALB
Decatur
WALTON
Monroe
Conyers
ROCKDALE
Covington
NEWTON
Madison
MORGAN
GREENE
Greensboro
TALIAFERRO
Crawfordville
McDUFFIE
Thomson
Appling
COLUMBIA
Augusta
Carrollton
CARROLL
CLAYTON
Jonesboro
McDonough
HENRY
Fayetteville
FAYETTE
Newnan
COWETA
HEARD
Franklin
SPALDING
Griffin
Jackson
BUTTS
JASPER
Monticello
PUTNAM
Eatonton
Warrenton
WARREN
RICHMOND
Sparta
HANCOCK
GLASCOCK
Gibson
JEFFERSON
Louisville
Waynesboro
BURKE
TROUP
La Grange
MERIWETHER
Greenville
PIKE
Zebulon
LAMAR
Barnesville
Forsyth
MONROE
JONES
Gray
Milledgeville
BALDWIN
Sandersville
WASHINGTON
JENKINS
Millen
Sylvania
SCREVEN
Thomaston
UPSON
Macon
BIBB
Irwinton
WILKINSON
JOHNSON
Wrightsville
Swainsboro
EMANUEL
Hamilton
HARRIS
TALBOT
Talbotton
Knoxville
CRAWFORD
Jeffersonville
TWIGGS
Dublin
LAURENS
Statesboro
BULLOCH
EFFINGHAM
Springfield
MUSCOGEE
Columbus
Butler
TAYLOR
Ft. Valley
PEACH
HOUSTON
Perry
BLECKLEY
Cochran
TREUTLEN
Soperton
Metter
CANDLER
CHATTAHOOCHEE
Cusseta
MARION
Buena Vista
MACON
Oglethorpe
SCHLEY
Ellaville
DOOLY
Vienna
Hawkinsville
PULASKI
Eastman
DODGE
Mt. Vernon
Alamo
WHEELER
MONTGOMERY
Lyons
TOOMBS
Reidsville
TATTNALL
Claxton
EVANS
Pembroke
BRYAN
Savannah
CHATHAM
STEWART
Lumpkin
WEBSTER
Preston
Americus
SUMTER
Cordele
CRISP
Abbeville
WILCOX
McRae
TELFAIR
Hazlehurst
JEFF DAVIS
Baxley
APPLING
LONG
Hinesville
LIBERTY
Ludowici
Georgetown
QUITMAN
Cuthbert
RANDOLPH
TERRELL
Dawson
LEE
Leesburg
TURNER
Ashburn
BEN HILL
Fitzgerald
Ocilla
IRWIN
COFFEE
Douglas
BACON
Alma
Jesup
WAYNE
McINTOSH
Darien
Ft. Gaines
CLAY
Morgan
CALHOUN
Albany
DOUGHERTY
WORTH
Sylvester
TIFT
Tifton
PIERCE
Blackshear
Blakely
EARLY
BAKER
Newton
Camilla
MITCHELL
COLQUITT
Moultrie
BERRIEN
Nashville
ATKINSON
Pearson
Waycross
WARE
Nahunta
BRANTLEY
GLYNN
Brunswick
Colquitt
MILLER
Adel
COOK
Lakeland
LANIER
Homerville
CLINCH
CAMDEN
Woodbine
SEMINOLE
Donalsonville
Bainbridge
DECATUR
GRADY
Cairo
THOMAS
Thomasville
BROOKS
Quitman
LOWNDES
Valdosta
ECHOLS
Statenville
CHARLTON
Folkston

Map	County Address	Date Formed Parent County/ies	Birth Marriage Death	Land Probate Court
G6	Appling 100 Oak Street Baxley 31513	1818 Creek lands	— 1869 —	1828 1879 1879
H5	Atkinson Pearson 31642	1918 Coffee/Clinch	1929 1919 1929	1919 1919 1919
G6	Bacon P.O. Box 376 Alma 31510	1914 Appling/Ware/Pearce	1915 1919 1915	1919 1919 1919
H2	Baker Newton 31770	1825 Early	— 1820 —	1850 1868 1879
D4	Baldwin Milledgeville 31061	1803 Creek lands/Hancock	— 1806 —	1861 1808 1861
B4	Banks P.O. Box 1686 Homer 30547	1858 Franklin/Habersham	— 1859 —	1859 1859 1859
B4	Barrow 310 Broad Street Winder 30680	1914 Jackson/Walton/Gwinnett	1915 1915 1915	1915 1915 1915
B2	Bartow P.O. Box 543 Cartersville 30120	1832 (as Cass; renamed, 1861) Cherokee	— 1836 —	1837 1853 1853
G4	Ben Hill Fitzgerald 31750	1906 Irwin/Wilcox	— 1906 —	1906 1906 1906
H5	Berrien P.O. Box 446 Nashville 31639	1856 Lowndes/Irwin/Coffee	1919 1856 1919	1850 1855 1856
E4	Bibb 601 Mulberry Street Macon 31201	1822 Jones/Monroe/ Twiggs/Houston	— 1823 —	1823 1823 1823
F4	Bleckley 306 S.E. Second Street Cochran 31014	1912 Pulaski	1919 1912 1919	1912 1912 1912
H7	Brantley Nahunta 31553	1920 Charlton/Pierce/Wayne	1921 1921 1921	1921 1921 1921
J4	Brooks Quitman 31643	1858 Lowndes/Thomas	— 1859 —	1857 1859 1859
F7	Bryan Pembroke 31321 *Fragmented records.*	1793 Chatham (enlarged with part of Effingham, 1794)	— 1865 —	1793 1790s 1794
F7	Bulloch Statesboro 30458	1796 Bryan/Screven	— 1796 —	1796 1816 1806

Map	County Address	Date Formed Parent County/ies	Birth Marriage Death	Land Probate Court
D7	Burke	1777	1927	1843
	P.O. Box 62	St. George Parish	1855	1856
	Waynesboro 30830		1927	1856
D3	Butts	1825	—	1825
	P.O. Box 320	Henry/Monroe	1826	1826
	Jackson 30233		—	1826
H2	Calhoun	1854	1928	1854
	Morgan 31766	Baker/Early	1854	1854
			1928	1854
J7	Camden	1777	—	1773
	P.O. Box 578	St. Mary Parish/	1819	1795
	Woodbine 31569	St. Thomas Parish	—	1790
	Campbell	1828 (became part of Fulton, 1932)	1919	1829
		Carroll/Coweta/DeKalb/Fayette	1829	1829
			1919	1829
F7	Candler	1914	1919	1915
	Metter 30439	Bulloch/Emanuel/Tattnall	1915	1915
			1919	1915
C1	Carroll	1826	1919	1827
	P.O. Box 1620	Indian lands	1827	1827
	Carrollton 30117		1919	1827
	Cass	1832 (renamed Bartow, 1861)		
A1	Catoosa	1853	—	1853
	206 E. Nashville Street	Walker/Whitfield	1853	1853
	Ringgold 30736		—	1853
J7	Charlton	1854	—	1878
	100 Third Street	Camden/Ware	1854	1878
	Folkston 31537		—	1879
F8	Chatham	1777	—	1785
	133 Montgomery	Christ Church Parish	1806	1777
	Savannah 31401		—	1783
F2	Chattahoochee	1854	—	1854
	P.O. Box 299	Muscogee/Marion	1854	1854
	Cusseta 31805		—	1854
A1	Chattooga	1838	—	1839
	P.O. Box 211	Floyd/Walker	1839	1839
	Summerville 30747		—	1839
B2	Cherokee	1831	—	1833
	100 North Street	Cherokee lands	1841	1833
	Canton 30114		—	1832
B4	Clarke	1801	—	1801
	300 E. Washington Street	Jackson	1801	1801
	Athens 30601		—	1801
H1	Clay	1854	—	1854
	P.O. Box 550	Early/Randolph	1854	1854
	Fort Gaines 31751		—	1854

Map	County Address	Date Formed Parent County/ies	Birth Marriage Death	Land Probate Court
C3	Clayton 121 S. McDonough Jonesboro 30236	1858 Fayette/Henry	— 1859 —	1859 1859 1859
J6	Clinch 100 Court Square Homerville 31634	1850 Ware/Lowndes	1919 1867 1919	1868 1867 1868
C2	Cobb 10 E. Park Square Marietta 30060 *Some earlier records survive.*	1832 Cherokee	— 1865 —	1865 1865 1865
H5	Coffee Douglas 31533	1854 Clinch/Irwin/Ware/Telfair	— 1854 —	1854 1854 1854
H4	Colquitt P.O. Box 886 Moultrie 31776	1856 Lowndes/Thomas	— 1881 —	1881 1881 1881
C6	Columbia P.O Box 11024 Martinez 30907	1790 Richmond	— 1787 —	1790 1790 1790
H4	Cook 103 N. Hutchinson Adel 31620	1918 Berrien	1919 1919 1919	1919 1919 1919
D2	Coweta P.O. Box 945 Newnan 30264	1826 Indian lands	1919 1828 1919	1827 1828 1828
E3	Crawford P.O. Box 420 Knoxville 31050	1822 Houston	— 1823 —	1830 1830 1830
G4	Crisp Cordele 31015	1905 Dooly	— — —	1905 1905 1905
A1	Dade P.O. Box 417 Trenton 30752 *Fragmented records.*	1837 Walker	— 1866 —	1849 1853 1854
A3	Dawson P.O. Box 192 Dawsonville 30534	1857 Lumpkin/Gilmer	1858 1858 1858	1858 1858 1858
J2	Decatur Bainbridge 31717	1823 Early	— 1824 —	1823 1823 1823
C3	DeKalb 556 N. Mcdonough Street Decatur 30030	1822 Henry	— 1842 —	1842 1842 1842
F5	Dodge P.O. Box 818 Eastman 31023	1870 Montgomery/Telfair/Pulaski	— 1871 —	1871 1871 1871

Map	County Address	Date Formed Parent County/ies	Birth Marriage Death	Land Probate Court
F4	Dooly P.O. Box 322 Vienna 31092	1821 Indian lands	— 1846 —	1847 1847 1847
H3	Dougherty 225 Pine Avenue Albany 31701	1852 Baker	— 1854 —	1854 1849 1854
C2	Douglas 6754 Broad Street Douglasville 30134	1870 Carroll/Campbell	— 1871 —	1871 1871 1871
H2	Early P.O. Box 525 Blakely 31723	1818 Creek lands	— 1820 —	1821 1824 1820
J5	Echols Statenville 31648 *Fragmented records.*	1858 Clinch/Lowndes	— 1898 —	1897 1897 1898
F8	Effingham Springfield 31329 *Fragmented records.*	1777 St. Matthew Parish/ St. Philip Parish	1927 1791 1927	1786 1796 1791
B5	Elbert Elberton 30635	1790 Wilkes	— 1791 —	1791 1791 1791
E6	Emanuel P.O. Box 787 Swainsboro 30401	1812 Montgomery/Bulloch	— 1812 —	1812 1812 1810
F7	Evans P.O. Box 711 Claxton 30417	1914 Bulloch/Tattnall	1915 1915 1915	1915 1915 1915
A2	Fannin Blue Ridge 30513	1854 Gilmer/Union	— 1854 —	1854 1854 1854
D2	Fayette 200 Court Square Fayetteville 30214	1812 Indian lands/Henry	— 1823 —	1823 1823 1823
B1	Floyd 201 Fifth Avenue Rome 30161	1832 Cherokee	— 1834 —	1840 1837 1840
B3	Forsyth P.O. Box 128 Cumming 30130	1832 Cherokee	— 1833 —	1832 1832 1832
A4	Franklin P.O. Box 70 Carnesville 30521	1784 Cherokee lands	— 1806 —	1786 1786 1798
C2	Fulton 165 Central Avenue S.W. Atlanta 30303 *Campbell and Milton counties became part of Fulton in 1932.*	1853 DeKalb	— 1854 —	1854 1854 1854
A2	Gilmer 1 Westside Square Ellijay 30540	1832 Cherokee	— 1836 —	1833 1833 1833

Map	County Address	Date Formed Parent County/ies	Birth Marriage Death	Land Probate Court
D6	Glascock P.O. Box 231 Gibson 30810	1857 Warren	— 1858 —	1858 1858 1858
H8	Glynn Brunswick 31521 *Fragmented, damaged records.*	1777 St. David Parish/ St. Patrick Parish	— 1818 —	1787 1792 1810
A2	Gordon P.O. Box 580 Calhoun 30701	1850 Bartow/Floyd	— 1864 —	1850 1856 1850
J3	Grady 250 N. Broad Street Cairo 31728	1905 Decatur/Thomas	— 1906 —	1906 1906 1906
C5	Greene 201 N. Main Street Greensboro 30642	1786 Washington	— 1805 —	1785 1785 1785
B3	Gwinnett 240 Oaks Street Lawrenceville 30245 *Fragmented records.*	1818 Cherokee lands/Jackson	— 1871 —	1871 1818 1858
A4	Habersham P.O. Box 227 Clarkesville 30523	1818 Cherokee lands/Franklin	— 1824 —	1819 1819 1819
B3	Hall P.O. Box 1435 Gainesville 30503 *Fragmented records.*	1818 Cherokee lands/ Jackson/Franklin	— 1819 —	1819 1819 1819
D5	Hancock Sparta 31087	1793 Greene/Washington	— 1806 —	1794 1794 1794
C1	Haralson P.O. Box 488 Buchanan 30113 *Fragmented records.*	1856 Carroll/Polk	— 1865 —	1856 1856 1856
E2	Harris P.O. Box 528 Hamilton 31811	1827 Muscogee/Troup	— 1828 —	1828 1828 1828
B5	Hart P.O. Box 128 Hartwell 30643	1853 Elbert/Franklin	— 1854 —	1856 1854 1854
D1	Heard N. River Street Franklin 30217	1830 Carroll/Coweta/Troup	1927 1886 1927	1894 1894 1894
D3	Henry 345 Phillips Drive McDonough 30253	1821 Indian lands	— 1822 —	1822 1822 1822
F4	Houston 200 Carl Vinson Parkway Warner Robins 31088	1821 Indian lands	— 1822 —	1822 1822 1822

Map	County Address	Date Formed Parent County/ies	Birth Marriage Death	Land Probate Court
G5	Irwin P.O. Box 287 Ocilla 31774	1818 Indian lands	— 1838 —	1821 1821 1820
B4	Jackson Jefferson 30549	1796 Franklin	— 1805 —	1796 1796 1796
D4	Jasper Monticello 31064	1807 (as Randolph (old); renamed, 1812) Baldwin	— 1808 —	1808 1809 1808
G6	Jeff Davis Hazlehurst 31539	1905 Appling/Coffee	— 1905 —	1905 1905 1905
D6	Jefferson P.O. Box 658 Louisville 30434	1796 Burke/Warren	— 1803 —	1865 1796 1796
E7	Jenkins P.O. Box 797 Millen 30442	1905 Bullock/Burke/ Emanuel/Screven	— 1905 —	1905 1905 1905
E5	Johnson P.O. Box 269 Wrightsville 31096	1858 Emanuel/Laurens/ Washington	— 1859 —	1859 1859 1859
D4	Jones Gray 31032	1807 Baldwin	— 1811 —	1808 1808 1808
D3	Lamar 326 Thomaston Street Barnesville 30204	1920 Monroe/Pike	1921 1921 1921	1921 1921 1921
J5	Lanier 100 Main Street Lakeland 31635	1919 Berrien/Lowndes/Clinch	1921 1921 1921	1921 1921 1921
F5	Laurens Dublin 31040 *Fragmented records.*	1807 Montgomery/Washington/ Wilkinson	— 1809 —	1807 1808 1808
G3	Lee P.O. Box 56 Leesburg 31763	1826 Indian lands	— 1867 —	1858 1858 1858
G8	Liberty P.O. Box 81 Hinesville 31313 *Fragmented records.*	1777 St. Andrew Parish/ St. James Parish/ St. John Parish	— ? —	1784 1786 1784
C6	Lincoln P.O. Box 340 Lincolnton 30817	1796 Wilkes	— 1796 —	1796 1796 1796
G7	Long Ludowici 31316	1920 Liberty	1920 1920 1920	1920 1920 1920
J5	Lowndes P.O. Box 1349 Valdosta 31603	1825 Irwin	— 1870 —	1858 1862 1862

Map	County Address	Date Formed Parent County/ies	Birth Marriage Death	Land Probate Court
A3	Lumpkin 280 Hill Dahlonega 30533	1832 Cherokee/Habersham/Hall	— 1833 —	1833 1833 1833
F3	Macon Oglethorpe 31068	1837 Houston/Marion	— 1858 —	1857 1857 1856
B4	Madison P.O. Box 147 Danielsville 30633	1811 Clarke/Elbert/Franklin/ Jackson/Oglethorpe	— 1812 —	1812 1811 1812
F2	Marion P.O. Box 481 Buena Vista 31803	1827 Lee/Muscogee/Stewart	— 1846 —	1846 1842 1846
C6	McDuffie P.O. Box 28 Thomson 30824	1870 Columbia/Warren	— 1871 —	1871 1871 1871
H8	McIntosh Darien 31305	1793 Liberty	— 1873 —	1873 1873 1873
E2	Meriwether Greenville 30222	1827 Troup	— 1828 —	1827 1825 1828
H2	Miller 155 S. First Street Colquitt 31737	1856 Baker/Early	— 1893 —	1873 1873 1873
	Milton	1857 (became part of Fulton, 1932) Cobb/Cherokee/Forsyth	— 1867 —	1858 1868 1858
H3	Mitchell P.O. Box 187 Camilla 31730	1857 Baker	— 1867 —	1858 1868 1858
D3	Monroe P.O. Box 817 Forsyth 31029	1821 Indian lands	— 1824 —	1822 1824 1824
F6	Montgomery P.O. Box 295 Mount Vernon 30445	1793 Telfair/Washington	1918 1807 1918	1793 1806 1794
C4	Morgan 141 E. Jefferson Street Madison 30650	1807 Baldwin	— 1808 —	1807 1808 1808
A2	Murray Third Avenue Chatsworth 30705	1832 Cherokee	1924 1842 1924	1833 1840 1833
F2	Muscogee 1000 10th Street Columbus, GA 31901	1826 Creek lands	— 1838 —	1838 1838 1838
C3	Newton 1113 Usher Street Covington 30209	1821 Henry/Jasper/Walton	— 1822 —	1822 1822 1822

Map	County Address	Date Formed Parent County/ies	Birth Marriage Death	Land Probate Court
C4	Oconee P.O. Box 145 Watkinsville 30677	1875 Clarke	— 1875 —	1875 1875 1875
C5	Oglethorpe Lexington 30648	1793 Wilkes	— 1795 —	1794 1794 1794
B2	Paulding 116 Main Street Dallas 30132	1832 Cherokee	— 1833 —	1848 1850 1859
F4	Peach P.O. Box 468 Fort Valley 31030	1924 Houston/Macon	1925 1925 1925	1925 1925 1925
A2	Pickens 211-1 N. Main Street Jasper 30143	1853 Cherokee/Gilmer	1924 1854 1854	1854 1854 1854
H6	Pierce Blackshear 31516	1857 Appling/Ware	1926 1875 1924	1875 1875 1875
D3	Pike P.O. Box 377 Zebulon 30295	1822 Monroe	— 1822 —	1823 1823 1824
B1	Polk P.O. Box 268 Cedartown 30125	1851 Paulding/Floyd	— 1852 —	1852 1852 1852
F4	Pulaski P.O. Box 29 Hawkinsville 31036	1808 Laurens/Wilkinson	1935 1810 1810	1807 1810 1809
D4	Putnam Eatonton 31024	1807 Baldwin	1927 1919 1923	1806 1808 1807
G1	Quitman Georgetown 31754	1858 Randolph/Stewart	1927 1879 1923	1879 1879 1879
A4	Rabun P.O. Box 925 Clayton 30525	1819 Cherokee lands/Habersham	— 1820 —	1821 1826 1829
	Randolph (old)	1807 (renamed Jasper, 1812)		
G2	Randolph (present) Court Street Cuthbert 31740	1828 Baker/Lee	— 1835 —	1830 1835 1838
D7	Richmond 530 Green Street Augusta 30911	1777 St. Paul Parish	— 1785 —	1789 1782 1782
C3	Rockdale 922 Court Street Conyers 30207	1870 Henry/Newton	— 1871 —	1871 1871 1871

Map	County Address	Date Formed Parent County/ies	Birth Marriage Death	Land Probate Court
F3	Schley P.O. Box 352 Ellaville 31806	1857 Marion/Sumter	1927 1858 1927	1857 1857 1857
E7	Screven Sylvania 30467	1793 Burke/Effingham	1927 1817 1927	1794 1790 1811
J2	Seminole P.O. Box 458 Donalsonville 31745	1920 Decatur/Early	1921 1921 1921	1921 1921 1921
D3	Spalding 132 E. Solomon Street Griffin 30223	1851 Fayette/Henry/Pike	— 1852 —	1852 1852 1852
A4	Stephens P.O. Box 386 Toccoa 30577	1905 Franklin/Habersham	— 1906 —	1906 1906 1906
G2	Stewart P.O. Box 157 Lumpkin 31815	1830 Randolph	1927 1828 1927	1830 1830 1830
G3	Sumter Americus 31709	1831 Lee	— 1831 —	1831 1831 1831
E2	Talbot P.O. Box 155 Talbotton 31827	1827 Muscogee	— 1828 —	1828 1828 1828
C5	Taliaferro P.O. Box 114 Crawfordville 30631	1825 Green/Hancock/Oglethorpe/ Warren/Wilkes	1927 1826 1920	1826 1826 1826
G7	Tattnall Reidsville 30453	1801 Montgomery/Liberty	— 1806 —	1802 1802 1805
F3	Taylor P.O. Box 148 Butler 31006	1852 Marion/Talbot/Macon	— 1832 —	1852 1852 1852
G5	Telfair McRae 31055	1807 Wilkinson	— 1810 —	1809 1831 1810
G2	Terrell P.O. Box 525 Dawson 31742	1856 Lee/Randolph	— 1856 —	1856 1856 1856
J3	Thomas Thomasville 31799	1825 Decatur/Irwin	— 1826 —	1826 1826 1826
H4	Tift P.O. Box 826 Tifton 31793	1905 Berrien/Irwin/Worth	1905 1905 1905	1905 1905 1905
F6	Toombs Lyons 30436	1905 Emanuel/Tattnall/ Montgomery	1905 1905 1905	1905 1905 1905

Map	County Address	Date Formed Parent County/ies	Birth Marriage Death	Land Probate Court
A4	Towns P.O. Box 178 Hiawassee 30546	1856 Rabun/Union	— 1856 —	1856 1856 1856
F6	Treutlen P.O. Box 88 Soperton 30457	1917 Emanuel/Montgomery	1919 1919 1919	1919 1919 1919
D1	Troup 900 Dallas Street La Grange 30241	1826 Indian lands	— 1828 —	1827 1827 1827
G4	Turner Route 3 Ashburn 31714	1905 Dooly/Irwin/Wilcox/Worth	1906 1906 1906	1906 1906 1906
E4	Twiggs P.O. Box 202 Jeffersonville 31044	1809 Wilkinson	— 1901 —	1901 1901 1901
A3	Union Route 8 Blairsville 30512	1832 Cherokee	— 1833 —	1860 1851 1854
E3	Upson P.O. Box 889 Thomaston 30286	1824 Crawford/Pike	— 1825 —	1825 1825 1825
A1	Walker P.O. Box 445 LaFayette 30728	1833 Murray	— 1883 —	1883 1883 1883
	Walton (old) *The area of the original Walton County in Georgia is in what is now Transylvania County, North Carolina. When the boundary between Georgia and North Carolina was fixed, Walton was abolished. At that time, the settlement was adjacent to Buncombe County, North Carolina.*	1803 (abolished, 1812; now in North Carolina)		
C4	Walton (present) Court Street, Annex 1 Monroe 30655	1818 Cherokee lands	— 1825 —	1819 1820 1819
H6	Ware P.O. Box 1069 Waycross 31502	1824 Appling	— 1874 —	1874 1879 1874
D6	Warren P.O. Box 46 Warrenton 30828	1793 Columbia/Wilkes/ Richmond/Burke	— 1794 —	1796 1794 1794
E5	Washington P.O. Box 271 Sandersville 31082	1784 Indian lands	— 1865 —	1865 1865 1865
H7	Wayne Annex Jesup 31545	1803 Indian lands/Appling/ Glynn/Camden	— 1809 —	1809 1809 1809
G2	Webster P.O. Box 29 Preston 31824	1853 Stewart	— 1878 —	1860 1854 1854
H6	Wheeler Alamo 30411	1912 Montgomery	1927 1913 1927	1913 1913 1913

Map	County Address	Date Formed Parent County/ies	Birth Marriage Death	Land Probate Court
A4	White P.O. Box 185 Cleveland 30528	1857 Habersham	— 1858 —	1858 1858 1858
A2	Whitfield P.O. Box 248 Dalton 30722	1851 Murray	1927 1852 1852	1852 1852 1852
G4	Wilcox Abbeville 31001	1857 Dooly/Irwin/Pulaski	1919 1858 1919	1858 1858 1858
C5	Wilkes 23 E. Court Street Washington 30673	1777 Indian lands	— 1790 —	1777 1777 1778
E5	Wilkinson Irwinton 31042 *Fragmented records.*	1803 Creek cession	— 1820 —	1855 1820 1855
H3	Worth 201 N. Main Sylvester 31791	1852 Dooly/Irwin	— 1854 —	1892 1879 1879

HAWAII

Dwight A. Radford

The Hawaiian Islands were originally settled by Polynesians a thousand years prior to European contact. In 1778 Captain James Cook visited the Hawaiian Islands and named them the Sandwich Islands after the Earl of Sandwich, then the first Lord of the British Admiralty. The native Hawaiians identified Captain Cook with their god Lono. Although most of Captain Cook's encounter with the Hawaiians was positive and friendly, his return voyage in 1779 resulted in his death at Kealakekua Bay at the hands of the natives. Cook's discovery awakened international interest in the islands.

Between 1790 and 1810, King Kamehameha I, the first Hawaiian monarch, united the islands and established political and social control. The Hawaiian monarchy ended when Queen Liliuokalani was overthrown in 1893. During the first part of the monarchy, most of the Europeans and Americans to visit the islands were mainly crews of trading ships and whalers who stopped off for supplies on voyages to the Orient. The primary sources of information on this time period come from the reports of the voyages. Outside the ruling class, or *alii,* very few Hawaiian names are mentioned.

Next came the Protestant missionaries who arrived from New England in 1820 and converted many native Hawaiians to Protestant Christianity. Roman Catholic missionaries arrived seven years later but were expelled from Hawaii by the Protestant leaders in 1831. The missionaries developed a written Hawaiian language and used the printing press to create a fairly literate and educated society by the 1850s. King Kamehameha III agreed to a Western-style constitution in 1839. Roman Catholics were allowed religious freedom in 1839 after a blockade of Honolulu by the French. Mormon missionaries arrived from California in 1850 and were successful among the native Hawaiians as well as the white population. They were opposed by both the Catholics and Protestants. It was not until the arrival of Japanese immigrants in 1885 that the written history of Buddhism in Hawaii can be traced.

The huge sugar and pineapple plantations of Hawaii account for the majority of the immigration. Chinese contract laborers came as early as 1852 to work on the plantations. The Reciprocity Treaty of 1876 allowed for Hawaiian sugar to be exported to the United States duty-free. The Reciprocity Treaty led to closer ties between the Kingdom of Hawaii and the United States.

The sugar plantations recruited workers from many countries, in part because of local pressure against further importation of Chinese. Portuguese were brought to the islands in 1878, Japanese in 1884, Puerto Ricans in 1900–01, Koreans in 1903, and Filipinos in 1906.

While Hawaii was annexed to the United States in 1898, it was not formally organized as a territory until June 1900. America entered World War II as a result of the infamous bombing of Pearl Harbor on 7 December 1941. Prior to the war, Japanese-Americans had become part of the larger Hawaiian community and demonstrated their patriotism. During the war there was widespread prejudice against the Japanese-American community in Hawaii. Hawaii became the fiftieth state on 21 August 1959. New immigrants arrived in the 1960s from Korea, the Philippines, Samoa, and Tonga. Hawaii continues to be the crossroads of the Pacific.

Of all the states in America, Hawaii is probably the most diverse. Hawaii's population is a mixture of Asian, Polynesian, native Hawaiian, European, American, and Puerto Rican. Researching family history in Hawaii is challenging. Therefore, many different and diverse record sources, although not exhaustive, are given to provide the basic knowledge necessary to begin research in Hawaii.

Vital Records

Hawaii has birth and death records beginning in 1853. The records are incomplete, however, prior to 1896. Early vital records were kept by local government authorities and clergymen. There are a few missionary reports that date back as early as 1826. They are on file at the Hawaii State Archives, the Department of Health, and the Daughters of the American Revolution Library in Honolulu, and many are at the FHL in Salt Lake City.

Since 1911, delayed birth certificates can be applied for in Hawaii. They often contain valuable genealogical information. The FHL has seventy microfilm reels of delayed birth records for Hawaii. This collection contains 50,000 records with indexes and covers the period from 1859 to 1938.

The Hawaii State Health Department has birth, marriage, and death records from 1896 to the present, although some records date back to 1863. Copies of certified certificates are available for $2 and can be obtained by writing the State Department of Health, Research and Statistics Office, Vital Records Section, P.O. Box 3378, Honolulu, Hawaii 96801. This office is located in Room 103, 1250 Punchbowl Street, Honolulu, near the state capitol building. This office is not open to the public and requests directed to them should not be complex because of the heavy workload of the staff. It usually takes about ten days to process and return a request. Microfilm copies of death records, 1909–30, are available at the FHL.

The Hawaii State Archives (see Archives, Libraries, and Societies) collection of early Hawaii marriages extends from 1826 to 1929, with an index from 1826 to 1910. The FHL in Salt Lake City also has many of these records, as well as the index.

Divorce records were not registered by the State Department of Health until July 1951. Copies of these can be obtained by writing this office. Earlier divorce records were recorded by the circuit court in the county where the divorce was granted. A collection of divorce records from 1849 to 1915 is on file at the Hawaii State Archives. These are records from the five circuit courts and have been microfilmed by the Genealogical Society of Utah and are available through the FHL.

For a summary of vital records in Hawaii, see Charles G. Bennett's article "Vital Records in Hawaii," *Hawaii Medical Journal* 15 (November/December 1955).

Census Records

Federal

Population Schedules.

- Indexed—1910
- Soundex—1900, 1920

The Hawaiian Islands were annexed to the United States in 1898. The 1900 U. S. census was being taken of the island population when they became a U. S. territory on 14 June 1900. The 1900 U.S. census is arranged by island since there were no counties at the time. The island of Niihau was enumerated as E. D. 84 of Kauai; the island of Kahoolawe as E. D. 107, and Lanai as E. D. 100 of Maui.

Counties were established beginning in 1905. By 1910 these included Kauai County with Niihau as E.D. 16; Maui County with Kahoolawe as E.D. 91, Lanai as E.D. 95, and Molokai as E.D. 72; and Honolulu County with the Midway Islands as E.D. 135. The 1910 U. S. census of Hawaii is indexed and has been published. In 1910 Kalawao County (now part of Maui County) on the island of Molokai consisted of a leper colony.

Territorial and State

Censuses for portions of the Hawaiian Islands were enumerated in 1866, 1878, 1890, and 1896. The 1878 census covers the islands of Hawaii, Maui, and Oahu, and the 1896 census covers Honolulu only. Copies of these early census records are on file at the Hawaii State Archives and the FHL.

The Hawaii State Archives has two "census files" dating from 1840 to 1866, and from 1847 to 1896, which contain miscellaneous records such as school census, population lists, and vital record summaries. These are also on microfilm at the FHL.

Background Sources

Char, Tin-Yuke, and Wai Jane Char. *Chinese Historic Sites and Pioneer Families of the Island of Hawaii.* Honolulu, Hawaii: University of Hawaii Press, 1979. This work, published for the Hawaii Chinese History Center, provides valuable historical and genealogical information. A similar volume is published concerning the island of Kauai.

Fuchs, Lawrence H. *Hawaii Pono: A Social History.* New York, N.Y.: Harcourt, Brace & World, 1961. A historical account of the various ethnic groups in Hawaii, the volume discusses the problems each faced in the islands.

Handy, E. S. Craighill, and Mary Kawena Pukui. *The Polynesian Family System in Ka-'u, Hawaii.* Rutland, Vt.: Charles E. Tuttle Co., n.d. This book is valuable for the study of native Hawaiians. It provides an account of old style Hawaiian life based on the recollections of living informants.

Hunter, Louise H. *Buddhism in Hawaii: Its Impact on a Yankee Community.* Honolulu, Hawaii: University of Hawaii Press, 1971. This volume provides an excellent overview of the introduction and history of Buddhism in Hawaii. Interesting emphasis is given to the relationship between Buddhism and Christianity.

Kuykendall, Ralph S. *The Hawaiian Kingdom, 1778–1854: Foundation and Transformation.* Honolulu,

Hawaii: University of Hawaii Press, 1966. Volume 1 of a three volume definitive history of the Hawaiian Kingdom. It covers the beginning of Hawaii and the European discovery of the Islands. *The Hawaiian Kingdom, 1854–1874: Twenty Critical Years,* Volume 2 covers the middle period of the kingdom's history, between the close of the reign of Kamehameha III and the accession of Kalakaua. *The Hawaiian Kingdom, 1874–1893: The Kalakaua Dynasty,* Volume 3 of this history deals with the reigns of Kalakaua and Liliuokalani, the expansive reciprocity era, and the downfall of the monarchy.

Lind, Andrew W. *Hawaii's People.* Honolulu, Hawaii: University of Hawaii Press, 1971. Lind's book focuses on the life and immigration of ethnic groups in Hawaii and the native Hawaiians. Education and assimilation of the diverse Hawaiian communities is also featured in this work. The first two chapters recount the history and statistics of several groups.

Okahata, James H., ed. *A History of Japanese in Hawaii.* Honolulu, Hawaii: United Japanese Society of Hawaii, 1971. This work covers such topics as the different immigrations of Japanese to Hawaii, disputes between the Kingdom of Hawaii and Japan, the sugar industry and plantation life, the Japanese people's struggle for equality, the 1920 plantation strike, and anti-Japanese feelings in America and Hawaii during World War II.

Pukui, Mary Kawena, Samuel H. Elbert, and Esther T. Mookini. *Place Names of Hawaii.* Honolulu, Hawaii: University of Hawaii Press, 1974. This excellent work is a glossary of important place-names in Hawaii. These include the names of valleys, streams, mountains, land sections, towns, villages, and Honolulu streets and buildings.

Maps

The United States Geological Survey publishes a catalog of topographical maps (see page 4) covering the state of Hawaii (also American Samoa and Guam). Ask for the publications entitled "Hawaii Catalog of Topographical and other Published Maps" and "Hawaii Index to Topographical and other Map Coverage." The catalog lists over-the-counter dealers of USGS maps in Hawaii. Many libraries maintain reference files of the published maps of the Geological Survey. In Hawaii the maps are deposited in the library at the University of Hawaii at Hilo, the Hamilton Library at the University of Hawaii, Manoa, and at the Joseph F. Smith Learning Resource Center on the Brigham Young University—Hawaii Campus.

The Hawaii State Archives has detailed "fire maps" of Honolulu dating back to 1879. Urban areas on other islands also begin as early as 1912. These maps were made for fire insurance purposes and show the placement of buildings on lots and the type of construction.

Land Records

State-Land State

Prior to 1840 there were no land titles in Hawaii. The society was feudalistic and all land belonged to the king. King Kamehameha I conquered the entire Hawaiian Islands, partitioned the lands among his chiefs, and received revenue from them. The chiefs in turn did the same to persons under them by dividing out arable land among the common people. Under this system land allotments could be taken away at any time.

The advent of foreigners and foreign business methods created a change in the land system in Hawaii. This transitional period was called the "Great Mahele" of 1848 and provided the way for the acquisition of real estate. The Board of Commissioners to Quiet Land Titles was established in 1845. By decision of the king and the chiefs, the king was given his own property, and the remainder was divided equally between the government, the chiefs, and the tenants.

The land commission went to the various islands to meet the people and to prepare them for awarding their claims. This involved the hearing and taking of testimony in connection with nearly 12,000 individual claims. An index to these claims and the Hawaiian terms used in the claims is found in the volume entitled *Indices of Award Made by The Board of Commissioners To Quiet Land Titles in the Hawaiian Islands,* by the Office of the Commissioner of Public Lands of the Territory of Hawaii (Honolulu, Hawaii: Territorial Office Building, 1929). These claims cover the period of 1848 to 1852 and are valuable to native Hawaiians for the genealogical material contained in the actual records.

If the claim was approved by the land commission, the claimant received an award, which was then presented to the minister of the interior who issued a royal patent. The royal patent gave the individual sole ownership of the land once he paid an assessment of cash or land to the government.

The Bureau of Conveyances, 403 Queen Street, Honolulu, Hawaii 96813, has records of the original royal patents and the records of the "Great Mahele" of 1848. These records are for all islands, and since transfers were often made between parents and children or grandparents, statements of relationship are often in these records.

Records in this office begin in the 1840s and include the following record types: Grantors index books (1845–1961), with subsequent records on card file or in the daily entries book; recorded deeds in Libers (1845–1961), with subsequent records on card file or in the daily entries book; land court transfer certificates of title; document and land court maps, called the "file plan"; liens; and private abstractors. This office is open to the public. Many of these records have been microfilmed and are on file at the FHL and the Hawaii State Archives.

The state archives has a "land file" of letters and documents dating from the 1830s regardless of the office concerned. The "land file" covers the period of 1830 to 1900, is filed chronologically, and is one of the most completely translated and indexed group of records in the archives. This collection consists of letters addressed to the Commission to Quiet Land Titles, award books, testimony, and registers of the land documents.

The Department of Land and Natural Resources, 1151 Punchbowl Street, Honolulu, Hawaii 96813, has many early land records of Hawaii, including award books (1836–55); patents (1847–1961); foreign testimonies (1846–62); native testimonies (1844–54); native registers (1846–48); and patents upon confirmation of land commission (1847–1961). These are also on microfilm at the FHL.

Probate Records

Probates were filed with the circuit court, and the records begin during the 1840s. There are no earlier probates except for royal families. Many probates are on file at the Hawaii State Archives and on microfilm at the FHL from 1845 to 1900, although microfilm indexes run from 1814 to 1917. Additional records are available at the various county courthouses.

Probate records on file at the state archives and the FHL are as follows: First Circuit Court (Oahu), beginning in 1845; Second Circuit Court (Maui, including Molokai), beginning in 1849; Third and Fourth Circuit courts (Hawaii), beginning in 1849; Fifth Circuit Court (Kauai), beginning in 1851 (see Court Records below).

Court Records

The "Act to Organize the Judiciary" of 1847 set up four levels of courts in Hawaii: the supreme court, superior courts, circuit courts, and district courts. Each of these courts have records of genealogical value. Many of these court records are on file at the Hawaii State Archives and on microfilm at the FHL.

The supreme court in Hawaii has final appellate jurisdiction in all cases from inferior courts and original jurisdiction to issue all writs over its appellate jurisdiction. Supreme court cases prior to October 1904 are filed with the First Circuit Court records. If it was an appeal from the First Circuit, the records were filed with the original case; if the appeal was from another circuit, the case was given a First Circuit number according to the type of case. For example, if a probate was appealed from the Second, Third, Fourth, or Fifth Circuit, the appeal record will be filed and indexed as though it were a First Circuit case. Supreme court cases after October 1904 are filed with the supreme court clerk's office.

The superior court of law and equity is an appellate court for most cases and a court of origin primarily for cases involving the government, admiralty affairs, bankruptcy, and foreign officials. In 1852 the original supreme court was abolished and the superior court became the supreme court.

On 1 January 1893 the circuit court was organized into five districts as follows: First Circuit (Oahu); Second Circuit (Maui, Molokai, and Lanai); Third Circuit (Kau, Kohala, and Kona on Hawaii); Fourth Circuit (Hamakua, Hilo, and Puna on Hawaii); Fifth Circuit (Kauai and Niihau). This division continued until 1943 when the Third and Fourth circuits were combined; the Fourth Circuit was abolished and the Island of Hawaii once again became the Third Circuit Court. These courts are over criminal cases, probate cases, and divorce cases. Juvenile cases are under the circuit courts in a family court division.

Family court cases usually involve paternity, guardianship, adoption, FC (misdemeanors and felonies), UCCJ (Uniform Child Custody Jurisdiction), miscellaneous, and domestic abuse. The only type of family court records that are restricted and not open to the public are cases involving adoption and paternity and guardianship. Others can be viewed at the courthouses as long as they are not marked confidential.

There are four district courts (or justice courts) in Hawaii with divisions the same as the circuit courts. There are smaller districts on each island. Their jurisdiction involves minor criminal and civil cases.

Tax Records

The Hawaii State Archives has both personal and property tax records for Hawaii (1855–93); Kauai (1855–92); Lanai (1855–92); Maui (1887–92); Molokai (1855–92); and Oahu (1855–1929). These tax records are incomplete and are unindexed. The early tax records are a poll tax only. The tax records were taken on a division basis with each island divided into many divisions. It is necessary to know the correct division in order to search these records.

Property tax records and tax maps were moved from state to county control about 1980. Tax maps dating as early as the 1920s are on microfilm at the Real Property Assessment Office. The address for the City and County of Honolulu is 842 Bethel Street, Honolulu, Hawaii 96813.

The Hawaii State Tax Office has a map room with tax maps beginning in 1932. These tax maps give the names of owners, estate heirs, and field books. The field books give the title history and its book and page numbers, which are found in the Bureau of Conveyances.

Cemetery Records

Hawaii's unique mixture of ethnic groups has produced many fascinating and historic cemeteries. A few of the unique practices need to be understood in order to appreciate fully the various types of tombstones to be found on the islands. For example, when men were "lost at sea" or "buried at sea," tombstones were often raised as a memorial to them in Hawaii's cemeteries. Another example are Buddhist tombstones, which are found very close together because of the cremation practice of the culture. Chinese were often returned to China for burial. This practice and the practice of removal of the remains to be shipped to China are reflected in the sexton's records. Many of the Chinese and Japanese tombstones follow Confucian or Buddhist customs for memorializing ancestors. The use of posthumous names and lunar death dates is very common.

The Hawaiian Historical Society (see Archives, Libraries, and Societies) publishes a guide to cemetery research on the island of Oahu. Many Hawaiian cemeteries are currently being cataloged and indexed in a computer bank by the Cemetery Research Project at the society. Some cemeteries have been transcribed in the past by members of the Church of Jesus Christ of Latter-day Saints (Mormons) in Hawaii. Transcripts are available through the FHL.

Church Records

Hawaii's blend of cultures has led to a diverse religious community. New England Congregationalists first brought Protestant Christianity to the islands in 1820. Roman Catholic missionaries came to Hawaii in 1827 but were forced to leave by Protestant missionary leaders in 1831. Catholicism was allowed back into Hawaii. Quakers came in 1835, and Mormons came in 1850. Methodists came in 1855, and the Church of England arrived in the 1860s.

The history of Buddhism in Hawaii, as a matter of written record, can be traced to the arrival of Soryu Kagahi, a priest of the True Pure Land Sect and a native of Japan. He arrived at Honolulu Harbor in March 1889. Japanese Buddhist and Shinto ideas have been in Hawaii since laborers arrived in 1887. For a more detailed account of the development of the various religions and sects in the state, see John F. Mulholland's *Hawaii's Religions* (Rutland, Vt.: Charles E. Tuttle Co., 1970). Today, Hawaii's religious population is generally 33 percent Catholic, 30 percent Protestant, 20 percent Buddhist, and 17 percent in other faiths. Other religious groups, Christian and non-Christian, have been active in Hawaii in recent years. Among these are Jehovah's Witnesses, Baha'i, various Pentecostal faiths, Seventh Day Adventists, Lutherans, Baptists, Quakers, and many new religious sects exported from Japan.

The Roman Catholic church in Hawaii can be contacted by writing the Diocese of Honolulu, Chancery Office, 1184 Bishop Street, Honolulu, Hawaii 96813. They can provide direction on determining the correct parish and the address. For further reading on Catholicism in the islands see Robert Schoofs, *Pioneers of the Faith: History of the Catholic Mission in Hawaii (1827–1940)* (Hawaii: Sturgis Printing Co., 1978). The Catholic church today is the largest Christian denomination in Hawaii.

The Church of Jesus Christ of Latter-day Saints (Mormons) has grown rapidly in Hawaii since 1850 when missionaries were sent to the islands. The first Mormon colony was established at Lanai. When the Mormon Temple at Laie was completed in 1919, a group of native Hawaiians returned after spending a decade or two at Iosepa in Utah. For additional history on Mormonism in Hawaii see R. Lanier Britsch, *Mormona: The Mormons in Hawaii* (Laie, Hawaii: Institute for Polynesian Studies, 1989), and Joseph H. Spurrier, *Sandwich Island Saints* (Laie, Hawaii: Joseph H. Spurrier, 1989).

The Episcopal church arrived in Hawaii in 1866. Prior to that time, in 1862, the Church of England had established itself on the islands. The Episcopal Church in Hawaii, Queen Emma Square, Honolulu, Hawaii 96813, has records and photos of the church ministry beginning in 1862. Some of their collections are also on file at the state archives. The Episcopal Archives is open to the public.

The first Japanese immigrants to Hawaii probably brought Shinto ideas with them. The first Shinto temple was built in Hilo in 1898. Two recognized Shinto sects came to Hawaii: Shinto (Honkyoku) and Taishakyo. Other Shinto sects are active in Hawaii and several temples have been built. For information on various sects, contact the individual temples.

Guides such as *Brief History of Buddhist Temples* (Hilo, Hawaii: Big Island Buddhist Federation, 1979) can be helpful in locating the temples of various sects and their addresses. Several articles on Buddhism are filed with the Hawaiian and Pacific Collection, Sinclair Library, University of Hawaii.

Military Records

The Hawaii State Archives has a card list for deceased veterans of the Spanish-American War, Civil War, and World War I. Also in their collection is a list of Hawaiians who served in World War I and members of the Guard of the Republic of Hawaii. Prior to becoming a U.S. territory, Hawaii's army consisted of a royal household guard and militia units. A report and rosters of these groups are at the Hawaii State Archives along with records of the Hawaiian Navy and the treason trials held after the 1895 counter-revolution.

Periodicals, Newspapers, and Manuscript Collections

Periodicals

An excellent periodical published on Hawaii's history is *The Hawaiian Journal of History*, a scholarly journal published by the Hawaiian Historical Society in Honolulu. Between 1892 and 1940 the Hawaiian Historical Society published the *Hawaiian Historical Society Papers,* which were devoted to scholarly articles, genealogy, and early record sources. The Australian National University, Canberra, Australia, publishes *The Journal of Pacific History,* which has printed many articles on Hawaii. The Institute for Polynesian Studies at Brigham Young University—Hawaii publishes *Pacific Studies,* which also contains articles and book reviews on Hawaii.

Newspapers

The Hawaii State Archives has an index to many newspapers published in Hawaii from 1836 to 1950. This index includes the following: *Advertiser, Star Bulletin, Polynesian, Hawaiian Gazette,* and *Friend.* An index to marriages and deaths from English language newspapers in Hawaii (1836–1929) is also available at the archives.

During the history of Hawaii, many Hawaiian language newspapers were published. These newspapers were not only reflections of politics and culture but were primary instruments of movements and individuals. An indispensable guide to Hawaiian language newspapers is Esther K. Mookini's *The Hawaiian Newspapers* (Honolulu, Hawaii: Topgallant Publishing Co., 1974). This work will help in locating Hawaiian language newspapers and the dates published.

Native Hawaiian genealogies were published in Hawaiian language newspapers between 1834 and 1900 and are published in *Hawaiian Genealogies: Extracted From Hawaiian Language Newspapers* 2 vols. (Laie, Hawaii: Institute for Polynesian Studies, 1983, 1985), by Edith Kowelohea McKinzie with Ishmael W. Stagner II, editor.

Chinese newspapers can be helpful in reconstructing the Chinese experience in Hawaii. Unfortunately, many Chinese newspapers have not survived, and those that have were often organs for political groups, although vital material can be obtained from these newspapers. Chinese newspapers have been gathered and microfilmed by the University of Hawaii, Hamilton Library. The University of Hawaii, Sinclair Library also has several Chinese newspapers. Among these are the *United Chinese Press, Hawaiian Chinese Journal,* and the *Hawaii Chinese Weekly.*

The FHL has microfilm copies of many older Japanese newspapers in Hawaii. These include the *Nippon Jiji* (1896–1942) and *Hawaii Hochi* (also *Times,* 1912–42). These papers frequently published items on the arrival of immigrants as well as community affairs. The Bishop Museum (see Archives, Libraries, and Societies) and Hamilton Library at the University of Hawaii at Manoa have a good collection of early Japanese newspapers. The Hamilton Library also has various early Korean and Filipino newspapers.

Manuscripts

The Hawaiian Mission Children's Society Library (see Archives, Libraries, and Societies) has records of the nineteenth-century missionary families sent to Hawaii by the American Mission Board of Commissioners for Foreign Missions. This collection also has information on the early Hawaiian converts. The library is not open to the general public but will accommodate descendants. Fortunately, many of their records have been utilized in various publications over the years. One such publication is *Descendants of New England Protestant Missionaries to the Sandwich Islands (Hawaiian Islands) 1820–1900: An Alphabetically Arranged Copy of Births, Marriages, and Deaths from the Records of the Hawaiian Mission Children's Society Library, Honolulu, Hawaii* (Honolulu, Hawaii: Privately printed, Hawaiian State Regent, National Society of Daughters of the American Revolution, 1984). For a more detailed listing of the holdings of this library, see "The Hawaiian Mission Children's Society Library," *The Journal of Pacific History* 16 (1981): 1–2.

The Hawaii State Archives has supplemented many sources for early Hawaiian research. Some collections have been gathered from outside of Hawaii. Sources include the records for the British Consulate in Hawaii (1824–94); Admiralty and Foreign Office records in the Public Record Office, London (1824–75); and the portions of journals concerning Hawaii from Captain Cook's voyage. Other sources include a "Biographical File" which indexes the names of individuals who appear in both published and unpublished sources.

Several hundred Hawaiian and "haole" genealogies have been compiled by Bruce Cartwright in the Cartwright Collection at the Hawaii State Archives. Voters records are also available at the state archives. These include the "Great Register of Voters" (1887–88) which gives the name, age, place of birth, and occupation of the voter. This register is arranged by island and precinct. The "Oath and Certificates" of persons registering as voters in 1894, arranged by island, is also available. In some cases they give age and birthplace. Registers from 1900 to about 1960 are presently being organized and microfilmed for availability through the FHL.

The Cole-Jensen Collection at the archives consists of oral genealogies of the Pacific people, including Hawaii. The Kala Kana Collection consists of ancient Hawaiian chants, mythology concerning Hawaiian ancestry, and ancient Hawaiian pedigrees with ancestry of the Hawaiian royal families.

The Russian presence has been in Hawaii since the 1800s. Czarist Russian Consulates were in the U.S. port cities of Chicago, Honolulu, New York, Philadelphia, Portland, San Francisco, and Seattle, as well as the office in Nome, Alaska. The Russian Consular Records deposited at the National Archives in Suitland, Maryland (see page 9), have been microfilmed by the Genealogical Society of Utah. This collection has been indexed by the Jewish Genealogical Society of Greater Washington in Sallyann Amdur Sack and Susan Fishl Wynne's *The Russian Consular Records Index and Catalog* (New York, N.Y., and London, England: Garland Publishing, 1987). This valuable collection covers the period of 1849 to 1926, with the majority of documents dating from 1917 to 1926, and is on microfilm at the National Archives and the FHL.

The Hawaiian Historical Society in Honolulu has a collection of telephone books from 1909 to 1973 and city directories from 1880 to 1973.

Archives, Libraries, and Societies

Hawaii State Archives
Iolani Palace Grounds
478 South King Street
Honolulu, HI 96813

An excellent research repository for Hawaii, its many holdings have already been described above.

Hawaiian Historical Society
560 Kawaiahao Street
Honolulu, HI 96813

The society has an extensive collection of nineteenth century materials on Hawaii including manuscripts, maps, and photos.

University of Hawaii, Manoa Campus
Hamilton Library
Honolulu, HI 96822

This is a government document repository. The library has strong Hawaii and Pacific collections, serials, maps, and the largest genealogical book collection in the state.

Hawaiian Mission Children's Society Library
553 South King Street
Honolulu, HI 96813

Not open to the public, but accessible by mail or phone, their record holdings include journals and photos of early nineteenth century Congregational missionaries in Hawaii and the archives of the Congregational Church in Hawaii and the Pacific.

Bishop Museum Library
1525 Bernice Street
Honolulu, HI 96817

This repository has material on the Hawaiian Royal families and nobility, records of major sugar companies, and a large photographic collection.

Hawaii Chinese History Center
111 North King Street, Room 410
Honolulu, HI 96813

Materials relating to the Chinese in Hawaii, which include maps, genealogies, histories, photos, and rare documents, are located here.

Hawaii State Library
1390 Miller Street
Box 2360
Honolulu, Hawaii 96804

The library has large collections and materials on ethnic groups in Hawaii as well as guides on genealogical research.

Kona Historical Society
P.O. Box 398
Kona, HI 96704

Materials on the Kona section of the Island of Hawaii are among its holdings.

Maui Historical Society and Museum
2375-A Main Street
P.O. Box 1018
Wailuku, HI 96793

This organization has publications, newspaper clippings, and photos of historical value to the island of Maui.

Kauai Historical Society
4428 Rui Street
P.O. Box 1778
Lihue, HI 96766

Holdings here include newspapers, manuscripts, photos, oral histories, and various writings on Kauai Island. Some records for now defunct sugar plantations are also available.

Special Focus Categories

Immigration

The population of Hawaii is a blend of many ethnic groups. Immigrants came to Hawaii to work. The Chinese arrived in 1852, the Portuguese in 1878, the Japanese in 1884, the Koreans in 1903, and the Filipinos in 1906. The Japanese currently make up about 30 percent of the population and represent Hawaii's largest ethnic group.

Records concerning arrival prior to 1860 have been compiled in the valuable volume entitled *Voyages to Hawaii before 1860* by Bernice Judd (Honolulu, Hawaii: University of Hawaii, ca. 1974). This book is a compilation of narratives found in the libraries of the Hawaiian Mission Children's Society and the Hawaiian Historical Society.

Passenger lists for persons arriving in Hawaii have been microfilmed from 1843 to 1900. These include a separate index for Chinese arrivals (1854–1900); Japanese arrivals (1888–1900); Portuguese arrivals (1878–1900); and a general index for all others (early to 1900). These ship manifests and the index are on microfilm at the Hawaii State Archives and the FHL. For the time period after 1900 contact the state archives.

Although the Chinese arrivals in Hawaii are listed in the passenger lists (1854–1900), many arrivals were not recorded. The Board of Immigration in Hawaii recorded additional Chinese arrivals. This collection of records spans 1847 to 1880 and is on file at the Hawaii State Archives with microfilm copies at the FHL.

The Chinese Bureau of Hawaii collected records of Chinese entry permits (1888–98); card index to Chinese Passports (1884–98); Chinese work permits (1895–97); departures of Chinese from Hawaii (1852–1900); index to entry permits of Chinese minors (1891–98); labor permits of persons who died in Hawaii (1895–97); and special resident permits (1891). Many of these records provide the entry date of the immigrant as well as the vessel. The originals are at the Hawaii State Archives. They have been microfilmed and are also on file at the FHL.

Many passport registrations for Portuguese citizens have been published in Robert S. DeMello, *Passport Registrations Portuguese Immigrants from Azores to Sandwich Isles, 1879–1883* (Honolulu, Hawaii: DeMello Publishing Co., n.d.).

The Japanese Consulate General, 1742 Nuuanu Avenue, Honolulu, Hawaii 96817, has records of Japanese nationals who came to Hawaii between 1885 and 1910.

The Hawaiian Sugar Planters' Association, Experiment Station Library, 99-193 Aiea Heights Drive, P.O. Box 1057, Aiea, Hawaii 96701, has passenger manifests of Filipino contract laborers from 1906 to the present. Some early Korean immigrations can be found with the Chinese arrivals from 1 January 1900 to 28 December 1903.

Native Hawaiian

The ethnic group known as Hawaiian is generally reserved for descendants of the original Polynesian inhabitants of the Hawaiian Islands. The present interracial mixture of ethnic groups in the state of Hawaii makes the term Hawaiian ambiguous to the point that it is unclear who is a Hawaiian in the modern society of Hawaii.

Many native Hawaiian historical, genealogical, and cultural collections have been gathered and preserved in libraries in Hawaii. In Hawaiian families, the firstborn child, (hoiapo), whether male or female, became the inheritor of the family name. This means that in conducting Hawaiian genealogical research, it is often not possible to know the sex of the child. To complicate matters, it was often a common practice to name a child after an event, circumstance, or wish, without respect to sex. For additional information on Native Hawaiian records and record repositories, see David Kittleson, *The Hawaiians: An Annotated Bibliography* (Honolulu, Hawaii: University of Hawaii Press, 1985).

Other Ethnic Groups

Hawaii is a unique state because all racial groups are minorities, and the majority of the population has ancestry in the Pacific Islands or Asia rather than Europe or Africa. Ethnic sources to be examined in this section include those for the Chinese, Japanese, Filipinos, and Koreans. For additional information on the ethnic groups of Hawaii, see Eleanor C. Nordyke, *The Peopling of Hawaii* (Honolulu, Hawaii: University of Hawaii Press, ca. 1977), and Andrew W. Lind, *Hawaii's People* (Honolulu, Hawaii: University Press of Hawaii, 1971). Information on Asian research and repositories can be found in Greg Gubler's article, "Asian American Records and Research" in Jessie Carney Smith, *Ethnic Genealogy* (Westport, Conn.: Greenwood Press, 1983), pages 239–308.

For Chinese research in Hawaii, see the following reference works: Clarence E. Glick, *Sojourners and Settlers: Chinese Migrants in Hawaii* (Honolulu, Hawaii: University of Hawaii Press, 1980); Kum Pai Lai and Violet Lai, *Researching One's Chinese Roots* (Honolulu, Hawaii: Hawaii Chinese History Center, 1988); and Nancy Foon Young, *The Chinese in Hawaii: An Annotated Bibliography* (Honolulu, Hawaii: University Press of Hawaii, 1973).

For the Japanese, see the following references: Ronald Kotani, *The Japanese in Hawaii: A Century of Struggle* (Honolulu, Hawaii: Hawaii Hochi, 1985); Mitsugu Matsuda, *The Japanese in Hawaii* (Honolulu, Hawaii: University of Hawaii, 1975), revised by Dennis M. Ogawa, and Jerry Y. Fujioka; and Franklin Odo and Kazuko Shinoto, *A Pictorial History of the Japanese in Hawaii, 1885–1924,* (Honolulu, Hawaii: Bishop Museum, 1985).

Filipino resources include Ruben R. Alcantara, *The Filipinos in Hawaii: An Annotated Bibliography* (Honolulu, Hawaii: Social Research Institute, University of Hawaii, 1972).

For the early period of Korean immigration, see Wayne Patterson's *The Korean Frontier in America: Immigration to Hawaii, 1896–1910* (Honolulu, Hawaii: University Press of Hawaii, 1988).

County Resources

Many of the pre-1900 Hawaiian records are deposited at the state archives. Since territorial days, Hawaii has consisted of five counties: Hawaii, Honolulu, Kalawao, Kauai, and Maui. These were created on 1 July 1905, but their purpose does not include administration of land, probate, or court records. After 1900 probate records and court records are accessed through the Hawaii State Judiciary Court, 797 Punchbowl Street, Honolulu, Hawaii 96813. For land records contact the Bureau of Conveyances, 403 Queen Street, Honolulu, Hawaii 96813. The addresses that follow are for the individual counties, but in Hawaii the counties do not hold the records. For a more complete discussion as to the location of county record sources, see preceding sections.

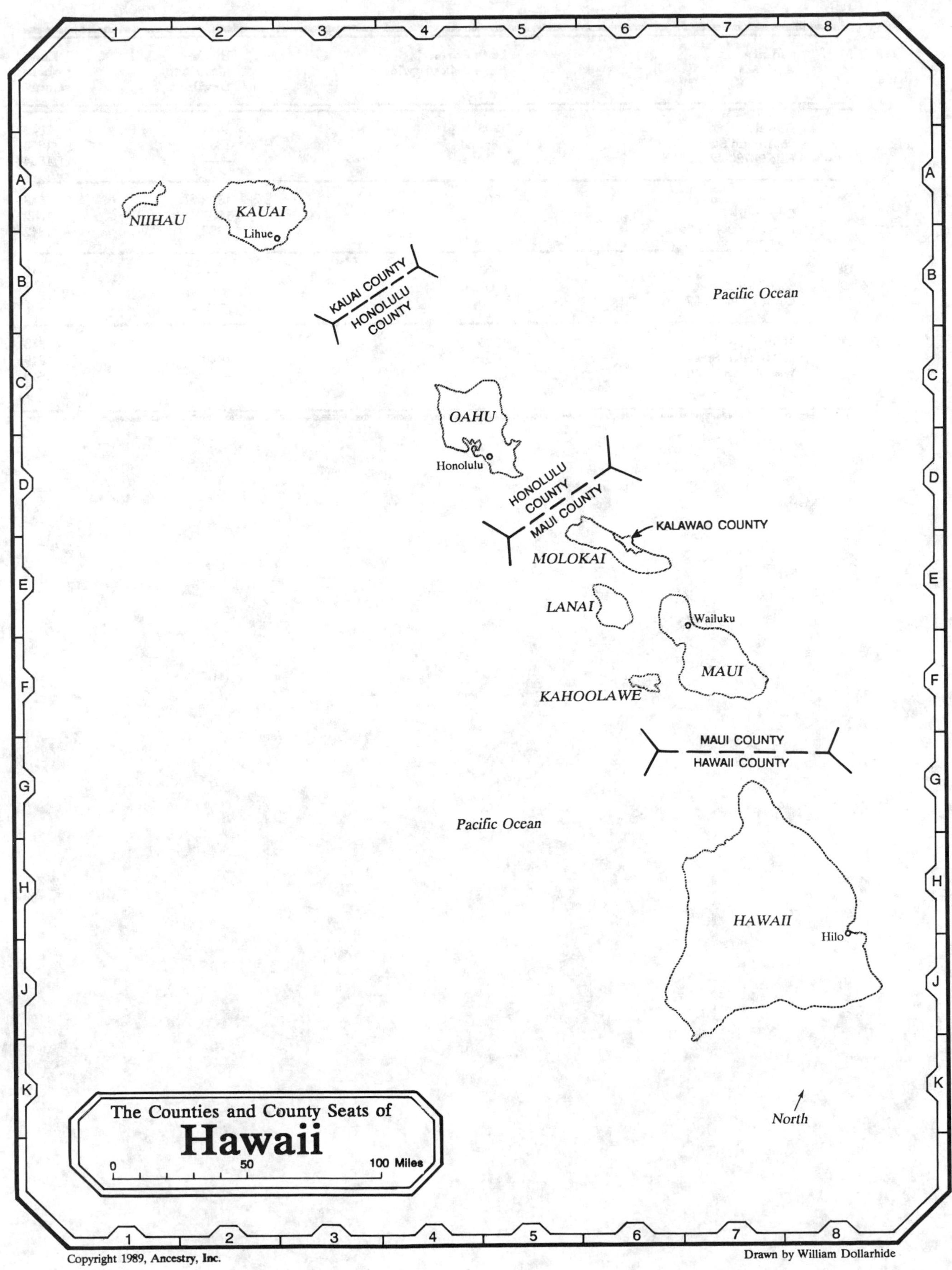

Drawn by William Dollarhide

Map	County Address	Date Formed Parent County/ies	Birth Marriage Death	Land Probate Court
J7	Hawaii 25 Aupuni Street Hilo 96720-4252	1905 original	1877 1832 —	1848 1854 1854
D4	Honolulu County City Hall Honolulu 96813-3014	1905 original	1863 1832 1862	1848 1842 1842
B3	Kauai 4396 Rice Street Lihue 96766-1337	1905 original	— 1826 —	1848 1851 1851
F6	Maui 200 S. High Street Wailuku 96793-2155	1905 original	— 1843 —	1848 1849 1849

IDAHO

Dwight A. Radford

The first permanent settlement of whites in Idaho country was the Mormon colony at Franklin in Cache Valley, but it was the lure of gold that brought the first major wave of settlers. Just three years after gold was discovered, the territory of Idaho was created, in 1863, consisting of ten counties. The new territory included what is now all of Montana and most of present-day Wyoming. At the peak of the mining boom as many as 70,000 whites may have been in Idaho Territory. By 1870, however, this number had dwindled to 15,000. Mining was Idaho's chief producer of wealth until the beginning of the twentieth century when agriculture became the number one industry.

In 1866 the first district land office in Idaho opened in Boise. Other district offices included Lewiston in 1866, Oxford in 1879, Hailey in 1883, Coeur d'Alene in 1884, and Blackfoot in 1886. After the Civil War, Confederate refugees settled in Idaho. Others came to Idaho during a renewed mining boom in the 1880s and 1890s and with the coming of the railroads to the farm land of southern Idaho.

Idaho's transition from a territory to statehood was long and difficult. When the new Idaho Constitution was drafted in 1889, territory officials sought to redress sectional antagonisms. The only exception was that a section in the constitution was written denying Mormons the right to vote and to hold public office. Many compromises had to be reached in order to set the boundaries of the new state. Idaho became a state on 3 July 1890.

Idaho was never a "melting pot" but did have its share of ethnic groups, such as Scandinavian converts to the Mormon faith who colonized in eastern Idaho. Coeur d'Alene mines attracted miners from Wales and immigrants from the Balkans, and the Finns settled in the high mountain valleys near Payette Lakes. Hundreds of Chinese came to Idaho in the 1860s and 1870s to work in the mines. The Basque migration from the Spanish Pyrenees came primarily to Idaho, northern Nevada, western Oregon, and California as sheepherders. Japanese immigrants began settling in southwestern Idaho prior to World War II. Other Japanese settled near Idaho Falls and Pocatello. Between 1900 and 1910, reclamation projects opened desert lands for farming. This brought a new wave of settlement from nearby states, especially Utah.

Idaho's Native American population lives on four reservations: Nez Perce Reservation and Coeur d'Alene Reservation in northern Idaho, Fort Hall Reservation north of Pocatello, and Duck Valley Reservation in Owyhee County. Many Kootenai Native Americans reside in an enclave near Bonners Ferry, and some Kalispell Native Americans live in an enclave at Cusick on the Idaho-Montana border.

Idaho's development was often turbulent and yet tolerant and just at times. The Mormon east, non-Mormon west, and the northern mining part of the state developed three distinct cultures that eventually grew and bonded into the state of Idaho.

Vital Records

The registration of births and deaths on the county level in Idaho was not required until 1907. Prior to that time, the only birth and death records were kept by churches, midwives, mortuaries, and physicians. These records are fragmentary at best. The County Resources section lists those vital records which were available on the county level before mandatory recording.

Beginning in 1907 the state of Idaho required that professional midwives and physicians record births. The registration of deaths was the responsibility of any clergyman, coroner, physician, or undertaker who had cared for the deceased during the last sickness or made arrangements for the burial. This information was reported to the county recorder. The law governing the registration of births and deaths was changed in 1911, at which time the county recorder was relieved of this responsibility. After 1911 all births and deaths were registered directly with the state.

The first laws in Idaho Territory concerning marriages and divorces were enacted in 1864. The first Territorial Legislative Assembly made provisions for books in which to record certificates issued by the person performing the marriage ceremony as well as contracts made by individuals. Under the law, the marriage contract did not have to be a written contract. If it was a written contract, there was no compulsion about making a public record of it. Although some early Idaho Territorial marriage contracts were recorded, most were not. Pre-1895 records located in the county courthouses of Idaho are certificates issued by the person performing the marriage ceremony—to the effect that such a ceremony was performed. Ricks College (see Archives, Libraries, and Societies) has an index to all pre-1900 marriages recorded in Idaho.

District courts in Idaho were given jurisdiction in divorce cases by an act passed by the first Territorial Legislative Assembly in 1864. Divorce and annulment actions were filed in the district court in the same manner as other civil cases.

Statewide records of Idaho's birth and death certificates begin in 1911, and marriage and divorce records begin in 1947. These certificates can be obtained by contacting the Vital Statistics Unit, Idaho Department of Health and Welfare, 450 West State Street, Statehouse Mall, Boise, Idaho 83720-9990.

It takes approximately three weeks to fill a request for a vital records search. The cost is $6 for a certified copy of a birth, marriage, death, or divorce record. Copies of certified delayed births, court ordered name changes, adoptions, and paternity actions and legitimation are $10 per record.

Certain restrictions apply when requesting vital records from the state of Idaho. Written authorization is needed from the individual, immediate relative, or legal representative to obtain a birth, marriage, or divorce certificate for persons other than one's own family. No written authorization is needed to verify vital records information if the exact information is supplied and no search is required. The cost for this is $4, and all these records are accessible in person. There are no published indexes for Idaho vital records held by the state.

Census Records

Federal

Population Schedules.

- Indexed—1870, 1880, 1910
- Soundex—1900, 1920

Mortality Schedules.

- 1870, 1880 (both indexed)

In 1860, Idaho north of 46 degrees north latitude was part of Spokane County, Washington Territory. The 1860 federal census appears to reflect no white population, and the 1860 federal census of Cache County, Utah Territory, included some persons living in what is now the southeastern corner of the Bear Lake area. The 1870 Idaho territorial census is extant for all counties and has been indexed, although the unorganized area of Kootenai was enumerated with Nez Perce County. A portion of Bear Lake and the Franklin County area was enumerated with Cache County, Utah. An index has been compiled by the Idaho State Historical Society (see Archives, Libraries, and Societies) entitled "Missing 1870 Census of Franklin and Bear Lake Counties Idaho Found in 1870 Census of Utah" (Boise, Idaho: Williams Printing Co., 1982). Any population in the Yellowstone National Park area of Idaho for 1880 was enumerated in the Wyoming census. An index to the 1910 federal population schedules was published by the Idaho Genealogical Society (see Archives, Libraries, and Societies).

Background Sources

Beal, Merrill. *A History of Southeastern Idaho: An Intimate Narrative of Peaceful Conquest by Empire Builders.* Caldwell, Idaho: Caxon Printers, 1942. This book outlines the history of an area which was influenced by Mormon Utah to the south, mining Montana to the north, and pioneer Oregon to the west.

———, and Merle W. Wells, *History of Idaho.* 3 vols. New York, N.Y.: Lewis Historical Publishing Co., 1959. Volumes one and two cover the history of the state. Volume three is especially noteworthy as it contains personal and family histories.

Bieter, Pat. "Reluctant Shepherds: The Basque of Idaho." *Idaho Yesterdays* 1 (Summer 1957): 10–15. A discussion of the characteristics of the Basque people and why they migrated and settled in Idaho is presented.

Bilbao, Julio B. "Basque of Early Idaho." *Idaho Yesterdays* 15 (Summer 1971): 26. Accounts of some of Idaho's earliest settlers who were Basque are provided.

Defenbach, Byron. *Idaho, the Place and Its People: A History of the Gem State from Prehistoric to Present Days.* 3 vols. Chicago, Ill.: American Historical Society, 1933. Volume one covers the history of the state, and volumes two and three contain biographical sketches.

Derig, Betty Belle. "Celestials in the Digging." *Idaho Yesterdays* 16 (Fall 1972): 2. A century ago, the typical Idaho miner was Chinese. By 1870, more than 4,000 Chinese had moved into Idaho. This article tells the story of the Chinese miners.

French, Hiram Taylor. *History of Idaho: A Narrative Account of Its Historical Progress, Its People, and Its Principle Interest.* 3 vols. Chicago, Ill.: Lewis Publishing Co., 1914. This three-volume set is very useful because volumes two and three are biographical sketches. Volume one is a history of the state.

Gazetteer of Cities, Villages, Unincorporated Communities and Landmark Sites in the State of Idaho. Idaho Department of Highways, 1966. Listed are 1,900 places in Idaho. It is especially useful to the researcher because each place is broken down into county, quadrants within the county, township, section, range, post office, highway, railroad, airport, stream, lake or reservoir, principal industry, and notes.

Hawley, James H., ed. *History of Idaho: The Gem of the Mountains.* 4 vols. Chicago, Ill.: S. J. Clarke Publishing Co., 1920. Volume one is a standard history of the state, while the other volumes consist of biographical sketches.

History of Idaho Territory: Showing Its Resources and Advantages; with Illustrations . . . From Original Drawings. San Francisco, Calif.: W. W. Elliott, 1884. Territorial newspapers were among the sources used for this compilation.

An Illustrated History of the State of Idaho: Containing a History of the State of Idaho from the Earliest Period of Its Discovery to the Present Time, Together With Glimpses of Its Auspicious Futures; Illustrations . . . and Biographical Mention of Many Pioneers and Prominent Citizens of Today. 4 vols. in 2. Chicago, Ill.: Lewis Publishing Co., 1899. This two-volume set covers the history of Idaho and contains biographical sketches.

Sims, Robert C. "The Japanese American Experience in Idaho." *Idaho Yesterdays* 22 (Spring 1978): 2. Japanese Americans make up an important chapter in Idaho's history, and this article tells of their journey.

Wunder, John. "The Courts and the Chinese in Frontier Idaho." *Idaho Yesterdays* 25 (Spring 1981): 23. Idaho's supreme court did not succumb to the anti-Chinese pressures present throughout the West. It upheld a tradition of fundamental fairness.

Maps

Maps are essential in conducting on-site research, locating towns and cemeteries, and plotting mining claims. Several maps are available for Idaho that are helpful in conducting on-site or historical research.

The United States Geological Survey (see page 4) maps are available for Idaho. Two catalogs will help locate the needed sections: "Idaho, Index to Topographical and Other Map Coverage" and "Idaho, Catalog of Topographic and Other Published Maps." These catalogs give the current cost of each topographical map and provide a listing of over-the-counter map sellers in Idaho.

Major libraries in Idaho have been designated by the U.S. Geological Survey as map depository libraries. They include Boise State University in Boise; University of Idaho in Moscow; Idaho State University in Pocatello; Public Library, 812 East Clark Street, in Pocatello; and Ricks College in Rexburg. The first three, along with the Library and Archives of the Idaho State Historical Society, are the major map repositories in the state.

Ralph N. Preston's *Maps of Early Idaho* (Corvallis, Oreg.: Western Guide Publishers, 1972) is an excellent collection of early Idaho maps, beginning with the 1804 Lewis and Clark trail map to a present-day map of the state. The various maps detailing the history of Idaho are valuable for genealogical research as they show overland stage routes, old military roads, Indian battle grounds, old forts, old mining areas, and early towns. Another set of historical maps has been published by the Idaho State Historical Society and annotated by Meryl W. Wells, *An Atlas of Idaho Territory, 1863–1890* (Boise, Idaho: Idaho State Historical Society, 1978).

Land Records

Public-Domain State

Idaho was a public land state, created from land that was public domain. The federal government administered most of the land that was settled through the GLO, which became the BLM. These land offices kept records of each land entry, including tract books and township plats. Tract books are records of transactions for each section of land. Township plat books are maps of land entries for each township.

Records for the BLM are on file at the National Archives-Pacific Northwest Region (see page 9) and the BLM Office at 3380 Americana Terrace, Boise, Idaho 83706. These land records cover the years 1868 to 1910. The following land office records are on microfiche in Seattle: Boise Land Office (1868–1910); Oxford Land Office (1879–1908); Oxford-Blackfoot Land Office (1879–1901); Blackfoot Land Office (1884–1940); Coeur d'Alene Land Office (1885–1908), Hailey Land Office (1883–1940), Lewiston (1874–1908); and Unidentified Land Office Records (1878–1917). Also on file are records for the Office of Surveyor General of Idaho (1913–50). There were two types of land entries in Idaho, cash entries and homesteads. For a more detailed discussion of these two land entries, see Washington—Land Records.

The above land office records include letters sent and received by state offices and suboffices, case files, township tract books, survey plats, registers, indexes of declaratory statements, entries, receipts, certificates of homesteads, mineral, and timber culture lands.

The custodian of subsequent land records on the county level in Idaho is the county recorder. The originals of these county records are on file at the local county courthouses. Many records in Idaho's county courthouses are microfilmed and available through the FHL.

Probate Records

Probate courts were established after Idaho became a state. For a more detailed account of probate courts, see the Court Records section. Idaho probate records include appraisals, claims, estate cases, fee books, final accounts, guardianships, inheritance tax records, inventories, letters, and wills. These records are available at the various county courthouses.

Those microfilmed are available through the FHL and the Library and Archives of the Idaho State Historical Society.

Court Records

The various Idaho courts that kept records of genealogical value were the district courts, probate courts, justice of the peace courts, and the magistrate divisions of district courts.

District courts have countywide civil and criminal jurisdiction, including naturalization, with some appellate jurisdiction.

Probate courts had jurisdiction over probates, adoptions, and minor civil matters until they were abolished in 1971, and their records and functions were assigned to the magistrate divisions of district courts.

Justice of the peace courts had jurisdiction over minor petty cases until 1971, when they were abolished, and their jurisdiction was assigned to the district courts.

Magistrate divisions of district courts are citywide courts assigned court cases by the various district courts. These cases generally include minor civil and criminal cases, probates, and juvenile matters.

Idaho court records are at the local county courthouses, although many are microfilmed and available through the FHL.

The Idaho State Historical Society has 1,200 boxes of Idaho Supreme Court case files from the territorial and state court covering 1863 to 1970.

Tax Records

Most of Idaho's county tax records are still located at the county courthouses. Many early territorial and pre-territorial tax rolls are on file at the Idaho State Historical Society with microfilm copies at the FHL.

Cemetery Records

Members of the Church of Jesus Christ of Latter-day Saints transcribed many Idaho cemetery records between 1952 and 1968. These records were published in a twelve-volume set that includes many of the cemeteries in the following counties: Ada, Adams, Bannock, Bear Lake, Bingham, Blaine, Bonneville, Boise, Bonner, Camas, Cassia, Canyon, Clark, Clearwater, Elmore, Franklin, Gem, Gooding, Idaho, Jefferson, Jerome, Kootenai, Lemhi, Madison, Minidoka, Nez Perce, Owyhee, Payette, Power, Twin Falls, Shoshone, Valley, and Washington.

The Idaho State Historical Society also has some transcribed cemetery records. A comprehensive listing of these holdings does not exist. For this reason, it is suggested that a researcher write the Idaho State Historical Society's genealogical department or call (208) 334-2305 and ask if records have been gathered for a specific area. An index of all cemetery records in Ada County has been completed by the Treasure Valley Chapter of the Idaho State Historical Society.

Church Records

Idaho has a rich and diverse religious culture. The Mormons settled along the Snake River in eastern Idaho and established farming communities. Among these farming communities was Franklin, the first permanent white settlement in Idaho. Catholic priests founded missions among the Coeur d'Alene Native Americans in 1853. Protestants such as the Methodists, Episcopalians, and the Christian church arrived during the gold mining era.

The largest religious organization in Idaho is the Church of Jesus Christ of Latter-day Saints (Mormons). Mormons colonized the eastern portion of Idaho by 1860. Due to friction caused by the practice of plural marriage by Mormons, many Mormon families that had originally moved from Utah to Idaho Territory continued their migration northward into Alberta, Canada, where the Mormon presence remains strong today. Mormon ward, branch, and mission records are available at the FHL. Ricks College is a Mormon institution in Rexburg, Idaho, and its Archives and Special Collections Department has manuscripts, photographs, and oral histories concerning the Mormon settlement in the Upper Snake River Valley.

Unlike the Mormons, early Protestant and Catholic efforts in Idaho were focused on converting the Native Americans to Christianity rather than settling the land. Methodists and Presbyterians arrived in the region before the Catholic fathers. Episcopalians soon followed. These efforts concentrated on northern Idaho with the Nez Perce and Flathead tribes. The Methodist mission board in 1834 took action to establish a mission among the Flathead tribe.

The first Episcopal clergy arrived in Boise and established St. Michael's Church (at the time, the only Episcopal church in Idaho, Montana, and Utah) a year after Idaho became a territory. The Episcopal faith spread across southern Idaho, and priests evangelized the Shoshoni-Bannock tribes at Fort Hall with success. Many Episcopal Church records in Idaho covering 110 years are microfilmed and deposited with the Idaho State Historical Society. Among the items filmed are church registers from Delamar, Fort Hall, and Silver City, as well as district and diocesan records between 1896 and 1924.

The emigration of Swedes and Norwegians to northern Idaho brought the Lutheran faith to the area. Other Scandinavians came from the Midwest in the early 1900s to work on irrigation canals in southern Idaho. Many remained to settle the land. Many Lutheran Finns settled in the Long Valley near Cascade and McCall.

The Catholic mission work in Idaho began in 1840 when Father Pierre Desmet was appointed to minister to the Native Americans. The Cataldo Mission near Kellogg was established in 1846, and the mission church still stands and is the oldest building in Idaho. When miners came in the 1860s, priests were assigned to pioneer white congregations. Currently, the Catholic church has the second largest membership. For information on the location of Catholic records contact the Diocese of Boise, Box 769, Boise, Idaho 83701.

It is uncertain how many Quakers lived in Idaho before the turn of the twentieth century, but by 1918 there were 763. A meeting was opened in Boise in 1898, but was briefly discontinued. At the turn of the century, a few Quakers resided in the Star area, a community about twenty miles from Boise. The promise of irrigation water brought many Quaker families to the Boise Valley. By 1906 the meetings in Fairview and Mountain View were organized into the Mountain View Monthly Meeting. The first Quarterly Meeting in Idaho (Boise Valley) was established in 1906 under the auspices of the Oregon Yearly Meeting. It consisted of New Hope (Star), Boise, and Mountain View Monthly Meeting.

In the last quarter of the nineteenth century, members of the Church of the Brethren began to settle in Idaho. They were attracted to the farm land of the Snake River Valley in southern Idaho and the Clearwater Plateau in northern Idaho. Railroad agents encouraged Brethren to settle in groups in Idaho. So many congregations were established between 1895 and 1910 that the Idaho and Western Montana District was organized. Early congregations were established in Moscow, Grafton-Clearwater, Nez Perce, Winchester, Nampa, Boise Valley, Boise, Bowmont, Payette, Weiser, Idaho Falls, Lost River, and Twin Falls. An excellent history of these early congregations is found in Roger E. Sappington, *The Brethren along the Snake River: A History of the Brethren in Idaho and Western Montana* (Elgin, Ill.: Brethren Press, 1966).

Jewish settlers in Idaho have contributed substantially to the society. During the territorial era, Jews became merchants serving the mining camps. The first synagogue, Temple Beth Israel, was constructed in 1895 in Boise. The only other synagogue is in Pocatello. Temple Beth Israel in Boise is the oldest continuous synagogue in existence west of the Mississippi. Idaho elected the first Jewish governor in U. S. history. A history of the Jewish community in Idaho is Juanita Brooks, *History of the Jews in Utah and Idaho* (Salt Lake City, Utah: Western Epics, 1973).

In 1940 the WPA printed a directory of religious organizations in Idaho entitled *Directory of Churches and Religious Organizations of Idaho* (Boise, Idaho: Idaho Historical Records Survey, 1940). The directory covers 1,100 church institutions, including 991 churches, and is an excellent tool for locating congregations for the time period. Most church records are still kept with the local congregation.

Military Records

Two military collections are on file at the Idaho State Historical Society that are of interest to the researcher. The first, "Soldier's Home" (AR 19), consists of applications for admission to the Idaho Soldier's Home from 1894 to 1983. Information contained in these applications includes record number, date of admission, name, age, nativity, company, regiment, rank, time served, pension, disabilities, county, occupation, social condition, and literacy. These applications are indexed.

The second collection is entitled "The Adjutant General—State of Idaho: Collection of Official Correspondence, Records, and Documents, 1877–1927" (AR 11). This collection is composed of requests to Governor Brayman for arms and ammunition from worried Idahoans during the Indian Wars of 1877–78, requests for discharge and/or pension benefits from said wars, the actual discharges for at least some Idaho volunteers from the Nez Perce and Bannock Wars, some muster rolls of the Idaho Volunteer Regiments, and other miscellaneous material. Material in this collection also includes various aspects of the draft during World War I and company rosters for the Idaho National Guard units who served during the Mexican Border campaign of 1916.

Periodicals, Newspapers, and Manuscript Collections

Periodicals

Three major periodicals are published in Idaho. The first is the *Idaho Genealogical Society Quarterly*, published by the Idaho Genealogical Society, 4620 Overland Road, Number 204, Boise, Idaho 83705-2867. This publication contains many articles of historical and genealogical value. The second publication is *Idaho Yesterdays: The Quarterly Journal of the Idaho State Historical Society*, an excellent source for a wide range of historical articles, including many concerning ethnic Idaho. The third publication is *Snake River Echoes*, which is published quarterly by the Upper Snake River Valley Historical Society, P.O. Box 244, Rexburg, Idaho 83440.

Newspapers

The Idaho State Historical Society has all available newspapers published in the state on microfilm. The current collection consists of 90 percent of the newspapers published since territorial days. From time to time new titles appear and are microfilmed and added to the society's collection. Filming of current newspapers is an ongoing project. Larger newspapers already on microfilm, such as the *Idaho Statesman* and the *Lewiston Morning Tribune*, are purchased by the Idaho State Historical Society and added to the collection. The society's newspaper collection is available through interlibrary loan with the exception of the *Idaho Statesman*.

Manuscripts

The Idaho State Historical Society has large record collections that are open to the public. Because of limited time and staff, there are limitations on mail requests. The staff is willing to search card indexes for particular names and will make photocopies of material for which a specific citation has been provided. They cannot do extensive research in their archive or manuscript collections.

A WPA project from 1935 to 1939 assembled material on biographies, reminiscences, narrative accounts, diaries, and documents pertinent to the history of Idaho. This WPA collection, MS 70, is indexed and is available at the Idaho State Historical Society.

Another indexed collection at the Idaho State Historical Society is a DAR collection of pioneer reminiscences, biographies, brief histories of Boise Basin towns, and other subjects relating to Idaho's territorial history. This collection is accessed under MS 455. The Pioneer chapter of the DAR compiled this collection between 1908 and 1934.

The remainder of the manuscript collections at the Idaho State Historical Society consist of over 2,000 collections, including 150 state and local governmental agencies, 600 large and 800 minor manuscript collections. Many collections relate primarily to Idaho and its history. Files of attorneys, defunct banks, labor organizations, lumber companies, ranches, merchants, church councils, mining companies, and newspapers comprise most of the nongovernment materials. These are indexed by individual or company name and to some extent by subject in the society's manuscript guide.

The "Joyce Dice Owen Collection" is on file at the FHL. This collection consists of Idaho genealogies extracted from the *Idaho Daily Statesman*, Boise, Idaho.

Archives, Libraries, and Societies

Idaho State Historical Society
The Library and Archives Genealogical Library
325 West State Street
Boise, ID 83702

Mailing address of genealogical library:
610 North Julia Davis Drive
Boise, ID 83702

Much of the society's excellent collection is already outlined above. A major genealogical collection is included, but the society's holdings are too large to store in one building. Write or call prior to making a trip to the society to make sure these collections are available during the time of the visit.

Idaho Genealogical Society
4620 Overland Road #204
Boise, ID 83705-2867

In addition to the statewide society, there are several local historical or genealogical societies and some chapters of the state society.

Two excellent resources for southeastern Idaho research are the Genealogical Library in the David O. McKay Resource Library at Ricks College in Rexburg, Idaho, and the Idaho Falls Family History Library in Idaho Falls, Idaho. The latter has all the area mortuary records, cemetery records, and the *Post Register* obituary index (to 1955).

Special Focus Categories

Immigration

There is no port of entry common to overseas immigrants who settled in Idaho. Prior to the migration of persons who stayed in Idaho, there were no railroads or emigration trails. It could be said that they crossed Idaho to the west coast. Those who remained in Idaho developed their society in relative isolation. Idaho had a port of entry at the Canadian border through which immigrants could migrate. By 1924 Idaho was under the jurisdiction of the Spokane, Washington, Office of the Bureau of Immigration. Port of entry was at Eastport, Idaho. Eastport records are filed with the Seattle passenger lists (1890–1957) at the National Archives (see page 8). These have been microfilmed but are not indexed. Additional information on people entering through Eastport, Idaho, may be obtained from a search of the St. Albans, Vermont District records (so-called, see Vermont—Immigration), which are indexed.

Native American

According to the 1900 U.S. census, the following tribal members were residing in Idaho: Bannocks, Cayuse, Coeur d'Alene, Colville, Cree, Crow, Flathead, Kalispell, Kootenai, Omaha, Seletze, Sheepeater, Snake, Spokane, and Umatilla.

Several agencies were set up by the federal government to administer to the affairs of Idaho's Native American population. These records are available at the National Archives-Pacific Northwest Region (see page 9) and the Idaho State Historical Society. Northern Idaho Agency records are also available at the FHL.

Fort Hall Agency, Fort Hall, Idaho (1889–1952). Records include school surveys and censuses, mining permits, grazing leases, ledgers and cards for accounts of individual Indians, records concerning owners of ceded land, irrigation, forestry, loans, and law suits. The Fort Hall Agency administered to the affairs of the Boise and Bruneau band of the Shoshone and Bannock tribes. Bannock tribal members from Wyoming came under the jurisdiction of the Fort Hall Agency in 1872.

Northern Idaho Agency, Lapwai, Idaho (1875–1964). Records include general correspondence and a decimal file, historical files, correspondence concerning Kutenai educational contracts, grazing and timber leases, ledgers for accounts of individual Indians, annuity payrolls, vital statistics, census records, Nez Perce tribal minutes, records concerning forestry, roads, and economic and social surveys. This agency administered to the affairs of the Coeur d'Alene, Kootenai, and Nez Perce Reservations.

In researching tribal records in Idaho, two school records and two other major collections should not be overlooked. The Chemawa Indian School in Chemawa, Oregon, and the Fort Shaw School in Cascade County, Montana, enrolled students from the whole of the northwestern United States. For more details, see the Native American Records sections for Montana and Oregon.

Two major Native American collections are the Major James McLaughlin Papers and the Pacific Northwest Tribes Missions Collection of the Oregon Province Archives of the Society of Jesus, 1853–1960. For additional details about these collections, see Montana—Native American.

For further explanation of Native American land ownership, see Oregon—Native American.

Other Ethnic Groups

Idaho had its share of ethnic minorities. Because Idaho was a frontier society, many ethnic groups did not readily blend into the society at large. Eastern Idaho was overwhelmingly part of the Mormon intermountain empire, made up mostly of Mormon converts from England and Scandinavia. The fact that the Mormons were distinctive in their religion and culture separated them from the mainstream frontier society. Their court system was administered by the Mormon theocracy, and therefore their dependence on Idaho territorial law was minimal.

The first Chinese came to Idaho in 1864 to mine the Oro Fino gold fields. They were brought from California to alleviate a shortage of labor, and soon every mining town in the territory had an ethnic Chinese community. By 1870 there were 4,274 Chinese in Idaho, which constituted 28.5 percent of Idaho's entire population. At one time, Boise had the largest Chinatown outside of San Francisco.

The Chinese came by steamers from San Francisco to Portland or Umatilla, and on to the Idaho placer mines by way of the Blue Mountains. Others came from Utah after the completion of the railroad, and a substantial number migrated from the Comstock Lode country of Nevada. An estimated 20 percent of the total number of Chinese came from British Columbia. Idaho's ethnic Chinese originally came from the city of Canton and province of Kuang-Tuang, which at the time was experiencing a great deal of political unrest as well as severe weather conditions that affected the economy and made migration to America attractive.

No regionally organized anti-Chinese groups emerged in Idaho, unlike neighboring states. Some rural violence did occur during the wave of anti-Chinese sentiments during 1885 and 1886. Eventually, legal matters concerning the Chinese were brought before the Idaho Supreme Court, which refused to imitate the hysteria that had swept Montana, Oregon, and Washington. Instead it sought to balance judiciously the interest of Idaho's Chinese and non-Chinese populations.

In 1880 there were 3,379 Chinese in Idaho. By 1890 the number had declined to 2,007, and in 1900 to 1,467. The bulk of the Chinese population in the latter part of the nineteenth century was in Boise County.

In the early 1970s the building belonging to the Hip Sing Association, a Chinese fraternity, was torn down in Boise, and a large collection of materials from the building were donated to the Idaho State Historical Society. The collection included both items and papers, and these papers, written in Chinese, are currently being inventoried. This is the only Chinese collection on file at the Idaho State Historical Society, and it will be available to the public at a future time.

The Japanese first came to Idaho in the decade following statehood in 1890, from which time they have constituted the state's largest ethnic group. By the end of the 1890s, Japanese settlements were common features along the length of the Oregon Short Line Railroad, especially in Nampa and Pocatello. By 1920 the number of Japanese in Idaho had reached 1,569.

World War II put the Japanese-American community's loyalty in question in the minds of many Americans. With the relocation of Japanese-Americans to camps set up by the U. S. government, the history of this ethnic group entered a new period. One of the ten camps was in Idaho. This camp, located in Hunt, Idaho, opened in August 1942 and became known as Camp Minidoka. Most of the residents in the camp were from Portland and Seattle. The effect of relocation on Idaho continued to be felt after the war as many Japanese-Americans chose to remain in Idaho rather than return to their former homes.

The Basque in Idaho came from the Spanish provinces of Guipuzcoa, Viscaya, Alava, and Navarre in the Pyrenees Mountains. Boise was the center of Basque immigration and probably has the largest Basque-American community in the American West. Young Basque left their homelands for California in 1876 because of Spanish suppression.

As the Basque people moved into southern Idaho, they sent word back to their homeland that jobs were available in the area. Basque came to the Boise Valley in their greatest numbers between 1900 and 1920. As their population grew, a serious religious problem surfaced. The Basque were Catholics who had found their homes in a predominantly Protestant society. The Catholic parishes in the Boise Valley were unable to minister to the immigrants as the Basque spoke very little, if any, English. In 1911 the

Bishop of the Boise diocese arranged for a Basque-speaking priest to be sent to Idaho. This was the beginning of a viable Basque community in Boise, which centered around a few boarding houses in the southeastern portion of the city. For a listing of Basque collections and sources, see Oregon—Other Ethnic Groups.

County Resources

Idaho's county resources can be found in the county seat. Land records are filed at the county recorder's office, probate records with the probate clerk, and court records with the district clerk of the court. A survey of the counties indicates that some hold vital records before the date of mandatory recording, and land records and court records, including judgments, minutes, and miscellaneous records, are available previous to county formation. In the list that follows the year of earliest known record is indicated. Naturalizations generally begin at the year of formation and are held by the clerk of the district court.

The Idaho State Historical Society library also holds microfilms of most of these records.

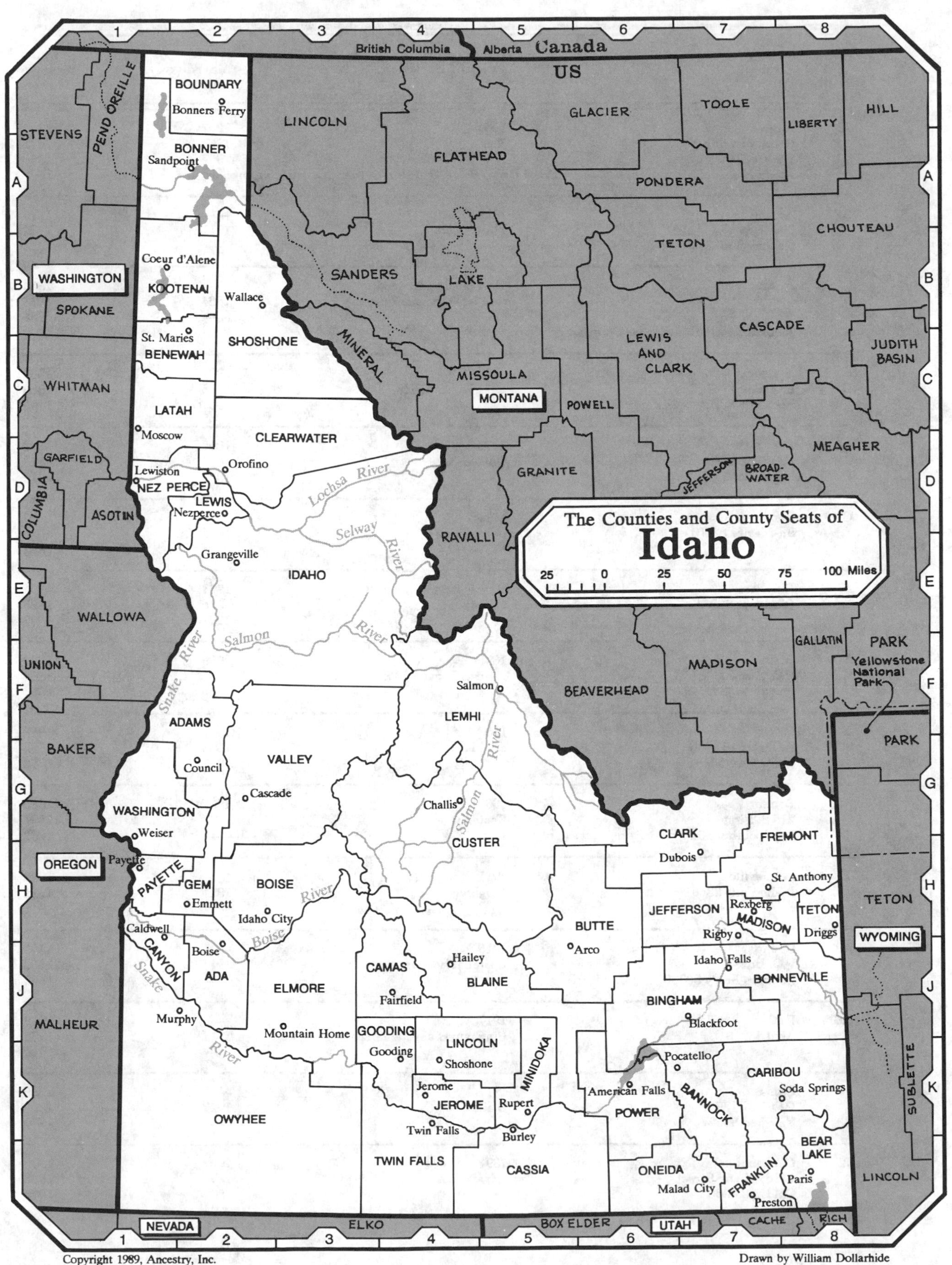

Drawn by William Dollarhide

Map	County Address	Date Formed Parent County/ies	Birth Marriage Death	Land Probate Court
J2	Ada County Building Boise 83702	1864 Boise	1907 1864 1907	1865 1873 1865
	Idaho Historical Society, 610 N. Julia Davis Drive, Boise 83706, holds Ada County land, probate, and court records.			
G2	Adams P.O. Box 48 Council 83612	1911 Washington	— 1911 —	1876 1889 1911
	Alturas	1864 (abolished, 1895 to create Blaine and Lincoln)	— 1864 —	1864 1883 1865
	Records available in Blaine County.			
K7	Bannock P.O. Box 4777 Pocatello 83201	1893 Bear Lake/Oneida	1907 1895 1907	1880 1888 1893
K8	Bear Lake P.O. Box 158 Paris 83261	1875 Oneida	1907 1875 1907	1876 1879 1875
C2	Benewah St. Maries 83861	1915 Kootenai	— 1915 —	1890 1915 1885
J7	Bingham Blackfoot 83221	1885 Oneida	1907 1866 1907	1865 1885 1866
J5	Blaine P.O. Box 400 Hailey 83333	1895 Alturas/Logan	1908 1866 1908	1895 1864 1901
H3	Boise P.O. Box 157 Idaho City 83631	1863 original	1907 1888 1907	1863 1863 1863
A2	Bonner 215 S. First Sandpoint 83864	1907 Kootenai	1907 1907 —	1885 1891 1882
J7	Bonneville Idaho Falls 83401	1911 Bingham	— 1911 —	1911 1911 1911
A2	Boundary P.O. Box 419 Bonners Ferry 83805	1915 Kootenai/Bonner	— 1915 —	1888 1892 1885
H6	Butte Arco 83213	1917 Bingham/Blaine/Jefferson	— 1917 —	1917 1886 1917
J4	Camas P.O. Box 127 Fairfield 83327	1917 Blaine	— 1917 —	1885 1897 1870
J2	Canyon 1115 Albany Street Caldwell 83605	1891 Ada/Owyhee	1907 1892 1907	1865 1885 1865

Map	County Address	Date Formed Parent County/ies	Birth Marriage Death	Land Probate Court
K8	Caribou Soda Springs 83376	1910 Bannock/Oneida	— 1919 —	1901 1914 1891
K5	Cassia Burley 83318	1879 Oneida	1907 1879 1907	1879 1879 1879
G6	Clark P.O. Box 205 Dubois 83423	1919 Fremont	— 1919 —	1866 1909 1893
D3	Clearwater P.O. Box 586 Orofino 83544	1911 Nez Perce	— 1911 —	1911 1911 1911
H4	Custer P.O. Box 385 Challis 83226	1881 Alturas	1907 1864 1907	1873 1879 1881
J3	Elmore 150 S. Fourth Street Mountain Home 83647	1889 Ada/Alturas	1907 1864 1907	1889 1892 1889
K7	Franklin P.O. Box 231 Preston 83263	1913 Oneida	— 1913 —	1874 1910 1878
G8	Fremont P.O. Box 248 St. Anthony 83445	1893 Bingham/Lemhi	1907 1893 1907	1880 1889 1885
H2	Gem 415 E. Main Emmett 83617	1915 Boise/Canyon	— 1915 —	1870 1896 1865
K4	Gooding Gooding 83330	1913 Lincoln	— 1913 —	1913 1913 1913
E3	Idaho Main Street #5 Grangeville 83530	1864 original	1907 1863 1907	1862 1865 1870
H7	Jefferson P.O. Box 275 Rigby 83442	1913 Fremont	— 1914 —	1913 1901 1891
K4	Jerome P.O. Box 407 Jerome 83338	1919 Gooding/Lincoln/Minidoka	— 1919 —	1919 1919 1894
B2	Kootenai 501 Government Way Coeur d'Alene 83814	1864 Nez Perce	1907 1881 1907	1881 1884 1884
C2	Latah P.O. Box 8068 Moscow 83843	1888 Nez Perce	1907 1888 1888	1888 1888 1888
F5	Lemhi 206 Courthouse Drive Salmon 83467	1869 Idaho	1907 1869 1907	1868 1870 1878

Map	County Address	Date Formed Parent County/ies	Birth Marriage Death	Land Probate Court
D2	Lewis	1911	—	1868
	P.O. Box 39	Nez Perce	1911	1911
	Nez Perce 83543		—	1890
K4	Lincoln	1895	1907	1879
	Shoshone 83352	Alturas/Logan	1895	1879
			1907	1883
	Logan	1889 (abolished, 1895 to	—	1879
		create Blaine and Lincoln)	—	—
	Records available in Blaine County.		—	1869
H7	Madison	1913	—	1913
	P.O. Box 389	Fremont	1914	1913
	Rexburg 83440		—	1912
K5	Minidoka	1913	—	1913
	P.O. Box 474	Lincoln	1913	1908
	Rupert 83350		—	1908
D2	Nez Perce	1864	1907	1864
	P.O. Box 896	original	1887	1877
	Lewiston 83501		1907	1864
K6	Oneida	1864	1907	1865
	P.O. Box 191	original	1887	1871
	Malad City 83252		1907	1865
K2	Owyhee	1863	1907	1865
	Murphy 83650	original	1876	1864
			1907	1873
H1	Payette	1917	—	1917
	1130 Third North	Canyon	1917	1896
	Fayette 83661		—	1917
K6	Power	1913	—	1913
	American Falls 83211	Bingham/Blaine/Oneida	1913	1900
			—	1913
B3	Shoshone	1864	1907	1871
	P.O. Box 1049	original	1885	1892
	Wallace 83873		1907	1866
H8	Teton	1915	—	1893
	P.O. Box 70	Bingham/Fremont/Madison	1915	1900
	Driggs 83422		—	1892
K4	Twin Falls	1907	1907	1880
	Twin Falls 83301	Cassia	1907	1907
			1907	1907
G3	Valley	1917	—	1879
	Cascade 83611	Boise/Idaho	1917	1917
			—	1892
G1	Washington	1879	1907	1879
	P.O. Box 670	Boise	1879	1878
	Weiser 83672		1907	1883

ILLINOIS

Carol L. Maki

When Louis Joliet and Father Jacques Marquette arrived in Illinois country in 1673, they found a settler's paradise: fertile soil, sweeping prairies, forests, and water. A traversable network of rivers, easy low-land portages, and the accessibility of Lake Michigan combined to make the future state of Illinois easy to explore. In 1680 Robert Cavelier, sieur de La Salle, with a vision of the economic promise of the area, erected Fort Crevecoeur at the site of Peoria. Henri de Tonti, an Italian, accompanied La Salle. Two years later the two explorers built Fort St. Louis. By 1691, Tonti, who had taken over the settlement when La Salle left in 1685, moved Fort St. Louis eighty miles downstream. The new fort, known as Fort Pimitoui, included several buildings, Father Marquette's mission, and a village of fur traders' European-native families. Cahokia was settled by Seminarian priests in 1699, Kaskaskia by Jesuits four years later. Settlement followed at Fort de Chartres, Prairie du Rocher, St. Phillipe, and Ste. Genevieve.

In 1717 Illinois country was placed under the French government of Louisiana. France then ceded all possessions east of the Mississippi in 1763, although the British did not take possession, at Fort de Chartres, until two years later. From 1778–82 the present state of Illinois was a territory of Virginia and known as the county of Illinois. The American Revolution and the Treaty of Paris in 1783 extended the American boundary to the Mississippi, thus making the present Illinois part of the United States.

The establishment of Northwest Territory in 1787 included Illinois land, but the area became part of Indiana Territory in 1800. Nine years later Illinois Territory was established, followed by statehood in 1818.

By 1800 the population of 2,000 included Americans from Virginia, Kentucky, Maryland, Tennessee, New York, New Jersey, Pennsylvania, and New England. In the spring of 1817 a group of English immigrants settled in Edwards County. Rhode Island farmers established a colony at Delavan, Tazewell County, in 1837. The state served as a conduit for the Underground Railroad before the Civil War.

Migration *from* Illinois was also significant and should not be overlooked by the genealogist. Kansas and Nebraska were the eventual homes of many Illinois settlers. The gold rush to California, the wagon trains of the Oregon Trail, and the open prairies of Iowa all tempted the populace of Illinois to venture further west.

From the late nineteenth century to the present, Chicago's accessibility and employment possibilities attracted a cross-section of all the nationalities. Many ethnic groups either settled in or passed through the state, leaving a great diversity of nationalities populating the city and state.

Vital Records

Marriage records were the first vital records kept by Illinois counties, some of them commencing with the formation of the county. Births and deaths were not generally recorded at the county level until 1877, although the practice was not universal before 1916. Some records existed in cities prior to 1877. The WPA *Guide to Public Vital Statistics Records in Illinois* was published in 1941 and outlines available records.

Births and deaths that were recorded prior to 1 January 1916 can be found at the county clerk's office. Birth and death records beginning 1916, with a statewide index from 1916 to the present, are available from the Illinois Department of Health, Division of Vital Records, 604 West Jefferson Street, Springfield, Illinois 62702. The fee for a search is $10. If the birth record is found, one certification or birth card is issued at no additional charge; additional certifications or birth cards are $2 each. The charge for a full certified copy is $15. Illinois law states that certifications or certified copies of birth records may be issued only upon the specific written request by the person or by a parent or other legal representative; by a department of the state, a municipal corporation, or the federal government; or by order of a court.

If the death record is found, one certification, including name, sex, place of death, date of death, date filed, and certificate number, is issued at no additional charge. Additional certifications are $2 each. The fee for a full certified copy (exact photographic copy of the original death certificate) is $15. The fee for a five-year search for genealogical research is $10. If found, one uncertified copy will be issued at no extra charge; each additional year searched is $1.

Indexes of marriage and divorce records have been kept by this office from 1962 through the present, but only verification will be made. Copies of the original record must be requested from the appropriate county official—county clerk for marriages and clerk of the circuit court for divorces. Individuals may not search the state records. It is interesting to note that in 1868, shortly after the end of the Civil War, the city of Chicago granted 400 divorces.

There are approximately 300,000 marriages representing portions of forty-three counties in the pre-1900 Illinois Statewide Marriage Index as of August, 1990. This is a continuing joint project of the Illinois State Archives and the Illinois State Genealogical Society (see Archives, Libraries, and Societies for both). The staff of the Illinois State Archives will search this index and send photocopies of any information found. Microfiche copies of this index may be used at the Illinois State Archives, Illinois Regional Archives Depositories (IRAD), and in each local genealogical society library in Illinois.

The Illinois State Archives has microfilm copies of records found in some Illinois county courthouses, mostly for southern Illinois. Researchers may use these microfilms at the archives and IRAD Centers. Staff will perform a limited amount of research in these county records in response to written requests. Inquiries may be addressed to the IRAD Coordinator, Illinois State Archives.

The *Illinois Statewide Death Index, 1916–38* has been microfilmed and is available at the Illinois State Archives and the FHL.

Census Records

Federal

Population Schedules.

- Indexed—1810 (only Randolph County), 1820, 1830, 1840, 1850, 1860, 1890 (fragment)
- Soundex—1880, 1900, 1910 (Miracode), 1920
- Unindexed—1870

Industry and Agriculture Schedules.

- 1850, 1860, 1870, 1880 (agriculture)

Mortality Schedules.

- 1850, 1860, 1870 (only counties Ke–Z), 1880

Edgar County lists county of births on the 1850 census. In addition to the three-volume 1860 AISI index (see page 2), a card index for Cook County developed by Bernice C. Richard is at the Illinois State Archives with microfilm copies at the Newberry Library (see Archives, Libraries, and Societies) and the National Archives-Great Lakes Region (see page 8). Printed indexes for the same census year have been published by local county organizations. Over 1,000 cards in the *O* section for the Soundex for the 1880 federal population schedules were omitted. All of the aforementioned are at the Illinois State Historical Library (see Archives, Libraries, and Societies). Only Mound Township of McDonough County survives from the 1890 census.

Territorial

Two territorial censuses were taken for Illinois populace in 1810 (as Indiana Territory) and 1818 (as Illinois Territory). The 1810 extant returns only include Randolph County in the southern portion of the state. What remains of both censuses have been indexed by AISI (see page 2). Originals are at the Illinois State Archives.

State

The state censuses will list only the head of family by name, followed by numerical totals in age categories for the balance of the household. The following enumerations were taken by the state and remain extant.

- 1820—Eighteen counties which included all of Illinois except Edwards County
- 1825—Edwards, Fulton, and Randolph counties only
- 1830—Morgan County only (includes present counties of Cass, Morgan, and Scott)
- 1835—Fayette, Fulton, Jasper, and Morgan counties (includes present counties of Cass, Morgan, and Scott)
- 1840—Thirty-five counties included. Consult *Descriptive Inventory of the Archives of the State of Illinois* (see Archives, Libraries, and Societies) for list of counties.
- 1845—Cass, Madison, Putnam, and Tazewell counties only

- 1855—For all counties except Carroll, Champaign, Franklin, Gallatin, Henry, Jefferson, Lake, Stark, Will, and Woodford
- 1865—For all counties except Gallatin, Mason, Monroe, and Tazewell (Elm Township in Tazewell County has survived)

The "Name Index to Early Illinois Records" (index to state and federal census records 1810–55 and other government documents) is available on interlibrary loan, by surname, from the Illinois State Library and through the FHL.

Some city census enumerations were made in Illinois in the 1930s. There is also a microfilmed military census, enumerated in 1862, by county, which lists men eighteen to forty-five years of age. It can be borrowed on interlibrary loan from the Illinois State Archives.

Background Sources

A good general history for the state is Robert P. Howard, *Illinois: A History of the Prairie State* (Grand Rapids, Mich.: W. B. Eerdman Publishing, 1972).

For several years the local and family history section of the Newberry Library in Chicago has been compiling a biography and industry card index. This index, part of an ongoing project, includes references to biographical sketches found in over twenty-five local histories and biographical compendia published in the nineteenth and early twentieth centuries. Most of the indexed works concentrate on Chicago and Cook County, although a few statewide biographical compendia containing a large number of Chicagoans have also been indexed as part of this project. Written requests for no more than three subjects per letter will be answered by the Newberry staff. For more detailed and original local sources, contact the local historical and genealogical groups and city and county libraries that may have regional history collections. The September 1988 *Illinois Libraries* (vol. 70, no. 7) is devoted to Illinois public libraries with genealogical collections, with emphasis on the unique features of each collection. An April 1986 issue (vol. 68, no. 4) of this same publication describes private genealogical collections, university libraries, governmental agencies, and the Shawnee Library System.

The scope of historical and genealogical research for the city of Chicago, founded in 1833, is extensive. The Chicago fire of 1871 complicates the search for accurate records prior to that year. Chicago research and resources, however, are thoroughly and expertly covered by Loretto Dennis Szucs in *Chicago and Cook County Sources: A Genealogical and Historical Guide* (Salt Lake City, Utah: Ancestry, 1986). This reference is highly recommended for anyone researching at any level in Chicago.

The Bicentennial Project sponsored by the Illinois Genealogical Society endeavored to index at least one history for each of the 102 Illinois counties. It was completed in 1976 by the Genealogy Projects Committee of the Winnetka Public Library. This index can be used at the Winnetka Public Library in Winnetka or at the Illinois State Archives where a search request can be made for no more than two specific individuals. If found, copies of the biographical sketches will be sent.

Maps

County atlases and plat books are at the Illinois State Historical Library (see Archives, Libraries, and Societies). They cover a period of ca. 1870 to 1930 and give details of each township and indicate ownership. Plat books may not be photocopied or loaned. Excellent map collections can also be found at the Illinois State Library; Galesburg Public Library (40 E. Simmons Street, Galesburg, Illinois 614010; Chicago Historical Society (North Avenue and Clark Street, Chicago, Illinois 60614); and the map library of the University of Illinois, Champaign-Urbana.

Illinois highway maps are available free through either of the following offices: Illinois Secretary of State, Communications Department, Springfield, Illinois 62756; or Department of Commerce and Community Affairs, 620 East Adams, Springfield, Illinois 62701.

The earliest Sanborn map (see page 4) for Illinois in this collection is 1884. Suggested references are:

Adams, James N. *Illinois Place Names.* Springfield, Ill.: Illinois State Historical Society, 1968. Addendum by Lowell M. Volkel. Springfield, Ill.: Illinois State Historical Library, 1989.

Mitchell, S. Augustus. *County and Township Map of the State of Illinois.* N.p., 1979.

Newberry Library. *Checklist of Printed Maps of the Middle West to 1900.* Boston, Mass.: G. K. Hall, 1980. The eleven volumes list all known pre-1900 plat maps and plat books for the state of Illinois.

Land Records

Public-Domain State

In 1791 a special act of Congress gave 400 acres to those who were heads of families in the year 1783 at Vincennes or in the Illinois country. This included the region west of Vincennes, Indiana, across the Wabash River. A later act in 1813 provided pre-emption rights to land occupied in the state.

But the major land distributions in Illinois occurred based on its status as a public-domain state. The first GLO opened at Kaskaskia in 1804 and began selling land ten years later. There were a total of ten land districts. The BLM Eastern States Land Office (see page 5) has patents, tract books, and township plats. Land-entry case files are at the National Archives, Washington, D.C.

Sale of public land was first conducted under a credit system, which proved to be unmanageable. Many purchasers overextended their ability to pay. In April of 1820 the credit system was abolished, requiring full payment for land at time of purchase. The same legislation reduced the minimum purchase from 160 acres to eighty acres and the minimum price per acre from $2.00 to $1.25. Several acts of Congress provided for further credit and extensions on the previously unpaid accounts. For further information on this aspect of land sales in Illinois (Record Group 952), see *Descriptive Inventory of the Archives of the State of Illinois* (cited under Archives, Libraries, and Societies). These files, listed as "U.S. General Land Office Records for Illinois" are extensive and include a wide variety of material from "Circulars Received from General Land Office" to lists of names of persons eligible for militia grants and ancient French and British grants affirmed by the Board of Commissioners.

An index created by the Illinois State Archives to the Illinois Public Domain Land Sale Records is in three parts: a statewide alphabetical listing by name of purchaser; a county-by-county listing arranged alphabetically by purchaser; and a geographic listing arranged by section, township, and range. Over a half million names appear in these records, including lands sold by the ten federal land district offices; lands sold by the Illinois Central Railroad; and certain school, canal, and internal improvement lands sold by the state. The alphabetical listing by purchaser is available for sale as a set of microfiche from the Illinois State Archives. Copies of the entire microfiche are found at the Newberry Library and at the National Archives-Great Lakes Region (see page 8).

For information on the War of 1812 bounty-land warrants military reserves in Illinois, see Lowell M. Volkel, *War of 1812 Bounty Lands in Illinois* (Thomson, Ill.: Heritage House, 1977), and Theodore L. Carlson, *Illinois Military Tract: A Study of Land Occupation, Utilization and Tenure* (Urbana, Ill.: University of Illinois Press, 1951).

In some counties there are county recorders to register all subsequent property transactions. Smaller counties give the responsibility to the county clerk. Land records usually have grantor and grantee indexes, with property records beginning with the creation of the county. Some indexes, notably Cook County's, are by legal description of land from the rectangular survey. Illinois Central Railroad land records are in the appropriate county courthouses.

Probate Records

Probate jurisdiction was initially granted in 1819 to the clerk of a county's commissioner's court, a court which served as administrators for the county. The duties included all matters involving estates and the guardianships of minors. The circuit court for that county had jurisdiction in probate cases when actions of the commissioners were appealed. In 1821 probate functions were moved from commissioners courts to the county's probate court.

When county courts (see Court Records) were established in 1848, jurisdiction of probate matters was transferred to them. Beginning in 1870, counties with a population of over 50,000 had probate courts separate from county courts. However, the minimum population number changed several times after that. Effective 1 January 1964, probate functions were turned over to circuit courts.

Illinois Regional Archives Depositories has an unusually large collection of probate records and continues to acquire these genealogically valuable resources. Their collection includes files beginning in 1813. Some very early estate records are included in the Kaskaskia Manuscripts and the Perrin Collection (see Manuscripts) in the Springfield depository.

Where extant, records not accessioned by the Illinois State Archives and the regional depositories presumably are at the office of the circuit court clerk serving that county.

Court Records

As the first nation to colonize Illinois, France was the first to organize its judiciary system. The commandant of Illinois, under the control of the governor of Louisiana, had jurisdiction for major criminal and civil cases, but appointed town judges for each settlement to handle lesser cases. The first court of which there is any record in Illinois is the Provincial Council, established in 1722 for the primary jurisdiction of civil and criminal cases.

Before statehood, the county court for all of what is now the state of Illinois was established in 1779 by Virginia for its "Illinois County". The court functioned within a revised version of the French law but with the influence of the English common law. Being in debt would have resulted in a jury trial and imprisonment. Although Virginia relinquished its "Illinois County" to the United States in 1784, no legal form of government replaced it until the Northwest Ordinance of 1787. From 1788 to 1805 and from 1809 to 1811, the courts of quarter sessions existed. From 1788 to 1809 and from 1811 to 1818, the courts of common pleas were in effect. Orphans' courts existed from 1795 to 1805. Justice's courts survived for the year 1818, and circuit courts existed from 1795 to 1812 and from 1814 to 1818.

A system of circuit courts was established by the Illinois state constitution in 1818. These courts were held by circuit-riding justices of the Illinois Supreme Court, each circuit court covering one or more counties. Jurisdiction for these courts included criminal cases, civil suits for more than $20, appeals from the justices of the peace, divorces, and some naturalizations. Additional responsibilities have been added through the years, including local, county, and state judicial elections.

Today the clerk of each circuit court is responsible for a wide variety of activities, among them selection of juries, maintaining court records, recording probate actions, and filing reports. Twenty-one circuit courts presently serve the state. Records of the circuit courts remain with their respective clerks except for those which have been archived or otherwise stored.

County courts were established in 1845 for only Cook and Jo Daviess counties. Three years later a statewide county court system was created. At that time county courts handled only probate cases (see Probate Records) and misdemeanors. Between 1848 and 1870 in counties not yet organized, the county judge also headed the county commissioners court, which served administrative functions of running daily county operations.

The constitution change in 1870 provided for uniformity in all Illinois county courts, with the exception of Cook County, which continues to have a uniquely functioning circuit court. Jurisdiction for county courts was restricted to probate, apprenticeship, and tax delinquency. Two years later the county courts received responsibility for misdemeanors and for hearing appeals from justices of the peace. Additional responsibilities were added frequently, including divorces and adoptions. However, in 1964 the county courts of Illinois were technically absorbed by the circuit court serving that county, with the county judge acting as an associate justice of the circuit court.

Some of the county court records before absorption have been transferred to the Illinois Regional Archives Depository (IRAD) collections. Records there for St. Clair County, for example, date back to the eighteenth century. A survey of some of these files indicates that the following types of cases may be included in county court records: criminal and common law proceedings, "feeble-minded" petitions and warrants of commitment, insanity proceedings and case files, bankruptcy inventories, and condemnation of property for railroad use. The depositories' collections include *limited* files from these courts, some predating 1800.

The highest level of judicial power in Illinois is the supreme court. It exercises appellate jurisdiction except in those cases in which it exercises original jurisdiction. Beginning in 1818, the supreme court convened at the seat of the state government. From 1848 to 1897 it met at one of the state's three grand divisions, and since 1897 it has held its sessions at Springfield. The Illinois State Archives holds numerous records from the supreme court.

Tax Records

The first known tax authorization in Illinois fell under the jurisdiction of the Territory of the United States North West of the Ohio River. The tax was based on every hundred acres of unimproved, uncleared prairie or wood land, divided into three classes based on quality of earth surface and soil. The rates were thirty, twenty, and ten cents, to be paid annually. Property with delinquent taxes was sold at public auction. There do not appear to be any surviving tax records from this territorial period.

Beginning with statehood, tax records form a large part of county archival material. The 1819 laws provided the first taxation process, imposing taxes on land, bank stock owned, slaves and indentured negroes or mulattoes, plus a poor tax. The tax was collected by the county with income divided between the county and state. Taxpayers lists were eliminated in 1824, and in 1825 a county road tax and school taxes were enacted.

Original and microfilmed tax records at Illinois Regional Archives Depositories include taxable land lists, assessors books, railroad tax books, road tax records, and collectors books, the earliest record dated 1817. Other county tax records are located in county seats.

Cemetery Records

The Genealogical Society of Utah and the DAR have compiled cemetery records for Illinois. *Soldiers' Burial Places in State of Illinois for Wars 1774–1898* is available on thirty-one reels of microfilm from the FHL. Local genealogical societies may have information and possible printed records of cemeteries in their locale.

The Illinois State Genealogical Society is currently coordinating a project statewide to create a directory of cemetery names and locations. The cemetery committee of that society can be contacted for additional information.

Church Records

Despite the early Catholic missionaries in Illinois, their church had almost totally disappeared from the state by the time of the American Revolution. Later migration of English-speaking Catholics reestablished the church in the state. In 1850 the largest religious denomination in Illinois was the Methodists. Baptists, Presbyterians, Roman Catholics, Lutherans, and Congregationalists followed. Episcopalians had organized in the state in 1835, the Disciples of Christ were in Illinois prior to 1830, and the Lutherans grew in numbers with the German and Scandinavian emigration of the 1840s.

In the spring of 1839 a group of five thousand Latter-day Saints, following their expulsion from Ohio and Missouri, were led into Illinois by Joseph Smith. At Nauvoo, originally called Venus and Commerce, they established their Mormon community. The population increased, prosperity increased, and opposition against the Mormons increased. This opposition and dissension within their church ended in the murder of Joseph Smith. In September of 1845 the Mormons were told they were being expelled from the state, an expulsion which led to their migration west.

The Bishop Hill colony of Henry County was founded by a group of Swedish immigrants. Fifteen hundred of them, led by Eric Janson, established a communal existence of a "Bible only" sect in 1846. The murder of Janson in 1853 led to the 1860 dissolution of this religious community. Most of the Jansonists eventually became Methodists.

Some of the local genealogical societies have published regional church records in their respective quarterlies.

Original forms for the inventory *Guide to Church Vital Statistics Records in Illinois; Historical Records Survey* (Chicago, Ill., 1942) are at the Illinois State Archives. Included in the published inventory are name of county and city/town; church name and address; denomination; date organized; date of lapse, if now defunct; description (by years, volumes, file boxes) of minute book, register book of baptisms, confirmations, marriages, members, and deaths; record book of Sunday school or other organization, and financial record; location and condition of records; general condition of all records; bibliographical information on any published or unpublished historical sketches of the church; and other information, particularly as to origins, history, and previous names of church. Files also include descriptions of records of orphanages, schools, and rest homes affiliated with the respective churches.

Military Records

The "Index to Compiled Service Records of Volunteer Union Soldiers who Served in Organizations from the State of Illinois," an index to the National Archives records, is located at the Newberry Library (NARA microfilm publication M539) and Allen County Public Library (see Indiana).

A recent addition at the Illinois State Archives is an 898-reel set of microfilmed Revolutionary War records based on the participation of American military, naval and marine, and enlisted men in the war. Most records date between 1800 and 1900 and come from files in National Archives Record Group 15, including "Selected Records from Revolutionary War Pension and Bounty-Land Warrant Application Files," NARA M805. This may be used at the Illinois State Archives and may be borrowed through the interlibrary loan service from the Illinois State Library (see Archives, Libraries, and Societies). Arrangement is alphabetical by surname of the veteran. Staff of the archives will also search these films upon request by mail and send photocopies of the documents. A billing statement will accompany the copies.

The Illinois State Archives has indexes to men serving in Illinois units during the Indian Wars, Black Hawk War, Mexican War, Civil War, and Spanish-American War. They will search a specified index and send reports on two soldiers. They will also search the *Honor Roll of Veterans Buried in Illinois* for two names (with county locations). The *Honor Roll* is a multivolume set organized by county and includes veteran's name, cemetery, war service, and grave location within cemetery.

A National Home for Disabled Volunteer Soldiers (Veterans Administration Center) was created at Danville, Illinois, in 1898. Records are located in National Archives in NARA Record Groups 15 and 231.

The World War I Selective Service Draft Registration Cards for Illinois are on microfilm, available at the Illinois State Archives. The *Records of the Selective Service Board . . . Illinois, Indiana, Michigan, Minnesota, Ohio and Wisconsin—1917–1919* (Record Group 163) are at the National Archives-Great Lakes Region (see page 8); the collection includes an Index to Delinquent and Deserter Forms (incomplete for some states).

Periodicals, Newspapers, and Manuscript Collections

Periodicals

Illinois State Genealogical Society Quarterly has been published quarterly since 1969 by the society, surveying Illinois original source material, family genealogies, and research questions.

Illinois Libraries is published monthly by Illinois State Libraries, often with genealogical collections information.

Illinois Historical Journal, formerly *Journal of the Illinois State Historical Society*, published four times a year since 1908, has excellent articles on local and state history.

Newspapers

The *Illinois Herald*, published at Kaskaskia in 1814, was the first Illinois newspaper. Numerous indexes of genealogically important data have been compiled from local and county newspapers. It is suggested that researchers contact appropriate local historical and/or genealogical societies to determine if, in fact, indexes are available to make newspaper research more efficient. As an example, the Newspaper Research Committee of the Chicago Genealogical Society has published *Vital Records from Chicago Newspapers, 1833–1839* (Chicago, Ill.: the society, 1971); *Vital Records from Chicago Newspapers, 1845* (Chicago, Ill.: the society, 1975); and *Vital Records from Chicago Newspapers, 1843–1844* (Chicago, Ill.: the society, 1974). Some suggested sources for more information on Illinois newspapers follow:

James, Edmund J. *A Bibliography of Newspapers Published in Illinois Prior to 1860.* Illinois State Historical Library Publications, Number 1. Springfield, Ill.: Phillips Brothers, 1899.

Stark, Sandra M. "Newspapers in the Illinois State Library," *Illinois Libraries* 70 (March–April 1988): 3–4. Updated publication in *Illinois Libraries* every three years.

University of Chicago. *Newspapers in the Libraries of Chicago.* Chicago, Ill.: University of Chicago Library, 1936.

Manuscripts

Some of the very earliest records of Illinois are included in the J. Nick Perrin Collection at the Illinois State Archives in Springfield. The collection is comprised of over 5,000 documents relating to the French, British, and American regimes at Cahokia and to early St. Clair County at Belleville, dating from 1737 to 1850. The earliest known official civil records in the West are included in this collection. The first entry in the oldest volume is a 1737 marriage contract. Births and deaths for 1840 to 1858 are recorded in one small volume. Land claims, tax records, road petitions, registers of slaves and free negroes, and probate records are only a few of the multitude of historically important documents.

The Kaskaskia Manuscripts, also at the Illinois State Archives, are another significant collection for Illinois research. The records, which begin in 1708, are almost entirely notarial transactions. Therefore, they include, among other agreements, acknowledgements of debt, marriage contracts, and land sales. Some clerk of court registers were included in the notary's files. If a notary was unavailable, a priest might draft documents to be filed with the notary's records.

See also Draper Manuscripts in Wisconsin—Manuscripts.

Archives, Libraries, and Societies

Illinois State Archives
Archives Building
Spring and Edwards
Springfield, IL 62756

Included in their extensive holdings are federal and state censuses, war records, land records, and other materials as described in the earlier sections of this chapter. Consult Victoria Irons and Patricia C. Brennan, *The Descriptive Inventory of the Archives of the State of Illinois* (Springfield, Ill., 1978), or request the Genealogical Records and Mail Research Policy brochure.

Illinois Regional Archives Depository [IRAD]
IRAD Coordinator
Illinois State Archives, Archives Building
Spring and Edwards
Springfield, IL 62756

As part of the state archives system, seven regional depositories at state universities include archival material from 102 counties. The records include original and microfilmed local government records. Write to the Coordinator or refer to Roy C. Turnbaugh, Jr., *A Guide to County Records in the Illinois Regional Archives* (Springfield, Ill.: Illinois State Archives, 1983), for a listing of repositories and holdings.

Illinois State Library
Second and Capitol Streets
Springfield, IL 62756

As the head of the public library system in the state, the library publishes *Illinois Libraries,* which frequently includes articles of genealogical interest. The library is the repository for federal and state documents; it holds all county histories and offers some research materials on interlibrary loan.

Illinois State Historical Library
Old State Capitol
Springfield, IL 62701

County histories, plat books, census indexes, cemetery indexes, city material, family and association files, microfilmed newspapers, manuscripts, and photographs are located beneath the restored old state capitol between 5th and 6th streets and Washington and Adams streets.

Illinois State Genealogical Society
P.O. Box 10195
Springfield, IL 62791

The organization publishes a newsletter and a quarterly. Physically, it is located at the Illinois State Archives and currently coordinates a statewide project to create a directory of cemetery names and locations.

Newberry Library
60 West Walton Street
Chicago, IL 60610

Peggy Tuck Sinko's *Guide to Local and Family History at the Newberry Library* (Salt Lake City, Utah: Ancestry, 1987) gives a comprehensive description of the sources, not limited to Illinois, available at this excellent repository.

Special Focus Categories

Naturalization

Although Illinois was not a direct "port of entry" for American immigrants, many individuals regarded it as their destination. Therefore, the number of applications for citizenship in Illinois are enormous. County circuit courts hold naturalization records prior to 1906. The Genealogical Society of Utah has microfilmed some Illinois naturalization records. Early Cook County naturalization files were destroyed in the Chicago Fire of 1871. Numerous Illinois naturalization records are located at the National Archives-Great Lakes Region, 7358 South Pulaski Road, Chicago Illinois 60629, (312) 581-7816; contact the Great Lakes Region for full particulars. Held by this repository is a Soundex Index (Records of Immigration and Naturalization Service, Record Group 85) for naturalizations for 1871–1950. The Index includes several northern Illinois counties (Cook County for 1871–1906) and has been microfilmed by the Genealogical Society of Utah. For any naturalizations that took place in this district court after 1959, contact the United States District Court—Chicago, Naturalization, Room 2062, 219 South Dearborn, Chicago, Illinois 60604. This court also maintains an index of all naturalizations in the court from 1871 to the present. Szucs' work, listed in Background Sources above, contains information on specific naturalization records from Calumet City and Chicago Heights.

Black American

Most people migrating to Illinois during the early years either came from or through the South. As a result, many black slaves arrived in Illinois with their white owners. In September 1807 the indenture law allowed black slaves aged fifteen and older to be brought into the state by their white owners. The law stated that they must be registered with the clerk of common pleas. Beginning on 8 December 1812 free blacks and "mulattoes" were required to register six months after they arrived in Illinois. These records are available through the Illinois State Archives. Many slaves were leased from slave owners in Kentucky and Tennessee to work the salt wells near Shawneetown.

In 1817 Governor Edwards agreed that the indenture law was illegal. The resulting constitutional compromise of 1818 put a one-year limit on new indenture contracts. The free blacks may have been issued freedom certificates after 17 January 1829, possibly recorded in the common pleas court files. Records of blacks in Illinois frequently gave places of origin in the slave state from which they came.

The parish records of the Immaculate Conception Church at Kaskaskia, St. Anne's at St. Charles, and St. Joseph's at Prairie du Rocher have records of baptisms, marriages, and deaths of blacks. The Illinois State Library has a few slave record books from various counties. These list indentured French slaves and freedmen before 1860. See W. Wesley Johnston, "Illinois Free Black Records," in *Illinois State Genealogical Society Quarterly* 14 (Summer 1982): 72–73, for a discussion of extant records.

For further study of black history in Illinois see the following:

Carlson, Shirley J. "Black Migration to Pulaski County, Illinois: 1860–1900," *Illinois Historical Journal* 80 (1987). Its focus is southern blacks who settled in rural areas of the North.

Harris, Norman Dwight. *The History of Negro Servitude in Illinois and of Slavery Agitation in that State, 1719–1864.* 1904. Reprint. New York, N.Y.: Haskell House, 1969. Also available on microfiche (LAC 12841) *Microbook Library of American Civilization.* Chicago, Ill.: Library Resources, 1970.

Hodges, Carl G. *Illinois Negro Historymakers.* Chicago, Ill.: Illinois Emancipation Centennial Commission, 1964.

Perrin, J. Nick, Collection: see Manuscripts above.

Tregillis, Helen Cox. *River Roads to Freedom: Fugitive Slave Notices and Sheriff Notices Found in Illinois Sources.* Bowie, Md.: Heritage Books, 1988.

Native American

When Europeans arrived in the Illinois country, the Illinewek or Illinois Indians were being dominated by the Iroquois of New York and were anxious to have the protection of a nearby fort or mission. In the Illinois valley region, they had once been the largest tribe, a loosely organized alliance of the Kaskaskia, Cahokia, Tamroa, Peoria, Michigamea, and Moingwena bands. Warfare and disease took their tolls, and by 1832 there were slightly more than two hundred of the tribe left in Illinois. The last land cession treaty in that year resulted in those few Native Americans being transferred to a Kansas reservation.

Included in the Illinois State Archives are the following: in Record Group 103.62, "Executive Section, Executive File," papers ca. 1824–32 concerning Native Americans in Illinois (copies of treaties and speeches made by Native Americans and government representatives at peace conferences, and depositions of Illinois citizens taken by state agents dealing with Indian depredations); and in Record Group 100, "Records of the Illinois Territory," there is material pertaining to speeches of, trade with, and treaties with natives, and mention of the Cherokee, Delaware, Fox, Kickapoo, Osage, Ottawa, Potawatomi, Sauk, and Shawnee tribes.

In regard to native lands, see Record Group 952.19, "Board of Commissioners, Ancient Grants Rejected," which lists names of original and present (ca. 1809) owners, including Indian claims. Also see Record Group 953.14, "Terrier of Grants Made to Potawatomi Indians," describing land grants made under the Treaty of Camp Tippecanoe on 20 October 1832; and Record Group 953.18, "Abstract of Conditions of Surveys of Indian Grants and Reservations," 1850. Other sources include:

Stewart Rafert, "American-Indian Genealogical Research in the Midwest: Resources and Perspectives," *National Genealogical Society Quarterly* 76 (September 1988): 212–24.

Tregillis, Helen Cox. *The Indians of Illinois.* Decorah, Iowa: Amundsen Publishing Co., 1983.

Other Ethnic Groups

Illinois has been the home of immigrants from many countries. Settlement patterns within the state frequently varied by nationality. One third of the foreign-born population in Illinois in 1850 was German. Religious, political, and economic factors had caused the massive migration. Cheap and fertile land in the Mississippi Valley brought them westward. Some of the earliest German settlements were in Dutch Hollow and Darmstadt, St. Clair County. One interesting perspective of early German settlers' lives is "Ferdinand Ernst and the Germany Colony at Vandalia" in *Illinois Historical Journal* 80 (Summer 1987), depicting this 1820 settlement in Fayette County.

Many German immigrants came to Illinois as affluent farmers, professionals, and artisans and were able to continue as such in America. There were also those who came with little or no money to spare. Immigrants came via the Great Lakes to Chicago. Working in the industries of the city, they could make good wages to buy their "American" farm. Unfortunately, living costs were high, savings grew slowly, and land values rose rapidly. The "farmer" often became a city dweller.

The Irish immigrant may have stayed in the cities, employed as a day laborer or factory worker. They moved from place to place within the state, but by 1860 the nucleus of the Irish immigrant community was in Chicago. Many Irish worked on the construction of the Illinois and Michigan canal system. When this project was temporarily abandoned in the early 1840s, large numbers of Irish became farmers.

There was considerable immigration from England, some of it prompted by the London Roman Catholic Emigration Society and the Mormon missionaries sent from Nauvoo by Joseph Smith. Kane County had a considerable Welsh population, and the lead mines brought the Cornish. In 1834 the Scottish began migrating to Illinois, their numbers in 1850 totalling 4,660.

The first Norwegian settlement in the Midwest was founded by a group from New York in 1834 along the Fox River near Ottawa. Five-hundred Swedes established themselves at Bishop Hill in Henry County, and the Mormons settled at Nauvoo. (See Church Records for further information on both these religious immigrant groups.)

Although there were scattered French-Canadians in Illinois country very early, there were few immigrants from France before 1830. Metamora in Woodford County was the first important French section, established in 1831, followed by several other French settlements. Bourbonnais, in Kankakee County, with a population of 1,719 in 1850, was a French-Canadian village that maintained Canadian customs for many years.

Colonies of religiously-exiled Portuguese immigrants were located at Springfield and Jacksonville in 1849. There was a cluster of Bavarian Jews in Chicago. Although few Swiss immigrated to Illinois, there were settlements in St. Clair County, in Galena, and in Madison County—the most important center of Swiss population in Illinois.

Szucs's publication, listed under Background Sources above, provides bibliographies of information on the following ethnic groups in Chicago: Afro-Americans, Bohemians, Chinese, Czechoslovakian, Dutch, German, Greeks, Irish, Italian, Japanese, Lithuanian, Mexican, Norwegian, Polish, Russian, Swedish, and Ukrainian. Szucs also states that "at different times in its history, Chicago has been the largest Lithuanian city, the second largest Bohemian city, the second largest Ukranian city, and the third largest Swedish, Irish, Polish, and Jewish city in the world."

Augustana College, Swenson Swedish Immigration Research, Rock Island, Illinois 61201, has immigrant letters, papers of church clergy including journals and correspondence, and a large collection of Swedish-American newspapers. The *Swedish Pioneer Historical Quarterly* is published by the Swedish-American Historical Society, 5125 North Spaulding Avenue, Chicago, Illinois 60625, an excellent research center for Swedish-American genealogy, particularly in Chicago. Their collections include letters, family histories, organization records, newspapers, diaries, books, oral histories, reference files, and photographs.

The University of Illinois, Urbana, Illinois 61801, holds a Czech-American collection of over 31,000 volumes of history, periodicals, original documents, and Czech-American newspapers. A collection of Czech family Bibles and 10,000 Czech history volumes are located at Illinois Benedictine College Library, 5700 College Road, Lisle, Illinois 60532.

For English and Irish ancestry research, contact the Newberry Library. For Irish, also contact the Irish American Heritage Center, 4626 North Knox Avenue, Chicago, Illinois 60630. DePaul University, Lincoln Park Campus Library, 2323 North Seminary, Chicago, Illinois 60614, has an Irish studies collection. Biographies and obituaries of Irish immigrants in Chicago may be found in an index compiled by John Corrigan (not published). See reference in Szucs (p. 152), cited in Background Sources.

When researching German ancestry in this state, contact the Palatines to America—Illinois Chapter, P.O. Box 3884, Quincy, Illinois 62305. Szucs (see Background Sources) states that the detailed church records of German-American churches must be utilized for that nationality in Cook County. Those with Polish ancestry should use the resources of the Polish Genealogical Society, 984 North Milwaukee Avenue, Chicago, Illinois 60622 and the Polish National Alliance Library-Archives, 1520 West Division Street, Chicago, Illinois 60622.

Other suggested sources include the Ukrainian National Museum, 2453 West Chicago Avenue, Chicago, Illinois 60622; Chicago Public Library, Chinatown Branch, 2314 South Wentworth, Chicago, Illinois 60616; Italians in Chicago Project, Department of History, University of Illinois at Chicago, Box 4348, Chicago, Illinois 60680; and the Balzekas Museum of Lithuanian Culture, 6500 South Pulaski, Chicago, Illinois 60629.

Also see Melvin G. Holli and Peter d'A. Jones, eds. *Ethnic Chicago* (Grand Rapids, Mich.: W. B. Eerdmans, ca. 1984), and Melvin G. Holli and Peter d'A. Jones, eds., *The Ethnic Frontier; Essays in the History of Group Survival in Chicago and the Midwest* (Grand Rapids, Mich.: W. B. Eerdmans, ca. 1977); and Mark Wyman's *Immigration History and Ethnicity in Illinois: A Guide* (Springfield, Ill.: Illinois State Historical Society, 1989).

County Resources

Wills, administrations, and probate matters are at the office of the circuit court. Deeds, mortgages, and leases are the responsibility of the recorder of deeds. In mailing requests to any Illinois county office, use the title of the appropriate county officer and "County Courthouse," with the address listed in the chart below.

For some counties there are two years for "Date Formed." The first is the year the county was created. The second is the year it was fully organized if it differs from the creation year. Under the heading "Parent County/ies," the name/s listed may be the county or counties from which the respective county was formed, or it may be the name by which the county was formerly known. "Unorganized" denotes that some formerly non-county area was included. A county name in parentheses is the county to which the unorganized land may have been attached at that time. Counties listed with an asterisk (*) are those in which you may also find records for the respective county since it may have been "attached" to that county for some period of time.

The date listed for each category of record is the earliest record known to exist in that county. It does not indicate that there are numerous records for that year and certainly does not indicate that all such events that year were actually registered.

The information on earliest dates of Illinois county births, marriages, deaths, land records, probate files, and county court records has been obtained through the courtesy of the Illinois Regional Archives. Karl R. Moore, supervisor of this repository, has been exceedingly kind in providing material for use in this publication. He was assisted in this project by Illinois Regional Archives Division staff members John Reinhardt and David Curtin. The basic sources of information used were the *Historical Records Survey* inventories, published and unpublished, which Moore feels are both thorough and accurate. The IRAD team used more recent data when available, comparing that with the Historical Records Survey findings, stating, "The sources cited in our report are always the most recent and authoritative that could be established without actually visiting the county courthouses and taking an inventory." Moore also explains, "We also gave especially close scrutiny to records whose beginning date fell after the date of county organization. Recording of births and deaths did not become mandatory in Illinois until 1877 . . . these records would seldom appear before that date, but marriage, probate, land sale, and court records should have been created from the beginning of a county." Many date discrepancies are explained, according to this report, by the loss of records in fires, floods, or other disasters. When this did not appear to be the explanation, the IRAD team again verified the accuracy of the beginning dates.

In regard to land records Moore states, "Deed records usually coincide with the beginning of a county, so earlier dates in the land sales column usually indicate transcribed records from a parent county, or land patent records that contain information on original land sales from the public domain." He explains, in regard to court records, "The earliest court records for Illinois counties created after 1818 are invariably records of the circuit court. Chancery, civil, and criminal cases are usually filed together at first." For counties created during the territorial period, the following gives the type of their earliest court: St. Clair: Court of the District of Cahokia; Randolph: French Provincial Council; Madison, Gallatin, and Johnson: court of common pleas; Edwards, White, Jackson, Pope, Monroe, Crawford, and Bond: county court; Franklin, Union and Washington: justices' court. Jackson, Cook and Franklin counties lost early court records in fires.

Ernest E. East's "Records Lost in Illinois Court House Fires," *Illinois Libraries* (October 1951): 376–79, provides an interesting history of courthouse fires in the state, plus an informative chart listing the counties, dates, and extent of record loss.

Sources for the county information pertaining to addresses and formation dates follow:

State Board of Elections. *State of Illinois, County Officers, 1988.* Springfield, Ill.: State of Illinois, 1988.

Edgar, Jim, Secretary of State. *Illinois Counties & Incorporated Municipalities.* Springfield, Ill: State of Illinois, 1988.

———. *Origin and Evolution of Illinois Counties.* Springfield, Ill: State of Illinois, 1987.

Drawn by William Dollarhide

Map	County Address	Date Formed Parent County/ies	Birth Marriage Death	Land Probate Court
E2	Adams 521 Vermont, Box 1169 Quincy 62306	1825 Pike/unorganized	1877 1825 1877	1817 1826 1825
K5	Alexander 2000 Washington Avenue Cairo 62914	1819 unorganized (Union)	1877 1819 1878	1818 1819 1821
G4	Bond P.O. Box 407 Greenville 62246	1817 Madison/Crawford/Edwards	1877 1817 1877	1817 1821 1817
A5	Boone 521 N. Main Street Belvidere 61008	1837 (1837) Winnebago *Jo Daviess	1877 1838 1877	1838 1840 1838
E2	Brown Mt. Sterling 62353	1839 Schuyler	1878 1839 1878	1817 1839 1837
C4	Bureau P.O. Box 366 Princeton 61356	1837 Putnam	1878 1837 1878	1817 1837 1837
G3	Calhoun P.O. Box 187 Hardin 62047	1825 Pike	1878 1825 1878	1825 1833 1825
A3	Carroll P.O. Box 152 Mt. Carroll 61053	1839 Jo Daviess	1877 1839 1877	1837 1839 1837
E3	Cass Virginia 62691	1837 Morgan	1878 1837 1874	1826 1837 1837
E6	Champaign Courthouse Annex 204 E. Elm Street Urbana 61801-3324	1833 Vermilion	1878 1833 1878	1833 1833 1836
F5	Christian P.O. Box 190 Taylorville 62568	1839 (as Dane; renamed, 1840) Montgomery/Sangamon/Dane	1877 1839 1877	1828 1839 1839
F7	Clark Marshall 62441	1819 Crawford	1865 1819 1865	1816 1820 1821
H6	Clay P.O. Box 160 Louisville 62858	1824 Fayette/Crawford/ Wayne/Lawrence	1877 1825 1877	1825 1827 1825
H4	Clinton Courthouse Square Carlyle 62231	1824 Washington/Fayette/Bond	1877 1825 1877	1818 1825 1825
F6	Coles P.O. Box 207 Charleston 61920	1830 Clark/Edgar	1878 1831 1877	1830 1830 1831

Map	County Address	Date Formed Parent County/ies	Birth Marriage Death	Land Probate Court
B7	Cook 118 N. Clark Street Room 434 Chicago 60602 **John Reinhardt, Illinois Regional Archives Depository assistant supervisor, states, "Since most of the major records for the county (Cook) were destroyed in the Chicago Fire of 1871, I will provide you with a listing of the earliest dates for several types of records within each category of records which do not appear (on the listing). I have not found an exact date for the earliest land sale or transaction. The Cook County Recorder's Office has these records from 1871 onward. Prior to 1871, the Chicago Title Insurance Company has ante-fire tract and copy books as abstracted from the original documents filed in the Cook County Recorder's Office and from the issuance of the first government land patents. The Illinois State Archives has the original documents related to the government land patents. Federal land sale began from the various land offices in Illinois in 1814. "Probate records present another case where there are several different records to choose from. According to Loretto Dennis Szucs's Chicago and Cook County Sources, a will index survives which begins in the year 1850. The Illinois Historical Records Survey lists a record series titled 'Documented Record of Wills' which begins in 1851 and a series titled 'Abstract of Probate Proceedings' beginning in 1861. All other probate records begin in 1871."*	1831 Putnam	1871 1856 1871	* * 1871
G7	Crawford P.O. Box 602 Robinson 62454	1816 Edwards	1877 1817 1877	1816 1818 1817
G6	Cumberland P.O. Box 146 Toledo 62468	1843 Coles	1885 1880 1844	1885 1884 1885
	Dane	1839 (renamed Christian, 1840)		
B6	DeKalb 110 E. Sycamore Street Sycamore 60178	1837 Kane	1877 1837 1878	1838 1837 1838
E5	DeWitt 201 W. Washington Street P.O. Box 439 Clinton 61727	1839 McLean/Macon	1877 1839 1878	1828 1839 1839
F6	Douglas 401 S. Center P.O. Box 67 Tuscola 61953	1859 Coles	1877 1859 1877	1830 1859 1859
B6	DuPage 421 N. County Farm Road Wheaton 60189	1839 Cook	1877 1839 1877	1835 1839 1839
F7	Edgar Paris 61944	1823 Clark	1877 1823 1877	1823 1823 1823
H7	Edwards Albion 62806	1814 Gallatin/Madison	1877 1815 1877	1815 1815 1815
G6	Effingham 101 N. Fourth P.O. Box 628 Effingham 62401	1831 (1833) Fayette/Crawford	1877 1833 1877	1833 1838 1833
G5	Fayette P.O. Box 401 Vandalia 62471	1821 Bond/Jefferson/Wayne/ Crawford/Clark	1860 1821 1877	1816 1821 1821
D6	Ford 200 W. State Street Paxton 60957	1859 unorganized (Vermilion)	1878 1859 1878	1834 1850 1859

Map	County Address	Date Formed Parent County/ies	Birth Marriage Death	Land Probate Court
J5	Franklin Benton 62812	1818 White/Gallatin/Johnson	1877 1836 1877	1835 1837 1836
D3	Fulton 100 N. Main Lewistown 61542	1823 unorganized (Pike)	1878 1824 1878	1817 1827 1824
J6	Gallatin P.O. Box K Shawneetown 62984	1812 Randolph	1878 1813 1878	1813 1814 1813
F3	Greene Carrollton 62016	1821 Madison	1877 1821 1877	1821 1821 1821
C6	Grundy 111 E. Washington Street Morris 60450	1841 LaSalle	1876 1841 1878	1832 1841 1837
J6	Hamilton McLeansboro 62859	1821 White	1878 1821 1878	1823 1821 1821
D2	Hancock P.O. Box 39 Carthage 62321	1825 unorganized (Pike) *Adams	1844 1829 1878	1817 1830 1829
K6	Hardin P.O. Box 187 Elizabethtown 62931	1839 Pope	1844 1884 1884	1814 1884 1878
D2	Henderson Oquawka 61469	1841 Warren	1877 1841 1878	1818 1839 1841
C3	Henry Cambridge 61238	1825 (1837) unorganized (Fulton) *Peoria/*Knox	1877 1837 1877	1836 1839 1837
	Highland	1847 (abolished, 1848) Adams/Marquette		
D7	Iroquois 550 S. 10th Street Watseka 60970	1833 (1834) unorganized (Vermilion)	1878 1866 1878	1834 1834 1834
J5	Jackson Murphysboro 62966	1816 Randolph/Johnson	1877 1843 1877	1814 1840 1843
G6	Jasper 100 W. Jourdan Street Newton 62448	1831 (1835) Crawford/Clay	1877 1835 1877	1835 1835 1835
J5	Jefferson Room 105 Mt. Vernon 62864	1819 Edwards/White	1877 1819 1877	1816 1820 1819
G3	Jersey 201 W. Pearl Street Jerseyville 62052	1839 Greene	1878 1839 1877	1822 1839 1839

Map	County Address	Date Formed Parent County/ies	Birth Marriage Death	Land Probate Court
A3	Jo Daviess 330 N. Bench Street Galena 61036	1827 Mercer/Henry/Putnam	1877 1830 1877	1828 1828 1827
K5	Johnson P.O. Box 96 Vienna 62995	1812 Randolph	1878 1835 1878	1809 1821 1812
A6	Kane 719 S. Batavia P.O. Box 70 Geneva 60134	1836 (1836) unorganized (LaSalle)/Cook	1877 1836 1877	1836 1836 1836
C7	Kankakee 450 E. Court Street Kankakee 60901	1853 Iroquois/Will	1877 1853 1877	1832 1853 1853
B6	Kendall 110 W. Ridge P.O. Box 549 Yorkville 60560	1841 LaSalle/Kane	1877 1835 1877	1839 1847 1841
D3	Knox 200 S. Cherry Street Galesburg 61401	1825 Fulton/unorganized *Peoria	1877 1830 1877	1818 1830 1836
A6	Lake 18 N. County Street Waukegan 60085	1839 McHenry	1877 1839 1877	1839 1839 1840
C5	LaSalle 707 Etna Road Ottawa 61350	1831 Putnam/unorganized	1868 1831 1870	1831 1831 1831
H7	Lawrence Lawrenceville 62439	1821 Crawford/Edwards	1878 1821 1878	1818 1821 1820
B4	Lee P.O. Box 385 Dixon 61021	1839 Ogle	1877 1839 1877	1838 1839 1840
C6	Livingston 112 W. Madison Street Pontiac 61764	1837 LaSalle/McLean/ unorganized (Vermilion)	1877 1837 1878	1835 1837 1839
E4	Logan Lincoln 62656	1839 Sangamon	1878 1857 1878	1829 1855 1857
E5	Macon 253 E. Wood Street Decatur 62523	1829 unorganized (Shelby)	1877 1829 1877	1827 1831 1829
G4	Macoupin Carlinville 62626	1829 unorganized (Madison)/ unorganized (Greene)	1877 1829 1877	1829 1829 1829
G4	Madison 155 N. Main Street Edwardsville 62025	1812 St. Clair/Randolph	1858 1813 1877	1802 1813 1803

Map	County Address	Date Formed Parent County/ies	Birth Marriage Death	Land Probate Court
H5	Marion P.O. Box 637 Salem 62881	1823 Fayette/Jefferson	1877 1823 1877	1819 1823 1823
	Marquette	1843 (abolished, 1847) Adams		
C4	Marshall 122 N. Prairie Lacon 61540	1839 Putnam	1870 1830 1877	1839 1830 1840
E4	Mason P.O. Box 90 Havana 62644	1841 Tazewell/Menard	1878 1841 1877	1827 1841 1841
K6	Massac P.O. Box 429 Metropolis 62960	1843 Pope/Johnson	1877 1843 1877	1843 1843 1843
D2	McDonough Macomb 61455	1826 unorganized (Schulyer)	1870 1830 1870	1817 1833 1830
A6	McHenry 2200 N. Seminary Avenue Woodstock 60098	1836 (1837) Cook/unorganized (LaSalle)	1877 1837 1877	1839 1840 1838
D5	McLean 104 W. Front Bloomington 61701	1830 Tazewell/unorganized	1877 1831 1877	1831 1831 1831
E4	Menard P.O. Box 456 Petersburg 62675	1839 Sangamon	1877 1839 1877	1821 1839 1839
C3	Mercer 604 N.E. Fifth Avenue P.O. Box 66 Aledo 61231	1825 (1835) unorganized (Pike) *Schulyer/*Peoria/*Warren	1877 1835 1877	1834 1837 1836
J3	Monroe 100 S. Main Street Waterloo 62298	1816 St. Clair/Randolph	1877 1816 1878	1816 1820 1816
G4	Montgomery Hillsboro 62049	1821 Bond/Madison	1862 1821 1877	1819 1821 1821
F3	Morgan 300 W. State Street Jacksonville 62650	1823 Sangamon/unorganized (Greene)	1851 1827 1851	1824 1824 1827
F6	Moultrie Sullivan 61951	1843 Shelby/Macon	1877 1843 1877	1831 1845 1840
A4	Ogle Washington and S. Fourth Street P.O. Box 357 Oregon 61061	1836 (1839) Jo Daviess/unorganized (LaSalle)	1878 1837 1878	1836 1836 1837
D4	Peoria 324 Main Street Peoria 61602	1825 Fulton/unorganized	1878 1825 1877	1818 1825 1825

Map	County Address	Date Formed Parent County/ies	Birth Marriage Death	Land Probate Court
J4	Perry 612 Virginia Court P.O. Box 438 Pinckneyville 62274	1827 Randolph/Jackson	1845 1827 1878	1817 1828 1827
E6	Piatt 101 W. Washington Street P.O. Box 150 Monticello 61856	1841 DeWitt/Macon	1877 1841 1877	1840 1843 1841
F2	Pike Pittsfield 62363	1821 Madison/Bond/Clark	1876 1827 1877	1818 1821 1819
K6	Pope Golconda 62938	1816 Johnson/Gallatin	1877 1813 1877	1816 1816 1817
K5	Pulaski P.O. Box 218 Mound City 62963	1843 Johnson/Alexander	1882 I861 1882	1843 1862 1857
C5	Putnam Hennepin 61327	1825 (1831) unorganized (Fulton) *Peoria	1877 1831 1877	1831 1831 1831
J4	Randolph Taylor Street Chester 62263	1795 (as a territorial county; became a state county, 1809) St. Clair	1877 1724 1877	1724 1722 1722
H6	Richland Olney 62450	1841 Clay/Lawrence	1877 1841 1877	1836 1841 1842
C2	Rock Island 1504 Third Avenue Rock Island 61201	1831 (1833) Jo Daviess	1861 1833 1877	1835 1835 1834
H4	St. Clair 10 Public Square Belleville 62220	1790 (as a territorial county; became a state county, 1809) unorganized	1830 1763 1832	1786 1772 1778
J6	Saline Harrisburg 62946	1847 (1852) Gallatin	1877 1845 1878	1817 1847 1848
F4	Sangamon 800 E. Monroe Room. 101 Springfield 62701	1821 Madison/Bond	1877 1821 1877	1822 1821 1821
E3	Schuyler P.O. Box 190 Rushville 62681	1825 unorganized (Pike)/Fulton	1877 1825 1877	1817 1825 1825
F3	Scott Winchester 62694	1839 Morgan	1877 1839 1877	1823 1839 1839
F5	Shelby Shelbyville 62565	1827 Fayette	1877 1827 1877	1827 1831 1827

Map	County Address	Date Formed Parent County/ies	Birth Marriage Death	Land Probate Court
C4	Stark 130 W. Main, Box 97 Toulon 61483	1839 Knox/Putnam	1877 1839 1877	1817 1839 1839
A4	Stephenson 15 N. Galena Avenue Freeport 61032	1837 (1837) Winnebago/Jo Daviess	1878 1837 1878	1837 1837 1837
D4	Tazewell McKenzie Building, Second Floor 4th and Court Streets Pekin 61554	1827 unorganized (Peoria)	1878 1827 1878	1825 1827 1827
K5	Union P.O. Box H Jonesboro 62952	1818 Johnson	1867 1818 1877	1818 1818 1817
E7	Vermilion 6 N. Vermilion Danville 61832	1826 unorganized (Clark)/ unorganized (Edgar)	1877 1826 1877	1826 1826 1826
H7	Wabash Fourth and Market Streets P.O. Box 277 Mt. Carmel 62863	1824 Edwards	1877 1857 1877	1857 1851 1857
D3	Warren Monmouth 61462	1825 (1831) unorganized (Pike) *Schulyer/*Peoria	1877 1831 1875	1800 1830 1832
H4	Washington St. Louis Street Nashville 62263	1818 St. Clair	1877 1831 1877	1815 1818 1818
	Wayne, Indiana Territory	1803 (abolished, 1803) Knox/St. Clair		
H6	Wayne P.O. Box 187 Fairfield 62837	1819 Edwards	1870 1850 1886	1865 1886 1819
J6	White P.O. Box 339 Carmi 62821	1815 Gallatin	1877 1816 1877	1816 1816 1816
B4	Whiteside 200 E. Knox Street Morrison 61270	1836 (1840) Jo Daviess *Ogle	1877 1857 1877	1838 1839 1838
B6	Will 302 N. Chicago Street Joliet 60431	1836 Cook/Iroquois/ unorganized (Vermilion)	1877 1836 1877	1835 1837 1836
K5	Williamson 200 Jefferson Marion 62959	1839 Franklin	1877 1839 1877	1818 1839 1840
A5	Winnebago 400 W. State Street Rockford 61101	1836 (1836) Jo Daviess/unorganized (LaSalle)	1877 1836 1877	1836 1837 1836
D5	Woodford P.O. Box 38 *Eureka 61530*	1841 McLean/Tazewell	1877 1841 1877	1831 1841 1841

INDIANA

Carol L. Maki

The settlement of Indiana was influenced by the area's great variability in terrain and in soil. While most of the southern one-third of the state is hilly and rough, with very poor soil, the central portion is generally level with deep fertile soil perfectly suited to productive farming. The northern area is paradoxically both flat and heavily glaciated, with considerable marsh land.

French explorers engaged in trapping and transporting furs in the early 1700s had the first contact with the major Native American tribes of this area, the Miami and Potawatomi. The French policy of mutual economic advantage and cooperation did not challenge the native inhabitants' occupation and/or use of the land. The French learned native ways and often married native women.

The French and Indian War in the mid-eighteenth century removed France as a serious threat to the British colonial expansion to the Mississippi. However, the resulting Proclamation of 1763 prohibited American colonists from settling west of the Appalachian Mountains since that land had been reserved for Native Americans and licensed fur traders. Great Britain took control of what would become Indiana, but during the Revolution, George Rogers Clark's expedition guaranteed the area for the United States with Virginia, Connecticut, and Massachusetts all making claims to the land.

At the close of the Revolution, some native tribes in the region chose to continue trade with the French and relocated west of the Mississippi, resulting in land speculators and settlers totally disregarding the earlier proclamation and heading west past the Appalachians. Indiana was first included in Northwest Territory in 1787. In 1790 all of the present state and part of Illinois were established as Knox County in Northwest Territory. Over the next twenty years, territorial jurisdiction went through several changes at the same time as natives, disillusioned with the incursion of settlers, mounted resistance.

Indiana Territory was established in 1800 out of Northwest Territory. Michigan and Illinois territories separated from Indiana Territory in 1805 and 1809, respectively. Statehood became a reality 11 December 1816.

Settlers from western Virginia, North Carolina, and eastern portions of Tennessee and Kentucky arrived in the southern part of Indiana in increasing numbers after the War of 1812. The majority of these settlers were farm families accustomed to frontier living and included many Scots-Irish and Germans who had earlier migrated south from Pennsylvania in the 1700s.

In the early nineteenth century migration to Indiana included upland southerners traveling across the Appalachians and emigrants from the Mid-Atlantic regions coming by land and the Ohio River. Most of the first farms and settlements in Indiana were necessarily located on the Ohio, Wabash, Whitewater, or White rivers or near the streams and creeks from which the rivers originated.

Northern Indiana was settled last because it was a final refuge for Native Americans and because of its more inaccessible terrain. Migration northward in the state was difficult because of the lack of land routes. Early roads traced native and animal trails or military expedition routes. The Michigan Road, from Michigan City in the north to Madison in the south, was opened in 1836, providing a vastly improved north-south land route. The National Road, a United States government endeavor to link the East and West, moved across Indiana in the 1830s. Three major canal projects, improved road systems, and a railroad line—all begun by the state government in 1836—immediately ceased with the financial panic and depression of 1837. However, the Wabash and Erie Canal, covering a distance of 468 miles, was completed in 1853 with assistance from the federal government. Railroads were developed from 1847 through the late 1850s, providing faster and more dependable transportation for people as well as agricultural products.

From the second half of the nineteenth century to the present, manufacturing began to take a firm position in the state's economy. The steel industry along the state's northern tier was a key component. Both Europeans and blacks from the South have significantly added to the state's ethnic composition of today.

Vital Records

The first law regulating marriages in Indiana was made in 1788, and marriage licenses became mandatory in 1800. The statutes of Northwest Territory required that (1) banns be read fifteen days before the marriage, (2) the male be seventeen years of age, and (3) the female be fourteen years of age.

Beginning with the formation of each respective county to the present, the county clerk's office has issued and kept marriage licenses and certificates. Both marriage transcripts (1882) and marriage applications, beginning in 1906 (with additional family information), may have been used in various counties. Prior to 1940 it was necessary for a couple to obtain a license from the county in which the female resided. If an ancestor's marriage record cannot be located in Indiana, check the Cincinnati marriage records. Cincinnati was a "Gretna Green" (no-questions-asked marriage locale) for Ohio, Kentucky, and Indiana.

Statewide collection of marriages from the counties did not begin until 1958. The *Indiana Marriage Index,* compiled by the State Board of Health, Division of Vital Records, 1330 West Michigan Street, Indianapolis, Indiana 46207, begins in 1958. Marriages are indexed by bride and groom, indicating county of license, marriage, and date. Annual indexes for 1958–65 are in book form; 1966–81 are on microfilm and available at the Indiana State Archives, Indiana Commission on Public Records (see Archives, Libraries, and Societies).

Birth and death records were recorded by the county health office beginning in 1882 where they remain before mandatory recording with the state board of health began in October 1907 for births and January 1900 for deaths. Certified copies may be obtained from either the county health department or the Division of Vital Records (address above).

The WPA began to index vital records, county-by-county, for the entire state, but the agency was abolished before the project was completed. Only sixty-eight of the ninety-two counties had their birth and death records (1882–1920) and marriages (generally 1850–1920) collected. The completed county indexes are available in print at the Indiana State Library and Allen County Public Library (see Archives, Libraries, and Societies), among others.

Several more recent projects have involved indexing marriage records for the state before 1955. *Indiana Marriages Thru 1820: In the Counties of Washington, Jefferson, Clark, Scott, Jackson, Jennings, Switzerland, Ripley* (Indianapolis, Ind.: Researchers of Indianapolis, 1981) and *The Hoosier Genealogist* (see Periodicals), which frequently publishes marriage abstracts, are two such projects.

Divorce records are kept in the office of the circuit court. It was not necessary until 1859 to be a resident of Indiana to file for a divorce in that state. Therefore, it is very possible to find divorce records for numerous individuals from other states in the Indiana files.

Census Records

Federal

Population Schedules.

- Indexed—1820 (Daviess County missing), 1830, 1840, 1850, 1860
- Soundex—1880, 1900, 1920
- Unindexed—1870 (index in process), 1910

Industry and Agriculture Schedules.

- 1850, 1860, 1870, 1880

Mortality Schedules.

- 1850, 1860, 1870, 1880

All of Indiana's federal census schedules through 1910 are available on microfilm at the Indiana State Library and the Allen County Public Library. Many rural families were missed during the enumeration of the 1850 U. S. census in Indiana because of poor weather and impassable trails. The agriculture schedule of that year was, however, taken at a different time of the year, and most of the rural residents were included in that enumeration.

Indiana Historical Society (see Archives, Libraries, and Societies) has recently completed on microfiche an every-name index for the 1860 census, available for purchase from the society. In addition, the entire census was computerized and indexed for all categories or variables. For example, it would be possible, through the historical society's computer printout, to locate by name all the ministers (occupation) born in North Carolina (place of birth). The society welcomes questions about their database and the program that produced it.

Territorial and State

Census for Indiana Territory for 1807, compiled by Rebah Fraustein, was published in Indianapolis by the Indiana Historical Society in 1980. No other state censuses exist, although state enumerations of males (without names) above age twenty-one were taken at various intervals beginning in 1820.

Background Sources

Sources for an overview of the state include:

Buley, R. Carlye. *The Old Northwest: Pioneer Period, 1815–1840.* 2 vols. (Bloomington, Ind.: Indiana University Press, 1951).

Cockrum, Col. William M. *Pioneer History of Indiana; Including Stories, Incidents and Customs of the Early Settlers.* Oakland City, Ind.: Press of the Oakland City Journal, 1907.

Dorrell, Ruth. *Pioneer Ancestors of Members of the Society of Indiana Pioneers.* Indianapolis, Ind.: Family History Section, Indiana Historical Society, 1983.

Madison, James H. *The Indiana Way: A State History.* Bloomington, Ind.: Indiana University Press and Indiana Historical Society, 1986.

Taylor, Robert M., Jr., et al. *Indiana: A New Historical Guide.* Indianapolis, Ind.: Indiana Historical Society, 1989.

An important indexing project, Indexes of Persons and Firms, was begun by the WPA and resumed in 1979 by the Indiana Historical Society. Copies of this typescript index to every name mentioned in biographical entries of each county's published histories are at the Indiana State Library, the Indiana Historical Society Library, and the Allen County Public Library and are available through the FHL. A later project on microfiche, *Indiana Biographical Index* (West Bountiful, Utah: Genealogical Indexing Associates, 1983), is a single alphabetical statewide index based on much of the same material as the Indexes of Persons and Firms, with some additions.

A recent source for statewide research is:

Beatty, John D. "Genealogical Research in Indiana," *National Genealogical Society Quarterly* 79, no. 2 (June 1991): 100–22.

Maps

County maps can be found in the surveyor's office of most courthouses and may sometimes be purchased or photocopied. They include historical county maps and contemporary county, township, and city maps.

A. T. Andreas, *Maps of Indiana Counties in 1876 . . .* (Indianapolis, Ind.: Indiana Historical Society, 1968), a reprint of the *1876 Illustrated Historical Atlas of the State of Indiana* (Chicago, Ill.: Baskin, Forster, 1876), has been published by the Indiana Historical Society. It is available for $10 from the Indiana Historical Society.

Indiana Topographical and Geological Survey Maps are available through the Indiana Department of Conservation, State Office Building, Indianapolis, Indiana 46204.

The earliest Sanborn Fire Insurance Map (see page 4) available for the state of Indiana is 1883. The Indiana State Library has a few Sanborn Fire Insurance Maps on microfilm; the Indiana University Geography and Map Library in Bloomington, however, has an almost complete collection of these maps. Atlas and plat maps for each county and township dating 1875 to the present are at the Indiana State Library, including county maps (ca. 1969) entitled Indiana Traffic Accident System that show roads, railroads, churches, cemeteries, schools, and radio towers.

Land Records

Public-Domain State

Following a 1795 treaty with the native residents, the first strip of land was surveyed in southeastern Indiana. In 1801 the Cincinnati Land Office was opened, the first such office to serve Indiana. Vincennes opened in 1807. *Indiana Land Entries,* 2 vols., by Margaret R. Waters (1948; reprint, Knightstown, Ind.: Bookmark, 1977), includes registers for the Cincinnati (1801–40) and Vincennes (1807–77) land districts. Five additional land offices opened as demand increased, principally following the conclusion of the War of 1812: Jeffersonville (1807), Brookville (1819—moved to Indianapolis in 1825), Terre Haute (1820—moved to Crawfordsville before 1828), Fort Wayne (1823), and LaPorte (1833—moved to Winamac in 1839). Registers are available on microfilm at the Indiana State Archives, the Allen County Public Library, and through the FHL. Indexes to some of the land registers have been published. Land was usually sold for under $2 per acre, was frequently sold at public auction, and could be purchased on an installment basis. Land patents were issued by the United States government when the total purchase price had been paid. Frequently, the documents recorded at the land offices included the purchaser's residence "outside of Indiana." Original land records for the years 1805–76, plus microfilmed copies, are at the Indiana State Archives.

Private land claims, which are first-title deeds surveyed outside the regular federal system of townships and ranges, also existed in Indiana. The legal description of these lands are in lot numbers assigned by the governor. The parcels of land are frequently long and narrow, giving each owner access to an adjacent river or road. Patents, copies of tract books, and township plats are available through the BLM Eastern States Office (see page 5). Land-entry case files are at the National Archives.

National Archives-Great Lakes Region (see page 8) has records of the GLO for Indiana 1808–76. These records include the cash certificate books denoting completion of purchase of land from the federal government. The records are arranged chronologically by land office.

A grant of land was provided for George Rogers Clark and his men for their service in the Revolutionary War. The property was situated in what is now Scott, Floyd, and Clark counties. Clarksville, established in 1784 on the northern bank of the Ohio River and within the grant, was the first American town to be laid out in the northwest. Most land owned by individuals prior to 1800 was either in Clark's Grant or at Vincennes. At Vincennes, between 1779 and 1783, the court would grant land, usually 400 acres, to every American immigrant who wanted property.

The recorder's office of the county courthouses has grantor and grantee indexes, land transfers, deeds, titles, mortgages (and releases and assignments of mortgages), and tract books of original land purchases from the U.S. government. The tract books include name of purchaser, purchase date, location (section number, township, and range), and number of acres.

Probate Records

The court jurisdiction responsible for probate changed a half dozen times in Indiana's history before finally settling in the county's circuit court. Thankfully, location of the records has remained with the clerk of the circuit court, although they are often stored in the county clerk's office. The records include wills, probate records, administration of estates, letters of administration, inventories of decedent's personal property, final record books, adoption papers, guardianship records, civil court records, records of minors, records of the insane, and naturalization records and proceedings. A statewide index to wills, *Indiana Wills Index through 1880*, 9 vols. (Indianapolis, Ind.: Ye Olde Genealogie Shoppe, 1983), is available.

Court Records

Indiana settlers wanted a government that was simple, democratic, and located close to the people. The county courthouse became the axis of politics and government that included a sheriff, coroner, circuit court clerk, recorder, and three county commissioners. The legal system was made up of a state supreme court, numerous circuit courts, and township justices of the peace who had jurisdiction for petty crimes and civil cases involving less than $50.

For additional information on local courts and the types of material they hold, see "Courthouse Research in Indiana" in *Genealogy* 7 (July 1974): 1–13; "Using County Records in Writing Your Community's History" by John Newman, in *Local History Today*... (Indianapolis, Ind.: Indiana Historical Society, 1979); and "Managing Your Research in Indiana Court Records" by John Newman, in *Genealogy* 62 (July 1981): 1–9. An important genealogical tool pertaining to immigrants in Indiana is *An Index to Indiana Naturalization Records Found in Various Order Books of the Ninety-Two Local Courts Prior to 1907*, published in Indianapolis by the Indiana Historical Society in 1981.

Tax Records

Records of county taxes were kept as early as 1842, although most were discarded. Remaining ones would be at the county courthouse.

National Archives-Great Lakes Region (see page 8) has records of the Internal Revenue Service for Indiana for 1867 to 1873. These are tax assessment records, arranged by district and then chronologically.

Cemetery Records

The commissioner's office of each Indiana county may have burial records for soldiers, sailors, and marines. If available, the records should include name, age, date of enlistment, discharge date, and death date. Records begin about 1862.

The Indiana State Library holds records of inscriptions from some Indiana cemeteries. The "Indiana Cemetery Locator File," compiled by the Genealogy Division, is an alphabetical listing of cemeteries, indicating the location in the state and the designation in the Genealogy Division of the Indiana State Library where inscriptions may be found. *Cemeteries of Indiana*, by Virgil A. Jewell (typescript, 1970), and *Indiana Cemetery Directory* (Cemetery Association of Indiana, 1961) may also be helpful.

In the 1940s, the American Legion and the Indiana Adjutant General's Office were responsible for the "Veteran's Grave Registration File." The state archives holds the original card file; it has been duplicated on thirteen microfilm reels. Included are soldiers buried in Indiana who fought in wars prior to and including World War I, and it includes fifty-one of the ninety-two counties.

Church Records

Although there was a Jesuit priest in Vincennes by 1749, the Catholic religion in Indiana declined in the late 1700s. Catholics in Vincennes and Fort Wayne were reorganized in the 1830s, and Irish and German immigrants added to the religion's number in the mid-1800s.

However, it was Protestantism that conformed to and enhanced the frontier existence of Indiana. The predominant denominations were Methodists, Baptists, and Presbyterians. A large group of Quakers migrated to the Whitewater Valley from North Carolina. German settlement areas were often Lutheran, but German-Americans established the United Brethren churches in Indiana. The Christian Church (Disciples of Christ) was created in the state in the early 1800s. By the mid-1800s, there were significant numbers of Jewish families in Indiana, most of them in the larger cities.

Of the predominant Protestant body, the Methodist denomination was the largest. The circuit rider, bringing religion to the scattered pioneers in their log cabins, and the camp meeting, with its religious fervor and social aspect, were precisely appropriate to that time and place.

Baptist records are found at Franklin College (in Franklin); Methodist at DePauw University (in Greencastle); Mennonite at Goshen College (in Goshen); Presbyterian at Hanover College (in Hanover); Disciples of Christ at their historical society in Nashville, Tennessee; and French Catholic in the Byron R. Lewis Collection at Vincennes University. There are also Catholic church histories and records at the Catholic Archives, University of Notre Dame, South Bend, Indiana. Quaker records are at Earlham College (in Richmond), and an excellent printed source exists: Willard Heiss, *Abstracts of the Records of the Society of Friends in Indiana,* 6 vols., with index (Indianapolis, Ind.: Indiana Historical Society, 1962–77). It is also available on microfiche from the society.

L. C. Rudolph and Judith E. Endelman, *Religion In Indiana; A Guide to Historical Resources* (Bloomington, Ind.: Indiana University Press, 1986), is organized in three sections: published books, articles, theses, and dissertations; primarily unpublished materials, listed by repository, which do not include individual congregations; and congregational histories listed by county.

The story of Harmony, a religious community of Pennsylvanian Germans that spawned the town by the same name, is covered in Karl J. R. Arndt, *A Documentary History of the Indiana Decade of the Harmony Society, 1814–1824,* 2 vols. (Indianapolis, Ind.: Indiana Historical Society, 1975, 1978).

Military Records

The Indiana State Archives, holds the following military records of interest to the genealogist:

Indiana State Militia, 1812–1851. Alphabetical index of officers commissioned, giving name, rank, and unit.

Card file of Indiana Civil War Volunteers. This may include name, rank, company, regiment, period of original enlistment, place and date of enrollment and muster, age, physical description, nativity, occupation, date, place and manner of leaving the service, information on promotions, and wounds.

Card file of Indiana Legion, which was the Civil War State Militia. This may include name, company, dates of active duty, age, and county and town where organized.

Card file of Civil War Substitutes. This includes the names of citizens who hired substitutes, the names of the substitutes, and the unit to which that person was assigned.

Veterans' Grave Registration. This includes a card file of veterans for fifty-one counties.

Veterans' Enrollments of 1886, 1890, and 1894. The books are arranged by county and township. They include name, company and regiment, state from which the veteran served, number of children under sixteen, medical problems, and physical condition.

The archives also has card files on Indiana Militia (1877–96), Mexican War Volunteer Index, Black Hawk War Militia Index, Gold Star Roll of Honor for 1914–18, Indiana Spanish-American War Volunteers microfilmed registration cards, and Registers of Visitors to the National Encampment of the Grand Army of the Republic at Indianapolis (4–9 September 1893). This repository has service records for all veterans who applied for the Indiana State Bonus for World War II and Korea; these records are restricted.

In addition to the Civil War material in the state archives, W. H. H. Terrell, comp., *Report of the Adjutant General of the State of Indiana,* 8 vols. (Indianapolis, Ind.: Indiana Adjutant General's Office, 1869), is a printed source of service records.

The National Archives-Great Lakes Region (see page 8) holds Records of the Selective Service Board (1917–19) for Indiana. The Index to Delinquent and Deserter Forms (incomplete for some areas) and docket books of registrants, arranged within state by county and division, are included.

Periodicals, Newspapers, and Manuscript Collections

Periodicals

The Hoosier Genealogist (Indianapolis, Ind.: Genealogical Section of the Indiana Historical Society) began printing Indiana genealogical information and extractions in January 1961; it is published quarterly. County, cemetery, church, and family records from this periodical have been published by Willard Heiss in *Indiana Source Book, Genealogical Material from the Hoosier Genealogist,* 3 vols., and index (Indianapolis, Ind.: Indiana Historical Society, 1977–83).

Indiana Magazine of History (Bloomington, Ind.: Department of History, Indiana University in cooperation with Indiana Historical Society) is published quarterly and includes well-written and documented state history articles, listings of recent pertinent publications, and reviews of books relevant to Indiana historical research. Elfreda Lang, *Indiana Magazine of History General Index,* vols. 51–75, 1955–79 (Bloomington, Ind.: Department of History, in cooperation with the Indiana Historical Society, 1982), available from the Indiana Historical Society, serves as an excellent printed index to the magazine. Also see Dorothy L. Riker, *Genealogical Sources Reprinted from the Genealogical Section, Indiana Magazine of History* (Indianapolis, Ind.: Indiana Historical Society, 1979), which includes marriages, will records, various county records, family Bible records, and cemetery and church records; it has a surname index.

Several genealogical societies publish periodicals as well. The Allen County Public Library is the headquarters for the extensive *PERiodical Source Index* (see below and page 7) which covers several thousand periodicals, not limited to Indiana.

Newspapers

Indiana's first newspaper, the *Indiana Gazette,* was published in Vincennes in 1804. The largest newspaper collections in the state are located in the Newspaper Division of the Indiana State Library and the Indiana University Library (see Archives, Libraries, and Societies). For an excellent Indiana newspaper history and finding guide, see John Miller, *Indiana Newspaper Bibliography* (Indianapolis, Ind.: Indiana Historical Society, 1982). It is alphabetically arranged within counties by name of town or city where published. It is indexed and includes listings of approximately 8,000 newspapers published between 1804 and 1980, with locations of all known original and/or microform copies.

Indiana has the unusual requirement of having their county recorders maintain, for public use, bound volumes of all newspapers published in their jurisdiction. These may begin as early as 1852. See also Margaret R. Waters, Dorothy Riker, and Doris Leistner, *Abstracts of Obituaries in the Western Christian Advocate, 1834–1850* (Indianapolis, Ind.: Indiana Historical Society, 1988), which includes all genealogical data found in more than 8,000 obituaries from this Methodist church newspaper. The entries are not, however, limited to Methodists, and they basically cover the states of Kentucky, Ohio, Indiana, and Illinois. There are surname and geographical indexes.

Manuscripts

The major manuscript collections include those at the Indiana Historical Society and the Indiana State Library, with a combined printed guide to both collections—see Pumroy Brockman, Eric Brockman, and Paul Brockman, comps. *A Guide to Manuscript Collections of the Indiana Historical Society and the Indiana State Library* (Indianapolis, Ind.: Indiana Historical Society, 1986). The manuscripts collections of the Indiana State Historical Society Library include the following: Francis Vigo (fur trader) Collection; William H. English Collection, 1741–1928; and Society of Friends Records (meetings minutes include records of marriages, births, deaths, removals, and new members).

Betty Jarboe and Katyrn Rumsey's bibliography, *Studies on Indiana; A Bibliography of Theses and Dissertations Submitted to Indiana Institutions of Higher Education for Advanced Degrees, 1902–1977* (Indianapolis, Ind.: Indiana Historical Bureau, 1980), includes, for example, "The Fur Trade Around Fort Wayne," "The History and Development of the Showers Brothers Furniture Company," "History of the French Lick Springs Hotel," and "Internal Migration in Indiana."

Local history collections exist in other libraries throughout the state. Many can be accessed through the National Union Catalog of Manuscript Collections (see page 8).

See also Wisconsin—Manuscripts—Draper Manuscripts.

Archives, Libraries, and Societies

Indiana State Library
140 North Senate Avenue
Indianapolis, IN 46204

The largest collection of research material in the state is centrally located at the state's capitol. The library's facility includes three major divisions of records: Indiana, Genealogy, and Newspaper. The Indiana State Archives is located in the library; the Indiana Historical Society is located adjacent to the library. The Indiana Division of the library provides the researcher with printed sources—county histories, church records, city directories. The Genealogy Division of the library holds the sizeable microfilm collection of records—vital, deed, probate, court, church, cemetery. Presently, more is being added to the microfilm collection, both here and at the FHL, by the County Records of Indiana Microfilm Project (CRIMP) which continues to film records in the county courthouses. Carolyn L. Miller's *Indiana Sources for Genealogical Research in the Indiana State Library* (Indianapolis, Ind.: Family History Section, Indiana Historical Society, 1984) provides an excellent guide to both of these divisions. In the Newspaper Division an attempt has been made to preserve all dailies and weeklies in the state. A published guide is available from the Indiana Historical Society.

Indiana State Archives,
Commission on Public Records
140 North Senate Avenue
Indianapolis, IN 46204

The keystone to this collection is its focus on military and federal land records, described earlier. Other holdings are described elsewhere in this chapter. A personal name index completed by the WPA can be found in the Indiana State Archives. The card file includes names in pre-1851 archives records including land office, judicial, military, treasury, and internal improvements.

Indiana Historical Society
315 West Ohio Street
Indianapolis, IN 46202

Founded in 1830 and adjacent to the Indiana State Library, the society's collections include rare books, manuscripts (see Manuscripts), over 100,000 images of people and scenes, early midwestern and Indiana maps pertaining to the history of Native Americans and the Old Northwest. The society has published or developed numerous guides and to records materials throughout the state, including the 1860 census project (see Census Records).

Allen County Public Library
Genealogy Department
900 Webster Street
Fort Wayne, IN 46802
Mailing address:
P.O. Box 2270
Fort Wayne, Indiana 46801

This department has thousands of family genealogies; research guides; state, county, and local histories; indexes to births, deaths, marriages, cemetery inscriptions, and wills; census microfilms; passenger lists; and city directories. The collection is particularly strong for all of midwestern local history and has other excellent regional collections as well. The *PERiodical Source Index* (*PERSI*) (see page 7) is compiled from the library's extensive periodical collection. The library is a noncirculating facility, but the staff will do limited research. Response to a written query for information is usually prompt and very thorough.

Indiana Genealogical Society
P.O. Box 10507
Fort Wayne, IN 46852

Southern Indiana Genealogical Society
P.O. Box 665
New Albany, IN 47150

The Newberry Library
60 West Walton Street
Chicago, IL 60610

This repository, although in Illinois, should be considered a source for Indiana research. Indiana holdings are among the library's strongest state collections. Records include indexes and transcripts of vital records, probates, deeds, cemetery records, naturalizations, church records, and extensive land records.

Special Focus Categories

Naturalization

Records, except bankruptcy cases, of the federal district courts of the United States for the state of Indiana have been transferred to the National Archives-Great Lakes Region. These include the Northern District (1879–1959), encompassing the divisions of Hammond, Ft. Wayne, South Bend, and the Southern District (1819–1959), with the divisions of Indianapolis, Terre Haute, Evansville, and New Albany.

Black American

Slavery was prohibited in the future state of Indiana by the Northwest Ordinance of 1787. However, slavery existed in the French households at Vincennes from the mid-1700s and continued despite the ordinance. In 1802 the territory requested a repeal from Congress, stating that a "slave state" would encourage more settlement. Although the petition was denied, in 1805 the territorial government allowed slaves to be brought into the area and held for "longer-than-life" indentures.

The sentiments concerning slavery changed as the government passed from a governor to the pre-state, forty-three delegate convention. An 1816 ruling prohibited slavery, but a "hereafter" clause in the state constitution provided justification for owners to keep their 190 slaves reported in the 1820 census in western counties. In the anti-slavery southeast area of Indiana, slavery of any kind was illegal. Early in the 1820s the Indiana Supreme Court made slavery, including pre-1816 indentures, illegal. There were a few slaves in the state in the 1830s. Despite the anti-slavery sentiments of the Indiana people, free blacks were not allowed to vote, testify in court, or marry whites; their intermarriage with Native Americans was fairly common in Indiana, particularly in the areas of the western frontier.

It is important, in researching blacks in Indiana, to make note of the commonality of intermarriage, the required registration of blacks in 1831, and the fact that many free blacks purchased land. Several underground railroad routes through Indiana helped many slaves escape to the North, although many remained in the state. The Emigrant Aid Society helped thousands of North Carolina blacks migrate to Indianapolis in the 1870s. Additional information can be found in:

McDougald, Lois. *Negro Migration into Indiana, 1800–1860*. Bloomington, Ind.: the author, 1945.

Lyda, John W. *The Negro History of Indiana*. Terre Haute, Ind.: the author, 1953.

Thornbrough, Emma Lou. *The Negro in Indiana: A Study of a Minority*. Vol. 37 of Indiana Historical Collections. Indianapolis, Ind.: Indiana Historical Bureau, 1957.

Witcher, Curt Bryan. *Bibliography of Sources for Black Family History in the Allen County Public Library Genealogy Department*. Fort Wayne, Ind.: Allen County Public Library, 1986.

Native American

In the New Purchase or St. Mary's Treaty of 1818, several tribes ceded the central portion of the state. The Delaware agreed to removal west of the Mississippi. The Miami and Potawatomi were the two major tribes remaining in Indiana after 1820. In 1826 the state obtained tribal land needed for the construction of the Michigan Road and the Wabash and Erie Canal. The federal Indian Removal Act of 1830 allowed the Indiana General Assembly to remove the remaining native inhabitants from the state. In 1838 the plans for removing the Potawatomi were in effect, but some of the tribe objected. Eight hundred were "escorted" to Kansas under an armed militia company in a disorganized and tragic march known as the "Trail of Death."

The Treaty of 1840 required that the Miami, the last tribe in Indiana, be removed to Kansas. The migration did not actually occur until 1846, although several chiefs and their families were given their own land near Fort Wayne. Other suggested sources are:

Dillion, J. B. *National Decline of the Miami Indians*. Indianapolis, Ind.: Indiana State Historical Society, 1897.

Rafert, Stewart. "American-Indian Genealogical Research in the Midwest: Resources and Perspectives." *National Genealogical Society Quarterly* 76 (September 1988): 212–24. See more detail in Wisconsin—Native American.

———. *The Hidden Community: The Miami Indians of Indiana, 1846–1940.* N.p.: the author, 1982.

Witcher, Curt Bryan. *Bibliography of Sources for Native American Family History in the Allen County Public Library Genealogy Department.* Fort Wayne, Ind.: Allen County Public Library, 1988.

Other Ethnic Groups

Beginning in 1850 and through 1920, the foreign born were never more than 10 percent of Indiana's population, the largest percentage coming from Germany. Schools, churches, and social clubs of German nationality helped maintain German culture in the state.

The Irish were the second largest immigrant group in Indiana, although their numbers were not large. Later immigrants, in the twentieth century, came primarily from southern and eastern Europe.

County Resources

During the Great Depression, Indiana pioneered the microfilming of records. A WPA project filmed vital records, court records, naturalizations, wills, slave registers, and some Revolutionary War pension files for at least sixteen counties in the state.

In the 1950s and 1960s, the Indiana State Library microfilmed many vital and court records. They received microfilm copies of Indiana county records via a joint effort with the Commission on Public Records, Indiana Historical Bureau, Indiana Historical Society, and the Genealogical Society of Utah. Twenty-eight of the ninety-two Indiana courthouses suffered courthouse fires; many of them were rebuilt only to be destroyed again by fire or natural disaster. The original county of Knox lost all records in a fire in 1814. *Hoosier Genealogist* 4 (1964) includes a listing of courthouse fires in Indiana.

Land records are located at the county recorder's office, and probates are at the clerk of the circuit court, along with other court records. County commissioner's records in Indiana courthouses are quite frequently the earliest official records of the organized governments in counties formed directly from Native American purchases. Records may include the names of road supervisors, payments made to individuals, appointments for tax collectors, business licenses, naturalization applications, and early justice of the peace dockets.

For some of the following counties there are two years listed for "Date Formed." The first is the year the county was created, the second is the year it was fully organized if it differs from the creation year. Under the heading "Parent County/ies," the name(s) listed may be the county or counties from which the respective county was formed, or they may be names by which the county was originally known. "Unorganized" denotes that it was formed from non-county lands. A county name in parentheses is the county to which the unorganized land may have been attached at that time. Counties listed with an asterisk (*) are those in which records may exist for the county in question. It may have been "attached" to that county for some period of time.

The date listed for each category of record is the earliest record known to exist in that county. It does not indicate that there are numerous records for that year and certainly does not indicate that all such events that year were actually registered.

Information for this section was obtained from Miller's *Indiana Sources* (cited previously under Indiana State Library's listing); Willard Heis, "Indiana," in Kenn Stryker-Rodda, ed., *Genealogical Research: Methods and Sources,* Vol. 2 (Washington D.C.: Amercian Society of Genealogists, 1983); and from those materials available through CRIMP at the Indiana State Library and the FHL.

Drawn by William Dollarhide

Map	County Address	Date Formed Parent County/ies	Birth Marriage Death	Land Probate Court
	Adams New Purchase	1820 (as Delaware New Purchase; renamed, 1827; abolished 1844) Delaware New Purchase		
C7	Adams 112 S. Second Decatur 46733	1835 (1836) Adams New Purchase/ (Allen/Delaware/Randolph)	1882 1836 1882	1837 1838 —
B7	Allen City County Building Fort Wayne 46802	1824 Delaware New Purchase/ unorganized land	1882 1824 1870	1824 1825 1824
G5	Bartholomew Columbus 47202	1821 Delaware New Purchase/Jackson	1883 1821 1882	1822 1821 1821
D2	Benton 700 E. Fifth Fowler 47944	1840 Jasper	1882 1840 1882	1840 1840 —
D6	Blackford Hartford City 47348	1838 (1839) Jay	— 1839 1882	1836 1839 —
E4	Boone 1 Courthouse Square Room 212 Lebanon 46052	1830 Wabash New Purchase/ (Hendricks)/Adams New Purchase/ (Hendricks/Marion)	1882 1831 1882	1856 1846 —
G4	Brown Nashville 47448 *Record loss, 1873.*	1836 Bartholomew/Jackson/Monroe	— 1836 1882	1873 1837 —
D3	Carroll Delphi 46923	1828 Adams New Purchase/(Hamilton)/ Wabash New Purchase/ (Fountain)/unorganized land	1882 1828 1882	1829 1829 —
C4	Cass 200 Court Park Logansport 46947	1829 unorganized land (Carroll)	1882 1829 1882	1830 1829 —
J5	Clark Court Avenue Jeffersonville 47130	1801 Knox	1882 1807 1882	1801 1801 1801
G2	Clay Brazil 47834 *Record loss, 1851.*	1825 Owen/Putnam/Vigo/Sullivan	1881 1851 1882	1825 1873 —
D4	Clinton Frankfort 46041	1830 Adams New Purchase/ (Tippecanoe)/Wabash New Purchase	1882 1830 1882	1829 1830 —
K4	Crawford P.O. Box 375 English 47118	1818 Harrison/Orange/Perry	1819 1818 —	1818 1818 —
H3	Daviess Washington 47501	1817 Knox	1882 1817 1882	1817 1817 —

Map	County Address	Date Formed Parent County/ies	Birth Marriage Death	Land Probate Court
A7	De Kalb Auburn 46706	1835 (1837) unorganized land/ (Allen/LaGrange)	1882 1837 1882	1837 1847 —
G7	Dearborn 550 Main Street Lawrenceburg 47025 *Record loss, 1826.*	1803 Clark	1882 1806 1882	1821 1824 1824
G6	Decatur 150 Courthouse Street, #5 Greensburg 47240	1822 unorganized land/Delaware New Purchase	1822 1822 —	1822 1822 1822
	Delaware New Purchase	1820 (renamed Adams New Purchase, 1827) unorganized land *Fayette/*Franklin/*Jackson/*Jennings/ *Randolph/*Ripley/*Wayne/*Bartholomew		
E6	Delaware P.O. Box 1089 Muncie 47305	1827 Delaware New Purchase *Randolph	1882 1827 1882	1829 1830 —
J3	Dubois Jasper 47546 *Record loss, 1839.*	1818 Pike	1882 1839 1882	1839 1840 —
A5	Elkhart Goshen 46526	1830 unorganized land/(Cass/Allen)	1882 1830 1882	1831 1830 —
F6	Fayette 401 Central Avenue Connersville 47331	1819 Franklin/Wayne/unorganized land	1883 1819 1829	1816 1819 —
J5	Floyd Room 235 New Albany 47150	1819 Clark/Harrison	1882 1819 1882	1818 1819 —
E2	Fountain Covington 47932	1826 Montgomery/Wabash New Purchase *Parke	1887 1826 1882	1827 1827 —
G7	Franklin 459 Main Street Brookville 47012	1811 Clark/Dearborn	1882 1811 1882	1811 1811 1811
B4	Fulton 815 Main Street Rochester 46975	1835 (1836) unorganized land/ (Cass/Elkhart/St. Joseph)	— 1836 1882	1836 1838 1836
J1	Gibson Princeton 47670	1813 Knox	1882 1813 1880	1836 1813 1813
D5	Grant Marion 46953	1831 Adams New Purchase/ (Randolph/ Delaware/ Madison)/ unorganized land/ (Cass)	— 1831 —	1831 1831 —
H3	Greene Bloomfield 47424	1821 Sullivan/unorganized land/(Daviess)	1885 1821 1893	1822 1823 —

Map	County Address	Date Formed Parent County/ies	Birth Marriage Death	Land Probate Court
E5	Hamilton Noblesville 46060	1823 Delaware New Purchase	1882 1833 1882	1825 1823 —
	Hamilton County, Northwest Territory, was formed in 1798 from territorial Knox County and included parts of Ohio and Indiana.			
F5	Hancock Greenfield 46140	1827 (1828) Madison	1882 1828 1882	1827 1828 —
K5	Harrison 300 N. Capital Avenue Corydon 47112	1808 Clark/Knox	1882 1809 1882	1807 1809 1809
F4	Hendricks Danville 46122	1824 Delaware New Purchase/ Wabash New Purchase	1882 1824 1882	1823 1822 —
E6	Henry New Castle 47362	1822 Delaware New Purchase	1882 1823 1882	1824 1822 —
D4	Howard Room 111 Kokomo 46901	1844 (as Richardville; renamed, 1846) unorganized land/(Carroll/Cass/Miami)	1875 1844 1875	1846 1844 —
C6	Huntington Huntington 46750	1832 (1834) Adams New Purchase/(Allen/Grant)	1875 1837 1882	1834 1841 —
H5	Jackson Brownstown 47220	1816 Clark/Jefferson/Washington	1882 1816 1882	1815 1817 —
B3	Jasper Rensselaer 47978 *Record loss, 1864.*	1835 (1838) Wabash New Purchase/ unorganized land/(Warren/White)	1882 1850 1882	1838 1864 —
D7	Jay Portland 47371	1835 (1836) Adams New Purchase/ (Delaware/Randolph)	1882 1837 1882	1836 — —
H6	Jefferson Madison 47250	1811 Clark/Dearborn	1882 1811 —	1811 1811 1811
H5	Jennings Vernon 47282	1817 Jackson/Jefferson	1882 1818 1882	1817 1818 1817
F4	Johnson 5 W. Jefferson Franklin 46131 *Record loss 1849 and 1874.*	1823 Delaware New Purchase	1882 1830 1882	1825 1821 —
H2	Knox 19 S. Ford Vincennes 47591	1790 (Indiana Territory 1800) unorganized land	1882 1806 1882	1783 1790 1801
	Knox County, Northwest Territory, was formed from non-county area in 1790. This included segments of present Illinois, Michigan, Ohio, Wisconsin, plus all of Indiana. Knox County became part of Indiana Territory in 1800 although much of the original county had been formed into other counties by that time. It became an Indiana county in 1816. Record loss, 1814.			

Map	County Address	Date Formed Parent County/ies	Birth Marriage Death	Land Probate Court
B5	Kosciusko 100 W. Center Street Warsaw 46580	1835 (1836) unorganized land/ (Cass/Elkhart/Grant)	1882 1830 1882	1834 1836 —
A3	La Porte La Porte 46350	1832 St. Joseph/unorganized land	1882 1832 1882	1831 1832 —
A6	Lagrange 114 W. Michigan Street Lagrange 46761	1832 unorganized land/(Allen/Elkhart)	1882 1832 1882	1832 1832 —
A2	Lake 2293 N. Main Crown Point 46307	1836 (1837) Porter/Newton	1882 1837 1882	1837 1854 —
H4	Lawrence Bedford 47421	1818 Orange	1882 1818 1882	1819 1818 —
E5	Madison 16 E. Ninth Street Anderson 46016 *Record loss, 1880.*	1823 Delaware New Purchase *Marion	1882 1853 1882	1822 1879 —
F4	Marion City-County Building Room W-122 Indianapolis 46204	1822 Delaware New Purchase	1882 1822 1882	1822 1822 —
B4	Marshall 501 N. Center Street Plymouth 46563	1835 unorganized land/(Cass/Elkhart/ St. Joseph)	— 1836 —	1834 1834 —
H3	Martin P.O. Box 170 Shoals 47581	1820 Daviess/Dubois	1882 1820 1882	1820 1821 —
C5	Miami 35 S. Broadway Peru 46970 *Record loss, 1843.*	1832 Cass/unorganized land	1882 1843 1882	1836 1843 —
G4	Monroe P.O. Box 547 Bloomington 47402	1818 Orange	1882 1818 1886	1817 1818 1854
E3	Montgomery Crawfordsville 47933	1823 Wabash New Purchase *Parke/*Putnam	1882 1823 1882	1821 1822 —
F4	Morgan Martinsville 46151 *Record loss, 1876.*	1822 Delaware New Purchase/ Wabash New Purchase	1882 1822 1899	1822 1822 —
	Newton (old)	1835 (abolished, 1839) unorganized land/(St. Joseph/Warren/White)		
C2	Newton (present) Kentland 47951	1859 (re-created) Jasper	1882 1860 1882	1838 1860 —

Map	County Address	Date Formed Parent County/ies	Birth Marriage Death	Land Probate Court
A6	Noble 101 N. Orange Street Albion 46701 *Record loss, 1859.*	1835 (1836) unorganized land/(Allen/Elkhart/ La Grange)	1882 1859 1882	1834 1854 —
H7	Ohio Main Street Rising Sun 47040	1844 (1844) Dearborn	1882 1844 1882	1844 1844 —
J4	Orange Paoli 47454	1816 Gibson/Knox/Washington	1882 1816 1882	1816 1816 —
G3	Owen Spencer 47460	1819 Daviess/Sullivan	1882 1819 1882	1819 1819 —
F2	Parke Rockville 47872 *Record loss, 1833.*	1821 Vigo/unorganized land/ Wabash New Purchase	1882 1829 1882	1816 1833 —
K3	Perry Cannelton 47520	1814 Gibson/Warrick	1882 1814 1882	1815 1813 1815
J2	Pike Main Street Petersburg 47567	1817 Gibson/Knox/Perry	1882 1817 1887	1817 1817 1817
A3	Porter 16 E. Lincoln Way Valparaiso 46383	1835 (1836) unorganized land/(St. Joseph)	1884 1836 1884	1833 1839 —
K1	Posey Mount Vernon 47620	1814 Warrick	1882 1814 1882	1812 1815 1815
B3	Pulaski Winamac 46996	1835 (1839) unorganized land/(Cass/White)	— 1839 1882	1840 1839 —
F3	Putnam Greencastle 46135	1822 Owen/Vigo/ Wabash New Purchase	1882 1820 1882	1824 1825 —
	Randolph (old) *Randolph County, Northwest Territory, was formed in 1795 from territorial St. Clair County. In 1800 Randolph became an Indiana territorial county. The present Randolph County was created in 1818. See below.*	1790 (Indiana Territory, 1800) (Illinois Territory, 1809) St. Clair—Northwest Territory		
E7	Randolph (present) Third Floor Winchester 47394 *Note also Randolph, Illinois Territory, above.*	1818 Wayne	1882 1819 1882	1820 1819 —
	Richardville	1844 (1844) (renamed Howard, 1846) unorganized land/(Carroll/Cass/Miami)		
G6	Ripley P.O. Box 177 Versailles 47042	1816 (1818) Dearborn/Jefferson *Jennings	1882 1818 1882	1818 1818 1818

Map	County Address	Date Formed Parent County/ies	Birth Marriage Death	Land Probate Court
F6	Rush Rushville 46173	1822 Delaware New Purchase	— 1822 1823	1822 1822 1822
	St. Clair	1790 (Indiana Territory, 1800) (Illinois Territory, 1809) unorganized land		
A4	St. Joseph Main Street South Bend 46601	1830 unorganized land/ (Carroll/Tippecanoe/Cass)	1882 1830 1882	1830 1830
J5	Scott Scottsburg 47170	1820 Clark/Jackson/Jefferson/ Jennings/Washington	1882 1820	1819 1820
F5	Shelby S. Harrison Street Shelbyville 46176	1822 Delaware New Purchase	1882 1822 1882	1822 1822 —
K3	Spencer P.O. Box 12 Rockport 47635	1818 Perry/Warrick	1882 1818 1882	1818 1818 —
B3	Starke Knox 46534	1835 (1850) St. Joseph/unorganized land/ (Starke/Cass/White)	1894 1840 1894	1850 1850 —
A7	Steuben S.E. Public Square Courthouse Annex Angola 46703	1835 (1837) unorganized land/(LaGrange)	— 1832 —	1836 1845 —
G2	Sullivan 936 N. State Street Sullivan 47882 *Record loss, 1850.*	1817 Knox	1882 1850 1880	1850 1844 —
H7	Switzerland Vevay 47043	1814 Dearborn/Jefferson	1882 1814 1882	1814 1814 —
D3	Tippecanoe 20 N. Third Street Lafayette 47901	1826 Wabash New Purchase/unorganized land	1882 1826 1882	1826 1825 —
D4	Tipton Tipton 46072	1844 (1844) Adams New Purchase/unorganized land (Cass/Hamilton/Miami)	— 1844 —	1844 1844 —
F7	Union 26 W. Union Street Liberty 47353	1821 Fayette/Franklin/Wayne	— 1821 —	1821 1821 —
K2	Vanderburgh County Courts Building, Room 216 Evansville 47708	1818 Gibson/Posey/Warrick	1882 1818 1882	1818 1821 1825
E2	Vermillion Newport 47966	1824 Parke/unorganized land/ Wabash New Purchase	1882 1824 1882	1824 1827 1825
G2	Vigo Third and Wabash, Room 22 Terre Haute 47807	1818 Sullivan	1882 1818 1882	1816 1818 —

Map	County Address	Date Formed Parent County/ies	Birth Marriage Death	Land Probate Court
	Wabash 650 Valleybrook Wabash 46992 *Record loss, 1870.*	1832 (1835) Adams New Purchase/(Grant)/ unorganized land/(Cass)	— 1835 —	1835 1847 —
C5	Wabash New Purchase Eliminated 1835	1820 unorganized land *Monroe/*Owen/*Vigo/*Parke		
D2	Warren Williamsport 47993	1827 Wabash New Purchase/ unorganized land/(Vermillion) *Fountain/	1882 1827 1882	1830 1829 —
K2	Warrick Room 105 Boonville 47601	1813 Knox	1882 1813 1882	1813 1814 1813
J4	Washington Salem 47167	1814 Clark/Harrison	1882 1815 1882	1814 1814 1814
E7	Wayne P.O. Box 1172 Richmond 47375 *See also Wayne County below.*	1811 Clark/Dearborn/Knox	1882 1811 1882	1816 1812 1811
	Wayne—Northwest Territory	1796 (abolished, 1800) Knox/unorganized land		
	Wayne County, Northwest Territory, was formed in 1796 from territorial Knox county and unorganized land. This included portions of modern Illinois, Michigan, Ohio, and Wisconsin. Wayne County, outside Northwest Territory, was eliminated in 1800. In 1803 Wayne County, Indiana Territory, was created from territorial Knox and St. Clair County and unorganized area. This included parts of today's Illinois, Indiana, Wisconsin, and most of Michigan. In 1811 Wayne County, Indiana Territory, was created from Clark, Dearborn, and Knox counties. This became an Indiana state county in 1816.			
C6	Wells Main and Market Bluffton 46714	1835 (1837) Adams New Purchase/ (Allen/Delaware/Randolph)	1883 1837 1883	1838 1838
C3	White Monticello 47960	1834 Wabash New Purchase/(Carroll)	1882 1834 1882	1834 1835 —
B6	Whitley 302 S. Chauncey Street Columbia City 46725	1835 (1838) unorganized land/(Allen/Elkhart/Grant) *Huntington	 1838 1882	1813 1839

IOWA

Carol L. Maki

From 1671 through 1689 the Iowa region was claimed for France by Sieur Saint-Lusson, Daniel de Greysolon Sieur de Luth (Du Luth), Robert Cavalier Sieur de la Salle, and Nicolas Perrot. Several jurisdictional changes occurred in Iowa's early history. France ceded the Iowa region to Spain in 1762, although it was returned in 1800 preceding the Louisiana Purchase in 1803, which made it United States territory. As part of the United States, Iowa was first included in Illinois Territory (1808) and then Missouri Territory (1812). Migrating groups from the states began the first settlements in 1832. Before statehood was established in 1846, these settlements were included in Michigan Territory (1834), Wisconsin Territory (1836), and finally its own territory in 1838.

Prior to 1800, Native Americans and French were the only residents of Iowa Territory. Julien DuBuque, a French Canadian, began mining lead in 1788 near present-day Dubuque, employing some of the normally unfriendly Fox tribal members in his mines. In 1796 DuBuque received a grant of land, including the lead mines, from the Spanish governor of Louisiana. The Spanish government gave additional grants. Louis Honore Tesson obtained 6,000 acres in 1799 in the present Lee County, and Basil Giard acquired land a year later in Clayton County. Meriwether Lewis and William Clark spent time near the Missouri River in Iowa in 1804. On 23 August 1805, the explorer Zebulon Pike raised the first American flag in Iowa, flying the stars and stripes from an area now on the southern edge of Burlington. A U.S. Army detachment from St. Louis built Fort Madison in 1808. Five years later, the fort was abandoned and burned by the departing troops whose exodus was caused by Chief Black Hawk and the War of 1812.

The year 1816 included the establishment of Fort Armstrong on Rock Island. Settlers from the east arrived as early as 1820. Danish immigrants settled in Lee County in 1832. A year later settlements were established by pioneers from Tennessee, Kentucky, Missouri, Illinois, Ohio, and Indiana.

With the creation of Iowa Territory in 1838, there was a great influx of settlers. The first territorial capital was established at Burlington. The new Iowans in the 1840s included Scandinavians, Dutch, Germans, Irish, Scots, and Welsh. New Englanders arrived in 1840, Quakers in 1841, and Mormons migrated across Iowa in 1846, the year Iowa became a state. The following year immigrants from the Netherlands settled at Pella. A large number of families migrated from Ohio to Iowa in 1854. From 1850 through 1880, there was a mass migration of Germans to the state. Migration *from* Iowa also occurred during this period, with a large exodus to California as a result of the gold rush beginning in 1849.

The steamboat industry peaked from 1850 to 1877, while the first railroad in the state was completed in 1855. Both had significant influence on the settlement of the state. By 1860 the state population was 674,913. Ten years later it was 1,194,020.

Most of the immigrants settling in Iowa during the latter part of the nineteenth century were from northwestern Europe. They could purchase land cheaply but found the thick prairie sod difficult to improve for farming. Because of the need for heavy equipment and cooperative drainage plans, farming was much more commercial than family-oriented. The commercial aspect necessitated an extensive railroad network, resulting in high freight prices and a response in the form of the Grange Movement rebelling against the railroads. Financial depressions in 1873, 1893, and the 1930s greatly affected Iowa. As the twentieth century brought more efficient farming methods for mass production, many of the families who had owned farms moved to the cities. Today, farming continues to be an important aspect of the economy and exists with a sizeable number of urban industries as well as the still rural ones like the community-owned Amana Colonies.

Vital Records

The Iowa vital records system originated on 1 July 1880 with legislation establishing a State Board of Health. A few events, primarily marriages, were recorded in the counties prior to 1880, but little information is included in those records. Early birth records contain only minimal data—name, date, place, and names of parents. Death certificates prior to 1904 do not include the names of the parents of the deceased.

It is estimated that between 1880 and 1921 only about 50 percent of the births and deaths were registered. However, because of a provision for delayed birth registration, almost 470,000 delayed birth records have been filed with the Bureau of Vital Statistics. Marriage record registration began in many areas with the organization of the county.

All *county* vital records in Iowa are accessible to the public by personal inspection or by a written request to the clerk of the district court in the county where the event occurred. *State* vital records are not open to the public. Copies of certificates, however, are issued to grandparents, parents, children, a spouse, brothers or sisters, legal guardians, or respective legal representatives. An applicant must have a direct and tangible interest in any specified record and must have the ability to present a direct lineal relationship to the registrant. The purpose for which a certificate is needed should also be indicated. A fee of $6 is required for each record search conducted by the state office, and one copy of a located certificate is provided. The fee is not refundable. If the exact name, date, and place of an event are not known, you must use an index schedule of rates. For the proper forms and the index schedule, contact the Iowa Department of Public Health, Bureau of Vital Records/Statistics, Lucas State Office Building, Des Moines, Iowa 50319.

The State Historical Society of Iowa (see Archives, Libraries, and Societies), in cooperation with the Genealogical Society of Utah, is involved in a statewide county records microfilming project. Records included in this project are vital statistics, probate, and land. Copies of these microfilms, with an index to records filmed in each county, are available for use at the State Historical Society's libraries and many are now in the FHL. Contact the State Historical Society of Iowa for current status on individual counties. State vital records, 75 years old or older, are now available, with some limitations, at the State Archives, a division of the State Historical Society of Iowa.

Many of the local chapters of the Iowa Genealogical Society (see Archives, Libraries, and Societies below) have publications of vital records in their respective counties. A statewide publication listing, with ordering information, is available through the state society.

Census Records

Federal

Population Schedules.

- Indexed—1840, 1850, 1860, 1870
- Soundex—1880, 1900, 1920
- Unindexed—1910

Industry and Agriculture Schedules.

- 1850, 1860, 1870, 1880

Mortality Schedules.

- 1850, 1860, 1870, 1880

The state archives at the State Historical Society of Iowa does hold, in addition to the above mentioned census records, the *manuscript state copies* of the 1850, 1860, 1870 federal censuses for Iowa, but they are only available for use on microfilm. The microfilmed state copies, however, make it possible to compare the microfilm edition of the *federal copy* from the National Archives for handwriting, spelling errors, completeness of the copy, or other problems suspected from the entry.

Territorial and State

In *Iowa History Sources: Census Data for Iowa,* No. 1 (Iowa City, Iowa: State Historical Society of Iowa, 1973), author Loren N. Horton states, "Iowa is rich in the number of censuses taken, probably because legislative apportionment was based upon them during the nineteenth century. This was a period of rapid migration into the area and rapid disposal of public lands, therefore it was thought necessary to have a census taken almost every election in order to maintain fairness in distributing legislative seats" (p. 1).

Although Iowa did indeed enumerate its population frequently, both in special and regular censuses, not all counties complied each time. Some enumerations are only for specific cities. Also, many of the censuses that were actually completed no longer exist. Because of this complexity, any research in these records should be preceded by obtaining the aforementioned publication by Loren N. Horton and the *Iowa Special Census* microfilm register from the research library of the State Historical Society of Iowa at Des Moines.

Taking into consideration that not all years include all counties, nor all townships of a county, and that in fact some are *very* limited, the following census enumerations are available for Iowa:

The Wisconsin Territorial Census for 1836 includes the original counties of Dubuque and Des Moines, Iowa. This is indexed, printed, microfilmed and available at the State

Historical Society of Iowa. A microfilm copy of the territorial census of 1836 is also held by the National Archives-Central Plains Region (see page 8) and may also be found in "The Territorial Census for 1836," *Collections of the State Historical Society of Wisconsin,* Volume XIII, edited by Reuben Gold Thwaites, (Madison, Wis.: Democrat Printing Co., State Printer 1895, pages 247–70).

Most of the following "head of households" census enumerations have been indexed in some form. They are held in manuscript form by the state archives at the State Historical Society of Iowa and are available for research on microfilm. They are listed by year and county: 1838—Van Buren; 1844—Keokuk; 1846—Louisa, Polk, and Wapello; 1847—Boone, Clinton, Davis, Louisa, Marion, Polk, Scott, Van Buren, and Wapello; 1849—Benton, Boone, Clinton, Louisa, Madison, Poweshiek, Scott, Van Buren, and Washington; 1851—Cedar, Clinton, Decatur, Guthrie, Iowa, Johnson, Madison, Mahaska, Page, Pottawattamie, Poweshiek, Scott, and Washington; 1852—forty-five counties included; 1853—Warren County for Allen, Greenfield, Lynn, and Richland townships only; 1854—fifty-two counties included; 1859—Carroll and Sac.

For the 1847 Iowa state census, additional details are indicated for some members of the Church of Jesus Christ of Latter-day Saints. The enumeration of its members in Pottawattamie includes the standard information but adds a count of wagons and guns; number of family members ill, aged, or infirm; and number of oxen, cattle, and horses. It is thought that the extended census information was part of a preparation for moving these families westward.

Clinton in Clinton County is enumerated for 1887 in two bound volumes. The following are Iowa Special Censuses on microfilm: 1881—Mason City, Cerro Gordo County; 1888—Algona, Kossuth County; 1889—Cherokee, Cherokee County; 1889—North part of Des Moines, Polk County; 1891—Emmetsburg, Emmet County; 1891—Spencer, Clay County; 1891—Villisca, Montgomery County; 1892—Carroll, Carroll County; 1892—Eagle Grove, Wright County; 1892—Estherville, Emmet County; 1892—Jefferson, Greene County; 1892—Tama, Tama County; 1893—Mystic, Appanoose County; 1893—Hampton, Franklin County; 1893—Ames, Story County; 1893—Bloomfield, Davis County; 1893—Nevada, Story County; 1893—West Union, Fayette County; 1895—Independence, Buchanan County; 1896—Oelwein, Fayette County; 1897—New Hampton, Chickasaw County.

Although censuses were taken in 1863, 1869, 1873 and 1875, the returns are not known to be extant. However, Henry County Genealogical Society (P.O. Box 81, Mount Pleasant, Iowa 52641) has located and printed the 1863 and 1869 censuses for their county only.

The state censuses for 1856, 1885, 1895, 1905, 1915, and 1925 include name, age, sex, color, birthplace, and occupation (age sixteen and up) for each member of each household. Additional information, listed by year of enumeration, is also listed:

1856—voter; native/naturalized/alien; owner of land; years in state; marital status.

1885—marital status; house number and street in towns, smallest legal description if rural; county of birth if born in Iowa; nativity of parents; foreign/native; alien who has/has not taken out first papers.

1895—marital status; births and deaths in household in 1894; county of birth if born in Iowa; nativity of parents; foreign/native; naturalized; Civil War service, including company, regiment and state; Mexican War soldiers, including regiment and state.

1905 and 1915—marital status; birthplace of parents;owner of home or farm, with value; naturalized; years in United States/Iowa; military service in Civil, Mexican, or Spanish War.

1925—marital status; birthplace of parents; names of parents, including maiden name of mother, place of birth and marriage; age of parents, if living; house number and street in cities and towns; years in United States/Iowa; amount for which each listed property owner's house was insured.

There is no statewide index for the censuses of 1856, 1885, 1895, 1905, 1915 or 1925. Indexes, however, for counties or portions of counties are becoming available through individuals, chapters of the Iowa Genealogical Society, *Hawkeye Heritage,* or the staff of the State Historical Society.

All extant state censuses are microfilmed, available for research at the State Historical Society of Iowa, and can be purchased; most years are available on interlibrary loan from the organization's branch in Iowa City.

Background Sources

Regional historical sources are most frequently found through local groups or individuals who have a working knowledge of the town or county records. It is possible to contact these people through historical or genealogical societies in the area or to use the query columns in their periodicals.

Many of the local chapters of the Iowa Genealogical Society have reprinted county histories, some with indexes. Most of them must be ordered through the local chapters. In addition, the following material includes useful background on Iowa history and its residents:

Dawson, Patricia, and David Hudson, comps. *Iowa History and Culture: A Bibliography of Materials Published Between 1952 and 1986.* Ames, Iowa: State Historical Society of Iowa in association with Iowa State University Press, 1989. Professional librarians spent more than ten years surveying Iowa's printed and unpublished dissertations and papers of historical accounts for this bibliography for the state of Iowa. Although family histories are not included, genealogical information may be located in the county, town, and church histories, in the biographies, and through the extensive name and subject indexes. Items in the Table of Contents such as "claim clubs," "pioneer life," and "defunct schools" could be helpful in developing an understanding of the historical context surrounding individuals and families.

Eckhardt, Patricia, comp. *Historical Organizations in Iowa, Iowa History Sources No. 2.* Iowa City, Iowa: Iowa Historical Department, Division of the State Historical Society, 1982.

Iowa Genealogical Society. *Surname Index.* 5 vols. Des Moines, Iowa: Iowa Genealogical Society, 1972–90. Includes a total of 149,000 surnames being researched by society members.

Morford, Charles. *Biographical Index to the County Histories of Iowa.* Vol. 1. Baltimore, Md.: Gateway Press, 1979. Provides surname indexes to numerous county histories.

Peterson, William J. *Iowa History Reference Guide.* Iowa City, Iowa: State Historical Society, 1952.

Sopp, Elsie L. *Personal Name Index to the 1856 City Directories of Iowa.* Gale Genealogy and Local History Series. Vol. 13. Detroit, Mich.: Gale Research Co., 1980.

Suggested references regarding migration to Iowa and its settlement include:

Bogue, Allan G. *From Prairie to Cornbelt: Farming on the Illinois and Iowa Prairies in the 19th Century.* Chicago, Ill.: University of Ohio Press, 1963.

Riley, Glenda. *Frontierswomen: The Iowa Experience.* Ames, Iowa: Iowa State University Press, 1983.

Maps

Among the standard map references for Iowa, in addition to the numerous county atlases for all areas of the state, is Alfred Theodore Andreas, *Illustrated Historical Atlas of the State of Iowa, 1875* (1875; reprint, Iowa City, Iowa: State Historical Society, 1970), which superbly illustrates towns and farms, specifically locating patrons to the publication. An indexed patron's list with place of residence, county and state of birth, and year of emigration is included.

The earliest Sanborn Fire Insurance map (see page 4) of Iowa is 1883. The State Historical Society of Iowa publishes and sells *Fire Insurance Maps of Iowa Cities and Towns: A List of Holdings,* compiled by Peter H. Curtis and assisted by Richard S. Green and Edward N. McConnell (Iowa City, Iowa: Iowa State History Department, 1983), which lists the society's collection. All fire insurance maps (Sanborn and others) have been compiled into one microfilm collection that is at both branches of the State Historical Society research library, the University of Iowa, and the Library of Congress. Of the approximately 4,000 Iowa maps included in both locations of the State Historical Society of Iowa library, the Des Moines branch has original plat maps created by the territorial land surveyors.

Newberry Library's *Checklist of Printed Maps of the Middle West to 1900,* 11 vols. (Boston, Mass.: G. K. Hall, 1980), lists all known pre-1900 plat maps and plat books for the state of Iowa.

Current county maps for Iowa can be ordered by sending check or money order to the Iowa Department of Transportation Office Supplies, Ames Storeroom, Ames, Iowa 50010. A "small" map is fifteen cents, the "larger" map is twenty-five cents. The larger map is 17 x 22 or 17 x 28 inches, depending on the particular county. The maps are fairly easy to read, divided by townships and sections, and show highways, railroads, cities and towns, and rivers and streams.

Land Records

Public-Domain State

Iowa was a public-domain state with one principal meridian which had been established in Arkansas in 1815. Original land disposition was made by the federal government and its agents. There were nine land districts in Iowa, the first two at Burlington and Dubuque in 1838.

However, over 20,000 settlers were in Iowa prior to the first land sales and thus had no legal title to their claims. To prevent speculators and latecomers from buying such improved lands at land office auctions, the settlers and speculators formed claims clubs to rig the auctions on grounds of first settlement.

Patents, tract books, and township plats are available at the BLM Eastern States Land Office (see page 5). Holdings for Iowa land records at the National Archives-Central Plains Region (see page 8) include abstracts of military warrants. More federal military bounty-land warrants were used in Iowa than any other state. It is estimated that half of Iowa was purchased with these authorizations. Locations on warrants for some or all acts of 1842–55 are for the district offices of Chariton, Kanesville, Council Bluffs, Decorah, Osage, Des Moines, Fort Des Moines, Dubuque, Marion, Burlington, Fairfield, Fort Dodge, Iowa City, and Sioux City. Other records of the register and receiver are held for these same counties. Records of homesteads including certificates, receipts, and entries, are held for Des Moines, Fort Dodge, and Sioux City.

Acquisitions of the Iowa State Archives that should be of great interest to the genealogist include land office copies of plats based on original land surveys (in color), ca. 1835–60. These twelve volumes, transferred from the secretary of state's vault, totally cover the state and include notes on Indian villages and trails, old roads, and pioneer dwellings. The "Auditor of State Abstracts of Original Land Entries," 1847–59, has been microfilmed and is available to researchers. The cooperative microfilming project of the Genealogical Society of Utah and the State Historical Society of Iowa has provided the preservation of land conveyances for almost every county. The records are available at the State Historical Society of Iowa's Des Moines research library. There are numerous tract books, receipt books, series of county plat books, etc., available for genealogical research in Iowa. Other references include:

Bogue, Allan G. "The Iowa Claims Clubs: Symbols and Substance." *Mississippi Valley Historical Review* 45 (1958): 231–35.

Lokken, Roscoe L. *Iowa Public Land Disposal.* Iowa City, Iowa: State Historical Society of Iowa, 1942.

Shambaugh, Benjamin F., ed. *Constitution and Records of the Claim Association of Johnson County, Iowa.* Iowa City, Iowa: University of Iowa Press, 1894.

Snedden, Howard E. "Auditor's Transfer Books: A Valuable Iowa Land Research Tool," *Hawkeye Heritage* 24 (Autumn 1989): 141–45. The Transfer Books, created in 1866, are sources of property transfers, arranged by land description instead of by grantor or grantee. The entries include the names of the parties involved, the transaction dates, and reference either deed books or plat books (varies with county). The Transfer Books are currently being microfilmed as well.

Swierenga, Robert P. *Pioneers and Profits: Land Speculation on the Iowa Frontier.* Ames, Iowa: Iowa University Press, 1968.

Following the federal disposal of land in Iowa, land purchases and sales were handled by the recorder of the respective county government, beginning with the establishment of that particular county.

Probate Records

Matters of probate, including wills, administrator or executor bonds, inventories, and guardianships, are kept by the clerk of the county district court. The Genealogical Society of Utah and the State Historical Society of Iowa are jointly microfilming probate records at the county level. In the case of Scott County, packets of original probate files in addition to the court's record books are included. Full particulars on which counties have which records can be obtained from the research library in Des Moines.

Court Records

The first instrument of government formulated in Iowa country is said to be the Miners' Compact, drawn up by the lead miners in 1830. When Iowa Territory was established in 1838 three district courts were created, which continued until statehood in 1846 when the three districts became one. In 1849 this district was divided into northern, middle, and southern divisions.

There was considerable redivision and reorganization through 1907. Holdings at the National Archives-Central Plains Region (see page 8) include files from the District of Iowa, 1845–82; Northern District, 1850–1959; and Southern District, 1842–1959.

At the county level, criminal and civil court records are filed with the county clerks. A few Iowa court records have been, and are being, transferred to the State Archives in Des Moines. A recent acquisition of interest to genealogists is the Supreme Court of Iowa Order Books, beginning with the formation of Iowa Territory in 1838, in four volumes through 1858. Order Book A contains twenty-one naturalizations between 1840 and 1851, for example.

Naturalizations, which are part of the district court records at the county level, are being microfilmed. Naturalizations for most counties have been filmed and are available at both State Historical Society of Iowa research libraries.

Tax Records

The tax rolls for personal property and real estate were kept by the auditor or the treasurer of each county. A few of these records have been microfilmed and are available at the State Historical Society of Iowa. Original county tax rolls are usually not transferred.

Old age pension tax is a resource genealogists should consider in Iowa. A 1934 directive to collect an old age assistance tax was based on a list of all persons over twenty-one years of age. Although the tax was discontinued in 1936, the information included could be important: name, address, sex, date of birth, place of birth, and names of both parents. Many counties have had these lists microfilmed and they are available through the FHL.

Cemetery Records

Many of the local chapters of the Iowa Genealogical Society have publications of cemetery records in their respective counties that can be ordered through the chapter. A statewide publication listing is available through the state society. A large number of cemetery transcription collections as well as records of funeral homes, casket lists, and obituary indexes are held by the FHL.

Church Records

Predominant church groups in Iowa include Catholic, Methodist, Lutheran, and Baptist. Smaller in size, but equally important in religious history in the state, are the Quakers, Mormons, Mennonites, and Congregationalists. The first church building in Iowa, a Methodist church built of logs, was constructed in Dubuque in 1834. A year later the Catholics erected a parish building in the same city. In 1843 the "Iowa Band" of Congregational and Presbyterian clergy began ministering to the settlers in Iowa. In 1854, a small group of the Community of True Inspiration arrived from Germany, settling along the Iowa River in the mid-section of the state. A year later additional members of their group joined them, establishing the unique Amana colonies of present-day Iowa.

For an extensive bibliography on religion and religious groups in Iowa, see Peterson (1952) and Dawson and Hudson (1989) described in Background Sources.

The microfilming project of the Genealogical Society of Utah and the State Historical Society of Iowa has preserved a large number of church baptismal and marriage records. The state society also has impressive collections of original religious records from various Iowa organizations. The University of Iowa in Iowa City, Iowa State University in Ames, and other educational institutions within the state have additional manuscript collections of church records.

Military Records

Military records at the State Archives, a division of the State Historical Society of Iowa, include the State Adjutant General's records of Iowa volunteers in the Mexican War, Civil War, and Spanish-American War. Included among those records are regimental muster rolls, enlistment papers, roster books, reports, pay books, and correspondence. There are indexes for some of these records. Index entries can be copied for a fee. There are no pension records for Iowa volunteer units. Records of the Grand Army of the Republic posts for many Iowa communities are available at the state archives. Casualty files for World War I and II have information, and sometimes photographs, of individual servicemen. Published sources include:

Iowa Adjutant General's Office. *Persons Subject to Military Duty, ca. 1862–1920.* 94 microfilm reels. Salt Lake City, Utah: Genealogical Society of Utah, 1978.

Iowa Adjutant General's Office. *Roster and Record of Iowa Soldiers in the War of the Rebellion: Together with Historical Sketches of Volunteer Organizations, 1861–1866.* 6 volumes. Des Moines, Iowa: E. H. English, State Printer, 1908–11.

Revolutionary War Soldiers and Patriots Buried in Iowa. Marceline, Mo.: Walworth, ca. 1978.

Snedden, Howard E. "A Unique Iowa Resource: The G.A.R. Card Index File." *Hawkeye Heritage* 21 (Summer 1986): 70:1.

———. "A Neglected Source: A Case in Point: The Civil War Draft Rolls of Iowa's Fifth Congressional District." *Hawkeye Heritage* 19 (Winter 1984): 185–89. Although this involves only the southwest quarter of the state, it includes "consolidated lists" of eligible men, names and descriptions of men drawn for the draft, and an interesting array of additional genealogical information. As indicated by the author, remarks such as "Gone to Nebraska City," "In Holmes Co., Ohio," or "deserted across the plains" will certainly give direction to research. These lists are part of Record Group 110, Provost Marshall General's Bureau (Civil War) at the National Archives.

United States Adjutant General's Office. *Index to Compiled Service Records of Volunteer Union Soldiers Who Served in Organizations from the State of Iowa.* Washington, D.C.: National Archives, 1964.

Periodicals, Newspapers, and Manuscript Collections

Periodicals

Iowa has several valuable historical periodicals. The State Historical Society of Iowa has published the *Annals of Iowa,* a scholarly quarterly in three series—1863–74, 1882–83, and 1893 to present; *Iowa Historical Record* (1885–1902); and the *Iowa Journal of History and Politics,* renamed *Iowa Journal of History,* 1903–61; and the *Palimpsest,* a popular quarterly, published continuously since 1920. Volume and cumulative indexes are available.

Hawkeye Heritage, the quarterly publication of the Iowa Genealogical Society, contains a wealth of local information from various parts of the state. For example, issues from 1987 included the following articles: "Iowans Allowed Pensions 02 March 1887"; "Tombstone Inscriptions in Cass Cemetery, Hamilton County"; "Genealogical Excerpts, Diary of Rev. Frederick C. Bauman" (German immigrant—excerpts were for 1890, 1891, 1892); and "Index to the 1856 Special Census of Franklin County, Iowa."

Newspapers

The *Du Buque Visitor,* Iowa's first newspaper, was published in 1836 at Dubuque, followed a year later by *The Western Adventurer* at Montrose. The State Historical Society of Iowa has been collecting the newspapers of the state extensively for quite some time. Currently archived are over 22,000 reels of microfilm. Papers cataloged as part of the United States Newspaper Project are on the OCLC database and can be obtained on interlibrary loan from either the Des Moines or Iowa City facilities. Suggested references include the following:

Cheever, L. D., comp. *Newspaper Collection of the State Historical Society of Iowa.* Iowa City, Iowa: State Historical Society of Iowa, 1969. An update file to this listing is available at the State Historical Library, Iowa City.

Iowa Pilot Project of the Organization of American Historians, The Library of Congress, United States Newspaper Project. *A Bibliography of Iowa Newspapers, 1836–1976.* Iowa City, Iowa: Iowa State Historical Department, 1979.

Petersen, W. J. *The Pageant of the Press, A Survey of 125 Years of Iowa Journalism.* Iowa City, Iowa: Iowa State Historical Society, 1962.

Pitman, Edward F. *Index to Bound Newspapers in Iowa State Department of History and Archives.* Des Moines, Iowa: State of Iowa, 1947.

Available for purchase from the State Historical Society of Iowa Library (Iowa City) is *Bibliography of Iowa Newspapers, 1836–1976* (Iowa State Historical Department, 1979).

Manuscripts

Civil War diaries, a Bond of Proper Conduct, papers of an 1866 Indian agent, and a witness to a presidential assassination are just a few of the items found in the Manuscript Department of the State Historical Society of Iowa. In *Guide to Manuscripts* (Iowa City, Iowa: State Historical Society of Iowa, 1973), compiler Katherine Harris lists numerous genealogical treasures in this collection. The book, very descriptive and well organized, is still only a sampling of the scope of the material available. A few examples are an 1840 bond of apprenticeship for Anne Brophy's sixteen-year-old son as apprentice mariner for five years; the 1841 proper conduct papers that allowed Francis and Maria Reno to be free blacks without paying a bond; three pages written by E. H. Sampson, a guard at Ford's Theatre the night Abraham Lincoln was shot; fifty-three folders and nine packages of records from Grace Episcopal Church, Cedar Rapids, for 1850–1967; numerous Civil War diaries, many without names; and the papers of Leander Clark, special Indian agent for the Sac and Fox in Tama County, 1866–74. The collection also includes various county government and court papers, vital records, property deeds, maps, photographs, and family genealogies.

Another large manuscript collection is located at the State Archives in Des Moines. There are numerous finding aids to these manuscripts although a published guide does not exist. Included in the collection are early land records, manuscript Civil War records for Iowa (muster rolls, clothing books, regimental reports, correspondence, volunteer enlistment), and records of schools and other institutions. This repository also has papers of private and public individuals, photographs, diaries, and journals. The record books of the Iowa Service Star Legion include nearly 1,100 completed questionnaires and photographs of World War I servicemen from Iowa.

Excellent manuscript collections will also be found in the libraries of the University of Iowa, Iowa State University, Luther College in Decorah, Loras College in Dubuque, Grinnell College in Grinnell, and Morningside College in Sioux City.

Frequently, manuscript collections in adjacent states should be seriously considered in tracing families, such as the James J. Hill papers, located at the James J. Hill Library, St. Paul, Minnesota. Hill is most widely known as the "Empire Builder" who created the giant Great Northern system from the St. Paul and Pacific Railroad and controlled railroads and property in Iowa. There is considerable Iowa material within this collection, most of it in twenty-six archival boxes labeled "Iowa Properties Papers." Because of the diversity of the Hill enterprises there is a broad spectrum of original source material. The papers of the Lehigh Supply Company, for example, provide information on boarding houses and miners' incomes and expenditures.

Iowa Territorial Papers, 1838–46, are held at the National Archives-Central Plains Region (see page 8; see also Wisconsin—Manuscripts—Draper Manuscripts).

Archives, Libraries, and Societies

State Historical Society of Iowa Library
Capitol Complex
Des Moines, IA 50319

This statewide organization encompasses all the state historical operations including the historical libraries (at the Des Moines address and at Iowa City—see below); state archives (including manuscript, maps, school and institutional records, and photographs); museum; and membership and development of publications. The extensive holdings of the research library at the Des Moines location are the largest in the state. The staff is very responsive to written request for general information (see list of publications under Periodicals).

State Historical Society of Iowa
Research Library
402 Iowa Avenue
Iowa City, IA 52240

The second largest research collection in the state is located at the Iowa City branch of the State Historical Society's research facilities. Holdings include local, state and national histories, biographies, government documents, and current historical periodicals not all identical to those at the facility at Des Moines. Microfilm holdings are loaned between the collections. Of specific interest to genealogists are county histories, census data, cemetery records, atlases, and plat books. Iowa newspapers, beginning in 1836, can be found in 10,000 bound volumes and 12,000 microfilm reels (microfilm available on interlibrary loan). Fire insurance maps include more than 700 Iowa communities. Over 100,000 photographic images can be located by standard subject headings, geographical designations, or the portrait index.

Iowa Genealogical Society
6000 Douglas
P.O. Box 7735
Des Moines, IA 50322

Maintains an extensive genealogical reference library (shelf list available), publishes the quarterly *Hawkeye Heritage*, a member newsletter and, in cooperation with its chapters, a variety of genealogical reference works, primarily Iowa vital records. State and national speakers are featured at the annual conference in Ames.

Newberry Library
60 West Walton Street
Chicago, IL 60610

Although in Illinois, this repository should be considered as a source for Iowa research. See Peggy Tuck Sinko, *Guide to Local and Family History at the Newberry Library* (Salt Lake City, Utah: Ancestry, 1987). The Iowa collection includes considerable genealogical and local history material, plus a number of very rare books and manuscripts included in the Graff Collection.

Resources of Iowa research can be found in a multitude of other locations in the state. County/city level archival programs exist, for example in Dubuque and both Polk and Scott counties. See the following to locate other valuable resource collections in the state of Iowa:

George, Shirley. *1990 Iowa Library Directory*. Des Moines, Iowa: State Library of Iowa, 1990.

Horton, Loren H., ed. *Historical Organizations in Iowa*. Iowa History Sources, No. 2. Iowa City, Iowa: Iowa Historical Department, Division of State Historical Society, 1982.

Ludwig, Cherie, comp.. *Iowa Genealogical and Historical Resources by County*. Iowa State Historical Department, Division of Historical Museum and Archives, 1978.

Special Focus Categories

Black Americans

In the 1840s only slightly more than 300 blacks were living in Iowa. Free blacks were discouraged, if not totally forbidden, from migrating to the state by a ruling in April of 1839. It stated that any black or "mulatto" must provide "a fair certificate of actual freedom under a seal of a judge and give bond of $500 as surety against becoming public charges" before being permitted to settle in Iowa. After 1865, however, the black population in the state tripled, most migrating from Missouri and other Mississippi and Ohio river areas. Very few histories of blacks in Iowa exist at this time. William J. Peterson's *Iowa History Reference Guide* (see Background Sources) lists numerous periodical articles and some books for Negro history in Iowa. The following are a brief sampling of those articles.

Bergmann, Leola Nelson. "The Negro in Iowa." *Iowa Journal of History* 46 (January 1948): 3–90.

Gallaher, Ruth A. "Slavery in Iowa." *Palimpsest* 28 (May 1947): 158–60.

Van Ek, Jacob. "Underground Railroad in Iowa." *Palimpsest* 2 (May 1921): 129–43.

Additional suggestions for reference on Black American history in Iowa include:

Iowa Bystander, 1894–1987, Des Moines. Renamed *New Iowa Bystander* in 1971, this newspaper was established for the black community in Iowa in 1894 by I. W. Williamson, Billy Colson, and Jack Logan. Some years are available on microfilm.

Schweider, Dorothy, Joseph Hraba, and Elmer Schweider. *Buxton: Work and Racial Equality in a Coal Mining Community*. Ames, Iowa: Iowa State University Press, 1987. Buxton, which existed as an integrated community coal camp in south-central Iowa during the 1900s, was referred to as "the black man's utopia in Iowa."

Native Americans

In 1781 the wife of Peosta, a Fox warrior, reported the discovery of lead deposits in the Iowa country. Seven years later Julien Dubuque, a fur trader, obtained sanction from the Indians to work lead mines near what is now Dubuque. The following time-line of the Native Americans in Iowa will provide a guideline to their disbursement within and beyond the state.

- **1824:** Half-Breed Tract established in present Lee County
- **1825:** Neutral lines established between Sioux, Sac, and Fox
- **1830:** Neutral ground is established between Sioux, Sac, and Fox
- **1832:** Black Hawk War terminates in cession of strip of lands west of Mississippi River known as Black Hawk Purchase; Winnebago tribe is given part of neutral ground
- **1833:** Title to Black Hawk Purchase is transferred to United States Government; Ottawa, Potawatomie, and Chippewa tribes are given lands in what is now southwestern Iowa
- **1834:** "Half-breeds" are given fee simple title to Half-Breed Tract by act of Congress
- **1836:** Sac and Fox cede Keokuk's Reserve of the United States
- **1837:** Sac and Fox cede to the United States 1,250,000 acres of land known as the second Black Hawk Purchase
- **1838:** Chief Black Hawk dies at his home near the Des Moines River in Davis County
- **1842:** Sac and Fox cede all remaining lands in Iowa
- **1843:** Sac and Fox vacate lands east of line passing north and south through the Red Rocks of Marion County
- **1845:** Sac and Fox withdraw from Iowa
- **1846:** Potawatomie relinquish lands in western Iowa
- **1848:** Removal of Winnebago tribe begins
- **1851:** Sioux cede lands in northern Iowa
- **1857:** Spirit Lake Massacre: Sioux attack settlers and kill thirty; small band of Sac and Fox return, permitted to buy eighty acres of land in Tama County; members

of these tribes still live on a semi-reservation north of the village of Tama

- **1862:** Blockhouses erected in northwestern Iowa for protection against the Sioux

See the following for Native American research in Iowa:

Rafert, Stewart. "American-Indian Genealogical Research in the Midwest: Resources and Perspectives." *National Genealogical Society Quarterly* 76 (September 1988): 212–24.

Other Ethnic Groups

The following sources are valuable in gaining an understanding of various ethnic groups in Iowa from both a historical and genealogical standpoint.

Foreman, Grant. "English Emigrants in Iowa." *Iowa Journal of History* 44 (October 1946): 385–420.

Calkin, Homer L. "The Coming of the Foreigners," *Annals of Iowa* 43 (April 1962). This issue of *Annals* deals exclusively with foreigners including those immigrants from Germany, Scandinavia, and the United Kingdom.

Christensen, Thomas P. "A German Forty-eighter in Iowa." *Annals of Iowa* 26 (April 1945): 245–53.

———. *A History of Danes in Iowa.* New York, N.Y.: Arno Press, 1979.

Van der Zee, Jacob. *The Hollanders of Iowa.* Iowa City, Iowa: State Historical Society of Iowa, 1912.

Wick, Barthinius Larson. *The Amish Mennonites: A Sketch of Their Origins, and of Their Settlement in Iowa, with Their Creed in an Appendix.* Iowa City, Iowa: State Historical Society, 1984.

———. "The Earliest Scandinavian Settlement in Iowa." *Annals of Iowa* 29 (October 1948): 468–72.

Luther College, Koren Library, Decorah, Iowa 52101, holds over 20,000 Norwegian manuscripts and 1,000 volumes of Norwegian American newspapers.

County Resources

For some counties there are two "Date Formed" years listed. The first is the year the county was created; the second is the year it was fully organized if it differs from the creation year.

Under the heading "Parent County/ies," the name/s listed may be the county or counties from which the respective county was formed, or it may be names by which the county was originally known.

"Unorganized" in this same column denotes that it was formed from non-county lands. The county name in parentheses is the county to which the unorganized land may have been attached at that time.

Counties listed with an asterisk (*) are those in which you may also find records concerning the county listed. It may have been "attached" to those county/ies for some period of time.

Iowa county governments recorded few vital statistics earlier than 1880. Marriage record registration began in many areas with the organization of the county. It is estimated that between 1880 and 1921 only about 50 percent of the births and deaths were registered.

Birth, marriage, death, and probate records are usually found in the office of the clerk of courts at the county seat. Land transactions are in the county recorder's office.

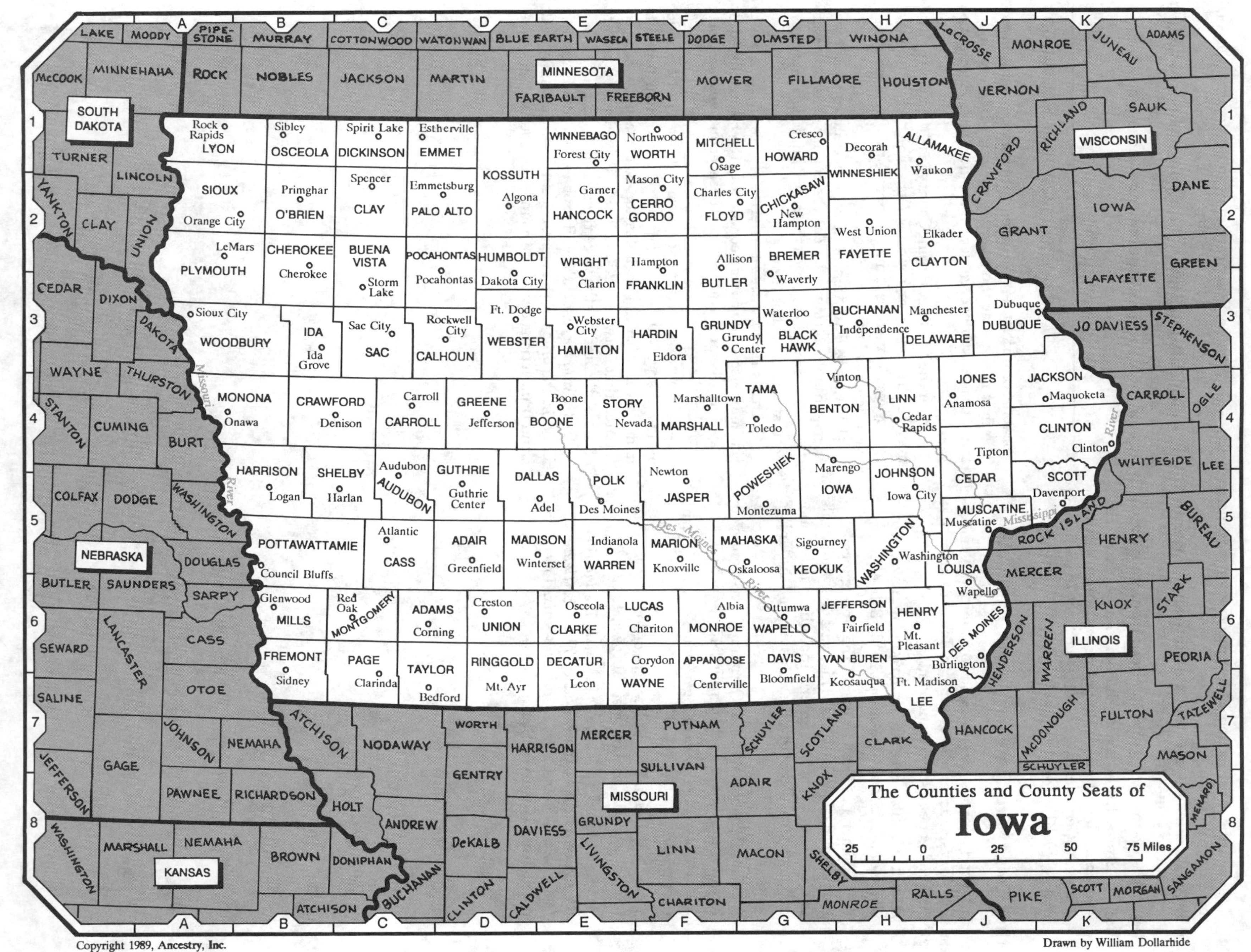
The Counties and County Seats of
Iowa
25 0 25 50 75 Miles
LYON Rock Rapids
OSCEOLA Sibley
DICKINSON Spirit Lake
EMMET Estherville
KOSSUTH Algona
WINNEBAGO Forest City
WORTH Northwood
MITCHELL Osage
HOWARD Cresco
WINNESHIEK Decorah
ALLAMAKEE Waukon
SIOUX Orange City
O'BRIEN Primghar
CLAY Spencer
PALO ALTO Emmetsburg
HANCOCK Garner
CERRO GORDO Mason City
FLOYD Charles City
CHICKASAW New Hampton
FAYETTE West Union
CLAYTON Elkader
PLYMOUTH LeMars
CHEROKEE Cherokee
BUENA VISTA Storm Lake
POCAHONTAS Pocahontas
HUMBOLDT Dakota City
WRIGHT Clarion
FRANKLIN Hampton
BUTLER Allison
BREMER Waverly
BLACK HAWK Waterloo
BUCHANAN Independence
DELAWARE Manchester
DUBUQUE Dubuque
WOODBURY Sioux City
IDA Ida Grove
SAC Sac City
CALHOUN Rockwell City
WEBSTER Ft. Dodge
HAMILTON Webster City
HARDIN Eldora
GRUNDY Grundy Center
TAMA Toledo
BENTON Vinton
LINN Cedar Rapids
JONES Anamosa
JACKSON Maquoketa
CLINTON Clinton
MONONA Onawa
CRAWFORD Denison
CARROLL Carroll
GREENE Jefferson
BOONE Boone
STORY Nevada
MARSHALL Marshalltown
IOWA Marengo
JOHNSON Iowa City
CEDAR Tipton
SCOTT Davenport
MUSCATINE Muscatine
HARRISON Logan
SHELBY Harlan
AUDUBON Audubon
GUTHRIE Guthrie Center
DALLAS Adel
POLK Des Moines
JASPER Newton
POWESHIEK Montezuma
POTTAWATTAMIE Council Bluffs
CASS Atlantic
ADAIR Greenfield
MADISON Winterset
WARREN Indianola
MARION Knoxville
MAHASKA Oskaloosa
KEOKUK Sigourney
WASHINGTON Washington
LOUISA Wapello
MILLS Glenwood
MONTGOMERY Red Oak
ADAMS Corning
UNION Creston
CLARKE Osceola
LUCAS Chariton
MONROE Albia
WAPELLO Ottumwa
JEFFERSON Fairfield
HENRY Mt. Pleasant
DES MOINES Burlington
FREMONT Sidney
PAGE Clarinda
TAYLOR Bedford
RINGGOLD Mt. Ayr
DECATUR Leon
WAYNE Corydon
APPANOOSE Centerville
DAVIS Bloomfield
VAN BUREN Keosauqua
LEE Ft. Madison
MINNESOTA
WISCONSIN
ILLINOIS
MISSOURI
NEBRASKA
SOUTH DAKOTA
KANSAS
Copyright 1989, Ancestry, Inc.
Drawn by William Dollarhide

Map	County Address	Date Formed Parent County/ies	Birth Marriage Death	Land Probate Court
C5	Adair Greenfield 50849	1851 (1854) Pottawattamie/unorganized (Dallas/Mahaska/Monroe/Polk) *Cass	1880 1854 1880	1854 1857 1887
C6	Adams Corning 50841	1851 (1853) Pottawattamie	1880 1855 1880	1853 1868 1857
H1	Allamakee Waukon 52172	1847 (1849) unorganized (Clayton)	1880 1849 1880	1851 1854 1849
F7	Appanoose Centerville 52544	1843 (1846) unorganized (VanBuren) *Davis	1880 1842 1880	1850 1846 1851
C5	Audubon Audubon 50025	1851 (1855) Pottawattamie/unorganized (Dallas/Mahaska/Monroe/Polk) *Cass	1880 1856 1880	1853 1871 1855
	Bancroft	1851 (abolished, 1855) unorganized (Delaware/Polk) *Boone		
G4	Benton Vinton 52349	1837 (1846) Dubuque *Jackson/*Linn	1880 1852 1880	1847 1856 1860
G3	Black Hawk 316 E. Fifth Street Waterloo 50703	1843 (1847) (1853) Buchanan *Delaware/*Benton	1880 1853 1880	1853 1853 1853?
E4	Boone Boone 50036	1846 (1849) unorganized (Linn) *Polk	1880 1848 1880	1849 1865 1867
G2	Bremer Waverly 50677	1851 (1853) unorganized (Delaware/Polk) *Buchanan	1880 1853 1880	1852 1852 1853
H3	Buchanan Independence 50644	1837 Dubuque *Delaware	1880 1848 1880	1846? 1851 1852
C2	Buena Vista P.O. Box 1186 Storm Lake 50588	1851 (1858) unorganized (Delaware/Polk) *Woodbury	1880 1877 1880	1869 1871 1877
	Buncombe	1851 (renamed Lyon, 1861) *Woodbury		
F3	Butler Allison 50602	1851 (1854) unorganized (Delaware/Polk) *Buchanen/*Blackhawk	ca. 1874 1854 1880	1854 1864 ?
D3	Calhoun Rockwell City 50579	1851 (as Fox; renamed, 1853) (1855) unorganized (Delaware/Polk) *Greene	1880 1857 1880	1855 1873 1860?

Map	County Address	Date Formed Parent County/ies	Birth Marriage Death	Land Probate Court
C4	Carroll P.O. Box 867 Carroll 51401	1851 (1855) Pottawattamie/ unorganized (Dallas/ Mahaska/Monroe/Polk) *Shelby/*Guthrie	1880 1855 1880	1855 1856 1855?
C5	Cass Atlantic 50022	1851 (1853) Pottawattamie	1880 1853 1880	1853 1880? 1880?
J4	Cedar Tipton 52772	1837 Dubuque	1880 1840 1880	1838 1839 1839
F2	Cerro Gordo Mason City 50401	1851 (1855) unorganized (Delaware/Polk) *Floyd	1880 1855 1880	1855 1857 1880?
B2	Cherokee Cherokee 51012	1851 (1858) unorganized (Delaware/Polk) *Woodbury	1880 1866 1880	1856 1859 1872
G2	Chickasaw New Hampton 50659	1851 (1853) unorganized (Delaware/Polk) *Fayette	1880 1853 1880	1851 1854 1853
E6	Clarke N. Main Street Osceola 50213	1846 (1851) unorganized (Kishkekosh)	1880 1852 1880	1849 1853 1854
C2	Clay P.O. Box 4104 Spencer 51301	1851 (1858) unorganized (Delaware/Polk) *Woodbury	1880 1866 1880	1858 1880? 1880?
H2	Clayton Elkader 52042	1837 Dubuque	1880 1865 1880	1839 1840 1850
K4	Clinton P.O. Box 157 Clinton 52732	1837 (1841) Dubuque *Scott	1880 1840 1880	1840 1851 1859
	Cook	1836 (abolished, 1838) Des Moines *Muscatine		
B4	Crawford P.O. Box 546 Denison 51442	1851 (1855) Pottawattamie/unorganized (Dallas/Mahaska/Monroe/Polk) *Shelby	1880 1853 1880	1855 1867 1868
	Crocker	1870 (abolished, 1871) Kossuth		
D5	Dallas 801 Court Street Adel 50003	1846 (1847) unorganized (Mahaska) *Polk	1880 1847 1880	1850 1851 1855
G6	Davis Bloomfield 52537	1843 (1844) unorganized (VanBuren)	1880 1844 1880	1847 1844 1844
E6	Decatur Leon 50144	1846 (1850) unorganized (Appanoose) *Davis	1880 1874 1880	1851 1871 1871

Map	County Address	Date Formed Parent County/ies	Birth Marriage Death	Land Probate Court
H3	Delaware Manchester 52037	1837 (1841) Dubuque	1880 1851 1880	1847 1853 1857?
J6	Des Moines 513 N. Main Street Burlington 52601	1834 (Michigan Territory) unorganized	1880 1835 1880	1837 1835 1835
C1	Dickinson Spirit Lake 51360	1851 (1857) unorganized (Delaware/Polk) *Woodbury	1880 1871 1880	1861 1880? 1880?
J3	Dubuque Seventh and Central Dubuque 52001 *No death records 1917–41; no birth records June 1940–September 1941.*	1834 (Michigan Territory) unorganized	1880 1835 1880	1834 1835 1834
D1	Emmet Estherville 51334	1851 (1859) unorganized (Delaware/Polk) *Boone/*Webster	1880 1876? 1880	1876 1877? 1859
H2	Fayette West Union 52175	1837 (1850) Dubuque *Clayton	1880 1851 ca. 1860	1851 1859 1859
F2	Floyd Charles City 50615	1851 (1854) unorganized (Delaware/Polk) *Fayette/*Chickasaw	1880 1880 1880	1855 1880? 1880?
	Fox	1851 (renamed Calhoun, 1853) unorganized (Delaware/Polk)		
F2	Franklin 12 First Avenue N.W. Hampton 50441	1851 (1856) unorganized (Delaware/Polk) *Fayette/*Chickasaw/*Hardin	1880 1855 1880	1855 1855 1856
B6	Fremont P.O. Box 549 Sidney 51652	1847 (1849) unorganized (Appanoose)	1880 1848 1880	1849 1880 1850
D4	Greene Jefferson 50129	1851 (1854) unorganized (Delaware/Polk) *Dallas	1880 1854 1880	1854 1854 ?
F3	Grundy Grundy Center 50638	1851 (1856) unorganized (Delaware/Polk) *Buchanan/*Blackhawk	1875 1856 1880	1863 1869 1871
D5	Guthrie Guthrie Center 50115 *Courthouse fire in 1963.*	1851 (1851) unorganized (Dallas)	1880 1852 1872	1852 1929? 1855
E3	Hamilton Webster City 50595	1857 Webster	1880 1857 1880	1854 1865 1868
E2	Hancock 855 State Street Garner 50438	1851 (1858) unorganized (Delaware/Polk) *Boone/*Webster	1880 1873 1880	1857 1859 1858
F3	Hardin Eldora 50627	1851 (1853) unorganized (Delaware/Polk) *Marshall	1880 1853 1880	1849 1854 1853

Map	County Address	Date Formed Parent County/ies	Birth Marriage Death	Land Probate Court
B4	Harrison Logan 51546	1851 (1853) Pottawattamie	1880 1853 1880	1853 1853? 1853?
H6	Henry Mount Pleasant 52641	1836 Des Moines	1880 1836 1880	1837 1837 1837
	Howard	1816 (became Missouri Territory) St. Louis/Washington/ unorganized (Saint Charles)		
G1	Howard Cresco 52136	1851 (1855) unorganized (Delaware/Polk) *Floyd	1880 1875 1880	1855 1873 1873
	Humboldt (old)	1851 (abolished, 1855) unorganized (Delaware/Polk) *Boone		
D2	Humboldt (present) Dakota City 50529	1857 Kossuth/Webster	1880 1858 1880	1855 1859 ?
B3	Ida 401 Moorehead Street Ida Grove 51445	1851 (1859) unorganized (Delaware/Polk) *Woodbury	1880 1868 1880	1856 1870 1875
H5	Iowa Marengo 52301	1843 (1845) Keokuk *Johnson	1880 1847 1880	1847 1848 1851
K4	Jackson 201 W. Platt Maquoketa 52060	1837 Dubuque	1880 1847 1880	1838 1838 1839
F5	Jasper P.O. Box 666 Newton 50208	1846 (1846) unorganized (Mahaska)	1880 1846 1880	1847 1846 1846
H6	Jefferson P.O. Box 984 Fairfield 52556	1839 (1839) Henry	1880 1839 1880	1838 1838 1840
H5	Johnson 404 Brown Street Iowa City 52240	1837 (1838) Cook/Dubuque/Muscatine *Cedar	1880 1839 1880	1839 1839 1839
J4	Jones Anamosa 52205	1837 (1839) Dubuque *Jackson	1880 1840 1880	1841? 1844 1848
G5	Keokuk Sigourney 52591	1837 (1844) Dubuque/unorganized *Cedar/*Johnson/*Washington	1880 1844 1880	1844 1844 1844
	Kishkekush	1843 (1845) (renamed Monroe, 1846) unorganized (Henry) *Jefferson/*Wapello		
D1	Kossuth Algona 50511	1851 (1856) unorganized (Delaware/Polk) *Boone/*Webster	1880 1857 1880	1855 ? ?

Map	County Address	Date Formed Parent County/ies	Birth Marriage Death	Land Probate Court
H7	Lee 701 Avenue F Fort Madison 52627 *and* Keokuk 52632 *County has two courthouses. Call for their respective holdings.*	1836 Des Moines	1880 1837 1880	1830 1841 1849
H4	Linn Third Avenue Bridge Cedar Rapids 52401	1837 (1839) Dubuque *Jackson	1880 1840 1880	1841 1840 1840
J6	Louisa Wapello 52653	1836 Des Moines	1880 1842 1880	1839 1838 1839
F6	Lucas Chariton 50049	1846 (1849) unorganized (Kishkekosh)	1880 1849 1880	1849 1850 1854
A1	Lyon Rock Rapids 51246	1851 (1872) (as Buncombe; renamed, 1861) unorganized (Delaware/Polk) *Woodbury	1880 1872 1880	1862 1885 1874
E5	Madison P.O. Box 152 Winterset 50273	1846 (1849) unorganized (Mahaska)	1880 1849 1880	1850 1852 1852
G5	Mahaska P.O. Box 30 Oskaloosa 52577	1843 (1844) unorganized (Washington)	1880 1844 1880	1845 1844 1844
F5	Marion P.O. Box 497 Knoxville 50138	1845 unorganized	1880 1845 1880	1846 1845 1854
F4	Marshall Marshalltown 50158	1846 (1849) unorganized (Linn) *Jasper	1880 1850 1880	1850 1851 1854
B6	Mills Glenwood 51534	1851 (1851) Pottawattamie	1880 1880 1880	1853 1852 1888
F1	Mitchell Osage 50461	1851 (1854) unorganized (Delaware/Polk) *Fayette/*Chickasaw	1880 1855 1880	1854 1855? 1855?
B4	Monona 61 Iowa Avenue Onawa 51040	1851 (1854) Pottawattamie/unorganized (Dallas/Mahaska/Monroe/Polk) *Harrison	1880 1856 1880	1858 1860 1926?
F6	Monroe Albia 52531	1843 (1845) (as Kishkekush; renamed, 1846) unorganized (Henry) *Jefferson/*Wapello	1880 1845 1880	1847 1848 1847
C6	Montgomery Red Oak 51545	1851 (1853) Pottawattamie *Adams	1880 1855 1880	1854 1868 1890?
J5	Muscatine Muscatine 52761	1836 Des Moines	1880 1837 1880	1838 1838 1839

Map	County Address	Date Formed Parent County/ies	Birth Marriage Death	Land Probate Court
B2	O'Brien Primghar 51245	1851 (1860) unorganized (Delaware/Polk) *Woodbury	1880 1860 1880	1857 1880? 1870
B1	Osceola Sibley 51249	1851 (1872) unorganized (Delaware/Polk) *Woodbury	1880 1872 1880	1869 1872 1873
C6	Page Clarinda 51632	1847 (1852) unorganized (Appanoose)	1880 1852 1880	1854 ? ?
D2	Palo Alto 11th and Broadway Emmetsburg 50536	1851 (1858) unorganized (Delaware/Polk) *Boone/*Webster	1880 1860 1880	1858? 1864 1870
A2	Plymouth Le Mars 51031	1851 (1858) unorganized (Delaware/Polk) *Woodbury	1880 1860 1880	1856 1871 1869
D2	Pocahontas Pocahontas 50574	1851 (1859) unorganized (Delaware/Polk) *Boone/*Webster	1880 1859 1897	1861 1867 1867
E5	Polk 111 Court Des Moines 50309	1846 (1846) unorganized (Mahaska)	1880 1846 1880	1846 1846 1846
B5	Pottawattamie 227 S. Sixth Street Council Bluffs 51501 *and* Avoca 51521 *County has two courthouses. Call for their respective holdings.*	1848 unorganized (Dallas/Mahaska/ Monroe/Polk)	1880 1848 1880	1849 1846 1876
G5	Poweshiek Montezuma 50171	1843 (1848) Keokuk *Iowa/*Johnson/*Mahaska	1880 1848 1880	1843 1849 1869
D7	Ringgold Mt. Ayr 50854	1847 (1855) unorganized (Appanoose) *Taylor	1880 1855 1880	1855 1858 ?
	Risley	1851 (abolished, 1853) unorganized (Delaware/Polk)		
C3	Sac P.O. Box 368 Sac City 50583	1851 (1856) unorganized (Delaware/Polk) *Woodbury/*Greene	1880 1864 1880	1856 1857 1869
K5	Scott 416 W. Fourth Davenport 52801	1837 Cook/Dubuque/Muscatine	1880 1838 1880	1838 1838 1838
C5	Shelby P.O. Box 431 Harlan 51537	1851 (1853) Pottawattamie	1880 1853 1880	1854 1869 1869
A2	Sioux Orange City 51041	1851 (1860) unorganized (Delaware/Polk) *Woodbury	1880 1871 1880	1856 1870 1871
	Slaughter	1838 (renamed Washington, 1839) Henry/Louisa/Muscatine/unorganized		

Map	County Address	Date Formed Parent County/ies	Birth Marriage Death	Land Probate Court
E4	Story Nevada 50201	1846 (1853) unorganized (Linn) *Polk/*Boone	1880 1854 1880	1853 1855 1865
G4	Tama P.O. Box 306 Toledo 52342	1843 (1853) Benton *Linn	1880 1853 1880	1853 1854 1850
C7	Taylor Bedford 50833	1847 (1851) unorganized (Appanoose)	1880 1851 1880	1855 1859 1875?
D6	Union Creston 50801	1851 (1853) Pottawattamie/unorganized (Dallas/ Mahaska/Monroe/Polk)	1880 1855 1880	1854 1880? 1880?
H6	Van Buren Keosauqua 52565	1836 Des Moines	1880 1837 1880	1837 1841 1837
	Wahkaw	1851 (renamed Woodbury, 1853) unorganized (Delaware/Polk)		
B6	Wapello Ottumwa 52501	1843 (1844) unorganized (Henry) *Jefferson	1880 1844 1880	1844 1844 1844
E5	Warren P.O. Box 379 Indianola 50125	1846 (1849) unorganized (Mahaska)	1880 1849 1880	1849 1850 1849
H5	Washington Washington 52353	1838 (as Slaughter; renamed, 1839) Henry/Louisa/Muscatine/ unorganized	1880 1839 1880	1839 1838 1868
F6	Wayne Corydon 50060	1846 (1851) unorganized (Appannose) *Davis	1880 1851 1880	1851 1851 1873
D3	Webster 703 Central Avenue Fort Dodge 50501	1853 (1853) Risley/Yell	1880 1853 1880	1856 1855 1864
E1	Winnebago Forest City 50436	1851 (1857) unorganized (Delaware/Polk) *Boone/*Webster	1880 1890 1880	1873 1900? 1900?
H1	Winneshiek 201 W. Main Decorah 52101	1847 (1851) unorganized (Clayton)	1880 1851 1880	1851 1852 1851
A3	Woodbury 101 Courthouse Sioux City 51101	1851 (1853) (as Wahkaw; renamed, 1853) unorganized (Delaware/Polk)	1880 1854 1880	1855 1856 1900?
F1	Worth Northwood 50459	1851 (1857) unorganized (Delaware/Polk) *Fayette/*Chickasaw/*Floyd/*Mitchell	1880 1858 1880	1857 1897 1863
E2	Wright P.O. Box 306 Clarion 50525	1851 (1855) unorganized (Delaware/Polk) *Boone/*Webster	1880 1855 1880	1855 1855 1857
	Yell	1851 (abolished, 1853) unorganized (Delaware, Polk)		

KANSAS

Marsha Hoffman Rising, C.G., C.G.L.

Kansas derives its name from a tribe of plains native peoples, the "Kansa," who lived in earth lodges along the Missouri, Kansas, and Blue rivers in the northeastern section of the state. Kansas, which was a segment of the vast area known as the Louisiana Purchase, became part of the United States in 1803. With the passage of the Kansas-Nebraska Act in 1854, it became Kansas Territory. On 29 January 1861 Kansas was admitted as a free state and became the thirty-fourth state in the Union.

Kansas was first designated as permanent Indian territory and became home for many of the displaced tribes from the states of Illinois, Indiana, Ohio, and Missouri as well as the remaining indigenous plains people. In 1825 the Kansa and Osage tribes were induced to give up part of their eastern Kansas lands to make way for those from the east: the Shawnee, Kickapoo, Delaware, Wea, Piankeshaw, and others. By 1846 nineteen reservations had been established within the boundaries of what is now Kansas. The first mission for Native Americans in what is now Kansas was Mission Neosho, established in 1824. A Methodist mission was founded for the benefit of the Shawnee in 1829.

It did not take long for the restless white settlers to desire permanent homes and farms in Kansas. This settlement, however, was spurred not so much by natural westward expansion as by the determination of both pro-slavery and anti-slavery factions to achieve a majority population. This struggle became an important part of the peopling of Kansas, and the genealogist with early Kansas ancestors will want to become familiar with the details.

Passage of the Kansas-Nebraska Act in 1854 only accentuated the difficulties, and this early civil war ultimately turned Kansas Territory into "bleeding Kansas." As each faction attempted to establish a majority, fraud became common. As an example, the 1855 Kansas territorial census showed fifty-three voters in the seventh district, but three months later, 253 votes were cast. From 200–300 men from Missouri went into the seventh district of Kansas territory in wagons and horseback on the day preceding the election. They were armed with pistols and other weapons and intended to vote to secure the election of pro-slavery members to the territorial legislature. These examples are typical of the stuffing of ballot boxes by residents of Missouri who were hoping to create a slave state. In 1859 slavery was prohibited by the Wyandotte Constitution, but this law did not go into effect until statehood in 1861. Kansas became a strong Republican force when it entered the Union. For the settler of Kansas, this period was a long, bloody, and difficult one. Bushwhackings, burnings, lootings, and murder became an inevitable part of life. Graphic testimony is offered in the *Reports of the Special Committee* (see Background Sources) and in the stories reported in surviving newspapers published along the Kansas-Missouri border.

The first act of the Kansas territorial legislature on 30 August 1855 was to designate thirty-three counties in the eastern section of the territory. The second act created Marion and Washington counties, and a third created Arapahoe County out of territory that would later become part of the territory of Colorado.

Kansas experienced its greatest population expansion at the end of the Civil War when peace brought development of the prairie lands. The construction of railroads and the availability of cheap lands through both the railroad companies and the federal government brought many settlers to the area. Kansas was not always hospitable; pioneers were visited by prairie fires, droughts, blizzards, dust storms, grasshopper plagues, cyclones, and floods. Many would-be settlers retreated saying, "In God We Trusted; In Kansas We Busted." Some early settlers returned to the safety of the east. The settlers who remained and those who came later established the farms, communities, and businesses that shaped Kansas history.

Vital Records

The recording of births and deaths began at the statewide level in July 1911. Some counties have records predating 1916. Marriage records are on file from 1 May 1913 as are divorces from 1 July 1951. These records are located in the Kansas Department of Health and Environment, Office of Vital Statistics, Landon State Office Building, 900 South Jackson, Topeka, Kansas 66612. The fee for these certificates as of 1990 was $6. Divorces that occurred prior to 1951 are in the office of the clerk of the district court in which the case was filed.

Territorial records of marriages and deaths located in Kansas newspapers from 1854–61 were published in several issues of Volume 18 of the *Kansas Historical Quarterly* (1960). Births and deaths were published in volume 19 (August and September 1961), and marriages were published in volume 21 (Summer 1955): 445–86. Reprints are available from the Midwest Historical Genealogical Society, Box 1121, Wichita, Kansas 67201, and Jefferson County Genealogical Society, P.O. Box 174, Oskaloosa, Kansas 66066. The *First Bicentennial Report of the State Board of Agriculture* also lists some vital statistics taken in the territory. Before statewide registration some births and deaths were kept at the county level. Compliance was inconsistent and sporadic. The researcher should consult the Historical Records Survey—Kansas, entitled *Guide to Public Vital Records in Kansas,* which lists the location of vital records *not* held by the Bureau of Vital Statistics. It is divided into type of record—birth, marriage, death, and divorce—and then by county.

As recently as 1987, Kansas law was changed to allow access to records of births, marriages, and deaths which occurred between 1885–1913. The Kansas State Historical Society is currently involved in a cooperative microfilming project with the Genealogical Society of Utah. As of July, 1990, twenty-five counties have had their records filmed. The film is available at the Kansas State Historical Society, Center for Historical Research (see Archives, Libraries, and Societies). Published indexes, abstracts, and transcriptions of vital records from a number of sources are in the collections at the society as well.

Census Records

Federal

Population Schedules.

- Indexed—1860, 1870
- Soundex—1880, 1900, 1910 (Miracode), 1920

Mortality Schedules.

- 1860, 1870, 1880 (indexed)

Industry and Agriculture Schedules.

- **Agriculture** 1870, 1880

The research center at the Kansas State Historical Society has all the federal population censuses for Kansas, as well as the 1880 and 1900 Soundex and the 1910 Miracode (see page 2).

Territorial and State

The census enumerations that were completed between 1855–59, inclusive, are actually voter's lists. The researcher must note that some voters boycotted elections, making the lists by no means complete. The 1857 Census of the Shawnee, Native and Adopted, is available in the state archives department at Kansas State Historical Society.

The 1860 Kansas territorial census was taken as part of the federal census. Two copies of it exist. The original copy was sent to Washington, with a transcription retained by the state. Both copies have been indexed and are available for research at the Kansas State Historical Society, Center for Historical Research, making it possible to check inconsistencies between the two returns. A county census was completed at the time of application for county organization. Many of these are extant, and some are housed at the Kansas State Historical Society, which can provide a list of availability.

Kansas completed state censuses in 1865, 1875, 1885, 1895, 1905, 1915, and 1925. They have been microfilmed, are available for research, and have been partly indexed by the Kansas State Historical Society. A list of those indexed is available from the society as are statistical rolls of the Board of Agriculture, which contain enumerations for the years 1873 and 1877, 1896–1904 (incomplete), 1918, 1920–24, 1925 (taken as part of state census), 1926–36, and from 1950 to 1979. These rolls only included the head of household until 1955; they must be used with caution as they are not complete, but this is a good source for recent data.

Background Sources

Anderson, Lorene, and Alan W. Farly. "Bibliography of Town and County Histories of Kansas." *Kansas Historical Quarterly* 21 (Autumn 1955): 513–51.

Barry, Louise. *The Beginnings of the West: Annals of the Kansas Gateway to the American West, 1540–1854.* 1972. Reprint. St. Louis, Mo.: Patrice Press, 1988. Chronological exploration in encyclopedia format of the pre-territorial lives and times of those who lived in Kansas.

Cutler, William G. *History of the State of Kansas.* 2 vols. Chicago, Ill.: A. T. Andreas, 1883.

Collections of the Kansas State Historical Society. 17 volumes. Topeka, Kans.: Kansas State Historical Society, 1881–1928. Historical documents for the state.

Owen, Jennie, and Kirche Mechem, eds. *The Annals of Kansas 1886–1925.* 2 vols. Topeka, Kans.: Kansas State Historical Society, 1954, 1956. A continuation of Wilder's book (see below).

Report of the Special Committee appointed to Investigate the Troubles in Kansas with the Views of the Minority of Said Committee—Report No. 200 to the 34th Congress. Washington, D.C.: Cornelius Wendell, 1856. This book was indexed in a two-volume separate publication by Robert Hodge, *An Index to the Report of the Special Committee Appointed to Investigate the Troubles in Kansas,* Vol. 1 (A–L) and Vol. 2 (M–Z) (Fredericksburg, Va.: the author, 1984). Testimonials and voting records regarding the slavery question in the settlement of Kansas.

Richmond, Robert W. Kansas: *A Land of Contrasts.* 3d ed. Arlington Heights, Ill.: Forum Press, 1989.

Rydjord, John. *Kansas Place Names.* Norman, Okla.: University of Oklahoma Press, 1972.

Stratton, Joanna L. *Pioneer Women: Voices from the Kansas Frontier.* New York, N.Y.: Simon and Schuster, 1981. Diaries of women in the early period of Kansas settlement.

Socolofsky, Homer E., and Huber Self. *Historical Atlas of Kansas.* Norman, Okla.: University of Oklahoma Press, 1972.

Wilder, Daniel W. *The Annals of Kansas.* 1886. Reprint ed. Topeka, Kans.: Kansas State Historical Society, 1975. Covers the pre-1886 era in Kansas. A new edition is in progress.

Maps

Robert W. Baughman's *Kansas In Maps,* 104 pages, first published in 1969 by the Kansas State Historical Society, contains ninety maps. It was reprinted in 1988 by the Patrice Press in St. Louis.

A good series of maps showing the expansion and development of Kansas counties was published in Kansas State Historical Society's volume 8 of *Transactions.* These maps were later reprinted by the Kansas Genealogical Society, Dodge City, in the *TreeSearcher,* April 1966–January 1967.

The map collection at Kansas State Historical Society includes 21,000 maps and architectural drawings. The maps were produced by government agencies, railroads, map publishers, and individuals. Researchers may request information regarding specific geographic locations and time periods, including the Kansas Dead Town List for those towns no longer in existence.

Land Records

Public-Domain State

Kansas was surveyed on the rectangular survey system (see pages 4–5) and was first officially opened for white settlement in 1854. Some of the early patent books for Kansas counties have been microfilmed by and are available through the FHL.

Kansas owes much of its growth to the passage and enactment of the Homestead Law, passed in 1862 and effective 1 January 1863. It offered "free" land to those who would live on and cultivate a tract. In order to make a claim, the individual had to (1) be twenty-one years old or head of a family, (2) be a United States citizen or have declared intention to become one, (3) *not* already own 320 acres of land, (4) *not* abandon land owned by him in the same state or territory, and (5) intend to use the homestead for himself and his family.

There were four classes of public lands opened for settlement. First, those owned by the federal government; second, those owned by institutions of higher learning; third, the common-school lands; and fourth, the railroad lands. The state was divided into nine land districts, and offices opened in Larned (Pawnee County), Oberlin (Decatur County), Topeka (Shawnee County), Kirwin (Phillips County), Independence (Montgomery County), Concordia (Cloud County), Salina (Saline County), Wakeeney (Trego County), Wichita (Sedgwick County), and Cherokee Strip lands and Osage Indian trust lands. Land was also sold through the railroad offices of the Missouri, Kansas and Texas Railway (headquarters at Parsons, Kansas), Atchison, Topeka and Santa Fe (headquarters in Topeka), and Kansas Division, Union Pacific Railroad (headquarters in Kansas City).

The Kansas State Historical Society has the Kansas tract books, plats, and tract maps, and the purchases from the Dodge City land office. It also has the land sales of the Sante Fe Railroad (mostly central Kansas) and the Kansas Town and Land Company (Rock Island Railroad), which sold land in Colorado, New Mexico, and Nebraska as well as in Kansas.

After initial purchase from the federal government, land records are kept at the county level in register of deeds offices.

Probate Records

Many probate records located at the county level are in the district court. One can expect to find an index to probate court papers, court records, executor's bonds, testamentary matters, inventories, sale bills, guardian and curators records, and court appointments. Usually the probate minute books, probate court records, and case files are also available. The researcher can check for the application letters for administration, executors and guardians, administrators and guardian's bonds, appraisement of estate, names and oaths of witnesses, sale bills, settlement records, orders of publication, term docket books, and wills and record of wills.

Court Records

The district court has general jurisdiction in all matters, both civil and criminal. Naturalization records may be filed here as well as in other courts of record. This court also holds jury lists, witness claims, alimony records, patent rights, judgments, and attorneys of records.

Tax Records

For the most part, tax records remain at the local level. Assessment and tax rolls are kept, permanently, by the county treasurer's office.

Cemetery Records

Two national cemeteries were established in Kansas: Leavenworth National Cemetery, P.O. Box 1694, Leavenworth, Kansas 66048, and Fort Scott National Cemetery, P.O. Box 917, Fort Scott, Kansas 66701.

There is no central registry of cemetery locations in Kansas. The Woman's Kansas Day Club recently completed a project to identify and locate many Kansas cemeteries. The project's results are at the Kansas State Historical Society, which has additional collections of published cemetery inscriptions, though not comprehensive, listed in their card catalog.

The register of deeds in each county is often able to assist in locating cemeteries. Certain maps distributed by the Kansas Department of Transportation, Docking Building, 8th Floor-Planning, Topeka, Kansas 66612, show the location of known cemeteries in relation to county roads.

Church Records

The earliest churches were established among the native tribes settled in Kansas long before it was organized as a territory. The Methodist, Baptist, Society of Friends, Roman Catholic, Presbyterian, and Congregational churches all had early missions which grew as the white settlers immigrated. Records of the Quakers can be found at Friends University in Wichita; United Brethren (Dunkards) at McPherson College in McPherson; Methodists at Baker University in Baldwin City; Mennonite at Bethel College in Newton; Lutheran, especially Swedish, at Bethany College in Lindsborg. Forsyth Library at Fort Hays University in Hays, Kansas 67601, holds numerous ethnic and religious group records. Volga German records here are outstanding.

The Kansas State Historical Society solicits church rolls, membership lists, records, and histories. The published material is located in the library; the unpublished material is located in the manuscript department. A few church records have been microfilmed.

Military Records

The records of the Kansas Adjutant General through World War II are located at the Kansas State Historical Society. Few are indexed. Virtually nothing has survived from the Territorial Militia, which was pro-slavery. The records of the unofficial "Free State Forces" are extant at the Kansas State Historical Society as are the records of the Kansas Adjutant General from 1861 to World War I. The Daughters of the American Revolution, John Haipt Chapter, have indexed the Kansas Civil War and Indian War militia. An index to the Kansas Adjutant General's report of 1861–65 is available. A list of soldiers killed in battle in Kansas regiments is given in Andreas's *History of Kansas*, pages 180–208 (see Background Sources).

Post-Civil War veteran's census records include the 1883 index to pensioners, veterans, their widows and orphans, and the 1930 veteran's census. The original Grand Army of the Republic Post Records are in the Kansas State Historical Society Library.

Good biographical information is available on Spanish-American and World War I veterans in the manuscript department of the Kansas State Historical Society. The Adjutant General report entitled *Index to Kansas Troops in the Volunteer Service of the United States in the Spanish and Philippine Wars* is also available for research. The Kansas State Historical Society holds the photostatic copies of World War I enlistment and discharge papers of Kansas military personnel (see also Cemeteries). The state archives at the state historical society has a list of military men who received a World War I bonus.

Periodicals, Newspapers, and Manuscript Collections

Periodicals

The Kansas State Historical Society publishes *Kansas History: A Journal of the Central Plains*, formerly called *Kansas Historical Quarterly* (1948–present). A directory to historical and genealogical societies is published annually indicating more than twenty genealogical periodicals published in the state.

Newspapers

The Kansas State Historical Society holds a superior collection of Kansas newspapers. As the historical society was founded by newspaper editors, they have copies of the vast majority of the newspapers published in Kansas. Their current goal is to microfilm all pre-1930 holdings. The newspapers are not currently available on interlibrary loan, although they may be purchased from the society.

The researcher will find an excellent reference in Aileen Anderson, ed. and comp., *Kansas Newspapers: A Directory of Newspaper Holdings in Kansas* (Kansas Library Network Board, 1984).

Manuscripts

In addition to newspapers, the Kansas State Historical Society has a diverse and rich manuscript collection, including letters, diaries, journals and photographs of early pioneers. Although there is no comprehensive guide to the manuscripts at the Kansas State Historical Society, there are finding guides to major and individual collections. A useful source is the original manuscripts and biographies of over 800 Kansas women collected by Lila Day Monroe, source material for Stratton's *Pioneer Women* (see Background Sources). Among the other materials at the society are records of the Atchison, Topeka, and Santa Fe Railroad, including payrolls; the papers of Indian missionaries, Isaac McCoy (1808–74) and Jotham Meeker (1825–64); and the papers of William Clark, superintendent of the St. Louis Indian Superintendency, which have been microfilmed. The state archives department in the society holds state prison records from the 1860s to the 1980s.

Genealogists with ancestors in the medical professions may be interested in the *Comprehensive Index to Kansas Physicians and Midwives 1887–1900* and *Index to Obituaries from the Kansas Medical Journal 1889–1966*. Both indexes were prepared by the Kansas State Historical Society. The material included is representative of the type of information included in its entire collection.

Several necrology indexes for hereditary and fraternal organizations are at the Kansas State Historical Society. They cover the period from the 1870s to the 1940s and give member's name and date of death. Organizations include Knights of Pythias, Ancient Order of United Workmen, Grand Lodge of Kansas, Masons, Odd Fellows, and Grand Army of the Republic.

A recent publication (1987) entitled *A Guide to Special Collections in Kansas* describes over 300 repositories including collections in university, public, and school libraries. It is available from the Special Collections Department, Ablah Library, Wichita State University, Wichita, Kansas 67208.

Archives, Libraries, and Societies

Kansas State Historical Society
120 West 10th Avenue
Topeka, KS 66612

The Center for Historical Research at the Society is composed of three sections: library, state archives, and manuscripts. The society also operates a museum at a different address. The society has published a listing of historical societies, genealogical societies, and museums throughout Kansas. It includes addresses, hours of operation, and descriptions of the collections. Individuals may purchase a copy from the Kansas State Historical Society.

Most extant territorial records, including census enumerations, are retained here. The researcher should review the specific category of records of interest for exact information. Included are territorial records pertaining to John Brown, the New England Emigrant Aid Company, and territorial military records as well as information about early settlers and pioneers.

Kansas Genealogical Society
700 Avenue G and Vine Street
P.O. Box 103
Dodge City, KS 67801

Topeka Genealogical Society
P.O. Box 4048
Topeka, KS 66604

In each April issue, the *Topeka Genealogical Society Quarterly* publishes a listing of all material on Kansas that has been published by the genealogical societies within the state during the year. This has been an annual listing since 1979. Back issues may be obtained from the society.

County Resources

The "County Address" indicates the address of the county courthouse in the county seat where inquiries regarding land (registry of deeds), probate (probate judge), and court (clerk of the district court) can be addressed. The county clerk at the same address holds birth and death records before statewide recording. Those years with an asterisk (*) are not complete. Those years with a double plus (++) are held either in book or microfilm form by the Kansas State Historical Society. Marriage records are held by the probate judge. The year indicated is the first known record continuing to the present. Sources for this information include the Kansas State Historical Society and the *Guide to Public Vital Records in Kansas* as indicated by the society.

Land, probate, and court records in Kansas generally begin with the organization of the county, although there will be variations. Records created soon after county organization may be incomplete. For some counties the date of government organization took place after the actual legislative formation of the county. In those cases, dates in parentheses in the "Date Formed" column are when the records begin. County seat names in parentheses are original names or county seats no longer functioning.

The appearance of a question mark (?) indicates that the information was not available, while dashes (——) indicate that no records are known to exist in this category.

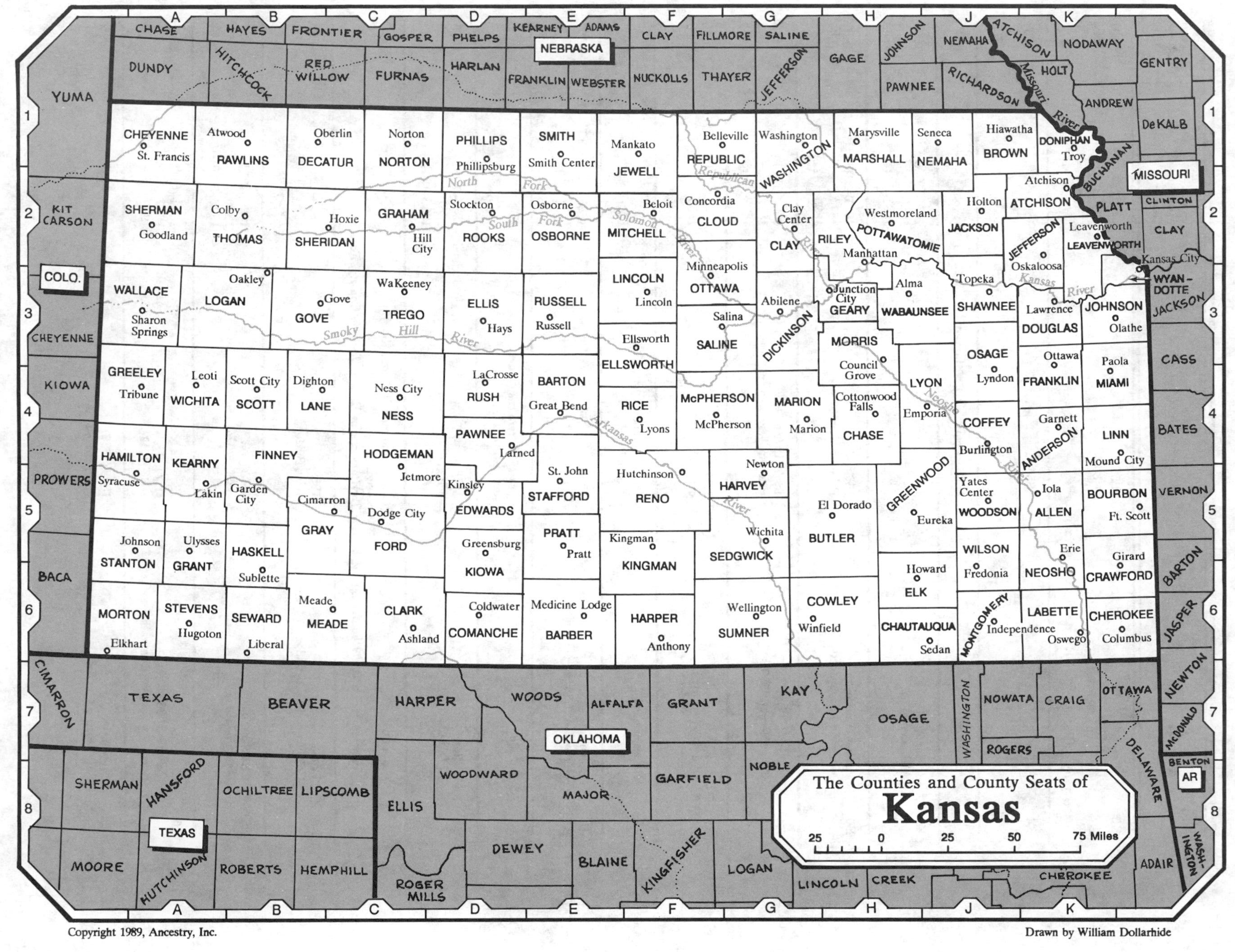
The Counties and County Seats of
Kansas
25 0 25 50 75 Miles
Copyright 1989, Ancestry, Inc.
Drawn by William Dollarhide
NEBRASKA
MISSOURI
OKLAHOMA
COLO.
TEXAS
AR
CHEYENNE St. Francis
RAWLINS Atwood
DECATUR Oberlin
NORTON Norton
PHILLIPS Phillipsburg
SMITH Smith Center
JEWELL Mankato
REPUBLIC Belleville
WASHINGTON Washington
MARSHALL Marysville
NEMAHA Seneca
BROWN Hiawatha
DONIPHAN Troy
SHERMAN Goodland
THOMAS Colby
SHERIDAN Hoxie
GRAHAM Hill City
ROOKS Stockton
OSBORNE Osborne
MITCHELL Beloit
CLOUD Concordia
CLAY Clay Center
RILEY Manhattan
POTTAWATOMIE Westmoreland
JACKSON Holton
ATCHISON Atchison
JEFFERSON Oskaloosa
LEAVENWORTH Leavenworth
WYANDOTTE Kansas City
WALLACE Sharon Springs
LOGAN Oakley
GOVE Gove
TREGO WaKeeney
ELLIS Hays
RUSSELL Russell
LINCOLN Lincoln
OTTAWA Minneapolis
SALINE Salina
DICKINSON Abilene
GEARY Junction City
WABAUNSEE Alma
SHAWNEE Topeka
DOUGLAS Lawrence
JOHNSON Olathe
GREELEY Tribune
WICHITA Leoti
SCOTT Scott City
LANE Dighton
NESS Ness City
RUSH LaCrosse
BARTON Great Bend
ELLSWORTH Ellsworth
RICE Lyons
McPHERSON McPherson
MARION Marion
MORRIS Council Grove
CHASE Cottonwood Falls
LYON Emporia
OSAGE Lyndon
FRANKLIN Ottawa
MIAMI Paola
HAMILTON Syracuse
KEARNY Lakin
FINNEY Garden City
HODGEMAN Jetmore
PAWNEE Larned
STAFFORD St. John
RENO Hutchinson
HARVEY Newton
BUTLER El Dorado
GREENWOOD Eureka
COFFEY Burlington
ANDERSON Garnett
LINN Mound City
STANTON Johnson
GRANT Ulysses
HASKELL Sublette
GRAY Cimarron
FORD Dodge City
EDWARDS Kinsley
KIOWA Greensburg
PRATT Pratt
KINGMAN Kingman
SEDGWICK Wichita
WOODSON Yates Center
ALLEN Iola
BOURBON Ft. Scott
MORTON Elkhart
STEVENS Hugoton
SEWARD Liberal
MEADE Meade
CLARK Ashland
COMANCHE Coldwater
BARBER Medicine Lodge
HARPER Anthony
SUMNER Wellington
COWLEY Winfield
ELK Howard
CHAUTAUQUA Sedan
WILSON Fredonia
MONTGOMERY Independence
NEOSHO Erie
LABETTE Oswego
CRAWFORD Girard
CHEROKEE Columbus

Map	County Address	Date Formed Parent County/ies	Birth Marriage Death	Land Probate Court
K5	Allen Iola 66749	1855 original	— 1856 —	1861 1858 1858
	Iola city clerk has birth, death, and burial records.			
K4	Anderson Garnett 66032	1855 original	1892–94* 1857–1913 1892–94*	1857 1855 1860
	Arapahoe	1855 (became part of the territory of Colorado, 1861)		
K2	Atchison Atchison 66002	1855 original	1891–1906 1855 1891–1911	1855 1855 1858
E6	Barber (Barbour) Medicine Lodge 67104	1867 Peketon Territory	1891–1911 1874 1899–1911	1867 1867 1874
E4	Barton Great Bend 67530	1867 (1872) Peketon Territory	1898–1911 1872 1892–1911	1872 1872 1873
K5	Bourbon Fort Scott 66701	1855 original	— 1855 —	1856 1855 1857
	Breckenridge	1855 (renamed Lyon, 1862) original		
J1	Brown Hiawatha 66434	1855 original	1885–90; ++1907–11 1857 1885–90; ++1907–11	1857 1857 1859
	Buffalo	pre-1880 (renamed Garfield, 1887) unorganized land		
G5	Butler El Dorado 67042	1855 original	1886–1911 1861 1886–1911	1855 1869 1860
	Calhoun	1855 (renamed Jackson, 1859) original		
	Early marriages of Calhoun County, Kansas Territory, are in Holton, Jackson County, Kansas.			
H4	Chase Cottonwood Falls 66845	1859 Wise/Butler	1885–1911 1860 1885–1911	1859 1859 1866
H6	Chautauqua Sedan 67361	1875 Godfrey/Howard	1886–1911* 1870 1896–98; 1910–11*	1875 1875 1871
K6	Cherokee Columbus 66725 (formerly Center, Centralia)	1855 (as McGee; renamed, 1866) original 1893–1911	1894–1911 1867 1868	1869 1872
A1	Cheyenne Saint Francis 67756	1873 (1886) unorganized land	— 1886 —	1886 1886 1886

Map	County Address	Date Formed Parent County/ies	Birth Marriage Death	Land Probate Court
C6	Clark Ashland 67831	1867 (abolished, 1883) (1885) Peketon Territory (reorganized from Ford County)	1904–11 1885 1904–11	1885 1885 1885
G2	Clay Clay Center 67432	1857 (1866) original	1885–1900; 1906–11 1864 1885–1911	1866 1866 1868
F2	Cloud Concordia 66901	1860 (as Shirley; renamed 1866) original	1885–1910 1867 1885–1911	1867 1867 1868
J4	Coffey Burlington 66839	1855 (1859) original	++1892–1908* 1858 1886–1910*	1858 1857 1858
D6	Comanche Coldwater 67029	1867 (1885) Peketon Territory	1891–1908 1885 1891–1905	1885 1885 1885
H6	Cowley Winfield 67156	1867 (as Hunter; renamed Cowley, 1870)	1885–1911 1870 1885–1911	1870 1870 1871
K6	Crawford Girard 66743	1867 Cherokee/Burbon	1887–1912 1867 1887–1911	1867 1870 1867
	Davis	1855 (renamed Geary, 1889) original		
B1	Decatur Oberlin 67749	1873 (1879) unorganized land	1889–1910 1880 1885–1910	1879 1900 1880
G3	Dickinson Abilene 67410	1855 (1857) original	1892–1911 1867 1892–1911	? ? 1882
K1	Doniphan Troy 66087	1855 original	1896–1911 1855 1895–1911	1856 1851 1858
	Dorn *Dorn was divided in 1867 into present counties of Neosho and Labette.*	1855 original		
K3	Douglas Lawrence 66044 *Records destroyed 21 August 1863 in Quantrill's raid. Some marriage records reconstructed.*	1855 original	1885–1907 1863 1885–97	1856 1856 1863
D5	Edwards Kinsley 67547 (Petersburg, Peter's City)	1874 Kiowa	1902–11* 1875 1902–11	1874 1874 1874
H6	Elk Howard 67349 *Courthouse burned 1906.*	1875 Howard	1885–1911 1875 1895–1911	1906 1906 1906
D3	Ellis Hays 67601	1867 unorganized land	1886–1911 1868 1885–1912	1871 1867 1868

Map	County Address	Date Formed Parent County/ies	Birth Marriage Death	Land Probate Court
F3	Ellsworth Ellsworth 67439	1867 unorganized land/Peketon Territory	1884–95; 1907–11 1867 1886–93; 1907–11	1867 1867 1867
B5	Finney Garden City 67846	1873 (as Sequoyah; renamed, 1883) Peketon Territory	1885–1910 1884 1886–1910*	1873 1873 1885
	Foote	1881 (renamed Gray, 1887) unorganized land		
C5	Ford Dodge City 67801	1867 (1873) Peketon Territory	1892–1904; ++1905–11 1874 1892–1904; ++1905–11	1873 1873 1874
K4	Franklin Ottawa 66067	1855 original	1892–1910 1858 1892–1911	1857 1856 1859
	Garfield	pre-1880 (as Buffalo; renamed,1887; became part of Finney, 1893) unorganized land		
H3	Geary Junction City 66441	1855 (as Davis; renamed, 1889) original	1905–11 1857 1871–1911	1858 1860 1861
	Godfrey	1855 (renamed Seward, 1861; then Howard) original		
B3	Gove Gove 67736	1868 (1886) unorganized land	1892–1911 1886 1892–1911	1886 1886 1887
C2	Graham Hill City 67642	1867 (1880) unorganized land	1892–1904; 1910–11 1880 1892–1904; 1910–11	1880 1880 1880
A5	Grant Ulysses 67880	1873 (abolished 1883) (1888) unorganized land	1890–1926 1888–98* 1892–1926	1888 1888 1888
B5	Gray Cimarron 67835 *County clerk has tax rolls from 1889.*	1881 (as Foote; renamed, 1887) unorganized land	— 1887 —	1886 1885 1887
A4	Greeley Tribune 67879	1873 (1889) unorganized land	1896–1904 1887 1897–1905	? ? 1880
H5	Greenwood Eureka 67045	1855 (1862) original	1885–1911 1859 1885–1911	1857 1865 1880
A5	Hamilton Syracuse 67878 (Hollidaysburg)	1873 (1886) unorganized land	1896–1911* 1886 1896–1911*	1884 1886 1885
F6	Harper Anthony 67003	1867 (1873) Peketon Territory	1892–1910* 1878 1891–1913	1873 1873 1878

Map	County Address	Date Formed Parent County/ies	Birth Marriage Death	Land Probate Court
G5	Harvey Newton 67114	1872 Sedgwick	1886–1911 1872 1886–1911	1872 1872 1872
B5	Haskell Sublette 67877 (Santa Fe)	1887 Finney	1888–97 1887 1888–97	1887 1887 1886
C5	Hodgeman (Hageman) Jetmore 67854 (Buckner)	1867 (1879) Peketon Territory	— 1880 —	1879 1887 1880
	Howard	1855 (as Godfrey; renamed Seward, 1861; then Howard, 1867) original		
	Howard was abolished in 1875 when it was divided into Elkland and Chautauqua.			
	Hunter	1867 (renamed Cowley, 1870) original		
J2	Jackson Holton 66436	1855 (organized, 1857, as Calhoun; renamed 1859) original	++1892; 1902–11 1855 ++1892; 1902–11	1858 1857 1861
K2	Jefferson Oskaloosa 66066	1855 original	1892–98* 1855 1892–98*	1854 1855 1858
F1	Jewell Mankato 66956 (Jewell City)	1867 (1870) unorganized land	1886–94 1871 1886–94	1870 1870 1872
K3	Johnson Olathe 66061	1855 original	— 1857 —	1857 1857 1858
	Kansas	1873 (abolished 1883; became Morton) unorganized land		
A5	Kearny (Kearney) Lakin 67860	1873 (abolished 1883) (1889) Peketon Territory	? 1888 ?	? ? 1888
F5	Kingman Kingman 67068	1869 (1874) Reno	1885–1911 1875 1885–1911	1890 1878 1878
D6	Kiowa Greensburg 67054	1867 (abolished, 1875) (re-created, 1886) Peketon Territory/Edwards	— 1886 —	? ? 1886
K6	Labette Oswego 67356	1857 (1867) Dorn/Neosho	1885–96 1867 1885–93	1867 1868 1865
B4	Lane Dighton 67839	1873 (1886) Peketon Territory/unorganized land	1888–1911 1886 1888–1911*	1886 1886 1886
K2	Leavenworth Leavenworth 66048	1855 original	1887–1911* 1855 1887–1911*	? ? 1855

Map	County Address	Date Formed Parent County/ies	Birth Marriage Death	Land Probate Court
F3	Lincoln Lincoln 67455 (Lincoln Center)	1867 (1870) unorganized land	1886–1910 1871 1885–1910	1871 1871 1871
K4	Linn Mound City 66056	1855 original	1885–1911* 1855 1885–1911*	1857 1855 1859
A3	Logan Oakley 67748 (Russell Springs)	1881 (as St. John; renamed, 1887) Wallace unorganized	—— 1888 ——	1885 1885 1888
	Lykins (see Miami)	1855 (renamed Miami, 1861) Original		
J4	Lyon Emporia 66801	1855 (as Breckenridge; renamed , 1862) (1859) original	1886–1911 1856 1885–1911	1859 1859 1858
	Madison *Madison was divided 1861–64 into Breckenridge (later Lyon) and Greenwood.*	1855		
G4	Marion Marion 66861	1855 (1860) Peketon Territory	1881–1911* 1865 1885–1911	? ? 1867
H1	Marshall Marysville 66508	1855 original	1885–1911 1856 1885–1911	1855 1855 1858
	McGee (see Cherokee)	1855 (renamed Cherokee, 1866)		
F4	McPherson McPherson 67460	1867 (1870) Peketon Territory	1887–1911 1870 1885–1900	1870 1870 1871
B6	Meade Meade 67864 (Skidmore, Meade Center)	1873 (abolished 1883) (1885) Peketon Territory	1886–1911 1886 1886–1911	1885 1885 1885
K4	Miami Paola 66071 (Peoria Village)	1855 (as Lykins; renamed, 1861) original	1885–1911 1857 1885–1911	1855 1857 1858
F2	Mitchell Beloit 67420 (Willow Springs) *†Records held by city clerk.*	1867 (1870) unorganized land	1891–1911† 1871 1891–1911†	1870 1870 1871
J6	Montgomery Independence 67301	1867 (1869) Wilson	1888–1911* 1870 1887–1911	1870 1870 1870
H3	Morris Council Grove 66846 *City clerk holds death records.*	1855 (as Wise; renamed, 1859) original	—— 1859 ——	1859 1859 1860
A6	Morton Elkhart 67950	1873 (1886) (became part of Seward, 1883; reoganized, 1886) Kansas	—— 1887 ——	1887 1887 1887

Map	County Address	Date Formed Parent County/ies	Birth Marriage Death	Land Probate Court
J1	Nemaha Seneca 66538	1855 original	1883–1904 1857 1883–1904	1855 1857 1859
K6	Neosho Erie 66733	1855 as Dorn (1864) original	1892–1905 1864 1892–1905	1868 1867 1867
C4	Ness Ness City 67560	1867 (abolished 1874) (1880) unorganized land/Peketon Territory	— 1880 —	? 1880 1880
C1	Norton Norton 67654	1867 (1872) unorganized land	1885–1911 1873 1885–1911	1872 1872 1874
J3	Osage Lyndon 66451	1855 (as Weller; renamed, 1869) original	1885–1911 1860 1885–1911	1859 1861 1861
E2	Osborne Osborne 67473	1867 (1871) unorganized land	1900–09 1872 1900–09	1871 1872 1872
	Otoe	1860 (abolished, 1867) original		
F3	Ottawa Minneapolis 67467 (Markley Mills)	1860 (1866) Saline	++1885–1911 1866 ++1895–1911	1866 1866 1869
D4	Pawnee Larned 67550	1867 (1872) Peketon Territory	1880–1911 1873 1897–1911	1872 1872 1873
	Peketon Territory	1854 (no population; abolished, 1867) original		
D1	Phillips Phillipsburg 67661	1867 (1872) unorganized land	— 1872 —	1872 1872 1873
H2	Pottawatomie Westmoreland 66549	1855 original	1885–1911 1855 1885–1911	1856 1856 1862
E5	Pratt Pratt 67124	1867 (1872–79) Peketon Territory	1888–1900 1879 1880–1900	1879 1879 1879
B1	Rawlins Atwood 67730 (Kelso and Pragg)	1873 (1881) unorganized land	— 1881 —	1881 1881 1881
F5	Reno Hutchinson 67501	1867 (1872) Peketon Territory	1890–1911 1872 1890–1911	1870 1873 1871
F1	Republic Belleville 66935	1860 (1868) original	1885–1911 1869 1885–1911	1868 1868 1871

Map	County Address	Date Formed Parent County/ies	Birth Marriage Death	Land Probate Court
F4	Rice Lyons 67554 (Atlanta and Brookdale)	1867 (1871) Peketon Territory	1895–1911* 1872 1892–1911	1871 1871 1872
	Richardson (see Wabaunsee)	1855 (renamed Wabaunsee, 1859) original		
H2	Riley Manhattan 66502	1855 original	1885–86; ++1892–1909* 1856 1885–86; ++1892–1909*	1855 1855 1859
D2	Rooks Stockton 67669	1867 (1872) unorganized land	1888–1901 1873 1888–1901	1872 1872 1873
D4	Rush LaCrosse 67548	1867 (1874) unorganized land/Peketon Territory	1895–1911 1876 1886–1911	1874 1874 1875
E3	Russell Russell 67665 (Fossil Station)	1867 (1872) unorganized land	1885–1911* 1872 1885–1911*	1872 1872 1872
	St. John	1881 (renamed Logan, 1887)		
F3	Saline Salina 67401	1859 original	1885–1915* 1860 1885–1915*	1859 1859 1965
	Sequoyah *Some records are in Ford County.*	1873 (renamed Finney, 1883)		
B4	Scott Scott City 67871	1873 (1886) unorganized land	1904–11 1886 1906–11	1886 1886 1886
G6	Sedgwick Wichita 66603 **At Wichita Historical Office.*	1867 (1870) Hunter/Otoe/Peketon Territory	1884–89; 1908–11 1870 1884–87; 1908–11*	1870 1870 1870
	Seward (old)	1855 (as Godfrey; renamed, 1861; renamed Howard, 1867 original		
B6	Seward (present) Liberal 67901	1873 (1886) unorganized land	— 1886 —	1886 1886 1886
J3	Shawnee 214 E. Seventh Street Topeka 66603	1855 original	1894–1910 1856 1894–1910	1859 1855 1858
B2	Sheridan Hoxie 67740	1873 (1880) unorganized land	1886–1911 1878 1887–1910	? ? 1873
A2	Sherman Goodland 67735 *†At city clerk Goodland.*	1873 (1886) unorganized land	++1888–1911 1886 ++1888–1911	1888 1886 1887
	Shirley	1860 (renamed Cloud, 1867) original		

Map	County Address	Date Formed Parent County/ies	Birth Marriage Death	Land Probate Court
E1	Smith Smith Center 66967	1867 (1872) unorganized land	1891–96 1872 1891–96	1872 1875 1872
E5	Stafford St. John 67576	1867 (1879) Peketon Territory	1886–93 1879 1886–89	1879 1879 1879
A5	Stanton Johnson 67855 (Veteran)	1873 (abolished, 1883) (1887) unorganized land	1887–1910* 1887 1889–1910*	1887 1887 1887
A6	Stevens Hugoton 67951	1873 (1886) unorganized land	— 1886 —	1886 1886 1886
G6	Sumner Wellington 67152	1867 (1871) Hunter/Peketon Territory	1885–91*; 1910–11 1871 1885–91*	1871 1871 1880
B2	Thomas Colby 67701	1873 (1885) unorganized land	1889–1910 1886 1886–1910	1885 1885 1885
C3	Trego WaKeeney 67672	1867 (1879) unorganized land	1899–1911* 1879 1899–1911*	1879 1879 1880
H3	Wabaunsee Alma 66401	1855 (as Richardson; renamed, 1859) original	1892–1911 1856 1892–1911	1859 1859 1860
A3	Wallace Sharon Springs 67758	1868 (abolished 1879) (1889) unorganized land	1891–1911 1880 1891–1911	? ? 1884
G1	Washington Washington 66968	1855 (1860) original	1887–1911 1861 1885–1911	1860 1860 1872
	Weller	1855 (renamed Osage, 1859) original		
A4	Wichita Leoti 67861 (Bonasa)	1873 (1886) unorganized land	1887–1909* 1887 1885–1909	1885 1887 1887
J5	Wilson Fredonia 66736	1855 (1867) original	1885–1909 1864 1889–1911	1866 1869 1866
	Wise	1855 (renamed Morris, 1859) original		
J5	Woodson Yates Center 66783	1855 original	1885–1911 1860 1885–92	1858 1864 1864
K3	Wyandotte Kansas City 66101	1855 (1859) original	1885–92 1859 1885–92	1859 1857 1859

KENTUCKY

Wendy L. Elliott, C.G., C.G.L.

Few American settlers had moved into the region of present-day Kentucky prior to the completion of the western portion of the border survey between Virginia and North Carolina in 1748. When the French and Indian War (Seven Years War) ended, the Ohio River was designated as the boundary between settlers and native inhabitants. Kentucky was under the jurisdiction of Augusta County, Virginia. Fincastle County, Virginia, was organized in 1772 to include all of present-day Kentucky with Harrodsburg designated the county seat. The following year the McAfee brothers and others surveyed land along the Salt River. In 1774, under James Harrod, Harrodsburg was founded as the first permanent English settlement in Kentucky by a group that arrived via the Ohio River.

That same year Richard Henderson purchased from the Native Americans all land lying between the Ohio, Kentucky, and Cumberland rivers for his Transylvania Company. John Finley's stories of Kentucky land precipitated Daniel Boone's subsequent exploration. Boone blazed the trail from the Cumberland Gap (at the junction of present-day Virginia, Kentucky, and Tennessee) to the interior. This path between the Cumberland Gap and central Kentucky became known, through the Transylvania Company's publicity, as the Wilderness Road. In 1775 Boonesborough was established as the headquarters of the Transylvania Company.

During the Revolutionary War the settlements in Kentucky were virtually ignored by the Virginia government. Troubles with native tribes, lack of military assistance, and isolation from the eastern portion of Virginia precipitated agitation for Kentucky's own statehood. Between 1784 and 1790, nine conventions met at Danville demanding separation from Virginia, but none of these were successful in gaining a division.

The Commonwealth of Kentucky was admitted to the Union as the fifteenth state on 1 June 1792 after the first constitution was drafted on 3 April of that year. Established as a commonwealth state, its first capital was at Danville. Early settlers included Revolutionary War veterans staking claim to bounty-land grants. They were joined by Scots-Irish, German, and English individuals and families from Virginia, Maryland, North Carolina, Pennsylvania, and Tennessee.

Ideology over the slave issue divided the populace before and during the Civil War. Many large land owners supported slavery, but the small farmers and mountain families did not. Officially, Kentucky, the birthplace of Abraham Lincoln, was neutral during the Civil War only until September 1861 when it actively began support of the Union, even though the Confederate States continued to act as if Kentucky were one of theirs.

Following the Civil War, tobacco and coal became leading commodities in Kentucky's economy. Kentucky's bluegrass pastures have produced an exceptional number of thoroughbred horses, leading to worldwide recognition in horse racing. Fort Knox, originally Camp Knox, began as a permanent military post and later became an official U.S. gold depository. In the twentieth century it has been a major training center for military recruits.

Genealogical research in the state is aided by excellent research facilities and printed materials on Kentucky's early settlement.

Vital Records

Although compliance was never complete, birth and death records for Kentucky begin as early as 1852 when statewide registration was first enacted. The requirement continued for only ten years. Some birth and deaths were recorded between 1874–79 and 1892–1910 as well, but observance was sporadic.

A few larger cities maintained separate birth and death records prior to 1911, but these too are incomplete. Louisville (1898–1911), Covington (1890–1911), Newport (1890–1911), and Lexington (1906–11) are four cities with registered births in their respective city health departments.

The Kentucky Department for Libraries and Archives and the Kentucky Historical Society (see Archives, Libraries and Societies) have early records for 1852–1910, arranged by counties. Jeffery M. Duff's *Inventory of Kentucky Birth, Marriage and Death Records, 1852–1910*, rev. ed. (Frankfort, Ky.: Department for Libraries and Archives, 1988), lists what is available by year and county at both of the repositories. Other repositories, including the Filson Club Library (see Archives, Libraries, and Societies) and the FHL, have some copies. No statewide index has been compiled of these early records, although the Kentucky Historical Society has a card index of both births and deaths for 1852–62. Some early records, which have been indexed by county, appear in various issues of the Kentucky Historical Society's *Register.*

Birth and death registration was enacted statewide on 1 January 1911 and generally adhered to by 1920. Indexes to births and deaths after 1911 are microfilmed; however, the actual records are not. Certificates of births and deaths after 1911 are only available at the Office of Vital Statistics, Department of Health Services, 275 East Main Street, Frankfort, Kentucky 40601. The microfilmed index can be used at the Kentucky Historical Society, University of Kentucky Library, Filson Club Library, and the FHL. The Kentucky Historical Society also maintains copies of delayed birth registrations and early city records.

Kentucky marriage records usually begin about the time of the respective county's establishment or within a few years of that date. Some counties have marriage records for dates prior to organization. Fayette, Jefferson, and Lincoln counties have marriage records as early as 1785. The respective county clerk has jurisdiction over marriage records. Beginning in 1958 statewide registration was required. Originals are filed in the counties and duplicates are available at the Office of Vital Statistics. The Office of Vital Statistics maintains an index to marriage records from 1958. Licenses and bonds may be filed separately from certificates. Published marriage records for Kentucky include the following:

Clift, G. Glenn, comp. *Kentucky Marriages, 1797–1865.* 1974. Reprint. Baltimore, Md.: Genealogical Publishing Co., 1987. Newspaper marriage notices previously published in *The Register of the Kentucky Historical Society.* Alphabetical by county and alphabetical within each county by groom's surname.

Kentucky's state legislature granted divorces from 1792 through 1849. Between 1849 and 1958, divorces were usually recorded by the circuit courts in the respective counties. Some early original circuit court records are available at the Kentucky Department for Libraries and Archives. The records of early divorces are included in the Acts of the General Assembly of the Commonwealth of Kentucky. These volumes, and a few microfilm copies of circuit court records, are available at the Kentucky Historical Society and Kentucky Department for Libraries and Archives. Statewide registration commenced in 1958. Divorces granted after statewide registration are available through the Office of Vital Statistics at the above address.

Census Records

Federal

Population Schedules.

- Indexed—1810, 1820, 1830, 1840, 1850, 1860, 1870
- Soundex—1880, 1900, 1910, 1920

Industry and Agriculture Schedules.

- 1850, 1860, 1870, 1880

Mortality Schedules.

- 1850, 1860, 1870, 1880

Slave Schedules.

- 1850, 1860

Union Veterans Schedules.

- 1890 (part)

Earlier U.S. censuses for Kentucky were destroyed, but published tax lists serve as a replacements for the lost 1790 and 1800 censuses. For substitutes see these works:

Clift, Garrett Glenn. *"Second Census" of Kentucky, 1800: A Privately Compiled and Published Enumeration of Tax Payers Appearing in the 79 Manuscript Volumes Extant of Tax Lists of the 42 Counties of Kentucky in Existence in 1800.* 1954. Reprint. Baltimore, Md.: Genealogical Publishing Co., 1982. Names of taxpayers are arranged alphabetically. Shows name, county, and date of tax list.

Early Kentucky Tax Records. Baltimore, Md.: Genealogical Publishing Co., 1987. Taken from the *Register of the Kentucky Historical Society* (see Periodicals) and indexed by Carol Lee Ford.

Heinemann, Charles Brunk. *"First Census" of Kentucky, 1790.* Baltimore, Md.: Genealogical Publishing Co., 1981. Privately compiled list of taxpayers arranged alphabetically assists in locating the proper county of residence. Provides name, county, and date of tax list.

This volume includes a map by Bayless Hardin depicting Kentucky in 1792 with the 1818 Jackson Purchase also noted.

Only returns for sixty-five Kentucky counties remain of the 1890 Union veterans and widows schedule of the federal census of Kentucky. Extracts and indexes for many of Kentucky's censuses have been compiled and published. Original or microfilm copies of the federal census returns are available at the Kentucky Department for Libraries and Archives. Several Kentucky indexes to censuses predate those published by AISI.

State School Census

Kentucky infrequently enumerated public school students beginning in 1888. Scattered records are at the office of the respective county Board of Health or Board of Education. Some are maintained by the Kentucky Department for Libraries and Archives and the Kentucky Historical Society.

Background Sources

Many county and state histories are available for Kentucky. Because Virginia was its parent state, some early Kentucky history through 1792 is recorded in Virginia documents. Historical material pertaining to Kentucky can be found in many excellent publications. A few include these:

Allen, William B. *A History of Kentucky.* 1872. Reprint. Ann Arbor, Mich.: University Microfilms, 1973.

Chinn, George Morgan. *Kentucky, Settlement and Statehood, 1750–1800.* Frankfort, Ky.: Kentucky Historical Society, 1975.

Clark, Thomas D. *Kentucky: Land of Contrast.* New York, N.Y.: Harper & Row, 1968.

Coleman, John Winston. *A Bibliography of Kentucky History.* Lexington, Ky.: University of Kentucky Press, 1949. Kentucky histories written prior to 1949 are listed in this bibliography.

Collins, Lewis, and Richard H. Collins. *History of Kentucky.* 2 vols. 1874. Reprint. Frankfort, Ky.: Kentucky Historical Society, 1979.

Filson, John. *The Discovery, Settlement, and Present State of Kentucky.* Wilmington, Del.: James Adams, 1784.

Kincaid, Robert Lee. *The Wilderness Road.* Harrogate, Tenn.: Lincoln Memorial University Press, 1955.

Littell, William. *The Statute Laws of Kentucky to 1816.* 5 vols. Frankfort, Ky.: William Hunter, 1809–19. Most important work concerning Kentucky laws.

Van Every, Dale. *Forth to the Wilderness, 1754–1774.* New York, N.Y.: Mentor Books, American Library, 1962. A good brief history of the struggle to conquer the Appalachians and settle the western frontier. Available in paperback.

A useful guide for research in the state is the following:

Schweitzer, George K. *Kentucky Genealogical Research.* Knoxville, Tenn.: the author, 1983. Contains a good discussion of Kentucky military records in addition to helpful information for statewide research.

Maps

One of the earliest known maps printed of Kentucky is John Filson's, dated 1784. A later detailed map of Kentucky watercourses, size twenty-two-by-forty-six inches, is published and sold by the Kentucky Cabinet for Economic Development, Maps and Publications Office, 133 Holmes Street, Frankfort, Kentucky 40601. This facility maintains a large collection of maps and atlases available for purchase. A map and publications price list, 1987, with ordering instructions, is available on request at no cost.

Helpful in locating early land grants is Luke Munsell's map printed in 1819 entitled "Map of the State of Kentucky together with parts of Indiana and Indian Territories." A copy of this map can be obtained from the Library of Congress, Photoduplication Service, Washington, D.C. 20540.

The Kentucky Department for Libraries and Archives houses a collection of Kentucky maps for the period 1784–1818, including agency-sponsored late nineteenth and early twentieth century maps, but this collection is largely unprocessed. Maps for the state are also available at the Kentucky Historical Society, University of Kentucky Library, and the Filson Club Library. These collections include state, county, and city maps.

Cadastral maps show land owners, drawn from official registers, used in conjunction with the appropriation of taxes, which list quantity, value, and ownership of real estate. Kentucky maps are included in:

Field, Thomas P. *Guide to Kentucky Place Names.* Lexington, Ky.: Kentucky Geological Survey, 1961. Early compilation on which some of Rennick's work (cited below) is based.

Rennick, Robert M. *Kentucky Place Names.* Lexington, Ky.: University Press of Kentucky, ca. 1984. A survey of Kentucky places was undertaken in 1971. This volume was published to publicize and stimulate interest in the survey. It catalogs approximately one-fourth of known places, usually only the largest, best known, and/or most important.

Stephenson, R. W. *Land Ownership Maps.* Washington, D.C.: Library of Congress, 1967. Contains maps of thirty-five Kentucky counties.

U.S. Geological Survey Maps (see page 4) for Kentucky are helpful in locating cemeteries.

Land Records

State-Land State

All early property in Kentucky was historically under Virginia's jurisdiction. In May 1779, Virginia passed an act which divided its western lands including Kentucky County, which consisted of all of the present-day state. Just eighteen months later, Kentucky County was discontinued, and Fayette, Lincoln, and Jefferson counties were organized from it. The only extant land entries for this time are those in Land Entry Books of Jefferson and Lincoln counties, but these include some Kentucky County records. Originals are kept by the county clerk of Jefferson County and are entitled "Land Entry Book No. A." Lincoln County records are at the Kentucky Land Office, Frankfort.

Like many other colonies prior to the Revolutionary War, Virginia had plenty of land, but little money. After the French and Indian War ended in 1763, Virginia found it necessary to pay the troops in bounty-land warrants. Military warrants were issued for military service and treasury warrants could be purchased. Warrants were issued authorizing surveys of property. The procedure was ineffective for it did not require a survey of the land prior to the issuance of the warrant. Instead, Virginia law required the person locate his land wherever he chose and then survey the property at his own cost. Unfortunately, the surveys were not reliable as most were not adept at surveying, and their attempts to do so sometimes resulted in conflicts in title and loss of the land.

Original surveys, patents, warrants and grants as well as indexes are filed in the Secretary of State's Office, Room 148, Capitol Building, Frankfort, Kentucky 40601. The Kentucky Historical Society and Kentucky Department for Libraries and Archives have microfilm copies of these records.

Land and property records for Kentucky include deeds, entries, warrants, surveys, mortgages, and indexes to these documents. Under the Kentucky Court of Appeals, which served as a court of record, deed books were maintained beginning in 1796. The first twenty-six books are designated as books *A* through *Z* for the period 1796 to 1835, although earlier deeds and documents, some dated as early as 1775, are recorded therein.

Within these twenty-six volumes are documents for residents of Virginia, Pennsylvania, Maryland, New York, New Jersey, and Louisiana, as well as some foreign countries. Books *A* through *C* comprise, for the most part, documents relating to the period 1775 through 1796, but other books also include early records.

When the Green River country opened, a law enacted in 1795 provided that each head of household would receive the maximum of 200 acres at the rate of $30 per hundred acres. The "In Fee Simple" title to the property was not to be given to the landholder until the price of the land was completely paid.

The following printed sources deal with Kentucky land records:

Brookes-Smith, Joan E. *Index for Old Kentucky Surveys and Grants.* Frankfort, Ky.: Kentucky Historical Society, 1975. Alphabetically arranged from the microfilm collection at the Kentucky Historical Society, the book includes volume number, original survey number, name, acreage, county, watercourse, survey date, original book and page, grantee, grant, and original book and page.

———. *Master Index: Grants which Were in What is Now Kentucky.* Frankfort, Ky.: Kentucky Historical Society, 1975. Compiled from thousands of original documents, includes original survey number, individual's name, acreage, county where filed, location on watercourse, survey, grantee to whom land was later transferred, date, and book and page.

———, comp. *Master Index: Virginia Surveys and Grants 1774–1791.* Frankfort, Ky.: Kentucky Historical Society, 1976. Contains data pertaining to bounty-land grants for service against the French and Indians. Includes Acts of the General Assembly of Kentucky pertaining to original land titles. Alphabetically arranged, includes Kentucky Historical Society volume number, original survey number, name, acreage, county, watercourse, survey date, original book and page, grantee, grant date, and original book and page.

Cook, Michael L., and Bettie A. Cook, *Kentucky Court of Appeals Deed Books.* 4 vols. Evansville, Ind.: Cook Publications, 1985. In a series of nine volumes of *Kentucky Records Series.* Deed Books cover periods 1796–1803, 1803–11, 1811–21, 1821–35. Volume 4 also includes supreme court records for the district of Kentucky, 1783–89.

———. *Fincastle & Kentucky County Virginia-Kentucky Records & History.* Vol. 1. Kentucky Records Series. Vol. 18. Evansville, Ind.: Cook Publications, 1987. Contains all known extant records for these counties, plus all acts of the Virginia legislature pertaining to Kentucky prior to 1792. Includes land entries for Lincoln and Jefferson counties pertaining to Kentucky County and Fincastle County land records.

Jillson, Willard Rouse. *The Kentucky Land Grants: A Systematic Index to All of the Land Grants Recorded in the State Land Office at Frankfort, Kentucky, 1782–1924.* 2 vols. 1925. Reprint. Baltimore, Md.: Genealogical Publishing Co., 1971. Vol. 1 [part 1] lists Kentucky land grants; Virginia grants, 1782–92; Old Kentucky grants, 1793–1856; Grants south of Green River, 1797–1866; Tellico Grants, 1803–53; Kentucky land warrants, 1816–73; Grants West of Tennessee River, 1822–58; and Grants south of Walker's line, 1825–1923. Vol. 2 [part 2] contains warrants for headright, 1827–49 (one page) and grants in county court records, 1836–1924. Originally published as Filson Club Publication Number 33.

———. *Old Kentucky Entries and Deeds: A Complete Index to All of the Earliest Land Entries, Military*

Warrants, Deeds and Wills of the Commonwealth of Kentucky. 1926. Reprint. Baltimore, Md.: Genealogical Publishing Co., 1987. This work is a companion volume to *Kentucky Land Grants* and indexes land records for the commonwealth of Kentucky. Records abstracted include manuscript documents of early civil land entries, military warrants, and state land office entries as well as first deeds, wills, and powers of attorney (relative to land) that were filed with the clerk of the court of appeals at Frankfort. Each section is arranged alphabetically and must be searched separately. Originally published as Filson Club Publication Number 34.

Sutherland, James F., comp. *Early Kentucky Landholders, 1787–1811.* Baltimore, Md.: Genealogical Publishing Co., 1986. A valuable tool for tracking elusive Kentucky land records. Contains data on over 17,000 landholders, representing forty-six of the fifty-four Kentucky counties extant in 1811.

Once county jurisdiction was established, land was to be surveyed and recorded at the county clerk's office. In most cases, original county land and property records are maintained by the respective county clerk's office, but microfilm copies are available at the Kentucky Department for Libraries and Archives, the University of Kentucky Library, Kentucky Historical Society, Filson Club Library, and the FHL. Some published land records are available in local, regional, historical. or genealogical society collections or libraries.

Probate Records

County probate records are filed at the respective county courthouse usually under the county clerk's jurisdiction. Probate records include wills, estates, administrators, executors, inventories, settlements, sales, accounts, guardianship, orphans, insolvent estates, bastardy, apprentices, and insanity. Documents pertaining to probate are recorded in volumes containing records of administrations, court proceedings, court minutes, estates, executors, guardians, inventories, probates, sales, settlements, and/or wills. Records may be filed under various titles. Loose papers are usually kept in folders or tied together in packets. Early estate records are frequently recorded along with regular proceedings of the county court. Circuit court records include inherited estate disputes. Some counties have transcribed early wills. The Kentucky Historical Society and the Filson Club Library have collections of these.

Some transcribed or microfilm copies of original probate records are available at the Kentucky Department for Libraries and Archives, Kentucky Historical Society, University of Kentucky Library, Filson Club Library, and the FHL. Some wills and inventories for the period of 1780 to 1788 are recorded in book *J* of the books maintained by the Kentucky Court of Appeals. These have been abstracted by Michael and Bettie Cook (see Land Records).

Unfortunately, many of the 120 Kentucky county courthouses have suffered record loss because of fire or other accidents. Even though fire may have destroyed records pertinent to the county in which research is being conducted, some records were re-recorded. Research must encompass several years beyond the time of the destruction of records.

Two sources are the following:

Jackson, Ronald, comp. *Index to Kentucky Wills to 1851.* Bountiful, Utah: Accelerated Indexing System, 1977.

King, Junie Estelle Stewart. *Abstracts of Early Kentucky Wills and Inventories.* 1933. Reprint. Baltimore, Md.: Genealogical Publishing Co., 1969.

Court Records

The first constitution gave judicial powers to the Kentucky Court of Appeals. Other courts of record in Kentucky included superior, county, chancery, quarterly, circuit, justice of peace, police, district, quarter sessions, oyer and terminer, and general. Court records include dockets, minutes, case files and orders. Land, tax, and probate matters may be included in Kentucky court records. Most court records are maintained at the respective county courthouse. Some original records are maintained in books, while other court-related documents are filed in folders in boxes or cabinets. Many of the books containing court records have been microfilmed, some have been abstracted and published, but the great majority of data filed in boxes, cabinets, and folders has not been copied in any form.

Courts and their jurisdiction have altered over time in Kentucky. Some early courts are no longer extant. Some have undergone name or jurisdictional changes. Early records may be filed in volumes or containers that may be mistitled, making it necessary to examine all court records for a county. County courts maintained jurisdiction over most matters, both civil and criminal, until 1852 when quarterly or circuit courts began handling criminal cases. Some circuit courts handled major civil and criminal matters as well as divorces. The circuit courts also served as appellate courts. Matters involving large sums of money were usually heard by the courts of quarter sessions from before statehood through the state's first ten years.

Microfilmed copies of county court records are at the Kentucky Department for Libraries and Archives. Many transcribed records are available at the University of Kentucky Library, the Kentucky Historical Society, Filson Club Library, and the FHL. Some published or transcribed records are at local and regional libraries.

Ireland, Robert M. *The County Courts in Antebellum Kentucky.* Lexington, Ky.: University of Kentucky Press, 1972. Includes data concerning court procedures and types of records created.

Richardson, William C. *An Administrative History of Kentucky Courts to 1850.* Frankfort, Ky.: Kentucky Department for Libraries and Archives, 1983.

Tax Records

One of the most valuable sources for early Kentucky until 1892 is its tax records. Most counties have yearly tax records from the date of organization. Some early tax schedules list watercourse, value and acreage of real estate, men over twenty-one, young men between sixteen and twenty-one, slaves, and horses. Extant county tax schedules from the date of organization of the county through 1892 have been microfilmed for most counties and are available from the Kentucky Department for Libraries and Archives and the FHL. Numerous original tax records from 1892 are available at the Kentucky Department for Libraries and Archives. The Kentucky Historical Society has tax records to 1875.

Kentucky tax lists are arranged by county and date. Within the counties, residents within its districts are grouped together and names usually arranged under the beginning letter of the surname, although these are not in strict alphabetical order. Some early tax records have been published and are available in research libraries (see Census Records).

Cemetery Records

Many collections of cemetery records are available for Kentucky. In 1977 the Kentucky Historical Society began computerizing extant cemetery records for the state. Cemetery tombstone transcriptions are included in the Ardery collection (see Manuscripts). The main repositories for cemetery compilations are the Kentucky Historical Society, University of Kentucky Library, Filson Club Library, DAR Library in Washington, D.C., local libraries, and the FHL. Kentucky regional libraries and some other large genealogical libraries outside the state have collections of Kentucky cemetery transcriptions. In addition, publications pertaining to Kentucky and Kentuckians frequently contain cemetery records for the state. See also:

Coyle, Malle B., and Lorena Eubanks. *Kentucky Cemetery Records.* Lexington, Ky.: Kentucky Society, Daughters of the American Revolution, 1960.

Johnson, Robert Foster. *Wilderness Road Cemeteries in Kentucky, Tennessee, and Virginia.* Owensboro, Ky.: McDowell Publications, 1981.

Wilson, V., M. B. Coyle, L. C. Mallows, and I. B. Gaines. *Kentucky Cemetery Records.* 5 vols. Florence, Ky.: Daughters of the American Revolution, 1960–72. The Coyle and Eubanks volume cited above is part of this series.

Church Records

Church membership of early Kentuckians include Baptist, Church of Christ, Episcopal, Lutheran, Methodist, Presbyterian, and Roman Catholic. Some church records were published, others were microfilmed, some are housed in church repositories, but many remain in the local church. Church records and histories may be found in periodicals pertaining to Kentucky. Repositories include the DAR Library, the FHL, Kentucky Historical Society, University of Kentucky Library, and Filson Club Library. The original Shane Manuscript Collection, which pertains to Kentucky Presbyterians, is housed at Presbyterian Historical Society, 425 Lombard Street, Philadelphia, Pennsylvania 19147. It has been microfilmed and is available at other libraries.

See also *Kentucky Bible Records,* 6 vols., from files of the Genealogical Records Committee, Kentucky Society of Daughters of the American Revolution. Volume 4 was compiled by Malle B. Coyle and Anne W. Fitzgerald for the Kentucky Records Research Committee (Florence, Ky.: Kentucky State Society Daughters of the American Revolution, 1966). Volume 5 was compiled by Malle B. Coyle and Lorena C. Eubanks (1981). Each volume is individually indexed. Most entries include only name, date, and name and address of the owner of the Bible at the time of publication. These are available at the Kentucky Historical Society. Local genealogical groups publish Kentucky Bible records in genealogical publications such as *Bluegrass Roots,* and *Kentucky Ancestors* (see Periodicals).

Military Records

Kentucky men served in all U.S. military conflicts. As with other states, many types of military records—service, pension, and bounty land—are maintained by the National Archives in Washington, D.C., and its regional centers (see page 7). The Military Records and Research Branch, Division of Veteran's Affairs, Pine Hill Plaza, 1121 Louisville Road, Frankfort, Kentucky 40601, maintains military service records from the Revolutionary War to the present. The Kentucky Department for Libraries and Archives and the Kentucky Historical Society have strong collections which cover service as well as pension and bounty-land records.

Although sparsely settled at the time, men from Kentucky served in the Revolutionary War. Many of the state's later residents served for Virginia and were allotted Kentucky land for their service. Anderson C. Quisenberry's *Revolutionary Soldiers in Kentucky* (Baltimore, Md.: Genealogical Publishing Co., 1968) covers a broad scope of service records. Names of many early Kentuckians and others who later obtained land grants in Kentucky can be found in records of the George Rogers Clark military expedition. A chronological compilation of name, rank, dates of enlistment and discharge, and payment are included in Margery Heberling Harding, *George Rogers Clark and His Men: Military Records, 1778–84* (Frankfort, Ky.: Kentucky Historical Society, n.d.).

Civil War rosters for Kentuckians who served in the Union and Confederate armies have been indexed and are available at the Kentucky Department for Libraries and

Archives. Kentucky provided its Confederate veterans and widows with pensions which can be located through the Kentucky Historical Society and Kentucky Department for Libraries and Archives. Alice Simpson, *Index of Kentucky Confederate Pension Applications* (Frankfort, Ky.: Division of Archives and Records Management, Department for Libraries and Archives, 1978), is helpful in locating these materials in Kentucky.

The Kentucky Historical Society has indexed rosters for Revolutionary Soldiers buried in Kentucky and Kentuckians who served in the Mexican War, 1846–48. The University of Kentucky and Kentucky Historical Society house the state Sons of the American Revolution organization papers, and Eastern Kentucky State University published rosters of Civil War regiments from Kentucky.

The following is a brief list of published works on Kentucky military records:

Burns, Annie Walker. *Abstracts of Pension Papers of Soldiers of the Revolutionary War, War of 1812, and Indian Wars Who Settled in Kentucky.* 20 vols. Washington, D.C.: the author, 1935–present.

Clift, G. Glenn. *The "Cornstalk" Militia of Kentucky, 1792–1811.* 1957. Reprint. Baltimore, Md.: Genealogical Publishing Co., 1982. Includes a history of the militia and lists of commissioned officers.

Cook, Michael L. *Index to Report of the Adjutant General of the State of Kentucky.* 4 vols. Owensboro, Ky.: Cook and McDowell Publications, 1979–82. Both volumes (Union and Confederate) of the original report are covered by these indexes.

Secretary of War Report. *Kentucky Pension Roll of 1835.* Baltimore, Md.: Southern Book Co., 1959.

Taylor, P. F. *A Calendar of the Warrants for Land in Kentucky for Service in the French and Indian War.* Baltimore, Md.: Genealogical Publishing Co., 1967. Good source for records of early military land warrants.

Wilson, Samuel M. *Catalogue of Revolutionary Soldiers and Sailors to Whom Land Bounty Warrants were Granted by Virginia.* Baltimore, Md.: Genealogical Publishing Co., 1967.

Periodicals, Newspapers, and Manuscript Collections

Periodicals

Several statewide, regional, and local genealogical publications are available for Kentucky. Most can be found at either the Kentucky Historical Society, the University of Kentucky Library, the Filson Club Library, regional libraries, or the FHL. Some local libraries maintain copies pertaining to their area. Many genealogical publications are maintained in the Kentucky Genealogical Society's collection housed at the Kentucky Department for Libraries and Archives.

Statewide or regional publications include the following:

Bluegrass Roots. (1973–present). Frankfort, Ky.: Kentucky Genealogical Society.

The Bulletin. (1968–present). Owensboro, Ky.: West-Central Kentucky Family Research Association.

The East Kentuckian: Journal of Genealogy and History. (1965–present). Lexington, Ky.: published privately by Clayton R. Cox.

Filson Club Historical Quarterly. (1926–present). Louisville, Ky.: Filson Club.

Kentucky Ancestors. (1965–present). Frankfort, Ky.: Kentucky Historical Society.

Kentucky Family Records. (1969–present). Owensboro, Ky.: West-Central Kentucky Family Research Association.

The Kentucky Genealogist. (1959–present). Louisville, Ky.: James R. Bentley, ed.

Kentucky Kinfolk. (1985–present). Lexington, Ky.: Kentucky Tree-Search.

Kentucky Pioneer Genealogy and Records. (1979–present). Evansville, Ind.: Cook and McDowell Publications.

The Register of the Kentucky Historical Society. (1903–present). Frankfort, Ky.: Kentucky Historical Society. A subject index is available for the first forty-three volumes.

South Central Kentucky Historical and Genealogical Society Quarterly. (1974–present). Glasgow, Ky.: South Central Kentucky Historical and Genealogical Society. Changed name to *Traces* in 1982.

Tree Shaker. (1982–present). Ashland, Ky.: Eastern Kentucky Genealogical Society.

Two sources combine information from noted periodicals for Kentucky:

Klotter, James, ed. *Genealogies of Kentucky Families From the Register of the Kentucky Historical Society and the Filson Club History Quarterly.* 4 vols. Frankfort, Ky.: Kentucky Historical Society, 1981. This indexed set includes all genealogies printed in the publications since 1903.

Trapp, Glenda K., and Michael L. Cook. *Kentucky Genealogical Index.* Vol. 1. Evansville, Ind.: Cook Publications, 1981. Every-name index to individuals mentioned in leading Kentucky genealogical publications.

Newspapers

The University of Kentucky Library is the major state repository for newspapers for the state. It participates in the United States newspaper project with holdings available from an on-line data base. The Kentucky Union List of 14,000 titles of early Kentucky papers that have been identified by a recent project is presently being microfilmed. When complete, all titles will be available through interlibrary loan.

The Kentucky Gazette, a Lexington newspaper, published news for most early Kentucky counties. Microfilm copies are available at many libraries in and out of the state and at the University of Kentucky Library in Lexington.

The *Louisville Courier* has been indexed for the years 1917 to 1977.

Some original and microfilmed newspapers are also available at the Kentucky Historical Society, the Filson Club Library, and the Lexington Public Library. The FHL and some regional libraries also have copies on microfilm.

Other helpful sources include:

Clift, G. Glenn, comp., ed. *Kentucky Obituaries, 1787–1854*. Reprint. Baltimore, Md.: Genealogical Publishing Co., 1984. Compiled from publications of *The Register of the Kentucky Historical Society*, from newspapers housed in the Lexington Public Library, from *The Kentucky Gazette*, and from *The Reporter*. Chronologically arranged.

Green, Karen Mauer. *The Kentucky Gazette: Genealogical and Historical Abstracts*. 2 vols. Baltimore, Md.: Gateway Press, 1983–85. Volume 1 covers 1787–1800; Volume 2 covers 1801–20. These volumes are extracts of names, events, and dates from *The Kentucky Gazette* and include entries for people from many Kentucky counties. Volumes are individually indexed; each have separate indexes for persons and places.

Manuscripts

The largest collections of manuscripts, many on microfilm, are at the University of Louisville, Western Kentucky University in Bowling Green, Kentucky Historical Society, University of Kentucky Library, and the Filson Club Library. Manuscript collections pertaining (all or in part) to Kentucky and Kentuckians include, among many, those of Ardery, Barton, and Draper.

The Ardery Collection contains abstracts of Kentucky and Virginia court, land, and Bible records as well as family history and correspondence. It is housed at University of Kentucky Library, has been microfilmed, and is available through the FHL. See also:

Ardery, Julia H. *Kentucky Records*. 2 vols. Baltimore, Md.: Genealogical Publishing Co., 1969.

The Barton Collection is housed at the University of Kentucky Library; most material in this collection pertains to Pendleton County, but other counties and states are represented. It is available on microfilm at the Kentucky Historical Society, the Kentucky Department for Libraries and Archives, and through the FHL.

The Draper Manuscripts, located at the State Historical Society of Wisconsin (see Wisconsin—Manuscripts for a guide), contain a wealth of information concerning Kentucky and Kentuckians. This exceptional collection of historical material has been microfilmed (134 reels) and is available for purchase or for interlibrary loan from that repository. Locally, the entire Draper collection is available on microfilm at the Kentucky Historical Society, the Kentucky Department for Libraries and Archives, and the University of Kentucky.

The DAR Collection includes transcriptions of Bible, cemetery, church, marriage, death, obituary, and probate records. It is housed at the DAR Library (see page 9) with microfilm copies of the originals available through the FHL.

In addition to *The Guide to Kentucky Archival and Manuscript Repositories*, cited under Archives, Libraries, and Societies, see also:

Brookes-Smith, Joan E. *Kentucky Historical Society: Microfilm Catalog: Excerpted Manuscripts*. 2 vols. Frankfort, Ky.: Kentucky Historical Society, 1975.

Clift, G. Glenn. *Guide to the Manuscripts of the Kentucky Historical Society*. Frankfort, Ky.: Kentucky Historical Society, 1955.

Talley, William M. *Talley's Northeastern Kentucky Papers*. Fort Worth, Tex.: American Reference Publishers, 1971.

Archives, Libraries, and Societies

Kentucky Department for Libraries and Archives
Public Records Division
300 Coffee Tree Road
Frankfort, KY 40601

The department serves as the statewide repository for microfilmed county records from the earliest date for all 120 counties. Some counties, without sufficient space, store either their original early or modern records here as well. Consequently research using original records for many counties can be conducted entirely at this repository. Correspondence with the department and the appropriate counties is recommended to clarify specific holdings.

Kentucky Historical Society
Old Capitol Annex
Broadway Street
Frankfort, KY 40601

For a dated description of some holdings in the Kentucky Historical Society Library, consult Brookes-Smith, Joan E. *Kentucky Historical Society Microfilm Catalog*, Vols. 3–4 (Frankfort, Ky.: Kentucky Historical Society, 1981).

Kentucky Genealogical Society
Box 153
Frankfort, KY 40602

University of Kentucky
Margaret King Library
Lexington, KY 40506

Filson Club Library
1310 S. Third Street
Louisville, KY 40205

A finding aid for names and addresses of Kentucky genealogical and historical societies is the following:

Kentucky Historical Society. *Directory of Historical Organizations and Speakers Bureau.* Frankfort, Ky.: Historical Confederation of Kentucky and Kentucky Historical Society, 1988. Guide to over 300 organizations, lists addresses and publications.

See also:

Kentucky Department for Libraries and Archives. *The Guide to Kentucky Archival and Manuscript Repositories.* Frankfort, Ky.: Public Records Division, 1986.

A valuable research tool is Kentucky Department for Libraries and Archives' *The Guide to Kentucky Archival and Manuscript Repositories* (Frankfort, Ky.: Public Records Division, 1986). Copyrighted by the Kentucky Department for Libraries and Archives, this compilation is based on data gathered by the Kentucky Guide Project. It contains an overview of 285 Kentucky repositories and their holdings.

Special Focus Categories

Black American

Both the Filson Club and the Kentucky Historical Society have extensive manuscripts and indexes of their collections, many of which include black families who migrated both as slaves and during Reconstruction (see also Virginia—Black American).

County Resources

Early Kentucky vital records, beginning from the dates indicated and until 1911 are held by the Kentucky Department of Libraries and Archives (see Vital Records). Land and probate records may be available at the office of the county clerk or at the Kentucky Department for Libraries and Archives.

Legal enactment dates for counties often vary from effective date of organization and beginning of record maintenance. The latter date is the one reflected in the following chart. Inventory sheets from the Kentucky Department for Libraries and Archives and the Kentucky Historical Society were used for beginning dates of some records. Land records may pre-date county organization because records were transferred from the parent county.

Dates given for court records may apply to one of many court records located in the county seat (see Court Records). Not all records are extant from the first date given.

For all records, it is advisable to direct correspondence to the county official at the county courthouse address listed below to determine present location and availability of records. In many cases, the Kentucky Department for Libraries and Archives will hold either the original or microfilm records.

The Historical Records Survey, *Guide to Public Vital Records in Kentucky* (Louisville, Ky.: Historical Records Survey, 1942), was used to extract some information found in the following county listing. County formation information comes from Wendell Holmes Rone, Sr., *An Historical Atlas of Kentucky and Her Counties* (Mayfield, Ky.: Mayfield Printing Co., 1965). It contains photographs, chronologically arranged maps, and historical data from 1772 through 1856. Campbell and Kenton counties have two county courthouses.

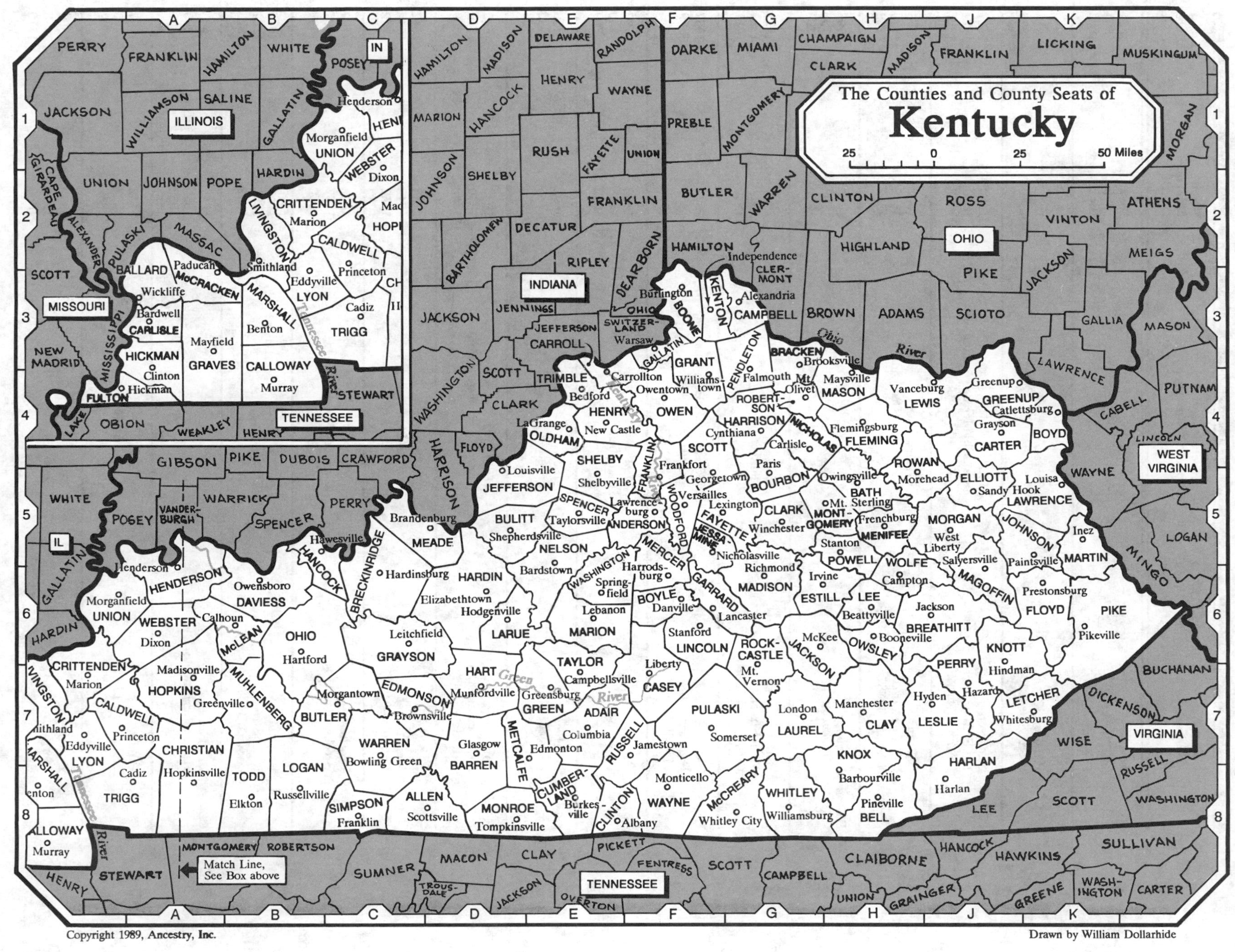
The Counties and County Seats of
Kentucky
25 0 25 50 Miles
Match Line, See Box above
Copyright 1989, Ancestry, Inc.
Drawn by William Dollarhide

Map	County Address	Effective Date Parent County/ies	Birth Marriage Death	Land Probate Court
E7	Adair Columbia 42728	1802 Green	1852 1802 1852	1801 1804 1802
D8	Allen P.O. Box 336 Scottsville 42164	1815 Barren/Warren	1862 1815 1852	1816 1815 1826
F5	Anderson 151 S. Main Street Lawrenceburg 40342	1827 Franklin/Mercer/Washington	1852 1831 1852	1827 1827 1827
A2	Ballard P.O. Box 145 Wickliffe 42087	1842 Hickman/McCracken	1852 1852 1852	1873 1879 1842
D7	Barren Glasgow 42141	1799 Green/Warren	1852 1799 1852	1795 1799 1799
H5	Bath Main Street Owingsville 40360	1811 Montgomery	1852 1811 1852	1811 1811 1811
H8	Bell P.O. Box 156 Pineville 40977	1867 (as Josh Bell; renamed, 1873) Knox/Harlan	1874 1867 1874	1867 1869 1867
F3	Boone Burlington 41005	1799 Campbell	1852 1798 1852	1799 1800 1799
G5	Bourbon Paris 40361	1786 Fayette	1852 1786 1852	1786 1786 1786
K4	Boyd 2800 Louisa Street Catlettsburg 41129	1860 Carter/Lawrence/Greenup	1859 1860 1859	1860 1860 1860
F6	Boyle Main Street Danville 40422	1842 Mercer/ Lincoln	1852 1842 1852	1842 1842 1842
G3	Bracken Brooksville 41104	1797 Campbell/Mason	1852 1797 1852	1797 1797 1798
J6	Breathitt Main Street Jackson 41339	1839 Clay/Estill/Perry	1852 1852 1852	1870 1884 1873
C6	Breckinridge Hardinsburg 40143	1800 Hardin	1852 1852 1852	1800 1800 1800
D5	Bullitt Shepherdsville 40165	1797 Jefferson/Nelson	1852 1797 1852	1797 1796 1797
C7	Butler Morgantown 42261	1810 Logan/Ohio	1852 1814 1852	1809 1812 1810

Map	County Address	Effective Date Parent County/ies	Birth Marriage Death	Land Probate Court
C2	Caldwell 100 E. Market Street Princeton 42445	1809 Livingston	1852 1809 1852	1809 1809 1809
B4	Calloway 101 S. Fifth Street Murray 42071 **This is the date of the earliest existing record, and records are not on microfilm.*	1821 Hickman	1852 1823 1852	1823 1836 1856*
G3	Campbell 24 W. Fourth Street Newport 41071 *and* Alexandria 41001	1795 Harrison/Mason/Scott	1852 1795 1852	1795 1794 1795
A3	Carlisle Bardwell 42023	1886 Graves/Ballard	1911 1886 1901	1886 1886 1886
E3	Carroll Carrollton 41008	1838 Gallatin/Henry/Trimble	1852 1837 1852	1795 1838 1838
J4	Carter Grayson 41143	1838 Greenup/Lawrence	1852 1838 1852	1838 1835 1838
F6	Casey Liberty 42539	1807 Lincoln	1852 1807 1852	1807 1809 1807
A8	Christian 511 S. Main Street Hopkinsville 42240	1797 Logan	1852 1797 1852	1797 1797 1797
G5	Clark Winchester 40391	1793 Bourbon/Fayette	1852 1793 1852	1793 1793 1793
H7	Clay P.O. Box 463 Manchester 40962	1807 Madison/Floyd/Knox	1852 1806 1852	1807 1826 1809
E8	Clinton Albany 42602	1836 Wayne/Cumberland	1852 1852 1852	1853 1863 1864
B2	Crittenden 107 S. Main Street Marion 42064	1842 Livingston	1852 1842 1852	1842 1833 1843
E8	Cumberland P.O. Box 826 Burkesville 42717	1799 Green	1852 1799 1852	1799 1815 1820
B6	Daviess P.O. Box 389 Owensboro 42302	1815 Ohio	1853 1815 1853	1815 1815 1815
C7	Edmonson Brownsville 42210	1825 Grayson/Hart/Warren	1852 1825 1852	1825 1826 1831

Map	County Address	Effective Date Parent County/ies	Birth Marriage Death	Land Probate Court
J5	Elliott P.O. Box 225 Sandy Hook 41171	1869 Carter/Lawrence/Morgan	1874 1874 1874	1869 1966 1958
H6	Estill Main Street Irvine 40336	1808 Clark/ Madison	1852 1808 1852	1808 1808 1808
G5	Fayette 162 E. Main Street Lexington 40507	1780 Kentucky County, Va.	1852 1785 1852	1782 1793 1782
H4	Fleming Courthouse Square Flemingsburg 41041	1798 Mason	1852 1798 1852	1798 1798 1798
K6	Floyd Prestonsburg 41653	1800 Fleming/Mason/Montgomery	1852 1808 1853	1810 1860 1808
F5	Franklin St. Clair Street Frankfort 40601	1795 Woodford/Mercer/Shelby	1852 1795 1852	1794 1795 1795
A4	Fulton P.O. Box 126 Hickman 42050	1845 Hickman	1852 1845 1852	1845 1845 1845
F3	Gallatin Warsaw 41095	1799 Franklin/Shelby	1852 1799 1852	1798 1800 1799
F6	Garrard Lancaster 40444	1797 Madison/Lincoln/Mercer	1852 1797 1852	1797 1797 1797
F4	Grant Williamstown 41097	1820 Pendleton	1852 1820 1852	1820 1820 1820
A3	Graves 902 W. Broadway Mayfield 42066 **This is the date of the earliest existing record, and records are not on microfilm.*	1824 Hickman	1852 1852 1852	1887 1887 1853*
C6	Grayson 100 Court Square Leitchfield 42754	1810 Hardin/Ohio	1852 1852 1852	1896 1896 1906
E7	Green 203 W. Court Street Greensburg 42743	1793 Lincoln/Nelson	1852 1793 1852	1793 1793 1794
J4	Greenup Greenup 41144	1804 Mason	1852 1803 1852	1811 1822 1838
B5	Hancock County Administration Building Hawesville 42348	1829 Daviess/Ohio/Breckinridge	1852 1829 1852	1829 1830 1834
D6	Hardin Dixie Highway Elizabethtown 42701	1793 Nelson	1852 1793 1852	1793 1793 1793

Map	County Address	Effective Date Parent County/ies	Birth Marriage Death	Land Probate Court
J8	Harlan First and Central Street Harlan 40831	1819 Knox	1852 1820 1852	1820 1850 1820
G4	Harrison Cynthiana 41031	1794 Bourbon/Scott	1852 1794 1852	1794 1794 1794
D7	Hart P.O. Box 277 Munfordville 42765	1819 Hardin/Barren	1852 1852 1852	1819 (tax) 1819
A6	Henderson Henderson 42420	1799 Christian	1852 1808 1852	1797 1799 1816
E4	Henry New Castle 40050	1799 Shelby	1852 1800 1852	1799 1800 1803
A4	Hickman Clinton 42031	1821 Caldwell/Livingston	1852 1822 1852	1822 1822 1822
A7	Hopkins Madisonville 42431	1807 Henderson	1852 1807 1852	1807 1806 1807
G6	Jackson P.O. Box 279 McKee 40447	1858 Rockcastle/Owsley/Madison/ Clay/Estill/Laurel	1858 1858 1858	1858 1860 1858
D5	Jefferson Louisville 40202	1780 Kentucky County, Va.	1852 1780 1852	1783 1784 1780
F5	Jessamine Nicholasville 40356	1799 Fayette	1852 1799 1852	1799 1799 1799
K5	Johnson Paintsville 41240	1843 Floyd/Morgan/Lawrence	1852 1843 1852	1843 1859 1843
	Josh Bell	1867 (renamed Bell, 1873) Knox/Harlan		
F3	Kenton Covington 41012 *and* Independence 41051	1840 Campbell	1852 1840 1852	1840 1840 1840
J7	Knott Hindman 41822	1884 Perry/Breathitt/Floyd/Letcher	1911 1884 1911	1883 1892 1888
H8	Knox P.O. Box 105 Barbourville 40906	1800 Lincoln	1852 1800 1852	1800 1803 1800
D6	Larue Hodgenville 42748	1843 Hardin	1852 1843 1852	1843 1843 1843

Map	County Address	Effective Date Parent County/ies	Birth Marriage Death	Land Probate Court
G7	Laurel London 40741	1826 Whitley/Clay/Knox/Rockcastle	1852 1826 1852	1826 1826 1826
K5	Lawrence 122 S. Main Cross Louisa 41230	1822 Floyd/Greenup	1852 1822 1852	1822 1824 1822
H6	Lee P.O. Box 417 Beattyville 41311	1870 Owsley/Breathitt/Wolfe/ Estill	1874 1870 1874	1870 1873 1870
J7	Leslie Hyden 41749	1878 Clay/Harlan/Perry	1878 1878 1878	1879 1884 1878
K7	Letcher Whitesburg 41858	1842 Perry/Harlan	1852 1842 1852	1844 1871 1866
H4	Lewis P.O. Box 129 Vanceburg 41179 **This is the date of the earliest existing record, and records are not on microfilm.*	1807 Mason	1852 1807 1852	1807 1807 1807*
F6	Lincoln Stanford 40484	1780 Kentucky County, Va.	1852 1781 1852	1780 1781 1781
K5	Livingston Smithland 42081	1798 Christian	1852 1799 1852	1800 1799 1798
B8	Logan Russellville 42276	1792 Lincoln	1852 1790 1853	1792 1795 1793
B3	Lyon P.O. Box 350 Eddyville 42038	1854 Caldwell	1853 1854 1853	1854 1847 1854
G6	Madison Main Street Richmond 40475	1786 Lincoln	1852 1786 1852	1787 1787 1786
J6	Magoffin P.O. Box 530 Salyersville 41465	1860 Floyd/Johnson/Morgan	1859 1860 1859	1860 1860 1860
E6	Marion Lebanon 40033	1834 Washington	1852 1852 1852	1863 1863 1863
B3	Marshall Benton 42025	1842 Calloway	1852 1848 1852	1848 1848 1848
K5	Martin P.O. Box 485 Inez 41224	1870 Lawrence/Floyd/Pike/ Johnson	1874 1871 1874	1870 1861 1870
H4	Mason Maysville 41056	1789 Bourbon	1852 1789 1852	1789 1791 1789

Map	County Address	Effective Date Parent County/ies	Birth Marriage Death	Land Probate Court
A2	McCracken Paducah 42002	1825 Hickman	1852 1825 1852	1825 1826 1825
G8	McCreary Whitley City 42653	1912 Wayne/Pulaski/Whitley	1912 1912 1912	1912 1912 1912
B6	McLean Calhoun 42327	1854 Muhlenberg/Daviess/Ohio	1854 1854 1854	1854 1854 1854
D5	Meade Brandenburg 40108	1824 Hardin/Breckinridge	1852 1824 1852	1824 1824 1824
H5	Menifee P.O. Box 123 Frenchburg 40322	1869 Powell/Wolfe/Bath/ Morgan/Montgomery	1874 1869 1874	1869 1870 1869
F6	Mercer Harrodsburg 40330	1786 Lincoln	1852 1786 1852	1786 1786 1786
E7	Metcalfe Edmonton 42129	1860 Monroe/Adair/Barren/ Cumberland/Green	1861 1867 1861	1868 1865 1868
D8	Monroe Tompkinsville 42167	1820 Barren/Cumberland	1852 1869 1852	1863 1861 1863
H5	Montgomery P.O. Box 414 Mount Sterling 40353	1797 Clark	1852 1852 1852	1797 1797 1841
J5	Morgan West Liberty 41472	1823 Floyd/Bath	1852 1823 1852	1823 1866 1823
B7	Muhlenberg Greenville 42345	1799 Christian/Logan	1852 1799 1852	1798 1801 1799
E5	Nelson Bardstown 40004	1785 Jefferson	1852 1785 1852	1784 1784 1785
G4	Nicholas Carlisle 40311	1800 Bourbon/Mason	1852 1800 1852	1800 1800 1800
B6	Ohio Hartford 42347	1799 Hardin	1852 1808 1852	1799 1801 1803
E4	Oldham La Grange 40031	1824 Henry/Shelby/Jefferson	1852 1824 1852	1824 1824 1823
F4	Owen Owenton 40359	1819 Scott/Franklin/Gallatin/Pendleton	1852 1819 1852	1819 1820 1819

Map	County Address	Effective Date Parent County/ies	Birth Marriage Death	Land Probate Court
H6	Owsley Booneville 41314	1843 Clay/Estill/Breathitt	1852 1852 1852	1929 1930 1923*
	**This is the date of the earliest existing record, and records are not on microfilm.*			
G3	Pendleton P.O. Box 129 Falmouth 41040	1799 Bracken/Campbell	1852 1799 1852	1798 1841 1799
J7	Perry P.O. Box 150 Hazard 41701	1821 Clay/Floyd	1852 1821 1852	1821 1901 1895
K6	Pike 320 Main Street Pikeville 41501	1822 Floyd	1852 1822 1852	1820 1839 1822
H5	Powell Stanton 40380	1852 Clark/Estill/Montgomery	1852 1852 1852	1864 1864 1864
F7	Pulaski P.O. Box 724 Somerset 42501	1799 Green/Lincoln	1852 1799 1852	1799 1801 1799
G4	Robertson Mount Olivet 41064	1867 Bracken/Nicholas/ Harrison/Mason	1874 1867 1874	1868 1864 1867
G6	Rockcastle Mount Vernon 40456	1810 Pulaski/Lincoln/ Knox/Madison	1852 1852 1852	1865 1855 1873
J5	Rowan Morehead 40351	1856 Fleming/Morgan	1856 1881 1856	1880 1853 1880
F7	Russell Jamestown 42629	1826 Cumberland/Adair/Wayne	1852 1826 1852	1826 1826 1826
F4	Scott Georgetown 40324	1792 Woodford	1852 1837 1852	1783 1792 1792
E5	Shelby 501 Main Street Shelbyville 40065	1792 Jefferson	1852 1792 1852	1792 1792 1804
C8	Simpson Franklin 42134	1819 Allen/Logan/Warren	1852 1852 1852	1822 1882 1816
E5	Spencer Taylorsville 40071	1824 Shelby/Bullitt/Nelson	1852 1824 1852	1824 1824 1824
E6	Taylor Campbellsville 42718	1848 Green	1852 1848 1852	1848 1848 1848
B8	Todd Elkton 42220	1820 Christian/Logan	1852 1820 1852	1820 1820 1820

Map	County Address	Effective Date Parent County/ies	Birth Marriage Death	Land Probate Court
C3	Trigg Cadiz 42211	1820 Christian/Caldwell	1852 1820 1852	1820 1820 1820
E4	Trimble Bedford 40006	1837 Henry/Oldham/Gallatin	1852 1837 1852	1837 1837 1837
C1	Union Morganfield 42437	1811 Henderson	1852 1811 1852	1811 1811 1823
C7	Warren 429 E. 10th Street Bowling Green 42101	1797 Logan	1852 1797 1852	1797 1796 1796
E5	Washington P.O. Box 446 Springfield 40069	1792 Nelson	1852 1792 1852	1792 1792 1792
F8	Wayne P.O. Box 565 Monticello 42633	1801 Pulaski/Cumberland	1852 1801 1852	1800 1801 1801
A6	Webster Dixon 42409	1860 Hopkins/Union/Henderson	1874 1860 1874	1860 1860 1860
G8	Whitley Williamsburg 40769	1818 Knox	1852 1860 1852	1818 1818 1818
H6	Wolfe P.O. Box 400 Campton 41301 **This is the date of the earliest existing record, and records are not on microfilm.*	1860 Owsley/Breathitt/Powell/Morgan	1861 1861 1861	1887 1887* 1818
F5	Woodford Main Street Versailles 40383	1789 Fayette	1852 1789 1852	1789 1789 1789

LOUISIANA

Sharon Sholars Brown, C.G.

The colony of Louisiana was founded in 1699 by two brothers, Pierre Le Moyne d'Iberville and Jean Baptiste Le Moyne de Bienville. Its boundaries stretched as far east as the Perdido River, about halfway between present-day Mobile, Alabama, and Pensacola, Florida. It stretched westward to the Red and Calcasieu rivers, next door to Spanish territory, and extended north all the way to Canada—which was a French possession. The vast boundaries of colonial Louisiana included part or all of at least ten states: Alabama (western part), Arkansas, Illinois, Kentucky, Louisiana (eastern part), Minnesota, Mississippi, Missouri, Oklahoma, and Tennessee.

France reigned over the Louisiana colony from 1699 until all North America holdings were lost in 1763, at the end of the Seven Years' War. Great Britain claimed all French territory east of the Mississippi River, and Spain claimed all French territory west of the Mississippi.

There is one quirk in this division important to the genealogist: New Orleans, built on the east bank of the Mississippi River, should have gone to Great Britain but went to Spain instead. The kings of France and Spain were cousins. In 1763 they connived together to keep New Orleans out of the hands of Great Britain, their common enemy. They obtained their victory by convincing the British negotiators that New Orleans was actually on the west bank and not the east.

The Spanish ruled Louisiana from 1763 until they gave it back to France in 1800. It is important to note that although Louisiana was once again a French possession, there was no change of affairs. Spanish officials continued to govern the colony while Napoleon secretly negotiated with Thomas Jefferson to sell Louisiana to the United States. Therefore, if an ancestor lived in colonial Louisiana between 1800 and 1803, search for him or her in the Spanish records, not the French.

Louisiana was one of the areas in the world most sought after by the three major powers of Europe: Spain, France, and Great Britain. Spain explored it first but withdrew in favor of richer lands farther south. Then France settled the land, but France's decaying monarchy had little regard for the colony, while it was obvious that the French statesmen who were interested had never dealt with the vast land upon which their policies were to operate. They did not comprehend the great extent of the country and were entirely ignorant of the means necessary for the successful cultivation of their lower Mississippi colony. Once the Spanish secured the colony, they were doing a magnificent job of building it when they were forced by Napoleon to relinquish control.

The struggle for Louisiana was finally won, not by one of the European nations which had plotted and fought for its permanent control for so long, but by the infant nation which had arisen on the eastern shores of North America. The United States took possession of Louisiana in December 1803 and began preparing the colony, which had never known a working democracy, for statehood. War broke out between England and the United States in 1812, and Great Britain began to plan the conquest of Louisiana, which failed when the Battle of New Orleans was lost. Less than four months later Louisiana celebrated its third anniversary as an American state.

Vital Records

The civil recording of births, marriages, and deaths did not begin in earnest until the early twentieth century. Laws were passed in the late nineteenth century requiring that vital events be recorded, but there was little compliance until later. Prior to that time, it was the responsibility of the churches to maintain this data.

The Roman Catholic church dominated Louisiana until the Louisiana Purchase in 1803. In fact, it was the only church in Louisiana until then. The Catholic churches throughout the state kept registers of christenings, marriages, and burials and were the recorders of Louisiana's early vital records. For important published works relating to marriages, see Church Records and the following:

DeVille, Winston. *The New Orleans French, 1720–1733: A Collection of Marriage Records Relating to the First Colonists of the Louisiana Province.* Baltimore, Md.: Genealogical Publishing Co., 1973.

Forsyth, Alice D. *Louisiana Marriages, 1784–1806.* New Orleans, La.: Polyanthos, 1977.

———, and Ghislaine Pleasonton. *Louisiana Marriage Contracts: 1725–1758.* New Orleans, La.: Polyanthos, 1980.

Mills, Elizabeth Shown. *Natchitoches Church Marriages, 1818–1850, Translated Abstracts from Registers of St. François des Natchitoches, Louisiana.* Vol. 6, Cane River Creole Series. Tuscaloosa, Ala.: Mills Historical Press, 1985.

The earliest city in Louisiana to exact civil registrations was New Orleans in 1790; however, registrations were only randomly made until the twentieth century. It was not until 1914 that civil recording began statewide. As of 1990, the Division of Archives, Records Management and History (see Archives, Libraries, and Societies) now stores all birth records over 100 years old, death and marriage records over fifty years old and will make them available to researchers for a standard fee (presently $5).

Some parish health departments have alphabetical birth and death indexes for their areas. They are not, however, complete listings of all births and deaths of that parish. Copies of these vital records can be ordered from the Division of Vital Records, Office of Health Services and Environmental Quality, P.O. Box 60630, New Orleans, Louisiana 70160. There are a few births from 1790 and deaths ca. 1803, but the majority of the records start in 1914. One must either show proof of kinship as a direct descendant or provide proper authorization to obtain a copy of any of these records.

Census Records

Federal

Population Schedules.

- Indexed—1810, 1820, 1830, 1840, 1850, 1860, 1870
- Soundex—1880, 1900, 1910, 1920

Industry and Agriculture Schedules.

- 1850, 1860, 1870, 1880

Mortality Schedules.

- 1850, 1860, 1870, 1880

Slave Schedules.

- 1850, 1860

Union Veterans Schedules.

- 1890

After the 1803 purchase of Louisiana it became an American possession; therefore, the first federal census report taken for the state was 1810.

Caution should be used particularly with the AISI indexes (see page 2) for Louisiana. Many of the French and Spanish names were transcribed wrong and numerous omissions exist. Many of these population schedules have been published:

Ardoin, Robert B. L. *Louisiana Census Records: 1810–1820.* 3 vols. Vols. 1 and 2 (Baltimore, Md.: Genealogical Publishing Co., 1970–72) and Vol. 3 (New Orleans, La.: Polyanthos, 1977). These cover more than fourteen of the early settled parishes.

Childs, Marleta, and John Ross, eds. *North Louisiana Census Reports, Volume II: 1830 and 1840 Schedules of Caddo, Claiborne and Natchitoches Parishes, Volume III: 1850 and 1860 Schedules of Union Parish.* New Orleans, La.: Polyanthos, 1977.

As early as 1860 the federal government began attempts to identify Native Americans. In 1900 and 1910 it created a special Indian schedule. The first page was the same as the population census only it had "Indian Population" as its heading. The second page provided for such important information as tribal affiliation, the tribe of each parent, the person's Indian blood quantum, and—if not full-blooded—their precise racial mixture. These schedules will be found at the end of the ward or district in which the Native American resided.

Some of the supplemental census schedules taken by the federal government are available for Louisiana at Duke University, Durham, North Carolina. Copies may also exist in Louisiana, but to date they have not been found. Louisiana's mortality schedules (1850–80) are on microfilm T655 at the National Archives, Washington, D.C.

Colonial

During the colonial period, Louisiana shifted from French to Spanish control. Both were diligent scribes, and many censuses exist for Louisianians. Some of the censuses for the colony's inhabitants are listed below:

French Period

Maduell, Charles R., Jr., comp., and trans. *Census Tables for the French Colony of Louisiana, 1699–1732.* Baltimore, Md.: Genealogical Publishing Co., 1972. Includes the following:

- **December 1699:** Census of the Inhabitants of the first settlement on the Gulf Coast, Fort Maurepas.
- **25 May 1700:** Census of the Officers, petty officers, sailors, Canadians, freebooters, and others located at Biloxi as of 25 May 1700.
- **1704:** List of marriageable girls who arrived aboard the *Pelican* at Biloxi in the year 1704.
- **1 August 1706:** Census of the inhabitants of Fort Louis de la Louisianne at Mobile, taken by Nicolas de la Salle.
- **1 August 1706:** Census of families and inhabitants of Louisiana, taken by Nicolas de la Salle.
- **1711:** Census of Fort Louis de la Mobile from the map of 1711.
- **25 October 1713:** List of officers commissioned at Fort Louis, Biloxi.
- **October 1713:** Persons mentioned in the colony by Antoine de la Mothe Cadillac.
- **24 November 1721:** General census of all the inhabitants of New Orleans and environs, as reported by Le Sieur Diron.
- **26 June 1721:** Census of the inhabitants in the area of Biloxi and Mobile, as reported by Le Sieur Diron.
- **13 May 1722:** Census of the inhabitants of the concessions along the Mississippi River; reported by Le Sieur Diron.
- **1 May 1722:** Census of the inhabitants of Natchitoches, Fort St. Jean Baptist, taken for Le Sieur Diron, General of the Troops.
- **1722:** Officials of the colony at Fort Louis, Biloxi, appointed in 1722.
- **8 April 1723:** Some colonists of Louisiana mentioned in a letter by de La Chaise.
- **18 October 1723:** Some colonists of Louisiana mentioned in a letter by de La Chaise.
- **12 November 1724:** Census of inhabitants of German villages located ten leagues above New Orleans along the river, under command of D'Arensbourg.
- **20 December 1724:** Census of inhabitants along the Mississippi River from New Orleans to Ouacha, or the German villages.
- **March 1725:** Census of the inhabitants of Dauphin Island, along the Mobile River, Cat Island, and Penscagoula (Pascagoula), compiled by M. Gorty.
- **1 January 1726:** General census of all the inhabitants of the colony of Louisiana, including the entire coast bordering the Gulf of Mexico, from Mobile to New Orleans, and the colonies along the Mississippi River, including the region known as Illinois.
- **October 1726:** List of those persons requesting Negroes from the company.
- **1 July 1727:** Census of New Orleans as reported by M. Perier, Commander General of Louisiana; also continuation of the census of M. Perier, being the inhabitants in the environs of New Orleans, along the river.
- **9 June 1730:** List of persons massacred at Natchez, 28 November 1729, as reported by R. P. Philibert, Capuchin priest.
- **1731:** List of property owners of New Orleans on the map published by Gonichon in 1731; census of inhabitants along the Mississippi River, unsigned, initialled N. S.; and list of landowners located along the Mississippi River from its mouth to the German villages, with indications of how they acquired the land. Date mentioned "after 1731."
- **January 1732:** Census of the inhabitants and property owners of New Orleans and census of the inhabitants of Illinois, both unsigned but initialled N. S.

For this time period, see also Jacqueline K. Voorhies, *Some Late Eighteenth Century Louisianians, 1758–1796* (Lafayette, La.: University of Southwestern Louisiana, 1973).

Spanish Period

Hill, Roscoe R. *Descriptive Catalogue of the Documents relating to the History of the United States in the Papeles Procedentes de Cuba deposited in the Archivo General de Indias.* 1916. Reprint. New York, N.Y.: Kraus Reprint Corporation, 1965. Lists the following:

Legajo 34.

- **1795:** Census of Baton Rouge and Manchak.

Legajo 81.

- **1770:** Reports of Eduardo Nugent and Juan Kelly on the number of inhabitants and livestock in the districts of Atakapas, Natchitoches, Opelousas, and Rapides.

Legajo 117.

- **1784 (?):** Census of the German Coast.

Legajo 121.

- **1790:** Census of Ouachita.

Legajo 142.

- **1805:** Census of Baton Rouge.

Legajo 187-b.

- **1766:** List of inhabitants of Pointe Coupee; census of Pointe Coupee; list of Cote des Allemands; general census of Pointe Coupee; general census of Villere at Allemands.

Legajo 188-1.

- **1772:** Left Bank of the Mississippi from Bayou de Placaminas to Ile au Marais; 1773 Rapides; 1774 negroes and mulattoes at Natchitoches.

Legajo 188-2.

- **1771:** Census of Atakapas and Opelousas.

Legajo 189-2.

- **1776 (dated incorrectly, 1766):** Census of parish of St. Charles (Allemands).

Legajo 193.

- **1782:** Census of Baton Rouge; 1786 census of Baton Rouge; 1798 census of the district of Nueva Feliciana; census of the district of la Metearie.

Legajo 198.

- **1785:** Census of Avoyelles.

Legajo 201.

- **1788 and 1789:** Census of Rapides; 1789 census of Natchitoches.

Legajo 205.

- **1772:** Census of Rapides.

Legajo 211.

- **1795 (slaves):** Census of Primer Cote des Allemand; census of the second and third wards of New Orleans; census of slaves at Allemands, Atakapas, Natchitoches; 1796 census of the Quartier de la Metairie of New Orleans.

Legajo 212.

- **1795 (slaves):** General census of slaves of New Orleans and masters who contributed to indemnity for slaves lost at Pointe Coupee; 1778 census of the third ward of New Orleans; 1803 census of Pointe Coupee.

Legajo 216.

- **1799:** Census of Allemands and Atakapas; general census of New Orleans.

Legajo 218.

- **1774:** Census of Atakapas.

Legajo 220.

- **1803:** Census of Atakapas (six documents).

Legajo 227-r.

- **1790:** *Recensements de la Pointe Coupee et Fausse Riviere.*

Legajo 2351.

- **1777:** Census of Louisiana.

Legajo 2357.

- **1771:** Census of Louisiana.

Legajo 2358.

- **1777:** Census of Atakapas and Opelousas.

Legajo 2360.

- **1786:** Census of Atakapas and Opelousas.

Legajo 2361.

- **1787:** Census of Pointe Coupee.

Legajo 2364.

- **1796:** Census of Opelousas.

Almost all of these censuses from the Spanish archives have been published in English by Voorhies (cited under French Period above) and by Elizabeth Shown Mills in *Natchitoches Colonials: Censuses, Military Rolls and Tax Lists, 1722–1803* (Chicago, Ill.: Adams Press, 1981).

Nuestra Señora del Pilar de los Adaes served as the Spanish capital of Texas from 1721–73. This presidio was located in present-day Natchitoches Parish, near Robeline, Louisiana. It was abandoned in 1773 and its inhabitants relocated in San Antonio, Texas. By 1779 many of these people moved back closer to their old home of Adaes and reestablished the mission at Nacogdoches, Texas. Yearly census reports exist for Nacogdoches for the years 1792–1806 and 1809. Many Louisiana ancestors can be found on these enumerations. See "Census Reports of the Village of Nuestra del Pilar de Nacogdoches," Bexar Archives, University of Texas Archives, Austin, Texas—copies also found in the Robert Bruce Collection, Vol. 18, pages 71–284, Ralph W. Steen Library, Special Collection, Stephen F. Austin University, Nacogdoches, Texas.

Background Sources

Researchers interested in Louisiana have a number of excellent histories, archival guides, and source references available to them. The following are particularly useful:

French Period

Conrad, Glenn R., and Carl A. Brasseaux, eds. *A Selected Bibliography of Scholarly Literature on Colonial Louisiana and New France.* Lafayette, La.: Center for Louisiana Studies, 1982.

———. *First Families of Louisiana.* 2 vols. Baton Rouge, La.: Claitor's Publishing Division, 1970.

Giraud, Marcel. *Historire de La Louisiane Française.* 4 vols. Paris, France: Presses Universitaires de France, 1953–74. The first volume of this series has been translated into English and is available as Joseph C. Lambert, trans., *A History of Louisiana, Vol. 1: The Reign of Louis XIV, 1698–1715* (Baton Rouge, La.: Louisiana State University Press, 1974).

Leland, Waldo G. *Guide to Materials for American History in the Libraries and Archives of France.* Washington, D.C.: Carnegie Institute, 1932.

Spanish Period

Bancroft Library. *Spain and Spanish America in the Libraries of the University of California.* 2 vols. Berkeley, Calif.: University of California, 1928 and 1930.

Bolton, Herbert Eugene. *Guide to Materials for the History of the United States in the Principal Archives of Mexico.* Washington, D.C.: Carnegie Institute, 1913.

Buckely, Eleanor Claire. "The Aguayo Expedition Into Texas and Louisiana, 1719–1721." *The Quarterly of the Texas State Historical Association* 9 (July 1911).

Castañeda, Carlos E. *Our Catholic Heritage in Texas.* 6 vols. 1936–50. Reprint. New York, N.Y.: Arno Press, 1976.

Cox, Isaac Joslin. "The Louisiana-Texas Frontier." *The Quarterly of the Texas State Historical Association* 10 (July 1906): 8–10.

Documents Pertaining to the Floridas Which Are Kept in Different Archives of Cuba. Appendix No. 1: Official List of Documentary Funds of the Floridas—New Territories of the States of Louisiana, Alabama, Mississippi, Georgia, and Florida. Havana, 1945. Kept in the National Archives.

Haggard, J. Villasano. *Handbook for Translators of Spanish Historical Documents.* Austin, Tex.: University of Texas, 1941.

Hill, Roscoe J. *Descriptive Catalogue of the Documents Relating to the History of the United States in the Papeles Procedentes de Cuba, deposited in the Archivo General de Indias, Seville.* Washington, D.C.: Carnegie Institute, 1916.

Holmes, Jack D. L. *A Guide to Spanish Louisiana, 1762–1806.* New Orleans, La.: Louisiana Collection Series, 1970.

Notre Dame University. *Guide to the Microfilm Edition of the Records of the Diocese of Louisiana and the Floridas, 1576–1803.* Notre Dame, Ind.: the compilers, 1967.

Statehood

Carter, Clarence E. *The Territory of Louisiana, 1803–1812.* In *The Territorial Papers of the United States.* 27 vols. Washington, D.C.: Government Printing Office, 1940.

Foote, Lucy B. *Bibliography of the Official Publications of Louisiana, 1803–1934.* Baton Rouge, La.: Hill Memorial Library, Louisiana State University, 1942.

Korn, Bertram Wallace. *The Early Jews of New Orleans.* Waltham, Mass.: American Jewish Historical Society, 1969.

Laws of the United Stales of America, from the 4th of March 1789 to the 4th of March 1815. Washington, D.C.: R. C. Weightman and Philadelphia, Pa.: W. John Duane, 1815.

Mills, Elizabeth Shown, and Gary B. Mills. *Tales of Old Natchitoches.* Vol. 3. Cane River Creole Series. Natchitoches, La.: Association for the Preservation of Historic Natchitoches, 1978.

Nolan, Charles A. *A Southern Catholic Heritage, Volume I: 1704–1813.* New Orleans, La.: Archdiocese of New Orleans, 1976.

Poret, Ory G. *History of Land Titles in the State of Louisiana.* Baton Rouge, La.: Louisiana Department of Natural Resources, 1972.

Guides

DeVille, Winston. "Louisiana," in Kenn Stryker-Rodda, ed. *Genealogical Research: Methods and Sources.* Vol. 2. Rev. ed. Washington, D.C.: American Society of Genealogists, 1983.

Maps

Most of the larger libraries (public and university) have excellent map collections. Superb maps can be found in the many historic and archive collections throughout the state — for example, the Historic New Orleans Collection in that city's French quarter includes the Bouligny Family Papers and the d'Auberville-Bouligny Family Papers, which document life during both the French and Spanish colonial regimes in Louisiana and have an extensive cartographic collection numbering more than 400 items.

Maps created during Louisiana's changing regimes, by Spanish, French, and American sovereignty, give information beyond that obtained from documents and books: the Pierre Clement de Laussat Papers and the Claude Perrin Victor Papers are good examples. Maps of the antebellum era reveal the settlement of population and the growth of transportation systems throughout the state. These also are a part of the Historic New Orleans Collection, one of many repositories in Louisiana.

The State Land Office, located in the State Land and Natural Resources Building in Baton Rouge, has all of the original and official field notes, survey plats, and maps made by early U.S. surveyors in Louisiana. Plat maps (showing ownership) can also be found in each parish in the clerk of courts office located in the parish courthouse.

Land Records

Public-Domain State

One of the most fantastic real estate deals of all time was made in 1803 when the infant United States acquired 544 million acres from France for the sum of $15 million. The land of the famous Louisiana Purchase was bought for approximately three cents per acre.

By the Act of March 26, 1804, Congress divided Louisiana into two parts: the Territory of Louisiana and the Territory of Orleans. The Territory of Louisiana consisted of that area above the 33rd degree latitude, and the Territory of Orleans covered that part below the 33rd latitude, or what is now basically the state of Louisiana.

The governor and his legislative council used the powers granted by the act to divide the Territory of Orleans into twelve counties: Acadia, Attakapas, Concordia, German Coast, Iberville, Lafourche, Natchitoches, Opelousas, Orleans, Ouachita, Pointe Coupee, and Rapides.

In 1807 the territory was redivided into nineteen parishes. These boundaries followed the old ecclesiastical boundaries used by the Spaniards. When Louisiana became a state in 1812, the state constitution referred to both counties and parishes. By the time of the 1845 state constitution the term counties had been dropped, and Louisiana became the only state to use the term parishes.

An act of congress of 2 March 1805 gave three important provisions:

First, it allowed individuals to obtain legal possession of their land or to acquire land. Congress appointed district land registers and opened the United States District Land Office in New Orleans for the eastern division of the Territory of Orleans and a land office at Opelousas for the western division of the Territory of Orleans. Later, for the convenience of inhabitants, other land offices were opened in Ouachita, Natchitoches, and Greensburg. These land districts are still used today for identifying land by districts.

Second, inhabitants with French, Spanish, or British land grants had to appear before a board of commissioners with their proof of ownership. If approved by the board, the evidence was then forwarded on to Washington.

Third, surveyors were to go to the Territory of Orleans to establish a system of subdividing the vacant public lands. By 1807 the United States surveyors had established a meridian and base line. Thus Louisiana land measurements changed from metes and bounds to section, township, and range.

Colonial grants can be found in various Louisiana parishes and in France, Spain, and England. As has been shown, after the Louisiana Purchase people had to prove their land ownership. *American State Papers: Documents Legislative and Executive of the United States,* 32 vols., and *Public Lands,* 7 vols. (Washington, D.C.: Gales and Seaton, 1832–61), are the best sources for these re-patented lands. A guide to these papers is Phillip W. McMullin, *Grassroots of America* (Salt Lake City, Utah: Gendex, 1972).

The state land office and the offices of clerks of courts in the parish courthouses have state and federal tract books listing the original landowners. These books are not in alphabetical order; the land record itself will have to be obtained from the State Land Office in Baton Rouge or from the National Archives Suitland Reference Branch (see page 9).

Land records may be found in notarial records or deeds. Each of the early communities had its own notary public that drafted wills, deeds, marriage contracts, and all estate papers. These transactions were filed loosely, and numbered consecutively as they happened, regardless of the type of record. Many of these records are now in the clerk's office in the parish courthouse, some are in the Division of Archives in Baton Rouge. The Notarial Archives of New Orleans are in the Civil Courts Building in New Orleans. Other land records in the courthouses will be found in the conveyance books.

Probate (Succession) Records

The succession record of Louisiana is much like the probate files of other states; if a will exists—which is rare in early Louisiana—it is filed with the succession. This is indeed a rich source for genealogists. The family meeting is one of the most important documents found in a succession. These are meetings held by family members and friends to discuss the estate and the fate of the minor heirs (should there be any). They name each person attending, give their relationship to the deceased and the minors, give the ages of the children; if there are married daughters they give the names of their husbands, and the name the widow and any former spouses, with their maiden names. Other documents found in a succession are notes owed the deceased by others, an inventory of all property and movables, a complete listing of all heirs (with maiden names of the females and spouses of the married daughters), ages of all minor heirs, date of death of the deceased, appraisal of all property, and a listing of the disbursement of said property.

If the heirs of the deceased are not known, the succession is called a "vacant succession." The testimonies of acquaintances either identify the missing heirs or state that there are none. If there are heirs, then the succession is left open until they are located. In this case the ancestral data compiled can be overwhelming.

Court Records

Under the French regime provincial power was held by the governor and the superior council, while the *cabildo* served the Spanish. A group of men was appointed to serve on the council/*cabildo*. They acted similar to a court of law but did not have the power of legislature. Most of the records created by, or sent to, the council/*cabildo* are still in New Orleans and are a part of four collections:

Superior Council Records. Housed at the Mint Building in New Orleans, this collection from the French period is an important resource for families in all corners of the colony. The files contain not only the judicial records of the city of New Orleans, but also those of all the outposts whose cases were appealed to New Orleans. Translated and very brief abstracts of these records were serialized in volumes 1–23 of the *Louisiana Historical Quarterly.*

Spanish Judicial Archives. This is a group of legal suits prosecuted at the various settlements and sent to New Orleans for final disposition in the Spanish era. These records are located in the Louisiana State Museum in the Old U.S. Mint Building in New Orleans. Between 1923 and 1949, translated abstracts of these records were published in the *Louisiana Historical Quarterly.*

Black Boxes. This is another Spanish collection housed at the Louisiana State Museum. Americans acquired these documents in 1803 and packed them away in black wooden boxes, hence the name. The museum has translated abstracts to these records, and a guide to this collection was printed over several years in the quarterly *New Orleans Genesis.*

Minutes of the Cabildo. These are the records created by the Spanish governing body. Translations of these documents are available at most major libraries (public and university) in Louisiana. Some of the original records belonging to this collection can be found at the New Orleans Public Library, Tulane University in New Orleans, and Louisiana State University in Baton Rouge.

For a better understanding of the court system and its laws of the nineteenth and twentieth centuries, see Albert Tate, Jr., "The Splendid Mystery of the Civil Code of Louisiana," *Louisiana Review* 2, no. 2 (1974). Also, Coleman Lindsey, *The Courts of Louisiana* (N.p., n.d.). To conduct genealogical research in the parish courthouse, it is necessary to know that the clerk of court's office has most of the records needed: notarial, marriage, divorce, will, succession, deeds, civil suits, discharge papers, etc.

Tax Records

Tax records are a valuable but little-used source. Almost everything was taxed: household and personal goods, livestock, slaves, and property. Tax lists can be used as a substitute census, to create complete neighborhoods for a neighborhood study, to establish relationships, and to locate land. Unfortunately, most of these lists no longer exist in Louisiana, but those that are extant are usually found in the tax assessor's office in the parish courthouse.

Cemetery Records

The recording of cemetery inscriptions in Louisiana has long been a project of the DAR and numerous genealogical societies. See Lela Cullon, *Louisiana Tombstone Inscriptions,* 11 vols. (Baton Rouge, La.: Louisiana DAR, 1957–60). Genealogical publications continually print these inscriptions in their issues. Indexes exist for some New Orleans cemeteries and can be found at the Louisiana State Museum Library (mailing address: 751 Chartes Street, New Orleans, Louisiana 70116).

Church Records

As previously stated, the Roman Catholic church was the only church in Louisiana until the 1803 Louisiana Purchase. Historian James D. Hardy, Jr., wrote that colonial Louisianians had to "be baptized, married and have their children baptized, and be buried as Catholics. A marriage performed anywhere but a Catholic Church was invalid, and the parties were living in sin. Their children were illegitimate . . . and their [marriage] contracts were unenforceable at law. Babies not given baptism were not people, and their births were unrecorded" (Quoted in Winston DeVille, *Gulf Coast Colonials* [Baltimore, Md.: Genealogical Publishing Co., 1968], page 11).

New recording requirements of the Catholic church in the early nineteenth century created a virtual goldmine of genealogical data. Not only did the priest list the names of the person or persons involved, and their parents, but he now named both sets of grandparents, place of nativity of each, and, as always, the maiden names of the females. Many church records still exist from both the French and the Spanish eras. Those of genealogical value are parish church registers and the bishops' records. Under the French, colonial Louisiana was part of the Diocese of Quebec. During the Spanish period, the Diocese of Havana served Louisiana until 1793. At this time the Diocese of Louisiana and the Floridas was founded, with New Orleans as its see. For most of the colonial period, the genealogist need not be concerned with the bishop's records; but for the period between 1793 and 1803, very valuable information can be found. One of the main sets of records within the bishop's files are the dispensations. These are mostly marital dispensations that ask for the church's permission to marry even though some impediment existed—for example, if the couple were first or second cousins or if one of the intended was not of the Catholic faith.

Most Catholic church registers are still in the local parish church. Many of them have been translated and published. See particularly:

Archdiocese of New Orleans. *Sacramental Records.* Vol. 1, *1718–1750.* Vol. 2, *1751–1771.* Vol. 3, *1772–1783.* New Orleans, La.: Archdiocese of New Orleans, 1987–89.

Diocese of Baton Rouge. *Catholic Church Records.* Vol. 1, *1707–1769.* Vol. 2, *1770–1802.* Baton Rouge, La.: Diocese of Baton Rouge, 1978–80.

Hébert, Donald. *Southwest Louisiana Records.* Vol. 1, *1756–1810.* Eunice, La., 1976.

Mills, Elizabeth Shown. *Natchitoches, 1729–1803, Abstracts of the Catholic Church Registers of the French and Spanish Post of St. Jean Baptiste des Natchitoches in Louisiana.* Vol. 2, Cane River Creole Series. New Orleans, La.: Polyanthos, 1977.

———. *Natchitoches, 1800–1826, Translated Abstracts of Register Number Five of the Catholic Church, Parish of St. François des Natchitoches in Louisiana.* Vol. 4. Cane River Creole Series. New Orleans, La.: Polyanthos, 1980.

Two important guides to Catholic church records are:

Hébert, Donald. *Guide to Church Records in Louisiana: 1720–1975.* Eunice, La.: the author, 1975.

Nolan, Charles E. *A Southern Catholic Heritage,* Vol. 1: *1704–1813.* New Orleans, La.: Archdiocese of New Orleans, 1976.

Military Records

Many military records exist for Louisiana soldiers. For the colonial period, a valuable collection is at the General Military Archives, Segovia, Spain. This voluminous archives has service records on all soldiers of the Spanish military from 1680–1920, listing much genealogical data, such as the soldier's name, rank, sometimes a description, the names of his parents, etc.

Two compiled lists of Louisiana soldiers serving in the American Revolution are these:

Churchill, E. Robert, comp., *Soldiers of the American Revolution Under Bernardo De Galvez.* Five copies of this book were originally printed: one was placed in the SAR Library housed in the Howard-Tilton Library at Tulane University, Louisiana; one was deposited in the DAR Library in Washington, D.C.; a third copy can be found in the Library of Congress.

Mills, Elizabeth Shown. *Natchitoches Colonials: Censuses, Military Rolls, and Tax Lists, 1722–1803.* Tuscaloosa, Ala.: Mills Historical Press, 1981.

The National Archives has many original military records for Louisiana, many of which have been microfilmed, for example: War of 1812—M229, 3 reels; Florida War of 1836—M239; War of 1836–38—M241; Confederate War Index—M378, 31 reels; Military Service Records—M320, 414 reels. See also:

Mills, Gary B. *Civil War Claims.* Vol. 1, *An Index to Cases Filed With the Southern Claims Commission.* Laguna Hills, Calif.: Aegean Park Press, 1980.

Periodicals, Newspapers, and Manuscript Collections

Periodicals

Many periodicals and quarterlies have been printed through the years, for example: *The Louisiana Genealogical Register* (compiled and published by the Louisina Genealogical and Historical Society), *The New Orleans Genesis,* the *Natchitoches Genealogist,* and others.

Newspapers

The earliest known Louisiana newspaper was *Le Moniteur,* published in New Orleans, but only a few issues still exist. Numerous guides have been compiled to Louisiana newspapers. See, for instance:

McMullan, Theodore N. *Louisiana Newspapers, 1794–1961.* Baton Rouge, La.: Louisiana State University Library, 1965.

Manuscripts

The manuscript collections of the large libraries, college and university libraries, and archives through out the state are numerous. Most of these institutions have guides to their holdings.

Archives, Libraries, and Societies

State of Louisiana Division of Archives, Records Management, and History
3851 Essen Lane
P.O. Box 94125
Baton Rouge, LA 70804
(504) 922-1200

In addition to the new storage of vital records (see Vital Records), the archives will be progressively storing an increasing number of records in their new facility from parish offices and courts.

Louisiana Genealogical and Historical Society
P.O. Box 3454
Baton Rouge, LA 70821

In addition to publishing *The Louisiana Genealogical Register,* the society holds an all-day seminar every April. It has no permanent headquarters.

Special Focus Categories

Immigration

The New Orleans Public Library has microfilm of nineteenth-century ship passenger lists. Glen Conrad published most of those for the French period as *First Families of Louisiana,* 2 vols. (La.: Claitor Publishing Co., 1970). The WPA published six volumes as *Ship Registers and Enrollments of New Orleans: 1804–1870* (New Orleans, La., 1931–42). A publication covering some of the lists from the middle period of the colonial era was done by Winston DeVille, *Louisiana Recruits: 1752–1758* (New Orleans, La.: Polyanthos, 1973).

Black American

An impressive array of primary source materials exists, in addition to the census materials cited above, in both parish offices and at the Louisiana State University collections in Baton Rouge (see *Black Genesis,* cited on page 10—this work contains a partial listing). In addition, a major ethnic group in Louisiana, the *Creoles de coulour,* have a unique place in its history. See Gary B. Mills, *The Forgotten People: Cane River's Creoles of Color* (Baton Rouge, La.: Louisiana State University Press, 1977).

Native American

Native peoples occupied Louisiana long before the first European explorers arrived. Many tribes have resided within and roamed across the state throughout the years. Louisiana's present Native American population are Choctaw, Chitimacha, Tunica-Biloxi, Houma, and Coushatta.

The genealogist tracing Native American ancestry usually gives up in frustration. If that ancestor is researched as any other nationality, many times it can be documented as such. Many records in Louisiana, both church and civil, have recorded native inhabitants by the correct ethnic designation.

See *U.S. Court of Claims, No. 12742: The Choctaw Nation of Indians v. The United States* (Washington, D.C., ca. 1895).

Parish Resources

Parishes, not counties, are the political jurisdictions for recording land (conveyances), probate (successions), marriage, and court records in Louisiana. Parish clerks hold the majority of these records, while some cities have these functions divided among registers of conveyances and district court clerks. The Louisiana Section of the State Library of Louisiana provided some of the information on parish formation.

Drawn by William Dollarhide

Map	Parish Address	Date Formed Parent Parish	Birth Marriage Death	Land Probate Court
E6	Acadia Crowley 70526	1886 St. Landry	— 1886 —	1886 1886 1886
D5	Allen Oberlin 70655	1912 Calcasieu	— 1913 —	1886 1913 1913
G6	Ascension Donaldsville 70346	1807 St. James	— 1763 —	1770 1800 1800
G7	Assumption Napoleonville 70390	1807 original	— 1800 —	1788 1788 1788
F4	Avoyelles Marksville 71351	1807 original (reorganized 1873)	— 1808 —	1808 1856 1856
	Baton Rouge	(see East Baton Rouge and West Baton Rouge)		
C5	Beaureguard DeRidder 70634	1913 Calcasieu	— 1913 —	1913 1913 1913
C2	Bienville Arcadia 71001	1848 Claiborne	— 1848 —	1848 1848 1848
C1	Bossier Benton 71006	1843 Claiborne	— 1843	1843 1843 1843
B1	Caddo Shreveport 71101	1838 Natchitoches	— 1835	1835 1835 1835
C6	Calcasieu Lake Charles 70601	1840 St. Landry	— 1910 —	1910 1910 1910
E2	Caldwell Columbia 71418	1838 Catahoula/Ouachita	— 1838 —	1838 1838 1838
C7	Cameron Cameron 70631	1870 Calcasieu/Vermillion	— 1870 —	1870 1870 1870
	Carroll *Divided into East Carroll and West Carroll, 1877.*	1832 Ouachita/Concordia		
F3	Catahoula Harrisonburg 71340	1808 original	— 1900s —	1900s 1900s 1900s
D1	Claiborne Homer 71040 *Record loss, 1949.*	1828 Natchitoches	— 1850 —	1850 1850 1850

Map	Parish Address	Date Formed Parent Parish	Birth Marriage Death	Land Probate Court
F4	Concordia Vidalia 71373	1805 Avoyelles	— 1840 —	1850 1850 1850
B2	De Soto Mansfield 71052	1843 Natchitoches/Caddo	— 1843 —	1843 1843 1843
G6	East Baton Rouge Baton Rouge 70801	1810 original	— 1840 —	1782 1782 1782
G1	East Carroll Lake Providence 71254	1877 Carroll	— 1832 —	1832 1832 1832
G5	East Feliciana Clinton 70722	1824 Feliciana	— 1824 —	1824 1824 1824
E5	Evangeline Ville Platte 70586	1911 St. Landry	— 1911 —	1911 1911 1911
	Feliciana *Divided into East Feliciana and West Feliciana, 1824.*	1810 original (from Spanish West Florida)		
F2	Franklin Winnsboro 71295	1843 Catahoula/Ouachita/Madison	— 1843 —	1843 1843 1843
D3	Grant Colfax 71417	1869 Rapides/Winn	— 1880 —	1880 1880 1880
F7	Iberia New Iberia 70560	1868 St. Martin/St. Mary	— 1868 —	1868 1868 1868
G7	Iberville Plaquemine 70764	1807 Assumption/Ascension	— 1770 —	1770 1807 1807
D2	Jackson Jonesboro 71251	1845 Claiborne/Ouachita/Union	— 1880 —	1880 1880 1880
J7	Jefferson Gretna 70072	1825 Orleans	— 1825 —	1825 1825 1825
D6	Jefferson Davis Jennings 70546	1913 Calcasieu	— 1913 —	1913 1913 1913
E6	Lafayette Lafayette 70501	1823 St. Martin	— 1823 —	1823 1823 1823
H8	Lafourche Thibodaux 70301	1807 original	— 1808 —	1808 1808 1808

Map	Parish Address	Date Formed Parent Parish	Birth Marriage Death	Land Probate Court
E3	LaSalle Jena 71342	1910 Catahoula	— 1910 —	1910 1910 1910
D1	Lincoln Ruston 71270	1873 Bienville/Jackson/Union/Claiborne	— 1873 —	1873 1873 1873
H6	Livingston Livingston 70754	1832 St. Helena	— 1875 —	1875 1875 1875
G2	Madison Tallulah 71282	1838 Concordia	— 1866 —	1839 1850 1882
F1	Morehouse Bastrop 71220	1844 Ouachita	— 1870 —	1844 1870 1870
C3	Natchitoches Natchitoches 71457	1807 original	— 1729	1732 1732 1732
J7	Orleans New Orleans 70112	1807 original	— 1718 —	1832 1805 1805
E2	Ouachita Monroe 71201	1807 original	— 1805 —	1805 1805 1805
K8	Plaquemines Pointe a la Hache 70082	1807 original	— 1807 —	1807 1807 1807
F5	Pointe Coupee New Roads 70760	1807 original	— 1735 —	1780 1780 1780
D4	Rapides Alexandria 71301	1807 original	— 1864 —	1864 1864 1864
C2	Red River Cochatta 71019	1871 Caddo/Bossier/Bienville/DeSoto/ Natchitoches	— 1871 —	1871 1871 1904
F2	Richland Rayville 71269	1869 Ouachita/Carroll/Franklin/Morehouse	— 1869 —	1869 1869 1869
C3	Sabine Many 71449	1843 Natchitoches	— 1843 —	1843 1843 1843
K7	St. Bernard Chalmette 70043	1807 original	— 1800s —	1800s 1800s 1800s
H7	St. Charles Hahnville 70057	1807 original	— 1739 —	1734 1734 1734

Map	Parish Address	Date Formed Parent Parish	Birth Marriage Death	Land Probate Court
H5	St. Helena Greensburg 70441	1810 original	— 1804 —	1804 1804 1804
G7	St. James Convent 70723	1807 original	— 1846 —	1809 1809 1809
H6	St. John the Baptist Edgard 70049	1807 original	— 1772 —	1770s 1770s 1770s
E5	St. Landry Opelousas 70570	1807 original	— 1756 —	1760s 1760s 1760s
F6	St. Martin St. Martinville 70582	1807 original	— 1756 —	1760 1700s 1800s
F8	St. Mary Franklin 70538	1811 Assumption	— 1800 —	1800 1800 1800
J6	St. Tammany Covington 70433	1810 St. Helena/Orleans	— 1812 —	1810 1812 1812
H6	Tangipahoa Amite 70422	1869 Livingston/St. Tammany/ St. Helena/Washington	— 1869 —	1869 1869 1869
G2	Tensas St. Joseph 71366	1843 Concordia	— 1843 —	1843 1843 1843
G8	Terrebonne Houma 70360	1822 La Fourche	— 1820 —	1820 1820 1820
E1	Union Farmerville 71241	1839 Ouachita	— 1839 —	1839 1839 1839
E7	Vermillion Abbeville 70510	1844 Lafayette	— 1885 —	1885 1885 1885
C4	Vernon Leesville 71446	1871 Nachitoches/Rapides/Sabine	— 1890 —	1871 1871 1871
J5	Washington Franklinton 70438	1819 St. Tammany	— 1897 —	1897 1897 1897
C1	Webster Minden 71055	1871 Claiborne/Bossier/Bienville	— 1871 —	1871 1871 1871
G6	West Baton Rouge Port Allen 70767	1807 Baton Rouge	— 1793 —	1800s 1800s 1800s

Map	Parish Address	Date Formed Parent Parish	Birth Marriage Death	Land Probate Court
F1	West Carroll Oak Grove 71263	1877 Carroll	— 1877 —	1833 1850 1898
F5	West Feliciana St. Francisville 70775	1824 Feliciana	— 1879 —	1811 1900 1900
D3	Winn Winnfield 71483	1851 Natchitoches/Rapides/Catchoula	— 1886 —	1886 1886 1886

MAINE

Alice Eichholz, Ph.D., C.G.

Maine, geographically the largest New England state, for nearly half of its history was an integral part of Massachusetts. The region, which first came to be known as the Province of Maine, was granted to Sir Ferdinando Gorges and Capt. John Mason in 1622. Wealthy business interests began the first settlements, although religious dissenters followed in settling what is now referred to as "Downeast." Attempts by the Massachusetts Bay Colony to expand its boundaries into Maine began by the 1640s. Absorption of the province was completed in the following decade, although official purchase from an heir of Gorges was not made until 1677. In the seventeenth century Puritan settlers were often forced to retreat back to Massachusetts Bay Colony settlements because of conflict with Native Americans, the influence of the French, the threat of war, and the difficult climate. The previously abandoned parts of Maine were eventually resettled, and expansion of new settlements began in the eighteenth century. Its homogeneous population began to vary with the addition of Scots-Irish (1718), Germans at Waldoboro (1740), and, after 1752, French Huguenots, Acadians, French-Canadians, and Irish.

Following the American Revolution, settlement was encouraged in hopes of generating revenues to counter the tremendous cost of the war to the new state of Massachusetts. Many people from Massachusetts and New Hampshire, including Revolutionary War soldiers, settled in Maine, assumed the land was theirs for the taking, and found themselves in disputes with original proprietors. They came to make use of Maine's natural resources, found an interior wilderness, and, as with the rest of northern New England, a harsh environment. By the mid-nineteenth century, however, a good portion was settled. Until statehood was achieved in 1820, Maine was a political part of Massachusetts. Today Maine attracts new residents for its "quality of life."

Geographically, Maine is vast and mountainous. The population is concentrated along the coast, with its islands and bays; along the border with New Hampshire; and in the lower third of the state along the Kennebec and Penobscot rivers. More than half of its land mass reaches above New Hampshire's northern latitude and remains chiefly wilderness. Political divisions in Maine are perhaps the most diverse in New England. There are 433 towns, twenty-two cities, thirty-six plantations, three Indian voting districts, twelve unorganized but populated townships, and approximately 200 land divisions, unpopulated and identified only by township and range. Border disputes existed with Maine's neighbors to the east and north in Canada. The same piece of land an ancestor lived on might be identified differently because borders, counties, and names changed. Genealogical research in Maine is challenging principally because of the numerous governmental changes affecting the way records have been kept.

Vital Records

Maine has the most uneven group of vital records in all of New England. The first settlements were dilatory in recording vital events. Only five towns (Biddeford, Kittery, Kennebunkport, York, and Wells) have such records from the seventeenth-century. By the eighteenth century, over 200 towns had begun recording vital events and kept doing so reasonably well until Maine became a separate state in 1820. Following statehood, records were not consistently kept at first, but most towns have good records of marriage intentions and births. Few deaths are recorded in town records.

After 1864 state legislation required that town clerks forward births, deaths, and marriages to the secretary of state. There was never total compliance, although all those that were sent *before* 1892 for about eighty towns are available at the Maine State Archives (see Archives, Libraries, and Societies).

By 1892 the State Board of Vital Statistics was established by the legislature as the depository for returns of vital events, and mandatory recording became a reality. The Maine State Archives presently holds the *original* 1892–1922 birth, death, and marriage records. Certified copies of records for that time period are obtained there. The archives also has the 1922–55 birth, death, and marriage records on microfilm with a helpful bride's index from 1892 to the present; groom's index, 1956–present; and death index, 1955–present.

Certified copies of all vital records after 1922 may be obtained from the State Board of Vital Statistics, State House, Station #11, Augusta, Maine 04330.

The New England Historic Genealogical Society (see page 9) has microfilm copies of Maine pre-1892 vital records, some additional reels through 1955, and death records through 1970. The FHL has the microfilm copies of records before 1892 and some after 1892, but they are not as current as those at Maine State Archives, which are updated regularly from the Office of Vital Records files.

A few of Maine's vital records have been published. A project undertaken by the Maine Historical Society (see Archives, Libraries, and Societies) issued all pre-1892 vital records for eighteen towns, which included sources outside the town clerk's office—diaries, church records, newspapers, gravestone information, family records, Bibles, and private records. Transcripts of town records for York 1681–1891 were published serially in *The New England Historical and Genealogical Register* from 1955–69.

Marriages for the early statehood period were sometimes recorded at the county level, as mandated by the legislature in 1828. Such records have not yet been fully assessed, although some are on microfilm at the Maine State Archives. The most complete listing of available Maine vital records continues to be the updated Microfilm List of Maine Town and Census Records (1980) distributed by the Maine State Archives. Recently funded by a grant from the National Historic Records Commission, the Maine State Archives will be broadening its scope to survey all of Maine's town records. In the Town Resource section at the end of this chapter, details from the most recent update are included to guide the researcher in finding vital records.

Census Records

Federal

Population Schedules.

- Indexed—1790, 1800, 1810, 1820, 1830, 1840, 1850, 1860
- Soundex—1880, 1900, 1920
- Unindexed—1870, 1910

Industry and Agriculture Schedules.

- 1850, 1860, 1870, 1880

Mortality Schedules.

- 1850, 1860, 1870, 1880

Union Veterans Schedules.

- 1890

Although Maine was part of Massachusetts until the 1820 census, for research purposes the National Archives catalogs the 1790, 1800, and 1810 federal censuses under Maine. The 1800 censuses for some towns in Hancock and Kennebec indicate where the person resided before immigrating to Maine. A date of immigration is given for some of Kennebec although this was not noted for Hancock. See Walter Goodwin Davis, "Part of Hancock County, Maine, in 1800," *The New England Historical and Genealogical Register* 105 (1951): 204–13, 276–91. All of the above census records are at the Maine State Archives on microfilm.

York County is incomplete on the 1800 census, half of Oxford County is missing in 1810, and Houlton Plantation returns are missing for Washington County, 1820.

Volunteers in some counties are in the process of indexing the 1860, 1870, and 1880 census records for those counties for the collection at the Maine State Archives. Waldo County is presently complete. The 1880 mortality schedule is presently being microfilmed and will be available at the Maine State Archives.

State

In 1837 a state census enumerating heads of households was taken, but only Bangor, Portland, and unincorporated towns survive on microfilm at the Maine State Archives. The Maine Historical Society (see Archives, Libraries, and Societies) holds the volume enumerating the town of Eliot.

Background Sources

Those town histories that have been published for Maine are good resources along with other excellent publications.

Atwood, Stanley B. *The Length and Breadth of Maine.* 1946. Reprint. Orono, Maine: University of Maine, 1973. The original place-name guide for Maine.

Clark, Charles E. *The Eastern Frontier: The Settlement of Northern New England, 1610–1763.* Hanover, N.H.: University Press of New England, 1987. Focuses primarily on Maine.

———, James S. Leamon, and Karen Bowden, eds. *Maine in the Early Republic.* Hanover, N.H.: University Press of New England, 1989. Essays by twelve local history professors cover the period following the Revolution to statehood in 1820.

Denis, Michael J. *Maine Towns and Counties: What Was What, Where and When.* Oakland, Maine: Danbury House Books, 1981. An indexed, updated survey of place-names.

Frost, John E. *Maine Genealogy: A Bibliographic Guide.* Portland, Maine: Maine Historical Society, 1985. A superb listing including printed probate records, maps, town histories, and numerous other sources. Organized by topic with thorough citations expediting interlibrary loan research.

Gray, Ruth, ed. *Maine Families in 1790,* Vol. 1. *Maine Genealogical Society Special Publication, No. 2.* Camden, Maine: Picton Press, 1988. Over 400 families are included in this first volume. The project hopes to cover two to three generations for all families in the state who were located in the 1790 census. Volume 2, as *Special Publication, No. 5,* was published by the same press in 1990.

Haskell, John D. *Maine: A Bibliography of its History.* 1977. Reprint. Hanover, N.H.: University Press of New England, 1983. Excellent focus on printed and published historical materials.

Noyes, Sybil, Charles T. Libby, and Walter G. Davis. *Genealogical Dictionary of Maine and New Hampshire.* 1928–39. Reprint. Baltimore, Md.: Genealogical Publishing Co., 1972, 1976, 1979. An excellent attempt at compiling family genealogies comprising every family established in New Hampshire and Maine by 1699; this is one of the first inclusive volumes with strong references to original source material.

Pope, Charles H. *The Pioneers of Maine and New Hampshire, 1623–1660.* 1908. Reprint. Baltimore, Md.: Genealogical Publishing Co., 1973. Focuses on earliest period; not on all families as in Noyes, et al.

Williamson, William D. *The History of the State of Maine.* 2 vols. Hallowell, Maine: Glazier, Master & Smith, 1839.

A guide to research in the state can be found in John Eldridge Frost, "Maine Genealogy: Some Distinctive Aspects," *The New England Historical and Genealogical Register* 131 (October 1977): 243–66, which includes a list of individual and multifamily genealogies. It is reprinted in Ralph J. Crandall, ed., *Genealogical Research in New England* (Baltimore, Md.: Genealogical Publishing Co., 1984).

Maps

One superb atlas can be extensively used for research and traveling, detailing town divisions, geographical details, road surface types, routes of transportation, and locations of cemeteries. It is The *Maine Atlas and Gazetteer,* which is published in updated versions by DeLorme Publishing of Freeport, Maine.

A bicentennial project edited by Gerald E. Morris entitled *The Maine Bicentennial Atlas and Historical Survey* (Portland, Maine: Maine Historical Society, 1976) is a superb composite of historical maps from the earliest grants and charters to the present. Railroad, lumbering, mining, recreation, population changes, court regions, and election districts illustrate the depth of this resource for genealogical purposes.

Atwood's *Length and Breadth of Maine* (see Background Sources above) includes helpful maps of towns. Maine State Archives has a computerized index of its fine map collection for Maine after statehood, but it is the Massachusetts State Archives (see Massachusetts) that holds the important lotting maps for the pre-statehood development of Maine. Included in many of the maps are the location of residences and the names of owners.

Saco Valley Publishing, 76 Main Street, Fryeburg, Maine 04037, has been reprinting excellent county editions of nineteenth-century maps indicating occupant's names for each structure.

Land Records

State-Land State

Maine obtained provincial status in New England under royal grants from England. In 1677 the Massachusetts Bay Colony purchased the area in Maine below the Kennebec River. The area east of the river became part of Massachusetts in 1691. As part of Massachusetts, the process of creating town grants for proprietors followed that of other Massachusetts towns (see Massachusetts—Land Records). All deeds before 1737 for the settled area in Maine have been transcribed verbatim and published in eighteen volumes entitled *York Deeds, 1642-1737* (Portland, Maine: Maine Historical Society, 1887–1910), available at most major libraries with a collection of New England materials.

Following the Revolution in 1783, under the auspices of the Massachusetts General Court, a Committee for the Sale of Eastern Lands began to survey and sell remaining unorganized portions of the state to help pay for the cost of the war. Land was disposed of in lotteries, a few war grants, tax sales, straight grants, and patents. All the original papers for the Eastern Lands are held in the Massachusetts State Archives (see Massachusetts), and there is a limited card index. Additionally, they have been published in *The Maine Historical and Genealogical Recorder,* Vols. 4–8. Between 1824–91, the Maine Land Office took over the work of the Massachusetts Committee for the Sale of Eastern Lands and distributed public land after separation from Massachusetts. Records are located at the Maine State Archives and include maps, field notes, and deeds starting with 1794 as Massachusetts deeds. A brochure entitled "Land Office Records in the Maine State Archives" is available from the archives. Land grant applications from Revolutionary War veterans are also available.

Land transactions are recorded on the county level and available at the county deed office.

Probate Records

The county seat is where an executor or petitioner would go to commence probate, adoption, or guardianship proceedings. The earliest of Maine's wills have been published in William Sargent's *Maine Wills, 1650–1760* (1887; reprint, Baltimore, Md.: Genealogical Publishing Co., 1972), which covers the entire state since there was only one place for instituting probate proceedings. William D. Patterson's *Probate Records of Lincoln County, Maine—1760–1800* (Portland, Maine: Maine Genealogical Society, 1895) extends Sargent by including all probate records, not just wills, and all of eastern Maine to 1789 when Hancock and Washington counties were set off from Lincoln. There were five probate courts by 1800.

Since probate records include more than wills, John E. Frost, *Maine Probate Abstracts*, 2 vols. (Camden, Maine: Picton Press, 1991), compiled the earlier material to complement the wills (volume 1 covers the period 1687–1775 and volume 2, 1775–1800). *Maine Probate Abstracts, 1687–1800* (Salt Lake City, Utah: Microfilm Service Corp., 1986–87) is a microfiche edition of all York County probate records for the time period and not just wills. It is presently available at the Maine Historical Society and the Maine State Library (see Archives, Libraries, and Societies for both); the New England Historic Genealogical Society; and the FHL. Maine State Archives hold the Somerset County probate records.

Court Records

An extensive array of courts have existed in Maine since the beginning of the settlements in the early 1600s. Jurisdictional changes are quite complicated. A detailed publication of the early records will be found in *Province and Court Records of Maine, 1639–1727,* 6 vols. (Portland, Maine: Maine Historical Society, 1928), as well as on microfilm through the FHL. All of the original court records for York County are at the Maine State Archives. Counties formed from York after 1760 (Cumberland and Lincoln) and 1789 (Washington) were under Massachusetts jurisdiction, although these records appear not to have been microfilmed. Most extant court records to 1929 for all counties except Lincoln can be found at the Maine State Archives. Lincoln County court records are at the courthouse in Wiscasset.

Before statehood, Maine's court of appeals was the Massachusetts Superior Court of Judicature (1692–1780). This also served as the original court for some other cases such as murders. Records for this court are filled as "Suffolk Files" at the Massachusetts State Archives (see Massachusetts) where they are indexed. The supreme judicial court replaced the superior court of judicature after 1780. According to the Massachusetts State Archives, their holdings include circuit court records for this court for Maine counties through 1793.

Tax Records

Maine participated in the U.S. Direct Tax of 1798, although the surviving lists do not cover the entire state. Landowners, renters, land and title boundaries, acreage, dwellings, value, and tax due, are included in the lists. The records can substitute for some missing towns on the 1800 census (see Massachusetts—Census Records and Tax Records). What survives is on microfilm with a printed inventory at the New England Historic Genealogical Society in Boston and the Maine State Archives.

Other tax lists exist throughout the years of Maine's history, both before and after statehood. No survey has been done to catalog these. Reading through town-meeting records may unearth what was recorded in the early nineteenth century. Later tax lists may be located at town offices.

Cemetery Records

Numerous transcripts of Maine cemeteries have been made, principally by the Maine Old Cemetery Association and DAR state and local chapters. There is a continuous indexing project of the transcripts being conducted by the Maine Old Cemetery Association. It is not only indexed but microfilmed and contains upwards of 200,000 records of people who were buried in Maine between 1650–1970. This alphabetical surname indexing project is held on microfilm at the Maine State Library in Augusta, with originals at the Farmingdale branch of the FHL in Maine. It can be accessed for a nominal fee by mail inquires addressed to the Maine State Library. A Revolutionary War Soldiers' graves project and a similar project underway for Civil War Soldiers' graves are included.

The Maine Historical Society, the New England Historic Genealogical Society, the Maine State Library, or the Bangor Public Library all have a complete set of DAR typescripts (see page 6).

Church Records

Few church records have been published or microfilmed for Maine, making it a major untapped source for genealogical research. No total survey of what exists has been made, but the Congregational church was the largest denomination and its records were usually quite comprehensive. According to John Frost, "Genealogy in Maine: A Pragmatic Approach," *Family History in the Northeast,* Vol. 1, Hartford '83 Conference (Hartford, Conn.: Connecticut Society of Genealogists, 1983), records for over two dozen Congregational churches are located at the Maine Historical Society, as well as thirteen Baptist, three Universalist, and ten Quaker meetings.

Literally hundreds more church records probably exist in various repositories or the churches themselves. The most likely genealogical material can be found in the lists of memberships with letters of admission or dismissal, and the baptisms.

A few church records, such as those from the Church of Christ in Buxton, 1763–1817, have been published in book form and others, such as Wells, are in periodicals such as *The New England Historical and Genealogical Register* (see page 7).

Military Records

For service in wars before statehood, refer to Massachusetts—Military Records. However, a few printed sources have attempted to extract Maine soldiers from the Massachusetts holdings, notably Charles J. House, *Names of Soldiers of the American Revolution who Applied for State Bounty . . . Land Office* (1893; reprint, Baltimore, Md.: Genealogical Publishing Co., 1967); Charles A. Flagg, *An Alphabetical Index of Revolutionary Pensioners Living in Maine* (1920; reprint, Baltimore, Md.: Genealogical Publishing Co., 1967); and Carleton Fisher and Sue Fisher, *Soldiers, Sailors and Patriots of the Revolutionary War—Maine* (Louisville, Ky.: National Society of Sons of the American Revolution, 1982).

The adjutant general's holdings for Maine, which include militia on state service in wars, published yearly reports on Civil War soldiers. World War I and II reports are held at Maine State Archives. The Spanish-American War service records are held but not published.

Maine State Archives has a card index of each Civil War soldier and grave records for Revolutionary, Civil War, and War of 1812 soldiers as well as service records through World War I. More recent records can be found at the Bureau of Veterans Services, State House Station #117, Augusta, Maine 04333.

Periodicals, Newspapers, and Manuscript Collections

Periodicals

Maine has some excellent periodical sources from the nineteenth century through the present period. Historical ones include *The Maine Genealogist and Biographer* (1875–78), primarily for Kennebec County; *The Maine Historical and Genealogical Recorder* (1884–98) for Cumberland and York counties; *Bangor Historical Magazine* (1885–95) for Penobscot Valley; *Sprague's Journal of Maine History* (1913–26) published in Dover, Maine; and, finally, what is known as *Maine Genealogies,* but is actually called *Genealogical and Family History of the State of Maine* (1909), 4 vols., which has been made somewhat obsolete by later research. Present periodicals include these:

Downeast Ancestry, P.O. Box 398, Biddeford Pool, Maine 04066; published six times a year beginning in 1977; has articles and queries.

Maine Genealogist (formerly *Maine Seine*), Maine Genealogical Society (see Archives, Libraries, and Societies for address); bimonthly publication available through membership.

Maine Historical Society Quarterly, Maine Historical Society; articles on Maine history, available through membership.

Newspapers

Local library and historical societies as well as the Maine Historical Society and Maine State Library have indexes to various newspaper vital statistics. The largest collection of microfilmed newspapers can be found at the University of Maine's Folger Library at Orono which has a computer printout listing of their holdings. They also supply a typescript, "Maine Newspapers in the Smaller Maine Public Libraries."

Manuscripts

Although it does not include acquisitions in the last forty years, Elizabeth Ring, *A Reference List of Manuscripts Relating to the History of Maine,* 3 vols. (Orono, Maine: University of Maine, 1938–41), is an excellent source. Volume 1 covers towns and manuscript materials related to them; volume 2 covers maps and collections of individuals, including the extensive collections at the Maine Historical Society of professional genealogists; and volume 3 is an index.

Both the Maine Historical Society and Maine State Library have excellent manuscript and single copy typescript collections for research in Maine genealogy.

Archives, Libraries, and Societies

Maine State Archives
State House Station 84
Augusta, ME 04333

Maine State Library
State House Station 64
Augusta, ME 04333

Located at the Maine Cultural Center, both of the above have been granted additional support for extending and organizing their already diverse collections. Maine State Archives is the central location in the state for vital records before 1922 and is the permanent "repository" for state documents. In addition, it holds all census records, adjutant general's records, court records, Maine Land Office records, county marriage returns, and the updated microfilm collection of extant Maine town records.

The east wing of the building houses the Maine State Library with the largest collection of town histories and family genealogies in the state, microfilm holdings of newspapers, town reports after 1902, and two collections of cemetery indexes.

Maine Historical Society Library
485 Congress Street
Portland, ME 04101

Open to nonmembers for a nominal fee, its superior collection includes extensive printed works on state and family history, and manuscripts (see above).

Maine Genealogical Society
P.O. Box 221
Farmington, ME 04938

The society has local chapters in the state and statewide meetings as well as a bimonthly publication *Maine Genealogist. Maine Families in 1790* is published and sold by the society, along with vital records of Mount Desert and the records of Rev. Edward Carter. The organization's library is presently at Cutler Memorial Library in Farmington.

University of Maine at Orono
Raymond H. Folger Library
Special Collections Department
Orono, ME 04469

In addition to focusing heavily on Orono, this is a good collection of state, county, and town histories as well as special collections of various Maine families.

Special Focus Categories

Immigration

Although Portland was a port of entry itself, with indexes to passengers arriving 1893–1954 in the National Archives collection with copies at National Archives-New England Region (see page 8), many Maine residents are descendants of the Irish and other nationalities who passed through immigration in Boston and New Brunswick (see Massachusetts—Immigration).

Native American

The Maine Bureau of Indian Affairs records are located at the Maine State Archives. They contain some tribal census information. See also:

Ray, Roger B. *The Indians of Maine and the Atlantic Provinces.* Portland, Maine: Maine Historical Society, 1972.

French-Canadian

Maine State Library. *Genealogy of French Canada, Acadia, and Franco-America at the Maine State Library.* Augusta, Maine: the author, 1977.

Baxter, Angus. *In Search of Your Canadian Roots.* Baltimore, Md.: Genealogical Publishing Co., 1989.

See also New Hampshire—Archives, Libraries, and Societies.

County Resources

Since Maine was part of Massachusetts for a long time, it should be expected that it would conform to a similar system for recording deeds, probates, and vital records. Such is the case. Deeds and probates were filed at the county seat and vital records at the town office. However, in Maine, marriages were to be submitted to the county clerk as mandated by the legislature in 1828, although the practice was never uniform and the results have not been completely assessed. The following chart reports what has been found regarding marriage returns on a county basis and where they are located (either at the Maine State Archives or with the county clerk). The Town Resources which follow will also have marriage records.

Map	County Address	Date Formed Parent County/ies	Marriage	Land Probate
C12	Androscoggin 2 Turner Street Auburn 04210	1854 Cumberland/Oxford/ Kennebec	1851–84 Maine State Archives	1854 1854
G3	Aroostook Court Street, Box 787, Houlton 04370	1839 Washington	1839–92 county clerk/FHL	1839 1839*
	**Previous deeds dealing with Washington County land from 1808, now in Aroostook, are located here as well.*			
B14	Cumberland 142 Federal Street Portland 04101	1760 York	See Portland under Towns	1760 1908
B8	Franklin Main Street, Farmington 04938	1838 Cumberland	1848–91 county clerk	1838 1838
H11	Hancock 60 State Street, Ellsworth 04605	1789 Lincoln	1842–91 county clerk	1790 1790
D12	Kennebec 95 State Street, Augusta 04330	1799 Lincoln	1828–87 Maine State Archives	1799 1799
F13	Knox 62 Union Street, Rockland 04841	1860 Lincoln/Waldo	1859–87 Maine State Archives	1860 1860
D13	Lincoln High Street, Wiscasset 04578	1760 York	1760–1865 county clerk	1763 1769
B11	Oxford 26 Western Avenue South Paris 04281	1805 York/Cumberland	1830–75 Maine State Archives	1805 1805
G8	Penobscot 97 Hammond Street, Bangor 04401	1816 Hancock	1827–88 Maine State Archives	1814 1816
E7	Piscataquis 51 E. Main Street Dover-Foxcroft, 04426	1838 Penobscot/Somerset	1839–89 Maine State Archives	1838 1838
D13	Sagadahoc 752 High, Bath 04530	1854 Lincoln	1852–87 Maine State Archives	1826* 1854
	**Includes Lincoln County earlier deeds.*			
C8	Somerset Corner and High Streets Skowhegan 04976	1809 Kennebec	1828–89 county clerk	1804 1830
F11	Waldo 73 Church Street, Belfast 04915	1827 Hancock	1828–87 Maine State Archives	1789 1827
	**Includes Hancock deeds covering Waldo land before county formation.*			
K10	Washington Court Street, Machias 04654	1789 Lincoln	1827–90 Maine State Archives	1784 1785
A15	York Court Street, Alfred 04002	1652 original	1771–94 county clerk 1833–87 county clerk	1642 1689

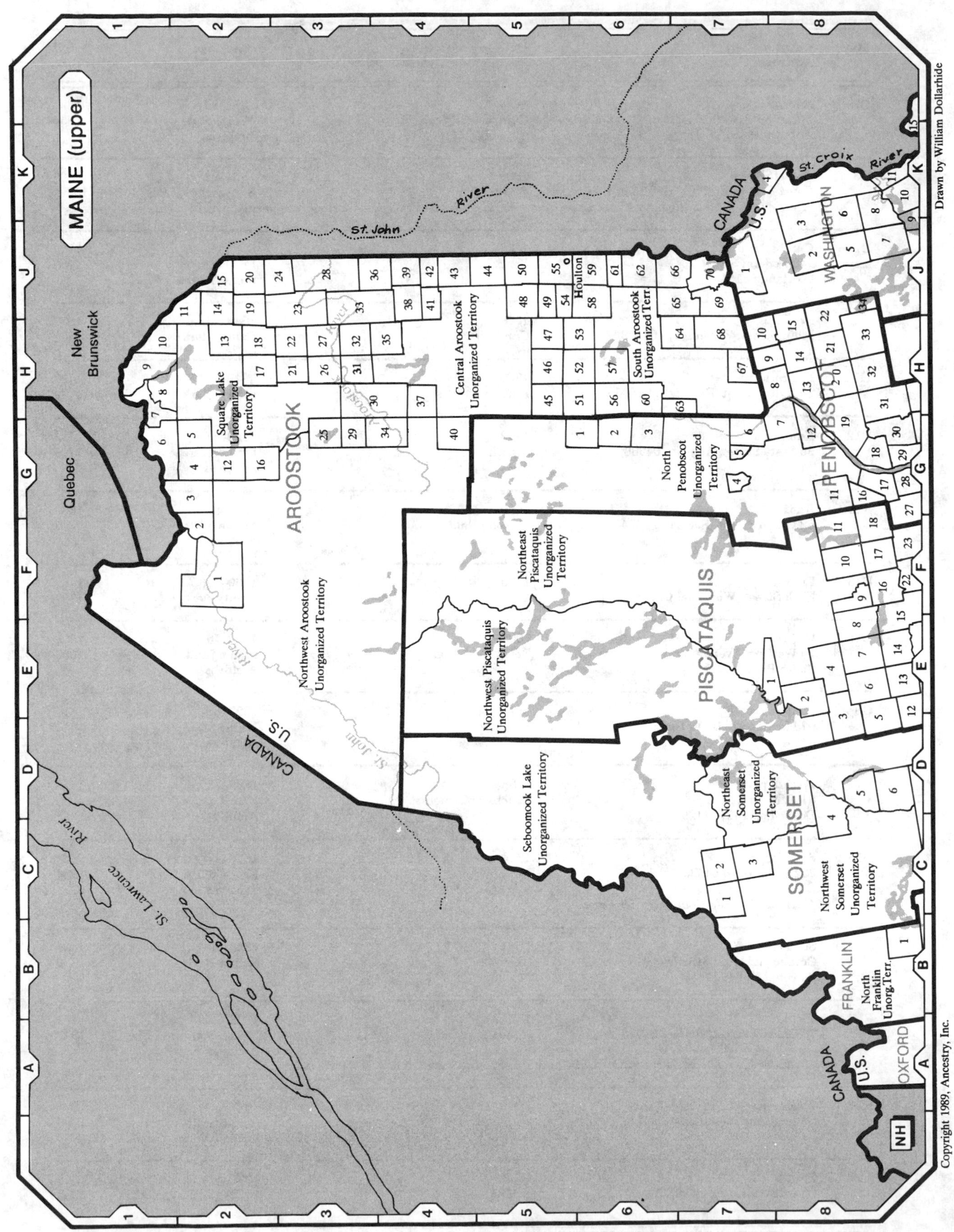
MAINE (upper)
Quebec
New Brunswick
CANADA
U.S.
St. John River
St. Lawrence River
St. Croix River
AROOSTOOK
Northwest Aroostook Unorganized Territory
Square Lake Unorganized Territory
Central Aroostook Unorganized Territory
South Aroostook Unorganized Terr.
Houlton
PISCATAQUIS
Northwest Piscataquis Unorganized Territory
Northeast Piscataquis Unorganized Territory
PENOBSCOT
North Penobscot Unorganized Territory
WASHINGTON
SOMERSET
Seboomook Lake Unorganized Territory
Northeast Somerset Unorganized Territory
Northwest Somerset Unorganized Territory
FRANKLIN
North Franklin Unorg. Terr.
OXFORD
NH
Copyright 1989, Ancestry, Inc.
Drawn by William Dollarhide

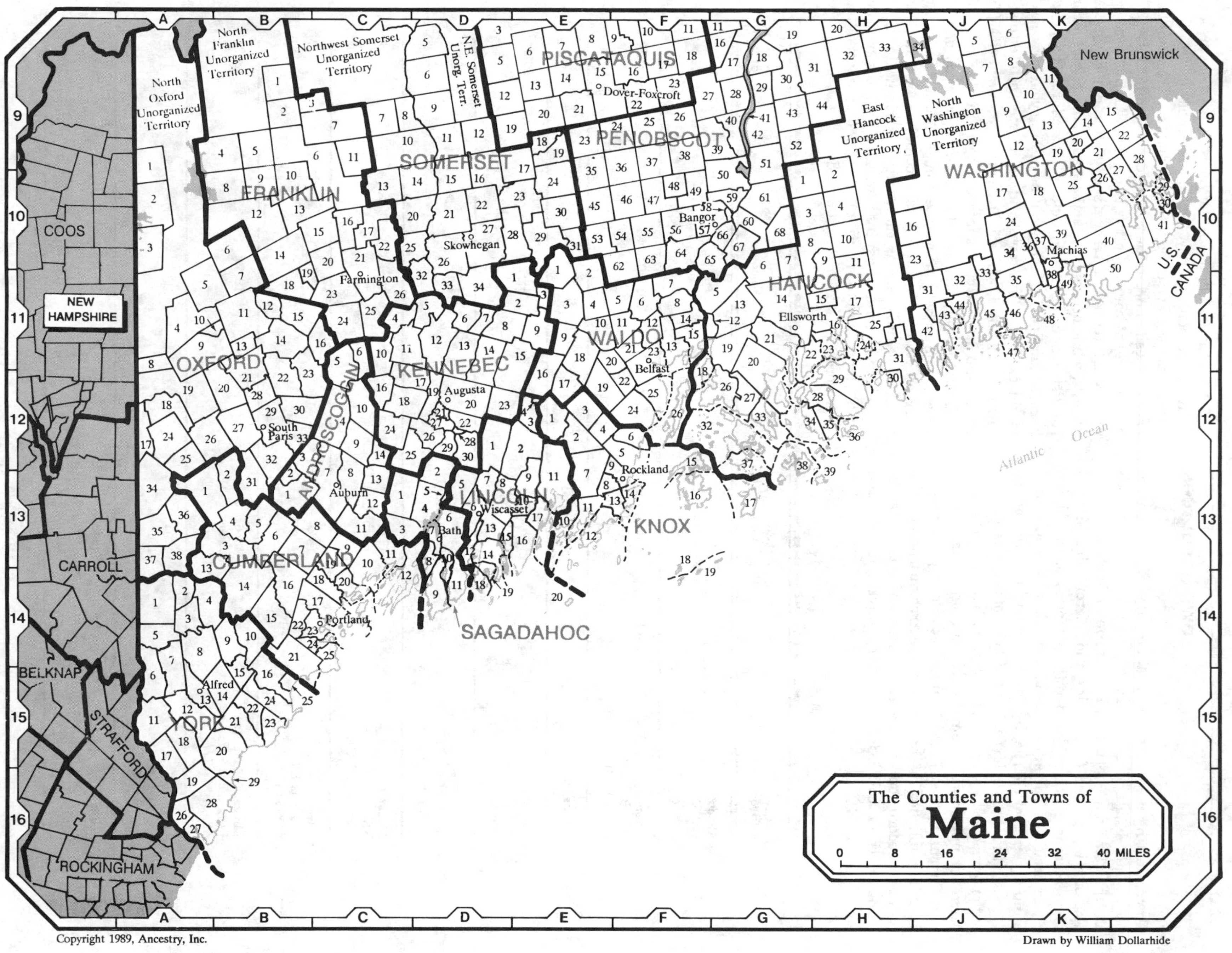
The Counties and Towns of
Maine
0 8 16 24 32 40 MILES
Drawn by William Dollarhide
Copyright 1989, Ancestry, Inc.
New Brunswick
CANADA
U.S.
Atlantic Ocean
NEW HAMPSHIRE
COOS
CARROLL
BELKNAP
STRAFFORD
ROCKINGHAM
North Oxford Unorganized Territory
North Franklin Unorganized Territory
Northwest Somerset Unorganized Territory
N.E. Somerset Unorg. Terr.
East Hancock Unorganized Territory
North Washington Unorganized Territory
WASHINGTON
HANCOCK
PENOBSCOT
PISCATAQUIS
SOMERSET
FRANKLIN
OXFORD
ANDROSCOGGIN
KENNEBEC
WALDO
KNOX
LINCOLN
SAGADAHOC
CUMBERLAND
YORK
Machias
Ellsworth
Bangor
Dover-Foxcroft
Skowhegan
Farmington
Belfast
Rockland
Augusta
Wiscasset
Bath
Auburn
South Paris
Portland
Alfred

Town Resources

Town meeting records have an abundance of information about New England ancestors. Maine is no exception, although some may not be located at the town clerk's office. The ongoing project for locating and microfilming Maine's town records continues under the auspices of the Maine State Archives. The addresses of town clerks are published annually, free of charge, by the Secretary of State's office. Those in the chart below are as of 1990. Some towns operate out of town clerk's homes and change with annual elections. Microfilm information from the 1980 edition of "Maine Town and Census Records" and "Public Records Repositories in Maine," published by the Maine State Archives, provide the dates for record sources. There are some more recent additions to their collection, but they have not yet been cataloged.

"Date Formed" indicates the year the town was organized with its present county listed underneath (see County Resources for previous county jurisdictions). The number in parentheses following the county corresponds to the town's number in the county on the state map. Many towns have their vital records interspersed with the town meeting records, while others have separate books for vital records. No distinction has been made in this chart. The purpose here is simply to indicate what beginning year a researcher might expect to find town and vital records in either the town clerk's office, which is indicated by an asterisk (*), or the Maine State Archives microfilm collection.

Unfortunately, fire has claimed many records since they were too often held in private homes. A question mark (?) suggests that information is incomplete or not certain. Dates of records earlier than formation indicate that the town holds records of parent towns. Some dates are considerably later than town organization, indicating that either the records are lost or have burned.

Town Address	Date Formed County (Map)	Vital Records	Town Records
Abbott P.O. Box 120 Abbott 04406	1827 Piscataquis (13)	1900	1900*
Acton P.O. Box 510 Acton 04001	1830 York (6)	1830	1830
Adams	(see Crawford)		
Addison P.O. Box 142 Addison 04606	1797 Washington (45)	1834*	1824*
Albion Route 1, Box 4250 Albion 04910	1804 Kennebec (9)	1802	1802
Alexander RR 1, Box 825 Alexander 04694	1825 Washington (13)	1784	?
Alfred P.O. Box 129 Alfred 04002	1808 York (13)	1803	?
Allagash Plantation RFD 1, Box 137 Allagash 04774	1886 Aroostook (1)	1892	1892*
Alna P.O. Box 265 Alna 04535	1794 Lincoln (7)	1795	1795
Alton RFD 1, Box 443 Alton 04468	1844 Penobscot (39)	1859	1844*
Amherst HC 31, Box 4720 Ellsworth 04605	1831 Hancock (3)	1783	1850*

Town Address	Date Formed County (Map)	Vital Records	Town Records
Amity General Delivery North Amity 04465	1836 Aroostook (62)	1862	1862
Andover P.O. Box 219 Andover 04216	1804 Oxford (5)	1795	?
Anson P.O. Box 298 North Anson 04958	1798 Somerset (20)	1798	1798
Appleton P.O. Box 622 Union 04862	1829 Knox (3)	1774	1820
Argyle (unorganized)	Penobscot (40)	1876	
Arrowsic P.O. Box 282, Old Stage Road Arrowsic 04530	1841 Sagadahoc (10)	1741	1892*
Arundel RR 1, 1375 Old Limerick Road Kennebunkport 04046	1915 York (22)	1916	1916
Ashland (Dalton 1869–76) P.O. Box A Ashland 04732	1862 Aroostook (30)	1863*	?
Athens P.O. Box 4137 Athens 04912	1804 Somerset (16)	1900	1900*
Atkinson RFD 3, Box 94 Dover-Foxcroft 04426	1819 Piscataquis (22)	1766	1888*
Auburn 45 Spring Street Auburn 04210	1842 Androscoggin (7)	1751	1840
Augusta 16 Cony Street Augusta 04330	1797 Kennebec (20)	1780	1900?*
Aurora Town Office Aurora 04408	1831 Hancock (4)	1945	—
Avon RFD 1, Box 1980 Phillips 04966	1802 Franklin (15)	1766	1917
Baileyville P.O. Box 370 Woodland 04694	1828 Washington (11)	1861	?
Baldwin Box 433, RFD 1 West Baldwin 04091	1802 Cumberland (13)	1802	1802

Town Address	Date Formed County (Map)	Vital Records	Town Records
Bancroft HCR 60, Box 80 Wytopitlock 04497	1878 Aroostook (69)	1892	1910*
Bangor 73 Harlow Street Bangor 04401	1791 Penobscot (57)	1775	1812
Bar Harbor (Eden 1913) 93 Cottage Street Bar Harbor 04609	1796 Hancock (29)	1796	1798
Baring Plantation RR1, Box 336 Baring 04694	1825 Washington (14)	1892	1892*
Barnard Plantation	1834 Piscataquis (9)	1921	1921*
Bath 55 Front Street Bath 04530	1781 Sagadahoc (7)	1757	1753*
Beals P.O. Box 93 Beals 04611	1925 Washington (47)	1925	1925*
Beaver Cove Plantation P.O. Box 2000 Greenville 04441	1975 Piscataquis (1)	1975	1975*
Beddington Box 85C, HCR 72 Beddington 04622	1833 Washington (16)	1792	1844*
Belfast 71 Church Street Belfast 04915	1773 Waldo (23)	1773	1773
Belgrade P.O. Box 96 Belgrade 04917	1796 Kennebec (12)	1758	1906*
Belmont HCR 80, Box 132 Belmont 04915	1814 Waldo (22)	1855	?
Benedicta	1873 Aroostook (63)	1928	1949*
Benton 200 Gogan Road Benton 04927	1842 Kennebec (2)	1841	?
Berwick P.O. Box 696 Berwick 03901	1713 York (17)	1701	1701
Bethel P.O. Box 108 Bethel 04217	1796 Oxford (9)	1745	1796*

Town Address	Date Formed County (Map)	Vital Records	Town Records
Biddeford P.O. Box 586 Biddeford 04005	1718 York (24)	1653	1653
Bingham P.O. Box 136 Bingham 04920	1812 Somerset (11)	1759	1812*
Blaine P.O. Box 190 Blaine 04734	1874 Aroostook (42)	1892	1942*
Blanchard Plantation	1831 Piscataquis (5)	1831	1831*
Blue Hill P.O. Box 433 Blue Hill 04614	1789 Hancock (20)	1785	1789?*
Boothbay RR 1, Box 464 Boothbay 04537	1764 Lincoln (14)	1763	1763*
Boothbay Harbor Box 117, 19 Townsend Avenue Boothbay Harbor 04538	1889 Lincoln (19)	1763	1889*
Bowdoin RR 2, Box 3822 Bowdoinham 04008	1788 Sagadahoc (1)	1763	1788*
Bowdoinham P.O. Box 85 Bowdoinham 04008	1762 Sagadahoc (4)	1776	1900*
Bowerbank P.O. Box 9 Sebec Village 04481	1839 Piscataquis (8)	1832	1966*
Bradford P.O. Box 26 Bradford 04410	1831 Penobscot (26)	1862	1819
Bradley P.O. Box M Bradley 04411	1835 Penobscot (61)	1805	1770
Bremen P.O. Box 171 Medomak 04551	1828 Lincoln (17)	1756	1828?
Brewer 80 N. Main Street Brewer 04412	1812 Penobscot (66)	1770	1743
Bridgewater P.O. Box 215 Bridgewater 04735	1858 Aroostook (43)	1894	1950*
Bridgton 48 Main Street Bridgton 04009	1794 Cumberland (1)	1785	1794

Town Address	Date Formed County (Map)	Vital Records	Town Records
Brighton Plantation P.O. Box 108 Athens 04912	1816 Somerset (12)	1840	1816
Bristol P.O. Box 147 Bristol 04539	1765 Lincoln (16)	1765	1765
Brooklin HCR 63, Box 324 Brooklin 04616	1849 Hancock (33)	1835	1849
Brooks RFD 2, Box 120 Brooks 04921	1816 Waldo (11)	1892	1930*
Brooksville Route 1 Box 56 Brooksville 04617	1817 Hancock (26)	1818	1966
Brownfield P.O. Box 100 Brownfield 04010	1802 Oxford (35)	1802	1800?
Brownville P.O. Box 659 Brownville 04414	1824 Piscataquis (10)	1812	?
Brunswick 28 Federal Street Brunswick 04011	1739 Cumberland (11)	1735	1735
Buckfield P.O. Box 179 Buckfield 04220	1793 Oxford (30)	1700	179-?
Bucksport P.O. Drawer X Bucksport 04416	1792 (as Buckstown) Hancock (5)	1775	1800
Burlington RR 2, Box 1800 Lincoln 04457	1832 Penobscot (31)	1769	1840
Burnham P.O. Box 55 Burnham 04922	1824 Waldo (1)	1821	1824?
Buxton RR 1, Box 189 West Buxton 04093	1772 York (10)	1773	1740
Byron SR 62, Box 51A Byron 04275	1833 Oxford (6)	1814	1814
Calais P.O. Box 413 Calais 04619	1809 Washington (15)	1824	1809
Cambridge Box 162, RFD 1 Cambridge 04923	1834 Somerset (18)	1792	1834*

Town Address	Date Formed County (Map)	Vital Records	Town Records
Camden P.O. Box 1207 Camden 04843	1791 Knox (6)	1783	1783
Canaan P.O. Box 68 Canaan 04924	1788 Somerset (28)	1776	1880?
Canton P.O. Box 669 Canton 04221	1821 Oxford (16)	1818*	?
Cape Elizabeth P.O. Box 6260, Town Hall Cape Elizabeth 04107	1765 Cumberland (25)	1765	1765
Cape Porpoise	(see Kennebunkport)		
Caratunk Plantation P.O. Box 44 Caratunk 04925	1840 Somerset (6)	1854	1854
Caribou 25 High Street Caribou 04736	1859 Aroostook (23)	1848	1848
Carmel P.O. Box 114 Carmel 04419	1811 Penobscot (55)	1760	1964*
Carrabassett Valley Town Office Carrabassett 04947	1972 Franklin (7)	?	1972*
Carroll Plantation RR 1, Box 196 Springfield 04487	1845 Penobscot (22)	1928	1928*
Carthage HCR 67, Box 220 Dixfield 04224	1826 Franklin (18)	1812	1826
Cary Plantation P.O. Box 1271 Houlton 04730	1878 Aroostook (61)	1862	1972*
Casco P.O. Box 60 Casco 04015	1841 Cumberland (5)	1841	1873*
Castine P.O. Box 204 Castine 04421	1796 Hancock (18)	1796	1796
Castle Hill P.O. Box 500 Mapleton 04757	1903 Aroostook (31)	1855	1940?*
Caswell Plantation HC 62, Box 48 Limestone 04750	1879 Aroostook (20)	1898	1945*

Town Address	Date Formed County (Map)	Vital Records	Town Records
Centerville RFD, Box 142 Columbia Falls 04623	1842 Washington (34)	1770	?
Central Hancock (unorganized)	Hancock (15)		
Central Somerset (unorganized)	Somerset (10)		
Chanderville	(see Detroit)		
Chapman P.O. Box 500 Mapleton 04757	1879 Aroostook (35)	1868	?
Charleston P.O. Box 120 Charleston 04422	1811 Penobscot (25)	1809	1809
Charlotte Route 214, Box 329 Charlotte 04666	1825 Washington (21)	1816	1821
Chelsea RR 6, Box 910 Gardiner 04345	1850 Kennebec (22)	1782	1851*
Cherryfield RFD 1, Box 3 Cherryfield 04622	1816 Washington (31)	1854	1842?
Chester RR 1, Box 379 Lincoln Center 04458	1834 Penobscot (12)	1788	1862*
Chesterville RR 2, Box 4190 Farmington 04938	1802 Franklin (25)	1788	1803
China RR 1, Box 970 South China 04358	1796 (as Harlem; renamed, 1818) Kennebec (15)	1785	1785
Clifton Rt. 180, P.O. Box 94 East Eddington 04428	1848 (as Maine; renamed, 1849) Penobscot (68)	1848	1860*
Clinton P.O. Box 219 Clinton 04927	1795 Kennebec (1)	1797	1892
Codyville Plantation Route 6 Topsfield 04490	1845 Washington (3)	1892	1922*
Columbia P.O. Box 22 Columbia 04623	1796 Washington (32)	1752	1752
Columbia Falls P.O. Box 82 Columbia Falls 04623	1863 Washington (33)	1863	1796
Connor (unorganized)	Aroostook (19)		

Town Address	Date Formed County (Map)	Vital Records	Town Records
Cooper Grove Post Office Cooper 04638	1822 Washington (19)	1878	1907*
Coplin Plantation P.O. Box 91 Stratton 04982	1895 Franklin (2)	1895	?
Corinna P.O. Box 1 Corinna 04928	1816 Penobscot (35)	1797	?
Corinth P.O. Box 309 East Corinth 04427	1811 Penobscot (37)	1785	1811*
Cornish P.O. Box 346 Cornish 04020	1794 York (2)	1857*	?
Cornville RFD 1, Box 3050 Cornville 04976	1798 Somerset (22)	1772	1794*
Coxhall	(see Lyman)		
Cranberry Isles P.O. Box 15 Islesford 04646	1830 Hancock (36)	1783	1830?*
Crawford RR 1, Box 1045 Crawford 04694	1828 Washington (12)	1827	1901
Criehaven (unorganized)	Knox (19)		
Crystal P.O. Box 40 Island Falls 04747	1901 Aroostook (56)	1854	1923*
Cumberland 12 Drowne Road, P.O. Box 128 Cumberland 04021	1821 Cumberland (18)	1720	1821*
Cushing HCR 68 Box 131 Cushing 04563	1789 Knox (11)	1735	1845*
Cutler P.O. Box 236 Cutler 04626	1826 Washington (50)	1844	1843?*
Cyr Plantation HCR 63 Box 51 Van Buren 04785	1870 Aroostook (14)	1892	1892*
Dallas Plantation P.O. Box 460 Rangeley 04970	1845 Franklin (5)	1892	1921*
Dalton	(see Ashland)		

Town Address	Date Formed County (Map)	Vital Records	Town Records
Damariscotta P.O. Box 218 Damariscotta 04543	1847 Lincoln (10)	1848	1864*
Danforth P.O. Box 117 Danforth 04424	1860 Washington (1)	1860	1936*
Dayton RFD 3, Box 362 Biddeford 04005	1854 York (15)	1832	1832
Deblois HCR 72, Box 32D Deblois 04622	1852 Washington (23)	1855*	1852*
Dedham P.O. Box 700 East Holden 04429	1837 Hancock (6)	1787	1932*
Deer Isle P.O. Box 43 Deer Isle 04627	1789 Hancock (32)	1768	1789*
Denmark P.O. Box 90 Denmark 04022	1807 Oxford (36)	1807*	1807*
Dennistown Plantation HCR 76, Box 125 Jackman 04945	1895 Somerset (1)	1840	1910*
Dennysville King Street, P.O. Box 142 Dennysville 04628	1818 Washington (26)	1790*	1818*
Detroit P.O. Box 147 Detroit 04929	1828 Somerset (31)	1780	1780
Dexter P.O. Box 313 Dexter 04930	1816 Penobscot (23)	1761	1816*
Dickeyville	(see Frenchville)		
Dixfield P.O. Box O Dixfield 04224	1803 Oxford (15)	1803	1803
Dixmont RFD 1, Box 205 Dixmont 04932	1807 Penobscot (62)	1800	1906*
Dover-Foxcroft 34 E. Main Street Dover-Foxcroft 04426	1822/1812 (merged, 1915) Piscataquis (15)	1792	1800s?
Dresden P.O. Box 4098, Calls Hill Road Dresden 04342	1794 Lincoln (5)	1771	1771

Town Address	Date Formed County (Map)	Vital Records	Town Records
Drew Plantation HCR 60 Wytopitlock 04497	1921 Penobscot (10)	1853	?
Durham RR 2, Box 1908 Lisbon Falls 04252	1789 Androscoggin (11)	1744	1961*
Dutton	(see Glenburn)		
Dyer Brook RFD 1, Box 104 Island Falls 04747	1891 Aroostook (52)	1895	?
E Plantation P.O. Box 94 Blaine 04734	1898 Aroostook (41)	?	1966*
Eagle Lake P.O. Box 287 Eagle Lake 04739	1870 Aroostook (12)	1867	1890*
East Central Franklin (unorganized)	Franklin (6)		
East Central Washington (unorganized)	Washington (18)		
East Livermore	(see Livermore Falls)		
East Machias P.O. Box 117 East Machias 04630	1826 Washington (39)	1709	1823*
East Millinocket 53 Main Street East Millinocket 04430	1907 Penobscot (5)	1907	1907*
East Thomaston	(see Rockland)		
Eastbrook RFD 1, Box 467 Franklin 04634	1837 Hancock (11)	1892	1892*
Easton P.O. Box 127 Easton 04740	1865 Aroostook (36)	1892	1896*
Eastport 78 High Street Eastport 04631	1798 Washington (30)	1778	?
Eddington P.O. Box 99 East Eddington 04428	1811 Penobscot (60)	1802	1805*
Eden	(see Bar Harbor)		
Edgecomb RR 1, Box 2140 North Edgecomb 04556	1774 Lincoln (13)	1774*	1774*
Edinburg HCR 66 Box 142 Howland 04448	1835 Penobscot (28)	1835	?

Town Address	Date Formed County (Map)	Vital Records	Town Records
Eliot 141 State Road Eliot 03903	1810 York (26)	1810	1810
Elliotsville Plantation	1835 Piscataquis (4)	1913	1960*
Ellsworth City Hall, P.O. Box 586 Ellsworth 04605	1800 Hancock (14)	1800?*	1933*
Embden P.O. Box 3160 North Anson 04958	1804 Somerset (14)	1783	1783
Enfield P.O. Box 28 Enfield 04433	1835 Penobscot (18)	1857*	1940*
Etna P.O. Box G Etna 04434	1820 Penobscot (54)	1742	1900?*
Eustis P.O. Box 350 Stratton 04982	1871 Franklin (1)	1871	?
Exeter P.O. Box 59 Exeter 04435	1811 Penobscot (36)	1808	1808
Fairfax	(see Albion)		
Fairfield P.O. Box 149 Fairfield 04937	1788 Somerset (34)	1788	1788*
Falmouth 271 Falmouth Road Falmouth 04105	1718 Cumberland (17)	1718	1718
Farmingdale 175 Maine Avenue Gardiner 04345	1852 Kennebec (27)	1852	1852*
Farmington 147 Lower Main Street Farmington 04938	1794 Franklin (21)	1741	1794*
Fayette RFD 1,Box 2180 Kents Hill 04349	1795 Kennebec (10)	1785	1795*
Forks Plantation P.O. Box 24 West Forks 04985	1895 Somerset (5)	?	?
Fort Fairfield P.O. Box 451 Fort Fairfield 04742	1858 Aroostook (28)	1847	1858*
Fort Kent 111 W. Main Street Fort Kent 04743	1869 Aroostook (6)	1892	1900*

Town Address	Date Formed County (Map)	Vital Records	Town Records
Fox Isle	(see North Haven)		
Foxcroft	(see Dover-Foxcroft)		
Frankfort P.O. Box 57 Frankfort 04438	1789 Waldo (8)	1903	1934*
Franklin P.O. Box 209 Franklin 04634	1825 Hancock (17)	1813*	1813*
Freedom Route 1, Box 860 Freedom 04941	1813 Waldo (9)	1777	1813*
Freeport 90 Pleasant Hill Road Freeport 04032	1789 Cumberland (10)	1795	1789*
Frenchboro 32 Harborside Drive Frenchboro 04635	? Hancock (39)		
Frenchville (Dickeyville) P.O. Box 146 Frenchville 04745	1869 Aroostook (7)	1869	1869
Friendship P.O. Box 136 Friendship 04547	1807 Knox (10)	1769	1824*
Fryeburg 2 Lovewell's Pond Road Fryeburg 04037	1777 Oxford (34)	1777	1777
Gardiner 6 Church Street Gardiner 04345	1803 Kennebec (29)	1800	?
Garfield Plantation RFD 1, Box 100 Ashland 04732	1895 Aroostook (34)	1892	1958
Garland P.O. Box 29 Garland 04939	1811 Penobscot (24)	1854	1936*
Georgetown P.O. Box 436 Georgetown 04548	1716 Sagadahoc (11)	1757	1757
Gilead P.O. Box 1310, RFD 2 Bethel 04217	1804 Oxford (8)	1757	1804?
Glenburn RFD 1, P.O. Box 1375 Bangor 04401	1822 Penobscot (49)	1800	1822*
Glenwood Plantation Star Route, P.O. Box 216 Wytopitlock 04497	1867 Aroostook (64)	1866*	1866*

Town Address	Date Formed County (Map)	Vital Records	Town Records
Gorham 270 Main Street Gorham 04038	1764 Cumberland (15)	1721	1733
Gouldsboro P.O. Box 68 Prospect Harbor 04669	1789 Hancock (31)	1772	1772
Grand Falls Plantation	1878 Penobscot (44)	?	?
Grand Isle P.O. Box 197 Grand Isle 04746	1869 Aroostook (10)	1892	1869
Grand Lake Stream Plantation P.O. Box 98 Grand Lake Stream 04637	1897 Washington (7)	?	?
Gray P.O. Box 258 Gray 04039	1778 Cumberland (7)	1700?*	1778*
Great Pond Plantation Great Pond Road Aurora 04408	1895 Hancock (2)	1910	1950*
Greenbush P.O. Box 210 Olamon 04467	1834 Penobscot (42)	1774	?
Greene P.O. Box 130 Green 04236	1788 Androscoggin (9)	1748	1788*
Greenfield HC 83, Box 563 Costigan 04423	1834 Penobscot (52)	1850	1848
Greenville P.O. Box 1109 Greenville 04441	1836 Piscataquis (2)	1820	1831*
Greenwood P.O. Box 180 Locke Mills 04255	1816 Oxford (20)	1797	1813
Guilford P.O. Box 750 Guilford 04443	1816 Piscataquis (14)	1770	1816*
Hallowell 1 Winthrop Street Hallowell 04347	1771 Kennebec (21)	1761	1761
Hamlin HCR 62, Box 38 Van Buren 04785	1870 Aroostook (15)	1892	?
Hammond Plantation P.O. Box 632 Houlton 04730	1886 Aroostook (48)	1864	1885*

Town Address	Date Formed County (Map)	Vital Records	Town Records
Hampden 106 Main Road N. Hampden 04444	1794 Penobscot (64)	1892	1794*
Hampton	(see Aurora)		
Hancock P.O. Box 68 Hancock 04640	1828 Hancock (16)	1828	1828
Hanover P.O. Box 33 Hanover 04237	1843 Oxford (10)	1807	?
Harlem	(see China)		
Harmony P.O. Box 94, Mill Hill Harmony 04942	1803 Somerset (17)	1764	1764
Harpswell RR 1, Box 103 Orr's Island 04066	1758 Cumberland (12)	1769	1900*
Harrington P.O. Box 165 Princeton 04643	1797 Washington (44)	1851	1837*
Harrison P.O. Box 300 Harrison 04040	1805 Cumberland (2)	1805	1805
Hartford RFD 1, Box 220 Canton 04221	1798 Oxford (23)	1800	1798*
Hartland 11 Academy Street, Box 281 Hartland 04943	1820 Somerset (23)	1772	1820*
Haynesville P.O. Box 21 Haynesville 04446	1876 Aroostook (65)	1892	?
Hebron RFD 1, Box 645 Hebron 04238	1792 Oxford (33)	1700	1700
Hermon RFD 3, Box 1206 Bangor 04401	1816 Penobscot (56)	1872	?
Hersey P.O. Box D Patten 04765	1873 Aroostook (51)	1862	1862
Hibberts Gore (unorganized)	Lincoln (4)		
Highland Plantation HCR 68, Box 445 N. New Portland 04961	1871 Somerset (7)	1972	1972*

Town Address	Date Formed County (Map)	Vital Records	Town Records
Hiram P.O. Box 49 South Hiram 04080	1814 Oxford (38)	1815	1804*
Hodgdon Route 4, Box 95 Houlton 04730	1832 Aroostook (59)	1837	1950*
Holden P.O. Box 490 East Holden 04429	1852 Penobscot (67)	1756	1852
Hollis P.O. Box 9 Hollis Center 04042	1798 York (9)	1781	1781
Hope RR 2, Box 6510 Union 04862	1804 Knox (4)	1795	?
Houlton 21 Water Street Houlton 04730	1831 Aroostook (55)	1892	1923*
Howard	(see Willimantic)		
Howland P.O. Box 445 Howland 04448	1826 Penobscot (17)	1798	1911*
Hudson P.O. Box 3 Hudson 04449	1825 Penobscot (38)	1856	1887*
Huntressville	(see Lowell)		
Indian Island Indian Reservation Community Building Indian Island 04468	1962? Penobscot (41)	1962	1940?
Indian Township Passamaquoddy Indian Reservation P.O. Box 503 Princeton 04668	1970 Washington (8)	?	
Industry RFD 1, Box 1308 Farmington 04938	1803 Franklin (22)	1738	1803*
Island Falls P.O. Box 100 Island Falls 04747	1872 Aroostook (57)	1910	1910*
Islandport	(see Long Island Plantation)		
Isle Au Haut P.O. Box 36 Isle au Haut 04645	1874 Knox (17)	1875*	1951*
Isleboro P.O. Box 75 Islesboro 04848	1789 Waldo (26)	1789*	1789*

Town Address	Date Formed County (Map)	Vital Records	Town Records
Jackman P.O. Box 269 Jackman 04945	1895 Somerset (3)	1892	1883
Jackson RFD 1, Box 2770 Brooks 04921	1818 Waldo (5)	1809	1818
Jay 99 Main Street Jay 04239	1795 Franklin (24)	1779	1779
Jefferson P.O. Box 237 Jefferson 04348	1807 Lincoln (2)	1757	1757
Jonesboro P.O. Box 59, Look's Point Road Jonesboro 04648	1809 Washington (35)	1766	1918
Jonesport P.O. Box 480 Jonesport 04649	1832 Washington (46)	1872	1854
Joy	(see Troy)		
Kenduskeag P.O. Box 308 Kenduskeag 04450	1852 Penobscot (48)	1852	1852
Kennebec	(see Manchester)		
Kennebunk 1 Summer Street Kennebunk 04043	1820 York (21)	1729	1850
Kennebunkport P.O. Box 566 Kennebunkport 04046	1653 York (23)	1678	1678
Kilmarnock	(see Medford)		
Kingfield RFD 1, Box 1585 Kingfield 04947	1816 Franklin (11)	1816	1816
Kingman (unorganized)	Penobscot (9)		
Kingsbury Plantation HC 31, Box 53 Kingsbury Plt. 04942	1836 Piscataquis (12)	1836	1836
Kingville	(see Troy)		
Kirkland	(see Hudson)		
Kittery P.O. Box 808 Kittery 03904	1652 York (27)	1674	1648
Knox RFD 1, Box 910 Thorndike 04986	1819 Waldo (10)	1777	1820

Town Address	Date Formed County (Map)	Vital Records	Town Records
Lagrange P.O. Box 40 Lagrange 04453	1832 Penobscot (27)	1833	1832
Lake View Plantation Route 2, Box 218A Milo 04463	1892 Piscataquis (11)	1892	1905
Lakeville P.O. Box 123 Springfield 04487	1868 Penobscot (33)	1862	1940
Lamoine RFD 2, Box 252A Ellsworth 04605	1870 Hancock (23)	1849	1870
Lebanon RFD 1, Box 828 E. Lebanon 04027	1767 York (11)	1765	1765
Lee P.O. Box 308 Lee 04455	1832 Penobscot (20)	1780	1780
Leeds RR 1, Box 170 Leeds 04263	1801 Androscoggin (10)	1785	1801
Levant P.O. Box 31 Levant 04456	1813 Penobscot (47)	1769	1920
Lewiston City Clerk's Office Lewiston 04240	1795 Androscoggin (8)	1750	1795
Liberty RR 1, Box 500 Liberty 04949	1827 Waldo (17)	1864	1856
Ligonier	(see Albion)		
Limerick RR 2, Box 878 Limerick 04048	1787 York (3)	?	?
Limestone 27 Church Street Limestone 04750	1869 Aroostook (24)	1862	1861
Limington P.O. Box 240 Limington 04049	1792 York (4)	1792	1792
Lincoln 75 Main Street Lincoln 04457	1829 Penobscot (19)	1829	1829
Lincoln Plantation HCR 10, Box 325 Wilsons Mills 03579	1875 Oxford (1)	1890	1875

Town Address	Date Formed County (Map)	Vital Records	Town Records
Lincolnville RR 1, Box 4660 Lincolnville 04849	1802 Waldo (24)	1786	1802
Linneus RFD 2, Box 126A Houlton 04730	1836 Aroostook (58)	1784	1840
Lisbon RR 2, Box 1908 Lisbon Falls 04252	1799 Androscoggin (12)	1782	1799
Litchfield Route 1, Box 1280 Litchfield 04350	1795 Kennebec (25)	1785	1785
Littleton Route 1, Box 70 Monticello 04760	1856 Aroostook (50)	1892	?
Livermore RFD 2, Box 2450 Livermore Falls 04254	1795 Androscoggin (5)	1762	1795
Livermore Falls 2 Main Street Livermore Falls 04254	1843 Androscoggin (6)	1892	1844
Long Island Plantation	1857 Hancock (?)	1900	1900
Lovell P.O. Box 236 Center Lovell 04016	1800 Oxford (24)	1785	1800
Lowell Box 91, Lowell Road Enfield 04433	1837 Penobscot (30)	1854	1900
Lubec 40 School Street Lubec 04652	1811 Washington (41)	1819	1820
Ludlow Route 1, Box 180 Houlton 04730	1864 Aroostook (49)	1840	1840
Lyman 1 South Waterboro Road Lyman 04005	1778 York (14)	1850	1850
Lyndon	(see Caribou)		
Machias P.O. Box 418 Machias 04654	1784 Washington (38)	1773	1773
Machiasport P.O. Box 295 Machiasport 04655	1826 Washington (49)	1859	1966
Machisses	(see East Machias)		

Town Address	Date Formed County (Map)	Vital Records	Town Records
Macwahoc Plantation Kingman P.O. Kingman 04451	1851 Aroostook (67)	1851	1851
Madawaska 98 St. Thomas Street Madawaska 04756	1869 Aroostook (9)	1871	1869
Madison P.O. Box 190 Madison 04950	1804 Somerset (21)	1939	1892
Madrid RFD 1 Phillips 04966	1836 Franklin (10)	1789	1956
Magalloway Plantation HCR 10, Box 260 Errol, NH 03579	1883 Oxford (2)	1952	1952
Maine	(see Clifton)		
Manchester P.O. Box 263 Manchester 04351	1850 Kennebec (19)	1808	1850
Mansel	(see Tremont)		
Mapleton P.O. Box 500 Mapleton 04757	1878 Aroostook (32)	1804	?
Mariaville RFD 4, Box 225 Ellsworth 04605	1836 Hancock (8)	1875*	1836*
Mars Hill RR 1, Box 13 Mars Hill 04758	1867 Aroostook (39)	1786	1880*
Marshfield HCR 71, Box 37 Machias 04654	1846 Washington (37)	1821	1846*
Masardis P.O. Box 6 Masardis 04759	1839 Aroostook (37)	1818*	1930*
Matinicus Isle Plantation P.O. Box 216 Matinicus 04851	1840 Knox (18)	1840	1840
Mattawamkeag P.O. Box 260 Mattawamkeag 04459	1860 Penobscot (8)	1860	1860*
Maxfield RFD 1, Box 29 Lagrange 04453	1824 Penobscot (16)	1825	1825
Mechanic Falls 90 Lewiston Street Mechanic Falls 04256	1893 Androscoggin (2)	1893*	1893*

Town Address	Date Formed County (Map)	Vital Records	Town Records
Meddybemps Route 214 Meddybemps 04657	1841 Washington (20)	1936	1946*
Medford 37 Main Street Milo 04463	1824 Piscataquis (18)	1844	?
Medway HCR 86, Box 320 Medway 04460	1875 Penobscot (6)	1856	1875*
Mercer RFD 2, Box 900 Norridgewock 04957	1804 Somerset (32)	1769	?
Merrill P.O. Box 54 Smyrna Mills 04780	1895 Aroostook (46)	1893*	1938*
Mexico P.O. Box 251, Main Street Mexico 04257	1818 Oxford (12)	1818*	1818*
Milbridge P.O. Box 66 Milbridge 04658	1848 Washington (43)	1848	1848
Milburn	(see Skowhegan)		
Milford P.O. Box 336 Milford 04461	1833 Penobscot (51)	1864	1952*
Millinocket 207 Penobscot Avenue Millincoket 04462	1901 Penobscot (4)	1898*	1901*
Milo P.O. Box 218 Milo 04463	1823 Piscataquis (17)	1802	1823
Milton (unorganized)	Oxford (13)		
Minot P.O. Box 67 Minot 04258	1823 Androscoggin (3)	1786	1802*
Monhegan Plantation P.O. Box 311 Monhegan Island 04852	1839 Lincoln (20)	1841	1841
Monmouth P.O. Box 270 Monmouth 04259	1792 Kennebec (24)	1774	1774
Monroe Jackson Road Monroe 04951	1818 Waldo (6)	1778	1820*
Monson P.O. Box 308, Main Street Monson 04464	1822 Piscataquis (6)	1635	1920*

Town Address	Date Formed County (Map)	Vital Records	Town Records
Montgomery	(see Troy)		
Monticello P.O. Box 99, Main Street Monticello 04760	1846 Aroostook (44)	1860	1860
Montville Route 2, Box 860 Thorndike 04986	1807 Waldo (18)	1785	1785
Moose River P.O. Box 269 Jackman 04945	1852 Somerset (2)	late 1800s*	1900
Moro Plantation Box 36, RFD 1 Smyrna Mills 04780	1850 Aroostook (45)	1896	1922
Morrill RR #1, Box 400 Morrill 04952	1855 Waldo (20)	1781	1816*
Moscow RFD 1, Box 1440 Bingham 04920	1816 Somerset (9)	1771	1816*
Mount Chase P.O. Box 318 Patten 04765	1864 Penobscot (1)	1871*	1951*
Mount Desert Municipal Office, Sea Street Northeast Harbor 04662	1789 Hancock (28)	1806	1900*
Mount Vernon RFD 1, Box 3340 Mount Vernon 04352	1792 Kennebec (11)	1775	1797*
Naples P.O. Box 6 Naples 04055	1834 Cumberland (4)	1834	1834*
Nashville Plantation Route 1, Box 162 Ashland 04732	1889 Aroostook (29)	1889*	1889*
New Canada RFD 2, Box 654 Fort Kent 04743	1881 Aroostook (5)	1892*	1892*
New Charleston	(see Charleston)		
New Gloucester P.O. Box 82 New Gloucester 04260	1774 Cumberland (8)	1771	1700
New Limerick General Delivery New Limerick 04761	1837 Aroostook (54)	1892*	1861
New Portland P.O. Box 204 N. New Portland 04961	1808 Somerset (13)	1770	1836*

Town Address	Date Formed County (Map)	Vital Records	Town Records
New Sharon RFD 1, Box 1950 New Sharon 04955	1794 Franklin (26)	1797	1800*
New Sweden East Road, P.O. Box 149 New Sweden 04762	1895 Aroostook (18)	1872*	?
New Vineyard RFD 1, Box 3430 New Vineyard 04956	1802 Franklin (17)	1892*	?
Newburgh RFD 1, Box 1513 Hampden 04444	1819 Penobscot (63)	1828	1814*
Newcastle P.O. Box 386 Newcastle 04553	1753 Lincoln (8)	1754	1754
Newfield P.O. Box 81 West Newfield 04095	1794 York (5)	1897*	1900*
Newport 7 Spring Street Newport 04953	1814 Penobscot (45)	1858	1835*
Newry HC 61, Box 78 Newry 04261	1805 Oxford (4)	1805	1805
Nobleboro P.O. Box 168 Nobleboro 04555	1788 Lincoln (9)	1788	1788
Norridgewock P.O. Box 7, Perkins Street Norridgewock 04957	1788 Somerset (26)	1674	1674
North Berwick P.O. Box 422 North Berwick 03906	1831 York (18)	1831	1831
North Haven P.O. Box 525 North Haven 04853	1846 Knox (15)	1802	1802
North Yarmouth 130 Walnut Hill Road Cumberland Center 04021	1732? Cumberland (19)	1720*	1732*
Northfield HCR 71, Box 224 Northfield 04654	1838 Washington (24)	1798	1938*
Northport Mounted Route Belfast 04915	1796 Waldo (25)	1896*	?
Northwest Hancock (unorganized)	Hancock (1)		

Town Address	Date Formed County (Map)	Vital Records	Town Records
Norway 26 Danforth Street Norway 04268	1797 Oxford (27)	1700	1856*
Number 14 Plantation	1895 Washington (25)		
Number 21 Plantation RR 1, Box 115 Princeton 04668	1895 Washington (9)	1892*	1899*
Oakfield P.O. Box 69 Oakfield 04763	1897 Aroostook (53)	1882	1897*
Oakland P.O. Box 187 Oakland 04963	1873 Kennebec (6)	1873*	1873*
Ogunquit P.O. Box 2122 Ogunquit 03907	1980 York (29)	1871*	?
Old Orchard Beach P.O. Box 234 Old Orchard Beach 04064	1883 York (25)	1883*	1883*
Old Town 51 N. Brunswick Street Old Town 04468	1840 Penobscot (50)	1820	1840*
Orient General Delivery Orient 04471	1856 Aroostook (66)	1892	?
Orland HCR 79, Box 36 Orland 04472	1800 Hancock (13)	1765	1792*
Orono P.O. Box 130 Orono 04473	1806 Penobscot (59)	1806	1806
Orrington P.O. Box 59 Orrington 04474	1788 Penobscot (65)	1643	1643
Osborn HCR 31, Box 2980 Ellsworth 04605	1895 Hancock (10)	1938*	?
Otis RR 4, Box 167AA Ellsworth 04605	1835 Hancock (7)	1835	1835
Otisfield Box 1160, Route 2 Oxford 04270	1798 Oxford (31)	1798*	1798*
Owl's Head Star Route 32 Owls Head 04854	1921 Knox (14)	1921*	1921*

Town Address	Date Formed County (Map)	Vital Records	Town Records
Oxbow Plantation P.O. Box 2 Oxbow 04764	1895 Aroostook (40)	1940*	1940*
Oxford P.O. Box 153 Oxford 04270	1829 Oxford (32)	1829	1892*
Palermo Main Street Palermo 04354	1804 Waldo (16)	1908*	1831*
Palmyra P.O. Box 6 Palmyra 04965	1807 Somerset (30)	1800	1807*
Paris 1 E. Main Street South Paris 04281	1793 Oxford (29)	1795	1793
Parkman RR 1, Box 181-B Guilford 04443	1822 Piscataquis (20)	1782	1822*
Parsonsfield P.O. Box C Kezar Falls 04047	1785 York (1)	1762	1774
Passadumkeag P.O. Box 45 Passadumkeag 04475	1835 Penobscot (29)	1844	1935*
Patten P.O. Box 260 Patten 04765	1841 Penobscot (2)	1821	1841*
Pembroke RFD 1, Box 32 Pembroke 04666	1832 Washington (27)	1831	1832*
Penobscot HC 79, Box 147 Orland 04472	1787 Hancock (19)	1732	1880*
Pepperrellborough	(see Saco)		
Perham RFD 1, Box 123AA Caribou 04736	1878 Aroostook (21)	1855	1897*
Perkins (unorganized)	Sagadahoc (5)		
Perry Shore Road Perry 04667	1818 Washington (28)	1780	1965
Peru P.O. Box 198 West Peru 04290	1821 Oxford (14)	1813	1821
Phillips P.O. Box 66 Phillips 04966	1812 Franklin (13)	1763	1812

Town Address	Date Formed County (Map)	Vital Records	Town Records
Phillipsburg	(see Hollis)		
Phippsburg HCR 31, Box 25 Phippsburg 04562	1814 Sagadahoc (9)	1825	1814
Pittsfield P.O. Box 579 Pittsfield 04967	1819 Somerset (29)	1815	1815
Pittston Rt. 2, Box 9A Gardiner 04345	1779 Kennebec (30)	1785	1785
Pleasant Point Indian Reservation P.O. Box 343 Perry 04667	Washington (29)		
Pleasant Ridge Plantation HCR 65, Box 80 Bingham 04920	1895 Somerset (8)	1852	1852
Plymouth P.O. Box 35 Plymouth 04969	1826 Penobscot (53)	1795	1932*
Poland P.O. Box 38 Poland 04273	1795 Androscoggin (1)	1780	1734
Port Watson	(see Brooklin)		
Portage Lake P.O. Box 255 Portage Lake 04768	1895 Aroostook (25)	1875	1875
Porter Main Street Kezar Falls 04047	1807 Oxford (37)	1892*	1829*
Portland 389 Congress Street Portland 04101	1786 Cumberland (23)	1712	1786
Pownal RR 1, Box 1034 Pownal 04069	1808 Cumberland (9)	1800	1800
Pownalborough	(see Wiscasset)		
Prentiss Plantation P.O. Box 156 Springfield 04487	1858 Penobscot (15)	1841	1900*
Presque Isle P.O. Box 1148 Presque Isle 04769	1859 Aroostook (33)	1859	1892
Princeton P.O. Box 408 Princeton 04668	1832 Washington (10)	1861	1960

Town Address	Date Formed County (Map)	Vital Records	Town Records
Prospect Route 1, Box 200 Stockton Springs 04981	1794 Waldo (14)	1756	1889*
Putnam	(see Washington)		
Randolph 128 Water Street Randolph 04345	1887 Kennebec (28)	1898*	1922*
Rangeley P.O. Box 1070 Rangeley 04970	1855 Franklin (4)	1795	1855*
Rangeley Plantation Rangeley 04970	1895 Franklin (8)	1910*	1900*
Raymond RR 1, Box 269 Raymond 04071	1803 Cumberland (6)	1745	1803*
Readfield Town Office, P.O. Box 97 Readfield 04355	1791 Kennebec (17)	1777	1790*
Reed Plantation P.O. Box 9 Wytopitlock 04497	1878 Aroostook (68)	1892*	1800*
Richmond P.O. Box 159 Richmond 04357	1823 Sagadahoc (2)	1782	1823*
Ripley RFD 3, Box 1470 Dexter 04930	1816 Somerset (19)	1783	1892*
Rockabema	(see Moro Plantation)		
Robbinston Box 240, Route 1 Robbinston 04671	1811 Washington (22)	1857	1886*
Rockland P.O. Box 546 Rockland 04841	1848 Knox (9)	1803	1854*
Rockport Town Office, P.O. Box 10 Rockport 04856	1891 Knox (5)	1783	1783
Rome Route 2, Box 1470 Norridgewock 04957	1804 Kennebec (5)	1776	1776
Roque Bluffs RR 1 Machias 04654	1891 Washington (48)	1892*	1891*
Roxbury P.O. Box 24 Roxbury 04275	1835 Oxford (7)	1892*	?

Town Address	Date Formed County (Map)	Vital Records	Town Records
Rumford Municipal Building Rumford 04276	1800 Oxford (11)	1800	1800*
Sabattus P.O. Box 12 Sabbattus 04280	1840 Androscoggin (13)	1892	1700*
Saco 300 Main Street Saco 04072	1762 York (16)	1717	1867*
St. Agatha Town Hall, P.O. Box 106 St. Agatha 04772	1899 Aroostook (8)	1889	1889
St. Albans RR 1, Box 4634 Street Albans 04971	1813 Somerset (24)	1785	1914*
St. Francis P.O. Box 98 St. Francis 04774	1870 Aroostook (2)	1892*	1892*
St. George P.O. Box 131 Tenants Harbor 04860	1803 Knox (12)	1737	1803*
St. John Plantation RFD #3, Box 440 Fort Kent 04743	1870 Aroostook (3)	1885*	1950*
Sandy River Plantation P.O. Box 589 Rangeley 04970	1905 Franklin (9)	1895	1905
Sanford 267 Main Street Sanford 04073	1768 York (12)	1769	1661
Sangerville P.O. Box 188 Sangerville 04479	1814 Piscataquis (21)	1793	1814*
Scarborough P.O. Box 360 Scarborough 04074	1658 Cumberland (21)	1725	1725
Searsmont P.O. Box 56 Searsmont 04973	1814 Waldo (19)	1854	1814*
Searsport P.O. Box 499 Searsport 04974	1845 Waldo (13)	1801	1845
Sebago P.O. Box 237 East Sebago 04029	1826 Cumberland (3)	1892*	?
Sebasticook	(see Benton)		

Town Address	Date Formed County (Map)	Vital Records	Town Records
Sebec RFD 2, Box 102 Dover-Foxcroft 04426	1812 Piscataquis (16)	1813	1794*
Seboeis Plantation P.O. Box 232 Howland 04448	1895 Penobscot (11)	1890*	1890*
Sedgwick RR 1, Box 6630 Sedgwick 04676	1789 Hancock (27)	1792	1789*
Shapleigh P.O. Box 26 Shapleigh 04076	1785 York (7)	1784	1784
Sherman P.O. Box 96 Sherman Mills 04776	1862 Aroostook (60)	1800	1904*
Shirley P.O. Box 40 Shirley 04485	1834 Piscataquis (3)	1797	1896*
Sidney RFD 3, Box 491 Augusta 04330	1792 Kennebec (13)	1772	1700*
Skowhegan 90 Water Street Skowhegan 04976	1823 Somerset (27)	1803	1814*
Smithfield P.O. Box 9 Smithfield 04978	1840 Somerset (33)	1775	1775
Smyrna P.O. Box 54 Smyrna 04780	1839 Aroostook (47)	1869	1869
Solon P.O. Box 284 Solon 04979	1809 Somerset (15)	1764	1804*
Somerville RR 1, Box 1402 Coopers Mills 04341	1858 Lincoln (3)	1798	1853*
Sorrento HCR 32, Box 161 Sorrento 04677	1895 Hancock (24)	1859*	1940*
South Berwick 180 Main Street S. Berwick 03908	1814 York (19)	1763	1763
South Bristol P.O. Box 65 South Bristol 04568	1915 Lincoln (15)	1916	1916
South Franklin (unorganized)	Franklin (19)		
South Oxford (unorganized)	Oxford (19)		

Town Address	Date Formed County (Map)	Vital Records	Town Records
South Portland 25 Cottage Road South Portland 04106	1895 Cumberland (24)	1748	1748
South Thomaston P.O. Box 147 South Thomaston 04858	1848 Knox (13)	1780	1780
Southeast (unorganized)	Piscataquis (23)		
Southport P.O. Box 53 Newagen 04552	1842 Lincoln (18)	1842	1842
Southwest Harbor P.O. Box 151 Southwest Harbor 04679	1905 Hancock (35)	1905	1905
Springfield P.O. Box 42, Route 6 Springfield 04487	1834 Penobscot (21)	1834	1834*
Stacyville P.O. Box 116 Sherman Station 04777	1883 Penobscot (3)	1860	1860
Standish P.O. Box 597 Standish 04084	1785 Cumberland (14)	1770	1785
Starks RFD 1, Box 300 Starks 04911	1795 Somerset (25)	1787	1796*
Stetson P.O. Box 85 Stetson 04488	1831 Penobscot (46)	1803	1900
Steuben P.O. Box 26 Steuben 04680	1795 Washington (42)	1769	1795*
Stockholm N. Main Street, P.O. Box 16 Stockholm 04783	1991 Aroostook (13)	1897*	1891*
Stockton Springs P.O. Box 339 Stockton Springs 04981	1857 Waldo (15)	1832	1857*
Stoneham Route 1, Box 95 East Stoneham 04231	1834 Oxford (18)	1837	1912*
Stonington P.O. Box 8 Stonington 04681	1897 Hancock (37)	1897*	1897*
Stow SR 68, Box 175 N. Fryeburg 04058	1833 Oxford (17)	1830*	1830*

Town Address	Date Formed County (Map)	Vital Records	Town Records
Strong P.O. Box 132 Strong 04983	1801 Franklin (16)	1779	1779
Stroudwater	(see Westbrook)		
Sullivan P.O. Box 67 West Sullivan 04689	1789 Hancock (25)	1745	1745
Summit (unorganized)	Penobscot (43)		
Sumner Star Route, Box 1330 West Sumner 04292	1798 Oxford (22)	1733	?
Surry P.O. Box 147 Surry 04684	1803 Hancock (21)	1790	1803*
Swan's Island P.O. Box 127 Swan's Island 04685	1897 Hancock (38)	1850*	1839*
Swanville RFD 2, Box 325 Belfast 04915	1818 Waldo (12)	1812	1814*
Sweden RFD 1, Box 580 Bridgton, 04009	1813 Oxford (26)	1953*	1953*
Talmadge P.O. Box 9 Waite 04492	1875 Washington (5)	1850	1850*
Temple RR 1, Box 67 Temple 04984	1803 Franklin (20)	1784	1803*
Thomaston P.O. Box 299 Thomaston 04861	1777 Knox (8)	1775	1776*
Thompsonborough	(see Lisbon)		
Thorndike P.O. Box 10 Thorndike 04986	1819 Waldo (4)	1776	1819*
Topsfield Star Route, Box 19 Topsfield 04490	1838 Washington (2)	1834	1860*
Topsham 22 Elm Street Topsham 04086	1764 Sagadahoc (3)	1892*	1926*
Townsend	(see Southport)		
Tremont P.O. Box 121 West Tremont 04690	1848 Hancock (34)	1825	1848*
Trenton P.O. Box 293-A Trenton 04605	1789 Hancock (22)	1786	1786

Town Address	Date Formed County (Map)	Vital Records	Town Records
Troy RR 1, Box 1970 Troy 04987	1812 Waldo (2)	1840	1812*
Turner P.O. Box 157 Turner 04282	1786 Androscoggin (4)	1740	1785*
Twombly (unorganized)	Penobscot (32)		
Union P.O. Box 186, Common Road Union 04862	1786 Knox (2)	1789	1788*
Unity (unorganized)	Kennebec (3)		
Unity P.O. Box 416 Unity 04988	1804 Waldo (3)	1797	1804*
Upton P.O. Box 680 Upton 04261	1860 Oxford (3)	1893	1830*
Usher	(see Stoneham)		
Van Buren 65 Main Street Van Buren 04785	1881 Aroostook (11)	1838	1881*
Vanceboro P.O. Box 25 Vanceboro 04491	1874 Washington (4)	1814*	1938*
Vassalboro P.O. Box 187 N. Vassalboro 04962	1771 Kennebec (14)	1764	1764
Veazie 1084 Main Street Veazie 04401	1853 Penobscot (58)	1852	1853*
Verona RFD 2, Box 147 Bucksport 04416	1861 Hancock (12)	1900*	1955*
Vienna P.O. Box 17 Vienna 04360	1802 Kennebec (4)	1752	1802*
Vinalhaven Pond Street Vinalhaven 04863	1789 Knox (16)	1785	1785
Wade RFD 1, Box 1340 Washburn 04786	1913 Aroostook (26)	1899*	1949*
Waite P.O. Box 37 Waite 04492	1876 Washington (6)	1892*	?
Waldo RFD #1, Box 2410 Morrill 04952	1845 Waldo (21)	1892*	?

Town Address	Date Formed County (Map)	Vital Records	Town Records
Waldoboro P.O. Box J Waldoboro 04572	1773 Lincoln (11)	1778	1778
Wales Route 1, Box 1765 Sabattus 04280	1816 Androscoggin (14)	1759	1836*
Wallagrass Plantation RFD 1, Box 1245 Soldier Pond 04781	1870 Aroostook (4)	1866	1866
Waltham Star Route HC 31, Box 2250 Ellsworth 04605	1833 Hancock (9)	1850*	1890*
Warren P.O. Box 116 Warren 04864	1776 Knox (7)	1795	1776*
Warsaw	(see Pittsfield)		
Washburn P.O. Box 504 Washburn 04786	1861 Aroostook (27)	1885	1912*
Washington P.O. Box 408 Washington 04574	1811 Knox (1)	1800	1811*
Waterboro P.O. Box 130 Waterboro 04087	1787 York (8)	1787	1787
Waterford RR 1, Box 1575 North Waterford 04267	1797 Oxford (26)	1762	1798*
Waterville City Hall Waterville 04901	1802 Kennebec (7)	1813	1802*
Wayne RFD 1, Box 515 Wayne 04284	1798 Kennebec (16)	1773	1773
Webster	(see Sabbatus)		
Webster Plantation RR 1, Box 170B Webster Plantation 04487	1856 Penobscot (14)	1840	1920*
Weld RFD 1, Box 210 Weld 04285	1816 Franklin (14)	1766	1844*
Wellington HCR 31, Box 114 Wellington 04942	1828 Piscataquis (19)	1823	1823
Wells P.O. Box 147 Wells 04090	1653 York (20)	1695	1700*

Town Address	Date Formed County (Map)	Vital Records	Town Records
Wesley HCR 71, Box 301 Wesley 04686	1833 Washington (17)	1840	1832*
West Bath RR 1, Box 420 West Bath 04530	1844 Sagadahoc (8)	1845	1914*
West Central Franklin (unorganized)	Franklin (12)		
West Forks Plantation P.O. Box 5 West Forks 04985	1893 Somerset (4)	1898	1898*
West Gardiner Route 3, Box 3690 Gardiner 04345	1850 Kennebec (26)	1848	??
West Paris P.O. Box 247 West Paris 04289	1957 Oxford (28)	1958*	1958*
West Pittston	(see Randolph)		
West Waterville	(see Oakland)		
Westbrook P.O. Box 648 Westbrook 04092	1814 Cumberland (22)	1800	1718*
Westfield P.O. Drawer C Westfield 04787	1905 Aroostook (38)	1892*	1894*
Westmanland Plantation RFD 1, Box 132 Stockholm 04783	1895 Aroostook (17)	1892	1940
Weston P.O. Box 28 Danforth 04424	1835 Aroostook (70)	1814	1835*
Westport RFD 2, Box 330 Wiscasset 04578	1828 Lincoln (12)	1761	1761
Whitefield P.O. Box 58 North Whitefield 04353	1809 Lincoln (1)	1748	1748
Whiting P.O. Box 101 Whiting 04691	1825 Washington (40)	1814	1817*
Whitney (unorganized)	Penobscot (34)		
Whitneyville P.O. Box 186 Whitneyville 04692	1845 Washington (36)	1861	1890*
Willimantic RR 2, Box 149 Guilford 04443	1881 Piscataquis (7)	1859	1881*

Town Address	Date Formed County (Map)	Vital Records	Town Records
Wilton P.O. Box 541 Wilton 04294	1803 Franklin (23)	1765	1765
Windham 8 School Road Windham 04062	1762 Cumberland (16)	1789	1823
Windsor RR 1, Box 1050 Windsor 04363	1809 Kennebec (23)	1797	1797
Winn P.O. Box 102 Winn 04495	1857 Penobscot (13)	1872	1892*
Winslow 16 Benton Avenue Winslow 04901	1771 Kennebec (8)	1771	1771
Winter Harbor P.O. Box 98 Winter Harbor 04693	1895 Hancock (30)	1895	1895
Winterport P.O. Box 559 Winterport 04496	1860 Waldo (7)	1860	1860*
Winterville Plantation General Delivery Winterville 04788	1895 Aroostook (16)	1876	1884*
Winthrop 57 Main Street Winthrop 04364	1771 Kennebec (18)	1720	1800*
Wiscasset P.O. Box 328 Wiscasset 04578	1760 Lincoln (6)	1752	1752
Woodland RFD 1, Box 83B Caribou 04736	1880 Aroostook (22)	1874	1875*
Woodstock P.O. Box 317 Woodstock 04219	1815 Oxford (21)	1814	1815
Woodville HCR 65, Box 828 Lincoln Ctr. 04458	1895 Penobscot (7)	1900*	1930*
Woolwich P.O. Box 1660 Woolwich 04579	1759 Sagadahoc (6)	1756	1760
Wyman (unorganized)	Franklin (3)		
Yarmouth P.O. Box 907 Yarmouth 04096	1849 Cumberland (20)	1830	1849
York P.O. Box 9 York 03909	1652 York (28)	1715	1897*

Maryland

Roger D. Joslyn, C.G., F.A.S.G.

In 1632 Maryland was granted to George Calvert, formerly secretary of state under King James I of England, but he could not hold public office after he espoused Catholicism in 1625. The Maryland Charter was issued to George's son, Cecilius, alias Cecil, Second Baron Baltimore, in 1632. However, it was Cecil's younger brother Leonard who brought the first colonists aboard the *Ark* and the *Dove*, landing in March 1634 at St. Clements Island near the future capital at St. Mary's. Named for Henrietta Maria, wife of King Charles I, the colony was called Maria's Land or Mariland. Agriculture and trading were quickly established with the help of laborers who worked off their passage to the new land, friendly Native Americans, and African slaves. The Europeans had good relations with the original inhabitants, although by the end of the century much of the native population had perished from disease, war, or liquor, and others were forced north or in some cases integrated with other groups.

A significant point in Maryland's history was the passage of the Act of Toleration in 1649, which encouraged settlement by many nonconformists, not only Catholics (in Calvert, Charles, and St. Mary's counties), but also dissenters from Virginia (in Anne Arundel County) and Friends (Quakers). The Protestant Revolution in England, however, spread unrest to Maryland, and the proprietary government was overthrown by the Crown in 1689. The Anglican church was established as the state church of Maryland, and the capital moved to a more central location at Annapolis. With the conversion of the young Lord Baltimore to Protestantism, the proprietorship was restored in 1715. In 1781 Catholics were disfranchised and barred from public office, but Jesuit Fathers quietly continued to serve a growing Catholic populace despite laws forbidding them to celebrate the Mass or perform the sacraments. A number of early Maryland gentry unions occurred through Catholic-Protestant marriages.

The earliest settlements congregated in southern Maryland on the western shore, in Anne Arundel, Calvert, Charles, and St. Mary's counties. By 1695, this included Prince George's County, which until 1748 stretched from Pennsylvania to Virginia. Virginia fur traders had settled at Kent Island prior to the arrival of Calvert's immigrants in 1634. On Maryland's eastern shore, Somerset County bordered Virginia, from which colony came the first settlers, soon joined by emigrants from St. Mary's and new arrivals from Britain. By the 1680s, Baltimore County, along the waterways of the Patapsco and Gunpowder rivers, was seated. Because of an uncertain border, evidence of many settlers in western Kent and southern and western Sussex counties in Delaware are found in Maryland records until the time of the Revolutionary War.

In the eighteenth century settlers left the Chesapeake region and began building homes among the hills and valleys of western Maryland. Beginning in the 1730s, Germans from bordering Pennsylvania counties poured into what were then Baltimore and Frederick counties; some Quaker groups came about this time from New Jersey. In the mid-1700s, many settlers came from Pennsylvania, and servants, felons, and Jacobite rebels numbered heavily among the eighteenth-century emigrants from Britain, with the Jacobites sold as laborers. Migrations out of Maryland in the eighteenth century included Catholics from St. Mary's into Kentucky and Moravians, most of whom went to Winston-Salem, North Carolina, in the 1760s to obtain free land. Other Germans, Ulster-Scots, and Quakers went south to Virginia and the Carolinas. With the completion of the National Road in 1818, migration westward through and out of Maryland was greatly increased. The building of the country's first railroad, the Baltimore and Ohio, as well as the canal system along the Potomac River also increased mobility within and out of the state.

Although British warships visited the Chesapeake in 1777, and there was a sizable number of Loyalists among the populace, no major battles were fought in Maryland during the American Revolution. The state was, however, the site for much action during the War of 1812. Although loyal to the Union during the Civil War, there was much sympathy for the South in southern and western shore counties and among the upper classes, and many fought for the Confederacy. After the war, many black Southerners fled to Maryland from their devastated homes. About this same time a large influx of Germans and eastern Europeans moved through Baltimore, one of the major eastern ports.

Vital Records

In 1640 the Maryland Assembly provided for the recording of births, marriages, and burials by the clerk of "every court," and banns were to be posted three days before the marriage, but very few of these records exist. Those that do are indexed at the Maryland State Archives (see Archives, Libraries, and Societies). When the Anglican church became the official church of the colony in 1692, the parishes were instructed to register the births, marriages, and deaths of all residents except blacks. Every county formed by 1770 has at least one pre-Revolution parish register, and many of these include blacks.

The first place to check for Maryland births, 1898–1950, including those for Baltimore City, 1875–1941, is the Maryland State Archives, which has microfilm of records and indexes. The state archives also has Maryland death records for 1898–1982 (indexes 1898–1968), with Baltimore City deaths for 1875–1982 (indexes 1875–1971). Self-service copies at the state archives are twenty-five cents; a search and copy by mail is $5. Birth and death records, but not corresponding indexes, are restricted—births for one hundred years and deaths for twenty years; however, "pertinent genealogical information" abstracted from a restricted record can be provided by the archives for a $5 fee. County civil marriage records from 1914 through 1950 are at the state archives but are indexed only to 1930. Maryland births from April 1898 with City of Baltimore births from January 1875, Maryland deaths occurring less than twenty years ago, and Maryland marriages from June 1951 are also available from the Division of Vital Records, State Department of Health and Mental Hygiene, 4201 Patterson Avenue, P.O. Box 13146, Baltimore, Maryland 21203-3146. The fee is currently $4, and a self-addressed, stamped envelope should be sent with each record request. Access at the Division of Vital Records is more restrictive than at the state archives.

Earlier marriages, usually from the 1770s to 1919, are either with the clerk of the circuit court where the license was issued or at the state archives. The latter also has film of most of these records, with an incomplete general index to records and licenses (1650–95 and 1777–1886) for the counties of Anne Arundel, Caroline, Charles, Dorchester, Frederick, Kent, Prince George's, and Somerset and an index to licenses for Baltimore City and County, 1777–1851. Marriage licenses for some counties have been published, and two volumes of *Maryland Marriages, 1634–1777* and *1778–1800*, compiled by Robert Barnes (Baltimore, Md.: Genealogical Publishing Co., 1975, 1978), were gathered from church and estate as well as public records. A similar compilation by F. Edward Wright is *Maryland Eastern Shore Vital Records*, 5 vols. (Silver Spring and Westminster, Md.: Family Line Publications, 1982–89), covering births, marriages, and deaths for 1648–1825 from church and court records.

Microfilms of early county vital records and a card file indexing some pre-state records entered in the county land and court records are at the state archives. These include records from the 1600s for Charles, Kent, Somerset, and Talbot counties; births, 1804–77, and deaths, 1865–80, for Anne Arundel County; births, 1898–1923, and deaths, 1898–1916, for Calvert County; births, 1865–73, for Kent County; and deaths, 1898–1916, for Annapolis. Another state archives index covers implied marriages from court, land, and probate records for the period from about 1674 to 1851, and other indexes cover vital records substitutes for various time periods from Bible, cemetery, and church records. Evidence of marriages found in Revolutionary War pension files was included in Newman's *Maryland Revolutionary Records* (see Military Records).

Although a few separations were granted, there were no divorces in Maryland before the Revolutionary War. From that time until 1842, divorces were granted by the state legislature; for these see Mary Keysor Meyer, *Divorces and Names Changed in Maryland by Act of the Legislature 1634–1854* (1970; reprint, Baltimore, Md.: Genealogical Publishing Co., 1972). Records of later divorces are with the clerk of the circuit court where the divorce was granted or at the state archives.

Census Records

Federal

Population Schedules.

- Indexed—1790, 1800, 1810, 1820, 1830, 1840, 1850
- Soundex—1880, 1900, 1920
- Unindexed—1860, 1870, 1910

Industry and Agriculture Schedules.

- 1850, 1860, 1870, 1880

Mortality Schedules.

- 1850, 1860 (1850 and 1860 indexed), 1870, 1880 (1870 and 1880 indexed for Eastern Shore)

Slave Schedules.

- 1850, 1860 (both indexed)

Union Veterans Schedules.

- 1890 (indexed)

Microfilm of the federal censuses, corresponding book and film indexes, and indexed mortality schedules are at the Maryland State Archives, the Maryland State Law Library (see Archives, Libraries, and Societies), and in other libraries. Missing schedules include 1790 for Allegany, Calvert, Somerset, and part of Dorchester counties (destroyed); 1800 for Baltimore County (never taken); and 1830 for Montgomery, Prince George's, Queen Anne's, Saint Mary's, and Somerset counties. An index to the 1860 slave schedules was compiled by Ralph Clayton in the *Maryland Genealogical Society Bulletin* 25 (1984): 92–112.

Non-population census schedules are at the state archives, which also has the original 1880 population schedules.

Colonial

A 1776 census was taken to determine population and is indexed at the Maryland State Archives, but it is not available for all counties. A 1778 "census" is a list of males over eighteen who, in some counties, signed the Oath of Fidelity and in others, did not. Of the few extant lists, those for nine counties were published by Gaius Marcus Brumbaugh in *Maryland Records: Colonial, Revolutionary, County and Church From Original Sources,* 2 vols. (1915–28; reprint, Baltimore, Md.: Genealogical Publishing Co., 1985). See also Bettie Stirling Carothers's compilations, *1776 Census of Maryland* and *1778 Census of Maryland* (Lutherville, Md.: the compiler, 1972). Both versions of the 1778 census published by Brumbaugh and Carothers contain transcription errors. Brumbaugh also published some of the 1778 Oaths of Fidelity (also indexed at the state archives); others were compiled and published in two volumes by Bettie Stirling Carothers (Lutherville, Md.: the compiler, 1975–78). A police census taken in Baltimore in 1868 is in the Baltimore City Archives (see Archives, Libraries, and Societies).

Among census substitutes is *Maryland Rent Rolls: Baltimore and Anne Arundel Counties, 1700–1707, 1705–1724* (Baltimore, Md.: Genealogical Publishing Co., 1976), taken from the *Maryland Historical Magazine.* See Tax Records for other lists.

Background Sources

J. Thomas Scharf, *History of Maryland,* 3 vols. (1879; reprint with new index, Hatboro, Pa.: Tradition Press, 1967), is one of the major, standard histories of the state. More modern and excellent works include Suzanne Ellery Greene Chappelle, and others, *Maryland: A History of its People* (Baltimore, Md.: Johns Hopkins University Press, 1986), and Robert J. Brugger, *Maryland: A Middle Temperament, 1634–1980* (Baltimore, Md.: Johns Hopkins Press, 1988). Hester Dorsey Richardson, *Side-Lights on Maryland History With Sketches of Some Families,* 2 vols. (1913), was reprinted in one volume by Tidewater Publishing of Cambridge, Md., 1967.

Matthew Page Andrews's *Tercentenary History of Maryland,* 4 vols. (Chicago, Ill., and Baltimore, Md.: S. J. Clarke Publishing Co., 1925), is really one volume of history and three of "mug book" biographies of twentieth-century Marylanders. The term mug book refers to those printed sources that present pictures and biographies of those who subscribed to the publication. Other mug book compilations, all of which must be used with caution, are *Portrait and Biographical Record of the Eastern Shore of Maryland* (New York, N.Y.: Chapman Publishing Co., 1898); *Men of Mark in Maryland,* 4 vols. (Washington, D.C.: B. F. Johnson, 1907–12); and *Genealogical and Memorial Encyclopedia of the State of Maryland,* 2 vols., edited by Richard H. Spencer (New York, N.Y.: American Historical Society, 1919).

Other useful works include *The Old Line State: A History of Maryland,* by Morris Leon Radoff and others (Annapolis, Md.: Hall of Records Commission, 1971), available from the Maryland State Archives for $5; Richard Walsh and William Lloyd Fox, eds., *Maryland: A History 1632–1974* (Baltimore, Md.: Maryland Historical Society, 1974); Clayton C. Hall, *The Lords of Baltimore and the Maryland Palatinate* (Baltimore, Md.: J. Murphy Co., 1902); and Harry Wright Newman, *The Flowering of the Maryland Palatinate: An Intimate and Objective History of the Province of Maryland to the overthrow of the Proprietary Rule in 1654* (1961; reprint, Baltimore, Md.: Genealogical Publishing Co., 1985). Newman also wrote on the manor system: *Seigniory in Early Maryland* (Washington, D.C.: Descendants of Lords of the Maryland Manors, 1949).

While seemingly limited in coverage, *A Biographical Dictionary of the Maryland Legislature, 1635–1789,* by Edward C. Papenfuse and others, 2 vols. (Annapolis, Md.: Johns Hopkins University Press, 1979–85), is quite useful since it covers a number of persons and families not found in other published works.

Two excellent works detailing large groups of persons are Grace L. Tracey and John P. Dern, *Pioneers of Old Monocacy: The Early Settlement of Frederick County, Maryland, 1721–1743* (Baltimore, Md.: Genealogical Publishing Co., 1987), and Robert W. Barnes, *Baltimore County Families, 1659–1759* (Baltimore, Md.: Genealogical Publishing Co., 1989), the latter of which also contains a very useful bibliography.

Local histories for Maryland's twenty-three counties have been published (see pages 3–4 for sources on local histories). Many books and articles have also been written on the histories of Maryland's cities and towns.

Guides

For excellent background reading, see the chapter on Maryland by John Frederick Dorman, F.A.S.G., in Milton Rubincam, ed., *Genealogical Research: Methods and Sources,* Vol. 1 (Washington, D.C.: American Society of Genealogists, 1980), pages 271–80.

Marion K. Kaminkow, *Maryland A to Z: A Topographical Dictionary* (Baltimore, Md.: Magna Carta Book Co., 1985), has a useful bibliography for the state and for each county. Henry Gannett, *A Gazetteer of Maryland and Delaware,* 2 vols. (1904; reprint in one vol., Baltimore, Md.: Genealogical Publishing Co., 1979), and Mary Keysor Meyer, *Genealogical Research in Maryland: A Guide,* 3d ed. (Baltimore, Md.: Maryland Historical Society, 1983), are also useful.

Eleanor P. Passano, *An Index to the Source Records of Maryland: Genealogical, Historical* (1940; reprint, Baltimore, Md.: Genealogical Publishing Co., 1984), indexes 20,000 Maryland surnames in published and manuscript works as well as various types of record sources located in the Maryland Historical Society, Library of Congress, DAR Library, and the Library of the Diocese of Maryland in Baltimore (now at the George Peabody Library at Johns Hopkins University). Richard J. Cox and Larry E. Sullivan, eds., *Guide to the Research Collections of the Maryland Historical Society* (Baltimore, Md.: Maryland Historical Society, 1981), is available from the society (see also the work by Pedley under Manuscripts).

A series of individual guides to microfilmed county and Baltimore City records, *A Guide to the Maryland State Archives Holdings,* is handy for obtaining microfilm through interlibrary loan. The individual guides are available for $5 each from the Maryland State Archives.

Maps

Reprints of county topographical maps are available from the Maryland Department of Natural Resources, Maryland Geological Survey, 2300 St. Paul Street, Baltimore, Maryland 21218. A good collection of maps, atlases, and plats is at the Maryland State Archives, where many are indexed by place and some by names of tracts and owners. Early maps of Maryland are in Russell Morrison, and others, *On the Map* (Chestertown, Md.: Washington College, 1983). Other fine and useful maps are at the Maryland Historical Society (see Archives, Libraries, and Societies). Mary Ross Brown, *An Illustrated Genealogy of the Counties of Maryland and the District of Columbia* (Silver Spring, Md.: the author, 1967), includes maps that show the county changes and also ward maps of Baltimore for 1850, 1860, 1870, and 1880. Atlases have been published for some of the counties, and county maps are to be found in most county histories.

For the best study of mapping in Maryland see Edward C. Papenfuse and Joseph M. Coale, III, *Atlas of Historical Maps of Maryland, 1608–1908* (Baltimore, Md.: Johns Hopkins University Press, 1982).

Land Records

State-Land State

The Maryland State Archives has land patents (from 1634) with indexes; quit rents (yearly payments to Lord Baltimore, similar to property taxes), 1749–61 (incomplete); rent rolls (the record of quit rent payments), 1639–1776 (incomplete); debt books (yearly compilations by Lord Baltimore's agent, giving the name of each tract and the amount owed), 1735–73; certificates of survey, 1705 to date; and warrants and assignments, 1634–1842. A separate index covers private and proprietary manors as found in the patent records. See Elizabeth Hartsook and Gust Skordas, *Land Office and Prerogative Court Records of Colonial Maryland* (1946; reprint, Baltimore, Md.: Genealogical Publishing Co., 1968 and 1989).

Beverly W. Bond's "The Quitrent System in Maryland," *Maryland Historical Magazine* 5 (1910): 350–65, describes the system whereby a rent was paid on land to the proprietor, and in volumes 19–26 of the same journal, some rent rolls were published. Some rent rolls are in the Calvert Papers at the Maryland Historical Society.

Other background information is in Clarence P. Gould, *The Land System in Maryland, 1720–1765* (Baltimore, Md.: Johns Hopkins Press, 1913); Paul H. Giddens, "Land Policies and Administration in Colonial Maryland, 1753–1769," *Maryland Historical Magazine* 28 (1933): 142–71; and Canville D. Benson, "Notes on the Preparation of Conveyances by Laymen in the Colony of Maryland," *Maryland Historical Magazine* 60 (1965): 428–38.

Prior to 1683, land was granted to those who transported settlers to the colony. The names of such immigrants found in the land patents, 1633–80, are listed in Gust Skordas, ed., *The Early Settlers of Maryland* (1968; reprint, Baltimore, Md.: Genealogical Publishing Co., 1986).

Other early land records have been published in separate volumes or in journals. For the names of Revolutionary soldiers to whom land in Allegany County was granted in 1781, see J. Thomas Scharf's *History of Western Maryland,* 2 vols. (1882; reprint, Baltimore, Md.: Regional Publishing Co., 1968). The names given tracts by their original owners are important because most have been retained and are a way of tracing a piece of property. The state archives has an index to tract names, and Donna Valley Russell's "Finding Land Tracts," *Western Maryland Genealogy* 3 (1987): 26–29, provides helpful background on the subject.

Deeds, mortgages, and bills of sale are recorded in the county circuit court, where standard indexes are also available. Mortgages were often recorded separately in later years. Films of all county land records are available at the state archives, which also has the original record books and indexes of many counties. At some courthouses there are films of earlier records that have been transferred to the state archives. A law enacted in 1784 required that abstracts of county deeds be sent to Annapolis. The extant records pertain mostly to counties whose early land records were destroyed, such as Calvert and St. Mary's.

Early deeds could be recorded in both county courts and the provincial and general courts. Indexes to the latter for 1658–1815, by name of person and tract, are available at the state archives.

When consolidated indexes to land records were prepared in the nineteenth century, other instruments recorded in the volumes, such as gifts of slaves, powers of attorney, and proofs of age, were often omitted; these must now be found by searching the index in each land record volume.

Probate Records

Before 1777 estates were recorded in the prerogative court, thus the records are "complete" despite courthouse fires and other losses at the county level. These include wills, inventories, accounts, balances of final distribution, and testamentary proceedings, all indexed at the Maryland State Archives. For the forty-one volumes of prerogative court wills (at the state archives and described in the work by Hartsook and Skordas cited under Land Records), see James M. Magruder, Jr., comp., *Index of Maryland Colonial Wills 1634–1777,* 3 vols. (1933; reprint in one vol., with additions by Louise E. Magruder, Baltimore, Md.: Genealogical Publishing Co., 1986). The wills through 1743 were abstracted by Jane Baldwin Cotton in *The Maryland Calendar of Wills,* 8 vols. (1904–28; reprint, Baltimore, Md.: Genealogical Publishing Co., 1968). Abstracts of later wills were provided by Annie Walker Burns, comp., *Abstracts of Maryland Wills* [1744–73], 15 parts (Annapolis, Md.: the compiler, 1938–45), and James M. Magruder, Jr., comp., *Maryland Colonial Abstracts: Wills, Accounts and Inventories 1772–1777,* 5 vols. (1934–39; reprint in one vol., Baltimore, Md.: Genealogical Publishing Co., 1968). Family Line Publications is publishing a new series of will abstracts for 1744–77, in the style of Cotton's work, that will correct errors in those produced by Burns. See also *Index to Inventories of Estates, 1718–1777* (Annapolis, Md.: Hall of Records Commission, 1947) and *Abstracts of the Inventories of the Prerogative Court of Maryland,* 12 vols., the latter by V. L. Skinner, Jr., (Westminster, Md.: Family Line Publications, 1988–91), covering 1733–77.

After 1777 probates were recorded in the county orphans' court. Indexes to wills kept in courthouses have been published for the counties of Allegany, Anne Arundel, Baltimore, Calvert, Charles, Garrett, Harford, Howard, Kent, Prince George's, St. Mary's, Somerset, and Washington. Abstracts of some county wills have been published, most notably the twenty volumes for Baltimore County, 1783–1845, compiled by Annie Walker Burns, but these should be checked with original records for accuracy. Some abstracts are found in journals such as those for Frederick County in *Western Maryland Genealogy,* as are indexes such as that for Carroll County in the *Carrolltonian* (1984). Other county estate records that have been published include administrations, inventories, guardianship bonds, and distributions.

While some early original will books and other record volumes of estate records have been retained in the counties, most of these have been transferred to the state archives where they are also available on microfilm. Films of early records are found in a few of the counties.

Court Records

In many cases, efforts to recover the early proprietary records of Maryland, which were privately kept by the Calvert family, have been successful, although some material has disappeared. The earliest surviving proprietary and royal papers for the period 1637 to 1785 were published in *Calendar of Maryland State Papers No. 1 The Black Books* (1943; reprint, Baltimore, Md.: Genealogical Publishing Co., 1967). Various records of and indexes to the provincial and general court (1658–1805) and the chancery (equity) court (1668–1851) are at the Maryland State Archives. An index to depositions from a variety of sources, 1668–1789, was published in the *Maryland Historical Magazine* 23 (1928): 101–54, 197–242, 293–343. Other early court and related records have been published and indexed, such as provincial and county records from 1637 to the 1780s in volumes of *The Archives of Maryland.* One interesting sample of information from county court records is Millard Millburn Rice, ed., *This Was the Life: Excerpts from the Judgment Records of Frederick County, Maryland 1748–1765* (1979; reprint, Baltimore, Md.: Genealogical Publishing Co., 1984).

Many twentieth-century court records are still in the counties, with earlier records or copies in the state archives. In some county circuit courts there are marriage records and licenses, divorces, naturalizations, land records, plats, and records of roads, but few civil and criminal court records. The clerk of the orphans' court is also the register of wills and other estate records. Taxes and road surveys are in the assessment office. An excellent guide to the county court records in the counties and the state archives (original documents, record books, and microfilm) and indispensable for Maryland research is Morris L. Radoff, Gust Skordas, and Phebe R. Jacobsen, *The County Courthouses and Records of Maryland. Part II. The Records* (Annapolis, Md.: Hall of Records Commission, 1963). Following a discussion of each type of record, a county-by-county listing covers what is available. Courthouse fires and other losses of records are mentioned. The guide also has pictures of the various types of indexing systems found throughout the counties. It should be noted, however, that much more material has been transferred from the counties to the state archives since the publication of the guide, and updated information should be sought in Annapolis.

Tax Records

A Maryland tax assessment of 1783 with index, which is "more complete" than the 1776 or 1778 "censuses" (see Census Records) is available at the Maryland State Archives. Robert W. Barnes and Bettie Stirling Carothers abstracted the *1783 Tax List of Baltimore County, Maryland* (Lutherville, Md.: Bettie Stirling Carothers, 1978); while it has some omissions, it serves as an index to photocopies of the originals published as *Maryland Tax List 1783 Baltimore County* from the collection of the Maryland Historical Society (Philadelphia, Pa.: Historic Publications, 1970). The counties of Calvert, Cecil, Harford, and Talbot are covered by Bettie Carothers, comp., *1783 Tax List of Maryland, Part I* (Lutherville, Md.: the compiler, 1977). Furthermore, there is a two-part index to the 1783 list at the state archives, one by names of property owners, the other by names of the tracts.

The earliest tax records are to be found among the proprietary papers, dating from the 1630s. Some early tax records have been published, such as Raymond B. Clark, Jr., and Sara Seth Clark, comps., *Baltimore County, Maryland Tax Lists, 1699–1706* (Washington, D.C.: Raymond B. Clark, Jr., 1964). A tax list for St. Anne's Parish, Anne Arundel County, 1764–66, is at the state archives, which also has the surviving 1798 U.S. Direct Tax records for Anne Arundel County (indexed), Baltimore County and City, and the counties of Caroline, Charles, Harford, Prince George's, Queen Anne's, Saint Mary's, Somerset, and Talbot. Richard J. Cox edited *A Name Index to the Baltimore City Tax Records, 1798–1808, of the Baltimore City Archives* (Baltimore, Md.: Baltimore City Archives and Records Management Office, 1981). Current tax records are found in the assessment office in the counties.

Cemetery Records

The Maryland State Archives has indexes to cemetery records for various time periods. Some have been published in the *Maryland Genealogical Society Bulletin* and other journals and in individual works covering large parts of Anne Arundel, Baltimore, Dorchester, Frederick, Garrett, St. Mary's, Somerset, Wicomico, and Worcester counties. A great number of grave marker inscriptions have been transcribed by members of the Maryland DAR and will be found at the Maryland Historical Society and the DAR Library in Washington, D.C. See also Helen W. Ridgely, *Historic Graves of Maryland and the District of Columbia* (1908; reprint, Baltimore, Md.: Genealogical Publishing Co., 1967).

Church Records

A search for church records should begin with Edna A. Kanely, comp. and ed., *Directory of Maryland Church Records* (Westminster, Md.: Family Line Publications, 1987), arranged by county and giving a range of dates of available records for over 2,600 churches with mailing addresses. Somewhat dated but still quite useful is the list in Passano (see Background Sources). Also helpful are Percy G. Skirven, *First Parishes of the Province of Maryland* (Baltimore, Md.: Norman, Remington Co., 1923), and Abdel Ross Wentz, *History of the Maryland Synod* (Harrisburg, Pa., 1920).

The largest collection of church records, with a consolidated index, is at the Maryland Historical Society, and many are at the Maryland State Archives, which has various original and microfilmed records, many with indexes. Some church records have been published in the *Maryland Genealogical Society Bulletin* or in individual books, such as those for St. Paul's in Baltimore and for many German churches in the western counties.

Although Catholicism is very important to the history of Maryland, the disenfranchisement of Catholics after the establishment of the Anglican church in 1692 largely contributed to the lack of record keeping prior to the Revolutionary War. One source for St. Mary's County in the 1700s, however, is Timothy J. O'Rourke's *Catholic Families of Southern Maryland* (1980; reprint, Baltimore, Md.: Genealogical Publishing Co., 1985). Records of the German churches and the Society of Friends are very good. The latter were early settlers of Maryland, along with Anglicans and Catholics. Phebe R. Jacobsen's *Quaker Records in Maryland* (Annapolis, Md.: Hall of Records Commission, 1966) is an excellent guide to the original and microfilmed Friends' records at the state archives. Some Quaker records were published in Kenneth Carroll, *Quakerism on the Eastern Shore* (Baltimore, Md.: Maryland Historical Society, 1970), and other records are at the Maryland Historical Society, the state archives, and the Friends Historical Library, Swarthmore, Pennsylvania.

Military Records

The Maryland State Archives has an incomplete index to colonial muster and payroll records for the period 1732 to 1772, as well as various records and indexes for the later wars and military units. Muster rolls and payrolls of colonial Maryland militia are included in Murtie June Clark's *Colonial Soldiers of the South, 1732–1774* (Baltimore, Md.: Genealogical Publishing Co., 1983). The National Archives-Mid Atlantic Region (see page 8) has microfilms of the Revolutionary War military service (with index) and pension records (arranged alphabetically), the index to War of 1812 and Spanish-American War service records, and name indexes to Union and Confederate soldiers in the Civil War. Lists of Revolutionary War muster rolls were published in *Archives of Maryland*, Vol. 18 (1900; reprint, Baltimore, Md.: Genealogical Publishing Co., 1972). Helpful for Revolutionary research are Raymond B. Clark, Jr., *Maryland Revolutionary Records: How To Find Them & Interpret Them* (St. Michaels, Md.: the author, 1976); S. Eugene Clements and F. Edward Wright, *Maryland Militia in the Revolutionary War* (Westminster, Md.: Family Line Publications, 1987); and Harry Wright Newman, comp., *Maryland Revolutionary Records: Data Obtained from 3,050 Pension Claims and Bounty Land Applications* (1938; reprint, Baltimore, Md.: Genealogical Publishing Co., 1987).

Much manuscript material is located through *An Inventory of Maryland State Papers, Volume I, The Era of the American Revolution, 1775–1789,* edited by Edward C. Papenfuse, and others (Annapolis, Md.: Hall of Records Commission, 1977). For Marylanders unsympathetic to the Revolution, see Richard Arthur Overfield's *The Loyalists of Maryland During the American Revolution,* thesis, University of Maryland (Ann Arbor, Mich.: University Microfilms, 1968).

For the nineteenth century, helpful published references include William M. Marine, *The British Invasion of Maryland 1812–1815* (1913; reprint, Hatboro, Pa.: Tradition Press, 1965; and Baltimore, Md.: Genealogical Publishing Co., 1977); F. Edward Wright, *Maryland Militia, War of 1812,* 7 vols. to date (Silver Spring, Md.: Family Line Publications, 1979–present); Thomas Huntsberry, *Western Maryland, Pennsylvania and Virginia Militia in Defense of Maryland, 1805 to 1815* (Baltimore, Md.: the author, 1983); L. Allison Wilmer, and others, *History and Roster of Maryland Volunteers, War of 1861–5,* 2 vols. (1898; reprint, Westminster, Md.: Family Line Publications, n.d.); William W. Goldsborough, *The Maryland Line in the Confederate Army 1861–1865,* 2d ed. (1900; reprint with index, Port Washington, N.Y.: Kennikat Press, 1972); and Daniel P. Hartzler, *Marylanders in the Confederacy* (Silver Spring, Md.: Family Line Publications, 1986).

World War I participants from Maryland are found in *Maryland in the World War: Military and Naval Records* (Baltimore, Md.: Maryland War Records Commission (Baltimore, 1933). The War Records Division of the Maryland Historical Society compiled 5 volumes of *Maryland in World War II, Register of Service Personnel* (Baltimore, Md., 1960–65). Some military history is available at the State of Maryland Military Department, Room B14, Fifth Regiment Armory, 219 29th Division Street, Baltimore, Maryland 21201-2288.

Periodicals, Newspapers, and Manuscript Collections

Periodicals

The Maryland Historical and Genealogical Bulletin was published privately in twenty-one volumes from 1930 to 1950. *The Maryland Genealogical Society Bulletin* has been published by the Maryland Genealogical Society since 1960 and has included the usual fare of genealogical records, including marriage licenses, cemetery and Bible records, wills, militia lists, naturalizations, railroad employees, slave lists, and vital records, as well as compiled genealogies.

Maryland Historical Magazine has been published by the Maryland Historical Society since 1906 and has included much historical and genealogical material. Like many other historical magazines, the *Maryland Historical Magazine* stopped publishing genealogical material for some years. In 1980 Genealogical Publishing Company of Baltimore, Maryland, issued two volumes of *Maryland Genealogies: A Consolidation of Articles from the Maryland Historical Magazine.*

The Maryland and Delaware Genealogist was introduced in 1959 by Raymond B. Clark, Jr., and his mother, Sara Seth Clark, who published the standard abstracts of records and genealogies. *The Maryland Original Research Society of Baltimore Bulletin* was published in Baltimore from 1906 to 1913 and included lists of early settlers, genealogies, cemetery and family Bible records, militia lists, and oaths of fidelity. A reprint in one volume, edited by Albert Levin Richardson, was published in 1979 by Genealogical Publishing Company, Baltimore, Maryland.

Western Maryland Genealogy, published by Catoctin Press, 709 East Main Street, Middletown, Maryland 21769, is a more recent addition to the periodical literature covering Allegany, Carroll, Frederick, Garrett, Montgomery, and Washington counties. Considerable Maryland material, including genealogies, newspaper abstracts, tax lists, records of servants, and other source records, can also be found in the *National Genealogical Society Quarterly* (see page 9).

Newspapers

One of first places to hunt for a Maryland newspaper is *Newspapers in Maryland Libraries: A Union List,* by Eleanore O. Hofstetter and M. S. Eustis (Baltimore, Md.: Maryland Department of Education, Division of Library Development, 1977). The Maryland State Archives has many newspapers as well as guides to and abstracts from them. See also *Newspapers of Maryland: A Guide to the Microfilm Collection of Newspapers in the Maryland State Archives* (Annapolis, Md.: Maryland State Archives, 1990).

Newspaper abstracts have been published for several localities, especially for Baltimore. These include Thomas L. Hollowak's two-volume *Index to Marriages and Deaths in the (Baltimore) Sun, 1837–1850 . . . 1851–1860* (Baltimore, Md.: Genealogical Publishing Co., 1978) and three works by Robert W. Barnes: *Marriages and Deaths from Baltimore Newspapers, 1796–1816* (Baltimore, Md.: Genealogical Publishing Co., 1973); *Marriages and Deaths from the Maryland Gazette, 1727–1839* (Baltimore, Md.: Genealogical Publishing Co., 1978); *and Gleanings From Maryland Newspapers 1727 . . . 1795,* 3 vols. (Lutherville, Md.: Bettie Carothers, 1975–76). Other large-scale compilations are those by F. Edward Wright: *Western Maryland Newspaper Abstracts 1786 . . . 1810,* 3 vols. (Silver Spring, Md.: Family Line Publications, 1985–87), and with I. Harper, *Maryland Eastern Shore Newspaper Abstracts . . . [1790–1834],* 8 vols. (Silver Spring, Md.: Family Line Publications, 1981–87). See also L. Tilden Moore, *Abstracts and Marriages and Deaths . . . in the Newspapers of Frederick and Montgomery Counties, Maryland, 1831–1840* (Bowie, Md.: Heritage Books, 1991), and Karen Mauer Green, comp., *The Maryland Gazette, 1727–1761: Genealogical and Historical Abstracts* (Galveston, Tex.: Frontier Press, 1990). The *Gazette* was Maryland's first newspaper and also included news about Delaware, Pennsylvania, and Virginia.

Manuscripts

Avril J. M. Pedley, comp., *The Manuscript Collections of The Maryland Historical Society* (Baltimore, Md.: Maryland Historical Society, 1968), supplements the Cox/Sullivan Guide (see Background Sources) and is updated in the *Maryland Historical Magazine* by notes of subsequent additions to the manuscript collection.

Indexes to many special collections, including the Calvert family collection (at the Maryland Historical Society) and other private papers, state documents, and census and election records as well as guides to photograph collections are at the Maryland State Archives.

Archives, Libraries, and Societies

Maryland State Archives
350 Rowe Boulevard
Annapolis, MD 21401

In a beautiful new building that opened in 1986, the Maryland State Archives, formerly the Hall of Records, is the central place for original source record research. Generally, one can expect to find all colonial governmental records as well as those from statehood up to 1900 and in many cases much later, as it is the official depository for all "state" records created before 28 April 1788 and for noncurrent records of state agencies, counties, and towns. Some service is available by mail; write for details and fees. *Bulletin No. 17: A Guide to the Index Holdings of the Maryland State Archives* is available for a nominal fee. The state archives lends microfilm to other libraries free of charge and sells microfilm of newspapers (see Newspapers).

Maryland Genealogical Society
201 West Monument Street
Baltimore, MD 21201

Not a library, the society publishes the *Maryland Genealogical Society Bulletin* (see Periodicals).

Maryland State Law Library
361 Rowe Avenue
Annapolis, MD 21401

Primarily a law library, it also has a large collection of useful books, maps, newspapers, the federal censuses and 1850 mortality schedules, and other items on microfilm. A guide to the library's genealogical holdings is available for a nominal fee.

Maryland Historical Society
201 West Monument Street
Baltimore, MD 21201

The society provides a free list of genealogists or, for a fee, will have a professional genealogist check their indexed holdings. The society publishes the *Maryland Historical Magazine* (see Periodicals). In 1883 it also began *The Archives of Maryland*, now published by the Maryland State Archives, which sells back issues. See also the published guide to the society's collection under Background Sources.

George Peabody Library of Johns Hopkins University
17 East Mount Vernon Place
Baltimore, MD 21202

Formerly the Peabody Institute Library, it is best known for its British collection of over 2,500 published English and Welsh parish registers and British and German heraldry. While its Maryland collection is not strong, the library has a wide variety of published material including periodicals for New England and the Mid-Atlantic regions.

Baltimore City Archives
211 East Pleasant Street, Room 201
Baltimore, MD 21202

This archives has a WPA-compiled name index to the municipal records for 1756–1938; indexes to Port of Baltimore ships' passenger arrivals kept by the city, 1833–66, and those from the National Archives for 1820–1909; and the index to naturalizations in the U.S. circuit and district courts for Maryland (Baltimore City), 1797–1951. These indexes can be searched for a fee of $4 per request. Other useful records here, dating from 1729, include maps, tax records from 1798, an 1868 police census (incomplete), and voter registrations for 1838, 1839, 1868, and 1877–89. For more detail, consult William G. LeFurgy, *The Records of A City: A Guide to the Baltimore City Archives* (Baltimore, Md.: City Archives and Records Management Office, 1984).

Special Focus Categories

Immigration

Ships' passenger arrival lists for the Port of Baltimore, 1891–1948 (earlier lists are in Washington, D.C.) and indexes to such lists for 1820–1952 are at the National Archives-Mid Atlantic Region. The index, 1820–1909, is also available at the Baltimore City Archives. For the early period, see Michael H. Tepper, ed., *Passenger Arrivals at the Port of Baltimore, 1820–1834*, transcribed by Elizabeth P. Bentley (Baltimore, Md.: Genealogical Publishing Co., 1982). Harry Wright Newman, *To Maryland From Overseas* (1982; reprint, Baltimore, Md.: Genealogical Publishing Co., 1986, 1991), lists some Jacobite rebels who were sold into service in Maryland.

Naturalization

Naturalizations granted in U.S. district and circuit courts in Maryland (Baltimore) are available on microfilm at the National Archives-Mid Atlantic Region in Philadelphia, with an index for the years 1797–1951. Some early naturalization petitions were destroyed by fire. The index is also available at the Baltimore City Archives and Maryland Historical Society. The Maryland State Archives has index/abstract cards for these courts for the period 1797–1906, as well as indexes for 1925–51, and for the naturalization of soldiers, 1918–23. Other naturalization records are available at the state archives and in the county courthouses. Citizenship was granted in the provincial period, 1634–1776, by the court, legislature, or the governor and council, and these records are indexed at the state archives. See also Jeffrey A. and Florence Leone Wyand, *Colonial Maryland Naturalizations* (Baltimore, Md.: Genealogical Publishing Co., 1975), for records, 1660–1775. Additional naturalizations from 1733, from Maryland Commission Book 82, were abstracted and published in *Maryland Historical Magazine,* vols. 26 and 27 (1931–32). The state archives also has an index to naturalizations, 1781–1906, granted by the general courts of the eastern and western shores and in certain county courts. There are separate indexes for naturalizations in Baltimore City (1793–1933) and Baltimore County (1872–1902). Records for some counties have been published, such as those for Frederick County, 1785–1850.

Black American

The Maryland State Archives has sale statistics, manumission records, certificates of freedom, and lists of slave owners for most counties with some limited indexes. From a different perspective, Maryland blacks who helped colonize Liberia and other places in Africa are discussed by Penelope Campbell in *The Maryland State Colonization Society, 1831–1857* (Urbana, Ill.: University of Illinois Press, 1971).

Not much has been published about slavery in Maryland, but Raphael Cassimere, Jr., *The Origins and Early Development of Slavery in Maryland, 1633 to 1715,* thesis, Lehigh University, (Ann Arbor, Mich.: University Microfilms, 1975), and Charles Lewis Wagndt, *Mighty Revolution: Negro Emancipation in Maryland, 1862–1864* (Baltimore, Md.: Johns Hopkins Press, 1964), provide studies from the two ends of the era. A very useful guide is *Researching Black Families at the Hall of Records,* by Phebe R. Jacobsen (Annapolis, Md.: Hall of Records Commission, 1984).

Native American

There is not much published material about Native Americans in Maryland. A general history is *Indians of Early Maryland* by Harold R. Manakee (Baltimore, Md.: Maryland Historical Society, 1959), and a more specific study is James A. McAllister's *Indian Lands in Dorchester County, Maryland: Selected Sources, 1669 to 1870* (Cambridge, Md.: the author, 1962).

Ethnic Groups

A number of books have been published about Maryland Friends (Quakers), Germans, and Jews. Some Quaker resources have been discussed above under Church Records. For Germans see *The Maryland Germans: A History,* by Dieter Cunz (1948; reprint, Port Washington, N.Y.: Kennikat Press, 1972), and *The Pennsylvania-German in the Settlement of Maryland,* by Daniel Wunderlich Nead (1914; reprint, Baltimore, Md.: Genealogical Publishing Co., 1985). For Jews, see "The Jews of Baltimore [to 1830], *American Jewish Historical Quarterly,* vols. 64 and 67, and *Generations,* the journal of the Jewish Historical Society of Maryland, published since 1978.

County Resources

Maryland has twenty-three counties and the city of Baltimore, which is not under county jurisdiction. Transfers of land, estates, and other records are recorded at the courthouses. The first column below indicates map coordinate. In the second column is the name of the county with the mailing address of the county circuit court clerk where deeds, mortgages, vital records, divorces, naturalizations, and other matters are recorded. In the third column is the date the county was created and the name or names of the parent county or counties. The date the earliest land deed was recorded appears in the fourth column. In the last column is the date when orphans' court records begin, followed by the mailing address of that court's clerk, called the register of wills, if different from the circuit court clerk. Other county offices not included below may have different mailing addresses. While some records are available in the counties, most original and/or microfilm copies of land, estate, vital, and court records have been transferred to the Maryland State Archives. As new county records are created, they will continue to be filmed and sent to the state archives.

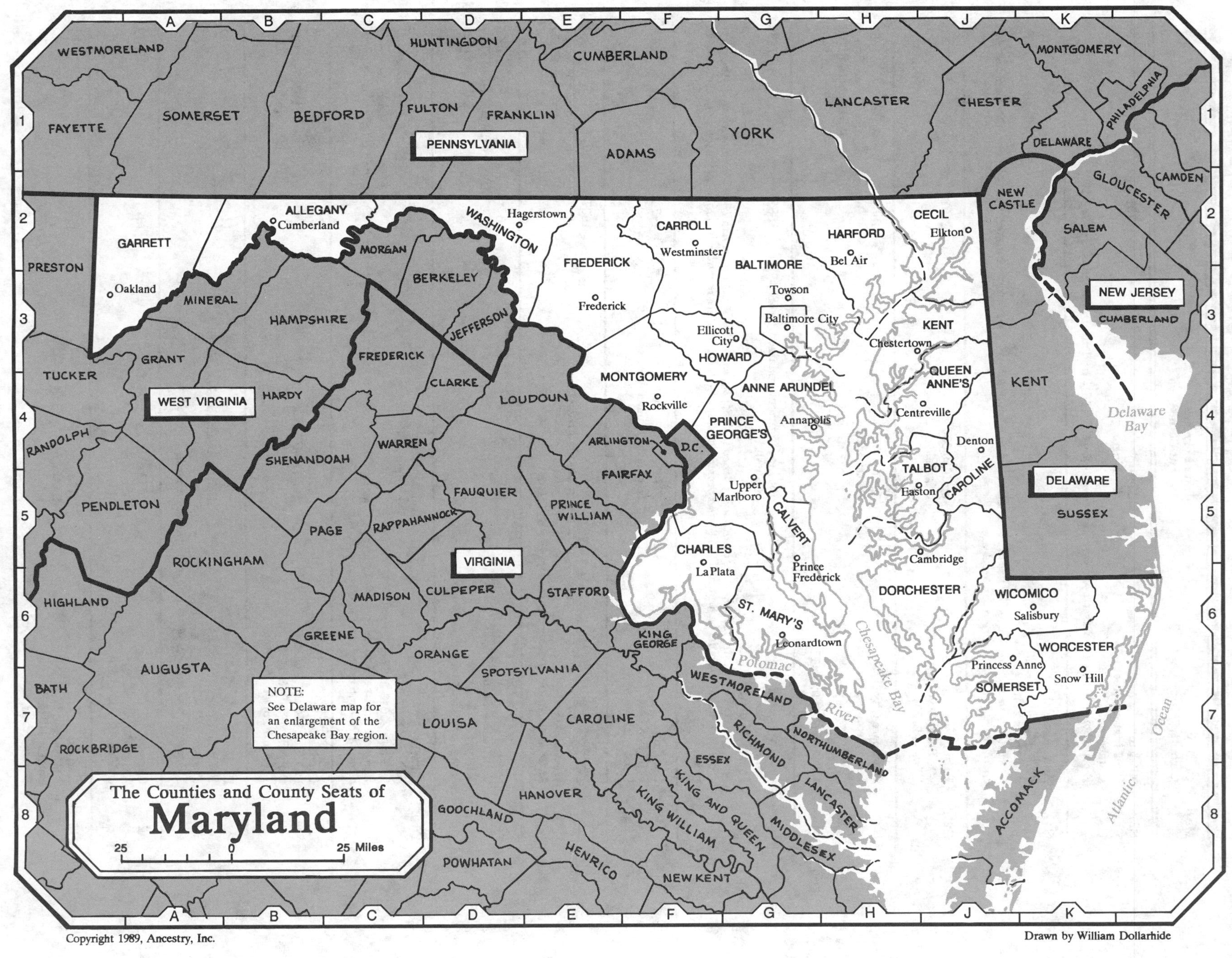
The Counties and County Seats of
Maryland
25 0 25 Miles
NOTE:
See Delaware map for
an enlargement of the
Chesapeake Bay region.
Copyright 1989, Ancestry, Inc.
Drawn by William Dollarhide
PENNSYLVANIA
NEW JERSEY
DELAWARE
WEST VIRGINIA
VIRGINIA
D.C.
GARRETT
Oakland
ALLEGANY
Cumberland
WASHINGTON
Hagerstown
FREDERICK
Frederick
CARROLL
Westminster
BALTIMORE
Towson
Baltimore City
HARFORD
Bel Air
CECIL
Elkton
KENT
Chestertown
QUEEN ANNE'S
Centreville
CAROLINE
Denton
TALBOT
Easton
DORCHESTER
Cambridge
WICOMICO
Salisbury
WORCESTER
Snow Hill
SOMERSET
Princess Anne
HOWARD
Ellicott City
MONTGOMERY
Rockville
ANNE ARUNDEL
Annapolis
PRINCE GEORGE'S
Upper Marlboro
CALVERT
Prince Frederick
CHARLES
La Plata
ST. MARY'S
Leonardtown
Chesapeake Bay
Delaware Bay
Atlantic Ocean
Potomac River
WESTMORELAND
FAYETTE
SOMERSET
BEDFORD
HUNTINGDON
FULTON
FRANKLIN
CUMBERLAND
ADAMS
YORK
LANCASTER
CHESTER
MONTGOMERY
DELAWARE
PHILADELPHIA
GLOUCESTER
CAMDEN
SALEM
CUMBERLAND
NEW CASTLE
KENT
SUSSEX
PRESTON
TUCKER
RANDOLPH
GRANT
MINERAL
HAMPSHIRE
HARDY
MORGAN
BERKELEY
JEFFERSON
FREDERICK
CLARKE
PENDLETON
HIGHLAND
BATH
ROCKBRIDGE
AUGUSTA
ROCKINGHAM
SHENANDOAH
WARREN
PAGE
LOUDOUN
ARLINGTON
FAIRFAX
PRINCE WILLIAM
FAUQUIER
RAPPAHANNOCK
MADISON
CULPEPER
GREENE
ORANGE
STAFFORD
KING GEORGE
SPOTSYLVANIA
LOUISA
CAROLINE
HANOVER
GOOCHLAND
POWHATAN
HENRICO
NEW KENT
KING WILLIAM
KING AND QUEEN
ESSEX
RICHMOND
WESTMORELAND
NORTHUMBERLAND
LANCASTER
MIDDLESEX
ACCOMACK

Map	County Circuit Court	Date Formed Parent County/ies	Deeds	Orphans' Court
B2	Allegany Washington Street Cumberland 21502 *A courthouse fire in 1893 destroyed marriage records for 1791–1847 and naturalizations for 1892–93.*	1789 Washington	1791	1790
G4	Anne Arundel 3 Church Circle Annapolis 21404 *The courthouse was destroyed by fire in 1704, with the loss of all but three court record volumes. Deeds before 1699 were lost, but there are five volumes of re-recorded deeds.*	1650 original	1653	1777
G2	Baltimore 401 Bosley Avenue Towson 21204	by 1659/60 original	1661	1666
G3	Baltimore City Land Records Division 100 N. Calvert Street Room 610 Baltimore 21202-3417	1851 Baltimore Co.	1851	1851 111 N. Calvert Street Baltimore 21202
G5	Calvert 175 Main Street Prince Frederick 20678 *Most records were destroyed when the courthouse burned in 1882, but some deeds dating back to 1840 were re-recorded. Abstracts of deeds sent to Annapolis beginning in 1784 and provincial court deeds/land office records also make up for some of the destroyed records.*	1654 (as Patuxent; renamed, 1858) original	1882	1882
J4	Caroline P. O. Box 356 Denton 21629-0356	1773 Dorchester/Queen Anne's	1774	1774
F2	Carroll P.O. Box 190 Westminster 21157 *Most early papers of the county court have been lost.*	1837 Baltimore/Frederick	1837	1837 55 N. Court Street Westminster 21157
J2	Cecil Courthouse, Second Floor Elkton 21921 *Many early court records have disappeared.*	1674 Baltimore	1674	1675 Courthouse, Third Floor Elkton 21921
F6	Charles P.O. Box B La Plata 20646-0167 *The state archives has the original index of Charles County court and land records before 1722, providing information about some of the contents of some lost record books.*	1658 original	1658	1665 Courthouse La Plata 20646
H6	Dorchester P.O. Box 150 Cambridge 21613-0150 *There are gaps in the court records. Some were probably lost in a fire in 1852.*	1669 Somerset/Talbot	1669	1852 P.O. Box 263 Cambridge 21613-0263
E2	Frederick 100 W. Patrick Street Frederick 21701 *There were two major fires, but no major loss of records.*	1748 Baltimore/Prince George's	1748	1751
A2	Garrett 203 S. Fourth Street Oakland 21550-1535	1872 Allegany	1873	1872
H2	Harford 20 Cortland W. Bel Air 21014 *Some records were destroyed in a fire in 1858.*	1773 Baltimore	1773	1774

Map	County Circuit Court	Date Formed Parent County/ies	Deeds	Orphans' Court
F3	Howard 8360 Court Avenue Ellicott City 21043	1850 Anne Arundel	1839	1840
	The county was formed in 1838 as Howard District of Anne Arundel Co., but did not gain full county status until 1850.			
J3	Kent Courthouse Chestertown 21620	by 1642 original	1648	1674
	A courthouse fire in 1720 destroyed some records.			
F3	Montgomery 50 Courthouse Square Rockville 20850	1776 Frederick	1777	1777
	A southern section of the county was set off in 1788 to form the District of Columbia.			
	Patuxent	1654 (renamed Calvert, 1658) original		
G5	Prince George's 14735 Main Street Upper Marlboro 20772	1696 Calvert/Charles	1696	1698 P.O. Box 368 Upper Marlboro 20772-0368
J4	Queen Anne's Courthouse Centreville 21617	1706 Dorchester/Talbot/Kent	1707	1706
G6	St. Mary's P.O. Box 308 Leonardtown 20650-0308	1637 original	1827	1658 P.O. Box 602 Leonardtown 20650-0602
	The courthouse was destroyed by fire in 1831. Some deeds were re-recorded back to 1781, and abstracts of deeds sent to Annapolis beginning in 1784 also make up for some of the records that were destroyed.			
J7	Somerset Courthouse Princess Anne 21853	1666 original	1665	1664
	The courthouse burned in 1831, but the records were saved.			
H5	Talbot P.O. Box 723 Easton 21601-0723	by 1661/2 original	1662	1668 P.O. Box 816 Easton 21601-0816
	Many court records have been lost.			
D2	Washington P.O. Box 229 Hagerstown 21740-0229	1776 Frederick	1777	1777
	Some records were lost in a courthouse fire in 1871.			
J6	Wicomico P.O. Box 198 Salisbury 21801-0198	1867 Somerset/Worcester	1867	1866 P.O. Box 787 Salisbury 21801-0787
K6	Worcester 104 Courthouse Snow Hill 21863-1296	1742 Somerset	1742	1742 102 Courthouse Snow Hill 21863-1296

Massachusetts

Alice Eichholz, Ph.D., C.G.

The Pilgrims landed on the outermost reaches of Cape Cod in 1620, considerably north of their original destination in Virginia. Providence would have it that they would create their colony based on the experimental ideals of religious freedom and self-government in a colder climate than they had expected. The colony's development, and that of its near neighbor to the north, Massachusetts Bay Colony, established ten years later, set a course for new models regarding the concept of community, political life, and records. During the "Great Migration" between 1630–42, an estimated twenty-thousand people left England and settled in these two colonies that eventually merged in 1691 to become the Province of Massachusetts.

Massachusetts was the stepping-stone for other settlements that developed along the New England coast and for thousands of immigrants who came in waves across the Atlantic over the last three centuries. Settlements grew first along the shores, then along the river banks, and later out of the forests rich with furs and lumber. These settlements existed in contrast to those of the native inhabitants and contained within themselves festering differences of opinion regarding religious and political views.

Some of those who dissented from their neighbors' views set out to begin their own communities, moving farther and farther west in the colony and sometimes migrating to other locations, including most of the eastern seaboard. They often took ideas with them about government and record keeping from their former Massachusetts communities.

Settlement continued steadily based on the peaceful accord between natives, represented particularly by agreement with Massasoit, chief of the Wampanoag, and settlers. All that changed in 1675 when Massasoit's son, King Philip (Metacom), declared open warfare, and raided fifty towns in the southeastern and central settlements. A year later, the warfare ended with the death of King Philip, but confidence in settlement was not immediately restored. In Great Britain, the Peace of Utrecht in 1713 brought sweeping changes to the political and economic enterprises in Europe, marking the beginning of Great Britain's colonial and commercial power, and stepping up the pace of emigration to New England again.

In the next two decades, more and more towns were established as the population grew in all of lower New England. Warfare reappeared in a long series of French and Indian wars throughout all the colonies, sending settlers scrambling for safety from the frontiers to the more securely established towns.

By the time of the American Revolution, nearly everyone still in Massachusetts could trace their ancestry to one of those 20,000 people in the first "Great Migration." Many of the French Huguenots, Irish, and Ulster-Scots who had also immigrated to Massachusetts before the American Revolution married into the English families who had arrived earlier. There were also a few Portuguese and some Germans in the early development of the colonies, but it was not until later that these ethnic groups immigrated in large numbers.

Long known for disagreements with the Crown, Massachusetts' ideals and strong voices became a catalyst for the American Revolution. Minutemen and Loyalists, sometimes in the same family, served their respective causes. They were supported on both sides by family members and former neighbors who had settled in all of the New England colonies. The conclusion of the war found some Loyalists from New England in the provinces of Canada or in the Port of New Orleans. An even larger number of patriots moved to the newly developing frontiers in northern New England and New York. Maine, which was still part of Massachusetts even after the Revolution, became a separate state in 1820.

The Commonwealth of Massachusetts was soon in the midst of the Industrial Revolution, which incorporated people with more cultural and linguistic differences. A glimpse of it could be seen as early as the mid-seventeenth century when hundreds of Scottish prisoners—cheap labor for the iron works in Braintree and Lynn—had arrived in Boston's harbor. Although the steady stream of immigrants to Boston's port continued over the next two centuries, the Irish Potato Famine widened that stream considerably in the 1840s and 1850s, providing the Industrial Revolution with a labor force previously unavailable in New England. Many other ethnic groups soon followed.

Massachusetts citizens fought another war of Northern ideals, sending its sons, and some daughters, to battlefields in the Civil War. New York eventually outdistanced Massachusetts as a port for immigration, but the industrial development and ethnic diversity of Massachusetts have had a profound impact on New England and left records of a rich history.

Vital Records

No state in the Union can boast the depth and breadth of vital records sources available in Massachusetts. Starting with the arrival of the Pilgrims, vital events have been diligently, although not completely, recorded, preserved, and published. Spurred by legislative order, over 200 (out of 364) towns have had all their vital records to 1850 published. The volume (or volumes) in the Systematic Series (those published as a direct result of legislation) for each town is divided into alphabetized sections of births, marriages, and deaths.

Some town vital records published before and after legislative order were printed verbatim and then indexed, making them more valuable than those in the Systematic Series for research purposes since original family groupings remain as recorded. Other towns' vital records have been published or microfilmed since publication of the Systematic Series. Original manuscript volumes of the Systematic Series are at the Massachusetts State Archives at Columbia Point (see Archives, Libraries, and Societies). Transcriptions of vital records for several western Massachusetts towns are in the Corbin Collection and those for the Braintree area are in the Sprague Collection, both at the New England Historic Genealogical Society (see Archives, Libraries, and Societies).

A listing indicating which towns have published vital records is that by Hanson and Rutherford in their chapter on Massachusetts research (see Background Sources). A code for locating vital records throughout different collections, individual publications, or the Systematic Series can be found in Marcia Wiswall Lindberg, *Genealogist's Handbook for New England Research* (Boston, Mass.: New England Historic Genealogical Society, 1985). Several towns, however, have published vital records since these lists were created. The year in which vital record registration begins for a town is indicated in the Town Resources section.

Microfiche of vital records for over 210 towns can be purchased from Archive Publishing (formerly Holbrook Research Institute), 57 Locust Street, Oxford, Massachusetts 01540. Those fiche of original records are listed in a microfiched "Bibliography of Massachusetts Vital Records 1620–1895," available from the company for $6 that provides complete information on this periodically expanding resource. Microfiche of individual towns' published Systematic Series are also available from the company.

Even though recording of vital events in towns was widespread in Massachusetts, the practice was still not universal. Most of the Systematic Series of published vital records additionally relied on documented material culled from other sources such as church records, cemetery inscriptions, and family Bibles.

There is no statewide index that includes all the towns' records for vital events before 1841. This makes it necessary to know the appropriate town in which to locate a record before that date. However, the IGI (see page 1) is adding birth and marriage records from the Massachusetts Systematic Series and other printed vital records into its master microfiche listing. At present it is not complete, but it may be helpful in locating or eliminating towns as potential targets for vital records research when the only information known is simply "born in Massachusetts."

There are some early vital records which were filed in counties as well as in towns for Suffolk, Middlesex, Essex, Plymouth (marriages only), and Hampshire (from private papers) counties. See Michael S. Hindus, *The Records of the Massachusetts Superior Court and Its Predecessors* (Boston, Mass.: Archives Division, Office of the Secretary of the Commonwealth, 1977), for a listing.

Beginning in 1841 the state mandated that a copy of each event recorded in a town or city be sent to the Secretary of the Commonwealth, which means that *two* sources exist for each event after that date—the town (or city) and the state. However, some towns were not in compliance until the late 1840s. The indexes for 1841–95 are in bound volumes, arranged in five-year periods, except for the first, which is 1841–50. They are available at the Massachusetts State Archives. Boston records are not duplicated in the state records until 1848, but all the city's vital records from 1630 are at Boston City Hall Archives, Boston, Massachusetts 02201. Published Boston vital records include births, deaths, and marriages, 1630–99; births, 1700–1800; and marriages, 1700–51 and 1752–1809.

The 1841–95 vital records books and indexes for the state are also available on microfilm at the New England Historic Genealogical Society and through the FHL, but verifying the original copy at the town clerk's office can be extremely important since the state records are copies and therefore subject to typical errors in transcription or omission from the original.

As of 1 January 1896 the Massachusetts Division of Health Statistics and Research, Registry of Vital Records and Statistics, 150 Tremont Street, Room B-3, Boston, Massachusetts 02111, is the repository for copies of town or city recorded vital records. The facility is open to the public, but marriage and birth records may be restricted. As with the bound ledger-style volumes for the 1841–95 period, indexes continue in five-year periods, separated into births, marriages, and deaths. Records and indexes are transferred to the Massachusetts State Archives every five years. The 1896–1900 grouping will begin the transfer process after December, 1991. Until individual death certificates were used in the 1900s, the name of the cemetery does not appear in the state copy, but it may be found in the town or city copy.

A statewide index to divorces after 1952 is available at the Registry of Vital Records, but no records are kept there (see Court Records for location of divorces prior to 1922 and Probate Records for those filed after that date). A descriptive sheet entitled "Massachusetts Divorce Records," by Roger D. Joslyn, which originally appeared in the *Massachusetts Genealogical Council Newsletter,* is available for a nominal fee from the council (MCG Reprints, 18 Martin's Cove Road, Hingham, Massachusetts 02043).

Census Records

Federal

Population Schedules.

- Indexed—1790, 1800, 1810, 1820, 1830, 1840, 1850, 1860 (Boston only)
- Soundex—1880, 1900, 1920
- Unindexed—1860 (except Boston), 1870, 1910

Industry and Agriculture Schedules.

- 1850, 1860, 1870

Mortality Schedules.

- 1850, 1860, 1870, 1880

Union Veterans Schedules.

- 1890

Original state copies and microfilm copies of the federal population, mortality, industry, and agriculture schedules are held by the Massachusetts State Archives; original schedules for 1850, 1860, and 1870 are available for research. The original 1880 schedule is available if the microfilm is not clear. The DAR prepared a typed, indexed transcript of the 1850 Massachusetts mortality schedule, a copy of which is at the New England Historic Genealogical Society. The Veterans enumeration is on microfilm at National Archives-New England Region (see page 8).

The 1800 census does not include enumerations for Boston or much of Suffolk County, but the published 1798 U.S. Direct Tax for Boston may be helpful (see Tax Records). The 1890 Union veterans schedule does not include Worcester County.

State

Massachusetts conducted two state census enumerations, 1855 and 1865, which contain information similar to the federal schedules. The originals are at the Massachusetts State Archives and transcripts with indexes are being published. Towns currently available are in Essex, Middlesex, and Plymouth counties. (Contact Ann Lainhart, P.O. Box 1487, Boston, Massachusetts 02117, for a brochure of available towns.) This makes it possible to follow a family in the census records for every five-year period 1850–70, a critical time given immigration and Industrial Revolution mobility.

Background Sources

Colony, town, county, and state histories abound for Massachusetts—a less than exhaustive list of the most helpful would outreach the limits of this book. The book loan program at the New England Historic Genealogical Society (see Archives listings) publishes a four-volume catalog of what circulates from its collection, with an extensive listing for Massachusetts. Periodical sources (see Periodicals) contain a wide variety of material on families, customs, and history of the state and New England in general.

Two comprehensive series provide a good background of understanding about both the Massachusetts Bay and Plymouth colonies: Nathaniel B. Shurtleff and David Pulsifer, eds., *Records of the Colony of New Plymouth in New England, 1620–1691,* 12 vols. (Boston, Mass.: Commonwealth Printer, 1855–61), and Nathaniel B. Shurtleff, ed., *Records of the Governor and Company of the Massachusetts Bay,* 5 vols. (Boston, Mass.: Commonwealth Printer, 1853–54). Eugene Aubrey Stratton, *Plymouth Colony: Its History & People 1620–1691* (Salt Lake City, Utah: Ancestry, 1986) provides a good social history with a genealogical perspective and includes biography, customs, history, and annotated bibliography on printed material covering the colony.

The following will be helpful in developing a more comprehensive history of the state:

Hart, Albert Bushnell, ed. *Commonwealth History of Massachusetts, Colony, Province and State, 1605–1930.* 5 vols. 1927–30. Reprint. New York, N.Y.: Russell and Russell, 1967. Provides an excellent history from disputed colonial claims through the last major immigration period in this century.

Haskell, John D. *Massachusetts: A Bibliography of Its History.* 1976. Reprint. Hanover, N.H.: University Press of New England, 1983. Surveys a broad scope of local historical material including those published in academia. Family genealogies are not included.

The following list includes three classic compilations of genealogical material for the state:

Pope, Charles Henry. *Pioneers of Massachusetts, a Descriptive List, Drawn from the Records of the Colonies, Towns and Churches and from Other Con-*

temporaneous Documents. 1900. Reprint. Baltimore, Md.: Genealogical Publishing Co., 1986. Similar to Savage (below) with important differences. It is essential to read the introduction to the book.

Savage, James. *A Genealogical Dictionary of the First Settlers of New England, Showing Three Generations of Those Who Came Before May 1692.* 4 vols. 1860–62. Reprint. Baltimore, Md.: Genealogical Publishing Co., 1986. Arranged alphabetically by male settlers in New England before 1692. Some documentation is provided for original sources and it is cross-indexed.

Society of Mayflower Descendants. *Mayflower Families Through Five Generations: Descendants of the Pilgrims Who Landed at Plymouth, Mass., December, 1620.* 4 vols. Plymouth, Mass.: Society of Mayflower Descendants, 1975–80, with separately published addenda. Not all passengers or their descendants have yet been covered in this ongoing series. Volume 3 is known to be quite unreliable. Recent publications by the society include *Mayflower Families in Progress,* a series of four-generation booklets for each Mayflower family. Issued by surname of the *Mayflower* passenger, they can be obtained from the society (see Archives, Libraries, and Societies). A few have been extended to five generations in separate publications.

A limited list of other examples of social history includes:

Cook, Edward M. *The Fathers of the Towns: Leadership and Community Structure in Eighteenth-Century New England.* Baltimore, Md.: Genealogical Publishing Co., 1976.

Jones, Douglas Lamar. *Village and Seaport: Migration and Society in Eighteenth Century Massachusetts.* Hanover, Mass.: University Press of New England, 1981. A study of Beverly and Wenham in Essex County.

Lockridge, Kenneth A. *A New England Town: The First Hundred Years, Dedham, Massachusetts, 1636–1736.* New York, N.Y.: W. W. Norton, 1985. A good example of using historical material for understanding social history.

Thompson, Roger. *Sex in Middlesex: Popular Mores in a Massachusetts County, 1649–1699.* Amherst, Mass.: University of Massachusetts Press, 1986. Informative study on the American family.

In addition to the Lindberg *Handbook* (see Vital Records), significant research guides for the state include:

Bowen, Richard LeBarron. *Massachusetts Records: A Handbook for Genealogists, Historians, Lawyers, and Other Researchers.* Rehoboth, Mass.: privately printed, 1957.

Coty, Ellen M. "Research Aids: Genealogy in Western Massachusetts." *Historical Journal of Western Massachusetts* 6 (Spring 1978): 42–47. Describes the excellent sources in county and library repositories in the western region of the state.

Davis, Charlotte P. *Directory of Massachusetts Place Names, Current and Obsolete.* Lexington, Mass.: Bay State News, 1988. Compiled by the state DAR, this lists 4,000 cities, towns, villages, and other sections, all cross-indexed.

Gardner-Wescott, Katherine A., ed. *Massachusetts Sources, Part I: Boston, New Bedford, Springfield, Worcester.* Boston, Mass.: Massachusetts Society of Genealogists, 1988. The first part of a series detailing each repository and the extent of materials held. Both public and private records are included.

Hanson, Edward W., and Homer Vincent Rutherford. "Genealogical Research in Massachusetts: A Survey and Bibliographical Guide." *The New England Historical and Genealogical Register* 135 (July 1981): 163–98. Covers in good detail many of the anomalies in Massachusetts public records and lists some basic town histories as well as single and multi-ancestor genealogies. This is reprinted, with additions to the listing of town vital records, in Ralph J. Crandall, ed., *Genealogical Research in New England.* Baltimore, Md.: Genealogical Publishing Co., 1984

Kaufman, Martin, John W. Ifkovic, and Joseph Carvalho, III, eds. *A Guide to the History of Massachusetts.* Westport, Conn.: Greenwood Press, 1988. Divided into historical periods and topics, this is an excellent bibliographic essay on the state's history and repository holdings.

Secretary of the Commonwealth. *Historical Data Relating to Counties, Cities and Towns in Massachusetts.* Boston, Mass.: the commonwealth, 1975. This substitutes for a place-name index for towns and cities, indicating towns no longer in existence and those that spawned new towns by division.

Sibbison, Wendy. *Directory for Research on the Pioneer Valley, Massachusetts: Franklin, Hampshire and Hampden Counties.* Greenfield, Mass.: Greenfield Community College, 1983. Focuses on western Massachusetts.

Schweitzer, George K. *Massachusetts Genealogical Research.* Knoxville, Tenn.: the author, 1990. Serves as a good guide for beginning researchers and those making a first research trip to the state.

Wright, Carroll D. *Report on the Custody and Condition of the Public Records of Parishes, Towns and Counties.* Boston, Mass.: Wright & Potter, State Printers, 1889.

Maps

Maps are critical to genealogical research. The Massachusetts State Archives has an eighteenth-century (1794–95) series of maps for the majority of Massachusetts towns as well as a series done in 1831 that were published and might be found in libraries elsewhere. Numerous town histories contain excellent maps that indicate dwelling places and owners at different points in the town's history.

As with most New England states, an *F. W. Beers Atlas* for each Massachusetts county was published in the 1870s. Presently only the Worcester County atlas is in print (Rutland, Vt.: Tuttle Books, 1971). Major research libraries generally have copies of these folio-sized maps that indicate residences, owners, schools, roads, churches, and cemeteries.

Excellent map collections of town lots and earlier land distribution exist at the Massachusetts State Archives. Good printed maps are available for research at the New England Historic Genealogical Society and many town offices. Saco Valley Printing (see Maine—Maps) is reissuing nineteenth-century editions of maps for Essex and Middlesex counties. These include structures and owners' names.

Land Records

State-Land State

Land ownership in Massachusetts descended initially from colony to proprietor and eventually to private ownership by individuals. The colonies of Plymouth and Massachusetts Bay were legally based on charters or patents from England to a company of business or trading associates. The general court for each colony (see Court Records), acting as a legislative body, established towns by granting to a group of proprietors blocks of land. The primary obligation of the proprietors was to divide the land among the settlers in the town based on family size, wealth, or both. Part of the land was held by town proprietors for the common good. See Roy Akagi, *The Town Proprietors of the New England Colonies* (1924; reprint, Gloucester, Mass.: P. Smith, 1963), for a discussion of the role of local proprietors in the development of towns.

Land was surveyed and plats drawn to identify who had a proprietorial share in each piece of land in town. The land itself was not actually sold in the early stages of town development. Having the use of a house lot and acreage for farming included a proprietorial right in the enterprise of the town and to further divisions of town land. See Stratton, *Plymouth Colony,* and Lockridge, *A New England Town* (both cited in Background Sources), for examples of the land acquisition process in individual towns. Native Americans, with a different concept and understanding of land than that of the colonists, often relinquished their land claims to colonists who found the land a desirable location for a town or useful for hunting, trapping, or farming. For an excellent discussion of differing perceptions of land, see William Cronon, *Changes on the Land,* cited under Native American.

Successive divisions of town land occurred, since not all the land was divided at one time. As families grew and newcomers arrived, shares of additional divisions were allocated to more people. Influx of the Great Migration period (1630–42), overcrowding, the desire for more land, and disagreements among inhabitants over religious, social, and political concerns all forced the development of new towns, and the process of land acquisition was repeated. Those who wished to form a new town petitioned the general court; the land was granted to the proprietors to divide as fit the needs of the new town. Published grants before county formation (1643 in Massachusetts Bay, 1685 in Plymouth) are found among the records of the colony (see Shurtleff and Pulsifer, *Records . . . New Plymouth,* and Shurtleff, *Records . . . Massachusetts Bay,* cited in Background Sources).

When a county system became established, land transactions became part of the county's records. Eventually, land was sold by proprietors to individuals and between individuals. Proprietors continued to keep records on "common and undivided lands" in a town—some well into the nineteenth century.

Deeds are recorded in the earliest records of the counties. Those for Suffolk County (1640–97), York County (now Maine) (1641–1737), and some of Plymouth Colony (1620–51) have been published. A series of abstracts for Plymouth Colony and County continues in the revived *Mayflower Descendant* (see Periodicals). Deeds are the purview of the county registry of deeds. Grantor and grantee indexes are available with date of recording, and sometimes the location (or town) is listed in the index, although this practice is not uniform. The first fourteen volumes of published Suffolk County deeds, entitled *Suffolk Deeds,* (1640–97) (Boston, Mass.: City Printers, 1880–1906), have, in addition to the grantor and grantee indexes, an every-name index. Original deeds through 1799 have an every-name index located at its registry office. These every-name indexes indicate all names in addition to grantor/grantee found in the deeds, such as witnesses and abutters.

In New England fashion, deeds generally indicate the residence of, and sometimes occupations for, both sets of parties and describe the land in either lot numbers, divisions, metes and bounds, or abutters—sometimes all four. There are conveyances for property, personal possessions, pews in churches, sale of slaves, indentures, mortgages, pre-nuptial agreements, and dower rights. Some conveyances for cemetery plots can be found in nineteenth- and twentieth-century transactions.

Deeds are available at the relevant county seat. There is usually a general deed index encompassing many deed books, although deed books may also have their own index in each volume. While the usual location for deeds is the county seat, larger counties were later divided up into districts to make the registry more convenient to the seller. The County Resources section clarifies the later divisions in counties. The FHL also has microfilm copies of early through mid-nineteenth-century deeds.

A frequently overlooked solution to genealogical problems is the use of land records. For two excellent examples of this technique using Massachusetts records, see the following articles:

Dearborn, David C. "The Family of William Curtis of Danvers, MA," in *A Tribute to John Insley Coddington,* edited by Neil D. Thompson and Robert C. Anderson,

31–46. (New York, N.Y.: Association for the Promotion of Scholarship in Genealogy, 1980).

Greene, David L. "Salem Witches I: Bridget Bishop." *The American Genealogist* 57 (1981): 129–38.

Probate Records

Probate proceedings had begun to apply to those with even minor personal property in England when the Great Migration occurred. Puritans pursued this practice with some vigor, but it was certainly not universal. Whether a person died with a will or without (intestate), complete probate proceedings regarding his or her estate were not automatic.

Probate records in Massachusetts are reasonably intact, but there are still gaps in what remains extant. In all cases there are two groups of records of concern: the original papers brought to court (such as original wills, affidavits of all kinds, and receipts from heirs) and those papers which were actually recorded in county probate books. Both of these exist in abundance for Massachusetts.

In Massachusetts the probate court jurisdictions follow county lines. Probate records have been published for Essex County (1635–81), Bristol County (1687–1745; 1745–62); wills for Suffolk County (1639–70); and indexes for the counties of Essex (1638–1841), Middlesex (1648–1909), Norfolk (1793–1900), Plymouth (1686–1881), Suffolk (1636–1910), and Worcester (1731–1910). Ruth Wilder Sherman and Robert S. Wakefield's *Plymouth Colony Probate Guide* (Warwick, R.I.: Plymouth Colony Research Group, 1983) is an alphabetical list of probate records and where they can be found for over 800 people who died in the colony from 1620 to 1691.

Each probate court has its own record books, with indexes of its original files usually arranged by file number. The Massachusetts State Archives, however, holds original probate files for Suffolk County (1636–1894), Middlesex County (1648–1871), and Plymouth County (1686–1881). Probate record books to the mid-nineteenth century are generally on microfilm through the FHL, but the original files are only at the probate court office or the Massachusetts State Archives. One exception is Middlesex County files which *are* available on microfilm at the FHL and the Boston Public Library, whose microfilm collection includes record books for Suffolk and Hampshire counties.

Beginning in 1922 divorces fell under the jurisdiction of both the superior court and probate court of the county (see Court Records). However, almost all cases after that date have been heard in probate court.

Court Records

During the seventeenth century, both colonies' court system included, from highest authority to the lowest: the colony's general court, a court of assistants, inferior quarter courts, and local magistrates. The general court met quarterly to create laws to insure religious, peaceful government. It was composed of chosen freemen of the colony, the governor, deputy-governor, and assistants. Functioning somewhat as an executive session of the general court, the governor, deputy-governor, and assistants formed the court of assistants which met more regularly, carried out general court business, and heard jury cases. Individually, assistants acted as local magistrates (justices of the peace) for civil suits in their respective towns. Additionally, magistrates who were not assistants were eventually added as the judicial need in towns arose.

Inferior quarter courts of first instance, later called county courts, were established in 1636 and were composed of the magistrates with a jury. This court's functions included civil actions, criminal actions, and administrative concerns. The three-tier court system (individual magistrates, county courts, and court of assistants) continued until reorganization in 1692 after Plymouth Colony and Massachusetts Bay Colony merged by executive order of the English Crown. Previous county court functions were divided between a court of general sessions (criminal actions) and a common pleas court (civil actions) for each county, with one superior court of judicature (1692–1780) overseeing the entire colony. The latter became the supreme judicial court after 1780, handling appeals from lower courts and originating actions in some capital offenses. The separate county sessions and common pleas courts were reorganized into county superior courts in 1859.

Comprehensive discussions of the court system can be found in George Lee Haskins, *Law and Authority in Early Massachusetts: A Study in Tradition and Design* (New York, N.Y.: Archon Books, 1968), and Catherine S. Menand, *A Research Guide to the Massachusetts Courts and Their Records* (Boston, Mass.: Massachusetts Supreme Judicial Court, Archives and Records Preservation, 1987). Michael S. Hindus, *Law in Colonial Massachusetts, 1630–1800,* in *Publications of Colonial Society of Massachusetts,* Vol. 62 (Boston, Mass.: Colonial Society of Massachusetts, 1984), lists various courts, their periods of operation, and what kinds of records were kept. An earlier publication by Hindus (see Vital Records) indicates what county court records might be found and where. However, with the transfer of pre-1860 judicial records to the Judicial Archives at the Massachusetts State Archives, and with much post-1859 material presently being held in storage, the Hindus listing is now very much dated and needs to be used accordingly.

Essex (1636–83), Suffolk (1671–80), Hampshire (1639–1702), and Plymouth (1686–1859, unindexed) county court records have been published, as well as those for Massachusetts Bay (1628–86) and Plymouth (1633–91) colonies. The Plymouth County court records are taken from the record books at the Pilgrim Society (see Archives, Libraries, and Societies) and are currently being indexed. The Hampshire County court records can be found in the William Pynchon papers, Joseph H. Smith, ed., *Colonial Justice in Western Massachusetts, 1639–1702* (Cambridge, Mass.: Harvard University Press, 1961). Essex County Quarterly

Court records, currently held at the Essex Institute (see Archives, Libraries, and Societies) are published in their eight-volume publication with an index. Those unpublished for 1687–93 are also at the Essex Institute with a WPA typescript index. *Mayflower Descendant* (see Periodicals) is serially indexing the Suffolk County Inferior Court (common pleas). The surviving Suffolk Quarterly Court records are published in volumes 29 and 30 of *Publications of the Colonial Society of Massachusetts* (Boston, Mass.: the society, 1933).

Towns issued "warnings out" to those poor for whom they would not assume responsibility. Although instituted by towns, the warnings were recorded in the county seat in Massachusetts. Those for Worcester County have been published. See *Worcester County Warnings Out, 1737–1788* (Worcester, Mass.: Franklin Rice, 1899). Others may also be in print.

Seventeenth century divorces were granted by the court of assistants until 1692 when authority transferred to the governor and council. The state's constitution gave that authority to the supreme judicial court in 1785. The county superior courts took over divorce cases from the supreme judicial court in 1887 and began sharing that authority with probate courts in 1922.

Tax Records

Tax records can be found at both the local and state levels. The Massachusetts State Archives has tax returns for 1768 and 1771. See Bettye Hobbs Pruitt, ed., *The Massachusetts Tax Valuation List of 1771* (Boston, Mass.: G. K. Hall, 1978). The archives also has some tax valuations for 1775, 1776, 1777, and 1778. The Massachusetts State Library holds them for 1780, 1783, 1784, 1791, 1792, 1793, 1800, 1801, 1810, and 1811.

Other tax lists may still be available at the town office. Boston's list for 1821 has been published in Lewis B. Rohrbach, *Boston Taxpayers in 1821* (1822; reprint, Camden, Maine: Picton Press, 1988), with a new index.

The U.S. Direct Tax of 1798 remains extant for most counties. See Michael H. Gorn, ed., *An Index and Guide to the Microfilm Edition of the Massachusetts and Maine Direct Tax Census of 1798* (Boston, Mass.: New England Historic Genealogical Society, 1979). The surviving originals are at the New England Historic Genealogical Society and are accessible on microfilm there and through the FHL.

Cemetery Records

Cemeteries were maintained by towns, churches, families and, later, private enterprises. Some records for Boston's oldest cemeteries, such as Central and Granary, have been published.

The state DAR annual volumes of cemetery records, including Bible, family, and church records transcribed by local chapters are helpful, but there is no central repository for maintaining them as is often the case for other states. Copies of some of the DAR volumes are at the New England Historic Genealogical Society.

Periodicals and repositories throughout the state have many examples of transcriptions; the most notable, such as the Corbin Collection (see Vital Records) are held in the Berkshire Athenaeum and the New England Historic Genealogical Society. The Systematic Series of town vital records (see Vital Records) included some information from gravestones.

Church Records

One expects an ample supply of church records in a state whose history is so interwoven with religious principles and dissension, and such is the case in Massachusetts. Many church records exist in published form either by themselves or in numerous periodicals or are noted in several inventories. Some early church records of vital events were included in the Systematic Series (see Vital Records). Church records often contain other genealogical information such as admissions and dismissals, which could indicate migration. Original records not held by the church itself are often deposited in central denominational libraries. The Corbin Collection (see Vital Records) includes many church records for the western part of the state. The following will guide the researcher to finding the appropriate records in Massachusetts for some of the historically largest or prominent denominations:

Baptist. Southern Baptist (1800–1960) church records for Boston are on microfilm at their national headquarters in Nashville, Tennessee. American Baptist (1699–1872) records are at their national headquarters in Rochester, New York.

Congregational. See Harold F. Worthley, *Inventory of the Records of Particular (Congregational) Churches of Massachusetts Gathered 1620–1805* (Cambridge, Mass.: Harvard University Press, 1970) and the Congregational Library, 14 Beacon Street, Boston, Massachusetts 02108.

Episcopal. See WPA, *Inventory of Church Archives of Massachusetts: Protestant Episcopal Church*, which was produced in 1942 by the WPA, and the Diocesan Library and Archives, 138 Tremont Street, Boston, Massachusetts 02135.

Jewish. Records can be found at the American Jewish Historical Society Library, 2 Thornton Road, Waltham, Massachusetts 02154, which is located on the campus of Brandeis University.

Methodist. See the Boston University School of Theology Library, 745 Commonwealth Avenue, Boston, Massachusetts 02215.

Roman Catholic. See James M. O'Toole, "Catholic Church Records: A Genealogical and Historical Resource," *The New England Historical and Genealogical Register* 132 (1978): 251–63, and Archives of the Archdiocese of Boston,

2121 Commonwealth Avenue, Brighton, Massachusetts 02135.

Society of Friends (Quakers). Essex Institute (see Archives, Libraries, and Societies) has a microfilm collection of Salem (Lynn) Monthly Meeting records, 1645–1819, a few group of family papers for Quakers in the area, and a collection of published materials. See also Rhode Island Historical Society (see Rhode Island).

Unitarian-Universalist. See *An Inventory of the Universalist Archives in Massachusetts,* compiled by the WPA in 1942, and Harvard Divinity School Library, 45 Francis Avenue, Cambridge, Massachusetts 02138.

Military Records

Armed conflict was as much a part of Massachusetts history as religious dissension. Military sources are just as plentiful as church records, but great quantities of them have been published.

Original extant records for the period 1643–1783 are at the Massachusetts State Archives, as well as some materials relating to Shays's Rebellion, the War of 1812, and the Spanish American War. Civil War and later records, including the Korean War, are at the Adjutant General's Office, War Records, 100 Cambridge Street, Boston, Massachusetts 02202.

The records in print for King Philip's War are covered in George M. Bodge's *Soldiers in King Philip's War* (1896; reprint, Baltimore, Md.: Genealogical Publishing Co., 1967). There are also five volumes jointly published by the Society of Colonial Wars in the Commonwealth of Massachusetts and the New England Historic Genealogical Society: Mary E. Donahue, ed., *Massachusetts Officers and Soldiers, 1702–1722* (1980); Myron O. Strachiw, ed., *Massachusetts Officers and Soldiers, 1723–1743: Dummer's War to the War of Jenkins' Ear* (1980); Robert E. Mackay, ed., *Massachusetts Soldiers in the French and Indian Wars, 1744-1755* (1978); Nancy S. Voye, ed., *Massachusetts Officers in the French and Indian Wars, 1748–1763* (1975); and Carol Doreski, ed., *Massachusetts Officers and Soldiers in the Seventeenth Century Conflicts* (1982).

Massachusetts Soldiers and Sailors of the Revolutionary War (Boston, Mass.: Commonwealth of Massachusetts, 1896–1908) is composed of seventeen volumes. Twenty-thousand names found after this work's publication were entered on cards and are on microfilm at the Massachusetts State Archives and the New England Historic Genealogical Society. Each listing, in both the published list and microfilmed card file, is alphabetical by occurrence of the name in a muster roll, report, or pay file, etc., along with a town residence of the man if it was obvious in the original record. No attempt was made to determine whether more than one record for the same name, in either the volumes or on the cards, is actually for the same person.

Numerous materials are available for Loyalist research in Massachusetts, including biographical studies. A comprehensive one is David E. Mass, ed., *Divided Hearts: Massachusetts Loyalists, 1765–1790, A Biographical Directory* (Boston, Mass.: New England Historic Genealogical Society, 1980).

For the War of 1812, see *Records of the Massachusetts Volunteer Militia Called Out by the Governor of Massachusetts to Suppress a Threatened Invasion during the War of 1812–14* (Boston, Mass.: Adjutant General's Office, 1913). For the Civil War, see *Massachusetts Soldiers, Sailors, and Marines in the Civil War* (Norwood, Mass.: Norwood Press, 1932).

In addition to the Adjutant General's Office, many towns have memorials to their residents who served in later wars. Records are generally kept at the town or city clerk's office.

The Massachusetts Military History Research Institute, 143 Speen Street, Natick, Massachusetts 01760, has an excellent collection of material from 1774 through the Vietnam War, with a heavy concentration on the Civil War.

Periodicals, Newspapers, and Manuscript Collections

Periodicals

Many periodicals are published concerning Massachusetts families and history. Among the more frequently used are:

The New England Historical and Genealogical Register, published since 1847 by the New England Historic Genealogical Society, serves all of New England and sets a standard for professional research with genealogies; local history; vital, church, and cemetery records; and important book reviews. Each volume has an annual every-name index. A cumulative index, *The New England Historical and Genealogical Register, Index of Persons,* 2 vols. (Camden, Maine: Picton Press, 1989), covers Vols. 1–50, and an abridged index covers Vols. 51–112.

The American Genealogist (*TAG*) is an independent quarterly founded by Donald Lines Jacobus in 1922; its primary focus is New England. Write Department A, 128 Massasoit Drive, Warwick, Rhode Island 02888.

Essex Institute Historical Collections (1859–present) and *Essex Antiquarian: A Quarterly Magazine Devoted to the Biography, Genealogy, History and Antiquities of Essex County, Massachusetts* (1897–1909) cover considerable primary and secondary source material for Essex County.

The Mayflower Descendant: A Quarterly Magazine of Pilgrim Genealogy and History (1899–1936; 1985–present) is published by the Massachusetts Society of Mayflower Descendants, 101 Newbury Street, Boston, Massachusetts 02116. It is indexed in separate volumes with a consolidated index for 1899–1936.

The Mayflower Quarterly (1935–present), published by the General Society of Mayflower Descendants (see

Archives, Libraries, and Societies) and has only annual indexes. Its focus is primarily on Plymouth Colony. Both *The Mayflower Quarterly* and *The Mayflower Descendant* (see above entry) are excellent publications for family articles and abstracts, particularly of vital and probate records.

Periodicals focused specifically on local genealogy are:

The Essex Genealogist (Essex, Mass., 1980–present): published by the Essex Society of Genealogists, c/o Lynnfield Public Library, 18 Summer Street, Lynnfield, Massachusetts 01940.

Berkshire Genealogist (1978–present): quarterly devoted to western Massachusetts, published by the Berkshire Family History Association, Box 1437, Pittsfield, Massachusetts 01201.

Other periodicals with historical material but no longer publishing include:

The Historical Collections of Danvers Historical Society: (Danvers, Mass., 1913–67).

The Dedham Historical Register (Dedham, Mass., 1890–1903).

The Medford Historical Register (Medford, Mass., 1898–1940).

Newspapers

Since 1704, Massachusetts newspapers have included some notices of deaths and marriages. A good number of these newspapers have been indexed in either published or typescript form. The New England Library Association's Bibliography Committee has produced *A Guide to Newspaper Indexes in New England* (Lynnfield, Mass.: the committee, 1978), which is extremely helpful. In more recent editions, *American Genealogical-Biographical Index* (see Connecticut—Background Sources) includes an index to the genealogical column of the defunct *Boston Evening Transcript* (see below).

The largest collection of microfilm copies of newspapers in the state can be found at the Boston Public Library (see Archives, Libraries, and Societies) and the Massachusetts State Library. But perhaps the most important newspaper for genealogical purposes, and one which should not be overlooked in Massachusetts research, is the *Boston Evening Transcript.* Between 1895 and 1941, it offered a genealogical column of queries, answers, and notes. Indexes to these valuable columns are available at the Boston Public Library and other New England repositories along with indexes of a similar column in the *Hartford Times* (see Connecticut—Newspapers).

Manuscripts

Rich manuscript sources exist in many excellent repositories in the state. In the eastern portion of the state, the New England Historic Genealogical Society; Massachusetts State Archives; Massachusetts Historical Society, which has a catalog of seven volumes; and the Essex Institute are key collections.

There are several collections in the western portion of the state, the largest of which are at the Berkshire Athenaeum and at the Connecticut Valley Historical Museum (see Archives, Libraries, and Societies for addresses).

Archives, Libraries, and Societies

New England Historic Genealogical Society
101 Newbury Street
Boston, MA 02116-3087

Founded in the mid-nineteenth century, the society is an extremely active center for New England family research, with an extensive collection of local and family histories, educational programs, and superior publications including *The New England Historical and Genealogical Register,* its quarterly periodical, and *Nexus,* its bimonthly newsletter, both distributed to the membership. Library facilities of open stacks (except for manuscripts and rare books) and microfilm collections of New England town and vital records are available on a per-day basis for a $10 fee (free for members). The book loan department makes materials available by mail to members for a small fee, and a four-volume catalog provides access to those circulating books. A research service is available to the general public for a fee.

Massachusetts Archives at Columbia Point
220 Morrissey Boulevard
Boston, MA 02125

Usually referred to as the Massachusetts State Archives, the repository holds all state copies of vital records (1841–95); passenger lists for the Port of Boston (1848–91); federal census records (state copies, 1850–70, with 1880 on microfilm) with all supplemental federal schedules and the state censuses for 1855 and 1865; legislative records from the general court with land grants, petitions, and tax records (1643–1787); Eastern land records for the settlement of Maine; human service institution records; all military records for the state through the Revolution; and Judicial Archives beginning with colony era courts to mid-nineteenth century courts (see Court Records).

State Library of Massachusetts
341 State House, Beacon Street
Boston, MA 02133

Its genealogical collection includes extensive newspaper collections and indexes, town and county histories, town and county maps and atlases, and city directories back to 1787. See Kenneth E. Flower, *A Guide to Massachusetts Genealogical Material in the State Library of Massachusetts* (Boston, Mass.: Massachusetts State Archives, 1978).

Boston Public Library
Copley Square
Boston, MA 02117

Both the Social Science Reference Department and Microtext Department have important collections for genealogical research. The former holds family genealogies and vertical file material not found elsewhere. Microtext has all federal census records for New England; copies of the National Archives' Boston ship passenger arrival lists 1820–91 and indexes for 1848–90 (see Immigration); probate records for Middlesex, Suffolk, and Hampshire counties; Suffolk Court of Common Pleas records; town records; newspapers including the *Boston Evening Transcript* and indexes; and city directories from over 200 cities and towns in the United States. For a descriptive listing, William H. Schoeffler's "Genealogical Research at the Boston Public Library," with an update by Alice Kane, is available for a nominal fee from MGC Reprints, 18 Martin's Cove Road, Hingham, Massachusetts 02043.

Connecticut Valley Historical Museum Library and Archives
Springfield Library Genealogy Department
194 State Street
Springfield, MA 01103

Serving the western portion of the state extremely well, this collection (formerly at the Springfield Public Library) holds an excellent local archives starting in 1636 for Springfield and vicinity and is one of the better collections of ethnic materials—French-Canadian, Irish, and black. Volunteers answer mail inquiries. Western Massachusetts Genealogical Society, Inc., Box 80206, Forest Park Station, Springfield, Massachusetts 01108, is a membership organization functioning in connection with the museum.

Berkshire Athenaeum
1 Wendell Avenue
Pittsfield, MA 01202

Their Cooke Collection of eighteenth and nineteenth century church and cemetery records also includes abstracts of newspaper notices of marriages and deaths, the personal records of ministers, and vital records which supplement the Systematic Series. Other collections include files of research notes collected by local researchers, and a 3 x 5 card file of vital records and notes throughout the state and the northeast. This includes Connecticut, Vermont, and Hudson Valley, New York, since the area was a major conduit for movement north and west. The Berkshire Family History Association, Box 1437, Pittsfield, Massachusetts 01201, is connected with the Athenaeum and provides a research service for its members.

Essex Institute Library
132-134 Essex Street
Salem, MA 01970

This is the largest collection of Essex County original source material, and there is a good collection of published genealogies and town histories for Essex County. This private library, open to annual membership or for a daily fee, currently has the pre-1800 Essex County court records; but no fee is charged for patrons using only these Essex County court records.

General Society of Mayflower Descendants
4 Winslow Street
Plymouth, MA 02360

The society is the national headquarters for the state organizations of descendants of Mayflower Pilgrims. It presently publishes the *Mayflower Quarterly* and the five-generation project (see Background Sources). There is a research library available.

Massachusetts Historical Society
1154 Boylston Street
Boston, MA 02215

Although not advertised as a genealogical library, the collection includes rare books; "personal papers"; manuscripts such as the Thwing Collection of Early Bostonians; and rare books focusing particularly on Boston, on Massachusetts, and on New England.

The Pilgrim Society
75 Court Street
Plymouth, MA 02360

Connected with the Pilgrim Hall Museum, which holds the Plymouth County Court record books from 1686–1859, the collection focuses on the Pilgrim experience in Plymouth.

American Antiquarian Society
185 Salisbury Street
Worcester, MA 01609

Superior collection specializing in printed sources of American history prior to 1877 and a fine newspaper collection.

Special Focus Categories

Immigration

Both immigration and naturalization records abound for Massachusetts since Boston was a major port of entry for thousands of people seeking refuge, food, land, economic opportunity, and religious and political freedom from points across the Atlantic. Smaller ports existed in other towns both north and south of Boston's wharfs. The seventeenth and nineteenth century records are well organized, but few of the eighteenth century records are as easily accessed.

Early Immigration. While literally hundreds of published lists exist, the most definitive resource to use for those lists actually discovered for the 1620–1700 period is Filby and Meyer's *Passenger and Immigration Lists Index* (see page 10), which serves this period well. However, the researcher *must* refer to the primary source after using the index since the index is derived from other published lists and not the primary material itself.

1800–Present. The nineteenth century brought massive numbers of immigrants to Massachusetts, creating a much more heterogeneous population than a century earlier. Fortunately, many passenger lists have been indexed for the period.

The Massachusetts State Archives has an alphabetical name index to the Port of Boston passenger lists from 1848–91, called the state list. The National Archives-New England Region has passenger lists from 1820–1925 and continues to obtain later ones from Washington, D.C. The National Archives in Washington, D.C., has copies of the Boston lists for 1820–91 (Record Group 36, M277), though some gaps in coverage appear in the microfilm copy of the lists. The microfilm index to passenger lists made by the National Archives in Washington, D.C., for 1848–91 (Record Group 36, M265) used the *state* lists to create the federal index for arrivals at the port of Boston. Consequently, people might appear on the microfilmed federal index but not on the federal lists, while they do appear on the state list at the Massachusetts State Archives.

The National Archives in Washington, D.C., also has an index to passenger lists for arrivals at Boston from 1902–20 (Record Group 85, T521; T617), book indexes to the Boston passenger lists by date of arrival from 1899–1940 (Record Group 85, T790), and passenger lists themselves for 1891–1943 (Record Group 85, T843).

Boston was only one port of entry open for immigrants to Massachusetts. There are lists for other ports in the state as well, generally covered by the National Archives index (Record Group 36, M334) for the Atlantic, Gulf, and Great Lakes ports, 1820–91.

In the Boston area, the Boston Public Library has microfilm copies of Boston passenger arrival lists, 1820–91, and indexes for 1848–91, as well as other immigration material.

Naturalization

The WPA developed an index of naturalizations found in numerous city, county, state, and federal courts in New England for the period 1786–1906, which is soundexed, microfilmed, and available through the National Archives (see page 8). The abstract cards used to create the microfilm for all of New England are at the National Archives-New England Region in Waltham, Massachusetts. For the period from 1906–70s, the abstract cards and an index for naturalization petitions from federal courts in Massachusetts have been moved to the National Archives-New England Region. In addition to the abstract cards and index, New England's regional branch of the archives holds dexigraphs of the actual records, making it possible to check the accuracy of the abstracts/index. Some have declarations of intention attached which may give more information about the immigrant.

The Massachusetts State Archives holds abstracts for state and local courts (1885–1931 with separate annual indexes), and also Essex County naturalization records (1901–82). Current petitions and index cards for the federal courts are at Immigration and Naturalization Service, U.S. Department of Justice, JFK Federal Building, Government Center, Boston, Massachusetts 02203.

Black American

From colonial beginnings, some slaves were recorded in the same town and county records as white settlers. The terms "black," "slave," "Negro," and "colored" are often included in Massachusetts seventeenth- and eighteenth-century primary source material including land, probate, court, and vital records, for example. Records of both slaves and free blacks are found in numerous repository collections for pre-revolutionary Massachusetts. However, little has been done to extract the information to make it more usable for genealogical research (see pages 10–11). One major exception is Joseph Carvalho, *Black Families in Hampden County, Massachusetts. 1650–1855* (Boston, Mass.: New England Historic Genealogical Society and the Institute on Massachusetts Studies, Westfield State College, 1984), which is an excellent study including families who migrated to Hampden County. See also:

Daniels, John. *In Freedom's Birthplace: A Study of the Boston Negroes.* 1914. Reprint. New York, N.Y.: Arno Press, 1969.

Moore, George H. *Notes on the History of Slavery in Massachusetts.* 1866. Reprint. New York, N.Y.: Negro University Press, 1968.

Pierson, William D. *Black Yankees: The Development of an Afro-American Subculture in Eighteenth Century New England.* Amherst, Mass.: University of Massachusetts Press, 1988.

Native American

For centuries before the Pilgrims' arrival, several tribes of Native Americans lived in what is now Massachusetts. In the early stages of European settlement, friendly relations existed. Following the migration, conflicts continued to escalate through the last part of the seventeenth century, the most well known of which is King Philip's War with the Wampanoag of Plymouth Colony. Before the end of those conflicts in the mid-eighteenth century, significantly fewer native inhabitants were left in the area, many having been killed, chased further to the north or west, or sold into slavery. See Howard S. Russell, *Indian New England Before the Mayflower* (Hanover, N.H.: University Press of New England, n.d.) and William Cronon, *Changes on the Land: Indians, Colonists, and the Ecology of New England* (New York, N.Y.: Hill and Wang, 1983).

Other Ethnic Groups

The large Irish and French-Canadian immigration in the mid-nineteenth century preceded the influx of eastern and southern European groups to Boston Harbor in the late nineteenth and early twentieth centuries. Latino and Southeast Asian immigrants have recently arrived.

The Irish American Research Association (commonly known as TIARA), P.O. Box 619, Sudbury, Massachusetts 01776, is a group which promotes cooperative research for both Protestant and Catholic Irish (see also New

Hampshire—American Canadian Genealogical Society and Rhode Island—American French Genealogical Society). The American Jewish Historical Society (see Church Records—Jewish) is an excellent resource for research on Jewish immigration, but not limited to Massachusetts.

County Resources

The following is a guide to beginning dates and locations of Massachusetts deeds, probates, and court records. Inquiries for land records should be addressed to the "Registry of Deeds" at the county (or district) seat. In some counties, division of the Registry of Deeds was created to make the location closer to the land involved in the transaction. Make sure the deed information sought falls in the appropriate district for the time period and the geography involved.

The "Probate Court Clerk" at the county seat should be addressed for probate records and the "Clerk of Courts" for civil court records.

Map	County Address	Date Formed Parent County/ies	Land Probate Court
J6	Barnstable Main Street Barnstable 02630	1685 as Barnstable County of Plymouth Colony	1827* 1686 1686
	**Fire destroyed nearly all early deed books and probate files, but probate books survived. Although the official deed books only begin in 1827, many deeds were re-recorded back to about 1783, though these are far from complete.*		
A3	Berkshire 44 Bank Row Pittsfield 01201	1761 Hampshire	1761 1761 1761
	Divided into three districts in 1788. The above office is the "parent" county seat, encompassing all the Berkshire towns between 1761–88. After that it was still the probate office for the county, but only the registry of deeds for the Middle District (see Town Resources for towns in each of Berkshire's three registry of deeds districts).		
	Berkshire Northern District 65 Park Street Adams 01220		1788
	Berkshire Southern District Great Barrington 01230		1788
G5	Bristol 11 Court Street Taunton 02780	1685 as Bristol County of Plymouth Colony	1685 1685 1685
	The county seat was Bristol until 1746 when succeeded by Taunton. The Taunton seat divided into three districts in 1837, with the above remaining as the probate office but only registry of deeds for the Northern District (see Town Resources for towns in each of Bristol's registry of deeds districts).		
	Bristol Southern District 25 N. Sixth Street New Bedford 02740		1837
	Bristol Fall River District 441 N. Main Street Fall River 02720		1837
H7	Dukes Edgartown 02539	1683 (as a New York County) 1695 (as a Mass. County)	1686 1696 1665
	Records from 1665 deal with Martha's Vineyard.		

Map	County Address	Date Formed Parent County/ies	Land Probate Court
H2	Essex 32 Federal Street Salem 01970	1643 original	1637 1635 1636
	The county was divided into two districts in 1869. The above office is the "parent" county seat. After that it remained the probate office for the county, but the registry of deeds for only the Southern District (see Town Resources for towns in each of the registry of deeds districts). This registry also has all the "old" Norfolk County (1637–1714) and Ipswich court deeds (1640–94). Essex court records to 1800 are at the Essex Institute (see Archives, Libraries, and Societies).		
	Essex Northern District 381 Common Street Lawrence 01840		1869
B2	Franklin 425 Main Street Greenfield 01310	1811 Hampshire	1787* 1812 1812
	**Earlier deeds for land now in Franklin County are at Springfield (see Hampden County). Abstracts of these deeds recorded at the Springfield registry from 1663–1786 are at Greenfield. Deeds for 1787 to present are in Greenfield, although between 1787–1812 they were recorded at the Deerfield registry, which was transferred to Greenfield in 1812. Probates before 1812 for towns now in Franklin County are at Northampton (see Hampshire County).*		
B4	Hampden 50 State Street Springfield 01103	1812 Hampshire	1636* 1812** 1812**
	**Although not established as the Hampden county until 1812, Springfield was the registry for Hampden's parent county, Hampshire, which was divided into three registries—Deerfield, Springfield, and Northampton — in 1787. Deerfield registry was transferred to Greenfield when Franklin County was established in 1811 (see Franklin and Hampshire). All deeds for land originally in Hampshire as well as Franklin and Hampden before their county division from Hampshire, are located at the Springfield registry.* ***Probates before 1812 for towns covered now by Hampden County are at the Hampshire Probate Office in Northampton. The bulk of the pre-1812 court records are also in Northampton.*		
C3	Hampshire 33 King Street Northampton 01060	1662 Middlesex	1812* 1660 1677
	**In 1787 three registry offices were created (Deerfield, Springfield, and Northampton) for Hampshire County corresponding with what eventually became the three present counties of Franklin, Hampden, and Hampshire, respectively. All deeds for the Northampton registry before it became what is now Hampshire County are located in the Springfield registry.*		
F2	Middlesex 208 Cambridge Street Cambridge 02141	1643 original	1649* 1654* 1643
	**Until 1649, records were kept in Boston. The county was divided into two districts in 1855. The above office is the "parent" county seat, encompassing all the Middlesex towns between 1643–1855. After that it was still the probate office for the county, but the registry of deeds for only the Southern District (see Town Resources for towns in each of Middlesex's two registry of deeds districts).*		
	Middlesex Northern District 360 Gorham Street Lowell 01852		1855
K7	Nantucket Broad Street Nantucket 02554	1695 Dukes	1695 1706 1721
	Norfolk "Old" Essex County Courthouse 32 Federal, Salem 01970	1643 (abolished 1680) original	1637–1714
	Exeter, Salisbury, Hampton, Haverhill, Dover, and Portsmouth (formerly Strawberry Banke) were in this county until it was abolished. All but Salisbury and Haverhill are now in New Hampshire. Probate and deed records for these towns in this period are located here.		
G4	Norfolk 649 High Street Dedham 02026	1793 Suffolk	1793 1793 1793
	Plymouth County towns of Hingham and Hull were part of Norfolk County from 1793–1803.		

Map	County Address	Date Formed Parent County/ies	Land Probate Court
H5	Plymouth S. Russell Street Plymouth 02360	1685 as Plymouth County of Plymouth Colony	1620 1633 1630
	Plymouth Colony divided into three counties in 1685. The entire colony joined with Massachusetts Bay Colony in 1691 to form the commonwealth. All earlier records that apply to Plymouth Colony are at the county commissioner's office above, bound in a separate series. The present probate and registry of deeds office is at the same address. Court record books (1686–1859) are at the Pilgrim Society, Court Street, Plymouth, MA 02360.		
H3	Suffolk Old Courthouse Pemberton Square Boston 02108	1643 original	1639 1636 1671
	In 1793 all that was Suffolk County except Boston, Chelsea, Hingham, and Hull became Norfolk County.		
E3	Worcester 2 Main Street Worcester 01608	1731 Middlesex/Suffolk	1731 1731 1731
	Worcester divided into two registries for deeds only in 1884 (see Town Resources for those towns that fall under this Worcester District registry after that date).		
	Worcester Northern District 84 Elm Street Fitchburg 01420		1884

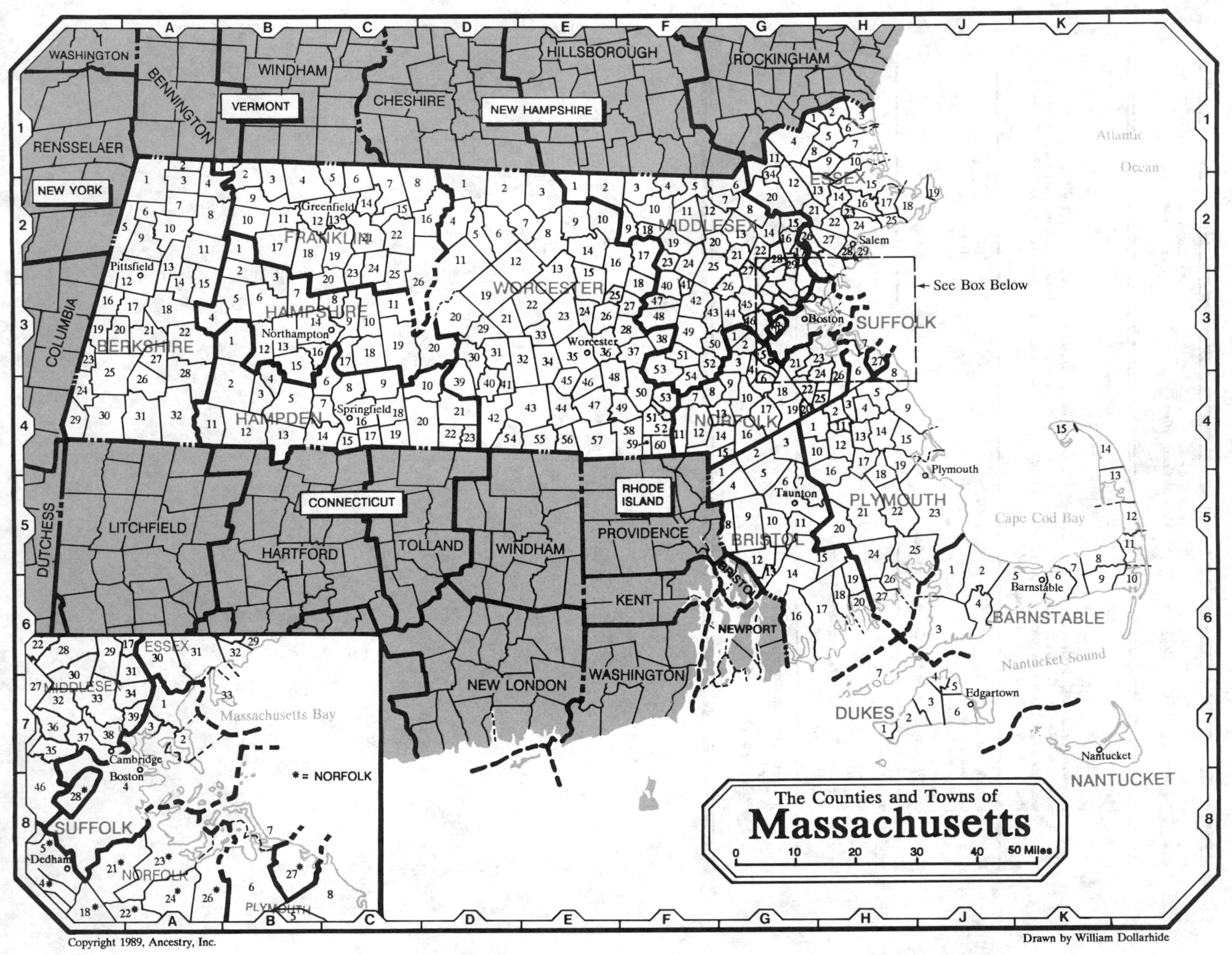

Copyright 1989, Ancestry, Inc.

Drawn by William Dollarhide

Town Resources

The *Historical Data Relating to Counties, Cities and Towns in Massachusetts,* cited in Background Sources above, provides some of the information which follows. Addresses are "Town Hall," unless otherwise indicated, and come from the most recent list of town clerks distributed by the secretary of state. The second column lists the date the town was established, town/s from which it was formed, and in parentheses, former names. The third column lists county, the town's number in that county on the map, and, if appropriate, registry of deeds district is indicated under the county.

Early records of town meetings have been published for a number of Massachusetts towns. See Ann S. Lainhart, "Town Records," *Essex Genealogist* 10 (February 1990): 3–10, for a list and discussion. Some are interspersed in the original vital record books on microfiche distributed by Archive Publishing, 57 Locust Street, Oxford, Massachusetts 01540. Those for Middlesex County towns are at the Boston Public Library, New England Historic Genealogical Society, or can be acquired through Early Massachusetts Records, Inc., 1154 Boylston, Boston, Massachusetts 02215. A descriptive guide to the collection was published in 1976 and can be obtained from that address.

The researcher should assume that vital records, whether in separate books or interspersed with other town records, begin with the formation of the town, as do the town records. See parent towns for earlier records; and the county (see County Resources) for beginning dates of deeds, probates, and court records. Clerks respond to inquires regarding vital records, since most have indexes available, but unindexed town records with details of town life—officers, tax lists, freeman's lists, cattle and hog marks, voting lists, warnings out, overseer's of the poor accounts, school records—must be searched in person either through microfilm or at the town's office.

Town Address	Date Formed Parent Town/s (Other Names)	County Land Records District
Abington P.O. Box 98 North Abington 02351	1712 Bridgewater	Plymouth (2)
Acushnet Acushnet 02743	1860 Fairhaven	Bristol (19) Southern
Acton Acton 01720	1735 Concord	Middlesex (24) Southern
Adams Adams 01220	1778 (East Hoosuck)	Berkshire (7) Northern
Agawam Agawam 01001	1855 West Springfield	Hampden (14)
Alford RFD 3, Box 184 Great Barrington 01230	1773 Great Barrington	Berkshire (23) Southern
Amesbury Amesbury 01913	1668 Salisbury	Essex (2) Southern
Amherst Amherst 01003	1759 Hadley	Hampshire (10) Northampton
Andover Andover 01810	1646	Essex (20) Northern
Arlington Arlington 02174	1807 Cambridge (West Cambridge, 1867)	Middlesex (32) Southern
Ashburnham Ashburnham 01430	1765 (Dorcester-Canada)	Worcester (3) Northern

Town Address	Date Formed Parent Town/s (Other Names)	County Land Records District
Ashby Main Street Ashby 01431	1767 Ashburnton/Fitchburg/Townsend	Middlesex (1) Southern
Ashfield Ashfield 01330	1765 (Huntstown Plantation)	Franklin (17) Greenfield (Deerfield)
Ashland Ashland 01721	1846 Framingham/Holliston/Hopkinton	Middlesex (51) Southern
Athol Athol 01331	1762 (Payquage Plantation)	Worcester (4) Worcester
Attleboro City Hall Attleboro 02703	1694 Rehoboth	Bristol (4) Northern
Auburn Auburn 01501	1778 (named Ward until 1837) Leicester/Oxford/Sutton/Worcester	Worcester (45) Worcester
Avon Buckley Center Avon 02322	1888 Stroughton	Norfolk (20)
Ayer Ayer 01432	1871 Groton/Shirley	Middlesex (18) Southern
Barnstable 364 Main Street Hyannis 02601	1638	Barnstable (5)
Barre Barre 01005	1753 Rutland (Rutland District, 1774; named Hutchinson until 1776)	Worcester (19) Worcester
Becket Becket 01223	1765 (No. 4 Plantation)	Berkshire (22) Middle
Bedford Bedford 01730	1729 Billerica/Concord	Middlesex (21) Southern
Belchertown 1 S. Main Street Belchertown 01007	1761 (Cold Spring Plantation)	Hampshire (19) Northampton
Bellingham Bellingham 02019	1719 Dedham/Mendon/Wrentham	Norfolk (11)
Belmont Belmont 02178	1859 Waltham/Watertown/West Cambridge (Arlington)	Middlesex (36) Southern
Berkley 145 Bryant Street Berkley 02780	1735 Dighton/Taunton	Bristol (11) Northern
Berlin Berlin 01503	1784 Bolton/Marlborough	Worcester (27) Worcester
Bernardston Bernardston 01337	1762 (as Falltown Plantation)	Franklin (6) Greenfield (Deerfield)

Town Address	Date Formed Parent Town/s (Other Names)	County Land Records District
Beverly City Hall Beverly 01915	1668 Salem	Essex (24) Southern
Billerica Billerica 01821	1655	Middlesex (13) Northern
Blackstone Blackstone 01504	1845 Mendon	Worcester (60) Worcester
Blandford Old Chester Road Blandford 01008	1741 (Suffield Equivalet) (Glasgow)	Hampden (2) Springfield
Bolton Bolton 01740	1738 Lancaster	Worcester (18) Worcester
Boston City Hall Boston 02201 *The following towns became part of Boston on the date indicated: East Boston (1637), South Boston (1804), Roxbury (1868), Dorchester (1870), Brighton (1874), Charlestown (1874), West Roxbury (1874), and Hyde Park (1912).*	1630	Suffolk (4)
Bourne Bourne 02532	1884 Sandwich	Barnstable (1)
Boxborough Boxborough 01780	1783 Harvard/Littletown/Stow	Middlesex (23) Southern
Boxford Boxford 01921	1694	Essex (13) Southern
Boylston Boylston 01505	1786 Shrewsbury	Worcester (26) Worcester
Bradford (became part of Haverhill, 1897)	1675 Southern	Essex
Braintree Braintree 02184	1640 Boston	Norfolk (24)
Brewster Brewster 02631	1803 Harwich	Barnstable (8)
Bridgewater Bridgewater 02324	1656	Plymouth (16)
Brighton (became part of Boston, 1874)	1817 Cambridge	Suffolk
Brimfield Brimfield 01010	1714 Original	Hampden (21) Springfield
Brockton City Hall Brockton 02401	1821 Bridgewater (North Bridgewater)	Plymouth (1)
Brookfield Brookfield 01506	1673	Worcester (40) Worcester

Town Address	Date Formed Parent Town/s (Other Names)	County Land Records District
Brookline 333 Washington Street Brookline 02147	1705 Boston	Norfolk (28)
Buckland 17 State Street Shelburne Falls 01370	1779 No-town Plantation/Charlemont	Franklin (11) Greenfield (Deerfield)
Burlington Burlington 01803	1799 Woburn	Middlesex (22) Southern
Cambridge City Hall Cambridge 02139	1631 (Newe Towne)	Middlesex (37) Southern
Canton Canton 02021	1797 Stoughton	Norfolk (18)
Carlisle Carlisle 01741	1780 Acton/Billerica/Chelmsford/Concord	Middlesex (20) Northern
Carver Carver 02330	1790 Plympton	Plymouth (22)
Charlemont Charlemont 01339	1765	Franklin (9) Greenfield (Deerfield)
Charlestown (became part of Boston, 1874)	1630	Suffolk
Charlton Charlton 01507	1754 Oxford	Worcester (43) Worcester
Chatham Chatham 02633	1712 (Manamoit Village)	Barnstable (10)
Chelmsford Chelmsford 01824	1655	Middlesex (12) Northern
Chelsea City Hall Chelsea 02150	1739 Boston (Winnissimet/ Rumney Marsh/Pullin Point)	Suffolk (3)
Cheshire Cheshire 01225	1793 Adams/Lanesborough/ Windsor/New Ashford District	Berkshire (10) Northern
Chester Chester 01011	1765 (Murrayfield)	Hampden (1) Northampton
Chesterfield Chesterfield 01012	1762 (New Hingham Plantation)	Hampshire (6) Northampton
Chicopee City Hall Chicopee 01013	1848 Springfield	Hampden (8)
Chilmark Chilmark 02535	1694	Dukes (2)

Town Address	Date Formed Parent Town/s (Other Names)	County Land Records District
Clarksburg Clarksburg 01247	1798	Berkshire (2) Northern
Clinton Clinton 01510	1850 Lancaster	Worcester (25) Worcester
Cohasset Cohasset 02025	1770 Hingham	Norfolk (27)
Colrain Colrain 01340	1761	Franklin (4) Greenfield (Deerfield)
Concord Concord 01742	1635 (Musketequid)	Middlesex (25) Southern
Conway Conway 01341	1767 Deerfield	Franklin (18) Greenfield (Deerfield)
Cummington Cummington 01026	1779 No. 5 Plantation	Hampshire (2) Northampton
Dalton Dalton 01226	1784 (Ashuelet Equivalent)	Berkshire (13) Middlesex
Dana (became part of Petersham, 1927)	1801 Greenwich/Hardwick/Petersham	Worcester Worcester
Danvers Danvers 01923	1752 Salem (Salem Village/Middle Parishes)	Essex (22) Southern
Dartmouth 249 Russell Mills Road South Dartmouth 02714	1652 (Acushena/Ponaganesett/Coaksett)	Bristol (17) Southern
Dedham Dedham 02026	1636	Norfolk (5)
Deerfield South Deerfield 01373	1677	Franklin (19) Greenfield (Deerfield)
Dennis P.O. Drawer D South Dennis 02660	1793 Yarmouth	Barnstable (7)
Dighton Dighton 02715	1712 Taunton	Bristol (10) Northern
Dorchester (became part of Boston, 1870)	1630 original	Suffolk
Douglas Douglas 01516	1746 (New Sherbourn)	Worcester (57) Worcester
Dover Dover 02030	1784 Dedham	Norfolk (3)
Dracut Dracut 01826	1702	Middlesex (6) Northern

Town Address	Date Formed Parent Town/s (Other Names)	County Land Records District
Dudley Dudley 01570	1732 Oxford	Worcester (55) Worcester
Dunstable Dunstable 01827	1673	Middlesex (4) Northern
Duxbury Duxbury 02332	1637	Plymouth (15)
East Bridgewater P.O. Box 387 Bridgewater 02333	1823 Bridgewater	Plymouth (12)
East Brookfield East Brookfield 01515	1920 Brookfield	Worcester (41)
East Longmeadow East Longmeadow 01028	1894 Longmeadow	Hampden (17)
Eastham Eastham 02642	1646 (Nawsett)	Barnstable (12)
Easthampton Easthampton 01027	1785 Northampton/Southampton	Hampshire (16) Northampton
Easton Easton 02334	1725 Norton	Bristol (3) Northern
Edgartown Edgartown 02539	1671 (Great Harbour)	Dukes (6)
Egremont P.O. Box 368 South Egremont 01258	1760	Berkshire (24) Southern
Enfield (became part of Belchertown/New Salem/Pelham/Ware, 1938)	1816 Belchertown/Greenwich	Hampshire Northampton
Erving Erving 01344	1838	Franklin (15) Greenfield
Essex Essex 01929	1819 Ipswich	Essex (17)
Everett City Hall Everett 02149	1870 Malden	Middlesex (39) Southern
Fairhaven Fairhaven 02719	1812 New Bedford	Bristol (20) Southern
Fall River City Hall Fall River 02722	1803 Freetown (Troy, 1834)	Bristol (14) Northern
Falmouth Falmouth 02540	1694	Barnstable (3)
Fitchburg Fitchburg 01420	1764 Lunenberg	Worcester (9) Northern

Town Address	Date Formed Parent Town/s (Other Names)	County Land Records District
Florida Post Office Drury 01343	1805 Barnardstone's Grant/Bullock's Grant	Berkshire (4) Northern
Foxborough Foxborough 02035	1778 Stoughton/Walpole/ Wrentham/Stoughtonham now named Sharon	Norfolk (16)
Framingham Framingham 01701	1675	Middlesex (49) Southern
Franklin Franklin 02038	1778 Wrentham	Norfolk (12)
Freetown Freetown 02702	1683	Bristol (15) Northern
Gardner City Hall Gardner 01440	1785 Ashburnham/Templeton/ Westminister/Winchendon	Worcester (7) Worcester
Gay Head Gay Head 02535	1855	Dukes (1)
Georgetown Georgetown 01830	1838 Rowley	Essex (9) Southern
Gill RFD Gill, Box 311 Turner Falls 01376	1793 Greenfield	Franklin (14) Greenfield (Deerfield)
Gloucester City Hall Gloucester 01930	1642 (Cape Ann)	Essex (18) Southern
Goshen Goshen 01032	1781 Chesterfield	Hampshire (3) Northampton
Gosnold Gosnold 02713	1864 Chilmark	Dukes (7)
Grafton Grafton 01519	1735 (Hassanamisco)	Worcester (48) Worcester
Granby Granby 01033	1768 South Hadley	Hampshire (18) Northampton
Granville Granville 01034	1754	Hampden (12) Springfield
Great Barrington Great Barrington 01230	1761 Sheffield	Berkshire (25)
Greenfield Greenfield 01301	1753 Deerfield	Franklin (13) Greenfield (Deerfield)
Greenwich (became part of Hardwick/New Salem/Petersham/Ware, 1938)	1754 (Quabbin Plantation)	Hampshire Northampton

Town Address	Date Formed Parent Town/s (Other Names)	County Land Records District
Groton Groton 01450	1655	Middlesex (10) Southern
Groveland Groveland 01830	1850 Bradford	Essex (8) Southern
Hadley Hadley 01035	1661 (New Plantation)	Hampshire (9) Northampton
Halifax Halifax 02338	1734 Middleborough/Pembroke/Plympton	Plymouth (17)
Hamilton Hamilton 01936	1793 Ipswich	Essex (16) Southern
Hampden Hampden 01036	1878 Wilbraham	Hampden (19)
Hancock Route 43, Hancock Road Williamstown 01267	1776 (Jericho Plantation)	Berkshire (5) Northern
Hanover Hanover 02339	1727 Abington/Scituate	Plymouth (4)
Hanson Hanson 02341	1820 Pembroke	Plymouth (13)
Hardwick Hardwick 01037	1739 (Lambstown Plantation)	Worcester (20) Worcester
Harvard Harvard 01451	1732 Groton/Lancaster/Stow	Worcester (17) Worcester
Harwich Harwich 02645	1694 (Stauckett)	Barnstable (9)
Hatfield Hatfield 01038	1670 Hadley	Hampshire (8)
Haverhill City Hall Haverhill 01830	1641	Essex (4) Southern
Hawley Hawley 01339	1792 (No. 7 Plantation)	Franklin (10) Greenfield (Deerfield)
Heath Heath 01346	1785 Charlemont	Franklin (3) Greenfield (Deerfield)
Hingham Hingham 02043	1635 (Barecove)	Plymouth (6) (Norfolk 1793–1803)
Hinsdale Hinsdale 01235	1804 Partridgefield/Dalton	Berkshire (14) Middle
Holbrook Holbrook 02343	1872 Randolph	Norfolk (25)

Town Address	Date Formed Parent Town/s (Other Names)	County Land Records District
Holden Holden 01520	1741 Worcester	Worcester (23) Worcester
Holland Holland 01550	1783 South Brimfield (Wales)	Hampden (23) Springfield
Holliston Holliston 01746	1724 Sherborn	Middlesex (54) Southern
Holyoke City Hall Holyoke 01040	1850 West Springfield	Hampden (6)
Hopedale Hopedale 01747	1886 Milford	Worcester (51) Worcester
Hopkinton Hopkinton 01748	1715 (Moguncoy)	Middlesex (53) Southern
Hubbardston Hubbardston 01452	1767 Rutland	Worcester (12) Worcester
Hudson Hudson 01749	1866 Marlborough/Stow	Middlesex (47) Southern
Hull Hull 02045	1644	Plymouth (7) (Norfolk 1793–1803)
Huntington Huntington 01050	1773 Murrayfield (Norwich)	Hampshire (12) Northampton
Ipswich Ipswich 02347	1634 (Aggawam)	Essex (15) Southern
Kingston Kingston 02360	1726 Plymouth	Plymouth (19)
Lakeville Lakeville 02347	1853 Middleborough	Plymouth (20)
Lancaster Lancaster 01523	1653	Worcester (16) Worcester
Lanesborough Lanesborough 01237	1765 (New Framingham Plantation)	Berkshire (9) Northern
Lawrence City Hall Lawrence 01840	1847 Andover/Methuen	Essex (34) Northern
Lee Lee 01238	1777 Great Barrington	Berkshire (21) Middle
Leicester Leicester 01524	1714	Worcester (34) Worcester
Lenox Lenox 01240	1767 Richmont	Berkshire (17) Middle

Town Address	Date Formed Parent Town/s (Other Names)	County Land Records District
Leominster City Hall Leominster 01453	1740 Lancaster	Worcester (14) Northern
Leverett 184 N. Leverett Road Leverett 01054	1774 Sunderland	Franklin (24) Greenfield (Deerfield)
Lexington Lexington 02173	1713 Cambridge	Middlesex (27) Southern
Leyden Leyden 01301	1784 Bernardston	Franklin (5) Greenfield (Deerfield)
Lincoln Lincoln 01773	1754 Concord/Lexington/Weston	Middlesex (26) Southern
Littleton Littleton 01460	1715 (Nashoba)	Middlesex (19) Southern (Northern 1856–60)
Longmeadow Longmeadow 01106	1783 Springfield	Hampden (15) Springfield
Lowell City Hall Lowell 01852	1826 Chelmsford	Middlesex (7) Northern
Ludlow Ludlow 01056	1774 Springfield	Hampden (9) Springfield
Lunenburg Lunenburg 01462	1728 Turkey Hills and land belonging to Woburn/ Dorchester/and Boardman's Farm	Worcester (10) Northern
Lynn City Hall Lynn 01901	1635 (Saugust)	Essex (31) Southern
Lynnfield Lynnfield 01940	1782 Lynn	Essex (26) Southern
Malden City Hall Malden 02148	1649	Middlesex (34) Southern
Manchester Manchester 01944	1645 Salem	Essex (25) Southern
Mansfield Mansfield 02048	1770 Norton	Bristol (2) Northern
Marblehead Marblehead 01945	1633	Essex (29) Southern
Marion Marion 02738	1852 Rochester	Plymouth (26)
Marlborough City Hall P.O. Box 47 Marlborough 01752	1660	Middlesex (48) Southern

Town Address	Date Formed Parent Town/s (Other Names)	County Land Records District
Marshfield Marshfield 02050	1640 (Green's Harbour) (Rexhame)	Plymouth (9)
Mashpee P.O. Box 1108 Mashpee 02649	1763	Barnstable (4)
Mattapoisett Mattapoisett 02739	1857 Rochester	Plymouth (27)
Maynard Maynard 01754	1871 Stow/Sudbury	Middlesex (41) Southern
Medfield Medfield 02052	1650 Dedham	Norfolk (9)
Medford City Hall Medford 02155	1630	Middlesex (33) Southern
Medway Medway 02053	1713 Medfield	Norfolk (7)
Melrose City Hall Melrose 02176	1850 Malden	Middlesex (31) Southern
Mendon P.O. Box 54 Mendon 01756	1667	Worcester (52) Worcester
Merrimac Merrimac 01860	1876 Amesbury	Essex (1) Southern
Methuen Methuen 01844	1725 Haverhill	Essex (11) Northern
Middleborough Middleborough 02346	1669 (Namassackett)	Plymouth (21)
Middlefield Middlefield 01243	1783 Becket/Chester/Washington/ Partridgefield/Worthington/ Prescott's Grant	Hampshire (4)
Middletown Middletown 01949	1728 Andover/Boxford/Salem/Topsfield	Essex (21) Southern
Milford Milford 01757	1780 Mendon	Worcester (53) Worcester
Millbury Millbury 01527	1813 Sutton	Worcester (46) Worcester
Millis Millis 02054	1885 Medway	Norfolk (8)
Millville Millville 01529	1916 Blackstone	Worcester (59) Worcester

Town Address	Date Formed Parent Town/s (Other Names)	County Land Records District
Milton Milton 02186	1662 Dorchester	Norfolk (21)
Monroe P.O. Box 6 Monroe 01350	1822 Rowe/The Gore	Franklin (1) Greenfield
Monson Monson 01057	1760 Brimfield	Hampden (20) Springfield
Montague 1 Avenue A Turners Falls 01376	1754 Sunderland	Franklin (21) Greenfield (Deerfield)
Monterey Monterey 01245	1847 Tyringham	Berkshire (26) Southern
Montgomery P.O. Box 109 Montgomery 01050	1780 Westfield/Norwich/Southampton	Hampden (4) Springfield
Mount Washington Route 3 Mount Washington 01258	1779 (Tauconnuck/Mountain Plantation)	Berkshire (29) Southern
Nahant Nahant 01908	1853 Lynn	Essex (33) Southern
Nantucket Nantucket 02554	1687 (Sherburn, 1713) (Tuckannock, 1795)	Nantucket
Natick Natick 01760	1650	Middlesex (50) Southern
Needham Needham 02192	1711 Dedham	Norfolk (2)
New Ashford New Ashford 01237	1781	Berkshire (6) Northern
New Bedford City Hall New Bedford 02740	1787 Dartmouth	Bristol (18) Southern
New Braintree New Braintree 01531	1751 Harwick/Brookfield	Worcester (29) Worcester
New Marlborough P.O. Box 64 Southfield 01259	1759	Berkshire (31) Southern
New Salem P.O. Box 46 New Salem 01355	1753	Franklin (26) Greenfield (Deerfield)
Newbury Newbury 01950	1635 (Wessacucon)	Essex (7) Southern
Newburyport City Hall Newburyport 01950	1764 Newbury	Essex (6) Southern

Town Address	Date Formed Parent Town/s (Other Names)	County Land Records District
Newton City Hall Newton 02159	1691 (Cambridge Village/New Cambridge)	Middlesex (46) Southern
Norfolk Norfolk 02056	1870 Franklin/Medway/Walpole/Wrentham	Norfolk (13)
North Adams City Hall North Adams 01247	1878 Adams	Berkshire (3)
North Andover North Andover 01845	1855 Andover	Essex (12) Northern
North Attleborough North Attleborough 02760	1887 Attleborough	Bristol (1)
North Brookfield North Brookfield 01535	1812 Brookfield	Worcester (31) Worcester
North Reading North Reading 01864	1853 Reading	Middlesex (15) Southern
Northampton City Hall Northampton 01060	1656	Hampshire (14)
Northborough Northborough 01532	1766 Westborough	Worcester (28) Worcester
Northbridge Northbridge 01588	1772 Uxbridge	Worcester (49) Worcester
Northfield Northfield 01360	1714 (Squakeag Plantation)	Franklin (7) Greenfield (Deerfield)
Norton Norton 02766	1710 Taunton	Bristol (5) Northern
Norwell P.O. Box 295, 345 Main Street Norwell 02061	1849 Scituate (South Scituate, 1888)	Plymouth (5)
Norwood Norwood 02062	1872 Dedham/Walpole	Norfolk (6)
Oak Bluffs P.O. Box 2490 Oak Bluffs 02557	1880 Edgartown (Cottage City)	Dukes (5)
Oakham Oakham 01068	1762 Rutland	Worcester (21) Worcester
Orange Orange 01364	1783 Athol/Royalston/Warwick/ Ervingshire tract	Franklin (16) Greenfield (Deerfield)
Orleans Orleans 02653	1797 Eastham	Barnstable (11)

Town Address	Date Formed Parent Town/s (Other Names)	County Land Records District
Otis Otis 01253	1773 Tryingham Equivalent (Loudon, 1810)	Berkshire (28) Middle
Oxford Oxford 01540	1693	Worcester (44) Worcester
Palmer Palmer 01069	1752 (The Elbows Plantation)	Hampden (10) Springfield
Paxton Paxton 01612	1765 Leicester/Rutland	Worcester (33) Worcester
Peabody City Hall Peabody 01960	1855 Danvers (South Danvers, 1868)	Essex (27) Southern
Pelham Route #2 Amherst 01002	1743 (New Lisburn tract)	Hampshire (11) Northampton
Pembroke Pembroke 02359	1712 Duxbury	Plymouth (14)
Pepperell Pepperell 01463	1753 Groton	Middlesex (3) Southern
Peru RFD 1 Peru Hinsdale 01235	1771 (Partridgefield, 1806)	Berkshire (15) Middle
Petersham Petersham 01366	1754 (Nichewoag Plantation)	Worcester (11) Worcester
Phillipston RFD 1 Athol Phillipston 01331	1786 Athol/Templeton (Gerry, 1814)	Worcester (5) Worcester
Pittsfield City Hall Pittsfield 01201	1761 (Pontoosuck Plant.)	Berkshire (12) Middle
Plainfield Main Street Plainfield 01070	1785 Cummington	Hampshire (1) Northampton
Plainville Plainville 02762	1905 Wrentham	Norfolk (15)
Plymouth Plymouth 02360	1620	Plymouth (23)
Plympton Plympton 02367	1707 Plymouth	Plymouth (18)
Prescott (became part of Pelham and New Salem, 1938)	1822 Pelham/New Salem	Worcester
Princeton Princeton 01541	1759 Rutland	Worcester (13) Worcester

Town Address	Date Formed Parent Town/s (Other Names)	County Land Records District
Provincetown Provincetown 02657	1727	Barnstable (15)
Quincy City Hall Quincy 02169	1792 Braintree/Dorchester	Norfolk (23)
Randolph Randolph 02368	1793 Braintree	Norfolk (22)
Raynham Raynham 02767	1731 Taunton	Bristol (7) Northern
Reading Reading 01867	1644 Lynn	Middlesex (16) Southern
Rehoboth Rehoboth 02769	1645 (as Seacunk)	Bristol (9) Northern
Revere City Hall Revere 02151	1846 Chelsea (North Chelsea)	Suffolk (1)
Richmond Route 49, Yokun Road Pittsfield 01201	1765 (Richmont)	Berkshire (16) Middle
Rochester Rochester 02770	1686 (Scippicam)	Plymouth (24)
Rockland Rockland 02370	1874 Abington	Plymouth (3)
Rockport Rockport 01969	1840 Gloucester	Essex (19) Southern
Rowe Rowe 01367	1785 (Myrefield)	Franklin (2) Greenfield (Deerfield)
Rowley Rowley 01969	1639	Essex (10) Southern
Roxbury (annexed to Boston, 1868)	1630	Suffolk
Royalston P.O. Box 111 Royalston 01368	1765 (Royalshire tract)	Worcester (1) Worcester
Russell Russell 01071	1792 Westfield/Montgomery	Hampden (3)
Rutland Rutland 01543	1714 (Naquag tract)	Worcester (22) Worcester
Salem City Hall Salem 01970	1630	Essex (28) Southern
Salisbury Salisbury 01950	1639 (Colchester)	Essex (3) Southern

Town Address	Date Formed Parent Town/s (Other Names)	County Land Records District
Sandisfield Sandisfield 01255	1762 (No. 3 Plantation)	Berkshire (32) Southern
Sandwich Sandwich 02563	1638	Barnstable (2)
Saugus Saugus 01906	1815 Lynn	Essex (30) Southern
Savoy Savoy 01256	1797	Berkshire (8) Northern
Scituate Scituate 02066	1633	Plymouth (8)
Seekonk Seekonk 02771	1812 Rehoboth	Bristol (8) Northern
Sharon Sharon 02067	1765 Stoughton (Stoughtonham)	Norfolk (17)
Sheffield Sheffield 01257	1733	Berkshire (30) Southern
Shelburne Shelburne 01370	1768 Deerfield	Franklin (12) Greenfield (Deerfield)
Sherborn Sherborn 01770	1674	Middlesex (52) Southern
Shirley Shirley 01464	1753 Groton	Middlesex (9) Southern
Shrewsbury Shrewsbury 01545	1720	Worcester (36) Worcester
Shutesbury Shutesbury 01072	1761 (Roadtown Plantation)	Franklin (25) Greenfield (Deerfield)
Somerset Somerset 02726	1790 Swansea	Bristol (13) Northern
Somerville City Hall Somerville 02143	1842 Charlestown	Middlesex (38) Southern
South Hadley South Hadley 01075	1753 Hadley	Hampshire (17) Northampton
Southampton Southampton 01073	1753 Northampton	Hampshire (15) Northampton
Southborough Southborough 01772	1727 Marlborough	Worcester (38) Worcester
Southbridge Southbridge 01550	1816 Charlton/Dudley/Sturbridge	Worcester (54) Worcester
Southwick Southwick 01077	1770 Westfield	Hampden (13) Springfield

Town Address	Date Formed Parent Town/s (Other Names)	County Land Records District
Spencer Spencer 01562	1753 Leicester	Worcester (32) Worcester
Springfield City Hall Springfield 01103	1641	Hampden (16) Springfield
Sterling Sterling 01564	1781 Lancaster	Worcester (15) Worcester
Stockbridge Stockbridge 01262	1739 (Indian Town Plantation)	Berkshire (20) Middle
Stoneham Stoneham 02180	1725 Charlestown	Middlesex (29) Southern
Stoughton Stoughton 02072	1726 Dorchester	Norfolk (19)
Stow Stow 01775	1683 (Pompositticut Plantation)	Middlesex (40) Southern
Sturbridge Sturbridge 01566	1738 (New Medfield tract)	Worcester (42) Worcester
Sudbury Sudbury 01776	1639	Middlesex (42) Southern
Sunderland Sunderland 01375	1714 (Swampfield)	Franklin (23) Greenfield (Deerfield)
Sutton Sutton 01527	1714	Worcester (47) Worcester
Swampscott Swampscott 01907	1852 Lynn	Essex (32) Southern
Swansea Swansea 02777	1667 Rehoboth (Wannamoisett)	Bristol (12) Northern
Taunton City Hall Taunton 02780	1639 (Cohannett)	Bristol (6) Northern
Templeton Templeton 01436	1762 (Narragansett No. 6 Plantation)	Worcester (6) Worcester
Tewksbury Tewksbury 01876	1734 Billerica	Middlesex (8) Northern
Tisbury Tisbury 02568	1671 (Middletowne)	Dukes (4)
Tolland S.R. Box 146 Tolland 01034	1810 Granville	Hampden (11) Springfield
Topsfield Topsfield 01983	1648 Ipswich	Essex (14) Southern

Town Address	Date Formed Parent Town/s (Other Names)	County Land Records District
Townsend Memorial Hall Main Street (Turkey Hills) P.O. Box 597 Townsend 01469	1732 Southern	Middlesex (2)
Truro Truro 02666	1709 (Pawmett tract)	Barnstable (14)
Tyngsborough Tyngsborough 01879	1789 Dunstable	Middlesex (5) Northern
Tyringham Tyringham Road Lee 01238	1762 (No. 1 Plantation)	Berkshire (27) Middle
Upton Upton 01568	1735 Hopkinton/Mendon/Sutton/Uxbridge	Worcester (50) Worcester
Uxbridge Uxbridge 01569	1727 Mendon	Worcester (58) Worcester
Wakefield Wakefield 01880	1812 Reading (South Reading)	Middlesex (17) Southern
Wales Wales 01081	1762 Brimfield (South Brimfield)	Hampden (22) Springfield
Walpole Walpole 02081	1724 Dedham	Norfolk (10)
Waltham City Hall Waltham 02154	1738 Watertown	Middlesex (45) Southern
Ware Ware 01082	1761 (Ware River Parish)	Hampshire (20) Northampton
Wareham Wareham 02571	1739 Rochester/Agawam Plantation	Plymouth (25)
Warren Warren 01083	1742 Brimfield/Brookfield/ Kingsfield (Western-1834)	Worcester (39) Worcester
Warwick Warwick 01364	1763 (Roxbury Canada Plantation)	Franklin (8) Greenfield (Deerfield)
Washington Washington 01223	1777 (Hartwood Plantation)	Berkshire (18) Middle
Watertown Watertown 02172	1630	Middlesex (35) Southern
Wayland Wayland 01778	1780 Sudbury (East Sudbury, 1835)	Middlesex (43) Southern
Webster Webster 01570	1832 Dudley/Oxford	Worcester (56) Worcester

Town Address	Date Formed Parent Town/s (Other Names)	County Land Records District
Wellesley Wellesley 02181	1881 Needham	Norfolk (1)
Wellfleet Wellfleet 02667	1763 Eastham	Barnstable (13)
Wendell Star Route 1 Wendell Depot 01380	1781 Shutesbury/Ervingshire	Franklin (22) Greenfield (Deerfield)
Wenham Wenham 01984	1643	Essex (23) Southern
West Boylston Public Works Building West Boylston 01583	1808 Boylston/Holden/Sterling	Worcester (24) Worcester
West Bridgewater West Bridgewater 02379	1822 Bridgewater	Plymouth (10)
West Brookfield West Brookfield 01585	1848 Brookfield	Worcester (30) Worcester
West Newbury West Newbury 01985	1819 Newbury (Parsons)	Essex (5) Southern
West Springfield West Springfield 01089	1774 Springfield	Hampden (7) Springfield
West Stockbridge West Stockbridge 01266	1774 Stockbridge	Berkshire (19) Southern
West Tisbury West Tisbury 02575	1892 Tisbury	Dukes (3)
Westborough Westborough 01581	1717 Marlborough	Worcester (37) Worcester
Westfield City Hall Westfield 01085	1669 Springfield	Hampden (5) Springfield
Westford Westford 01886	1729 Chelmsford	Middlesex (11) Northern
Westhampton Westhampton 01027	1778 Northampton	Hampshire (13) Northampton
Westminster Westminster 01473	1759 (Narragansett No. 2)	Worcester (8) Northern
Weston Weston 02193	1713 Watertown	Middlesex (44) Southern
Westport Westport 02790	1787 Dartmouth	Bristol (16) Southern
Westwood Westwood 02090	1897 Dedham	Norfolk (4)

Town Address	Date Formed Parent Town/s (Other Names)	County Land Records District
Weymouth Weymouth 02188	1635 (Wessaguscus)	Norfolk (26)
Whately Whately 01093	1771 Hatfield	Franklin (20) Greenfield (Deerfield)
Whitman Whitman 02188	1875 Abington/E. Bridgewater (South Abington)	Plymouth (11)
Wilbraham Wilbraham 01095	1763 Springfield	Hampden (18) Springfield
Williamsburg Williamsburg 01096	1771 Hatfield	Hampshire (7) Northampton
Williamstown Williamstown 01267	1765 (as West Hoosuck Plantation)	Berkshire (1) Northern
Wilmington Wilmington 01887	1730 Reading/Woburn	Middlesex (14) Northern
Winchendon Winchendon 01475	1764 (Ipswich Canada Plantation)	Worcester (2) Worcester
Winchester Winchester 01890	1850 Medford/Woburn/W. Cambridge	Middlesex (30) Southern
Windsor Windsor 01270	1771 (Gageborough)	Berkshire (11) Northern
Winthrop Winthrop 02152	1846 Chelsea (N. Chelsea)	Suffolk (2)
Woburn City Hall Woburn 01801	1642 (Charlestowne Village)	Middlesex (28) Southern
Worcester City Hall Worcester 01608	1684 (Quansigamond Plantation)	Worcester (35) Worcester
Worthington Worthington 01098	1768 (No. 3 Plantation)	Hampshire (5)
Wrentham Wrentham 02093	1673 (Wollonopaug)	Norfolk (14)
Yarmouth South Yarmouth 02664	1639 (Mattacheeset)	Barnstable (6)

MICHIGAN

Carol L. Maki

Water dominated Michigan's early history. The Great Lakes, the numerous inland lakes, and the extensive arrangement of rivers were means of transportation, sources of food supply, determinants of the climate, battlegrounds, the impetus for industry, and a strong force in the settlement patterns. Immigration was accelerated by the opening of the Erie Canal in 1825. Diverse soils and vast mineral deposits added their influence to the development of the area. Proximity to Canada also played a large part in the early exploration of the state.

The first French explorers arrived in the area between 1618 and 1622 and found approximately 15,000 Native Americans. Principally, the nations of the Chippewa or Ojibway, Potawatomi, Miami, Ottawa, and Huron or Wyandot had held claim to the land for generations.

The first European explorer thought to have actually visited the area that is now Michigan was Etienne Brule, sent from Canada by Samuel de Champlain, late in 1618 or early the following year. Another French-Canadian, Jean Nicolet, ventured into the area in 1634. The rationalization for French exploration of the land included adventure, visions of wealth and empire, and the determination of their missionaries. Catholic missions were established at Sault Ste. Marie in 1668 and at St. Ignace in 1671. French forts were built in the late seventeenth century. The French-Canadian families, brought by the fur trading industry and living in or near the forts, raised large families and enough crops for their own use.

The earliest permanent settlement, however, was made at Detroit in 1701, established by Antoine de la Mothe Cadillac. He arrived with a small group of followers to develop trade on the Great Lakes and defend the (then French) territory from the English.

During the eighteenth century, Michigan was involved in international wars, as the French, the English, and the American colonies fought for supremacy in the area, and many of the native tribes were involved in these battles. The British flag flew over Michigan from 1760 to 1796, although the United States had actually been ceded the area in 1783. Michigan was defined, although not named, in the Northwest Ordinance of 1787. From 1796 to 1800, Michigan was governed under the auspices of Northwest Territory. At that time the principal population settlements were at Detroit and Mackinac Island, and most inhabitants were of French ancestry. English and Scottish nationalities were most prevalent in the merchant class. Along the Raisin River, south of Detroit, was a community of French farmers. From 1800 to 1803, Michigan was considered both Indiana Territory and Northwest Territory, but from 1803 to 1805 it was totally included in Indiana Territory. On 11 January 1805, Michigan Territory was established. The War of 1812 again put Michigan in British hands, but it returned to the United States in 1813.

Michigan then became a lumbering and mining state. The new industries brought new people and new settlement. The first land office opened in 1818, but the difficulty of traveling to the territory hindered extensive migration. It was considered more dangerous to attempt to navigate Lake Erie than the Atlantic Ocean.

Federally funded lighthouses and harbor improvements, steam navigation on the Great Lakes, and the completion of the Erie Canal were instrumental in increasing the flow of Americans to Michigan. New Englanders and descendants of New Englanders, having previously migrated to New York, began moving to the area. New roads within the state and others connecting to adjacent states made Michigan even more accessible. For the most part, settlers came from New York, Ohio, and Indiana. They were not the very rich or the very poor and were typically farmers, generally young, and usually married.

There were, in addition to Yankees, several communities of settlers with German or Irish ancestry, many Quakers, and a few Southerners. The number of foreign-born immigrants was small before statehood.

In 1835 a state government was created, but the Toledo War delayed the actual statehood process. The "war" involved a border dispute between Michigan and Ohio which led to mobilization of armed men. There were no fatalities, and Ohio received the disputed land, with Michigan receiving land that is now the Upper Peninsula. Although the state government functioned during that period, Congress officially declared Michigan a state on 26 January 1837.

Lumber, copper, and iron-ore industries became a major attraction for immigrants between the 1840s and 1880s, augmenting the population with Irish, Finns, Norwegians, Swedes, Italians, and Poles. A group of religious refugees from Holland brought their skilled crafts and farming experience.

By the beginning of the twentieth century, when the iron had been heavily worked and the forests cut, the automobile industry generated a new commodity for Michigan's economy, bringing eastern Europeans and blacks from the South. The Detroit area, the site of Cadillac's settlement, remains the most densely populated in the state.

Vital Records

Marriages, recorded in the county where they occurred, are the earliest public vital records in Michigan since a marriage registration law was enacted in 1805. A later law required marriages to be collected by the county clerk after 1 April 1867 and forwarded to the secretary of state. Birth and death records begin in January 1867, although registration of all vital records was not totally enforced. A 1905 law was much more effective. Divorce records begin in 1897.

Photocopies of these registrations can be ordered from the Michigan Department of Public Health, Office of the State Registrar and Center for Health Statistics, P.O. Box 30035, Lansing, Michigan 48909. Birth records in Michigan are available only to the individual to whom the record pertains, the parent(s) named on the record, any heir, legal guardian, or any legal representative of an eligible person. Relationship to the person named on the birth record, and date and place of death for the person named on the birth record, must be supplied. Photocopies of death, marriage, and divorce records are available to any individual or agency upon written application and payment of the fee.

Official forms are required for either a certified copy of any vital record or genealogical research copy of a marriage, death, or divorce record. Fees for either type of copy are the following: first record request, including three year search—$10; duplicates of certified copies—$3; additional genealogical research requests, submitted at the same time in the same envelope—$6 each; and additional years searched per record request—$3 per year.

Marriages registered before mandatory recording (1867) in some counties (see County Resources) may be ordered from the appropriate county clerk. Charges for searches and/or copies will vary from county to county but must not exceed the state fees. Some township clerks also recorded births and deaths.

The Michigan Death Record Project, a joint endeavor between the Michigan Department of Public Health and the Michigan Genealogical Council, is in a developmental stage. The resulting index of some 500,000 early death registrations will include name of the deceased, book number, date of death, and county of death. Project managers hope to release the index to the public in increments, very likely in a microform format.

Microfilm copies of indexes to specific groups of Michigan vital records are at the Library of Michigan, State Archives of Michigan, Burton Historical Collection of the Detroit Public Library, and the Allen County Public Library in Fort Wayne, Indiana (see Archives, Libraries, and Societies for location of all four repositories):

Michigan. State Department of Health. *Index of Death Records, 1867–1914.* 13 reels.

Michigan. State Department of Health. *Index to Marriage Records, 1872–1921.* 21 reels.

The government archive records at the Burton Historical Collection include the forms for Wayne County Marriage Returns. Completed by a minister or civil authority, the forms were sent to the county clerk between 1818–88, although most are dated 1860–77. The forms include the date of the marriage and names of the bride and groom with their color, residence, age, place of birth, and occupation.

Census Records

Federal

Population Schedules.

- Indexed—1820 (six counties and Detroit), 1830, 1840, 1850, 1860
- Soundex—1880, 1900, 1910, 1920
- Unindexed—1870 (some counties have individually printed indexes, statewide index in progress)

Industry and Agriculture Schedules.

- 1850, 1860, 1870, 1880

Mortality Schedules.

- 1850, 1860, 1870, 1880

Union Veterans Schedules.

- 1890

A complete set of federal population and supplemental schedules are available on microfilm at the State Archives of Michigan along with available AISI indexes. Other repositories in the state have population schedules, Soundex, and indexes, while the Burton Historical Collection in Detroit and the Allen County Public Library in Fort Wayne, Indiana, hold those for Michigan and numerous other states as well.

Territorial and State

Numerous state and territorial censuses were taken in Michigan, although few are extant. In 1710 the French compiled the first Michigan census. This, plus others through the year 1792, were basically of the Detroit area. Fort St. Joseph had a census taken in 1780 (*Michigan Pioneer and Historical Collections,* Vol. 10, 1908, pages 406–07), as did Wayne County in 1796, which was printed in *National Genealogical Society Quarterly* 64 (1981): 185–94. A tax list of Wayne County in 1802 and a list of residents of Detroit in 1805 may be considered early enumerations of Michigan population. Sources discussing the state censuses more comprehensively include Donna Valley Russell, *Michigan Censuses 1710–1830 Under the French, British, and Americans* (Detroit, Mich.: Detroit Society for Genealogical Research, 1982), and "State Censuses of Michigan: A Tragedy of Lost Treasures," *Family Trails* 6 (Summer–Fall, 1978).

Microfilm copies of the state census schedules for 1845, 1854, 1864, 1874, 1884, and 1894 are held by the State Archives of Michigan. Some of these are partial and/or incomplete. The Library of Michigan in Lansing and the Allen County Public Library in Fort Wayne, Indiana, also hold Michigan state census records. Prior to 1884 the state census names only the head of the household. The 1884 census, however, will identify those in each household that have married within the census year, giving the month of and the location of the marriage. There are also mortality schedules with the 1884 and 1894 state censuses. A special Civil War Veteran Census was taken by the state in 1888; the manuscript of this census is at the state archives. See State Archives Circular No. 9, *State Census Records in the State Archives,* available from the archives.

McGinnis' publication (see Background Sources below) has a county by county listing of the state and territorial censuses that do exist. A list and location of schedules is also available from Bentley Historical Library, University of Michigan (see Archives, Libraries, and Societies).

Background Sources

An abundance of county histories and the many volumes of *Michigan Pioneer and Historical Collections* are suggested as sources of early local history. The latter, frequently listed as *Michigan Historical Collections,* was published between 1877 and 1929 by the Pioneer Society of the State of Michigan. Included in the forty volumes are proceedings of the society, biographical sketches, obituaries, genealogies, and other historical material. A finding aid to the *Collections* was originally developed by the WPA: Michigan Historical Society, *Classified Finding List of the Collections of the Michigan Pioneer and Historical Society* (Detroit, Mich.: Wayne State University Press, 1952).

Two sources for genealogical information and research in the state of Michigan are:

Callard, Carol, ed. *Sourcebook of the Michigan Census, County Histories and Vital Records.* Lansing, Mich.: Library of Michigan, 1987.

McGinnis, Carol. *Michigan Genealogy Sources and Resources* Baltimore, Md.: Genealogical Publishing Co., 1987.

The above two sources provide information on the availability of vital and government records. McGinnis's has sections on genealogical collections and historical and genealogical societies, arranged by county.

Maps

A John Farmer 1855 Wayne County plat map was the first Michigan map to show land ownership. H. F. Wallings' 1873 Atlas for the entire state was reprinted in 1977 by The Bookmark, in Knightstown, Indiana. Many county maps indicating ownership were published as part of the 1876 centennial. Extensive map collections are available at the Library of Michigan and the Burton Historical Collection.

Consult Robert W. Karrow, *Checklist of Printed Maps of the Middle West to 1900* (Chicago, Ill.: Newberry Library, n.d.). This fourteen-volume set lists all known pre-1900 plat maps and plat books for eleven states, including Michigan.

The earliest Sanborn map (see page 4) for Michigan is the year 1868 for the community of Lansing.

Land Records

Public-Domain State

Private land claims based on grants made prior to U.S. sovereignty are found for Mackinac and Detroit. These records are in the National Archives (see page 5). Most were "ribbon farms," very narrow but very long to ensure river frontage. Consult Silas Farmer, *History of Detroit and Wayne County and Early Michigan* (Detroit, Mich.: Silas Farmer and Co., 1890), or D. B. Reynolds, *Early Land Claims in Michigan* (Lansing, Mich.: Michigan Department of Conservation, 1940), for information on private land claims.

The first public-domain land was purchased by settlers in Michigan in 1818. The Ordinance of 1785 had provided the methods for dividing and selling the recently ceded regions. The land was first surveyed into six-mile-square townships, each containing thirty-six sections. The townships were surveyed from an east-west line called a "base line" and a north-south line called a "principal meridian." These public-domain lands were offered at the first land office, in Detroit, for $2 per acre, with a minimum purchase required. "Installment plans" were available. In 1820 the cost per acre was lowered to $1.25, with "cash only" and a minimum purchase of eighty acres. Land was usually paid for with silver, gold, bank notes, or drafts. A "patent," usually signed by a clerk, for the U.S. president, would be sent to the landowner, giving title to the previously federal property. A "pre-emption law" in 1841 gave "squatters" the right to purchase 160 acres at a minimum price.

Microfilm copies of the federal land patent records are at the Library of Michigan. These provide information on the first ownership of all federal lands in the state. The Office of the Great Seal, Department of State, 717 West Allegan, Lansing, Michigan 48918, has the original state land patent records. It is necessary to have an exact legal description of the property to utilize either of these valuable sources.

The State Archives of Michigan has numerous records of land transactions. They include the following sources of information (not inclusive) under various departments: tract books of swamp lands purchases, original maps prepared by federal surveyors that show cultural and physical features as they existed between about 1815 and 1855, abstracts of land grants ca. 1837–1900, surveys of private claims as early as 1807, and land tract books from 1818–1962. See Circular No. 2, *Land Records,* published by the State Archives of Michigan, for more complete information.

Subsequent land transactions, no longer under federal control, are recorded in the appropriate county register of deed's office. Deeds for southeastern Michigan's "Toledo Strip," encompassing portions of Monroe, Lenawee, and Hillsdale counties, may have been recorded in Ohio and Michigan.

The State Archives of Michigan indicates that a long-range goal of publishing "First Land Owners" volumes for each of the counties has been undertaken by either the Michigan Genealogy Council or Col. Paul Peck. To date, about thirteen have been completed.

Probate Records

Probate records are the responsibility of the probate court office or the office of the probate judge in each county. There is no state index to these records, but see County Resources for earliest records available. Some probate court records, estate case files in particular, have been deposited at the state archives or at a regional depository. Consult State Archives Circular No. 6, *Probate Court Records,* for a listing of counties and dates of these original and microfilmed files.

Court Records

County circuit court records are kept by the county clerk or the circuit court clerk in the appropriate county office. There are no state indexes to these records.

National Archives-Great Lakes Region (see page 8) holds federal district court records as follows: Eastern District (Flint), 1895–1962; Bay City, 1894–1962; Detroit, 1837–1962; Western District (Grand Rapids), 1863–1962; and Marquette, 1878–1962. An inventory of holdings is available at the archives in Chicago. Documentation of shipwrecks on the Great Lakes, filed in the admiralty case files, are included in these records.

Tax Records

Property tax records at the county level usually date back to the first land records. Either the county treasurer or the register of deeds will be the custodian of these records.

Numerous early tax assessment and general tax rolls are available at the State Archives of Michigan. Organized by county, the records include the name of the owner or occupant of the property, legal description and number of acres, value of land and personal estate, and amount of tax levied. There are tax rolls for some counties for the late 1830s, but most are for the last half of the nineteenth century. A complete list of these extensive rolls can be obtained from the State Archives Circular No. 1, *Tax/Assessment Rolls at the State Archives.* This circular also lists those tax rolls kept at the archives regional depositories (see Archives, Libraries, and Societies). Because of the complicated nature of tax records, in person research at the archives is encouraged.

National Archives-Great Lakes Region in Chicago (see page 8) holds numerous federal personal property and corporate tax assessment lists for the state of Michigan.

Cemetery Records

The Library of Michigan in Lansing and the Burton Historical Collection have over 1,000 books of transcribed or published tombstone readings from Michigan cemeteries. To locate a cemetery in the state, consult the *Michigan Cemetery Compendium* (Spring Arbor, Mich.: HAR-AL, 1979). It lists most cemeteries in Michigan.

Church Records

The earliest religious denomination in Michigan was the Roman Catholic church, established through a mission in 1668 at Sault Ste. Marie. Ste. Anne's, in Detroit, has parish records beginning in 1703. The Moravians, the first Protestant group in Michigan, assembled in Mount Clemens in the late 1770s. They were followed by the Congregationalists in 1800 and the first Michigan Methodist minister in 1803.

Michigan Historical Collections in Ann Arbor holds large collections from the Presbyterian church and the Protestant Episcopal church, in addition to other denominations. Dutch Reformed church records are at Calvin College and Seminary Library in Grand Rapids; Finnish church records are deposited at the Finnish-American Historical Archives at Suomi College in Hancock. The Upjohn Library at Kalamazoo College in Kalamazoo has a large collection of Baptist archive material.

Many early Detroit churches have their records deposited at the Burton Historical Collection—Detroit Public Library. The records for the Central Methodist Church and St. Paul's Cathedral begin in 1820. The St. Joseph, Michigan Catholic Mission records of 1720–72 are at this repository.

The Michigan Historical Records Survey, WPA, completed an *Inventory of the Church Archives of Michigan*, and many of the church records from this inventory were published from 1936 through 1942. Several unpublished inventories are held by the Burton Historical Collection—Detroit Public Library.

Military Records

The State Archives of Michigan is the repository for military records in the state. Mail inquiries are answered. The Descriptive Rolls of Michigan Units, 1838–1919, are available for any individual serving in a Michigan unit during that time period. Their files also include records of fraternal organizations for veterans of the Civil War and the Spanish-American War. Muster rolls of these organizations include names of members and their military history. A census of Civil War veterans taken in 1888 includes county, name of soldier, rank, military unit, and post office address. The state archives has extensive information on the Veterans' Facility, initially called the Soldier and Sailors' Home. It was established for Civil War veterans, but now serves veterans of all wars in which the United States has been involved. Records, many of which are indexed, span a period of 1885–1986. Individuals in those records are inhabitants of the facility; wives, widows, and mothers of veterans; and ex-nurses. The case files may include complete application forms with military and family information.

The State Archives of Michigan has no pension records for Civil War veterans (see National Archives holdings, page 7). They do have, however, a file of grave registrations gathered by the Civil War Centennial Observance Commission. The forms, filed by county and by name of soldier, include name, enlistment and service records, place and date of birth and death, name and location of cemetery, and additional remarks. They also have Muster Rolls of the Grand Army of the Republic Posts in Michigan. The archives has portraits of Civil War Soldiers, indexed by unit and by surname.

In the state archives collection, classified as Civil War Manuscripts, certificates, diaries, discharges, journals, letters, and miscellaneous documents can be found. The following published finding aids can be obtained from the state archives for their military collections: Archival #1—*Records of the Michigan Military Establishment, 1838–1941;* Archival #15—*Records of the Grand Army of the Republic, Michigan Department;* Archival #17—*Records of the Michigan Veteran's Facility;* Circular No. 20, *Civil War Manuscripts.*

The Burton Historical Collection holds extensive records for Civil War soldiers, but they are not cross indexed. One group of their records is for U.S. General Hospital (1864–65), which includes a register of sick and wounded soldiers taken to Harper, St. Mary's, and the Post Hospital in Detroit.

George H. Brown, as Adjutant General, published *Record of Service of Michigan Volunteers in the Civil War, 1861–1865,* often referred to as *Michigan Soldiers and Sailors* (Kalamazoo, Mich.: Ihling Brothers and Everard, 1903–15). This forty-six volume set includes an alphabetical index. An index compiled by Colman C. Vaughn lists Michigan individuals who served in the Civil War: *Alphabetical General Index to Public Library Sets of 85,271 Names of Michigan Soldiers and Sailors Individual Records* (Lansing, Mich.: Wynkoop, Hallenbeck, Crawford, Co., 1915).

The state archives also has unpublished indexes for the Spanish-American War and World War I.

Periodicals, Newspapers, and Manuscript Collections

Periodicals

The *Detroit Society for Genealogical Research Magazine,* published by the society, with a mailing address at the Burton Historical Collection of the Detroit Public Library, has been published since 1937. It is not limited to Detroit but also publishes family histories and source material for the entire state, as well as states or areas from which Michigan residents came: New York, New England, Pennsylvania, and Canada, particularly Ontario and Quebec.

Also see:

Quigley, Maud. *Index to Michigan Research Found in Genealogical Periodicals.* Grand Rapids, Mich.: Western Michigan Genealogical Society, 1979.

Michigan History. Published bimonthly by the Bureau of History, Michigan Department of State, this contains state history articles, book reviews, and information pertinent to historical research.

Newspapers

Michigan's first newspaper, *The Michigan Essay or Impartial Observer,* was published in Detroit on 31 August 1809 for one single edition. Continuous newspaper publishing began in July of 1817 with the *Detroit Gazette.* The most important articles in this English-language publication were also printed in French on the last page. The Library of Michigan has an extensive collection of microfilmed Michigan newspapers, which are available for use at the library or through interlibrary loan to other Michigan libraries. The Michigan Historical Collections in Ann Arbor and the Detroit Public Library also have large Michigan newspaper collections. Following are two references that may be helpful in locating newspapers:

Brown, Elizabeth Reed. *A Union List of Newspapers Published in Michigan Based on the Principal Newspaper Collections in the State with Notes Concerning Papers Not Located.* Ann Arbor, Mich.: University of Michigan, Department of Library Science, 1954.

Michigan Newspapers on Microfilm, With a Description of the Michigan Newspapers on Microfilm Project. 4th ed. Lansing, Mich.: Michigan Bureau of Library Services, 1973.

Manuscripts

Included in the genealogical and historical collections of the University Archives and Historical Collections of Michigan State University, Main Library EG13, East Lansing, Michigan 48824-1048, are numerous original papers, diaries, and manuscripts. Significant in the latter category are the John Harvey Kellogg papers, the REO Motor Company records, the Land Grant Research Collection, and the Hackley and Hume papers, business records and personal papers associated with the lumber industry.

The Burton Historical Collection has over twelve million items in its manuscript archives. Bernice Cox Sprenger's *Guide to the Manuscripts in the Burton Historical Collection, Detroit Public Library* (Detroit, Mich.: Burton Historical Collection, 1985) details these personal papers and records of churches, businesses, and organizations. Examples of genealogically important items listed in this collection include the Charles Kanter Papers' record book of an early Detroit German-American bank; the book indicates the German birthplaces of depositors. The papers of the Children's Aid Society for 1860–1942 could be an important resource for tracing a Detroit ancestry, especially since the organization functioned as an orphan home and an adoption agency. Also at this library is the Register of Prisoners for the House of Corrections (Detroit); the Register (1861–1983), indexed, gives the place of birth of each prisoner. See also Draper Manuscripts in Wisconsin—Manuscripts.

Archives, Libraries, and Societies

State Archives of Michigan
717 West Allegan Street
Lansing, MI 48918

Original material generated by government offices at the state and/or local level, including census records, tax assessment rolls, military records, and photographs are among the extensive holdings. They also have some naturalization files, correctional facility records, school records, and depression era agency files. Information circulars on many topics are distributed by the archives. The circulars act as finding aids to their extensive collection. Some of these are described in the various sections of this chapter.

Library of Michigan
Michigan Library and Historical Center
717 Allegan Street
Lansing, MI 48909

Holdings here include an extensive genealogical and historical collection including books, microforms, manuscripts, newspapers, surname index, Centennial and Sesquicentennial Certificate applications, and diaries. Records are housed in a new building with card catalog on 100 computer terminals. Limited reference service to mail requests.

Burton Historical Collection
Detroit Public Library
5201 Woodward Avenue
Detroit, MI 48202

This is the largest collection in Michigan. It includes diverse and extensive holdings of original, printed, and micrographic historical and genealogical material. The emphasis of the collection is on Detroit and Michigan beginning with the seventeenth century. Refer to Joseph Oldenburg's *A Genealogical Guide to the Burton Historical Collection—Detroit Public Library* (Salt Lake City, Utah: Ancestry, 1988).

Allen County Public Library
Reynolds Historical Genealogy Collection
P.O. Box 2270
900 Webster Street
Fort Wayne, IN 46801

As a major repository for the midwest as well as other areas of the country, the collection includes significant Michigan source material (see Indiana—Archives, Libraries, and Societies) as described in sections of this chapter.

Michigan Historical Collections
Bentley Historical Library
University of Michigan
1150 Beal Avenue
Ann Arbor, MI 48109-2113

The focus for genealogical work in this collection is original source materials for Michigan history and church records for almost all Protestant denominations, including discontinued churches.

Regional Depository Archives

According to LeRoy Barnett, Reference Archivist at the State Archives of Michigan, it is imperative that genealogical research in Michigan include the regional repositories. Each facility includes many of the following in their collections: Michigan military records, manuscripts and diaries, microfilmed newspapers, county and local history books, family genealogies, cemetery records, DAR records, maps and atlases, church records, city directories, federal and state census records, and assessment and tax rolls. Contact the individual library for hours; limited replies are given to written queries.

Clarke Historical Library
Central Michigan University
Mt. Pleasant, MI 48859
Phone number (517) 774-3352

Resources of particular interest to genealogists in this repository include records of Native Americans in Michigan, extensive material on Isabella County, and the James Jesse Strang Mormon Collection. (Strang, a follower of Joseph Smith, expelled from the church by Brigham Young, formed the Strangite sect in Wisconsin and Michigan.)

Archives and Regional History Collections
Western Michigan University
Kalamazoo, MI 49008
Phone number (616) 387-3990

This collection includes township and county records from Allegan, Barry, Berrien, Branch, Cass, Calhoun, St. Joseph, Kalamazoo, Kent, Muskegon, Ottawa, and Van Buren counties and 8,000 catalogued photographs.

Archives and Historical Collections
Michigan Technological University
1400 Townsend Drive
Houghton, MI 49931
Phone number (906) 487-2505

This depository is responsible for Gogebic, Ontonagon, Houghton, Keweenaw, Baraga, and Iron counties; it currently holds vital records for Houghton and Keweenaw counties, but has inventories for and will be acquiring records of the other counties. Special collections include those of the Michigan Technological University and the Copper County Historical Collection, the latter containing records of the mining companies and benevolent societies.

Michigan Room, Grand Rapids Public Library
60 Library Plaza
Grand Rapids, MI 49503
Phone number (616) 456-3640

This library has local history books, microforms, newspapers, cemetery records, manuscripts, diaries, and considerable material on Kent County history and people.

Other Libraries

There are literally dozens of local libraries with historical and/or genealogical collections and genealogical societies in the state (see McGinnis—Background Sources). The scope of the material in the majority of the libraries is very impressive, and includes books, microforms, original local manuscripts, church and cemetery records, maps, photographs, family genealogies, newspapers, diaries, and oral histories.

Special Focus Categories

Naturalization

Beginning in the 1840s and burgeoning near the end of the century, immigrants from northern and eastern Europe journeyed to Michigan for employment opportunities and religious freedom. Naturalization records for Michigan are organized by county, some with indexes. Declarations of intentions are usually arranged by surname while other documents for the citizenship process are chronological. Records for sixteen of Michigan's counties are cataloged by the State Archives of Michigan: Cass, Genesee, Gladwin, Hillsdale, Ingham, Ionia, Kalamazoo, Kent, Keweenaw, Luce, Marquette, Monroe, Montcalm, Muskegon, Saginaw, and Wayne.

Black American

Among the 500 residents in Detroit in 1796, both Native American and black slaves are listed along with some free blacks. During the 1840s and 1850s, several religious denominations in Michigan crusaded against slavery, and the "Underground Railroad" assistance to fleeing slaves included a well-established course through the state to Canada. Some blacks chose to settle in Michigan. In February of 1855 the state legislature passed a "personal liberty law" to block the recovery of escaped slaves who were in Michigan. Southerners who attempted to retrieve their slaves in Michigan were met with delay and violence.

In the twentieth century, large numbers of blacks, displaced by agri-business in the south, gravitated to Detroit for employment opportunities in the automotive industry.

For additional information and background, see black family manuscripts at the Burton Historical Collection: Malcolm Dade (1831–1976), Northcross Family (1899–1973), and the Pelham Family (1851–1948).

Also see:

Banner, Melvin E. *The Black Pioneer in Michigan.* Midland, Mich.: Pendall Publishing Co., 1973.

Larrie, Reginald. *Black Experiences in Michigan History.* Lansing, Mich.: Michigan History Division, Michigan Department of State, 1975.

State Archives of Michigan. Circular No. 29, *African-Americans.* Lansing, Mich.

Native American

Michigan had a Native American population of 15,000 to 20,000 when the first French explorers entered the state in the 1600s. Early in 1825 President Monroe proposed the removal of the indigenous population from Michigan. In August of that year the first treaty was signed with the Sioux, Winnebago, and Chippewa tribes.

In the early 1800s the Miami nation moved outside the present boundaries of Michigan. The Huron were first given a southeastern Michigan tract of land and then moved to 4,996 acres along the Huron River. The tribe eventually left Michigan when an 1842 treaty surrendered all their property rights in that state.

The Potawatomi Indian nation ceded its final reservations in Michigan to the United States by the Treaty of Chicago in 1833, agreeing to move to assigned lands west of the Mississippi. Beginning in 1838 members of the tribe started westward, first to Missouri, then to Iowa, and finally to Kansas. However, significant numbers of the tribe did not leave Michigan and eluded the government agents or escaped during the journey to return to Michigan.

The State Archives of Michigan catalogs a variety of documents relating to Native Americans in the state. A finding aid in their reading room details the holdings and how to use them.

The Burton Historical Collection has the 1908 census of the Chippewa Indians of Michigan, known as the Durant Roll. It names "all persons and their descendants who were on the roll of the Ottawa and Chippewa Tribe in 1870 and living on March 4, 1907." The census lists each name, relationship to the head of the family, age, sex, band, and place of residence.

The National Archives-Great Lakes Region (see page 8) has sizable holdings of the Bureau of Indian Affairs, including census and annuity rolls for Michigan beginning in the 1880s. Their collection includes financial records for individual Indians at the Mackinac Agency and correspondence from the Mount Pleasant Indian School.

National Archives Record Group 75, Records of the Bureau of Indian Affairs, includes correspondence, documents relating to negotiation of treaties, letter books, and special files. Records of the Superintendent of Indian Affairs for Michigan, 1814–51, are on seventy-one reels of microfilm designated as M1 in Record Group 75. Record Group 11, U.S. Government, General Records, M668, includes the actual ratified Indian treaties for the years 1722 through 1869.

For additional information, see A. Felch's "The Indians of Michigan and the Cession of Their Lands to the United States by Treaties," in *Michigan Pioneer and Historical Collections* 16 (1894–95): 274–97.

Other Ethnic Groups

The French were the first Europeans to inhabit present-day Michigan. Christian Denissen's *Genealogy of French Families of the Detroit River Region, 1701–1911*, 2 vols., edited by Harold F. Powell (Detroit, Mich.: Detroit Society for Genealogical Research, 1976), was revised in 1987 to include families through 1937. The Burton Historical Collection holds typed transcriptions of twenty-two volumes of French Notarial Records for Montreal (1682–1822) and four volumes of the Detroit Notarial Records (1737–95). Included are business contracts, indentures, apprentice and servant contracts, and fur trade transactions. Michigan French-Canadian descendants definitely should attempt to utilize the extensive available Canadian provincial and religious records in all repositories.

Membership in the French-Canadian Heritage Society of Michigan (Library of Michigan, 735 East Michigan Avenue, Lansing, Michigan 48913) includes five newsletters per year and the quarterly journal, *Michigan's Habitant Heritage.*

Michigan attracted a large number of immigrants. Entries for collections on various groups can be found in all of the repositories' holdings. One example is in Michigan Historical Collections in Ann Arbor, which holds letters sent by Swedish immigrants to entice others to come, as well as Swedish-language newspapers published in Michigan. *Ethnic Groups in Detroit* (Wayne State University, Department of Sociology and Anthropology, 1951) was published as part of the city's 250th anniversary. Included is a discussion of forty-three ethnic groups.

County Resources

Records at the county level are the responsibility of different offices—office of the county clerk: birth, death, and marriage; register of deeds: land records; office of the probate judge: probate files; and circuit court office or office of the county clerk: circuit court records.

Callard's *Sourcebook* (see Background Sources) provides a bibliography for each of the eighty-three Michigan counties. It is available for $6 from the Department of Management and Budget, Office Services Division Publications, State Secondary Complex, 7481 Crowner Drive, P.O. Box 30026, Lansing, Michigan 48909.

For some counties on the chart there are two years listed for "Date Formed." The first is the year the county was created, the second is the year it was fully organized if it differs from the creation year. Under the heading "Parent County/ies," the name/s listed may be the county or counties from which the respective county was formed, or it may be names by which the county was originally known. "Unorganized" denotes that it was formed from non-county lands. A county name in parentheses is the county to which the unorganized land may have been attached at that time. Counties listed with an asterisk (*) are those in which you may also find records for the respective county. It may have been "attached" to that county for some period of time.

The date listed for each category of record is the earliest record known to exist in that county. It does not indicate that there are numerous records for that year and certainly does not indicate that all such events that year were actually registered.

In addition to the sources listed on page 11, Callard (1987) and McGinnis (1987), described in Background Sources, were used for the following guide to county information. Where disagreement exists, an attempt has been made to verify the date with either the county or the state archives.

Drawn by William Dollarhide

Map	County Address	Date Formed Parent County/ies	Birth Marriage Death	Land Probate Court
	Aischum	1840 (renamed Lake, 1843) Mackinac *Ottawa		
F7	Alcona 106 5th Street Harrisville 48740	1840 (1869) (as Negwegon; renamed, 1843) unorganized land *Mackinac/*Cheboygan/*Aplena/*Iosco	1869 1869 1869	1869 1869 1872
C4	Alger 101 Court Street Munising 49862	1885 Schoolcraft	1884 1887 1884	1884 1889 1885
J5	Allegan 113 Chestnut Street Allegan 49010	1831 (1835) Barry/unorganized land	1867 1850 1867	1835 1839 1837
E7	Alpena 720 Chisholm Street Alpena 49707	1840 (1857) (as Anamickee; renamed, 1843) Mackinac *Cheboygan	1870 1871 1871	1858 1858 1871
	Anamickee	1840 (renamed Alpena, 1843) Mackinac/unorganized land		
E5	Antrim 208 E. Cayuga Street Bellaire 49615	1840 (1863) (as Meegisee; renamed, 1843) Mackinac *Grand Traverse	1867 1867 1867	1867 1863 1867
G7	Arenac Standish 48658 *Arenac was abolished in 1857 and re-created 1883 from Bay County.*	1831 (1883) unorganized land *Saginaw	1883 1883 1883	1882 1883 1883
B2	Baraga L'Anse 49946	1875 Houghton	1875 1875 1875	1875 1876 1875
J5	Barry Hastings 49058	1829 (1839) unorganized land *St. Joseph/*Kalamazoo	1867 1839 1867	1834 1862 1850
G7	Bay 515 Center Avenue Bay City 48706	1857 Midland/Saginaw/Arenac	1868 1857 1867	1835? 1857 1883
F4	Benzie Beulah 49617	1863 (1869) Leelanau *Grand Traverse	1868 1857 1868	1854 1870 1869
K4	Berrien 811 Port Street St. Joseph 49085	1829 (1831) unorganized land *Cass	1867 1831 1867	1831 1834 1833
	Bleeker	1861 (renamed Menominee, 1863) unorganized land		
K6	Branch 31 Division Street Coldwater 49036	1829 (1833) unorganized land *St. Joseph	1867 1833 1867	1833 1833 1850
	Brown *Became part of Wisconsin Territory in 1836; now in Wisconsin.*	1818 unorganized land		

Map	County Address	Date Formed Parent County/ies	Birth Marriage Death	Land Probate Court
J6	Calhoun 315 W. Green Street Marshall 49068	1829 (1833) unorganized land *St. Joseph/*Kalamazoo	1867 1848 1867	1833 1835 1867
K5	Cass 120 N. Broadway Cassopolis 49013	1829 (1829) unorganized land	1867 1830 1867	1829 1829 1831
	Charlevoix (old)	1840 (as Keskkauko; renamed, 1843; became part of Emmet, 1853) Mackinac		
E6	Charlevoix (present) Charlevoix 49720	1869 Antrim/Emmet/Otsego	1867 1868 1868	1869 1881 1869
D6	Cheboygan Cheboygan 49721	1840 (1853) Mackinac	1867 1867 1867	1854 1854 1884
	Cheonoquet	1840 (renamed Montmorency, 1843) Mackinac/unorganized land		
C6	Chippewa Sault Ste. Marie 49783	1827 Michilimackinac	1869 1868 1870	1826 1828 1860?
G6	Clare P.O. Box 438 Harrison 48625	1840 (1871) (as Kayakee; renamed, 1843) Mackinac *Midland/*Isabella/*Mecosta	1870 1871 1878	1865 1872 1871
H6	Clinton 100 E. State Street St. Johns 48879	1831 (1839) unorganized land *Kent	1867 1840 1867	1837 1840 1860?
	Crawford *Became part of Wisconsin Territory in 1836; now in Wisconsin.*	1818 (Michigan Territory) unorganized land		
F6	Crawford 200 W. Michigan Avenue Grayling 49738	1840 (1879) (as Shawono; renamed, 1843) Mackinac *Cheboygan/*Iosco/*Antrim/*Kalkasa	1879 1887 1878	1863 1881 1881
D4	Delta 310 Ludington Street Escanaba 49829	1843 (1861) Mackinac/unorganized land	1869 1869 1869	1843 1843 1869
	Des Moines *Became part of Wisconsin Territory in 1836; now in Iowa.*	1834 unorganized land		
C3	Dickinson Iron Mountain 49801	1891 Iron/Marquette/Menominee	1891 1891 1891	1891 1891 1891
	Dubuque *Became part of Wisconsin Territory in 1836; now in Iowa.*	1834 unorganized land		
J6	Eaton 1045 Independence Boulevard Charlotte 48813	1829 (1837) unorganized land *St. Joseph/*Kalamazoo	1867 1838 1867	1835 1835 1848

Map	County Address	Date Formed Parent County/ies	Birth Marriage Death	Land Probate Court
D6	Emmet 1457 Atkins Road Petoskey 49770	1840 (1853) (as Tonedagana; renamed, 1843) Mackinac	1867 1867 1867	1843 1867 1867
	Forest	1913 (abolished) Cheboygan/Presque Isle		
H7	Genesee Room 202 Flint 48502	1835 (1836) Lapeer/Saginaw/Shiawassee *Oakland	1867 1835 1867	1819 1836 1835
G6	Gladwin 401 West Cedar Street Gladwin 48624	1831 (1875) unorganized land *Saginaw/*Midland	1880 1880 1880	1886 1889 1880
C1	Gogebic Bessemer 49911	1887 Ontonagon	1887 1887 1887	1887 1887 1887
E5	Grand Traverse 400 Boardman Avenue Traverse City 49684	1851 Omeena	1858 1853 1867	1853 1875 1882
H6	Gratiot Ithaca 48847	1831 (1855) unorganized land *Saginaw/*Clinton	1867 1867 1867	1847 1867 1867
K6	Hillsdale Hillsdale 49242	1829 (1835) unorganized land *Lenawee	1835 1829 1829	1835 1835 1846
B2	Houghton 401 E. Houghton Avenue Houghton 49931	1845 Marquette/Ontonagon	1867 1848 1867	1848 1872 1848
G8	Huron 250 E. Huron Avenue Bad Axe 48413	1840 (1859) Sanilac *St. Clair/*Sanilac/*Tuscola	1867 1867 1867	1837 1861 1867
J7	Ingham 366 S. Jefferson Street Mason 48854	1829 (1838) Shiawassee/Washtenaw/unorganized land	1867 1838 1867	1835 1835 1839
H6	Ionia Ionia 48846	1831 (1837) Michilimackinac *Kent	1867 1838 1867	1836 1835 1845
F7	Iosco P.O. Box 838 Tawas City 48763	1840 (1857) (as Kanotin; renamed, 1843) unorganized land *Cheboygan/*Saginaw	1867 1858 1867	1840 1859 1859
	Iowa *Became part of Wisconsin Territory in 1836; now in Wisconsin.*	1830 Crawford		
C2	Iron 2 S. Sixth Street Crystal Falls 49920	1885 Marquette/Menominee	1895 1895 1895	1855 1886 1895
G6	Isabella 200 N. Main Street Mount Pleasant 48858	1831 (1859) Michilimackinac/unorganized land *Saginaw/*Ionia/*Midland	1880 1880 1880	1838 1859 1880

Map	County Address	Date Formed Parent County/ies	Birth Marriage Death	Land Probate Court
	Isle Royale	1875 (attached to Houghton, 1885; abolished, became part of Keweenaw, 1897) Keweenaw		
J6	Jackson 120 W. Michigan Avenue Jackson 49201	1829 (1832) Washtenaw/unorganized land *Washtenaw	1867 1830 1867	1830 1834 1830?
J5	Kalamazoo 201 W. Kalamazoo Avenue Kalamazoo 49006	1829 (1830) unorganized land *St. Joseph	1867 1831 1867	1824 1830 1847
F6	Kalkaska 605 N. Birch Kalkaska 49646	1840 (1871) (as Wabassee; renamed, 1843) Mackinac *Grand Traverse/*Antrim	1871 1871 1871	1853 1874 1871
	Kanotin	1840 (renamed Iosco, 1843) unorganized land *Mackinac		
	Kautawaubet (aka Kautawbet)	1840 (renamed Wexford, 1843) Mackinac		
	Kayakee (aka Kaykakee)	1840 (renamed Clare, 1843) Mackinac/unorganized land *Saginaw		
H5	Kent 300 Monroe N.W. Grand Rapids 49502	1831 (1836) Michilimackinac/unorganized land	1867 1845 1867	1860 1898 1854
	Keskkauko (aka Keshkauko, aka Reshkauko)	1840 (renamed Charlevoix 1843) Mackinac		
A3	Keweenaw Eagle River 49924	1861 (1861) Houghton	1867 1867 1867	1861 1866 1861
G5	Lake P.O. Box B Baldwin 49304	1840 (as Aischum renamed, 1843) (1871) Mackinac *Mason/*Newaygo	1870 1872 1870	1872 1872 1871
H8	Lapeer Lapeer 48446	1822 (1835) Oakland/St. Clair/unorganized land	1867 1835 1867	1835 1838 1835
E5	Leelanau Leland 49654	1840 (1863) Mackinac *Grand Traverse	1867 1867 1867	1847 1882 1879
K7	Lenawee 425 N. Main Street Adrian 49221	1822 (1826) Monroe	1867 1867 1867	1827 1827 1870
J7	Livingston Howell 48843	1833 (1836) Shiawassee/Washtenaw *Oakland	1867 1836 1867	1834 1837 1837
C5	Luce E. Court Street Newberry 49868	1887 Chippewa/Mackinac	1887 1887 1887	1887 1888 1887

Map	County Address	Date Formed Parent County/ies	Birth Marriage Death	Land Probate Court
C6	Mackinac 100 Marley Street Saint Ignace 49781	1818 (as Michilimackinac; renamed, 1837) Wayne	1873 1821 1873	1785 1851 1808
J8	Macomb 40 N. Gratiot Mount Clemens 48043	1818 Wayne	1867 1839 1867	1818 1849 1818
F5	Manistee 415 Third Street Manistee 49660	1840 (1855) Mackinac *Ottawa/*Grand Traverse	1867 1855 1867	1868 1881 1855
	Manitou	1855 (abolished, 1895)* Emmet/Leelanau		
	** In 1861 the county government was disorganized, and Manitou was attached to Mackinac. In 1865 it was attached to Leelanau, then again attached to Mackinac in 1869. Finally, in 1895, Manitou was abolished and was absorbed by Charlevoix and Leelanau counties.*			
C3	Marquette 232 W. Baraga Avenue Marquette 49855	1843 (1848) Chippewa/Mackinac *Houghton	1867 1850 1867	1851 1854 1852
G4	Mason Ludington 49431	1840 (1855) (as Notipekago; renamed, 1843) Mackinac *Ottawa	1867 1867 1867	1840 1855 1867
G5	Mecosta 400 Elm Street Big Rapids 49307	1840 (1859) Mackinac/Oceana *Kent/*Newaygo	1867 1867 1867	1867 1867 1859
	Meegisee	1840 (renamed Antrim, 1843) Mackinac		
D3	Menominee Menominee 49858	1861 (as Bleeker; renamed, 1863) unorganized land	1868 1868 1868	1850 1868 1861
	Michilimackinac	1818 (renamed Mackinac, 1837) Wayne		
G6	Midland 301 W. Main Street Midland 48640	1831 (1850) Saginaw/unorganized land	1867 1867 1867	1855 1856 1839
	Mikenauk	1840 (renamed Roscommon, 1843) Mackinac/unorganized land		
	Milwaukee	1834 (1835) Brown		
	Became part of Wisconsin Territory in 1836; now in Wisconsin.			
F6	Missaukee Lake City 49651	1840 (1871) Mackinac *Manistee/*Wexford/*Grand Traverse	1870 1871 1871	1871 1871 1872
K7	Monroe 106 E. First Monroe 48161	1817 Wayne	1874 1818 1867	1806 1817 1805
H6	Montcalm Stanton 48888	1831 (1850) Michilimackinac/unorganized land *Ionia	1867 1867 1867	1838 1855 1860?
E7	Montmorency P.O. Box 415 Atlanta 49709	1840 (1881) (as Cheonoquet; renamed, 1843) Mackinac/unorganized land *Cheboygan/*Alpena	1881 1887 1881	1943 1943 1940

Map	County Address	Date Formed Parent County/ies	Birth Marriage Death	Land Probate Court
H4	Muskegon 990 Terrace Street Muskegon 49440	1859 Ottawa/unorganized land	1867 1867 1867	1839 1867 1856
G5	Newaygo 1087 Newell Street White Cloud 49349	1840 (1851) Oceana/Mackinac *Kent/*Ottawa	1867 1866 1867	1840 1880 1893
	Negwegon (aka Neewago)	1840 (renamed Alcona, 1843) unorganized land *Mackinac		
	Notipekago (aka Nontipekago)	1840 (renamed Mason, 1843) Mackinac *Ottawa		
J8	Oakland 1200 N. Telegraph Road Pontiac 48053	1820 Macomb	1867 1827 1867	1821 1822 1826
G4	Oceana P.O. Box 153 Hart 49420	1831 (1851) Michilimackinac *Kent/*Ottawa	1867 1857 1868	1846 1900 1859
F7	Ogemaw West Branch 48661	1840 (1875) unorganized land *Mackinac/*Cheboygan/*Iosco	1879 1876 1876	1876 1877 1876
	In 1867 Ogemaw was abolished and absorbed by Iosco. In 1873 it was re-created from part of Iosco.			
	Okkuddo (aka Okkudo)	1840 (renamed Otsego, 1843) Mackinac		
	Omeena	1840 (abolished, 1853; became part of Grand Traverse) Mackinac		
B1	Ontonagon 725 Greeland Road Ontonagon 49953	1843 (1848) Chippewa/Mackinac *Houghton	1868 1861 1868	1850 1853 1854
G5	Osceola 301 W. Upton Reed City 49677	1840 (1869) (as Unwattin; renamed, 1843) Mackinac *Mason/*Newaygo/*Mecosta	1869 1869 1869	1853 1870 1870
F7	Oscoda 1190 Cauchy Mio 48647	1840 (1881) Mackinac *Iosco/*Cheboygan/*Alpena/*Alcona/	1881 1881 1881	1850 1881 1881
E6	Otsego 225 W. Main Street Gaylord 49735	1840 (1875) (as Okkuddo; renamed, 1843) Mackinac *Cheboygan/*Alpena/*Antrim	1875 1875 1887	1864 1876 1875
H5	Ottawa 414 Washington Street Grand Haven 49417	1831 (1837) Michilimackinac/unorganized land *Kent	1866 1847 1867	1834 1844 1839
E7	Presque Isle 151 E. Huron Street Rogers City 49779	1840 (1871) Mackinac *Cheboygan/*Alpena	1871 1872 1871	1856 1874 1872
	Reshkauko (see Keskkauko)			
F6	Roscommon Roscommon 48653	1840 (1875) (as Mikenauk; renamed, 1843) Mackinac *Cheboygan/*Midland	1874 1875 1874	1875 1875 1875

Map	County Address	Date Formed Parent County/ies	Birth Marriage Death	Land Probate Court
H7	Saginaw 111 S. Michigan Saginaw 48602	1822 (1835) St. Clair/unorganized land *Oakland	1867 1867 1868	1836 1800? 1843
H8	St. Clair 201 McMorran Blvd. Port Huron 48060	1820 (1821) Macomb	1867 1834 1868	1821 1828 1833
K5	St. Joseph P.O. Box 189 Centreville 49032	1829 (1829) unorganized land	1867 1844 1867	1830 1832 1842
G8	Sanilac 67 W. Sanilac Avenue Sandusky 48471	1822 (1848) St. Clair/unorganized land *Lapeer/*Oakland	1860 1870 1860	1834 1857 1850
C5	Schoolcraft 300 Walnut Street Manistique 49854	1843 (1871) Chippewa/Mackinac Marquette/*Houghton	1870 1870 1870	1871 1874 1881
	Shawono (aka Shawano, aka Shawona)	1840 (renamed Crawford, 1843) Mackinac		
H7	Shiawassee Corunna 48817	1822 (1837) Oakland/St. Clair/unorganized land *Genesee	1867 1867 1867	1836 1840 1848
	Tonedagana	1840 (renamed Emmet, 1843) Mackinac		
H8	Tuscola 440 N. State Street Caro 48723	1840 (1850) Sanilac *Saginaw	1867 1851 1867	1850 1852 1887
	Unwattin	1840 (renamed Osceola, 1843) Mackinac *Ottawa		
J5	Van Buren Paw Paw 49079	1829 (1837) unorganized land *Lenawee/*Cass	1867 1836 1867	1836 1837 1844
	Wabassee	1840 (renamed Kalkaska, 1843) Mackinac		
	Washington	1867 (declared unconstitutional) Marquette		
J7	Washtenaw P.O. Box 8645 Ann Arbor 48108	1822 (1826) Wayne/Oakland	1867 1833 1867	1835 1827 1835
J8	Wayne 728 City County Building Detroit 48226 *In 1796 Wayne County was created as part of the Northwest Territory from unnamed country; in 1815 it became part of the Michigan Territory.*	1796 original	1867 1818 1867	1703 1797 1818
F5	Wexford Cadillac 49601	1840 (1869) (as Kautawaubet; renamed, 1843) Mackinac *Grand Traverse/*Manistee	1868 1869 1869	1869 1869 1869
	Wyandot	1840 (abolished, 1853; became part of Cheboygan) Mackinac		

MINNESOTA

Carol L. Maki

Minnesota has been claimed by four nations since the first Europeans explored its terrain. Nine different territories or government subdivisions of the United States have maintained jurisdiction over its land. Understanding its multiple dominions and authorities is essential in researching early Minnesota residents.

With the erection and blessing of a great wooden cross at Sault Ste. Marie on 14 June 1671, Simon Francois Daumont, Sieur de St. Lusson, claimed for the King of France an area that included present-day Minnesota. French exploration followed, forts were built, and the fur trading industry created economic and family relationships between the French and the Native Americans.

The Minnesota country west of the Mississippi River was secretly ceded to Spain by France in 1762, resulting in the twin cities of St. Paul and Minneapolis briefly being French and Spanish. History intervened the following year when England acquired territory east of the river and free navigation on it by England by the Treaty of Paris. By proclamation northeastern Minnesota was forbidden trade and settlement. In 1774 that same area became part of the Province of Quebec and ten years later a United States territory. It remained unorganized until Northwest Territory was created in 1787 and became part of Indiana Territory in 1800. A northwestern section of the future state remained English until 1818. The southwestern section was Spanish until 1800 when it was ceded to France for another three years. It then became part of the District of Louisiana and subsequently Louisiana Territory from 1804–12.

The northeastern section of Minnesota, which was Indiana Territory, became part of Illinois Territory in 1809 and Michigan Territory in 1818. The balance of the state was in Missouri Territory from 1812 through 1821 but unorganized from then until 1834 when all of Minnesota country was attached to Michigan Territory. This temporary arrangement lasted two years. It became Wisconsin Territory in 1836.

Two years later Minnesota divided again and placed the country west of the Mississippi River into Iowa Territory until 1846. The eastern section remained part of Wisconsin Territory until 1848. On 29 May of that year, Wisconsin obtained statehood, with the western border being essentially the St. Croix River. This made Minnesota an abandoned area without any organized government. Despite a couple of false starts, the "Stillwater Convention of 1848" produced a document organizing Minnesota Territory. In March of 1849 the proposal was passed by Congress, and Minnesota finally came into existence. Included was part of what is now eastern North and South Dakota. Minnesota was admitted to the Union as the thirty-second state in May of 1858.

Early settlement in Minnesota was affected by several factors. The fur trading industry, the Catholic missions, and the military all brought European settlers to the area. The first American military post was the primitive Cantonment New Hope near Mendota, established in 1819 by Col. Henry Leavenworth and the Fifth United States Infantry. The camp, renamed Camp Coldwater, was moved to higher ground in the spring of 1820 and shortly thereafter replaced by a permanent stone fort originally called Fort St. Anthony, but renamed to Fort Snelling in 1825. It became a nucleus from which early Minnesota settlements evolved. Refugees from the Selkirk Colony in Canada tried to make new homes on or near the military reservation, and French-Canadian traders and voyagers settled their families at Mendota across the river from the Fort. Indian treaties in 1837 opened an area in 1838 between the Mississippi and St. Croix rivers, the first available Minnesota real estate. The logging industry and the evolving sawmills established a St. Croix River valley community, the second location of European settlement in Minnesota. On the east bank of the Mississippi River at St. Anthony Falls, the third center of pre-territorial population developed, eventually becoming the city of Minneapolis.

Treaties of Traverse des Sioux and Mendota in 1851 opened the territory west of the Mississippi River to settlers, and the Rock Island Railroad opening in 1854 brought many new Americans. Later, the Homestead Act of 1862 was a very positive incentive for immigration to Minnesota.

Minnesota immigrants from 1820 through 1890 were basically from the British Isles, Germany, and Scandinavia, although there were small groups of Czech and Polish farmers and those from Switzerland, the Netherlands, and Belgium. All these groups continued to arrive in Minnesota after 1890, but beginning in 1890 and continuing through 1920 there was also a new group of immigrants—those basically without financial means to purchase property but eager to fill the employment opportunities in the new industries and in the transportation systems. Their nationalities varied, many coming from the Russian and Austro-Hungarian empires. There were also Italians, Greeks, Germans from Russia, Poles, Jews, Ukrainians, and Finns.

Vital Records

Legislation ordering the recording of county vital records was passed in 1870. In some counties marriage registrations began before that date, but all of these early records are somewhat incomplete. Researchers may request birth, death, or marriage records from the office of the court administrator or clerk of district court in the respective county courthouse. Some counties have recently begun to transfer their birth, death and marriage records to the office of the county recorder. St. Paul births and deaths recorded after 1870 are available at the Bureau of Health, 555 Cedar Street, St. Paul, Minnesota 55101. Charges for birth, marriage, and death records from the county are consistent with the state rates, listed below.

In 1907 the Minnesota Vital Records law was enacted, giving the state the responsibility of keeping birth and death records. Their records for births start in 1900 and deaths in 1908. Both are indexed to the present but not available for research in person. There is no statewide marriage index until 1958. The fee ($11 for a birth record and $8 for a marriage or death record) will include a search and a copy of the requested record or a statement that the record is not on file. Send to the Minnesota Department of Health, Section of Vital Statistics, P.O. Box 9441, 717 Delaware Street S.E., Minneapolis, Minnesota 55440.

Some limited county vital record registers have been transferred to the Minnesota Historical Society Research Center (see Archives, Libraries, and Societies), although access is restricted. The center holds justice of the peace (marriage) records from some counties and coroner's inquest (death) registers. Other alternate sources for vital records may include local genealogical societies that have transcribed and indexed vital records and obituaries for their respective counties. Alfred J. Dahlquist, *Minnesota Genealogical Journal* (see County Resources), has transcriptions of marriages from several Minnesota counties. This publication also has printed extractions of marriage records, which include Minnesota people in Pierce and St. Croix counties, Wisconsin.

The WPA Historical Records Survey of township vital records was published in *Guide to Public Vital Statistics Records in Minnesota.* Many of these records have since been transferred to the Minnesota Historical Society.

Township records may include some vital statistics. Deaths and births may have been reported to townships or cities from 1870 through 1953. If these records are extant (and many are not), they frequently will contain more information than the county or state record. Many of these locally created vital records are at the Minnesota Historical Society Research Center.

School records, although not vital registrations, may help determine the age of an individual. Many of these are also at the Minnesota Historical Society Research Center.

Census Records

Federal

Population Schedules.

- Indexed—1850, 1860 (Minnesota Historical Society), 1870, 1890 (fragment)
- Soundex—1880, 1900, 1920
- Unindexed—1910

Industry and Agriculture Schedules.

- 1850, 1860, 1870, 1880

Mortality Schedules.

- 1850, 1860, 1870, 1880

Union Veterans Schedules.

- 1890 (indexed)

Although not a state at the time, Minnesota residents were enumerated in 1850 as part of the regular federal enumeration process. Both the 1850 and 1860 schedules have been indexed in addition to those generated by AISI (see page 2). See Patricia C. Harpole and Mary D. Nagle, *Minnesota Territorial Census, 1850* (St. Paul, Minn.: Minnesota Historical Society, 1972), and Dennis Meissner, *Guide to the Use of the 1860 Minnesota Population Census Schedules and Index* (St. Paul, Minn.: Minnesota Historical Society, 1978).

Much of the federal copy of Minnesota's 1870 federal census was destroyed. Only the schedules for Stearns, Steele, Stevens, St. Louis, Todd, Wabasha, Wadena, Waseca, Washington, Watonwan, Wilkin, Winona, and

Wright counties still exist. However, a duplicate of the entire census (state copy) retained by the Minnesota Historical Society was microfilmed. There are, therefore, two versions of the 1870 federal census for the state of Minnesota. The extant 1890 federal census includes one page of Rockford township in Wright County. A state copy for the 1890 federal return of Rockville Township, Stearns County, is at the Minnesota Historical Society Research Center.

The extensive early logging industry in Minnesota may make it difficult to locate ancestors involved in that particular labor force. They may be counted in the lumber camps or at the numerous boarding houses in the river cities and towns. It is also important to note that the steamboat crews on the rivers were often enumerated in the city in which the boat was temporarily docked.

Federal non-population schedules for Minnesota for 1860–80 (agriculture, industry, mortality, and social statistics) can be purchased on microfilm through the Minnesota Historical Society order department.

Territorial

Minnesota inhabitants were first enumerated in Michigan Territory 1820 census and the 1836 census of Wisconsin Territory. For the 1840 federal census, the areas of present-day Minnesota that were east of the Mississippi River were included in the St. Croix County, Wisconsin, federal census, while the western portion was included in the 1840 enumeration of Clayton County, Iowa. A census of Minnesota Territory was ordered in 1849, which included the name of head of household and number of males and females in that household. See Wiley R. Pope, *Minnesota Genealogical Index: Vol. 1* (St. Paul, Minn.: Minnesota Family Trees, 1984), and Minnesota (Territory), Legislative Assembly, *Journal of the House of Representatives, First Session of the Territory of Minnesota,* 1850, Appendices C and D, pages 195–215.

A very incomplete 1853 Minnesota census exists for limited areas. Some schedules only indicate head of household, number of children, and total number in household, but a few include names of all inhabitants. The state census for heads of household in 1855 has been largely lost. The published schedule for Wright County has survived, as have manuscript copies for the counties of Chisago, Doty, and Superior. Winona, however, has an unusual "inhabitants by building" enumeration for that year. The Minnesota Historical Society holds these 1853 and 1855 limited schedules.

The 1857 Minnesota territorial census was mandated for statehood qualification and apparently included fictitious names in seven counties to boost the population (see Arthur L. Finnell, "Southwest Minnesota's 1857 State Census: Notes on a Forgery," *Minnesota Genealogist* 17 [June 1986]: 76–78, and Robert J. Forrest, "Mythical Cities of Southwestern Minnesota," *Minnesota History* 14 [September 1933]: 243–62). The census includes name, age, sex, color, birthplace, voting status of male (native or naturalized), and occupation of each male over the age of fifteen. This census has been indexed by last name and a microfilm edition is available.

State

State censuses were also taken in 1865, 1875, 1885, 1895, and 1905. Each of the state census enumerations includes all members of the household. In 1865 "Soldier in service on June 1, 1865" was included. The 1875 states the birthplaces of father and mother. The 1895 and 1905 censuses may be especially helpful to the genealogist as they include the length of time an individual has lived in the state and the district. Microfilmed copies of the state censuses are at the Minnesota Historical Society in St. Paul. They may be purchased or obtained on interlibrary loan through the society.

The 1918 Alien Registration and Declaration of Holdings, under the auspices of the Minnesota Commission of Public Safety, is an alternate source for locating an immigrant ancestor in Minnesota in the twentieth century. The registration forms, completed by noncitizen adults in the state in February 1918, are filed by county. An every-name index, in progress, is complete except for St. Louis and Hennepin counties. Questions on the form include place of birth, years in the country, port of entry, date of arrival, occupation, name of spouse, and names of children. Originals of these forms are at the Minnesota Historical Society.

Alternates to census records in determining the location of a particular ancestor at a particular time include city directories, especially in St. Paul (from 1856) and Minneapolis (from 1859). Some are in original form; some are on microfilm at the Minnesota Historical Society.

Background Sources

Local history resources in Minnesota include the printed and archival collections of the Minnesota Historical Society, the library of the Minnesota Genealogical Society (see Archives, Libraries, and Societies), other private and public libraries, and county and local historical and genealogical societies. Each of these have unique material for research. The following printed sources are recommended:

Brook, Michael. *Reference Guide to Minnesota History: A Subject Bibliography of Books, Pamphlets and Articles in English.* St. Paul, Minn.: Minnesota Historical Society, 1974. Arranged by subject and indexed.

———, and Sarah P. Rubenstein. *A Supplement to Reference Guide to Minnesota History: A Subject Bibliography, 1970–80.* St. Paul, Minn.: Minnesota Historical Society, 1983. Arranged by subject and indexed.

Upham, Warren, and Rose Barteaw Dunlap, comps. *Collections of the Minnesota Historical Society.* Vol. 14. St. Paul, Minn.: Minnesota Historical Society, 1912. This is an 892-page index of Minnesota biographies, 1655–1912. The sources include 250 national and state printed biographical collections, Minnesota pamphlets, histories and military records of the state, magazines and journals, personal memoirs, scrapbooks, and state newspapers. A brief biographical sketch plus the reference from which the data was extracted is provided for each individual.

Folwell, William Watts. *A History of Minnesota.* 4 vols. St. Paul, Minn.: Minnesota Historical Society, 1921–30.

Kirkeby, Lucille L. *Holdings of Genealogical Value in Minnesota's County Museums*. Brainerd, Minn.: the author, 1986. This organizes the local historical societies by county, lists their hours, and gives descriptions of collections that would be of interest to a family researcher.

Pope, Wiley R. *Tracing Your Ancestors in Minnesota: A Guide to Sources*. St. Paul, Minn.: Minnesota Family Trees, various years. This is a series of research guides for Minnesota genealogical research. The first volume is a general statewide guide, but other volumes cover specific sections of the state. The sectional guides list resources in the county government centers, the Minnesota Historical Society, regional research centers, and county historical repositories.

Warren, Paula Stuart. "Genealogical Research in Minnesota," *National Genealogical Society Quarterly* 77 (March 1989): 22–42. A valuable, concise Minnesota guide to research.

Maps

A. T. Andreas, *An Illustrated Historical Atlas of the State of Minnesota* (Chicago, Ill.: the author, 1874), was the first county atlas of Minnesota. It includes the county maps, cities and townships, illustrations of private homes and businesses in the state, portrait sketches of important citizens, and statistical information. The original atlas is quite scarce, with the only existing copies sometimes available through dealers of rare books. It has, however, been republished as Winona County Historical Society's *Atlas of the State of Minnesota, Andreas, 1874* (Evansville, Ind.: Unigraphic, 1976), providing an excellent genealogical reference tool. A companion to it is Paul J. Ostendorf, *Every Person's Name Index to An Illustrated Historical Atlas of the State of Minnesota* (Winona, Minn.: St. Mary's College, 1979).

County atlases for Minnesota include maps for the respective county and for townships within that county. The names of property owners are frequently included on these maps. The Minnesota Historical Society has microfilmed many of these atlases, which makes them accessible on interlibrary loan.

Library of Congress Fire Insurance Maps in the Library of Congress; Plans of North American Cities and Towns Produced by the Sanborn Map Company (Washington D.C.: Library of Congress, 1981) states that the earliest map of this type for Minnesota is for 1884. There is, however, a Sanborn map for the city of St. Paul for 1875; this map is located at the map library of the Minnesota Historical Society.

The map collection of the Minnesota Historical Society consists of over 35,000 individual maps and 1,300 atlases, the majority of these for Minnesota and the Midwest. The society is a five-state, regional depository for the U.S. Geological Survey maps (see page 4). They have extensive collections of Minnesota territory and state maps, county and city maps, and fire insurance maps of over 950 Minnesota towns and cities. There are random maps and plat maps in the county records at the Minnesota Historical Society Research Center. The map library of the Wilson Library at the University of Minnesota, Minneapolis, is an outstanding cartographic repository, not restricted to Minnesota. It includes worldwide maps and associated material. For further information see the following references:

Upham, Warren. *Minnesota Geographic Names: Their Origin and Historic Significance.* 1920. Reprint. St. Paul, Minn.: Minnesota Historical Society, 1969.

Treude, Mai. *Windows to the Past: A Bibliography of Minnesota County Atlases.* Minneapolis, Minn.: University of Minnesota, Center for Urban and Regional Affairs, 1980.

The Minnesota Department of Transportation, Room B-20, St. Paul, Minnesota 55155, provides a series of current state, county, and city maps.

Land Records

Public-Domain State

Minnesota is a public-domain state, with twelve GLO districts, the first opening in 1848 at Falls St. Croix River, Wisconsin. However, pioneers were staking their claims long before that. Immediately following the tribal treaties of 1838, the European settlers built homes and sawmills, logged the white pine, and generally took possession of land that was not legally available. The federal government was, apparently, exceedingly slow to begin land surveys in the territory. The pressure of settlers and investors finally resulted in that process in 1847. The Pre-Emption Act of 1841 allowed home-seekers to purchase up to 160 acres of surveyed public lands at $1.25 per acre.

Numerous land records are held by the Minnesota Historical Society including tract books on microfilm; records of the state auditor; land department's state land sale correspondence, sales and accounting records; and U.S. GLO files comprised of correspondence, accounting records, and location records (which include homestead records and preemption sales). The earliest records are for the Stillwater district, beginning in 1848. The Minnesota Historical Society Research Center also has duplicates of the records of the U.S. Surveyor General's Office and a list of lands allotted to the White Earth Reservation in 1901. *A Guide to the Records of Minnesota's Public Lands* (St. Paul, Minn.:

Minnesota Historical Society, 1985), by George Kinney and Lydia Lucas, indicates holdings at the research center.

At the county level in Minnesota, land records are kept by the county recorder. This office will have deed and mortgage records, grantor-grantee indexes, township and village plats, and various records pertaining to power of attorney, contracts, and leases.

Probate Records

The probate office in county courthouses will usually have all those records pertaining to estates and wills, guardianships, juvenile court records, and insanity records. Probate case files for Freeborn, Pope, Washington, and Winona counties are at the Minnesota Historical Society Research Center. This repository also holds probate summary volumes (not the files) for numerous other counties in the state. Probate records will frequently pre-date death records in Minnesota counties.

Court Records

The first term of the district court in Minnesota convened in the second floor of John McKusick's store on 1 June 1847 in Stillwater.

The district court may include civil and criminal cases with indexes, coroner's records, professional registrations, and oaths and bonds. Civil cases may include monetary suits, change of name, divorce, garnishments, and adoptions. The district court records for Wright County at Minnesota Historical Society Research Center include, for example, court minutes, 1858–1929; criminal case files and dockets for 1858–1928; judgement dockets, 1857–66; and register of civil actions, ca. 1879–99. The court records at this repository vary considerably by county and type of record. Some counties have not transferred any of these files but retain them at the district court office in the county seat.

Tax Records

The Minnesota Historical Society holds large numbers of county property tax records, filed under the respective county. Some of the tax records are for specific municipalities. No determination has been made concerning tax record holdings in the county courthouse.

Cemetery Records

The Minnesota Genealogical Society's Cemetery Project is compiling the names and sites of all cemeteries in Minnesota indicating which have been transcribed and where the transcription can be located. Many cemetery records have been published in the *Minnesota Genealogist*, the quarterly publication of that society. Several regional groups have published records of their local cemeteries. Also see Wiley R. Pope, *Minnesota Cemeteries in Print: A Bibliography of Minnesota Published Cemetery Inscriptions, and Burials, etc.* (St. Paul, Minn.: Minnesota Family Trees, 1986); Minnesota Historical Society Research Center for the WPA papers for cemeteries in Minnesota; and Wiley R. Pope, *Minnesota Cemetery Locations* (St. Paul, Minn.: Minnesota Family Trees, 1988).

Church Records

Detailed background on Minnesota church history is found in numerous published denominational histories. Religion of the European settlers was first brought to Native Americans in what is now Minnesota with the Catholic missionaries and the French explorers. In 1656 Groseilliers and Radisson built a chapel at Prairie Island, near present-day Hastings. The Mission of St. Michael the Archangel was established at Fort Beauharnois on Lake Pepin (Mississippi River) in 1727.

In June of 1839, the Right Reverend Mathias Loras, first Bishop of Dubuque, Iowa, visited Mendota (then known as St. Peter's), finding 185 Catholics among the French, English, and Sioux. Arrangements were made for the establishment of a parish. James Michael Reardon, *The Catholic Church in the Diocese of St. Paul, from Earliest Origin to Centennial Achievement* (St. Paul, Minn.: North Central Publishing Co., 1952), provides background on the development of this parish.

Sacramental records for all parishes within the Roman Catholic Archdiocese of St. Paul and Minneapolis are presently being microfilmed. The staff will provide limited research upon written request directed to the Archdiocese of St. Paul and Minneapolis, 226 Summit Avenue, St. Paul, Minnesota 55102.

For Catholic parishes in Minnesota (and North and South Dakota), there is the Minnesota Historical Society collection for the Archdiocese of St. Paul and Minneapolis parish questionnaires and related papers. The questionnaires were from the 1930s and 1940s; however, additions were made through the 1970s when the collection was microfilmed.

During the 1850s the number of churches increased rapidly in the new territory with at least fifteen congregations in St. Paul, eight in Minneapolis, and seven in St. Anthony by 1859. Episcopal, Presbyterian, Methodist, Baptist, Congregational, and Catholic were the most prevalent at that time. Chisago Lakes and Vasa, both Scandinavian settlements, had Lutheran churches in the mid-1850s. Quakers were active in Minneapolis at this time, while the first Jewish service was held in St. Paul in 1856.

Numerous church records are deposited at the Minnesota Historical Society. Some are originals; some are microfilms. There are significant collections for Quakers and for the

United Church of Christ. Anne A. Hage, *Church Records in Minnesota: A Guide to Parish Records of Congregational, Evangelical, Reformed, and United Church of Christ Churches, 1851–1981* (Minneapolis, Minn.: Minnesota Conference, United Church of Christ, 1983), helps in locating record sources, while the Minnesota Historical Society is the official repository for the Protestant Episcopal Church.

Luther Northwestern Seminary in St. Paul is the archives repository of the Region Three Archives of the Evangelical Lutheran Church in America and for some American-Lutheran Church records. The seminary is at 2481 Como Avenue, St. Paul, Minnesota 55108.

Microfilmed records of the Minnesota Conference of the old Augustana Synod (Swedish-American) are at the American Swedish Institute in Minneapolis. Archives of the Minnesota South District of the Lutheran Church—Missouri Synod are at Concordia College in St. Paul. There are records of Swedish-American Lutheran Churches at Gustavus Adolphus College, Folke Bernadotte Memorial Library, St. Peter, Minnesota.

The WPA Minnesota Papers "Historical Records Survey, Churches," held by the Minnesota Historical Society, gives information on locations of individual church records in the 1930s and limited histories of the congregations. The papers are filed by county, name of community, and church.

The Minnesota Historical Society Research Center has guidebooks to the center's *Minnesota Historic Resources Survey* completed between 1973–79 and organized by county and 300 historic organizations on seven reels of microfilm. They indicate location of church records in local historical societies or other manuscript repositories. The state archives section has secretary of state notebooks for articles of incorporation of churches and religious organizations.

Military Records

Initial research on a Minnesota volunteer in the Civil War should include the two-volume Board of Commissioners on Publication of History in Civil and Indian Wars' *Minnesota in the Civil and Indian Wars, 1861–1865* (St. Paul, Minn.: Pioneer Press Co., 1890–93 and 1891–99). The first volume includes regimental rosters and narratives. The second contains reports and correspondence. *Minnesota in the Civil and Indian Wars: An Index to the Rosters* was compiled in 1936 for the Minnesota Historical Society by the WPA and is available on microfilm at the society.

The society's reference library has an incomplete file "in progress" of veterans of these periods of warfare, including those who moved to Minnesota after the wars. The information, which may include residence, death date, widow's name, pension file number, regiment and company, has been accumulated from a variety of sources, including the 1890 federal census of Union veterans, pension registers, names of participants in GAR parades, the reports noting deaths during the years, and a few biographical sketches.

Minnesota Historical Society Research Center holds numerous diaries of Civil War veterans, some regimental records, Grand Army of the Republic records, microfilms of service cards for Minnesota State Militia in federal military service in the Civil War, and Civil War Pension Registers of letters sent from the Adjutant General for 1877 through 1949. The name of the veteran, date of the letter, and amount awarded is included on the cards. Board of Auditors files at the research center includes minutes and registers of claims and certificates relating to the Dakota Conflict (Sioux Uprising) of 1862.

World War I military service cards for people who entered the service through the Minnesota National Guard are also at the research center along with photographic copies of original draft lists, induction lists, and Soldiers' Bonus Records. This file includes over 120,000 bonus applications for Minnesota soldiers, marines, sailors, and medical personnel who served in World War I. It is *not* indexed, but the fifty-one questions on the application include name, place and date of birth, names and residence of nearest relative, draft information, present residence and occupation, name of employer, business address, name and address of parents at time of enlistment, length of residence in Minnesota, and marital status.

The Public Safety Commission Gold Star Roll Records at the Minnesota Historical Research Center pertain to men and women from Minnesota who died in World War I. The four page form includes biographical information and *may* include family photographs, letters, and clippings.

Other military records at the Minnesota Historical Society Research Center include the following: Camp Ripley records for 1842–43, Mexican border service payroll records from the early twentieth century, Minnesota Soldiers' Home Records beginning in 1891, membership applications for the Sons of American Revolution, and information from the Mexican-American and Spanish-American wars.

Periodicals, Newspapers, and Manuscript Collections

Periodicals

The *Minnesota Genealogist*, quarterly publication of the Minnesota Genealogical Society, includes a variety of genealogical articles, cemetery readings, newspaper and vital records extractions, book reviews, queries, and miscellaneous information of interest to the Minnesota researcher. Indexes are available through the society.

Minnesota History usually contains three to four full-length historical articles. It is indexed and published quarterly by the Minnesota Historical Society.

Newspapers

George S. Hage, *Newspapers on the Minnesota Frontier, 1849–50* (St. Paul, Minn.: Minnesota Historical Society, 1967), provides an excellent source for the historical development of Minnesota's newspapers. The Minnesota

Historical Society was chartered as a repository for these territorial "day-books of history" beginning in 1849. On 28 April 1849, the first issue of the *Minnesota Pioneer* was published by James Madison Goodhue. By 14 July of that year Minnesota had three newspapers, all printed in St. Paul. The *St. Anthony Express*, the earliest newspaper in what is now Minneapolis, was first printed in 1851. The prime objective of all the early papers was to attract settlers to the territory.

There are two reference sources available for locating information in the *Minnesota Pioneer*. The *Minnesota Pioneer Index* is a card file located at the Minnesota Historical Society that covers the newspaper through 4 Sept 1851. Alfred J. Dahlquist, *Minnesota Genealogical Journal* (see County Resources), includes important extractions from the same newspaper through 4 April 1854. Obituaries, probate notices, lists of arrivals at St. Paul hotels, and letters remaining at the post office are covered.

The Minnesota Biography File is an extensive ongoing alphabetical card file index citing obituaries and other biographical details from newspapers, serials, books, and microfilmed scrapbooks in the collection at the Minnesota Historical Society.

Both Minneapolis and St. Paul city libraries have printed contemporary indexes of their respective major newspapers. The Minnesota Regional Research Centers and local historical and genealogical groups may have indexing projects of community newspapers underway.

Two other sources are the Babcock Newspaper Index to articles in Minnesota newspapers, 1849–58, which is a card index located at the Minnesota Historical Society Research Center and the University of Minnesota, and the Immigration History Research Center, *Newspapers on Microfilm* (St. Paul, Minn.: Immigration History Research Center, 1978). The latter is for ethnic newspapers.

Manuscripts

The Minnesota Historical Society has manuscript collections for almost every aspect of Minnesota territorial and state history. Many of these are listed in a series of three guides:

Nute, Grace Lee, and Gertrude W. Ackermann, comps. *Guide to the Personal Papers in the Manuscript Collections of the Minnesota Historical Society*. St. Paul, Minn.: Minnesota Historical Society, 1935.

Kane, Lucile M., and Kathryn A. Johnson, comps. *Manuscripts Collections of the Minnesota Historical Society, Guide Number 2*. St. Paul, Minn.: Minnesota Historical Society, 1955.

Lucas, Lydia A., comp. *Manuscripts Collections of the Minnesota Historical Society, Guide Number 3*. St. Paul, Minn.: Minnesota Historical Society, 1977.

Significant collections at the Minnesota Historical Society include the historical records of the Northern Pacific and Great Northern railways for 1854 through 1970. Personnel files are limited. The Mission File Index (Nute) is an index to copies of manuscript materials about missionaries and pre-twentieth century life in Minnesota.

The Minnesota Historical Society also has an immense number of fur trade papers. These are described, although not inclusively, in Bruce M. White, *The Fur Trade in Minnesota: An Introductory Guide to Manuscript Sources* (St. Paul, Minn.: Minnesota Historical Society Press, 1977).

Manuscript collections of value can be found at the Iron Range Research Center, Minnesota Regional Research Centers (see Archives, Libraries, and Societies), Immigration History Research Center of the University of Minnesota, and university and religiously affiliated libraries in the state. Some repositories have printed guides or bibliographies.

Archives, Libraries, and Societies

Minnesota Historical Society
690 Cedar Street
St. Paul, MN 55101

The Minnesota Historical Society has been collecting, preserving, and interpreting the history of Minnesota since 1849, which makes the society older than the state it represents. The collections are currently located in three locations: the Minnesota Historical Society (address above), Fort Snelling History Center (Archaeology, Historic Sites, and State Historic Preservation), and the Minnesota Historical Society Research Center (address below). In 1992 the material from all three locations will be housed in the new Minnesota History Center. See Minnesota Historical Society Library and Archives Division, *Genealogical Resources of the Minnesota Historical Society: A Guide* (St. Paul, Minn.: Minnesota Historical Society Press, 1989), for an excellent guide to the multitude of sources in their collection. This handbook alphabetically lists resources, cross-referenced, with a description of contents, location within the society's departments, and means of access.

At the above location are the audio-visual library (genealogists will appreciate the photograph collection of approximately 200,000 images, indexed by subject and name); the map library; the newspaper library (over 3 million issues of approximately 6,500 newspapers); reference library (over 500,000 books, pamphlets, periodicals, microforms, and documents); the largest collection of published Minnesota materials; extensive holdings on railroads, Canadian history, the fur trade, Scandinavians, and Native Americans in Minnesota; and publication offices.

Minnesota Historical Society Research Center
1500 Mississippi Street
St. Paul, MN 55101

At this location there are two major collections of records:

State Archives. Records created by state or local governments in the state of Minnesota. There is an ongoing program of transferring these records to the Minnesota Historical Society Research Center. The collection is immense, covering a broad spectrum of Minnesota history beginning in 1849. Representative of the collections to be found are the State Board of Auditors for the adjustment of claims for war expenditures, 1862–68; supreme court naturalization records, 1858–1906; and Stillwater State Prison, 1853–1976. References to numerous items at this location are included under various subjects covered in this chapter.

Manuscript Collections. Holds primary research materials that document Minnesota and its people. There are over 6,000 manuscript collections in this division of the Minnesota Historical Society, including diaries, letters, account books, scrapbooks, business papers, and personal papers of politicians and farmers.

Minnesota Genealogical Society
P.O. Box 16069
St. Paul, MN 55116

Membership includes the quarterly *Minnesota Genealogist* and the *MGS Newsletter*. Meetings are held quarterly, with state and national speakers. The Minnesota Genealogical Society Library at 1101 Fort Road (West 7th Street), St. Paul, Minnesota 55116, contains over 3,000 reference books, research materials on Indian and Metis groups, and the books and research materials of several of the branches of the society. Special interest groups within the main society include Northwest Territory Canadian and French Heritage Center, Computer Interest Group, Czechoslovak Genealogical Society, Douglas County Genealogical Society, English Genealogical Society, German Interest Group, Irish Genealogical Society, The Scandinavian-American Genealogical Society, Danish-American Genealogical Society, Finnish Genealogy Group, Icelandic Genealogy Group, Norwegian Genealogy Group, Swedish Genealogy Group, Scottish Genealogical Society, and Yankee Interest Group.

The Minnesota Genealogical Society office and library are staffed by volunteers, and hours are limited. Classes are provided for beginning and advanced genealogists.

Iron Range Research Center
Highway 169 West
P.O. Box 392
Chisholm, MN 55719

Located at the Iron Range Interpretative Center with a full-time library and archives staff, it is designated as the government records repository for Iron Range communities and includes manuscripts, oral histories, and photographs.

Minnesota Regional Research Centers

This network was originally established by the Minnesota Historical Society. James E. Fogerty states in *Preliminary Guide to the Holdings of the Minnesota Regional Research Centers* (St. Paul, Minn.: Minnesota Historical Society, 1975) that its purpose was to expand research possibilities within the state by collecting and preserving sources at various locations in the state. See also, James Fogerty, *Manuscript Collection of the Minnesota Regional Research Centers: Guide Number 2* (St. Paul, Minn.: Division of Archives and Manuscripts, Minnesota Historical Society, 1980).

The centers, which are located on the campuses of, and now associated with, colleges and universities in the state, concentrate on topics of regional importance. They are not all staffed on a full-time basis. Material varies at individual centers from information on the Stephen H. Long expedition of 1823 to the account of an auto trip from Minnesota to California and back in 1929. There are oral history interviews and such items as the register of a nineteenth century inn on the Mississippi River.

The eight centers and the counties they cover are as follows:

Central Minnesota Historical Center
Centennial Hall, Room 148
St. Cloud University
St. Cloud, MN 56301

Serves Aitkin, Benton, Chisago, Crow Wing, Isanti, Kanabec, Mille Lacs, Morrison, Pine, Sherburne, Stearns, Todd, Wadena, and Wright counties.

North Central Minnesota Historical Center
The A. C. Clark Library
Bemidji State University
Bemidji, MN 56601

Serves Beltrami, Cass, Clearwater, Hubbard, Itasca, Koochiching, and Lake of the Woods counties.

Northeast Minnesota Historical Center
University of Minnesota-Duluth
Library 375
Duluth, MN 55812

Serves Carlton, Cook, Lake, and St. Louis counties.

Northwest Minnesota Historical Center
Livingston Lord Library
Moorhead State University
Moorhead, MN 56560

Serves Becker, Clay, Kittson, Mahnomen, Marshall, Norman, Otter Tail, Pennington, Polk, Red Lake, Roseau, and Wilkin counties.

Southern Minnesota Historical Center
Mankato State University
Mankato, MN 56001

Serves Blue Earth, Brown, Fairbault, Freeborn, Le Sueur, Martin, Nicollet, Rice, Sibley, Steele, Waseca, and Watonwan counties.

Southwest Minnesota Historical Center
Southwest State University - BA 509
Marshall, MN 56258

Serves Cottonwood, Jackson, Kandiyohi, Lac qui Parle, Lincoln, Lyon, McLeod, Meeker, Murray, Nobles, Pipestone, Redwood, Renville, Rock, and Yellow Medicine counties.

West Central Minnesota Historical Center
University of Minnesota - Morris
Morris, MN 56267

Serves Big Stone, Chippewa, Douglas, Grant, Pope, Stevens, Swift, and Traverse counties.

Minnesota Historical Society Research Center
1500 Mississippi Street
St. Paul, MN 55101
(612) 296-6980
(formerly located at Winona State University)

Serves Dodge, Fillmore, Goodhue, Houston, Mower, Olmsted, Wabasha and Winona counties.

Special Focus Categories

Immigration

The only direct immigration to Minnesota would have been across the United States-Canadian border by land, railroad, or waterways. According to the Immigration and Naturalization Service, St. Paul, it was not until 1890 that port of entry records were kept for people entering from Canada. Passenger lists were not required on the lakes and rivers of Minnesota although some lists do exist. They may be found in diaries, letters, records of ship personnel, newspapers, or shipping company business papers. Their rarity makes them an uncommon source for genealogical research. For extensive information on the availability of river vessel records, see Ann H. Peterson's comprehensive, "Finding River People on Western Waters," *National Genealogical Society Quarterly* 78 (Dec. 1990): 245–61. Although focused on crews of steamboats, her listed sources could be helpful for research involving Midwest river travel.

Naturalization

Naturalization records are located at the district court office of the county or at the Minnesota Historical Society Research Center. Availability varies by county and will continue to shift as more counties transfer their files to the center. Supreme court naturalization records, 1858–1906, are found at the center. After 1906, naturalization was granted by the U.S. Federal District Court.

Black American

Minnesota counted very few blacks in the population prior to the Civil War. Those who were in the state were basically in two groups, either servants of officers at Fort Snelling or engaged in the fur trading industry. The latter, hired mainly by the fur companies in St. Louis, were some of the earliest blacks in Minnesota. The Minnesota territorial census of 1849 listed forty free persons of African descent, thirty of those living in St. Paul in seven family groups. After 1860 the black population increased two fold, including over 500 men, women, and children arriving by steamboats from St. Louis to St. Paul in May of 1863. The Minnesota Historical Society has numerous manuscript collections pertaining to blacks in Minnesota. Some of these have been documented in various articles in *Minnesota History*. See also:

Spangler, Earl. *Bibliography of Negro History: Selected and Annotated Entries, General and Minnesota.* Minneapolis, Minn.: Ross and Haines, 1963. Excellent bibliography.

Taylor, David Vassar. "The Blacks." In Holmquist, June Drenning, ed., *They Chose Minnesota: A Survey of the State's Ethnic Groups.* St. Paul, Minn.: Minnesota Historical Society Press, 1981, pages 73–91. Included are detailed endnotes.

———. *Blacks in Minnesota: A Preliminary Guide to Historical Sources.* St. Paul, Minn.: Publications of the Minnesota Historical Society, 1976.

Native American

Minnesota's two major native nations were the Dakota (or Sioux), originally from the southern prairie, and the Ojibway (or Chippewa) of the northern pine forests, both seminomadic societies based on hunting and gathering. In 1805 the United States purchased two small parcels of land in Minnesota—one piece for a military post, Fort Snelling; all other land belonged to the Native Americans. Intertribal fighting for northern Minnesota existed until 1825 when the Dakota and Ojibway agreed to a tribal diagonal demarcation almost across the center of the state.

Massive cessions of Native American land to European settlement began in Minnesota country in 1837 when an area between the St. Croix and Mississippi rivers was relinquished by the Dakota and Ojibway. After the chiefs signed the treaty, they headed north to the lands for which they thought they had given only timber rights. It was not until 1849 that they realized they had indeed sold their native land.

In 1847 land west of the Mississippi in central Minnesota was provided by treaty for the Winnebago and Menominee, although neither tribe ever occupied the area. Four years later, at Traverse des Sioux and Mendota, the Dakota signed treaties that gave the United States most of southern Minnesota. In treaties of 1854, 1855, 1863, and 1866, the Ojibway gave up much of their northern Minnesota land.

During the 1850s and 1860s, the Dakota treaties brought about a tragic and sorrowful chapter of Minnesota history. The reservations were not established as promised, and the various bands refused to move to the provisional reserves in the mid-1850s. Late annuity payments, the restriction of reservation life, and the nonexistence of promised agricultural aid led many Dakota families to return to their original lands, now the homes of settlers. In 1857 settlers were killed in Spirit Lake, Iowa, and in Jackson County, Minnesota. A treaty in 1858 providing for Dakota self-government and land allotments failed, resulting in the Sioux Conflict of 1862, after which many either fled to Dakota Territory or Canada or were moved to Crow Creek (now South Dakota). The unsatisfactory conditions at Crow Creek resulted in many deaths before the tribe was moved to Nebraska in 1866.

Minnesota's Ojibway were not involved in armed conflict with the settlers, but the United States acquired most of their land and tried to confine them to reservations within the state. Small intertribal treaty parcels were consolidated, and some Ojibway refused to move to these larger reservations.

However, by 1980 there were nearly twice as many Native Americans in Minnesota as when the Europeans first visited this area. The metropolis of St. Paul and Minneapolis has the third largest urban concentration of Native Americans in the United States. The Ojibway in the northern part of the state occupy one of the few unallotted and unceded reservations in the country.

For an excellent explanation of the Native Americans in Minnesota in the twentieth century, see Mitchell E. Rubenstein and Alan R. Woolworth, "The Dakota and Ojibway," in Holmquist's *They Chose Minnesota* (cited previously). An article specifically directed at the family researcher of Native American records is Virginia Rogers, "The Indians and the Metis: Genealogical Sources on Minnesota's Earliest Settlers," in *Minnesota History* (Fall 1979): 286–96. Rogers has directed her research on Ojibway born prior to 1850, including the use of Canadian genealogical volumes and extensive study of missionary manuscript sources. These include early parish records, with baptisms at St. Ignace de Michilimackinac as early as 1712.

Helpful aids at the Minnesota Historical Society include the society's *Chippewa and Dakota Indians: A Subject Catalogue of Books, Pamphlets, Periodical Articles, and Manuscripts in the Minnesota Historical Society* (St. Paul, Minn.: Minnesota Historical Society, 1969) and their original source material: U.S. Office of Indian Affairs, Chippewa Annuity Rolls, 1849–1935; U.S. Office of Indian Affairs, Sioux Annuity Rolls, 1849–1935; White Earth Indian Reservation, St. Columba Parish Register, 1853–1933; and Philip C. Bantin, *Guide to Catholic Indian Mission and School Records in Midwest Repositories* (Milwaukee, Wis.: Marquette University Libraries, Department of Special Collections and University Archives, 1984).

Other Ethnic Groups

Nineteenth-century French-Canadians as fur traders, as lumbermen, and as priests in the Catholic church, were the first immigrants to Minnesota. Later other French-Canadians followed, locating their new homes in the river valleys. The first French-Canadian communities at Fort Snelling and Mendota were both at the junction of the Mississippi and Minnesota rivers. Minnesota has a larger French-Canadian population in the late twentieth century than any state outside of New England.

Of the approximate 32 million total immigrants to the United States from 1820 through 1950, it is estimated that at least 1 million made their way to or through Minnesota. They came to the state for the available land; they came with tickets purchased for them by earlier U.S. immigrants; and they came to the support and security of ethnic communities already established in the counties and small towns. Most came via Canada and the Red River trails, up the Mississippi on steamboats, and overland. Eventually they arrived by train.

For excellent and thorough discussions of all the immigrant groups to Minnesota see June Drenning Holmquist's *They Chose Minnesota* (cited previously).

There are several research repositories for ethnic groups in Minnesota. The Immigration History Research Center was founded at the University of Minnesota (826 Berry Street, St. Paul, Minnesota 55114) in 1965. Its dual purpose is to encourage the study of the role of immigration and to collect the records of twenty-four American ethnic groups originating from Eastern, Central, and Southern Europe and the Near East. The collection includes newspapers, books, periodicals, the records of churches, cultural societies, political and fraternal organizations, and the personal papers of immigrants. The American Letters (1880–1964), a microfilmed collection of some 15,000 letters sent by immigrants to friends and relatives in Finland, is an example of the type of items in the collection.

The Norwegian-American Historical Association, St. Olaf College, Northfield, Minnesota 55057, has a collection on immigration including letters, diaries, business records, family histories, photographs, oral histories, and obituary and newspaper indexes.

The Minnesota Historical Society has a large collection of Norwegian immigration materials including guidebooks written for prospective emigrants, about 10,000 manuscripts, an excellent printed and periodical collection for Swedish-Americans, and several ethnic collections which include artifacts and manuscripts listed in the society's *Historic Resources in Minnesota: A Report on their Extent, Location, and Need for Preservation* (St. Paul, Minn.: Minnesota Historical Society, 1979).

The American Swedish Institute, 2600 Park Avenue, Minneapolis, Minnesota 55407, focuses on the settlement of Swedes in America. Its collection includes family and personal papers, oral history, correspondence and record books of Swedish immigrant organizations, Bibles, genealogies, photographs, and microfilm copies of Swedish church records in Minnesota.

The emphasis of the Celtic Collection, O'Shaughnessy Library, College of St. Thomas, 2115 Summit Avenue, St. Paul, Minnesota 55105, is on Welsh, Scottish, and Irish history, folklore, language, and literature.

County Resources

Records at the county level are the responsibility of the following offices: office of the court administrator—birth, death, and marriage; county recorder—land records; office of the probate judge—probate files; and office of the court administrator—criminal and civil court records. Although birth, marriage, and death records are the earliest located in that county, it cannot be considered that all records exist from date of formation. The earliest land records may be deeds, mortgages, or grantor-grantee/grantee-grantor indexes, but all do not necessarily start with that year. The earliest year for probate records may be probate files or wills. Court records may be civil and/or criminal. In some counties, the earlier criminal files may be found in the civil court files.

For some counties there are two years for date of formation listed. The first is the year the county was created. The date in parentheses is the year it was fully organized if it differs from the creation year. Under the heading "Parent County/ies," the name/s listed without an asterisk (*) are the county or counties from which the respective county was formed. "Unorganized" denotes that it was formed from non-county area. Counties listed with an asterisk (*) are not parent counties but other counties in which you may also find records for the respective county since it may have been "attached" to that county for some period of time.

In addition to other sources listed on page 11; the files of the Minnesota Historical Society Research Center; Pope's *Tracing Your Ancestors in Minnesota* (see Background Sources), which draws heavily on the WPA guides developed fifty years ago, with record sources changing in the interim; and the following have been consulted for county information:

Dalquist, Alfred J. *Minnesota Genealogical Journal.* Brooklyn Park, Minn.: Park Genealogical Book Co., 1984–87.

The Minnesota Legislative Manual, 1989–90. St. Paul, Minn.: Election Division, Secretary of State, 1989.

What follows is a guide to the various record sources after the inception of Minnesota Territory in 1849. It is not to be considered a definitive explanation for the peculiarities of each county's holdings.

Drawn by William Dollarhide

Map	County Address	Date Formed Parent County/ies	Birth Marriage Death	Land Probate Court
D4	Aitkin 209 Second Street N.W. Aitkin 56431 *Aitkin County was spelled Aiken until 1872.*	1857 (1885) Pine/Ramsey *Crow Wing/*Morrison	1874 1885 1887	1872 1890 1862
	Andy Johnson	1858 (as Toombs; renamed, 1862; deorganized, 1864; renamed Wilkin, 1868) Pembina *Stearns/*Crow Wing/*Douglas		
F5	Anoka 325 E. Main Street Anoka 55303	1857 Ramsey	1870 1858 1870	1857 1858 1858
D2	Becker 915 Lake Avenue Detroit Lakes 56501	1858 (1871) Cass/Pembina *Stearns/*Crow Wing/*Douglas	1871 1871 1871	1872 1872 1871
B3	Beltrami 619 Beltrami Avenue N.W. Bemidji 56601	1866 (1897) Itasca/Pembina/Polk/ unorganized land *Becker	1896 1897 1896	1874 1896 1897
F4	Benton R.R. 2 Foley 56329	1849 St. Croix/unorganized land	1865 1850 1867	1850 1852 1850
	Big Sioux	1857 (abolished, 1858) Brown		
F1	Big Stone 20 S.E. Second Street Ortonville 56278	1862 (1881) Pierce *Renville/*Stevens	1881 1881 1881	1873 1881 1881
J3	Blue Earth 204 S. Fifth Street Mankato 56001	1853 Dahkota	1870 1865 1870	1853 1858 1854
	Breckenridge	1858 (renamed Clay, 1862) Pembina		
B3	Brown New Ulm 56073	1855 (1856) Blue Earth	1870 1857 1870	1857 1856 1857
	Buchanen	1857 (abolished, 1861; became part of Pine) Pine *Chisago/*St. Louis		
D5	Carlton Carlton 55718	1857 (1870) Pine/St. Louis *St. Louis	1870 1871 1870	— — 1871
G4	Carver 600 E. Fourth Street Chaska 55318	1855 (1855) Hennepin/Sibley	1870 1856 1870	1856 1857 1854
D3	Cass Walker 56484	1851 (1872) (deorganized, 1876; became part of Crow Wing) (reorganized, 1897) Dakota/Pembina/Mahkato/Wahnahta *Benton/ *Stearns/ *Crow Wing/ *Morrison	1896 1897 1896	1864 1897 1888

Map	County Address	Date Formed Parent County/ies	Birth Marriage Death	Land Probate Court
G2	Chippewa 629 N. 11th Street Montevideo 56265	1862 (1869) Davis/Pierce *Renville	1870 1870 1870	1870 1872 1870
F5	Chisago Center City 55012	1851 (1852) Ramsey/Washington	1870 1858 1870	1852 1857 1858
D1	Clay 807 11th Street N. Moorhead 56560	1858 (as Breckenridge; renamed, 1862) (1872) Pembina *Stearns/*Crow Wing/*Douglas/*Becker	1872 1872 1872	1864 1872 1872
C2	Clearwater Bagley 56621	1902 Beltrami	1898 1903 1903	1903 1903 1903
B8	Cook Grand Marais 55604	1874 (1897) Lake *St. Louis	1897 1897 1897	 1892
H2	Cottonwood 900 Third Avenue Windom 56101	1857 (1873) Brown *Brown/*Redwood/*Watonwan	1871 1871 1871	1871 1871 1871
D4	Crow Wing Brainerd 56401	1857 (deorganized, 1858) (1866) (deorganized, 1867) (1871) Ramsey *Morrison	1873 1871 1874	1857 1874 1871
	In 1858 Cass was deorganized and attached to Morrison; in 1866 it was fully organized; again deorganized in 1867 and attached to Morrison; in 1871 it was fully organized.			
H5	Dakota 1560 Highway 55 W. Hastings 55093	1849 (1853) unorganized land *Ramsey	1870 1853 1870	1852 1863 1853
	Davis	1855 (abolished, 1862; became part of Chippewa and Lac Qui Parle) Cass/Nicolet/Pierce/Sibley *Stearns		
J5	Dodge P.O. Box 38 Mantorville 55955	1855 (1855) Rice/unorganized land	1870 1858 1870	1856 1857 1859
	Doty	1855 (renamed Newton, 1855; abolished, 1856; became part of St. Louis) Itasca		
E2	Douglas 305 Eighth Avenue W. Alexandria 56308	1858 Cass/Pembina	1870 1870 1870	1862 1868 1867
J4	Faribault N. Main Blue Earth 56013	1855 (1857) Blue Earth	1870 1870 1870	1854 1858 1870
J6	Fillmore Preston 55965	1853 Wabasha	1870 1856 1870	1853 1857 1856
J5	Freeborn 411 S. Broadway Albert Lea 56007	1855 (1857) Blue Earth/Rice	1870 1857 1870	1854 1866 1857

Map	County Address	Date Formed Parent County/ies	Birth Marriage Death	Land Probate Court
H5	Goodhue Room 310 Red Wing 55066	1853 (1854) Dakota/Wabasha	1870 1854 1870	1853 1854 1854
E1	Grant P.O. Box 59 Elbow Lake 56531	1868 (1883) Stevens/Traverse/Wilkin *Douglas	1877 1869 1879	1872 1875 1872
G4	Hennepin 300 S. Sixth Street Minneapolis 55487	1852 (1852) Dakota *Ramsey	1870 1853 1870	1848 1855 1853
J7	Houston 304 S. Marshall Caledonia 55921	1854 Fillmore	1870 1854 1870	1856 1867 1857
C3	Hubbard Park Rapids 56470	1883 (1887) Cass *Wadena	1885 1884 1887	1883 1884 1884
F5	Isanti 237 S.W. Second Avenue Cambridge 55008	1857 (deorganized, 1858; reorganized, 1871) Ramsey *St. Louis/*Anoka	1873 1871 1873	1857 1868 1880
C4	Itasca Grand Rapids 55744	1849 (1857) (deorganized, 1858; reorganized, 1891) unorganized land *Washington/*Benton/*Chisago/ *Crow Wing/*Morrison/*St. Louis/*Aitkin	1893 1891 1894	1868 1898 1891
J2	Jackson Jackson 56143	1857 (abolished, due to Sioux uprising, 1862; reorganized, 1866) Brown *Martin	1870 1868 1870	1866 1867 1871
E5	Kanabec 18 N. Vine Mora 55051	1858 (1881) Pine *Chisago/*Pine	1880 1885 1880	1859 1888 1882
G3	Kandiyohi P.O. Box 936 Wilmer 56201	1858 (deorganized, 1866; reorganized, 1871) Davis/Meeker/Pierce/Renville *Meeker	1870 1880 1870	1858 1867 1871
A1	Kittson 410 S. Fifth Street Hallock 56728	1849 (as Pembina; renamed, 1878 (1897) unorganized land *Benton/*Morrison/*Crow Wing/*Douglas/ *Becker/*Clay/*Polk	1877 1881 1881	1879 1899 1897
A4	Koochiching International Falls 56649	1906 Itasca	1906 1906 1906	1907 1907 1907
	Lac Qui Parle (old)	1862 (abolished, 1868; became part of Chippewa) Davis/Pierce *Renville		
G1	Lac Qui Parle (present) 600 Sixth Street Madison 56256	1871 (1873) Redwood	1872 1872 1872	1871 1868 1885
B7	Lake 601 Third Avenue Two Harbors 55616	1855 (as Superior; renamed St. Louis, 1855; renamed Lake, 1856) (1891) Itasca *Benton/*St. Louis	1891 1888 1891	 1874

Map	County Address	Date Formed Parent County/ies	Birth Marriage Death	Land Probate Court
A3	Lake of the Woods P.O. Box 808 Baudette 56623	1922 Beltrami	1922 1923 1923	1896 1923 1922
H4	Le Sueur P.O. Box 10 Le Center 56057	1853 Dakota	1870 1854 1870	1856 1853 1853
	Lincoln (old)	1861 (abolished, 1868; became part of Renville) Renville *McLeod		
H1	Lincoln (present) Ivanhoe 56142	1873 (1881) Lyon *Redwood/*Lyon	1879 1879 1879	1874 1878 1880
H2	Lyon 607 W. Main Marshall 56258	1868 (1870) (deorganized, 1873; reorganized, 1875) Redwood	1874 1871 1874	1870 1890 1875
G3	McLeod 830 11th East Glencoe 55336	1856 Carver/Sibley	1870 1865 1870	1856 1864 1867
	Mahkahto	1849 (abolished, 1851; became part of Cass and Pembina) unorganized land *Ramsey		
C2	Mahnomen P.O. Box 379 Mahnomen 56557	1906 Norman	1907 1907 1907	1904 1907 1907
	Manomin	1857 (deorganized, 1858; abolished, 1869; became part of Anoka) Ramsey *St. Louis/*Anoka/*Hennepin		
A1	Marshall 208 E. Colbin Avenue Warren 56762	1879 (1881) Kittson *Polk	1884 1881 1884	 1882
J3	Martin Fairmont 56013	1857 Brown/Faribault	1870 1862 1870	1857 1864 1861
G3	Meeker P.O. Box 881 Litchfield 55355	1856 (deorganized, 1856; reorganized, 1866) Davis *Carver	1869 1859 1869	1856 1858 1858
	Midway	1857 (abolished, 1858) (see South Dakota) Brown		
E4	Mille Lacs 635 Second Street S.E. Milaca 56353	1857 (1860) Ramsey *Morrison	1871 1868 1872	1849 1875 1861
	Monongalia	1861 (1861) (deorganized, 1865; abolished, 1870; became part of Kandiyohi) Davis/ Pierce/unorganized land *Stearns/*Meeker		
	See Arthur L. Finnell, The Extant Records of Monongalia County, Minnesota, 1858–1870 (Marshall, Minn.: Finnell-Richter and Assoc. 1980).			
E3	Morrison Little Falls 56345	1856 (1856) Benton	1870 1866 1870	1856 1860 1857

Map	County Address	Date Formed Parent County/ies	Birth Marriage Death	Land Probate Court
J5	Mower 201 First Street N.E. Austin 55912	1855 (1856) Rice	1870 1870 1870	1856 1877 1858
H2	Murray 2500 28th Street Slayton 56172	1857 (1879) Brown *Redwood/*Watonwan/*Cottonwood	1873 1872 1873	1873 — 1879
	Newton	1855 (as Doty; renamed, 1855; abolished, 1856; became part of St. Louis)		
H4	Nicollet 510 S. Minnesota St. Peter 56082	1853 Dahkota	1870 1852 1870	1853 1862 1850
J2	Nobles P.O. Box 757 Worthington 56187	1857 (1870) Brown *Martin	1869 1872 1870	1872 1873 1874
C1	Norman 16 E. Third Avenue Ada 56510	1881 Polk	1881 1882 1881	1885 1882 1882
J6	Olmsted 515 Second Street S.W. Rochester 55902	1855 (1855) Fillmore/Rice/ Wabasha/unorganized land	1871 1855 1871	1855 1864 1858
D2	Otter Tail 121 W. Junius Avenue Fergus Falls 56537	1858 (1870) Cass/Pembina *Stearns/*Crow Wing/*Douglas	1871 1869 1871	1867 1872 1871
	Pembina	1849 (1852) (renamed to Kittson, 1878) unorganized land *Benton/*Morrison/*Crow Wing/ *Douglas/*Becker/*Clay		
B1	Pennington Thief River Falls 56701	1910 Red Lake	1910 1910 1910	1880 1910 1910
	Pierce	1853 (abolished, 1862; became part of six counties) Dakota *Nicolet		
E5	Pine Pine City 55063	1856 (1857) (deorganized, 1858; reorganized, 1871) Chisago/Ramsey *Chisago	1871 1871 1871	 1875 1871
H1	Pipestone P.O. Box 455 Pipestone 56164	1857 (exchanged names with Rock, 1862) (1879) Brown *Big Sioux/*Redwood/*Watonwan/ *Cottonwood/*Rock	1877 1879 1877	1879 1880 1879
B1	Polk 612 N. Broadway Crookston 56716	1858 (1879) Pembina *Crow Wing/*Douglas/*Becker/*Clay	1873 1873 1873	1873 1877 1879
F2	Pope 131 E. Minnesota Avenue Glenwood 56334	1862 (1866) Cass/Pierce/unorganized land	1868 1869 1870	1866 1867 1868

Map	County Address	Date Formed Parent County/ies	Birth Marriage Death	Land Probate Court
G5	Ramsey Room 286 15 W. Kellogg Boulevard St. Paul 55102	1849 St. Croix (old)/unorganized land	1870 1849 1870	1844 1849 1849
B1	Red Lake Red Lake Falls 56750	1896 (1897) Polk	1897 1897 1897	1873 1897 1897
H2	Redwood P.O. Box 130 Redwood Falls 56283	1862 (1865) Brown	1864 1865 1869	1865 1877 1868
G3	Renville 500 E. DePue Olivia 56277	1855 (1866) Nicollet/Pierce/Sibley *Nicollet	1870 1867 1870	1864 1893 1870
H5	Rice 218 N.W. Third Street Faribault 55021	1853 (1855) Dakota/Wabasha	1870 1856 1870	1853 1858 1858
J1	Rock Luverne 56156	1857 (exchanged names with Pipestone, 1862) (1874) Brown *Brown/*Martin/*Nobles	1870 1872 1870	1871 1873 1874
A2	Roseau 216 Center Street Roseau 56751	1894 (1896) Beltrami/Kittson	1895 1895 1895	1892 1894 1895
	St. Croix (old)	1840 (Wisconsin Territory) (eliminated, 1849)		
	St. Louis (old)	1855 (as Superior; renamed St. Louis, 1855; renamed Lake, 1856) Itasca		
C5	St. Louis (present) 100 N. Fifth Avenue W. Duluth 55802	1856 (1857) Itasca/Newton *Benton	1870 1870 1870	 1869
G4	Scott 428 S. Holmes Street Shakopee 55379	1853 Dakota	1871 1856 1871	1853 1853
F4	Sherburne 13880 Highway 10 Elk River 55330	1856 (1862) Benton	1870 1858 1870	1856 1857 1861
H4	Sibley 400 Court Street Gaylord 55334	1853 (1854) Dakota *Hennepin	1870 1865 1870	1855 1895 1866
F3	Stearns P.O. Box 548 St. Cloud 56302	1855 (1855) Cass/Nicollet/ Pierce/Sibley	1870 1870 1870	1855 1859 1857
J5	Steele Owatonna 55060	1855 (1856) Blue Earth/LeSueur/ Rice	1870 1856 1870	1856 1858 1856
F1	Stevens Fifth and Colorado P.O. Box 107 Morris 56267	1862 (1871) Pierce/unorganized land *Stearns/*Douglas/*Pope	1872 1869 1872	1871 1875 1870

Map	County Address	Date Formed Parent County/ies	Birth Marriage Death	Land Probate Court
	Superior	1855 (renamed St. Louis [old]) Itasca		
F2	Swift P.O. Box 110 Benson 56215	1870 (1897) Chippewa *Pope/*Chippewa/*Kandiyohi	1871 1871 1870	1871 1873 1874
E3	Todd 215 First Avenue S. Long Prairie 56347	1855 (1873) Cass *Stearns/*Morrison	1869 1867 1870	1867 1876 1868
	Toombs	1858 (renamed Andy Johnson, 1862; renamed Wilkin, 1868) Pembina		
F1	Traverse P.O. Box 428 Wheaton 56296	1862 (1881) Pierce/unorganized land *Chippewa/*Stearns/*Douglas/*Pope/ *Stevens	1881 1881 1881	1872 1880 1881
H6	Wabasha 625 Jefferson Avenue Wabasha 55981	1849 (1853) unorganized land *Washington	1870 1865 1870	1853 1856 1860
D3	Wadena 415 S. Jefferson Wadena 56482	1858 (1881) Cass/Todd *Crow Wing/*Morrison	1873 1873 1880	1873 1889 1881
	Wahnahta Seventh Street and Second Avenue P.O. Box 518 St. James 56081	1849 (abolished, 1851; became part of Cass, Dakota, and Pembina) unorganized land *Ramsey		
J4	Waseca N. State Street Waseca 56093	1857 Steele	1870 1857 1870	1856 1871 1857
G5	Washington 14900 N. 61 Street Stillwater 55082	1849 St. Croix (old)/ unorganized land	1870 1843 1870	1856 1849 1847
J3	Watonwan Seventh Street and Second Avenue St. James 56081	1860 (1871) Brown *Blue Earth	1870 1867 1870	1859 1890 1885
E1	Wilkin Breckenridge 56520	1868 (as Toombs; renamed Andy Johnson, 1862; renamed Wilkin, 1868) (1872) Pembina	1880 1884 1885	1871 1888 1884
	1n 1864, Andy Johnson was deorganized and attached to Stearn, then Crow Wing, then Douglas, then Otter Tail.			
J7	Winona 171 W. Third Winona 55987	1854 Fillmore/Wabasha	1870 1854 1870	1853 1856 1855
G4	Wright 10 N.W. Second Street Buffalo 55313	1855 (1855) Cass/Sibley	1868 1856 1868	1856 1854 1858
G2	Yellow Medicine 415 Ninth Avenue Granite Falls 56214	1871 (1874) Redwood	1872 1872 1872	1861 1874 1872

MISSISSIPPI

Kathleen Stanton Hutchison

The first written record of Mississippi history began in 1540 when the Spaniard Hernando de Soto and his men later crossed its boundaries to discover the Mississippi River. Yet long before these first Europeans came, there were Native Americans who existed in this natural habitat with its gentle climate, fertile soil, and plentiful food environment. Mississippi was home to many tribes; in the early days there was a larger population of Native Americans there than in any other state in the Southeast. Some of the major tribes include the Natchez on the lower Mississippi, the Chickasaw in the north and northeast, and the Choctaw in the central and southern part.

Mississippi history may be divided into four distinct jurisdictional periods: French Colonial (1699–1763), British Provincial (1763–79), Spanish Provincial (1779–98), and American Territorial and Statehood (1798–present). The year 1699 saw the French establish the colony of Biloxi, the first permanent settlement in this part of the Lower Mississippi Valley. Later this colony was moved to Mobile, and Natchez was established as the seat of government in 1716. Towards the end of the Seven Years War (or French and Indian Wars) in 1763, France ceded this province to Britain, beginning the immigration of Protestant, land-loving British who contrasted with the remaining Roman-Catholic French. Sixteen years later in 1779, the British yielded control of the Natchez District to the Spanish, who remained until pro-American sentiment prevailed.

When Mississippi Territory was formed in 1798 by the U.S. Congress, the territory included lands north of the 31st parallel and south of Tennessee lying between the Chattahoochee and the Mississippi rivers. During this period there were only two significant regions of settlement: the Natchez District found in the southern part of the state along the Mississippi River, and the St. Stephens District in the eastern section on the Tombigbee River. At the time, Spain controlled the Gulf Coast and the Choctaw, Creek, and Chickasaw tribes owned more land than did the white settlers, who numbered fewer than 5,000 in 1798.

With the opening of the territory in that year, there was a surge of immigration that sparked a recurring division and formation of county boundaries. The fact that the present state of Alabama was part of Mississippi Territory now and then causes confusion for the researcher. The present Alabama counties of Washington, Madison, Baldwin, Clarke, Monroe, Mobile, and Montgomery were organized as counties in Mississippi Territory. County names have been duplicated in Mississippi and Alabama of all these except for Baldwin and Mobile counties. The coastal area of Mississippi Territory was part of British West Florida (1763–79) and later of Spanish West Florida (1779–1810) until after the War of 1812. Actually, the land encompassing the Mississippi counties of Hancock, Harrison, and Jackson was made a part of Mississippi Territory in 1812, following the West Florida Revolution of 1810.

Ambiguous application of land grant distribution through the Treaty of Paris in 1783 and Pinckney Treaty of 1795, coupled with politics of the era, produced a sometimes muddled trail of land titles. Early Mississippi history may be characterized as one of white settlers moving onto lands that were previously owned by natives. The acquisition of this land by treaties is more fully explained in Goodspeed's *Biographical and Historical Memoirs of Mississippi* (see Background Sources for additional references). Some of the problems encountered with these treaties may be better understood by reviewing Clarence Edwin Carter, comp. and ed., *Territorial Papers of the United States: The Territory of*

Mississippi, vol. 6 (Washington, D.C.: Government Printing Office, 1938).

The thrust of immigration and settlement pushed the territory towards statehood in 1817. In 1832, through treaties made with the Choctaw and Chickasaw, all land in the present state of Mississippi was opened for settlement. Offering opportunities for a richer life, the divergent cultures from the past came together as one. Cotton became king, and the state of Mississippi flourished at an astonishing pace for decades preceding the Civil War, aided by the labors of many blacks, both slave and free.

Mississippi voted to secede from the Union on 9 January 1861, putting into motion events that led to Mississippi's involvement in the Civil War. The harsh period of Reconstruction that followed left a long-standing bitterness that further strengthened Mississippi's political stand regarding states' rights. The Jim Crow laws, legislation put into effect by the white electorate, guaranteed that the freed blacks would continue in a condition of servitude, poverty, and ignorance. Sharecropping sprang into being for blacks and whites alike, leading once again to an economic dependence on cotton. Because of its persistence in clinging to an agricultural society, Mississippi was well into the twentieth century before attempting to join an industrialized America. The records created after 1940 reflect political, economic, and cultural changes that dramatically altered Mississippi life.

Vital Records

By law, the State of Mississippi was not required to keep birth or death certificates until 1 November 1912. Birth and death records since 1912 have been kept by the Bureau of Vital Statistics, P.O. Box 1700, Jackson, Mississippi 39205. The bureau will respond to mail requests; however, the requests must be submitted on the appropriate, required form. After the Civil War, separate books for black marriages were kept, although when looking for *any* marriage in Mississippi *all* marriage volumes in the county should be checked.

The Mississippi Department of Archives and History (see Archives, Libraries, and Societies) maintains microfilm copies of marriage records held in the county courthouses. The records held are often sporadic depending upon the years of courthouse fires. The Mississippi Genealogical Society, *Survey of Mississippi Courthouses* (Jackson, Miss.: the society, 1957), although outdated, provides important holdings information about surviving court records kept in each courthouse. In addition to the marriage records in each county, there is a statewide index listed by groom's name on microfilm for those marriages prior to 1926. This index includes name of the bride and groom, date marriage took place or when the license was secured, name of the county, and book and page number of the marriage record. Also, some counties have original marriage records indexed by bride's name.

Before 1859, divorce proceedings were introduced as private bills in the legislature. References to these are found in Index to Session Acts, an unpublished guide found in the Mississippi Department of Archives and History. Since 1859, divorce proceedings are filed in the chancery clerk's office of the county in which the divorce took place. Copies of these later records are not found at the state archives.

Census Records

Federal

Population Schedules.

- Indexed—1820, 1830 (part), 1840, 1850, 1860 (part), 1870
- Soundex—1880, 1900, 1910, 1920

Industry and Agriculture Schedules.

- 1850, 1860, 1870, 1880

Mortality Schedules.

- 1850, 1860, 1870, 1880

Slave Schedules.

- 1850, 1860 (part)

Union Veterans Schedules.

- 1890

In 1817 Mississippi became the twentieth state to enter the union; therefore, the first federal population census available is that of 1820. Variations of this census appear in three printed forms, none of which include slave or miscellaneous information. Both the *Mississippi 1820 Census* and the *Mississippi 1830 Census* have been published by Irene and Norman Gillis, Shreveport, Louisiana. Enumerations for Pike County are missing in 1830, but the Gillis index used extant tax records to supplement their index. Transcriptions are subject to error; use these reprints simply as a *guide* to the original records. A significant addition to the 1840 census supplies the names and ages of pensioners (see page 3). Schedules are missing for Hancock, Sunflower, and Washington counties in 1860. By 1870, with slavery abolished, all blacks, natives, and Chinese were included, along with information regarding citizenship. With the destruction of the 1890 population schedules (see page 2), only the schedules enumerating Union veterans are available for Mississippi.

Aside from those indexes produced by AISI (see page 2), two other indexes include Irene S. Gillis, comp. *Mississippi 1850 Census Surname Index*, 3 vols. (Shreveport, La.: the compiler, 1972), and Kathryn Rose Bonner, comp., *Mississippi 1860 United States Census Index*, 3 vols. (Mariana, Ark.: the compiler, n.d.).

Microfilm copies of all federal census schedules and the original state copies of the 1850–80 schedules are located at the Mississippi Department of Archives and History. Some of the original agriculture and industry schedules were lost after microfilming. Scattered reels of census schedules are available at other repositories in the state. Microfilm copies of federal censuses for Mississippi are available through national organizations (see pages 2–3).

Colonial

An early census of the Natchez District, taken in 1792 from the Spanish Provincial records, has been printed in Dunbar Rowland, *History of Mississippi, The Heart of the South,* 4 vols. (Chicago, Ill.: S. J. Clark Publishing Co., 1925). Other censuses from the Spanish Colonial period (1784, 1787, 1788, and 1794) can be found in the *Papeles Procedentes de Cuba* (The Cuban Papers) located at the General Archives of the Indies in Seville, Spain. See Roscoe R. Hill, *Descriptive Catalogue of the Documents Relating to the History of the United States in the Papeles Procedentes de Cuba* (Washington, D.C.: Carnegie Institute of Washington, 1916).

Territorial and State

Territorial census reports were authorized by the legislature of Mississippi Territory at different intervals from 1798 until 1817. A useful start with territorial census information may be found in Norman E. Gillis, *Early Inhabitants of the Natchez District* (Shreveport, La.: the author, 1963). Although the information was gathered from secondary sources, it still remains a helpful tool. The original records are housed at the Mississippi Department of Archives and History. These census records are available for research purposes at the Mississippi Department of Archives and History and for purchase on microfilm from Micro Security, P.O. Box 1723, Hutchinson, Kansas 67504-1723.

One other special census known as the "Armstrong Roll of 1831" (see Alabama—Census Records) was taken following the signing of the Choctaw "Treaty of Dancing Rabbit Creek," the last major land concession made by the native Americans to the Europeans. Some of the information on this roll includes names of the Choctaw tribal members, whites who married Choctaw natives, and slaves.

An indirect source giving census information is the Educable Children Records, a census of school age children taken by county. Although the Mississippi Department of Archives and History has some of these records, many are still located at each county superintendent of education's office. These records are arranged at the archives by county with no index available.

Background Sources

To begin researching Mississippi records, there are two publications of particular note that provide useful overviews of resources in the state. See Richard S. Lackey, "Mississippi" in Kenn Stryker-Rodda, ed., *Genealogical Research Methods and Sources,* vol. 2, rev. ed. (Washington, D.C.: American Society of Genealogists, 1983): 188–218, and Ruth Land Hatten, "Genealogical Research in Mississippi," *National Genealogical Society Quarterly* 76 (March 1988): 25–51. For a broad historical account of the development of Mississippi, consult Richard A. McLemore, *A History of Mississippi,* 2 vols. (Jackson, Miss.: University and College Press of Mississippi, 1973). All three were consulted as resources in developing this chapter.

An excellent interpretive history is John Ray Skates, *Mississippi: A Bicentennial History* (New York, N.Y.: W. W. Norton & Co., and Nashville, Tenn.: American Association for State and Local History, 1979). A good, short bibliographic essay at the end suggests other Mississippi history to read.

In the later part of the nineteenth century, a historical and biographical compilation of information about Mississippi was put together in Goodspeed's *Biographical and Historical Memoirs of Mississippi,* 2 vols. (Chicago, Ill.: Goodspeed Publishing Co., 1891), reproduced by Bell and Howell (Wooster, Ohio: Micropublishers, Micro Photo Division, n.d.). Information for these volumes was taken from oral histories, but the publication offers a genuine "flavor" of Mississippi.

With eighty-two counties in the state, it would be impractical to formulate a listing of all local histories. For a current listing, see P. William Filby's *A Bibliography of American County Histories* (see page 3).

Original folders of the WPA County Files, completed in the late 1930s, provide an introspective view of a county through a variety of sources found in each folder. Both the folders and a microfilm copy are at the Mississippi Department of Archives and History. The Mississippi Library Commission, P.O. Box 10700, Jackson, Mississippi 39209-0700, has microfilm copies as well.

The Biographical Index found at the Mississippi Department of Archives and History is a card index to information on Mississippians during the territorial and early statehood days. The genealogical sources indexed include territorial census and tax rolls, Secretary of State's Register of Commissions (lists of state and county office holders), select Mississippi newspaper notices, and Goodspeed's *Memoirs,* cited previously. Also indexed are Mississippi soldiers who participated in the War of 1812 and the Mexican War.

For the best explanation of Mississippi military participation, see Dunbar Rowland, *Military History of Mississippi, 1803–1898* (1898; reprint, Spartanburg, S.C.: Reprint Co., 1978). James F. Brieger, *Hometown Mississippi* (2d ed., n.p., 1980), provides an extensive listing of Mississippi places with a brief historical passage and can be important in locating communities that no longer exist.

Maps

Historical maps found at the Mississippi Department of Archives and History can be accessed through the Chronological Listing arranged by date and situation of the map. Included in this list are numerous maps dating from 1500 to 1984. This selection contains all accessioned maps, including some produced by governmental agencies such as the U.S. Geological Survey (see page 4) and the Mississippi

State Highway Department. Sanborn Fire Insurance Maps (see page 4) help identify location of structures.

County highway maps, produced by the Mississippi State Highway Department, Map Sales, P.O. Box 1850, Jackson, Mississippi, 39215-1850, are available for a nominal fee. These maps are useful when trying to locate cemeteries in the state (see Cemetery Records).

Information in respect to state and federal legislation of land is uncovered in the Mississippi Historical Records Survey, *State and County Boundaries of Mississippi* (Jackson, Miss.: Historical Records Survey, 1942). This publication presents, in summary form, all the laws affecting the boundaries of the state of Mississippi, the counties in the state, and the judicial districts that were changed either by law, treaty, or proclamation.

Land Records

Public-Domain State

At different times, early Mississippi land records were granted by four different jurisdictions: France, Britain, Spain, and the state of Georgia. These four all owned parts of Mississippi before the area became part of the United States in 1798. Ownership of land based on a grant from a former jurisdiction is called a private land claim, and each landowner of these claims was required to file it with the federal government after Mississippi came under U.S. jurisdiction. These private land claim records are on microfilm (RG 28 SG 1) at the Mississippi Department of Archives and History and can be accessed by consulting the department's guide, "Index to Private Claims and Field Notes in Mississippi." Further information is given in E. K. Kirkham, *The Land Records of America . . .* (see page 4) and *Guide to Genealogical Research in the National Archives* (see page 5).

Mississippi is a public land state, which means that initial (first-grant) disposition of public owned land after 1798 became the responsibility of the federal government under the GLO (now BLM). Kinds of records contained here are field notes and surveys, tract books, official monthly abstracts, patents, and entry records. For the individual buying land directly from the United States government, the transaction was recorded in local federal land offices, and the legal description was entered into tract books. Mississippi's eight land office districts and the chronological periods of operation within the state of Mississippi as described in Harry P. Yoshpe and Philip P. Brower, Preliminary Inventory, No. 22 (see page 5) were the following:

St. Stephens (or district east of the Pearl River) (26 December 1806–17) was the first opened land office district, and it was the first closed. The district was located in what is now Washington County, Alabama. Transactions covered those for the southeastern district, including land Georgia ceded to the federal government in 1798 and 1802. Augusta became the land office serving the area.

The Washington land office (Adams County) (or district west of the Pearl River) (1807–61) covered land including Choctaw sales of individual reserves.

The federal land office at Huntsville, Alabama (1810–present), was created for the purpose of managing those lands acquired by treaties with the Chickasaw in 1805 and Cherokee in 1806, the office is located in Madison County, Alabama. See Marilyn Davis Barefield, comp., *Old Huntsville Land Office Records and Military Warrants, 1810–1854* (Easley, S.C.: Southern Historical Press, 1985).

Between 1827–36, the Jackson land office (Hinds County) (1823–27, 1836–61, 1866–1925) was located at Mt. Salus and regulated land sales in west-central Mississippi.

The office at August (Perry County) (1820–59) was moved to Paulding (Jasper County) in 1860–61, having jurisdiction over lands in the lower portion of east-central Mississippi.

The Columbus district (Lowndes County) (1833–61) encompassed lands in the northern portion of east-central Mississippi.

The Chocchuma land office (now Grenada County) (1833–40) was located in the Choctaw District on the Yalobusha River. It moved to Grenada after 1840 where it continued operating until 1860, serving land in the vicinity of northwest Mississippi.

The Pontotoc office (Pontotoc County) (1836–61) served lands roughly in the extreme northeast of Mississippi. By 1869, all were consolidated to one in Jackson.

When the land offices closed in Mississippi, the land records were sent to the BLM (see page 5); however, the original field notes and plat books are housed at the Secretary of State's Office. Inquiries may be sent to the Public Lands Division, 401 Mississippi Street, Jackson, Mississippi 39205. This office is open to those who want to do research, but there is a fee for research done by the staff.

The best genealogical information pulled from the first-grant land records may be found in the various types of entry records. The private land claim, as previously explained, was the entry record which recorded claims to land from foreign governments. Military bounty land was issued as a reward for military service. Credit entries were simply those lands purchased with the intent of paying later, and the Cash entry signified those lands sold after 1820 when land was sold for cash only. Those lands given by the government for specific reasons were called donation entries. Homestead entries were created under the Homestead Act of 1862, which gave certain stipulations to settlers in exchange for land. Aid in deciphering these records may be found in Richard S. Lackey, "Credit Land Sales, 1811–1815: Mississippi Entries of the Pearl," (Master's thesis, University of Southern Mississippi, 1975: 185–222); and Robert V. Haynes, "Disposal of Lands in Mississippi Territory," *Journal of Mississippi History* 24 (1962): 226–52.

Another type of land transaction involves the buying and selling of property among private citizens (subsequent sales). In Mississippi, these transactions are recorded as deeds at the county courthouse and filed by the chancery clerk, although the Mississippi Department of Archives and

History and the FHL have large collections of these land records on microfilm, filed by county.

The Mississippi Department of Archives and History has copies of records taken from both the land commissioner's office (first-grants) and the offices of chancery clerks (subsequent sales). The Congressional Records in the archives provide a considerable amount of information about land legislation including petitions from individuals, land companies, and state and local governments regarding land claims from 1795 to 1872. Located in these documents are also copies of treaties with Native Americans regarding land cessions. Other information is dispersed throughout the provincial, territorial, state and federal records found in the collection. The map file includes extensive land surveys for the area of the lower Mississippi Valley.

The documentation of ownership of land offers valuable information to the researcher, but it can be a complicated process in Mississippi. For a better working knowledge in the use of such records, see Elizabeth Shown Mills, "Backtracking Hardy Hunter: A Case Study of Genealogical Problem Solving Via the Preponderance of Evidence Principle," *Association of Professional Genealogists Quarterly* 1 (Spring 1986): 1–19; continued in 1 (Summer 1986): 1–20; and her "Land Titles: A Neglected Key to Solving Genealogical Problems—A Case Study," *Louisiana Genealogical Register* 31 (June 1984): 103–23.

Probate Records

Although Mississippi Territory had influences from different European countries, it was English law that it looked to for guidance even from the beginning; this law separated courts of law and equity as Mississippi distinguished the chancery court from the circuit court.

Courts of probate were originally created by the state constitution in 1817 as "orphans' courts," with responsibilities encompassing probate matters and guardianship. By 1832, the actual name had become "probate court" and was administered by the "chancery clerk." An amendment passed in 1857 abolished all chancery courts, with probate function then coming under the jurisdiction of the circuit courts. And so it remained until 1869 when the chancery courts were reinstated.

The chancery court in Mississippi encompasses a wide range of duties. One responsibility of the clerk of the chancery court was to act as judge of probate, keeping records of wills and testaments that are probated. Other functions include claims against an estate being administered; taking proof of wills and admitting wills to probate; and appointing guardians for minors, people of unsound minds, and convicts. These records are on file at the county courthouse, and many are also on microfilm at the Mississippi Department of Archives and History.

Record books are only one source of material in Mississippi. Loose papers associated with the estate are also located in some county courthouses, with scattered microfilm copies at the Mississippi Department of Archives and History.

Court Records

It is important to make the distinction that probate records are maintained by the chancery court, but that the chancery court has additional responsibilities for other records. These tasks include keeping official records of land titles, mortgages, and other documents customarily recorded at the courthouse.

The term "circuit" developed in 1817 when the state set up judges to rotate in a particular geographic area to make determinations in civil matters. These courts have not deviated greatly from their earliest mission. Marriage licenses, voter registrations, declarations and naturalizations, criminal court minutes, and in some cases the coroner's book are maintained by the circuit court. These records are available to the public at the county courthouse and may also be found on microfilm at the Mississippi Department of Archives and History and through the FHL.

Tax Records

Local county courthouses maintain original tax records, both real and personal. Microfilm copies of the earlier records are found in the Mississippi Department of Archives and History where the collection is extensive, but there are gaps. Although not many, some counties have published selected years of tax rolls.

Cemetery Records

The card catalog at the Mississippi Department of Archives and History provides access to the numerous cemetery books that have been published for many counties throughout the state. Another card index of value provides volume-by-volume access to *Mississippi Cemetery and Bible Records*, an ongoing publication project by the Mississippi Genealogical Society since 1949. Individual volumes, without the card index, are on the shelves of many local libraries throughout the state.

The Bible and Cemetery Records Collection, prepared by the DAR, is very useful but is not thoroughly indexed. Although records of individual cemeteries are scattered throughout these compilations, some volumes concentrate on the cemeteries of one county, such as Hinds, Adams, or Bolivar.

Another source to consult is the Genealogical and Cemetery File, which consists of an upright file of folders arranged by county and includes, among other items, unpublished cemetery records donated to the archives by researchers.

To facilitate the process of finding a cemetery in the state, the typescript of "State Cemeteries" located at the Mississippi Department of Archives and History lists public and private cemeteries giving section, township, and range. This finding aid and the WPA cemetery list, a typescript listing of public and private cemeteries by county, which also includes the section, township, and range, can be used in conjunction with county maps (see Maps).

Also on microfilm are the Mississippi Grave Registrations, which could help in the location of a veteran who was buried in Mississippi. However, this list is not complete.

All of the above resources are available at the Mississippi Department of Archives and History (see Maps about location of cemeteries in the state).

Church Records

The Spanish Dominion brought the strong influence of Catholicism into colonial Mississippi, but Mississippi as a territory witnessed the development of other organized religions that were predominantly Protestant faiths. In actuality, the priest left with the Spanish as the U.S. officially claimed Mississippi Territory, leaving only a handful of Catholic families in the area. For a general interpretation of this period, see James J. Pillar, "Religious and Cultural Life, 1817–1860," in McLemore, *A History of Mississippi*, pages 378–410, vol. 1, cited in Background Sources.

In 1798 the remaining Roman Catholic populace was administered to occasionally by priests from Louisiana and Mobile. More specific information about Catholic records in colonial and territorial times may be found in Elizabeth Shown Mills, "Spanish Records: Locating Anglo and Latin Ancestry in the Colonial Southeast," *National Genealogical Society Quarterly* 73 (December 1985): 243–61; and in *Records of the Diocese of Louisiana and the Floridas, 1576–1803*, 12 reels (South Bend, Ind.: University of Notre Dame Archives Microfilm Publications, 1967). There was no real growth in the church until after the 1840s when there was a rush of Irish immigrants into the state. A separate diocese was created in 1837, located in Natchez, but ultimately was moved to Jackson. Archival material housed in the Catholic Diocese of Jackson Archives (P.O. Box 2248, 237 East Amite Street, Jackson, Mississippi 39205) includes clipping files (1850–present); papers of all prior bishops of the Mississippi Catholic Church (1837–present); property deeds and microfilmed sacramental record books of all parishes in the diocese; national Catholic directories (1843–present); and books dealing with Mississippi history and Southern church history.

Although there was not rapid progression of any church during territorial and early statehood days, the Methodist church became the largest antebellum religious group. See Gene R. Miller, *A History of North Mississippi Methodism, 1820–1900* (Nashville, Tenn.: Parthenon Press, 1966), for a general history of this denomination. The J. B. Cain Archives of Mississippi Methodism (Millsaps-Wilson Library, Millsaps College, Jackson, Mississippi 39210) contains an archival collection that features the history and development of the Methodist church in Mississippi from the Methodist Episcopal Church to the United Methodist Church. The materials include church histories, manuscript items from the early nineteenth century, various conference minutes beginning in 1817, and some periodicals. Most of these materials do not circulate, but photocopy services are available depending on the condition of the item. The United Methodist Archive Center, Drew University, Madison, New Jersey 07940, also holds a significant records collection.

Beginning in 1791 the Baptist church in Mississippi showed early signs of strength after the preacher Richard Curtis brought together the first group of Baptists at Coles Creek near Natchez. The Mississippi Baptist Association was formed as early as 1806 with a total of six churches and 706 members. Now it claims the largest membership in the state. For a broad overview see Richard A. McLemore, *A History of Mississippi Baptists, 1780–1970* (Jackson, Miss.: Mississippi Baptist Convention Board, 1971), and Gordon A. Cotton, *Of Primitive Faith and Order: A History of the Mississippi Primitive Baptist Church, 1780–1974* (Raymond, Miss.: Keith Press, 1974). Historical materials focusing on the development of the church are housed at the Mississippi Baptist Historical Commission, Mississippi College Library, P.O. Box 51, Clinton, Mississippi 39060-0051. The collection contains minutes of churches, a clipping and genealogical file dating to the late eighteenth century, local histories, manuscript materials, newspapers and newsletters, photographs, and other select church related records. There are no restrictions on use of the materials.

The formation of the Presbyterian church in 1800 is attributed to three missionaries: James Hall, William Montgomery, and James Bowman who were sent by the Synod of the Carolinas to preach. The first established Presbyterian church in Mississippi was Bethel at Uniontown in Jefferson County. The Synod of Mississippi was formed in 1835. For information on the synod, see Walter B. Posey, *The Presbyterian Church in the Old Southwest, 1778–1838* (Richmond, Va.: John Knox Press, 1952), and "Documentary Material Relating to the Early History of the Presbyterian Church in Mississippi," *Journal of the Presbyterian Historical Society* 21 (December 1943): 196–200. Some historical records may be found in the Belhaven College, Hood Library, 1500 Peachtree Street, Jackson, Mississippi 39202. There are no restrictions on the use of the materials. Other records may be located through the Historical Foundation of the Presbyterian and Reformed Churches, Assembly Drive, Box 847, Montreat, North Carolina 28757.

Episcopal church services were held in the Mississippi region in 1790. However, the first church, named Christ Church (at Church Hill in Jefferson County) was not organized until 1815 when it was founded by Adam Cloud. The Episcopal Diocese of Mississippi was organized in 1826 with churches located in Church Hill, Natchez, Port Gibson, and Woodville. No central repository exists for these church records. For more detail, see Nash K. Burger and Charlotte

Capers, "Episcopal Clergy of Mississippi, 1790–1940," *Journal of Mississippi History* 8 (April 1946): 59–66.

The Lutheran church was the last protestant church to organize in the state. The New Hope Lutheran Church was first formed in 1846 near Sallis in Attala County. However, in 1855 the Mississippi Synod was assembled as part of the United Synod of the South. There were nine Lutheran churches at the time. The repository for the southern states is the Lutheran Southern Seminary, 4201 North Main Street, Columbia, South Carolina 29203.

In addition to records found in local churches, researchers should look at the WPA publication, *Guide to Vital Statistics Records in Mississippi, Vol. II, Church Archives* (Mississippi Historical Records Survey, 1942). Compiled by Donna Pannell, *Church Records in the Mississippi Department of Archives and History* (1986), a bound computer printout, makes available materials such as manuscript papers, journals, minutes, and organization records found in both the library and the manuscript section of the department.

Military Records

Revolutionary War. At the beginning of the Revolutionary War, the region that was later to become Mississippi Territory was a province of Great Britain. In 1779 a patriot by the name of James Willing led attacks along the Mississippi, confiscating and destroying property belonging to the British. The significance of this action preambles later events which led to the Spanish taking control of British West Florida. Primary source material regarding these events may be uncovered through the British Provincial records found in the Mississippi Department of Archives and History. Of special interest is the Fifth Series (covering America and the West Indies), 582–97. Another helpful source from the National Archives is the Oliver Pollack Papers from Record Group 360, Records of the Continental Congress. These records were obtained in London through the British Public Record Office. For a better understanding of the period, see Robert V. Haynes, *The Natchez District and the American Revolution* (Jackson, Miss.: University Press of Mississippi, 1976).

Veterans of the Revolutionary War pioneered their way into this land and some can be traced through *Family Records: Mississippi Revolutionary Soldiers,* published by the Mississippi Society of the DAR. Information found here is not considered official proof but does offer good leads to what may otherwise have been lost. This publication does have errors, but it is well indexed. Because Mississippi was not part of the United States at the time, the Mississippi Department of Archives and History has no official Revolutionary War records on file. The grave registrations, however, include revolutionary soldiers who are buried in Mississippi (see Cemetery Records).

War of 1812. Research about the War of 1812 in Mississippi should begin with Eron O. M. Rowland's article, "Mississippi Territory in the War of 1812," found in volume four (Centenary Series) of Dunbar Rowland, ed., *Publications of the Mississippi Historical Society* (Jackson, Miss.: the society, 1921). The Mississippi Department of Archives and History has available copies of National Archives microfilm of both index and service records for Mississippians who served in this war. In addition, grave registrations should be checked (see Cemetery Records).

Mexican War. For an overview of the Mexican War as it related to Mississippi, see Lynda J. Lasswell, "First Regiment of Mississippi Infantry in the Mexican War" (Master's thesis, Rice University, 1969). National Archives microfilm of Mississippians' service records for the war are available at the Mississippi Department of Archives and History, along with Mississippi Grave Registrations (see Cemetery Records).

Civil War. Of particular value are the chapters in Rowland's *Military History*. . . (see Background Sources). It includes the numerical listing of the state's units that served in the Army of Northern Virginia, and the other listing of those that served in the Western Theater of Operations, Army of Tennessee. For a publication citing original materials pertaining to the Civil War, see Patti Carr Black and Maxyne Madden Grimes, comps., *Guide to Civil War Source Material in the Department of Archives and History, State of Mississippi* (Jackson, Miss.: Mississippi Department of Archives and History, 1962).

National Archives microfilm of Mississippi confederate military records, which include both muster rolls and some pension applications, are found at the Mississippi Department of Archives and History. The military record gives the name, rank, and organization of Mississippi soldiers who served in the Confederate States Army, and the pension application, made by the veteran or widow of a veteran, gives more genealogical data. There is also a listing of Union Volunteers from Mississippi. All of these compilations are indexed. The state's archives also has a microfilm copy of "Selected Records of the War Department Relating to Confederate Prisoners of War, 1861–1865," which are part of the War Department Collection of Confederate Records, Record Group 109.

Some county courthouses conducted and kept an enumeration of confederate soldiers in 1907. The Vicksburg National Military Park, Park Historian, 3201 Clay Street, Vicksburg, Mississippi 39180, has a listing of all known Union soldiers buried in their National Military Cemetery along with some family members that were buried there after 1866. This list is available at the park and at the Old Courthouse Museum in Vicksburg. Confederate Soldiers are buried at the Cedar Hill Cemetery, whose office has recorded lot purchasers beginning in 1840 and has a listing arranged alphabetically by state of confederate soldiers buried there. Inquiries may be addressed to P.O. Box 150, Vicksburg, Mississippi 39180.

Later Wars. With privacy restrictions placed on some later military records, availability becomes more difficult. Some records found in the Mississippi Department of Archives and History include World War I records (which include an alphabetical typescript index of Mississippi veterans). The National Archives-Southeast Region (see page 8) has World War I draft registration cards. The state's archives has an alphabetical index to Mississippi soldiers who fought in the Korean Conflict (Record Group 33), and in Official Records, Mississippians killed in World War I, World War II, the Korean Conflict, and the Vietnam Conflict. Grave Registrations for those buried in Mississippi include the following wars: Revolutionary War, War of 1812, Indian Wars, Mexican War, Civil War, Philippine Insurrection, World War I, World War II, and the Korean Conflict—though helpful, the source is not exhaustive.

Periodicals, Newspapers, and Manuscript Collections

Periodicals

A selected listing of genealogical and historical periodicals for Mississippi include the following:

Publications of the Mississippi Historical Society (1898–1914), published by the society (see Archives, Libraries, and Societies). Additional publications from the society continued to 1925 before *The Journal of Mississippi History* (1939–present), P.O. Box 571, Jackson, Mississippi 39205, published by the organization, began.

Family Trails (1977–1990), published quarterly by the Historical and Genealogical Association of Mississippi (see Archives, Libraries, and Societies).

Mississippi Coast Historical and Genealogical Society Quarterly (1968–present), P.O. Box 513, Biloxi, Mississippi 39533.

Mississippi Genealogical Exchange (1955–87), P.O. Box 16609, Jackson, Mississippi 39211.

Mississippi Genealogy and Local History (1969–70; 1974–79).

There are many good periodicals and newsletters published by local historical societies throughout the state. A listing of these organizations is kept at the Mississippi Department of Archives and History.

Newspapers

Over 2,000 newspaper titles have been published in Mississippi since the first paper, the *Mississippi Gazette,* appeared in Natchez in 1799. With the completion of the Mississippi Newspaper Project, a grant initiated by the Mississippi Department of Archives and History and funded by the National Endowment for the Humanities, surviving titles were identified, located, and microfilmed for preservation and research purposes. General bibliographic information was gathered along with detailed holdings data for courthouses, museums, and all types of libraries throughout the state. This information may be accessed through OCLC, a national online database found in many public and academic libraries, or through the Mississippi Union List of Newspapers. See also, George Lewis's reference guide, *Mississippiana: Union List of Newspapers* (Jackson, Miss.: Mississippi Library Commission, 1971).

Since it records documented events including births, deaths, and marriages, the newspaper is a source that should not be overlooked by researchers. Some have been indexed in Betty Couch Wiltshire, *Marriages and Deaths from Mississippi Newspapers, 1837–1863,* Vol. 1 (Bowie, Md.: Heritage Books, 1987); *1801–1850,* Vol. 2 (ca. 1989); and *1813–1850,* Vol. 3 (ca. 1989). Furthermore, some titles of newspapers are the only surviving documentation of the existence of a community or town.

Manuscripts

The Private Manuscript Collection found at the Mississippi Department of Archives and History consists of private papers from the 1700s to the present donated to the archives by families and individuals. There is genealogical information scattered throughout the collection; however, access can be a problem. The in-house finding aid is arranged alphabetically by title, which is usually the name of the donor, and contains a brief description of the papers. For a nominal fee, this narrative can be computer searched by using key words. The types of materials located consist of letters, business papers, plantation journals, diaries, church minute books and records, and even school and bank reports. The photograph collection encompasses some 50,000 images of portraits, architecture, scenes, and events. The WPA county collection is also found here. Access is provided through a card file arranged alphabetically by subject.

Archives, Libraries, and Societies

Mississippi Department of Archives and History
P.O. Box 571
Jackson, MS 39205

Major holdings of the department are outlined in its 1977 catalog, compiled by Thomas W. Henderson and Ronald E. Tomlin, *Guide to Official Records in the Mississippi Department of Archives and History,* which lists collections by record group number and itemizes county records available on the premises in microfilm form. Holdings acquired since 1977 have been described in its annual and biennial reports. Some records are restricted (for example, those of the insane asylums and charity hospitals), but an archivist usually will provide a copy of available data on a specific individual.

Mississippi Historical Society
100 South State Street
Jackson, MS 39205

Historical and Genealogical Association of Mississippi
618 Avalon Road
Jackson, MS 39206

Mississippi Genealogical Society
P.O. Box 5301
Jackson, MS 39216

L. W. Anderson Genealogical Library
P.O. Box 1647
Gulfport, MS 39501

Lauderdale County Department of Archives and History, Inc.
P.O. Box 5511
Meridian, MS 39302

University of Southern Mississippi
McCain Library and Archives
Hattiesburg, MS 39410

Among the largest holdings in the state of printed sources, not limited to Mississippi specifically, are located here.

Millsaps College
Millsaps-Wilson Library
P.O. Box
Jackson, MS 39210

Mississippi State University, Special Collections
P.O. Box 5408
Mississippi State, MS 39762

Microfilm of the collection's newspapers are available on interlibrary loan.

University of Mississippi, Archives and Special Collections
John Davis Williams Library
University, MS 38677

A general summary of the holdings found in the above institutions is found in the publication compiled and edited by Sandra E. Boyd and Julia Marks Young, *Mississippi's Historical Heritage: A Directory of Libraries, Archives, and Organizations.* (Hattiesburg, Miss.: Society of Mississippi Archivists, 1990). It provides an alphabetical listing of institutions by county, their current address, and a general summary of their published and unpublished historical materials.

Special Focus Categories

Immigration

The ports of New Orleans and then Mobile were main ports of entry for those nineteenth century immigrants who later came to settle in Mississippi. Gulfport, Harrison County, has served as port of entry in the twentieth century.

National land passports were issued to those passing through Native American lands or foreign-held land. Occasionally they give a description of the person and an explanation as to their reason of passage. For publication of these types of passports pertaining to Mississippi, see Dorothy Williams Potter, *Passports of Southeastern Pioneers, 1770–1823: Indian, Spanish and Other Land Passports for Tennessee, Kentucky, Georgia, Mississippi, Virginia, North and South Carolina* (Baltimore, Md.: Gateway Press, 1982).

Naturalization

Before 28 September 1906, all naturalization proceedings took place in any state court. Access to these earlier records may be obtained through the typescript index created by the WPA in 1942, "Index to Naturalization Records in Mississippi Courts, 1798–1906." Preparation of this index involved a massive combing of courthouse records in both chancery and circuit courts that located some material that had previously been considered lost. This index gives information leading to the location of declarations of intention, petitions, and minutes, noting the administration of oaths of allegiance.

Following 1906, all naturalization matters were conducted by the federal district courts. These records are housed at the National Archives-Southeast Region (see page 8).

Black American

Materials previously described in this chapter may be used in black genealogical research. In addition, there are other resources for the study of both free and slave black families in Mississippi's history. See Vernon L. Wharton, *The Negro in Mississippi, 1865–1890* (Chapel Hill, N.C.: University of North Carolina Press, 1947), for a classic study of that time period. There are the more specialized collections that are associated with black history or genealogy, and then there are areas in scattered collections that reveal a variety of useful information.

A voluminous collection also housed at the National Archives contains the papers pertaining to the Bureau of Refugees, Freedmen, and Abandoned Lands (RG 105), commonly referred to as the Freedman's Bureau collection. The Mississippi Department of Archives and History has a microfilm copy of these records and has created the only existing index for Mississippi labor contracts found within the collection. This bureau supervised issues relating to refugees, freedmen, and abandoned property. The labor contracts have been computer indexed by plantation, planter's name, freedman's name, and county. The researcher should be aware of the fact that there were approximately 300,000 freed slaves, but the index provides only 36,000 names. Not all freedmen entered into labor contracts. Another segment of the Freedman's Bureau includes the custody papers of the abandoned property owned by Confederates. Signed loyalty oaths or presidential pardons are held here if the property was restored to an individual.

Apart from slave enumerations in the federal censuses, the slave schedules of 1850 and 1860, and the indication of "race" in later censuses when each person in the household was named, county records of all kinds reveal some black genealogical information interspersed in tax rolls and marriage, probate (some records specifically noting names and ages of slaves in the estate), and court records. The researcher should take note that the distinction of race was not always marked in some of these records.

Other information may be gathered from school censuses, plantation journals, church records, cemetery records, and even newspapers. For a recently published guide to black press materials, see Julius E. Thompson, *The Black Press in Mississippi, 1865–1985: A Directory* (West Cornwall, Conn.: Locust Hill Press, 1988). With an intended historical purpose, this work directly renders a listing of newspapers, magazines, and newsletters printed by blacks in Mississippi from 1865 to 1985.

One collection that focuses on the black population is the Slave Impressments—Confederacy. These records are located at the National Archives (RG 109) and are hard to access since they are not indexed, microfilmed, or published. For the years 1864–65, this material gives a physical description, identification of the owner, the slave's value, and the date and name of person to whom the slave was sent for work detail.

The WPA ex-slave narrative project has particular genealogical interest. Mississippi was one of several states where the WPA conducted interviews with these black freedmen. These interviews have been published (see page 10) and are available at the Mississippi Department of Archives and History. Apart from these narratives, the manuscript collection at the department also contains oral histories of historical as well as genealogical value. Another collection found in the state archives library, with a limited finding aid, is the Alfred Stone Papers, which encompass a large compilation of published materials pertaining to black history.

The Newsfilm Collection draws together a more recent historical period of unedited news footage for the years 1954 to 1971. The significance of this collection is found in the documentation of the Civil Rights Movement in Mississippi including events like the arrival of the Freedom Riders, the Capitol Street Boycott, lunch counter sit-ins, demonstrations, James Meredith's enrollment at the University of Mississippi, and the desegregation of schools. The Coleman Library at Tougaloo College near Jackson maintains a significant collection focusing on the history of the Civil Rights Movement in Mississippi. Private papers of some Civil Rights leaders are found here along with papers from the NAACP Legal Defence Fund, the Lawyers Committee for Civil Rights Under Law, and the Lawyers Constitutional Defense Committee.

Another repository of special interest is the University of Mississippi Blues Archives which houses an extensive collection of historical materials pertaining to the blues. In addition to the recordings there is extensive biographical information on blues musicians including interviews, posters, and photographs.

Native American

Mississippi records relating to Native Americans did not give actual names until the nineteenth century. For a good explanation of the structure of kinship see Charles M. Hudson, *Southeastern Indians* (Knoxville, Tenn.: University of Tennessee Press, 1976), pages 185–96. Census records such as the "Armstrong Roll of 1831" (see Census Records) is a good place to begin, along with the papers kept by the Bureau of Indian Affairs (see page 11). The Mississippi Department of Archives and History has some of the records of the BIA on microfilm. There is also a select collection of genealogical sources located at the Choctaw reservation. Inquiries may be directed to Tribal Historian, Mississippi Band of the Choctaw, Route 7, Box 21, Philadelphia, Mississippi 39350.

Treaties are another genealogical source to be considered. See Charles J. Kappler, comp., *Indian Affairs: Laws and Treaties* 1779–1803, Vol. 2. (1904; reprint, New York, N.Y.: Interland Publishing Co., 1972). A valuable source with listings of Choctaw names is found in the Master's thesis by Samuel James Wells, "Choctaw Mixed Bloods and the Advent of Removal" (University of Southern Mississippi, 1987). A copy of the printed form or microfilm may be found at the Mississippi Department of Archives and History. Early native trading post records are found in the Papers of Panton, Leslie, and Company, a multi-reel microfilm edition covering 1738–1853 is available at the archives.

A bibliography of works published on the Choctaw is Clara Sue Kidwell and Charles Roberts, *The Choctaws: A Critical Bibliography* (Bloomington, Ind.: Indiana University Press, 1980). See also Sharon Sholars Brown, "The Jena Choctaw: A Case Study in the Documentation of Indian Tribal Identity," *National Genealogical Society Quarterly* 75 (September 1987): 180–93, and Arthur H. DeRosier, *The Removal of the Choctaw Indians* (Knoxville, Tenn.: University of Tennessee Press, 1970).

Many records relating to Native Americans were created by early colonial Americans as found in the Provincial Records (RG 24–26—see Provincial Records, below), in the Mississippi Department of Archives and History. However, evidence found in the records provides mostly background understanding of native and colonialists relations.

Provincial Records

These original records are divided according to the historical powers that ruled Mississippi during its early development. The French Provincial Records, covering the French Dominion date from 1678–1763 and are housed in Paris, France, at the Archives du Ministers du Colonies, Series C13a. A description of these papers may be found in the *Fifth Annual Report of the Mississippi Department of Archives and History, 1905–1906*, pages 61–151. For a translation of these records see *Mississippi Provincial Archives French*

Dominion, 1729–1748, 5 vols. (Baton Rouge, La.: Louisiana State University Press, 1927–84).

The English Provincial Records, dating from 1763 through 1783, cover the term of British Dominion and are at the British Public Records Office in London. For a listing of these records, see Charles M. Andrews, *Guide to the Materials for American History to 1783 in the Public Record Office of Great Britain,* Vols. I and II (Washington, D.C.: Carnegie Institute, 1965).

The Spanish Provincial Records are located in Seville, Madrid, and Simancas in Spain. Transcripts and microfilm copies of selections of all of these colonial records are found at the Mississippi Department of Archives and History and are known as the Provincial Records (RG 24–26).

County Resources

Microfilm and original copies of a large, although not complete, collection of Mississippi county records are in the collection held by the Mississippi Department of Archives and History. Microfilm copies are also generally available through the FHL. Researchers will still want to consult county courthouses for those materials that have either not been transferred or microfilmed, including, but not limited to, marriage licenses, probate files, court records, etc.

In 1798 when Mississippi became a territory, Adams, Pickering, and Washington counties were organized. Pickering was renamed Jefferson in 1802. As new counties were formed in the territory, some counties in both Alabama and Mississippi duplicated names from territorial days. For a visual representation of this county formation problem, see William Thorndale and William Dollarhide, *Map Guide to U.S. Federal Census Records, 1790–1920* (Baltimore, Md.: Genealogical Publishing Co., 1987).

Dates in the chart which follows indicate those materials jointly held by the Mississippi Department of Archives and History and the FHL. Known record losses from fires and other causes are indicated.

Deeds, probate records, and marriages may be found at the chancery clerk at the county courthouse. Microfilmed marriage books for both whites and blacks (see Vital Records) are indicated, in that order, under "Marriages." Court records may be found in the appropriate clerk's office at the courthouse.

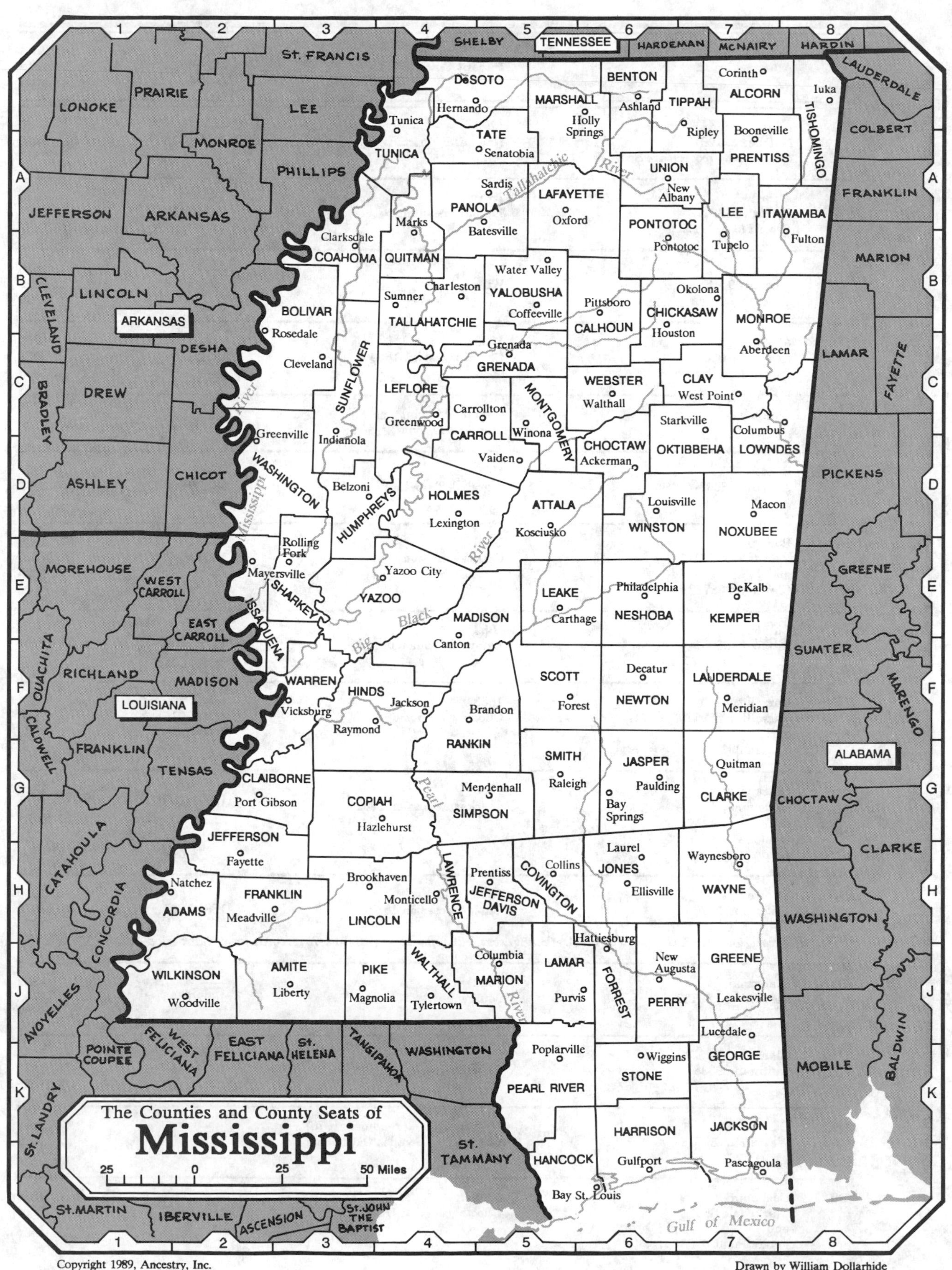

 Drawn by William Dollarhide

Map	County Address	Date Formed Parent County/ies	Birth Marriage Death	Land Probate Court
H2	Adams Natchez 39120 **Some early records are Spanish.*	1799 Natchez District	— 1802/1866 —	1780 1800 1781*
A7	Alcorn Corinth 38834 *Record loss, 1917.*	1870 Tippah/Tishomingo	— 1876/1871 —	1870 ? 1881
J3	Amite Liberty 39645	1809 Wilkinson	— 1809/1866	1810 1809 1809
D5	Attala Kosciusko 39090 *Record loss, 1858 and 1896.*	1833 Choctaw cession 1830	— 1892/1892 —	1858 1858 1858
	Bainbridge	(renamed Covington) Lawrence/Wayne		
A6	Benton Ashland 38603	1870 Marshall/Tippah	— 1870/1909 —	1870 1871 ?
B3	Bolivar Rosedale 38769 *and* Cleveland 38732	1836 Choctaw cession 1830	— 1866 —	1836 1861? 1836
B6	Calhoun Pittsboro 38951 *Record loss, 1922.*	1852 Lafayette/Yalobusha	— ? —	? ? ?
D5	Carroll Carrollton 38917 *and* Vaiden 39176	1833 Choctaw cession 1830	— 1834/1915 —	1834 1834 1834
B6	Chickasaw Houston 38851 *and* Okalona 38860 *Record loss, 1863.*	1836 Chickasaw cession 1832	— 1863/1863 —	1836 1863 1863
D6	Choctaw Ackerman 39765 *Record loss, 1888. Chester was the first county seat, but suffered several fires. No records from that period extant.*	1833 Choctaw cession 1830	— 1881/1881 —	1880 1879 1881
G2	Claiborne Port Gibson 39150	1802 Jefferson	— 1802/1805 —	1802 1802 1805
G7	Clarke Quitman 39335	1833 Choctaw cession 1830	— 1853/1865 —	1834 1837 1867?
C7	Clay West Point 39773	1871 (as Colfax; renamed, 1876) Chickasaw/Lowndes/Oktibbeha	— 1872 —	1872 1872 1872
B3	Coahoma Clarksdale 38614 and Friars Point 38631	1836 Choctaw cession 1830	— 1849/1849 —	1839 1856? ?

Map	County Address	Date Formed Parent County/ies	Birth Marriage Death	Land Probate Court
	Colfax	1871 (renamed Clay, 1876) Chickasaw/Lowndes/Oktibbeha		
G3	Copiah Hazlehurst 39083	1823 Choctaw cession 1820	— 1823 —	1823 1823 1856?
H5	Covington Collins 39428 *Record loss, 1904.*	1819 (as Bainbridge; renamed) Lawrence/Wayne	— 1904/1904 —	1853 1854 1857
A4	DeSoto Hernando 38632 *Record loss, 1940.*	1836 Chickasaw cession 1832	— 1845/1866 —	1836 1836 1854
J6	Forrest Hattiesburg 39401	1906 Perry	— 1906 —	1906 1906 ?
H2	Franklin Meadville 39653 *Record loss, 1877.*	1809 Adams	— 1825/1825	1842* 1842 1836
K7	George Lucedale 39452	1910 Greene/Jackson	— 1910/1910 —	1910 1910 1910
J7	Greene Leakesville 39451 *Record loss, 1875.*	1811 Amite/Franklin/Wayne	— 1874/1910 —	1876 1878 1898
C5	Grenada Grenada 38520 **Earlier records from parent counties are included.*	1870 Carroll/Yalobuska/ Choctaw/Tallahatchie	— 1870/1880 —	1834* 1870 1870
K5	Hancock Bay St. Louis 39520 *Record loss, 1853.*	1812 Mobile District	— 1853 —	1853 1853 1853
H6	Harrison Gulfport 39501 *Record loss, 1916.*	1841 Hancock/Jackson/Perry	— 1841/1907 —	1841 1853 ?
F3	Hinds Raymond 39154 *and* Jackson 39201 **Index and partial records begin 1854 with fragments earlier.*	1821 Choctaw cession 1820	— 1870/1871 —	1870 1823 1854*
D4	Holmes Lexington 39095	1833 Yazoo	— 1884 —	1833 1833 ?
D3	Humphreys Belzoni 39038	1918 Holmes/Washington/ Yazoo/Sunflower	— 1918? —	1918? 1918? 1918?
E2	Issaquena Mayersville 39113	1844 Washington	— 1866 —	1843 1849 1849

Map	County Address	Date Formed Parent County/ies	Birth Marriage Death	Land Probate Court
B8	Itawamba Fulton 38843	1836 Chickasaw cession 1832	— 1837 —	1836 1854 1854
K7	Jackson Pascagoula 39567 *Record loss, 1875.*	1812 Mobile District	— 1875 —	1875 1874 1875
G6	Jasper Paulding 39348 *and* Bay Springs 39422 *Record loss, 1932. *Indexes available for earlier dates.*	1833 Choctaw cession 1830	— 1906/1906	1904* 1904*
H2	Jefferson Fayette 39069 *Record loss, 1904.*	1799 (as Pickering; renamed, 1802) Natchez District	— 1805/1869 —	1798 1805 1802
H5	Jefferson Davis Prentiss 39474	1906 Covington/Lawrence	— 1906/1906	1906 1906 1906
H6	Jones Ellisville 39437 *and* Laurel 39440 *Record loss.*	1826 Covington/Wayne	— 1882/1888 —	1828 1894 1857
E7	Kemper DeKalb 39328 *Record loss, 1882.*	1833 Choctaw cession 1830	— 1912/1912 —	1881 1881 1881
A5	Lafayette Oxford 38655	1836 Chickasaw cession 1832	— 1850/1876 —	1836 1836 1836
J5	Lamar Purvis 39475 **Includes former Marion county records.* *Record loss, 1934.*	1904 Marion/Pearl River	— 1903 —	1836* 1901 ?
F7	Lauderdale Meridian 39301	1833 Choctaw cession 1830	— 1839/1870 —	1837 1849 1856
H4	Lawrence Monticello 39654 *Record loss.*	1814 Marion	— 1818/1910 —	1815 1836 1815
E5	Leake Carthage 39051	1833 Choctaw cession 1830	— 1836 —	1834 1852 1844
B7	Lee Tupelo 38801	1866 Itawamba/Pontotoc	— 1867/1867 —	1867 1867 1867
C4	Leflore Greenwood 38930 **Includes records from parent counties.*	1871 Carroll/Sunflower/Tallahatchie	— 1844/1894 —	1837* 1845* ?
H3	Lincoln Brookhaven 39601	1870 Franklin/Lawrence/ Copiah/Pike/Amite	— 1893/1893 —	1894 1893 ?

Map	County Address	Date Formed Parent County/ies	Birth Marriage Death	Land Probate Court
D7	Lowndes Columbus 39701	1830 Monroe	— 1830/1881 —	1830 1830 1837
F4	Madison Canton 39046	1828 Yazoo	— 1830 —	1828 1828 1828
J5	Marion Columbia 39429	1811 Amite/Wayne/Franklin	— 1812/1908 —	1821? 1812 1812
A5	Marshall Holly Springs 38635 **Two early deed books missing.*	1836 Chickasaw cession 1832	— 1836 —	1856* 1836 1839
B7	Monroe Aberdeen 39730	1821 Chickasaw cession 1816	— 1821 —	1821 1825 1825
C5	Montgomery Winona 38967 *Record loss, 1903.*	1871 Carroll/Choctaw	— 1891/1901 —	1871 1872 1872
E6	Neshoba Philadelphia 39350	1833 Choctaw cession 1830	— 1877/1895 —	1835 1837 1859
F6	Newton Decatur 39327 *Record loss, 1877 and 1910.*	1836 Neshoba	— 1872/1876 —	1876 1876 1876
D7	Noxubee Macon 39341	1833 Choctaw cession 1830	— 1834/1834 —	1834 1834 1834
D7	Oktibbeha Starkville 39759 *Record loss, 1880.*	1833 Choctaw cession 1830	— 1861/1861 —	1834 1880 1836
A4	Panola Sardis 38666 *Record loss, 1886.*	1836 Chickaswa cession 1832	— 1871/1884 —	1836 1845 1836
K5	Pearl River Poplarville 39470	1890 Hancock/Marion	— 1890/1909 —	1890 1899 1890
J6	Perry New Augusta 39462 *Record loss, 1877.*	1820 Greene	— 1877/1892 —	1862 1889 ?
	Pickering	1799 (renamed Jefferson, 1802) Natchez District		
J4	Pike Magnolia 39652 *Record loss, 1882.*	1815 Marion	— 1882/1882 —	1882 1882 1882
B6	Pontotoc Pontotoc 38863	1836 Chickasaw cession 1832	— 1849/1880 —	1836 1836 1872?

Map	County Address	Date Formed Parent County/ies	Birth Marriage Death	Land Probate Court
A7	Prentiss Booneville 38829 *Record loss, 1912. *Earlier deeds from parent county.*	1870 Tishomingo	— 1870 —	1836* 1870 1872
B4	Quitman Marks 38646	1877 Panola/Coahoma/Tunic/Tallahatchie	— 1877/1877	1877 1878 1878
F4	Rankin Brandon 39042	1828 Hinds	— 1828 —	1824 1828 1819
F5	Scott Forest 39074	1833 Choctaw cession 1830	— 1872/1865 —	1835 1835 1867?
E3	Sharkey Rolling Fork 39159	1876 Washington/Issaquena	— 1876 —	1876 1877 1877
G4	Simpson Mendenhall 38114 *Record loss, 1840, 1872. *Plat [Tract] book from 1832.*	1824 Choctaw cession 1820	— 1872/1872 —	1872* 1872 1872
G5	Smith Raleigh 39153 *Record loss, 1892, 1915.*	1833 Choctaw cession 1830	— 1912 —	1892 1893 ?
K6	Stone Wiggins 39577 *Records not on microfilm.*	1917 Harrison	— ? —	1917? 1917? 1917?
	Sumner	1874 (renamed Webster, 1882) Montgomery/Choctaw		
C3	Sunflower Indianola 38751 **Record loss, 1870.*	1844 Bolivar/Washington	— 1871/1871 —	1817* 1884 1844
B4	Tallahatchie Charleston 38921 *and* Sumner 38957 *Record loss at Sumner, 1908.*	1830 Choctaw cession 1830	— 1856/1880 —	1835 1834 1841
A4	Tate Senatobia 38668 **Transcripts from parent counties available.*	1873 Marshall/Tunica/DeSoto	— 1873/1873 —	1873* 1873 1873
A6	Tippah Ripley 38663 *Record loss, 1863.*	1836 Chickasaw cession 1832	— 1858/1888 —	1836 1855 1849
A8	Tishomingo Iuka 38852	1836 Chickasaw cession 1832	— 1842/1866 —	1836 1836 1856
A4	Tunica Tunica 38676	1836 Chickasaw cession 1832	— 1858 —	1836 1839 1839
A6	Union New Albany 38652 *Record loss, 1882. School Commisser Minutes 1846-59.*	1836 Pontotoc/Tippah	— 1878/1892 —	1872 ? ?

Map	County Address	Date Formed Parent County/ies	Birth Marriage Death	Land Probate Court
J4	Walthall Tylertown 39667	1914 Marion/Pike	— 1914/1914 —	1913 1913 1913
F3	Warren Vicksburg 39180	1809 Natchez District	— 1846/1860 —	1810 1810 1810
D2	Washington Greenville 38701	1827 Warren/Yazoo	— 1891/1858 —	1828 1839 ?
H7	Wayne Waynesboro 39367 *Record loss, 1892.*	1809 Washington	— 1881 —	? 1879 ?
C6	Webster Walthall 39771	1874 (as Sumner; renamed, 1882) Montgomery/Choctaw	— 1874/1909 —	1873 1874 1879
J1	Wilkinson Woodville 39669	1802 Adams	— 1804/1823 —	1803 1808 1822
D6	Winston Louisville 39339	1833 Choctaw cession 1830	— 1834/1908 —	1835 1834 1856
B5	Yalobusha Water Valley 38965 *and* Coffeeville 38922	1833 Choctaw cession 1830	— 1847/1866 —	1834 1834 1834
E4	Yazoo Yazoo City 39194	1823 Choctaw cession 1820	— 1845 —	1824 1834 1867?

Missouri

Marsha Hoffman Rising, C.G., C.G.L.

Missouri became the twenty-fourth state with its admission to the Union on 10 August 1821. Its central location, navigable waterways, and variable terrain attracted settlers from every part of the country, as well as from abroad. Missouri was settled by people from New England, the Ohio Valley, the Appalachian region, and the upper South, as well as from Germany and other European nations.

Four major migrations influenced Missouri's settlement. The first wave began during the Spanish and French control when American settlement was encouraged due to the fear of British encroachment. A colony came with Colonel George Morgan and settled near New Madrid, which was known as the first distinctly American settlement. In 1797 Moses Austin helped develop a sizeable settlement near the lead mine at the town of Mine á Breton, and in 1798 Daniel Boone was offered land if he would move to Missouri and bring new settlers with him. Boone's group settled in 1798 in what is now the area of St. Charles County. That same year a group of German-Swiss from North Carolina settled near the Whitewater Creek bottoms in present-day Cape Girardeau and Bollinger counties.

The second wave of settlers came with the acquisition of the territory by the United States in 1803. The population of the state grew from 10,000 people in 1804 to over 65,680 by 1821 when the state was admitted to the Union. During this time period, boundaries were changing rapidly, and the researcher will find it necessary to follow these changes in order to locate required records.

The third major wave was between 1820 and 1860 when the Ohio-Mississippi-Missouri river system and the extension of the Cumberland Road to the Mississippi River brought thousands of immigrants from the upper South and lower Midwest into Missouri, pushing the frontier to the Kansas border. During this period, the largest number of settlers came from Kentucky, followed by Tennessee, Virginia, Ohio, Indiana, and Illinois. The mountaineers from middle or east Tennessee and North Carolina were especially attracted to the Ozarks. Many of the Missouri and Mississippi river settlements were established by Southerners who maintained their political sympathies, slavery, and Democratic politics. They settled along the Mississippi River well north of St. Louis and across the Missouri Valley. A large proportion of settlers in the middle prairie regions came from Kentucky, while the people from Ohio, Indiana, and Illinois concentrated along the northern border and the Mississippi River. During this period, a large number of Germans settled in St. Louis and along the river counties west.

The researcher working between 1803–50 in Missouri should be familiar with the rapidly changing county boundaries and names. Much of the land purchased during this period was acquired through the federal land offices located in strategic positions throughout the state. The first land offices were established in 1818 at Jackson, Franklin, and St. Louis.

Immigration, for all intents and purposes, came to a standstill during the Civil War, but with peace, the fourth wave of settlers arrived. With the help of the railroads,

Europeans as well as pioneers from the prairie states of Ohio, Indiana, Illinois, and Iowa provided the major portion of newcomers. Northerners outnumbered Southerners nearly two to one. They occupied most of the remaining land north of the Missouri River, along the Kansas border, and along the Osage and Springfield plains. During this period the cities of St. Louis, Kansas City, Joplin, Springfield, and Jefferson City also grew rapidly. By 1890 the population of Missouri had reached 2,679,185.

Vital Records

No vital records were kept on the state level before 16 August 1909. For those filed after that date, requests should be made to Missouri Department of Health, Bureau of Vital Records, P.O. Box 570, Jefferson City, Missouri 65102. The 1991 fee for these records was $4.

A non-compulsory birth registration law was adopted in Missouri in 1863 and provided that county recorders of deeds could record births upon request. These births are recorded in the regular deed books (or in marriage books) and are not indexed. Registration was sporadic.

In the city of St. Louis, deaths were recorded from 1850–1910 and births from 12 July 1870 through 1910. It is estimated that only about 60 percent of the births and deaths that occurred during this period were recorded. They can be requested by writing to St. Louis City Vital Records, P.O. Box 14702, St. Louis, Missouri 63178. Kansas City also has intermittent early birth and death records. The address for inquiry is Kansas City Vital Records, 414 East 12th Street, Kansas City, Missouri 64106.

In 1883 Missouri passed a state law requiring the recording of births and deaths at the county level. Ten years later this law was inadvertently repealed. Compliance was poor. Most counties do have these registers, but there is enormous variation as to how complete and/or comprehensive they are. "A Guide to Public Vital Statistics Records in Missouri" (deaths) was published in the *Missouri State Genealogical Association Journal* in the fall issue of 1984. The Historical Records Survey, *Guide to Public Vital Statistics in Missouri* (St. Louis, Mo.: Historical Records Survey, 1941), will also aid the researcher. Many of these early county vital records have been microfilmed and are available through the Missouri State Archives.

Marriage records are held by the county recorder of deeds. Prior to 26 June 1881, no marriage license was required; the marriage was recorded at any convenient courthouse.

Divorce records are held by the clerk of the circuit court of the county in which the divorce occurred, except in St. Louis where they are held by the City Circuit Court Clerk, City Hall, 12th and Market, St. Louis, Missouri 63103; and in Kansas City by the Judicial Records Department, Jackson County Courthouse, 415 East 12th Street, Kansas City, Missouri 64106.

Census Records

Federal

Population Schedules.

- Indexed—1830, 1840, 1850, 1860, 1870
- Soundex—1880, 1900, 1910, 1920

Industry and Agriculture Schedules.

- 1850, 1860, 1870, 1880

Mortality Schedules.

- 1850, 1860, 1870, 1880

Slave Schedules.

- 1850, 1860

Union Veterans Schedules.

- 1890 (all except Daviess and DeKalb counties; some inadvertently included Confederate veterans)

The State Historical Society of Missouri in Columbia (see Archives, Libraries, and Societies) holds microfilmed copies of all available federal population censuses for Missouri and will loan them on interlibrary loan. The censuses for the years 1810 and 1820 are lost for all districts. All the remaining population censuses (except for 1890) have survived. The Missouri State Archives (see Archives, Libraries, and Societies) also holds microfilmed copies of all federal censuses for Missouri including the Soundex. The Missouri State Archives knows of no *state* copies of the federal population schedules that survived the capitol building fire of 1911. It does hold the original *federal* supplement to the 1880 population census that enumerated the defective, delinquent, and dependent classes. Called Supplemental Schedules Numbers 1–7, this part of the census enumerated those labeled "Insane, Idiots, Deaf-mutes and Blind, Homeless Children, Prisoners, Paupers and Indigents." Institutions were inventoried as well as private households. Since the county or state listed was one of the legal residences, the listing for the inhabitants of various institutions will give their residence before moving into the institution. The Missouri Historical Society in St. Louis has the original agriculture, industry, slave, and mortality schedules. The State Historical Society of Missouri in Columbia has microfilmed copies of some, but not all have been filmed.

Territorial and State

Censuses were taken during the territorial period in 1814, 1817, and 1819, but only statistical summaries remain. There are listings of heads of families of New Madrid for 1797 and 1803. Heads of families were enumerated for St. Charles in 1817 and 1819 only. Some of the early Spanish censuses of Upper Louisiana have been retrieved from the archives in Seville, Spain, and were published in Louis Houck's *The Spanish Regime in Missouri*, 2 vols. (Chicago, Ill.: R. R. Donnelley and Sons, 1909). This publication is an excellent documentary history of the period between 1770–1804.

Although Missouri conducted a number of state censuses, most of the individual schedules are lost; only the statistical abstracts remain. The state did compile a census corresponding to the 1840 U.S. census. Nine of those enumerations survived the capitol building fire of 1911; they are the counties of New Madrid, Newton, Pike, Randolph, Ray, Shelby, Stoddard, Warren, and Rives (now Henry). The originals are located in the Missouri State Archives. A few listings remain for the state censuses of 1844, 1852, 1856, and 1868. Most of these are statistical abstracts only. The state census of 1876 exists for Benton, Butler, Callaway, Cape Girardeau, Christian, Franklin, Greene, Holt, Howard, Iron, McDonald, Montgomery, Osage, Phelps, Reynolds, St. Francois, and Texas counties. The originals of these censuses remain in the county, but microfilmed copies have been made by the Missouri State Archives and can be searched there. Schuyler County took a special census in 1880. These censuses are not individual enumerations but are by age group, similar to the federal population schedules before 1850. They include the number of deaf, dumb, blind, insane, the number of livestock, and some agricultural items.

Background Sources

The following publications will be helpful to the Missouri researcher:

Foley, William E. *A History of Missouri.* Vol. I: 1673–1820. Missouri Sesquicentennial Edition. William E. Parrish, ed. Columbia, Mo.: University of Missouri Press, 1971.

Gerlach, Russell L. "Population Origins in Rural Missouri." *Missouri Historical Review* 71 (October 1976): 1–21.

———. *Settlement Patterns in Missouri: A Study of Population Origins, with a Wall Map.* Columbia, Mo.: University of Missouri Press, 1986.

Houck, Louis. *History of Missouri: From the Earliest Explorations and Settlements until the Admission of the State Into the Union.* 3 vols. Chicago, Ill.: R. R. Donnelley and Co., 1908.

March, Daniel. *The History of Missouri.* 4 vols. New York, N.Y.: Lewis Historical Publishing Co., 1967. Volumes 3 and 4 contain personal and family records.

Meyer, Duane. *The Heritage of Missouri.* Columbia, Mo.: University of Missouri Press, 1967.

Ohman, Marian M. "Missouri County Organization 1812–1876." *Missouri Historical Review* 76 (April 1982): 253–81.

———. *A History of Missouri's Counties, County Seats, and Courthouse Squares.* Columbia, Mo.: University of Missouri-Columbia Extension Division, 1983.

Schroeder, Walter A. *Bibliography of Missouri Geography.* Columbia, Mo.: University of Missouri-Columbia Extension Division, 1977. An excellent annotated listing of geographic materials including atlases. A must for the serious researcher.

Shortridge, James R. "The Expansion of the Settlement Frontier in Missouri." *Missouri Historical Review* 75 (October 1980): 64–90.

Maps

One of the best publications for Missouri maps is Milton D. Rafferty, *Historical Atlas of Missouri* (Norman, Okla.: University of Oklahoma Press, 1981). Detailed county maps showing cemeteries, houses, churches, schools, and all county roads are available from the Missouri State Highway Department, Division of Planning, Jefferson City, Missouri 65101. The researcher should ask for "General Highway Map of _____ County." The cost is minimal.

Other maps which will be helpful to the Missouri researcher are:

Campbell, R. A. *Gazetteer of Missouri.* St. Louis, Mo.: R. A. Campbell, 1874.

Ramsey, Robert L. *Our Storehouse of Missouri Place Names.* 1952. Reprint. Columbia, Mo.: University of Missouri Press, 1973.

Selby, Paul O. "A Bibliography of Missouri County Histories and Atlases." 2d ed. Kirksville, Mo.: *Bulletin of the Northeast Missouri State Teachers College* 66, no. 12 (1966).

Wetmore, Alphonso. *Gazetteer of the State of Missouri.* St. Louis, Mo.: C. Keemle, 1837.

Land Records

Public-Domain State

Land in Missouri was granted by three nations—France, Spain, and the United States. The original papers, as well as microfilmed copies, of the Spanish and French land grants are retained by the Missouri State Archives. Recording by the United States government of clear land titles granted by the Spanish and French governments actually began in St. Louis on 16 September 1805. An index to the land grants (Books A–D) has been published by the St. Louis Genealogical Society in the *St. Louis Genealogical Quarterly* 8 (September 1975): 53–58. The original minutes are housed in the Missouri State Archives.

Two good printed sources that describe the attempts to settle the early land conflicts are *Missouri Land Claims,* reprinted by Polyanthos Press, and Walter Lowrie, *Early Settlers of Missouri as Taken From Land Claims in the Missouri Territory* (1834; reprint, Easley, S.C.: Southern Historical Press, 1986). The former publication is the 1832 report from the Commissioner of the General Land Office to the 24th Congress. The disputed land claims began as early as 1787. The latter publication is or records compiled and indexed from the *American State Papers*.

The United States land offices began granting land in Missouri in 1818. For a brief history of locations and land policies in Missouri, see "Missouri's Public Domain: United States Land Sales, 1819–1922," *Archives Information Bulletin*, Vol. II, no. 3 (July 1980), produced in a separate publication by the Office of the Missouri Secretary of State. *Index of Purchasers of U.S. Land Sales 1817–1837* (Volumes 1–3) and *Springfield Land Office Abstracts 1835–1846* can be obtained from the Ozarks Genealogical Society, P.O. Box 3494, Glenstone Station, Springfield, Missouri 65808. The original records of the United States Land Sales have been microfilmed on seventeen reels and are located in Record Group 5 at the Missouri State Archives. A complete name index is on each reel. They are available for purchase at $5 per reel.

If the researcher knows the land description of the property of interest, copies of the original land patents granted by the United States government can be obtained from United States Department of the Interior, BLM, Eastern States Land Office (see page 5).

The Missouri State Archives also holds other land records of interest to the genealogical researcher. These include an alphabetical index to War of 1812 military lands of north Missouri; the Savannah Land Grants from 1845 through 1857 (indexed); the Platte Purchase records (with an index available at the archives); the Land Office Reports, microfilmed copies of *American State Papers*, volumes 1 through 8; and the United States General Land Office Reports, 1828–59. Other records of interest, which are indexed, include the township school lands, seminary lands, saline lands, and swamp lands, all of which were patented by the state.

Each county has a recorder of deeds. Here the researcher can expect to find the direct and indirect index to deeds, a transcript of deeds, warranty deeds, administrator's deeds, quit claim deeds, sheriff's deed records, index to mortgages, mortgages, school fund mortgage records, chattel mortgages, deeds of trust, patent records, plat books, the index to marriage records, marriage records, applications for marriage licenses, records of certificates of marriage, records of marriage of persons of color (from 1865 to the twentieth century in separate registers), and military discharge papers. Note that in Missouri all marriage records are held by the recorder of deeds (see Vital Records).

Probate Records

These are retained at the county level although many have been microfilmed by the Genealogical Society of Utah, in cooperation with the Missouri State Archives and the Missouri Supreme Court. Fortunately for the genealogist, special emphasis is placed on microfilming the estate files. One can expect to find an index to probate court papers, court records, executor's bonds, testamentary matters, inventories, sale bills, guardian and curators records, and court appointments. Usually the probate minute books, probate court records, and case files are also available. The researcher can check for the application letters for administration, executors and guardians, administrators and guardian's bonds, appraisement of estate, names and oaths of witnesses, sale bills, settlement records, orders of publication, term docket books, wills, and records of wills.

Court Records

The clerk of the county court holds an index to common pleas, records of all extant proceedings, chancery minute books, records of births and deaths, county court records, right-of-way and road records, as well as surveyor's records (including field notes and plats made by the county surveyor). This office usually holds the county treasurer's notes, bonds and commissions, records of marks and brands, wolf scalps, stray notices, real estate assessments, and tax books. The researcher needs to be aware that, in some counties, early terms for this court included "chancery" or the "court of common pleas."

The clerk of the circuit court holds the direct index to records such as divorces, debt, dissolution of partnerships, adoptions, judgment, and tax fee books including direct and indirect indexes. They also retain the index to criminal records and criminal files of the circuit court. Adoptions are under the jurisdiction of the circuit court. Naturalization records, including petitions, declarations of intention, certificates, and certificates of allegiance, and the granting of citizenship, are also located in the clerk's office, as well as an index to civil case files. Some naturalization records, however, have been found with the deeds.

Federal records that pertain to Missouri citizens are located at the National Archives-Central Plains Region (see page 8). The U.S. circuit and district court records beginning as early as 1822 include case file indexes, records books, dockets, and judgment books that have been microfilmed.

Tax Records

The Missouri Historical Society has some original tax records; others can be found in the Western Historical Manuscript Collection at the University of Missouri-Columbia, but most extant records remain in the office of the clerk of the county court. The Missouri State Archives has microfilmed some tax records for the counties of Boone, Callaway, Cape Girardeau, Chariton, Clay, Cooper, Franklin, Howard, Marion, Monroe, Montgomery, St. Charles, St. Francois, and Ste. Genevieve.

Prior to 1850, purchasers of the federal lands in Missouri were exempt from land taxes for five years after purchase. If one finds an ancestor on a Missouri tax list with livestock, etc., but no land being taxed, the individual may have purchased his land from the government within the preceding five years.

Some early delinquent tax lists were sent to the state auditor's office and are now located in the Capitol Fire Documents held by the Missouri State Archives (see Manuscripts).

Cemetery Records

The following national cemeteries are located in Missouri:

Springfield National Cemetery, 1702 East Seminole Street, Springfield, Missouri 65804. All known soldiers buried there, including those transferred from towns throughout southwest Missouri, were published in *Ozar'kin,* published by the Ozarks Genealogical Society in the four issues of volume 8, 1986.

Jefferson Barracks National Cemetery, 101 Memorial Drive, St. Louis, Missouri 63125. There is a card file reference to persons interred there. Inquiries may be made by phone or mail.

Jefferson City National Cemetery, 1024 E. McCarty Street, Jefferson City, Missouri 65101. The researcher may phone or write the Jefferson Barracks for information.

There is no central registry for cemeteries located in Missouri. Several projects are currently underway to locate and describe the private and public cemeteries. The Missouri State Genealogical Association (see Archives, Libraries, and Societies) has designated an individual to handle correspondence and maintain a card file on cemeteries that have been located. This list is regularly updated, and a publication is planned for the future.

An Index to Cemetery Locations in the Missouri Ozarks is available from the Ozark Genealogical Society (see Land Records for address) for $20. Recently released, the publication covers a forty-one-county area south of the Missouri River, listing over 5,000 cemeteries by name and location.

Church Records

The Missouri State Archives has published *A Brief Guide to Church Records on Microfilm,* which is a county by county listing, but it is currently out of print. The available church records can be located by using the archives's Manuscript Register. Church microfilm reels are not available for purchase without written consent of the individual church and must otherwise be used at the Missouri State Archives. The Western Historical Manuscript Collection on the University of Missouri-Columbia campus holds some church records. These can be located by using their descriptive catalogue or microfiche guide (see Manuscripts). Most church records in Missouri are scattered and remain in private hands.

The William E. Partee Center for Baptist Historical Studies is located in the Curry Library, William Jewell College, Liberty, Missouri 64068.

Military Records

The best source for military records now is the Missouri State Archives. Many of the records previously held by the Office of the Adjutant General have been transferred. Service records are indexed and maintained for the following wars: War of 1812, Indian Wars (1832–38), Seminole War (1837), Mormon War (1838), Iowa or Honey War (1839), Mexican War (1846–47), and Civil War—both Union and Confederate. Confederate pension applications and applications for admission to the Confederate Homes are also among these holdings. Accumulated files number approximately one-half of the reported 40,000 men who served from Missouri. Alphabetical indexes for the Spanish-American War (1898) are also extant.

Records subsequent to 1917, including those from World War I (1917–19), Missouri National Guard (1900–40), and World War II (1941–45), remain in the Office of the Adjutant General, 1717 Industrial Boulevard, Jefferson City, Missouri 65101.

The Loyalty Oaths (often called "The Ironclad Oath") administered after the Civil War can sometimes be located in local historical societies, county offices, or in manuscript collections (see below). A few of these oaths are among the records of the General Assembly in the Missouri State Archives.

A list of the Revolutionary War soldiers buried in Missouri is not complete, but a listing was published in the *Missouri State Genealogical Association Journal,* Vol. 5, nos. 3 and 4, and Vol. 6, no. 2. The known 1812 soldiers buried in Missouri were published in the same quarterly, Vol. 6, nos. 1 and 2.

Periodicals, Newspapers, and Manuscript Collections

Periodicals

Statewide and locally, many genealogical periodicals are published in Missouri. Both the *Missouri Historical Review* and the *Missouri State Genealogical Association Journal* cover the state on a broader spectrum. The active local organizations can be contacted regarding their current publications and activities. To determine available material of a local nature, refer to the *Directory* published by State Historical Society of Missouri (see Archives, Libraries, and Societies).

Newspapers

The State Historical Society of Missouri in Columbia holds the most complete newspaper collection. The earliest extant is the *Missouri Gazette,* 1808–14, which has been microfilmed. The society has published *Guide to Missouri Newspapers: When and Where 1808–1963,* compiled by

William H. Taft (Columbia, Mo.: State Historical Society of Missouri, 1964). In addition, *A Catalogue of Missouri Newspapers on Microfilm* is also available from the society for $10. The society will loan their microfilmed newspapers through the interlibrary loan system.

Several early newspapers have been abstracted for their genealogical material. These include *The Liberty Tribune, The Springfield Advertiser,* and *The St. Louis Christian Advocate.* Abstracts from various newspapers appear in *Death Records From Missouri Newspapers 1810–1857, Death Records of Missouri Men,* and *Death Records of Missouri Pioneer Women.* These have been privately published and are available in many libraries.

The State Historical Society of Missouri in Columbia has indexed some of its newspapers, particularly those located in their immediate geographic area and will check that index on request. The list of these counties (as of 1984) was published as "Newspapers Indexed for Obituaries," *Missouri State Genealogical Association Journal* 16 (Fall 1984): 185. The Missouri Historical Society in St. Louis has a unique obituary clippings collection which began over one hundred years ago. This collection concentrates on newspapers published in the eastern part of the state.

Manuscripts

The Joint Collection of the University of Missouri Western Historical Manuscript Collection and the State Historical Society of Missouri are located at 23 Elmer Ellis Library, University of Missouri-Columbia, Columbia, Missouri 65201. The State Historical Society of Missouri published a *Joint Collection Guide for the Manuscript Repositories* (July 1985) to aid researchers. It includes summary information on 3,414 of its manuscript holdings. The guide is arranged into thirty-eight distinct lists according to the subject classifications of the manuscript collections. Among the subjects are family and personal papers, genealogy, local history, military, pioneer and frontier life, travel, and women. Each manuscript collection is listed in as many subject areas as necessary to provide full access to that collection. Microfiche copies are $10 and microfilm orders $17.50. These may be ordered from the Joint Collection at the address above. The Joint Collection also houses the records of the Missouri Historical Records Survey (1936–42), which includes transcriptions of early court records.

The records which survived the devastating fire of the capitol building in 1911 were combined into a collection called the Capitol Fire Documents at the State Historical Society of Missouri, which has been indexed and microfilmed. The collection consists of thirteen reels of the index and 242 reels of documents. The original records and another set of microfilmed copies are in the Missouri State Archives.

The House and Senate journals are also in the Missouri State Archives. They have been microfilmed and are available for purchase. Items of interest in the records of the General Assembly include private acts, early divorces, petitions, and compensation for individuals.

Archives, Libraries, and Societies

Missouri Historical Society
Jefferson Memorial Building
Forest Park
St. Louis, MO 63103.

This private historical society holds an extensive collection of colonial materials; original copies of agricultural, slave, and mortality schedules; family papers with indexes; and extensive manuscript collections. There is a daily research fee of $5 for nonmembers.

State Historical Society of Missouri
1020 Lowry Street
Columbia, MO 65201

Located in the Ellis Library, University of Missouri-Columbia, this is a public institution. They hold federal population censuses, newspapers, county histories, genealogies, city directories, and county atlases in their wide collection. A guide entitled *Directory of Local Historical, Museums and Genealogical Agencies in Missouri* is published annually and is available for purchase. The directory lists addresses, hours, special collections, and publications of these various organizations, most of which exist on a county level and publish their own materials.

Missouri State Archives
Mailing Address: P.O. Box 778
Jefferson City, MO 65102

Located at 600 West Main in Jefferson City, the archives is the official repository for state materials. The archives has an extensive microfilm collection of county records (see County Resources). In addition to original records, they house some county histories, cemetery records, genealogies, and other published local records.

Missouri State Genealogical Association
P.O. Box 833
Columbia, MO 65205

This is the statewide organization, although many counties have their own local genealogical societies. They publish the *Missouri State Genealogical Association Journal* on a quarterly basis.

National Park Service
Wilson Creek National Battlefield Park
Springfield, MO 65807

Because of space limitations, the researcher should call ahead for an appointment to use this excellent Civil War library.

Special Focus Categories

Territorial Records

Many of the best sources for the early time period of Missouri history are inventoried in Milton Rubincam, ed., *Genealogical Research: Methods and Sources,* Vol. II, revised edition published by the American Society of Genealogists in 1983. Many of the colonial records are housed in the Missouri Historical Society in St. Louis (see Archives, Libraries, and Societies). Most of the early civil records and manuscripts concerning early colonial and St. Louis families are also there. The Chouteau Papers, which include the records of the American Fur Trading Company and the papers of the French and Spanish colonial archives, are just two of the society's major holdings. Real estate transactions from the St. Louis colonial archives were copied, in both French and English, into volumes maintained by the recorder of deeds in St. Louis. These volumes are indexed, and microfilmed copies are available at the Missouri State Archives. The researcher may also be assisted by the Historical Records Survey publication, *Early Missouri Archives,* published in 1941.

Original and microfilmed copies of the French and Spanish Land Grant papers are held at the Missouri State Archives. The papers have been partially indexed (see Land Records). A must for pre-statehood research is the book, *Index to the Minutes of the First and Second Board of Land Commissioners* (St. Louis, Mo.: St. Louis Genealogical Society, 1981).

The Missouri State Archives holds microfilmed copies of the early court records of Randolph County, Illinois; the Kaskaskia Manuscripts from 1718–1841; and the Randolph County, Illinois, Circuit Court papers. Copies of the Cahokia Parish Records, now St. Clair County, Illinois, extending from the years 1784 to 1809, are also held by the Missouri State Archives. Many of the early settlers traveled back and forth across the Mississippi River with great ease and may have recorded marriages and baptisms with whichever priest or county office that was in the area in which they were trading or visiting. The researcher should check in both Missouri and Illinois for records of these early pioneers.

Two sources helpful to the genealogist working in this time period are *The American State Papers: Documents Legislative and Executive of the Congress of the United States,* 38 volumes, indexed in *Grassroots of America,* edited by Philip W. McMullen and published in 1971 by Gendex Corporation in Salt Lake City. The genealogist will be particularly interested in the section that pertains to public lands. The researcher should also consult Clarence Edwin Carter's *The Territorial Papers of the United States,* Vol. XIII—Territory of Louisiana-Missouri, 1803–06; Vol. XIV, 1806–14; and Vol. XV, Territory of Missouri, 1815–21 (Washington, D.C.: General Services Administration, 1951). All are indexed. These publications are located in major genealogical and historical collections as well as in most university libraries.

Both original and microfilmed copies of the general court records (Territory of Louisiana), 1804–12, and superior court records (Territory of Missouri), 1812–21, are located in the Missouri State Archives and are in the process of being indexed and cataloged. Other territorial records available at the Missouri State Archives are found in Record Groups 1 and 2. These consist of some early tax lists, licenses for fur traders, and other miscellaneous records.

Black American

Although Missouri was a slave-holding state, the geography determined whether slaves were present in significant numbers. The slave population was distributed along the Mississippi and Missouri rivers. The greatest concentration was in the area called "Little Dixie" because it was settled by Southerners before the Civil War. The core area of "Little Dixie" includes the present-day counties of Howard, Cooper, Boone, Callaway, Audrain, Randolph, Monroe, Ralls, and Pike. The best general history for Missouri's black population is Lorenzo J. Greene, Gary R. Kremer, and Anthony F. Holland's, *Missouri's Black Heritage* (St. Louis, Mo.: Forum Press, 1980). The slave schedules for 1850 and 1860 for Missouri are extant and available on microfilm through the National Archives (see page 10).

County Resources

County records are retained at the local county level. The Missouri State Archives is making an extensive effort to microfilm many of these county records. A microfilm reel entitled *A Roll by Roll Listing of County Records on Microfilm* is available from the Missouri State Archives. This enables the researcher to ascertain the exact number of the reel desired. Microfilmed copies of county records are currently available at $5 per reel.

Note that in Missouri all marriage records are held by the recorder of deeds, even though they are listed here with other vital records sources. The year given is the earliest recorded, but there was no official requirement for records until 1881. Those birth and death records that do exist before statewide recording began in 1909 are held at the clerk of the county court in the county seat. The time period these cover is indicated below.

Dates given in the chart are the earliest ones for which records are held in a particular category. The researcher should be aware this does not mean all records in that category are extant. For instance, there may be letters of administration for a county as early as 1833, but the guardianships may not begin until 1845. Some of these early records are not indexed.

Correspondence may be addressed to the recorder of deeds, probate clerk, clerk of the circuit court, or clerk of the county court at the county courthouse as indicated below. Street addresses are necessary for some larger counties.

 Drawn by William Dollarhide

Map	County Address	Date Formed Parent County/ies	Birth Marriage Death	Land Probate Court
B4	Adair	1841	1883-93	1841
	Kirksville 63501	Macon	1841	1841
			—	1841
B1	Andrew	1841	1883-95	1841
	Savannah 64485	Platte Purchase	1841	1841
			1883-93	1841
	Arkansas	1806 (abolished, 1819; when it became Arkansas Territory)		
		New Madrid		
B1	Atchison	1845	1883-93	1845
	P.O. Box J	Platte Purchase/Holt	1845	1845
	Rock Port 64482		1883-93	1845
D5	Audrain	1836	1883-86	1837
	Mexico 65265	Callaway/Monroe/Ralls	1837	1837
			1883-86	1837
H3	Barry	1835	1883-85	1835
	Cassville 65625	Greene	1837	1835
			1883-85	1872
G2	Barton	1855	1883-96	1857
	Lamar 64759	Jasper	1866	1866
			1883-99	1866
E2	Bates	1841	1883-1907	1839
	Butler 64730	Cass	1860	1845
			1883-93	1858
	Courthouse burned 1861.			
E3	Benton	1835	1883-90	1837
	P.O. Box 1238	Pettis/Greene	1839	1836
	Warsaw 65355		1883-90	1835
G7	Bollinger	1851	1883-91	1851
	P.O. Box 46	Cape Girardeau/Madison/	1865	1866
	Courthouse burned 1866, 1884.	Stoddard/Wayne	1883-92	1866
D5	Boone	1820	—	1821
	701 E. Broadway	Howard	1821	1821
	Columbia 65201		—	1821
C1	Buchanan	1838	—	1839
	Fifth and Jules	Platte Purchase	1839	1839
	St. Joseph 64501		1883-93	1839
H7	Butler	1849	1883-93	1849
	Poplar Bluff 63901	Wayne	1878	1849
			1883-93	1849
C2	Caldwell	1836	—	1835
	Kingston 64650	Ray	1860	1856
	Courthouse burned 1860, 1896.		—	1859
D5	Callaway	1820	1883-88	1821
	Fulton 65251	Boone/Howard/Montgomery	1821	1821
			1883-88	1821
	Clerk of the county court has state census of 1844 and 1876.			

Map	County Address	Date Formed Parent County/ies	Birth Marriage Death	Land Probate Court
F4	Camden P.O. Box 960 Camdenton 65020 *Courthouse burned 1902.*	1841 (as Kinderhook; renamed, 1843) Benton/Morgan/Pulaski	— 1902 —	1849 1902 1902
G8	Cape Girardeau 1 Barton Square Jackson 63755 *Courthouse burned 1870; state census 1868, 1876.*	1812 original	1883-93 1805 1883-93	1805 1805 1815
C3	Carroll P.O. Box 245 Carrollton 64633	1833 Ray	1883-85 1833 1883-90	1833 1833 1833
H6	Carter Van Buren 63965	1859 Oregon/Reynolds/Ripley/Shannon	— 1861 —	1845 1859 1866
E2	Cass Harrisonville 64701	1835 (as Van Buren; renamed, 1849) Jackson	1883-1903 1836 —	1837 1835 1835
F3	Cedar P.O. Box 126 Stockton 65785	1845 Dade/St. Clair	1883-89 1845 1883-86	1845 1845 1845
C4	Chariton Keytesville 65261 *Courthouse burned 1864, 1973.*	1820 Howard	1883-87 1821 1883-87	1826 1861 1820
G3	Christian P.O. Box 549 Ozark 65721 *Courthouse burned 1865. Clerk of the county court has state census for 1876.*	1859 Greene/Taney/Webster	1840-1904 1866 1883-84	1861 1864 1865
	Clark (old)	1818 (abolished, 1819 when it became part of Arkansas Territory)		
B5	Clark (present) Kahoka 63445	1836 Lewis	1830-40; 1883-92 1836 1883-92	1833 1836 1837
D2	Clay Administration Building Liberty 64068	1822 Ray	1883-84 1822 1883-84	1822 1821 1822
C2	Clinton P.O. Box 245 Plattsburg 64477	1833 Clay	1863-79; 1883-88 1847 1883-88	1833 1833 1836
E5	Cole P.O. Box 353 Jefferson City 65101	1820 Cooper	1883-1906 1821 1883-1906	1821 1834 1821
D4	Cooper P.O. Box 8 Boonville 65233	1818 Howard	1883-94 1819 1883-89	1819 1819 1821
F6	Crawford P.O. Box 484 Steelville 65565 *Courthouse burned 1873, 1884.*	1829 Gasconade	1879-1903 1829 1883-91; 1942-43	1832 1832 1831

Map	County Address	Date Formed Parent County/ies	Birth Marriage Death	Land Probate Court
G3	Dade Greenfield 65661 *Courthouse burned 1863.*	1841 Barry/Polk	1883-85 1863 1883-85	1841 1841 1846
F4	Dallas P.O. Box 436 Buffalo 65622 *Courthouse burned 1863, 1864, 1867.*	1841 (as Niangua; renamed, 1844) Polk	1883-1908 1867 1883-1924	1867 1867 1867
C2	Daviess P.O. Box 334 Gallatin 64640	1836 Ray	1883-91 1837 1883-91	1838 1890 1837
	Decatur	1841 (as Ozark; renamed 1843; renamed Ozark again, 1845)		
C2	DeKalb P.O. Box 248 Maysville 64469 *Courthouse burned 1864.*	1845 Clinton	1883-93 1845 1883-91; 1942-43	1836 1877 1856
F6	Dent Salem 65560 *Courthouse burned 1864; earlier deeds re-created.*	1851 Crawford/Shannon	1883-84 1851 1883-84	1851 (1866) 1866 1866
	Dodge	1849/50 (abolished, 1853; became part of Putnam)		
H4	Douglas P.O. Box 398 Ava 65608 *Courthouse burned 1886.*	1857 Ozark	— 1877 1886-94	1858 1886 1886
J8	Dunklin P.O. Box 188 Kennett 63857 *Courthouse burned 1872 deeds 1872-76 re-created.*	1845 Stoddard	— 1872 —	1859 1865 1872
E6	Franklin P.O. Box 391 Union 63084 *County clerk has 1876 state census.*	1818 St. Louis	1862-92 1819 —	1819 1819 1819
E6	Gasconade P.O. Box 241 Hermann 65041	1820 Franklin	1867-96 1822 1883-96	1821 1825 1821
B2	Gentry Albany 64402 *Courthouse burned 1885. County clerk reports Feb. 1989 that earliest records for * categories is 1885.*	1845 Clinton	1867-93 1859 1883-93	1859* 1859* 1859*
G3	Greene 940 Boonville Springfield 65803 *Courthouse burned 1861. County clerk has state census for 1844 and 1876.*	1833 Crawford/Wayne	1883-1901 1833 1883-1902	1833 1832 1833
B3	Grundy 700 Main, Second Floor Trenton 64683	1841 Livingston	1847-66, 1883-93 1841 1883-93	1841 1863 1841
B2	Harrison P.O. Box 27 Bethany 64424 *Courthouse burned 1874.*	1845 Daviess	1883-89 1845 1883-93	1845 1853 1845

Map	County Address	Date Formed Parent County/ies	Birth Marriage Death	Land Probate Court
	Hempstead	1818 (abolished, 1819 when it became part of Arkansas Territory) New Madrid		
E3	Henry Clinton 64735	1834 (as Rives; renamed, 1841) Lillard	1883-90 1835 scattered	1835 1834 1835
F3	Hickory P.O. Box 3 Hermitage 65668 *Courthouse burned 1852, 1881.*	1845 Benton/Polk	1883-98 1872 1883-89	1846 1845 1845
B1	Holt Oregon 64473 *Courthouse burned, 1965. County court clerk has state census 1876.*	1841 (as Nodaway; renamed, 1841) Platte Purchase	1883-89 1841 1883-89	1841 1837 1841
D4	Howard Fayette 65248 *Courthouse burned 1887. County court clerk has state census 1876.*	1816 St. Charles/St. Louis	1883-93 1816 1883-88	1816 1818 1816
H5	Howell West Plains 65775 *Courthouse burned 1866.*	1857 Oregon	1883-95 1867 1883-95	1866 1862 1857
F7	Iron 250 S. Main Street Ironton 63650	1857 Madison/St. Francois/Reynolds/ Washington/Wayne	1883-96 1857 1883-87	1814 1857 1857
D2	Jackson 415 E. 12th Street Kansas City 64106	1826 Lillard	1883-95 1827 1883-93	1827 1828 1828
G2	Jasper Carthage 64836 *Courthouse burned 1863 and 1883.*	1841 Barry	1883-1900 1841 1883-97	1841 1841 1841
E7	Jefferson P.O. Box 100 Hillsboro 63050	1818 St. Louis/Ste. Genevieve	1883-92 1825 1883-92	1819 1820 1819
E3	Johnson Warrensburg 64093	1834 Lillard	1883-94 1835 1883-94	1832 1835 1835
	Kinderhook	1841 (renamed Camden, 1843) Benton/Pulaski/Morgan		
B5	Knox Edina 63537	1845 Scotland	1883-1939 1845 1883-93	1845 1845 1845
F4	Laclede Second and Adams Lebanon 65536	1849 Camden/Pulaski/Wright	1883-93 1855 —	1849 1848 1845
D3	Lafayette P.O. Box 416 Lexington 64067	1820 (as Lillard; renamed, 1825) Cooper	— 1821 —	1820 1821 1821
	Lawrence (old)	1815 (abolished, 1819; when it became part of Arkansas Territory) New Madrid		

Map	County Address	Date Formed Parent County/ies	Birth Marriage Death	Land Probate Court
G3	Lawrence (present) Mt. Vernon 65712	1845 Barry/Dade	1883-93 1845 1883-93	1845 1843 1845
B5	Lewis P.O. Box 67 Monticello 63457	1833 Marion	1883-87 1833 1883-87	1833 1833 1833
	Lillard	1820 (renamed Lafayette, 1825)		
D6	Lincoln 201 Main Street Troy 63379	1818 St. Charles	— 1825 1883-84	1819 1820 1819
C4	Linn Linneus 64653	1837 Chariton	1822-88; 1907 1857 1883-87	1836 1840 1837
C3	Livingston P.O. Box 803 Chillicothe 64601	1837 Carroll	1883-91 1837 1883-90	1837 1837 1837
H2	McDonald P.O. Box 665 Pineville 64856 *Courthouse burned 1863. Deeds before 1863 re-created; county court clerk has state census 1876.*	1849 (as Seneca; renamed, 1849) Newton	1856-94 1865 —	1853 1865 1855
C4	Macon P.O. Box 382 Macon 63552	1837 Chariton/Randolph	1883-93 1837 1883-93	1837 1838 1837
G7	Madison Fredericktown 63645	1818 Cape Girardeau/Ste. Genevieve	1883-1900 1821 1883-1900	1819 1821 1827
F5	Maries Vienna 65582 *Courthouse burned 1868.*	1855 Osage/Pulaski	1883-84 1869 1883 only	1855 1866 1866
C5	Marion Palmyra 63461 **Also births 1927-30 and deaths 1927-30.*	1826 Ralls	1883-90* 1827 1883-89*	1827 1827 1827
B3	Mercer Princeton 64673 *Courthouse burned 1898.*	1845 Grundy	1883-94 1898 1883-94	1846 1849 1868
E4	Miller P.O. Box 12 Tuscumbia 65082	1837 Cole/Pulaski	1883-91 1837 1883-1904	1837 1837 1837
H8	Mississippi P.O. Box 304 Charleston 63834	1845 Scott	— 1845 —	1823 1845 1845
E4	Moniteau California 65018 *County clerk has state census 1876.*	1845 Cole/Morgan	1883-94 1845 1883-87	1845 1845 1845
C5	Monroe Paris 65275	1831 Ralls	1883-85 1831 1883-85	1831 1832 1831

Map	County Address	Date Formed Parent County/ies	Birth Marriage Death	Land Probate Court
D6	Montgomery 211 E. Third Montgomery City 63361	1818 St. Charles	—— 1864	1839 1889
	Courthouse burned 1864, 1901. County Clerk has State Census 1876; copies of the orginal early deeds are in Jones Abstract Company in Montgomery City.			
E4	Morgan Versailles 65084	1833 Cooper	1841-63; 1883-86 1833 1883-86	1834 1834 1833
	Courthouse burned 1887.			
H8	New Madrid P.O. Box 68 New Madrid 63869	1812 original	—— 1847 ——	1805 1800 1805
H2	Newton Neosho 64850	1838 Barry	1883-85 1865 1883-85	1839 1839 1939
	Courthouse burned 1862.			
	Niangua	1841 (renamed Dallas, 1844) Polk		
B1	Nodaway Third and Main Maryville 64468	1845 Andrew	1883-90 1845 1883-93	1845 1845 1845
H6	Oregon P.O. Box 406 Alton 65606	1845 Ripley	1883-90 1845-61; 1877 1883-89	1845 1854 1845-59; 1872
	Courthouse burned during Civil War.			
E5	Osage P.O. Box E Linn 65051	1841 Gasconade	1883-98 1841 1883-94	1841 1841 1841
	Courthouse burned 1880. County clerk has 1876 state census.			
H4	Ozark P.O. Box 36 Gainesville 65655	1841 (renamed Decatur, 1843; renamed Ozark, 1845) Taney	1884-90 1858 1887-89	1858 1865 1858
J8	Pemiscot Caruthersville 63830	1851 New Madrid	1883-84 1882 ——	1881 1865 1883
	Courthouse burned 1883. Deed index from 1833 survived fire.			
F8	Perry Perryville 63775	1820 Ste. Genevieve	1883-94 1830 1883-94	1821 1821 1821
E3	Pettis 415 S. Ohio Sedalia 65301	1833 Cooper/Saline	1883-85 1833 1883-85	1833 1833 1833
F5	Phelps Third and Rolla Rolla 65401	1857 Crawford	1883-90 1857 1883-90	1857 1858 1857
	County clerk has 1876 state census.			
C6	Pike 115 W. Main Bowling Green 63334	1818 St. Charles	1883-84 1825	1819 1825 1819
C1	Platte P.O. Box 70CH Platte City 64079	1838 Platte Purchase	1883-87 1839 1883-87	1839 1839 1839

Map	County Address	Date Formed Parent County/ies	Birth Marriage Death	Land Probate Court
F3	Polk Bolivar 65613	1835 Greene	1872-1900 1836 1883-90	1837 1835 1836
F5	Pulaski Waynesville 65583 *Courthouse burned 1903.*	1833 Crawford	— 1903 —	1903 1833 1903
B4	Putnam Unionville 63565	1845 Adair/Sullivan	1878-1907 1849 1887-1907	1847 1853 1855
C6	Ralls New London 63459	1820 Pike	1883-93 1821 1883-86	1821 1821 1821
C4	Randolph Main Street Huntsville 65259 *Courthouse burned 1880. Deed index from 1829 survived fire.*	1829 Chariton/Ralls	1883-89 1829 1883-89	1841 1829 1858
D2	Ray Richmond 64085	1820 Howard	1883-90 1820 1883-89	1820 1821 1821
G6	Reynolds P.O. Box 76 Centerville 63633 *Courthouse burned, 1872. State census, 1876.*	1845 Shannon	1883-86 1872 1883-86	1872 1872 1872
H7	Ripley Doniphan 63935	1833 Wayne	1883-97 1833 1883-93	1833 1856 1867
	Rives	1834 (renamed Henry, 1841)		
D7	St. Charles 188 N. Second Street St. Charles 63301 *City Clerk has birth and death records 1883-1952.*	1812 original	1867-90 1807 —	1804 1805 1808
F3	St. Clair P.O. Box 405 Osceola 64776	1841 Rives	1883-1903 1855 1883-90	1841 1865 1841
F7	St. Francois Farmington 63640 *County clerk has state census for 1876.*	1821 Jefferson/Washington/Ste. Genevieve	1883-93 1836 1883-90	1822 1822 1822
E7	St. Louis 7900 Forsythe Boulevard Clayton 63105 **Public Vital Records before State Recording: Department of Community Health, 121 S. Meramec, Clayton 63102.*	1876 original/St. Louis City	1876-* 1876-* 1883-*	1876 1876 1876
E7	St. Louis (City) 1200 Market Street St. Louis 63100 *Public Vital Records before State Recording: City of St. Louis, Vital Records, P.O. Box 14702, St. Louis 63178. Some births and deaths were recorded back as far as 1825, but they are far from complete; card index from 1870 for births and 1850 for deaths, but this is not available for public research.*	1804 (1764) original	1825-* 1766 1825-*	1766 1766 1766
F7	Ste. Genevieve P.O. Box 46 Ste. Genevieve 63670 **Also Misc. Records (Concessions, Contracts, Deeds, Slave Deeds) 1761-.*	1812 original	1883-92 1807 1883-92	1804* 1807 1804

Map	County Address	Date Formed Parent County/ies	Birth Marriage Death	Land Probate Court
D3	Saline Marshall 65340 *Courthouse burned during Civil War.*	1820 Cooper	1883-85 1835 1883-85	1821 1821 1821
B4	Schuyler P.O. Box 186 Lancaster 63548 *County court clerk has state census 1880.*	1845 Adair	1883-93 1845 1883-91	1845 1845 1846
B5	Scotland Memphis 63555 *Clerk of the county court has census of 1850, 1860, 1870.*	1841 Clark/Lewis/Shelby	1883-89 1841 1883-89	1836 1842 1841
G8	Scott P.O. Box 188 Benton 63736	1821 New Madrid	1883-86 1840 1883-86	1822 1825 1822
	Seneca	1849 (renamed McDonald, 1849)		
G6	Shannon P.O. Box 148 Eminence 65466 *Courthouse burned 1863, 1871, 1938; recorder's office burned 1893.*	1841 Ripley	— 1881 —	1859 1869 1872
C5	Shelby P.O. Box 176 Shelbyville 63469	1835 Marion	1883-87 1835 1883-87	1835 1836 1835
H8	Stoddard P.O. Box 25 Bloomfield 63825 *Courthouse burned 1864.*	1835 New Madrid	1883-87 1863 1883-86	1835 1835 1835
H3	Stone P.O. Box 45 Galena 65656	1851 Taney	— 1851 —	1854 1848 1851
B4	Sullivan Milan 63556 **Also Birth records 1883-92.*	1845 Linn	1835-71* 1845 1883-99	1845 1849 1845
H4	Taney P.O. Box 335 Forsythe 65653 *Courthouse burned 1885.*	1837 Greene	— 1885 —	1881 1888 1887
G5	Texas 210 N. Grand Houston 65483 *Courthouse burned 1932. County clerk has 1876 state census.*	1845 Shannon/Wright	1883-87 1855 1883-90	1843 1870 1858
	Van Buren	1835 (renamed Cass, 1849)		
F2	Vernon Nevada 64772 *Courthouse burned during Civil War.*	1855 Bates	1883-97 1855 1883-1904	1855 1855 1856
D6	Warren 116 W. Main Warrenton 63383	1833 Montgomery	1883-89 1833 1884-94	1833 1833 1833
F6	Washington 102 N. Missouri Street Potosi 63664	1813 Ste. Genevieve	1883-95 1815 1883-95; 1974-76	1813 1813 1819

Map	County Address	Date Formed Parent County/ies	Birth Marriage Death	Land Probate Court
G7	Wayne P.O. Box 187 Greenville 63944 *Courthouse burned 1854, 1891.*	1818 Cape Girardeau/Lawrence	— 1892 —	1849 1869 1893
G4	Webster Marshfield 65706 *Courthouse burned 1863; destroyed by tornado 1881.*	1855 Greene	1883-93 1855 1883-84	1854 1856 1855
B2	Worth P.O. Box H Grant City 64456	1861 Gentry	1883-93 1861 1883-93	1849 1861 1861
B4	Wright P.O. Box 39 Hartville 65667 *Courthouse burned 1864, 1897.*	1841 Pulaski	— 1897 —	1853 1853 1895

MONTANA

Dwight A. Radford

The first wave of migration and settlement in Montana occurred when gold was discovered in Bannack (1862) and Alder Gulch (1863), south of Butte. Montana became a fusion of frontiers that included settlers who had originally gone to California and Oregon in the 1850s. The migration of eastern settlers, southern-born Civil War veterans, and foreign-born such as the Chinese came at the same time.

Montana was created as a territory in 1864. The area was formed from Washington Territory west of the Continental Divide and Nebraska Territory east of the Continental Divide. Statehood was granted in 1889

After 1865, cargo and people destined for the gold camps arrived in Montana by steamboat up the Missouri River. Steamers usually left St. Louis or Sioux City in late March or early April and arrived at Ft. Benton, Montana, between May and July. The Mullan Road began in Ft. Benton and continued to the mines some 100 to 200 miles away. In 1867 the total number of people entering and leaving Montana by way of the Missouri River and Mullan Road routes was about 5,000.

Beginning in 1869 Montana territorial officials began advertising for settlers. An agent in New York was contracted to print pamphlets on the territory for distribution in Germany and Scandinavian countries. According to the 1870 U.S. census, Montana's population consisted of 18,306 whites, 1,949 Chinese, and 183 blacks. The estimated Native American population was 19,300. By 1872 the Montana Immigration Society was established in Helena, and by 1875 another immigration society was holding meetings in Bozeman. The agent for Bozeman was commissioned to bring immigrants to Big Horn and Yellowstone counties.

By 1883 the Northern Pacific Railroad was completed. From 1882 to 1883, the railroad sent out 2.5 million pieces of literature advertising land for sale. Though only a few came, immigrants from northern Europe were sought, as it was thought they could adapt to the climate and conditions of Montana. English colonies were established in Helena and the Yellowstone Valley in 1882; a few French came to Missoula County; and a few Dutch families settled in the Gallatin Valley in 1893. The most notable settlement was that of Finnish lumbermen east of Missoula in 1892. Italians and Germans settled in Fergus and Park counties, and many Germans came from North Dakota and Canada.

The cattlemen of Montana were primarily English and Scottish; the cattle they drove were owned by the Germans. The sheepmen were also of English and Scottish origin.

American migrations included 506 individuals from Ripon, Wisconsin. This group of 115 families settled near Billings in 1882. Many Southerners came to the state and settled in the Bitterroot Valley, and many immigrants from Oregon arrived driving cattle.

The smelters and mills of the Anaconda Copper Mining Company in Anaconda and Great Falls at first drew Scandinavian and Irish workers to the area. After 1900 a heavy influx of workers from the Balkan countries arrived. The Montana coal mines of Cascade, Carbon, and Musselshell counties were worked by the Irish, Poles, and Italians.

Vital Records

Prior to 1895 there were no legal requirements for keeping birth records in Montana. In 1895 the legislative assembly passed a law requiring all physicians and midwives to keep a register of all births. All pre-1907 birth records are filed with the county clerk in the county where the child was born (see County Resources). Montana began recording births and deaths on the state level in 1907. It was not until about 1915 that mandatory registration of births became more complete. By 1922 about 90 percent of the births were being registered.

The 1895 law governing births also pertained to deaths. At that time the registration of deaths was the responsibility of clergymen, coroners, physicians, sextons, and undertakers. Registration of deaths on the state level began in 1907. By 1910 the registration of deaths reached about 90 percent. It was not until about 1915 that the registration of Montana deaths became reasonably complete.

Certified copies of birth and death certificates dated 1907 and later can be obtained for $5 by writing the Department of Health and Environmental Sciences, Bureau of Records and Statistics, Cogswell Building, Helena, Montana 59620.

When ordering a certified copy of a birth certificate, send the full name of the individual, date and place of birth, father's name, and mother's maiden name. The bureau will provide a five-year search when the exact information is unknown. Genealogical use of the birth certificate will be accommodated by the Bureau of Records and Statistics only if proof is provided of the death for the individual named on the birth certificate.

When requesting a death certificate, the place and date of death are required. Genealogical use of the death certificate will be accommodated provided it is satisfied that the requester is engaged in legitimate genealogical activity. Searches and issuance of copies will be conducted thirty years after the date of death.

The Bureau of Records and Statistics has forms available for ordering certified copies of birth and death records. It is best to request a form prior to ordering certified copies. When writing for vital records, it is good policy to include your relationship and the purpose for the request. If the request is on behalf of another party, send a signed letter from the individual with your request giving you permission to obtain the certificate. Montana state vital records are not open to the public. They prefer to have customers fill out application forms and leave them. Orders filed this way will be filled at the earliest convenience of the staff. There are no published indexes to Montana state vital records. It takes approximately ten days to two weeks to fill requests by mail.

Marriage and divorce records are not available through the Bureau of Records and Statistics. These records may be obtained from the clerk of the district court in the county where the license or decree was issued. Divorces were registered on the state level beginning in July 1943. The Bureau of Records and Statistics may be able to forward requests for information on records after that date to the appropriate court.

The most thorough survey of what vital records exist for each county can be found in the Historical Records Survey, WPA, *A Guide to Vital Records for Montana* (Bozeman, Mont.: Montana State College, 1941). This WPA program inventoried the availability of birth, marriage, and divorce records of the state.

Census Records

Federal

Population Schedules.

- Indexed—1870, 1880
- Soundex—1880, 1900, 1920
- Unindexed—1910 (see below)

Industry and Agriculture Schedules.

- 1870, 1880

Mortality Schedules.

- 1870, 1880

Union Veterans Schedules.

- 1890 (indexed)

In 1860 the area of Montana that lies east of the Continental Divide was part of Nebraska Territory. People residing in this area were enumerated in the unorganized part of Nebraska Territory. The only exceptions to this were two trading posts, Fort Alexander and Fort Union, which were enumerated with unorganized Dakota. The area of Montana west of the Continental Divide was enumerated as the Bitterroot Valley and the Ponderay Mountains in Spokane County, Washington Territory.

A "census" of miners taken during 1862–63 can be found in "List of Early Settlers: A List of All Persons (Except Indians) Who Were in What is Now Montana During the Winter of 1862–63, Which Was the First Winter After the Gold Mines of This Region Had Become Noised Abroad," *Contributions to the Historical Society of Montana*, vol. 1. (Helena, Mont.: Rocky Mountain Publishing Co., 1876).

Yellowstone National Park was created in 1872, and all residents of the area were enumerated in the Wyoming census for 1880.

A partial index to the 1910 census is available from Barbara Van DePete, 8430 Highway 2 West, Havre, Montana 59501.

Background Sources

In Montana, genealogy and history are intertwined. For this reason, many published history books are also valuable genealogical sources.

Burlingame, Merrill G. and K. Ross Toole, eds. *A History of Montana*. New York, N.Y.: Lewis Historical Publishing Co., 1957. A three-volume set, volumes one and two are a history of Montana. Volume three provides valuable biographical sketches.

Brown, Mark H. *The Plainsmen of the Yellowstone: A History of the Yellowstone Basin*. New York, N.Y.: G. P. Putnam's Sons, 1961. A history of the Yellowstone Basin; it includes early maps of the area and maps of the Crow and Cheyenne reservations.

Hamilton, James McClellan. *History of Montana from Wilderness to Statehood.* 2d ed. Edited by Merrill G. Burlingame. Portland, Oreg.: Binfords and Mort, 1970. This state history has illustrations, maps, portraits, and references.

Koury, Michael J. *The Military Posts of Montana.* Bellevue, Nebr.: Old Army Press, 1970. This is an introduction to the army posts of Montana. Included are Camp Cooke, Fort C. F. Smith, Fort Shaw, Fort Ellis, Camp Baker, Fort Logan, Fort Benton, Fort Custer, Fort Keogh, Fort Missoula, Fort Maginnis, and Fort Assiniboine.

Merrian, Harold Guy. "Ethnic Settlement of Montana." *Pacific Historical Review* 12 (June 1943): 157–68. This article is a brief overview of the immigration of foreign born settlers into Montana.

Richards, Dennis L. *Montana's Genealogical and Local History Records, A Selected List of Books, Manuscripts, and Periodicals.* Detroit, Mich.: Gale Research Co., 1981. One of the best guides to history and genealogical works, this volume lists historical and genealogical sources for the territorial and state periods of Montana.

Spence, Clark C. *Montana: A Bicentennial History.* States and the Nations series. New York, N.Y.: W. W. Norton and Co., 1978. This volume contains a history of the state with illustrations, maps, and photographs.

Wolle, Muriel Vincent Sibell. *Montana Pay Dirt: A Guide to Mining Camps of the Treasure State.* Denver, Colo.: Sage, 1963. Included are maps, illustrations, and a selected bibliography.

Maps

Maps can be very useful in conducting Montana research, especially in light of the now extinct communities. Several kinds of maps are available that can help in locating land, mining claims, ghost towns, or ranches.

The U. S. Geological Survey topographical maps for Montana (see page 4) can be ordered from the two following publications: "Montana, Catalog of Topographical and Other Published Maps" and "Montana, Index to Topographic and Other Map Coverage." The catalog will provide the current cost for each topographical map and a listing of over-the-counter map dealers in Montana.

The libraries in the state designated by the U. S. Geological Survey as map depository libraries are Eastern Montana College, Billings; Montana State University, Bozeman; Montana College of Mineral Science and Technology, Butte; Northern Montana College, Havre; Montana Historical Society and Montana State Library, Helena; Lewistown City Library, Lewistown; and the University of Montana, Missoula.

The state lacks a historical atlas; however, Roberta Cheney, *Names on the Face of Montana,* rev. ed. (Missoula, Mont.: Mountain Press, 1987), can prove helpful in locating places during specific time periods.

Land Records

Public-Domain State

Montana federal land offices were originally located in Bozeman, Glasgow, Great Falls, Helena, Kalispell, Lewistown, Miles City, and Missoula. All of these offices were eliminated by 1950, leaving Billings as the only land office at present.

The land entries for the Montana area from 1800 to 1908 are filed by state, land office, kind of entry, and certificate number. There is no name index prior to 1908 for Montana. To access a federal land entry either the certificate number or the legal description of the land, such as range, township, and section, must be known. The description can be obtained from the county clerk and recorder.

Public land records can be accessed through the Department of the Interior. Major federal land records include survey plats and field notes, tract books, register's returns, case files or land-entry papers, and patent records. The survey plats, tract books, and patent records prior to 1908 are available at the BLM, Granite Tower, 222 North 32nd Street, P.O. Box 36800, Billings, Montana 59107. BLM district offices are located in Butte, Lewistown, and Miles City.

Patent records after 1908 and case files or land-entry papers prior to 1908 are available through the National Archives system (see pages 8–9). Both the Seattle and Denver centers hold Montana research materials. The case files are the most important genealogically as they often contain military papers, naturalization records, and other documentation.

Subsequent land transactions after the initial federal grant are filed with the respective county clerk and recorder.

Probate Records

Probate courts in Montana existed from 1864 to 1889. These courts had jurisdiction over adoptions, marriages, probates, and various civil suits and criminal matters. After 1889 jurisdiction was transferred to the district courts. Montana probate records are filed at the county courthouses.

Court Records

The Montana court records system has records of genealogical value. These records are found in the district courts, probate courts, and the supreme court.

District courts are district-wide courts with each county having its own clerk of the court. As major trial courts, their jurisdictions cover appeals, criminal cases, debts, divorces, guardianships, juvenile matters, naturalizations, and probates (since 1889).

Probate courts were disbanded in 1889 when their functions were transferred to the district courts. Prior to that time district court jurisdiction covered minor civil and criminal matters, marriages, and probates.

The supreme court served as a statewide appellate court. Microfiche copies of supreme court dockets are available through interlibrary loan for cases dating from 1868 to approximately 1983. Supreme court records are on microfilm at the Montana Historical Society (see Archives, Libraries, and Societies).

Court records can be obtained on the county level at the courthouses in the clerk of court's office.

Tax Records

Property taxes in Montana consisted of the name of the individual and a description of the property. Delinquent tax records included the delinquency date, penalty, interest, and amount due. Tax records are arranged by range, township, and section number, and can be obtained by contacting the clerk and recorder at the county courthouse.

Cemetery Records

Montana does not have a complete listing of all known cemeteries, nor does it have an agency over cemeteries. Some cemetery records are kept by the county clerk and recorder; in other cases, the county has a cemetery board which is responsible for record keeping. Many cemeteries have no records, and others kept records only of who purchased the lot and the name of the individual buried there. The policy varies with each cemetery. Some Montana genealogical societies have transcribed cemetery records in their counties.

Church Records

Church records in Montana vary according to denomination. Many churches recorded transfers of membership, thus making it possible to trace the migration of a family. Before 1900 the largest religious groups were the Roman Catholic, Methodist, Episcopal, and Presbyterian churches. Each group arrived during the territorial period to proselytize among the Native Americans and the miners. Minority faiths included various Latter-day Saint movements, Baptist, Brethren, Hutterites, Lutheran, and Disciples of Christ.

A listing of Montana churches was compiled in 1941, entitled *A Directory of Churches and Religious Organizations in Montana* (Bozeman, Mont.: Historical Records Survey, 1941). This listing does not include the numerous independent congregations, but it is a useful guide in determining the location of a particular denomination in Montana.

Many denominational histories are on file at the University of Montana, Mansfield Library, Missoula. These include Assemblies of God, Baptist, Brethren Church, Catholic, Disciples of Christ, Episcopal, Hutterite, Methodist, Mormon, and Presbyterian faiths.

Patricia M. McKinney's *Presbyterian in Montana: Its First Hundred Years, 1872–1972* (Helena, Mont.: Thurbers, n.d.) provides a list of churches in Montana including Native American congregations both extant and defunct.

Catholic records can be obtained by writing the Diocese of Great Falls, 121 23rd Street South, P.O. Box 1399, Great Falls, Montana 59403, and the Diocese of Helena, 515 North Ewing, P.O. Box 1729, Helena, Montana 59624. They will advise as to the location of parish registers.

Mormons living in Idaho crossed into Montana to obtain employment. They began freighting goods and produce from Idaho and Utah into Montana in the late 1870s. As early as 1880, Montana politicians took advantage of popular prejudice in trying to eliminate the Mormon vote in some precincts. Montana was not an official church missionary field until 1896. All ward, branch, and mission records are on file at the FHL.

The first Mennonite mission was established on the Northern Cheyenne Reservation at Bushy in 1904. In 1906 the Lame Deer mission was established eighteen miles away. Other Cheyenne communities asked the Mennonite missionaries to preach to them, and over 500 Cheyennes were baptized when the missions first opened. The Montana Mennonite congregations are part of the General Conference Mennonite Church. A history of this movement is found in Lois R. Habegger's *Cheyenne Trails: A History of Mennonites and Cheyennes in Montana* (Newton, Kans.: Mennonite Publication Office, 1959).

The Methodist church reached Montana in 1864 as miners brought their faith to the gold mines. For a history of Methodism in Montana see Doris Whithorn, *Bicentennial Tapestry of the Yellowstone Conference* (Livingston, Mont.: Livingston Enterprise, 1984). A major records repository for the United Methodist Church is located at the Montana Conference Depository, Paul M. Adams Memorial Library, Rocky Mountain College, Billings, Montana 59101.

In the last quarter of the nineteenth century, members of the Church of the Brethren began to settle in Idaho and then moved up the Snake River Valley into Montana. Many congregations were established in Idaho and Western Montana between 1895 and 1910. The history of this settlement entitled *The Brethren Along the Snake River: A History of the Brethren in Idaho and Western Montana* (Elgin, Ill.: Brethren Press, 1966), by Roger Sappington, should be utilized when searching and identifying congregations in western Montana.

Military Records

Many original military records for the state of Montana are on file at the Montana Historical Society in Helena. These include World War I and World War II records and early National Guard enlistment records. These records are filed on sixty thousand cards arranged alphabetically by surname. The information on these cards includes name, service number, place of enlistment and date, age at entrance, rate, home address, service record history, remarks, and discharge information.

An inventory of military records and the Veterans Administration was conducted by the WPA and can be found in the following publications: *Inventory of Federal Archives in the States,* series 4, Department of War, No. 25; Montana (Bozeman, Mont.: Historical Records Survey Project, 1941) and *Inventory of Federal Archives in the States,* series 12, Veteran Administration, No. 25; Montana (Bozeman, Mont.: Historical Records Survey Project, 1940). These volumes detail the founding of the Fort Harrison Facility in Helena from 1895 to the subsequent growth of the Veterans Administration at the facility. Records kept through Fort Harrison include Canadian claims, compensation claims, guardianship cases, insurance claims, leave cards, medical records, patient funds, patients' registers, pensions, salary records, travel orders, and a veterans index.

Periodicals, Newspapers, and Manuscript Collections

Periodicals

Montana: The Magazine of Western History is published quarterly by the Montana Historical Society and *Western Montana Genealogical Society Bulletin* is published quarterly by the Western Montana Genealogical Society in Missoula. An important but defunct publication is *Contributions to the Historical Society of Montana with its Transactions,* published irregularly between 1876 and 1940. Copies are available at the Montana Historical Society. It is an excellent source of history and genealogy. An excellent source for information on newspapers, city/county records, cemetery records, church records, military records, and indexes to local histories and other books, magazines, and newsletters is *The Montana Historical and Genealogical Data Index,* which was compiled by Paulette Parpart and Donald Spritzer.

Many historical and genealogical periodicals are published in Montana. The largest quarterlies published by several Montana genealogical societies are:

Smoke Signals—Havre Genealogical Society

Central Montana Wagon Trails—Lewistown Genealogical Society

Faded Genes—Lewis and Clark Genealogical Society

Tri-County Searcher—Broken Mountains Genealogical Society

Treasure State Lines—Great Falls Genealogical Society

Trees and Trails—Flathead Genealogical Society

Gallatin Trails—Gallatin Genealogical Society

The Last Leaf—Dawson County Tree Branches

Newspapers

For information on newspaper holdings, the Montana Historical Society should be contacted as they have the largest collection in the state. Many newspapers are on microfilm at Montana State University and the University of Montana. Rex S. Blazer and John L. Washmuth's "Bibliography of Sources for the Study of Montana Mining Camps, 1860–1910" (1977) is an unpublished, typewritten manuscript covering the holdings of the University of Montana, Montana Historical Society, Montana State University, and the Montana College of Mineral Science and Technology, Butte.

Manuscripts

Since 1865 the Montana Historical Society has been collecting manuscripts for the state and other areas. Many manuscript collections in their possession cover areas such as agriculture, banking, early exploration, fur trading, government, the military, mining, and Native Americans. These manuscripts can be accessed through the following three indexes: "The Cumulative Name Index," "The Cumulative Subject Index," and "The Cumulative Place Name Index."

The staff at the Montana Historical Society has been indexing collections and manuscripts within the "Cumulative Subject Index" under the title "Population—Genealogical Sources." This growing collection includes Montana Territorial census enumerations, church records, military records, poll lists, publications, and institutional records.

Significant collections concerning Montana are announced in the Library of Congress *National Union Catalog of Manuscript Collections.* Inventories of many manuscript collections are available on microfiche through Chadwyck-Healey's *National Inventory of Documentary Sources in the United States.*

Other repositories housing manuscripts are Butte-Silver Bow Public Archives (P.O. Box 81, 17 West Quartz Street, Butte, Montana 59703), which houses both municipal and private papers and records concerning Butte; the Cascade County Historical Museum and Archives (Paris Gibson Square, 1400 1st Avenue, North Great Falls, Montana 59401); the Historical Museum at Fort Missoula (Building 322, Fort Missoula, Montana 59801); and the Powell County Museum (1119 Main Street, Deer Lodge, Montana 59722), which holds some prison records.

Archives, Libraries, and Societies

Montana Historical Society
225 North Roberts
Helena, MT 59601

The Montana Historical Society has served as the official archives for the records of the state of Montana since 1969. In that capacity, it has obtained state and territorial records from 1864 to the present.

Among these are papers of the governors, state prison, and other institutions, the legislative assembly, and the supreme court. Box-and-folder-level inventories are available for processed manuscripts and state records through a single name, subject, and place-name index.

A good reference tool for those interested in researching specific localities in Montana is *A Guide to Montana Museums, Art Centers, and Historical Organizations* (1982. Reprint. Helena, Mont.: Department of Education, Montana Historical Society, 1990). This guide also lists names and addresses of genealogical societies.

Montana State Genealogical Society
6400 43rd Street S.W.
Great Falls, MT 59404

Special Focus Categories

Immigration

Most of the foreign immigrants who settled in Montana arrived through the port of New York, although immigrants also came from Canada. The ports of entry from Canada were Sweetgrass, Gateway, and Roosville. Sweetgrass was established as a port of entry in 1903, Gateway in 1908, and Roosville in 1930. The WPA conducted an inventory of the Immigration and Naturalization Service records, including these ports of entry, in the volume Inventory of Federal Archives in the States—Series XI, Department of Labor, No. 25: Montana (Bozeman, Mont.: Historical Records Survey Project, 1942). Other records inventoried in this booklet were Canadian steamship arrivals, Chinese arrests, Chinese laborers, Chinese natives, Japanese and Korean aliens and deportations, passports, smuggling of aliens, and warrants for alien arrests.

The Montana ports of entry are filed with the Seattle passenger lists, which have been microfilmed and are at the National Archives and the FHL. Additional information on persons entering through Montana ports-of-entry may be found in the St. Albans, Vermont District records (so-called, see Vermont—Immigration), which are indexed.

Native American

Some Native American Agency records are microfilmed and can be examined through the National Archives-Pacific Northwest Region (see page 9); FHL in Salt Lake City; and the University of Montana in Missoula, Montana. These agency records are very important and should not be overlooked when conducting Native American research. For a discussion of Native American ownership of land, see the Native American section for Oregon, which will explain some of the terms used below.

Billings Area Office, Billings, Montana (1912–52). These records document the activities of the federal government as trustee of tribal lands and resources. Record sources include general decimal files, grazing leases, records concerning education, health, tribal enactments, irrigation, land transactions, forestry, soil conservation, agricultural extension, and road construction.

Blackfeet Agency, Browning, Montana (1875–1959). Records include general correspondence, grazing permits, oil and gas production reports, census records, birth and health records, ledgers, abstracts of accounts of individual Indians, tribal council records, records concerning education, road, forestry, irrigation, credit, welfare, and rehabilitation programs. This agency was established in 1855 for the three bands of the Siksika Native Americans.

Crow Agency, Crow Agency, Montana (1874–1959). This agency was established in 1869 and administered the affairs of the Mountain and River Crows. The River Crows were originally under the control of the Fort Peck Agency, but they gradually came under the control of the Crow Agency. Record sources include general correspondence and decimal files, student case files, school censuses, tractbooks, maps of the Crow reservations, grazing leases, building plans, annuity payrolls, ledgers for accounts of individual Indians, records of goods issued to Indians, census rolls, Indian court dockets, records concerning irrigation, forestry, Civilian Conservation Corps, and road programs.

Flathead Agency, St. Ignatius, Montana (1875–1960). Records include general correspondence and decimal files; correspondence; reports and censuses concerning schools; grazing permits; leases; records concerning allotments, land transactions, and other records concerning land, irrigation, Civilian Conservation Corps, engineering, and road and forestry programs; ledgers for accounts of individual Indians; census reports; records concerning relief, welfare projects and cases; Indian police and court records; credit program files; tribal accounts; and annuity payrolls. This agency was established in 1854 principally for the Flathead, Upper Pend d'Oreille, and Kutenai tribes. Lower Kalispells moved onto the Flathead Reservation in 1887, and Spokane moved to the reservation in 1894. In time, the distinctions became ignored and all were known as Flatheads.

Fort Belknap Agency, Harlem, Montana (1877–1969). Records include general correspondence and decimal files, correspondence concerning education, school reports and applications, grazing permits, leases, ledgers for accounts of individual Indians, correspondence and reports about health and welfare, census rolls, family history cards, traders' licenses, police and court records concerning roads, land sales, Civilian Conservation Corps work, and financial matters. This agency was established in 1873 and had jurisdiction over the Gros Ventre and Upper Assiniboine along the Milk River.

Fort Peck Agency, Popular, Montana (1871–1959), formally known as the Milk River Agency. Agency records include general correspondence and decimal files, school reports, records of 4-H activities, grazing permits, mining leases, ledgers for accounts of individual Indians, credit rehabilitation ledgers, industrial status reports, census records, medical reports, registers of Indians, birth and death records, welfare relief case files, tribal council records, and records concerning land allotments and sales, forestry and range management, irrigation, and road construction. This agency had jurisdiction over the Lower Assiniboine and Sioux, principally Yanktonai, Native Americans.

Indian schools were set up to further the education of the Native American youth. Two important schools whose records should not be overlooked are the Chemawa Indian School in Chemawa, Oregon, and the Fort Shaw School in Cascade County, Montana. These schools attracted students from many states. (For a more detailed account of the Chemawa Indian School, see Oregon—Native American.) The Fort Shaw School was established in Fort Shaw in 1892 as a non-reservation school and closed in 1910. Its records consist of letters received, registers of pupils, rosters of employees, and cashbooks. A major Native American Collection is the James McLaughlin Papers. Major James McLaughlin was an Indian agent for some time in the Dakotas, Montana, and Wyoming Territory. He kept careful records of his dealings with many tribes. His papers include Native American family data and locations of specific families. Many families had become scattered during their subsequent relocation to reservations. Therefore, the James McLaughlin Papers are an excellent source for locating many of these scattered families. This collection consists of 30,000 pages with an index containing 15,675 cross-reference cards.

A guide to the James McLaughlin Papers is published and entitled *Guide to the Microfilm Edition of the Major James McLaughlin Papers,* by Rev. Louis Pfaller (Richardson, N.Dak.: Assumption College, 1969).

A very important Native American collection for Montana, as well as Idaho, Oregon, and Washington, is the Pacific Northwest Tribes Missions Collection of the Oregon Province Archives of the Society of Jesus, 1853–1960. This massive collection of Jesuit records includes births, marriages, deaths, censuses, land records, church records, histories, and newspaper clippings. The following tribes are recorded in these records: Blackfoot, Cheyenne, Coeur d'Alene, Colville, Crow, Flathead, Kalispell, Kootenai, Nez Perce, Spokane, and Umatilla.

The following Jesuit missions are part of this collection: St. Mary's Mission (1841–1908), located in Stevensville, Montana, served the Flathead; St. Ignatius Mission, Montana (1854–1960), in the Flathead Valley, served the Kalispell along with the Flathead Reservation; St. Peter's Mission, Montana (1859–98), which was near the Blackfoot Reservation; Holy Family Mission, Montana (1890–1914), which was located on Two Medicine River a few miles from the Blackfoot Agency at Badger Creek; St. Joseph Labre Mission, Montana (1883–97), served the Northern Cheyenne near the present town of Harlem; St. Francis Xavier Mission, Montana (1887–1960), worked among the Crow; Sacred Heart Mission, Idaho (1842–1960), worked among the Coeur d'Alene and was located near the town of De Smet; St. Joseph's Mission, Idaho (1874–1958), served the Nez Perce; St. Ignatius Mission, Washington (1845–55), on the Pend Oreille River, served the Kalispell (later removed to Flathead Valley of Montana); St. Paul Mission, Washington (1845–65), near Kettle Falls on the Upper Columbia River, ministered to the Kettle (or Colville); St. Francis Regis Mission, Washington (1845–1945), worked among the Chewelah; St. Mary's Mission, Washington (1886–1960), near Ellisford, served the Okanogan and Colville; and St. Andrew's Mission, Oregon (1888–1960), in the Pendleton area.

These records are on microfilm with a copy at the FHL with the originals at the Crosby Library, Gonzaga University, Spokane, Washington, which is where the Oregon Province Archives is now located. For a guide to the microfilm collection, see Robert C. Carriker and Eleanor R. Carriker, *Guide to the Microfilm Edition of the Pacific Northwest Tribes Missions Collection of the Oregon Province Archives of the Society of Jesus* (Wilmington, Del.: Scholarly Resources, 1987).

Other Ethnic Groups

The discovery of gold in Montana brought many Chinese into the region during the early 1860s. These Chinese were from the province of Kwangtung around the Canton area. The 1870 U.S. census of Montana Territory counted 1,943 Chinese, representing about 10 percent of the total population. By 1880 the number had declined to 1,765, but by 1890 it had risen to 2,532.

By the 1870s there were a number of Chinese mining operations in western Montana. As placer mining declined during the late 1870s and 1880s, the Chinese moved into other fields such as railroad construction and business, which served not only the Chinese population but the white majority as well. Montana's largest communities of Chinese were in Butte and Helena.

The most important institution in the Chinese community was the Joss House or Temple, which served the religious (Confucianism) as well as the social needs of the community. Butte's Chinatown had two Joss Houses. Another important institution was the Masonic Temple.

The Chinese contributed much to the development of Montana, especially in the building of the Northern Pacific Railroad, which opened the state up to further development. Little remains of Montana's Chinese era. The failure of the community was due to racism, discriminatory laws, immigration laws, as well as the shortage of Chinese female emigrants in western America. For an excellent treatment of Montana's Chinese, see Robert R. Swartout, Jr., "Kwangtung to Big Sky: The Chinese in Montana, 1864–1900," *Montana: The Magazine of Western History* 1 (Winter 1988): 42–53. The best method of researching the Chinese in Montana is through county sources such as land, tax, and court records and federal census enumerations.

Finnish immigrants came to Montana in 1892 to work in the lumber mills and settled in Milltown, five miles east of Missoula. After 1900 Finnish immigrants came directly from Finland, and achieved a population of 570 in 1915.

County Resources

County seats in Montana are the location of the county clerk and recorder (vital records and deeds) and the clerk of the district court (probate and court records). The latter includes civil and criminal files and naturalizations. Correspondence should be addressed to the appropriate official at the county seat address.

The Counties and County Seats of
Montana
25 0 25 50 75 100 Miles
British Columbia
Alberta
Saskatchewan
Canada
U.S.
LINCOLN
Libby
FLATHEAD
Kalispell
GLACIER
Cut Bank
TOOLE
Shelby
LIBERTY
Chester
HILL
Havre
Chinook
BLAINE
Malta
PHILLIPS
VALLEY
Glasgow
Scobey
DANIELS
Plentywood
SHERIDAN
ROOSEVELT
Wolf Point
PONDERA
Conrad
TETON
Choteau
CHOUTEAU
Fort Benton
Thompson Falls
SANDERS
Polson
LAKE
MINERAL
Superior
MISSOULA
Missoula
LEWIS AND CLARK
Great Falls
CASCADE
Stanford
JUDITH BASIN
FERGUS
Lewistown
PETROLEUM
Winnett
Jordan
GARFIELD
McCONE
Circle
RICHLAND
Sidney
DAWSON
Glendive
Wibaux
WIBAUX
PRAIRIE
Terry
POWELL
Helena
Deer Lodge
GRANITE
Philipsburg
Hamilton
RAVALLI
Anaconda
DEER LODGE
Butte
SILVER BOW
Boulder
JEFFERSON
BROADWATER
Townsend
MEAGHER
White Sulphur Springs
WHEATLAND
Harlowton
GOLDEN VALLEY
Ryegate
MUSSELSHELL
Roundup
ROSEBUD
Hysham
TREASURE
Forsyth
Miles City
CUSTER
Baker
FALLON
GALLATIN
Bozeman
SWEET GRASS
Big Timber
Livingston
PARK
YELLOWSTONE
Billings
STILLWATER
Columbus
CARBON
Red Lodge
Hardin
BIG HORN
Ekalaka
CARTER
Broadus
POWDER RIVER
MADISON
Virginia City
Dillon
BEAVERHEAD
Flathead River
Clark Fork
Bitterroot River
Teton River
Missouri River
Milk River
Musselshell River
Yellowstone River
Bighorn River
Little Bighorn
BOUNDARY
BONNER
SHOSHONE
CLEARWATER
IDAHO
IDAHO
LEMHI
VALLEY
CUSTER
BOISE
ELMORE
CAMAS
BLAINE
BUTTE
CLARK
FREMONT
JEFFERSON
MADISON
TETON
BONNEVILLE
BINGHAM
Yellowstone National Park
PARK
WYOMING
BIG HORN
SHERIDAN
JOHNSON
CAMPBELL
CROOK
TETON
HOT SPRINGS
FREMONT
NATRONA
CONVERSE
NIOBRARA
WESTON
SOUTH DAKOTA
BUTTE
LAWRENCE
CUSTER
HARDING
BOWMAN
SLOPE
GOLDEN VALLEY
McKENZIE
NORTH DAKOTA
WILLIAMS
DIVIDE
Copyright 1989, Ancestry, Inc.
Drawn by William Dollarhide

Map	County Address	Date Formed Parent County/ies	Birth Marriage Death	Deeds Probate Court
B6	Beaverhead 2 S. Pacific Dillon 59725	1865 original	1901 1877 1901	1876 1865 1865
	Big Horn (old)	1865 (renamed Custer, 1877) original		
G6	Big Horn (present) P.O. Box H Hardin 59034	1913 Rosebud/Yellowstone	— 1913 —	1913 1913 1913
F2	Blaine P.O. Box 278 Chinook 59523	1912 Chouteau	— 1912 —	1912 1912 1912
D5	Broadwater P.O. Box 489 Townsend 59644	1897 Jefferson/Meagher	1894 1897 1903	1866 1897 1897
F6	Carbon P.O. Box 887 Red Lodge 59068	1895 Park/Yellowstone/Custer	1904 1895 1895	1888 1895 1895
K6	Carter P.O. Box 315 Ekalaka 59324	1917 Custer	— 1917 —	1917 1917 1917
D4	Cascade P.O. Box 2867 Great Falls 59403	1887 Chouteau/Meagher/Lewis and Clark	1892 1888 1893	1889 1889 1889
E2	Chouteau P.O. Box 459 Fort Benton 59422	1865 original	1895 1882 1895	1872 1880 1895
J5	Custer 1010 Main Street Miles City 59301	1865 (as Big Horn; renamed, 1877) original	1895 1887 1895	1877 1883 1879
J1	Daniels P.O. Box 247 Scobey 59263	1920 Sheridan/Valley	— 1920 —	1920 1920 1910
K3	Dawson 207 W. Bell Glendive 59330	1865 original	1895 1882 1895	1881 1883 1883
B5	Deer Lodge 800 S. Main Anaconda 59711	1865 original	1903 1865 1895	1864 1871 1865
	Edgerton	1865 (renamed Lewis and Clark, 1867) original		
K5	Fallon 10 W. Fallon Baker 59313	1913 Custer	— 1912 —	1889 1914 1914
F3	Fergus 712 W. Main Street Lewistown 59457	1885 Meagher/Chouteau	1904 1885 1904	1888 1888 1888

Map	County Address	Date Formed Parent County/ies	Birth Marriage Death	Deeds Probate Court
A2	Flathead 800 S. Main Street Kalispell 59901	1893 Missoula	1896 1892 —	1884 1893 1893
D6	Gallatin 615 S. 16th Street Bozeman 59715	1865 original	1895 1865 1895	1862 1886 1886
H3	Garfield P.O. Box 7 Jordan 59337	1919 Dawson	— 1919 —	1919 1919 1919
B1	Glacier 512 E. Main Street Cut Bank 59427	1919 Teton	— 1910 —	1919 1919 1919
F5	Golden Valley County Courthouse Ryegate 59074	1920 Musselshell/Sweet Grass	— — —	1920 1920 1920
B4	Granite P.O. Box B Philipsburg 59858	1893 Deer Lodge	1895 1893 1895	1866 1893 1893
E1	Hill 315 Fourth Street Havre 59501	1912 Chouteau	1898 1912 1897	1912 1912 1912
C5	Jefferson P.O. Box H Boulder 59632	1865 original	1895 1887 1895	1865 1869 1869
E4	Judith Basin P.O. Box 485 Stanford 59479	1920 Cascade/Fergus	— 1920 —	1921 1921 1921
A3	Lake 106 Fourth Avenue, E. Polson 59860	1923 Flathead/Missoula	— 1923 —	1923 1923 1923
C4	Lewis and Clark 316 N. Park Avenue Helena 59623	1865 (as Edgerton; renamed 1867) original	1895 1865 1895	1865 1895 1867
D2	Liberty P.O. Box 549 Chester 59522	1920 Chouteau/Hill	— 1920 —	1920 1920 1920
A1	Lincoln 512 California Avenue Libby 59923	1909 Flathead	1897 1896 1897	1909 1909 1909
J3	McCone P.O. Box 199 Circle 59215	1919 Dawson/Richland	— 1919 —	1919 1919 1919
C6	Madison P.O. Box 278 Virginia City 59755	1865 original	1903 1887 1903	1863 1864 1864
D4	Meagher P.O. Box 309 White Sulphur Springs 59465	1867 original	1895 1866 1895	1866 1866 1867

Map	County Address	Date Formed Parent County/ies	Birth Marriage Death	Deeds Probate Court
A3	Mineral	1914	—	1914
	P.O. Box 550	Missoula	1887	1914
	Superior 59872		—	1914
B4	Missoula	1865	1895	1868
	201 W. Broadway	original	1865	1867
	Missoula 59802		1895	1867
G5	Musselshell	1911	—	1911
	P.O. Box 686	Fergus/Yellowstone	1895	1911
	Roundup 59072		—	1911
E6	Park	1887	1889	1887
	414 E. Callender	Gallatin	1887	1886
	Livingston 59047		1892	1886
G4	Petroleum	1925	—	1925
	P.O. Box 226	Fergus	1925	1925
	Winnett 59087		—	1925
G2	Phillips	1915	—	1915
	P.O. Box U	Blaine/Valley	1915	1915
	Malta 59538		—	1915
C2	Pondera	1919	—	1919
	20 Fourth Avenue, S.W.	Chouteau/Teton	1919	1919
	Conrad 59425		—	1919
J6	Powder River	1919	—	1919
	Box J	Custer	1919	1919
	Broadus 59317		—	1919
C5	Powell	1901	—	1901
	409 Missouri Avenue	Deer Lodge	1901	1901
	Deer Lodge 59722		—	1901
J4	Prairie	1915	—	1915
	P.O. Box 125	Custer/Dawson/Fallon	1915	1915
	Terry 59349		—	1915
A5	Ravalli	1893	—	1866
	P.O. Box 5001	Missoula	1893	1893
	Hamilton 59840		—	1893
K3	Richland	1914	—	1914
	201 W. Main	Dawson	1914	1914
	Sidney 59270		—	1914
K2	Roosevelt	1919	—	1919
	400 Second Avenue, South	Sheridan	1913	1919
	Wolf Point 59201		—	1919
H4	Rosebud	1901	1893	1877
	P.O. Box 47	Custer	1901	1901
	Forsyth 59327		1909	1901
A3	Sanders	1906	—	1885
	P.O. Box 519	Missoula	1906	1906
	Thompson Falls 59873		—	1906
K1	Sheridan	1913	—	1913
	100 W. Laurel Avenue	Valley	1913	1913
	Plentywood 59254		—	1913

Map	County Address	Date Formed Parent County/ies	Birth Marriage Death	Deeds Probate Court
C5	Silver Bow 155 W. Granite Butte 59701	1881 Deer Lodge	1878 1881 1890	1881 1881 1881
F6	Stillwater P.O. Box 147 Columbus 59019	1913 Carbon/Sweet Grass/Yellowstone	1887 1913 —	1913 1913 1913
E5	Sweet Grass P.O. Box 460 Big Timber 59011	1895 Meagher/Park/Yellowstone	1895 1895 1895	1895 1895 1895
C3	Teton P.O. Box 610 Choteau 59422	1893 Chouteau	1897 1893 —	1893 1890 1895
D1	Toole 226 First Street, S. Shelby 59474	1914 Hill/Teton	— 1914 —	1914 1914 1914
H5	Treasure P.O. Box 392 Hysham 59038	1919 Rosebud	— 1919 —	1879 1919 1919
H2	Valley P.O. Box 311 Glasgow 59230	1893 Dawson	— 1893 —	1893 1893 1893
E5	Wheatland County Courthouse Harlowton 59036	1917 Meagher/Sweet Grass	— 1917 —	1917 1917 1917
K4	Wibaux P.O. Box 207 Wibaux 59353	1914 Dawson/Fallon	— 1914 —	1914 1914 1914
G5	Yellowstone P.O. Box 35000 Billings 59107	1883 Custer/Gallatin	1884 1895 1884	1881 1890 1884

NEBRASKA

Marsha Hoffman Rising, C.G., C.G.L.

Nebraska was part of the Louisiana Purchase acquired from France in 1803. Before the 1860s most pioneers passed through Nebraska along the Platte River Valley on their way to Oregon and California. First attempts to form Nebraska Territory were begun in 1851, but territorial status was not achieved until three years later. Nebraska Territory was created in 1854 as a result of the Kansas-Nebraska Act, a political compromise regarding the expansion of slavery. Although this act officially opened the area for white settlement, the real impetus to organizing the territory was the building of a Pacific railroad, not colonization. At that time Nebraska Territory extended to the Canadian border. The center of government was located in Omaha, which sits on the Missouri River. As the population grew, migration worked its way westward along the rivers, such as the Platte, and via the rapidly developing railroads.

The first federal land office was established in 1855, but it was not until after the Civil War that extensive settlement began, leading to Nebraska's admission to the United States on 1 March 1867. The Homestead Acts of 1862 and 1866 governed the disposal of the public land, but those acts do not account for the large migration to the state. The settlement of Nebraska required a new view of the economics of an unfamiliar geography and an advance in technology. The former obstacle was overcome by the cattle ranchers whose animals grazed the vast prairie, and the technology came with the invention of farming implements. These agricultural innovations included barbed wire, the steel plow, the spring harrow, and the windmills—inventions that did not come into widespread usage until the years between 1870–90. It was during that period that the Great Plains experienced its tremendous growth in population. By 1880 the years of good weather and new productivity in farming equipment had brought the population growth in Nebraska to more than 450,000.

Not only farmers, but merchants, capitalizing on expanding markets, moved to Nebraska and created small towns, especially along the developing railroads. In fact, between 1860–70 the city population of Nebraska increased 416.6 percent, indicating that not all ancestors in Nebraska lived on farms.

Both natives and foreigners were attracted by the government promotion of the land acts, advertising by the railroads and steamship companies, and immigration efforts by the federal government. European groups that settled Nebraska include individuals and families from Russia, Bohemia, Germany, Sweden, Denmark, and the British Isles.

Years of unprecedented growth and frontier expansion soon gave way to negative repercussions. Abysmal living conditions, inflated land prices, low profits on produce, and poor weather brought a reversal of fortunes and mounting dissatisfaction with economic and political conditions. From that discontent, came the agrarian political movements.

Genealogical research in Nebraska must be completed at both the state and county level. Few statewide Nebraska indexes exist. The researcher will find it necessary to do a great deal of family research at the county level where the individual family resided.

Vital Records

The statewide requirement for registration of births and deaths began late in 1904, and marriages and divorces in 1909. However, compliance was not total for several years.

The available records can be ordered from the Bureau of Vital Statistics, State Department of Health, 301 Centennial Mall South, P.O. Box 95007, Lincoln, Nebraska 68509. The most recent fee was $6 for birth records and $5 for marriage and death records.

With the exception of some delayed birth registrations located in the office of the county clerk, Nebraska did not record births and deaths at the county level. Divorce records before 1909 are at the county clerk of the district court.

Several genealogical societies have compiled indexes to the early marriage records of their county, and some are at the Nebraska State Historical Society. The early marriage records of Lancaster County have been indexed and published in 2 volumes, Vol. 1 (1866–93), and Vol. 2 (1893–1906) by the Lincoln-Lancaster County Genealogical Society, P.O. Box 30055, Lincoln, Nebraska 68503-0055. A third volume was due to be published in 1991.

Census Records

Federal

Population Schedules.

- Indexed—1860, 1870
- Soundex—1880, 1900, 1920
- Unindexed—1910

Industry and Agriculture Schedules.

- 1860, 1870, 1880

Mortality Schedules.

- 1860, 1870, 1880

Union Veterans Schedules.

- 1890

Territorial and State

The Nebraska State Historical Society has a copy of the 1860 federal schedules and the 1860–80 agriculture, industry, and mortality schedules.

The society holds microfilmed copies of the 1910 federal population schedule of Nebraska, but the census has not been indexed. The researcher can use a street guide to the larger towns of Omaha and Lincoln, which will aid in searching. City directories of Lincoln and Omaha are also helpful.

The Nebraska State Historical Society has the original enumerations for the territorial censuses. Territorial Census are available for 1854, 1855, and 1856 and indexed in *Nebraska and Midwest Genealogical Records.* All volumes of this now defunct publication are at the Nebraska State Historical Society. A few counties were recorded in censuses taken in 1867, 1874, 1875, 1878–79. Lancaster County was indexed and published in the *Historical Records of Lancaster County Nebraska,* Series 3, Vols. 1–13 (Lincoln, Nebr.: Genealogical Records Committee of the Deborah Avery Chapter of the Daughters of the American Revolution, under sponsorship of the Nebraska State Historical Society, 1939.). A census for Otoe and Cuming counties was taken in 1865 and for Butler and Stanton counties in 1869. For details, request Reference Information Guide #2 from the Nebraska State Historical Society.

Microfilmed copies of the 1885 state census are at the Nebraska State Historical Society and the National Archives. The original 1885 population and special schedules are housed at the National Archives. It includes the names of all members of the household and encompasses agricultural, industrial, and mortality schedules. Although this census is not indexed, the researcher can use the *1886 Nebraska Gazetteer and Business Directory Index,* on microfilm at the Nebraska State Historical Society, as a fairly accurate guide to the 1885 census. This is an alphabetical index listing farmers and businessmen in Nebraska. There is also an 1890 *Nebraska Gazetteer and Business Directory,* which lists farmers and businessmen by towns and counties. Microfilmed copies of these gazetteers are available by interlibrary loan.

School Censuses

Required by law, school censuses are taken every year in Nebraska. Those available at the Nebraska State Historical Society are for all of Adams (1875–77), Buffalo (1902–04), Cass (1860–1977), Chase (1910–77), Clay (1872–1912), Lancaster (1875–1972), and York (1905–73) counties; also available are portions of Burt, Butler, Dawson, Gage, Hall, Harlan, Jefferson, Johnson, Kearney, Madison, Nuckolls, Otoe, Saunders, Sherman and Washington counties for various years. A special school census for Lancaster County, taken in 1905, is partially indexed in *Historical Records of Lancaster County Nebraska,* cited previously.

Background Sources

The best printed sources for the territorial period are the following:

Territorial Papers of the United States Senate—Nebraska 1853–1867. Record Group 46, Reel 16. This publication is available in many historical societies and university libraries.

White, John B., comp. *Published Sources on Territorial Nebraska.* Vol. 23, Nebraska State Historical Society Publications. Lincoln, Nebr.: Nebraska State Historical Society, 1956. This may be purchased from the society for $3.

U.S. Department of State. *State Department Territorial Papers, Nebraska, December 31, 1854–March 27, 1867.* Washington, D.C.: National Archives and Records Service, General Services Administration, 1955. This publication is available on NARA microfilm M228.

Published sources for Nebraska are the following:

Berry, Myrtle D. "Local Nebraska History—A Bibliography." *Nebraska History* 26 (April–June 1945): 104–15.

Compendium of Historical Reminiscence and Biography of Western Nebraska Containing . . . Biographical Sketches of Hundreds of Prominent Old Settlers. Chicago, Ill.: Alden Publishing, 1909 and 1912 (1912 contains entire state).

History of the State of Nebraska. 2 vols. Reprinted with index by Raymond E. Dale. Lincoln, Nebr.: Nebraska State Historical Society, 1962. Originally published by A. T. Andreas in 1882 in Chicago. Also reprinted, with index, in 1975 by Unigraphic, Evanston, Indiana, and available from McDowell Publishing (often referred to as "Andreas").

Nebraska State Genealogical Society. *Nebraska: A Guide to Genealogical Research.* Lincoln, Nebr.: the society, 1984.

Perkey, Elton A. *Perkey's Nebraska Place Names.* Lincoln, Nebr.: Nebraska State Historical Society, 1982. Available for purchase from the society for $6.95.

White, John Browning. *Published Sources on Territorial Nebraska: An Essay and Bibliography.* Vol. 23, Nebraska State Historical Society Publications. Lincoln, Nebr.: Nebraska State Historical Society, 1956. Available for $3.

Many counties have published county histories and have donated copies to the Nebraska State Historical Society. Request the Reference Information Guide No. 4 from the Nebraska State Historical Society for a complete list of "Basic Sources on Nebraska History."

For background on those who immigrated to Nebraska between 1865–90, see Frederick C. Luebke, *Ethnicity on the Great Plains* (Lincoln, Nebr.: University of Nebraska Press, 1980).

"The Agrarian Revolt, 1873-1896," in *Westward Expansion: A History of the American Frontier* (5th ed. New York, N.Y.: Macmillan Publishing Co., 1982), by Ray Allen Billington and Martin Ridge, may be helpful to the researcher with family living on the frontier plains during the latter part of the nineteenth century.

Maps

The Nebraska State Historical Society holds the Sanborn Fire Insurance Maps for Nebraska. Early county atlases are on microfilm for all counties except Arthur, Banner, Blaine, Garden, Hooker, Kimball, Logan, McPherson, and Thomas.

Everts and Kirk. *The 1885 Official State Atlas of Nebraska.* Reprinted in 1976 with 10,000 name index by Margie Sobotka. Fremont, Nebr.: Eastern Nebraska Genealogical Society, 1976.

Nimmo, Sylvia. *Maps Showing County Boundaries of Nebraska 1854–1925.* Papillion, Nebr.: the author, 1978. It is available from 6201 Kentucky Road, Route 21, Papillion, Nebraska 68133.

Land Records

Public-Domain State

Nebraska is a public domain state in which land was initially granted by the federal government. The first homestead claim in the United States was made on 1 January 1863, nine miles west of Beatrice in Gage County by Daniel Freeman. His homestead is now the location of Homestead National Monument. Many of the settlers of Nebraska were Civil War veterans from the northern states of Ohio, New York, Pennsylvania, Illinois, Indiana, and Iowa. Many were eager to obtain the inexpensive farm land available from the federal government.

The researcher should be familiar with the boundaries of the early land offices in Nebraska from 22 July 1854, when the first office opened in Omaha, until 1933 when the last closed at Alliance. Two good sources are Addison Erwin Sheldon, *Land Systems and Land Policies in Nebraska,* Vol. 22 (Lincoln, Nebr.: Nebraska State Historical Society Publications, 1936), and Homer Socolofsky, "Land Disposal in Nebraska 1854–1906: The Homestead Story," in *Nebraska History* 48 (1967): 225–48.

Another helpful reference available from the Nebraska State Historical Society is the Reference Information Guide No. 7, "U.S. Government Land Laws in Nebraska 1854–1907," by James E. Potter. This may be obtained upon request.

The Nebraska State Historical Society has records from the land offices and microfilmed copies of all the tract books. Some of these entries are indexed. If the exact land description is known, land patents for Nebraska may be obtained from the BLM, Wyoming State Office, 2515 Warren Avenue, Box 1828, Cheyenne, Wyoming 82003.

The researcher should be aware that the railroads acquired nearly a tenth of Nebraska land from the federal government and sold it cheaply to settlers to encourage settlement and the development of commerce. The farm, which may have been called "the old homestead" in family tradition, may have first been farmed by this family but was actually acquired from the railroad at an early date. Therefore, it is best to chain the title back using the exact land description in the register of deed's office before going to the federal records. Most of the original records of railroad land sales were destroyed by fire, but the Nebraska Historical Society holds land records of the Burlington and Missouri River Railroad in Nebraska.

After the first land purchase from the government, transfers of land are located in the individual county in the register of deeds office. Here, the researcher can search deeds, indexed by grantee-grantor, mortgages, and cemetery record deed books. Some offices hold the register of entries made at the land office in Lincoln under the Homestead Act of 1862. Many abstracts and claims are also located at the county level.

Probate Records

Probate records are located in the office of the clerk of the county court. In these records, the researcher can expect to find wills, estate records, guardianships, bonds, and probate books. Although adoption records are located in this office, they are legally closed to the public.

Court Records

In the office of the clerk of the district court, available records include felony cases, cases of appeal, marriage, divorce, civil cases, and naturalization records. The naturalization records should include declarations of intention, petitions for naturalization, and second or final papers.

Tax Records

Many tax records are still held at the county level; many taken before 1912 have been sent to the Nebraska State Historical Society. The society is continually collecting county records. At present they have tax records for forty-three counties and assessment records for many others, all for various periods of time. The researcher should contact the archives at the society to learn of its holdings for a particular county before contacting the county. County tax records, real and personal, are located in the office of the county treasurer at the county seat.

Cemetery Records

In the counties for which a research guide is available, the genealogist will find a list of cemeteries, their locations, and whether the listing has been published. Many of these publications also contain names and addresses of funeral homes and mortuaries.

Many cemeteries in Nebraska have been transcribed, and the records are housed at the Nebraska State Historical Society. Records have been compiled for part or all of all but one or two counties.

The Daughters of the American Revolution Library in Washington, D.C., holds a nineteen-volume collection from over 150 cemeteries located in Nebraska.

The National Cemetery in Nebraska is the Fort McPherson National Cemetery, HCO 1 Box 67, Maxwell, Nebraska 69151.

Church Records

The Nebraska State Historical Society holds a number of early church records in its manuscript division. For a complete list of the counties, communities, inclusive dates, and name of the church, the researcher should request the Reference Information Guide No. 6 from the society. Included in the collection are records from selected churches representing the Baptist, Presbyterian, Congregational, Lutheran, Evangelical United Brethren, Methodist, Episcopal, and Society of Friends denominations.

Researchers interested in Nebraska Synod Lutheran records should write for information to Archives of the Nebraska Synod, Suite 204, 124 South 24th Street, Omaha, Nebraska 68102. Missouri Synod Lutheran materials are at the District office, P.O. Box 407, 152 South Columbia, Seward, Nebraska 68434. Those interested in the Methodist or Evangelical United Brethren church can obtain information from Historical Center Nebraska Conference Depository, Lucas Library Building, Nebraska Wesleyan University, Lincoln, Nebraska 68504.

Regional and some national and international materials for the Seventh Day Adventist church are held at the Union College Library, 3800 South 48th Street, Lincoln, NE 68506.

Many people of the Roman Catholic faith settled in Nebraska. The state is divided into the Omaha Diocese, the Lincoln Diocese, and the Grand Island Diocese. The archivist for the Lincoln Diocese is located at 3400 Sheridan Boulevard, Lincoln, Nebraska 68506. The Chancery Office for the Omaha Diocese is located at 100 North 62nd Street, Omaha, Nebraska 68132.

Military Records

The following records that pertain to the military are located at the Nebraska State Historical Society:

The Grand Army of the Republic Membership Rosters (the Nebraska Department of the Grand Army of the Republic Membership Files) give the name of each member, dates of military service, the unit and state from which he served, Grand Army of the Republic post number, and Nebraska post office address of union Civil War Veterans.

The Grand Army of the Republic Burial Records is an alphabetical file of Civil War veterans buried in Nebraska, which lists the military unit in which the veteran served, date of death, place of burial, and often the place of birth.

Rosters of Nebraska Soldiers in the Civil War (1861–65) were published in Andreas' 1882, *History of Nebraska* (see Background Sources). It includes rosters of those persons serving in Nebraska units and Indian Campaigns on the Plains, 1861–69. These rosters list names, dates of service, Nebraska residence, and remarks.

Rosters of Soldiers, Sailors, and Marines (1887–1925) were printed and published by the secretary of state from information furnished by county clerks and assessors. These rosters give name, unit designation, and post office address.

The war service cards for the 1898 Spanish-American War provide name, birthplace, age or birth date, residence, dates of service and assigned unit of Nebraskans. Included in these records are the enlistment and service records for Nebraskans who served in the Philippine War and the Insurrection that followed (1898–1902). World War I service cards are also available and provide name, serial number, residence, age or birth date, and dates of service of Nebraskans. A World War II servicemen index cites references to Nebraska servicemen from local newspapers in the state.

Periodicals, Newspapers, and Manuscript Collections

Periodicals

Nebraska History is published quarterly by the Nebraska State Historical Society. A subscription is included with the annual membership fee of $15. The complete series, from 1918 to present, may be purchased from University Microfilm International, 300 North Zeeb Road, Ann Arbor, Michigan 48103.

Nebraska Ancestree, a quarterly, is published by the Nebraska State Genealogical Society. It contains genealogical data such as cemetery readings, early marriage records, newspaper abstracts, and queries. Back issues of their earlier publication are available: *Nebraska and Midwest Genealogical Records*, Volumes 1–22, published from 1923–44.

Many of the genealogical societies in Nebraska publish monthly newsletters.

Newspapers

The Nebraska State Historical Society has over 27,000 reels of Nebraska newspapers on microfilm dating from the territorial period to the present. A Guide to the Newspaper Collection of the State Archives—*Nebraska State Historical Society* (Lincoln, Nebr.: Nebraska State Historical Society, 1977) has been compiled by Anne P. Diffendal. This may be purchased from the society for $4. Microfilmed newspapers are not available for loan but can be purchased from the Nebraska State Historical Society. Prices and necessary ordering information are available from the society upon request. The society has many reels of microfilmed local foreign language newspapers that are not listed in this guide. Contact the society concerning special newspaper collections. Three specific incidents from the newspapers on microfilm will be checked by historical society staff (if the exact name and date are known) for a minimum fee of $5.

The following resources are available at the Nebraska State Historical Society for use with Nebraska newspapers:

Newspaper notices of births, deaths, and marriages appearing in *The Nebraska State Journal*, 1867–86, published in the *Historical Records of Lancaster County 1855–1905*, Series 2, Vols. 1–3. These records were compiled by the DAR and the WPA.

An *Index of Surnames for Which Information Has Been Found in the Nebraska State Journal from May 1873–December 1899* by Melvin Sittler (now called "The Sittler Index") contains birth, marriage and death notices, town of residence, pension applications and other items from across the state. Indexed by surname, in 4 volumes: 1, A–D; 2, E–K; 3, L–R; 4, S–Z; it is published by the Lincoln-Lancaster County Genealogical Society, P.O. Box 30055, Lincoln, Nebraska 68503.

Indexes for early newspapers include *Beatrice Express* (1871–77), (Brownville) *Nebraska Advertiser* (1856–65), *Fremont Herald* (1880–85), *Gering Weekly* (1887–92), *Hamilton County News* (1877–80), *Hastings Newspaper* (1872–1938), *Niobrara Pioneer* (1874–81), *North Bend Newspaper* (1894–1907), (Plattsmouth) *Nebraska Herald* (1865–72), *Tecumseh Chieftain* (1873–1900).

There is a 1950–80 card file index for *The Lincoln Journal, The Lincoln Star*, and the Sunday edition of the *Omaha-World Herald*.

Nebraska Newspaper Abstracts, 1870, 1880, 1890, and 1900 Series, have been compiled by the Nebraska State Genealogical Society (see Archives, Libraries, and Societies).

Golden Weddings of Nebraskans, by Martha Adamson Cline (431 South 56th Street, Lincoln, Nebraska 68510), is a 1986, 125-page typed index to notices in the *Nebraska Farmer* of over 6,400 Nebraska couples who celebrated fifty or more years of marriage between 1930–70. The index lists the anniversary date, place of residence on anniversary, and date of notice in that newspaper. Copies can also be found at the Library of Congress and DAR Library in Washington, D.C.

The Nebraska State Historical Society and the Nebraska State Genealogical Society are currently engaged in a joint project to computerize existing data found in some early newspapers.

The *Omaha World-Herald* Clipping File, a subject and biographic file with 400,000 subject files (including over five million clippings between 1907–83), is held at the Douglas County Historical Society, General Crook House, P.O. Box 11398, 30th & Fort Streets, Omaha, Nebraska 68111. The researcher should correspond with the society for information concerning fees.

Manuscripts

A Guide to Manuscript Division of the State Archives, Nebraska State Historical Society (Lincoln, Nebr., 1978 and 1983) is an excellent aid to finding material deposited at the society. The 1978 guide can be purchased for $10; the 1983 edition, compiled by Andrea I. Paul, is available for purchase from the society for $3. Family papers, church records, railroad collections, diaries, fraternal lodges, and other papers related to pioneer life may all be found in the manuscript collection. Some of these records have been microfilmed and are available for purchase.

Additional materials are being added to the collection on a continuing basis. The researcher is advised to contact the society concerning specific areas of interest and to notify staff a few days in advance of a visit to allow the materials to be accessed.

Archives, Libraries, and Societies

Nebraska State Historical Society
P.O. Box 82554
1500 R Street
Lincoln, NE 68501

The state archives, museum, and library are all entities of the society. Its holdings include an extensive photo collection, indexed by surname on microfiche, and many family histories and biographical accounts of Nebraskans in various references.

Nebraska State Genealogical Society
Box 5608
Lincoln, NE 68505

Publishes county record source guides and is compiling a computerized statewide cemetery index in collaboration with the historical society.

The State DAR Library
Lue R. Spencer Genealogical Library
at the Edith Abbott Memorial Library
2nd and Washington Streets
Grand Island, NE 68801

Holdings include DAR Cemetery Records of Nebraska and originals of Nebraska DAR Ancestors Registry. Books will be loaned to DAR members for a small shipping fee. The ninety-eight-page catalog is available for $3.

American Historical Society of Germans from Russia
631 D Street
Lincoln, NE 68502

Their collection includes special indexes, obituaries, and materials relating to Germans from Russia.

There are currently over forty-six genealogical societies and 150 historical societies operating in Nebraska. For a complete list, request Reference Information Guide No. 5 and No. 8, respectively, from the Nebraska State Historical Society.

Special Focus Categories

Naturalization

A card index to pre-1906 naturalizations for all the counties in Nebraska, western Iowa, and some counties in eastern Iowa in the 1930s and 1940s was compiled as a WPA project. This index has been microfilmed and can be searched at the Nebraska State Historical Society. Each card contains the name, country of origin, date of naturalization, and the court, county, and state of naturalization. The researcher should be aware that the name of the state does not appear on cards for many Nebraska counties. The reverse side contains the type of naturalization and the volume and page number where the record is located. This index includes only those who received their final papers in Nebraska. It does not report those who only declared their intention in Nebraska.

Ethnic Groups

Czech bibliographical materials can be found in the archives at the Nebraska State Historical Society and in general stacks at Love Library on the University of Nebraska campus which has a policy of not assisting in genealogical queries. These materials must be searched by the individual.

A special census of Germans from Russia living in Lincoln, 1913–14, is available on microfilm at the Nebraska State Historical Society under MS 451 (H. P. Williams Collection).

County Resources

The Nebraska State Genealogical Society has published *Research Guides for Genealogical Data* for thirty-six of Nebraska's counties. These guides, available from the society, describe early history, place-names, records available in the county offices, libraries, maps, cemeteries, churches, and newspapers. Some guides cover adjacent counties. The counties for which guides exist are Adams, Banner, Box Butte, Buffalo, Chase, Cherry, Cheyenne, Clay, Dawes, Deuel, Fillmore, Franklin, Gage, Garden, Grant, Hamilton, Hooker, Jefferson, Johnson, Kimball, Lancaster, Lincoln, Morrill, Nemaha, Nuckolls, Pawnee, Perkins, Phelps, Richardson, Saline, Scotts Bluff, Sheridan, Sioux, Thomas, Webster, and York. Soon to be available is a guide for Kearney County. This ongoing project will publish additional guides in the future.

In the office of the county clerk, the researcher should check county commissioners' minutes, notary records, and delayed birth registrations. Other records of interest to the researcher include Military Discharges, Motor Vehicle and Voter Registrations, estray notices, marks and brands, physician's registers, farm home and ranch names, and school registers. A few minutes of county commissioners' are at the Nebraska State Historical Society.

Dates on the chart are based on the Nebraska State Historical Society's claim that Nebraska has experienced no major loss of records at the county level. With some individual variation, the researcher should look for probate, land, and marriage records to begin within a year or two of the county's formation.

No births or deaths were kept before statewide recording (see Vital Records). Marriages are at the county clerk, deeds at the register of deeds, and probates at the clerk of the county court, as are court records dealing with civil matters.

Dates in parentheses indicate date organized as opposed to date formed. "Original" counties were established when territorial government was created. "Unorganized land" refers to counties added later from land not organized under territorial government.

The Counties and County Seats of
Nebraska
25 0 25 50 75 Miles
SOUTH DAKOTA
IOWA
MN
MO
KANSAS
COLORADO
WY
SIOUX
Harrison
DAWES
Chadron
BOX BUTTE
Alliance
SHERIDAN
Rushville
SCOTTS BLUFF
Gering
BANNER
Harrisburg
MORRILL
Bridgeport
KIMBALL
Kimball
CHEYENNE
Sidney
GARDEN
Oshkosh
DEUEL
Chappell
GRANT
Hyannis
ARTHUR
Arthur
KEITH
Ogallala
PERKINS
Grant
CHASE
Imperial
DUNDY
Benkelman
CHERRY
Valentine
HOOKER
Mullen
McPHERSON
Tryon
THOMAS
Thedford
LOGAN
Stapleton
LINCOLN
North Platte
HAYES
Hayes Center
HITCHCOCK
Trenton
FRONTIER
Stockville
RED WILLOW
McCook
KEYA PAHA
Springview
BROWN
Ainsworth
ROCK
Bassett
BLAINE
Brewster
LOUP
Taylor
CUSTER
Broken Bow
DAWSON
Lexington
GOSPER
Elwood
FURNAS
Beaver City
PHELPS
Holdrege
HARLAN
Alma
BOYD
Butte
HOLT
O'Neill
GARFIELD
Burwell
WHEELER
Bartlett
VALLEY
Ord
GREELEY
Greeley
SHERMAN
Loup City
HOWARD
St. Paul
BUFFALO
Kearney
KEARNEY
Minden
FRANKLIN
Franklin
HALL
Grand Island
ADAMS
Hastings
WEBSTER
Red Cloud
KNOX
Center
ANTELOPE
Neligh
BOONE
Albion
NANCE
Fullerton
MERRICK
Central City
HAMILTON
Aurora
CLAY
Clay Center
NUCKOLLS
Nelson
CEDAR
Hartington
PIERCE
Pierce
MADISON
Madison
PLATTE
Columbus
POLK
Osceola
YORK
York
FILLMORE
Geneva
THAYER
Hebron
DIXON
Ponca
WAYNE
Wayne
STANTON
Stanton
COLFAX
Schuyler
BUTLER
David City
SEWARD
Seward
SALINE
Wilber
JEFFERSON
Fairbury
DAKOTA
Dakota City
THURSTON
Pender
CUMING
West Point
BURT
Tekamah
DODGE
Fremont
WASHINGTON
Blair
SAUNDERS
Wahoo
DOUGLAS
Omaha
SARPY
Papillion
LANCASTER
Lincoln
CASS
Plattsmouth
OTOE
Nebraska City
JOHNSON
Tecumseh
NEMAHA
Auburn
GAGE
Beatrice
PAWNEE
Pawnee City
RICHARDSON
Falls City
Niobrara River
Missouri River
Elkhorn River
North Loup River
Middle Loup
South Loup
North Platte River
South Platte River
Platte River
Republican River
Big Blue
CUSTER
FALL RIVER
SHANNON (Attached to FALL RIVER)
WASHABAUGH (Attached to JACKSON)
BENNETT
MELLETTE
TODD (Attached to TRIPP)
TRIPP
LYMAN
BRULE
AURORA
DAVISON
HANSON
McCOOK
MINNEHAHA
ROCK
DOUGLAS
CHARLES MIX
GREGORY
HUTCHINSON
TURNER
LINCOLN
BON HOMME
YANKTON
CLAY
UNION
LYON
OSCEOLA
DICKINSON
SIOUX
O'BRIEN
CLAY
PLYMOUTH
CHEROKEE
BUENA VISTA
WOODBURY
IDA
SAC
MONONA
CRAWFORD
HARRISON
SHELBY
POTTAWATTAMIE
MILLS
MONTGOMERY
FREMONT
PAGE
ATCHISON
HOLT
NIOBRARA
GOSHEN
LARAMIE
WELD
LOGAN
SEDGWICK
PHILLIPS
MORGAN
WASHINGTON
YUMA
ADAMS
ARAPAHOE
ELBERT
KIT CARSON
LINCOLN
CHEYENNE
CHEYENNE
RAWLINS
DECATUR
NORTON
PHILLIPS
SMITH
JEWELL
REPUBLIC
WASHINGTON
MARSHALL
NEMAHA
BROWN
SHERMAN
THOMAS
SHERIDAN
GRAHAM
ROOKS
OSBORNE
MITCHELL
CLOUD
CLAY
RILEY
POTTAWATAMIE
JACKSON
ATCHISON
JEFFERSON
DOUGLAS
WALLACE
LOGAN
GOVE
TREGO
ELLIS
RUSSELL
ELLSWORTH
SALINE
DICKINSON
MORRIS
LYON
OSAGE
Copyright 1989, Ancestry, Inc.
Drawn by William Dollarhide

Map	County Address	Date Formed Parent County/ies	Birth Marriage Death	Land Probate Court
G6	Adams Hastings 68901	1867 unorganized land	— 1871 —	1871 1871 1871
H3	Antelope Neligh 68756	1871 unorganized land/L'Eau Qui Court	— 1871 —	1871 1871 1871
C4	Arthur Arthur 69121 **Earlier records, before county government formed, are in McPherson County.*	1887 (1913*) unorganized land	— 1913 —	1913 1913 1913
A4	Banner Harrisburg 69345	1888 Cheyenne	— 1881 —	1888 1888 1888
	Blackbird *Became Omaha Reservation in 1857 and Thurston County in 1889. From 1884–89 administered by Dakota County.*	1855 Burt		
E2	Blaine Brewster 68821	1885 unorganized land	— 1885 —	1885 1885 1885
H4	Boone Albion 68620	1871 unorganized land	— 1871 —	1871 1871 1871
A2	Box Butte Alliance 69301	1887 Dawes	— 1886 —	1886 1886 1886
G1	Boyd Butte 68722	1891 unorganized land	— 1891 —	1891 1891 1891
E2	Brown Ainsworth 69210	1883 unorganized land	— 1883 —	1883 1883 1883
F5	Buffalo Kearney 68847	1855 (1870) original	— 1870 —	1870 1870 1870
K3	Burt Tekamah 68061	1854 original	— 1854 —	1854 1854 1854
J4	Butler David City 68632	1856 Green	— 1856 —	1856 1856 1856
	Calhoun	1856 (renamed Saunders, 1862) Lancaster		
K5	Cass Plattsmouth 68048	1855 original	— 1855 —	1855 1855 1855
J2	Cedar Hartington 68739	1857 Dixon	— 1857 —	1857 1857 1857

Map	County Address	Date Formed Parent County/ies	Birth Marriage Death	Land Probate Court
C6	Chase Imperial 69033	1873 unorganized land	— 1887 —	1887 1887 1887
D2	Cherry Valentine 69201	1883 unorganized land	— 1883 —	1883 1883 1883
A4	Cheyenne Sidney 69162	1867 unorganized land	— 1871 —	1871 1871 1871
G6	Clay Clay Center 68933	1855 original	— 1871 —	1871 1871 1871
J4	Colfax Schuyler 68661	1869 Platte	— 1869 —	1869 1869 1869
J3	Cuming West Point 68788	1855 Burt	— 1855 —	1855 1855 1855
E4	Custer Broken Bow 68822	1877 unorganized land	— 1877 —	1877 1877 1877
J2	Dakota Dakota City 68731	1855 Burt	— 1855 —	1855 1855 1855
A2	Dawes Chadron 69337	1885 Sioux	— 1886 —	1885 1885 1885
E5	Dawson Lexington 68850	1860 unorganized land	— 1871 —	1871 1871 1871
B5	Deuel Chappell 69129	1888 Cheyenne	— 1889 —	1889 1889 1889
J2	Dixon Ponca 68770	1856 Izard/Blackbird/unorganized land	— 1858 —	1858 1858 1858
J4	Dodge Fremont 68025	1855 Cass	— 1855 —	1855 1855 1855
K4	Douglas Omaha 68102	1854 original	— 1856 —	1854 1857 1854
C6	Dundy Benkelman 69021	1873 unorganized land	— 1873 —	1873 1873 1873
H6	Fillmore Geneva 68361	1855 (as Jackson; renamed, 1856) (1871) original	— 1871 —	1871 1871 1871

Map	County Address	Date Formed Parent County/ies	Birth Marriage Death	Land Probate Court
	Forney	1854 (renamed Nemaha, 1855) original		
F6	Franklin Franklin 68939	1867 Kearney	— 1871 —	1871 1871 1871
D6	Frontier Stockville 69042	1872 unorganized land	— 1872 —	1872 1872 1872
E6	Furnas Beaver City 68926	1873 unorganized land	— 1873 —	1873 1873 1873
J6	Gage Beatrice 68310	1855 original	— 1855 —	1855 1855 1855
B4	Garden Oshkosh 69154	1909 Deuel	— 1909 —	1909 1909 1909
F3	Garfield Burwell 68823	1884 Wheeler	— 1881 —	1881 1881 1881
E6	Gosper Elwood 68937	1873 unorganized land/Kearney	— 1873 —	1873 1873 1873
C3	Grant Hyannis 69350	1887 unorganized land	— 1888 —	1888 1888 1888
G4	Greeley Greeley 68842	1871 unorganized land	— 1871 —	1871 1871 1871
	Greene	1855 (renamed Seward, 1862) Cass		
G5	Hall Grand Island 68801	1858 Buffalo/unorganized land	— 1858 —	1858 1858 1858
	A special issue on Hall County was published by the Nebraska State Historical Society by William Stolley, 1946.			
H5	Hamilton Aurora 68818	1867 unorganized land	— 1871 —	1871 1871 1871
F6	Harlan Alma 68920	1871 Kearney	— 1871 —	1871 1871 1871
D6	Hayes Hayes Center 69032	1877 unorganized land	— 1877 —	1877 1877 1877
D6	Hitchcock Trenton 69044	1873 unorganized land	— 1873 —	1873 1873 1873

Map	County Address	Date Formed Parent County/ies	Birth Marriage Death	Land Probate Court
G2	Holt O'Neill 68763	1860 (as West; renamed, 1862) unorganized land	— 1862 —	1862 1862 1862
D3	Hooker Mullen 69152	1889 unorganized land	— 1889 —	1889 1889 1889
G4	Howard St. Paul 68873	1871 Hall	— 1871 —	1871 1871 1871
	Izard	1855 (renamed Stanton, 1862) Burt		
	Jackson	1855 (renamed Fillmore, 1856) original		
J6	Jefferson Fairbury 68352	1856 (1864) unorganized land	— 1864 —	1864 1864 1864
K6	Johnson Tecumseh 68450	1857 Nemaha/Pawnee	— 1855 —	1855 1855 1855
	Johnston	1855 (renamed Saline, 1856) original		
	Jones	1856 (abolished 1867; became part of Jefferson) unorganized land		
F6	Kearney Minden 68958	1860 unorganized land	— 1860 —	1860 1860 1860
C4	Keith Ogallala 69153	1873 unorganized land	— 1873 —	1873 1873 1873
E1	Keya Paha Springview 68778	1884 Brown	— 1884 —	1884 1884 1884
A4	Kimball Kimball 69145	1888 Cheyenne	— 1888 —	1888 1888 1888
H2	Knox Center 68724	1857 (as L'Eau Qui Court; renamed, 1873) Pierce/unorganized land	— 1857 —	1857 1857 1857
J5	Lancaster Lincoln 68508	1855 Cass/Pierce (old)	— 1866 —	1867 1869 1880
	L'Eau Qui Court	1857 (renamed Knox, 1873) Pierce/unorganized land		
D5	Lincoln North Platte 69101	1860 (as Shorter; renamed, 1861) unorganized land	— 1860 —	1860 1860 1860

Map	County Address	Date Formed Parent County/ies	Birth Marriage Death	Land Probate Court
D4	Logan Stapleton 69163	1885 unorganized land	— 1885 —	1885 1885 1885
	Loup (old)	1855 (abolished, 1856; became part of Madison, Izard, Monroe, Platte) Burt		
F6	Loup (present) Taylor 68879	1883 unorganized land	— 1855 —	1855 1855 1855
H3	Madison Madison 68748	1856 (1867) McNeale/Loup (old)	— 1867 —	1867 1867 1867
	McNeale	1855 (abolished, 1856; became part of Madison) Burt		
D4	McPherson Tryon 69167	1887 (1890) unorganized land	— 1890 —	1890 1890 1890
H4	Merrick Central City 68826	1858 unorganized land	— 1858 —	1858 1858 1858
	Monroe	1856 (abolished, 1860; became part of Platte) Loup		
A3	Morrill Bridgeport 69336	1908 Cheyenne	— 1908 —	1908 1908 1908
H4	Nance Fullerton 68638	1879 Pawnee Reservation	— 1879 —	1879 1879 1879
K6	Nemaha Auburn 68305	1854 (as Forney; renamed, 1855) original	— 1855 —	1855 1859 1855
H6	Nuckolls Nelson 68961	1860 (1871) unorganized land	— 1871 —	1869 1871 1871
K5	Otoe Nebraska City 68410	1855 Cass/Pierce (old)	— 1855 —	1855 1855 1855
K6	Pawnee Pawnee City 68420	1855 Richardson	— 1855 —	1855 1855 1855
C5	Perkins Grant 69140	1887 Keith	— 1887 —	1887 1887 1887
F6	Phelps Holdrege 68949	1873 Kearney	— 1873 —	1873 1886 1873

Map	County Address	Date Formed Parent County/ies	Birth Marriage Death	Land Probate Court
	Pierce (old)	1854 (abolished, 1855) original		
H2	Pierce (present) Pierce 68767	1856 Izard/unorganized land	— 1856 —	1856 1856 1856
H4	Platte Columbus 68601	1856 Loup (old)	— 1856 —	1856 1856 1856
H4	Polk Osceola 68651	1856 (1870) York/unorganized land	— 1870 —	1870 1870 1870
D6	Red Willow McCook 69001	1873 unorganized land	— 1873 —	1873 1873 1873
K6	Richardson Falls City 68355	1854 (1855) original	— 1854 —	1854 1858 1854
F2	Rock Bassett 68714	1888 Brown	— 1888 —	1888 1888 1888
J6	Saline Wilber 68465	1855 (as Johnston; renamed, 1856) original	— 1866 —	1867 1867 1867
K4	Sarpy Papillion 68046	1857 Douglas	— 1857 —	1857 1857 1857
J4	Saunders Wahoo 68066	1856 (as Calhoun; renamed, 1862) Lancaster	— 1856 —	1856 1856 1856
A3	Scotts Bluff Gering 69341	1888 Cheyenne	— 1888 —	1888 1888 1888
J5	Seward Seward 68434	1855 (as Greene; renamed, 1862) Cass	— 1856 —	1856 1856 1856
B2	Sheridan Rushville 69360	1885 Sioux	— 1885 —	1885 1885 1885
F2	Sherman Loup City 68853	1871 unorganized land/Buffalo	— 1871 —	1871 1871 1871
	Shorter	1860 (renamed Lincoln, 1861) unorganized land		
A2	Sioux Harrison 69346	1877 unorganized land	— 1877 —	1877 1877 1877

Map	County Address	Date Formed Parent County/ies	Birth Marriage Death	Land Probate Court
J3	Stanton Stanton 68779	1855 (as Izard; renamed, 1862) Burt	— 1862 —	1862 1862 1862
	Taylor *Unorganized county in western section enumerated as part of Lincoln in 1870 census. Name discontinued. Area became Cheyenne County.*			
H6	Thayer Hebron 68370	1871 Jefferson	— 1871 —	1871 1871 1871
D3	Thomas Thedford 69166	1887 unorganized land	— 1887 —	1887 1887 188
J3	Thurston Pender 68047 *From 1857–89, Thurston was part of the Omaha Reservation.*	1855 (as Blackbird; renamed, 1889) Burt	— 1855 —	1855 1855 1855
F4	Valley Ord 68862	1871 unorganized land	— 1871 —	1871 1871 1871
K4	Washington Blair 68008	1855 original	— 1855 —	1856 1855 1855
J3	Wayne Wayne 68787	1871 unorganized land	— 1871 —	1871 1871 1871
G6	Webster Red Cloud 68970	1867 unorganized land	— 1867 —	1867 1867 1867
	West	1860 (renamed Holt, 1862) unorganized land		
G3	Wheeler Bartlett 68622	1877 unorganized land	— 1877 —	1877 1877 1877
H5	York York 68467	1855 Cass/Pierce (old)	— 1870 —	1870 1870 1870

NEVADA

Nell Sachse Woodard

Beginning in the 1820s, trailblazers such as Jedediah S. Smith, Peter Skene Ogden, Kit Carson, and Gen. John C. Fremont crossed Nevada's miles of trackless wilderness, laying the footpaths for pioneers who would follow in the next two decades. The Donner Party followed the Humboldt and Truckee rivers in the winter of 1846 on the way to their historic and tragic encampment in the Sierras. By 1848, lands encompassing Nevada were ceded to the United States by Mexico. The Mormon Station, the first permanent settlement at what is now Genoa in the Carson Valley, was established at the same time that Utah Territory was formed in 1850. The territory included all of the present state of Utah, Nevada (except the southern tip that was in New Mexico Territory), the western third of Colorado, and a small corner of southwestern Wyoming.

The decade that followed brought the discovery of gold and silver and the opening of the Comstock Mine in Virginia City in 1859. Carson City was founded the same year with a burgeoning population of gold-seekers, many from California and Europe.

The Comstock Mine brought about the settlement of the state and its rapid economic growth. Nevada became a territory in 1861, and three years later Nevada's natural resources were incorporated into the United States as the thirty-sixth state. Nevada suffered a severe economic depression when the Comstock Lode petered out and until minerals were discovered at Tonopah in 1900.

An expansion of the sheep farming industry near the turn of the twentieth century was attempted for improvement of a slackened economy. What it produced was an active conflict between cattlemen and sheepmen, which proved to be grist for many popular movies about the west. The Taylor Grazing Act settled the conflict by dividing the open range in 1934. The sheep industry added to the ethnic diversity of the population, bringing English, Scots, Mexicans, Irish, Chinese, and Basques.

In modern times, the state has been traversed by three major continental railroads and several airline companies. With the advent of legalized gambling in 1931, its two principal cities—Reno and Las Vegas—became meccas for the nation's gamblers, augmenting their already established eminence in granting divorces for people in a hurry who could not quickly obtain a decree in their own state.

In addition to its gambling interests, the state still carries on mining and, in recent decades, has become a magnet for recreational purposes, particularly with mountain resorts and skiing, or boating at Lake Mead, an adjunct to Boulder Dam. Nevada has extensive farming that, for the most part, is irrigated. It contributed its share of inhabitants for the wars in which America has been engaged and has been the site of much nuclear testing since the advent of the first atomic bomb during World War II.

Vital Records

Birth and death records are at the Nevada State Department of Human Resources, State Health Division, Section of Vital Statistics, 505 East King Street, Carson City, Nevada 89710. These records date from 1911 to the present. Some counties have available birth and death registers beginning in 1887, a few of which have been deposited with the Section of Vital Statistics. Most of those that still exist are in the county recorder's office. None of the pre-1911 birth and death records are included in the statewide index, which begins in 1911 and has restricted access.

Although vital statistics are held by county recorders or health officers, those officers are restricted by law from providing certified copies of such documents. Only the Vital Statistics Section can provide certified copies of birth or death records. Abbreviated birth certificates, which contain birth date, sex, race, and birthplace of the person, are provided. An applicant for a copy of a birth or death certificate must have a direct and tangible interest in the matter recorded. The only available sources for births before 1887 are the extant newspapers or church baptismal records (see Church Records).

County coroners issued burial certificates based on death certificates issued by physicians or, if no physician had been in attendance, based on the facts of the death. It was the duty of the county coroner to file all physicians' certificates and memoranda of burial permits issued and turn them over to the successor in office. Incorporated cities required burial permits from the county coroner's offices between 1879 and 1911. These exist for Virginia City and Gold Hill, 1879–1887, and Carson City, 1893–1896. Nevada State Library and Archives, Division of Archives and Records (see Archives, Libraries, and Societies), has the Ormsby County Coroner's burial permit register for 1893–1896, which includes Carson City's permits and Storey County's coroners' records. There is a compilation of names from the coroner's records at the Nevada State Library.

The Vital Statistics Office also has marriage and divorce records after 1969. Prior to that date, marriage records are located in the county recorder's office where the license was originally obtained.

Divorce records are in the district court office for the county. The indexes of divorce records for the territorial period for Carson County and both Utah and Nevada territories are at the Nevada State Library and Archives, Division of Archives and Records.

Census Records

Federal

Population Schedules.

- Indexed—1850 (part of Utah Territory), 1860 (part of Utah Territory), 1870, 1900, 1910
- Soundex—1880, 1900, 1920

Industry and Agriculture Schedules.

- 1870, 1880

Mortality Schedules.

- 1850 (part of Utah Territory), 1860 (part of Utah Territory), 1870, 1880

Union Veterans Schedules.

- 1890

For census purposes, the counties of Carson, Humboldt and St. Mary's were in Utah Territory in 1860. All of the Nevada federal censuses through 1910 are available on microfilm in both units of the Nevada State Library, Nevada Historical Society, and the Las Vegas Family History Center.

The mortality, industry (1870, 1880), and agriculture (1870) schedules are located at the Nevada Historical Society. The Nevada State Library has the 1880 agriculture schedule and a typescript of the 1870 mortality schedule, which is indexed. AISI publishes indexes to all the population and mortality schedules (see page 2).

Territorial and State

At the Division of Archives and Records, there is a partial census for the territory for 1862 and 1863; there is a full one available for 1875. The 1875 census includes all members of the household and is published in the *Appendix to Journals of Senate and Assembly, of the Eighth Session of the Legislature of the State of Nevada, 1877,* volumes two and three, and the microfiche index. These are available in the Las Vegas Family History Center as well.

Background Sources

For the person doing research in Nevada, useful books are the following: Russell R. Elliott and William D. Rowley, *History of Nevada*, 2d ed., rev. (Lincoln, Nebr., and London, England: University of Nebraska Press, 1987); Stanley W. Paher, *Nevada, An Annotated Bibliography* (Las Vegas, Nev.: Nevada Publications, 1980); Myron F. Angel, *History of Nevada with Illustrations and Biographical Sketches of its Prominent Men and Pioneers* (Oakland, Calif.: Thompson and West, 1881). Angel's History was not published with an index, but this was rectified by Helen J. Poulton, *Index to Thompson and West's History of Nevada* (Reno, Nev.: University of Nevada Press, 1966). See also Robert Laxalt, *Nevada: Bicentennial History* (New York, N.Y.: W.W. Norton & Co., 1977); the Oral History Program, *Master Index to the Collection of University of Nevada Oral History Program 1965–1986* (Reno, Nev.: Oral History Program, 1987), distributed by the University of Nevada Press; and J. Carlyle Parker and Janet Parker, comps., *Nevada Biographical and Genealogical Sketch Index* (Turlock, Calif.: Marietta Publishing Co, 1986).

For place-names, see Rufus Wood Leigh, *Nevada Place Names: Their Origin and Significance* (Salt Lake City, Utah: Deseret News Press, 1964), and Helen S. Carlson, *Nevada Place Names, A Geographical Dictionary* (Reno, Nev.: University of Nevada Press, 1974).

Maps

A wide variety of maps are offered by the Nevada Department of Transportation, Map Section, Room 206, 1263 South Stewart Street, Carson City, Nevada 89712. They will send a catalog and price list of the maps that they have available. There are thirty-minute quadrangle maps of the entire state, a bound volume of all of these and others comprising an atlas of 168 maps, a geographic names directory containing 11,000 place-names, area maps, and maps of the following cities: Boulder City, Caliente, Carlin, Elko, Ely, Fallon, Gabbs, Lovelock, Wells, Winnemucca, and Yerington.

The United States Geological Survey will supply any of their maps for a nominal fee (see page 4). Addresses of local map reference libraries and local map dealers are available from them as well. Request their index for Nevada and then determine which maps will be of assistance.

Land Records

Public-Domain State

Nevada was among the states that received federal land grants. On 1 January 1863 the Homestead Act, passed by the U.S. Congress, became effective. The first U.S. District Land Office was opened in Carson City, Nevada, in 1864. In addition to those records held by the National Archives (see page 5), the BLM, 300 Booth Street, Box 12000, Reno, Nevada 89520, has records involving transactions through Nevada's land offices. The Nevada State Library, Division of Archives and Records, has Carson County (Utah Territory) land records and land patents for the state.

The Comstock Mine's minerals, including gold and silver, were claimed in 1859. The result was the first influx of population into the state that would continue until the substantial depletion of its mineral resources late in the nineteenth century. Mining dominated the economy and politics of the state for a half century. In 1866 alone, there were 200 mining districts that acted roughly as a court system in that they recorded deeds, transferred titles to claims, drew abstracts, and recorded a variety of land instruments. Documents related to mining and minerals may be found on the county level at the Nevada State Library, Division of Archives and Records.

The archives has mining corporation papers, 1861–1926. Those after 1926 are at the Nevada Secretary of State's Office. Other holdings at the archives include state mine inspection records, 1909–74, for operating mines. These records include information regarding name; county and mine supervisor; licenses of hoist operators, 1922–71; and mining accidents, both fatal and nonfatal, 1909–71.

In each individual county in Nevada, records pertaining to land after initial grant are usually located in the respective office of the county recorder.

Probate Records

Probate records for Nevada are located at the office of the county clerk of the respective county and include guardianships, estate files, and the like.

Court Records

Shortly after the territory of Nevada came into being on 2 March 1861, President Lincoln named James Nye as governor and appointed three newly designated federal district judgeships. The bulk of the cases involved the handling of litigation regarding mines and mining, but there were some criminal cases as well.

In general, the modern court system follows the pattern of the other southwestern states. There are four levels of jurisprudence, beginning with the municipal court, which handles only civil cases against city/local ordinances. Currently there are twenty-three judges of these courts. The next step upward is the justice court, composed of sixty-two judges. They also have jurisdiction over civil cases, but this includes injunctions in domestic problems as well. This level is followed by the district court, which has thirty-four judges. These courts handle both civil and criminal cases, divorces, probate, minors, and appeals from the lower courts. The highest court is the Nevada State Supreme Court, made up of five justices who hear appeals from the lower courts, review district court cases, and accept writs.

Each level of the court system has its own offices, clerks, and records maintenance. Thus if a case is pursued at any of these courts, the search must be made in the office holding jurisdiction over the respective records. The Director, Administrative Office of the Courts, 400 West King Street, Suite 406, Carson City, Nevada 89710, will provide the proper court and its address.

Tax Records

The county courthouse where the property was located is the best place to search for tax records. The tax assessment rolls are also at the same place. The assessment rolls are published annually in the local newspapers and should be on file where the newspapers are currently held, either the actual newspaper or the microfilm. The Nevada State Library and Archives, Division of Archives and Records, holds duplicate assessment rolls for all counties for 1891–92, and Ormsby County's assessment rolls from 1862–1950.

Cemetery Records

Cemetery records for almost every county in the state of Nevada can be found on microfilm through the FHL and at the Las Vegas Family History Center. Richard B. Taylor's *The Nevada Tombstone Record Book*, Vol. I (Las Vegas, Nev.: Nevada Families Project, 1986) covers most of Southern Nevada with the promise that Volume II will cover the rest of the state when it is published.

Church Records

Historically, Nevada was built on the lure of mineral wealth; the populace shifted with each succeeding strike. Establishing churches and bringing religion to this transient group of people was not only difficult but compounded by the fire destruction of numerous early frame churches. Mormon, Catholic, Methodist, Episcopalian, Congregationalist, and Jewish congregations all have had some historical part in the establishment of religion in Nevada. A description of early churches is found in Marjorie A. Hanes, *Early Nevada Churches* (Reno, Nev.: Nevada State Society, Daughters of the American Revolution, 1974).

Two possible locations for baptismal records are the Nevada Historical Society for the Protestant Episcopal Church, Nevada Diocese, 1862–1969, and the Nevada Diocese of the Catholic Church, Catholic Chancery Office, 515 Court Street, Reno, Nevada 89501.

The records of the Church of Jesus Christ of Latter-day Saints for Nevada have been microfilmed and are found in the FHL and are also available at the Las Vegas Family History Center. Most other religious bodies have local affiliations and can help researchers.

Military Records

In 1861 the Union was able to raise a volunteer regiment of infantry that served with California troops. In 1862 headquarters were established at Fort Churchill for the military district of Utah and Nevada, and in 1863 six companies of cavalry and a like number of infantry outfits were raised. These Union soldiers did not serve outside their own region. The militia was under the jurisdiction of the legislature. The National Archives has indexes of the army volunteers from the state (NARA microfilm publication M548); these are also available through the FHL. For soldiers buried under the jurisdiction of the Veterans Administration, write the Cemetery Service, National Cemetery System, Veterans Administration, 810 Vermont Avenue, Washington, D.C. 20420.

Although the Nevada State Library, Division of Archives and Records, has service records for World War I through 1972 and copies of discharge papers, access is restricted to the person of record or immediate family.

Periodicals, Newspapers, and Manuscript Collections

Periodicals

Nevada Historical Society Quarterly is published by the Nevada Historical Society. *The Prospector* has been published since 1976 by Clark County Genealogical Society (see Archives, Libraries, and Societies).

Newspapers

Newspapers for a great many cities are on microfilm at the Nevada State Library, Nevada Historical Society, and the University of Nevada in both Reno and Las Vegas. The *Territorial Enterprise* had its advent at Genoa in 1858 but was shortly moved to Carson City and then to Virginia City. Mark Twain used this newspaper to cut his journalistic teeth, so these publications were not just politics and mining but literary endeavors as well.

The *Silver Age* superseded the *Enterprise* at Carson City. *The Daily Independent* began publishing in Carson City in 1863, but it did not survive after October 1864. *The Daily Evening Post* was also a short-lived publication. A number of early papers were started only to end or to move from one location to another. A standard reference to those and subsequent undertakings is Richard E. Lingenfelter and Karen Rix Gash, *The Newspapers of Nevada: A History and Bibliography, 1854–1979* (Reno, Nev.: University of Nevada Press, 1984).

Below is a listing of indexes of Nevada newspapers as reported in May 1985 showing the name of the newspaper, the dates for which it has been indexed, and the location of that index.

Carson Daily Appeal: 1865–66, 1869–70, 1881, 1885–1886; Nevada State Library.

Carson Valley News: 1875–1900; Douglas County Library in Minden.

Copper Ore: 1910; White Pine County Library in Ely.

Daily Inland Empire: 1867–70; White Pine County Library.

Douglas County Banner: Oct.–Dec. 1865; Nevada State Library.

Eastern Slope: 1865–68; Nevada Historical Society.

Elko Daily Free Press: 1883–1962; Northeast Nevada Museum in Elko.

Elko Independent: 1883–1962; Northeast Nevada Museum.

Eureka Daily Sentinel: 1873–74; White Pine County Library.

Eureka Sentinel: 18(?)–1871; White Pine County Library.

Kimberly News: 1910; White Pine County Library.

Las Vegas Age: 1905–40; Nevada State Museum and Historical Society, 700 Twin Lakes Drive, Las Vegas, Nevada 89107.

Las Vegas Review-Journal: 1972–present; Nevada State Museum and Historical Society (see Archives, Libraries, and Societies) and most libraries of Clark County including the Las Vegas Family History Center.

Las Vegas Sun: 1972–present; Las Vegas Public Library.

Nevada Appeal: 1980–present; Nevada State Library.

Nevada State Journal: 1870–76, 1880–1884; Nevada Historical Society.

Pioche Weekly Record: 1872–1904; Nevada State Museum and Historical Society.

Reese River Reveille: 1863–68; White Pine County Library.

Reno Crescent: July 1868–March 1874; Nevada Historical Society.

Territorial Enterprise: 1859–81; Nevada Historical Society.

Ward Miner: 1876–77; White Pine County Library.

Washoe Times: 1862–63; Nevada Historical Society.

Washoe Weekly Star: 1864–65; Nevada Historical Society.

Washoe Weekly Times: 1865–68; Nevada Historical Society.

White Pine Evening Telegram: 1869; White Pine County Library.

White Pine News: 1869–1906; White Pine County Library.

The University of Nevada at Reno's special collection includes substantial numbers of available newspapers on microfilm. There is an index to the *Territorial Enterprise* at the Nevada Historical Society. Microfilm copies of various newspapers are available on interlibrary loan from the Nevada State Library. Newspapers are not located at the Division of Archives.

Manuscripts

The Nevada Historical Society, a major historical depository, has an excellent collection of old newspapers, manuscripts, and diaries.

A special collection at the University of Nevada at Las Vegas contains major historical records, manuscripts, diaries, and photographs, especially of Clark County.

Outside the state, one should consult the Bancroft Library of the University of California at Berkeley, California, as well as the Utah State Archives and the Utah State Historical Society (see Utah). All of these have important historical manuscript materials, particularly for the territorial and pre-state eras.

Archives, Libraries, and Societies

Nevada State Library and Archives
Library:
Capitol Complex
401 North Carson Street
Carson City, NV 89710

Archives:
Division of Archives and Records
101 South Fall Street
Carson City, NV 89710

This institution has a library and an archives, each with good research collections, though the archives concerns itself with statewide oriented research material.

Nevada State Museum and Historical Society
700 Twin Lakes Drive
Las Vegas, NV 89107

Las Vegas Family History Center
509 South Ninth Street
Las Vegas, NV 89101
A branch of the FHL, it holds a variety of materials for research pertaining to Nevada.

The state is still not a largely populated one, but there are a few county genealogical and historical societies in addition to the two thriving statewide societies, both operating in Reno.

Nevada State Genealogical Society
Box 20666
Reno, NV 89515

Nevada Historical Society
1650 North Virginia Street
Reno, NV 89503

Clark County Genealogical Society
P.O. Box 1929
Las Vegas, NV 89125
The largest county genealogical society in the state; it publishes *The Prospector.*

Special Focus Categories

Native American

At the onset of emigration into the state, there were four major tribes occupying lands in present-day Nevada: Northern and Southern Paiute, the Shoshone, and the Washo. Today, there are twenty-three reservations; although most of the state's native people have never lived on one. For further information on twentieth-century tribes, contact the Inter-Tribal Council of Nevada, 806 Holman Way, Sparks, Nevada 89431.

Two fine accounts of native life, including personal historical accounts and writing are the following:

Forbes, Jack D. *The Nevada Indian Speaks.* Reno, Nev.: University of Nevada Press, 1967.

Hopkins, Sarah Winnemucca. *Life Among the Piutes.* Boston, Mass.: Putnam Publishers, 1883.

Other Ethnic Groups

Nevada has a large foreign-born population whose history is covered in Wilbur S. Shepperson, *Restless Strangers: Nevada's Immigrants and Their Interpreters* (Reno, Nev.:

University of Nevada Press, 1970), which draws from newspaper accounts, interviews, and census records.

The Yugoslavians and the Basques are two important ethnic groups in the history of Nevada. The following will be helpful background material: Adam S. Eterovich, *Yugoslavs in Nevada, 1859–1900* (San Francisco, Calif.: R and E Research Associates, 1973), and William A. Douglass and Jon Bilbao, *Amerikanuak, Basques in the New World* (Reno, Nev.: University of Nevada Press, 1975).

County Resources

The following indicates what vital, land, probate, and court records are in each county. The dates indicated are the first known records for each county. They do not imply that all records are extant to the present.

According to the Nevada State Library, Division of Archives and Records, there has been considerable record loss because of fires (Virginia City, 1875); changes in county seat locations with only Ormsby (now Carson City), Clark, Elko, Mineral, Pershing, and Storey counties retaining their original county seats; and lack of adequate funds to care for the records.

The Nevada State Library, Division of Archives and Records holds many statewide and territorial records, including the territorial records for Carson County, Utah Territory, and Nevada Territory with not only deeds and their indexes but also probate, inquests, and divorces. A calendar of these records has also been published: Marion Ellison, comp., *An Inventory & Index to the Records of Carson City, Utah & Nevada Territories, 1855–1861* (Reno, Nev.: Grace Dangberg Foundation, 1984).

The nineteenth-century county records (land, probate, court, etc.) have recently been microfilmed for Douglas, Lyon, Ormsby, and Washo. Microfilm copies are at the Nevada State Library, Division of Archives and Records, the Nevada State Historical Society, and the Nevada State Museum and Historical Society.

County recorders hold land records, except in two cases where the county assessor's office handles them. County clerks have probate records, and the clerk of the courts maintains court records.

In addition to the county officials and the other sources listed on page 11, Elliott and Rowley's *History of Nevada* (cited under Background Sources) was used as a reference.

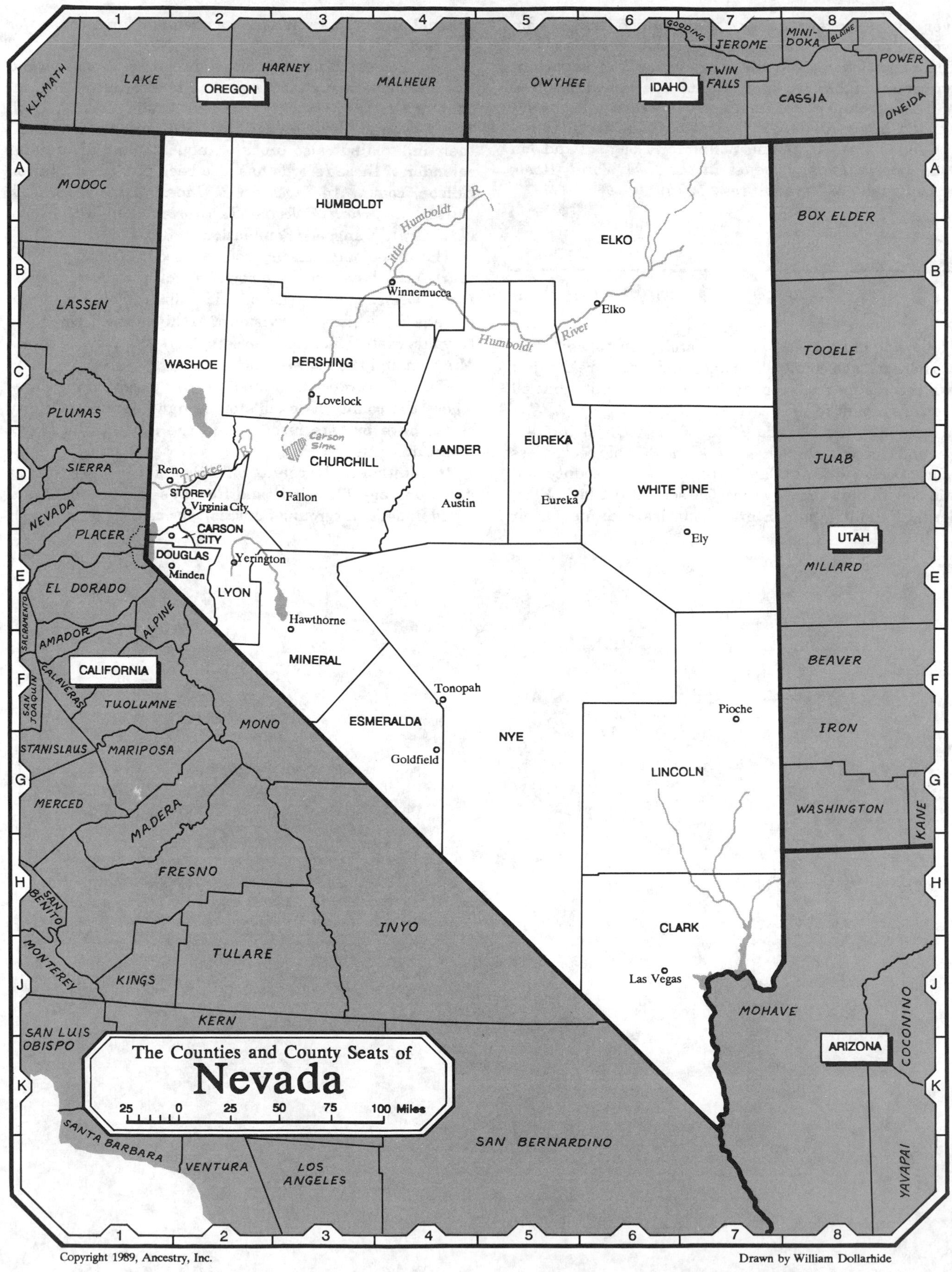

Drawn by William Dollarhide

Map	County Address	Date Formed Parent County/ies	Birth Marriage Death	Land Probate Court
	Carson	1853 (abolished, 1861; became part of Washoe, Churchill, Storey, Lyon, Douglas, and Humboldt)		
		Utah Territory		
	As part of Utah Territory, it included Carson City, Genoa, and Virginia City, but it was abolished when Nevada Territory counties were formed.			
E2	Carson City	1969	1887	1862
	198 N. Carson Street	Ormsby	1855	1864
	Carson City 09701		1891	1864
	Ormsby County was consolidated with Carson City, 1969, to form an independent city.			
D3	Churchill	1861	1888–1969	1864
	10 W. Williams Avenue	original	1864	1904
	Fallon 89406		1888–1968	1904
J7	Clark	1909	1909	1909
	309 S. Third Street	Lincoln	1909	1909
	Las Vegas 89101		1909	1909
	District Health Department, 625 Shadow Lane, Las Vegas, has births and death from 1955 for Las Vegas.			
E2	Douglas	1861	1887–1923	1855
	P.O. Box 218	original	1802	1887
	Minden 89423		1887–1933	1887
	Courthouse fire, 1910.			
B6	Elko	1869	1887–1915	1869
	Courthouse, Room 103	St. Mary's/Lander	1869	1869
	Elko 89801		1887–1915	1869
G4	Esmeralda	1861	1907–11	1863
	P.O. Box 491	original	1898	1881
	Goldfield 89013		1907–11	1908
D5	Eureka	1873	1873–1929	1873
	P.O. Box 556	Lander	1873	1873
	Eureka 89316		1887	1873
A3	Humboldt	1861	1888–1911	1861*
	25 W. Fourth Street	original	1862	1863
	Winnemucca 89445		1888–1911	1862
	**Deeds to 1864 are not indexed; index is available after 1864.*			
D4	Lander	1862	?	1862?
	P.O. Box 909	original	1862?	1862?
	Battle Mountain 89820		?	1862?
G6	Lincoln	1866	1887	1865
	P.O. Box 218	Nye	1872	1855
	Pioche 89043		1887	1873
	Some records were damaged or lost when moving into the new courthouse.			
E2	Lyon	1861	1887–1911	1862
	P.O. Box 927	original	1862	1867*
	Yerington 89447		1887–1911	1867
	**Record loss, 1911. These are not complete.*			
E3	Mineral	1911	1911*	1911
	P.O. Box 1447	Esmeralda	1911	1911
	Hawthorne 89415		1911*	1911
	**Held at the state, Dept. of Human Resources (see Vital Records).*			
F5	Nye	1864	1887	1864
	P.O. Box 1111	Esmeralda	1864	1865
	Tonopah 89049		1887	1864

Map	County Address	Date Formed Parent County/ies	Birth Marriage Death	Land Probate Court
	Ormsby	1861 (became part of Carson City, 1969) original		
	Pahute	1864 (abolished, 1871; became part of Lincoln and later Clark) Arizona Territory		
C3	Pershing P.O. Box 736 Lovelock 89419	1919 Humboldt	1919 1919 1919	1919 1919 1919
	Roop	1870 (annexed to Washoe, 1883)		
	St. Mary's	1860 (abolished, 1869; became Elko)		
D2	Storey P.O. Box 493 Virginia City 89440 **County Assessor's Office.* *Courthouse fire, 1875.*	1861 original	1887–1942 1874 1887	1876* 1886 1861
B2	Washoe P.O. Box 11130 Reno 89520 **At Washoe County Health Department, 1001 E. Ninth Street, Reno 89520.*	1861 original	1887* 1861? 1887*	1870 1870 1870
D7	White Pine P.O. Box 68 Ely 89301 *Courthouse fire, 1885. *Deeds at County Assessor's Office.*	1869 Millard, Utah Territory/ St. Mary's (Elko)/Nye	1887? 1869? 1887?	1885* 1885 1885

NEW HAMPSHIRE

Alice Eichholz, Ph.D., C.G., and George F. Sanborn, Jr.

The first permanent European settlements in what is now New Hampshire occurred along the Piscataqua River in 1623, when two groups of families associated with the Fishmonger's Company of London located on Dover Neck and Little Harbor (now part of Portsmouth). It is highly probable that European fishermen had visited the Isles of Shoals and adjacent parts of the mainland for many years prior to 1623. Following these two settlements, towns sprang up in Exeter (1637) and Hampton (1638). For many years, New Hampshire consisted of these four communities. As their populations grew, the large tracts of land that comprised the four towns were subdivided until they included the many coastal communities seen today. The lands not claimed by the towns were covered by various patents granted to English entrepreneurs, whose heirs were still struggling over the titles decades later.

New Hampshire was a Royal Province until 1771 except for two short periods, 1642–79 and 1690–92, when it was under the control of Massachusetts. Because of New Hampshire's status as a Royal Province, it was in the peculiar position of separating the two parts of the Massachusetts Bay Colony, present-day Maine and Massachusetts.

People began migrating at a very early date from Middlesex and Essex counties, Massachusetts, into the seacoast area and the Merrimack River Valley, while settlers from Connecticut and central and western Massachusetts were pushing their way up into what is now Cheshire County, with many settling as far inland as the interior parts of Grafton County.

A significant number of Ulster Scots settled in south central New Hampshire in 1718 and again in 1723. They had close familial ties with other Ulster Scots settlements in New England and Cherry Valley, then on the New York frontier, southwest of Albany. Originally settling in the old town of Londonderry, they spread out to found numerous other towns across the southern tier of New Hampshire.

Settlement of the interior of New Hampshire was effected largely by two waves of migrations. People from the seacoast were primarily responsible for settling the Lakes Region, the Upper Merrimack Valley, and "along the edge of Maine," whereas settlers from southern New England were primarily responsible for settling western and southwestern New Hampshire, with a mixture of both groups peopling the North Country. The settlers with seacoast origins had a further tendency to continue westward out of New Hampshire.

By the middle of the nineteenth century, French-Canadians began to move southward into New Hampshire to work in the mill towns and in the lumber industry. Migration from Quebec and later from the Maritime Provinces became very heavy between 1880 and 1920 and now accounts for over one-third of New Hampshire's population. Large numbers of Irish settlers came to the larger towns and cities following the potato famine and now comprise a significant portion of the population, while migrations of other ethnic groups to particular areas, often to work in specific trades, have added to the rich mosaic of New Hampshire's population. Such groups include the Poles of Franklin, the Greeks of Manchester and Laconia, as well as the Italians brought to New Hampshire to work as masons or road builders.

Vital Records

The town or city clerk's office is the place where vital events are officially recorded in New Hampshire. Today each town or city sends copies of its vital events to the Bureau of Vital Records and Health Statistics, 6 Hazen Drive, Concord, New Hampshire 03301. Statewide compilation, however, did not begin until a law was passed in 1866 requiring the secretary of state to make a report of all vital events for each of the towns. Total compliance with the law was not accomplished until the 1880s, and even then the practice of sending a copy of the vital event to the secretary of state was not uniform. By 1905, when the Bureau of Vital Records was established, regular statewide recording became a reality.

A statewide compilation, gathered from earlier town vital records, generated the alphabetical arrangement which exists today in the card file at the bureau and in the microfilm collections at the New England Historic Genealogical Society (see Massachusetts) and the FHL. This alphabetical compilation is incomplete since some towns did not send all their pre-1905 vital records to the bureau. It is therefore important to check the town clerk's official records directly if no event is found in the bureau's compilation.

Births that were recorded before 1901 and deaths, marriages, and those divorce records from the 1870s to 1938, can be personally searched at the bureau. The current price for a copy, in person or by mail, is $10, but phone orders are accepted at an additional charge if a credit card is used (see Court Records).

The alphabetical arrangement of the compilation at the bureau and consequently on microfilm requires some explanation. The system used was an early version of a soundex. Vital records are broken down into type of event (birth, marriage, death) and time period and then by the first and third letter of the last name to determine the proper card file drawer in which to search for the event. Cards exist for grooms, but brides before 1947 are on a separate microfilm index since they are not included on separate cards in the compilation. After 1901 for births and 1938 for deaths, marriages, and divorces, a researcher has to demonstrate a direct interest in the event to view or receive a copy of the record.

Children not named at birth later had their names added in the town or city office records. This practice, particularly prevalent in the last half of the nineteenth century, meant that the name eventually given did not always get sent in to the state compilation. French-Canadian families might have used the baptismal names of "Joseph" or "Marie" in the copy sent to the state.

There are printed versions of New Hampshire vital records for some towns including Colebrook (1873–86), Danville (1760–1886), Dover (1640–1850), Hampton Falls to 1899, Keene (1742–1881), Laconia marriages (1826–92), Londonderry to 1910, and South Hampton (1743–1886). A large number of typescripts of southeastern town vital records were prepared by Priscilla Hammond and others and are located at the New Hampshire Historical Society (see Archives, Libraries, and Societies), with some at the New England Historic Genealogical Society.

When the microfilming of New Hampshire town records, which included vital records, was accomplished, an every-name index created by the WPA for town records kept before approximately 1850 was microfilmed as well. Births, deaths, and marriages were included in the records as early as 1640 although there is no consistency, and they are far from complete. The original card index is held by the New Hampshire State Library (see Archives, Libraries, and Societies). Both the town records and the WPA index are on microfilm through the FHL and are at the New England Historic Genealogical Society. A notable omission in the index is the town of Exeter, which was completely overlooked.

Census Records

Federal

Population Schedules.

- Indexed—1790, 1800 (part), 1810, 1820 (part), 1830, 1840, 1850, 1860
- Soundex—1880, 1900, 1920
- Unindexed—1870, 1910

Industry and Agriculture Schedules.

- 1850, 1860, 1870, 1880

Mortality Schedules.

- 1850, 1860, 1870, 1880

Union Veterans Schedules.

- 1890

Part of the 1800 and 1820 census records for New Hampshire are no longer in existence. Towns in Rockingham County in 1800 not included are Atkinson, Greenland, Hampton, Hampton Falls, Londonderry, Northampton, Pelham, Plaistow, Salem, Seabrook, Stratham, and Windham. Strafford County towns missing for that census are Alton, Barnstead, Brookfield, Effingham, Gilmanton, Middleton, New Durham, Ossipee, Tuftonboro, Wakefield, and Wolfeborough. However, *The 1798 U.S. Direct Tax* has been found for only nine of these towns and published by Heritage Books: Alton, Brookfield, Effingham, Middleton, New Durham, Ossipee, Tuftonboro, Wakefield and Wolfeborough. This is an excellent alternative source to the lost census returns (see Tax Records). *Heads of Family at the Second Census of the United States Taken in the Year 1800* was privately published by John Brooks Threlfall (Madison, Wisc., 1973). Except for the missing towns, the entire census enumerations are in this volume distributed through Adams Press in Chicago, Illinois.

All of the census records for 1820 for Grafton County and parts of Rockingham (Gosport, Greenland, New Castle, Newington, Portsmouth, and Rye) are lost. Only Center Harbor, Gilford, Moultonborough, New Hampton, and Sanbornton records are available for Strafford County.

The original records (1850, 1860, 1870, and 1880 for the entire state, and 1840 for Rockingham, Merrimack, and Strafford county towns) are now held by the New Hampshire Division of Records Management and Archives (see Archives, Libraries, and Societies).

With large numbers of French-Canadians in the state by the time of the 1850 census, care should be taken to use alternate spellings when using any indexes.

Provincial

For the provincial period various enumerations exist for the years 1732, 1744, 1767, and 1776. All are available at the New Hampshire Records and Archives, and except for 1732, appear in the multivolume set of *New Hampshire State Papers* (see Background Sources below). There are reprints of some with additional material used for supplements. It should be noted that none of the following listings are censuses in strict terms:

Holbrook, Jay Mack. *New Hampshire Residents 1633–1699*. Oxford, Mass.: Holbrook Research Institute, 1979. For Dover, Exeter, Portsmouth, Hampton (and Kingston), Isles of Shoals. An alphabetical listing compiled from tax lists, land grants, probates, church records, and other sources. Each listing gives the original source for checking accuracy.

———. *New Hampshire 1732 Census*. Oxford, Mass.: Holbrook Research Institute, 1981. Lists 3,500 heads of households by town with number of males over sixteen enumerated and covers a period of years, not just 1732.

———. *New Hampshire 1776 Census*. Oxford, Mass.: Holbrook, 1976. Over 9,000 males listed by place of residence and whether for or against revolution. Original spellings are used.

Background Sources

Town histories are abundant, particularly for southwestern towns of New Hampshire, with over 100 containing excellent genealogies of families stretching the generations back to the point of debarkation. The largest collections are held by the New Hampshire State Library and the New Hampshire Historical Society located next door to each other (see Archives, Libraries and Societies for addresses).

Jeremy Belknap, *The History of New Hampshire*, 3 vols. (1784–96), is an excellent history of the state including the complicated and conflicting land grants up the 1796. It has been reprinted many times and is available on microfilm. The second edition (1812) included all three volumes, but John Farmer revised the first two volumes in one (Dover, Del., 1831), with copious notes added to the text. This one-volume edition was reprinted in 1862. Volume 3 of the 1812 edition has been recently reprinted as Gary T. Lord, ed., *Belknap's New Hampshire History: An Account of the State in 1792* (Hampton, N.H.: Peter Randall, 1973), with a new introduction and notes on this classic perspective of New Hampshire history.

Copeley, William. *Index to Genealogies in New Hampshire Town Histories*. Concord, N.H.: New Hampshire Historical Society, 1988. Updated and comprehensive, this index lists any family for whom more than three generations are covered in New Hampshire published town histories.

Hanrahan, E. J., ed. *Hammond's Check List of New Hampshire History*. Somersworth, N.H.: New Hampshire Publishing Co., 1971. This bibliography of published New Hampshire history has been superseded by Haskell and Bassett (see below), but some items were not carried over.

Haskell, John D., and T. D. Seymour Bassett, eds. *New Hampshire: A Bibliography of Its History*. Hanover, N.H.: University Press of New England, 1979. A scholarly bibliography, it indicates background sources of value to genealogists.

Hunt, Elmer M. *New Hampshire Town Names and Whence They Came*. Peterborough, N.H.: Noone House, 1970. This gazetteer provides a good place-name index indicating etymology.

New Hampshire State Papers. 40 vols. Concord and Manchester, N.H., 1867-1943. Although published under various titles, its official title is *Documents and Records Relating to New Hampshire, 1623–1800*, as described in R. Stuart Wallace, "The State Papers? A Descriptive Guide," *Historical New Hampshire* 31 (1976): 119–28. Published versions of numerous records are included in the extensive forty-volume collection. Probate (to 1771), town, and military records are among them. Wallace's descriptive guide can provide a general overview.

Noyes, Sybil, Charles T. Libby, and Walter G. Davis. *Genealogical Dictionary of Maine and New Hampshire*. 1928–29. Reprint. Baltimore, Md.: Genealogical Publishing Co., 1983. This is a highly creditable attempt at compiling family genealogies of every family established in New Hampshire and Maine by 1699.

Turner, Lynn Warner. *The Ninth State: New Hampshire's Formative Years*. Chapel Hill, N.C.: University of North Carolina Press, 1983. Covered in this readable text are the events and developments after the Revolution.

Excellent county histories and gazetteers can aid in locating particular family surnames and providing good background for local research. Some notable ones are:

Child, Hamilton. *Child's Cheshire County Gazetteer, 1736–1885*. Syracuse, N.Y.: Journal, 1885.

———. *Child's Grafton County Gazetteer, 1709–1886*. Syracuse, N.Y.: Journal, 1886.

Merrill, Georgia Drew. *History of Carroll County.* 1889. Reprint. Somersworth, N.H.: New Hampshire Publishing Co., 1972.

———. *History of Coos County.* 1888. Reprint. Somersworth, N.H.: New Hampshire Publishing Co., 1971.

Hurd, D. Hamilton. *History of Hillsborough County, New Hampshire.* Philadelphia, Pa.: J. W. Lewis & Co., 1885.

Guides which will be helpful for genealogical research in the state include:

Dearborn, David C., "New Hampshire Genealogy: A Perspective." *The New England Historical and Genealogical Register* 130 (October 1976): 244-58. An interesting perspective on migration is included.

Lindberg, Marcia Wiswall, ed. *Genealogist's Handbook for New England Research.* Boston, Mass.: New England Historic Genealogical Society, 1985. Major collections, repositories, and town formation information are presented.

Towle, Laird C., and Ann M. Brown. *New Hampshire Genealogical Research Guide.* Bowie, Md.: Heritage Books, 1983. Details of resources available are provided.

Maps

New Hampshire is a state with excellent map sources, making it possible to follow migration trails with the use of political divisions and geographic features. David A. Cobb, *New Hampshire Maps to 1900: An Annotated Checklist* (Concord, N.H.: New Hampshire Historical Society, 1981), helps to identify and locate many maps for research purposes.

An excellent, currently published atlas for the entire state is *The New Hampshire Atlas and Gazetteer* (Freeport, Maine: DeLorme Publishing, 1986). It is continually updated and has excellent cartography of New Hampshire features including roads (indicating type of surface), structures, some cemeteries, and churches. Although slightly oversized for easy carrying, its usefulness outweighs this hindrance.

Statewide nineteenth-century maps are also excellent. D. H. Hurd and Co., *Town and City Atlas of the State of New Hampshire* (Boston, 1892), indicates occupants' names for structures and treats each town on a separate page with close-up maps for more populated areas. Saco Valley Publishing, 76 Main Street, Fryeburg, Maine 04037, has been reprinting excellent county editions of these in a handy notebook size.

Early folio size maps were published by H. F. Wallings and Charles H. Hitchcock in *Atlas of the State of New Hampshire* (New York, 1877). Although individual structures are not shown on these maps, such detail can be found on the large county maps done by Wallings, Chase, and others in the 1850s.

As with other New England states, obtaining a copy of the town's lotting map (the way land was divided before being granted or sold) can be extremely beneficial in solving genealogical problems. The most comprehensive collection of these can be found at the New Hampshire Records and Archives. The layouts are cataloged by town and include the numbering process of lots and, in many cases, name of the original proprietor, which can help backtrack land holdings and provide a chain of title for problem solving. Many of these are found in the *New Hampshire State Papers* (see Background Sources) as well.

Land Records

State-Land State

All New Hampshire deeds for the provincial period before 1771 were filed in Exeter, or the Ipswich deeds and the Old Norfolk County deeds in Salem, Massachusetts. Microfilms of the first 100 volumes of those filed in Exeter, called Province Deeds, now reside, along with a card file index, at the New Hampshire Records and Archives. The original books are deposited there as well.

Counties were formed in 1769, with each county seat becoming the location for recording land transactions in that county, but in actuality the practice did not begin until 1771, except Strafford County, which, due to delays in constructing a new courthouse, did not commence until 1773. Indexes at county offices are in grantor and grantee volumes, by time period, and often include the name of the town where the land is located. Since there are numerous towns in each county, this detail in the index can be helpful in searching land held by those with a common surname. When details of property description are given in the deed, they are usually either metes and bounds or lot identification.

New Hampshire Records and Archives holds the original books and an index to Rockingham County deeds (1771–1824), which includes transactions in Strafford County for the years 1771–73. Early books of Grafton County Deeds (through volume 16) are also at the New Hampshire Records and Archives, but can be viewed on microfilm at the Grafton County Courthouse in Woodsville. For all others, one can use either the books or microfilms in the county seat or microfilm of deeds to ca. 1850 at the FHL and the New England Historic Genealogical Society.

Because of geographic and boundary considerations, some early deeds involving land transactions in the Cheshire County area might have been recorded in Massachusetts. Consequently, Hampden County Courthouse in Springfield (see Massachusetts—County Resources) should be consulted. Conversely, it is possible that land granted by New Hampshire in what is now Vermont may be mentioned in the Province Deeds.

Probate Records

Probate records covering the colonial period from 1636–1771, originally filed in Portsmouth and Exeter, are in the collection at the New Hampshire Records and Archives, and abstracts have been published in volumes 31–39 of the *New Hampshire State Papers* (see Background Sources). Probate records for residents of towns along the Massachusetts border may be found in Massachusetts counties. For those in Rockingham County, see *Essex County (Mass.) Probate Index, 1636–1840* (see Massachusetts—Probate Records).

After the formation of counties, probates were filed at county seats. All probate records, except for Coos County whose records were burned prior to 1887, are extant. *Abstracts of Probate Records of Strafford County New Hampshire, 1771–1799* (Bedford, N.H.: the author, 1973), compiled by Helen Evans, and the *Hillsborough County Register of Probate Index, 1771–1884* (Nashua, N.H., 1973) are available.

Abstracts and indexes are only the tip of the iceberg in probate records, however. Each county holds original files that include letters, affidavits, bills, receipts, original wills, and inventories. Not all material in the file was recorded in probate books. Consequently, a probate search is not complete without surveying the materials in the original files.

Court Records

Each county, in addition to having a registry of probate and of deeds, has court records. At different times there were inferior courts of common pleas, superior courts, and courts of general sessions of the peace which dealt with civil and criminal cases, equity and naturalizations. Divorces, although indexed beginning in the 1870s at the Bureau of Vital Records, are all filed at the county superior court. Some earlier ones are in legislative petitions.

The province court records to 1771 are card indexed at the New Hampshire Records and Archives. After that time, the county seat traditionally housed court records. In a few cases, card indexes to plaintiff and defendant are available to guide the search. Original county court records now at the New Hampshire Records and Archives instead of the county seat include Hillsborough to 1880, Merrimack to 1870, Rockingham 1772–1860, Strafford 1773–1850, and Sullivan to 1880. Microfilm of Grafton, Merrimack, and Strafford court record copy and docket books are at the New Hampshire State Library.

New Hampshire State Papers, volume 40, contains court records from the Dover-Portsmouth Quarterly Court, 1640–92, and there are some general court records and indexes both at the New Hampshire Records and Archives and on microfilm at the FHL for the colonial period. After statehood, the court system became established along county lines. The only court records which have been abstracted or published for the post-colonial period are abstracts of Strafford County Inferior Court records, 1773–83.

Tax Records

No thorough survey has yet been attempted to locate all the annual tax lists for New Hampshire towns. They can be found in manuscript collections in public libraries, in town clerk's offices among the pages of the annual town meeting minutes, and at the archives and other repositories. Both residents and nonresidents who owned property or businesses might be listed on the annual assessment, which would indicate the number of voting-age males as polls, and such items as the type and acreage of land, animals, and milling products. Following annual tax lists can provide important clues for ages of males (nearly always 21–50 and occasionally 16–60) and for men moving to or leaving a town, since non-landowners were listed as well, although a few officials were usually exempt.

One important collection of tax records, which has been microfilmed from the originals held at the New Hampshire Records and Archives, is the multivolume nonresident tax lists from 1849–74.

In 1798 a U.S. direct tax was ordered. Heritage Books has printed the returns which have been located for nine New Hampshire towns located at that time in Strafford County.

Cemetery Records

Few cemetery records have been published and most exist in manuscript form in various repositories. There is an extensive typescript collection augmented annually by the local chapters of the DAR. A copy of each volume is deposited at the New Hampshire Historical Society, whose growing collection of cemetery inscriptions from all sources is being microfilmed. There are numerous typed and indexed cemetery transcriptions at the New Hampshire Historical Society, including many for southeastern towns.

Contributions to genealogical periodicals often contain cemetery inscriptions, and an increasing number of cemetery records have been published by local historical societies in recent years.

A project well under way to index all cemetery records statewide is being directed by Louise Tallman of Rye, New Hampshire.

Church Records

The New Hampshire Historical Society has an excellent manuscript collection of original church records, and a typescript collection of church records that indicates when members were admitted, date and reason for leaving the church, baptisms, marriages, and burials. The New

Hampshire Society of Genealogists (see Archives, Libraries, and Societies) is compiling an inventory of all New Hampshire church records. A considerable number of church records which were published in *The New Hampshire Genealogical Record* have been recently indexed and reprinted by Heritage Books of Bowie, Maryland.

The American Baptist Historical Society, 1106 South Goodman Street, Rochester, New York 14620, and the Historical Commission of the Southern Baptist Convention, 910 Commerce Street, Suite 400, Nashville, Tennessee 37203, both have a microfilm collection of some early church records from New Hampshire towns. They are available for purchase.

Military Records

Because men tended to enroll in service units close to their homes and with neighbors, using military lists can be helpful in tracing migration patterns. Muster rolls, pay receipts, and other service records are complete for New Hampshire residents from the colonial period through the Civil War and are available in three published collections.

Ayling, August D. *Revised Register of the Soldiers and Sailors of New Hampshire in the War of Rebellion, 1861–1866.* Concord, N.H., 1895.

New Hampshire State Papers. Vols. 5, 6, 14, 16. Include records of those who served in the French and Indian Wars for New Hampshire. Vols. 14–17 include "Rolls of Documents Relating to Soldiers in the Revolutionary War." Indexes available (see Background Sources).

Potter, Chandler E. *The Military History of the State of New Hampshire, 1623–1861.* 2 vols. 1866, 1868. Reprint (2 vols. in 1). Baltimore, Md.: Genealogical Publishing Co., 1972.

The New Hampshire Records and Archives has Civil War enlistment papers in a microfiche edition, and this is also available at the New England Historic Genealogical Society.

The New Hampshire Historical Society has a name index and abstracts in seventy-one volumes of all New Hampshire residents who received pensions, regardless of residence. A microfilm of these volumes and index is at the New England Historic Genealogical Society. The original applications and records are in Washington, D.C., at the National Archives, with microfilm copies in Waltham, Massachusetts, at the New England Branch (see 8).

Periodicals, Newspapers, and Manuscript Collections

Periodicals

The New Hampshire Genealogical Record, Dover, N.H., 1903–10, originally short-lived (only seven volumes were published), has been revived under the auspices of the New Hampshire Society of Genealogists. Publication resumed in July 1990. It is devoted to compiled genealogies, source records, book reviews, and the like.

The New Hampshire Historical Society has published *Historical New Hampshire* since 1944 in quarterly editions as a magazine of state and local history.

The Granite Monthly, a sixty-two volume magazine published between 1877–1930, does not concentrate on family history but is a rich source of local and state history and includes some marriage records and other genealogical data. It is indexed in Jacobus (see page 7).

The Genealogist is the quarterly publication distributed to members of the American-Canadian Genealogical Society in Manchester, publishing materials and articles concentrating on Canadian-American (Quebec and New England, principally) research.

Newspapers

No newspapers were published in New Hampshire before the 1750s, although items referring to residents before that date may be found in Massachusetts newspapers (see Massachusetts—Newspapers). For the provincial period, the Boston Anthenaeum's *Index of Obituaries in Boston Newspapers, 1704–1800,* 3 vols. (Boston, 1968), may prove helpful.

The New Hampshire Historical Society is the principal repository for pre-1900 newspapers in the state, holding what remains extant of the Granite State's newspapers beginning with the *New-Hampshire Gazette* in 1758 until 1900. The society has a grant to microfilm the most fragile pre-1900 newspapers in their collection. Post-1900 newspapers are often on microfilm at the New Hampshire State Library along with some pre-1900 microfilms. Original newspapers between 1900–45 may not be used.

Hammond, Otis G. *Notices from the New Hampshire Gazette, 1765–1800.* Lambertville, N.J.: Hunterton House, 1971. Vital events appearing in the first newspaper and a valuable place-name index are included.

Young, David C. and Robert L. Taylor. *Death Notices from Freewill Baptist Publications, 1811–1851.* Bowie, Md.: Heritage Books, 1985. A similar publication to the above, it covers the denomination's newspaper and publications for all geographical areas.

Manuscripts

The three major sources of collections in New Hampshire can be found at the New Hampshire Records and Archives, New Hampshire State Library, and New Hampshire Historical Society.

Baker Library at Dartmouth College in Hanover, New Hampshire, has a significant manuscript collection, but other helpful collections exist around the state as well, notably: Dimond Library at the University of New Hampshire in Durham, the Exeter Historical Society,

Exeter, New Hampshire, and the Agnes Bartlett Collection on Portsmouth families, available on microfilm at the New Hampshire Historical Society and New England Historic Genealogical Society. The latter institution is also the repository for some of the finest New Hampshire genealogical manuscripts and original source records, rivalling the New Hampshire Historical Society.

Archives, Libraries, and Societies

New Hampshire Division of Records Management and Archives
71 South Fruit Street
Concord, NH 03301

Often referred to as the New Hampshire Records and Archives, it holds the provincial (court, probate, and deed) records before 1771 (and some after that date), maps, military records, and state copies of the federal censuses. Many records were published in the *New Hampshire State Papers* (see Background Sources), including original records before 1771 that are cataloged and accessible in the archives. Additionally, this office also has many original town records and all legislative petitions.

New Hampshire Historical Society
30 Park Street
Concord, NH 03301

The society includes a library, museum, and gift shop with superb collections of New Hampshire research materials and a large collection of local history and family genealogies. Microfilm copies of the Province Deeds and Probate records are located here. A strong point is the magnificent manuscript collection.

New Hampshire State Library
20 Park Street
Concord, NH 03301

All the microfilm collections for town records, post-1900 original newspapers, and census records are housed here, as is the WPA index to town records (see Vital Records and Town Resources).

New Hampshire Society of Genealogists
P.O. Box 633
Exeter, NH 03833

Semi-annual state meetings are held. The society publishes a newsletter of current events and news, and *The New Hampshire Genealogical Record*, a journal of scholarly articles, compiled genealogies, and abstracts of records. A family register for all individuals and families known to have lived in New Hampshire before 1901 is maintained by the society. Inquiries concerning the family register can be sent by mail.

American Canadian Genealogical Society Library
Mailing Address: P.O. Box 668
South Manchester, NH 03103
Library: 378 Notre Dame Avenue
Manchester, NH 03102

This unique repository has an extensive microfilm collection of early Canadian original source material. Individual help is offered the researcher on site. It is one of the only major sources of French-Canadian research in the United States and serves both the Maritimes and Lower Canada (Quebec).

Special Focus Categories

Immigration

New Hampshire was not a significant port of immigration, even though thirty-two of its miles are on the Atlantic coast. In addition to a sizeable French-Canadian and Atlantic-Canadian migration, however, many of Boston's immigrants found their way to New Hampshire for work in manufacturing in the late nineteenth century. The collections of the New Hampshire Historical Society and New Hampshire State Library are excellent sources for research.

Native American

The early history of New Hampshire is filled with conflict between settlers and Native Americans. Little remains in the provincial records for reclaiming information on native inhabitants who participated in those conflicts, beginning in 1675 with King Philip's War. Those who survived were eventually pushed west and north into Canada.

County Resources

New Hampshire deeds and probates are recorded on the county level. An act forming counties was passed in 1769, but the Province continued to record deeds and probates until 1771. Strafford did not organize as quickly as the other original counties, beginning its functions in 1773. After 1771, deeds are located at the county registry of deeds and probate records are located at the county registry of probate. Both registries are located at the county seat. Deeds and probate records on microfilm at the New Hampshire Historical Society and at the New Hampshire Division of Records and Archives go through 1771, with Rockingham County deeds at the archives through 1824. At the FHL and the New England Historic Genealogical Society they go from inception to ca. 1850. Later records are only available at the appropriate county office unless otherwise indicated below.

Map	County Address	Date Formed Parent County/ies	Deeds	Probate
G4	Belknap 64 Court Street Laconia 03246 *County courthouse has copies of Strafford County deeds covering land, which became part of Belknap after formation in 1840.*	1841 Strafford/Merrimack	1841	1841
E5	Carroll Ossipee 03864	1841 Strafford/Grafton	1841	1841
K2	Cheshire 12 Court Street Keene 03431	1771 original	1771	1771
B5	Coos 148 Main Street Lancaster 03584 ** Fire damaged thirty-three volumes of the pre-1887 deeds and all of the probate records before that date. Damaged deeds were transcribed when possible and are retained in the courthouse. Seven volumes of Grafton deeds relating to Coos County before formation are kept in a separate series with separate indexes covering 1772–1803.*	1803 Grafton	1803*	1887
E3	Grafton Woodsville 03774 *The county seat is officially Haverhill, but the post office address for location of records is Woodsville.*	1771 original	1773	1773
J3	Hillsborough 19 Temple Street Nashua 03061 *There is a published index to the 1771–1884 probates.*	1771 original	1771	1773
H3	Merrimack 163 N. Main Street Concord 03301	1823 Rockingham/Hillsborough	1823	1823
J5	Rockingham Administration Building Exeter 03833 *County was the provincial courthouse and therefore has copies of the original deeds in a collection at the courthouse and microfilm collection for deeds before 1771 located in the FHL. An index to the pre-1900 probates will soon be privately published and will include colonial pre-1771 records as well.*	1771 original	1630	1639
H5	Strafford Justice and Administration Building County Farm Road, Dover 03820	1773 original	1769	1769
H2	Sullivan 24 Main Street Newport 03773 *Early deeds were damaged by fire. A separate series of "burned deeds," consisting of copies of surviving portions of the burned volumes with a separate index, is at the registry.*	1827 Cheshire	1827	1827

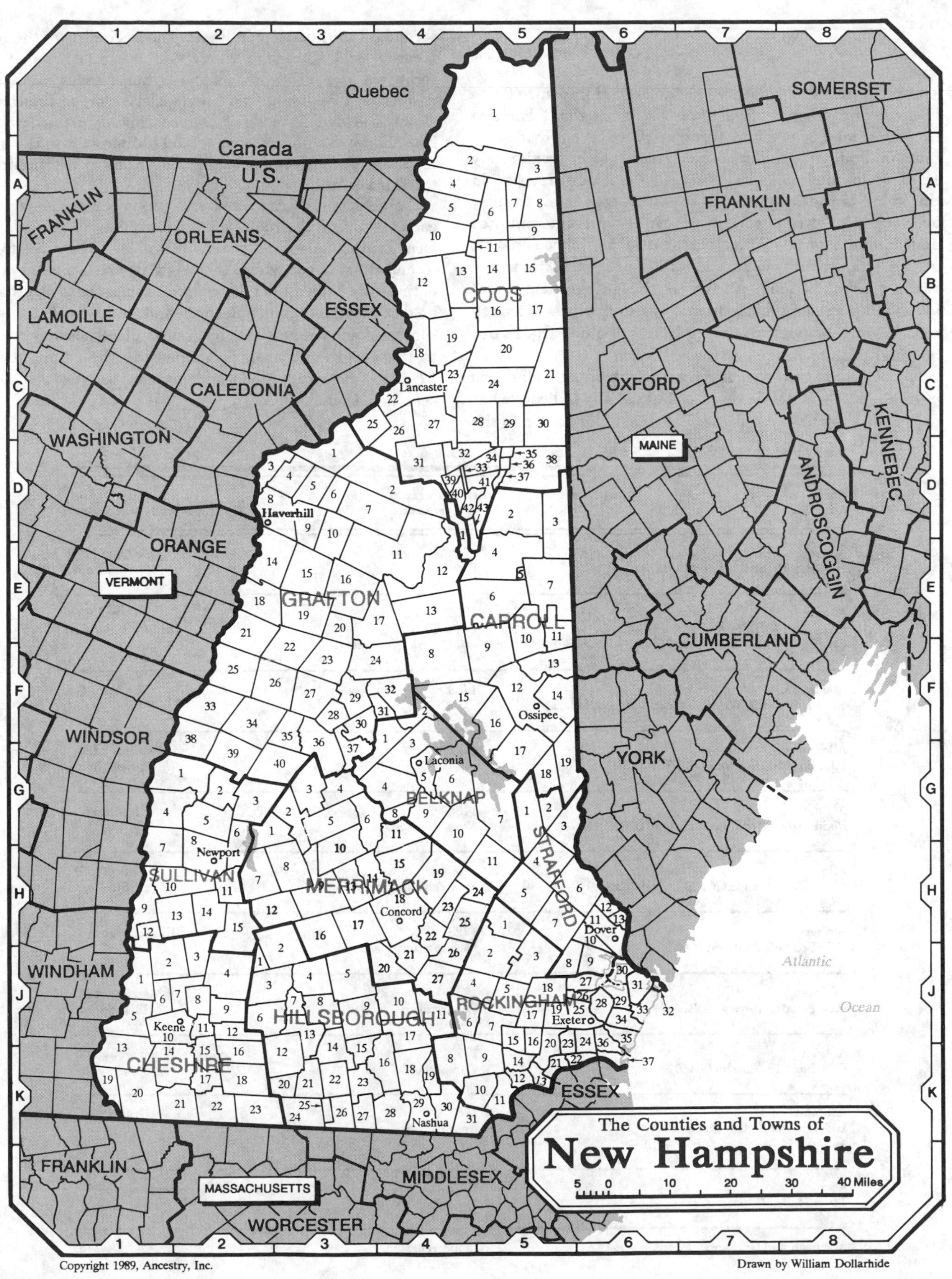

 Drawn by William Dollarhide

Town Resources

The WPA index, also located at the New Hampshire State Library and on microfilm at the New England Historic Genealogical Society and through the FHL, provides an unusual statewide index of town records to approximately 1850, which includes vital records. (A notable omission in the index is the town of Exeter, which was inadvertently overlooked.) Town officers, tax records, warrants, minutes and accounts of town meetings, cattle and sheep marks, voting lists, warnings out, and militia are usually found at town clerks' offices, although the information and availability varies greatly from town to town. A thorough search for genealogical material must include the record holdings of the appropriate town.

On the chart below, addresses are for town/city clerks as of 1990. Most will not do research but usually indicate what materials they have available. The date of formation in the second column usually indicates the beginning of the town records, and therefore when vital records began to be recorded (see Vital Records). "Other Names" indicates names used earlier in the town's history or, in the case of "from," the town from which it was formed. The third column lists the town's parent county and its number on the state map. The parent county/ies are listed on the second line of the third column.

To determine what deed and probate records exist for each town, find the name on the town list, note the date of formation, county, and parent counties. Then refer to the county chart to see where the originals are located. For the entire state before 1771, both deeds and probate records are held at New Hampshire Records and Archives. This means that to extend the research back through all possible records in the geographic area encompassing the county before 1771, the Province deeds and probate records need to be searched as well.

Town Address	Date Formed Other Names	County (Map) Parent County
Acworth P.O. Box 15, South Acworth 03607	1735/36 Burnet	Sullivan (13) Cheshire
Albany P.O. Box 1767, Conway 03818 *Originally in Grafton County until 1810, then in Strafford until Carroll was created.*	1766 Burton	Carroll (6) Grafton/Strafford
Alexandria RFD 1, Box 807, Washburn Road, Bristol 03222	1753	Grafton (36)
Allenstown P.O. Box 231, Suncook 03275	1722	Merrimack (26) Rockingham
Alstead Main Street, Town Hall, Alstead 03602	1735/36 No. 4/ Newton	Cheshire (2)
Alton Alton Town Hall, Route 11, Alton 03809	1796 New Durham Gore	Belknap (7) Strafford
Amherst P.O. Box 960, Amherst 03031	1728 Narragansett No. 3	Hillsborough (16)
Andover P.O. Box 61, Andover 03216	1751 Emerystown	Merrimack (5) Hillsborough
Antrim P.O. Box 248, Antrim 03440	1777 Cumberland	Hillsborough (3)
Ashland 10 Highland Street, Box 499 Ashland 03217	1868 from Holderness	Grafton (31)
Atkinson Town Hall, Atkinson 03811	1767 from Plaistow	Rockingham (12)
Atkinson and Gilmanton Grant	unincorporated	Coos (3)

Town Address	Date Formed Other Names	County (Map) Parent County
Auburn P.O. Box 309, Auburn 03032	1845 from Chester	Rockingham (6)
Barnstead P.O. Box 11, Center Barnstead 03225	1727	Belknap (11) Strafford
Barrington Star Route, Province Lane, Barrington 03825	1722	Strafford (7)
Bartlett RFD 1, Box 50, Intervale 03845	1790 Strafford	Carroll (4) Grafton/Coos
Bath Town Office, Bath 03740	1761	Grafton (8)
Bean's Grant	unincorporated	Coos (40)
Bean's Purchase	unincorporated	Coos (38)
Bedford 24 N. Amherst Road, Bedford 03102	1733/34 Narragansett No. 5	Hillsborough (17)
Belmont Main Street, P.O. Box 67, Belmont 03220 *Belmont inherited the original Gilmanton town records when the towns separated.*	1859 from Gilmanton	Belknap (9) Strafford
Bennington Town Hall, School Street, Bennington 03442	1842 from Hancock/Deering/Greenfield	Hillsborough (7)
Benton RFD 2, Woodsville 03785	1764 from Coventry	Grafton (15)
Berlin City Clerk Main Street, Berlin 03570	1771 Maynesborough	Coos (24) Grafton
Bethlehem Main Street, Bethlehem 03574	1774	Grafton (2)
Boscawen 17 High Street, Boscawen 03303	1732 Contoocock	Merrimack (14) Hillsborough
Bow 10 Grandview Road, Bow 03301	1727	Merrimack (21) Rockingham
Bradford Main Street, Town Hall, Bradford 03221	1735/36 New Bradford/Bradfordton	Merrimack (12) Hillsborough
Brentwood RFD 1, Dalton Road Exeter 03833	1744 from Exeter	Rockingham (19)
Bridgewater RFD 2, River Road, Plymouth, 03264	1788 from New Chester	Grafton (30)
Bristol 71 Lake Street, P.O. Box 297, Bristol 03222	1819 from Hill/Bridgewater	Grafton (37)
Brookfield Cedar Park, 8 Piney Road, Brookfield 03872	1794 from Middelton	Carroll (18) Strafford
Brookline Meeting House Road, Brookline 03033	1769	Hillsborough (27)

Town Address	Date Formed Other Names	County (Map) Parent County
Cambridge	1773	Coos (17) Grafton
Campton P.O. Box 127, Main Street, Campton 03223	1761	Grafton (24) Strafford
Canaan P.O. Box 38, Church Road, Canaan 03741	1761	Grafton (34)
Candia 74 High Street Candia 03034	1763 from Chester Charmingfare	Rockingham (4)
Canterbury P.O. Box 500, Hackleboro Road, Canterbury 03224	1727	Merrimack (15) Rockingham
Carroll P.O. Box 88, Twin Mountain 03595	1772 Bretton Woods	Coos (31) Grafton
Center Harbor P.O. Box 140, Center Harbor 03226	1797 from New Hampton, "Moultonborough Addition"	Belknap (2) Strafford
Chandler's Purchase	1835	Coos (33)
Charlestown P.O. Box 834, Railroad Street, Charlestown 03603	1735	Sullivan (9) Cheshire
Chatham P.O. Box 241, Center Conway 03813	1767	Carroll (3) Grafton/Coos/ Strafford
Chester P.O. Box 275, Chester 03036	1720	Rockingham (7)
Chesterfield P.O. Box 56, Chesterfield 03443	1735 No. 1	Cheshire (13)
Chichester Town Hall, Main Street, Chichester 03263	1727	Merrimack (23) Rockingham
Claremont City Clerk City Hall, Claremont 03743	1764	Sullivan (7) Cheshire
Clarksville Town Hall, RFD 1, Box 460 Pittsburg 03592	1792 Dartmouth College Grant	Coos (2) Grafton
Colebrook Town Hall, 10 Bridge Street Colebrook 03576	1762 Dryden	Coos (5) Grafton
Columbia RFD 1, Box 523 Colebrook 03576	1762 Preston/Cockburntown	Coos (10) Grafton
Concord City Clerk 41 Green Street, Concord 03301	1659 Penacock/Rumford	Merrimack (18) Rockingham
Conway P.O. Box 70, Center Conway 03813	1765	Carroll (7) Grafton/ Strafford

Town Address	Date Formed Other Names	County (Map) Parent County
Cornish P.O. Box 176, Cornish Flat 03746	1763	Sullivan (4) Cheshire
Crawford's Purchase and Crawford's Notch	1834	Coos (39)
Croydon RFD 1, Box 307, Newport 03773	1763	Sullivan (5) Cheshire
Cutt's Grant	unincorporated	Coos (42)
Dalton RFD 2, Box 143, Whitefield 03598	1784 from Littleton	Coos (25) Grafton
Danbury Box 96A-Ragged Mountain Road Danbury 03230	1795 from Alexandria	Merrimack (3) Grafton
Danville RFD 1, Box 423, Fremont 03044	1760 from Kingston Hawke	Rockingham (16)
Deerfield P.O. Box 159 Deerfield 03037	1766 Nottingham	Rockingham (2)
Deering RFD 1 Box 62, Hillsborough 03244	1774	Hillsborough (4)
Derry 48 E. Broadway, Derry 03038	1827 from Londonderry	Rockingham (9)
Dixville Dixville Notch 03576	unincorporated	Coos (6) Grafton
Dix's Grant	unincorporated	Coos (7)
Dorchester RFD 1, Box 490, Rumney 03266	1761	Grafton (26)
Dover City Clerk City Hall, 288 Central Avenue, Dover 03820 **Not formally granted as a town.*	1623*	Strafford (11)
Dublin Town Hall, P.O. Box 62, Dublin 03444	1749 Monadnock	Cheshire (16)
Dummer RFD 1, Milan 03588	1773	Coos (16) Grafton
Dunbarton RFD 2 Box 244 Dunbarton 03301	1735 Gorhamstown/Starkstown	Merrimack (20) Hillsborough
Durham Town Office, Durham 03824	1732 Dover Parish	Strafford (9)
East Kingston 7 Main Street, East Kingston 03827	1738 Kingston	Rockingham (23)
Easton RFD 1, Box 75A, Franconia 03580	1876	Grafton (10)

Town Address	Date Formed Other Names	County (Map) Parent County
Eaton Town Hall, P.O. Box 42, Eaton Center 03832	1766	Carroll (11) Strafford
Effingham P.O. Box 48, South Effingham 03882	1749	Carroll (14) Strafford
Ellsworth RFD Box 128, Plymouth 03264	1769 Trecothick	Grafton (20)
Enfield Whitney Hall, Main Street, Enfield 03748	1761	Grafton (39)
Epping Town Hall, RFD, Epping 03042	1741/42 from Exeter	Rockingham (18)
Epsom Route 4, Town Hall, Epsom 03234	1727	Merrimack (25) Rockingham
Errol Route 26, Errol 03579	1774	Coos (15) Grafton
Erving's Grant	unincorporated	Coos (11)
Exeter 10 Front Street, Exeter 03833 **Not formally granted as a town.*	1638*	Rockingham (25)
Farmington Town Hall, Farmington 03835	1798 from Rochester North Rochester	Strafford (4)
Fitzwilliam Village Green, P.O. Box 504, Fitzwilliam 03447	1752 Monadnock No. 4	Cheshire (22)
Francestown King Hall Road, Francestown 03043	1772	Hillsborough (8)
Franconia Box F, Sawmill Lane Franconia 03580	1764 Indian Head/Morristown	Grafton (7)
Franklin City Clerk P.O. Box 235, Franklin 03235	1828 Pemigewasset	Merrimack (6) Rockingham
Freedom Maple Street, Freedom 03836	1831 N. Effingham	Carroll (13) Strafford
Fremont 168 Scribner, Fremont 03044	1764 from Exeter Poplin	Rockingham (17)
Gilford 47 Cherry Valley Road Gilford 03246	1812 Gunstock Parish of Gilmanton	Belknap (6) Strafford
Gilmanton Town Hall, Route 107, Gilmanton 03837	1727	Belknap (10) Strafford
Gilsum P.O. Box 66, Hammond Hollow, Gilsum 03448	1752 Boyle	Cheshire (7)

Town Address	Date Formed Other Names	County (Map) Parent County
Goffstown 16 Main Street, Goffstown 03045	1733/34 Narragansett No. 5	Hillsborough (10)
Gorham Park Street, Gorham 03581	1770 from Shelburne	Coos (29) Grafton
Goshen P.O. Box 710, Goshen 03752	1791 Sunapee	Sullivan (11) Cheshire
Grafton Route 4, Grafton 03240	1761	Grafton (40)
Grantham P.O. Box 135, Grantham 03753	1761	Sullivan (2) Cheshire
Greenfield P.O. Box 16, Town Office Building, Greenfield 03047	1791 Lyndefield Addition	Hillsborough (13)
Greenland 575 Portsmouth, Greenland 03840	1721 from Portsmouth	Rockingham (29)
Greenville Main Street, Box 354, Greenville 03048	1872	Hillsborough (25)
Green's Grant	unincorporated	Coos (36)
Groton N. Groton Road, Hebron 03241	1761 Cockermouth	Grafton (27)
Hadley's Purchase	unincorporated	Coos (43)
Hale's Location	unincorporated	Carroll (5)
Hampstead P.O. Box 338, Hampstead 03841	1749 Timberlane Parish of Haverhill, Massachusetts	Rockingham (14)
Hampton P.O. Box 1, Hampton 03842	1638	Rockingham (35)
Hampton Falls 1 Drinkwater Road Hampton Falls 03844	1726 from Hampton Hampton Falls Parish or Fallside Parish from 1712	Rockingham (36)
Hancock P.O. Box 23, Hancock 03449	1779	Hillsborough (6)
Hanover P.O. Box 483, 41 S. Main Street, Hanover 03755	1761	Grafton (33)
Harrisville P.O. Box 250, Harrisville 03450	1870 Twitchellville	Cheshire (12)
Hart's Location Route 302, Hart's Location 03812	1772	Carroll (1) Grafton
Haverhill Court Street, Woodsville 03785	1763 Lower Coos	Grafton (14)

Town Address	Date Formed Other Names	County (Map) Parent County
Hebron Selectmen's Building East Hebron 03232	1792 from Cockermouth	Grafton (28)
Henniker P.O. Box 485, Henniker 03242	1735/36 No. 6	Merrimack (16) Hillsborough
Hill Old Shop Road, Hill 03243	1753 New Chester	Merrimack (4) Grafton
Hillsborough P.O. Box 1699, Hillsborough 03244	1735/36 No. 7	Hillsborough (2)
Hinsdale P.O. Box 3, Main Street, Hinsdale 03451	1753	Cheshire (19)
Holderness Route 3, Town Hall, Holderness 03245	1751	Grafton (32) Strafford
Hollis P.O. Box 509, Hollis 03049	1746	Hillsborough (28)
Hooksett 16 Main Street, Hooksett 03106	1822 Chester Woods/Rowe's Corner	Merrimack (27) Hillsborough
Hopkinton P.O. Box 169, Fountain Square, Contoocook 03229	1735/36 No. 5	Merrimack (17) Hillsborough
Hudson 12 School Street, Hudson 03051	1746 Nottingham West	Hillsborough (30)
Jackson P.O. Box 336, Town Hall, Jackson 03846	1800 New Madbury/ Adams	Carroll (2) Grafton/Coos/
Jaffrey P.O. Box 390, 69 Main Street, Jaffrey 03452	1749 Rowley Canada	Cheshire (18)
Jefferson RFD 1, Box 162A, Jefferson 03583	1765	Coos (27) Grafton
Keene City Clerk 3 Washington Street, Keene 03431	1733 Upper Ashuelot	Cheshire (10)
Kensington 95 Amesbury Road, Kensington 03833	1737	Rockingham (24)
Kilkenny	1774	Coos (23) Grafton
Kingston P.O. Box 657, Kingston 03848	1694	Rockingham (20)
Laconia City Clerk P.O. Box 489, Laconia 03246	1855 from Meredith/Gilford/Gilmanton Meredith Bridge	Belknap (5)
Lancaster P.O. Box 151, Lancaster 03584	1763	Coos (22) Grafton
Landaff Center Hill Road, Lisbon 03585	1764	Grafton (9)

Town Address	Date Formed Other Names	County (Map) Parent County
Langdon Town Hall, Langdon 03602	1787	Sullivan (12) Cheshire
Lebanon City Clerk 51 N. Park Street, Lebanon 03766	1761	Grafton (38)
Lee 7 Mast Road, Durham 03824	1766	Strafford (8)
Lempster Route 10, Town Hall, East Lempster 03605	1735/36 No. 9/Dupplin	Sullivan (14) Cheshire
Lincoln P.O. Box 25, Lincoln 03251	1764	Grafton (11)
Lisbon 21 School Street, Lisbon 03585	1763 Concord/Chiswick/ Gunthwaite	Grafton (5)
Litchfield 255 Charles Bancroft Highway Hudson 03051	1729 Naticock	Hillsborough (19)
Littleton 1 Union Street, Littleton 03561	1764 Lisbon	Grafton (1)
Livermore	1876	Grafton (12)
Londonderry 268 Mammoth Road, Londonderry 03053	1722	Rockingham (8)
Loudon P.O. Box 7837, Loudon 03301	1773 from Canterbury	Merrimack (19) Rockingham
Lowe and Burbank Grant	unincorporated	Coos (32)
Lyman RR 1, Lisbon 03585	1761	Grafton (4)
Lyme Town Clerk's Office, Lyme 03768	1761	Grafton (25)
Lyndeborough P.O. Box 164, Lyndeborough 03082	1735	Hillsborough (14)
Madbury 254 Littleworth Road, Madbury 03820	1755 from Durham	Strafford (10)
Madison P.O. Box 248, Route 113, Madison 03849	1852 from Eaton/Albany	Carroll (10)
Manchester City Clerk 904 Elm Street, Manchester 03101	1735 Harrytown/Tyngsborough/Derryfield	Hillsborough (11)
Marlborough Municipal Building, Box 515 Marlborough 03455	1752 Monadnock No. 5/ Oxford/ New Marlborough	Cheshire (15)
Marlow P.O. Box 16, Forest Road, Marlow 03456	1753 Addison	Cheshire (3)
Martin's Location	unincorporated	Coos (35)

Town Address	Date Formed Other Names	County (Map) Parent County
Mason Fitchburg Road, Mason 03048	1749 No. 1	Hillsborough (26)
Meredith Main Street, Meredith 03253	1748 Palmer's Town/New Salem	Belknap (3) Strafford
Merrimack Baboosic Lake Road, Box 27, Merrimack 03054	1746 from Nashua	Hillsborough (18)
Middleton Town Hall, Middleton 03887	1749	Strafford (2)
Milan 158 Bridge Street, Milan 03588	1771 from Paulsborough	Coos (20) Grafton
Milford Town Hall, Milford 03055	1794 from Munson	Hillsborough (23)
Millsfield P.O. Box 48, Errol 03579	1774	Coos (14) Grafton
Milton N. Main Street, Town Building, Milton 03851	1802 from Rochester	Strafford (3)
Monroe RFD 1, Box 279, Monroe 03771	1854 from Lyman	Grafton (3)
Mont Vernon Town Office, Mont Vernon 03057	1803 from Amherst	Hillsborough (15)
Moultonborough P.O. Box 15, Moultonborough 03254	1763	Carroll (15) Strafford
Nashua City Clerk City Hall, 229 Main Street, Nashua 03061	1746 Dunstable	Hillsborough (29)
Nelson Old Brick School Road, Nelson 03457	1752 Monadnock No. 6/Packersfield	Cheshire (9)
New Boston Town Office Building, New Boston 03070	1735/36	Hillsborough (9)
New Castle Main Street, Box 367, New Castle 03854	1693 from Portsmouth	Rockingham (32)
New Durham Town Hall, Main Street, New Durham 03855	1749 Cocheco Township	Strafford (1)
New Hampton Main Street, New Hampton 03256	1765 Moultonborough Addition	Belknap (1) Strafford
New Ipswich Main Street, Town Office Bldg., New Ipswich 03071	1735/36	Hillsborough (24)
New London P.O. Box 314, New London 03257	1753 Heidleberg/Alexandria Addition	Merrimack (1) Hillsborough
Newbury Route 103, Old Newbury Road, South Newbury 03255	1753 Dantzig/Hereford,	Merrimack (7) Cheshire/ Hillsborough

Town Address	Date Formed Other Names	County (Map) Parent County
Newfields P.O. Box 45, Newfields 03856	1849 from Newmarket South New Market	Rockingham (26)
Newington 205 Nimble Hill Road, Newington 03801	1764	Rockingham (30)
Newmarket Main Street, Town Hall, Newmarket 03857	1727 from Exeter	Rockingham (27)
Newport 15 Sunapee Street, Newport 03773	1753 Grenville	Sullivan (8) Cheshire
Newton Town Hall, Box 85, Newton 03858	1749 from South Hampton	Rockingham (21)
North Hampton P.O. Box 141, North Hampton 03862	1738 from Hampton North Hill/North Parish of Hampton	Rockingham (34)
Northfield 21 Summer, Tilton 03276	1780 from Canterbury	Merrimack (11) Rockingham
Northumberland 2 State Street, Groveton 03582	1761 Stonington	Coos (18) Grafton
Northwood Town Hall, Box 314, Northwood 03261	1773 from Nottingham	Rockingham (1)
Nottingham Town Hall, P.O. Box 114, Nottingham 03290	1722	Rockingham (3)
Odell	unincorporated	Coos (13)
Orange RFD 2, Peaske Road, Orange 03741	1769 Cardigan/Bradford/Middletown/Liscomb	Grafton (35)
Orford Orford 03777	1761	Grafton (21)
Ossipee P.O. Box 67, Center Ossipee 03814	1785 New Garden	Carroll (12) Strafford
Pelham 6 Main Street, Pelham 03076	1746	Hillsborough (31) Rockingham
Pembroke 311 Pembroke Street, Pembroke 03275	1728 Lovewell's Town/Suncock/Buckstreet	Merrimack (22) Rockingham
Peterborough 1 Grove Street, Peterborough 03458	1737/38	Hillsborough (12)
Piermont Library Building, Route 10, Piermont 03779	1764	Grafton (18)
Pinkham's Grant & Pinkham's Notch	unincorporated	Coos (37)
Pittsburg P.O. Box 127, Pittsburg 03592	1840 Indian Stream Territory	Coos (1)
Pittsfield Town Office, Pittsfield 03263	1782 from Chichester	Merrimack (24) Rockingham

Town Address	Date Formed Other Names	County (Map) Parent County
Plainfield Town Office, HC 64, Box 164, Meriden 03770	1761	Sullivan (1) Cheshire
Plaistow Town Office, 145 Main Street, Plaistow 03865	1749 from Haverhill, Massachusetts	Rockingham (13)
Plymouth Courthouse, Plymouth 03264	1763 New Plymouth	Grafton (29)
Portsmouth City Clerk 1 Jenkins Avenue, P.O. Box 62, Portsmouth 03801	1631 Piscataqua/Strawberry Banke	Rockingham (31)
Randolph Route US 2, Randolph 03570	1772 Durand	Coos (28) Grafton
Raymond Epping Street, Raymond 03077	1764 from Chester Freetown	Rockingham (5)
Richmond RFD, 125 Old Homestead, Richmond 03470	1735 Sylvester Canada	Cheshire (21)
Rindge Payson Hill Road, P.O. Box 11, Rindge 03461	1736/37 from Rowley Canada	Cheshire (23)
Rochester City Clerk 31 Wakefield, Rochester 03867	1722	Strafford (6)
Rollinsford Town Hall, P.O. Box 427, Rollinsford 03869	1849 from Somersworth	Strafford (13)
Roxbury RFD 4 Box 236, Roxbury 03431	1812 from Marlborough	Cheshire (11)
Rumney Quincy Road, Rumney 03266	1761	Grafton (23)
Rye 10 Central Road, Rye 03870	1726 from Portsmouth	Rockingham (33)
Salem Municipal Building, 33 Geremonty, Salem 03079	1750 North Parish of Methuen, Massachusetts	Rockingham (11)
Salisbury Franklin Road, Salisbury 03268	1736/37 Baker's Town/Stevenstown/Gerrishtown	Merrimack (10) Hillsborough
Sanbornton P.O. Box 124, Route 132, Sanbornton 03269	1748	Belknap (4) Strafford
Sandown Town Hall, Sandown 03873	1756 from Kingston	Rockingham (15)
Sandwich P.O. Box 191, Main Street, Center Sandwich 03227	1763	Carroll (8) Strafford
Sargent's Purchase	unincorporated	Coos (41)
Seabrook 99 Lafayette Road, Seabrook 03874	1768 from Hampton Falls/South Hampton	Rockingham (37)
Second College Grant	unincorporated	Coos (8)

Town Address	Date Formed Other Names	County (Map) Parent County
Sharon 3 Sliptown Road Sharon 03458	1791 from Peterborough	Hillsborough (20)
Shelburne North Road, Shelburne 03581	1769	Coos (30) Grafton
Somersworth City Clerk 157 Main, Somersworth 03878	1754 from Dover	Strafford (12)
South Hampton RFD 2, Main Avenue South Hampton 03827	1742 from Amesbury and Salisbury, Massachusetts	Rockingham (22)
Springfield P.O. Box 87, Springfield 03284	1769 Protectworth	Sullivan (3) Cheshire
Stark RFD 1, Town Hall, Box 388, Groveton 03582	1774 Percy	Coos (19) Grafton
Stewartstown P.O. Box 35, West Stewartstown 03597	1770	Coos (4) Grafton
Stoddard RT 9, Stoddard 03464	1752 Monadnock No. 7/Limerick	Cheshire (4)
Strafford Route 202A, Center Strafford 03815	1820	Strafford (5)
Stratford P.O. Box 366, Main Street, North Stratford 03590	1762 Woodbury	Coos (12) Grafton
Stratham 115 Portsmouth Avenue, Box 115, Stratham 03885	1715/16	Rockingham (28)
Success	1773	Coos (21) Grafton
Sugar Hill Main Street, Box 74, Sugar Hill 03585	1962 from Lisbon	Grafton (6)
Sullivan HCR 33, Box 228, Keene 03431	1787	Cheshire (8)
Sunapee Main Street, Box 303, Sunapee 03782	1768 Saville/Wendell	Sullivan (6) Cheshire
Surry HCR 32, Box 178, Surry 03431	1769	Cheshire (6)
Sutton Fox Chase Road South Sutton 03273	1749 Perrystown	Merrimack (8) Hillsborough
Swanzey Route 32, Box 9, East Swanzey 03446	1733	Cheshire (14)
Tamworth P.O. Box 279, Tamworth 03886	1766	Carroll (9) Strafford
Temple P.O. Box 216, Temple 03084	1750 Peterborough Slip	Hillsborough (21)

Town Address	Date Formed Other Names	County (Map) Parent County
Thompson and Meserve's Purchase	unincorporated	Coos (34)
Thornton RFD 1, Campton 03223	1763	Grafton (17)
Tilton 145 Main Street, Tilton 03276	1869 from Sanbornton East Sanbornton	Belknap (8)
Troy Town Hall, Troy 03465	1815 from Marlborough	Cheshire (17)
Tuftonborough Route 109A, Center Tuftonborough 03816	1750	Carroll (16) Strafford
Unity HCR 66, Box 176, Newport 03773	1753 Buckingham	Sullivan (10) Cheshire
Wakefield P.O. Box 279, Main Street East Wakefield 03830	1749 Ham's-town/East-town/ Watertown	Carroll (19) Strafford
Walpole P.O. Box 729, Elm Street, Walpole 03608	1736 Bellowstown	Cheshire (1)
Warner RD 2, Box 265 Warner 03278	1735/36 New Amesbury/Jennesstown/ Waterloo/Ryetown	Merrimack (9) Hillsborough
Warren Studio Road, P.O. Box 98, Warren 03279	1763	Grafton (19)
Washington P.O. Box 109 Washington 03280	1735/36 Monadnock No. 8/ New Concord/Camden	Sullivan (15) Cheshire
Waterville Valley P.O. Box 267, Waterville Valley 03223	1829 Waterville	Grafton (13)
Weare P.O. Box 90, Weare 03281	1735 Beverly Canada/Haletown/ Robiestown/Wearestown	Hillsborough (5)
Webster RFD 5, Long Street, Penacook 03303	1860 from Boscawen	Merrimack (13)
Wentworth P.O. Box 44, Town Hall, Wentworth 03282	1766	Grafton (22)
Wentworth's Location Route 16, Errol 03579	1797	Coos (9) Grafton
Westmoreland Town Hall, Westmorland 03467	1735/36 Great Meadows	Cheshire (5)
Whitefield 7 Jefferson Road, Whitefield 03598	1774 Grafton	Coos (26) Grafton
Wilmot Cross Hill Road, Wilmot 03287	1807 from Mt. Kearsarge Gore	Merrimack (2) Hillsborough

Town Address	Date Formed Other Names	County (Map) Parent County
Wilton Town Hall, Wilton 03086	1749 No. 2	Hillsborough (22)
Winchester Old Westport Road, Winchester 03470	1733	Cheshire (20)
Windham 3 N. Lowell Road., Windham 03087	1741/42	Rockingham (10)
Windsor Route 31, Windsor 03244	1798 Campbell's Gore	Hillsborough (1)
Wolfeborough P.O. Box 1207, Wolfeborough 03894	1759	Carroll (17) Strafford
Woodstock Lost River Road North Woodstock 03262	1763 Peeling/Fairfield	Grafton (16)

NEW JERSEY

Roger D. Joslyn, C.G., F.A.S.G.

After Henry Hudson's initial explorations of the Delaware River area, some Dutch settlements were attempted in New Jersey as early as 1618 but were soon abandoned because of real or imagined threats from the Lenni-Lenape (or Delaware), the original inhabitants. A more lasting settlement was made from 1638 to 1655 by the Swedes and Finns along the Delaware as part of New Sweden, which continued to flourish although the Dutch eventually gained control over this area and made it part of New Netherland. From 1660 to the end of the century, many Dutch from New York established farms in northern New Jersey. Throughout the colonial period, only the English outnumbered the Dutch in New Jersey. When England conquered the Dutch in 1664, King Charles II gave his brother, the Duke of York (later King James II), all of New York and New Jersey. The duke in turn granted New Jersey to two of his creditors, Lord John Berkeley and Sir George Carteret. The land was named Nova Caesaria for the Isle of Jersey, Carteret's home. Within the year that England took control, there was a large influx of English from New England and Long Island who, for want of more or better land, settled the East Jersey towns of Elizabethtown, Middletown, Piscataway, Shrewsbury, and Woodbridge. A year later, Newark was founded by migrants from Connecticut. In 1685 a large group of Scots came to Perth Amboy, but they were not part of the great wave of Ulster-Scots who in the 1720s began their immigration to the New World, including New Jersey. The Dutch regained New Jersey and New York for a brief period in 1673–74, but control soon reverted back to the English.

The southern part of the state drew English Quakers, some of whom spilled over from the Philadelphia area. They gained control of the southern part when it was sold by Lord Berkeley to Quaker John Fenwick. In 1676 New Jersey was divided into two provinces, East and West, controlled by proprietors, with capitals at Perth Amboy and Burlington, respectively. William Penn, a proprietor of both provinces, forced the setting of a boundary. It was poorly surveyed and cut across the state so that all of the more settled southern part fell in West Jersey. For two years beginning in April 1688, New Jersey was, with New York, part of the Dominion of New England, but no significant records of New Jersey seem to have been generated in the capital, which was Boston. The proprietors of both provinces gave up their right to rule in 1702 but continued to control first sales of the land. New Jersey was then under united rule by the royal governor of New York until 1738, after which it had its own royal governor.

Significant migrations and immigrations continued into the eighteenth century. These included French Huguenots fleeing France and Long Islanders who settled at Cape May in the 1690s and Morris County in the 1730s. Many of the Palatines who immigrated to New York in 1709 came to New Jersey, as did Germans who entered through Philadelphia throughout the 1700s. Descendants of some of these families migrated to northwestern New Jersey.

New Jersey was a major battleground during the Revolutionary War. American and British troops passed through the colony, to and from New York and Pennsylvania, all of which caused some destruction of records. Like New York, New Jersey was quite divided by the war, and a large number of Loyalists left for Canada.

Throughout the nineteenth century, the state continued to grow through increased development of transportation, including the completion of a canal in 1834 connecting the Delaware and Raritan rivers, enabling faster travel between Philadelphia and New York. Except for its forty-eight-mile border with New York, New Jersey is completely surrounded by water, which remains one of its major modes of transportation. Today, the railroads and roadways make New Jersey the major corridor between the northeast and the south. The 1800s saw New Jersey develop industrially, starting with the establishment of the nation's first factory town at what is today Paterson. New Jersey is one of the more densely populated states in the country, with many of its residents commuting to work to neighboring New York and Pennsylvania.

Vital Records

Among the Mid-Atlantic states, New Jersey has the longest continuing run of statewide registration of births, marriages, and deaths, which begin in May 1848. The New Jersey State Archives (see Archives, Libraries, and Societies) has these records with indexes through 1923 for births and through 1940 for marriages and deaths. Transcriptions of vital records only for May 1848 to May 1878 can be requested by mail for the current fee of $4. For the period 1848 to 1878, there are consolidated indexes by event, but they vary in the type and amount of identifying detail they provide. There are also consolidated indexes for births and marriages, 1878–1903 (but for grooms only, 1901–03). All death indexes are arranged by place within the registration period July through June, with an alphabetical index for 1901–03. Since 1903, records are filed yearly in alphabetical order for each event, with marriages arranged by name of groom.

Requests for certificates of records after May 1878 should be submitted on form H2843 to the State Registrar of Vital Statistics, together with the required current fee of $4. Write the State Registrar—Search Unit, New Jersey State Department of Health, CN-360, Trenton, New Jersey 08625-0360. Vital records at the local level (city, borough, township) are usually in abbreviated form, and most inquirers will probably be directed to Trenton.

Like the other Mid-Atlantic States, New Jersey had a colonial law that provided for the recording of births, marriages, and deaths in town records from about the 1670s, but this was rarely followed, nor was a later law of 1799. The only known early records are those for Woodbridge and Piscataway. The former begin in the 1660s and were published to 1750 in *Woodbridge and Vicinity* by the Rev. Joseph W. Dally (New Brunswick, N.J.: A. E. Gordon, 1873), pages 315–57, and reprinted as *Vital Records of Woodbridge, New Jersey* (Lambertville, N.J.: Hunterdon House, 1983). Those for Piscataway were published in *Proceedings of the New Jersey Historical Society*, 3d Ser., beginning at vol. 2 (1896), page 73, although the original records do not seem to have survived. Other early public vital records include marriage bonds for the period 1711–95, available at the New Jersey State Archives. Information from these bonds, together with some church and other marriage records, was published as volume 22 of *Documents Relating to the Colonial History of New Jersey*, 1st Ser., 42 vols. (Newark, Paterson, and Trenton, N. J., 1880–1949), popularly known as the "New Jersey Archives." It was reprinted as William Nelson, *New Jersey Marriage Records, 1665–1800* (Baltimore, Md.: Genealogical Publishing Co., 1967), and these should be supplemented by the bonds published for 1727–51 by Charles Carroll Gardner in *The Genealogical Magazine of New Jersey*, vols. 14–23, and by the originals at the state archives. The originals often show additional information not included in the published version, such as the names of bondsmen, and, although rarely, parents' consent for a minor, or a prior marriage. Marriages were also to be kept by the county clerks from 1795. Most of these are available in published books or on film at the state archives, which also has the originals for Atlantic (volume 1 missing), Cumberland, and Somerset counties. The originals for Middlesex County are in the Department of Special Collections and Archives, Alexander Library, Rutgers University (see Archives, Libraries, and Societies). Individual books of marriage records have been published for Atlantic, Bergen, Burlington, Camden, Cape May, Cumberland, Gloucester, Hunterdon, Monmouth, and Salem counties. Others have been published in *The Genealogical Magazine of New Jersey* (earliest records for Essex, Monmouth, and Morris) and the *Somerset County Historical Quarterly* (Somerset). For Cape May, Cumberland, Gloucester, and Salem counties, see also H. Stanley Craig, comp., *South Jersey Marriages* (Merchantville, N.J.: the compiler, n.d.). Some records of slave births that were mostly recorded in the counties in the early 1800s are at the state archives. The slave birth records for Monmouth County were published by that county's clerk as *Black Birth Book of Monmouth County, New Jersey, 1804–1848* (1989); see also *The Genealogical Magazine of New Jersey* 54 (1979): 83–94 for slave births for Sussex and Warren counties. The *Guide to Vital Statistics Records In New Jersey*, compiled by the New Jersey Historical Records Survey, 2 vols. (Newark, N.J.: WPA, 1941), while dated, is helpful in determining what records existed for what communities.

For the period 1743 to 1850, divorces in New Jersey were granted by the chancery court or act of the legislature and are available at the state archives. Legislative divorces for 1778–1844 are indexed in John Hood, *Index of Colonial and State Laws of New Jersey Between the Years 1663–1903 Inclusive* (Camden, N.J.: Sinnickson, Chew and Sons, 1905), pages 390–94, available at the New Jersey State Library, county law libraries, and elsewhere. This list is also found in George E. McCracken, "New Jersey Legislative Divorces, 1778–1844," *The American Genealogist* 34 (1958): 107–12. The original laws up to the 1830s are on microfilm at the state archives and state library. Inquiries about later divorces should be addressed to Clerk of the Superior Court, Matrimonial Section, Hughes Justice Complex, CN 971, Trenton, New Jersey 08625-0971.

Census Records

Federal

Population Schedules.

- Indexed—1800 (Cumberland County only), 1830, 1840, 1850, 1860, 1870 (Hudson, Passaic, and Mercer counties only), 1890 (fragment)
- Soundex—1880, 1900, 1920
- Unindexed—1870 (except for those counties cited above), 1910

Agriculture and Industry Schedules.

- 1850, 1860, 1870, 1880

Mortality Schedules.

- 1850, 1860, 1870, 1880

Union Veterans Schedules.

- 1890 (Indexed)

The New Jersey State Archives, the New Jersey Historical Society (see Archives, Libraries, and Societies), Rutgers University, and the Newark Public Library all have microfilm copies of New Jersey census records and printed indexes.

There are problems with the AISI indexes for 1830 (shows Atlantic for Bergen County entries), 1850 (does not include Winslow Township, Camden County), and 1860 (excludes parts of Middlesex County).

The state copies of the federal censuses for 1850–80 are at the New Jersey State Library. The county copy of the 1850 and the abbreviated copy of the 1880 federal censuses for Essex County are in the county clerk's vault in Newark. Ocean County's abbreviated 1880 census is at the state archives. The originals and films of the corresponding mortality, agriculture, and industry/manufacturing schedules are available at the state library and on film at the state archives. *New Jersey 1850 Mortality Schedule Index* was compiled by Shirley J. George and Sandra E. Glenn (Columbus, N.J.: G. & G. Genealogical Book Co., 1982), and these records are being published in *The Genealogical Magazine of New Jersey,* beginning in volume 54 (1979), page 64. Also in *The Genealogical Magazine of New Jersey,* beginning in volume 52 (1977), page 71, are 1850 mortality schedules of other states, listing those persons whose birthplace was New Jersey. Among the few surviving schedules of the 1890 federal census are some for Jersey City, Hudson County.

State

State censuses were also taken in New Jersey every ten years from 1855 through 1915 and are available at the New Jersey State Archives, the New Jersey State Library, Rutgers, the New Jersey Historical Society (1855–85), and the Newark Public Library (the latter of which has a street guide to Newark's wards, as does the state archives and Rutgers). Unfortunately, they are not complete for 1855, 1865, and 1875, and none are indexed. The information in these censuses is similar to that found in federal censuses, except that most of the 1855 and 1865 censuses list only the head of the household. The original state censuses for Essex County, 1855–75, are in the county clerk's vault in Newark.

Censuses taken of Paterson residents from 1824 to 1832 by the Rev. Samuel Fisher were published by AISI (see page 2). Two earlier "censuses" have been published for New Jersey: Kenn Stryker-Rodda, *Revolutionary Census of New Jersey* (1972; reprint, Lambertville, N.J.: Hunterdon House, 1986), was constructed from tax records, and James S. Norton, *New Jersey in 1793* (Salt Lake City, Utah: the author, 1973), was taken from militia rosters, with tax records substituting for those counties with missing militia lists.

Background Sources

There is a sizeable amount of published material on the history of New Jersey. Richard P. McCormick, *New Jersey from Colony to State, 1609–1789* (1964; revised, Newark, N.J.: New Jersey Historical Society, 1981), gives excellent coverage of the first 180 years. Samuel Smith, *The History of The Colony of Nova-Caesaria, or New Jersey* (Burlington, N.J.: James Parker, 1765), still considered one of the old standards, has lengthy quotes from records. It was first reprinted in 1877 (Trenton, N.J.: Wm. S. Sharp) and as recently as 1975 (Spartanburg, S.C.: Reprint Co.). Francis Bazley Lee, *New Jersey As A Colony and As a State,* 4 vols. (New York, N.Y.: Publishing Society of New Jersey, 1902), is also one of the standard works. *The Outline History of New Jersey,* by Harold F. Wilson and others (New Brunswick, N.J.: Rutgers University Press, 1950), was intended for students and serves as a quick and helpful reference, with a long bibliography.

New Jersey has its share of "mug" books, which must be used with caution, and some also contain a history of the state. The term mug book refers to printed sources that present pictures and biographies of those who subscribed to the publication. Some examples are *The Biographical Encyclopaedia of New Jersey of The Nineteenth Century* (Philadelphia, Pa.: Galaxy Publishing Co., 1877); *Biographical and Portrait Cyclopedia of the Third Congressional District of New Jersey* (Philadelphia, Pa.: Biographical Publishing Co., 1896); *Biographical, Genealogical and Descriptive History of the First Congressional District of New Jersey,* 2 vols. (New York, N.Y.: Lewis Publishing Co., 1900); William Brown, ed., *Biographical, Genealogical, and Descriptive History of the State of New Jersey* (Newark, N.J.: New Jersey Historical Publishing Co., 1900); Samuel Fowler Bigelow, *The Biographical Cyclopedia of New Jersey,* 2 vols. (New York, N.Y.: National Americana Society, 1909); Francis Bazley Lee, comp. and ed., *Genealogical and Memorial History of the State of New Jersey,* 4 vols. (New York, N.Y.: Lewis Historical Publishing Co., 1910); *Nelson's Biographical Cyclopaedia of New Jersey,* 2 vols. (New York, N.Y.: Eastern Historical Publishing Society, 1913); Mary Depue Ogden, ed., *Memorial Cyclopedia of New Jersey,* 4 vols. (Newark, N.J.: Memorial

History Co., 1915–17); *Cyclopedia of New Jersey Biography,* 3 vols. (Newark, N.J.: Memorial History Co., 1916); Irving S. Kull, ed., *New Jersey: A History,* 5 vols. (New York, N.Y.: American Historical Society, 1930); and William Starr Myers, ed., *The Story of New Jersey,* 5 vols. (New York, N.Y.: Lewis Historical Publishing Co., 1945).

Of more narrow focus are three works covering the proprietary period. Two are by John E. Pomfret: *The Province of West New Jersey* and *The Province of East New Jersey, 1609–1702: The Rebellious Proprietary* (Princeton, N.J.: Princeton Press, 1956, 1962). The other is by William A. Whitehead, *East Jersey Under the Proprietary Governments,* New Jersey Historical Society Collections, Vol. 1 (Newark, N.J.: Martin R. Dennis, 1875). With these works, one should consult *The Minutes of the Board of Proprietors of the Eastern Division of New Jersey, 1685–1794,* 4 vols., edited by George J. Miller, Maxine N. Lurie, and Joanne R. Walroth, with the first three volumes published by the General Board of Proprietors of the Eastern Division of New Jersey (Perth Amboy, 1949–60) and the fourth by the New Jersey Historical Society (Newark, 1985).

Adrian C. Leiby, *The Early Dutch and Swedish Settlers of New Jersey* (Princeton, N.J.: D. Van Nostrand Co., 1964), is but one example covering a part of New Jersey's colonial history. Other works dealing with the Dutch and Swedes are listed in the New York, Pennsylvania, and Delaware chapters.

There are many more titles concentrating on certain aspects of New Jersey history that help trace persons and families and provide important historical background. One example is *From Indian Trail to Iron Horse: Travel and Transportation in New Jersey 1620–1860* by Wheaton J. Lane (Princeton, N.J.: Princeton University Press, 1939).

Several town and city histories have been published in addition to county histories (see pages 3–4 for sources on local histories). John Stillwell, *Historical and Genealogical Miscellany: Data Relating to the Settlement and Settlers of New York and New Jersey,* 5 vols. (1903–32; reprint, Baltimore, Md.: Genealogical Publishing Co., 1970), contains source material and genealogies, mostly relating to Monmouth County, New Jersey, and Staten Island, New York. *Scotland and Its First American Colony, 1683–1765,* by Ned C. Landsman (Princeton, N.J.: Princeton University Press, 1985), is among the modern, scholarly works and concerns lowland Scots settlers in eastern and central New Jersey.

Some works particularly need to be verified in original records. High on this list is Orra Eugene Monnette, *First Settlers of Ye Plantations of Piscataway and Woodbridge . . . 1664–1714,* 7 vols. (Los Angeles, Calif.: Leroy Carmen Press, 1930–35). In spite of its length, it must be used very cautiously, for even Monnette's transcriptions of source records are filled with errors (see *The American Genealogist* 34 [1958]: 213–15). In the "useful for clues but undocumented category" is John Littell, *Family Records, or Genealogies of the First Settlers of Passaic Valley (And Vicinity)* (1852; reprint, Baltimore, Md.: Genealogical Publishing Co., 1981). Typed indexes by Mabel Day Parker and Elmer T. Hutchinson are at the state library, the New Jersey Historical Society, and Rutgers. Another example is *Pioneer Families of Northwestern New Jersey* (Lambertville, N.J.: Hunterdon House, 1979), assembled in the 1930s from ninety-four newspaper articles from various contributors and edited by William C. Armstrong.

Guides

Kenn Stryker-Rodda's chapter on New Jersey in Milton Rubincam, ed., *Genealogical Research: Methods and Sources,* Vol. 1 (revised, Washington, D.C.: American Society of Genealogists, 1980), pages 221–33, is excellent for good background reading. Earlier materials by Stryker-Rodda, just as useful and delightful to read, are *New Jersey: Digging for Ancestors in the Garden State* (Detroit, Mich.: Detroit Society for Genealogical Research, 1970); "New Jersey Records: A Genealogical Haystack Full of Needles," *The Pennsylvania Genealogical Magazine* 24 (1965): 3–14; "Genealogical Spadework in the Garden State," *Proceedings of the New Jersey Historical Society* 79 (1961): 264–81; and "That Genealogical Quagmire: New Jersey," *National Genealogical Society Quarterly* 48 (1960): 59–71.

John P. Snyder, *The Story of New Jersey's Civil Boundaries 1606–1968,* 1st ed. (Trenton, N.J.: Bureau of Geology and Topography, 1969), Bulletin 67, clearly shows county, township, and city boundary changes, enhanced with maps.

Henry A. Gannett's *A Geographical Dictionary of New Jersey* (1894; reprint, Baltimore, Md.: Genealogical Publishing Co., 1978) and Thomas F. Gordon's *Gazetteer of the State of New Jersey* (1834; reprint, Cottonport, La.: Polyanthos, 1977), while earlier works, are necessary for early place-names. *New Jersey Local Names, Municipalities and Counties,* issued by the State Department of Transportation (Trenton, N.J., 1982), gives a more modern list of New Jersey places.

Bette Marie Barker, Daniel P. Jones, and Karl J. Niederer, comps., *Guide to Family History Sources in the New Jersey State Archives,* 2d ed. (Trenton, N.J.: Division of Archives and Records Management, 1990), is an excellent update of an older guide to a wonderful collection of original source material and is available for $5 from the publication section of the archives.

Dated, but still a useful bibliography is William Nelson, *The Public Archives of New Jersey* (Washington, D.C.: Government Printing Office, 1904), reprinted from the Annual Report of the American Historical Association 1 (1903): 479–541. Nelson was then chairman of the Public Record Commission of New Jersey. This work covers deeds and other land records, wills, marriage licenses, court and military records, and catalogs the contents of the two "New Jersey Archives" series published up to that time.

An Analytical Index to the Colonial Documents of New Jersey in the State Paper Offices of England, compiled by Henry Stevens and edited by William A. Whitehead, New Jersey Historical Society Collections, Vol. 5 (New York, N.Y.: D. Appleton and Co., 1858), is also dated but identifies some New Jersey sources not in this country.

Not to be overlooked is Rosalie Bailey's guide to Dutch naming systems (see New York—Background Sources).

Maps

John Snyder, *The Story of New Jersey's Civil Boundaries 1606–1968* (see Guides above) includes very helpful maps. Useful highway maps are available in all or most counties, and older maps have been published, mostly from the 1840s to the 1880s, in county histories, atlases, and in individual sheets. Excellent collections of maps are at the New Jersey Historical Society, the New Jersey State Library, and the New Jersey State Archives. Some modern city maps marked to show ward boundaries are at the state library. These are helpful for locating persons in census records when an address is known. The state archives has many maps for locating roads described in the county road returns.

Land Records

State-Land State

The earliest sales of land in New Jersey were by the proprietors of East and West Jersey, who still hold some land today and maintain their records, although those for West Jersey are on film at the New Jersey State Archives. Until the Land Act of 1785 transferred the recording of deeds to the counties, land conveyances after the initial grants from the proprietors were recorded in the East and West New Jersey capitals, Perth Amboy and Burlington, and in 1795 transferred to Trenton, where they became known as the Secretary of State's Deeds. These deeds, dating 1664 to the 1800s, are at the state archives and are indexed in *Colonial Conveyances: Provinces of East & West New Jersey 1664–1794,* 2 vols. (Summit, N.J.: Crestview Lawyers Service, 1974). Published abstracts of the earliest deeds, surveys, and patents are in William Nelson, ed., *Patents and Deeds and Other Early Records of New Jersey, 1664–1703* (Baltimore, Md.: Genealogical Publishing Co., 1982), originally volume 21 of the "New Jersey Archives" 1st Series. It has been estimated that only a quarter of colonial land transfers were recorded. For more information about the proprietary period, see John Edwin Pomfret, *The New Jersey Proprietors and Their Lands, 1664–1776* (Princeton, N.J.: Van Nostrand, 1964), and related works listed under Background Sources.

The usual deeds and mortgages are found at the county level with corresponding indexes to each type of record. These records begin for most counties at two stages. Mortgages have been recorded with the county clerk from 1766 and deeds from 1785, and generally one would expect to find such records for all counties established by these dates. There is, however, some variance, and some counties recorded deeds in earlier years. At least two counties, Hudson and Passaic, have abstracts of deeds pre-dating the formation of the county that pertain to lands previously in parent counties. Microfilm of deeds recorded to about 1900 and mortgages to about 1850, for almost all New Jersey counties, are available at the state archives. The county clerk also has divisions or partitions of lands that include descriptions and often maps showing how the real property of a person who died intestate was divided among his or her heirs (see also Probate Records). Many unrecorded deeds are found at the state archives, the New Jersey Historical Society, Rutgers University, and in several local historical societies.

Probate Records

As in New York, the county court with jurisdiction over estates is called the surrogate's court (where the modern petition for probate is called the "complaint"). A typical "Surrogate's General Index," however, refers to docket books, where a summary of the action on an estate is entered, with reference to the estate file and to the record volumes. Depending on the action, some information will be found in orphans' court records. Also with the county surrogate (and usually with the county clerk as well) are records of divisions or partitions of lands that include descriptions and often maps showing how the real property of a person who died intestate was divided among his or her heirs. These records have been published for the following counties: Essex (1793–1881), Middlesex (1780–1870), Morris (1785–1907), Somerset and Hunterdon (1809–1904), Sussex (1789–1918), and Warren (1824–1924).

In New Jersey, *original* wills and inventories up to 1901 are on file at the New Jersey State Archives and are identified through *Index of Wills, Inventories, Etc. In the Office of the Secretary of State Prior to 1901,* 3 vols. (1912–13), reprinted with the inadequate title *New Jersey Index of Wills* (Baltimore, Md.: Genealogical Publishing Co., 1969). This set is arranged by county and then alphabetically by name of the estate, with separate sections for wills proved in the prerogative court (precursor to the surrogate's courts) and for unrecorded wills. Each estate has a number that relates to the file at the state archives where these records can be examined on microfilm. Note that this index does *not* cover estate records in the county surrogate's courts. A comprehensive index, alphabetical for the entire state, is not without errors: Lee Smeal and Ronald Vern Jackson, eds., *Index to New Jersey Wills, 1689–1890* [*sic*], *the Testators* (Salt Lake City, Utah: Accelerated Indexing Systems, 1979). The records in Trenton, which for the 1700s to 1804 also include some other estate papers such as administration bonds, accounts, and guardianships, were abstracted and published up through the year 1817 in the "New Jersey Archives" 1st Ser., vols. 23, 30, and 32–42. These should be checked against the original records for accuracy but are useful for their every-name indexes (which do not, however, include the alphabetically arranged names of the decedents or wards). From 1901, original wills and inventories are filed with the Clerk of the Superior Court, Hughes Justice Complex, CN-971, Trenton, New Jersey 08625-0971.

By a law of 1784, orphans' courts were established with jurisdiction over estate matters, which until that time had been the responsibility of the prerogative court (the prerogative became an appellate court). Surrogate's courts were established in 1804, but action on estates should also be checked in orphans' court records. Prior to 1804, estates were handled in the proprietary capitals of Perth Amboy, East Jersey, and Burlington, West Jersey, but the records were sent to Trenton after it became the capital in 1790.

If an estate is not found in the indexes mentioned above, there still may be some record of it at the county level. The *recorded* wills and inventories, as well as the original and recorded bonds, accounts, guardianships, and other estate papers, will be found in the surrogate's court. Many of these county records have been filmed and are available at the state archives. Some colonial New Jersey estates may not be found either in Trenton or in the counties because they were proved in New York, Pennsylvania, or Delaware, and conversely some estates for these adjacent colonies were proved in New Jersey.

The Gloucester County Historical Society has published some estate material for southern New Jersey including three works by Stanley H. Craig: *Genealogical Data from Cumberland County, New Jersey, Wills*; *Salem County Wills Recorded in the Office of the Surrogate at Salem, New Jersey*; and *Petitions for Guardians from the Minutes of the Salem County, New Jersey, Orphans' Court* (Woodbury, N.J., 1981, 1986). This society also published Doris Cole Rogers's *Gloucester County Wills, 1818–1836* (Woodbury, N.J., 1988).

Court Records

New Jersey county clerks are responsible for land records including deeds and mortgages, naturalizations, marriages (usually 1795–1840s), and various county court records. A few original county justice of the peace dockets are at the New Jersey State Archives. Estate matters are handled in the surrogate's and orphans' courts.

The state archives has minute books, indexes, and some case files for records of the prerogative court, 1830s–1900 (some scattered earlier); chancery court, 1780–1850 (some scattered back to 1743); and supreme court, 1681–1844 (indexes to 1947); court of errors and appeals dockets, 1869–1949 (some files prior to 1869); and records of the court of common pleas for some counties for the eighteenth and nineteenth centuries. Later records are with the Superior Court of New Jersey, R. J. Hughes Justice Complex, CN-971, Trenton, New Jersey 08625-0971. Some state court records for the 1800s were destroyed in a fire in 1980.

Records of federal courts in New Jersey are at the National Archives-Northeast Region, and some of these are on microfilm. These include the U.S. District Court for 1789–1960 and U.S. Circuit Court for 1790–1911.

At least two important volumes of court records for the proprietary period have been published: Preston W. Edsall, ed., *Journal of the Courts of Common Right and Chancery of East New Jersey 1683–1702* (Philadelphia, Pa.: American Legal Historical Society, 1937), and H. Clay Reed and George J. Miller, eds., *The Burlington* [County] *Court Book: A Record of Quaker Jurisprudence in West New Jersey 1680–1709* (Washington, D.C.: American Historical Association, 1944).

Tax Records

Because New Jersey's pre-1830 federal censuses have not survived, tax records are quite an important substitute for placing persons and families prior to that time. Tax lists arranged by township are available for 1773–1822. The originals, at the New Jersey State Archives, show heads of households, landowners, and single adult males, with information about their property that was taxable, including land, horses, cattle, slaves, and mills. Only about half of the 1773–74 lists are extant, and for some places, such as Sussex County, coverage is very slight. Microfilms of these records are at the state archives, the New Jersey Historical Society, Rutgers University, and the New York Genealogical and Biographical Society (see New York). A six-volume index published by AISI in 1981 is available in these places and elsewhere, but it contains transcription errors and does not include the lists for Hunterdon County, most of Burlington County, and most if not all of Bergen and Middlesex counties. The early tax lists have been published in *The Genealogical Magazine of New Jersey*, beginning in volume 36, and those for the period 1773–86 were used to construct a "Revolutionary census" (see Census Records). The 1784 tax lists for thirty-eight municipalities (predominantly in southern New Jersey) are the only ones to indicate the size of a household, with a column for number of whites and a column for number of slaves. Abstracts of these 1784 ratables are intended for publication in *The Genealogical Magazine of New Jersey*. The published index problems have been partially corrected by *Hunterdon County, New Jersey Taxpayers, 1778–1797* and *Bergen County, New Jersey Taxpayers, 1777–1797*, both compiled and published by T. L. C. Genealogy (Miami Beach, Fla., 1990).

Later tax records are found in the counties starting about 1869–70. Tax lists for some extinct New Jersey municipalities are at the state archives.

Cemetery Records

The important work of grave marker transcribing has been the goal of the Genealogical Society of New Jersey (see Archives, Libraries, and Societies), which was originally formed by "Tombstone Hounds." Their core collection is at Rutgers University, where there is a card index by county and name of the cemetery as well as a "master index" arranged alphabetically by surname but only for selected cemeteries. Many of the society's transcriptions have been published in their journal, *The Genealogical Magazine of New Jersey*. Another large collection of cemetery records is that gathered by the New Jersey DAR chapters, with copies deposited at the New Jersey State Library and the New Jersey Historical Society. Both these places have other cemetery records, as do the Genealogical Society of Pennsylvania (see Pennsylvania) and the New York Public Library (see New York). Some individual books of cemetery inscriptions have been published (such as the one for Whippany and Hanover, Morris County), and some are found in *The New York Genealogical and Biographical Record.* Some early burial records for Elizabeth's First Presbyterian Church were even published in *The New England Historical and Genealogical Register* 44 (1890): 264–69.

Church Records

Church records are just as important in New Jersey as in the other Mid-Atlantic states, but many have been lost or destroyed. One of the first places to look for them, however, is the twenty-volume *Directory of Churches in New Jersey,* (Newark, N.J.: WPA, 1940–41) and, for individual denominations, the eleven-volume *Guide to the Church Archives of New Jersey* (Newark, N.J.: WPA, 1938–41), both by the Historical Records Survey. William Nelson, *Church Records in New Jersey* (Paterson, N.J.: Paterson History Club, 1904), was originally published in the *Journal of the Presbyterian Historical Society* 2 (1904): 173–88, 251–66. It is arranged by name of place and, while dated, is still very helpful in locating church records in the Garden State. Another list of church records is in the Holland Society's *Yearbook* for 1912.

Many New Jersey church records have been published in state historical and genealogical journals, such as *The Genealogical Magazine of New Jersey, Proceedings of the New Jersey Historical Society,* volumes 1 and 2 of John Stillwell's *Historical and Genealogical Miscellany* (see Background Sources), and the *Somerset County Historical Quarterly,* as well as in New York and Pennsylvania publications. Original and transcribed material is to be found at the New Jersey Historical Society (including the DAR collection), Rutgers University, the Gloucester County Historical Society (see Archives, Libraries, and Societies), and elsewhere in New Jersey, and in New York, Delaware, and Pennsylvania sources and libraries, particularly in the Collections of the Genealogical Society of Pennsylvania.

Some volumes of records of individual churches have been published, such as those for the Presbyterian churches of Madison, Morristown, and Freehold; and Dutch church records of Bergen, Hackensack, Schraalenburgh, and Acquackanonk (Passaic). Volume 2 of William Wade Hinshaw, *Encyclopedia of American Quaker Genealogy* (1938; reprint, Baltimore, Md.: Genealogical Publishing Co., 1969, 1991), contains records from only two monthly meetings in New Jersey—Salem and Burlington. Other Quaker records, in original form and transcript, are found at the New Jersey Historical Society, Rutgers University, the Friends Historical Library in Swarthmore, the New York Genealogical and Biographical Society, and the Genealogical Society of Pennsylvania. Records of other meetings, particularly Philadelphia, should be checked for New Jersey ancestors. Early Catholic records are scarce, but see Janet Drumm Dirnberger, *New Jersey Catholic Baptismal Records from 1759–1781* (Searbrook, Tex.: Brambles, 1981), which is an index to 285 baptismal records taken from Rev. Joseph M. Flynn, *The Catholic Church in New Jersey.* Unfortunately, the sources Flynn used for his work are no longer extant.

The Historical Society of the Reformed Church in America, 21 Seminary Place, New Brunswick, New Jersey 08901, has published *Guide to Local Church Records in the Reformed Church in America and to Genealogical Resources in the Gardner Sage Library, New Brunswick Theological Seminary,* Local Church Archive Group Special Guide No. 1, edited by Russell L. Gasero (New Brunswick, N.J., 1979).

University Archives, Steton Hall University, South Orange Avenue, South Orange, New Jersey 07079, maintains microfilm copies of parish registers from 1832 to 1914 for the Archdiocese of Newark, which until 1881 included all of New Jersey. A small research fee is charged for inquiries. Records after 1914 are in the individual parishes but are not open for research. In 1881 the archdiocese was divided, and the Southern Archdiocese in Trenton lost most of its records in a fire in 1956. Another split in 1937 created archdioceses at Paterson and Camden, but Trenton and Camden have no archives.

Diocesan House of the Episcopal Church, 808 West State Street, Trenton, New Jersey 08618, has copies of baptismal and confirmation records from individual churches. The church archives has a full run of diocesan journals, which are not indexed but are useful for tracing clergy and convention delegates, the church newspaper, published and manuscript church histories, and fragmentary records for only eighteen of the eighty or more extinct churches.

The Methodist church has an archives for each of its two state conferences: United Methodist Church Archives, Northern New Jersey Conference, Drew University, 36 Madison Avenue, Madison, New Jersey 07940, and United Methodist Church Archives, Southern New Jersey Conference, Bishop's Building, Pennington School, 40 Delaware Avenue, Pennington, New Jersey 08534.

Inquiries about Presbyterian records should be made to the History Department, Presbyterian Church in the U.S.A. (see Pennsylvania—Church Records). Inquiries about Baptist records should be made to the American Baptist Historical Society, 1106 South Goodman Street, Rochester, New York 14620.

In 1986–89, Ronald L. Becker conducted a survey of New Jersey synagogue records, and the results are expected to be published in a guide. In the meantime, the information can be used at the Special Collections and Archives in Rutgers, if one first obtains Becker's permission.

Military Records

Pre-World War I material on New Jersey's military activities is mostly found at the New Jersey State Archives, with later records at the New Jersey Department of Military and Veterans' Affairs, Eggert Crossing Road, CN-340, Trenton, New Jersey 08625-0340. Some material has been published, but there is little on the colonial period. A typescript, "Military Lists from the Office of the Adjutant General, Trenton, New Jersey," copied by Albert F. and Sara Morton Koehler (N.p., 1962), is available at the New York Genealogical and Biographical Society, and a small amount of colonial military material is available at the state archives. See also "Abstracts of New Jersey Commissions, Civil and Military . . . [1703–1769]," in *Publications of th Genealogical Society of Pennsylvania*, vols. 6, 7, and 10.

For the Revolutionary period, there is the *Official Register of the Officers and Men of New Jersey in the Revolutionary War*, compiled by Adjutant General William S. Stryker (1872; reprint, Baltimore, Md.: Genealogical Publishing Co., 1967). An index compiled by the WPA in 1941 was reprinted: *Index of the Official Register of the Officers and Men of New Jersey in the Revolutionary War* (Baltimore, Md.: Clearfield Co., 1989). This work has only about a third of all the names; other material should be sought at the state archives (where there are alphabetical card files to the New Jersey "patriots" and the New Jersey Loyalist regiment) and the National Archives (see page 7). Background reading is available in *New Jersey in the American Revolution 1763–1783: A Documentary History*, edited by Larry R. Gerlack (Trenton, N.J.: New Jersey Historical Commission, 1975). E. Alfred Jones, *The Loyalists of New Jersey: Their Memorials, Petitions, Claims, etc. from English Records* (1927; reprint, Lambertville, N.J.: Hunterdon House, 1988), originally published in New Jersey Historical Society Collections, volume 10, should be supplemented with other sources. A list of eligible men age eighteen to forty-five who did not serve in the Revolution or in the militia of another state is found in James S. Norton, *New Jersey in 1793* (see Census Records). The state archives also has war damage claims filed by the British and Americans, 1776–82.

Records of Officers and Men of New Jersey in the Wars 1791–1815, compiled by the Adjutant General's Office (1909; reprint, Baltimore, Md.: Genealogical Publishing Co., 1970), mostly covers the War of 1812 period. Later nineteenth-century conflicts are treated in *Record of Officers and Men of New Jersey in the War with Mexico, 1846–1848* (Trenton, N.J., 1900) and *Record of Officers and Men of New Jersey in the Civil War, 1861–1865*, compiled by William S. Stryker, 2 vols. (Trenton, N.J.: John L. Murphy, 1876).

The National Archives microfilm "Index to Compiled Service Records of Volunteer Union Soldiers Who Served . . . from New Jersey" is at the Northeast Region (see page 8). The state archives also has indexes to the Spanish-American War and some other pre-World War I military service, as well as unindexed material on the War of 1812, Mexican War, Spanish-American War, the State Militia (1789–1947), and the National Guard (to about 1910). Modern military records are with the New Jersey Department of Military and Veterans' Affairs (address above).

Periodicals, Newspapers, and Manuscript Collections

Periodicals

The Genealogical Magazine of New Jersey was introduced in 1925 by the Genealogical Society of New Jersey and has carried many cemetery marker inscriptions, county marriages, tax lists, church records, and other source material, but only a little compiled genealogy. Kenn Stryker-Rodda produced four volumes of a *Given Name Index* covering the first fifty volumes of the journal (Cottonport and New Orleans, La.: Polyanthos, and Lambertville, N.J.: Hunterdon House, 1973–82), and Donald A. Sinclair compiled a subject and author index to the first thirty-five volumes, published by the genealogical society in 1962. See also Elizabeth M. Perinchief's *Index to Cemetery Transcriptions, Baptismal, Burial, Church and Marriage Records in the Genealogical Magazine of New Jersey through 1980* (Mount Holly, N.J.: Burlington County Library, 1981).

The New Jersey Historical Society's journal was first issued in 1845 as *Proceedings of the New Jersey Historical Society*, comprising ten volumes through 1866. From 1867 to 1895, thirteen volumes were issued with the designation Second Series; from 1896 to 1915, ten volumes were published as the Third Series; and from 1916 to 1966, eighty-four volumes comprised the New Series. The journal was retitled *New Jersey History* in 1965 but continued the volume numbering from the New Series of *Proceedings*. A subject index to the first thirty-six volumes published 1845–1919 was printed in volume 5 of the New Series (1920). Basic genealogical material was dropped from the publication after 1951, but earlier there were many excellent features including source records and genealogies.

The New Jersey Genesis was published in twenty volumes from 1953 to 1973 and included source records (some of which were published elsewhere), queries, and other material. An index compiled by the New Mexico Genealogical Society was published in 1973.

Among the regional periodicals that have appeared are *The Jerseyman*, published in Flemington in eleven volumes from 1891 to 1905. It included church records, genealogies, and local history, mostly for Hunterdon and bordering counties. Another older publication, the *Somerset County Historical Quarterly*, was published in eight volumes from 1912 to 1919 and has been reprinted by Hunterdon House (Lambertville, N.J., 1977–89); *A Subject-and-Author Index* to this quarterly, by Donald A. Sinclair, was published by the Genealogical Society of New Jersey in 1991. Its most valuable contents were source records, especially Dutch church records, and some of its coverage was devoted to Hunterdon County. A newer periodical for this area, the *Somerset County Genealogical Quarterly*, is excellent for its source material. Two other important journals are *The Vineland Historical Magazine*, begun in 1916 and concerning Cumberland County, and *The Cape May Magazine of History and Genealogy*, begun in 1931.

Much New Jersey information is also to be found in the periodical literature of its neighbors such as *The New York Genealogical and Biographical Record, Publications of The Genealogical Society of Pennsylvania* and its successor *The Pennsylvania Genealogical Magazine,* and *The Pennsylvania Magazine of History and Biography.*

Newspapers

The first newspaper published in New Jersey was in 1777 and extracts to 1782 from this and from a second early newspaper were published in the five volumes of the "New Jersey Archives," 2d Ser. (Trenton, N.J., 1901–17), and continued in Thomas B. Wilson, *Notices From New Jersey Newspapers 1781–1790 . . . Volume I* (Lambertville, N.J.: Hunterdon House, 1988). Published extracts of items concerning New Jersey in the period 1704 to 1782 found in newspapers in other colonies appeared in eleven volumes of the "New Jersey Archives" 1st Series. For locating New Jersey newspapers, consult William C. Wright and Paul A. Stellhorn, eds., *Directory of New Jersey Newspapers, 1765–1970* (Trenton, N.J.: New Jersey Historical Commission, 1977).

Large collections of newspapers are at the New Jersey State Archives and the New Jersey Historical Society. Notices of marriages, deaths, and other items have been extracted from New Jersey newspapers and are found in such places as the "Biographical" card file at the historical society (which includes information from some church publications), an index at the state archives for Trenton newspaper marriages and deaths for 1777–1900, and the Hutchinson Collection of New Brunswick Newspaper Extracts, 1792–1865, at Rutgers.

Manuscripts

Mary R. Murrin, comp., *New Jersey Historical Manuscripts: A Guide to Collections in the State* (Trenton, N.J.: New Jersey Historical Commission, 1987), is a general guide to 263 repositories. Don C. Skemer and Robert C. Morris, comps., *Guide to the Manuscript Collections of the New Jersey Historical Collection,* New Jersey Historical Society Collections, Vol. 15 (Newark, N.J.: New Jersey Historical Society, 1979), includes family and personal papers as well as a wealth of other useful material.

Herbert F. Smith's, *A Guide to the Manuscript Collection of the Rutgers University Library* (New Brunswick, N.J.: Rutgers University Press, 1964), while outdated, can be a useful starting point for this impressive collection, and much important material has been added.

Other significant manuscript collections include those in southern New Jersey such as those at Glassboro State College in Glassboro and the Gloucester County Historical Society (see Archives, Libraries, and Societies).

Historical Records Survey, *Calendar of the New Jersey State Library Manuscript Collection* (Newark, N.J.: WPA, 1939), covers a small collection that was numbered and indexed and is now located in the New Jersey State Archives.

The Charles Carroll Gardner Collection, at the New Jersey Historical Society and Rutgers University and on microfilm elsewhere, is strongest on Essex County families. Gardner set out to publish some of his work in *The Genealogical Magazine of New Jersey,* under the title "A Genealogical Dictionary of New Jersey," but unfortunately the series only got through some surnames beginning with the letter *A* (vols. 10–27). Other collections include those of Charles E. Sheppard at Vineland and the John P. Dornan files at Rutgers, both for southern New Jersey, and the Hiram E. Deats collection at Flemington for Hunterdon County. Collections of the Genealogical Society of Pennsylvania should not be overlooked, particularly for southern New Jersey, such as the Gilbert Cope collection. New York sources should also be considered, such as the Alfred Vail and Josephine C. Frost collections at The New York Genealogical and Biographical Society and the John E. Stillwell material at the New-York Historical Society.

Archives, Libraries, and Societies

Department of State
Division of Archives and Records Management
Bureau of Archives and Records Preservation
State Library Building
185 West State Street, CN-307
Trenton, NJ 08625-0307

The New Jersey State Archives has many of the basic research materials for the state such as federal and state census records; probate, land, and court records; newspapers; and vital records. Mail requests are accepted for only some of the collections. For more information, refer to the guide to its holdings mentioned above (see Background Sources).

New Jersey State Library
State Library Building
185 West State Street, CN-520
Trenton, NJ 08625-0520

The New Jersey State Library essentially has the published complement to the New Jersey State Archives including genealogies, histories, periodicals, guidebooks, maps, atlases, and indexes. Its collection, however, is stronger for the southern and central parts of the state than for northern New Jersey. There are also newspaper clipping files, phone books, directories, and folders of material and correspondence arranged by family name, as well as microfilms of the federal and state censuses. The state library is one of the two depositories for the state's DAR collection.

New Jersey Historical Society
230 Broadway
Newark, NJ 07104

There is a $1, nonmember fee to use the library, which has an excellent collection of published material, microfilms of New Jersey federal and state censuses (1855–85), tax rateables (and published index), and much more. The New

Jersey Historical Society is one of the two depositories for the state's DAR compilations and houses much manuscript material including maps, cemetery and church records, family Bibles, and genealogies, as well as thousands of other original documents and papers. The society's quarterly, *New Jersey History,* was issued as *Proceedings of The New Jersey Historical Society* until 1967 (see Periodicals). The society has also published a number of books on New Jersey history, many of which are mentioned in this chapter. See also Maude E. Johnson, "Genealogical-Index to Books, Pamphlets, MSS., Etc., in The New Jersey Historical Society Library," *Proceedings,* New Series 8 (1923): 81–88 and "Supplement" 14 (1929): 129–44. A more modern guide to the society's manuscript collection is listed under Manuscripts. The Genealogy Club of the Library of the New Jersey Historical Society meets here.

Genealogical Society of New Jersey
P. O. Box 1291
New Brunswick NJ 08903-1291

The Genealogical Society of New Jersey has published *The Genealogical Magazine of New Jersey* since 1925. The society houses its collection of genealogical materials including cemetery transcriptions, family Bibles (over 4,800), military records, and notes of genealogists in the A. S. Alexander Library at Rutgers University.

Rutgers University Library
Department of Special Collections and Archives
New Brunswick, NJ 08903

Perhaps holding the best published collection of New Jersey material, Rutgers also has a wealth of manuscripts including the collections of the Genealogical Society of New Jersey.

Other Repositories

Many significant genealogical collections are elsewhere throughout the state, including the Gloucester County Historical Society, 17 Hunter Street, P.O. Box 409 Woodbury, New Jersey 08096-0409; the Monmouth County Historical Association, 70 Court Street, Freehold, New Jersey 07728; and the Joint Free Library of Morristown and Morris Township, 1 Miller Road, P.O. Box 267M, Morristown, New Jersey 07960.

For a list of historical societies in New Jersey, see *Historical Organizations in New Jersey: A Directory,* by Mary Alice Quigley and others (Trenton, N.J.: League of Historical Societies of New Jersey, 1983).

Special Focus Categories

Immigration

Most nineteenth- and twentieth-century immigration to New Jersey by ship was through the ports of New York and Philadelphia. There were some ship arrivals, however, in New Jersey directly, and federal passenger lists of these are available at the National Archives (see page 10) for Perth Amboy, 1801–37 (with gaps); Bridgetown and Cape May, 1828; Little Egg Harbor, 1831; and Newark, 1836. These are indexed in the National Archives microfilm publication "A Supplemental Index to Passenger Lists of Vessels Arriving at Atlantic and Gulf Coast Ports." See also Carl Boyer, ed., *Ship Passenger Lists: New York and New Jersey 1600–1825* (Newhall, Calif.: the editor, 1978).

Naturalization

A search for New Jersey naturalization records should usually begin with the county clerk. A guide to these records for 1702–1886 was prepared by the WPA: *Naturalization Records in New Jersey* (Newark, N.J.: New Jersey Historical Records Program, 1941). U.S. District Court naturalization records for Camden, Camp Fort Dix, Newark, and Trenton, for various periods 1838 to 1981, arranged alphabetically or indexed, are at the National Archives-Northeast Region. The earliest of these U.S. District Court records were abstracted by Kenneth Scott in "New Jersey Naturalizations, 1838–1844," *National Genealogical Society Quarterly* 69 (1981): 27–33.

For the 1700s and 1800s, naturalization records are at the New Jersey State Archives, where there are also microfilms of many of the county records up to 1906. Some of the earliest records were published in *Laws of the Royal Colony of New Jersey, 1703–1775,* volumes 2–5 of the "New Jersey Archives" 3d Series (Trenton, N.J.: Division of Archives and Records Management, 1977–86). See also John R. Stevenson, "Persons Naturalized in New Jersey Between 1702 and 1776," *The New York Genealogical and Biographical Record* 28 (1897): 86–89. It is important to keep in mind that many New Jersey residents may have become naturalized or at least filed a declaration of intention in New York City or Philadelphia if they stayed long enough in those port cities before settling in the Garden State.

Ethnic Groups

David Steven Cohen, comp., *New Jersey Ethnic History: A Bibliography* (Newark, N.J.: New Jersey Historical Society, 1986), lists over 600 books, articles, and theses covering Afro-Americans, Cubans, Dutch, Germans, Hungarians, Irish, Italians, Japanese, Jews, Native Americans, Portuguese, Quakers, and Swedes. Another interesting work by Cohen is *The Ramapo Mountain People* (New Brunswick, N.J.: Rutgers University Press, 1974).

Theodore F. Chambers, *The Early Germans of New Jersey* (1895; reprint, Lambertville, N.J.: Hunterdon House and Baltimore, Md.: Genealogical Publishing Co., 1982), has information on non-German families as well as on northwestern New Jersey, but it is one of those unreliable works that must be used with great caution.

Dennis J. Starr, *The Italians of New Jersey: A Historical Introduction and Bibliography,* New Jersey Historical Society Collections, Vol. 20 (Newark, N.J.: New Jersey Historical Society, 1985), discusses the largest ethnic group of the state and is helpful for finding other sources on the subject.

Clement Alexander Price, comp. and ed., *Freedom Not Far Distant: A Documentary History of Afro-Americans in New Jersey,* New Jersey Historical Society Collections, Vol. 16 (Newark, N.J.: New Jersey Historical Society, 1980), is based heavily on original source material.

Herbert C. Kraft, *The Lenape: Archaeology, History, and Ethnography,* New Jersey Historical Society Collections, Vol. 21 (Newark, N.J.: New Jersey Historical Society, 1986), is a study of the so-called Delaware Indians who lived in what are now New Jersey, Delaware, Pennsylvania, and New York. In an earlier work, William Nelson compiled a referenced work, *Personal Names of Indians of New Jersey* (Paterson, N.J.: Paterson History Club, 1904), listing 650 names, mostly from seventeenth-century deeds.

County Resources

The state of New Jersey is divided into twenty-one counties that have recorded transfers of land, estates, court, and other records (see Court Records). Each county is governed by a Board of Freeholders whose records should not be overlooked. Other useful county records may be located in the courthouses or at the New Jersey State Archives including justice of the peace dockets; tavern, peddler's, and shopkeeper's licenses; road books; and slave births and manumissions.

Some New Jersey counties have established or are establishing county record centers and archives where older records may be transferred for better preservation and use by researchers. Such facilities, in one stage or another, exist in the counties of Bergen, Cape May, Hudson, Middlesex, Monmouth, Morris, Ocean, and Somerset. Most clerks still retain custody over such material and should be contacted first about the location of and access to a particular record.

Most municipal records are still in the townships, boroughs, and cities, but some are at the state archives and the New Jersey Historical Society. These records (and some county records) list indigents, elected officials, stray animals, and earmarks. The *Records of the Town of Newark, New Jersey . . . 1666, To . . . 1836* (Newark, N.J.: New Jersey Historical Society, 1864) was published as volume 6 of the *Collections* of the New Jersey Historical Society, with a supplement issued two years later that included genealogical notes of the first settlers by Samuel H. Congar.

Based on an act by the state legislature in 1979, New Jersey has a system of local historians who are "to promote and preserve the history of the municipality/ies." Such historians *may* be appointed in the counties, townships, and boroughs, and thus the coverage is less than it should be. In 1989, for example, only ten county historians had been appointed. A list of historians can be obtained from the New Jersey Historical Commission, 4 North Broad Street, CN-305, Trenton, New Jersey 08625-0305.

The first column of the following table contains the map coordinate for the state map. In the second column is shown the name of the county with the mailing address of the county clerk where deeds, mortgages, early marriages, naturalizations, and other matters are recorded. In the third column is given the date the county was created and the name or names of the parent county or counties. The date the earliest land deed was recorded appears in the fourth column; where two years appear, the first refers to mortgages, the second to deeds. Under New Jersey law, mortgages were first recorded in the counties in 1766 and deeds in 1785. Some counties have abstracts of earlier deeds from their parent counties (see Land Records). In the last column is shown the date when surrogate's records began, followed by the mailing address of the county surrogate's court, if different from the county clerk. Where two years are given, the first is the date when orphans' court minutes began, the second when surrogate's records and files began (see Probate Records).

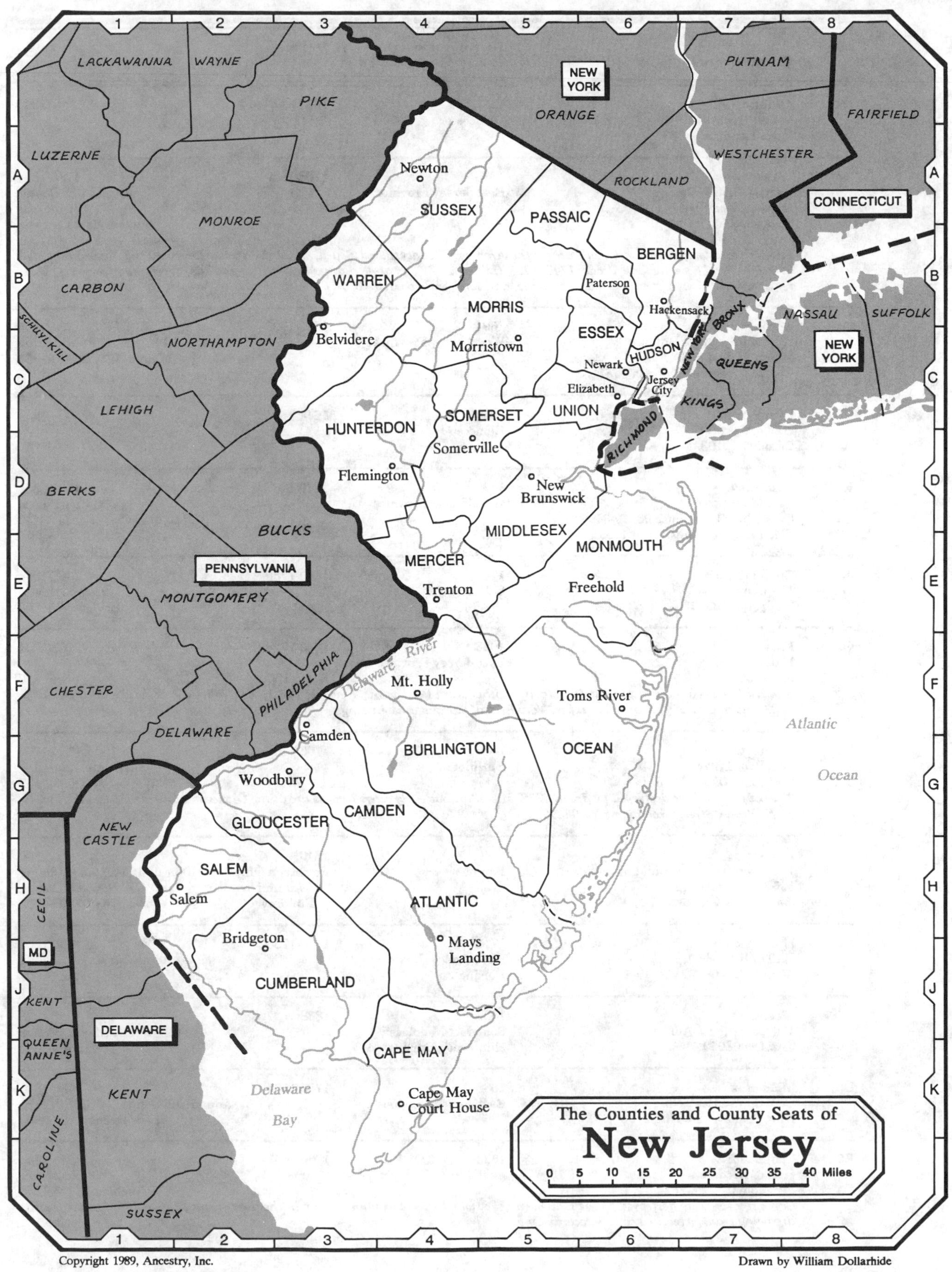

Drawn by William Dollarhide

Map	County County Clerk	Date Formed Parent County/ies	Deeds	Surrogates' Court
H4	Atlantic Main Street Mays Landing 08330	1837 Gloucester	1837	1837
B6	Bergen County Justice Center Main & Essex Streets Hackensack 07601-7691	1683 East Jersey Province	1766/1829	1785/1804 County Justice Center Room 211 Main & Essex Streets Hackensack 07601-7691
	Earlier records of the county clerk are in the Archives, County Plaza South, 21 Main Street, Room 203W, Hackensack, NJ 07601-7000. These include deeds 1707–1828 (Libers A–Z2), chattel mortgages, soldier burials, freeholders records, voter registrations, slave births and manumissions, and some early court records.			
G4	Burlington 103 County Office Building Mount Holly 08060-1384 *Courts were established in 1681.*	1694 West Jersey Province	1766/1785	1785/1804 116 County Office Building Mount Holly 08060-1384
G3	Camden Hall of Justice Camden 08103	1844 Gloucester	1844	1844
K4	Cape May 7 N. Main Street Cape May Courthouse 08210-3096 *Courts were established in 1685.*	1692 West Jersey Province	1770/1785	1786/1804 122 Courthouse Cape May Courthouse 08210
J2	Cumberland 117 Courthouse Bridgeton 08302	1748 Salem	1766/1785	1785/1804 108 Courthouse Bridgeton 08302
C6	Essex Hall of Records Room 240	1683 East Jersey Province	1783/1728 Room 130	1783/1804 Room 213
	The Hall of Records is located at 465 Martin Luther King Boulevard., Newark, NJ 07102. Volume A of deeds, dating back to 1688, was reportedly destroyed in a fire. Volume A of mortgages is missing.			
G2	Gloucester 1 N. Broad Street Woodbury 08096-7376	1686 Burlington	1766/1785	1785/1804 Surrogate's Building Woodbury 08096-7177
	The courthouse was destroyed by fire in 1786. Miscellaneous early court records are at the Gloucester County Historical Society, 58 N. Broad Street, Woodbury, NJ 08096.			
C6	Hudson 101 Administration Building 595 Newark Avenue Jersey City 07306-2301	1840 Bergen	1840 Register's Office 104 Administration Building	1840 106 Administration Building 595 Newark Avenue Jersey City 07306-2301
D3	Hunterdon Hall of Records Flemington 08822	1714 West Jersey Province/ Burlington	1766/1785	1785/1804 Administration Building Flemington 08822
E4	Mercer 100 Courthouse Annex Trenton 08650	1838 Somerset/Middlesex/ Hunterdon/Burlington	1838	1838 310 Courthouse Annex Trenton 08650
D5	Middlesex Courthouse East Wing New Brunswick 08903-2153	1683 East Jersey Province	1766/1785	1786/1804 Administration Building, 7th floor New Brunswick 08903
E6	Monmouth Hall of Records Freehold 07728-1251	1683 East Jersey Province	1766/1667	1785/1804 Hall of Records Freehold 07728-1265
	Some records were destroyed by the British in 1778, which might explain the gap in the deeds from 1756 to 1785. Older records are being transferred to a county records center.			

Map	County County Clerk	Date Formed Parent County/ies	Deeds	Surrogates' Court
B5	Morris CN-900 Morristown 07960	1739 Hunterdon	1765/1785	1785/1804 New Hall of Records Morristown 07960
	Early surrogates' files and books, circuit court and court of common pleas records, naturalizations, marriages (1795–1876), and other material are located at the Morris County Records Center and Archives, 300 Mendham Road, Morristown, NJ 07960, which should be contacted before a visit.			
F6	Ocean 105 Courthouse CN-2191 Toms River 08754	1850 Monmouth	1850	1850 211 Courthouse CN-2191 Toms River 08754
A5	Passaic 77 Hamilton Street Paterson 07505-2018	1837 Bergen/Essex	1837	1837 71 Hamilton Street Paterson 07505
H2	Salem 92 Market Street, P.O. Box 18 Salem 08079-0018 *Courts were established in 1681.*	1694 West Jersey Province	1766/1786	1785/1804 92 Market Street Salem 08079-1913
D4	Somerset 110 Administration Building P.O. Box 3000 Somerville 08876-3000 *In 1779 the courthouse, then at Millstone, was burned.*	1688 Middlesex	1765/1785	1794/1804 112 Administration Building P.O. Box 3000 Somerville 08876-3000
A4	Sussex 4 Park Place Newton 07860	1753 Morris	1766/1785	1804
C5	Union Courthouse, 1st Floor Elizabeth 07207-2204	1857 Essex	1857	1857 Courthouse, 2d Floor Elizabeth 07207-2204
B3	Warren 118 Courthouse Belvidere 07823	1824 Sussex	1825	1825 116 Courthouse Belvidere 07823

NEW MEXICO

Margaret L. Windham, C.G., and Nell Sachse Woodard

Among the western states, it can be said that New Mexico is unique. It had celebrated its sesquicentennial before the first presidio was erected in Alta California, and its bicentennial before Brigham Young would gaze on the sagebrush in the valley of the Great Salt Lake.

Coronado traveled across New Mexico from Arizona in 1540, going as far north as Kansas. Four decades later, Rodriquez explored what is now New Mexico, with the Espejo and Oñate expeditions following suit. Oñate's first Spanish settlement in the Rio Grande Valley was established in 1598. Santa Fe was established in the early seventeenth century, bringing the Spanish speaking population to 2,400 by 1680. That same year Native Americans revolted, reclaiming their homeland, but by 1693 New Mexico was reconquered and reoccupied.

Over a century passed before Mexico revolted against Spain and became independent in 1821. The new country included what is now New Mexico. In 1844 New Mexico land was divided into three districts: Central, Northern and Southeastern. In 1850 the Central District was divided into the counties of Santa Fe, Santa Ana and San Miguel; the Northern District into Rio Arriba and Taos counties; and the Southeastern District into Valencia and Bernalillo.

United States expansionism helped provoke the Mexican War in 1846 with General Kearny occupying Santa Fe. When the war ended in 1848, Mexico ceded the Guadalupe Hidalgo Treaty territories, including almost all of the southwestern lands, and New Mexico became a part of the United States. Two years later, in 1850, Congress created the Territory of New Mexico, setting up a territorial government within a year. The Gadsden Purchase in 1854 established the present southern border of New Mexico. In 1877 telegraph lines were erected from New Mexico to San Diego, providing the communication needed for more settlement.

The reason for New Mexico's early settlement was simply that it was easily reached by anyone coming from the Spanish and Mexican strongholds via the Rio Grande. The river was not only a means of access but also life blood for the weary traveler, and it insured the growth of crops. Between defending themselves against marauding natives, aggressive Texans who looked wistfully to the west for expansion, and their own indifferent public officials, the citizens of New Mexico had to be a flexible lot in order to endure from the founding of Santa Fe in 1610 to the celebration of statehood in 1912.

The population reached 300,000 as New Mexico entered the Union in 1912. Most were living on small land holdings. In recognition of the entry of the state into the modern technological world, the county of Los Alamos came into being in March 1949. It was there during World War II with the development of the atom bomb that the country prepared to bring the war to its eventual conclusion.

Today, New Mexico is a mixture of cultures and political philosophies, a center for both nuclear, technological research, and new-age living, set on a backdrop of Native American and Mexican cultures.

Vital Records

New Mexico's vital records are divided between a statewide index for births and deaths and county clerks' offices where marriage records are filed. Statewide recording began in

1920, although there are some earlier death records that may be found as part of real estate transactions in some counties.

Access to the statewide index of births and deaths is through the New Mexico Health and Environment Department, Health Services Division, Vital Statistics Office, 1190 St. Francis, Santa Fe, New Mexico 87503. They will accept phone requests and charge fees to MasterCard or Visa.

Requests for county records of marriage should go to the respective county clerk in which the event occurred.

Divorces are filed through the district court serving the county. Records before 1912 are located in court dockets at the New Mexico Records Center and Archives (see Archives, Libraries, and Societies).

Census Records

Federal

Population Schedules.

- Indexed—1850, 1860, 1870
- Soundex—1880, 1900, 1920
- Unindexed—1910

Union Veterans Schedules.

- 1890

Microfilm population schedules and printed index copies of all of the federal censuses for New Mexico are located at the New Mexico Records Center and Archives. Originals include the years 1850–70.

The 1850 census is available in print:

Windham, Margaret Leonard. *New Mexico 1850 Territorial Census.* 4 vols. Albuquerque, N.Mex.: New Mexico Genealogical Society, 1976.

Territorial

There are Spanish and Mexican colonial censuses that can be found at the New Mexico Records Center and Archives (see Archives, Libraries, and Societies for address). The originals are in Spanish, but the New Mexico Genealogical Society has published *Spanish and Mexican Censuses of New Mexico, 1750–1830,* translated by Virginia L. Olmsted. Copies are available at the Albuquerque Public Library, Special Collections; University of New Mexico, the Center for Southwest Research, Special Collections; and the FHL Family History Center in Albuquerque, as well as many other libraries.

The New Mexico State Records Center and Archives also houses the 1885 state census, which was actually a federally taken census and includes all members of the household. However, some schedules are missing. It is also available through the Albuquerque Public Library, Special Collections; University of New Mexico, Special Collections; the National Archives; and the FHL.

Background Sources

The definitive book to be consulted is Hubert Howe Bancroft's *History of Arizona and New Mexico, 1530–1888* (San Francisco, Calif.: History Publishing, 1888), followed by Ralph Emerson Twitchell's *The Leading Facts of New Mexican History,* 2 vols. (1911; reprint, Albuquerque, N.Mex.: Horn and Wallace, 1963). A good overview of the state can be obtained by using the extensive bibliography of Warren A. Beck's *New Mexico: A History of Four Centuries* (Norman, Okla.: University of Oklahoma Press, 1962).

More recent publications include Christine Myers, *New Mexico Local and County Histories: A Bibliography* (Albuquerque, N.Mex.: New Mexico Library Association, 1983); Marc Simmons, *New Mexico: A Bicentennial History* (New York, N.Y.: W. W. Norton, 1977); Calvin A. Roberts and Susan A. Roberts, *A History of New Mexico* (Albuquerque, N.Mex.: University of New Mexico Press, 1986). An important reprint is Ralph Emerson Twitchell, *The Spanish Archives of New Mexico.* 2 vols. (1914; reprint, New York, N.Y.: Arno Press, 1976).

If further information is needed about the territorial period, see Howard Robert Lamar's *The Far Southwest, 1846–1912: A Territorial History* (New Haven, Conn.: Yale University Press, 1966).

Those with Hispanic heritage will want to consult George R. Ryskamp, *Tracing Your Hispanic Heritage* (Riverside, Calif.: Hispanic Family History Research, 1984), and Fray Angelico Chavez, *Origins of New Mexico Families in the Spanish Colonial Period* (1954; reprint, Santa Fe, N.Mex.: William Gannon, 1975).

Maps

Both a good atlas and place-name index exist for research in New Mexico:

Beck, Warren, and Ynez D. Haase. *Historical Atlas of New Mexico.* Norman, Okla.: University of Oklahoma Press, 1969.

Pearce, T. M. *New Mexico Place Names: A Geographical Dictionary.* Albuquerque, N.Mex.: University of New Mexico Press, 1965.

Land Records

Public-Domain State

When New Mexico became a part of the United States, the land laws applied to it just as they did to the other more established states. New Mexico was admitted as a territory on 9 September 1850 and became a state on 6 January 1912.

The New Mexico State Records Center and Archives has large holdings of land records going back to 1693. Spanish land grants date from that time and continue to 1821. Mexican land holdings begin in 1821 and go to 1845. These original records are in Spanish but some have been translated.

Information regarding homestead lands for New Mexico is located at the BLM, the Department of the Interior, Field

Office, South Federal Place, P.O. Box 1449, Santa Fe, New Mexico 87504-1449.

In addition, there are deed books from 1850 to 1912 for most of the counties. There are also numerous mining deeds from 1850 to 1920. Both sets of deeds are indexed. Land records are also obtained in the respective counties where complete records are maintained by the county clerk for those people having business in a particular county.

Probate Records

Many early probates may be found at the New Mexico Records Center and Archives. Formal probate records are filed by the district court that serves a particular county, or by informal probate in the county clerk's office. The size and complexity of the estate determines whether it would be handled as a formal or informal practice.

There are thirteen judicial districts in the state, each covering one or more counties. In order to locate the work of the probate court, write to the clerk of the respective court in the county of focus for the research problem. Addresses are found in the section under court records. However, the county clerk's office may need to be contacted since laws change from time to time and probate records can be found there as well.

Court Records

The judicial system of New Mexico is much like the other states in this region. All have courts that are close to their people and by steps progress to the more complicated and further removed.

The supreme court reviews death penalty cases and necessary writs; it may review cases of the courts of appeal. The courts of appeal hear the mandatory review of death penalty cases and may review other criminal cases and extraordinary writs. The district courts are arranged into thirteen districts as listed below.

- First Judicial District includes Santa Fe, Los Alamos, and Rio Arriba counties: Court Clerk, P.O. Box 2268, Santa Fe 87504-2268.
- Second Judicial District includes Bernalillo County: Court Clerk, P.O. Box 488, Albuquerque 87103.
- Third Judicial District includes Dona Ana County: Court Clerk, 134 East Organ, Las Cruces 88001.
- Fourth Judicial District includes Guadalupe, Mora, and San Miguel counties: Court Clerk, Bin N, Las Vegas, New Mexico 87701.
- Fifth Judicial District includes Lea, Eddy, and Chaves counties: Court Clerk, P.O. Box 1776, Roswell 88201; P.O. Box 98, Carlsbad 88220; Court Clerk, Lea County Courthouse, Lovington 88260.
- Sixth Judicial District includes Grant, Hidalgo, and Luna counties: Court Clerk, P.O. Box 2339, Silver City 88061; Court Clerk, Drawer E, Lordsburg 88045; Court Clerk, Luna County Courthouse, Deming 88030.
- Seventh Judicial District includes Catron, Sierra, Socorro, and Torrance counties: Court Clerk, Drawer 32, Truth or Consequences 87901; Court Clerk, P.O. Box 1127, Socorro 87801; and Court Clerk, P.O. Box 78, Estancia 87016.
- Eighth Judicial District includes Colfax, Union, and Taos counties: Court Clerk, P.O. Box 160, Raton 87740; Court Clerk, P.O. Box 310, Clayton 88415; Court Clerk, P.O. Box 1715, Taos 87571.
- Ninth Judicial District includes Curry and Roosevelt counties: Court Clerk, Curry County Courthouse, Clovis 88101; Court Clerk, Roosevelt County Courthouse, Portales 88130.
- Tenth Judicial District includes Quay, De Baca, and Harding counties: Court Clerk, P.O. Box 1067, Tucumcari 88401; Court Clerk, P.O. Box 910, Fort Sumner 88119; Court Clerk, Harding County Courthouse, Mosquero 87733.
- Eleventh Judicial District includes McKinley and San Juan counties: Court Clerk, P.O. Box 460, Gallup 87301; Court Clerk, 103 South Oliver, Aztec 87410.
- Twelfth Judicial District includes Lincoln and Otero counties: Court Clerk, Drawer T, Alamogordo 88310; and Court Clerk, P.O. Box 725, Carrizozo 88301.
- Thirteenth Judicial District includes Sandoval, Cibola, and Valencia counties: Court Clerk, P.O. Box 1089, Los Lunas 87031; Court Clerk, P.O. Box 130, Bernalillo 87004; Court Clerk, P.O. Box 58, Grants 87020.

Below the district courts, magistrate courts handle civil cases; probate courts handle probates, guardianships, and adoptions for each of the judicial districts outlined above; and finally, metropolitan and municipal courts of record handle city violations. Court records before 1912 are archived at the New Mexico Records Center and Archives.

Tax Records

The New Mexico Records Center and Archives has property tax records for the whole state beginning in the 1870s and continuing to 1912. From 1884 to 1912, the records have been microfilmed. The remaining portion are original documents.

Individual counties have the property tax books from 1913 to the present.

Cemetery Records

The New Mexico Records Center and Archives also has some records of Catholic burials for the northern half of New Mexico, which began very early and extend to 1955. It also has records for the Fairview Cemetery in Santa Fe from 1871 to the present. Albuquerque Public Library has cemetery records that have been copied by New Mexico Genealogical Society members. The *New Mexico Genealogist* has published many while others are in book form. The History Library for the Museum of New Mexico has necrology files compiled by the Historical Society of New

Mexico. If one seeks Hispanic ancestors or relatives in New Mexico, it would be well to consult the works of Ryskamp and Beers for specific assistance and to study Bancroft for background (see Background Sources).

Church Records

By and large, the population of the state was both Spanish speaking and Catholic; thus an excursion into the diocesan records of the towns and villages presents an important avenue of research. The New Mexico State Records Center and Archives has early Catholic records from the archives of the Archdiocese of Santa Fe. Others may be found at the FHL. The records begin in the late 1600s and continue to 1955. They include baptisms, marriages, burials, and census records among other things. These also include some records for Native Americans and Mexicans. A reference to church holdings is Fray Angelico Chavez, *Archives of the Archdiocese of Santa Fe, 1678–1900* (St. Paul, Minn.: North Central Publishing Co., 1957). New Mexico Genealogical Society published *Albuquerque Baptisms, Archdiocese of Santa Fe, 1706–1850,* while other scattered birth records can be found in the *New Mexico Genealogist.*

The archives does not have Protestant church records as such, but it does have some Evangelical Navajo Indian records for about 1850. For Protestant records, almost all of which will be after 1850, one should consult the local churches in the area where the ancestor resided.

Military Records

The New Mexico Records Center and Archives' holdings of the Spanish and Mexican Archives includes military records for those respective eras. Territorial records from 1847–97 in this repository include Indian Wars of the 1850s, Union militia muster rolls and some records of Confederates, as well as the Spanish-American War.

On 23 April 1898 President William McKinley called for 125,000 troops to serve in the Spanish-American War. New Mexico was asked to supply 340 men for "special duty," but Governor Otero responded with not only this request but added both cavalry and mounted riflemen as well. The regiment was commanded by Captain Leonard Wood and Lieutenant Colonel Theodore Roosevelt. The troops were first mustered in at Santa Fe and joined the regiment at San Antonio, Texas. On 14 June 1898 they sailed from Tampa, Florida. They served on Cuban soil and were mustered out on 15 September 1898. These men would go down in the history books as Teddy Roosevelt's famed "Rough Riders."

For a roster of the men and information about their regiment, write Las Vegas Rough Rider's and City Museum, P.O. Box 179, Las Vegas, New Mexico 87701; and see Ralph Emerson Twitchell's *The Leading Facts of New Mexican History,* Vol. 2, pp. 530–43 (cited under Background Sources). The New Mexico Records Center and Archives has Union militia muster rolls for the Civil War period as well as some Spanish-American records and information for World War I and World War II.

The archives has thirteen folders of Confederate data. The Confederate Research Center at Hill Junior College, P.O. Box 619, Hillsboro, Texas 76645, has microfilm copies of the National Archives holdings for New Mexicans who served the confederate cause. For Union records of the Civil War, consult the National Archives records (see page 7) that have been microfilmed. There are four reels of indexes for New Mexico volunteers. The reference number is M242. For the compiled military service records, there are forty-six reels available, and the number is M427. For the records of any soldier and/or veteran who is buried in New Mexico, under federal jurisdiction, write the Cemetery Service of the National Cemetery System, Veterans Administration, 810 Vermont Avenue, Washington, D.C. 20420. These records begin in 1861.

Twentieth-century holdings at the state archives include World War I and II (service and discharges), and some Korean and Vietnam era records.

Periodicals, Newspapers, and Manuscript Collections

Periodicals

The New Mexico Historical Review has been printed since 1926 and is fully indexed. According to the editor it is a magazine of history that contains materials possibly helpful to genealogists in providing background information. Write to *The New Mexico Historical Review,* University of New Mexico, Albuquerque, New Mexico 87131. *La Cronica* is issued by the Historical Society of New Mexico, Box 5819, Santa Fe, New Mexico 87502. The New Mexico Genealogical Society publishes the *New Mexico Genealogist,* and Eddy County Genealogical Society publishes *Pecos Trails. Southwestern Association on Indian Affairs Quarterly* has been published by the association, 320 Galisteo, Suite 600, Santa Fe, New Mexico 87501, since 1954.

Newspapers

The following newspapers are presented to give the researcher a representative selection of publications covering several areas of the state and is not definitive: *Albuquerque Journal* (Albuquerque, 1880); *Las Cruces Sun-News* (Las Cruces, 1882); *Raton Range* (Raton, 1881); *Roswell Daily Record* (Roswell, 1888); and *Santa Fe New Mexican* (Santa Fe, 1849).

The state archivist recommends a definitive work: *New Mexico Newspapers,* edited by Pearce S. Grove, Becky J. Barnett, and Sandra J. Hansen (Albuquerque, N.Mex.: University of New Mexico Press, 1975).

Manuscripts

The New Mexico State Records Center and Archives has manuscript materials, very few newspapers, extensive collections of historical data, and family and corporate records available. One secondary source, described by the state archivist as being of especial importance, is *The Lucero de Godoi Family Tree,* which begins in the early 1600s and extends to 1870. Because of the work's scope, marriage records, and index, it is unique to the state. Moreover, the archives' special collections contain numerous biographical, historical, corporate, and personal papers, many of which have been donated by both corporate and private owners.

Of equal importance at the archives are the records of the Archdiocese of Santa Fe, which also began in the 1600s and continued to 1955, available on microfilm. They are extensive and include many baptisms, marriages, burials, and census records. In additon, there are some newspapers; three Spanish Period documents dated 1621, 1636, and 1664; and a number of documents from 1680 to 1821. *The Spanish Archives,* series 1, about one-third of the entire collection, covers the dates 1701–1820 and is especially useful to genealogists as it contains both wills and land transfers of that early period. Series 2 is less valuable as these records are civil documents, treaty instruments, etc.

Archives, Libraries, and Societies

New Mexico Records Center and Archives
404 Montezuma
Santa Fe, NM 87503

In 1959 the state passed the "Public Records Act" which created the State Records Center and Archives. The archives contains records of the Spanish-Mexican period as well as of the territorial and statehood eras. It also has judicial records and an extensive collection of private papers. The center is open to the public during regular business hours.

New Mexico Genealogical Society
P.O. Box 8283
Albuquerque, NM 87198-8283
Publishes *New Mexico Genealogist.*

Historical Society of New Mexico
Box 5819
Santa Fe, NM 87502
Publishes *La Cronica.*

Center for Southwest Research
Special Collections Department, General Library
University of New Mexico
Albuquerque, NM 87131

Collections include books, periodicals, microforms, manuscripts, archives, photographs, Western Americana and New Mexicana, and a rare book room.

Albuquerque Public Library, Special Collections
423 Central Avenue, N.E.
Albuquerque, NM 87102

Collection includes all New Mexico censuses and special censuses of New Mexico's Native population; part of the microfilmed Spanish, Mexican and Territorial Archives; indexes to Albuquerque obituaries; and extensive New Mexico and U.S. genealogical collections.

History Library, Palace of Governors
Museum of New Mexico
P.O. Box 2087
Santa Fe, NM 87504

Eddy County Genealogical Society
P.O. Box 461
Carlsbad, NM 88220
Publishes *Pecos Trails*

Special Focus Categories

Native American

Native to New Mexico are the Navajo, Mescalero Apache, and Jicarilla Apache, as well as pueblo dwellers—Taos, Zuni, Acoma, Santo Domingo, Isleta and others. Federal records concerning pueblo Native Americans are in the National Archives-Rocky Mountain Region in Denver, Colorado (see page 8). Records concerning the Apache and Navajo are at the National Archives-Pacific Southwest Region in Laguna Niguel, California (see page 9). The Bureau of Indian Affairs, 1570 Pacheco Street, Santa Fe, New Mexico 87501, has incomplete Indian Censuses for the eight northern pueblos from 1904.

County Resources

Land records including deeds, surveys and plats; marriage records; and some probate records are at the county clerk's office at the county seat. Military discharges, liens (mechanics, federal tax and judgement), mortgages, powers of attorney, and miscellaneous affidavits may also be found there. Probate records may be found in either the county clerk's office or the state district court clerk's office (see Court Records for appropriate court for county in question).

Counties may have sub-offices in towns other than the seat, but they have no permanent custody of records. The sub-offices were set up for conveniently transporting documents to the seat for permanent recording.

A number of counties still have territorial and, occasionally, Mexican era records in their custody. This explains record holdings earlier than formal organization for those counties. Earlier records not in counties should be available at the New Mexico State Records Center. Former county seats are in parentheses below the address.

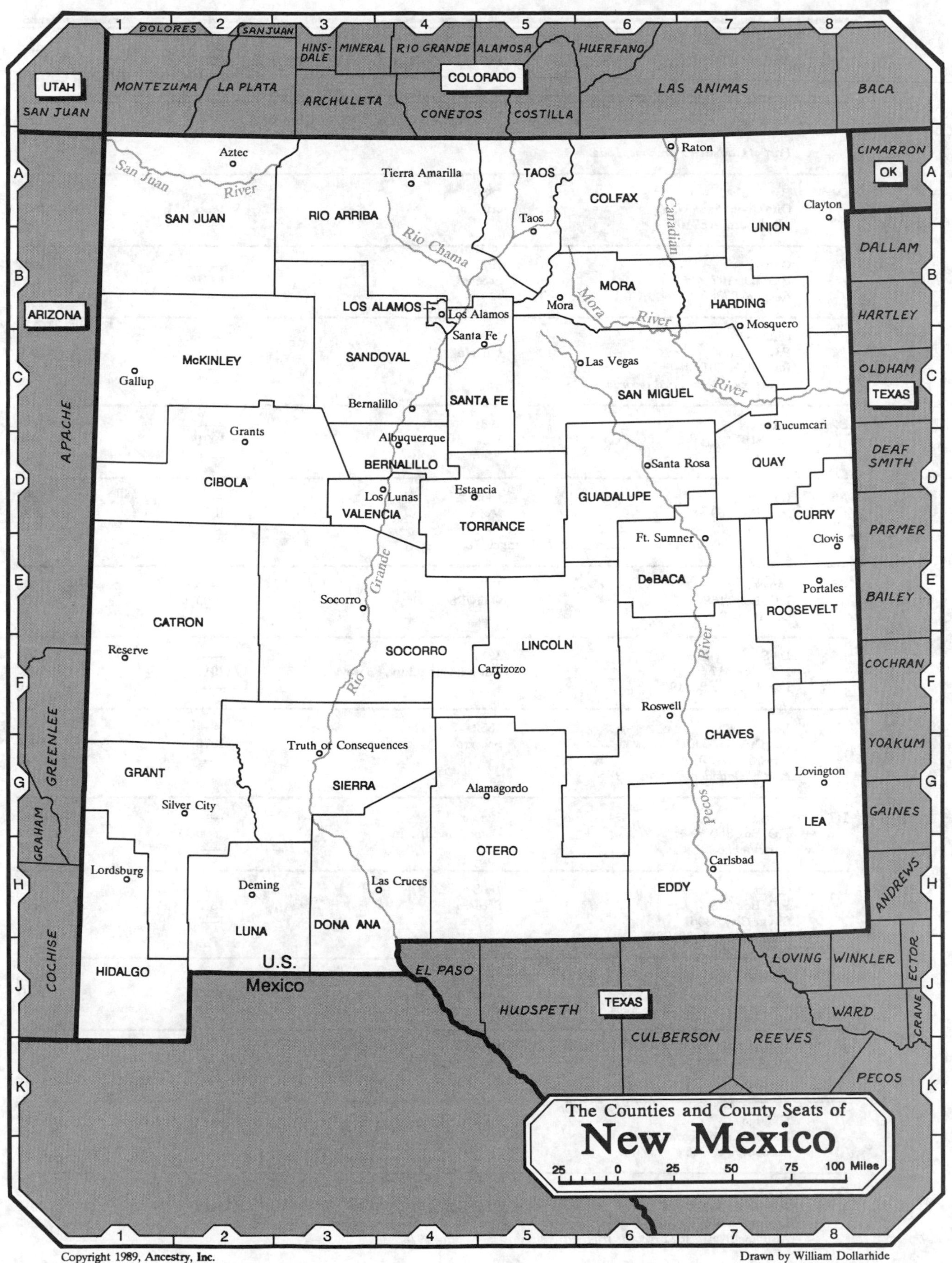

 Drawn by William Dollarhide

Map	County Address	Date Formed Parent County/ies	Birth Marriage Death	Land Probate District Court #
	Arizona *Part of Gadsden Purchase, 1854.*	1859 (became part of Dona Ana 1861–62) Tubac		
D4	Bernalillo One Civic Plaza N.W. Albuquerque 87102	1850 original	— 1885 —	1873 1902 #2
E2	Catron P.O. Box 197 Reserve 87830	1921 Socorro	— 1921? —	1921? 1921* #7
F7	Chaves P.O. Box 580 Roswell 88201 *Holds some territorial records.*	1889 Lincoln	— 1881 —	1887 1900 #5
D2	Cibola Box 816 Grants 87020	1981 Valencia	— 1981 —	1981 1981 #13
A6	Colfax P.O. Box 159 Raton 87740 (Elizabeth Town, 1869; Cimarron, 1872; Springer, 1882)	1869 Mora	— 1869 —	1864 1884 #8
D8	Curry P.O. Box 1168 Clovis 88101	1909 Quay/Roosevelt	— 1905 —	1903 1909 #3
E7	De Baca P.O. Box 347 Fort Sumner 88119	1917 Chaves/Guadalupe/Roosevelt	— 1917 —	1917 1917 #10
H3	Dona Ana Las Cruces 88001 (Mesilla, 1856) *Part of Gadsden Purchase, 1854.*	1852 Socorro	— 1870 —	1803 1833 #3
H7	Eddy P.O. Box 850 Carlsbad 88221	1889 Dona Ana/Lincoln	— 1895 —	1884 1912 #5
G1	Grant P.O. Box 898 Silver City 88061 (Pinos Altos, 1869–72)	1868 Socorro	— 1872 —	1872 1887 #6
D6	Guadalupe Santa Rosa 88435	1891 Lincoln/San Miguel	— 1893 —	1893 1907 #4
B7	Harding Mosquero 87733	1921 Mora/Union	— 1921 —	1921 1921 #10
J1	Hidalgo 300 S. Shakespeare Street Lordsburg 88045	1919 Grant	— 1895 —	1879 1920 #6
G8	Lea P.O. Box 1507 Lovington 88260 *Also has transcribed records from parent counties starting 1913.*	1917 Chaves/Eddy	— 1917 —	1918 1917 #5

Map	County Address	Date Formed Parent County/ies	Birth Marriage Death	Land Probate District Court #
F5	Lincoln	1869	—	1869
	P.O. Box 338	Socorro	1882	1881
	Carrizozo 88301		—	#12
	(Rio Bonito, formerly called Los Placitas then Lincoln, 1869–70)			
	County clerk has complete indexes for all records.			
B4	Los Alamos	1949	—	1949
	Los Alamos 87544	Sandoval/Santa Fe	1949	1950
			—	#1
H2	Luna	1901	—	pre-1901
	P.O. Box 1838	Dona Ana/Grant	1901	1901
	Deming 88031		—	#6
C1	McKinley	1899	—	1901
	P.O. Box 1268	Bernalillo/Valencia/	1901	1901
	Gallup 87301	San Juan/Ria Arriba	—	#11
B6	Mora	1860	—	1861
	P.O. Box 360	San Miguel	1891	1920s
	Mora 87732		—	#4
H5	Otero	1899	—	1890s
	P.O. Box 780	Dona Ana/Lincoln/Socorro	1899	1890s
	Alamogordo 88310		—	#12
D7	Quay	1903	—	1903
	P.O. Box 1225	Guadalupe/Union	1904	1892
	Tucumcari 88401		—	#10
A3	Rio Arriba	1850	—	1852
	P.O. Box 158	original	1852	1852
	Tierra Amarilla 87575		—	#1
E8	Roosevelt	1903	—	1892
	Portales 88130	Chaves/Guadalupe	1903	1903
			—	#9
C3	Sandoval	1903	—	1926
	P.O. Box 40	Rio Arriba	1926	1926
	Bernalillo 87004		—	#13
	Record loss, 1926.			
A1	San Juan	1887	—	1887
	P.O. Box 550	Rio Arriba	1887	1909
	Aztec 87410		—	#11
C6	San Miguel	1850	—	1887
	Las Vegas 87701	original	1905	1939
	(San Miguel, 1852–64)		—	#4
	Santa Ana	1850 (became part of Bernalillo, 1876)		
	(Pina Blanca, 1852–76)	original		
C4	Santa Fe	1850	—	1848
	P.O. Box 1985	original	1900	1894
	Santa Fe 87501		—	#1
	**First book of marriage records, 1863–99, is at the New Mexico Record Center and Archives (see Archives, Libraries, and Societies).*			
G3	Sierra	1884	—	1884
	300 Date Street	Socorro/Dona Ana/Grant	1884	1884
	Truth or Consequences 87901		—	#7
	(Hillsborough, 1884; Truth or Consequences, originally called Hot Springs)			

Map	County Address	Date Formed Parent County/ies	Birth Marriage Death	Land Probate District Court #
E3	Socorro P.O. Box 1 Socorro 87801 (Limitar, 1854–67)	1852 Valencia	 1887	1912* 1912* #7
	** Original records before 1912 are at the state records center.*			
A5	Taos Taos 87571	1850 original	— 1905* —	1880s 1912 #8
	**First book of marriage records, 1863–1905, is at the New Mexico Record Center and Archives (see Archives, Libraries, and Societies).*			
D5	Torrance P.O. Box 48 Estancia 87016	1903 Lincoln/San Miguel/ Socorro/Santa Fe/Valencia	— 1910 —	1910 1910 #7
A7	Union P.O. Box 430 Clayton 88415	1893 Colfax/Mora/San Miguel	— 1894 —	1894 1911 #8
D3	Valencia P.O. Box 969 Los Lunas 87031	1850 original	— 1880s —	1880s 1910 #13
	Original territorial records were filed at Valencia, 1852–72; Tome, 1872–74; Belen, 1874–76.			

NEW YORK

Roger D. Joslyn, C.G., F.A.S.G.

In 1609 Henry Hudson explored the river that bears his name, and in the 1620s the Dutch West India Company established settlements at Fort Orange (Albany) and Manhattan, influencing immigration by other northern Europeans. English, mostly from New England, came to Long Island where the boundary between New Netherland and New England had to be settled by treaty in 1650. The Dutch claimed New Netherland from the Connecticut to the Delaware rivers but were overthrown in 1664 by the English, who renamed the colony for the Duke of York. A brief comeback was staged by the Dutch in 1673, but after a year New York reverted to English control. In 1688–90 New York was part of the Dominion of New England, and some documents were generated in Boston.

By the time of the Revolutionary War, New Englanders had crossed westward into the eastern counties of New York, and settlers from Long Island and New Jersey had migrated to the lower Hudson valley. Huguenots had settled in New York City, New Rochelle, and elsewhere in the late 1600s, and Ulster Scots came to the Hudson area and settled in Orange and Ulster counties. The first major immigration of Germans to New York was in 1710, when 847 Palatine families settled in the Hudson Valley.

The Revolution was a major part of New York's history. The British occupied New York City and controlled all of Long Island and part of Westchester County. This provided a refuge for many Loyalists, including some from New Jersey, while patriots fled from Long Island to Connecticut and from elsewhere up the Hudson. Major battles were fought upstate and every effort was made to prevent the British from taking control of the Hudson Valley and dividing the colonies.

Up to the time of the Revolutionary War, New York had been slower to expand beyond its original settlements than most of the other colonies. Much of the land had been held by only a few people, and Native Americans threatened settlement west of the Hudson and Mohawk valleys. After the war, however, New York grew dramatically. Migrations and immigrations increased at a rapid pace, with only a slight interruption during the War of 1812. Immigration was fueled particularly by Europeans sailing to the port of New York. The state became the principal gateway for those heading west, mostly from New England to the Great Lakes and beyond, although a great number remained as families made "chain migrations" across New York (see David Paul Davenport, "The Yankee Settlement of New York, 1783–1820," *Genealogical Journal* 17 [1988/89]: 63–88, especially 70). Important to settlement were the Old Military Tract and St. Lawrence Ten Towns in the north; the Military Tract, Chenango Ten Towns, and Boston Ten Towns in the central region; and the Phelps-Gorham and Holland purchases further west. Travel was greatly enhanced by the completion of the Erie Canal in 1825, by which one could get from New York City to Buffalo in less than three weeks. The Hudson River was linked with Lake Champlain by a canal in the northeast and with the Delaware River by another canal in the southeast. By the mid-1800s, a busy system of stage lines and a network of railroads carried migrants, business people, and goods over the entire state, which promoted growth of cities and villages along their paths.

In the nineteenth century, immigrants swarmed through the port of New York, particularly the Irish and Germans in the mid-1800s, followed by Italians, Poles, Jews, and others by the turn of the century. Large numbers of blacks came north after the Civil War and more so after the world wars, followed by a sizeable Puerto Rican immigration after World War II. Today, many in New York City, if not born abroad themselves, have at least one parent who was.

New York had disputed areas with Massachusetts in Columbia County and over six million upstate acres, with Connecticut in Dutchess County, and with Vermont over the counties of Gloucester, Cumberland, and part of Charlotte. Earlier, New York lost two of its original twelve counties to Massachusetts: Cornwall to Maine in 1686 and Dukes in 1692. There was also disagreement over borders with New Jersey and Pennsylvania. Staten Island, long claimed by New Jersey, was not fully relinquished until 1855.

Under the Reorganization Act of 7 March 1788, New York was divided into 120 towns (not townships), many of which were already in existence. (In parts of New York, particularly in the west, land was often *surveyed* into townships, and many people today still use the term colloquially.) Towns are the primary point at which many records are kept and their number has increased greatly since 1788. Cities and incorporated villages are not part of towns, but a town may have several hamlets and other communities included in its own government.

The modern city of New York, since the turn of the century, has been comprised of five boroughs with coterminous counties. While often identified synonymously with the state of New York, the city is an entity of its own and some state laws concerning record keeping do not apply.

Vital Records

Not until the mid-nineteenth century was any attempt made by the state of New York to mandate the keeping of vital records. This makes the use of substitutes, such as church, cemetery, census, and newspaper records that much more important. A few vital records were entered into some early town records on Long Island and later in some towns along the eastern border, the latter evidently by New England settlers bringing with them a long standing tradition of such practice. However, the mass migration into New York just after the Revolution took place at a time when vital event recording slacked off greatly, even in New England.

The earliest items that might be classified as civil vital records in New York were marriage bonds, issued from 1639 to 1783. Names of the parties and the date of the bond were published in *Names of Persons for Whom Marriage Licenses Were Issued by the Secretary of the Province of New York, Previous to 1784* (1860; reprint with supplements, Baltimore, Md.: Genealogical Publishing Co., 1984), commonly referred to as "New York Marriages." This work did not include all the important information in the bonds, many of which were destroyed or damaged in the 1911 fire at the New York State Library (see Archives, Libraries, and Societies). From those that survived, Kenneth Scott compiled *Marriage Bonds of Colonial New York, 1753–1784* (New York, N.Y.: Saint Nicholas Society of the City of New York, 1972). Some records of marriages performed by justices of the peace have survived, of which a few have been published in *Tree Talks* and *The New York Genealogical and Biographical Record* (see Periodicals).

In 1847 a law was enacted requiring school districts to keep records of births, marriages, and deaths. While not a complete failure, compliance was scattered, and some towns that began to record vital events quickly stopped. Those that were kept are incomplete, and the latest that records were continued was 1852. The New York State Archives (see Archives, Libraries, and Societies) has originals of a few of these records; others are still with the town clerks or have been placed in historical societies. Some records have been published in *Tree Talks* and in the Cemetery, Church, and Town Records volumes compiled by the Daughters of the American Revolution in the State of New York (see Cemetery Records). Also useful for the nineteenth century are the marriages and deaths listed in the 1865 and 1875 New York state censuses for the census period ending 31 May of those years (the 1865 census also included deaths of officers and enlisted men). Marriages and deaths were also recorded in the 1855 state census but without names. The statistics of births, marriages, and deaths for each household in the 1825, 1835, and 1845 censuses can sometimes be used to advantage (see Census Records).

Another attempt by the state to require the keeping of vital records was made in 1880, and this law is the basis for the recording of births, marriages, and deaths in New York today. The original record is made in the town, village, or city in which the event took place, and a copy is sent to Albany where alphabetical indexes of names are arranged by event and thereunder by year. Each index entry lists the name, date of event, place, and certificate number; no maiden names, marital status, or ages are shown. Marriages are indexed by the name of each party, but there is no cross-referencing. Indexes for marriages for 1908 through 1914 are arranged by a Soundex code. It should be kept in mind that compliance with the 1880 law was slow, and many events were not recorded.

Copies of vital record certificates, marked "for genealogical research only," can be issued at the state or local level for the current fee of $11 each. This applies only to births recorded at least seventy-five years ago and to marriages and deaths recorded fifty years ago and earlier. Indexes to these records are available at the state archives in Albany, which also has a list of local registrars from which copies of the records may be obtained. Copies can also be obtained from the New York Department of Health, Vital Records Section, Genealogy Unit, Corning Tower Building, Empire State Plaza, Albany, New York 12237-0023, but a long delay for a response is likely because of the large backlog of requests. *Certified* copies of birth and death certificates, at the local or state level, are currently $15 each, and marriage certificates are $5 each.

Some cities kept vital records earlier than those sent to Albany under the 1880 law. These include Albany, Buffalo,

Rochester, Syracuse, Utica, Yonkers, and New York City. For Albany, Buffalo, and Yonkers, birth and death records before 1914 and marriages before 1908 should be sought from those cities' registrar of vital statistics, as copies were not sent to the state until those years. For the period 1908 through 1935, marriages were recorded with the county clerk, with copies sent to Albany, although some counties do not have these records for all of this time period.

Copies of vital records for New York City are *not* duplicated in Albany except for those areas annexed to the cities of New York or Brooklyn after 1880, such as Staten Island (Richmond County), the present Queens County, and certain parts of Bronx and Kings counties. For early vital records of New York City (Manhattan, Brooklyn, Queens, the Bronx, and Staten Island), contact the New York City Municipal Archives (see Archives, Libraries, and Societies). Births through 1897, marriages through 1937 (currently only for Manhattan and Brooklyn), and deaths through 1929 can be obtained by mail for $10 each ($5 if the certificate number is known), or one may visit the archives and search indexes and films of the records for a $5 daily search fee (copies of desired records would then be an additional $5 each). Later birth and death records should be obtained from the New York City Department of Health, Bureau of Vital Records, 125 Worth Street, New York, New York 10013; the current cost is $15 for each record. Marriage records for the Bronx, Queens, and Staten Island, and for Manhattan and Brooklyn after 1937 should be obtained from the appropriate borough office of the city clerk; the current fee is $10. Printed New York City vital records indexes (from 1888 for Manhattan and from 1898 for the other boroughs) are available at the New York Public Library (see Archives, Libraries, and Societies) for births and deaths to 1982 and for marriages to 1937. These are also available at the New York Genealogical and Biographical Society (see Archives, Libraries, and Societies) from about 1900 to the early 1930s. For more detail about availability of New York City vital records, see *Genealogical Resources in the New York Metropolitan Area* under Background Sources.

While there is no contemporary, comprehensive guide to New York State vital records, a nearly complete inventory of what existed in the early 1940s was compiled by the Historical Records Survey, *Guide to Public Vital Statistics Records in New York State (Including New York City)*, 3 vols. (Albany, N.Y.: Historical Records Survey, 1942). This guide includes existing records for the period 1847–52.

Since 1847 divorce actions in New York have been handled in the supreme court for the county in which the divorce was heard. New York divorce files, however, are sealed for one hundred years. In colonial times, petitions for divorce had to be made to the governor or legislature, and only a few were granted. The court of chancery granted divorces from 1787 to 1847. These older records are in the state archives or for the New York City area at the New York County Clerk's Office, Division of Old Records, 31 Chambers Street, 7th Floor, New York, New York 10007. See also Matteo Spalletta, "Divorce in Colonial New York," *The New-York Historical Society Quarterly* 39 (1955): 422–40.

Census Records

Federal

Population Schedules.

- Indexed—1790, 1800, 1810, 1820, 1830, 1840, 1850, 1860, 1870 (only Long Island), 1890 (fragment)
- Soundex—1880, 1900, 1920
- Unindexed—1870 (except Long Island), 1910

Industry and Agriculture Schedules.

- 1850, 1860, 1870, 1880

Mortality Schedules.

- 1850, 1860, 1870, 1880

Union Veterans Schedules.

- 1890 (indexed)

Microfilms of the federal censuses for New York, 1790–1920, and corresponding book and microfilm indexes are available in several places throughout the state and country (see pages 2–3). There are three published indexes for the 1800 census. The 1850 index published by AISI covers only half of the towns for Westchester County, as the other half were indexed in error from the 1860 census. Some counties have their "short form" copies of the 1880 census, which serve as complete indexes (by district) to that census (see the Douglas-Yates guide mentioned below). Within the state, the National Archives-Northeast Region (see page 8) has complete sets of these records as does the New York Public Library, the New York State Library, and the Onondaga County Public Library (see Archives, Libraries, and Societies). The New York Genealogical and Biographical Society has the census through 1880 for New York and 1900 for New York City. Most of these collections include the 1910 street indexes to enumeration districts for the New York City boroughs of Manhattan and Brooklyn. Many libraries with genealogical collections have films of most or all the censuses for their particular county and often for surrounding counties. Several early New York censuses have been published, many in *Tree Talks*, some in *The New York Genealogical and Biographical Record*, and in the volumes by Ralph Van Wood for Cayuga, Herkimer, Oneida, and Ontario counties. Two enumerations were taken in New York City in 1870. Parts of the enumerations for the towns of Eastchester (Westchester County) and Brookhaven (Suffolk County) are among the few surviving schedules of the 1890 federal census. A Manhattan 1890 police census, available at the Municipal Archives, also fills part of the void of the destroyed federal census. Damaged and missing censuses include the following:

- **1810:** Cortland and part of Broome County—missing
- **1860:** Chenango and Columbia counties—damaged
- **1880:** Suffolk County and New York City Wards 21 and 22—damaged

The corresponding federal mortality, agricultural, industry/manufacturing, and other schedules are available at the New York State Library, and films of these records are also at the Queensborough Library in Jamaica, Long Island.

Colonial and State

Some important censuses were taken in colonial New York, some of which have been extracted and published (see Background Sources). Others have been published in journals such as *The New York Genealogical and Biographical Record* and the *National Genealogical Society Quarterly*.

Of almost greater value in New York than the federal are the state censuses, taken every ten years from 1825 to 1875, in 1892, and again in 1905, 1915, and 1925 (pre-1825 state censuses were destroyed in the 1911 state library fire). Most of these censuses that have survived can be found with the county clerk, although some are with the county historian or in other locations. For a list of the whereabouts of these censuses, consult Marilyn Douglas and Melinda Yates, comps., *New York State Census Records, 1790–1925,* Bibliography Bulletin 88 of the New York State Library (Albany, 1981), which has some errors and omissions. Films of many of the 1855, 1865, and 1875 censuses are at the New York Genealogical and Biographical Society, and the New York Public Library has most films for 1855. The New York State Library has microfilms of all the 1915 and 1925 censuses for the entire state and many of the earlier state censuses.

Indexes have been prepared for some of the state censuses and are usually found with the county historian or at the county historical society. Some of these indexes are mentioned in the Douglas-Yates guide; others are listed in David Paul Davenport's "The State Censuses of New York, 1825–75," *Genealogical Journal* 14 (1985–86): 172–97. The Douglas-Yates guide also shows the existence of the *county* copies of the federal censuses available locally, which are useful for checking against the *federal* copies as filmed by the National Archives. The *state* copies of the census perished in the 1911 New York State Library fire.

The 1825, 1835, and 1845 state censuses are similar to pre-1850 federal censuses in that only the name of the head of the household is listed, although there is valuable information about the composition of the household, its agriculture and commerce, and so forth. Beginning in 1855, every person is listed, with his or her relationship to the head of the household, and, if a native New Yorker, the county of birth is shown. Years of residency in the town or city in which enumerated are also given, as is citizenship status for adult males. The 1865 census dropped the years residency column but added ones for parents of how many children and number of times married. It also listed active and veteran servicemen. Later state censuses provide similar information, although the schedules for 1892 listed only name, sex, color, age, country of birth, whether or not a U.S. citizen, and occupation. The date and court of naturalization for naturalized citizens was a feature of the 1925 census. For more details, consult the Douglas-Yates guide.

The surviving 1790 *state* census schedules for Albany County were compiled by Kenneth Scott in *New York: State Census of Albany County Towns in 1790* (1975; reprint, Baltimore, Md.: Clearfield Co., 1991). In his work, Scott also compared these schedules with the 1790 *federal* census for Albany County.

The New York State Library has some original census records and copies of others; consult the Douglas-Yates guide for more information, but note that the schedules for Albany County are now in the County Hall of Records, 250 South Pearl Street, Albany, New York 12202.

Background Sources

New York state abounds in published history, so much so that only a few representative titles can be listed here. These include Alexander C. Flick, ed., *History of the State of New York,* 10 vols. (1933–37; reprint, Port Washington, N.Y.: Kennikat Press, 1962); David M. Ellis, et al., *A History of New York State,* rev. ed. (Ithaca, N.Y.: Cornell University Press, 1967); Bruce Bliven, Jr., *New York: A Bicentennial History* (New York, N.Y.: Norton, 1981); and Michael G. Kammen, *Colonial New York: A History* (New York, N.Y.: Scribners, 1975).

For the earlier period one should not overlook Edmund B. O'Callaghan, ed., *Documentary History of the State of New-York,* 4 vols. (1849–51; reprint, Vol. 1, West Jordan, Utah: Stemmons Publications, 1984), which concerns the seventeenth and eighteenth centuries but is not indexed. Various lists of persons from these volumes were reprinted as *Lists of Inhabitants of Colonial New York* (Baltimore, Md.: Genealogical Publishing Co., 1989).

O'Callaghan also edited *Calendar of Historical Manuscripts in the Office of Secretary of State, Albany, N.Y.* 2 vols. (1865–66; reprint, Ridgewood, N.J.: Gregg Press, 1968). Volume 1 covers the Dutch period, 1632–64, and volume 2 covers the English, 1664–1776. Some of these documents were lost or damaged in the state library fire in 1911. O'Callaghan translated a great many of the Dutch documents, but most remained unpublished. With Berthold Fernow, he edited the fifteen-volume *Documents Relating to the Colonial History of the State of New-York* (1853–87; reprint, New York, N.Y.: A.M.S. Press, 1969). The first ten volumes were compiled from records in Amsterdam, Paris, and London, with volume 11 serving as the index. Volumes 12–14 cover documents found in New York state, and volume 15 covers the Revolutionary War (see Military Records). Since the 1970s, the surviving original Dutch and English material up to 1700 is being published in the series titled *New York Historical Manuscripts,* although some of the volumes to date, under various editors and publishers, have included material not in O'Callaghan's *Calendar,* such as the Brooklyn Dutch Church records and records of the New Amsterdam notary, Salomon Lachaire.

A major contribution focusing on one immigrant group is Henry Z Jones, Jr., *The Palatine Families of New York: A Study of the German Immigrants Who Arrived in Colonial*

New York in 1710, 2 vols. (Universal City, Calif.: the author, 1985).

More recent scholarship and reinterpretations of New York history are found in articles in *New York History, The New-York Historical Society Quarterly* (defunct), and *The William and Mary Quarterly* (see Virginia).

Much of the state's regional history consists of three- or four-volume works, the first two or three volumes of which are the "history" and the rest "mug" books. The term mug book refers to those printed sources which present pictures and biographies of those who subscribed to the publication. The latter are useful for clues about families, but they are not always factual. A long list of works on regional New York history and genealogy is found in Austin's "Genealogical Research in Upstate New York" (see under Guides below).

Guides

For a good overview, see the New York chapters in *Genealogical Research: Methods and Sources,* Vol. 1, rev. ed., edited by Milton Rubincam (Washington, D.C.: American Society of Genealogists, 1980). Kenn Stryker-Rodda wrote chapters on New Netherland, Long Island, Staten Island, and the Hudson Valley counties (pages 168–95), and Mary J. Sibley on "Upstate New York," updated by Gerald J. Parsons (pages 195–220).

George K. Schweitzer, *New York Genealogical Research* (Knoxville, Tenn.: the author, 1988), is a good, inexpensive New York guide.

Florence Clint, *New York Area Key* (Elizabeth, Colo.: Keyline Publishers, 1979), while it has many errors and omissions, can help one prepare for on-site research. It lists FHL films of state censuses.

Kate Burke, *Searching in New York: A Reference Guide to Public and Private Records* (Costa Mesa, Calif.: ISC Publications, 1987), includes libraries and hospitals and is useful for adoptees. Some information is not current or sufficiently detailed.

John Austin, "Genealogical Research in Upstate New York, An Informal Finding List of Published Materials" (1983), is out of print but a very useful guide to such things as items in *Tree Talks* and abstracts of and indexes to wills.

Gateway to America: Genealogical Research in the New York State Library, 2d ed., rev. (Albany, N.Y.: New York State Library, 1982), is available from the library for $3.

Guide to Records in the New York State Archives (Albany, N.Y.: State Archives, 1981) is out of print but is being revised.

"Research in Progress in New York History," a feature in *New York History,* indexing books and articles since 1952, was continued in 1968 as *Research and Publications in New York State History,* published by the University of the State of New York.

Estelle M. Guzik, ed., *Genealogical Resources in the New York Metropolitan Area* (New York, N.Y.: Jewish Genealogical Society, 1989), is the best guide to most nineteenth- and twentieth-century New York City sources, as well as New York City area Jewish research. It should be supplemented by Rosalie Fellows Bailey, *Guide to Genealogical and Biographical Sources for New York City (Manhattan) 1783–1898* (New York, N.Y.: the author, 1954), which concerns many other and earlier records, some covering more than just Manhattan. Bailey's guide was revised from its original publication in *The New England Historical and Genealogical Register* 106–08 (1952–54).

Arlene H. Eakle and L. Ray Gunn, *Descriptive Inventory of the New York Collection,* Number 4 of Finding Aids to the Microfilmed Manuscript Collection of the Genealogical Society of Utah, edited by Roger M. Haigh (Salt Lake City, Utah: University of Utah Press, 1980), does not include film numbers, and much has been added since its publication.

J. H. French, *Gazetteer of the State of New York* (1860; reprint, Interlaken, N.Y.: Heart of the Lakes Publishing, 1980), is the best of several gazetteers and should be used with Frank Place, II, comp., *Index of Persons and Names in J. H. French's Gazetteer of the State of New York (1860)* (Cortland, N.Y.: Cortland County Historical Society, 1962), and *Supplementary Index of Names and Places* (Albany, N.Y.: University of the State of New York, 1966). For a modern list of New York places, consult *Gazetteer of the State of New York,* rev. ed. (Albany, N.Y.: Health Education Series, 1980).

Herbert F. Seversmith and Kenn Stryker-Rodda, *Long Island Genealogical Source Material,* National Genealogical Society Special Publication 24, 2d printing (Washington, D.C.: National Genealogical Society, 1980), is an excellent bibliography of about 850 published and manuscript sources in 125 libraries throughout the country.

Rosalie Fellows Bailey, *Dutch Systems in Family Naming: New York-New Jersey,* National Genealogical Society Special Publication 12, 3d printing (Washington, D.C.: National Genealogical Society, 1978), covers a difficult subject.

Maps

The first place to obtain a map is in each county, usually in the county treasurer's office for a dollar or two. Most maps are large enough to show all county roads, and a further benefit is that most show the towns in different colors, making them easily distinguishable. Many more maps can be found at the courthouse in the county clerk's or tax offices. They can be useful for locating a specific piece of property; but the further back in time, the fewer maps will be available. A map is sometimes included with a recorded deed. More detailed maps are available for cities, villages, and towns, and a good place to look for these would be local libraries. U. S. topographical maps (see page 4) are useful for locating cemeteries. Excellent map collections are at the New York Public Library, the New York State Archives, and the New-York Historical Society.

Numerous county maps are found in county histories and county atlases. For a list of these, see Albert Hazen Wright, *A Check List of New York State County Maps Published 1779–1945* (Ithaca, N.Y.: Cornell University, 1965).

On a larger scale, David H. Burr's *An Atlas of the State of New York* (New York, N.Y.: David H. Burr, 1829) and Joseph R. Bien's *Atlas of the State of New York* (New York, N.Y.: J. Bien & Co., 1895) are useful; the latter work includes some original land patents. For patents, 1624–1800, and a series of maps showing county formations and migration routes, consult the excellent *Richards Atlas of New York State,* 2d ed., edited by Robert J. Rayback (Phoenix, N.Y.: Frank E. Richards, 1965). A state map showing all counties and towns can be obtained from the New York State Department of Environmental Conservation.

David Kendall Martin, "The Districts of Albany County, New York, 1772–1784," *The NYG&B Newsletter* 1 (1990): 9, 12–13, while covering only one section of the province, includes maps that help show that county's divisions prior to the creation of towns in 1788.

A "Map of the Meetings constituting New-York Yearly Meeting of Friends," 1821, by Dr. Shadrach Ricketson, is found facing page 263 in volume 45 of *The New York Genealogical and Biographical Record* (1914).

Land Records

State-Land State

Colonial and state government records of patents, grants, and deeds are at the New York State Archives and identified in *Public Records Relating to Land in New York State* (Albany, N.Y.: New York State Archives, 1979). See also *Calendar of N.Y. Colonial Manuscripts Indorsed Land Papers . . . 1643–1803* (1864; reprint, Harrison, N.Y.: Harbor Hill Books, 1987). The Secretary of State Deeds, dating from colonial times and including many private conveyances up to about 1775 (fewer to about 1830), are on microfilm at the state archives, with the usual grantor and grantee indexes. Charles F. Grim's *An Essay Towards an Improved Register of Deeds, City and County of New York to December 31, 1799 "Inclusive"* (New York, N.Y.: Gould, Banks & Co., 1832) indexes those Secretary of States Deeds pertaining to New York City property.

Abstracts of early deeds for Kings and Westchester counties have been published in *The New York Genealogical and Biographical Record,* beginning in volumes 48 and 50 respectively. Fred Q. Bowman, *Landholders of Northeastern New York, 1739–1802* (Baltimore, Md.: Genealogical Publishing Co., 1983), covers the counties of Clinton, Essex, Franklin, Warren, and Washington.

Isaac N. P. Stokes's superb *Iconography of Manhattan Island 1498–1909,* 6 vols. (1915–28; reprint, New York, N.Y.: Arno Press, 1967), is based heavily on land records and includes detailed maps. It is well indexed.

Bounty land in the central part of the state was awarded by lottery to New York Revolutionary War soldiers, although most sold their allotments rather than settle on them. The successful drawers are listed in *The Balloting Book, and Other Documents Relating to Military Bounty Lands in the State of New York* (Albany, N.Y.: Packard & Van Benthuysen, 1825).

To help understand the settlement of western New York, see Orsamus Turner, *History of Pioneer Settlement of Phelps and Gorham Purchase and Morris' Reserve* (1851; reprint with supplements and indexes by LaVerne C. Cooley and George E. Lookup, Interlaken, N.Y.: Heart of the Lakes Publishing, 1976). Turner also wrote *Pioneer History of the Holland Land Purchase of Western New York* (1850; reprint with Cooley's index, Interlaken, N.Y.: Heart of the Lakes Publishing, 1976, and Bowie, Md.: Heritage Books, 1991). See also William Chazanof, *Joseph Ellicott and the Holland Land Company: The Opening of Western New York* (Syracuse, N.Y.: Syracuse University Press, 1970); Ruth L. Higgins, *Expansion in New York* (1931; reprint, Philadelphia, Pa.: Porcupine Press, 1974); and William Wyckoff, *The Developer's Frontier: The Making of the Western New York Landscape* (New Haven, Conn.: Yale University Press, 1988). Microfilm of the archives of the Holland Land Company is available at the Daniel E. Reed Library, State University at Fredonia, Fredonia, New York 14063; Research Guide No. 55 explains these records. Karen E. Livsey's *Western New York Land Transactions, 1804–1824* (Baltimore, Md.: Genealogical Publishing Co., 1991) is an index to early Holland Company sales. Other land company records are in the state library in Albany and scattered among other repositories.

In the counties are deeds and mortgages and corresponding indexes to each type of record (published indexes covering into the nineteenth century are available for New York and Albany counties). These records in the county clerk's office begin mostly with the formation of the county, but many colonial deeds were recorded in town records. Also, many land transactions were not recorded in earlier times since it was a long way to the courthouse, or the family moved on before the document could get recorded. Furthermore, with some New York lands in dispute, deed holders were reluctant to bring them in for recording. Sometimes deeds were recorded in the neighboring county, as its courthouse was closer to the party or parties involved. Many early New Yorkers simply leased land from individuals or families who held vast acreage. Evidence of residency in those cases might be found in the private papers of manorial families such as the Livingstons, Van Rensselaers, and Van Cortlandts. Unfortunately, there is no guide to the location of all manorial records, but for the Van Cortlandts, Sung Bok Kim's *Landlord and Tenant in Colonial New York* (Chapel Hill, N.C.: University of North Carolina Press, 1978) includes a good bibliography. The Livingston papers are available at the Historic Hudson Valley Library in Tarrytown, New York, and on film at the FHL, and the Van Rensselaer papers are in the state archives in Albany.

Probate Records

Estate records have been handled in New York in the surrogate's court since 1787 when a system of county surrogate's courts was established. Prior to that time most estates were handled in New York City, the capital until 1797. Abstracts of most of the earlier records are found in *Abstracts of Wills on File in the Surrogate's Office, County of New York, 1665–1800,* in volumes 25–41 of the New-York Historical Society Collections (New York, 1892–1909), usually referred to as "New York Wills," and in Berthold Fernow, comp. and ed., *Calendar of Wills on File and Recorded in the Offices of the Court of Appeals, of the County Clerk at Albany and of the Secretary of State 1626–1836* (1896; reprint, Baltimore, Md.: Clearfield Co., 1991). Only the first of these includes letters of administration, but both contain errors (the former set actually includes two volumes of corrections and additions). Also, there is some overlap between these sources, so both should be consulted. Other material has been published in abstract form in Kenneth Scott: *Genealogical Data from New York Administration Bonds 1753–1799,* volume 10 of the New York Genealogical and Biographical Society Collections (New York, 1969); *Genealogical Data From Further New York Administration Bonds 1791–1798,* volume 11 of the New York Genealogical and Biographical Society Collections (New York, 1971); *Genealogical Data from Administration Papers in the New York State Court of Appeals in Albany* (New York, N.Y.: National Society of Colonial Dames of the State of New York, 1972); *Records of the Chancery Court, Province and State of New York: Guardianships, 1691–1815* (New York, N.Y.: Holland Society of New York, 1971); and with James A. Owre, *Genealogical Data From Inventories Of New York Estates 1666–1825* (New York, N.Y.: New York Genealogical and Biographical Society, 1970). Scott also published articles on New York wills, guardianships, and inventories in the *National Genealogical Society Quarterly,* 51:90; 54:98, 246; 55:119; and 56:51. Many original wills are available on microfilm at the New York Genealogical and Biographical Society.

Before 1787, some wills were recorded in the counties and occasionally in town records. See Gustave Anjou, *Ulster County, N.Y. Probate Records,* 2 vols. (New York, N.Y.: the author, 1906), covering records 1663–1766 and 1792–1827, and the two volumes by William S. Pelletreau, *Early Long Island Wills of Suffolk County, 1691–1703* and *Early Wills of Westchester County New York from 1664 to 1784* (New York, N.Y.: Francis P. Harper, 1897, 1898). The former does not include those in Suffolk County sessions records (which are in manuscript at the New York Genealogical and Biographical Society) or a few in early county deed books. Better abstracts of the Westchester County wills are found in Pelletreau's *Abstracts of Wills on File* (see also below for Westchester County). Other early New York wills have been published in *The New York Genealogical and Biographical Record,* such as those for Kings County mostly from deeds, 1684–1719, in volume 47; Queens County wills from deeds, 1683–1744, in volume 65; Dutchess County wills in volume 61; and Westchester County wills in volume 55. For the period 1688–90, New York was part of the Dominion of New England, and during that time estates valued at over £50 were to be probated in Boston. Seventeen wills of New York residents were brought to Boston, and abstracts of these are found in volumes 12 and 13 of *The American Genealogist* (see page 7).

Beginning in 1830, a New York law required that the petition for probate include a list of each legal heir—whether or not there was a will, and whether or not he or she was named in the will—his or her relationship to the deceased, and his or her residence. This is often the single most important document in an estate file, but it is not generally found in the record books until modern times.

Most counties have consolidated indexes to all estate matters, including wills, administrations, guardianships, and so forth. In some counties, however, the types of estates may be indexed separately. Likewise, all the documents pertaining to a particular estate may not be filed together but separately according to type of action such as bonds, accounts, and inventories, and thereunder by date of filing. Many counties have particularly separated the original wills—many early ones are not on file—from the rest of the documents pertaining to an estate. Some early letters of administration give the relationship of the administrator to the deceased, and some early letters of guardianship provide the date of birth of the minor.

A New York law permits clerks of the surrogate court to impose a stiff fee (currently $70) to search for an estate over twenty-five years old (Surrogate's Procedure Act Section 2402, item 14), and the cost of copies of the documents can be extra. Some indexes to wills, administrations, and guardianships, and some abstracts of these records for many counties, can be found in the New York State Library, the New York Public Library, the New York Genealogical and Biographical Society, and in other libraries. Many such indexes and abstracts were prepared by the late Gertrude A. Barber of Brooklyn or by one of her sisters, Ray C. Sawyer and Minnie Cowen. The indexes and abstracts serve as guides only and should be verified in the original record books and files. Abstracts of New York state wills to about 1830, with an all-name index by W. A. D. Eardeley, at the Brooklyn Historical Society are also helpful. Abstracts of wills and letters of administration and guardianship have been published in such journals as *Tree Talks* and *The New York Genealogical and Biographical Record.*

An excellent discussion of early New York estates is Harry Macy, Jr., "New York Probate Records Before 1787," *The NYG&B Newsletter* 2 (1991): 11–15.

Court Records

The county clerk is the keeper of most civil and criminal trial court records, naturalizations, marriages (1908–35), censuses (county copies of the federal census and the state censuses), as well as deeds and mortgages. Estate matters are recorded with the clerk of the county surrogate court (see Probate Records), but before 1847 cases involving property of minor heirs and incompetents were often heard in the court of chancery. The *Inventory of the County Archives of New York State,* taken by the Historical Records Survey, 6 vols. (Albany N.Y., and New York, N.Y.: WPA, 1937–40), was published only for Albany, Broome, Cattaraugus, Chautauqua, Chemung, and Ulster counties. Unpublished material, excluding that for the five counties of New York City, is at the New York State Archives.

Much state court record material is at the state archives and the Division of Old Records, New York County Clerk's Office (see Vital Records). An excellent guide to some of these records is James D. Folts and others, *"Duely & Constantly Kept": A History of the New York Supreme Court, 1691–1847 and An Inventory of Its Records (Albany, Utica, and Geneva Offices), 1797-1847* (Albany, N.Y.: New York State Court of Appeals and the New York State Archives and Records Administration, 1991). Federal court records are at the National Archives-Northeast Region (see page 8), covering the U.S. district and circuit courts in New York for various periods from 1789 to 1967 and early admiralty courts from 1685 to 1838.

Tax Records

Scattered town and precinct tax records for a few years in the 1770s and 1780s and nearly complete lists for the whole state, 1799–1804, are at the New York State Archives, although for the latter period the surviving 1804 rolls cover only delinquent taxes of nonresidents. New York City tax records are at the Municipal Archives (see Archives, Libraries, and Societies). Some early assessment rolls have been published in *The New York Genealogical and Biographical Record,* such as those for New York City, 1730, in volume 95; New Rochelle, 1767, in volume 107; and Ulster County, 1709–21, in volume 62. See also volumes 43–44 of the New-York Historical Society's *Collections* for New York City assessments 1695–99. A few counties, such as Ontario, have retained their early tax records, but most do not have them until about 1850 or even later. Many old tax lists are to be found in manuscript collections. Dutchess County is fortunate to have a long series of eighteenth century tax records. See Clifford M. Buck, *Dutchess County, NY Tax Lists 1718–1787 with Rombout Precinct by William Willis Reese,* edited by Arthur and Nancy Kelly (Rhinebeck, N.Y.: Kinship, 1990).

Some of the 1798 U.S. Direct Tax records survive for New York. Two examples are David Kendall Martin, "A 1798 United States Assessment List for Northern New York State [Plattsburgh]," *The New York Genealogical and Biographical Record* 113 (1982): 93–102; and C. R. Carey, "Town of Deer Park 1798 Assessment Records," *Orange County Historical Society Publication No. 8* (Goshen, 1978–79), 13–25.

Cemetery Records

The largest number of New York cemetery records (the bulk of which are actually transcriptions of cemetery marker inscriptions) is found in the multivolume collection of the Daughters of the American Revolution in the State of New York Cemetery, Church, and Town Records, located at the New York State Library, the New York Public Library, and the DAR Library in Washington, D.C. Scattered volumes are found in other libraries, including many local libraries in the area in which a particular cemetery is located. To determine which cemeteries have been covered, consult the *Master Index,* 3d ed., compiled by Constance M. Whitacre, and her *Master Index Supplement 1972–1978 Records and Corrections* (Albany, N.Y.: the compiler, 1978). There is also a master card catalog index to the collection, arranged by place, at the New York State Library. While these DAR collections are useful, it is unfortunate that most of the cemetery inscriptions have been alphabetized, thus destroying important clues based on the location of the grave markers.

Some counties have had many or nearly all of their cemetery records published. These include Putnam, Dutchess, and Ulster counties along the Hudson River, and Genesee County in the west. Another large published collection is *Some Cemeteries of the Between-the-Lakes Country,* 3 vols. (Trumansburg, N.Y.: Chief Taughannock Chapter, DAR, 1974), covering part of the counties of Seneca, Schuyler, and Tompkins. The Orange County Genealogical Society is publishing that county's cemetery records, a volume for each town. Published cemetery records are also found in *Tree Talks, The New York Genealogical and Biographical Record,* and other genealogical journals. Many transcriptions are in manuscript form, such as those by Gertrude A. Barber and her sisters, Ray C. Sawyer and Minnie Cowen. Local libraries and historical societies throughout the state are likely to have collections of cemetery records for their area. A list of New York City area cemeteries, with addresses and telephone numbers, is available from the Municipal Archives.

Church Records

Particularly useful as vital records substitutes among the surviving New York church records are those of the Dutch Reformed, Lutheran, Anglican, and Quaker groups. For a general background about New York churches, consult *Ecclesiastical Records, State of New York,* 7 vols. (Albany, N.Y.: James B. Lyon, 1901–05, 1916). Volume 7 is an index.

For the records themselves, see *Guide to Vital Statistics Records in New York State Churches (Exclusive of New York City),* 2 vols. (Albany, N.Y.: Historical Records Survey, 1942), and *Guide to Vital Statistics Records in the City of New York, Boroughs of the Bronx, Brooklyn, Manhattan,*

Queens, Richmond. Churches, 5 vols. (New York, N.Y.: Historical Records Survey, 1942). There are also several volumes arranged by denomination. These guides, although dated, are still useful for learning what existed and where.

The largest collection of New York church records is probably that of the Daughters of the American Revolution in the State of New York Cemetery, Church, and Town Records (see Cemetery Records above). Scattered volumes may be found in local libraries for the area in which a particular church is located. To determine what records have been covered, consult the *Master Index* and *Supplement* (see Cemetery Records). A card catalog at the state library indexes this collection by county and thereunder by town, village, or other municipality.

Another large collection was commissioned by the New York Genealogical and Biographical Society and is known by the name of its editor, Royden Woodward Vosburgh. Its 101 volumes cover mostly Dutch, German-Lutheran, and Presbyterian records, but not all are indexed. Besides the New York Genealogical and Biographical Society, these volumes are available at the Connecticut State Library and on film at the New York Public Library, the FHL, and in other libraries. Some of the Vosburgh Collection, particularly for Hudson Valley churches, has been published by Arthur C. M. Kelly and Jean D. Worden. Kelly has also published church records that were not part of the Vosburgh series.

For western New York there is a collection of church records compiled by the Study Center for Early Religious Life in Western New York at Ithaca College. The study center is now defunct, but the collection is at the Department of Manuscripts and University Archives, Cornell University, Ithaca, New York 14853-5310. A published list of the records is available.

Quakers are treated in John Cox, Jr., "Quaker Records in New York," *The New York Genealogical and Biographical Record* 45 (1914): 263–69, 366–73. Some Quaker records are published such as those for New York City and Long Island in volume 3 of William Wade Hinshaw's *Encyclopedia of American Quaker Genealogy* (1940; reprint, Baltimore, Md.: Genealogical Publishing Co., 1969, 1991) and Shirley V. Anson and Laura M. Jenkins, comps., *Quaker History and Genealogy of the Marlborough Monthly Meeting, Ulster County, N.Y. 1804–1900+* (Baltimore, Md.: Gateway Press, 1980). See also Loren V. Fay, ed., *Quaker Census of 1828* (Rhinebeck, N.Y.: Kinship, 1989). Original and full copies of New York state Quaker records from 1663 are at the Haviland Records Room, Society of Friends, 222 East 16th Street, New York, New York 10003, and many films and abstracts are at the New York Genealogical and Biographical Society.

A very helpful guide for Jewish genealogical sources in the New York City area is Estelle M. Guzik, ed., *Genealogical Resources in the New York Metropolitan Area* (see Background Sources).

Many church records, mostly early and particularly for Long Island, New York City, and the Hudson River Valley, have been published in *The New York Genealogical and Biographical Record* with a large collection of unpublished records maintained by the New York Genealogical and Biographical Society and by other repositories with manuscript collections.

Military Records

Most pre-twentieth-century New York military records are at the New York State Archives, although some were destroyed or damaged in the 1911 fire at the New York State Library.

Volumes 2 and 3 of the *Annual Report of the State Historian* (Albany and New York, 1896, 1897) contain collected lists of colonial militia. See also Edward F. DeLancey, ed., *Muster Rolls of New York Provincial Troops 1755–1764,* Vol. 24 of the New-York Historical Society Collections (1892; reprint, Bowie, Md.: Heritage Books, 1990), in which the age, birthplace, and occupation are given for many soldiers.

Berthold Fernow, *New York in the Revolution,* Vol. 1 (New Orleans, La.: Polyanthos, 1972), was originally volume 15 of *Documents Relative to the Colonial History of the State of New York* (Albany, N.Y.: Weed, Parsons and Co., 1887). Additional names are in *New York in the Revolution as Colony and State,* 2 vols., and *Supplement* (Albany, N.Y.: J. B. Lyon, 1901, 1904), and in *Calendar of Historical Manuscripts Relating to the War of the Revolution,* 2 vols. (Albany, N.Y.: Weed, Parsons and Co., 1868), both compiled by the New York [State] Comptroller's Office. To find other material at the state archives, consult Stefan Bielinski, ed., *A Guide to the Revolutionary War Manuscripts in the New York State Library* (Albany, N.Y.: New York State American Bicentennial Commission, 1976). See also Milton M. Klein, comp., *New York in the American Revolution: A Bibliography* (Albany, N.Y.: New York State American Revolution Bicentennial Commission, 1974). A lot of Revolutionary War material burned in the 1911 state library fire, but the remaining charred fragments are at last being microfilmed and made available for research. The state archives is preparing a computerized name index to New York soldiers and other individuals mentioned in the surviving Revolutionary War manuscripts. Other Revolutionary War material sent to Washington before the 1911 fire should be sought in the National Archives (see *The New York Genealogical and Biographical Record* 120 [1989]: 66).

There is much published and manuscript material on New York Loyalists. One of the best works is Harry B. Yoshpe, *Disposition of Loyalist Estates in the Southern District of the State of New York* (New York, N.Y.: Columbia University Press, 1939). Some Loyalist material is at the New York Public Library and the state archives.

Hugh Hastings, ed., *Military Minutes of the Council of Appointment of the State of New York, 1783–1821,* 4 vols. (Albany, N.Y.: J. B. Lyon, 1901–04) (volume 4 is an index), lists local officers and is useful for determining the area from which a War of 1812 soldier probably served when only his unit commander's name is known. Published material on New Yorkers in the War of 1812 is scarce, but one published list put out by the New York [State] Adjutant General's Office is *Index of Awards on Claims of the Soldiers of the War of 1860* (1860; reprint, Baltimore, Md.: Genealogical Publishing Co., 1969). The original claims that survived are at the state archives.

There is a typescript index of Civil War participants from New York at the state archives, and if the regiment is known, see *Register of New York Regiments in the War of the Rebellion,* 43 vols., issued as supplementary reports to the *Annual Report* of the state adjutant general for 1893–1905 (Albany, N.Y.: J. B. Lyon and others, 1894–1906). *A Record of Commissioned Officers, Non-Commissioned Officers and Privates . . . in Suppressing the Rebellion,* 8 vols. (Albany, N.Y.: Comstock & Cassidy, 1864–68), and *Registers . . . the War of the Rebellion* (Albany, N.Y.: J. B. Lyon, 1894), not indexed by name, were compiled by the New York Adjutant General's Office. Frederick Phisterer, comp., *New York in the War of the Rebellion 1861–1865,* 6 vols. (Albany, N.Y.: J. B. Lyon, 1912), lists officers only. The National Archives-Northeast Region and the state archives have the microfilm index of compiled service records of New York volunteer soldiers in the Union Army. The state archives has much material on the Civil War, including town clerk's registers, which often show the soldier's full name, date and place of birth, and names of parents, including mother's maiden name. Civil War soldiers and deaths of officers and enlisted men were also noted in the population schedules of the 1865 State Census, and veterans or their widows were listed in a special 1890 Census (see Census Records).

Richard H. Saldaña, *Index to the New York Spanish-American War Veterans, 1898,* 2 vols. (North Salt Lake City, Utah: AISI Publishers, 1987), is a reprint with an index of the original three-volume report issued by the state adjutant general in 1900, arranged by regiment. For world wars, there are card files of New York state servicemen at the state archives.

Periodicals, Newspapers, and Manuscript Collections

Periodicals

The New York Genealogical and Biographical Record is the oldest continuing genealogical periodical in the state. Published since 1870, it is the quarterly of the New York Genealogical and Biographical Society and has printed numerous source records, compiled genealogies, and other fine articles concerning New York history and genealogy. Some of the journal's more extensive coverage has extended to New England and New Jersey. There is no every-name index, but typescript indexes to surnames are available for volumes 1–94. See also Jean D. Worden's *Master Index* to this journal for 1870–1982 (Franklin, Ohio: the author, 1983).

The Central New York Genealogical Society began *Tree Talks* in 1961. Except for some information articles, it is essentially a journal of mostly pre-1850 source records, arranged by county, with coverage for most of the state except New York City and Long Island, with concentration on upstate New York. Its contents include abstracts of censuses, wills, administrations, guardianships, marriages and deaths from newspapers, cemetery marker transcripts, church records, family Bibles, naturalizations, tax records, and town records.

The *Western New York Genealogical Society Journal* is the periodical of that organization. Published since 1974, it includes sources of records and other material pertaining to the eight western counties of Allegany, Cattaraugus, Chautauqua, Erie, Genesee, Niagara, Orleans, and Wyoming.

Among the many periodicals covering one New York county are a series of "Valley Quarterlies" published by Arthur C. M. Kelly (60 Cedar Heights Road, Rhinebeck, New York 12572): *The Capital* (Albany and Rensselaer counties), *The Columbia* (Columbia County), *The Mohawk* (Montgomery and Schenectady counties), and *The Saratoga* (Saratoga County), all with helpful abstracts of source records.

Janet W. Foley's *Early Settlers of New York State: Their Ancestors and Descendants* 9 vols. (Akron, N.Y., 1934–42), contain source records and queries with concentration on central and western New York.

De Halve Maen is the journal of the Holland Society of New York, published since 1922. It contains articles about early Dutch in the state and has some genealogies tracing the origins of Dutch immigrants.

Important quarterlies with more historical focus are *The New-York Historical Society Quarterly* (1917–80) and *New York History,* begun in 1919 by the New York State Historical Association in Cooperstown. The seventeen volumes of *Proceedings* (1902–17) of the association should also be mentioned.

Journals published outside the state should not be overlooked for New York material. These include *The New England Historical and Genealogical Register, National Genealogical Society Quarterly, The American Genealogist, The Genealogical Magazine of New Jersey,* and *The Detroit Society for Genealogical Research Magazine.*

Newspapers

The "Newspaper Project" at New York State Library seeks to identify and preserve newspapers throughout the state. While this project is underway, consult *Bibliographies and Lists of New York State Newspapers: An Annotated Guide,* Bibliography Bulletin 87 of the New York State Library (Albany, 1981), available for $4 and *A Checklist of Newspapers in Microform in the New York State Library* (Albany, 1979), available for $3. Sylvia G. Faibisoff and Wendell Tripp, comps., *A Bibliography of Newspapers in Fourteen New York Counties* (Cooperstown, N.Y.: New York Historical Association, 1978), covers Allegany, Broome, Cayuga, Chemung, Chenango, Cortland, Delaware, Otsego, Schuyler, Seneca, Steuben, Tioga, Tompkins, and Yates counties.

Many libraries and historical societies have important collections of newspapers and often have abstracts of or indexes to newspaper items, mostly notices of marriages and deaths. Among those published items are the following:

Bowman, Fred Q. *10,000 Vital Records of Western New York, 1809–1850;... of Central New York, 1813–1850;* and... *of Eastern New York, 1777–1834.* Baltimore, Md.: Genealogical Publishing Co., 1985, 1986, 1987. These are three separate, useful volumes. For a continuation of the latter book, see "1,100 Vital Records of Northeastern New York 1835–1850" in volumes 118 and 119 of *The New York Genealogical and Biographical Record.*

Gavit, Joseph. *American Deaths and Marriages, 1784–1829.* This is a microfilm of alphabetized abstracts from New York newspapers, for which Kenneth Scott prepared *Index to Non-principal Names* (New Orleans, La.: Polyanthos, 1976).

Maher, James P., comp. *Index to Marriages and Deaths in the New York Herald 1835–1855.* Baltimore, Md.: Genealogical Publishing Co., 1987. Coverage extends beyond the New York City area.

Reynolds, Helen W. *Notices of Marriages and Deaths . . . Published in Newspapers Printed in Poughkeepsie . . . , 1778–1825.* Volume 4 of Dutchess County Historical Society Collections. Poughkeepsie, N.Y., 1930. A card file at the Adriance Library, Poughkeepsie, takes these abstracts further into the nineteenth century.

Scott, Kenneth. *Genealogical Data From Colonial New York Newspapers.* Reprinted from *The New York Genealogical and Biographical Record.* Baltimore, Md.: Genealogical Publishing Co., 1982.

———, and Kristin Lunde Gibbons, eds. *The New-York Magazine Marriages and Deaths: 1790–1797.* New Orleans, La.: Polyanthos, 1975.

Nineteenth-century marriage and death notices from the *New York Evening Post* and *Brooklyn Eagle,* both abstracted by Gertrude A. Barber, are also to be checked. For a more complete list of New York City and Long Island area abstracts, see Henry B. Hoff's "Marriage and Death Notices in New York City Newspapers" and "Marriage and Death Notices in Long Island Newspapers" *The NYG&B Newsletter* 2 (1991): 3–5 and 20–21, respectively.

Manuscripts

A substantial amount of manuscript material is located in the New York State Archives, the New York State Library, and the New York Genealogical and Biographical Society. Other major collections are determined through the following published guides:

Beton, Arthur J. *A Guide to the Manuscript Collections of The New-York Historical Society.* 2 vols. Westport, Conn.: Greenwood Press, 1972. Covers the society's many holdings of newspapers, maps, photos, and business records.

WPS. *Guides to Depositories of Manuscript Collections in New York State.* New York, N.Y.: Historical Records Survey, 1941–44.

Mango, Karin R., comp. *The Long Island Historical Society Calendar of Manuscripts: 1763–1783.* Brooklyn, N.Y.: Long Island Historical Society, 1980. Now called the Brooklyn Historical Society.

New York Historical Resources Center. *Guide to Historical Resources in . . . County, New York Repositories.* Ithaca, N.Y.: Cornell University Press, 1978–present. Sometimes called "the Red Books," this series has at least one volume for each county. Public records are not represented, and the project ended before all New York City and Long Island information was published.

The New York Public Library Research Libraries Dictionary Catalog of the Manuscript Division. 2 vols. Boston, Mass.: G. K. Hall, 1967.

Archives, Libraries, and Societies

New York State Archives and Records Administration
The State Education Department
Cultural Education Center, 11th Floor
Empire State Plaza
Albany, NY 12230

Referred to here as the New York State Archives for brevity, it was the last such archives to be established in the United States. It houses land and court records, some 1847–52 vital records, military and tax records, and legislative records. The out-of-date published guide to the holdings is being revised.

New York State Library, Humanities/History
Cultural Education Center, 7th Floor
Empire State Plaza
Albany, NY 12230

The state library has a large collection of published and manuscript material on New York, including genealogies and local histories, federal and state censuses, city directories, and periodicals. It is also one of the two depositories for the State of New York DAR collection. There is a published guide to the library called *Gateway to America* (see Background Sources). *The Eighth Annual Report of the New York State Education Department* and the *New York (State) State Library Annual Report 94th,* both for 1911, reported the loss and salvage following the library's disastrous fire that year. An annotated copy of the latter is in the manuscript division of the state library.

The New-York Historical Society
170 Central Park West
New York, NY 10024-5194

Probably best known to genealogists for its manuscript collection, the New-York Historical Society has newspapers, city directories, maps, original deeds and other documents, and prints and photographs. The guide to its manuscript collections is currently out of print. Some of the society's holdings were published in its *Collections* from 1892 to 1908. From 1917 to 1980, the society also published *The New-York Historical Society Quarterly.*

The New York Public Library
5th Avenue and 42nd Street
New York, NY 10018

The New York Public Library is not only a tremendous library for New York research, but also contains substantial amounts of material on the rest of the country and the world. Besides genealogy and local history, the public library has newspapers, federal and state censuses, church records, city and telephone directories, and divisions for maps, manuscripts, Jewish, and other material. For the published and some of the manuscript material, see *Dictionary Catalog of the Local History and Genealogy Division,* 18 vols. (Boston, Mass.: G. K. Hall, 1974), and four supplements. More current acquisitions are accessed through computer terminals at the library. Timothy Field Beard, a former reference librarian in the Local History and Genealogy Division, with Denise Demong compiled *How to Find Your Family Roots* (New York, N.Y.: McGraw Hill, 1977), which includes New York Public Library call numbers in its bibliography. A list of area researchers is available from the library on request.

The New York Genealogical and Biographical Society
122 East 58th Street
New York, NY 10022-1939

A private society, the New York Genealogical and Biographical Society publishes a quarterly, *The New York Genealogical and Biographical Record.* Its library holds much New York State and related material, both for New England and the Mid-Atlantic states. For New York there are censuses, federal and state; a large manuscript collection of church, cemetery, Bible, and other records; and an extensive amount of published family and local histories. Nonmembers may use the library for a small fee, but only members have access to the stacks, manuscripts, and microforms. The library provides a list of area researchers.

Municipal Archives
Department of Records and Special Services
31 Chambers Street
New York, NY 10007

Holdings of early New York City records are described in various sections of this chapter.

Onondaga County Public Library
447 South Salina Street
Syracuse, NY 13202-2494

With one of the largest collections of genealogical material in the state, it has a fine collection of published works, manuscripts, and specialized indexes.

Central New York Genealogical Society
Box 104
Colvin Station
Syracuse, NY 13205

While the society does not maintain a library, it publishes *Tree Talks,* a very fine journal of source material.

Western New York Genealogical Society, Inc.
5859 South Park Avenue
P.O. Box 338
Hamburg, NY 14075-0338

Their journal consists of many useful source records and articles about the eight counties it covers (see Periodicals).

Among the other libraries in the state with large collections of New York material are Brooklyn Historical Society, 128 Pierpont Street, Brooklyn, New York 11201; Buffalo and Erie County Historical Society, 25 Nottingham Court, Buffalo, New York 14216; Montgomery County Department of History and Archives, Old Courthouse, Railroad Street, Fonda, New York 12068; New York State Historical Association, West Lake Road, P.O. Box 800, Cooperstown, New York, 13326-0800; and Rochester Public Library, 115 South Avenue, Rochester, New York 14604.

Special Focus Categories

Immigration

Microfilm lists of ships' passenger arrivals at the port of New York are at the National Archives-Northeast Region for 1820–1909 and 1943–52, and at the New York Public Library for 1820–1910. The archives has name indexes for 1820–46 and 1897–48, and the public library has them for 1820–46 and 1897–1943. A portion of the gap in the unindexed period, 1847–97, has been filled by Ira Glazier, ed., *The Famine Immigrants . . . 1846–1851,* 8 vols. (Baltimore, Md.: Genealogical Publishing Co., 1983–86); Robert P. Swierenga, comp., *Dutch Immigrants in U.S. Ship Passenger Manifests, 1820–1880,* 2 vols. (Wilmington, Del.: Scholarly Resources, 1983); Nils William Olsen, *Swedish Passenger Arrivals in New York 1820–1850* (Chicago, Ill.: Swedish Pioneer Historical Society, 1967); Ira A. Glazier and P. William Filby, eds., *Germans to America . . . 1850–93* (Wilmington, Del.: Scholarly Resources, 1988–); Gary J. Zimmerman and Marion Wolfert, *German Immigrants . . . from Bremen to New York, 1847–1867,* 3 vols. (Baltimore, Md.: Genealogical Publishing Co., 1985–88); and Trudy Schenk and Ruth Froelke, *The Wuerttemberg Emigration Index,* 5 vols. (Salt Lake City, Utah: Ancestry, 1986–88). For a critical evaluation of two of these works, see Gordon L. Remington, "Feast or Famine: Problems in the Genealogical Use of *The Famine Immigrants* and *Germans to America,*" *National Genealogical Society Quarterly* 78 (1990):135–46.

Naturalization

County naturalization records are kept by the county clerk. U.S. court records are in federal buildings in Buffalo and Albany, with most downstate records to the 1940s or 1950s at the National Archives-Northeast Region. At the latter is a WPA-created card index, arranged by Soundex, for all naturalizations (but not declarations of intention) performed in all courts in all five New York City boroughs, 1792–1906, together with dexigraphs (photostats) of the original records. Until the late 1800s and early 1900s, these records provide little information; upstate records up to the mid-1800s are generally more informative. For some early records, see two compilations by Kenneth Scott: *Early New York Naturalizations . . . 1792–1840* (Baltimore, Md.: Genealogical Publishing Co., 1981), from federal, state, and local court records, and with Kenn Stryker-Rodda, *Denizations, Naturalizations and Oaths of Allegiance in Colonial New York* (Baltimore, Md.: Genealogical Publishing Co., 1975). See also "Naturalizations in Federal Courts, New York District, 1790–1828," by Mrs. Edward J. Chapin, in volume 97 of *The New York Genealogical and Biographical Record* (1966); Kenneth Scott, "New York City Naturalizations, 1795–1799," *National Genealogical Society Quarterly* 71 (1983): 280–83; and "List of Immigrants 1802–1814" in the Emmet Collection in the New York Public Library manuscript department.

A somewhat related work in this category is Kenneth Scott and Rosanne Conway, *New York Alien Residents, 1825–1848* (1978; reprint, Baltimore, Md.: Clearfield Co., 1991).

Black American

The best bibliography of material on Black American genealogy in New York is *Black Genesis* (see page 10). Not to be overlooked is the New York Public Library's Schomburg Center for Research in Black Culture, 515 Lenox Avenue, New York, New York 10037, with an extensive collection.

Native American

The two major Native American groups in New York were the Iroquois Five (later Six) Nations and their enemies, the Algonquins. Other groups were in the southeast and on Long Island. Among several works on the subject, research can begin in H. Leon Abrams, Jr., *A Partial Working Bibliography on the Amerindians of New York* (Greeley, Colo.: University of Northern Colorado, Museum of Anthropology, 1979); Russell A. Judkins, ed., *Iroquois Studies: A Guide to Documentary and Ethnographic Records from Western New York and the Genesee Valley* (Geneseo, N.Y.: Department of Anthropology, State University of New York and the Geneseo Foundation, 1987); and "Problems of American Indian Research in New York State," from a talk by Elma Patterson, Indian Affairs Specialist for the New York State Department of Social Services, *Western New York Genealogical Society Journal* 12 (1985): 107–12. See also E. M. Ruttenber, "Indian Geographical Names," issued as a supplement and bound in the back of the New York State Historical Association's *Proceedings* for 1906.

County Resources

Since 1919 New York has had a system of local historians who are appointed to collect and preserve old records. While each county, town, and village should have a historian, not all vacancies are always filled, and of those that are, the knowledge and helpfulness in answering inquiries varies. In most cases it is best to start with the county historian, whose office may contain original or transcribed county, church, cemetery, newspaper, and other material, and in some cases, specialized indexes to these and other types of records. See *Directory of New York State County and Municipal Historians* (N.p., 1991), available for $20 from Directory, RFD 2, Box 228, Bath, New York 14810.

Publication of town records is not widespread, with the exception of those for Queens (including Nassau), Suffolk, and Westchester counties. Various items from town records have been presented in *Tree Talks* (see Periodicals). See also Harlod Nestler, *A Bibliography of New York State Communities: Counties, Towns, Villages* (Port Washington, N.Y.: Ira J. Friedman, 1968).

Some New York counties have set up record centers or archives, as found in Broome, Cayuga, Montgomery, Ontario, Washington, and Westchester counties. While most initial inquiries about records should be made with the county clerk and county surrogate's clerk, the information sought might actually now be housed in a county records center/archives. This practice will doubtless continue in New York, especially for older records.

All the counties in New York, past and present, are listed below. The name of the county and the mailing address of the county clerk, who is in charge of deeds, mortgages, marriages (1908–35), divorces, court records, state censuses, and other records is in the second column. Next, the year the county was created follows and, where applicable, the parent county or counties from which it was formed. The date the earliest deed was recorded is in the fourth column. County deeds and mortgages not found with the county clerk are also indicated here. The last column shows the date of the earliest county surrogate court record, followed by the mailing address of the county surrogate's clerk, if not the same as that of the county clerk. Some counties have copies or abstracts of earlier deeds and wills from parent counties.

It should be kept in mind that the names of the parent county or counties are those from which the new county was first formed in the year indicated. Many changes took place later, at which times whole towns or parts of them were annexed to or from the newer county. For example, Yates County was created in 1823 from part of Ontario County; the following year two towns were added to Yates from Steuben County. For the specifics of other changes, consult gazetteers, county directories, and county histories.

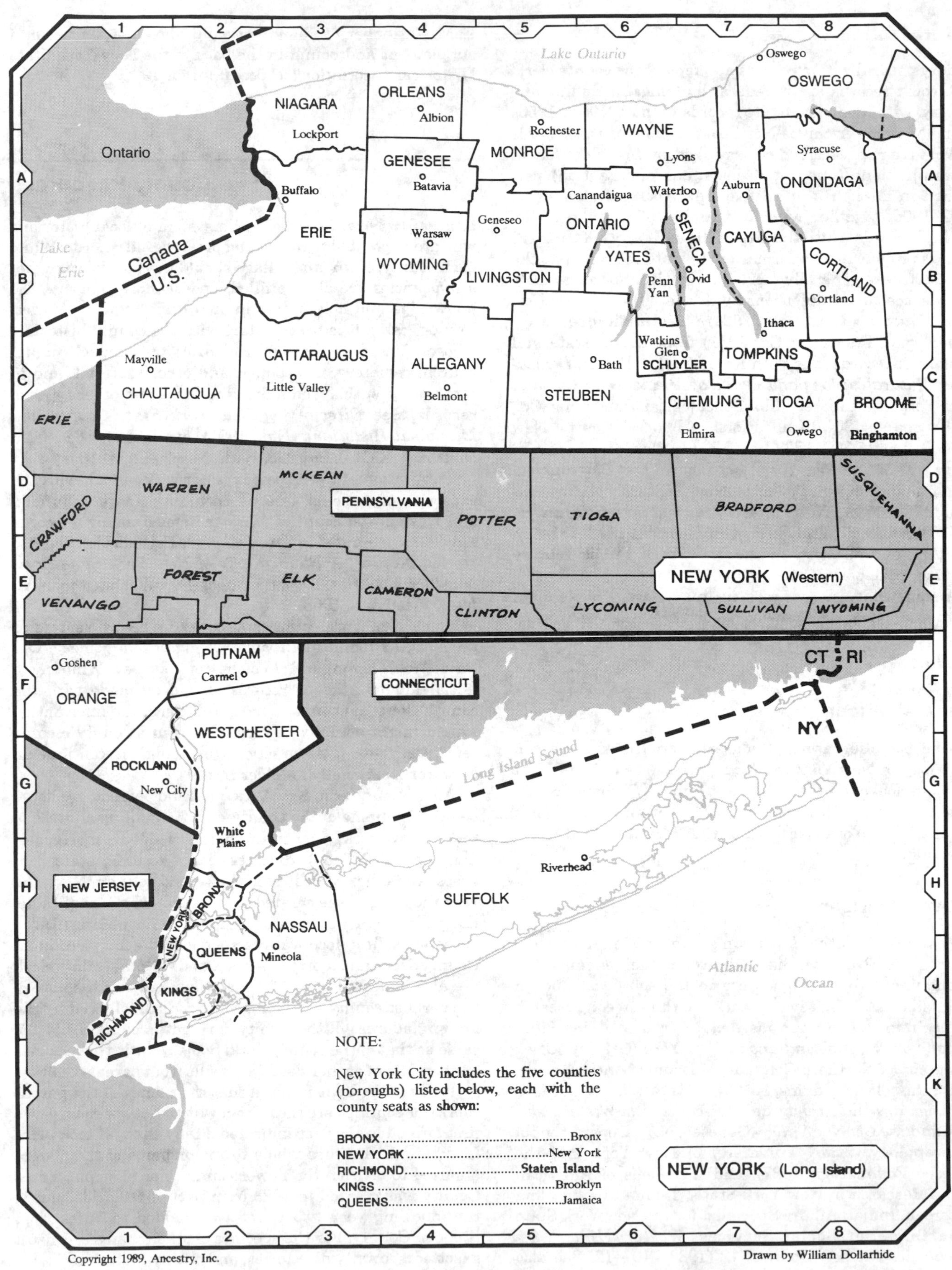

Drawn by William Dollarhide

Drawn by William Dollarhide

Map	County Clerk's Address	Date Formed Parent County/ies	Deeds	Surrogate's Court
Q15	Albany 16 Eagle Street, Room 128 Albany 12207-1019	1683 original	1656	1787 16 Eagle Street Albany 12207-1019
C4	Allegany Courthouse Belmont 14813	1806 Genesee	1807	1807
H2	Bronx 851 Grand Concourse Room 118 Bronx 10451-2937	1914 New York (New York County annexed part of Westchester, 1873, which is now part of the Bronx)	1914*	1914 851 Grand Concourse Room 317 Bronx 10451-2937
	** At the City Register's Office, 1932 Arthur Avenue, Bronx 10457*			
S11	Broome P. O. Box 2062 Binghamton 13902-2062	1806 Tioga	1806	1806 Courthouse Binghamton 13901
C3	Cattaraugus 303 Court Street Little Valley 14755-1028	1808 Genesee	1817	1817
	Cattaraugus had no county government until 1817. Its records were first kept in Buffalo, but they were destroyed in 1813 when the British burned the courthouse. In 1812 Cattaraugus became part of Allegany County, and from 1814–17 county records for the eastern towns of Olean and Ischua were kept in Belmont and for the western town of Perry, in Buffalo.			
Q10	Cayuga County Office Building Box 616 Auburn 13021-0616	1799 Onondaga	1799	1799 Courthouse Auburn 13021-3471
	Charlotte	1772 (renamed Washington, 1784) Albany		
C1	Chautauqua P. O. Box 292 Mayville 14757-0292	1808 Genesee	1811	1811 Box C Mayville 14757
	Chautauqua was attached to Niagara County until 1811, but records kept in Buffalo were burned by the British in 1813.			
S10	Chemung 210 Lake Street P.O. Box 588 Elmira 14902-0588	1836 Tioga	1836	1836 224 Lake Street P.O. Box 588 Elmira 14902-0588
R12	Chenango 5 Court Street Norwich 13815	1798 Herkimer/Tioga	1798	1798
L16	Clinton 137 Margaret Street Plattsburgh 12901-2933	1788 Washington	1788	1790
R16	Columbia Courthouse Hudson 12534	1786 Albany	1786	1787
	Cornwall	1683 original		
	Located in Maine, this county became part of Massachusetts in 1686, but no longer exists in name. See Collections of the Maine Historical Society [first series], Vol. 5 (1857).			
Q11	Cortland P.O. Box 5590 Cortland 13045-5590	1808 Onondaga	1808	1808

Map	County Clerk's Address	Date Formed Parent County/ies	Deeds	Surrogate's Court Address
	Cumberland	1766 Albany		
	Disallowed the year after it was formed, Cumberland was re-established in 1768 and ceased to exist 1777–78 when Vermont declared itself a republic.			
S13	Delaware P.O. Box 426 Delhi 13753-0426	1797 Ulster/Otsego	1797	1797 Courthouse Delhi 13753
	Dukes	1683 original		
	Dukes County became part of Massachusetts in 1692 (see Massachusetts).			
T15	Dutchess 22 Market Street Poughkeepsie 12601	1683 original	1718	1752 10 Market Street Poughkeepsie 12601
	Almost uninhabited until 1701, Dutchess was administered by Ulster County from that time until at least 1713. Some older records, including marriages, 1908–35; state and federal censuses; tax records, 1854–1954; and the "Ancient Documents" series are at the Couty Records Center and Archives, 27 High Street, Poughkeepsie 12601.			
B3	Erie 25 Delaware Avenue Buffalo 14202	1821 Niagara	1808	1800 92 Franklin Street Buffalo 14202
	In 1813, the British burned the courthouse in Buffalo, which was then the seat of Niagara County, destroying records that also included Cattaraugus and Chautauqua counties.			
M15	Essex Government Complex Court Street Elizabethtown 12932	1799 Clinton	1799	1803
L14	Franklin 63 W. Main Street Malone 12953-1817	1808 Clinton	1808	1809
P14	Fulton P.O. Box 485 Johnstown 12095-0485	1838 Montgomery	1838	1838 County Building Johnstown 12095
A4	Genesee P.O. Box 379 Batavia 14021-0379	1802 Ontario	1803	1805 P.O. Box 462 Batavia 14020-0462
	Gloucester	1770 Cumberland		
	This county ceased to exist when Vermont declared itself a republic, 1777–78.			
R15	Greene P.O. Box 446 Catskill 12414-0446	1800 Ulster/Albany	1800	1803 P.O. Box 469 Catskill 12414-0469
O14	Hamilton County Office Building Lake Pleasant 12108	1816 Montgomery	1797	1861 P.O. Box 780 Indian Lake 12842-0780
	Hamilton remained attached to Montgomery County until 1838 and then briefly to Fulton County. Earlier surrogate's records are evidently in Montgomery, Fulton, and St. Lawrence counties. See Tree Talks 20 (1980): 166.			
P13	Herkimer County Office Building P.O. Box 111 Herkimer 13350-0111	1791 Montgomery	1804 1791–98*	1792 P.O. Box 550 Herkimer 13350-0550
	**Deeds 1791–98 for what became Oneida County are in Utica.*			
M11	Jefferson 175 Arsenal Street Watertown 13601-2522	1805 Oneida	1805	1805

Map	County Clerk's Address	Date Formed Parent County/ies	Deeds	Surrogate's Court
J2	Kings Room 189 360 Adams Street Brooklyn 11201-3712	1683 original	1683*	1787 Room 109 2 Johnson Street Brooklyn 11201
	** At the City Register's Office, 210 Joralemon Street, Brooklyn 11201. Many surrogate's files before about 1870 are now at the NYC Archives and on microfilm at the FHL.*			
N12	Lewis 7660 State Street Lowville 13367-1432	1805 Oneida	1805	1805
B5	Livingston 2 Court Street Geneseo 14454-1048	1821 Genesee/Ontario	1821	1821
Q11	Madison P.O. Box 668 Wampsville 13163-0668	1806 Chenango	1806	1806 P.O. Box 607 Wampsville 13163-0607
A5	Monroe 39 W. Main Street Rochester 14614	1821 Genesee/Ontario	1821	1824 Hall of Justice Room 304 Rochester 14614
Q14	Montgomery Record Room Fonda 12068	1772 (as Tryon; renamed, 1784) Albany	1777	1787 New Courthouse Fonda 12068
H3	Nassau Room 109 240 Old Country Road Mineola 11501	1899 Queens	1899	1899 3rd Floor 240 Old Country Mineola 11501
J2	New York Room 103B 60 Centre Street New York 10007-1402	1683 original	1654*	1665** Room 402 31 Chambers Street New York 10007
	** At the City Register's Office, Rooms 203–205, 31 Chambers Street, New York 10007. Early records of the county clerk are in Division of Old Records, 7th Floor. **Pre-1830 surrogate's files and inventories are not known to have survived.*			
A3	Niagara 175 Hawley Street P.O. Box 461 Lockport 14094-0461	1821 Genesee	1821	1821 Courthouse Lockport 14094
	Records for the period 1813–21 are in Buffalo, which was the county seat of Niagara until Erie was created; earlier records were destroyed when the British burned the Buffalo courthouse in 1813.			
P12	Oneida 800 Park Avenue Utica 13501-2939	1798 Herkimer	1791–1885*	1798 Elizabeth Street Utica 13501
	** At the B-1 Records Center, 800 Park Avenue, Utica 13501. Deeds 1886 to present are with the county clerk.*			
P11	Onondaga 401 Montgomery Street Room 200 Syracuse 13202	1794 Herkimer	1784	1796 401 Montgomery Street Room 209 Syracuse 13202
A6	Ontario 25 Pleasant Street Canandaigua 14424	1789 Montgomery	1789–1915*	1789–1926*
	**These records–and mortgages to 1920–are at Records Center, 3907 County Road 46, Canandaigua 14424; later deeds and all indexes are at the county clerk's; later surrogate's court records at the Courthouse, Canandaigua 14424.*			
U14	Orange 255-275 Main Street Goshen 10924-1621	1683 original	1703	1787 Park Place Goshen 10924

Map	County Clerk's Address	Date Formed Parent County/ies	Deeds	Surrogate's Court Address
A4	Orleans 1 Main Street Albion 14411-1449	1824 Genesee	1824	1824 Courthouse Square Albion 14411
O11	Oswego 46 E. Bridge Street Oswego 13126-2123	1816 Oneida/Onondaga	1791	1816 E. Oneida Street Oswego 13126
Q13	Otsego P.O. Box 710 Cooperstown 13326-0710	1791 Montgomery	1791	1791 197 Main Street Cooperstown 13326-1129
U15	Putnam 2 County Center Carmel 10512	1812 Dutchess	1812	1812
J2	Queens Room 105 88-11 Sutphin Boulevard Jamaica 11435 ** At the City Register's Office, 90-27 Sutphin Boulevard, Jamaica 11435.* *** Most or all pre-1830 surrogate's files were lost or destroyed.*	1683 original	1683*	1787** Seventh Floor 88-11 Sutphin Boulevard Jamaica 11435
Q16	Rensselaer Congress and Second Street Troy 12180	1791 Albany	1791	1794
J1	Richmond 18 Richmond Terrace Staten Island 10301-1935 **Same address as county clerk, but Room 201.*	1683 original	1683	1787*
U15	Rockland 27 New Hempstead Road New City 10956-3526	1798 Orange	1798	1798 Main Street New City 10956
L13	Saint Lawrence Court Street Canton 13617	1802 Clinton/Herkimer/Montgomery	1802	1803
P15	Saratoga 40 McMaster Street Ballston Spa 12020-1908	1791 Albany	1791	1791 Municipal Center Ballston Spa 12020
Q15	Schenectady 620 State Street Schenectady 12307-2113	1809 Albany	1809	1809 Judicial Building Schenectady 12307
R14	Schoharie 300 Main Street P.O. Box 549 Schoharie 12157-0549	1795 Albany/Otsego	1795	1795 P.O. Box 669 Schoharie 12157-0669
R9	Schuyler P.O. Box 9 Watkins Glen 14891-0009	1854 Tompkins/Steuben/Chemung	1854	1854 Courthouse Watkins Glen 14891
B7	Seneca P.O. Box 310 Waterloo 13165-0310	1804 Cayuga	1804	1804 48 W. Williams Street Waterloo 13165-1338
C6	Steuben 13 E. Pulteney Square Bath 14810	1796 Ontario	1796	1796

Map	County Clerk's Address	Date Formed Parent County/ies	Deeds	Surrogate's Court
H5	Suffolk County Center Riverhead 11901-3398	1683 original	1683	1787
T13	Sullivan 100 North Street Monticello 12701 *A fire in 1909 destroyed will volumes 1–7 but all or most of the files survived.*	1809 Ulster	1809	1811
S10	Tioga 16 Court Street P. O. Box 307 Owego 13827-0307 *The explanation for the nine-year delay in the surrogate's records is not fully known, but some estate records during this period may have perished in an early fire in Spencer, once the county seat.*	1791 Montgomery	1791	1798 P.O. Box 10 Owego 13827-0010
R10	Tompkins 320 N. Tioga Street Ithaca 14850-4284	1817 Cayuga/Seneca	1817	1817
	Tryon	1772 (renamed Montgomery, 1784) Albany		
S14	Ulster 244 Fair Street P.O. Box 1800 Kingston 12401-1800	1683 original	1684	1787 P.O. Box 1800 Kingston 12477-1800
O15	Warren 1 Municipal Center Lake George 12845	1813 Washington	1813	1813
P16	Washington County Office Building Upper Broadway Fort Edward 12828 *The eastern part of the county became a part of Vermont when it declared itself a republic in 1777–78.*	1772 (as Charlotte; renamed, 1784) Albany	1774	1787 East Broadway Salem 12865
A6	Wayne P.O. Box 183 Lyons 14489-0183	1823 Ontario/ Seneca	1823	1823 26 Church Street Lyons 14489-1134
U15	Westchester 110 Grove Street White Plains 10601 **These records, with indexes 1680-1898, are held at the Records Center and Archives, 2199 Saw Mill River Road, Elmsford 10523. Later deed records are with the county clerk (address above).* ***Later surrogate court records are at 111 Grove Street, Room 702, White Plains 10601.*	1683 original	1667–1825*	files, 1775–1865; original wills to 1942; and record books, 1777–1885**
B4	Wyoming P.O. Box 70 Warsaw 14569-0070	1841 Genesee	1841	1841 143 N. Main Street Warsaw 14569-1123
B6	Yates 110 Court Street Penn Yan 14527	1823 Ontario	1823	1823 108 Court Street Penn Yan 14527

North Carolina

Johni Cerny and Gareth L. Mark, A.G.

The first permanent English settlers in North Carolina were Virginians who heard glowing reports of fertile bottom lands, abundant timber resources, and an excellent climate. They moved into the Albemarle Sound area about 1650, purchasing land from the local Indian tribes. The Virginia Assembly also granted land along the Chowan and Roanoke rivers to Roger Green in 1653. By 1657, Nathaniel Batts had a house at the western end of Albemarle Sound.

English claims on North Carolina date to 1497 when John Cabot visited the New World and claimed the area for King Henry VII. These claims were the basis for Charles I's 1629 grant of "Carolana" to Sir Robert Heath, who failed to settle Carolina before the execution of Charles I in 1649. During the Commonwealth period in England, many citizens remained loyal to Charles II. At his ascension to the throne of England in 1660, eight men pressed their claims for a reward: Edward Hyde, Earl of Clarendon; George Monck, Duke of Albemarle; Lord William Craven; Lord John Berkeley; Lord Anthony Ashley Cooper, Earl of Shaftesbury; Sir George Carteret; Sir William Berkeley; and Sir John Colleton. Charles II granted Carolina to the eight Lords Proprietors in 1663. After the claims of Heath's successors had been disposed of, the grant was revised and extended in 1665.

Two factors heavily influenced the development of North Carolina. Its stormy coastline, known as the "graveyard of the Atlantic," does not include a natural harbor to promote commerce. The Cape Fear River is the only river that empties into the Atlantic Ocean, and its approaches are endangered by the Frying Pan Shoals. Except for Highland Scots, immigrants to North Carolina generally arrived by overland routes. The second factor influencing North Carolina's development was the presence of approximately 35,000 Native Americans. They taught the European settlers important agricultural techniques such as planting row crops and fertilizing plants. The Europeans also learned the natives' techniques of wilderness war. But the presence of the whites eventually destroyed the native civilization through disease, forceful removal to reservations, and war.

New Bern was founded in 1710 by colonists from Germany, Switzerland, and England under the leadership of Christopher de Graffenried. The colonists landed in Virginia and trekked overland to North Carolina, arriving too late to plant and harvest crops. The settlement survived and flourished, however, and New Bern became the largest town in North Carolina during the colonial period. The New Bern settlement, however, was located in the Tuscarora hunting grounds, and the Cary Rebellion in 1711 left the colonists open to attack. The Tuscarora Indian War (1711–15) was the result.

In 1729 the Lords Proprietors, except for John Carteret, Earl Granville, sold their shares in the provinces of North and South Carolina to King James II of England, ending the proprietary period. North Carolina was the most sparsely settled English colony in America at that time. The end of the proprietary period marked the beginning of a period of great expansion and growth. Scots-Irish and German immigrants traveled over the Great Wagon Road from Pensylvania through the Shenandoah Valley of Virginia to North Carolina. Highland Scots, the only significant migration that sailed directly to North Carolina, settled in the Cape Fear River valley. The Moravians purchased nearly

100,000 acres in present-day Forsyth County from Earl Granville in 1753 and settled the tract they called "Wachovia."

The movement for independence was strong in North Carolina, and a provincial congress met in New Bern in 1774. Yet not all North Carolinians supported the revolution. The Highland Scots, in particular, remained loyal to the crown and recruited Loyalist military units.

In 1789, North Carolina ratified the United States Constitution and ceded its western lands, now known as Tennessee, to the federal government. The site for the state capital was located and named Raleigh three years later. Dissatisfaction with the state constitution of 1776, which heavily favored the eastern counties and towns, resulted in the constitutional convention of 1835 and the adoption of a new state constitution.

North Carolina was not ardently secessionist in 1860, but when the federal government requested troops to quell the rebellion, Gov. John W. Ellis refused, and North Carolina soon joined the Confederacy. North Carolina supplied about 125,000 troops to the Confederacy, more than any other southern state, and over 14,000 North Carolinians were killed in action.

From the end of the Civil War, North Carolina rapidly developed as an industrial state. Governmental support fostered the growth of the textile, tobacco, and furniture industries for which North Carolina is known.

See Powell, *North Carolina through Four Centuries,* cited in Background Sources, for a more comprehensive history of the Tarheel State.

Vital Records

On 10 March 1913, the North Carolina General Assembly ratified an act requiring the registration of births and deaths in the state; virtually full compliance was achieved by 1920, with some delayed birth records for earlier dates eventually added. The indexes to these records are available in the county where the event took place or on microfilm at the North Carolina State Archives and the FHL.

Original copies of birth certificates can be obtained from Department of Environmental, Health and Natural Resources, Vital Records Section, P.O. Box 29537, Raleigh, North Carolina 27626. The register of deeds in the county where the birth was filed also may be able to provide a copy of the birth certificate.

Copies of death records filed at the county register of deeds office and dated before 1930 are at the North Carolina State Archives, Archives and Records Section (see Archives, Libraries, and Societies). Death records dated from 1930 are at the Vital Records Section cited above. However, counties maintain copies as well.

Most marriages before 1868 were not recorded. A 1669 law required that each marriage be registered, but compliance was apparently low. Marriages could be solemnized by Church of England ministers or any member of the Council, including the Governor; in 1741, the right to perform marriages was extended to justices of the peace. Citizens were required to publish banns three times or obtain a marriage license; most marriages were by publication of banns. When the marriage was by license, the groom executed a marriage bond in the bride's county of residence; some marriage bonds have survived for about half of North Carolina's counties. *Index to Marriage Bonds Filed in the North Carolina State Archives* is a microfiche index to both brides and grooms of marriage bonds available at the North Carolina State Archives. The index may be used in the Search Room at the Archives, and a copy is available through the FHL. See Archives, Libraries, and Societies for information about searches by mail at the North Carolina State Archives.

After 1868, the register of deeds in each county was given the task of issuing marriage licenses. These licenses and their accompanying certificates offer a wealth of information, including age when married, parents' names, if the parents were living, parents' residences, and consent when required. Marriage records from 1868 to 1962 are on file with the register of deeds in the county where the marriage took place. Most North Carolina marriage records dating from 1868 to 1950 have been microfilmed and are available at the North Carolina State Archives and the FHL. Marriage records dating from 1962 are available at the Division of Health Services.

The superior court in each county has granted divorce decrees since 1814. Details about divorces that were not included in court minutes are very valuable to researchers. They include "loose papers" that discuss reasons for the divorce, details of the family's composition, children's ages, and other information. Copies of pre-1868 divorce records are at the North Carolina State Archives; records dating from 1868 are available from each county's superior court clerk.

Census Records

Federal

Population Schedules.

- Indexed—1790 (incomplete), 1800, 1810 (incomplete), 1820 (incomplete), 1830, 1840, 1850, 1860, 1870, 1890 (fragments)
- Soundex—1880, 1900, 1910 (Miracode), 1920

Industry and Agriculture Schedules.

- 1850, 1860, 1870, 1880

Mortality Schedules.

- 1850, 1860, 1870, 1880

Union Veterans Schedules.

- 1890

Slave Schedules.

- 1850, 1860

The first federal census was taken in 1790 and all of North Carolina's enumerations survive except Caswell,

Granville, and Orange counties. The 1810 U.S. census of North Carolina is complete except for Craven, Greene, New Hanover, and Wake counties. The 1820 census is missing Currituck, Franklin, Martin, Montgomery, Randolph, and Wake counties. Those schedules surviving for the 1890 population schedules are South Point and River Ben townships in Gaston County and Township No. 2 in Cleveland County. The North Carolina State Archives has either bound original copies or microfilm copies of the extant federal censuses of North Carolina.

State

Apparently there was no colonial census of North Carolina, but tax records, used judiciously, may be substituted (see Tax Records). A census was conducted in 1775 by direction of the Continental Congress, and the enumeration of Pitt County has survived. See Jean Anderson, "The Census of 1775 as Seen in Pitt County, NC," *The North Carolina Genealogical Society Journal* 7, no. 4 (November 1981): 186–96. In 1784 the North Carolina General Assembly requested that a list of inhabitants be taken. Age and sex categories for whites and blacks are included. Compliance was slow and apparently incomplete, with some counties not responding until 1786. There is some evidence that another census was conducted in 1787; the so-called 1784–87 state census may be two censuses intermingled. Extant portions of the 1784–87 state censuses are in Alvaretta K. Register, *State Census of North Carolina, 1784–1787,* 2d ed., rev. (1971; reprint, Baltimore, Md.: Genealogical Publishing Co., 1978). Additional portions of the 1784–87 censuses have been located since the Register's publication. See Helen F. M. Leary, comp., "Bertie Co., N.C., 1787 State Census," *The North Carolina Genealogical Society Journal* 9, no. 1 (February 1983): 32–34, and Jonathan B. Butcher, "1787 Census Return for Pearson's Company, Rowan County, NC," *The North Carolina Genealogical Society Journal* 11, no. 4 (November 1985): 253–54.

Background Sources

An essential guide for research in North Carolina is Helen F. M. Leary and Maurice R. Stirewalt, eds., *North Carolina Research: Genealogy and Local History* (Raleigh, N.C.: North Carolina Genealogical Society, 1980). In addition to being specific about the locations of sources, it provides excellent suggestions for research strategies and the interpretation of records in their historical context. See also Helen F. M. Leary, "A Master Plan for North Carolina Research," *National Genealogical Society Quarterly* 75 (1987):15–36.

A recently published history of North Carolina by William S. Powell, *North Carolina Through Four Centuries* (Chapel Hill, N.C., and London, England: University of North Carolina Press, 1989), is a new standard textbook for college level work and very readable for the general public.

The laws of North Carolina are available in many publications. The most accessible is James Iredell, comp., *Laws of the State of North Carolina* (Edenton, N.C.: James Iredell, 1791), reprinted as *The First Laws of the State of North Carolina* (Wilmington, Del.: Michael Glazier, 1984).

The North Carolina Department of Archives and History has published several guides to its holdings, the most notable of which is *Guide to Research Materials in the North Carolina State Archives, Section B: County Records* (10th rev. ed., 2d printing, Raleigh, N.C.: North Carolina Department of Archives and History, 1990). It details both original and microfilmed records held by the agency and available for purchase on microfilm. A catalog of other publications is also available from the North Carolina State Archives.

The University of North Carolina Press offers excellent materials for placing ancestors in the context of local history in the state. A copy of their catalog can be obtained from P.O. Box 2288, Chapel Hill, North Carolina 27514. A useful publication is Sydney Nathans, ed., *The Way We Lived in North Carolina* (Chapel Hill, N.C.: University of North Carolina Press, 1983), a five volume series, with each volume covering a different time period. Volume 1 covers the period before 1770 and is Elizabeth A. Fenn and Peter H. Wood's *Native and Newcomers;* volume 2 (1770–1820) is Harry L. Wilson's *An Independent People;* volume 3 (1820–70) is Thomas H. Clayton's *Close to the Land;* volume 4 (1870–1920) is Sydney Nathans's *The Quest for Progress;* and volume 5 (1920–70) is Thomas C. Parramore's *Express Lanes and Country Roads.*

Maps

Excellent maps, atlases, and gazetteers for North Carolina are readily available. The best gazetteer available for North Carolina is William Stevens Powell, *The North Carolina Gazetteer: A Dictionary of Tar Heel Places* (Chapel Hill, N.C.: University of North Carolina Press, 1968). The *Gazetteer* includes historical definitions, derivations of place-names, and exact locations. It is cross-indexed well and gives references for the first use of place-names. An important historical publication is Richard Edwards, ed., *Statistical Gazetteer of the States of Virginia and North Carolina* (Richmond, Va.: Published for the Proprietor, 1856).

There are several excellent atlases and map guides available for North Carolina. James W. Clay, Douglas M. Orr, Jr., and Alfred W. Stuart, eds., *North Carolina Atlas: Portrait of a Changing Southern State.* (Chapel Hill, N.C.: University of North Carolina Press, 1975), is perhaps the best atlas available. Fifteen North Carolina maps are included in William P. Cummings, *North Carolina in Maps,* (Raleigh, N.C.: State Department of Archives and History, 1966). See also Garland P. Stout, *Historical Research Maps: North Carolina Counties,* 5 vols. (Greensboro, N.C.: Garland P. Stout, 1973).

The North Carolina Department of Archives and History has revised David Leroy Corbitt, *The Formation of the North Carolina Counties, 1663–1943* (1950; reprint with supplementary data and corrections, Raleigh, N.C.: State Department of Archives and History, 1969). This guide is essential for determining the historical boundaries of North Carolina's counties.

Land Records

State-Land State

The availability of land helped attract settlers to North Carolina. Until the border survey was begun in 1728, grants of land in North Carolina occasionally were made by Virginia. Surviving Virginia grants may be found in Nell Marion Nugent, *Cavaliers and Pioneers, Abstracts of Virginia Land Patents and Grants*, 3 vols. (1934; reprint, Baltimore, Md.: Genealogical Publishing Co., 1983).

The process of patenting land in North Carolina was not complex. The person wishing to patent land first made application, also called a land entry, to a land office. The land officer then issued a warrant. Land officers included the secretary of state (1669–1776), the agents of Earl Granville (1748–76), or the county entry taker (1778–present). The warrant was taken to a surveyor who surveyed the land and sketched a plat (map) of the claim. The plat was then filed in the land office or, after 1777, recorded by the county register of deeds, and a patent for the land was issued and recorded. The land grants of North Carolina are indexed in the *Master Card File Index to North Carolina Land Grants, 1679–1959*, available from the Land Grant Office, Office of the Secretary of State, 300 North Salisbury Street, Raleigh, North Carolina 27603. When writing, furnish the full name of the grantee and the county in which the grant was made.

During the proprietary period (1663–1729) the Lords Proprietors relied on a headright system to distribute land grants. The standard headright of fifty acres per person established in Virginia was adopted in the Carolinas about 1697; before that time a sliding scale was used that granted one hundred acres to heads of families but only six acres to women servants when their terms expired. The governor also was allowed to sell tracts of 640 acres or less to those without headrights, or who had used their headrights for free land. To keep people in North Carolina, the assembly forbade the sale of headrights until the claimant had been in the colony for two years. The proprietary land patents are available at the North Carolina State Archives and on microfilm at the FHL. See Margaret M. Hofmann, *Province of North Carolina: 1663–1729, Abstracts of Land Patents* (Weldon, N.C.: Roanoke News Co., 1983), for abstracts of over 3,400 land patents made between 1663 and 1729. See Jo White Linn and Thornton W. Mitchell, "Headrights in North Carolina," *The North Carolina Genealogical Society Journal* 15 (February 1989): 2–11, for detailed information on the headright system used in North Carolina.

Seven of the original proprietary shares were sold to King George II in 1729, and North Carolina became a royal colony. Only John Carteret, second Earl Granville, chose not to sell the share he had inherited. The Crown continued the headright system instituted by the Lords Proprietors, but modified the system in 1741 to allow one hundred acres for the head-of-household. The Crown land office first opened in 1735, six years after the Crown purchased the province. Abstracts of Crown land patents are in Margaret M. Hofmann, *Colony of North Carolina, 1735–1764, Abstracts of Land Patents* and *Colony of North Carolina, 1765–1775, Abstracts of Land Patents* (Weldon, N.C.: Roanoke News Co., 1983–84).

The Granville District, an area that encompassed the upper half of present-day North Carolina, was created and partially surveyed in 1744 for John Carteret, second Earl Granville. Unlike the early proprietors, Granville owned all unsettled lands but had no right to govern the area. Earl Granville never visited North Carolina, but appointed agents there as representatives to grant land, collect rents, and conduct his business. The Granville land office opened in 1748. See Margaret M. Hofmann, *The Granville District of North Carolina, 1748–1763: Abstracts of Land Grants*, Vol. 1– (Roanoke Rapids, N.C.: the author, 1986–), which is a continuing project, presently with four volumes. The Granville land records are indexed in full in the Lord Granville Index in the Land Grant Office of the Secretary of State. The North Carolina State Archives also has a group of Granville land office records in the Granville Grant Card File.

After the Revolutionary War the state of North Carolina granted land formerly owned by the Crown and Earl Granville. A settler could claim as much as 640 acres of unsettled land for himself and an additional hundred acres for his wife and each minor child for a fee of two pounds ten shillings per hundred acres. If the amount of land claimed exceeded the above allotment, the additional land cost five pounds per hundred acres. Most of the state grants have been microfilmed and are available at the North Carolina State Archives and the FHL, along with grants made in Tennessee to veterans who served in the Revolutionary War.

When land was sold by individuals, the transaction generally was recorded in county deed books. Most deed books are partially indexed, but, to facilitate research, most North Carolina counties also have general indexes to grantees and grantors. Descriptions of land follow the "metes and bounds" survey system (see page 5). Copies of deeds may be obtained from the county register of deeds, but many North Carolina county records have been microfilmed and are available at the North Carolina State Archives and the FHL. Additionally, many early North Carolina deed books have been abstracted and published. Copies of these publications may be found in libraries with genealogical collections.

Probate Records

Probate records are generally of two types: wills and estate records. Estate records include both recorded and "loose" documents relating to a decedent's estate, such as inventories, divisions of estates, sales of real or personal property, and other documents. Some of this material is recorded in bound books under various titles. Although bound books generally remain in the county, many have been microfilmed and are available at the North Carolina State Archives and the FHL. However, for each county there may be surviving original wills and loose estate papers which have been transferred to the North Carolina State Archives. They are filed by county alphabetically by the surname of the decedent, and may be examined in the Search Room of the archives.

North Carolina early wills were filed with the secretary of state prior to 1760. For summarized abstracts, see J. B. Grimes, *Abstracts of North Carolina Wills, 1690 to 1760* (reprint; Baltimore, Md.: Genealogical Publishing Co., 1967), and William Perry Johnson, "Grimes Wills: Major Additions and Corrections," *Journal of North Carolina Genealogy* 11 (1965) and 12 (1966) and *North Carolina Genealogy* 13 (1967) and 14 (1968).

After 1760 wills were recorded in North Carolina counties, with the county court assuming the jurisdiction over probate matters from 1760 to 1868. After 1868, probate jurisdiction was transferred to the clerk of the superior court in each county. Some early probate records can be obtained from the clerk of the superior court in individual counties; however, pre-1868 original records have been sent to the North Carolina State Archives for preservation and copies of all records are available there. The FHL also has an extensive collection of wills and other probate records on microfilm. Thornton W. Mitchell, *North Carolina Wills: A Testator Index, 1665–1900,* 2 vols. (Raleigh, N.C.: the author, 1987), is a statewide index to all known wills probated during that period.

Court Records

Court of Pleas and Quarter Sessions (ca. 1670–1868). The court of pleas and quarter sessions was the basic court of North Carolina's counties. As such, it was often called the county court or precinct court before 1739 and the inferior court after 1806.

The county court was presided over by justices of the peace and handled minor civil matters (usually dealing with indebtedness), misdemeanors, probate, levying and expending of local taxes, matters dealing with public works (buildings, roads, bridges, ferries, and mills), summoning and selection of jurors, and a host of other local matters. See Raymond A. Winslow, Jr., "The County Court," *The North Carolina Genealogical Society Journal* 10 (1984): 70–79 and 134–43, for an in-depth examination of the county court. The court of pleas and quarter sessions was abolished under the constitution of 1868, and the county superior court took over its functions.

The county court minutes often are not indexed but are one of the richest sources of genealogical information available. Gaps in local records may be filled in by examination of the Supreme Court of North Carolina case files (see below).

General Court (1670–1754). The general court, sometimes called the court of grand council, the grand court, and the Court of Albemarle, was the court of appeals for the county court. Additionally, the general court was the court of origin in all criminal cases punishable by loss of life or limb. The court often handled probate of large estates or estates that included land in several counties. Three district courts were added to the general court in 1739, and the court was replaced in 1754 by district courts.

District Courts (1754–1806). District courts, sometimes called district superior courts, replaced the general court in 1754. In 1782 district courts acquired jurisdiction over all equity cases. From 1771–78 the district courts did not function. When the courts were reestablished in 1778, their probate authority was transferred to the county courts. District courts were replaced in 1806 by superior courts in each county.

Superior Court (1806–present). In 1806 each county received a superior court to share the judicial burden until the constitution of 1868 abolished the county court. Initially, superior courts heard cases involving large sums of money or serious criminal charges, and then took over all county-level court jurisdiction in 1868.

Court of Chancery (1663–1776). The governor and council were members of the court of chancery. During its period of operation, this court was the only court with jurisdiction over equity cases, such as division of land between partners, enforcement of contracts, and other non-criminal cases. In 1782 the North Carolina legislature vested jurisdiction over equity cases in the district courts. The equity system was abolished by the constitution of 1868.

Court of Conference (1799–1805) and Supreme Court of North Carolina (1805–present). The supreme court is the highest judicial level in the state. It was originally formed by the judges of the district superior courts, but election of supreme court justices began in 1818. Before the twentieth century, if a case was appealed to the supreme court, the entire case file often was transferred from the lower court to the supreme court. See Loren D. Austin, "Genealogy in North Carolina's Supreme Court Cases," *The North Carolina Genealogical Society Journal* 7 (August 1981): 124–32.

The North Carolina State Archives maintains most original pre-1900 court records, and microfilm copies are available at the FHL. See Leary and Stirewalt, *North Carolina Research* (cited in Background Sources) for a more thorough discussion of North Carolina's court system. An information circular, "North Carolina Courts of Law and Equity Prior to 1868," is available from the North Carolina State Archives for a fee.

Tax Records

That all governments require money to operate was well known to those who established North Carolina's civil administration. They decided to follow existing methods of taxation by placing levies on people. Prior to 1777, people who were taxed were usually called taxables, tithables, or polls; in essence they were paying a head tax. A 1715 law enacted by the general assembly defined taxables as all free males sixteen years of age and over and all slaves, male and female, aged twelve and over. The law was revised in 1749 and included all white males aged sixteen and over, as well as negroes, mulattoes, mustees or octoroons (offspring of a white and a quadroon), and all persons of mixed blood to the fourth generation, both male and female, who were twelve years of age and older.

Tax rules remained fairly constant from 1749 until 1777 when the state began applying different criteria, such as restricting the poll tax to freemen who did not own a minimum amount of property, exempting soldiers, changing the minimum age to twenty-one, or taxing only unmarried men. By 1784 the legislature settled on taxing freemen and male servants twenty-one and over and all slaves (male and female) between twelve and fifty. In 1801 all free males over fifty were exempted from the poll tax, and then in 1817 the exemption age was lowered to forty-five. A constitutional amendment in 1835 set age limits at twenty-one to forty-five for free males and twelve to fifty for slaves. The constitution of 1868 included all males between the ages of twenty-one and fifty. Poll taxes were abolished in North Carolina in 1970. Property taxes were levied in North Carolina from 1715 through 1722 and then abolished. They were reinstated in 1777 and remain in effect today. See Raymond A. Winslow, Jr., "Tax and Fiscal Records," *North Carolina Research* (see Background Sources).

North Carolina tax lists have survived better than those for many states. The lists date from the first decade of the eighteenth century to the present. Microfilmed copies are available at the North Carolina State Archives and the FHL. Many transcriptions are found in the pages of North Carolina's periodicals (see Periodicals).

Cemetery Records

An index to many pre-1914 gravestone inscriptions in North Carolina cemeteries is in the Search Room at the North Carolina State Archives. A microfilm copy of the index is available at the FHL.

Church Records

Quakers. William Edmundson and George Fox were Quaker missionaries who brought the Society of Friends (Quakers) to North Carolina in 1672. The tide of Quaker migration from Pennsylvania, Maryland, and Virginia was enough to make the Society of Friends one of the larger religious group in North Carolina during the eighteenth and early nineteenth centuries. By the start of the Civil War, the majority of Quaker families had moved to Ohio and Indiana where they hoped to escape the effects of slavery and the conflict they thought it would cause. Quakers kept excellent records, and originals of the North Carolina monthly meeting minutes and records are among the Quaker Collection at Guilford College Library in Greensboro, North Carolina. The collection consists of over 6,000 manuscript volumes of minutes and records from 1680 to the present. Early records from monthly meetings in East Tennessee, Georgia, and South Carolina that were affiliated with the North Carolina Yearly Meeting also are found there. Many North Carolina Quaker records are published in part in William W. Hinshaw, *Encyclopedia of American Quaker Genealogy*, vol. 1 (1936; reprint, Baltimore, Md.: Genealogical Publishing Co., 1978).

Church of England. The second denomination to establish a congregation in North Carolina was the Church of England in 1700. As elsewhere, that group became known as Episcopalians some years after the American Revolution. There are no surviving eighteenth century Church of England parish registers for North Carolina.

Moravian. Known also as United Brethren, a group from Pennsylvania purchased nearly 100,000 acres in 1753 and called the tract "Wachovia." Their first three towns were Bethabara, Bethlehem, and Salem. They, like the Quakers, kept excellent records. Write the Moravian Archives, Southern Province of the Moravian Church in America, Drawer M, Salem Station, Winston-Salem, North Carolina 27108. The collection contains historical books and manuscripts concerning Moravians in North Carolina. Early congregational diaries have been translated and published in Adelaide L. Fries, et al., eds., *The Records of the Moravians in North Carolina*, 11 vols. (Raleigh, N.C.: State Department of Archives and History, 1922–69).

Baptists. The Baptists reached North Carolina during the mid-eighteenth century, and the Sandy Creek Church, called the "Mother of Southern Baptist Churches," was founded in 1755. Over the next two centuries, the Baptist church became the leading religious denomination in the state. Baptist church records do not offer the wealth of information found in Quaker or Moravian records, but useful historical details and migrational clues sometimes are found in their records. Many types of Baptist churches split off from the host denomination.

The principal depository of Baptist records is the Baptist Historical Collection of the Z. Smith Reynolds Library at Wake Forest University. Write to P.O. Box 7777, Reynolds Station, Winston-Salem, North Carolina 27106. For records of the Free-Will Baptists, write to the Free-Will Baptist Historical Collection, Moye Library, Mount Olive Junior College, Mount Olive, North Carolina 28365. Primitive Baptist records are found at the Primitive Baptist Library, Route 2, Elon College, North Carolina 27244.

Other denominations. A plethora of religious groups exists in North Carolina today, but few of them were influential during the state's early history. The Presbyterians, Lutherans, and the Moravians constituted the largest minority denominations during the eighteenth and nineteenth centuries.

Presbyterianism came with the Highland Scots families who settled in the Cape Fear River area in the 1730s and the Scots-Irish who came down into North Carolina from Pennsylvania and Virginia. Write to the Presbyterian Historical Foundation, P.O. Box 847, Montreat, North Carolina 27410.

Lutheranism came into North Carolina with the Germans who first arrived in Pennsylvania early in the eighteenth century and then moved into Virginia's Shenandoah Valley before continuing south to North Carolina, where they joined the descendants of the Germanna colonists from Orange and Spotsylvania counties of north-central Virginia. Write to Archives of the North Carolina Synod, P.O. Box 2049, Salisbury, North Carolina 28144.

Military Records

North Carolina's war record begins with the Chowanoc Indian War (1675–77) and continues with the Tuscarora Indian War (1711–15), but virtually no records survive to tell of the participants. Then came the War of Jenkins's Ear (1739–44) and King George's War (1744–48) between England, France, and Spain. Some North Carolinians served in these wars, but only a few muster rolls remain. The French and Indian War began in 1755 and ended in 1763; that North Carolinians served in this war is certain, but little remains to document a soldier's service. The surviving muster rolls and militia officer lists are available at the North Carolina State Archives and are published in Murtie June Clark, *Colonial Soldiers of the South, 1732–1774* (Baltimore, Md.: Genealogical Publishing Co., 1986).

Revolutionary War. Some of the original service records for the Revolutionary War were destroyed by fire, but those remaining are on file at the National Archives, compiled primarily from rosters and rolls of soldiers serving in North Carolina's militia units. See the published list of North Carolina soldiers in *Roster of Soldiers from North Carolina in the American Revolution* (1932; reprint, Baltimore, Md.: Genealogical Publishing Co., 1977). However, the comprehensive index to Revolutionary War Records on fifty-eight reels of microfilm is available at the National Archives and its branches, the FHL and its branches, and other selected libraries.

The new states were required to raise quotas of soldiers to serve in the Continental Line during the Revolutionary War, and land was offered as an inducement. North Carolinians who volunteered to serve for at least two years were given bounty-land warrants that could be exchanged for land in what was to become Tennessee. The North Carolina State Archives has records of soldiers serving in the Continental Line.

Many North Carolinians remained loyal to the Crown during the Revolutionary War. See Murtie June Clark, *Loyalists in the Southern Campaign of the Revolutionary War* (Baltimore, Md.: Genealogical Publishing Co., 1980).

War of 1812. Information included in service records for the War of 1812 is similar to that in the same records of soldiers in the Revolutionary War. *Muster Rolls of the Soldiers of the War of 1812: Detached from the Militia of North Carolina, in 1812 and 1814* (1851; reprint, Baltimore, Md.: Genealogical Publishing Co., 1976) is the most comprehensive list available of soldiers from North Carolina. Unfortunately, *Muster Rolls* contains many errors and must be carefully verified in original records. There are War of 1812 pay vouchers for twenty-eight counties arranged alphabetically and an alphabetical list of all vouchers available in the Search Room of the North Carolina State Archives.

Civil War. Many service records are available at the North Carolina State Archives, including enlistment bounty payrolls. The most comprehensive publication on North Carolina's Confederate soldiers is Louis H. Manarin and Weymouth T. Jordan, comps., *North Carolina Troops, 1861–1865, A Roster,* 12 vols. (Raleigh, N.C.: State Department of Archives and History, 1981–present). *North Carolina Troops* includes both unit histories and some excellent biographies.

North Carolina offered pensions to Confederate veterans and their widows beginning in 1885. The 1885 pension law offered pensions to veterans and widows of veterans disabled by the loss of a limb or an eye; an 1887 amendment provided pensions for widows of veterans who died of disease while serving the Confederacy. A new law was enacted in 1889 and revised in 1901 that required a twelve-month residence in North Carolina and required that widows had married the veteran before April 1865. Original pension records and the accompanying index are available at the North Carolina State Archives; the index is available on microfilm at the FHL.

Spanish American War. An unindexed, printed *Roster of the North Carolina Volunteers in the Spanish American War* is available in the Search Room of the North Carolina State Archives.

For a more in-depth look at how military, veterans', and pension records apply in North Carolina, see George Stevenson, "Military Records" and Raymond A. Winslow, Jr., "Military Service and Veterans Records" in Leary and Stirewalt, *North Carolina Research* (see Background Sources).

Periodicals, Newspapers, and Manuscript Collections

Periodicals

A host of excellent periodicals regarding North Carolina genealogy have been or are currently being published, including *The North Carolina Genealogical Society Journal* (Raleigh, N.C.: North Carolina Genealogical Society, 1975–present) and *North Carolina Genealogy,* formerly *The North Carolinian* (Raleigh, N.C.: W. P. Johnson, 1955–75). These two periodicals provide an extensive array of instructive articles and transcriptions of original source material, making it important for the researcher to keep abreast of their contents. The North Carolina Department of Archives and History and the FHL have copies of these and other periodicals of interest to the researcher.

Newspapers

North Carolina Gazette, the first newspaper published in North Carolina, appeared in August 1751. Other newspapers followed and are detailed in H. G. Jones and Julius H. Avant, *Union List of North Carolina Newspapers, 1751–1900* (Raleigh, N.C.: State Department of Archives and History, 1963). The most extensive collection of early North Carolina newspapers on microfilm is at the North Carolina State Archives; however, many other public and academic libraries have newspapers on microfilm. See Roger C. Jones, comp., *Guide to North Carolina Newspapers on Microfilm: Titles Available from the Division of Archives and History,* 6th ed., rev. (Raleigh, N.C.: Division of Archives and History, 1984).

Manuscripts

There are superior manuscript collections in North Carolina with comprehensive guides:

Blosser, Susan Sokol, and Clyde Norman Wilson, Jr. *The Southern Historical Collection: A Guide to Manuscripts.* Chapel Hill, N.C.: University of North Carolina Press, 1970, supplemented by Everard H. Smith, III. *The Southern Historical Collection: Supplementary Guide to Manuscripts, 1970–1975.* Chapel Hill, N.C.: University of North Carolina Library, 1976. Both guides catalog the Southern Historical Collection of the University of North Carolina Library at Chapel Hill. The collection includes, but is not limited to, family papers, records on slavery, blacks, and plantations. The two guides are supplemented by a computer index located with the collection.

Cain, Barbara T., Ellen Z. McGrew, and Charles E. Morris, comps. *Guide to Private Manuscript Collections in the North Carolina State Archives.* 3d rev. ed. Raleigh, N.C.: State Department of Archives and History, 1981.

Davis, Richard C., and Linda A. Miller. *Guide to the Cataloged Collections in the Manuscript Department of the William R. Perkins Library, Duke University.* Santa Barbara, Calif., and Oxford, England: Clio Books, 1980. The collection includes private family papers, which in turn include bills of sale, names of free blacks, and plantation journals and records that are helpful in slave research.

Midgette, Susan R., and Martha G. Elmore. *An Index to Manuscript Bulletins, 1–10.* Greenville, N.C.: East Carolina University Manuscript Collection, 1988.

The Society of North Carolina Archivists is revising their publication, *Archival and Manuscript Repositories in North Carolina: A Directory,* which will provide information on numerous archival resources in the state.

Another important manuscript source for North Carolina is the Draper Collection held by the State Historical Society of Wisconsin (see Wisconsin—Manuscripts). Microfilm copies of the collection may be found at University of North Carolina at Chapel Hill and the North Carolina State Archives, as well as other repositories.

Archives, Libraries, and Societies

North Carolina Division of Archives and History
109 East Jones Street
Raleigh, NC 27611

The North Carolina State Archives maintains and provides public access to a voluminous collection of original and microfilmed material that ranges from the sixteenth century to the present. It publishes *North Carolina Historical Review,* as well as many guides to their collections (see Background Sources) and other books. Microfilm copies of some of its holdings are available for purchase.

The archives has a fine facility for in-person research, and provided the following information in January 1991 on searches by mail:

"A $5 fee is required for each letter received from out-of-state correspondents for which the Archives staff will answer one question about one person. The fee must accompany the letter. A legal-sized, stamped, self-addressed envelope should be enclosed with every inquiry. The search or handling fee does *not* apply to the cost of copies of documents which may subsequently be ordered. Checks or money orders, rather than cash, should be sent by mail."

The one question allowed should be specific, i.e., "Do you have a will for John Doe, died about 1741 in Perquimans County?" rather than general, i.e. "Do you have a will for John Doe?"

Genealogical Services Branch,
Division of North Carolina State Library
109 East Jones Street
Raleigh, NC 27611

Located in the same building as the North Carolina State Archives, the Genealogical Services Branch includes an extensive array of published and printed sources for genealogical research as well as microfilmed census records for many states.

North Carolina Genealogical Society
P.O. Box 1492
Raleigh, NC 27602

The society publishes *The North Carolina Genealogical Society Journal* (see Periodicals).

University of North Carolina
Chapel Hill, NC 27514

In addition to an extensive list of publications coming from its press, the university houses the Southern Historical Collection (see Manuscripts) and the North Carolina Collection, an exceptional and extensive collection of printed material on the state.

Duke University
William R. Perkins Library
Durham, NC 27701

This fine collection focuses on, but is not limited to, the southeastern part of the state (see Black American).

Smaller collections of genealogical and historical material exist throughout the state in local genealogical and public repositories. See Jo Ann Williford and Elizabeth F. Buford, eds., *A Directory of North Carolina Historical Organizations* (Raleigh, N.C.: Department of Cultural Resources for the Federation of North Carolina Historical Societies, 1982), for descriptions of member organizations.

Special Focus Categories

Black American

Duke University Library in Durham and the University of North Carolina Library at Chapel Hill have excellent collections of materials relating to blacks in North Carolina, in addition to that available through the National Archives (see page 10). The North Carolina Department of Archives and History and the Moravian Archives in Winston-Salem also have sources in their collections pertaining to blacks and slavery. See Thornton W. Mitchell, comp., *Preliminary Guide to Records Relating to Blacks in the North Carolina State Archives,* Archives Information Circular, No. 17 (Raleigh, N.C.: State Department of Archives and History, 1980).

A basic guide to Black American research in North Carolina is Ransom McBride, "Searching for the Past of the North Carolina Black Family in Local, Regional, and Federal Record Resources," *The North Carolina Genealogical Society Journal* 9 (May 1983): 66–77.

Native American

By 1838 the majority of North Carolina's Native American population had been destroyed or relocated to other areas. The Tuscarora moved up to New York after the Tuscarora War (1711–15), and most of the remaining Cherokee were removed to what would become Oklahoma. A significant number of tribal members who did not want to move hid out in the mountains of North Carolina and became the Eastern Band of Cherokee. Another group of Cherokees remained in the state by petitioning to become citizens. Certificates allowing them to stay were issued if they proved they could care for themselves.

Most Cherokee records were created and are presently maintained by the federal government. The National Archives has a register of Cherokees who petitioned to remain in the East, registers of Indians who decided to migrate to the West between 1817 and 1838, and the Cherokee census of 1835 (called the Henderson Roll). The census includes a list of members of the Cherokee Nation in North Carolina, Tennessee, Alabama, and Georgia. Consult also the *Eastern Cherokee Reservation Census Rolls, 1898 to 1939* and other removal records available at the National Archives (see page 11).

An Act of Congress approved on 1 July 1902 gave the U.S. Court of Claims jurisdiction over any claim arising from treaty stipulations that the Cherokees had against the United States and vice versa. Three suits were brought before the court and each was decided in favor of the Cherokees. The secretary of the interior was instructed to identify those persons of Cherokee descent entitled to a portion of the more than one million dollars appropriated by Congress for use in payment of claims.

The court established that payment was to be made to all Eastern and Western Cherokees who were alive on 28 May 1906 and who could establish that they were members or descendants of members of the Eastern Cherokee Tribe at the time the treaties were made before 1845. Claims were to be filed with the claims agent on or before 31 August 1907. By that deadline nearly 46,000 applications were on file, representing about 90,000 individual claimants. Roughly one-third of these were entitled to a share. Census lists and rolls compiled by other special agents between 1835 and 1884 were used to determine eligibility and create a new 1910 Eastern Cherokee Enrollment.

Congress authorized the allotment of land to the Five Civilized Tribes on 3 March 1893 and appointed a commission to determine who was eligible to receive land. Over 200,000 applications for land selection were received. Cherokee allotments began in 1903. Applicants were required to submit documents and affidavits as proof of Cherokee citizenship.

Some records pertaining to the Cherokees from North Carolina are housed at the Indian Archives in the Oklahoma Historical Society, Oklahoma City. The collection, which covers the Five Civilized Tribes, contains approximately three million pages of manuscripts and 6,000 bound volumes—the largest collection of Native American documents outside of the National Archives.

Native American records available at the North Carolina State Archives are detailed in Donna Spindel, ed., *Introductory Guide to Indian-Related Records (to 1876) in the North Carolina State Archives* (Raleigh, N.C.: State Division of Archives and History, 1977).

County Resources

The Lords Proprietors planned three counties in Carolina in 1664: Albemarle, Clarendon, and Craven. Craven County lay in South Carolina, and Clarendon County was abandoned in 1667 after achieving a population of about 800. Albemarle County included too large an area to provide adequate local government, so it was subdivided into Berkeley, Carteret, and Shaftesbury precincts about 1668. About 1681, the three original precincts were divided and renamed Chowan, Currituck, Pasquotank, and Perquimans precincts. By about 1689 the four precincts functioned as *de facto* counties. In 1696 Bath County was formed; it was divided into Archedale, Pamptecough, and Wickham precincts in 1705. The Provincial Government of North Carolina recognized the *de facto* status of the precincts and declared all precincts to be counties in their own right in 1739, and Albemarle and Bath counties were abolished.

Research in North Carolina county records can begin with the microfilmed North Carolina material at a central collection, such as the North Carolina State Archives, Allen County Public Library (see Indiana), the FHL, or other repositories with the North Carolina Core Collection. However, county seats still may hold additional material, including original deed and will books. What follows is an outline of beginning dates of extant records of each county. When counties were formed in North Carolina, many county clerks copied appropriate records from the parent county. In other cases, records pertaining to the land and families of the new county were transferred wholesale. Most counties therefore have some records that pre-date the formation of the county. The register of deeds at the county seat holds land and vital records, the clerk of the superior court holds probate records and court records if they have not been transferred to the state archives in Raleigh. Land records may include deeds, grants, plats, and other miscellaneous items. Probate records include not only wills, but also loose estates records, most of which have not been microfilmed. Court records may include apprentice bonds, bastardy bonds, and officials' or constables' bonds in addition to dockets, fee and account books, and court minutes and orders. The beginning dates do not imply that all records are extant since some of North Carolina's county records have been lost due to fire and other causes.

County records information is quoted from *Guide to Research Materials in the North Carolina State Archives, Section B: County Records* (10th rev. ed., Raleigh, N.C.: North Carolina Department of Archives and History, 1988). County formation information is derived from the above *Guide*, David Leroy Corbitt, *The Formation of the North Carolina Counties 1663–1943* (1950; 2d printing, Raleigh, N.C.: State Department of Archives and History, 1969); George K. Schweitzer, *North Carolina Genealogical Research* (Knoxville, Tenn.: the author, 1984); and William Perry Johnson, "North Carolina Precincts and Counties, 1663–1911," *The North Carolinian* 2, no. 2 (June 1956): 165–72.

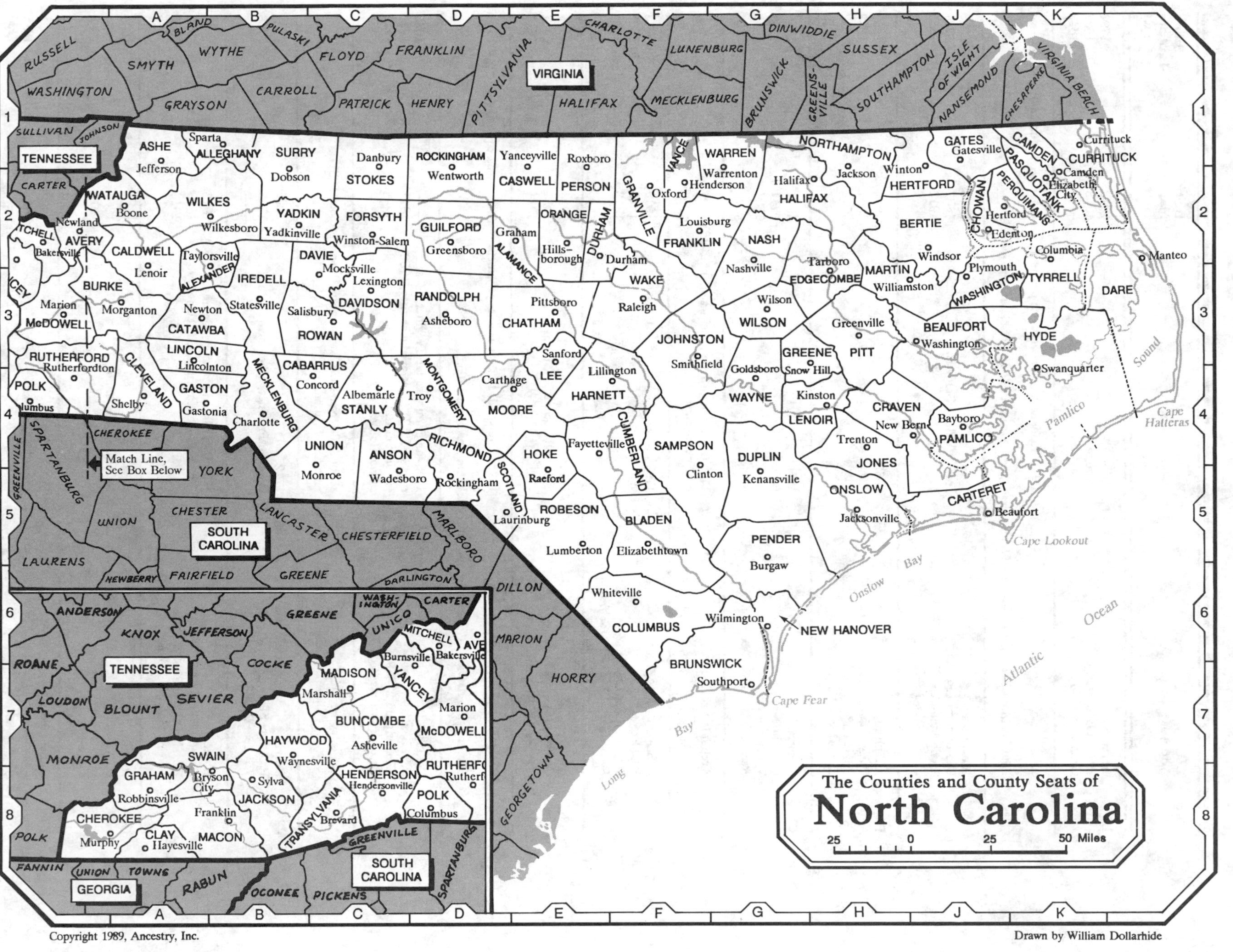
The Counties and County Seats of
North Carolina
25 0 25 50 Miles
Drawn by William Dollarhide
Copyright 1989, Ancestry, Inc.
VIRGINIA
TENNESSEE
SOUTH CAROLINA
GEORGIA
Match Line, See Box Below
ASHE Jefferson
ALLEGHANY Sparta
SURRY Dobson
STOKES Danbury
ROCKINGHAM Wentworth
CASWELL Yanceyville
PERSON Roxboro
GRANVILLE Oxford
VANCE Henderson
WARREN Warrenton
NORTHAMPTON Jackson
HERTFORD Winton
GATES Gatesville
CAMDEN Camden
CURRITUCK Currituck
PASQUOTANK Elizabeth City
PERQUIMANS Hertford
CHOWAN Edenton
BERTIE Windsor
HALIFAX Halifax
NASH Nashville
EDGECOMBE Tarboro
MARTIN Williamston
WASHINGTON Plymouth
TYRRELL Columbia
DARE Manteo
HYDE Swanquarter
BEAUFORT Washington
PITT Greenville
WILSON Wilson
FRANKLIN Louisburg
WAKE Raleigh
DURHAM Durham
ORANGE Hillsborough
ALAMANCE Graham
GUILFORD Greensboro
FORSYTH Winston-Salem
YADKIN Yadkinville
WILKES Wilkesboro
WATAUGA Boone
AVERY Newland
MITCHELL Bakersville
CALDWELL Lenoir
ALEXANDER Taylorsville
IREDELL Statesville
DAVIE Mocksville
DAVIDSON Lexington
RANDOLPH Asheboro
CHATHAM Pittsboro
LEE Sanford
JOHNSTON Smithfield
WAYNE Goldsboro
GREENE Snow Hill
LENOIR Kinston
CRAVEN New Bern
PAMLICO Bayboro
CARTERET Beaufort
JONES Trenton
ONSLOW Jacksonville
DUPLIN Kenansville
SAMPSON Clinton
HARNETT Lillington
CUMBERLAND Fayetteville
MOORE Carthage
MONTGOMERY Troy
STANLY Albemarle
ROWAN Salisbury
CABARRUS Concord
MECKLENBURG Charlotte
UNION Monroe
ANSON Wadesboro
RICHMOND Rockingham
SCOTLAND Laurinburg
HOKE Raeford
ROBESON Lumberton
BLADEN Elizabethtown
PENDER Burgaw
NEW HANOVER Wilmington
BRUNSWICK Southport
COLUMBUS Whiteville
CATAWBA Newton
LINCOLN Lincolnton
GASTON Gastonia
CLEVELAND Shelby
BURKE Morganton
McDOWELL Marion
RUTHERFORD Rutherfordton
POLK Columbus
YANCEY Burnsville
MADISON Marshall
BUNCOMBE Asheville
HAYWOOD Waynesville
HENDERSON Hendersonville
TRANSYLVANIA Brevard
JACKSON Sylva
SWAIN Bryson City
MACON Franklin
GRAHAM Robbinsville
CLAY Hayesville
CHEROKEE Murphy
Cape Hatteras
Cape Lookout
Cape Fear
Pamlico Sound
Atlantic Ocean
Onslow Bay
Long Bay

Map	County Address	Date Formed Parent County/ies	Birth Marriage Death	Land Probate Court
E2	Alamance 124 W. Elm Street Graham 27253	1849 Orange	1913 1853 —	1793 1832 1849
	Albemarle	1664 (abolished, 1739, when its precincts were declared counties) original		
	Divided into Carteret, Berkeley, and Shaftesbury precincts about 1668. Miscellaneous records, 1678-1737.			
A2	Alexander 255 Liledoun Road Taylorsville 28681 *Record loss, 1865.*	1847 Iredell/Wilkes/Caldwell	1913 1867 1913	1833 1847 1853
B1	Alleghany County Office Building Sparta 28675 *Record loss, 1932.*	1859 Ashe	1914 1861 1914	1859 1859 1862
C5	Anson Courthouse Wadesboro 28170 *Record loss, 1868. Records fragmented.*	1750 Bladen	1921 1741 1921	1749 1751 1771
	Archdale Precinct	1705 (renamed Craven Precinct about 1712) precinct of Bath		
A1	Ashe P.O. Box 633 Jefferson 28640 *Record loss, 1865. Records fragmented.*	1799 Wilkes	1913 1828 1913	1778 1801 1805
A2	Avery Courthouse Newland 28657	1911 Caldwell/Mitchell/Watauga	1914 1911 1914	1911 1911 1911
	Bath	1696 (abolished, 1739, when its precincts were declared counties) original		
	Divided into Archedale, Pamptecough, and Wickham precincts, 1705.			
J3	Beaufort P.O. Box 1027 Washington 27889 *Records fragmented. Delayed birth certificates are available.*	1705 (as Pamptecough Precinct; renamed, 1712; declared a county, 1739) precinct of Bath	— 1847 —	1695 1720 1744
	Berkeley Precinct	about 1668 (renamed Perquimans Precinct about 1681) precinct of Albemarle		
J2	Bertie P.O. Box 530 Windsor 27983	1722 Chowan Precinct, Albemarle County	— 1762 —	1721 1728 1724
F5	Bladen Courthouse Elizabethtown 28337 *Record losses, 1800 and 1893. Also called Pelham Precinct.*	1734 (as Pelham Precinct; renamed, 1734) New Hanover Precinct, Bath County	1913 1868 1913	1784 1766 1866
G6	Brunswick P.O. Box 249 Bolivia 28422 *Record loss, 1865.*	1764 New Hanover/Bladen	1914 1804 1914	1764 1764 1782
C7	Buncombe Courthouse Asheville 28801 *Record losses, 1830 and 1865. Records fragmented.*	1791 Burke/Rutherford	1887 1842 —	1791 1815 1790

Map	County Address	Date Formed Parent County/ies	Birth Marriage Death	Land Probate Court
A3	Burke P.O. Box 219 Morganton 28655 *Record loss, 1865.*	1777 Rowan	1913 1780 1913	1770 1776 1755
	Bute *Records transferred to Warren and Franklin counties.*	1764 (abolished, 1779) Granville	— — —	1778 1760 1764
C4	Cabarrus 65 Church Street, S.E. P.O. Box 707 *Concord 28025* *Record loss, 1876.*	1792 Mecklenburg	1914 1792 —	1784 1793 1793
A2	Caldwell 905 West Avenue, N.W. P.O. Box 2200 Lenoir 28645	1841 Burke/Wilkes	1914 1841 1914	1840 1830 1838
K1	Camden 117 N. 343 Camden 27921 *Records fragmented.*	1777 Pasquotank	1913 1848 1913	1739 1766 1802
J5	Carteret Courthouse Square Beaufort 28516	1722 Craven Precinct, Bath County	1912 1746 1912	1721 1744 1723
	Carteret Precinct *Divided into Currituck and Pasquotank Precincts about 1681.*	about 1668 (abolished about 1681) precinct of Albemarle		
E1	Caswell Courthouse Yanceyville 27379	1777 Orange	1913 1775 1913	1777 1771 1767
A3	Catawba P.O. Box 389 Newton 28658	1842 Lincoln	1913 1843 1913	1837 1843 1843
E3	Chatham P.O. Box 87 Pittsboro 27312	1770/1771 Orange	— 1772 —	1771 1771 1757
A8	Cherokee Courthouse Murphy 28906 *Record losses, 1865, 1895, and 1926.*	1839 Macon	1913 1837 1913	1838 1848 1846
J2	Chowan P.O. Box 1030 Edenton 27932 *Record loss, 1848. Records fragmented.* ** Formed as Shaftsbury Precinct about 1681, it was renamed Chowan about 1681 and declared a county, 1739)*	about 1668 (as Shaftsbury precinct)* precinct of Albemarle	1913 1747 1913	1678 1694 1715
	Clarendon	1664 (abolished, 1667) original		
A8	Clay Courthouse Hayesville 28904 *Record loss, 1870. Early records fragmented.*	1861 Cherokee	1913 1870 1913	1845 1862 1868

Map	County Address	Date Formed Parent County/ies	Birth Marriage Death	Land Probate Court
A4	Cleveland 100 Justice Place Shelby 28150	1841 Rutherford/Lincoln	1908 1851 1913	1792 1795 1838
F6	Columbus Administrative Building Whiteville 28472	1808 Bladen/Brunswick	1913 1867 1913	1802 1808 1817
H4	Craven P.O. Box 1425 New Bern 28563	1705 (as Archdale Precinct)* precinct of Bath	— 1740 —	1710 1737 1712
	Formed as Archdale Precinct, it was renamed Craven about 1712 and declared a county in 1739.			
F4	Cumberland 117 Dick Street Fayetteville 28302	1754 Bladen	1913 1800 1913	1752 1757 1755
K1	Currituck Courthouse Currituck 27929 *Record loss.*	about 1681 (as a precinct; declared a county, 1739) Carteret Precinct, Albemarle County	1914 1851 1914	1735 1772 1799
K3	Dare Administrative Building Manteo 27954	1870 Currituck/Tyrrell/Hyde	— 1870 —	1804 1832 1869
	Davidson (Tenn.)	1783 Washington, Tenn.		
	Ceded to the United States in 1790 as part of the Southwest Territory (later Tennessee).			
C3	Davidson Courthouse Annex Lexington 27292 *Record loss, 1866.*	1822 Rowan	1914 1822 1914	1808 1817 1820
C2	Davie 123 S. Main Street Mocksville 27028	1836 Rowan	1913 1851 1913	1792 1808 1829
	Dobbs *Divided into Glasgow and Lenoir counties, 1791.*	1758 (abolished, 1791) Johnston	— 1785 —	1746 — —
G5	Duplin P.O. Box 158 Kenansville 28349 *Records fragmented.*	1750 New Hanover	1914 1755 1914	1754 1759 1784
E2	Durham County Judicial Building Durham 27701	1881 Orange/Wake	— 1881 —	1881 1875 1881
H2	Edgecombe P.O. Box 10 Tarboro 27886	1741 Bertie	1914 1760 1914	1732 1730 1744
	Land records prior to 1759 are among those of Halifax County.			
	Fayette *Formation repealed 1784.*	1784 (abolished, 1784) Cumberland		
C2	Forsyth 700 Hall of Justice Winston-Salem 27101	1849 Stokes	— 1849 —	1849 1845 1848

Map	County Address	Date Formed Parent County/ies	Birth Marriage Death	Land Probate Court
F2	Franklin 215 E. Nash Street Louisburg 27549	1779 Bute	1913 1789 1913	1781 1776 1774
A4	Gaston P.O. Box 1578 Gastonia 28053 *Record loss, 1874. Records fragmented.*	1846 Lincoln	— 1848 —	1846 1839 1847
J1	Gates Courthouse Gatesville 27938	1779 Chowan/Hertford/Perquimans	1913 1779 1913	1776 1762 1768
	Glasgow	1791 (renamed Greene, 1799) Dobbs		
A8	Graham Courthouse Robbinsville 28771	1872 Cherokee	1913 1873 1913	1789 1847 1864
F2	Granville P.O. Box 906 Oxford 25765	1746 Edgecombe	1913 1758 1913	1746 1746 1742
	Greene (Tenn.) *Ceded to the United States in 1790 as part of the Southwest Territory (later Tennessee).*	1783 Washington, Tenn.		
H3	Greene P.O. Box 675 Snow Hill 28580 *Record loss, 1876. Records fragmented.*	1791 (as Glasgow; renamed, 1799) Dobbs	1913 1875 1913	1857 1809 1861
D2	Guilford 301 W. Market Street P.O. Box 3427 Greensboro 27402	1770/1771 Rowan/Orange	1913 1770 1913	1771 1771 1774
H2	Halifax P.O. Box 38 Halifax 27839	1758 Edgecombe	1913 1770 1913	1716 1759 1759
E4	Harnett P.O. Box 759 Lillington 27546 *Record losses, 1892 and 1894. Records fragmented.*	1855 Cumberland	1914 1892 1914	1855 1854 1875
	Hawkins (Tenn.) *Ceded to the United States in 1790 as part of the Southwest Territory (later Tennessee).*	1787 Sullivan, Tenn.		
B7	Haywood Courthouse Waynesville 28786	1808 Buncombe	1913 1808 1913	1786 1803 1809
C8	Henderson 100 N. King Street Hendersonville 28792	1838 Buncombe	1914 1838 1913	1835 1838 1838
J2	Hertford County Office Building #1 P.O. Box 116 Winton 27986 *Record losses, 1830 and 1862. Records fragmented.*	1759 Chowan/Bertie/Northampton	1911 1868 1911	1862 1868 1830

Map	County Address	Date Formed Parent County/ies	Birth Marriage Death	Land Probate Court
E4	Hoke 277 N. Main Street Raeford 28376	1911 Cumberland/Robeson	1911 1911 1911	1911 1911 1911
K3	Hyde Courthouse Swan Quarter 27885	1705 (as Wickham Precinct; renamed, 1712; declared a county, 1739) precinct of Bath	1877 1742 1877	1736 1745 1713
B3	Iredell P.O. Box 788 Statesville 28677 *Record loss, 1854.*	1788 Rowan	1913 1788 1913	1788 1787 1786
B8	Jackson 8 Ridgeway Street Sylva 28779 *Records fragmented. Delayed birth certificates are available.*	1851 Haywood/Macon	— 1853 —	1853 1853 1853
F3	Johnston P.O. Box 1049 Smithfield 27577 *Records fragmented.*	1746 Craven	1914 1746 1914	1748 1760 1759
H4	Jones P.O. Box 266 Trenton 28585 *Record loss, 1862.*	1779 Craven	1914 1851 1914	1779 1760 1807
E3	Lee P.O. Box 1968 Sanford 27331-1968	1907 Chatham/Moore	1913 1908 1913	1908 1906 1908
H4	Lenoir P.O. Box 3289 Kinston 28501 *Record losses, 1878 and 1880. Records fragmented.*	1791 Dobbs	1914 1791 1914	1737 1869 1874
A3	Lincoln 115 W. Main Street Lincolnton 28092 *Records fragmented.*	1779 Tryon	1913 1779 1913	1763 1765 1771
B8	Macon Courthouse Franklin 28734	1828 Haywood	1913 1828 1913	1820 1830 1822
C7	Madison P.O. Box 579 Marshall 28753	1851 Buncombe/Yancey	1913 1851 1913	1851 1851 1837
H3	Martin P.O. Box 668 Williamston 27892 *Records loss, 1884. Records fragmented.*	1774 Halifax/Tyrrell	1913 1872 1913	1774 1774 1809
D7, A3	McDowell County Administrative Building Marion 28752	1842 Burke/Rutherford	1914 1842 1914	1813 1841 1822
B4	Mecklenburg 600 E. Fourth Street P.O. Box 31787 Charlotte 28231	1762 Anson	1913 1783 1913	1762 1713 1774

Map	County Address	Date Formed Parent County/ies	Birth Marriage Death	Land Probate Court
D6, A2	Mitchell Courthouse Annex Bakersville 28705 *Record loss, 1907.*	1861 Burke/Caldwell/McDowell/ Watauga/Yancey	1913 1861 1913	1789 1823 1861
D4	Montgomery P.O. Box 425 Troy 27371 *Record loss, 1835. Records fragmented.*	1779 Anson	1913 1779 1913	1769 1785 1807
E4	Moore Courthouse Carthage 28327 *Record loss, 1889. Records fragmented.*	1784 Cumberland	1913 1851 1913	1787 1783 1784
G2	Nash Courthouse Nashville 27856	1777 Edgecombe	1913 1777 1913	1739 1770 1751
G6	New Hanover 320 Chestnut Street Wilmington 28401 *Records fragmented.*	1729 (as a precinct; declared a county, 1739) Craven Precinct, Bath County	1879 1741 1879	1729 1732 1738
H1	Northampton P.O. Box 808 Jackson 27845	1741 Bertie	1917 1811 1917	1741 1759 1771
H5	Onslow 521 Mill Avenue Jacksonville 28540-4259 *Record losses, 1752 and 1786.*	1734 New Hanover Precinct, Bath County	1914 1745 1914	1712 1735 1732
E2	Orange 106 E. Margaret Lane Hillsborough 27278	1752 Bladen/Granville/Johnston	1913 1779 1913	1752 1752 1752
J4	Pamlico P.O. Box 776 Bayboro 28515	1872 Beaufort/Craven	1913 1872 1913	1869 1872 1872
	Pamptecough Precinct	1705 (renamed Beaufort Precinct, 1712) precinct of Bath		
K2	Pasquotank Courthouse Room E201 Elizabeth City 27909	about 1681 (as a precinct; declared a county, 1739) Carteret Precinct, Albemarle County	1691 1691 1691	1666 1709 1737
	Pelham Precinct	1734 (renamed Bladen Precinct, 1734) New Hanover Precinct, Bath County		
G5	Pender P.O. Box 5 Burgaw 28425	1875 New Hanover	1913 1875 1913	1875 1875 1875
K2	Perquimans P.O. Box 45 Hertford 27944	about 1668 (as Berkeley precinct; renamed about 1681; declared a county, 1739) precinct of Albemarle	1659 1659 1913	1681 1709 1688
E1	Person Courthouse Roxboro 27573	1791 Caswell	1913 1791 1913	1774 1792 1775

Map	County Address	Date Formed Parent County/ies	Birth Marriage Death	Land Probate Court
H3	Pitt 1717 W. Fifth Street Greenville 27834 *Record loss, 1857. Records fragmented.*	1760 Beaufort	1913 1826 1913	1762 1836 1850
D8, A4	Polk P.O. Box 308 Columbus 28722	1855 Henderson/Rutherford	— 1855 —	1830 1851 1847
D3	Randolph 707 McDowell Road P.O. Box 4728 Asheboro 27204-4728	1779 Guilford	1913 1779 1913	1779 1773 1772
D4	Richmond P.O. Box 504 Rockingham 28379	1779 Anson	1914 1779 1914	1762 1772 1772
E5	Robeson Courthouse Lumberton 28358	1787 Bladen	1913 1803 1913	1782 1783 1795
D1	Rockingham Courthouse Highway 65 Wentworth 27375	1785 Guilford	1913 1785 1913	1785 1772 1786
C3	Rowan 202 N. Main Street Salisbury 28144 *Record loss, 1865.*	1753 Anson	1913 1753 1913	1753 1743 1753
D8, A4	Rutherford 601 N. Main Street Rutherfordton 28139 *Record loss, 1907.*	1779 Tryon	1913 1774 1913	1768 1782 1779
F4	Sampson County Office Building Rowan Street Clinton 28328 *Record losses, 1865 and 1921.*	1784 Duplin	1913 1867 1913	1752 1778 1790
D5	Scotland P.O. Box 489 Laurinburg 28352	1899 Richmond	1913 1900 1913	1900 1887 1887
	Shaftesbury Precinct	about 1668 (renamed Chowan Precinct about 1681) precinct of Albemarle		
C4	Stanly Courthouse Albemarle 28001	1841 Montgomery	1913 1850 1913	1840 1839 1841
C1	Stokes Government Center Danbury 27016	1789 Surry	1913 1790 1913	1760 1753 1782
	Sullivan (Tenn.) *Ceded to the United States in 1790 as part of the Southwest Territory (later Tennessee).*	1779 Washington, Tenn.		
	Sumner (Tenn.) *Ceded to the United States in 1790 as part of the Southwest Territory (later Tennessee).*	1787 Davidson, Tenn.		

Map	County Address	Date Formed Parent County/ies	Birth Marriage Death	Land Probate Court
B1	Surry P.O. Box 706 Dobson 27017	1770 Rowan	1912 1778 1912	1771 1770 1770
A7	Swain P.O. Drawer A Bryson City 28713 *Record loss, 1879. Delayed birth certificates are available.*	1871 Jackson/Macon	— 1871 —	1871 1871 1871
	Tennessee (Tenn.) *Ceded to the United States in 1790 as part of the Southwest Territory (later Tennessee).*	1788 Davidson, Tenn.		
C8	Transylvania 208 E. Main Street Brevard 28712	1861 Henderson/Jackson	1913 1861 1913	1861 1861 1861
	Tryon *Divided into Lincoln and Rutherford Counties in 1779. Records transferred to Lincoln County.*	1768 Mecklenburg	— — —	1769 — 1769
K3	Tyrrell County Office Building Water Street Columbia 27925	1729 Bertie/Chowan, Currituck, Pasquotank precincts, Albemarle County	1913 1742 1913	1736 1739 1735
C4	Union P.O. Box 218 Monroe 28110	1842 Anson/Mecklenburg	1913 1842 1913	1842 1837 1843
F1	Vance Courthouse Young Street Henderson 27536	1881 Granville/Franklin/Warren	1913 1881 1913	1849 1881 1881
F3	Wake P.O. Box 550 Raleigh 27602	1770 Cumberland/Orange/Johnston	— 1770 —	1774 1770 1769
	Walton (Ga.) *Was a settlement of Georgia but was actually in North Carolina; see Walton (old), Georgia.*	1803 (abolished, 1812)		
G1	Warren P.O. Box 619 Warrenton 27589	1779 Bute	1914 1779 1914	1764 1763 1769
	Washington District *Ceded to the United States in 1790 as part of the Southwest Territory (later Tennessee).*	1776 original		
J3	Washington P.O. Box 1007 Plymouth 27962 *Record losses, 1862, 1869, and 1881.*	1799 Tyrrell	1912 1851 1912	1779 1795 1815
A2	Watauga P.O. Box 1 Boone 28607 *Record loss, 1873. Records fragmented.*	1849 Ashe/Caldwell/Wilkes/Yancey	1914 1873 1914	1830 1858 1873
G4	Wayne P.O. Box 227 Goldsboro 27530	1779 Dobbs	1913 1790 1913	1780 1776 1782

Map	County Address	Date Formed Parent County/ies	Birth Marriage Death	Land Probate Court
	Wickham Precinct	1705 (became Hyde Precinct, 1712) Bath		
B2	Wilkes County Office Building Wilkesboro 28697	1777 Surry/Washington District	1913 1778 1913	1741 1777 1761
G3	Wilson P.O. Box 1728 Wilson 27893	1855 Edgecombe/Nash/Johnston/Wayne	1913 1855 1913	1836 1840 1850
B2	Yadkin P.O. Box 146 Yadkinville 27055	1850 Surry	1914 1850 1914	1793 1836 1845
D7, A2	Yancey Courthouse Room 11 Burnsville 28714	1833 Buncombe/Burke	1913 1851 1913	1831 1838 1834

North Dakota

Beth H. Bauman and Marsha Hoffman Rising, C.G., C.G.L.

The first Europeans in the area arrived the last part of the eighteenth century and were fur traders employed by the Missouri Fur Company. The peopling of the area quickly followed the first exploration with settlements in Selkirk Colony, on the Red and Assiniboine rivers, and the Pembina settlement. Both were established in 1812, but conditions were so difficult that by 1823 Selkirk had become part of the Hudson Bay Company settlement, and Pembina had been abandoned.

The indigenous tribes of the Dakotas were the Mandans and Arikaras. Eastern tribes which were moved into the area included Hidatsas, Crows, Cheyennes, Creeks, Assiniboines, Yanktonai Dakotas, Teton Dakotas, and Chippewas. The smallpox epidemics in 1782 and 1786 wiped out three-fourths of the Mandans and half of the Hidatsas. The epidemic of 1837, probably introduced by the white fur traders, had an additional devastating effect on the native population.

Composing the largest settlement at the Red River were the "half-breeds" (called métis) who were the offspring of European fathers (French, Canadian, Scottish, and English) and Native American mothers (Chippewa, Creek, Assiniboine). Many area residents claimed French-Chippewa ancestry. By 1850 more than half of the five to six thousand people living at Fort Garry were métis, with a large percentage being Canadian-born.

Settlers began moving into the region in 1849 with the organization of Minnesota Territory and the settlement of Iowa and Minnesota. This immigration brought a number of settlers to southeastern Dakota. Dakota Territory was created by an act of Congress on 2 March 1861 from the area that had previously been Nebraska and Minnesota territories. Overland migration to Montana brought settlers in conflict with the Native Americans and several wagon trains were attacked. The government reacted by constructing a number of additional forts including Rice, Buford, Stevenson, Totten, and Ransom. Fort Pembina was established in 1870.

Steamboats improved transportation after 1871, but it was the railroads that truly opened North Dakota to the outside world. With the treaties signed by the Sioux in 1867 and 1868, the population of North Dakota increased from 16,000 people to 191,000 during the Dakota Boom years of 1879–86.

Many of these settlers arrived in community groups: a group from Lansing, Michigan, settled in McIntosh County; a German-Russian group of fifty families settled Morton County; another of seventy-five families located in Emmons County; an Iowa colony settled in Logan County; and a group of 100 Pole families settled at Crystal Springs in Kidder County. For further information see Harold E. Briggs, "The Great Dakota Boom 1879–1886," *North Dakota Historical Quarterly* 4 (January 1930): 78–108.

Land could be purchased from either the Northern Pacific Railroad or directly from the federal government land offices under the Homestead or Timber Culture acts. The Pembina land office was opened in 1871; by 1890, 19,500 settlers had purchased three million acres under the 1841 pre-emption law. The speculation frenzy during the boom period was followed by retrenchment and abandonment. Those who stayed faced economic problems, drought, and low farm prices.

The genealogical researcher with ancestors in North Dakota should be aware of the three major themes in its history: its remoteness, which resulted in late development and a dependence on outside influences and economic changes; the cool, sub-humid climate that required major adaptation by the immigrating families; and an economy with low farm income and little manufacturing.

Major efforts encouraged immigration to North Dakota after statehood was obtained on 2 November 1889, creating a second population boom period. Articles describing mineral resources, timber, land, climate, livestock, and religious denominations were widely published. Of the approximately forty-five million acres of land, three-fourths were advertised as still susceptible to profitable tillage, and thirty million acres were still idle in 1892. Beginning in 1898 and ending with World War I, some 250,000 immigrants moved to the state, many of these foreign born. Most of this settlement occurred along the Great Northern Railroad, the Missouri Plateau, and the Drift Prairie. Again, more people immigrated to the area than could be sustained, and later years brought more outward migration from the state.

Vital Records

A state law passed in 1893 made it mandatory to file vital records with township clerks. It was repealed in 1895 but re-enacted in 1899.

The State Department of Vital Records was formed in 1923; all copies of prior birth and death information were required to be sent there. Copies of birth and death records beginning 1 July 1893 may be obtained from the Division of Vital Records, State Department of Health, First Floor, Capitol Building, Bismarck, North Dakota 58505. Relationship information must be provided when requesting these records.

Marriage records generally dating from county organization can be obtained from the county judge of the county where the license was issued. Only marriage records after 1 July 1925 are on file at the Division of Vital Records in Bismarck.

All divorce proceedings are recorded by the clerk of the district court in each county.

The records from the Bureau of Indian Affairs include vital records such as birth, death, and marriages from the agencies of Fort Totten, Turtle Mountain, Standing Rock, and Fort Bethold. The National Archives-Central Plains Region (see page 8) maintains these records.

Census Records

Federal

Population Schedules.

- Indexed—1850 as Pembina County, Minnesota Territory; 1860, as unorganized Dakota; 1870, Dakota Territory; 1900
- Soundex—1880, 1900, 1920
- Unindexed—Special 1885, 1910

Industry and Agriculture Schedules.

- Agriculture—1870, 1880

Mortality Schedules.

- 1860, 1870, 1880 Indexed as Dakota Territory; 1885

Union Veterans Schedules.

- 1890

The first federal census records available for this area can be found with the 1836 Iowa Territory census. North Dakota State Archives and Historical Research Library of the State Historical Society of North Dakota (see Archives, Libraries, and Societies) holds microfilmed copies of 1850 Pembina County Minnesota; 1860, 1870, and 1880 of Dakota Territory; the 1890 Union veterans and widows census; the 1900 census, including Soundex; and 1910 census. Dakota Territory agriculture schedules for 1870 and 1880 are on microfilm at the South Dakota State Historical Society.

State

The 1857 census for Pembina County, then part of Minnesota Territory, is located at the State Archives and Historical Research Library.

Part of the special, pre-statehood, federal 1885 census is available in print (see *Collections* under Background Sources). Only part of the indexing has been completed by AISI. This schedule included a special veterans and mortality return. This and the unindexed 1915 and 1925 state censuses are available on microfilm at the State Archives and Historical Research Library and through interlibrary loan.

Native American

There were several series of censuses taken at reservations. Indexing is variable. Unless otherwise indicated, the State Archives and Historical Research Library retains these censuses:

- Fort Totten Reservation: 1885–1905, 1910–39
- Fort Berthold Reservation: 1889–93, 1895–1939
- Standing Rock Reservation: 1885–1913, 1915–39 (located at National Archives-Central Plains Region in Kansas City)
- Turtle Mountain Reservation: 1885–1905 (with Fort Totten Reservation), 1910–39
- Digger Indians: 1899–1904, 1915–20

Background Sources

Aberle, George. *Pioneers and Their Sons: 165 Family Histories.* 2 vols. Bismarck, N.Dak.: Tumbleweed Press, 1980.

Bye, John E. *Guide to Manuscripts and Archives.* Fargo, N.Dak.: North Dakota Institute for Regional Studies, 1985.

Collections of the State Historical Society of North Dakota. 7 vols. Bismarck, N.Dak.: North Dakota Historical Society, 1906–25. Volume 4 (1913) contains a transcription of the 1885 census for some counties.

Hennesey, W. B. *Compendium of History and Biography of North Dakota.* Chicago, Ill.: George A. Ogle & Co., 1900.

———. *History of North Dakota.* Bismarck, N.Dak.: Bismarck Tribune, 1910.

Lounsberry, Clement Augustus. *North Dakota History and People: Outlines of American History.* 3 vols. Chicago, Ill.: S. J. Clarke, ca. 1916.

Miller, Michael M. *Researching Germans from Russia: An Annotated Bibliography.* Fargo, N.Dak.: North Dakota Institute for Regional Studies, 1987.

Robinson, Elwyn B. "The Themes of North Dakota History." *North Dakota History* 26 (January–October 1959): 5–24.

———. *History of North Dakota.* Lincoln, Nebr.: University of Nebraska Press, 1966.

Ulvestad, Martin. *Norwegians in America.* 2 vols. (in Norwegian). This publication discusses Norwegian migration to North America and specifically North Dakota.

Wick, Douglas A. *North Dakota Place Names.* Bismarck, N.Dak.: Hedemarken Collectibles, 1988.

Williams, Mary Ann Barnes. *Origins of North Dakota Place Names.* Washburn, N.Dak.: the author, 1966.

Maps

The State Archives and Historical Research Library holds a one-reel microfilm index (series 1121) to *Cartographic Records of North Dakota* that are in the custody of the Bureau of Indian Affairs.

County plat books and atlases from 1884, including Andreas's *Historical Atlas of Dakota,* are also housed at the archives as well as other repositories with North Dakota collections.

See William C. Sherman, *Prairie Mosaic: An Ethnic Atlas of Rural North Dakota* (Fargo, N.Dak.: North Dakota Institute for Regional Studies, 1983), which will be most helpful, as will *Northwestern Gazetteer: Minnesota, North and South Dakota and Montana Gazetteer and Business Directory* (St. Paul, Minn.: R. L. Polk and Co., 1914).

Land Records

Public-Domain State

The State Archives and Historical Research Library holds a few original records of the GLO for North Dakota and a microfilmed copy of the BLM's original tract books and survey plats. The North Dakota Water Commission, State Office Building, 900 East Boulevard Avenue, Bismark, North Dakota 58505, maintains original township plats although patents and copies of tract books and plats are located at the BLM, P.O. Box 222, Billings, Montana 59107.

After initial purchase, the records of transfer of land at the county level remain in the office of the register of deeds. Most land records in North Dakota are extant at the county level from the time the county was organized.

Probate Records

The district court has original jurisdiction for probate and testamentary matters, the appointment and removal of administrators and guardians, and other probate action. Marriage licenses are issued by the county judge, who keeps those records on file. Request these records from the county clerk of court. Insanity records are also maintained in the office of the county judge.

Court Records

The State Archives and Historical Research Library holds some federal district court records for Dakota Territory from 1861 through 1889 on microfilm and some county level courts records. However, the county's clerk of the district court is responsible for juvenile court records, naturalization records, coroner's juries and records, civil actions, jury lists, justice of the peace records, liquor applications for medical use, judgment records, and criminal proceedings.

Tax Records

The county auditors have possession of the tax rolls in North Dakota. Some rolls date from statehood and/or organization of the county and may be available at the State Archives and Historical Research Library and the special collection at the Chester Fritz Library (see Archives, Libraries, and Societies).

Cemetery Records

The North Dakota Bureau of Vital Statistics holds an index to cemetery names (not individuals buried there), location, and date of organization of cemeteries in the state. Many cemetery transcripts have been compiled by local genealogical societies in separate publications or periodicals. They may be found in one of several North Dakota libraries.

Seventeen volumes of cemetery records were compiled by the Red River Valley Genealogical Society (formerly the Fargo Genealogical Society). Some have been microfilmed and are available for research through the FHL.

Church Records

Religious denominations which have been predominant in North Dakota history are Roman Catholic, Lutheran, Methodist, Episcopal, and Presbyterian. Most extant records remain with the local church. Some records in manuscript, microfilm, or printed form can be found at the State Archives and Historical Research Library, the Chester Fritz Library, the North Dakota Institute for Regional Studies (see Archives, Libraries, and Societies), and the FHL.

Military Records

The Historical Research Library has the National Archives microfilm index to service records of Union soldiers in North Dakota.

The researcher should also check the *Official Roster of North Dakota Soldiers, Sailors and Marines in World War I, 1917–1918,* 4 vols. (Bismarck, N.Dak.: North Dakota State Historical Society, 1931). Other rosters exist for World War II and the Korean and Vietnam eras. Contact the Office of the Adjutant General, P.O. Box 551, Attention, SIDPERS, Bismark, North Dakota 58502.

Periodicals, Newspapers, and Manuscript Collections

Periodicals

North Dakota History (formerly *North Dakota Historical Quarterly*) is published by the State Historical Society of North Dakota. This is the major statewide periodical for historical material, publishing helpful background for research.

Newspapers

Newspapers from across the state have been collected at the State Archives and Historical Research Library since the turn of the century. All have been microfilmed and are available on interlibrary loan. An index of newspapers, arranged by county name and city name, is available.

Between 5 April 1931 and 28 October 1934, the *Fargo Forum* printed 173 profiles of pioneer women of North Dakota under the title "Quarter Sections and Wide Horizons." With few exceptions, all were living in Dakota Territory prior to statehood in 1889. The stories were written by Angela Boyelin, editor of the *North Dakota Clubwoman.*

Manuscripts

Three major manuscript collections exist in North Dakota. The first of these is located in the State Archives and Historical Research Library. David P. Gray's *Guide to Manuscripts* [of North Dakota] (Bismarck, N.Dak.: State Historical Society of North Dakota, 1985) serves as a directory to the state historical society's manuscript collections. Of note are the following groups of materials at the library:

Historical Data Project (WPA) Biography contains biographical information and consists of over 5,000 files gathered in the 1930s and organized by individual name and county. These files are microfilmed and available on interlibrary loan from the library.

The Necrology of North Dakota consists of six scrapbooks and obituaries from the years 1920 to 1926 and is held in the manuscript division of the state archives.

Photo Archives has over 60,000 black and white images from 1865 to present. Reprints can be made for a nominal fee.

Pioneer Mothers Project, indexed by individual name, was created by the North Dakota Federation of Women's Clubs in the 1930s and contains family histories, biographical entries, obituaries, and some lineage charts.

Chester Fritz Library's *Guide to Orin G. Libby Manuscript Collection* consists of three volumes, providing access to this second large group of materials on North Dakota. Volume one was compiled by John B. Davenport in 1975, volume two by Colleen A. Oihus in 1983, and volume three by Sandra J. Beidler in 1985.

The third collection includes a statewide biographical index of over 500 volumes and is located at the North Dakota Institute of Regional Studies.

Archives, Libraries, and Societies

State Archives and Historical Research Library
State Historical Society of North Dakota
612 East Boulevard Avenue
Bismarck, ND 58505-0179

The archives and historical research library is operated as one unit by the State Historical Society of North Dakota and holds several categories of records that are discussed elsewhere. The staff will do a limited search in censuses and newspapers if specific information is known. *Guide to the North Dakota State Archives* (Bismarck, N.Dak.: State Historical Society of North Dakota, North Dakota Heritage Center, State Capitol Grounds, 1985) is available to assist in using the library's collection.

Many of the territorial records for the Dakotas are housed at the State Archives of North Dakota including Dakota Territorial Papers 1877–86, the Office of Indian Affairs Correspondence for the years 1824–87, and the Indian Treaty negotiations between 1801–69.

North Dakota State Library
Liberty Memorial Building
Capitol Grounds
Bismarck, ND 58505

The State Library holds printed volumes of source materials, as it is the primary library, coordinating the various libraries throughout the state. While its collection for genealogical research is limited, it does have county histories and other similar printed sources that circulate on interlibrary loan.

Chester Fritz Library
University of North Dakota
Grand Forks, ND 58202-9000

The family history room holds a variety of national and North Dakota printed source materials in addition to those cited in various sections above.

North Dakota Institute for Regional Studies
North Dakota State University Library
Fargo, ND 58105

Manuscript sources here constitute one of the major collections in the state and include the Germans from Russia collection.

Bismarck-Mandan Historical and Genealogical Society
P.O. Box 485
Bismarck, ND 58502-0485

As one of three genealogical societies producing publications, this association makes state research possible through the Historical Research Library. Other societies at Fargo (Red River Valley Genealogical Society) and Minot (Mouse River Loop Genealogical Society) have a more limited scope.

Special Focus Categories

Naturalizations

Most of North Dakota's naturalization records have been transferred from the clerk of the district court offices in each county to the State Archives and Historical Research Library. These records represent the bulk of documentation pertaining to immigration and naturalization proceedings in the state. The records document individuals who became, or applied to become, citizens between 1873 and 1952. Indexes for forty counties are presently available and others are in process.

Ethnic Groups

North Dakota settlers who were immigrants to America came primarily from Norway and Canada, but others were from Germany, England, Ireland, Sweden, and Russia. By 1890 the foreign-born settlers made up 43 percent of the population. These people together with the children of foreign parents actually comprised 69 percent of North Dakota's families. In 1910, 21 percent of the residents were Norwegian, 20 percent were German (with about half of these from Russia), 12 percent were English and Celtic (Irish, Scottish, and Welsh), and 5 percent were descendants of earlier immigrants.

The Germans from Russia Heritage Society, 1008 E. Central Avenue, P.O. Box 1671, Bismarck, North Dakota 58501, has an in-depth collection of family files, obituaries, immigration records, and family and county histories for those with a German heritage through Russia. Both North Dakota and national records are included. Another collection for this ethnic group is located at the North Dakota Institute for Regional Studies (see Archives, Libraries, and Societies), but, in addition, its biographical index identifies books and publications dealing with this group of immigrants.

The Bygdeboker (Bygde Books) that discuss Norwegian immigrants are located at the Chester Fritz Library and are available on interlibrary loan if they have been microfilmed.

County Resources

The FHL holds the *Historical Records Survey of North Dakota* (Bismarck, N.Dak.: WPA, 1939). Although outdated, it remains a helpful guide. County records including land, court, tax, probate and township records for North Dakota may be extant from time of formation. There may, however, be individual discrepancies, and the researcher will need to check with the local office for exact reference. The county judge holds marriage and probate records, the register of deeds holds land records, and the clerk of the district court holds civil court records.

Some records have been transferred to the State Archives and Historical Research Library (see *Preliminary Guide to Local Government Records at the State Historical Society of North Dakota* (1983). Since this is a continuing process, correspondence should be addressed to the county *first,* and if the records have been transferred, the letter will be forwarded. County offices can normally be addressed in care of the county courthouse; however, in the list below, addresses or post office boxes for registers of deeds are given.

For some counties on the chart there are two years listed for "Date Formed." The first is the year that the county was created; the second is the year it was fully organized if it differs from creation year. Under the heading "Parent County/ies," unorganized land denotes that it was formed from non-county lands, and counties listed with an asterisk (*) are those to which the county was at one time "attached" before organization.

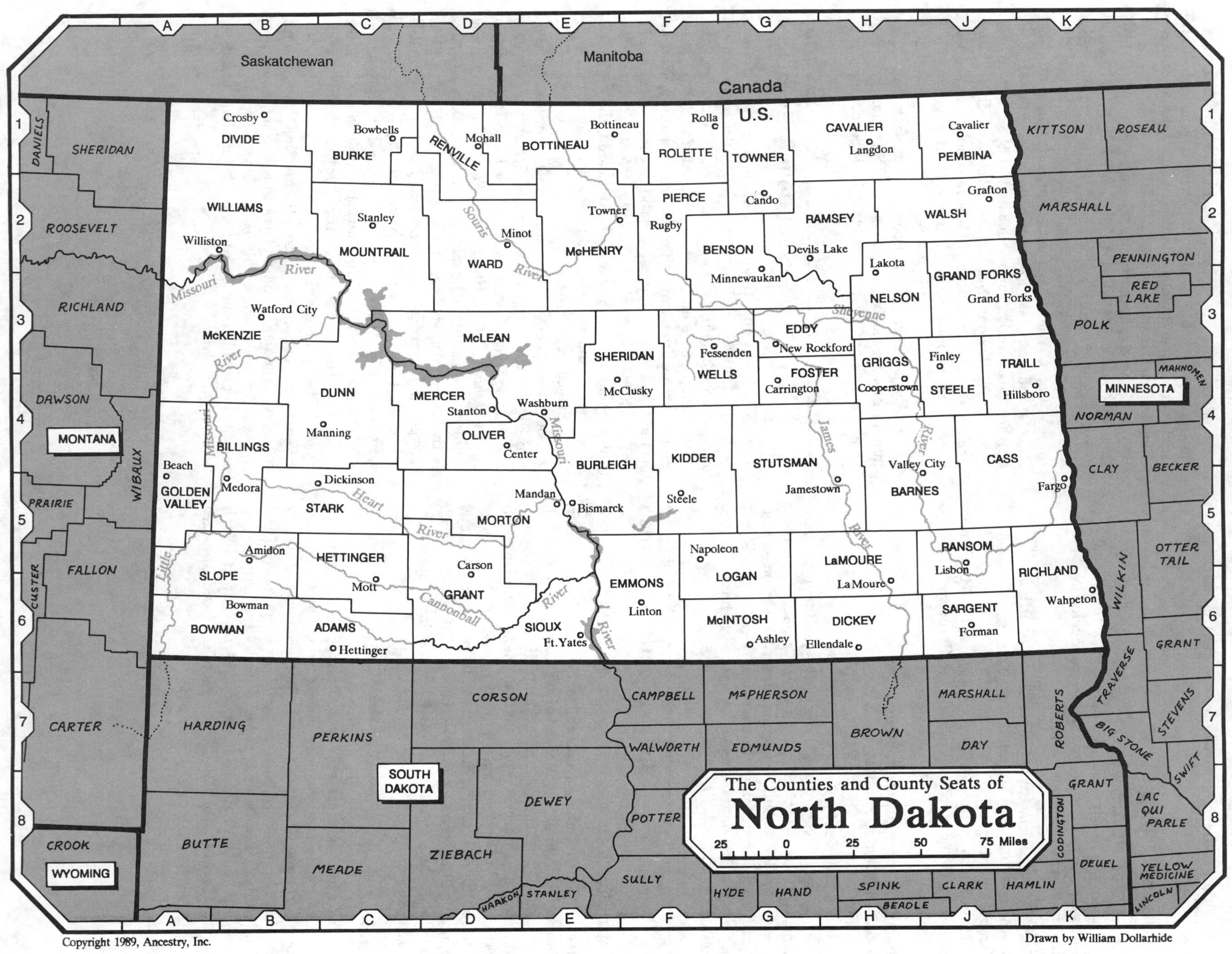
The Counties and County Seats of
North Dakota
25 0 25 50 75 Miles
Saskatchewan
Manitoba
Canada
U.S.
MINNESOTA
MONTANA
SOUTH DAKOTA
WYOMING
Crosby
DIVIDE
Bowbells
BURKE
Mohall
RENVILLE
Bottineau
BOTTINEAU
Rolla
ROLETTE
TOWNER
Cando
CAVALIER
Langdon
Cavalier
PEMBINA
WILLIAMS
Williston
Stanley
MOUNTRAIL
Minot
WARD
Towner
McHENRY
PIERCE
Rugby
BENSON
Minnewaukan
RAMSEY
Devils Lake
WALSH
Grafton
Lakota
NELSON
GRAND FORKS
Grand Forks
Watford City
McKENZIE
McLEAN
SHERIDAN
McClusky
Fessenden
WELLS
EDDY
New Rockford
FOSTER
Carrington
GRIGGS
Cooperstown
Finley
STEELE
TRAILL
Hillsboro
DUNN
Manning
MERCER
Stanton
Washburn
OLIVER
Center
BILLINGS
Beach
GOLDEN VALLEY
Medora
Dickinson
STARK
Mandan
Bismarck
MORTON
BURLEIGH
KIDDER
Steele
STUTSMAN
Jamestown
Valley City
BARNES
CASS
Fargo
Amidon
SLOPE
HETTINGER
Mott
Carson
GRANT
EMMONS
Linton
Napoleon
LOGAN
LaMOURE
La Moure
RANSOM
Lisbon
RICHLAND
Wahpeton
Bowman
BOWMAN
ADAMS
Hettinger
SIOUX
Ft. Yates
McINTOSH
Ashley
DICKEY
Ellendale
SARGENT
Forman
Missouri River
Souris River
Sheyenne
James River
Heart River
Cannonball River
Little Missouri River
DANIELS
SHERIDAN
ROOSEVELT
RICHLAND
DAWSON
WIBAUX
PRAIRIE
FALLON
CUSTER
CARTER
CROOK
KITTSON
ROSEAU
MARSHALL
PENNINGTON
RED LAKE
POLK
MAHNOMEN
NORMAN
CLAY
BECKER
WILKIN
OTTER TAIL
GRANT
TRAVERSE
STEVENS
BIG STONE
SWIFT
LAC QUI PARLE
YELLOW MEDICINE
LINCOLN
HARDING
PERKINS
CORSON
CAMPBELL
McPHERSON
MARSHALL
WALWORTH
EDMUNDS
BROWN
DAY
ROBERTS
GRANT
CODINGTON
DEUEL
BUTTE
MEADE
ZIEBACH
DEWEY
POTTER
SULLY
HAAKON
STANLEY
HYDE
HAND
SPINK
BEADLE
CLARK
HAMLIN
Copyright 1989, Ancestry, Inc.
Drawn by William Dollarhide

Map	County Address	Date Formed Parent County/ies	Birth Marriage Death	Land Probate Court
C6	Adams P.O. Box 469 Hettinger 58639	1907 Hettinger	— 1907 —	1907 1907 1907
	Allred	1883 Howard		
	In 1896 Allred became a part of Billings; in 1901 Allred was re-created from Billings; in 1903 it was attached to Williams; and in 1905 it was abolished when it became part of McKenzie.			
H5	Barnes Register of Deeds P.O. Box 684 Valley City 58072	1873 (as Burbank; renamed Barnes, 1875) Pembina	1893–1910 1882 1893–1910	1875 1875 1875
G2	Benson 311 B Avenue Minnewaukan 58351	1883 Ramsey/De Smet	1903 1885 1903	1883 1883 1883
B4	Billings P.O. Box 138 Medora 58645	1879 (1886) unorganized land/Howard	— 1887 —	1879 1879 1879
E1	Bottineau 818 Kersten Bottineau 58318	1873 (1884) Buffalo	— 1884 —	1884 1884 1884
A6	Bowman P.O. Box 379 Bowman 58623	1883 (1907) Billings	? 1907 ?	1883 1883 1883
	In 1896 Bowman became part of Billings; in 1901 Bowman was re-created from Billings; in 1903 it was attached to Stark; and in 1907 it became fully organized.			
	Buffalo	1864 (1871) unorganized land/Bruguier/Charles Mix *Bon Homme		
	In 1873 Buffalo lost land to twenty-five counties in Dakota Territory; in 1889 Buffalo became a county in the newly created state of South Dakota.			
	Buford	1883 Wallette		
	In 1891 Buford was attached to Ward; in 1892 it was abolished and became part of Williams.			
	Burbank	1873 (renamed Barnes, 1875) Pembina		
C1	Burke P.O. Box 219 Bowbells 58721	1910 Ward	— 1910 —	1910 1910 1910
E5	Burleigh Clerk of District Court *and* Clerk of County Court 514 E. Thayer Avenue Bismarck 58501 *and* Register of Deeds 221 N. Fifth Street Bismarck 58501	1873 Buffalo	— 1898 1880; 1901*	1873 1873 1873
J5	Cass P.O. Box 2806 Fargo 58108 **1889–1920 at Fargo.*	1873 Pembina	— 1872 1884–87*	1873 1873 1873

Map	County Address	Date Formed Parent County/ies	Birth Marriage Death	Land Probate Court
H1	Cavalier 901 Third Street Langdon 58249	1873 (1884) Pembina	1884–1908 1887 1884–1908	1873 1873 1873
	De Smet *In 1887 De Smet was abolished and became part of Pierce.*	1873 (as French; renamed De Smet, 1875) Buffalo		
H6	Dickey Register of Deeds P.O. Box 148 Ellendale 58436 **Incomplete.*	1881 (1882) La Moure/Ransom/unorganized land	1894–1900 1883 1894–1900*	1881 1881 1881
B1	Divide P.O. Box 68 Crosby 58730	1910 Williams	— 1910 —	1910 1910 1910
	Dunn (old)	1883 (became part of Stark, 1896) Howard		
C4	Dunn (present) P.O. Box 106 Manning 58642	1901 (1908) Stark	— 1908 —	1908 1908 1908
G3	Eddy 524 Central Avenue New Rockford 58356	1885 Foster	1889–1926 1887 1893–1907	1885 1885 1885
F6	Emmons P.O. Box 905 Linton 58552	1879 (1883) unorganized land/Burleigh	1903 1888 1903	1879 1879 1879
	Flannery *In 1891 Flannery was attached to Ward; in 1892 it was abolished and became part of Williams.*	1883 Wallette		
G4	Foster P.O. Box 257 Carrington 58421	1873 (1883) Pembina	— 1883 —	1873 1873 1873
A5	Golden Valley P.O. Box 596 Beach 58621	1912 Billings	— 1912 —	1912 1912 1912
J3	Grand Forks Register of Deeds P.O. Box 6 Grand Forks 58206 **Coroner's records and inquests for deaths; county judge has index to marriage certificates from 1875.*	1873 (1875) Pembina	— 1887* 1891*	1873 1873 1873
D6	Grant P.O. Box 258 Carson 58529	1916 Morton	— 1916 —	1916 1916 1916
H4	Griggs P.O. Box 326 Cooperstown 58425	1881 Foster/Barnes/Traill	1901–07 1883 1900–07	1881 1881 1881
	Gringras	1873 (renamed Wells, 1881) Buffalo		

Map	County Address	Date Formed Parent County/ies	Birth Marriage Death	Land Probate Court
C6	Hettinger P.O. Box 668 Mott 58646	1883 (1907) Stark	— 1907 —	1883 1883 1883
	In 1896 Hettinger was abolished and became part of Stark; in 1901 it was re-created from Stark but remained attached to Stark until it was fully organized in 1907.			
	Howard	1873 (abolished, 1883; became part of Allred, Dunn, McKenzie, Wallace) unorganized land		
F4	Kidder P.O. Box 66 Steele 58482	1873 (1881) Buffalo	1899–1907 1886 1885–1907	1873 1873 1873
H6	La Moure 202 Fourth Avenue N.E. La Moure 58458 **City auditor.*	1873 (1881) Pembina	1903–23* 1887 1903–23*	1873 1873 1873
G6	Logan P.O. Box 6 Napoleon 58561	1873 (1884) Buffalo	1883–1923 1890 1883–1923	1873 1873 1873
E2	McHenry Register of Deeds P.O. Box 57 Towner 58788	1873 (1885) Buffalo	1889–1907 1905 1889–1907	1873 1873 1873
G6	McIntosh P.O. Box 179 Ashley 58413	1883 (1884) Logan/unorganized land	1899–1908 1885 1899–1908	1883 1883 1883
	McKenzie (old)	1883 (abolished, 1896; became part of Billings) Howard		
B3	McKenzie (present) Register of Deeds P.O. Box 523 Watford City 58854	1901 (1905) Billings	1905–08 1906 1905–08	1905 1905 1905
	In 1901 McKenzie was re-created but remained attached to Stark until it was fully organized in 1905.			
D3	McLean Register of Deeds P.O. Box 119 Washburn 58577	1883 Burleigh/Stevens/Sheridan	1884–1907 1887 1884–1907	1883 1883 1883
D4	Mercer P.O. Box 39 Stanton 58571 **Coroner's reports.*	1875 (1884) unorganized land	— 1885 1909*	1875 1875 1875
D5	Morton 210 Second Avenue N.W. Mandan 58554	1873 (1881) unorganized land	1893–95 1882 1893–1908	1873 1873 1873
C2	Mountrail P.O. Box 69 Stanley 58784	1873 Buffalo	— 1909 —	1909 1909 1909
	In 1891 Mountrail was attached to Ward; in 1892 it was abolished and became part of Ward; in 1909 it was re-created from Ward.			
H3	Nelson P.O. Box 565 Lakota 58344	1883 Foster/Grand Forks/Ramsey	? 1885 ?	1883 1883 1883

Map	County Address	Date Formed Parent County/ies	Birth Marriage Death	Land Probate Court
D4	Oliver P.O. Box 125 Center 58530	1885 Mercer	— 1885 —	1885 1885 1885
J1	Pembina Register of Deeds P.O. Box 147 Cavalier 58220 **Also births and deaths, 1899–1907.*	1867 unorganized land	1893–95* 1872 1893–95*	1867 1867 1867
F2	Pierce 240 S.E. Second Street Rugby 58368	1887 (1889) Bottineau/De Smet/McHenry/Rollette	1893–1903 1888 1893–1903	1887 1887 1887
G2	Ramsey P.O. Box 863 Devils Lake 58301	1873 (1885) Pembina	1903–09 1887 1903–09	1873 1873 1873
J5	Ransom Register of Deeds P.O. Box 666 Lisbon 58054 **Also coroner's records, 1883.*	1873 (1881) Pembina	— 1882 1892–1902*	1873 1873 1873
	Renville (old)	1873 Buffalo (attached to Ward, 1891; abolished 1892; became part of Bottineau and Ward)		
D1	Renville (present) P.O. Box 68 Mohall 58761	1910 Ward	— 1910 —	1919 1919 1919
K6	Richland Register of Deeds P.O. Box 995 Wahpeton 58075 *and* Clerk of the County Court 413 Third Avenue N. Wahpeton 58075 **Coroner's inquests.*	1873 (1875) unorganized land/Pembina	— 1877 1883*	1873 1873 1873
F1	Rolette Register of Deeds P.O. Box 276 Rolla 58367	1873 (1884) Buffalo	1894–1929 1884 1894–1915	1873 1873 1873
J6	Sargent P.O. Box 176 Forman 58032 **Also coroner's inquests from 1899.*	1883 Ransom/unorganized land	— 1886 1888*	1883 1883 1883
	Sheridan (old)	1873 Buffalo (abolished 1892; became part of McLean)		
F3	Sheridan (present) P.O. Box 668 McClusky 58463	1908 McLean	— 1909 —	1909 1909 1909
E6	Sioux P.O. Box 345 Fort Yates 58538 **Superintendent of Indian reservation.*	1914 Standing Rock Reservation	1902* 1916 1902*	1915 1915 1915

Map	County Address	Date Formed Parent County/ies	Birth Marriage Death	Land Probate Court
B6	Slope P.O. Box JJ Amidon 58620	1914 (1915) Billings	— 1915 —	1915 1915 1915
B5	Stark P.O. Box 130 Dickinson 58601	1879 (1883) Howard/Williams/unorganized land	— 1887 1893–94	1873 1873 1873
J4	Steele P.O. Box 296 Finley 58230	1883 Griggs/Traill	— 1884 —	1884 1884 1884
	Stevens	1873 Buffalo		
	The original Stevens County was created in 1862 from unorganized land but was abolished in 1863. This Stevens County was attached to Ward in 1891 and was abolished in 1892 when it became part of McLean and Ward.			
G5	Stutsman 511 Second Avenue S.E. Jamestown 58401 **Clerk of district court.*	1873 Pembina/Buffalo	— 1884 1881*	1873 1873 1873
G1	Towner Towner County Courthouse Cando 58324	1883 (1884) Rolette/Cavalier	1903–07 1888 1903–27	1883 1883 1883
J4	Traill Register of Deeds P.O. Box 399 Hillsboro 58045 **Mayville only.*	1875 Grand Forks/Burbank/Cass	— 1880 1891*	1875 1875 1875
	Wallace	1883 Howard		
	In 1896 Wallace was abolished and became part of Billings and Stark; in 1901 it was re-created from Billings and Stark but remained attached to Stark; in 1905 it was abolished again and became part of McKenzie.			
	Wallette	1873 (abolished 1883; became part of Buford and Flannery) Buffalo		
J2	Walsh 600 Cooper Avenue Grafton 58237 **Filed in state records.*	1881 Grand Forks/Pembina	—* 1882 —*	1881 1881 1881
D2	Ward Ward County Courthouse Minot 58701 **Coroner reports, clerk of district court.*	1885 Renville/Stevens	— 1888 1888–*	1885 1885 1885
F3	Wells Register of Deeds P.O. Box 125 Fessenden 58438	1873 (as Gingras; renamed, 1881) Buffalo	1893–1913 1887 1893–1913	1873 1873 1873
	Williams (old)	1873 (abolished 1892; became part of Mercer) unorganized land		
B2	Williams (present) P.O. Box 2047 Williston 58801	1892 (1903) Buford/Flanery	— 1892 —	1890 1890 1890

Ohio

Carol L. Maki

René Robert Cavelier, Sieur de la Salle, the French explorer, traveled through Ohio land in 1667 and is thought to have been the first white person to see the Ohio River. Eighty years later, in 1747, the Ohio Company of Virginia was organized to colonize the Ohio River Valley, leading to the creation of the Ohio Land Company two years later. Great Britain gained control of the region following the French and Indian War in 1763 but lost it again in 1779.

The establishment of Northwest Territory in 1787 marked the beginning of a steady stream of migration. Scots-Irish from Virginia, Kentucky, and Pennsylvania settled mainly in Marietta in Washington County. New Englanders and Revolutionary War soldiers, most of them from Massachusetts and Connecticut, arrived in that same area followed by Essex County, New Jersey, people, who settled in Cincinnati in an area called the Symmes Purchase. French immigrants settled in Gallipolis, Gallia County, from 1790 through 1791. Additional Connecticut migrations occurred in 1796–97, settling in the Connecticut Western Reserve. Others from Connecticut and Vermont settled in what became Geauga County three years later. Clermont County was the new home of those from Maine in 1796, the same year that emigrants from Scotland arrived in Montgomery County. In 1796 the Refugee Tract was established in Columbus for Canadians who sympathized with the American Revolution. Three years later Ohio Territory was created, followed in 1800 by the first Ohio territorial census and the opening of the first land offices at Marietta, Steubenville, Chillicothe, and Cincinnati. The territory became a state in 1803.

The influx of new settlers continued, with Germans and Welsh from Pennsylvania, plus additional migrations from Kentucky and Virginia. Statehood was rapidly achieved in 1803. Three years later the United Society of Believers of Christ's Second Appearing (Shakers) migrated to Warren County. Germans settled in Brown and Tuscarawas counties from 1814 through 1824. The opening of the Erie Canal in 1825 was an opportunity for those in the northeastern United States to migrate to Ohio. The Mormons (see Church Records) arrived in Ohio in 1831. English and Irish emigrated to Ohio for railroad construction employment in the 1840s. By 1860, Ohio's extensive railroad construction provided more miles of track than any other state.

Ohio was intensely involved with the abolitionist movement prior to the Civil War having considerable activity in the Underground Railroad along Lake Erie and the Ohio River. Following the Civil War, the state gained national political power, producing seven United States presidents. As an agricultural and industrial state, some early industries were barrel-making and meat packing. The American Federation of Labor formed there in the 1880s. The industrialization and urbanization of Ohio brought new residents from eastern and southern Europe and blacks from southern states. Mining became increasingly important with products of coal, limestone, and salt.

The twentieth century brought continued industrial strength under the power of capitalists like Benjamin F. Goodrich, Charles Franklin Kettering, and John D. Rockefeller. The multitude of Ohio manufacturers of this century produce a diverse range of items from steam shovels to matches.

Vital Records

Ohio enacted a statute in 1856–57 that required birth, death, and marriage registration, a law that was generally disregarded. Ann Fenley states in *The Ohio Open Records Law and Genealogy* (Dayton, Ohio: Ohio Connection, 1989) that the two types of "death records" known to be in existence before 1867 are records of cholera deaths, registered during some epidemics, and veterans' deaths. A later 1867 law again required registration of birth and death records. Some of these have survived. The third law, in 1908, established the more complete records now maintained.

For death and birth registration prior to 20 December 1908, contact the county. For birth registrations beginning 20 December 1908 and death registrations after 31 December 1936, write to the State Department of Health, Division of Vital Statistics, Ohio Departments Building, Room G-20, 65 Front Street, Columbus, Ohio 43266-0333. A certified photocopy of either record is $7; uncertified, $1.10. If exact date and place of birth or death cannot be provided with the request, they will search statewide indexes for the information for a fee of $3 per hour. Approximately ten years of indexes can be searched for one name in an hour. Unused finds are returned. It is not necessary to prove a relationship to obtain a birth or death record photocopy. Some city health departments may have city birth and death records *if* separate records were kept.

The State Department of Health has registered births and deaths since 20 December 1908. Early in 1989 all Ohio death records for 20 December 1908 through 31 December 1936 and the respective indexes plus death indexes, for 1937–38 were transferred to the State Archives of Ohio housed by the Ohio Historical Society (see Archives, Libraries, and Societies). Actual death records for 1937–38 were not transferred. The Ohio Historical Society will search the aforementioned records for $7. The nonrefundable fee will cover a search of eight years and an uncertified copy of the record, if found. Certified copies require two $7 checks, the first to the Ohio Historical Society, the second made out to the Ohio Division of Vital Statistics. The Ohio Historical Society will forward that check and the certificate to Vital Statistics for certification. The second check will be returned if no record is found. Only one name with one spelling variation will be accepted in each request. One letter per patron per week is the limit, and a two to three month response time should be anticipated.

Marriage records were kept by the office of the county probate clerks until 7 Sept 1949, when it became a state registration procedure. The statewide index to marriages begins with that date. Certified abstracts of marriages were filed with the state beginning 7 September 1949. The Division of Vital Statistics will search indexes of these abstracts for $3 per hour and indicate the county where the marriage occurred (the search covers about a ten-year period). However, certified copies of marriage records may only be obtained from the probate court of the county that issued the license (see County Resources).

Ohio marriages to approximately 1865 are included in the IGI (see pages 1–2) of the FHL. The marriages in years between 1865 and 1949 are not indexed. Marriage records in Ohio *usually* include the following information: names of bride and groom, date of marriage, county and possibly the specific location, officiating party, and ages and residences of the bride and groom.

The Ohio Historical Society and the Ohio Network of American History Research Centers (see Archives, Libraries, and Societies) are collecting centers for early birth, marriage, and death records and may need to be contacted regarding their holdings in addition to the county courthouse.

Hamilton County has the jurisdiction for the registration of marriages for Cincinnati. However, many of those records were lost in a courthouse fire. Records that survived were indexed by the WPA and include applications, licenses, and returns. Genealogists have reconstructed marriage records from ministers' daybooks, original certificates, and newspaper accounts.

Marriage records from family and local sources have been collected by the DAR. The State Library of Ohio is the official depository for the state copies of DAR compilations. These records are listed in Carol W. Bell, *Master Index Ohio D.A.R. Genealogical and Historical Records*, Vol. 1 (Westlake, Ohio: Mrs. Thomas B. Clark, 1985). Local genealogical societies have compiled numerous vital records indexes.

Cincinnati was also a "Gretna Green" (meaning, no questions asked) marriage locale. Although the records for Cincinnati are incomplete, they should be checked for a marriage not otherwise found in Ohio, Indiana, or Kentucky.

An index of some Ohio marriages is Marjorie Smith, ed., *Ohio Marriages 1790–1897* (1977; reprint, Baltimore, Md.: Genealogical Publishing Co., 1986). The information is extracted from the *Old Northwest Genealogical Quarterly*. Marriages, listed alphabetically by bride and groom, are from fifteen volumes of this periodical and begin in the early 1800s. This includes records from only nine counties.

Since 1851, divorces have been handled by the county court of common pleas. Prior to 1851 the records were found in either the supreme court, the chancery court, or the court of common pleas, and then appealed through the legislature. See David G. Null's, "Ohio Divorces, 1803–1852," *National Genealogical Society Quarterly* 69 (March 1981): 109–14, for a list of people granted divorces by the legislature between 1795 and 1852.

Census Records

Federal

Population Schedules.

- Indexed—1800 (Washington County only), 1810 (Washington County only—others burned 1812), 1820 (Franklin and Wood counties missing), 1830, 1840, 1850, 1860, 1870 (Cincinnati and Cleveland only), 1890 (fragment)

- Soundex—1880, 1900, 1910 (Miracode), 1920
- Unindexed—1870 (except Cincinnati and Cleveland)

Industry and Agriculture Schedules.

- 1850, 1860, 1870, 1880 (lists do not exist for all counties for each year); manufacturer's—1820 (very limited)

Mortality Schedules.

- 1850 for counties H–W (published), 1860 all counties (published), 1870 (Seneca County only), 1880 (Adams to Geaugan counties only)

Union Veterans Schedules.

- 1890

The Ohio Historical Society suggests that the duplicate tax lists of Ohio counties may be used as a substitute for the missing 1810 census. In addition to the indexes published by AISI (see page 2), the 1850 and 1860 census records indexed and published by Lida Flint Harshman in 1979 are recommended. The Ohio Genealogical Society (see Archives, Libraries, and Societies) has completed an every-name surname index from the original 1880 census which it has in its possession.

The 1890 population census exists only for Cincinnati (Hamilton County) and Wayne Township (Clinton County) and is indexed in the microfilm index provided by the National Archives for the remaining 1890 census returns.

State

Ohio had no state census records. There are scattered county census records taken for militia purposes, plus personal and real estate tax lists, all of which have been incorrectly referred to as state census records. There are quadrennial enumerations taken every four years from 1803 to 1911 to determine voting districts. These include males (white only prior to 1863) over twenty-one years of age residing in a county, showing address, race, occupation, and whether a freeholder of land. Not all counties are available for each four year period, nor is each township for each county included. A list of the available records can be obtained from the Ohio Historical Society, where the enumerations are either on microfilm or in original form. This repository also holds "enumerations of school-aged youth" for selected years and counties. Contact the society for details.

The "Special Enumeration of Blacks Immigrating to Ohio, 1861–1863 by the Auditor of the State," State Archives Series 2261 is microfilmed and can be purchased from the Ohio Historical Society Microfilm Department. The microfilm includes a four-part index, by name, previous residence, questionable names, and county of those blacks who had migrated to the state between 1 March 1861 and 3 March 1863. Forty-seven counties scattered around the state responded with at least one name, resulting in a total of 1,375 names. The Ohio Genealogical Society has published many of these enumerations in its chapter's newsletters.

Background Sources

Ohio has a very active statewide genealogical society, with local chapters throughout the state and several out-of-state chapters (see Archives, Libraries, and Societies). Contact the state or local groups for guidance in researching an ancestral area. The response is generally outstanding with letters answered promptly and courteously, sometimes being forwarded to possible "connections."

The Ohio Historical Society has an extensive collection of Ohio county histories, many of which are included in their Ohio County History Surname Index. An information sheet regarding the microfilmed edition and its index is available from the Ohio Historical Society.

For additional information see:

Bell, Carol Willsey. *Ohio Guide to Genealogical Sources.* Baltimore, Md.: Genealogical Publishing Co., 1988.

———. *Ohio Genealogical Guide.* 5th ed. Youngstown, Ohio: the author, 1990.

Colket, Meredith B., Jr. "Genealogical Material Relating to the Western Reserve." *National Genealogical Society Quarterly* 59 (1971): 281–82.

Dickore, Marie. "Genealogical Resources in the Cincinnati, Ohio Area." *National Genealogical Society Quarterly* 43 (1955): 1–5.

Fenley, Ann. *The Ohio Connection Formula for Finding Elusive Ancestors.* Dayton, Ohio: Ohio Connection, 1985.

Fess, Simeon D. *Ohio: A Four-Volume Reference Library on the History of a Great State.* Chicago, Ill.: Lewis Publishing Co., 1937.

Harter, Stuart, comp. *Ohio Genealogy and Local History Sources Index.* Fort Wayne, Ind.: the compiler, 1986

Khouw, P., et al. *County by County in Ohio Genealogy.* Columbus, Ohio: State Library of Ohio, 1978.

Robson, Charles, ed. *Biographical Encyclopedia of Ohio in the Nineteenth Century.* Cincinnati, Ohio: Galaxy Publishing Co., 1876.

Sperry, Kip. "Genealogical Research in Ohio." *National Genealogical Society Quarterly* 75 (1987): 81–104.

Upton, Harriet Taylor. *History of the Western Reserve.* 3 vols. Chicago, Ill.: Lewis Publishing Co., 1910.

Maps

The earliest Sanborn Map for Ohio is an 1875 map for Zanesville, held by the Ohio Historical Society. Consult the Newberry Library *Checklist of Printed Maps of the Middle West to 1800* (2 vols. Boston, Mass.: G. K. Hall, 1980), although this is not an inclusive listing for maps in Ohio. It does not, for example include those held by the Western Reserve Historical Society (see Archives, Libraries, and Societies). Other excellent sources include:

Brown, Lloyd A. *Early Maps of the Ohio Valley: A Selection of Maps, Plans and Views Made by Indians and Colonials From 1673–1783.* Pittsburgh, Pa.: University of Pittsburgh Press, 1959.

Kilbourn, John. *The Ohio Gazetteer, Or, Topographical Dictionary Containing A Description of the Several Counties, Towns, Etc.* Columbus, Ohio: J. Kilbourn, 1826.

Smith, Thomas H. *The Mapping of Ohio.* Kent, Ohio: Kent State University Press, 1977.

Walling, Henry F. *Atlas of the State of Ohio.* 1867. Reprint. Knightstown, Ind.: Bookmark, 1983. Delineates townships, railroads, roads, and geographical features as of 1868.

Land Records

Public-Domain State

Virginia, New York, Connecticut, and Massachusetts claimed portions of land in this part of Northwest Territory based on charters granted by the kings of England. In 1778 the Congressional Committee proposed that these states cede their western lands. New York ceded in 1781, Virginia in 1784, Massachusetts in 1785, and Connecticut in 1786 and 1800. Both Virginia and Connecticut reserved lands in Ohio as part of the cession compromise.

In 1784 the first Congressional Committee was appointed to prepare a plan for disposal of federal lands north of the Ohio River. The Land Act of 20 May 1785 set up a rectangular survey system (see pages 4–5) reserving one section in each township of thirty-six sections for the support of public schools. Originally, section twenty-nine in each township was reserved for religious purposes until 1833 when Congress authorized the State of Ohio to sell these sections.

The following is a list and description of Ohio's land tracts that were the basis of initial government-to-individual transfers of land:

Virginia Military District. Land in twenty-three Ohio counties from the Ohio River north between the Scioto and Little Miami Rivers was reserved by Virginia to satisfy its military bounty warrants. One of the original nine major subdivisions in Ohio, it is the only one not using a rectangular survey system. In 1852 Virginia ceded all unclaimed lands to the federal government which in turn ceded these remaining lands to Ohio in 1875. Soldiers' applications are filed in the Virginia State Library in Richmond (see Virginia). Volume four (in two parts) of Clifford Neal Smith's *Federal Land Series* (see page 5) deals exclusively with land in the Virginia Military District.

Connecticut Western Reserve. Fourteen northeastern counties starting at the Pennsylvania line, bordered by Lake Erie to the north, and west 120 miles, including the Fire Lands (see below), encompassed this agreement with Connecticut. Records are at the Connecticut State Library (see Connecticut), although the Western Reserve Historical Society has an extensive collection.

Fire Lands. This area, including the west end of the Connecticut Western Reserve, was given to Connecticut supporters of the American Revolution who suffered losses because of destruction of nine Connecticut towns by the British and Tories.

Seven Ranges. Located in southeastern Ohio on the Ohio River, these were the first public lands to be surveyed in the United States.

Moravian Indian Grants. Three separate tracts of 4,000 acres each in Tuscarawas County were reserved in 1785 for the "use of the Christian Indians who formerly settled there, or the remains of that society" because of the slaughter of nine innocent Christian Indians in 1782 in retaliation for hostile raids on settlers in West Pennsylvania and Virginia.

Refugee Tract. Located in central Ohio, it runs forty-two miles east from the Scioto River and was granted to Canadian (1783) and Nova Scotian (1785) refugees who abandoned their settlements and fled to the United States to aid the colonial cause during the Revolutionary War.

Dohrman Tract. Arnold Henry Dohrman was granted this tract in 1787 to compensate for disallowed expenditures and his humanitarian efforts as an agent of the United States for the revolutionary cause.

The Ohio Company. Over 1.5 million acres were negotiated from the federal government in southeastern Ohio in 1787 by the Ohio Company. But only 750,000 were included when the company failed to raise money for the whole piece (first purchase). A second purchase of over 200,000 acres was added in 1792. Records are at Marietta College Library, Marietta, Ohio.

Donation Tract. One hundred thousand acres were granted in 100 acre lots to any male, eighteen or older, who would settle on the land at the time of the conveyance. It was to be a buffer between the settlers in the Ohio Company and the native population.

Symmes Purchase. Known also as the Miami Purchase, it was acquired in 1794 and privately surveyed in southwestern Ohio from the Ohio River twenty-four miles northward between the Great Miami and the Little Miami Rivers. Fire destroyed records, although the Hamilton County Recorder's Office has two extant volumes.

French Grants. The first grant, in Scioto County on the Ohio River, consisted of 24,000 acres given to the French in 1795 who were swindled by the Scioto Company. An additional, smaller grant was made in 1798.

U.S. Military District. Bounty land granted the Continental Army officers and soldiers in 1796 containing 2.5 million acres was bounded north by the Greenville Treaty Line, east by the Seven Ranges, south by the Refugee Tract and Congress Lands, and west by the Scioto River.

Zane's Tracts. Three tracts of land, 640 acres each, were granted to Ebenezer Zane for laying out a road (Zane's Trace) from Wheeling, Virginia (now West Virginia) to Limestone (now Maysville), Kentucky.

Congressional Lands. After other sales and grants, Congress had two remaining tracts—one east of the Scioto River, one west of the Miami River.

The Auditor of the State, 88 E. Broad Street, 5th Floor, Columbus, Ohio 43266-0541; the National Archives; and the BLM, Eastern States Office in Alexandria, Virginia (see page 5) all have records dealing with some aspect of government-to-individual transfers of land.

For explanations of greater detail, see William E. Peters, "Ohio Lands and Their History," *Bulletin of the History and Philosophy Society of Ohio* 15 (1957): 340–48; his *Ohio Lands and Their Subdivision,* 2d ed. (Athens, Ohio.: the author, 1918); and his seventeen-volume typescript, "Code of Land Titles in Ohio. A Compilation from Official Records of All Charters, Indian Treaties, Grants . . ." (1935). See also Kenneth Duckett, "Ohio Land Patents," *Ohio History* 72 (1963): 51–60. *Ohio Lands: A Short History,* a short information booklet and *The Building of Ohio,* a small map showing all the land grants in Ohio, were published by and are available free from the state auditor.

Mayburt Stephenson Reigel's *Early Ohioans' Residences from the Land Grant Records* (Mansfield, Ohio: Ohio Genealogical Society, 1976) concerns some records which are in the state archives section of the Ohio Historical Society and not those in the custody of the auditor of the state. The author searched twenty-four volumes of records, including those for land offices at Cincinnati, Steubenville, Chillicothe, Canton-Wooster, Zanesville, and Marietta, plus the Refugee Tract and the Donation Tract Lands. The first mention of each name, in each place of residence, and in each land office, is listed; the place of residence may assist a genealogist in determining from where the ancestor migrated. Researchers must be aware in using this source that it includes very limited extractions from the twenty-four volumes.

Ellen T. Berry and David A. Berry, *Early Ohio Settlers: Purchasers of Land in Southeastern Ohio, 1800–1840* (Baltimore, Md.: Genealogical Publishing Co., 1984), also summarizes the records of the Marietta Land Office. The alphabetically arranged entry gives the date, name, and residence of the purchaser, and the location of the land. Also, see the following by the same authors and publisher: *Early Ohio Settlers, Purchasers of Land in South Western Ohio* (1986), which indexes the records of the Cincinnati Land Office, and *Early Ohio Settlers, Purchasers of Land in East and East Central Ohio* (1989). Carol Willsey Bell, *Ohio Lands: Steubenville Land Office, 1800–1820* (Youngstown, Ohio: the author, 1983), includes an every-name index to this series of records.

Marie Clark Taylor compiled two helpful books: *Ohio Lands South of the Indian Boundary Line* (Chillicothe, Ohio: the compiler, 1984) and *Ohio Lands: Chillicothe Land Office, 1800–1829* (Chillicothe, Ohio: the compiler, 1984).

The Newberry Library in Chicago has very good resources on land records and boundary disputes for Ohio. Included in its collection are works on the Scioto Land Company and the Ohio Company, plus the microfilmed Ohio Land Grant Records, 1788–1820.

Once granted by the federal government, subsequent transactions involving that land are recorded at the county recorder's office in deed books.

Probate Records

The court of common pleas was responsible for probate and estate records beginning in 1797. Since 1851 probate functions have been under the jurisdiction of the probate court. Indexes are available in each probate office. Some probate records are on microfilm at the Ohio Historical Society and the FHL. The county probate court holds guardianship, name changes, insanity proceedings, naturalization, marriage records from the beginning of the county, and birth and death records 1867–1908.

Adoptions in Ohio are processed through the probate court. Access to adoption records is restricted. For those prior to 1939, the probate court must be petitioned. From 1 January 1939 to 1 January 1964, adopted persons or their lineal descendants can obtain information from the Supervisor of Special Records in the State Department of Health in Columbus (see Vital Records).

Indexes are available in each probate office, while some records are accessible on microfilm at the Ohio Historical Society and the FHL. An excellent source is Carol Willsey Bell, *Ohio Wills and Estates to 1850: An Index* (Columbus, Ohio: the author, 1981), which includes an excellent introduction, cites entries for records no longer in existence, and references documents in county courthouses. An index is in progress for 1851–1900 Ohio wills. A county records manager, or similar office, has been created in some Ohio counties. This office may hold records generated by chancery courts, petition to partition land to settle an estate, probate journals, and probate case files.

Court Records

From the time of the Northwest Ordinance in 1787 until 1802, three judges held courts in Ohio Territory, but the records are scarce. In 1804, a year after statehood, the territory was organized as one district court at Chillicothe. Considerable reorganization, divisions, and transfers later occurred in the system.

Many Ohio records are found in county court records not intended for that particular purpose. Vital records, naturalizations (in probate court after 1851), and military pension applications are examples of items possibly found in the county court of common pleas located at the county seat until 1851 and later in the state supreme court files. Land records, deeds, and miscellaneous volumes can at times include records of court proceedings.

Bell's *Ohio Guide to Genealogical Sources* (see Background Sources) details the various county court records that can be located at each county seat, many of which are available on microfilm through either the Ohio Historical

Society or the FHL. The County Resource section below indicates only the first known court record of any kind for the county.

Some court records may be deposited at the Ohio Network of American History Research Centers. See David Levine, "Ohio's Court System," in Ohio Genealogical Society, *The Report* 20 (Winter 1980): 171–74.

Some holdings for the Ohio circuit court are at the National Archives-Great Lakes Region. Refer to their inventory for details on the Northern division: Cleveland (1855–1962) and Toledo (1869–1962); and the Southern division: Cincinnati (1803–1962), Columbus (1877–1962), and Dayton (1915–62).

Tax Records

Tax records for Ohio began as early as 1800. The archives section of the Ohio Historical Society has a collection of original Ohio tax lists from the state auditor's office. They include lists from the county's organization to 1838, usually arranged by county and township. They are not indexed. Esther Weygandt Powell has included many of them in *Early Ohio Tax Records* (Akron, Ohio: the author, 1971), beginning about 1800. The book does not include all the tax lists at the archives, nor does it include tax lists for all counties. It does, however, provide an excellent source to document many early Ohio families. The reprint of this book (Baltimore, Md.: Genealogical Publishing Co., 1985) includes a surname index. County courthouses hold various tax records that have not been inventoried. They are in the office of the county auditor or the county records manager.

The FHL has microfilm copies of all known extant tax records 1800–38 for Ohio. AISI produced *Index to Ohio Tax Lists, 1800–10* (Bountiful, Utah: AISI, 1977) and Gerald Petty has compiled *Ohio 1825 Tax Duplicates* (Columbus, Ohio: Petty's Press, 1897). A similar volume by Petty for 1835 is also available.

The National Archives-Great Lakes Region (see page 8) retains numerous federal tax records for Ohio. These include assessment books for 1867–73 and corporate and personal records for District 10, Toledo, and District 11, Columbus.

Cemetery Records

According to the Ohio Genealogical Society, the majority of Ohio counties have published cemetery records in one form or another. They suggest contacting local societies or one of the major genealogical libraries in the state.

Ohio Cemeteries (Ohio Genealogical Society, 1978), edited by Maxine Hartmann Smith, is a listing comprising all known cemeteries included in several sources. It is organized by county and by township, alphabetically, with an index by cemetery name. Included are concise locations of the cemetery and publication information. *Ohio Cemeteries: Addendum* (Baltimore, Md.: Gateway Press, 1990), edited by Teresa L. M. Klaieber, includes updates and revisions to the previous volume. County chapters of the Ohio Genealogical Society can be contacted regarding cemetery information in their counties.

See also *Ohio Cemetery Records: Extracted from the "Old Northwest" Genealogical Quarterly* (Baltimore, Md.: Genealogical Publishing Co., 1984), which includes an every-name index by Elizabeth P. Bentley and covers northeastern and central Ohio, and the Ohio Adjutant General's Office, *Grave Registration of Soldiers Buried in Ohio* (Salt Lake City, Utah: Genealogical Society of Utah, 1958).

Church Records

Religion in Ohio was an early and important factor in settlement. The first Moravian mission was established in 1772. Presbyterians and Quakers were in the state at an early date, the latter having established forty-three monthly meetings and settlements between 1801 and 1883. The Presbyterians founded seventeen towns between 1784 and 1799. Baptists, Congregationalists, several reformed groups, Lutherans, Disciples of Christ, United Brethren, Methodists, and Catholics arrived prior to 1850. By 1890 the latter two denominations were the largest in the state. The Methodist circuit in Ohio was organized in 1798, with circuit riders traveling from log cabins to camp meetings across the territory. In 1831 the Church of Jesus Christ of Latter-day Saints migrated from New York to Kirtland in Lake County. No thorough survey exists of any of the holdings of individual churches in Ohio, although many are on microfilm through the FHL. The Ohio Genealogical Society is presently undertaking a church records survey.

Historical Records Survey for Ohio produced an *Inventory of the Church Archives of Ohio Presbyterian Churches* (Salt Lake City, Utah: Genealogical Society of Utah, 1967). Records of the Quakers in the Miami Valley and the Church of the Brethren of the Southern District of Ohio are available on microfilm through the FHL. Some Ohio Quaker records may be found in William Wade Hinshaw, *Encyclopedia of American Quakers* (Ann Arbor, Mich.: Edwards Brothers, 1936). The Western Reserve Historical Society has an extensive Shaker manuscript collection. Bluffton College in Bluffton, Ohio, has Mennonite records.

Military Records

There is a long list of published (printed and/or microfilmed) Ohio military records that are available through the FHL and throughout many genealogical libraries. These include records from the Civil War, Mexican War, American Revolution, War of 1812, Spanish-American War, and World War I. An excellent listing can be found in Bell's *Ohio Guide to Genealogical Sources* (see Background Sources).

Loyalist records are an important resource in Ohio. A large concentration of loyalist material is available at the Ohio Historical Society, the Blegen Library at the University of Cincinnati, and Miami University in Oxford, Ohio.

Ohio did not grant state pensions, but the office of the State of Ohio, Adjutant General's Department, Room 11, State House Annex, Columbus, Ohio 43266-0605, holds the records for those who served in of the War of 1812 through the Vietnam era. They consist only of wartime records with no published indexes available across its holdings. The office does not hold information on national pension records. The Civil War index is on microfilm and is available through the FHL.

Information from service records will be supplied for an individual at no charge, but full name, birth date, and other available information should be submitted if possible. Records for the War of 1812 are sketchy. A sample provided by the Adjutant General's Department gave the roll of various companies, giving the service dates of the unit and the members of the company, with their rank. The Ohio Society, Daughters of 1812, is computerizing data from some original militia rolls, 1810–20. A service number for World War II and Korea is very helpful. For Vietnam, a social security number is necessary.

The Ohio Historical Society holds a number of Civil War regimental histories on microfilm that may be purchased from the society. A genealogically important and impressive, although not inclusive, resource is the "Graves Registration File" at the society, which includes several hundred microfilm reels with information on Ohio burial places for Veterans through the Vietnam era. Microfilm cards state name, war of service, date of death and burial site, and occasionally additional details on military service or family. The society will search the reference for a fee.

Military records located at the county level may include soldiers' discharge and/or burial information.

Periodicals, Newspapers, and Manuscript Collections

Periodicals

Ohio History is published by the Ohio Historical Society. It was previously called *Ohio Archaeological and Historical Quarterly* and *Ohio Historical Quarterly*.

The Report and *Ohio Records and Pioneer Families* are published by the Ohio Genealogical Society with excellent local history, problem solving techniques, and original source material.

Also see:

Bell, Carol Willsey. *Ohio Genealogical Periodical Index: A County Guide*. Youngstown, Ohio: privately published, 1987. Subject index to publications of genealogical and historical societies.

Newspapers

The *Centinel of the North-Western Territory* was published in Cincinnati ten years before Ohio became a state. Its first issue was dated 9 November 1793. This newspaper, and some issues of the *Chillicothe Gazette*, the oldest paper in continuous publication west of the Alleghenies, are available at the Ohio Historical Society, along with a limited number of newspaper indexes.

Many local historical societies and public libraries have obituary files. The German Immigrant Society of Cincinnati has a clipping collection of 1,700 obituaries.

There have been several projects for the compilation and indexing of newspapers in Ohio. These are primarily done on an individual newspaper or county basis. Some may be obtained by contacting county historical or genealogical societies. A microfiche catalog of newspapers available at the Ohio Historical Society, published in 1990, may be purchased from the society.

Also consult Karen Mauer Green, *Pioneer Ohio Newspapers, 1802–1818* (Galveston, Tex.: Frontier Press, 1988), a compilation of abstracts of genealogical data and "mentions" of people from six Ohio newspapers. It includes articles from newly formed settlements in Indiana, Illinois, and Michigan. The book has an every-name, place-name, and subject index. Green has also published *Pioneer Ohio Newspapers, 1793–1810* (Galveston, Tex.: Frontier Press, 1986), which covers five early Ohio newspapers. The cities most prevalent in these indexes are Chillicothe, Cincinnati, Marietta, and Steubenville. Further information is in Stephen Gutgesell, *Guide to Ohio Newspapers 1793–1973, Union Bibliography of Ohio Newspapers Available in Ohio Libraries* (Columbus, Ohio: Ohio Historical Society, 1974). The Ohio Historical Society provides microfilmed newspapers on an interlibrary loan basis. A microfiche catalog of newspapers available may be ordered from the society.

Manuscripts

The manuscript division of the Ohio Historical Society includes as primary subjects: Northwest Territory and early statehood, the Civil War, religion, blacks, women, labor, politics, and mass communication. Particularly notable are the Wilbur Siebert Collection, which includes American Loyalists and the Underground Railroad; land grants signed by George Washington and Thomas Jefferson; Henry O. Dwight's watercolor drawings of the Civil War; and Ohio AFL-CIO records. For details see Andrew D. Lentz, ed., *A Guide to Manuscripts at the Ohio Historical Society* (Columbus, Ohio: Ohio Historical Society, 1972).

Kermit J. Pike, *A Guide to the Manuscripts and Archives of the Western Reserve Historical Society* (Cleveland, Ohio: Western Reserve Historical Society, 1972), surveys this excellent collection including oral histories of Western Reserve women.

The Ohio Genealogical Society's manuscript collection includes Bible records and First Family of Ohio applications, the latter proving ancestry in Ohio prior to 1820.

See also Draper Manuscripts under Wisconsin —Manuscripts.

Ohio Network Centers should be contacted for their pertinent manuscript collections.

Archives, Libraries, and Societies

Ohio Genealogical Society
34 Sturges Avenue
P.O. Box 2625
Mansfield, OH 44906

Membership includes a quarterly, *The Report,* and the monthly *OGS Newsletter.* The society has annual meetings, one hundred county chapters, the Families of Ohio lineage society, and publishes various items of genealogical and historical interest. This library contains over 15,000 volumes, family vertical files, Bible records, ancestors cards, manuscript files, census microfilm, and a broad variety of other valuable resources for research in Ohio. A response to a written request for general and specific information is answered promptly, cordially, and *very* thoroughly.

Ohio Historical Society, Archives-Library Division
1985 Velma Avenue
Columbus, OH 43211

The society's library collections document the history of Ohio and its people, including 125,000 books and pamphlets and 40,000 reels of newspaper microfilm and 20,000 volumes of original newspapers. The newspaper collection is one of the nation's largest. Their audiovisual collections are outstanding, including nearly 7,500 photographs of locomotives and railroad subjects in the G. Hayes Coleman series. Major works on the settlement and government of Northwest Territory are in the rare books division.

The society houses (at the above address) the State Archives of Ohio, with more than 30,000 cubic feet of state and local government records. The society also serves the central Ohio counties as part of the Ohio Network of American History Research Centers. The *Directory of Historical Organizations in Ohio* can be obtained from the society for $10.

State Library of Ohio
Genealogy Division
65 South Front Street
Columbus OH 43215

The Genealogy Division holds microfilm; printed, typescript, and manuscript collections, including family and local histories; atlases; cemetery records; city directories; military records; censuses and census indexes; and transcribed records provided by the Ohio chapters of the DAR. See "The State Library of Ohio," in the Ohio Genealogical Society's *The Report* 23 (Winter 1983): 187–88, for a description of the holdings of the State Library of Ohio.

Western Reserve Historical Society
10825 East Boulevard
Cleveland, OH 44106

Its extensive manuscript collection (published guide available by mail) is supplemented by an equally extensive microfilm collection of federal census returns and the National Archives Revolutionary War Pension records. The society serves as the network center (see below) for its area and charges a per-day fee for nonmembers.

Ohio Network of American History Research Centers

Established in 1970 to aid in the collection, preservation, and accessibility of research materials related to Ohio history, the network is composed of seven institutions —Ohio's two largest historical societies and five state universities. A central feature of the network is the division of the entire state into seven distinct geographical areas for research. Each center collects county records for its area.

Archives Services
Bierce Library
University of Akron
Akron, OH 44325-1750
Serves Region 1—east central Ohio.

Center for Archival Collections
Bowling Green State University
Bowling Green, OH 43403-0175
Serves Region 2—northwest Ohio.

Archives and Rare Books Department
Blegen Library
University of Cincinnati
Cincinnati, OH 45221-0113
Serves Region 3—southwest Ohio.

Archives-Library Division
Ohio Historical Society
1985 Velma Avenue
Columbus, OH 43211
Serves Region 4—central Ohio.

Archives and Special Collections
Alden Library
Ohio University
Athens, OH 45701-2978
Serves Region 5—southeast Ohio.

Western Reserve Historical Society
10825 East Boulevard
Cleveland, OH 44106
Serves Region 6—northeast Ohio.

Archives and Special Collections
Wright State University Library
Dayton, OH 45435-0001
Serves Region 7—west central Ohio.

For information about the network and service of its centers, contact either the specific center or headquarters at the Ohio Historical Society.

Special Focus Categories

Black American

Consult the following when researching black Americans in Ohio:

Alilunas, Leo. "Fugitive Slave Cases in Ohio Prior to 1850." *Ohio State Archaeological and Historical Quarterly* 69 (1940): 160–84. See other issues of this particular periodical for additional articles on blacks in Ohio.

Fuller, Sara, ed. *The Ohio Black History Guide.* Columbus, Ohio: Ohio Historical Society, 1975.

Gerber, David Allison. *Black Ohio and the Color Line, 1860–1915.* Urbana, Ill.: University of Illinois Press, ca. 1976.

Hickock, Charles Thomas. *The Negro in Ohio, 1802–1870.* 1896. Reprint. New York, N.Y.: AMS Press, 1975.

Nitchman, Paul E. *Blacks in Ohio.* 7 vols. Ft. Mead, Md.: the author, 1987.

Turpin, Joan. *Register of Black, Mulatto and Poor Persons in Four Ohio Counties, 1791–1861.* Bowie, Md.: Heritage Books, 1985.

Wesley, Charles Harris. *Ohio Negroes in the Civil War.* Publications of the Ohio Civil War Centennial Commission, no. 6. Columbus, Ohio: Ohio Historical Society, 1962.

The Archives-Library Division of Ohio Historical Society publishes *Selected Bibliography of Black History Sources at the Ohio Historical Society* and holds the state auditor's "Special Enumeration of Blacks Immigrating to Ohio 1861–1863," State Archives Series 2261, and the *Palladium of Liberty,* the state's first black newspaper (see Census Records section for information on 1863 census of blacks).

The Afro-American Museum, Wilberforce, Ohio 45385, is the first national museum of its kind.

Native American

Twelve to fifteen thousand native inhabitants were said to have been living in Ohio country when the first European settlers arrived. The Miami lived in the western part of Ohio, and the Wyandotte were in the northwest. The Huron, the Ottawa, and the Seneca were also in the northwest. The Shawnee tribe was located in the lower Scioto Valley, the Delaware in the Muskingum Valley, the Tuscarora in the northeastern section of that valley, and the Mingo occupied the east.

In the mid-1700s, the French and the English began their long struggle for possession of the region. The English victory was followed by the battles of the American Revolution; the native inhabitants of Ohio were tragically involved in both of these wars. When the bloodshed was over between the two European factions, the contest for the land began in earnest between white and native. By the end of the Revolutionary War, still unwilling to give up their domain, the natives struggled to maintain their lands for twelve long years. In the summer of 1794, at the battle at Fallen Timbers, Anthony Wayne and his well-trained troops totally defeated the Native Americans of Ohio. The following year, in August of 1795, a treaty was negotiated—the final step in taking away native home lands. The last group of Native Americans left northwestern Ohio in 1833.

See Stewart Rafert, "American-Indian Genealogical Research in the Midwest: Resources and Perspectives," *National Genealogical Society Quarterly* 76 (September 1988): 212–24. See also Wisconsin—Native American Records.

Other Ethnic Groups

The introductory section of this chapter identified some of the various ethnic groups that settled in Ohio. Western Reserve Historical Society is notable in its collection of materials on the ethnic immigrants to Ohio. Two helpful sources are:

Maxwell, Fay. *Irish Refugee Tract Abstract Data and History of Irish Acadians.* Columbus, Ohio: Maxwell Publications, ca. 1974.

Smith, Clifford Neal. *Early Nineteenth Century German Settlers in Ohio, Kentucky and Other States.* McNeal, Ariz.: Westland Publications, 1984.

County Resources

Ohio generally does not have any birth and death records prior to 1867. From 1867 to 1908 birth and death records were recorded at the probate court office in the county where the event occurred. After 1908 the event was recorded at the county's health department and also with the Vital Records Office in Columbus. A marriage record before 1949 (see Vital Records) will be found in the probate court office of the county where the event occurred. Deeds will be found in the county recorders office from the county's formation to the present.

In mailing requests to any Ohio county office, use the name of the county and "County Courthouse" with the address listed below. The address given is that listed as the county government building. In some cases, some records are located at another address. Ann Fenley lists some of these in *The Ohio Open Records Law and Genealogy* (Dayton, Ohio: Ohio Connection, 1989). Carol Willsey Bell, *Ohio Wills and Estates to 1850: An Index* (Columbus, Ohio: the author, 1980), lists several courthouses known to have had destructive fires. Note, however, that not all records were destroyed in these fires and that there may have been other fires or disasters. Before making any presumptions that the records have been lost, request the records needed. The courthouse fires listed by Bell are as follows:

Adams, 1910; Belmont, 1980; Brown, 1977; Champaign, 1948; Columbiana, 1976; Crawford, 1831; Delaware, 1835; Fayette, 1828; Franklin, 1879; Fulton, before 1860; Gallia, 1981; Hamilton, 1814, 1849, 1884; Henry, 1847; Licking,

1875; Monroe, 1840, 1867; Seneca, 1841; and Trumbull, 1895.

The following list of counties indicates the county seat; year the county was created; if different, the year it was fully organized for record keeping (in parentheses); and the parent county from which it was formed. Under parent county are some county names with an (*) indicating records may also be found there since the county may have been "attached" to those other counties for some period in its history.

The date listed for each record category is the earliest record known to exist in that county. It does not indicate that there are numerous records for that year and certainly does not indicate that all such events that year were actually registered. In some cases there may be lapses in records *after* the beginning year listed. For example, Adams County has birth and death records beginning in 1888—but only through 1893.

In addition to sources listed on page 11, information for the County Resources section was obtained from Bell's *Ohio Guide to Genealogical Sources* (see Background Sources) and the following:

Fenley, Ann. *Ohio Open Records Law and Genealogy.* Dayton, Ohio: Ohio Connection, 1989.

State Board of Elections. State of Ohio, County Officers, 1988.

Drawn by William Dollarhide

Map	County Address	Date Formed Parent County/ies	Birth Marriage Death	Land Probate Court
H3	Adams 110 West Main West Union 45693	1797 Hamilton/Washington	1888 1910 1888	1797 1849 —
C2	Allen 301 N. Main Street Lima 45802	1820 (1831) Shelby/Logan *Mercer	1867 1831 1867	1831 1835 1831
C5	Ashland W. Second Street Ashland 44805	1846 Huron/Lorain/Richland/Wayne	— 1846 —	1846 — 1846
A8	Ashtabula 25 W. Jefferson Street Jefferson 44047	1808 (1811) Geauga/Trumbull	1867 1812 1867	1798 1811 —
G6	Athens Athens 45701	1805 Washington	1867 1817 1867	1792 1800 1807
D2	Auglaize R.R. 3 Wapakoneta 45895	1848 Allen/Mercer	1867 1848 1867	1835 1852 1848
E8	Belmont 101 W. Main Street St. Clairsville 43950	1801 Jefferson/Washington	1867 1803 1867	1800 1804 1804
H2	Brown Georgetown 45121	1818 Adams/Clermont	1867 1818 1867	1818 1817 1818
G1	Butler 130 High Street Hamilton 45012	1803 Hamilton	1856 1803 1856	1803 1851 1803
D7	Carroll Public Square Carrollton 44615	1833 Columbiana/Harrison/ Jefferson/Stark/Tuscarawas	1867 1833 1867	1826 1833 1833
E3	Champaign Main and Court Street Urbana 43078	1805 Franklin/Greene	1867 1805 1867	1806 1804 1805
E3	Clark 31 N. Limestone P.O. Box 10008 Springfield 45502	1818 Champaign/Greene/Madison	1867 1818 1867	1818 1818 1818
H2	Clermont 76 South Riverside Batavia 45103	1800 Hamilton	1856 1801 1856	1800 1810 1801
G3	Clinton 46 S. South Street Wilmington 45177	1810 Highland/Warren	1868 1817 1867	1806 1810 1810
C8	Columbiana 105 S. Market Street Lisbon 44432	1803 Jefferson	1867 1803 1867	1798 1803 1803
E6	Coshocton 349 1/2 Main Street Coshocton 43812	1810 (1811) Muskingum/Tuscarawas	1867 1811 1867	1800 1811 1811

Map	County Address	Date Formed Parent County/ies	Birth Marriage Death	Land Probate Court
C4	Crawford 7585 Millboro Road Bucyrus 44820	1820 (1826) Delaware *Seneca*/Sandusky/*Marion	1866 1831 1868	1816 1831 1831
B6	Cuyahoga 1219 Ontario Street Cleveland 44113	1808 (1810) Geauga	1867 1810 1868	1810 1811 1823
E1	Darke Fourth and Broadway Greenville 45331	1809 (1817) Miami	1867 1817 1867	1822 1818 1817
B1	Defiance 500 Court Street Defiance 43512	1845 Henry/Paulding/Williams	1867 1845 1867	1823 1845 1845
E4	Delaware 91 N. Sandusky Delaware 43015	1808 Franklin	1867 1835 1867	— 1812 1818
B5	Erie Sandusky 44870	1838 (1838) Huron/Sandusky	1856 1838 1856	1837 1838 1838
F5	Fairfield 224 E. Main Lancaster 43130	1800 Ross/Washington	1867 1803 1867	1801 1803 1801
F3	Fayette 110 East Court Washington Courthouse 43160	1810 Highland/Ross	1867 1810 1868	1810 1810 1882
E4	Franklin 369 S. High Street Columbus 43215	1803 Ross/unorganized land	1867 1803 1867	1800 1805 1803
A2	Fulton 210 South Fulton Wauseon 43567	1850 Henry/Lucas/Williams	1867 1864 1867	1835 1853 —
H5	Gallia Locust Street Gallipolis 45613	1803 Washington	1864 1803 1867	1803 1803 1811
B7	Geauga Chardon 44024	1806 Trumbull	1867 1803 1867	1795 1806 1806
F2	Greene 45 N. Detroit Street Xenia 45385	1803 Hamilton/Ross/	1869 1803 1870	1798 1803 1802
E7	Guernsey Wheeling Avenue Cambridge 43725	1810 Belmont/Muskingum	1867 1810 1867	1802 1812 1810
G1	Hamilton 1000 Main Street Cincinnati 45202	1790 original	1863 1808 1881	1787 1790 1844
C3	Hancock 300 South Main Findlay 45840	1820 (1828) Logan/Delaware *Wood	1867 1828 1867	1820 1828 1828

Map	County Address	Date Formed Parent County/ies	Birth Marriage Death	Land Probate Court
D3	Hardin Kenton 43326	1820 (1833) Logan/Delaware	1867 1833 1867	1831 1830 1833
E7	Harrison Cadiz 43907	1813 Jefferson/Tuscarawas	1867 1813 1867	1812 1813 ——
B2	Henry 660 N. Perry Napoleon 43545	1820 (1834) Logan/Shelby *Wood/*Williams	1867 1847 1867	1846 1847 1847
G3	Highland P.O. Box 825 Hillsboro 45135	1805 Adams/Clermont/Ross	1867 1805 1868	1804 1809 1805
F5	Hocking 1 E. Main Street Logan 43138	1818 Athens/Ross/Fairfield	1867 1818 1867	1818 1819 1818
D6	Holmes Millersburg 44654	1824 (1825) Coshocton/Tuscarawas/Wayne	1867 1821 1867	1808 1825 1825
B5	Huron 180 Milan Avenue Norwalk 44857	1809 (1815) Portage/Geauga *Cuyahoga	1867 1818 1867	1809 1815 1818
H5	Jackson Jackson 45640	1816 Athens/Gallia/Ross/Scioto	1867 1816 1867	1816 1819 1816
D8	Jefferson 301 Market Street Steubenville 43952	1797 Washington	1867 1803 1867	1795 1798 1803
D5	Knox 111 E. High Street Mt. Vernon 43050	1808 Fairfield/Franklin	1867 1808 1867	1808 1808 1808
A7	Lake P.O. Box 480 Painesville 44077	1840 (1840) Cuyahoga/Geauga	1867 1840 1867	1839 1853 1840
J5	Lawrence Fifth and Park Avenue Ironton 45638	1815 (1817) Gallia/Scioto	1864 1817 1867	1818 1846 1817
E5	Licking 9309 Reynolds Road, N.E. Newark 43055	1808 Fairfield	1875 1809 1875	1800 1875 1809
D3	Logan P.O. Box 429 Bellefontaine 43311	1818 Champaign	1867 1818 1867	1810 1851 1804
B5	Lorain 306 Second Street Elyria 44035	1822 (1824) Cuyahoga/Huron/Medina	1867 1824 1867	—— 1840 1824
A3	Lucas 1 Government Circle Suite 800 Toledo 43624	1835 Wood/Sandusky	1867 1835 1868	1808 1835 1835

Map	County Address	Date Formed Parent County/ies	Birth Marriage Death	Land Probate Court
F3	Madison London 43140	1810 Franklin	1867 1810 1888	1810 1810 1810
C8	Mahoning 120 Market Street Youngstown 44503	1846 Columbiana/Trumbull	1856 1846 1856	1795 1846 1847
D4	Marion 114 N. Main Street Marion 43302	1820 (1824) Delaware	1867 1824 1867	1821 1825 1824
C6	Medina 93 Public Square Medina 43302	1812 (1818) Portage	1867 1818 1867	1818 1818 1818
G6	Meigs Second Street Pomeroy 45769	1819 Athens/Gallia	1867 1819 1867	1819 1820 1819
D1	Mercer Courthouse Room 107 Celina 45822	1820 (1824) Darke/Shelby	1867 1838 1867	1823 1824 1824
E2	Miami 201 W. Main Street Troy 45373	1807 Montgomery	1853 1807 1867	1807 1807 1804
F7	Monroe Woodsfield 43793	1813 (1815) Belmont/Guernsey/Washington	1867 1866 1867	1836 — 1818
F2	Montgomery 451 W. Third Street Dayton 45402	1803 Hamilton	1867 1803 1866	1805 1803 1803
F6	Morgan 19 E. Main Street McConnelsville 43756	1817 (1819) Guernsey/Muskingum/Washington	1867 1819 1867	1795 1819 1819
D4	Morrow Mt. Gilead 43338	1848 Delaware/Knox/Marion/Richland	1867 1848 1867	1848 1848 1848
E6	Muskingum Zanesville 43701	1804 Fairfield/Washington	1867 1804 1867	1800 1804 1804
F7	Noble Caldwell 43724	1851 Guernsey/Monroe/Morgan/ Washington	1867 1851 1867	1851 1851 1851
B4	Ottawa 315 Madison Street Port Clinton 43452	1840 Erie/Lucas/Sandusky	1867 1840 1869	1820 1840 1840
C1	Paulding Paulding 45879	1820 (1839) Shelby/Darke *Williams/*Wood	1867 1839 1867	1835 1842 1839
F5	Perry New Lexington 43764	1818 Fairfield/Muskingum/Washington	1867 1818 1867	1818 1817 1818

Map	County Address	Date Formed Parent County/ies	Birth Marriage Death	Land Probate Court
F4	Pickaway Circleville 43113	1810 Fairfield/Franklin/Ross	1867 1810 1867	1810 1810 1810
G4	Pike 100 E. Second Waverly 45690	1815 Adams/Ross/Scioto	1867 1815 1867	1799 1817 1815
B7	Portage 203 W. Main Ravenna 44266	1808 Trumbull	1867 1808 1867	1795 1803 1809
F1	Preble Eaton 45320	1808 Butler/Montgomery	1867 1808 1867	1805 1808 1808
C2	Putnam 245 E. Main Street Ottawa 45875	1820 (1834) Shelby/Logan *Wood/*Williams	1857 1834 1867	1830 1835 1834
C5	Richland 50 Park Avenue, East Mansfield 44903	1808 (1813) Franklin *Knox	1856 1813 1890	1814 1813 1819
G4	Ross Chillicothe 45601	1798 Adams/Hamilton/Washington	1867 1798 1867	1797 1797 1798
B4	Sandusky 100 N. Park Fremont 43420	1820 Huron	1867 1820 1867	1822 1820 1820
H4	Scioto 602 Seventh Street Portsmouth 45662	1803 Adams	1856 1804 1856	1803 1810 1809
B4	Seneca 81 Jefferson Street Tiffin 44883	1820 (1824) Huron/Sandusky	1867 1841 1867	1821 1828 1824
D2	Shelby Sidney 45365	1819 Miami	1867 1824 1867	1819 1825 1819
C7	Stark County Office Building Canton 44702	1808 (1809) Columbiana/Muskingum	1867 1809 1867	1809 1810 1809
B7	Summit 175 S. Main Street Akron 44308	1840 (1840) Medina/Portage/Stark	1866 1840 1870	1840 1839 1840
B8	Trumbull 160 High Street, N.W. Warren 44483	1800 Jefferson/ Wayne County of Northwest Territory	1867 1803 1867	1795 1803 1807
D7	Tuscarawas Public Square New Philadelphia 44663	1808 Muskingum	1867 1808 1867	— 1809 1808
D4	Union Marysville 43040	1820 Delaware/Franklin/Logan/Madison	1867 1820 1867	1811 1820 1820

Map	County Address	Date Formed Parent County/ies	Birth Marriage Death	Land Probate Court
C1	Van Wert Van Wert 45891	1820 (1837) Darke/Shelby *Mercer	1867 1840 1867	1824 1840 1837
G5	Vinton McArthur 45651	1850 Athens/Gallia/Hocking/ Jackson/Ross	1867 1850 1867	1850 1852 1850
G2	Warren 320 E. Silver Street Lebanon 45036	1803 Hamilton	1867 1803 1867	1795 1803 1803
F7	Washington 205 Puynam Street Marietta 45750	1788 unorganized land	1867 1789 1867	1788 1789 1790
C6	Wayne 428 West Liberty Wooster 44691	1808 (1812) *Columbiana/*Stark	1867 1813 1867	1813 1817 1812
A1	Williams Bryan 43506	1820 (1824) Darke/Shelby *Wood	1867 1824 1867	1824 1825 1824
B3	Wood 1 Courthouse Square Bowling Green 43402	1820 Logan	1867 1820 1867	1820 1820 1823
C3	Wyandot Upper Sandusky 43351	1845 Crawford/Hancock/Hardin/Marion	1867 1845 *1867*	1826 1845 *1845*

OKLAHOMA

Wendy L. Elliott, C.G., C.G.L.

Oklahoma's background, formation, and organization are unique among the states. Developed out of two separate territories, Indian and Oklahoma, numerous changes have occurred in Oklahoma jurisdictions and boundaries.

The region alternated between French and Spanish possession until 1803 when it became part of the United States' Louisiana Purchase from France. A few forts and settlements cropped up along the Red River as the area successively fell under the territorial jurisdiction of Indiana (1803), Missouri (1812) and Arkansas (1819).

As early as 1804, efforts were made to negotiate the removal of southeastern tribes to west of the Mississippi River. The period of largest removal occurred between 1825–42 when the federal government forced relocation to what eventually became western Arkansas and eastern Oklahoma. The region was established as a home, "as long as the grass shall grow and rivers run," for the Five Civilized Tribes (Creek, Cherokee, Chickasaw, Choctaw, and Seminole) displaced from their previous homes in the south and southeast by the U.S. government and its citizens. The route traveled became known as the "Trail of Tears" because of the grief and loss experienced by Native Americans during their uprootings. Once relocated, the five tribes again set up their own governments as they had in their previous homes, established a newspaper, built towns, and organized schools and farms. Forts Gibson, Washita, and Towson were erected to protect the Native Americans from intruding U.S. citizens and raiding plains tribes.

When the United States acquired the Republic of Texas in 1845, what would later become Oklahoma's panhandle ostensibly belonged to Texas. In 1850 Congress purchased the panhandle strip, but this "No Man's Land" remained separate from Indian Territory or any other territory or state. During the 1850s, railway companies pressured the government to open the unassigned lands of the panhandle strip, but Congress confined Indian Territory to present-day Oklahoma in 1854, excluding the panhandle strip. Prior to the Civil War, the Chickasaw and Choctaw nations had leased the southwestern third of the present-day state to the United States as hunting grounds for the plains tribes.

During the Civil War, internal dissention among the tribes arose as some members served the Union, while others supported the Confederate cause, and still others tried to stay neutral. A much larger percentage favored the Confederate cause, and the Five Civilized Tribes officially supported the Confederacy.

At the conclusion of the Civil War, the federal government, partly to make provision for free blacks to own land and partly as a response to Native American support of the Confederacy, demanded a new set of treaties in 1866. These treaties reduced the original size of the reservations and permitted other tribes to be moved into the territory. Within the next seventeen years, many other tribes were relocated to Oklahoma. The greater part of the Cherokee Outlet (along the northern border with Kansas) and a desirable tract in the center of Oklahoma remained "Unassigned."

Between 1865 and 1889, cattlemen, railroaders, soldiers, and settlers lived within Indian Territory's borders before settlement was legally permitted. Some had taken advantage of the loopholes in the law allowing artisans and professionals to contract with tribes for labor.

In 1872 the first railroad was established through the area connecting Missouri, Kansas, and Texas. Indian Territory was called "the promised land" as it offered fine grazing land and the possibility of free land. Major trails such as the Chisholm, Great Western, East Shawnee, West

Shawnee, Couch, Payne, and Plummer ran between cattle land in Texas and grazing and farm land in Kansas.

In April 1880, in defiance of federal authorities, David L. Payne crossed the Kansas/Oklahoma border and marched with a band of twenty-one "Boomers" (those who promoted opening of the territory for settlement) to the center of Indian Territory, commonly called "Oklahoma country." The trail they blazed was followed by other Boomers over the next five years.

A major settlement transition occurred in 1889. The previous sixty years had marked the arrival in Indian Territory of sixty-five different tribes, including the Five Civilized Tribes. However, agitation for opening these lands to nonnative settlement increased until the federal government purchased a clear title to the central tract, called "Unassigned Lands," and on 22 April 1889 the first official "run" for these homestead lands occurred. Prospective homesteaders lined up along the South Canadian River and Indian Territory boundary lines to await the signal to begin. Others, called "Sooners" (because they did not wait), jumped the gun. This contributed to many court cases where land ownership was contested and also gave rise to the state's nickname—the Sooner State.

An estimated 50,000 people settled the tract in a day, marking the shift from native to nonnative settlement. Oklahoma City became a tent colony with over 10,000 people. Other large towns settled that day were Guthrie, Kingfisher, and Norman.

Many land run trails into the area led southward from Kansas. These included the Wild Horse, Ponca, Black Bear, and Caldwell trails. Stage routes ran south from Kansas, west from Arkansas, and east from Fort Reno. The Butterfield Stage route left Fort Smith, Arkansas, and ran southwest to the Red River. A wagon road closely followed the North Canadian River through Potawatomie land. Through a joint effort of a number of railroad companies, a line was completed from Guthrie to Kingfisher and beyond to Seward.

The present-day state of Oklahoma was divided into two governmental divisions, Oklahoma Territory and Indian Territory, in May 1890. Indian Territory encompassed the eastern half of the state and the Cherokee Outlet along the Kansas border. Oklahoma Territory included the panhandle, called "No Man's Land," and an area that stretched from the southwestern section, including Greer County northeast to the Kansas border, called "Unassigned Lands." County governments began to emerge in Oklahoma Territory.

During the 1890s cattlemen were prohibited from the practice of leasing grazing grounds from the tribes. Congress forced the Native Americans to accept individual land allotments for each member of their tribes instead of holding the land in common. The Dawes Commission was established in 1893 to register individual Native Americans, allot the land, and assist and supervise the government in changing from a tribal to a state organization. In response to vehement demand, additional tracts were opened for land runs or homesteading in 1891, 1892, 1895, 1904, and 1906.

By 1900 Oklahoma Territory had burgeoned to encompass more than the western half of the present state, while Indian Territory was dwindling to a smaller part of the eastern section. Greer County, formerly under Texas jurisdiction, became legally attached to Oklahoma Territory in 1896. In June 1906 Congress provided for the admission of Oklahoma Territory and Indian Territory to the Union as one state, if both nonnatives and natives approved. On 16 November 1907, President Theodore Roosevelt proclaimed Oklahoma the forty-sixth state. Oklahoma City supplanted Guthrie as the capital in 1910.

Mineral and ore deposits drew many settlers, some directly from Europe. Coal and petroleum products still represent a large portion of the state's output. With the spectacular rise of the petroleum industry, the state entered a prosperous era that helped it survive declines in the livestock industry and in the value of dry-farming produce. By the 1930s, six railroads served the state, converging in Oklahoma City.

The state's population of those with Native American heritage remains one of the highest in the United States. The dual history of native relocation and nonnative settlement remains important in the use of records kept for genealogical research.

Vital Records

Statewide recording of births and deaths began in October 1908, although compliance was incomplete for several years in most counties and for two decades or longer in others. Registration was mandated in 1917, but it was another decade before 90 percent compliance was attained. Although county clerks record births and deaths and provide information on request, certificates are available only from the Vital Records Section, State Department of Health, 1000 Northeast Tenth Street, P.O. Box 53551, Oklahoma City, Oklahoma 73152. Purpose and relationship statements are required. Early birth certificates contain much less information than those recorded presently.

Tribal records at the Oklahoma Historical Society (see Archives, Libraries, and Societies) contain some earlier birth records in relationship to land allotments (see Land Records) as well as death records. Children of mixed marriages may be included in the births.

Some marriage records for the Five Civilized Tribes and some other tribes are also at the Oklahoma Historical Society. Others are at the National Archives-Southwest Region (see page 8). Nonnative settlers whose marriages were recorded in U.S. Federal District Court records for Indian Territory are included. Marriage records (June 1890–1907) in Indian Territory, which predate statehood, may be located in the office of the court clerk in either Muskogee or Pittsburg counties. After 1895, pre-statehood marriage records in Indian Territory may additionally be found in county court clerk offices in Carter or Craig. Still others may be found in Atoka, Bryan, Latimore, and LeFlore counties. Creek County marriages may have been recorded in the cities of Bristow, Drumright, Sapulpa, or Muskogee, now in Muskogee County. There is no centralized index for these marriages.

Some marriage records are also available at the county level for Oklahoma Territory before statehood. Some of these have been published, such as Frances Murphy Bode, *Oklahoma Territory Weddings* (Geary, Okla.: Blaine County People and Places, Pioneer Book Committee, 1983), based on newspaper notices and county records for Blaine, Caddo, and Kingfisher counties.

After statehood, marriage and divorce records are available from the clerk of the court in the county in which the license was issued or divorce granted.

Census Records

Federal

Population Schedules.

- Indexed—1860
- Soundex—1900, 1910 (Miracode), 1920

Slave Schedules.

- 1860

Union Veterans Schedules.

- 1890

Those who were not Native American but who were residing in Indian Territory were enumerated in the federal census of 1860. These schedules are recorded under "Indian Lands" and follow the enumeration for Yell County, Arkansas, in the microfilm editions. Some natives were also included in the slave schedules of 1860. See Sharron Standifer Ashton's "1860 Slave Schedules: Indian Lands West of Arkansas," *Oklahoma Genealogical Society Quarterly* 36 (June 1991): 67–71, and Frances Wood, *Indian Lands West of Arkansas (Oklahoma) Population Schedule of the United States Census of 1860* (N.p.: Arrow Printing Co., 1964).

In the 1890 and 1900 census enumerations, the present-day state was divided into Oklahoma Territory and Indian Territory. None of the population returns for 1890 survived, but returns for both territories in the special schedule enumerating Union veterans and widows of Union veterans of the Civil War in 1890 are available on one microfilm reel. The only extant population census enumerations for 1890 for Indian Territory is for the Cherokee Nation (see Census Records—Native American, below).

Census enumerations for 1900 for both Oklahoma and Indian territories are on separate microfilm reels. Reel numbers for the area called "Oklahoma" follow those for Ohio but include only schedules for Oklahoma Territory counties, Oklahoma Territory Indian Reservation, and military and naval jurisdictions. The 1900 census for Indian Territory is grouped separately in microfilm reels following the territories of Wyoming, Alaska, and Hawaii. Indicating a final resolution to the dispute over jurisdiction of Greer County, which functioned as part of Texas between 1886 and 1896, Greer County was included in the 1900 Oklahoma Territory census. In 1910 the first federal census for the state of Oklahoma was enumerated.

Microfilm copies of all these federal census returns are at the Oklahoma Historical Society.

Native American

- Cherokee—1880, 1890, 1896

The Cherokee Nation took its own censuses in 1880 and 1890, and according to the Indian Archives at the Oklahoma Historical Society, the censuses are considered fairly accurate. The originals are at the Indian Archives where microfilm copies are available for sale but not for interlibrary loan. Other repositories may have copies. In 1896, in association with the Dawes Commission in determining Cherokee citizenship, another census was taken but is not considered as accurate, with many claims of citizenship eventually overturned.

Other enumerations are included at the Indian Archives, Oklahoma Historical Society, and among the Bureau of Indian Affairs (see page 11) resources. Some published censuses of Native Americans include:

1851 Census Drennen Roll of Cherokee and Court Claims Records. Tulsa, Okla.: Indian Nations Press.

Wagner, Rosalie, comp. *Cherokee Nation 1890 Census, Index of Persons Living Under Permit in the Coo-Wee-Scoo-Wee and Delaware Districts.* Vinita, Okla.: Northeast Oklahoma Genealogical Society, 1986.

Territorial

An Oklahoma Territory census was taken in June 1890 for the seven territorial counties. Finding aids include a card index at the Oklahoma Historical Society and James W. Smith, *Smith's First Directory of Oklahoma Territory: For the Year Commencing August 1st, 1890* (Guthrie, Okla.: the author, 1890). In 1907 a census was recorded, but the only remaining schedule is for Seminole County.

Some school censuses are available at the respective county's superintendent of schools. These records may contain full name of student, birth date, and parents' names.

Background Sources

An understanding of the development of both Indian and Oklahoma Territories is essential in Oklahoma research. Sources include:

Gibson, Arrell Morgan. *Oklahoma: A History of Five Centuries*, 1965. Reprint. 2d ed., Norman, Okla.: Harlow Publishing Corp., 1981. A standard, well-known history.

Gittinger, Roy. *The Formation of the State of Oklahoma, 1803–1906.* 1917. Reprint. Norman, Okla.: University of Oklahoma Press, 1939. Relates the historical events under French, Spanish, and Mexican jurisdiction and the territorial periods.

Goble, Danny. *Progressive Oklahoma: The Making of a New Kind of State*. Norman, Okla.: University of Oklahoma Press, 1980.

Hill, Luther B. *A History of the State of Oklahoma*. 2 vols. Chicago, Ill.: Lewis Publishing Co., 1908. Details the history of the territories up to statehood.

Jackson, A. P., and E. C. Cole. *Oklahoma! Politically and Topographically Described*. Kansas City, Mo.: Miller and Hudson, 1885.

McReynolds, Edwin C., Alice Marriott, and Estelle Faulconer. *Oklahoma: A History of the State and Its People*. Rev. ed. Norman, Okla.: University of Oklahoma Press, 1971.

Morgan, H. Wayne, and Anne Hodges Morgan. *Oklahoma: A Bicentennial History*. New York, N.Y.: W. W. Norton, and Nashville, Tenn.: American Association for State and Local History, 1977. Includes a good bibliographic essay on various aspects of the state's history.

———. *Oklahoma: New Views of the Forty-Sixth State*. Norman, Okla.: University of Oklahoma Press, 1982.

Thoburn, Joseph B. and Wright, Muriel H. *Oklahoma—A History of the State and Its People*. 4 vols. 1929. Reprint. Tucson, Ariz.: W. C. Cox, 1974.

Zellner, William W., and Ruth L. Laird, eds. *Oklahoma: The First Hundred Years*. Ada, Okla.: Galaxy Publications, n.d.

Writings on Native American history and culture in the state are extensive, but a good place to start is with Angie Debo, *A History of the Indians of the United States* (Norman, Okla.: University of Oklahoma Press, 1970), which has a fine bibliography for more comprehensive reading. See also Debo's "Major Indian Record Collections in Oklahoma" in *Indian-White Relations: A Persistent Paradox*, edited by Jane Smith and Robert Kvasnicka (Washington, D.C.: Howard University Press, 1976). Other suggested readings include:

Carlson, L. A. *Indians, Bureaucrats, and Land*. Westport, Conn.: Greenwood Press, 1981. Concerns Oklahoma Native Americans and land policy.

Coffer, William E. [Koi Hosh]. *Phoenix: The Decline and Rebirth of the Indian People*. New York, N.Y.: Van Nostrand Reinhold, 1980.

Foreman, Grant. *Indian Removal: The Emigration of the Five Civilized Tribes*. 1953. Reprint. Norman, Okla.: University of Oklahoma Press, 1969.

King, Duane H., ed. *The Cherokee Indian Nation: A Troubled History*. Knoxville, Tenn.: University of Tennessee Press, 1979. Provides historical glimpses of the Cherokees before, during, and after removal.

Smith, Robert E., ed. *Oklahoma's Forgotten Indians*. Oklahoma City, Okla.: Oklahoma Historical Society, 1981. Volume 15 in the society's *The Oklahoma Series*.

Tyler, Lyman S. *A History of Indian Policy*. Washington, D.C.: Government Printing Office, 1973. Details policy and its constant changes.

Wright, Muriel Hazel. *A Guide to the Indian Tribes of Oklahoma*. Norman, Okla.: University of Oklahoma Press, 1951.

For reading on the land runs see:

Hoig, Stan. *The Oklahoma Land Rush of 1889*. Oklahoma City, Okla.: Oklahoma Historical Society, 1984. Provides a historical overview of the land rush including its problems and opportunities.

Thiel, Sidney, comp. *The Oklahoma Land Rush*, Washington, D.C.: Historical Records Commission, n.d.

Wood, S. N. *The Boomers or the True Story of Oklahoma*, Topeka, Kans.: Bond and Neill, 1885.

Background reading in the role those of African-American descent played in Oklahoma settlement is available in Gene Aldrich, *Black Heritage of Oklahoma* (Edmond, Okla.: Thompson Book & Supply Co., 1973). (See also Special Focus Categories.)

The most recently published, thorough guide for doing research in the Twin Territories is Bradford Koplowitz, *Guide to the Historical Records of Oklahoma* (Bowie, Md.: Heritage Books, 1990). This guide lists numerous records and repositories in which specific records are maintained for all counties, many municipalities, and five general repositories.

A helpful, although not completely current, publication for Oklahoma research is Patrick J. Blessing, *Oklahoma Records and Archives* (Tulsa, Okla.: University of Tulsa Publications in American Social History, No. 1, 1978). This guide includes maps and access information for vital records statewide. Record holdings described are those of the Secretary of State, Commissioner of Land Office, Department of Interior, State Election Board, WPA, Historical Records Surveys, Vital Statistics, miscellaneous, theses, dissertations, Public Works, and guides.

Maps

Maps are particularly important in identifying the previous jurisdictions of the two territories that preceded present-day Oklahoma. The University of Oklahoma Library's Manuscripts Division (see Archives, Libraries, and Societies) and the Oklahoma State University Library at Stillwater, Oklahoma, maintain excellent collections for the state and its earlier territories. A *Guide to Cartographic Records in the National Archives* (Washington, D.C.: National Archives and Records Service, 1971) indicates availability of GLO maps which are particularly helpful for Indian Territory.

County maps may be purchased from the Oklahoma Department of Transportation, Reproduction Branch, 200

N.E. 21st Street, Oklahoma City, Oklahoma 73105-3204. Fees are minimal.

Some valuable compilations have been published including these:

Morris, John Wesley, ed. *Boundaries of Oklahoma.* Oklahoma City, Okla.: Oklahoma Historical Society, 1980. Explains the changing borders within the territory and state.

———. *Ghost Towns of Oklahoma.* Norman, Okla.: University of Oklahoma Press, 1978.

———, Charles R. Goins, and Edwin C. McReynolds. *The Historical Atlas of Oklahoma.* 2d ed. Norman, Okla.: University of Oklahoma Press, ca. 1986. Historical data and accompanying maps for the various developmental stages of the territory and state.

Oklahoma Department of Highways. *Town and Place Locations.* Oklahoma City, Okla.: Oklahoma Department of Highways, 1975. Alphabetically arranged listing showing place-name, county, section, township, and range. Includes towns and cities of today as well as towns that have vanished, names of known landmarks, road junctions, or railroad sidings. Lists over 4,200 places in Oklahoma.

Shirk, George H. *Oklahoma Place Names.* 1965. 2d ed. Norman, Okla.: University of Oklahoma Press, 1974. Alphabetically arranged, it begins with "A County" and concludes with "Zybra."

Land Records

Public-Domain State

Before 1889, the first year Oklahoma was officially opened for nonnative settlement, many nonnatives contracted for labor with the Five Civilized Tribes in exchange for land tenancy. Land records for the nations were filed under their respective Bureau of Indian Affairs (BIA) agency.

After some areas were opened for nonnative settlement, the common holdings of the tribes were divided into individual allotments to tribal members, with the federal government remaining guardian over the allotments. This freed up other land that was then made available to nonnative settlers. No centralized repository exists for the land allotments given the natives, but original allotments for all but the Five Civilized Tribes are on microfilm at the Indian Archives at the Oklahoma Historical Society. Outright payments made for land in the Cherokee Outlet are included in this microfilm. Arrell Morgan Gibson, *Oklahoma: A History of Five Centuries* (1965; reprint, Norman, Okla.: University of Oklahoma Press, 1981), describes allotment history and details for several tribes.

Land allotments given to Native Americans between 1889–1906 freed more land for nonnatives. The Indian Archives at the Oklahoma Historical Society holds land descriptions and plat maps for some of these allotments, although originals are either at the BIA in Muskogee, Oklahoma, or the National Archives-Southwest Region (see page 8). Related publications include:

Chapman, B. B. "Cherokee Allotments in the Outlet," *The Chronicles of Oklahoma.* 59 (Winter 1981–82): 401–21.

Cook, Fredrea, and Marlyn Hermann, *Forgotten Oklahoma Records: Cherokee Land Allotment Book.* Vol. 1. Cullman, Ala.: Gregath Co., 1981.

A majority of the nonnative settlers in the territory of Oklahoma obtained their lands through homestead claims. Case entry files, original tract books, and plat maps for homestead claims are maintained by the BLM (see page 5). Patents and copies of both tract books and plat maps are at the BLM New Mexico State Office, Federal Building, Box 1449, Santa Fe, New Mexico 87501. The Oklahoma Historical Society has seventy-two volumes of Oklahoma Federal Tract Books on microfilm that can be used in determining land descriptions to obtain homestead files. These are records of the homesteaders in Oklahoma Territory and a relatively few homesteaders (volume 63) for Ottawa and Delaware counties. Although not indexed by name, but by land description, a surname index has been compiled for each reel. A statewide index is currently being developed.

Homestead papers associated with the claim usually contain some genealogical information, including details such as age, birthplace, marital status, and number of family members, along with data concerning land use and improvements. If the homestead applicant was a naturalized citizen or in the process of becoming one, the homestead files will include a copy of the naturalization papers. If the homesteader was a Union veteran, the file may contain a copy of the discharge paper.

To locate homestead claims in the BLM records (see page 5) which were finalized prior to 1908, either the land description from the tract books (including county, township, range, etc.) or the date of entry and name of land office is required. For claims finalized after 1908, the number assigned to the case at the time that the land was patented is required. It is best to include a legal description of the property. In all cases, the full name of the homesteader must accompany the request for file copies.

A legal description of the land or the number assigned to the case may also be on file with the respective county clerk's office in which the land was originally located. These records are filed separately in the county but are usually fully indexed by landowner's name.

Land was, and continues to be, identified according to the rectangular survey method of measurement (see page 5). Records from Oklahoma's several local land offices (open from 1889–1927) are housed at the Division of Archives and Records, Oklahoma Department of Libraries (see Archives, Libraries, and Societies).

Since statehood in 1907, the respective clerk of the court or registrar maintains land and property transactions between individuals. Oklahoma land records usually include an abstract of title (property ownership) from the date of patent or first sale.

Probate Records

Probate records filed with the various tribal governments and Indian Agencies for the Five Civilized Tribes and some other Native American tribes in Oklahoma are maintained by the Oklahoma Historical Society. Other tribes' records are in the National Archives-Southwest Region (see page 8).

Territorial probate records were processed and filed under the jurisdiction of the U.S. district court. Most original federal district court probate records are also in the National Archives-Southwest Region, although the Oklahoma Historical Society has some federal district court probate records on microfilm.

Some probate packets for the northern section of Cherokee Territory were filed in the U.S. district court. These are indexed and identified in the following volume:

Wever, Orpha Jewell. *Probate Records, 1892–1908, Northern District Cherokee Nation.* 2 vols. Vinita, Okla.: Northeast Oklahoma Genealogical Society, 1982–83.

Since statehood, the respective county clerk of the court has maintained probate records. County probate records may include some wills recorded during the territorial period.

Court Records

The western district of Arkansas at Ft. Smith covered present-day Oklahoma as early as 1844. U.S. Federal District Courts served as the official criminal and civil courts for non-Native Americans until land was opened in 1889. Congress established federal courts at Muskogee in 1889 for crimes except those punishable by death or imprisonment. Cases for felonies were tried at either Ft. Smith, Arkansas; Paris, Texas; or Ft. Scott, Kansas. For nonnatives, the laws of Arkansas were applicable.

Between 1890–95, federal law divided Indian Territory into the three judicial districts of South McAlester (Choctaw Nation), Ardmore (Chickasaw and Seminole nations), and Muskogee (Cherokee and Creek nations and the Quapaw Agency). Judges from these three jurisdictions heard all appellate cases including those from Ft. Smith, Paris, and Ft. Scott. Until 1898, tribal courts continued hearing cases in which both parties were Native Americans. Thereafter, all persons, no matter their race, in Indian Territory were subject to federal laws and the laws of Arkansas.

In 1883 Congress changed the jurisdiction for the northern half of the western section of Indian Territory to that of the U.S. District Court of Kansas. The U.S. District Court, Northern District of Texas, was authorized to extend its jurisdiction to the southern half of the western part of Indian Territory.

During the first few years, a district court in Oklahoma Territory frequently served more than one county.

Most original, pre-statehood, district court records are in the National Archives-Southwest Region. Some are on microfilm at the Oklahoma Historical Society, Archives and Manuscripts Division.

Civil and criminal court records after statehood are available from the clerk of the court for the respective county. They maintain records such as proceedings, dockets, cases, and indexes to civil court matters. Jurisdiction may include probate, felony, civil, divorce, adoption, naturalization, small claims, licenses, juvenile, notary, minister's credentials, traffic, and misdemeanor cases. The appellate courts for Oklahoma are the state supreme court, court of appeals, and the court of criminal appeals.

Some early court records may include non-court related records. A volume stored in the basement of the Logan County courthouse contains the first court minutes, but the frontispiece lists a few marriages that occurred during that period.

Tax Records

Heavy spring rains with severe flooding in 1902 awakened Oklahoma's citizens to the need for better roads. Territorial laws placed responsibility with townships, and a road overseer was to be elected for each district. General property tax and some funds from liquor licenses collected by counties and townships were used to finance the building of public roads along section lines. A road tax was required, along with the requirement that all males between the ages of twenty-one and forty-five donate four eight-hour days a year to work on highways. Those who did not work or provide a substitute were fined $5 for each absence.

The county treasurer or assessor may have tax or assessment records. Some tax records are stored in museums, historical, and/or genealogical societies' repositories. Published tax records for Oklahoma are almost nonexistent. Some duplicated copies of county tax records are stored in the Oklahoma Department of Libraries, State Archives Division for security purposes, but are not available for research. Koplowitz, *Guide to the Historical Records of Oklahoma* (cited in Background Sources), indicates location of county records, including those of tax and assessments.

Cemetery Records

The Oklahoma Historical Society Library has the state copies of cemetery transcriptions completed by the state DAR, although this group of compilations is by no means comprehensive. A card file index at the library lists cemeteries in the DAR collection and some other cemeteries that have been canvased. The card index is alphabetical by name of county and indicates the cemetery.

Many other cemetery records exist that are not on the card file. Published records include some for Carter, Garfield, LeFlore, Murray, Muskogee, Payne, Roger Mills, Sequoyah, and Woodward counties. The FHL has *Cemetery Records of Oklahoma*. 9 vols. (Salt Lake City, Utah: Genealogical Society of Utah, 1959–62). Also see James W. Tyner and Alice Tyner Timmons, *Our People and Where They Rest*, 10 vols. (Norman, Okla.: University of Oklahoma, 1969–78), and Madeline S. Mills and Helen R. Mullenax, *Relocated Cemeteries in Oklahoma and Parts of Arkansas-Kansas-Texas* (Tulsa, Okla.: the authors, 1974).

Church Records

A Methodist church was organized at Pecan Point, in present-day McCurtain County, in 1818. It was the first Protestant church in the territory. Prior to statehood the largest numbers of citizens were Baptist, Roman Catholic, Disciples of Christ, or Methodist. Church records are among the most-difficult-to-locate sources in Oklahoma. Some are on microfilm at the Oklahoma Historical Society; others are maintained by members of the congregation and are housed in private homes rather than in church repositories. Still others are stored in the respective church. Some church records are deposited in the denominations' archives. A Historical Records Survey inventory was created relating to various church records in the counties. See WPA, Historical Records Survey. *Preliminary List of Churches and Religious Organizations in Oklahoma* (Oklahoma City, Okla.: Historical Records Survey, 1942).

The Chronicles of Oklahoma (see Periodicals) frequently publishes articles concerning specific churches or denominations. An example is Walter N. Vernon, "Methodist Beginnings Among Southwest Oklahoma Indians," *The Chronicles of Oklahoma* 58 (1980): 392–411.

Numerous missions provided through the Presbyterian, Baptist, and Moravian churches were established to serve Native Americans. Both teachers and missionaries constituted part of the nonnative population in Indian Territory. Some records are on microfilm in the Archives and Manuscript Division of the Oklahoma Historical Society. Others are maintained by denominational archives.

Records for Methodists, Catholics, and Baptists are housed in state facilities:

United Methodist, Box 1138, Bristow, Oklahoma 74010.

Roman Catholic Chancery Office, 1521 North Hudson, Oklahoma City, Oklahoma 63103

Oklahoma Baptist University Library, Shawnee, Oklahoma 74801. Privately funded, the library collection contains some materials and histories of the Baptist church.

Oklahoma City University, Oklahoma City, Oklahoma 73106. Founded in 1911 at Guthrie, it is affiliated with the Methodist Episcopal church. After uniting with Epworth University, it was relocated to Oklahoma City.

Military Records

Military records are available for Oklahoma prior to statehood. Bounty-land and military service records are located either at the National Archives or the Southwest Region branch in Fort Worth (see page 8). See also Odie B. Faulk, Kenny A. Franks, and Paul F. Lambert, eds., *Early Military Forts and Posts in Oklahoma* (Oklahoma City, Okla.: Oklahoma Historical Society, 1978). Troops who accompanied Native Americans during the federal government's forced removal of tribes can be found in U.S. Senate Document 512.

Confederate and Union service as well as other military service records are available from the National Archives (see pages 8–9). Some Civil War applications for pensions and pension records are extant at the Oklahoma Department of Libraries, State Archives Division (see Archives, Libraries, and Societies). Included are records for Confederate veterans (and their widows) who served elsewhere but were residents of Oklahoma when allocated pensions. These are filed numerically and indexed separately. See Oklahoma Board of Pension Commissioners, *Confederate Pension Applications for Soldiers and Sailors* (Oklahoma City, Okla.: Archives and Records Division, Oklahoma Department of Libraries, n.d.). Data on a Confederate pension from Oklahoma may be obtained from the Oklahoma Department of Welfare, Capitol Office Building, Oklahoma City, Oklahoma 73103.

Index to Applications for Pensions from the State of Oklahoma Submitted by Confederate Soldiers, Sailors and their Widows (Oklahoma City, Okla.: Oklahoma Genealogical Society, 1969), Special Publication No. 2, gives veteran's name, application number, and number of the reel for locating the pension file on microfilm.

Native American military units were part of Texas organizations, and are filed with those units, not as separate units for Indian Territory. Some confederate service records may be filed with the State Adjutant General's Office or the Oklahoma Historical Society, Archives and Manuscripts Division. See also Grant Foreman, *History of the Service and List of Individuals of the Five Civilized Tribes in the Confederate Army*, 2 vols. (Oklahoma City, Okla.: Oklahoma Historical Society, 1948).

The Oklahoma Historical Society maintains a card file of veterans buried in Oklahoma. These data cards may include full name, birth date, death date, burial place, and military service unit data. The Oklahoma Historical Society has the records, although incomplete, of the Confederate Home located in Ardmore, Oklahoma. Other records at the historical society include those for Native Americans that are contained in the Indian Archives section. Muster rolls of the Indian Home Guard are on microfilm. These are arranged by tribe, then by unit.

Periodicals, Newspapers, and Manuscript Collections

Periodicals

The Chronicles of Oklahoma is a valuable periodical published by the Oklahoma Historical Society since 1921. This ongoing series contains information about all aspects of life in the state and records created by and for its people. Volume 23 includes an article on the Edward Palmer Collection housed in the Carnegie Library in Enid, Oklahoma. Two cumulative indexes exist:

Chronicles of Oklahoma Cumulative Index, Volumes 1–37, 1921–1959. Vol. 1. Oklahoma City, Okla.: Oklahoma Historical Society, 1961.

Chronicles of Oklahoma Cumulative Index, Volumes 38–57, 1960–1979. Vol. 2. Oklahoma City, Okla.: Oklahoma Historical Society, 1983.

As many as fifty distinct publications are available for Oklahoma counties, regions, special interests, or the state. The Federation of Oklahoma Genealogical Societies publishes a quarterly *Newsletter*; and the *Oklahoma Genealogical Society Quarterly*, which began in 1961 (formerly called *The Bulletin*, beginning in 1955) as the publication for the Oklahoma Genealogical Society (see Archives, Libraries, and Societies for addresses).

Newspapers

The Oklahoma Historical Society has an extensive collection of newspapers published in Indian Territory, Oklahoma Territory, and the state of Oklahoma, dating back to the *Cherokee Advocate*, which ran from 1845–1901 in Tahlequah, Cherokee Nation, Indian Territory. Another newspaper was the *Indian Chieftain*, which was published between 1884–1900 in Vinita, Cherokee Nation, Indian Territory. Most are on microfilm (which can be purchased), and some indexes are available. A smaller collection is at the Oklahoma Department of Libraries (see Archives, Libraries, and Societies). The Muskogee Genealogical Society indexed all Muskogee newspapers. These index cards are maintained by the Muskogee Public Library, Muskogee, Oklahoma 74401. See also:

Ray, Grace. *Early Oklahoma Newspapers: History and Description of Publications from Earliest Beginnings to 1889.* Norman, Okla.: University of Oklahoma Press, 1928.

Parker, Doris Whitehall. *Footprints on the Osage Reservation.* 2 vols. Pawhuska, Okla.: the author, 1984. These are newspaper abstracts for 1894–1907.

Manuscripts

Large manuscript collections pertaining to Oklahoma's history and people are housed at the Oklahoma Historical Society in the Archives and Manuscript Division, including the Indian Archives, which maintains an extensive manuscript collection of records pertaining to the state's Native Americans. The Division consists of a large number of individual collections. Among the outstanding are the Grant Foreman Collection, principally dealing with the Five Civilized Tribes; the Joseph Thoburn Collection, concentrating on anthropology, archeology and history; and the Muriel Wright Collection, Wright being the former editor of *Chronicles of Oklahoma*, with correspondence dealing with Choctaw and Oklahoma history and families.

The WPA's Project S-149, Indian-Pioneer Papers (called the Indian-Pioneer History Collection), is located both at the Oklahoma Historical Society and the Western History Collection at the University of Oklahoma (see Archives, Libraries, and Societies). The project includes interviews of a large number of native and nonnative (both white and black) pioneers about their experiences and lives in Oklahoma. Included in these records are details of birth dates and places, parents' names, and other genealogical pertinent information. Each repository, however, has indexed this collection separately.

In addition to the University of Oklahoma, other university libraries in the state have significant collections. The Angie Debo Collection at Special Collections, Oklahoma State University in Stillwater contains the personal papers, correspondence, and recollections of this important professor of history in the state. In addition to Blessing, *Oklahoma Records and Archives*, and Koplowitz, *Guide to the Historical Records of Oklahoma* (both cited in Background Sources), which indicate general manuscript holdings, guides for specific manuscript collections include:

Stewart, John, and Kenny Franks. *State Records, Manuscripts, and Newspapers at the Oklahoma State Archives and Oklahoma Historical Society.* Oklahoma City, Okla.: State Department of Libraries and Oklahoma Historical Society, 1975.

Gibson, Arrell Morgan. *A Guide to Regional Manuscript Collections in the Division of Manuscripts, University of Oklahoma Library.* Norman, Okla.: University of Oklahoma Press, 1960.

Archives, Libraries, and Societies

Oklahoma Historical Society
2100 North Lincoln Boulevard
Oklahoma City, OK 73105

The society has a museum and a library with several major collections that do not circulate. It has federal census records, nearly 50,000 books including, but not limited to, the extensive collection of printed volumes belonging to the State Library of the Oklahoma Society of the National Society of the Daughters of the American Revolution, the collection of the Oklahoma Genealogical Society, and other standard genealogical reference materials. It has the largest collection of newspapers for the state, Oklahoma state records, and land records. The strength of its printed collections, however, concerns the counties formed from Oklahoma Territory. It maintains a surname file and a good collection of family histories. The Fred S. Bard Collection of genealogical material concerning pioneers and history is included. The Archives and Manuscripts Division houses some records for the counties of Comanche, Greer, Johnston, Kiowa, Logan, Muskogee, Osage, Payne, Potawatomie, and Swanson. The Indian Archives section of the division houses excellent resources for Native American research (see Special Focus Categories).

University of Oklahoma Library
630 Parrington Oval
Monnet Hall
Norman, OK 73019

Genealogical materials including histories and general reference materials for public use are among the accessions for the library. Special interests are history of the West, development of the Trans-Mississippi West, and Native American cultures. Its Western History Collection includes the WPA Indian-Pioneer Papers (see Manuscripts). It maintains more than 1,500 collections pertaining to Oklahoma, Native Americans, and western frontier history. The Manuscripts Division houses over 5,000 maps of Indian Territory, Oklahoma Territory, and the Trans-Mississippi West. It also has more than 1,000 sound recordings, including the Doris Duke Indian Oral History Collection and other interviews with Oklahoma's pioneers and leaders.

Oklahoma Department of Libraries
Division of State Archives and Records
200 N.E. 18th Street
Oklahoma City, OK 75105

The agency holds the original permanent records generated by state government including Confederate pension applications and transcripts of minutes of the boards of county commissioners for forty-seven counties for 1886–89. The Records Center, a few blocks away at 125 N.E. 21st Street, maintains the non-permanent records for state government and has some records for Cleveland County.

Oklahoma Genealogical Society
P.O. Box 314
Oklahoma City 73101

Publishes a quarterly (see Periodicals).

The Oklahoma Territorial Museum
107 East Oklahoma
Guthrie, OK 73044

It has a collection of early Oklahoma microfilmed records as well as a small collection of histories of the area.

Oklahoma City Public Library
131 Northwest Third Street
Oklahoma City, OK 73102

The library has a genealogical collection. On request, the staff will check family histories free of charge, and materials are available through interlibrary loan.

Many county and city libraries have some genealogical collections, and most counties have genealogical or historical societies. The Federation of Oklahoma Genealogical Societies, P.O. Box 2531, Ponca City, Oklahoma 74602, can help locate currently operating ones (also see pages 8–10).

Special Focus Categories

Native American

Because of the federal government's removal policy, sixty-five different tribes have made their home in present-day Oklahoma. The sources for research are enormously varied from the kinds of materials generally associated with county-state record patterns. In addition to the sources held in the National Archives and its Southwest regional branch in Ft. Worth (see page 8), materials for research on both natives and nonnatives who lived in the Twin Territories can be found at all agencies of the Bureau of Indian Affairs (see page 11), including those in Anadarko, Ardmore, Concho, Okmulgee, Pawhuska, Pawnee, Miami, Shawnee, Tahlequah, Talihina, Wewoka, and Stewart. What is covered here are some general categories of records found regarding Native Americans in the state. For a more extensive and detailed discussion see Blessing, *Oklahoma Records and Archives,* and Koplowitz *Guide to the Historical Records of Oklahoma* (both cited under Background Sources), or George J. Nixon, "Records Relating to Native American Research: The Five Civilized Tribes," in *The Source* (see page 11).

Some copies of census records on Native Americans are available at the Oklahoma Historical Society library and the FHL. These censuses are alphabetically arranged by BIA agency, then tribal name, and then date of enumeration. Since agency changes were made, a specific tribe may have been under the jurisdiction of two or more agencies. Beginning about 1916, the registration of individuals' names may be alphabetically arranged within the tribe's census schedule.

Land allotment records can be a valuable source for Native American ancestors. To obtain a parcel of land, each applicant had to include documentation of descent. Final rolls list those who received land allotments. When the land was to be sold or the individual died, all heirs were identified since transfer of land required permission from all heirs. This data usually was registered in allotment or family registers. Later lists of heirs may be located in records entitled "Heirship Records." Each person is usually identified by age or birth date and relationship. Most allotted land eventually returned to tribal jurisdiction, for few individuals received patents to their holdings (see also Land Records).

Enrollment records, on which land allotments were based, were drawn up by the Dawes Commission for the Five Civilized Tribes. Under the Dawes Commission, information was abstracted onto data cards entitled *Enrollments Cards for the Five Civilized Tribes: 1898–1914* (Washington,

D.C.: National Archives, 1981). Cards were made from both approved and rejected applications of Cherokee, Choctaw, Chickasaw, Creek, and Seminole tribe members. Microfilm of these packets and records is available at the Oklahoma Historical Society, the National Archives, and the FHL. Original applications are housed at the National Archives-Southwest Region in Fort Worth. A guide and index to these records is included in the Commission to the Five Civilized Tribes' publication, *The Final Rolls of Citizens and Freedmen of the Five Civilized Tribes in Indian Territory,* 2 vols. (Washington, D.C.: Government Printing Office, n.d.).

Another valuable source is the Guion Miller records, which are contained on 348 reels of microfilm entitled *Eastern Cherokee Applications of the U.S. Court of Claims, 1906–1909* (Washington, D.C.: National Archives, 1981). A separate index is available for this collection of court records for individuals who applied for government compensation for lands confiscated from the Eastern Cherokees during the 1800s, mainly in North Carolina. Claims include data with documentation showing claimant's lineage back to the Eastern Cherokee. It was also required that the claimant prove no other tribal affiliation.

Second only to the National Archives in Native American research for Oklahoma is the Indian Archives Division of the Oklahoma Historical Society. Included are federal and state government records and private collections, particularly the extensive work of Grant Foreman (also see Manuscripts). The society's collection is listed and described in Lawrence Kelly's "Indian Records in the Oklahoma Historical Society Archives," *The Chronicles of Oklahoma* 54 (1976): 227–44. Other issues include data relating to the Native Americans in Oklahoma and their records. Among many such articles are "Public Land Policy of the Five Civilized Tribes" 23 (1945): 107–18; "Provincial Indian Society in Eastern Oklahoma" 23 (1945): 323–37; and "Cherokee Allotments in the Outlet" 59 (1981): 401–21.

The Archives and Manuscripts Division of the Oklahoma Historical Society has approximately 3,000,000 pages and 6,000 bound volumes from Indian Agencies in Oklahoma for 1870 through 1930. The archives is the national repository for records of the Cherokee, Chickasaw, Choctaw, Creek, and Seminole nations for the period 1860 through 1906. The archives also maintains agency records for Cheyenne, Cantonment, Pawnee, Quapaw, Chilocoo, Shawnee, Kiowa, and Arapaho, as well as Mekusukey Academy records and many special collections. There are 1,400 volumes of the Executive Library Cherokee Nation in the collection. The newspaper collection includes *The Cherokee Advocate* which began publication in 1844.

The Bureau of Indian Affairs, Muskogee Agency, 4th Floor, Federal Building, Muskogee, Oklahoma 74401, maintains records of the Cherokee and other tribes. The Cherokee Registration Office, P.O. Box 119, Tahlequah, Oklahoma, 74464, has records pertaining to the Cherokees.

A few selected private collections in the Indian Archives Division, Oklahoma Historical Society include transcripts of the Office of Commissioner Indian Affairs and Superintendent of the Five Civilized tribes in the Grant Foreman transcripts, Frederick B. Severs Collection for the Creek Nation, Grant Foreman's numerous collections and WPA project interviews, John H. Adair Collection of early Cherokees, and the G. A. Root collection of newspaper clippings for Oklahoma Land openings.

The following publications include valuable source material:

Baker, Jack D. *Cherokee Emigration Rolls, 1817–1835.* Oklahoma City, Okla.: Baker Publishing Co., ca. 1977.

Bogle, Dixie. *Cherokee Nation Births and Deaths, 1884–1901.* Owensboro, Ky.: Cook and McDowell Publications, 1980. This publication was sponsored by the Northeast Oklahoma Genealogical Society and contains abstracts from two newspapers, *Indian Chieftain* and *Daily Chieftain.*

Bogle, Dixie, and Dorothy Nix. *Cherokee Nation Marriages, 1884–1901.* Owensboro, Ky.: Cook and McDowell Publications, 1980. This publication was sponsored by Abraham Coryell Chapter, National Society Daughters of the American Revolution, and it contains abstracts taken from *Indian Chieftain* newspapers.

Campbell, John Bert. *Campbell's Abstract of Creek Indian Census Cards and Index.* Muskogee, Okla.: Phoenix Job Printing, 1981.

———. *Campbell's Abstract of Seminole Indian Census Cards and Index.* Muskogee, Okla.: Oklahoma Printing, 1925.

Chase, Marybelle W., comp. *1842 Cherokee Claims: Tahlequah District.* Nashville, Tenn.: Tennessee State Library and Archives, 1989. This volume is reproductions of handwritten records and is indexed.

———. *A Survey of Tribal Records in the Archives of the United States Government in Oklahoma.* N.p., n.d.

Kelly, Lawrence. "Indian Records in the Oklahoma Historical Society Archives." *The Chronicles of Oklahoma* 54 (Summer 1976): 227–44.

Oklahoma Genealogical Society. *A Compilation of Records from the Choctaw Nation, Indian Territory.* Oklahoma City, Okla.: Oklahoma Genealogical Society, ca. 1976.

Sober, Nancy Hope. *The Intruders: The Illegal Residents of Cherokee Nation, 1866–1907.* Ponca City, Okla.: Cherokee Books, ca. 1991.

Other Ethnic Groups

A series entitled "Newcomers to a New Land" was sponsored by the Department of Libraries and the Oklahoma Library Association. These books analyze the role and impact of major ethnic groups in the state. The following are among volumes in the series:

Bernard, Richard. *The Poles in Oklahoma.* Norman, Okla.: University of Oklahoma Press, 1980.

Bicha, Karel D. *The Czechs in Oklahoma.* Norman, Okla.: University of Oklahoma Press, 1980.

Blessing, Patrick J. *The British and Irish in Oklahoma.* Norman, Okla.: University of Oklahoma Press, 1980.

Brown, Kenny L. *The Italians in Oklahoma.* Norman, Okla.: University of Oklahoma Press, 1980.

Hale, Douglas. *The Germans from Russia in Oklahoma.* Norman, Okla.: University of Oklahoma Press, 1980.

Rohrs, Richard C. *The Germans in Oklahoma.* Norman, Okla.: University of Oklahoma Press, 1980.

Smith, Michael M. *The Mexicans in Oklahoma.* Norman, Okla.: University of Oklahoma Press, 1980.

Tobias, Henry J. *The Jews in Oklahoma.* Norman, Okla.: University of Oklahoma Press, 1980.

For Czechs in Oklahoma, see also:

Lynch, Russell Wilford. "Czech Farmers in Oklahoma." *Oklahoma A & M College Bulletin* 39, no. 13 (June 1942).

For blacks in Oklahoma, see also:

Franklin, Jimmie Lewis. *The Blacks in Oklahoma.* Norman, Okla.: University of Oklahoma Press, 1980.

———. *Journey Toward Hope: A History of Blacks in Oklahoma.* Norman, Okla.: University of Oklahoma Press, 1982.

Tolson, Arthur L. *The Black Oklahomans: A History, 1541–1972.* New Orleans, La.: Edwards Print Co., 1974.

County Resources

Oklahoma deeds, probates, and civil court records are located at the county clerk's or clerk of the courts office. Marriage records before statewide recording may be found at the county clerk as well, but records of births and deaths are not available until statewide recording began. Official certificates come from the State Department of Health (see Vital Records). The State Election Board, Oklahoma Museum of Election History, Oklahoma City, Oklahoma 73105, holds precinct registers and/or other records for thirty-four counties.

The largest percentage of Oklahoma's extant public records were generated in the twentieth century and are generally intact. Send inquiries to the county official at the courthouse address for the appropriate county. Some dates in the following chart were obtained from Blessing, *Oklahoma Records and Archives,* and Koplowitz, *Guide to Historical Records of Oklahoma* (both cited in Background Sources). There are a few discrepancies in county record beginning dates between Koplowitz and Blessing; in such instances, Koplowitz's dates have been used.

Drawn by William Dollarhide

Map	County Address	Date Formed Parent County/ies	Birth Marriage Death	Land Probate Court
K3	Adair Stilwell 74960	1907 Cherokee lands	1908 1907 1908	1907 1907 1907
F2	Alfalfa Cherokee 73728	1907 Woods	1908 1807 1908	1895 1907 1907
J5	Atoka 201 E. Court Atoka 74525	1907 Choctaw lands	1908 1892 1908	1907 1897 1913
C1	Beaver P.O. Box 338 Beaver 73932	1890 original	1908 1890 1908	1890 1890 1891
D4	Beckham P.O. Box 67 Sayre 73662	1907 Roger Mills	1908 1907 1908	1900 1907 1907
F3	Blaine P.O. Box 138 Watonga 73772	1892 original	1908 1892 1908	1892 1892 1892
H6	Bryan 402 W. Evergreen Durant 74701	1907 Choctaw lands	1908 1902 1908	1903 1912 1902
F4	Caddo P.O. Box 68 Anadarko 73005	1901 original	1908 1902 1908	1902 1901 1901
F3	Canadian El Reno 73036	1889 original	1908 1890 1908	1890 1890 1890
G5	Carter First and B Street, S.W. Ardmore 73401	1907 Chickasaw lands	1930 1895 1930	1907 1895 1895
K3	Cherokee 213 W. Delaware Tahlequah 74464	1907 Cherokee lands	1908 1907 1908	1907 1907 1907
J6	Choctaw Hugo 74743	1907 Choctaw lands	1908 1907 1908	1907 1907 1907
A1	Cimarron Boise City 73933	1907 Beaver	1908 1908 1908	1908 1908 1908
G4	Cleveland 201 S. Jones Norman 73069	1889 unassigned lands	1908 1890 1908	1890 1893 1891
H5	Coal 3 N. Main Street Coalgate 74538	1907 Choctaw lands	1908 1907 1908	1904 1907 1907
F5	Comanche Lawton 73501	1901 Kiowa/Comanche/Apache lands	1906 1901 1906	1901 1901 1901

Map	County Address	Date Formed Parent County/ies	Birth Marriage Death	Land Probate Court
F5	Cotton 301 N. Broadway Street Walters 73572	1912 Comanche	1917 1912 1918	1902 1912 1912
K1	Craig Vinita 74301	1907 Cherokee lands	1908 1902 1908	1907 1907 1907
H3	Creek Sapulpa 74066	1907 Creek lands	1908 1907 1908	1898 1907 1917
E3	Custer Arapaho 73620	1892 Cheyenne/ Arapaho lands	1908 1895 1908	1896 1900 1896
	Day	1892 (abolished 1907; now Ellis County area) Cheyenne/ Arapaho lands		
K2	Delaware P.O. Box 309 Jay 74346	1907 Cherokee	1908 1911 1908	1905 1911 1911
E3	Dewey P.O. Box 368 Taloga 73667	1892 original	1908 1895 1908	1892 1902 1904
D3	Ellis 100 S. Washington Arnett 73832	1907 Day/Woodward	1908 1892 1908	1896 1901 1907
F2	Garfield Enid 73701	1893 Cherokee	1908 1893 1908	1893 1907 1907
G5	Garvin Pauls Valley 73075	1907 Chickasaw lands	1908 1907 1908	1906 1907 1907
F4	Grady P.O. Box 1009 Chickasha 73018	1907 Caddo/Comanche	1908 1907 1908	1903 1907 1907
F2	Grant Medford 73759	1893 original	1908 1893 1908	1893 1893 1893
D4	Greer Mangum 73554	(organized by Texas, 1886; became part of Oklahoma, 1896)	1908 1901 1908	1900 1901 1901
D5	Harmon Hollis 73550	1909 Greer/Jackson	1909 1909 1909	1909 1909 1909
D1	Harper P.O. Box 369 Buffalo 73834	1907 Indian lands/Woods/Woodward	1908 1907 1908	1900 1907 1907
K4	Haskell 202 W. Main Stigler 74462	1908 Choctaw lands	1908 1907 1908	1905 1907 1907

Map	County Address	Date Formed Parent County/ies	Birth Marriage Death	Land Probate Court
H4	Hughes Holdenville 74848	1907 Creek lands	1908 1907 1908	1907 1907 1907
D5	Jackson Altus 73521	1907 Greer	1908 1907 1908	1907 1910 1907
F6	Jefferson 220 N. Main Waurika 73573	1907 Comanche/Chickasaw	1908 1907 1908	1907 1907 1907
H5	Johnston Tishomingo 73460	1907 Chickasaw lands	1908 1907 1908	1907 1907 1907
G1	Kay Newkirk 74647	1895 Cherokee outlet	1908 1893 1908	1893 1893 1893
F3	Kingfisher P.O. Box 118 Kingfisher 73750	1890 original	1908 1900 1908	1890 1900 1896
E4	Kiowa Hobart 73651	1901 Kiowa/Comanche/Apache lands	1908 1901 1908	1901 1901 1901
K4	Latimer 109 N. Central Wilburton 74578	1902 Choctaw lands	1908 1907 1908	1906 1908 1908
K4	Le Flore P.O. Box 607 Poteau 74953	1907 Choctaw lands	1908 1897 1908	1907 1897 1907
H3	Lincoln P.O. Box 126 Chandler 74834	1891 Iowa Kickapoo/Sac-Fox lands	1908 1891 1900	1891 1893 1891
G3	Logan Guthrie 73044	1890 original	1908 1890 1908	1895 1890 1890
G6	Love 405 W. Main Street Marietta 73448	1907 Chickasaw lands	1908 1907 1908	1903 1907 1907
F2	Major E. Broadway Fairview 73737	1907 Woods	1908 1893 1908	1893 1907 1907
H6	Marshall Madill 73446	1907 Chickasaw lands	1908 1907 1908	1907 1907 1907
K2	Mayes Pryor 74361	1907 Cherokee lands	1908 1907 1908	1903 1907 1907
G4	McClain P.O. Box 629 Purcell 73080	1907 Chickasaw lands	1908 1907 1883	1891 1895 1895

Map	County Address	Date Formed Parent County/ies	Birth Marriage Death	Land Probate Court
K6	McCurtain P.O. Box 1078 Idabel 74745	1907 Choctaw lands	1908 1907 1908	1907 1917 1907
J4	McIntosh P.O. Box 108 Eufaula 74432	1907 (Creek) Indian lands	1905 1907 1905	1907 1907 1907
G5	Murray P.O. Box 240 Sulphur 73086	1907 Chickasaw lands	1908 1907 1908	1906 1907 1907
K3	Muskogee P.O. Box 2307 Muskogee 74401	1898 Creek	1908 1908 1908	1901 1908 1908
G2	Noble P.O. Box 409 Perry 73077	1893 Cherokee Outlet	1908 1896 1908	1893 1896 1896
J1	Nowata 229 N. Maple Street Nowata 74048	1907 Cherokee lands	1908 1907 1908	1909 1907 1907
H3	Okfuskee P.O. Box 26 Okemah 74859	1907 Creek lands	1909 1907 1909	1907 1910 1907
G3	Oklahoma 320 N.W. Robert S. Kerr Oklahoma City 73102	1890 original	1908 1889 1908	1890 1890 1890
J3	Okmulgee Okmulgee 74447	1907 Creek lands	1908 1907 1908	1907 1907 1907
H2	Osage P.O. Box 87 Pawhuska 74056	1907 Osage Indian lands	1908 1907 1908	1906 1907 1897
K1	Ottawa Miami 74354	1907 Cherokee nation	1908 1907 1908	1895 1907 1907
H2	Pawnee Pawnee 74058	1893 Cherokee Outlet	1908 1897 1908	1894 1897 1897
G3	Payne 6th and Husband Streets Stillwater 74074	1890 Cherokee Outlet	1876 1894 1876	1895 1889 1894
J4	Pittsburg McAlester 74501	1907 Choctaw lands	1908 1890 1908	1907 1907 1909
H5	Pontotoc 13th and Broadway Ada 74820	1907 Chickasaw lands	1908 1907 1908	pre-1907 1907 1907
H4	Pottawatomie 325 N. Broadway Shawnee 74801	1891 Pottawatomie-Shawnee lands	1908 1892 1908	1895 1892 1892

Map	County Address	Date Formed Parent County/ies	Birth Marriage Death	Land Probate Court
K5	Pushmataha 203 S.W. 3rd Antlers 74523	1907 Choctaw lands	1917 1907 1917	1907 1907 1907
D3	Roger Mills P.O. Box 708 Cheyenne 73628	1892 Cheyenne-Arapaho lands	1908 1893 1908	1892 1907 1894
J2	Rogers 219 S. Missouri Claremore 74017	1907 Cherokee Nation	1915 1907 1915	1907 1907 1907
H4	Seminole Wewoka 74884	1907 Seminole lands	1908 1907 1908	pre-1907 1909 1915
K3	Sequoyah 120 E. Chickasaw Street Sallisaw 74955	1907 Cherokee lands	1907 1907 1907	1907 1907 1907
F5	Stephens Duncan 73533	1907 Comanche	1908 1907 1908	1907 1907 1907
B1	Texas P.O. Box 197 Guymon 73942	1907 Beaver	1908 1907 1908	1889 1907 1909
E5	Tillman P.O. Box 992 Frederick 73542	1907 Comanche lands	1908 1907 1908	1907 1907 1907
J3	Tulsa 500 S. Denver Tulsa 74100	1905 Creek lands	1908 1907 1908	1907 1906 1906
J3	Wagoner 307 E. Cherokee Wagoner 74467	1908 Creek lands	1908 1908 1908	1906 1907 1907
J1	Washington 420 S. Johnstone Bartlesville 74003	1897 Cherokee lands	1908 1907 1908	1900 1907 1907
E4	Washita P.O. Box 380 Cordell 73632	1900 Cheyenne-Arapaho lands	1908 1892 1908	1907 1903 1892
E2	Woods P.O. Box 386 Alva 73717	1893 Cherokee Outlet	1908 1890 1908	1894 1890 1890
E2	Woodward 1600 Main Street Woodward 73801	1893 Cherokee Outlet	1908 1897 1908	1894 1900 1894

OREGON

Dwight A. Radford

The settlement of Oregon began in 1829 when retired French-Canadian fur trappers from the Hudson Bay Company started farming on the banks of the Willamette River at Champoeg near present-day St. Paul. By the 1840s, American missionaries had established settlements in the Oregon Country. Missions were sponsored by the Congregational, Presbyterian, Methodist, and Catholic churches.

Immigration encouraged by the missionaries began in the early 1840s. Most of the early settlers in Oregon were farmers from the Mississippi, Missouri, and Ohio river valleys. The promise of free land and a better life brought 53,000 immigrants to Oregon between 1840 and 1860. The Oregon Donation Land Act of 1850 provided from 160 to 320 acres of free land to white male settlers. Wives could receive an additional 160 to 320 acres in their own right.

The first city in Oregon, Willamette Falls, later called Oregon City, was established in 1829 by Dr. John McLoughlin, chief factor of the Hudson Bay Company. The city of Portland was started in 1844 when sixteen blocks were plotted out along the Willamette River bank. During the California gold rush, Portland became a place where wagons could meet sea-faring ships to exchange commodities. In 1850 gold was discovered in the Rogue River valley and led to the founding of Jacksonville in 1852. The town of Roseburg began in 1852 as a way station on the California-Oregon trail. During the years 1847–50, 1851–53, and 1855–56, conflicts between the immigrants and the natives plagued the routes and settlements in southern and northeastern Oregon. Statehood was obtained in 1859.

Gold mining in Baker and Grant counties during 1862 and 1865 brought prosperity to the entire region. Cattle drives across the Cascades from the valleys to the mines were more substantial to the economy. This gave rise to the cattle-baron empires and cattle towns such as Burns, Lakeview, and Prineville. The sheep industry followed the cattle empires in northeastern Oregon between The Dalles and the Umatilla and contributed to the growth of towns such as Condon, Heppner, and Pendleton.

European immigrants came to Oregon in the 1870s. Scandinavians drawn by fishing settled in coastal areas, and a large number of Finns settled at Astoria. Swiss immigrants settled at Tillamook and began the cheese industry in the area.

Portland became a major port, and during the 1870s attained status as one of the major wheat ports of the world. Portland's thriving economy drew a wide range of foreign immigrants including Chinese, Germans, Irish, Jews, Scandinavians, and Scots.

Vital Records

The state of Oregon began recording births and deaths in 1903 and marriages in 1906. Divorces were recorded at the state level beginning in 1925. Vital records may be obtained by writing the Oregon State Health Division, Vital Records Unit, P.O. Box 116, Portland, Oregon 97207-0116.

When ordering vital records from Oregon, the following information is required: name of record, name of spouse (death, marriage, divorce only), date of event, place of event, father's name, mother's first and maiden name, name of agency or person ordering record, your relationship to person on record, and your address and phone number. The cost for obtaining a record is $10 per copy.

Only immediate family members or legal representatives may order a birth record. Anyone with an interest may order a death, marriage, or divorce record. It takes about two weeks for the Oregon State Health Division to answer a mail request. It is possible to request a certificate in person and receive it the same day. According to Oregon State law, birth records (including indexes) have a 100 year access restriction. Therefore, birth indexes are not available to the public.

Some death, divorce, and marriage indexes have been microfilmed. They include deaths from 1903–89; divorces from 1946–60 and 1966–89; and marriages from 1906–24, 1946–60, and 1966–89. A complete set is available at the Oregon State Archives, Oregon State Library, and the Oregon Historical Society (see Archives, Libraries, and Societies). The Oregon Historical Society also has a complete death index and the later divorce and marriage indexes. Other libraries throughout Oregon and the FHL in Salt Lake City have portions of the indexes.

The early death indexes are known to be incomplete, and other sources should be checked, such as the county clerk for the county where the death was recorded, the Oregon State Archives, newspaper indexes, and cemetery records.

The Oregon State Archives in Salem has vital records from fifteen of the thirty-six counties. These include Benton, Clackamas, Columbia, Douglas, Jackson, Lincoln, Linn, Marion, Multnomah (and the city of Portland), Polk, Tillamook, Umatilla, Wasco, Washington, and Yamhill. Pre-1903/06 vital records also exist for a few counties/cities at the state archives (see County Resources).

Census Records

Federal

Population Schedules.

- Indexed—1850, 1860, 1870
- Soundex—1880, 1900, 1920
- Unindexed—1910

Industry and Agriculture Schedules.

- 1850, 1860, 1870, 1880

Mortality Schedules.

- 1850, 1860, 1870, 1880

Union Veterans Schedules.

- 1890 (indexed)

The Oregon State Archives, Oregon State Library, and Oregon Historical Society Library hold microfilm copies of federal Oregon censuses. The supplemental schedules are at the Oregon Historical Society Library.

Territorial and State

Territorial and state census records reflect the rapid growth of the Oregon country. These census enumerations were taken in 1842, 1843, 1845, 1849, 1853, 1854, 1855, 1856, 1857, 1858, 1859, 1865, 1875, 1885, 1895, and 1905. Only portions of some of these enumerations have survived. Most of these censuses include only the name of the head of household, although the 1895 and 1905 censuses include some information on all members of the household.

The following census rolls are on file at the Oregon State Library, the Oregon Historical Society, the University of Oregon Library, and the FHL.

- **1845:** Champoeg, Clackamas, Clatsop, Tuality (now Washington County), Yamhill
- **1849:** Benton, Champoeg (now Marion), Clackamas, Lewis (now in Washington State), Linn, Polk, Tualatin (now Washington County), Vancouver (now in Washington State), Yamhill
- **1853:** Marion, Polk, Umpqua (now Douglas), Washington, Benton
- **1854:** Clatsop, Jackson
- **1855:** Coos, Jackson
- **1856:** Clackamas, Curry, Jackson, Polk, Washington
- **1857:** Clackamas, Coos, Curry, Douglas, Jackson, Tillamook, Umpqua (now Douglas), Washington
- **1858:** Clatsop, Coos, Curry, Umpqua (now Douglas)
- **1859:** Clatsop, Umpqua (now Douglas)
- **1895:** Marion
- **1905:** Baker, Linn, Lane, Marion

AISI (see page 2) has published a comprehensive index for the territorial/state censuses from 1841 through 1859.

Background Sources

Bailey, Barbara Ruth. *Main Street, Northeastern Oregon: The Founding and Development of Small Towns.* Portland, Oreg.: Oregon Historical Society, 1982. This volume examines all the towns, except Baker and LaGrande, founded within the northeastern section of Oregon.

Bowen, William A. *The Willamette Valley: Migration and Settlement on the Oregon Frontier.* Seattle, Wash.: University of Washington Press, 1978. The creative approach to this place and time period makes it an unusual and important discussion.

Brandt, Patricia. *Oregon Biographical Index.* Corvallis, Oreg.: Oregon State University, 1976. This is an important publication that indexes forty-seven historical volumes which are either entirely devoted to biographies or have large self-contained biographical sections.

Carey, Charles Henry. *History of Oregon.* Chicago, Ill.: Pioneer History Publishing Co., 1922. Three volumes detailing the discovery, settlement, and development of Oregon country.

Clarke, S. A. *Pioneers of Oregon History.* Portland, Oreg.: J. K. Gill, 1905. This two-volume work deals with early exploration of the Oregon region, the Native American population, arrival of Protestant and Catholic missionaries, overland emigration, and the early political history of Oregon.

Gaston, Joseph. *The Centennial History of Oregon, 1811–1912; With Notice of Antecedent Explorations.* Chicago, Ill.: S. J. Clarke Publishing Co., 1912. This two-volume work covers the history of the northwest Pacific coast, the fur trading industry, the founding of Portland, Indian wars, government, religion, agriculture, industry, and politics. The second volume is dedicated to biographical sketches of Oregonians.

Gray, W. H. *A History of Oregon, 1792–1849.* Tucson, Ariz.: W. C. Cox Co., 1974. Originally published in 1870, this volume covers the failure of Protestant missions, the Indian wars, early settlers and settlements, and the mining and agricultural industries.

Hawthorne, Julian. *The Story of Oregon: A History With Portraits and Biographies.* Salt Lake City, Utah: Genealogical Society of Utah, 1964. Compiled in a two-volume set, the most valuable portion is the autobiographical section in volume two. These autobiographies were contributed by a number of living Oregon residents.

Hines, Harvey K. *An Illustrated History of the State of Oregon.* Chicago, Ill.: Lewis Publishing Co., 1893. This history of Oregon contains full-page portraits and biographical material on many of the prominent citizens of the period.

Lenzen, Connie. "Genealogical Research in Oregon," *National Genealogical Society Quarterly* 79 (March 1991). Details of genealogical resources in Oregon are presented in this excellent article.

Lang, Herbert O. *History of the Willamette Valley.* Salt Lake City, Utah: Genealogical Society of Utah, 1985. The purpose of this volume, which was originally published in 1885, was to arrange and preserve the scattered records and recollections of the Willamette Valley. The newspapers of the valley contributed information.

The Oregonian's Handbook of the Pacific Northwest, Portland: Oregonian Publishing Co., 1894. This important travel guide, published by the newspaper *The Oregonian,* gathers information on Oregon, Washington, Idaho, and western Montana, as well as British Columbia and Alaska. Information was gathered through personal visits by the staff of *The Oregonian.*

Portrait and Biographical Record of the Willamette Valley, Oregon: Containing Original Sketches of Many Well Known Citizens of the Past and Present. Chicago, Ill.: Chapman Publishing Co., 1903. A great deal of genealogical information is provided in these excellent sketches of Willamette Valley residents.

Portrait and Biographical Record of Western Oregon: Containing Original Sketches of Many Well Known Citizens of the Past and Present. Tucson, Ariz.: W. C. Cox, 1974. This volume originally published in 1904 records biographies of the men who contributed to the development and progress of western Oregon. Many pioneers are listed.

Preston, Ralph N. *Historical Oregon: Overland Stage Routes, Old Military Roads, Indian Battle Grounds, Old Forts, Old Gold Mines.* Portland, Oreg.: Binford & Mort, 1978. A compilation of historical maps of Oregon from the Lewis and Clark expedition map to modern maps.

Wojcik, Donna M. *The Brazen Overlanders of 1845.* Portland, Oreg.: the author. A history of the 1845 overland migration to Oregon country. Sources for the book were drawn from newspapers, censuses, historical and genealogical records, diaries, and letters.

Maps

Maps are essential in conducting on-site research, in plotting mining claims, and in discovering cemeteries and towns. Several helpful maps are available for Oregon.

Ralph N. Preston's *Historical Oregon: Overland Stage Routes, Old Military Roads, Indian Battle Grounds, Old Forts, Old Gold Mines* (Portland, Oreg.: Binford & Mort, 1978), is an excellent collection of early Oregon maps beginning with the 1804 Lewis and Clark trail map to a present-day map of the state. This collection is valuable for genealogical research because it shows overland stage routes, old military roads, native battle grounds, old forts, and old mining areas.

Two other important works should be referred to: Erma S. Brown's *Oregon County Boundary Change Maps, 1843–1916* (Salem, Oreg.: the author, 1970) shows the changes in county boundaries, and Lewis A. McArthur's *Oregon Geographic Names,* 5th ed. (Portland, Oreg.: Oregon Historical Society, 1982), lists Oregon place-names and gives location and history.

City and county maps of Oregon can be obtained by writing the Oregon Department of Transportation, State Highway Division, Map Distribution Unit, Transportation Building, Salem, Oregon 97310.

The United States Geological Survey (see page 4) will send a free index and catalog of their topographical maps. To obtain these booklets for Oregon, ask for the following two publications: "Oregon, Index to Topographical and Other Map Coverage" and "Oregon, Catalog of Topographic and Other Published Maps." The catalog has the current cost for each topographical map, as well as a listing of over-the-counter map sellers in Oregon.

Major libraries in Oregon have been designated by the U.S. Geological Survey as map depository libraries. They include Southern Oregon State College in Ashland; Central Oregon Community College in Bend; Oregon State University in Corvallis; University of Oregon, Law Library and Map Library in Eugene; Pacific University in Forest Grove; Oregon Institute of Technology in Klamath Falls; Eastern Oregon State College in La Grande; Linfield College in

McMinnville; Western Oregon State College in Monmouth; Lewis and Clark College, Library Association of Portland, Oregon Historical Society Library, and Portland State University, all in Portland; and the Oregon State Library, State Library Building in Salem.

Land Records

Public-Domain State

Land records for the Oregon territorial period of 1844 to 1857 were kept with the territorial recorder. These records are indexed and in the Oregon State Archives. Early settlers who were in Oregon by 1855 may have received grants called Donation Land Claims. Claims often provide valuable genealogical information such as a person's year and place of birth, date and place of marriage, given name of the wife, record of migration to Oregon, record of settlement of the land, citizenship, and names of witnesses and those who testified in behalf of the claimant.

Under the terms of an act of Congress approved on 27 September 1850, certain white and "half-breed" Native American settlers in Oregon Territory were entitled to land. This also applied to certain settlers arriving in the territory between 1 December 1850 and 1 December 1853. The number of acres granted to the settlers varied between 160 and 640 acres, depending upon marital status and date of settlement. Settlers were required to live on and cultivate the land for four years. Donation Claims, filed with each land office, have been abstracted, indexed, and published by the Genealogical Forum of Oregon (see Archives, Libraries, and Societies). Indexing is by both name and geographical location. The Forum's published editions are available in many genealogical libraries. The Oregon State Archives has a microfilm copy of the U.S. BLM, Oregon Donation Land Claim Files, National Archives Microcopy (M815).

Public Land Offices were opened in the following towns: Oregon City, pre-1855 to 1905; Winchester, 1855 to 1859; Roseburg, 1860 to an unknown closing date; Burns, 1889 to 1925; Le Grande, 1867 to 1925; Linkville, 1873 to 1877; Lakeview, 1877 to an unknown closing date; The Dalles, 1875 to an unknown closing date; and Portland, 1905 to 1925. Records generated through these land offices included cash entries, homestead final certificates, canceled homestead entries, timber-culture final certificates, canceled timber-culture entries, desert-land final certificates, canceled desert-land entries, town lots, Indian allotments, and notifications to the surveyor general of Oregon of settlers on unsurveyed lands. The Genealogical Forum of Oregon Library has a microfilm series of the BLM tract books, plat books, and survey notes for Oregon.

In 1862, under the Five-year Homestead Act, Congress provided for a gift of up to 160 acres to persons who would settle on and cultivate the lands and reside upon them for five years. This requirement was reduced to three years in 1912. The original Oregon homestead applications have been moved to the National Archives-Pacific Northwest Region (see page 9). They contain names of those persons whose claims were canceled. The indexes and record books have been microfilmed and are available through the FHL.

Subsequent land records, including deeds and mortgages, were recorded in each county beginning at the creation of the county. For information concerning local land records, write to the county courthouse, attention "Deeds."

Probate Records

Probate records in Oregon were kept by county courts or circuit courts. Territorial probate records from 1841 to 1845 may be deposited at the Oregon State Archives. The majority of probate records such as estate inventories, guardianships, and wills are still deposited at the various county courthouses. For a listing of the probate records deposited at the state archives, write to the archives and ask for their leaflet entitled, "Probate Records in the Oregon State Archives."

Court Records

Most Oregon court records are either deposited at the state archives or remain at local county courthouses. The Oregon court system is divided as follows: circuit courts, county courts, district courts, justice courts, municipal or city courts, and the supreme court.

Circuit courts are major trial courts. In Oregon they have countywide jurisdiction over criminal cases, probate matters, guardianships, divorces, and some administrative functions. County courts, where they exist, have countywide jurisdiction in juvenile cases, and in some probate matters. District courts have countywide jurisdiction over minor criminal cases. Justice courts have concurrent countywide jurisdiction with circuit courts over minor criminal cases. Municipal or city courts have jurisdiction over municipal law violations or liquor control law violations. The supreme court has the final appellate jurisdiction for the entire state.

The State of Oregon took over jurisdiction of the court system in 1983. At that time, a separation was made between the duties of the county clerks, the recorders offices, and the circuit courts. Therefore, to improve the chances of getting correspondence to the proper office, it is best for genealogists or family historians to write to "Marriage Records," "Probate Records," "Deeds," etc.

Since the Oregon State Archives has some county records, it is wise to contact them first to see if they have the records and time periods needed for research.

Tax Records

Some assessment or tax rolls from 1845 to 1900 are deposited at the Oregon State Archives, but most tax records are still at county courthouses. The archives also has a useful research tool from the state treasurer entitled, "Reports of Estates, 1903–1913," which contains the date of death and the names of heirs of those who died testate. This record is arranged by county, then by year.

Oregon counties are required to keep their tax rolls through 1905. All subsequent records must be kept for fifty years before they are destroyed. The exception to this is for years ending in *0* or *5*, which are kept for research samples.

Cemetery Records

An important source in identifying and locating Oregon cemeteries is *Oregon Cemetery Survey* (Salem, Oreg.: Oregon Department of Transportation, 1978). This volume records the location of every known cemetery in Oregon by utilizing modern highway maps of each county to show the location of each cemetery. Published and microfilmed cemetery records are at the Oregon State Library, various public libraries, and genealogical societies throughout the state.

Church Records

Before the turn of the twentieth century, the largest religious groups in Oregon were Roman Catholic, Methodist, Episcopal, Presbyterian, Baptist, and Christian Church. Most church registers are still housed at the original churches, although some records have been transferred to a central archives. The WPA published a directory of Oregon religious bodies entitled *Directory of Churches and Religious Organizations, State of Oregon* (Portland, Oreg.: Oregon Historical Records Survey, 1940) that lists about 2,000 churches in Oregon. Even though this volume was printed in 1940, it is a valuable genealogical tool for locating and identifying various congregations on a county level.

In 1834 Methodist missionaries led the settlement of the Willamette Valley in Marion County. Earl Howell's *Methodism in the Northwest* (Nashville, Tenn.: Parthenon Press, 1966) outlines the church's experience in the Pacific Northwest. Early Methodist vital records are incomplete and scattered. Archives collections are located at Willamette University in Salem and at the Oregon Historical Society in Portland.

Presbyterians under the leadership of Marcus Whitman established churches in Walla Walla (now in Washington) in 1836. The first Presbyterian church in present-day Oregon was in the home of William H. Gray on Clatsop Plains between Astoria and Seaside. The first service was held in 1846. The Oregon State Library has on file a WPA inventory of Presbyterian Churches in Oregon, indexed by the Presbyterian Historical Society in Philadelphia. These inventories consist of churches affiliated with the Presbyterian Church in the United States, United Presbyterian Church of North America, Cumberland Presbyterian Church, and Reformed Presbyterian Church, and are not complete. The inventories are in the form of questionnaires that asked for the date the congregation was organized and which church records are available, and only congregations in eleven Oregon counties are listed. The Presbyterian Historical Society prepared four indexes: by county name, by place-name, in chronological order according to the organizational date of the congregation, and by church name. The indexes and the inventories are on microfilm at the FHL.

The first permanent Episcopalian minister was Rev. St. Michael Fackler who came to Oregon City in 1847. The vital records of the Episcopal Diocese of Eastern Oregon were gathered by their historian. These have been microfilmed and are at the Oregon State Library, along with an index to baptisms from 1873 to 1956 extracted from the records and interfiled in the "Oregon Collection" catalog.

The Episcopal Diocese of Oregon, P.O. Box 467, Lake Oswego, Oregon 97034, has an archives that includes records of defunct parishes and diaries of bishops of the diocese dating back to 1841.

The Quakers arrived in Oregon prior to the Civil War and founded the first Friends Sunday School in Ashland during the early 1850s. No communities or meetings were developed until the 1870s due to the fact that Quaker families were scattered throughout the region. From the 1870s onward, the migration of Quaker families into Oregon was rapid, and the Oregon Yearly Meeting was established in 1893. Most of the early Oregon Friends were representatives of Orthodox, Gurneyite Quakerism. By 1890, there were slightly less than 1,000 Quakers in Oregon. For a history of Oregon's Quaker community, see Ralph K. Beebe, *A Garden of the Lord: A History of Oregon Yearly Meetings of Friends Church* (N.p., ca. 1968). A repository of Quaker records is at George Fox College, Newberg, Oregon.

Two Catholic priests from Quebec arrived in what is now Oregon in 1838. They established a mission at St. Paul, north of Salem, on what is called the French Prairie where Hudson Bay fur trappers had a settlement. They also traveled the Pacific Northwest, establishing missions and churches. The early Oregon Catholic records are well preserved and have been transcribed by Harriet Duncan Minnick in her seven volumes of *Catholic Church Records of the Pacific Northwest* (Portland, Oreg.: Binford & Mort, 1972–89). Catholic repositories include Diocese of Baker, Box 879, Baker City, Oregon 97814; and Archdiocese of Portland in Oregon, Archives, 2838 East Burnside, Portland, Oregon 97214.

There is a Mennonite collection on file at the Oregon Historical Society's Oral History Collection entitled "Pacific Northwest Mennonite Oral History Project." It consists of twenty-four hours of recorded cassette tape.

Mormon missionaries first arrived in Oregon in 1857 but were met with opposition. For this reason, missionary work was postponed until later in the century. In 1890 the Oregon

Lumber Company was organized at Sumter Valley, which brought an influx of Mormon families into Oregon. The Amalgamated Sugar Factory was built in 1897 and lured people seeking employment from Idaho and Utah, including many Mormons from southern Utah. Malheur County has a large Mormon population dating back to the 1880s. Ward, branch, and mission records of the Church of Jesus Christ of Latter-day Saints are deposited at the FHL. For specific information on Mormonism in Oregon, see "Mormons in Oregon and Montana," *Daughters of the Utah Pioneer Magazine* (March 1952).

The Lutheran Church-Missouri Synod, Northwest District, 1700 N.E. Knott, Portland, Oregon 97212, has archival holdings relating to the history of the denomination, biographical material, and congregational records.

Jewish settlers came to Oregon early. Oregon's first synagogue was the Congregation Beth Israel, organized in Portland in 1858. Other congregations soon followed, among them the Congregation Ahavath Achim, organized in Portland in 1911. This synagogue was composed of Sephardic Jews who came from Turkey and the island of Rhodes.

The Jewish Historical Society of Oregon, 6651 S.W. Capitol Highway, Portland, Oregon 97219, operates a library collection of documents, photographs, and record books pertaining to Jewish life in Oregon. Also included are some synagogue and Hebrew school records and transcripts of interviews with members of the local Jewish community. The library is open by appointment only.

Military Records

The Oregon State Archives has early military records of soldiers from the Indian Wars and the Oregon National Guard. Write for their leaflet, "Records of the Oregon Military Department, 1847–1968." The archives also has the records of the Roseburg State Soldier's Home. A published list of war deaths reported to the Oregon Department of the Grand Army of the Republic has been compiled by Jane Myers, *Honor Roll of Oregon Grand Army of the Republic 1881–1935* (Cottage Grove, Oreg.: Cottage Grove Genealogical Society, 1980).

M. A. Parker and Edna Mingus's roster of volunteers, *Soldiers Who Served in the Oregon Volunteers Civil War Period Infantry and Cavalry* (Portland, Oreg.: Genealogical Forum of Oregon, 1961), provides the name of the soldier, rank, date of service, place of enlistment, place of birth, age, occupation, and company.

The Official Records of the Oregon Volunteers in the Spanish War and Philippine Insurrection by C. U. Gantenbein (Salem, Oreg.: J. R. Whitney, State Printers, 1903) is a roster of soldiers providing age, place of birth, occupation, physical description, and time of service.

World War I records on file at the Oregon State Archives include an index to all World War I veterans who served from Oregon, World War I files from the state historian of the Defense Council, records of state bonuses, and loan applications of veterans. World War I files include some biographical questionnaires and are useful in genealogical research.

The archives also has a casualty index to those who served in Korea, 1950 to 1954, and an index to the Oregon State Reserve in World War II, 1940 to 1945.

Periodicals, Newspapers, and Manuscript Collections

Periodicals

The periodical collections at the Oregon State Library and at the Oregon Historical Society include publications of local and county historical societies in Oregon. Major Oregon periodicals include *Oregon Historical Quarterly*, published by the Oregon Historical Society in Portland; *Bulletin*, published by the Genealogical Forum of Oregon in Portland; *Beaver Briefs*, published by the Willamette Valley Genealogical Society, P.O. Box 2083, Salem, Oregon 97308; *Oregon Genealogical Society Quarterly*, published by the Oregon Genealogical Society in Eugene; *Timber Trails*, published by Yamhill County Genealogical Society, P.O. Box 568, McMinnville, Oregon 97128; *Rogue Digger*, published by Rogue Valley Genealogical Society, 133 South Central Ave., Medford, Oregon 97501; and *Douglas County Pioneer*, published by Douglas County Genealogical Society, P.O. Box 579, Roseburg, Oregon 97970.

Newspapers

The largest Oregon newspaper collection is on microfilm at the University of Oregon's Newspaper Library. Rory Funke, *Oregon Newspapers in Microfilm*, reprinted by Genealogical Council of Oregon in 1990, lists the newspapers available and the years included. The second largest newspaper collection is at the Oregon Historical Society.

Manuscripts

The Oregon State Library has manuscripts in their microfilm collection. Betty Book, *Manuscripts on Microfilm at Oregon State Library*, reprinted by Genealogical Council of Oregon in 1990, provides the titles and major topic of each manuscript.

The WPA organized large quantities of documents. Included in these projects were unpublished county manuscripts containing biographical sketches, church histories, cemetery information, interviews, town histories, etc. These are deposited at the University of Oregon, Eugene, and the Oregon State Library, Salem.

The University of Oregon Manuscript and Rare Book Collection, located in the Knight Library, University of Oregon, Eugene, Oregon 97403, has a large number of manuscripts dealing with Oregon history and development. These collections have been indexed in Martin Schmitt, *Catalogue of Manuscripts in the University of Oregon Library* (Eugene, Oreg.: University of Oregon Books, 1971).

The Oregon Historical Society has several biographical aids to assist the researcher. One such collection is the vertical file, consisting of newspaper clippings including 4,000 subjects on state and local history and 1,500 biographies and genealogies of prominent Oregonians. Also covered in these files are historic structures, ethnic groups, cities, counties, Portland neighborhoods, railroads, and maritime history. This collection is indexed.

The library also has a "Biography Card File" which contains information from books, newspapers, scrapbooks, and Indian War pension papers. Information from the society's scrapbooks is very fragile and must be copied by hand.

Another collection at the Oregon Historical Society is the "Pioneer Card File" which provides data on early immigrants. The "DAR Card File" indexes material in the DAR books on file at the society.

The work compiled by the Oregon Daughters of the American Revolution is on thirty-three reels of microfilm at the FHL. The collection consists of Bible records, cemetery records, wills, marriage records, divorce records, records of pioneers, church records, donation land claims, compiled genealogies, and military records. It is divided by county and general Oregon state items.

Records for Hudson Bay Company are available on interlibrary loan from the Hudson Bay Company Archives, Provincial Archives of Manitoba, 200 Vaughn Street, Winnipeg, Manitoba, Canada R3C 1T5.

Archives, Libraries, and Societies

Oregon State Archives
800 Summer Street NE
Salem, OR 97310

The vast holdings of this major state repository are discussed in various sections above. Printed guides to many groups of holdings—census, county, probate and vital records among them—can be obtained from the archives.

Oregon State Library
Summer and Court Streets
Salem, OR 97310

An extensive collection of genealogical and historical resources is located here.

Oregon Historical Society Library
1230 S.W. Park Avenue
Portland, OR 97205

The largest repository in the state encompasses a variety of research materials, including the records of the Oregon Pioneer Association as one of the major collections indexed.

University of Oregon
Knight Library
Eugene, OR 97403

Manuscripts, rare books, newspapers, and the Oregon Collection Room here all are good resources for research in the state.

Multnomah County Library
801 S.W. 10th Avenue
Portland, OR 97205

Genealogical Council of Oregon, Inc.
P.O. Box 15169
Portland, OR 97215

There are several county and local genealogical societies in Oregon in addition to those noted with their publications under Periodicals. The statewide council can direct researchers to functioning societies in a specific area.

Genealogical Forum of Oregon, Inc.
1410 S.W. Morrison, Suite 812
Portland, OR 97205

Oregon Genealogical Society
P.O. Box 10306
Eugene, OR 97440

Special Focus Categories

Immigration

Immigrants arrived in Oregon at six ports: Astoria, Newport, North Bend, Portland, Reedsport, and Tillamook. Records concerning the port of Portland are on file at the National Archives-Pacific Northwest Region in Seattle and include records of the Immigration and Naturalization Service, Portland Office, and the Portland Collector of Customs. No passenger lists for the port of Portland or the smaller ports have yet been found.

Naturalization

Foreign-born residents could become naturalized in any court of record. Records created prior to 1906 may still be in the county. Some records were not kept in separate naturalization books but in court journals or court minutes, making them difficult to locate. The Oregon State Archives has some naturalization records and publishes a naturalization records leaflet.

Native American

The history of Oregon's Native American population is similar to that of Washington. Coastal tribes were little affected by the Spaniards in California or the fur traders. However, from the mid-nineteenth century onward, the Native Americans of Oregon were rapidly dispossessed and placed upon reservations as follows: most of the Chinookan tribes were placed on the Warm Springs and Grande Ronde reservations and on Yakima Reservation in Washington; all of the Athapascan tribes were placed on the Siletz Reservation; the Umpqua went to the Grand Ronde; the Kusan and Yakonan tribes were placed on the Siletz Reservation; the Salishan population of Oregon was placed on the Grande Ronde and Siletz reservations; most of the Kalapooian peoples went to the Grand Ronde and a few on the Siletz; most of the Molala went to the Grande Ronde; the Klamath went to Klamath Reserve; the Modoc went mostly on the Klamath Reserve, but a few went to the Quapaw Reservation in Oklahoma; the Shahaptian tribes of Oregon went to the Umatilla Reservation; and the Northern Paiutes went to the Klamath Reservation.

Past and present ownership of land by Native Americans can be divided into four categories: tribal trust lands, allotment, fee-patent allotments, and surplus lands. In tribal trust lands, the title to the land is shared by the tribe and the United States, and the United States manages the land for the tribe. Not only does the federal government oversee the land base, it also is responsible for the timber, mineral, and water resources on the reserved trust land. Allotments are tracts of individually owned land held in trust by the United States. Usually, allotments are inside the reservation boundaries. Fee-patent allotments are tracts of land no longer in trust by the United States. No restrictions apply and these lands may be owned by persons who are not Native Americans. Surplus lands are adjacent to present-day reservations and formerly belonged to the tribe.

For a more detailed history of each Oregon reservation and land definitions, see Jeff Zucker, *Oregon Indians: Culture, History and Current Affairs, An Atlas and Introduction* (Portland, Oreg.: Oregon Historical Society, ca. 1983).

Many Native Americans converted to Catholicism, and the early parish and mission registers have been printed. An excellent source of Native American family genealogies is Charles E. McChesney, et al., *Rolls of Certain Indian Tribes In Washington and Oregon* (Fairfield, Wash.: Ye Galleon Press, 1969). For a more detailed explanation of this valuable source, see Washington—Native American.

Many Native American records are microfilmed and are on file at the National Archives-Pacific Northwest Region (see page 9); some are on file at the FHL. The following agency records are available:

Grand Ronde-Siletz Agency, Toledo, Oregon (1863–1954). Records include general correspondence and decimal files, school records, heirship cards, maps, annuity payrolls, ledgers for accounts of individual Indians, vital statistics and census rolls, health reports, social service case files, court records, tribal constitutions, records concerning land allotments and sales, forestry, Civilian Conservation Corps work, and relief and rehabilitation. This agency was established in 1856 for Native Americans living on the Coast Reservation who had been moved from other parts of Oregon. The principal tribes under this agency were the Joshua, Sixes (Kwatami), Chetco, Rogue River, Chastacosta, and Klamath.

Klamath Indian Agency, Klamath Falls, Oregon (1865–1960). Records include general subject files, tribal election ballots, business committee and general council minutes, Klamath Loan Board files, records concerning irrigation, allotments and other land transactions, forestry, grazing, agricultural extension, accounts of individual Indians, law and order, annuities, and medical care. Klamath was made a full agency in 1872, with the Klamath, Modoc, "Snake," Pit River, and Shoshoni tribes under its jurisdiction.

Portland Area Office, Portland, Oregon (1902–64). Records include program planning records, minutes of the Columbia Basin Inter-Agency Committee, correspondence and reports concerning schools, grazing permits, welfare case files, tribal constitutions, legal case files, allotment ledgers, records concerning land allotments and sales, land classification, heirship, forestry, irrigation, road construction, tribal welfare, and health.

Umatilla Indian Agency, Pendleton, Oregon (1862–1964). Records include general correspondence, school records, tribal rolls, records concerning farming and grazing leases, the Civilian Conservation Corps program, individual Indian accounts, land allotments, heirship, family histories, medical treatment, law enforcement, court cases, and economic and social surveys. This agency was established in 1861 for the Umatilla, Cayuse, and Walla Walla tribes. Other tribes were later transferred to this agency.

Warm Springs Indian Agency, Warm Springs, Oregon (1861–1952). Records include general correspondence, decimal files, school attendance records, land and survey field notes, a tract book, cattle sales reports, ledgers and abstracts of individual Indian accounts, appropriation land allotment ledgers, censuses, a family history record, individual Indian history cards, court dockets, birth and death registers, medical reports, tribal council records, records concerning lease payments, forestry, Civilian Conservation Corps programs, roads, and per capita payments. This agency was established in 1851 for the Warm Springs, Wasco, Tenino, John Day, and Northern Paiute tribes.

A valuable source for Native American research is the Chemawa Indian School records, a non-reservation school established in Forest Grove, Oregon, in 1880. In 1885 it was moved to a site north of Salem known as Chemawa and has been called both Chemawa and Salem. The school is important because it enrolled students from all over the Pacific Northwest. The school records include general correspondence, decimal files, descriptive statements about children, applications for admission, attendance records, student health cards, student and graduate student case files, and ledgers for accounts of individual Indians. These school records are on file at the National Archives-Pacific Northwest Region and the FHL.

Two major sources for Native American research are the Major James McLaughlin Papers and the Pacific Northwest Tribes Missions Collection of the Oregon Province Archives of the Society of Jesus, 1853–1960. For additional details about these two collections, see Montana—Native American.

Other Ethnic Groups

The southeast corner of Oregon has a large population of Basque, who arrived in the latter 1800s and early 1900s. Basques usually entered America at Ellis Island and drifted across the country. Principal Basque settlements in Oregon were McDermitt, on the northern Nevada border; Jordan Valley; Andrews, 125 miles south of Crane; Fields, fifteen miles further south; and Ontario, Oregon, at the junction of the Malheur River and the Snake River.

In 1925 McDermitt was almost completely a Basque town, and by 1945 Jordan Valley had the largest Basque settlement in southeast Oregon with two-thirds of the population of Basque descent. The University of Nevada has major Basque collections which include 12,000 volumes concerning the Basque in America. They can be contacted by writing Basque Studies Program, University of Nevada, Getchell Library, Room 274, Reno, Nevada 89557.

During the 1880s, Oregon's Chinese population greatly increased as a result of extensive railroad construction in the area. Tension rose against the Asiatics in the Pacific Northwest. Shortly after the riots against Seattle and Tacoma's Chinatowns in November 1885, Portland held an anti-Chinese convention in which resolutions were adopted requiring the Chinese population to relocate to San Francisco within thirty days. The first group of Chinese laborers coming directly to Portland arrived in 1888.

The Chinese played a vital role in the development of eastern Oregon. Eastern Oregon's growth was dependent on the railroad and mining for which the Chinese provided the majority of labor. By 1857 the Chinese began moving north from California to Oregon to begin mining. Migrants began to move eastward from southern Oregon when gold was discovered on the Powder River in Oregon and the Salmon River in Idaho. By 1880 many Chinese mining companies were in operation at John Day in Grant County. Christopher Howard Edson, *The Chinese in Eastern Oregon, 1860–1890* (San Francisco, Calif.: R and E Research Associates, 1974), is an excellent study of the contributions of the Chinese community to the settlement and development of eastern Oregon.

A few Japanese entered Oregon between 1880 and 1890, but the greatest migration came during subsequent decades. Japanese immigrants generally worked as railroad hands, sawmill workers, and agricultural laborers. A total of 2,501 Japanese were recorded in the 1900 U.S. census of Oregon. By 1930 the Japanese population in Oregon had doubled. During World War II, hysteria swept America and Oregon's Japanese community came under suspicion. Many Japanese-Americans were relocated to camps in Idaho where they remained until the war was over. For more details, see Idaho—Other Ethnic Groups. Two articles will provide additional background information: Marvin Gavin Pursinger, "The Japanese Settle Oregon: 1880–1920," *Journal of the West* 5 (April 1966): 251, which outlines the decision to open Japan for contact with the west as well as the settlement of Japanese in Oregon, and Marjorie R. Stearns, "The Settlement of the Japanese in Oregon," *Oregon Historical Quarterly* 39 (September 1938): 262–69, which details the history of the Japanese immigration to Oregon. Since it was written in 1939, it does not include the interment of Japanese in camps during World War II.

County Resources

Vital records, prior to statewide recording, were filed at the county clerk's office. The dates of the first known of these for each county are listed below. Earlier birth and death records exist for only a few counties/cities, and these are on microfilm and housed at the Oregon State Archives and indicated by an asterisk (*). Land records subsequent to the Donation Land Claims, including deeds and mortgages, were also recorded at the county clerk's office beginning at the creation of the county. For information concerning local land records, write to the county courthouse, attention "Deeds." Probate records during the territorial period, generally, from 1841 to 1845 are deposited at the Oregon State Archives, but after that they are located at the appropriate county or circuit court in the county seat, as were the court records described above. If the early probate records can be found at the Oregon State Archives, they are indicated by an asterisk (*), although later ones are at the county seat. Both agencies should be addressed to assure thoroughness in research.

Drawn by William Dollarhide

Map	County Address	Date Formed Parent County/ies	Birth Marriage Death	Deeds Probate Court
H3	Baker 1995 Third Street Baker City 97814	1862 Wasco	— 1862 —	1863 1860 1860
B3	Benton 120 N.W. Fourth Corvallis 97330	1847 Polk	1897 1850 1897	1850 1852* 1852
	Champoeg	1843 (renamed Marion, 1849) original		
C2	Clackamas 906 Main Street Oregon City 97045	1843 original	— 1853 —	1851 1847* 1850
A1	Clatsop 749 Commercial Astoria 9710	1844 Tuality	— 1851 —	1849 1848* 1850
B1	Columbia Strand Street Saint Helens 97051	1854 Washington	— 1854* —	1865 1880* 1860
A5	Coos Second and Baxter Coquille 97423	1853 Jackson/Umpqua	— 1855 —	1854 1854 1854
E4	Crook 300 E. Third Prineville 97754	1882 Wasco	— 1882 —	1882 1883 1891
A7	Curry 450 N. Ellensburg Gold Beach 97444	1855 Coos	— 1876 —	1856 1856* 1901
D4	Deschutes 1164 N.W. Bond Bend 97701	1916 Crook	— — —	1916 1917 1916
B5	Douglas 1036 S.E. Douglas Roseburg 97470	1852 Umpqua	— 1852* —	1852 1852 1852
E2	Gilliam 221 S. Oregon Street Condon 97823	1885 Wasco/Morrow	— 1885 —	1874 1885
G3	Grant 200 S. Canyon City Boulevard Canyon City 97820	1864 Umatilla/Wasco	— 1872 —	1864 1864 1864
G6	Harney 450 N. Buena Vista Burns 97720	1889 Grant	— 1889 —	1889 1889 1889
D1	Hood River 309 State Street Hood River 97031	1908 Wasco	— — —	1859 1908 1908
B7	Jackson 100 S. Oakdale Medford 97501	1852 Umpqua	— — —	— 1856* 1851

Map	County Address	Date Formed Parent County/ies	Birth Marriage Death	Deeds Probate Court
D3	Jefferson 657 C Street Madras 97741	1914 Crook	— 1914 —	1914 1915 1915
A7	Josephine N.W. Sixth and C Grants Pass 97526	1856 Jackson	— 1857 —	1880 1855* 1908
D6	Klamath 316 Main Street Klamath Falls 97601	1882 Lake	— 1882 —	1871 1882 1882
E6	Lake 513 Center Street Lakeview 97630	1874 Jackson/Wasco	— 1875 —	1896 1896 1896
B4	Lane 125 E. Eighth Avenue Eugene 97401	1851 Linn/Umpqua/Benton	1882 1852 1882	1855 1852* 1856
A3	Lincoln 225 W. Olive Street Newport 97365	1893 Benton/Polk	— 1893 —	1893 1893 1893
C3	Linn 300 Fourth Avenue N.W. Albany 97321	1847 Champoeg	— 1850* —	1850 1850* 1863
J6	Malheur 251 B Street W. Vale 97918	1887 Baker	— 1887 —	1887 1887 1887
B2	Marion 100 High Street N.E. Salem 97301	1843 (as Champoeg; renamed, 1849) original	1871* 1849 1894	1855 1849* 1850
F1	Morrow Court Street Heppner 97836	1885 Umatilla	— 1885 —	1862 1885 1885
C1	Multnomah 1021 S.W. Fourth Avenue Portland 97204	1854 Clackamas/Washington	1864 (Portland)* 1855 1862 (Portland)*	1849 1856* 1855
B3	Polk 850 Main Street Dallas 97338	1845 Yamhill	— 1849* —	1856 1853* 1893
E2	Sherman 500 Court Street Moro 97039	1889 Wasco	— 1889 —	1860 1889 1889
A2	Tillamook 201 Laurel Avenue Tillamook 97141	1853 Clatsop/Yamhill/Polk	— 1855 —	1860 1859* 1860
	Tuality	1843 (renamed Washington, 1849) original		
G1	Umatilla 216 S.E. 4th Pendleton 97801	1862 Wasco	— 1860 —	1862 1890 1890

Map	County Address	Date Formed Parent County/ies	Birth Marriage Death	Deeds Probate Court
	Umpqua	1851 (became part of Douglas, 1862) Benton		
H2	Union 1100 L Avenue La Grande 97850	1864 Baker	— 1877 —	1893 1895 1894
G1	Wallowa 101 S. River Enterprise 97828	1887 Union	— 1887 —	1875 1887 1887
D2	Wasco Fifth and Washington The Dalles 97058	1854 Marion/Clackamas/Linn	— 1856* —	1856 1854* 1854
B1	Washington 150 N. First Hillsboro 97123	1843 (as Tuality; renamed, 1849) original	— 1849 —	1844 1844* 1849
F3	Wheeler Fourth and Adams Fossil 97830	1899 Crook/Gilliam/Grant	1899 1899 1899	1866 1870 1899
B2	Yamhill 525 East Fifth McMinnville 97128	1843 original	1875 1857* —	1853 1849* —

PENNSYLVANIA

Roger D. Joslyn, C.G., F.A.S.G.

The Dutch first came to the region now known as Pennsylvania following Henry Hudson's exploration of the Delaware River, the state's waterway to the Atlantic, but they did little more than establish trading posts. Swedes arrived in 1638 and, with the Finns who came about the same time, spilled over into what is now the Philadelphia area. The Dutch gained control of New Sweden in 1655, but nine years later England conquered New Netherland, and Pennsylvania became a part of the Duke of York's new territory, which included New York, New Jersey, and Delaware. In 1673–74 the Dutch regained control, but soon the colony was back under English rule.

None of these early settlements had as lasting an impression on Pennsylvania as did that of the colony of William Penn. Chartered in 1681 by King Charles II to Penn, a Quaker, Pennsylvania received this new governor aboard the *Welcome* the following year. The new immigrants were primarily English Quakers, although some were of Welsh, Scottish, and Irish ancestry. Pennsylvania became a royal province briefly in 1692–94 when Penn lost his power over the conflict between the proprietary and popular elements, but the proprietary government resumed and survived until the American Revolution. Penn and his descendants had a long-standing influence, especially in governing, in dealing with the native population, and in providing a climate of religious tolerance.

Penn's "Holy Experiment" attracted throngs of immigrants in the next century. The two largest groups were the Ulster-Scots, who first came in 1707 and in greater numbers from 1728 on, and the Germans, who first arrived in 1683. The Germans, mostly from the principalities bordering the Rhine, included subgroups that characterize those who have become known, more culturally than ethnically, as the "Pennsylvania Dutch"—Amish, Dunkers, Mennonites, Moravians, and Schwenkfelders, although the majority of Pennsylvania Germans were Lutheran, Reformed, or Roman Catholic. They first settled beyond the Quaker belt around Philadelphia—in Lancaster, Northampton, Berks, and Lehigh counties—eventually moving west along a more central route. The Ulster-Scots tended to settle the frontier beyond the Germans, first in the Cumberland Valley, and then west, where they populated southwestern Pennsylvania. The westward movements were made despite the Allegheny mountains that diagonally divide the rectangular-shaped state, and early settlements were chiefly made in the valleys such as the Cumberland, Lebanon, and Lehigh. Other immigrants in the 1700s included Welsh (some of whom were Quakers), French (including Huguenots, later Acadians, and at the end of the century refugees from revolutionary-torn France and Haiti), Irish, Jews, and blacks. In spite of the strong, early Quaker influence, slavery did exist in Pennsylvania, but of the 10,000 blacks there in 1790, over half were free, and slavery was phased out by the early 1800s.

Most of Pennsylvania's western settlers migrated from the eastern part of the province. Some came up from Maryland and Virginia, such as Ulster-Scots and Germans, many of whom had ventured south from Pennsylvania earlier. The territory of the Holland Land Company extended into the Northwestern part of Pennsylvania, where New Yorkers met Pennsylvanians coming north from Washington, Allegheny, and other southwestern counties.

It has generally been believed that the Penns dealt fairly with the Native Americans, peacefully acquiring additional territory through treaties and purchase; however, some historians question this. As settlers pushed westward, however, they forced the natives ahead of them, and the resulting hostilities peaked during the last French and Indian War. This conflict caused Pennsylvania to increase its militia in order to defend the frontier settlements.

Connecticut claimed northeastern Pennsylvania and began sending settlers there in the 1750s. A bitter conflict ensued until Connecticut relinquished its claim by the Decree of Trenton in 1782. Other boundary disputes took place with New York and, in the southwest, with Virginia. The most famous, however, was the early and lengthy controversy between the Penns and Lord Baltimore. A temporary line was drawn with Maryland in 1739, but the fixed boundary was not settled until Charles Mason and Jeremiah Dixon's work was ratified in 1769, creating what became the historic slave/free state division between the North and the South.

At the time of the Revolutionary War, Pennsylvania was the "keystone" (hence its nickname) between the northern and southern colonies, and many important events took place in Philadelphia that shaped the emerging nation. The state's charter referred to the "Commonwealth" of Pennsylvania, to help express democracy. The British invaded Philadelphia and defeated the patriots at Germantown in 1776, but Pennsylvania is probably best remembered for the harsh winter of 1777–78, which Washington's poorly trained army spent at Valley Forge. During the War of 1812 Pennsylvanians were instrumental in Commodore Perry's victory on Lake Erie. The "Erie Triangle," now Erie County, was purchased from Native Americans in 1792 to provide the commonwealth with a port on the lake. Pennsylvania's other inland port is Pittsburgh, whose early development was the result of its location on the Ohio River. The commonwealth was greatly involved in the Civil War, and here occurred the Battle of Gettysburg, a major turning point for the Union Army.

In the nineteenth century, Pennsylvania experienced the same growth through transportation systems of canals, roads, and railroads, as did the other mid-Atlantic states. Like her neighbors, she also received a large influx of new immigrants, such as Irish and Germans, followed by Italians, Poles, Scandinavians, Russians, and others. Many of these groups, as well as blacks migrating north, took part in the tremendous industrial growth of the commonwealth—in the steel production in Bethlehem and Pittsburgh, the coal mining around Scranton and Wilkes-Barre, and the drilling of oil fields in the northwest.

Vital Records

Although a colonial law of 1682 provided for the recording of births, marriages, and burials in Pennsylvania, few if any of these events were ever entered in civil records. A new law in the mid-nineteenth century required these events to be recorded by the county register of wills, with copies sent to Harrisburg. Some of these records are still in the courthouses, and others are at the Pennsylvania State Archives (see Archives, Libraries, and Societies), where microfilms of many are available. Indexes to these records are arranged first by county, then by event, then by year. Films of some of these records are also available at the Historical Society of Pennsylvania (see Archives, Libraries, and Societies). From 1860 through 1893, and in some cases to a later date, births and deaths were recorded in Philadelphia and other cities—Allegheny, Easton, Harrisburg, Pottsville, Pittsburgh, and Williamsport—although there are gaps. Since 1885 the clerk of the orphans' court in each county has had the responsibility of recording marriages. Films of some of these records are at the state archives and the Historical Society of Pennsylvania. Births and deaths in Pennsylvania were also recorded in the county orphans' courts for the period 1893 through 1905, as were delayed birth records for events occurring as far back as the 1860s. The state archives has films of some of these records; the Historical Society of Pennsylvania has those for Philadelphia.

Statewide registration of births and deaths has occurred since 1906, although compliance with the law was scattered for at least the first ten years. To request these records, complete form H105.102 and submit it with the current fee of $4 for a birth record or $3 for a death record to the Division of Vital Statistics, State Department of Health, Central Building, 101 South Mercer Street, P.O. Box 1528, New Castle, Pennsylvania 16103-1528. Application can also be made at one of the following five Division of Vital Records branch offices: Room 129, Health and Welfare Building, Foster Street and Commonwealth Avenue, P.O. Box 90, Harrisburg, Pennsylvania 17120-0090; Room 920, 401 North Broad Street, Philadelphia, Pennsylvania 19108; Room 512, 300 Liberty Avenue, Pittsburgh, Pennsylvania 15222; 3832 Liberty Street, Erie, Pennsylvania 16509; or 100 Lackawanna Avenue, Scranton, Pennsylvania 18503.

Marriage licenses were not required in colonial Pennsylvania, but information from surviving marriage bonds for 1760–90 was published in *Pennsylvania Archives,* series 2, volume 2, and reprinted with some other records as *Pennsylvania Marriages Prior To 1790* (Baltimore, Md.: Genealogical Publishing Co., 1984). These records provide the names of the couple and the date of the bond. See also "List of Marriage Licenses Issued in the Secretary's Office, from August 1755 through April 1759" in *Pennsylvania Genealogical Magazine* 21 (1960):312–27. Many early church marriage records were published in *Pennsylvania Archives,* series 2, vols. 8 and 9, and reprinted as *Record of Pennsylvania Marriages Prior to 1810,* 2 vols. (Baltimore, Md.: Genealogical Publishing Co., 1987). The three-volume *Pennsylvania Vital Records* (Baltimore, Md.: Genealogical Publishing Co., 1983) reprints a number of articles containing births, baptisms, marriages, and deaths from *The Pennsylvania Magazine of History and Biography* and *The Pennsylvania Genealogical Magazine.*

Besides the exceptions noted above and marriages recorded from 1885 in the county orphans' courts, nineteenth-century civil vital records in Pennsylvania are practically nonexistent. It is important, therefore, to make use of substitutes such as church and justice of the peace records, grave marker inscriptions and burial records, newspaper marriage and death notices, and censuses.

Most Pennsylvania divorce records from 1804 are found in the county court of common pleas, where the prothonotary is usually the clerk with custody of the records. Only two divorces are found in the *Pennsylvania Statutes at Large* for the colonial period—one granted in 1769 and a second voided in 1772. Divorces were granted, mostly for adultery, by the General Assembly during and following the Revolutionary War, for which one should consult *Statutes at Large of Pennsylvania,* beginning with volume 7. The assembly had jurisdiction from 1776 to 1847 (see Candy Crocker Livengood, *Genealogical Abstracts of Pennsylvania & the Statutes at Large* [Westminster, Md.: Family Line Publications, 1990]). The supreme court had concurrent jurisdiction of granting divorces from 1785 to 1804, and its records to 1801 were published in *Publications of The Genealogical Society of Pennsylvania* 1 (1898): 185–92. The state archives has divorce papers for 1786–1815 from the records of the supreme court.

Census Records

Federal

Population Schedules.

- Indexed—1790, 1800, 1810, 1820, 1830, 1840, 1850, 1860, 1870 (Berks County, Philadelphia, and Pittsburgh)
- Soundex—1880, 1900, 1910 (Miracode), 1920
- Unindexed—1870 (except as listed above)

Industry and Agriculture Schedules.

- 1850, 1860, 1870, 1880

Mortality Schedules.

- 1850, 1860, 1870, 1880 (1880 not indexed)

Veterans Schedules.

- 1890

From the first federal census of 1790, the records are nearly complete for Pennsylvania, and microfilms of the federal copies are widely available at the National Archives-Mid Atlantic Region (see page 8), the Pennsylvania State Archives, the Historical Society of Pennsylvania, the Pennsylvania State Library (see Archives, Libraries, and Societies), and other libraries. Two enumerations were taken in Philadelphia in 1870. Gaps in the records are the following: 1800 (part of Westmoreland County); 1810 (parts of Bedford, Cumberland, and Philadelphia counties); and 1820 (parts of Lancaster and Luzerne counties).

There are three indexes for the 1800 census and two for 1810. The 1850 census also has two indexes, one arranged by county. For the 1910 Miracode, Philadelphia County is indexed apart from the rest of the commonwealth. After it was filmed by the National Archives, the 1880 census was sent to the University of Pittsburgh. The state copies of the 1840–70 censuses are no longer extant, but a few county copies are known to exist. Microfilms of the non-population and mortality schedules for 1850–80 are at the state library and at the National Archives-Mid Atlantic Region.

Pennsylvania took no state censuses, but an enumeration of taxpayers compiled every seven years from 1779 through 1863 is commonly called the Septennial Census. These records have only survived in small numbers and are available at the state archives.

Background Sources

Many of Pennsylvania's early government records were published in two groups. The first of these were the *Minutes of the Provincial Council* and *The Supreme Executive Council of Pennsylvania,* usually referred to as *The Colonial Records,* 16 vols. (1838–53; reprint, New York, N.Y.: A.M.S. Press, 1971). Beginning in 1852 the first of nine series of *Pennsylvania Archives* was published. The published archives include records concerning military service and pensions, land warrants, naturalizations, baptisms and marriages, tax lists, ships' lists, Native Americans, boundary disputes, Provincial Assembly journals, and actions of governors, as well as maps. Not all the volumes are indexed and much of the original material from which they were prepared is now gone, but there are helpful guides which should be consulted. Among these are Henry Howard Eddy and Martha L. Simonetti, eds., *Guide to the Published Archives of Pennsylvania,* (Harrisburg, Pa.: Historical and Museum Commission, 1949; reprint, 1976); Sally A. Weikel, comp., *Genealogical Research in the Published Pennsylvania Archives* (Harrisburg, Pa.: State Library of Pennsylvania, 1976); and Jean S. Morris, comp., *Use of the Published Pennsylvania Archives in Genealogical Research* (Pittsburgh, Pa.: Western Pennsylvania Genealogical Society, 1978). See also Frank B. Evans, "The Many Faces of the Pennsylvania Archives," *American Archivist* 27 (1964): 271, and Roland M. Baumann, "Dr. Sheuk's Missing Series of the Published Pennsylvania Archives," *Pennsylvania Magazine of History and Biography* 103 (1979):415–31.

Norman B. Wilkinson, comp., *Bibliography of Pennsylvania History,* 2d ed., S. K. Stevens and Donald H. Kent, eds. (Harrisburg, Pa.: Pennsylvania Historical and Museum Commission, 1957), is a large work divided into sections for state, county, local, and topical history. *A Supplement* (Harrisburg, Pa.: Pennsylvania Historical and Museum Commission), edited by Carol Wall, was published in 1976, and updates through 1985, compiled by John B. B. Trussell, Jr., appeared in six volumes as *Pennsylvania Historical Bibliography* (Harrisburg, Pa.: Pennsylvania Historical and Museum Commission). The bibliography is now being continued in *Pennsylvania History,* beginning in volume 56 (1989).

George P. Donehoo, *Pennsylvania: A History,* 11 vols. (New York, N.Y.: Lewis Historical Publishing Co., 1926), is one the better large works, with volumes 5–11 containing biographical data.

Philip F. Klein and Ari Hoogenboom, *A History of Pennsylvania*, 2d ed. (University Park, Pa., and London, England: Pennsylvania State University Press, 1986), is another useful work.

No study of Pennsylvania is complete without *The Papers of William Penn*, edited by Mary Maples Dunn and others, 5 volumes published in Philadelphia by the University of Pennsylvania Press, 1981–86. Each volume is indexed separately.

Other titles include Paul A. W. Wallace, *Pennsylvania, Seed of a Nation* (New York, N.Y.: Harper & Row, 1962); Joseph J. Kelley, Jr., *Pennsylvania: The Colonial Years 1681–1776* (Garden City, N.Y.: Doubleday & Co., 1980), which has a useful bibliography; and the following works by Sylvester Kirby Stevens: *Pennsylvania, The Keystone State*, 2 vols. (New York, N.Y.: American Historical Co., 1956); *Pennsylvania, Birthplace of a Nation* (New York, N.Y.: Random House, 1964); and *Pennsylvania, The Heritage of a Commonwealth*, 4 vols. (West Palm Beach, Fla.: American Historical Co., 1968), of which volume 4 is biographical.

As for other states, "mug books" are common for Pennsylvania and must be used with care, but they are too numerous to name here. The term mug book refers to those printed sources that present pictures and biographies of the those who subscribed to the publication. The largest set, however, is the *Encyclopedia of Pennsylvania Biography*, published by Lewis Historical Publishing Company of New York in 32 volumes (1914–67). A somewhat better group is *Colonial and Revolutionary Families of Pennsylvania*, 17 vols. (1911–65; reprint, Baltimore, Md.: Genealogical Publishing Co., 1968).

Guides

One of the best overviews is Milton Rubincam's chapter on Pennsylvania in *Genealogical Research: Methods and Sources*, Vol. 1, rev. ed. (Washington, D.C.: American Society of Genealogists, 1980).

Thomas F. Gordon, *A Gazetteer of the State of Pennsylvania* (1832; reprint, New Orleans, La.: Polyanthos, 1975), is helpful for the early period. A later, related work that is basic on the subject is A. Howry Espenshade, *Pennsylvania Place Names* (1925; reprint, Baltimore, Md.: Clearfield Publishing Co., 1991). Many places not named in these works can be located in *Pennsylvania Postal History* (Lawrence, Mass.: Quarterman Publications, 1976), by John L. Kay and Chester M. Smith, Jr.

How Pennsylvania Acquired Its Present Boundaries, by William A. Russ, Jr. (University Park, Pa.: Pennsylvania Historical Association, 1966), covers the colony's boundary disputes.

Pennsylvania Genealogical Research, by George K. Schweitzer (Knoxville, Tenn.: the author, 1986), is a good, basic, inexpensive guide, although it has errors and should be used with caution.

Florence Clint, *Pennsylvania Area Key*, 2d ed. (Logan, Utah: Everton Publishers, 1976), is helpful when preparing for on-site research, such as understanding county record book indexing systems. More detailed *Area Keys* were also published for each of the commonwealth's sixty-seven counties, but these and the state *Area Key* are somewhat dated.

Pennsylvania Line: A Research Guide to Pennsylvania Genealogy and Local History, 4th ed. (Laughlintown, Pa.: Southwest Pennsylvania Genealogical Services, 1990), contains a wide variety of helpful information, such as place-names; maps of the counties, townships, and cities; and lists of available published and microfilmed books, newspapers, and censuses.

For the western part of the commonwealth, see Raymond Martin Bell, *Searching in Western Pennsylvania* (Detroit, Mich.: Detroit Society for Genealogical Research, 1977), and Bell's *Mother Cumberland: Tracing Your Ancestors in South-Central Pennsylvania* (Bowie, Md.: Heritage Books, 1989); George Swetnam and Helen Smith, *A Guidebook to Historic Western Pennsylvania* (Pittsburgh, Pa.: University of Pittsburgh Press, 1976); and *Western Pennsylvania Genealogical Quarterly*, vol. 8 (1982).

John Daly has produced *Descriptive Inventory of the Archives of the City of Philadelphia* (Philadelphia, Pa.: Department of Records, 1970), and with Allen Weinberg, *Genealogy of Philadelphia County Subdivisions*, 2d ed. (Philadelphia, Pa.: Department of Records, 1966), which explains, with maps, the changes of the state's largest city/county.

Floyd G. Hoenstine, *Guide to Genealogical and Historical Research in Pennsylvania*, 4th ed. (Hollidaysburg, Pa.: the author, 1978), with supplements for 1985 and 1990, provides a surname index to many published works.

Maps

County road maps are available in most if not all courthouses. Older maps are in published county histories, county atlases, and in manuscript collections such as at the Historical Society of Pennsylvania, the state library, and the state archives. For the latter see Martha L. Simonetti, comp., *Descriptive List of the Map Collection in the Pennsylvania State Archives*, edited by Donald H. Kent and Harry E. Whipkey (Harrisburg, Pa.: Pennsylvania Historical and Museum Commission, 1976). Useful city maps can sometimes be found in city directories. An interesting map showing the development of the commonwealth's counties is available for a nominal fee from the land records office (see Land Records). See also Henry F. Walling and O. W. Gray, *1872 Historical Topographical Atlas of the State of Pennsylvania* (1872; reprint, Knightstown, Ind.: Bookmark, 1977), which has business directories and a place-name index.

Available at the state archives, with copies at the state library and the respective county recorder of deeds, are warrantee maps for twenty-four counties. Those for Fayette, Greene, and Washington were also published and indexed in volume 3 of *The Horn Papers* by W. F. Horn (New York, N.Y.: Hagstrom Co., 1945), but the preceding two volumes of text are mostly fiction (see *William & Mary Quarterly*, series three, 4 [1947]: 409–45]).

Land Records

State-Land State

The Land Records Office, formerly the Bureau of Land Records (see below), came into operation in 1682, keeping records about state boundaries, land granted by William Penn and the commonwealth, and land still owned by Pennsylvania. Of greatest value are the warrants, surveys, and patents, including warrantee maps (see Maps), all available by mail for a modest fee from their current repository in the state archives.

Some of the earliest records of Pennsylvania grants are indexed in *Warrants and Surveys of the Province of Pennsylvania including the Three Lower Counties 1759*, compiled by Allen Weinberg and Thomas E. Slattery (1965; reprint, Knightstown, Ind.: Bookmark, 1975). The "Lower Counties" were those that are now the state of Delaware. Warrantees of land for several counties for 1682–1898 are listed in *Pennsylvania Archives*, 3d series, vols. 2, 3, and 24–26. This series is indexed in volumes 27–30. See also William H. Egle, *Early Pennsylvania Land Records: Minutes of the Board of Property of the Province of Pennsylvania, 1687–1732* (Baltimore, Md.: Genealogical Publishing Co., 1976), reprinted from the *Pennsylvania Archives*, 2d series, vol. 19.

The southwest corner of Pennsylvania was contested with Virginia, and many records for this area are to be found at the Virginia State Archives in Richmond and at the University of West Virginia in Morgantown. For further research refer to "Virginia Claims to Land in Pennsylvania" in *Pennsylvania Archives*, 3d series, vol. 3, pages 483–574; Boyd Crumrine, *Virginia Court Records in Southwestern Pennsylvania . . . 1775–1780* (1902–05; reprint with index, Baltimore, Md.: Genealogical Publishing Co., 1974); and articles by Dr. Raymond Martin Bell in the *National Genealogical Society Quarterly* 45 (1957): 132–36, and *The Virginia Genealogist* 7 (1963): 78–83, 103–07, 158–62, and 11 (1967):126–27.

Settlers from Connecticut came to the Upper Delaware and Wyoming valleys claimed by Connecticut from about 1753 to 1782. The records of the Delaware Company have not survived, but see *The Susquehanna Company Papers* by Julian P. Boyd and Robert J. Taylor, 11 vols. (Wilkes-Barre, Pa.: Wyoming Historical and Geological Society; Ithaca, N.Y.: Cornell University Press, 1930–71); William Henry Egle, *Documents Relating to the Connecticut Settlement in the Wyoming Valley (of Pennsylvania)* (1890; reprint, Bowie, Md.: Heritage Books, 1990); and Donna Bingham Munger, "Following Connecticut Ancestors to Pennsylvania: Susquehanna Company Settlers," *The New England Historical and Genealogical Register* 139 (1985): 112–25. Other material is at the Connecticut State Library and the Wyoming Historical and Geological Society in Wilkes-Barre.

Tax-free land in the western part of the state, called the "Donation Lands," was offered to Revolutionary War soldiers of the Pennsylvania Line of the Continental Army. Also in this section of Pennsylvania were "Depreciation Lands," sold at reduced prices to Revolutionary War veterans or available to them instead of payment if they redeemed their Depreciation Certificates. The claims to these lands were published with maps in volumes 3 and 7 of *Pennsylvania Archives*, 3d series. A helpful discussion of both of these land groups by John E. Winner appeared in *the Western Pennsylvania Historical Magazine* 8 (1925): 1–11. See also "The Depreciation and Donation Lands" compiled by Nell Y. Herchenroether in *Western Pennsylvania Genealogical Quarterly* 7 (1981):127–33.

Most research in Pennsylvania land records will begin in the deeds and mortgages found with the recorder of deeds (who in smaller counties is also the register of wills). Here will also be found the seller and buyer (grantor and grantee) indexes, most often arranged by the somewhat cumbersome Russell system, which is explained in *Pennsylvania Area Key*, pages 41–43 (see Guides above). In Pennsylvania, deeds and mortgages are more often than not indexed separately. Chattel mortgages are also found with the recorder of deeds. Most county deeds recorded to about 1850 and corresponding indexes are available on microfilm at the Pennsylvania State Archives and the Historical Society of Pennsylvania. Some unrecorded deeds may be found in courthouses, and many have found their way from private hands into archives, historical societies, and libraries. Keep in mind that in Pennsylvania, as elsewhere, a deed may have been recorded long after its execution and acknowledgment. In the southwestern part of the state, for example, some original deeds surfaced for recording when titles were being cleared for petroleum rights around the beginning of the twentieth century—some deeds dated over 100 years earlier. In earlier times many clerks were careful to copy German signatures into the deed books. This practice is of particular value as in the text of the deed the name was usually anglicized.

Research on Pennsylvania land is incomplete without consulting Donna Bingham Munger, *Pennsylvania Land Records: A History and Guide for Research* (Wilmington, Del.: Scholarly Resources, 1991).

Probate Records

The Pennsylvania General Assembly passed an act in 1682 which required the recording of wills and letters of administration. The first place to seek a will or other type of estate record in the Keystone State is with the county register of wills. Here are files of original papers pertaining to an estate as well as the record books in which were copied wills, letters of administration, inventories, accounts, and other related records. In some counties the original papers may be arranged by type of document—will, bond, or account—and thereunder by date of filing. Most filming of estate records has concentrated on will books, but the files must not be passed up even where there is a will. The clerk of the orphans' court in each county (who is often the register of wills and in smaller counties the recorder of deeds as well) is responsible for keeping such records that concern the division of estates, guardians of minor children, and similar matters. Indexes to records in both the register of wills and clerk of the orphans' court offices should both be checked, as often there will be action on an estate in both places. Most county indexes will lead to a docket book that in turn will summarize the existing documents and record book entries. Besides the availability of many Pennsylvania estate records on microfilm and some in abstract form in periodicals, such as *Publications of the Genealogical Society of Pennsylvania* and *Your Family Tree*, or in separate publications, published indexes for many counties are widely available, usually up to about 1900. Some of these indexes cover both wills and letters of administration and provide the year of the first action on the estate, the volume and page for the will or letters of administration, and the file number of the original papers, if a number has been assigned. Films of the indexes and record books are at the Pennsylvania State Archives and the Historical Society of Pennsylvania.

In counties with large German populations, such as Berks, Lancaster, and York, it is common to find original wills written in German, with English translations.

Court Records

Sylvester K. Stevens and Donald H. Kent, *County Government and Archives in Pennsylvania* (Harrisburg, Pa.: Pennsylvania Historical and Museum Commission, 1947), while a bit dated, explains the development of the counties and the responsibilities of the various county offices, with a good description of the county court.

The prothonotary has been the clerk of court of common pleas since 1707. Court records here include divorces, naturalizations, peddlers' licenses, registration of attorneys, oaths of county officers, equity, sheriff's sales, juror lists, some tax records, and some civil court records. Other court records are with the clerk of courts.

The register of wills and clerk of orphans' court (for estate records) are often the same person, sometimes sharing the responsibility of the recorder of deeds and clerk of courts as well. Counties are classed by population, which determines the number of hats worn by one or more clerks (see County Resources).

Other courts exist in Pennsylvania, although their jurisdictions are less likely to have genealogical impact. These include supreme court (1722–present), superior court (1895–present), and commonwealth court (1970–present), with mostly appellate but some original jurisdiction.

Tax Records

Late eighteenth-century tax records for various counties, 1765–91, were published in *Pennsylvania Archives*, 3d series, vols. 11–22; some of these lists are being reprinted by Family Line Publications of Westminster, Maryland. The 1781 tax list for Washington County in volume 22 was actually taken in 1782 (see Jane M. Fulcher and Raymond Martin Bell, "Washington County, Pennsylvania Intestate Records 1789–1806," *The Pennsylvania Genealogical Magazine* 31 [1979]: 51).

John "D" Stemmons and E. Diane Stemmons, comps., *Pennsylvania in 1780* (Salt Lake City, Utah: the compilers, 1978), indexes 1779 and 1780 tax lists published in the *Pennsylvania Archives*, 3d series, volumes 12–18 and 20–22, as well as unpublished lists for Northampton County 1780 and Westmoreland County 1776–80.

Among the few surviving 1798 U.S. Direct Tax lists are those for Pennsylvania. They were microfilmed by the National Archives and are available at the Mid Atlantic Region in Philadelphia and at the Pennsylvania State Archives. Indexes have been published for Washington and Lancaster counties.

Tax records are typically found in the county tax assessment offices but may also be in the county commissioners's office or with the prothonotary. The state archives has microfilms for some of these records (1715–1930s). Some assessment records have found their way into manuscript collections of county historical societies and the Historical Society of Pennsylvania, as well as the Philadelphia City Archives (see Archives, Libraries, and Societies).

Cemetery Records

Large collections of cemetery records are located at the Historical Society of Pennsylvania, and at many local libraries and historical societies. The Pennsylvania State Library maintains the state's DAR cemetery collection (see page 6). Several funeral director records for Philadelphia are in the Collections of the Genealogical Society of Pennsylvania.

The Pennsylvania State Department of Military Affairs (see Military Records below) has records of veterans' graves and burials. The Genealogical Society of Pennsylvania (see Archives, Libraries, and Societies) is currently in the process of microfilming cemetery records throughout the commonwealth.

Church Records

The Historical Records Survey produced an inventory of the church archives in Pennsylvania, but it was never published. Arranged by county, the inventory is located in the state archives. A good number of church records have been published individually and in periodicals such as *The Pennsylvania Genealogical Magazine*. Many copies exist in manuscript at the Historical Society of Pennsylvania, the Pennsylvania State Library (DAR collection), and in other libraries. A good portion of the published material concerns German churches and Quaker meetings.

Among the useful published works are *The Mennonite Encyclopedia*, 4 vols. (Hillsboro, Kans.: Mennonite Brethren

Publishing House, 1955–59); Howard Weigner Kriebel, *The Schwenkfelders in Pennsylvania, A Historical Sketch* (Lancaster, Pa.: Pennsylvania-German Society, 1904); Samuel Kriebel Brecht, ed., *The Genealogical Record of the Schwenkfelder Families* (New York, N.Y., and Chicago, Ill.: Rand McNally & Co., 1923); *The Brethren Encyclopedia,* 3 vols. (Philadelphia, Pa.: Brethren Encyclopedia, 1983); and *History of the Church of the Brethren of the Eastern District of Pennsylvania* (Lancaster, Pa.: Era Printing Co., 1915), which has much genealogical material.

Some major religious bodies have libraries in the commonwealth with collections that include not only Pennsylvania church records, but for other states as well. These include the following:

The collection at the Friends Historical Library, Swarthmore College, Swarthmore, Pennsylvania 19081, is defined in four publications: *Catalog of the Book and Serials Collections of the Friends Historical Library,* 6 vols. (Boston, Mass.: G. K. Hall, 1982); *Guide to the Manuscript Collections of the Friends Historical Library* (Swarthmore, Pa.: Friends Historical Library, 1982); *Inventory of Church Archives: Society of Friends in Pennsylvania,* compiled by the Pennsylvania Historical Survey (Philadelphia, Pa.: Friends Historical Association, 1941); and *Guide to the Records of Philadelphia Yearly Meeting,* compiled by Jack Eckert (Haverford, Pa.: Haverford College, 1989). The library has original and microfilmed Quaker records, mostly for Pennsylvania, New Jersey, Maryland, and some for Virginia, including those for fourteen Pennsylvania meetings copied by Hinshaw (see below) but never published. See Ethel D. Williams, *Know Your Ancestors* (Rutland, Vt.: Charles E. Tuttle Co., 1960), pages 125–27, 136. While the basic meeting records are located at Swarthmore, other material, particularly that of the "Orthodox" rather than "Hicksite" Friends (the latter at Swarthmore), can be found at Haverford College Library, Quaker Collection, Haverford, Pennsylvania 19041-1392.

Some Pennsylvania Quaker records have been published. The most significant are those in William Wade Hinshaw, *Encyclopedia of American Quaker Genealogy,* Vol. 2, covering the two oldest monthly meetings in the Philadelphia area, and volume 4 covering three southwestern Pennsylvania monthly meeting records (1938 and 1946; reprint, Baltimore, Md.: Genealogical Publishing Co., 1969, 1991).

The Lancaster Mennonite Historical Society, 2215 Millstream Road, Lancaster, Pennsylvania 16702-1499, has a handout entitled *Genealogical Resources at the Lancaster Mennonite Historical Society.* A research fee is charged for mail inquiries. The society also publishes a quarterly, *Pennsylvania Mennonite Heritage.*

The Evangelical and Reformed Historical Society of the United Church of Christ, 555 West James Street, Lancaster, Pennsylvania 17603, loans microfilm of church records ($5 per reel), covering German churches in Adams, Berks, Bucks, Chester, Columbia, Dauphin, Lancaster, Lebanon, Lehigh, Monroe, Montgomery, Northampton, Northumberland, Perry, Philadelphia, Schuylkill, and York counties, as well as a few for Maryland and Virginia.

Many German church records, particularly for the German Reformed and Evangelical church, have been published in books and periodicals. Charles H. Glatfelder, in *German Lutheran and Reformed Churches in the Pennsylvania Field, 1717–1793,* 2 vols. (Breingsville, Pa.: Pennsylvania-German Society, 1980, 1981), provides the location and history of the early churches and pastors of these two denominations. For a large collection of Evangelical records (births, baptisms, marriages, burials, etc.), see *Pennsylvania German Church Records,* 3 vols. (Baltimore, Md.: Genealogical Publishing Co., 1983), reprinted from *Proceedings and Addresses of the Pennsylvania German Society.*

The History Department, Presbyterian Church in the U.S.A. (formerly the Presbyterian Historical Society), 425 Lombard Street, Philadelphia, Pennsylvania 19147, has records of over 20,000 churches and has published the *Journal of Presbyterian History* since 1901.

The Historical Society of Pennsylvania has a microfilm collection of Jewish synagogue and cemetery records; other related material is at the Philadelphia Jewish Archives Center at the Balch Institute, 18 South 7th Street, Philadelphia, Pennsylvania 19106.

Other important archives are kept by the Moravians at 66 West Church Street, Bethlehem, Pennsylvania 18018; by the Schwenkfelders at Pennsburg, Pennsylvania 18073; and by the Lutherans at Abdel Ross Wentz Library, Gettysburg, Pennsylvania 17325, and at the Lutheran Theological Seminary, 7301 Germantown Avenue, Philadelphia, Pennsylvania 19119.

Military Records

Because of the Quaker influence, Pennsylvania had only intermittent militia until the Seven Years' War, the last of the French and Indian Wars, when it became necessary to defend its citizens on the western frontier. Most original military records up through World War II are in the Pennsylvania State Archives. Later records are with the Adjutant General's Office, Department of Military Affairs, Fort Indiantown Gap, Annville, Pennsylvania 17003. Information since World War II is restricted.

Many names of soldiers and sailors, from the period of the French and Indian Wars through the Mexican War, are found in the volumes of *Pennsylvania Archives,* particularly in the 2d and 5th series, although research in these should be supplemented by records at the state archives and the National Archives. For the specific *Pennsylvania Archives* volumes, consult the guides listed under Background Sources. For this period, see also the following:

Cope, Harry E., comp. *List of Soldiers and Widows of Soldiers Granted Revolutionary War Pensions by Commonwealth of Pennsylvania.* Edited by Mrs. Daniel L. Whitehead. Greensburg, Pa.: Phoebe Bayard Chapter DAR, 1976. Indexes acts of the Pennsylvania General Assembly.

Laverty, Bruce. *Colonial Muster Rolls at the Historical Society of Pennsylvania.* Philadelphia, Pa.: Historical

Society of Pennsylvania, 1983. Reproduces copies of original with name index.

Muster Rolls of the Pennsylvania Volunteers in the War of 1812–1814. Reprinted from *Pennsylvania Archives.* 2d series, Vol. 12. Baltimore, Md.: Genealogical Publishing Co., 1967. Only officers are indexed.

Stevens, S. K., et al. *The Papers of Henry Bouquet.* 5 vols. Harrisburg, Pa.: Pennsylvania Historical and Museum Commission, 1951–78.

The following should be consulted for background reading:

Jackson, John W. *The Pennsylvania Navy, 1775–1781.* New Brunswick, N.J.: Rutgers University Press, 1974.

Kent, Donald H. *The French Invasion of Western Pennsylvania.* Harrisburg, Pa.: Pennsylvania Historical and Museum Commission, 1981.

Roach, Hannah Benner. "The Pennsylvania Militia in 1777." *The Pennsylvania Genealogical Magazine* 23 (1964): 161–229. Reprinted as pamphlet with name index, 1975.

Sipe, C. Hale. *The Indian Wars of Pennsylvania.* 2d ed., with *A Supplement.* Harrisburg, Pa.: Telegraph Press, 1931.

Trussell, John B. B., Jr. *The Pennsylvania Line: Regimental Organization and Operations, 1775–1783.* Harrisburg, Pa.: Pennsylvania Historical and Museum Commission, 1977.

Much interesting material is located at the David Library of the American Revolution, River Road, Box 48, Washington Crossing, Pennsylvania 18977-0048, which has a guide to its microform holdings.

Like the other Mid-Atlantic colonies, there were Loyalists in Pennsylvania, mostly in the southeastern part of the colony, many of whom left for England or Canada. Some are identified in Anne M. Ousterhouk, "Opponents of the Revolution Whose Pennsylvania Estates were Confiscated," *Pennsylvania Genealogical Magazine* 30 (1978): 237–53. See also "Forfeited Estates Accounts" in *Pennsylvania Archives,* 6th series, vols. 12–13. For a detailed study see Wilbur H. Siebert, "The Loyalists of Pennsylvania," *Ohio State University Bulletin* 24 (1920; reprint, Boston, Mass.: Gregg, 1972). Copies of muster rolls of the Pennsylvania Loyalist Regiment are at the Public Archives of Canada and the Library of Congress.

Samuel P. Bates, *History of Pennsylvania Volunteers, 1861–65,* 5 vols. (Harrisburg, Pa.: B. Singerly, 1869–71), is arranged by regiment but only indexes officers. For all names, consult the National Archives microfilm, *Index to Compiled Service Records of Volunteer Union Soldiers in Pennsylvania Organizations,* available at the National Archives-Mid Atlantic Region and the Pennsylvania State Library. There is also a separate, every-name index in the state archives. *Record of Pennsylvania Volunteers in the Spanish-American War, 1898,* 2d ed. (Philadelphia, Pa.: Wm. Stanley Ray, 1901), was compiled by the Pennsylvania Adjutant General's Office.

Soldier discharges from the time of the Civil War are usually in the office of the county recorder of deeds. Veterans' grave and burial records are kept in the county commissioners' office and at the Department of Military Affairs.

Periodicals, Newspapers, and Manuscript Collections

Periodicals

The Pennsylvania Genealogical Magazine, published by the Genealogical Society of Pennsylvania since 1948, tends to focus on the Philadelphia area with some coverage of New Jersey, Delaware, and Maryland. The first issue was numbered volume 16, as it succeeded the society's *Publications of the Genealogical Society of Pennsylvania,* started in 1895. Reprinted from these two journals was *Genealogies of Pennsylvania Families,* 3 vols. (Baltimore, Md.: Genealogical Publishing Co., 1982).

The Pennsylvania Magazine of History and Biography is the publication of the Historical Society of Pennsylvania. It contains excellent articles on Pennsylvania subjects, although mostly with a historical focus, and since 1936 without "genealogical" material. Volume 1 was published in 1877, and in 1954 the society issued a consolidated index to the first seventy-five volumes, *The Pennsylvania Magazine of History and Biography Index Volumes 1–75 (1877–1951)* (Philadelphia, Pa.: Historical Society of Pennsylvania, 1954), edited by Eugene E. Doll, but it does not include names from "genealogical" articles. Volumes 30–67 (1906–43) were reprinted by Johnson Reprint Corp. of New York in 1969. In 1981 Genealogical Publishing Company of Baltimore reprinted a volume of *Genealogies of Pennsylvania Families* from *The Pennsylvania Magazine.*

The Western Pennsylvania Genealogical Society has published the *Western Pennsylvania Genealogical Quarterly* since 1974. It is one of the more important regional journals since it covers a large area and has many fine articles and abstracts of source records.

Another journal that concerns the central and western parts of the commonwealth was *Your Family Tree,* produced 1948–83. Besides queries, it featured abstracts of wills, tax lists, grave marker inscriptions, and newspaper items.

Publications of the Pennsylvania German Folklore Society was issued in twenty-eight volumes from 1963–66, when it merged with the *Pennsylvania German Society Proceedings,* which since 1891 had produced sixty-three volumes. Many emigration and church records have been published in these periodicals.

More historical than genealogical, but still quite useful, is *Pennsylvania History,* published by the Pennsylvania Historical Association since 1934. A cumulative index for volumes 1–28 is available at the Genealogical Society of Pennsylvania.

Much Pennsylvania material has been published in the *National Genealogical Society Quarterly* (see page 9). There are also numerous one-county, one-township, and regional publications that should not be overlooked.

Newspapers

In 1976 the Pennsylvania State Library (Harrisburg, 1984) published a list of Pennsylvania newspapers that included selected out-of-state papers arranged by county, locality, and title. See also Glenora Rossell, ed., *Pennsylvania Newspapers: A Bibliography and Union List,* 2d ed. (Pittsburgh, Pa.: Pennsylvania Library Association, 1978). This updates the earlier edition by Ruth Salisbury, but the most current information is available through Online Computer Library Center. The commonwealth sponsored a newspaper project to identify, catalog, preserve, and microfilm old newspapers. The state library, with the largest collection, makes microfilms available through interlibrary loan.

Several volumes of newspaper abstracts have been published. Some representative titles are:

Hawbaker, Gary T., ed. *Runaways, Rascals, and Rouges: Missing Spouses, Servants and Slaves.* Hershey, Pa.: the author, 1987.

Hocker, Edward W. *Genealogical Data Relating to the German Settlers in Pennsylvania and Adjacent Territory: From Advertisements in German Newspapers Published in Philadelphia and Germantown 1743–1800.* Baltimore, Md.: Genealogical Publishing Co., 1980.

Scott, Kenneth. *Genealogical Data from The Pennsylvania Chronicle, 1767–1774.* National Genealogical Society Special Publication No. 37. Washington, D.C.: National Genealogical Society, 1980.

Manuscripts

Many wonderful collections of manuscript material at the Historical Society of Pennsylvania are on microfilm at the FHL, such as those of Gilbert Cope, Alfred R. Justice, Israel D. Rupp, and many others. Nearly every repository in the commonwealth has extensive, helpful collections (see below). For a beginning guide to some of these, see Irwin Richman, comp., *Historical Manuscript Depositories in Pennsylvania* (Harrisburg, Pa.: Pennsylvania Historical Museum Commission, 1965), which is arranged by place.

Archives, Libraries, and Societies

Bureau of Archives and History
Pennsylvania Historical and Museum Commission
William Penn Memorial Museum and Archives Building
3rd and Forster Streets, P.O. Box 1026
Harrisburg, PA 17108-1026

Referred to as the Pennsylvania State Archives, the bureau holds various source materials, including vital records, censuses, maps, and tax lists. See Robert M. Dructor, *A Guide to Genealogical Sources At the Pennsylvania State Archives* (Harrisburg, Pa.: Pennsylvania Historical and Museum Commission, 1981). This should be supplemented with four titles also published by the Historical and Museum Commission:

Bauman, Roland M., and Diana S. Wallace, comps. and eds. *Guide to the Microfilm Collections in the Pennsylvania State Archives.* 1980.

Fortna, Nancy L. P., and Frank M. Suran, comps. and eds. *Guide to County and Municipal Records on Microfilm In the Pennsylvania State Archives.* 1982. This guide is outdated and may be revised in the near future.

Suran, Frank M., comp. and ed. *Guide to the Record Groups in the Pennsylvania State Archives.* 1980.

Whipkey, Harry E., comp. *Guide to the Manuscript Groups in the Pennsylvania State Archives.* 1976.

The commission also publishes a number of books on Pennsylvania, detailed in their catalog.

State Library of Pennsylvania
Commonwealth Avenue and Walnut Street
P.O. Box 1601
Harrisburg, PA 17105-1601

Genealogies, local histories, maps, censuses, newspapers, periodicals, and city directories are at the state library. Of particular use is the Genealogical Surname Index, described by Janice B. Newman in "Genealogical Research at the State Library of Pennsylvania," *Pennsylvania Genealogical Magazine* 35 (1988): 199–212. Also to be consulted is *A Guide to the Genealogy/Local History Section of the State Library of Pennsylvania* (Harrisburg, Pa.: State Library of Pennsylvania, 1989).

The Historical Society of Pennsylvania Library
1300 Locust Street
Philadelphia, PA 19107

Founded in 1824, the historical society has published the *Pennsylvania Magazine of History and Biography* since 1877. In 1892 a group of society members formed the adjunct Genealogical Society of Pennsylvania, now a separate body, although it has offices in the building of the historical society (see below). See *Guide to Manuscript Collections of Historical Society of Pennsylvania.* 2d ed. (Philadelphia, Pa.: Historical Society of Pennsylvania, 1949).

The Genealogical Society of Pennsylvania Library
1300 Locust Street
Philadelphia, PA 19107

Beginning in 1895, the society produced *Publications of the Genealogical Society of Pennsylvania,* renamed *Pennsylvania Genealogical Magazine* in 1948. Helen Hutchinson Woodroffe compiled "A Genealogist's Guide to Pennsylvania Records." Beginning in volume 31 (1979), it is a listing of the county material in the Historical Society of Pennsylvania's extensive collection, with the library's call numbers. See also J. Carlyle Parker, comp., *A User's Guide to the Manuscript Collection of the Genealogical Society of Pennsylvania . . . Microfilmed by the Genealogical Department of Salt Lake City* (Turlock, Calif.: Marietta Publishing Co., 1986). The society charges a research fee for mail inquiries.

Historical Society of Western Pennsylvania and Western Pennsylvania Genealogical Society
4338 Bigelow Boulevard
Pittsburgh, PA 15213-2695

Covering the western half of the commonwealth, the historical society has published *The Western Pennsylvania Historical Magazine* since 1918, with cumulative indexes for volumes 1–43 and 44–53. The genealogical society, which has no formal office or library, publishes *Western Pennsylvania Genealogical Quarterly*. For a list of the holdings of the historical society, see volumes 4 and 6 of the genealogical society's *Quarterly*.

The South Central Pennsylvania Genealogical Society, Inc.
P.O. Box 1824
York, PA 17405-1824

This society has distinguished itself through the publication of many source records, including Bible records, tax lists, private vital records, cemetery inscriptions, and naturalizations.

Many Pennsylvania counties have fine historical societies which should be checked for their manuscript collections. These include Adams, Berks, Bucks, Chester, Crawford, Lancaster, and York counties. See also *Directory Pennsylvania 1990* by the Library Development of the State Library of Pennsylvania (Harrisburgh, Pa., 1990).

Special Focus Categories

Immigration

Two works take up the coming of Pennsylvania's first immigrants to the Penn colony: *Passengers and Ships Prior to 1684*, compiled and edited by Walter Lee Sheppard, Jr. (1970; reprint, Bowie, Md.: Heritage Books, 1985), which is basically synthesized passenger lists; and George E. McCracken, *The Welcome Claimants: Proved, Disproved and Doubtful* (1970; reprint, Bowie, Md.: Heritage Books, 1985).

The most important work on the mass immigration of Germans is Ralph B. Strassburger, *Pennsylvania German Pioneers*, edited by William J. Hinke, 3 vols. (1934; reprint of volumes 1 and 3, Baltimore, Md.: Genealogical Publishing Co., 1980), covering arrivals at Philadelphia of thousands of Palatines and others, 1727–1808. It is regrettable the reprint did not include volume 2, which has facsimile signatures of the passengers who signed an oath to the province. See also the "Annotations" to this work by Dr. Friedrich Krebs in *The Pennsylvania Genealogical Magazine* 21 (1960): 235–48. Two other volumes, edited by Don Yoder, supplement Strassburger/Hinke: *Pennsylvania German Immigrants 1709–1786* (Baltimore, Md.: Genealogical Publishing Co., 1984), reprinted from the Pennsylvania German Folklore Society *Yearbooks*, and *Rhineland Emigrants* (Baltimore, Md.: Genealogical Publishing Co., 1981), reprinted from *Pennsylvania Folklife*.

Other early records were published in *Pennsylvania Archives*, 2d Series, vol. 17, pages 521–667; Michael Tepper, ed., *Emigrants to Pennsylvania, 1641–1819* (Baltimore, Md.: Genealogical Publishing Co., 1975), consolidated from passenger lists published in *The Pennsylvania Magazine of History and Biography;* and Carl Boyer, III, ed., *Ship Passenger Lists: Pennsylvania and Delaware (1641–1825)* (Newhall, Calif.: the compiler, 1980).

Passenger lists for the port of Philadelphia, 1800–1945, and indexes, 1800–1948, are available at the National Archives-Mid Atlantic Region. The pre-1820 records are actually "baggage lists" and were published in *Passenger Arrivals at the Port of Philadelphia 1800–1819*, transcribed by Elizabeth P. Bentley and edited by Michael H. Tepper (Baltimore, Md.: Genealogical Publishing Co., 1986).

While not classified as immigration records, crew and vessel lists for the port of Philadelphia, 1789–1880, are available in indexed typescript volumes at the Historical Society of Pennsylvania and the Free Library of Philadelphia, Logan Square, Philadelphia, Pennsylvania 19103.

Naturalization

Most county naturalizations are in the office of the prothonotary, although some are in city or county archives, such as those for Philadelphia and Chester counties. A few of these records have been published, such as those for Allegheny (1798–1891), Bucks (1802–1906), and Westmoreland (1802–52). Provincial, state, and other records are in the state archives, including those of the supreme court, most of which were published in *Pennsylvania Archives*, 2d series, vol. 2, and reprinted as *Persons Naturalized in the Province of Pennsylvania 1740–1773* (Baltimore, Md.: Genealogical Publishing Co., 1967, 1991). For other records at the archives, see Ductor's *Guide* listed under Archives, Libraries, and Societies.

Non-British subjects in Pennsylvania were required to take an oath to the province, and their names are found in Strassburger/Hinke noted above and in Thompson Wescott, *Names of Persons Who Took the Oath of Allegiance to the State of Pennsylvania Between . . . 1777 and 1789* (1865; reprint, Baltimore, Md.: Genealogical Publishing Co., 1965). Many nineteenth-century Philadelphia records are located through P. William Filby, ed., *Philadelphia Naturalizations: Records of Aliens' Declarations of Intention and/or Oaths of Allegiance 1789–1880* (Detroit, Mich.: Gale Research Co., 1982), which reproduced an earlier compilation by the Historical Records Survey (1941).This should be used with "The WPA Index of Naturalizations: An Explanation," *The Pennsylvania Genealogical Magazine* 36 (1989): 109–16.

Federal court naturalizations are at the National Archives-Mid Atlantic Region in Philadelphia. These cover the Eastern District (Philadelphia) petitions (1790–1960s), indexed (1795–1951); Western District (Pittsburgh) petitions (1820–50s), indexed (1820–1906); and Middle District (Scranton and Harrisburg) petitions (1906–50s), indexed (1901–84).

Black American

See David McBride, *The Afro-American in Pennsylvania: A Critical Guide to Sources in the Pennsylvania State Archives*

(Harrisburg, Pa.: Pennsylvania Historical and Museum Commission, 1979). McBride also edited *Blacks in Pennsylvania History: Research and Educational Perspectives* (Harrisburg, Pa.: Pennsylvania Historical and Museum Commission, 1983). Charles L. Blockson, *Pennsylvania's Black History* (Philadelphia, Pa.: Portfolio Association, 1975), is another useful work. For other sources see also *Black Genesis*, pages 176–81, cited on page 10.

Native American

Among the tribes in Pennsylvania were the Lenni-Lenape (or Delaware) in the east, the Susquehannock and Shawnee along the Susquehanna River, and the Iroquois Five Nations who migrated down from New York in the west. See Barry Kent's, *Susquehanna's Indians* (1984), Paul A. W. Wallace's, *Indians of Pennsylvania*, 2d ed. (1986), and Wallace's *Indian Paths of Pennsylvania* (1987), all published by the Pennsylvania Historical and Museum Commission, Harrisburg, Pennsylvania. (See also Kraft's *The Lenape* under New Jersey—Special Focus Categories.)

Other Ethnic Groups

John E. Bodnar, *Ethnic History in Pennsylvania: A Selected Bibliography* (Harrisburg, Pa.: Pennsylvania Historical and Museum Commission, 1974), covers published and manuscript material. Also useful is David E. Washburn, comp. and ed., *The Peoples of Pennsylvania: An Annotated Bibliography of Resource Materials* (Pittsburgh, Pa.: University for International Studies, University of Pittsburgh, 1981). One of the best research centers, not limited to Pennsylvania, is the Balch Institute for Ethnic Studies, 18 South 7th Street, Philadelphia, Pennsylvania 19106.

The "big three" colonial Pennsylvania immigrant groups have all been covered in great detail in published material. Some selected titles are the following:

William Wistar Comfort, *The Quakers* (University Park, Pa.: Pennsylvania Historical Association, 1948), while brief, includes a helpful bibliography; and see Albert Cook Myers, *Immigration of the Irish Quakers into Pennsylvania 1682–1750* (1902; reprint, Baltimore, Md.: Genealogical Publishing Co., 1969), and Hugh Barbour and J. William Frost, *The Quakers* (New York, N.Y.: Greenwood Press, 1988).

Emil Meynen, *Bibliography on German Settlements in Colonial North America, Especially on the Pennsylvania Germans and Their Descendants, 1683–1933* (1937; reprint, Gale Research Corp., 1966), is useful, and Russell Wieder Gilbert, *A Picture of the Pennsylvania Germans* (University Park, Pa.: Pennsylvania Historical Association, 1962), has a bibliography.

John A. Hostetler, *Amish Society* (Baltimore, Md.: Johns Hopkins University Press, 1983), explains the beliefs and practices of this group.

For the Ulster Scots, see Wayland F. Dunaway, *The Scotch-Irish of Colonial Pennsylvania* (1944; reprint, Baltimore, Md.: Genealogical Publishing Co., 1985); and Charles K. Bolton, *Scotch Irish Pioneers of Ulster and America* (1910; reprint, Baltimore, Md.: Genealogical Publishing Co., 1972).

For information on the early Swedes in Pennsylvania, see the titles listed under Delaware—Background Sources.

Another early immigrant group is covered in Albert Bernhardt Faust and Gaius Marcus Brumbaugh's *Lists of Swiss Immigrants in the Eighteenth Century to the American Colonies*, 2 vols. in 1 (1920–25; reprint, Baltimore, Md.: Genealogical Publishing Co., 1991).

While not one of the major three immigrant groups, the Welsh have received good treatment in print. See works by Thomas Allen Glenn: *Merion in the Welsh Tract* (1896; reprint, Baltimore, Md.: Genealogical Publishing Co., 1970) and *Welsh Families of Pennsylvania*, 2 vols. (1911–13; reprinted in one volume, Baltimore, Md.: Genealogical Publishing Co., 1970, 1991). Although some of his other publications may have been less than reliable, Charles H. Browning's *Welsh Settlement of Pennsylvania* (1912; reprint, Baltimore, Md.: Genealogical Publishing Co., 1970) is a worthwhile work. It also includes Welsh Quakers.

County Resources

The township is the basic political unit in the county and may have within its boundaries incorporated towns, boroughs, and cities, although these would have their own local governments. Useful records generated at these levels include vital records, taxes, and voter registration.

The commonwealth of Pennsylvania is comprised of sixty-seven counties where records of land, estates, vital events, divorces, naturalizations, and court actions can be found. It is mandated that each county support a historical society. In 1952, an archives was founded in Philadelphia, the oldest city archives in the country. John Daly compiled a *Descriptive Inventory* of its holdings in 1970. The first county archives was established in Chester County in 1982 and is considered the model for the commonwealth. Other county archives are underway at various stages in Bucks, Delaware, Lancaster, Montgomery, Northampton, Schuylkill, Westmoreland, and York counties. For more detail about county office holdings, see the *County Records Survey, Record Series Inventory, 1985–86*, available on microfiche from the Pennsylvania Historical and Museum Commission, Division of Archives and Manuscripts in Harrisburg; however, Philadelphia is not included, and Monroe County follows Montgomery, out of alphabetical sequence. This survey updates the more detailed inventories prepared by the WPA. See also Stevens and Kent's *County Government Archives* cited under Court Records.

The first column below indicates the map coordinate. In the second column is the name of the county and the mailing address of the recorder of deeds, where deeds and mortgages are found. The third column shows the date of county formation, with the name or names of the parent county or counties. The fourth column gives the date the earliest deed was recorded. The last column gives the mailing address of the register of wills, if different from the recorder. Estate records are found in the register's office or orphans' court. (See Court Records for other county offices.)

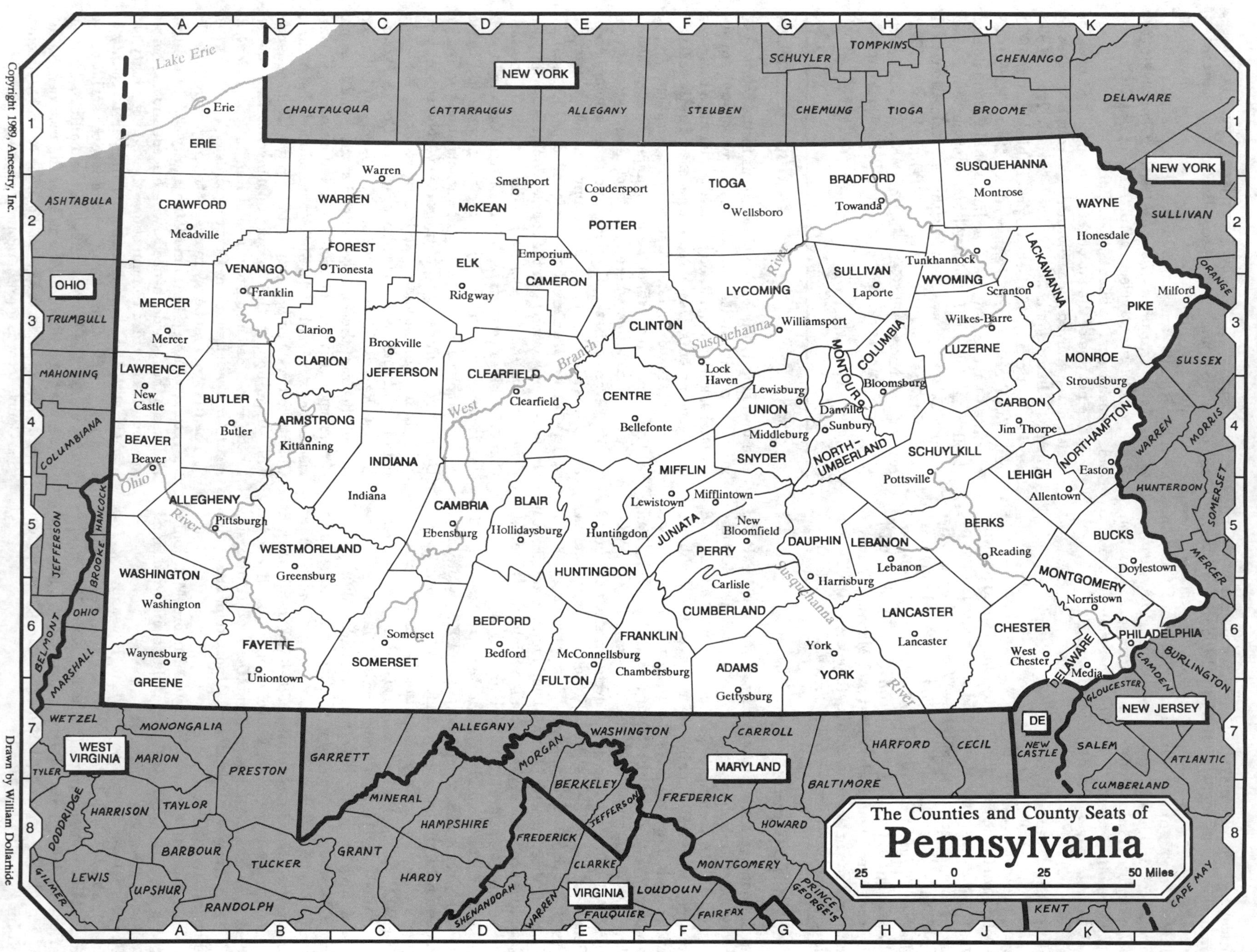

Drawn by William Dollarhide

Map	County Recorder of Deeds	Date Formed Parent County/ies	Deeds	Register of Wills
G6	Adams Courthouse, Room 102 Gettysburg 17325-2398	1800 York	1800	1800
A5	Allegheny County Office Building Ross Street Pittsburgh 15219	1788 Washington/Westmoreland	1788	1789 City County Building Pittsburgh 15219
B4	Armstrong Market Street Kittanning 16201 *Armstrong was attached to Westmoreland County until 1805.*	1800 Allegheny/Lycoming/Westmoreland	1805	1805
A4	Beaver P.O. Box 537 Beaver 15009-0537 *Beaver was attached to Allegheny County until 1803.*	1800 Allegheny/Washington	1803	1800 Courthouse Beaver 15009
D6	Bedford 200 S. Juliana Street Bedford 15522-1714	1771 Cumberland	1771	1771
J5	Berks 33 N. Sixth Street Reading 19601-3594 *There are unrecorded deeds back to 1717 on microfilm at the Historical Society of Pennsylvania.*	1752 Chester/Lancaster/Philadelphia	1752	1752
E5	Blair 423 Allegheny Street Hollidaysburg 16648-2022	1846 Huntingdon/ Bedford	1846	1846
H2	Bradford 301 Main Street Towanda 18848-1824	1810 (as Ontario; renamed and formally organized, 1812) Luzerne/Lycoming	1812	1812
K5	Bucks Court and Main Streets Doylestown 18901	1682 original	1684	1683
B4	Butler S. Main Street Butler 16001 *Butler was attached to Allegheny County until 1803.*	1800 Allegheny	1804	1804
D5	Cambria P.O. Box 240 Ebensburg 15931-0240 *Cambria was attached to Somerset County until 1807.*	1804 Somerset/Huntingdon	1846	1819 P.O. Box 298 Ebensburg 15931-0298
E3	Cameron E. Fifth Street Emporium 15834	1860 Clinton/Elk/McKean/Potter	1860	1863
J4	Carbon Broadway Jim Thorpe 18229	1843 Monroe/Northampton	1843	1843
E4	Centre Courthouse Bellefonte 16823-3003	1800 Lycoming/Mifflin/Northumberland/ Huntingdon	1801	1800

Map	County Recorder of Deeds	Date Formed Parent County/ies	Deeds	Register of Wills
J6	Chester High and Market Streets West Chester 19380 **Located at Chester County Archives and Records Service, 117 West Gay Street, West Chester 19380.*	1682 original	1688	1924 1714–1923*
B3	Clarion Main Street Clarion 16214	1839 Venango/Armstrong	1840	1840
D4	Clearfield P.O. Box 361 Clearfield 16830-0361 *Not organized for judiciary purposes until 1822; Clearfield functioned as a part of Centre County.*	1804 Lycoming/Huntingdon	1805	1823
F3	Clinton P.O. Box 943 Lock Haven 17745-0943	1839 Lycoming/Centre	1839	1839
H3	Columbia P.O. Box 380 Bloomsburg 17815-0380	1813 Northumerland/Luzerne	1813	1813
A2	Crawford 903 Diamond Park Meadville 16335	1800 Allegheny	1800	1800
G6	Cumberland Hanover Street Carlisle 17013-2677	1750 Lancaster	1750	1750
H5	Dauphin P.O. Box 12000 Harrisburg 17108	1785 Lancaster	1785	1785 Front and Market Streets Harrisburg 17101
K6	Delaware Government Administration Building W. Front Street Media 19063	1789 Chester	1789	1789
D2	Elk P.O. Box 314 Ridgway 15853-0314	1843 Jefferson/McKean/Clearfield	1844	1844
A1	Erie 140 W. Sixth Street Erie 16501 *Erie was attached to Crawford County until 1803. A courthouse fire destroyed pre-1823 records.*	1800 Allegheny	1823	1823
B6	Fayette 61 E. Main Street Uniontown 15401-3514	1783 Westmoreland	1784	1784
C2	Forest P.O. Box 423 Tionesta 16353-0423 *Forest was attached to Jefferson County until 1857.*	1848 Jefferson	1857	1855
E6	Franklin 157 Lincoln Way E. Chambersburg 17201-2211	1784 Cumberland	1784	1784
E6	Fulton Courthouse N. Second Street McConnellsburg 17233	1850 Bedford	1850	1851

Map	County Recorder of Deeds	Date Formed Parent County/ies	Deeds	Register of Wills
A6	Greene Courthouse Waynesburg 15370	1796 Washington	1796	1796
E5	Huntingdon Courthouse, Penn Street Huntingdon 16652	1787 Bedford	1786	1787
C4	Indiana 825 Philadelphia Street Indiana 15701-3934 *Indiana was attached to Westmoreland County until 1806.*	1803 Lycoming/Westmoreland	1806	1803
C3	Jefferson 200 Main Street Brookville 15825-1236 *Jefferson was attached to Westmoreland County until 1806 and to Indiana County until 1830.*	1804 Lycoming	1828	1832
F5	Juniata P.O. Box 68 Mifflintown 17059-0068	1831 Mifflin	1831	1831
J3	Lackawanna Courthouse North Washington Avenue Scranton 18503	1878 Luzerne	1878	1878
J6	Lancaster 50 N. Duke Street Lancaster 17602-2805 *Some early court records have been transferred to the Lancaster County Historical Society, 230 North President Avenue, Lancaster 17603.*	1729 Chester	1729	1729
A4	Lawrence County Government Center Court Street New Castle 16101	1849 Beaver/Mercer	1849	1849
H5	Lebanon 107 Municipal Building 400 S. Eighth Street Lebanon 17042-6794	1813 Dauphin/Lancaster	1813	1813 105 Municipal Building 400 S. Eighth Street Lebanon 17042-6794
J4	Lehigh 455 Hamilton Street Allentown 18101	1812 Northampton	1812	1812
J3	Luzerne Courthouse 600 N. River Street Wilkes-Barre 18702-2685 *A flood in 1972 destroyed some estate files.*	1786 Northumberland	1787	1786
G3	Lycoming 48 W. Third Street Williamsport 17701-6519	1795 Northumberland	1795	1795
D2	McKean P.O. Box 3426 Smethport 16749-3426 *Attached to Centre County until 1814 and to Lycoming County until 1826 for judicial and elective purposes; McKean was not fully organized until 1826.*	1804 Lycoming	1827	1827 P.O. Box 202 Smethport 16749-0202

Map	County Recorder of Deeds	Date Formed Parent County/ies	Deeds	Register of Wills
A3	Mercer Box 109, Courthouse Mercer 16137-0109 *Attached to Crawford County until 1803.*	1800 Allegheny	1803	1804 Box 112, Courthouse Mercer 16137-0112
F5	Mifflin 20 N. Wayne Street Lewistown 17044-1770	1789 Cumberland/Northumberland	1789	1789
K3	Monroe Courthouse Square Stroudsburg 18360	1836 Pike/Northampton	1836	1836
K5	Montgomery Courthouse Norristown 19404 ** Some early deed books are in the Montgomery County Archives Center, 1880 Markley Street, Norristown 19401, and the county historical society.* *** Most records through the mid-1980s are in the county archives.*	1784 Philadelphia	1784*	1784**
H3	Montour 29 Mill Street Danville 17821-1945	1850 Columbia	1850	1850
K4	Northampton Government Center Seventh and Washington Streets Easton 18042-7401	1752 Bucks	1752	1752
G4	Northumberland Courthouse Second and Market Streets Sunbury 17801-3408	1772 Lancaster/Berks/Bedford/Cumberland/ Northampton	1770	1771
	Ontario	1810 (renamed Bradford, 1812)		
G5	Perry P.O. Box 223 New Bloomfield 17068-0223	1820 Cumberland	1820	1820
K6	Philadelphia City Hall Philadelphia 19107-3209 *The city and county of Philadelphia were combined in 1854 and city and county offices merged in 1952. The orphans' court is in Room 415 of City Hall, and the City Archives is located at 401 North Broad Street, Philadelphia 19108.*	1682 original	1684	1682 City Hall Philadelphia 19107 (for indexes) 34 S. 11th Street Philadelphia 19107 (for records)
K3	Pike 412 Broad Street Milford 18337	1814 Wayne	1814	1814
E2	Potter Courthouse Coudersport 16915 *Attached to Lycoming County until 1826 and to McKean County until 1835 for judicial purposes, Potter was not fully organized until 1835.*	1804 Lycoming	1806	1836
H4	Schuylkill Second and Laurel Streets Pottsville 17901	1811 Berks/Northampton	1811	1811

Map	County Recorder of Deeds	Date Formed Parent County/ies	Deeds	Register of Wills
G4	Snyder P.O. Box 217 Middleburg 17842-0217	1855 Union	1855	1855
C6	Somerset P.O. Box 568 Somerset 15501-0568	1795 Bedford	1795	1795 P.O. Box 186 Somerset 15501-0186
H3	Sullivan Courthouse Laporte 18626 *Sullivan was attached to Lycoming until 1848.*	1847 Lycoming	1848	1847
J2	Susquehanna Courthouse Montrose 18801 *Susquehanna was attached to Luzerne County until 1812.*	1810 Luzerne	1812	1812
F2	Tioga 116 Main Street Wellsboro 16901-1410 *Tioga was attached to Lycoming until 1812.*	1804 Lycoming	1806	1806
G4	Union 103 S. Second Street Lewisburg 17837-1903	1813 Northumberland	1813	1813
B3	Venango Courthouse Liberty Street Franklin 16323 *Venango was attached to Crawford County until 1805.*	1800 Allegheny/Lycoming	1805	1806
C2	Warren 204 Fourth Street Warren 16365-2318 *Attached to Crawford County until 1805 and then to Venango, until Warren was formally organized in 1819.*	1800 Allegheny/Lycoming	1819	1820
A6	Washington 100 W. Beau Street Washington 15301-4402	1781 Westmoreland	1781	1781
K2	Wayne Courthouse, Court Street Honesdale 18431-9517	1798 Northampton	1798	1798
B5	Westmoreland P.O. Box 160 Greensburg 15601-0160	1773 Bedford	1773	1773 301 Courthouse Square Greensburg 15601
J2	Wyoming Courthouse Square Tunkhannock 18657-1216	1842 Luzerne	1842	1843
H6	York 28 E. Market Street York 17401-1501	1749 Lancaster	1749	1749

RHODE ISLAND

Alice Eichholz, Ph.D., C.G.

Named when Roger Williams referred to Aquidneck Island as the isle of roses, bedecked by rhododendrons and owned by the native inhabitants, Rhode Island had its beginnings as a haven for religious dissenters expelled by Massachusetts Bay and Plymouth colonies. Williams's unceasing belief in religious freedom probably helped establish a long, collaborative relationship with the Narragansetts. In 1636, the only place he had to run was south, out of reach of both Massachusetts colonies and not yet within the Puritan strongholds of Connecticut's colonies. He purchased from the native inhabitants what became Providence Plantations in 1637, and a group associated with Anne Hutchinson purchased Aquidneck Island in 1638. Renamed "Rhode Island," it now encompasses Portsmouth, Middletown, and the city of Newport.

Geographically, the settlements might have met economic disaster had it not been for the enterprise of sea trade. Not having the rich natural resources that the other colonies had, a few wealthy planters in part of the colony capitalized on their excellent location relative to the sailing currents of the Atlantic. They developed import trade in sugar, fruit, rum, slaves, and exports from the other colonies to build an impressive plantation system. Throughout the state's history this has provided a highly mobile and much more ethnically diverse population than other New England states. Individuals from other New England locations may have broken loose from their moorings and headed to Newport for adventure and livelihood on the sea. Transients in town for a year or two were not uncommon.

More and more land was purchased from the native inhabitants, and groups of Quakers from England and Jews from Portugal and Spain arrived in the colony where they were accorded the status of freemen by the general assembly. At the outbreak of King Philip's War in 1675, despite an attempt to remain neutral, Rhode Island and Providence Plantations were swept into it when major battles were fought there. When this first of the colonial wars ended, more and more land was purchased from the indigenous tribes, and conflicts developed with both Massachusetts and Connecticut colonies over land claims.

The towns in Rhode Island remained reasonably separate and distinct groups that coexisted despite considerable differences. As such, no county system of government developed until the eighteenth century, and even then its function was chiefly for court proceedings. The general assembly and the general court dealt with the colonial matters usually conducted by counties.

During the Revolution, the British captured and occupied the Island of Aquidneck. The British Navy used Narragansett Bay as a strategic harbor, just as the United States Navy does today. Portuguese Jews, French settlers, and African slaves all found their way to Narragansett Bay in the seventeenth and eighteenth centuries. The port of Providence brought hundreds of Irish and French-Canadians in the nineteenth century, and Italians, Germans, Russians, and Poles in the early twentieth century.

Good collections of Rhode Island records, the indexing of early materials, and the short distance from one end of the state to another, all make Rhode Island an excellent site for genealogical research.

Vital Records

Although many vital events before 1853 were not recorded, those that were are fairly easy to locate. The general assembly mandated that marriage intentions be recorded beginning in 1647, although the law was not enforced. More often, marriages were reported by ministers to town clerks. Births were often recorded in family groups at different times in a family's life. Not all births were recorded even when some in the family were. James N. Arnold's *Vital Record of Rhode Island, 1636–1850,* 21 vols. (Providence, R.I.: Narragansett Historical Publishing Co., 1891–1912), whose title is in the singular, is a compilation of Rhode Island research materials, the first six volumes of which are alphabetized extracts of vital events from town records. The volumes can usually be located at major research libraries holding New England resources and are in the FHL collection. Births, deaths, and marriages (both bride and groom listed separately) are recorded from the earliest settlement to 1850 and are organized according to county and town. More information is often given under the groom's entry. Some of the rest of the volumes contain vital events from sources other than the town records (see Church Records), although individual entries are documented, making it possible to check the original source. Towns, for the most part, still hold all of these originals in the clerk's office (see Town Resources).

Arnold stops in 1850, and statewide reporting did not begin until 1853. For the three years, 1850–53, vital events must be searched for in town records.

Copies of vital events recorded in towns beginning in 1853 were sent to the Rhode Island Division of Vital Statistics, Department of Health, Cannon Building, Room 101, 75 Davis Street, Providence, Rhode Island 02908. The records for this time period have been stored at the Records Center, 1 Capitol Hill, Providence, Rhode Island 02903, although births are still at the Health Department along with the indexes for both births and deaths. There are computerized indexes to marriages and deaths to 1900 at the Rhode Island Historical Society.

A more recent publication is Alden G. Beaman's *Vital Records of Rhode Island, New Series* (Princeton, Mass.: the author, 1975–present), presently in thirteen volumes with more to follow published by his daughter. Using probates and gravestones, Beaman supplements Arnold with information on vital events not found in the town's vital records. This is an alphabetical arrangement for an entire county, with the town of residence indicated. Washington, Newport, and Kent counties are included in what has already been published.

Vital records for Providence from 1850–1945 are in print in thirty-two volumes, usually available at research centers with good New England collections or on microfilm.

Divorces were granted through all of the courts. Those granted before 1962 are at the various county superior courts. After 1962 records can be obtained—with some restrictions—from Family Court, 22 Hayes Street, Providence, Rhode Island 02908, or by writing the Supreme Court Judicial Records Center (see Court Records).

Census Records

Federal

Population Schedules.

- Indexed—1790, 1800, 1810, 1820, 1830, 1840, 1850, 1860, 1870
- Soundex—1880, 1900, 1920
- Unindexed—1910

Industry and Agriculture Schedules.

- 1850, 1860, 1870, 1880

Mortality Schedules.

- 1850, 1860, 1870, 1880

Union Veterans Schedules.

- 1890

Provincial

Before statehood Rhode Island took several censuses for a variety of purposes. These are supplemented by the freemen's lists indicating all those admitted to that status between 1747–55. The originals and a card index are at the Rhode Island State Archives, but they have been published in Bruce C. MacGunnigle, *Rhode Island Freemen, 1747–1755* (Baltimore, Md.: Genealogical Publishing Co., 1977).

Some censuses were ordered as early as 1706, but the earliest extant is for 1730, although only Portsmouth and part of South Kingston returns have been located. Blacks and whites are enumerated and identified as such in the publication of the lists transcribed by Mildred Mosher Chamberlain in *Rhode Island Roots* 7 (1981): 16–17 and 10 (1984):1.

The 1774 census has survived for nearly all towns and was indexed and published. Only New Shoreham (Block Island) is missing. Since this is a pre-Revolutionary War list, its value is in locating these families before the decline in population and the economic and political changes caused by the war. Original returns are at Rhode Island State Archives, but their publication makes them more accessible. See John R. Bartlett, *Census of the Inhabitants of the Colony of Rhode Island and Providence Plantations* (1858; reprint, Baltimore, Md.: Genealogical Publishing Co., 1969).

A military census falls chronologically between the 1774 and 1782 census (see Military Records). The last census before the federal censuses begin can be found indexed in Jay Mack Holbrook's, *Rhode Island 1782 Census* (Oxford, Mass.: Holbrook Research Institute, 1979). Returns for some of the towns were lost. This is a reconstructed census using original manuscripts and tax lists to replace those lost records. Returns for North Providence and Smithfield are not extant. There is a breakdown by age, sex, and race (see also Military Records).

State

Rhode Island is the only New England state with extensive state census records taken every ten years between 1865–1935 (1895 is missing). Similar to the federal census, the 1865 state census is microfilmed and every-name indexed at the Rhode Island Historical Society. The 1875, 1885, 1915, and 1925 census records are at Rhode Island State Archives with an index in process. The 1905 and 1935 records are currently being restored by the State Records Center in Providence (see Vital Records), with transfer to the State Archives scheduled for 1991.

Background Sources

Comprehensive town histories with genealogies, abundantly found in other New England states, do not exist to the same extent in Rhode Island. Particularly for the seventeenth century, much of Rhode Island's local history is found in the town council records available in print (see Town Resources). However, there are good general history materials for the state, genealogical research guides, and compendium family genealogies such as:

Andrews, Charles M. *The Colonial Period of American History*. 2 vols. New Haven, Conn.: Yale University Press, 1938. Presents a good view of history useful to genealogists.

Arnold, Samuel Greene. *History of Rhode Island and Providence Plantations*. 2 vols. New York, N.Y.: D. Appleton & Co., 1859–60. Detailed chronological history of the state.

Austin, John O. *Genealogical Dictionary of Rhode Island*. 1887. Reprint. Baltimore, Md.: Genealogical Publishing Co., 1969. Comprehensive in its coverage of 485 families for three or four generations. No references are indicated, but the researcher can often surmise the source and thus check the original. The reprint edition supplements the original and has corrections.

Bartlett, John Russell, ed. *Records of the Colony of Rhode Island and Providence Plantations in New England*. 7 vols. Providence, R.I.: A. Crawford Greene and Brother, 1856–62. A helpful edited transcript of the General Assembly proceedings.

Bridenbaugh, Carl. *Fat Mutton and Liberty of Conscience: Society in Rhode Island, 1636–1690*. Providence, R.I.: Brown University Press, 1974. A social history of the seventeenth century.

Coleman, Peter J. *The Transformation of Rhode Island—1790–1860*. Providence, R.I.: Brown University Press, 1963. Is a comprehensive portrait of the effects of social and political life in the state during early statehood until the Civil War.

Fiske, Jane Fletcher. "Genealogical Research in Rhode Island." *The New England Historical and Genealogical Register* 136 (July 1982): 173–219. A superb guide to research in Rhode Island that follows the types of resources century by century. It is reprinted in Ralph J. Crandall, ed., *Genealogical Research in New England* (Baltimore, Md.: Genealogical Publishing Co., 1984).

Gannett, Henry. *A Geographic Dictionary of Connecticut and Rhode Island*. 2 vols. in 1. 1984. Reprint. Baltimore, Md.: Genealogical Publishing Co., 1987. Serves as a place-name guide for the state.

Genealogies of Rhode Island Families from the New England Historical and Genealogical Register. 2 vols. Baltimore, Md.: Genealogical Publishing Co., 1989. A second set of similar material is published from Rhode Island periodicals (see Periodicals).

Parks, Roger, ed. *Rhode Island: A Bibliography of its History*. Hanover, N.H.: University Press of New England, 1985. An excellent, comprehensive bibliography.

Sherman, Ruth Wilder. *Peleg Burroughs's Journal, 1778–1798: The Tiverton, R.I. Years of the Humbly Bold Baptist Minister*. Warwick, R.I.: Rhode Island Genealogical Society, 1981. An extraordinary example of day-to-day living in the late eighteenth century, including genealogical information and social history.

Sperry, Kip. *Rhode Island Sources for Family Historians and Genealogists*. Logan, Utah: Everton, 1986. Alphabetical organization of source records that can be found, with basic research maps, in the state and in the FHL.

Maps

An excellent map of Rhode Island and Providence Plantations, 1636–65, makes clear the location and dates of purchase for all of the early settlements. Land disputes and dates of boundaries of resolution are included. A copy can be found in James Truslow Adams, ed., *Atlas of American History* (New York, N.Y.: Charles Scribner's Sons, 1943). Two other excellent published map resources are John Hutchins Cady, *Rhode Island Boundaries, 1636–1936* (Providence, R.I.: State of Rhode Island and Providence Plantations, 1936), and Marion I. Wright and Robert J. Sullivan, *Rhode Island Atlas* (Providence, R.I.: Rhode Island Publications Society, 1982).

Perhaps the largest collection of maps in the state can be found at the Rhode Island Historical Society, although some of these are on microfilm through the FHL. A "Chronological Checklist of Maps in Rhode Island in the Rhode Island Historical Society Library," published in *Rhode Island Historical Collections* 11 (1918): 47–55, continues serially through the next several volumes. Among the more relevant to genealogical research are the Wallings Series and the *Beers' Atlas* of 1870, the first one produced for the state. Over 200 categories of maps are listed in the checklist.

Town offices usually have lot maps, although no statewide survey exists.

Land Records

State-Land State

From the beginning of the settlement, as in Connecticut and Vermont, land transactions in Rhode Island were filed in the town office in either proprietors' records or deed books. Indexes to the records are just as varied as they are in the rest of New England. Some grantor/grantee indexes are by surname only, some by surname and first initial instead of full name. Land was divided by proprietors in a pattern of lots. Metes and bounds were the usual land descriptions when the transaction did not involve an easily identified part of the lot or full lot.

One group of land records was recorded by the colony during the seventeenth century. Such transactions produced a multivolume collection entitled "Rhode Island Land Evidence," which is located at the Rhode Island State Archives. Volume 1 has been abstracted and published as *Rhode Island Land Evidence, Volume 1* (1921; reprint, Baltimore, Md.: Genealogical Publishing Co., 1970). Abstracts of volumes 2, 3, 4, and 5 have been printed in *Rhode Island Roots* (see Periodicals).

Some unindexed, unpublished deeds from the 1640s which did not appear in the first volume of *Records of the Colony of Rhode Island* (see Background Sources) are at the Rhode Island Archives.

Probate Records

Unlike any other state in New England, from colonial times probate functions have been organized by town, not county or separate probate district. The town council, in addition to its normal function, handled probate matters in Rhode Island. Wills were accepted and challenged, executors authorized, administrators appointed, inventories ordered, and estates distributed, although the town council book, probate book, or will book differed from town to town. It was not until much later that a certain uniformity began to take hold in the recording procedures, dividing town functions into separate books instead of locating them on whatever blank parchment space was available in the office or home of a council member.

Court Records

Courts kept the only countywide records in Rhode Island, and that has been the case since the inception of counties in 1729. Previous to that the general court of trials existed for the entire state along with several lower courts. All the colonial court records from colonial and state courts from 1645–1900 are located at the Rhode Island Superior Court Judicial Records Center, 1 Hill Street, Pawtucket, Rhode Island 02860. This is intended as a temporary repository until the state has a new archives building. Records are presently open only to scholarly researchers by permission. Eventually it is hoped they will be more accessible for genealogical research. Clarence S. Brigham's "Report on the Archives of Rhode Island," made in 1903 to the American Historical Society annual meeting, indicates what was extant then. A few have been lost or damaged since that time. Beginning in 1729 with the formation of counties, a superior court of judicature (criminal) and inferior court of common pleas (civil) as well as a supreme court were established, similar to those in Massachusetts. Debts, divorces, and trespass claims are found within the court records for each county.

Court records that are or will be in print shortly include records of the general court of trials: *Rhode Island Court Records: Records of the Court of Trials of the Colony of Providence Plantations,* 2 vols. (Providence, R.I.: Rhode Island Historical Society, 1920, 1922), which covers 1647–70, and *Gleanings from Newport Court Files,* Vol. 1 (through 1730) to be published by Jane F. Fiske in 1991.

Tax Records

Tax records pre-date the Revolution and may be found at the town clerk's office, Rhode Island State Archives, or the Rhode Island Historical Society. The clerk's office usually has an inventory of tax list holdings. No other attempt has been made to catalog or inventory tax records, though when they exist on a year-by-year basis, they provide good evidence for the social status of a family and its presence in a town when no land is owned.

Cemetery Records

Rhode Island cemetery records exist in abundance. As with other New England states, the local DAR chapters have been collecting gravestone inscriptions and indexing them in typed volumes annually. A complete set of their work can be found at the DAR Library in Washington and the Rhode Island Historical Society.

James N. Arnold gathered gravestone inscriptions from many Rhode Island cemeteries. Part of his collection of handwritten bound manuscripts is at the Rhode Island Historical Society, while the notebooks with a card index are at the Knight Memorial Library, 275 Elmwood Avenue, Providence, Rhode Island 02907.

Another excellent collection on microfilm at the Rhode Island Historical Society is the Benns Collection at the East Greenwich Public Library, 82 Pierce Street, East Greenwich, Rhode Island 02818. Newport Historical Society (see Archives, Libraries, and Societies), has some cemetery records as well. David Dumas, "Rhode Island Grave

Records," *Rhode Island Roots* 3 (1977):1–6, is an excellent guide to locating many of the manuscript and typescript collections. The Historic Graves Commission for Rhode Island has devised a list of all cemeteries declared "historical." The Rhode Island State Archives holds the Graves Registration List, organized by town, of historical cemeteries.

Church Records

Quakers, Anglicans, and Baptists all managed to develop a strong presence in Rhode Island and Providence Plantations. Although church records never reach quite the comprehensiveness that is characteristic of Massachusetts in the seventeenth century, there are strong collections in the state, many still held and maintained by the local organization. A WPA survey of church records conducted in 1939 was updated to 1970 by the Rhode Island State Archives when the microfilming was completed for the FHL. Information may be obtained by request addressed to the Rhode Island State Archives (see Archives, Libraries, and Societies).

Baptist. In a colony founded by Roger Williams, this is the historical home of the Baptists in this country. Since infant baptism was not practiced, the earliest church records have more social than genealogical value. The Newport Historical Society Library has some of these records. Ministers often carried their own records with them that included marriages. Some of these are printed in Arnold (see Vital Records). Later Baptist records can be found at the Rhode Island Historical Society and the local church.

Society of Friends. Arnold's volume 7 (see Vital Records) is devoted to the vital records for Narragansett and Rhode Island Friends. An index rather than a transcript of the records, some of the valuable items such as witnesses to marriages are not included and need to be found in the original records. Those for the settlements on the island of Rhode Island are at the Newport Historical Society. Rhode Island Historical Society's manuscript department has a curator for the Friends materials for the rest of the colony. Many Rhode Island Quaker families migrated to Monmouth County, New Jersey, as well as Dutchess County, New York, and North Carolina. Some others moved with the sea trade to the Caribbean.

Episcopal. Three Episcopal congregations were established in Rhode Island by the early eighteenth century. Volume 10 of Arnold has the earliest extant baptisms and marriages for Trinity Church at Newport with the originals now at the Newport Historical Society. Wilkins Updike's *History of the Episcopal Church at Narragansett*, 3 vols. (Boston, Mass.: D. B. Updike, 1907) is a complete transcription of that church's records from 1718 to 1774, whereas Arnold's Volume 10 reports just the vital records for the church up to 1875.

Roman Catholic. Both French and Irish Catholic churches developed in the nineteenth century. See Patrick T. Conley and Matthew J. Smith, *Catholicism in Rhode Island: The Formative Era* (Providence, R.I.: Diocese of Providence, 1976). Records can be located at the Diocesan Archives, 1 Cathedral Square, Providence, Rhode Island 02903, or at the individual parishes. A few of the early Irish records are at the Chancery Archives of the Archdiocese of Boston (see Massachusetts—Church Records).

Military Records

Shipwrecks, privateering, slave trading, and smuggling were all part of everyday life in colonial Rhode Island. Many materials illustrative of military service concerning these events are housed at the Rhode Island State Archives, but there is no cumulative index. The first published material on military service in the state is Joseph J. Smith's *Civil and Military List of Rhode Island, 1647–1850*, 3 vols. (Providence, R.I.: Preston and Rounds, 1900–07), with a full index published in the last volume. Unfortunately, only officers are included for the Revolutionary War. George M. Bodge's *Soldiers of King Philip's War* (1906; reprint, Baltimore, Md.: Genealogical Publishing Co., 1976) deals with all of New England. However, Rhode Island was heavily involved in all of the colonial wars since it depended so heavily on sea trade with England and other European countries. Rhode Island State Archives material concerning the colonial wars is published by the Rhode Island Historical Society in Providence in three volumes by Howard M. Chapin, *Rhode Island in the Colonial Wars: A List of Rhode Island Soldiers and Sailors in King George's War, 1740–48; Rhode Island Privateers in King George's War, 1739–48;* and *Rhode Island Soldiers and Sailors in the Old French and Indian War, 1755–62.*

In a more complete form than Smith's, revolutionary records appear in volume 12 of Arnold and in Benjamin Cowell's *Spirit of '76 in Rhode Island* (1850; reprint, Baltimore, Md.: Genealogical Publishing Co., 1973). In addition, Mildred M. Chamberlain's *The Rhode Island 1777 Military Census* (Baltimore, Md.: Genealogical Publishing Co., 1985) lists men in age categories 16–50, 50–60, and over 60, and whether they were able for service. But, since Portsmouth, Middletown, and Newport were occupied by the British at the time, no returns exist for those towns. Those for Exeter, Little Compton, and New Shoreham appear to be lost. A card file at the Rhode Island State Archives indexes men who served in the Revolution.

Adjutant General's Office records before 1865 are now located at the Rhode Island State Archives, although the report entitled *Annual Report . . . for the Year 1865, Official Register, Rhode Island Officers and Enlisted Men, U.S. Army and Navy*, 2 vols. (Providence, R.I.: State Printer, 1893–95), is usually available in research libraries with New England collections and is the official register for the Civil War.

Military records for service from the Civil War through World War I can be obtained from the Adjutant General's Office, 1051 North Main Street, Providence, Rhode Island 02904.

Periodicals, Newspapers, and Manuscript Collections

Periodicals

Rhode Island Roots is the quarterly of the Rhode Island Genealogical Society. Transcriptions of early Rhode Island records and family genealogies are the focus of its material.

Rhode Island Genealogical Register is an independent journal (P.O. Box 585, East Princeton, Massachusetts 01517) devoted to publishing original source material for Rhode Island.

Several periodicals were published in the past including *The Newport Historical Magazine* (1880–84), *The Rhode Island Historical Magazine* (1844–87), *Rhode Island Historical Tracts* (1877–96), *Rhode Island Historical Society Collections* (1827–1914), *Rhode Island Historical Society Publications* (1893–1900).

Genealogical material from the old journals is reprinted in *Genealogies of Rhode Island Families from Rhode Island Periodicals,* 2 vols. (Baltimore, Md.: Genealogical Publishing Co., 1983).

Newspapers

The first newspaper, the *Gazette,* was published in Newport in 1732. Because of Rhode Island's unique position as one of the early "jumping off" points in a highly mobile community moving west and south, its newspapers tended to carry marriage and death notices for many former residents. Arnold's volumes 12 through 21 carry abstracts of many of these records.

The Rhode Island Historical Society is the official repository in the state for all published newspapers; however, abstracts of vital records from them may be found in several other repositories. The Rhode Island Historical Society itself has some abstracts and indexes. One is a microfilm card index to the *Providence Journal* and the *Providence Bulletin.*

Manuscripts

While many town and city libraries have manuscript collections consisting of personal and business papers both from the broader community and professional genealogists, the three largest are at Rhode Island Historical Society, Newport Historical Society (see Archives, Libraries, and Societies), and Brown University, John Hay Library, 1 Prospect Street, Providence, Rhode Island 02912, which is particularly strong in nineteenth-century material.

Archives, Libraries, and Societies

Rhode Island State Archives
337 Westminster Street
Providence, RI 02903

Service can be obtained by mail and appointment. The archives holds the state's census, military records, colonial petitions, and correspondence. Much of the material is also available on microfilm through the FHL.

Rhode Island Historical Society
121 Hope Street
Providence, RI 02906

The society publishes *A Guide to Genealogical Materials at the Rhode Island Historical Society Library,* which lists such things as the federal and state census records, Quaker meeting records for all of New England, extensive gravestone records, and manuscripts.

Rhode Island Genealogical Society
13 Countryside Drive
Cumberland, RI 02864

The above is the address of the recording secretary and is subject to change. *Rhode Island Roots* is included quarterly with membership.

Newport Historical Society
82 Touro Street
Newport, Rhode Island 02840

Library holdings include church, early town, and cemetery records for Newport and a good manuscript collection with ship logs.

Special Focus Categories

Immigration

Newport, Bristol and, to a lesser extent, Providence, were ports of entry for the slave trade (see Black American, below) in the colony's early history and the choice for later immigrants. Immigration records are held by the National Archives and available regionally at the National Archives-New England Region (see page 8).

U.S. Customs Service passenger records for the ports of Providence (1820–67), Newport (1820-57), and Bristol and Warren (1820-71) are included in NARA microfilm publication M575 and are held regionally at the National Archives-New England Region (see page 8). *Index to Passengers Arriving at Providence, R.I., June 18, 1911–October 5, 1954* (NARA microfilm publication T518) as well as the passenger lists to 1943 are available on microfilm at the National Archives.

Naturalization

Naturalizations granted (1842–1904) by the Federal District Court at Providence are included in the soundex cards for all of New England (1790–1906) held at the National Archives-New England Region (see Massachusetts—Naturalization).

Since naturalizations were also granted by other courts, both at the county and state level, they can be hard to find. Court records previously at the Providence College Library have been moved to the superior court at the Rhode Island Superior Court Judicial Records Center, 1 Hill Street, Pawtucket, Rhode Island 02860. Both the Records Center and the State Archives have a personal name index to these records from 1793–1900 on microfilm.

Black American

As part of the "Triangular Slave Trade" with the South and the Caribbean, Rhode Island's economy was heavily reliant on slave trade. However, slavery waned in acceptance during the Revolutionary War. Despite the slave trade, Rhode Island had one of the first anti-slavery laws. Records of blacks as both slaves and free citizens exist in abundance in Rhode Island, integrated in all varieties of public records. The Rhode Island State Archives has numerous collections that document the role of black soldiers in the Revolutionary War. Not much has been published, however.

The Rhode Island Historical Society, in its large collection of manuscript material, has many records on blacks, although they have not been inventoried for genealogical research purposes. The Rhode Island Black Heritage Society, 45 Hamilton Street, Providence, Rhode Island 02907, is at work developing such research materials. Membership is open, and mail inquiries are answered.

Native American

Rhode Island's native population sold their land to the outcasts from Plymouth and Massachusetts Bay colonies to create the earliest settlements in the state. The early manuscript holdings in the Rhode Island State Archives contain information on Narragansetts and their descendants who managed to stay in the state long after the demise, through either death or slavery after King Philip's War, of most other tribes in New England. "Indian" is a term found often in all categories of records for the state. As with black slaves, natives often took the names of their owners or those to whom they were indentured, making it critical to follow white families of the same surnames. For excellent historical background see Sydney S. Rider, *The Lands of Rhode Island as They were Known to Canonicus and Miantunnomu* (Providence, R.I.: the author, 1904).

Other Ethnic Groups

French, Jewish, and Portuguese communities have existed in the state from an early time. For Jewish research, Rhode Island Jewish Historical Society, 130 Sessions Street, Providence, Rhode Island 02906, offers annual state and local meetings and projects. It publishes *Rhode Island Jewish Historical Notes* with a query column.

The early French were Huguenots soon integrated into Rhode Island's population. The American-French Genealogical Society, P.O. Box 2113, Pawtucket, Rhode Island 02861, is primarily concerned with French-Canadians who came for work in the nineteenth century mills. Membership is open to French-Canadian or French researchers, but inquiries regarding the society's library are answered by mail for a per surname fee. The society publishes *Je Me Souviens* with membership. See also Albert K. Aubin, *The French in Rhode Island* (Pawtucket, R.I.: American French Genealogical Society, 1981).

County Resources

The major genealogical use for counties in Rhode Island is the pursuit of court records and federal census returns. Before 1729 there were no county courts in Rhode Island. Two counties became incorporated in 1703, Providence and Newport. By 1750 all of Rhode Island's present counties existed, and no more developed after these were formed. Bristol became a county in 1746–47 when five towns, originally belonging to Massachusetts, were ceded to Rhode Island. Probably because the rest of the country is so oriented to counties, some of the vital records have been published in "county" groups, but the records themselves only exist on a town level.

Modern court records are at the superior court at the county seat; earlier ones have been moved (see Court Records).

Map	County Address	Date Formed Parent County/ies	Encompassed Towns
E7	Bristol Bristol 02809	1746/47 Bristol County, Mass.	Barrington, Bristol, Warren
E4	Kent East Greenwich 02818	1750 Providence	Coventry, East Greenwich, Warwick, West Greenwich, West Warwick
G6	Newport Newport 02840	1703 original	Jamestown, Little Compton, Middletown, Newport, New Shoreham (Block Island), Portsmouth, Tiverton
C3	Providence Providence 02903	1703 original	Burrillville, Central Falls, Cranston, Cumberland, East Providence, Foster, Glocester, Johnston, Lincoln, North Providence, North Smithfield, Pawtucket Providence, Scituate,Smithfield, Woonsocket
H3	Washington West Kingston 02892	1729 Narragansett Country	Charlestown, Exeter, Hopkinton, North Kingston, Narragansett, Richmond, South Kingston, Westerly

Drawn by William Dollarhide

Town Resources

No other state has the emphasis on the town that Rhode Island enjoys. Town resources are extensive, and what follows is only a brief summary. In Rhode Island, the "town records" are usually found in the town council book or the town meeting records. Brigham's inventory (see Court Records), Fiske's article (see Background Sources), and the WPA Historical Records Survey for the state all contain excellent summaries of what records are available for each town. The chart that follows draws on that material. The first column lists town (or city) and address. All correspondence concerning deeds and probates should be directed to the town or city clerk at that address. Since so much of the early material is already in print, it is wise to consult those sources first. The second column lists the date formed and the parent town/s. There are no parent counties, as such, in Rhode Island. The "Date Formed" also indicates the year one can expect to find the *first* recorded vital records in that town. Fiske's article indicates which volume of Arnold (see Vital Records) corresponds to that town's vital records. The last column indicates the beginning dates that land and probate records can be found and where the court records for that town can be located.

Some early records for the four original towns, Portsmouth, Providence, Newport, and Warwick are in print. An additional reference for town and county resources is:

Lindberg, Marcia Wiswall. *Genealogist's Handbook for New England Research.* Boston, Mass.: New England Historic Genealogical Society, 1985.

Town Address	Date Formed Parent Town/s	Land Probate Court
Barrington 283 County Road Barrington 02806	1770 Barrington, Massachusetts	1770 1770 Bristol
Originally created in 1717 as Barrington, Massachusetts, it was ceded to Rhode Island in 1747 as part of the town of Warren. Barrington, R.I., a new town, was set off from Warren in 1770. Barrington, Massachusetts records between 1717 and 1747 are in Bristol County; 1747–70 in Warren town clerk's office. This office has the town meeting records for the town since 1718.		
Bristol 10 Court Street Bristol 02809	1747 Bristol, Massachusetts	1747 1747 Bristol
Part of Plymouth Colony, 1681–86, then Bristol Co. Massachusetts. Ceded to Rhode Island, 1747. See Taunton, Massachusetts, for earlier records.		
Burrillville 70 Main Street Harrisville 02830	1806 Glocester	1806 1806 Providence
Central Falls 580 Broad Street Central Falls 02863	1895 (incorporated) Lincoln	1895 1895 Providence
Early Smithfield records are in this office.		
Charlestown P.O. Box 849 Charlestown 02813	1738 Westerly	1738 1738 Washington
Coventry 670 Flat River Road Coventry 02816	1741 Warwick	1741 1741 Kent
Cranston City Hall, 869 Park Avenue Cranston 02910	1754 Providence	1754 1754 Providence
Cumberland 45 Broad Street Cumberland 02864	1747 Attleboro Gore, Massachusetts	1747 1747 Providence
Earlier records, 1692–1747, are in Bristol County, Massachusetts, at Taunton.		
East Greenwich P.O. Box 111 East Greenwich 02818	1677 (called Dedford or Deptford, 1686–89)	1679 1679 Kent

Town Address	Date Formed Parent Town/s	Land Probate Court
East Providence 145 Taunton Avenue E. Providence 02914	1862 Rehoboth and Seekonk, Mass.	1862 1862 Providence
See Rehoboth and Seekonk, Bristol County, Massachusetts, for earlier records.		
Exeter Victory Highway Exeter 02822	1743 North Kingstown	1742 1742 Washington
Foster South Killingly Road Foster 02825	1781 Scituate	1781 1781 Providence
Glocester Main Street Chepachet 02814	1731 Providence	1731 1731 Providence
Hopkinton Town House Road Hopkinton 02833	1757 Westerly	1757 1757 Washington
Jamestown 71 Narragansett Avenue Jamestown 02835	1678 Native lands, Conanicut	1678 1678 Newport
Johnston 1385 Hartford Avenue Johnston 02919	1759 Providence	1759 1759 Providence
Probates to 1898 at Providence City Archives, Providence 02903.		
Lincoln 100 Old River Road Lincoln 02865	1871 Smithfield	1871 1871 Providence
Records before 1895 in Central Falls City Clerk's Office		
Little Compton Little Compton 02837	1682 (part of Plymouth Colony)	1747 1747 Newport
Became part of Rhode Island in 1747. Earlier records are at Plymouth Colony and Bristol County offices (see Massachusetts).		
Middletown 350 E. Main Road Middletown 02840	1743 Newport	1743 1743 Newport
Narragansett 25 Fifth Avenue Narragansett 02882	1901 South Kingston District, 1888	1888 1901 Washington
Was a district before becoming a town; 1888–1901 records in S. Kingston. Proprietor's records are in print: James Arnold, The Fones Record (1894; reprint, Baltimore, Md.: Genealogical Publishing Co., 1990).		
Newport City Clerk Newport 02840	1639 original	1639 1639 Newport
Records before 1783 at Newport Historical Society.		
New Shoreham P.O. Drawer 220 Block Island 02807	1661 (admitted to colony, 1664 as Block Island; renamed, 1672)	1672 1672 Washington
Part of Newport County until 1963.		
North Kingstown 80 Boston Neck Road Wickford 02852	1641 (renamed Kingstown, 1674; Rochester, 1686–89; North Kingstown after 1723)	1674 1674 Washington
Fire damaged all records in 1870; they are being restored.		

Town Address	Date Formed Parent Town/s	Land Probate Court
North Providence City Hall, 2008 Smith Street North Providence 02911	1765 Providence	1765 1765 Providence
North Smithfield Slatersville 02876	1871 Smithfield	1871 1871 Providence
Pawtucket City Hall, 137 Roosevelt Avenue Pawtucket 02860	1862 Pawtucket, Mass., North Providence, R.I.	1862 1862 Providence
Incorporated 1885. See Seekonk, Bristol County Massachusetts, Northern District for earlier records.		
Portsmouth 2200 E. Main Road Portsmouth 02871	1638 (called Pocasset, 1639) original	1636 1636 Newport
Pocasset proprietor's records are in manuscript form at New Bedford Massachusetts Public Library.		
Providence 25 Dorrance Street Providence 02903	1636 original	1636 1636 Providence
Providence City Archives has earlier deeds and vital records for Providence and Johnston; probates to 1898		
Richmond P.O. Box 318 Wyoming 02898	1747 Charlestown	1747 1747 Washington
Scituate Main Street N. Scituate 02857	1731 Providence	1731 1731 Providence
Smithfield 64 Farnum Pike Esmond 02917	1731 Providence	1731 1731 Providence
Records to 1870 are in city clerk's office, Central Falls 02863.		
South Kingstown 66 High Street Wakefield 02879	1723 Kingstown	1674 1674 Washington
Kingstown divided into North and South in 1723. Records before that date were in North Kingston, but damaged in 1870. Copies are here.		
Tiverton 343 Highlands Road Tiverton 02878	1747 Dartmouth and Freetown, Mass.	1747 1747 Newport
Earlier records are in Bristol County offices in Taunton, Massachusetts.		
Warren 514 Main Street Warren 02885	1747 Barrington, Rehoboth, and Swansea, Mass.	1747 1747 Bristol
See Bristol County, Northern District, Taunton, Massachusetts, for earlier records.		
Warwick 3275 Post Road Apponaug 02886	1643 (as Shawomet; renamed, 1648) original	1642 1642 Kent
Westerly Westerly 02891	1669 (called Haversham, 1686–89) original	1669 1669 Washington
West Greenwich Victory Highway, RR 2 West Greenwich 02816	1741 East Greenwich	1741 1741 Kent

Town Address	Date Formed Parent Town/s	Land Probate Court
West Warwick 1170 Main Street West Warwick 02893	1913 Warwick	1913 1913 Kent
Woonsocket City Hall, 169 Main Street Woonsocket 02895 *City hall has copies of earlier deeds from parent towns beginning 1847.*	1867 Cumberland/Smithfield	1867 1867 Providence

South Carolina

Johni Cerny and Gareth L. Mark, A.G.

English claims on the area now called South Carolina dated to 1497 when John Cabot visited the New World and claimed the area for King Henry VII. These claims were the basis for Charles I's 1629 grant of "Carolana" to Sir Robert Heath, who failed to settle Carolina before the execution of Charles I in 1649. During the Commonwealth period in England, many citizens remained loyal to Charles II. At his ascension to the throne of England in 1660, eight men pressed their claims for a reward: Edward Hyde, Earl of Clarendon; George Monck, Duke of Albemarle; Lord William Craven; Lord John Berkeley; Lord Anthony Ashley Cooper, Earl of Shaftesbury; Sir George Carteret; Sir William Berkeley; and Sir John Colleton.

Charles II granted Carolina to the eight Lords Proprietors in 1663. After the claims of Heath's successors had been disposed of, the grant was revised and extended in 1665. In August 1669, over a hundred colonists sailed under the temporary command of Captain Joseph West and reached Barbados by November. Two of the original ships were lost in storms, but on 15 March 1670, the *Carolina* anchored in what is now called Bull's Bay. Permanent settlement of South Carolina had finally begun.

The first settlement, called "Old Town," was on the western side of the Ashley River at its mouth. The original settlers were entitled to headright grants, but they chose security over land, surrounding their houses with a palisade and confining themselves to ten-acre plots. Their precaution proved wise because three Spanish frigates attacked the town in August 1670; bad weather forced the Spanish to withdraw.

A new town was laid out at Oyster Point on the neck of land between the Ashley and Cooper rivers, with streets intersecting at right angles. One of the first pre-planned cities in North America, Charles Town was settled in 1680. Renamed Charleston in 1783, it was the only repository for South Carolina's public records until 1785 and remained the capital of South Carolina until the legislature moved the capital to Columbia in 1790.

South Carolinians first found economic stability in the deerskin trade, but the resulting encroachment on the territory of the Yemassee Indians led to war in 1715. South Carolina also was a leading producer of naval stores, such as pitch and tar. This trade attracted pirates to South Carolina's shores; a welcome business in the seventeenth century, it became a real problem after the Yemassee Indian War. Blackbeard sailed four ships toward Charles Town in June 1718, stopped ships at leisure, and took hostages whom he traded for medical supplies. The South Carolina assembly had repeatedly requested the crown to protect the province, and about half of the free white men—nearly 600 individuals—signed a petition to that effect in 1717. The ineffectual policies of the Lords Proprietors and their apparent inability to defend the colony led to further disaffection. When a rumor reached Charles Town in 1719 that the Spanish were readying a fleet to attack the city, revolution broke out. While not bloody, the revolution of 1719 nonetheless effectively ended the rule of the Lords Proprietors, and the crown established a provisional royal government in 1721. When the crown bought out seven of the eight proprietors in 1729, South Carolina became a royal colony.

South Carolina is divided, culturally and topographically, into Up-Country and Low Country. The topographical division runs along the fall line, approximately from Aiken to Columbia to Camden to Cheraw. Culturally, Charleston and the surrounding Tidewater region is the Low Country. Residents of the Low Country tended toward large rice or indigo plantations with great numbers of slaves. Residents of the Up-Country tended to work small farms and in general had few slaves. The government was seated at Charleston, and residents of the Up-Country often complained of unfair representation. This was based at least in part on the lack of local government.

During the three decades from the 1730s into the 1760s, the frontier families of the Up-Country frequently rebelled against the provincial government. The Low Country elite promised representation, protection against outlaws and Indian attacks, and churches and schools, but they neglected to deliver on their promises. As a result of isolation, hardships, and a growing divergence from the Low Country, residents of the Up-Country seldom bothered to travel to Charles Town, except to petition for land. The Stamp Act of 1765, which imposed taxes on many official and unofficial papers, including not only legal documents but also playing cards, affected the pocket books of the Low Country planters. While they had the political power in South Carolina, residents of the Low Country needed the support, and numbers, of Up-Country frontiersmen to resist the Stamp Act. Some autonomy was granted in the District Circuit Court Act of 1769, which divided the province into seven judicial districts. About 1772, the first courts were held outside of Charleston. See County Resources for a full explanation.

The Revolutionary War found a deeply divided South Carolina. Charlestonians planned to resist the importation of tea, and the Boston Tea Party strengthened their resolve; Up-Country Loyalists were equally resolved and attacked a fort at Ninety-Six in November 1775. The war raged throughout South Carolina for seven years. The British attacked Charleston in June 1776 but were forced to withdraw. Then, in July 1776, a Cherokee War broke out in the Up-Country. Militia from South and North Carolina, Georgia, and Virginia defeated the tribe, and the northwest corner of South Carolina was ceded by the Cherokees in the treaty of May 1777. Between 1776 and 1779, Patriots and Loyalists fought skirmishes and continued marauding attacks on each other in the Up-Country, although the Loyalists were largely suppressed. In May 1778, the British once again moved against Charleston, laying siege to the city. Charleston capitulated on 12 May 1780, and the British began moving into the Up-Country, establishing a series of outposts. Meanwhile, the suppressed Loyalists began guerilla raids on Patriot farms, and local civil war broke out in several areas. The Patriots also formed guerilla bands and harassed both the Loyalists and the British. Finally, the Patriot partisans began driving the British out of the Up-Country, with major battles at Camden (May 1781), Ninety-Six (May–June 1781), and Eutaw Springs (September 1781); the British were so weakened that they and the Loyalists were forced to withdraw to Charleston. When the British finally evacuated Charleston on 14 December 1782, over four thousand Loyalists went with them.

Rice and indigo provided economic stability to South Carolina during much of the eighteenth century; the debts accrued during the Revolutionary War and the loss of bounties to support indigo production threatened to ruin the economy. Loyalists returning from exile in the Bahamas brought a new strain of cotton that thrived in the southeast. Then, in 1793, Eli Whitney improved the cotton gin. Within a decade, short-staple cotton transformed the Up-Country into a prosperous region.

Like rice and indigo before it, cotton was a labor-intensive crop. A shortage of laborers temporarily led South Carolina to reopen the slave trade in 1803; 40,000 blacks were imported in five years. As cotton pushed its way westward, political and journalistic battles over the slavery issue divided the United States into increasingly antagonistic factions. South Carolina and its neighbors felt threatened by the north's abolitionist movement, and when Abraham Lincoln was elected to the Presidency, South Carolina called a secession convention on 17 December 1860. As the first state to secede, the first state to ratify the Constitution of the Confederate States of America, and the first state to fire shots during the Civil War, South Carolina received particularly harsh treatment when Union General William T. Sherman and his troops subdued her in 1864. Virtually destroyed, South Carolina faced difficult decades of racial and economic strife, but she recovered and today is a prosperous and healthy state.

Vital Records

A law mandating registration of all births and deaths in South Carolina was signed into law on 1 September 1914. Actual registration began in 1915, and South Carolina achieved ninety percent compliance within a few years. Original copies of birth and death certificates are filed with the state, and copies can be obtained by writing to South Carolina Department of Health and Environmental Control, Office of Vital Records and Public Health Statistics, 2600 Bull Street, Columbia, South Carolina 29201.

The above office accepts Visa or MasterCard for payment for requests made by phone. There is an additional fee for this service including postal costs. Each South Carolina county has a copy of the state's records, and a few cities have records pre-dating the statewide registration requirement: Charleston began keeping birth records in 1877 and death records in 1821, and Georgetown was authorized to establish a vital records registration system in 1883. The Church of England parishes created in 1706 recorded christenings, marriages, and burials, and these registers can serve as vital records for much of the colonial period (see Church Records).

South Carolina had no law requiring marriage licenses or registration until 1911. Assembly Act No. 70, "An Act to require Marriage Licenses and Regulate their Issuances," became effective on 1 July 1911. Licenses are on file with the judge of probate in each county. Prior to 1911, marriages were legal if performed according to canonical law; common law marriages also were recognized. Many churches recorded marriages, but when compared with the vast number of marriages that took place, the number of documented marriages is small. Marriage settlements, made by a widow and her second husband to protect the heirs of her first husband, and pre-marital agreements, not necessarily involving widows, were popular for a while. These records date from about 1760 to about 1890 and may be found in county conveyance books or the South Carolina Department of Archives and History and on microfilm at the FHL. Newspaper accounts of marriages from 1732 to the present are a primary source of marriage documentation (see Newspapers).

Until 1949, divorce was illegal in South Carolina. Since then, divorces are the province of the county court, and all inquiries should be directed to the county clerk of court.

Census Records

Federal

Population Schedules.

- Indexed—1790, 1800, 1810, 1820, 1830, 1840, 1850, 1860, 1870
- Soundex—1880, 1900, 1910, 1920

Industry and Agriculture Schedules.

- 1850, 1860, 1870, 1880

Mortality Schedules.

- 1850 (indexed), 1860 (indexed), 1870, 1880

Slave Schedules.

- 1850, 1860

Union Veterans.

- 1890

The South Carolina Department of Archives and History holds all of the federal census records either in original or microfilm form. Part of the 1800 census for Richland District is missing. The 1850 census of York and Lexington districts indicates county of birth as well as state for each person.

State

There are fragments of state census returns available at the South Carolina Department of Archives and History. The 1829 state census of Fairfield and Laurens districts and the 1839 state census of Kershaw and Chesterfield districts are extant. The population returns for the 1869 state census are complete except for Clarendon, Oconee, and Spartanburg counties. The 1875 state census returns are available for Clarendon, Newberry, and Marlboro counties, as are partial returns for Abbeville, Beaufort, Fairfield, Lancaster, and Sumter counties. The original returns are found at the South Carolina Department of Archives and History; some of the returns have been published in South Carolina's historical and genealogical periodicals.

Background Sources

Successful research in South Carolina requires the researcher to be familiar with three things: (1) the cultural and topographical division of the state into Up-Country and Low Country (see above), (2) the checkered history of local government formation (see County Resources), and (3) the laws of the state. The most comprehensive collection of South Carolina laws is found in Thomas Cooper and David J. McCord, eds., *The Statutes at Large of South Carolina,* 10 vols. (Columbia, S.C., 1836–41). See also John D. Cushing, comp., *The First Laws of the State of South Carolina* (Wilmington, Del.: Michael Glazier, 1981).

Robert M. Weir, *Colonial South Carolina—A History* (Millwood, N.Y.: KTO Press, 1983), covers South Carolina's colonial history. Researchers should consult Richard N. Coté, comp., *Local and Family History in South Carolina: A Bibliography* (Easley, S.C.: Southern Historical Press, 1981), for a comprehensive list of publications. See also John Hammond Moore, *Research Materials in South Carolina* (Columbia, S.C.: University of South Carolina Press, 1967).

Brent Howard Holcomb, *A Guide to South Carolina Genealogical Research and Records* (Columbia, S.C.: the author, 1986), and George K. Schweitzer, *South Carolina Genealogical Research* (Knoxville, Tenn.: the author, 1985), serve as guides for research in South Carolina.

No researcher can afford to overlook the Combined Alphabetical Index of the South Carolina Department of Archives and History. The Department's free pamphlet describing this resource says that it "is a computer-generated microfilm finding aid to many early and important record series held by the South Carolina Department of Archives and History. With this index the researcher can find listed in alphabetical order in one place persons and places from all the record series currently covered." Records indexed (as of January 1991) include plats, ca. 1680 to ca. 1926; colonial land grants, 1694–1776; memorials, 1731–75; conveyances, 1719–85; petitions to practice law, 1752–1867 (broken series); renunciations of dower, 1726–1887; Court of Common Pleas Summary Process Rolls, 1783–90; Court of Common Pleas Judgement Rolls, 1703–1839; Tax Returns, 1824; bills of sale, 1773–1840 and 1843–72; and Accounts Audited of Claims Growing Out of the Revolution, 1778–1804. Not all series are indexed to the same depth, and not all series cover the entire province or state; nonetheless, the Combined Alphabetical Index is one of the most valuable resources in South Carolina. See Land Records, Court Records, and Military Records (Revolutionary War) for descriptions of some of these records.

Maps

Early South Carolina maps are crucial for locating families. The South Caroliniana Library of the University of South Carolina at Columbia has the best collection of early South Carolina maps (see also Manuscripts). The South Carolina

Department of Archives and History publishes a free pamphlet, "The Formation of Counties in South Carolina," which traces the evolution of political subdivisions in the state. The Department also publishes a set of ten guide maps illustrating the development of parishes, districts, and counties.

There is no gazetteer for South Carolina, but a useful substitute is Claude Henry Neuffer, ed., *Names in South Carolina*, 30 vols. (1954–83; reprint, 4 vols., Spartanburg, S.C.: Reprint Co., 1976–84). See also Joseph B. Martin III, "Guide to Presbyterian Ecclesiastical Names and Places in South Carolina 1685–1985," *South Carolina Historical Magazine* 90 (October 1989): 4–215; and WPA, *Palmetto Place Names* (1945; reprint, Spartenberg, S.C.: Reprint Co., 1975).

Robert Mills, *Atlas of the State of South Carolina* (1825; reprint, Easley, S.C.: Southern Historical Press, 1980), is fully indexed and mentions many landowners. Thorndale and Dollarhide, *Map Guide* (see page 11) illustrate the changing boundaries of South Carolina's districts and counties at each decennial census and include census districts in 1790 and 1800 that were not legal polities. The *Map of the States of North & South Carolina* published in 1831 by Hinton & Simpkin & Marshall has been reproduced by Jonathan Sheppard Books (Box 2020, Albany, NY 12220).

Land Records

State-Land State

Land and property records, in combination with court records, are often the key to solving difficult research problems. South Carolina's colonial land records are among the most complete of the thirteen original colonies, probably because all records were maintained in Charleston, and Charleston was not destroyed during the Revolutionary War.

Land in South Carolina was granted by headright and bounty. Headrights were the "right" to free land of every "head" settling in the colony. Settlers who arrived with the first fleet were authorized headrights of 150 acres for every male aged sixteen and above and a hundred acres for every female and every male aged under sixteen. Heads-of-household could claim land for their slaves and servants as well as family members. Settlers who arrived after the first fleet and before 1756 were authorized fifty acres for each member of the household. After 1755, heads-of-household could receive a hundred acres plus an additional fifty acres for every other member of the household.

The prospective grantee first petitioned the Grand Council (see Court Records) for a warrant. The petition had to be made in person by the head-of-household; he had to give his name, the number of acres requested, and the location of the land. While there was no requirement to request all of the land due to the family, the household had to have as many persons as claimed. Petitions occasionally include names and ages of spouses and children or other genealogically valuable information. The date of petition or application is often called the precept, warrant, or pursuant date. The petitions are found at the South Carolina Department of Archives and History in one of two sets of volumes: *Records of the Grand Council*, 1671–1692, in two volumes and *Records of His Majesty's Council* in twenty-seven volumes covering the entire colonial period. These twenty-nine volumes are in chronological order and are unindexed; the precept date is required to locate the petition. See also Alexander S. Salley, Jr., and R. N. Olsberg, eds., *Warrants for Land in South Carolina, 1672–1721* (Columbia, S.C.: University of South Carolina Press, 1977), and Alexander S. Salley, Jr., *Records of the Secretary of the Province and the Register of the Province of South Carolina, 1671–1675* (Columbia, S.C.: Historical Commission of South Carolina, 1944).

After receiving a warrant, the prospective grantee carried it to a surveyor who surveyed the land and drew a plat, or map, of its boundaries. Recorded plats have important information including the precept date, necessary to locate the original petition; the survey (or certified) date; the recording date; and a full description of the land, including watercourses and location. Recorded plats are indexed in the Combined Alphabetical Index (see Background Sources).

When the plat was returned to the Surveyor General's office, the prospective grant was checked against other plats to ensure that only one person was claiming the same land. If there were no problems, grant papers were sent to the Governor for his signature and seal. Recorded grants are indexed in the Combined Alphabetical Index (see Background Sources).

Once the land was finally granted, the owner was responsible for paying a quitrent. The first quitrent payment came due within two years on headright grants and within ten years on bounty-land grants. The quitrent was a land tax that had its roots in English manorial society where "the land obligations due the manor, such as plowing and haying the lord's land, were commuted to an annual money payment. Upon payment, the obligations were 'quit' for the year."

Another important land record is the memorial. From 1731 through 1775, those who had obtained land were given the task of preparing a memorial attesting to the location, quantity, names of adjacent land owners, and the boundaries of the land. Memorials also included a chain of title, often from the original patentee to the current owner. Original memorials are located at the South Carolina Department of Archives and History and are indexed in the Combined Alphabetical Index (see Background Sources). Some memorials have been microfilmed and are available at the FHL. The following published volumes are useful:

Esker, Katie-Prince Ward. *South Carolina Memorials, 1731–1776: Abstracts of Selected Land Records from a Collection in the Department of Archives and History.* 2 vols. New Orleans, La.: Polyanthos, 1973–77.

Jackson, Ronald Vern, Gary Ronald Teeples, and David Schaefermeyer, eds., *Index to South Carolina Land Grants, 1784–1800.* Bountiful, Utah: Accelerated Indexing Systems, 1977.

Langley, Clara A. *South Carolina Deed Abstracts, 1719–1772.* 4 vols. Easley, S.C.: Southern Historical Press, 1983–84.

Lucas, Silas E., Jr., *An Index to Deeds of the Province and State of South Carolina, 1719–1785, and Charleston District, 1785–1800.* Easley, S.C.: Southern Historical Press, 1977.

The boundary between South Carolina and North Carolina was first surveyed in 1772, and a final agreement was reached in 1815. Land previously thought to be in Mecklenburg and Tryon counties, North Carolina, was found to be in South Carolina. Records of both Carolinas should be examined for colonial inhabitants of the area encompassed by present-day Cherokee, Greenville, Spartanburg, and York Counties. See Brent Howard Holcomb, comp., *North Carolina Land Grants in South Carolina* (Greenville, S.C.: A Press, 1980).

In South Carolina, deeds are often called *mesne conveyances*, or conveyances, and are recorded in the office of the register of mesne conveyance. Original records are found in each county's clerk of court office, and microfilmed copies of most pre-1865 records are available at the South Carolina Department of Archives and History and the FHL.

Probate Records

Probate records include wills, inventories, guardianship papers, estate papers, settlements, newspaper announcements, and numerous other documents. Researchers should be familiar with four terms: testate, intestate, primogeniture, and dower (see pages 5–6)—all have importance in South Carolina research.

During the colonial period, the rule of primogeniture operated in South Carolina. Under primogeniture, land automatically descended to the eldest male heir; if there were no male heirs, all female heirs shared the land equally. In South Carolina primogeniture was abolished in 1791. The division of intestate estates during the colonial period was based on an English statute of 1670, formally adopted into South Carolina law in 1712. The division of the estate after payment of all just debts and expenses was as follows: the widow, if any, received one-third of all real estate for life; the heir-at-law (eldest son) received the title to all real estate, including the widow's dower, which he inherited at her death; the widow received one-third of the personal property, and the children shared equally in the other two-thirds. If there were no widow, the children shared the personal property equally. If there were no children, the widow received one-half of the estate, and the other half was divided equally among the siblings of the deceased. Any property, real or personal, that was not bequeathed or devised in a valid will was divided according to the law.

Initially, the governor and the grand council were the only court of ordinary (probate) in the province; the secretary of the province also began functioning as a court of ordinary by 1692 (see Court Records). See Caroline T. Moore and Agatha Aimar Simmons, *Abstracts of the Wills of State of South Carolina, 1670–1800,* 4 vols. (Columbia, S.C.: R. L. Bryan, 1960–74); Caroline T. Moore, comp., *Records of the Secretary of the Province of South Carolina, 1692–1721* (Columbia, S.C.: R. L. Bryan, 1978); Brent Howard Holcomb, comp., *Probate Records of South Carolina,* 3 vols. (Easley, S.C.: Southern Historical Press, 1977); and Alexander S. Salley, Jr., "Abstracts from the Records, Court of Ordinary (Probate)," in *South Carolina Historical and Genealogical Magazine,* 8–13 (1907–12).

In 1781, the seven circuit court districts (see County Resources) were given courts of ordinary, but the only surviving records are those of Camden, Charleston, and Ninety-Six districts. See Brent Howard Holcomb and Elmer O. Parker, comps., *Old Camden District Wills and Administrations, 1781–1787* (Easley, S.C.: Southern Historical Press, 1981); Brent Howard Holcomb, comp., *Ninety-Six District Journal of the Court of Ordinary, Inventory Book, Will Book, 1781–1786* (Easley, S.C.: Southern Historical Press, 1978); and Pauline Young, comp., *Abstracts of Old Ninety-Six and Abbeville District: Wills, Bonds, Administrations, 1774–1860* (1950; reprint, Easley, S.C.: Southern Historical Press, 1977).

In 1785 the circuit court districts were subdivided into counties; courts of ordinary were established in functioning counties beginning in 1787. During the fifteen years that counties in circuit court districts existed, probate actions could be conducted in the courts of ordinary in both the county and its circuit court district. When the counties and districts were replaced by twenty-five districts (counties) in 1800, courts of ordinary were established in each district. Probate records from 1800 to the present and records of the counties and circuit court districts from 1785–1800 are found in the county's judge of probate office. See Martha Lou Houston, comp., *Indexes to the County Wills of South Carolina* (1939; reprint, Baltimore, Md.: Genealogical Publishing Co., 1970); Charleston Free Library, *Index to the Wills of Charleston County, South Carolina, 1671–1868* (Baltimore, Md.: Genealogical Publishing Co., 1974); and Pauline Young, comp., *A Genealogical Collection of South Carolina Wills and Records,* 2 vols. (1955; reprint, Easley, S.C.: Southern Historical Press, 1981).

Many probate records are among the records of the equity court. Established in 1791 and mostly disbanded by 1821, the equity courts handled partitions of property, among other probate actions (see Court Records). Maps illustrating the equity court districts are found with a brief explanation of the equity court records in Brent Howard Holcomb, "South Carolina Equity Records" *The South Carolina Magazine of Ancestral Research* 6 (1978): 235–38).

Court Records

Understanding South Carolina's court system is challenging.

Grand Council/His Majesty's Council. While South Carolina was a proprietary and crown colony, its government was centralized, and all civil administration took place at Charleston. The grand council, composed of the governor and councillors, sat as the general court, the court of chancery (equity), the court of common pleas, the court of general sessions (assize), the court of admiralty, the court of probate, and the court of appeals. Restructuring during the eighteenth century led to appointments of judges for many of these courts. All records were created and maintained in Charleston, and the extant original records are at the South Carolina Department of Archives and History.

General Court. The general court handled all cases that did not have a specific court; one of its important functions was hearing petitions for headright grants (see Land Records). The records of the general court are included in *Journals of the Grand Council,* 1671–92, and *His Majesty's Council Journals,* 1721–74, original records maintained at the South Carolina Department of Archives and History.

Court of Chancery. Established in 1721, the court of chancery handled equity cases. Prior to 1791, most cases were tried in Charleston, and all records were kept there. The South Carolina Department of Archives and History maintains the original records of the court of chancery, and there is an index to the extant cases. The court of chancery was replaced by equity circuit courts in 1791.

Equity Circuit Courts (1791–1821). The equity court, also called the chancery court, handled cases for which there were no remedies specified in South Carolina law. For example, the equitable division of a tract of land among heirs cannot be mandated in a law that would cover all cases; each division must take into account many variables, including the quality of the land.

In 1791 South Carolina was divided into three equity circuits: (1) the Upper Circuit included Ninety-Six and Washington Circuit Court districts and Spartanburg and Union counties in Pinckney Circuit Court District; (2) the Middle Circuit included the remaining counties in Pinckney Circuit Court District, plus all of Camden, Cheraws, and Orangeburgh Circuit Court districts; (3) the Lower Circuit included Beaufort, Charleston, and Georgetown Circuit Court districts.

Another division in 1799 produced four districts, each of which was divided in half; there were eight district seats. A further division in 1808 produced nine districts. By 1821, all districts/counties had their own equity court, except Cheraws District. In 1868, the equity or chancery court was combined with the court of ordinary or probate and became the court of probate.

Maps of the equity circuits are essential to understanding the locations of the districts. See Holcomb, "South Carolina Equity Records," cited under Probate Records.

Known record locations include Middle Circuit (1791–99) and Camden Circuit (1808–21) records housed in Camden County; Lower Circuit (1791–99) and Charleston Circuit (1808–21) records housed in Charleston County, Columbia Circuit (1808–21) records housed in Richland County; Western Circuit (1799–1808) and Pinckney Circuit (1808–21) records housed in Union County. The records have not been located for Upper Circuit (1791–99); Southern, Northern, Eastern, and the lower half of Western circuits (1799–1808); and Cheraws, Georgetown, Ninety-Six, Orangeburgh, and Washington circuits (1808–21).

Court of Common Pleas. This is the civil court of South Carolina. A civil court handles all cases involving private citizens or organizations against private citizens or organizations. The court of common pleas was one of the functions of the grand council during most of the colonial period. Until 1772, the court of common pleas was held in Charleston, but by 1772 courts of common pleas had been established in each of the circuit court districts (see County Resources), with records maintained in Charleston until 1785. Each of the counties within the circuit court districts formed in 1785 was authorized a court of common pleas. The counties in Beaufort, Charleston, and Georgetown districts did not function, and the counties in Orangeburgh District only functioned until about 1791. From 1785 until 1800, courts of common pleas operated at both the county and district level; extant records of both must be examined. When districts (counties) were formed in 1800, each was authorized its own court of common pleas.

The records of the court of common pleas generally include guardianship records, such as petitions, reports, and orders; renunciations of dower; and Revolutionary War pension applications. The records will be found in the clerk of court's office. Most pre-1865 court of common pleas records have been microfilmed and are available at the South Carolina Department of Archives and History and the FHL.

Court of General Sessions of the Peace, Oyer and Terminer, Assize and General Gaol Delivery. This is the criminal court of South Carolina and is generally called the court of general sessions or court of assize. The court of general sessions was one of the functions of the grand council during most of the colonial period. Until 1772, the court of general sessions was held in Charleston; by 1772 courts of general sessions had been established in each of the circuit court districts (see County Resources), with records maintained in Charleston until 1785. Each of the counties within the circuit court districts formed in 1785 was authorized a court of general sessions. The counties in Beaufort, Charleston, and Georgetown districts did not function, and the counties in Orangeburgh District only functioned until about 1791. From 1785 until 1800, courts of general sessions operated at both the county and district level; extant records of both must be examined. When districts (counties) were formed in 1800, each was authorized its own court of general sessions.

Court of Ordinary. During the colonial period, the governor acted as ordinary for the province of South Carolina, with power to grant probates and administrations; the secretary of the colony also began acting as an ordinary by 1692. Courts of ordinary were established in the circuit court districts in 1781 and in functioning counties within the circuit districts in 1787. When districts (counties) were formed in 1800, each was authorized its own court of ordinary. In 1868, the court of ordinary was combined with the court of equity (chancery) and became the court of probate.

Circuit Courts (1769–1800). Circuit courts were established by the South Carolina Assembly in 1769. The circuit courts were courts of record and included both the court of common pleas and the court of general sessions of the peace, oyer and terminer, assize and general gaol delivery. Clerks, sheriffs, and commissioners were appointed for each district. As courts of record, the circuit courts created records that were maintained in Charleston until 1785. From 1785 through 1800 the circuit courts' records were kept in the district seat. In 1800 the circuit court districts were abolished, and their records were transferred to the district/county that included the circuit court district seat. See County Resources—Circuit Court Districts, for a complete listing of the circuit court districts, their locations, and their records.

Precinct Courts. Precinct courts, also called county courts, were established in 1721. The five courts were held outside Charleston and staffed by local justices of the peace who tried minor criminal cases and civil suits. There are no extant records for the precinct courts according to the South Carolina Department of Archives and History.

County Courts. County courts were first established in 1785. The county courts were directed to maintain records of their proceedings, prove and record conveyances and renunciations of dower (see Land Records and Probate Records), license tavern-keepers, and levy taxes. Many county courts did not function until 1800, and others functioned only for a few years from 1785–91. When districts (counties) were established in 1800, the county court became the primary judicial body in the district, with three offices: the register of mesne conveyance (see Land Records); the court of common pleas; and the court of general sessions.

Many court records have been microfilmed and are available at the South Carolina Department of Archives and History and the FHL. Most libraries and archives with genealogical collections have some printed abstracts of court records.

Tax Records

With the exception of a single tax list from 1733 and occasional lists of tax collectors, no colonial tax records of South Carolina have survived. Parishes and townships functioned as tax districts until 1800; circuit court districts and their counties also functioned as tax districts from 1785–1800. The known tax lists, 1783–99, are as follows: Christ Church Parish, 1784, 1786, 1788, and 1793–99; Prince Frederick's Parish, 1784 and 1786; Prince George's Parish, 1786–87; Prince William's Parish, 1798; St. Andrew's Parish, 1784–85, 1787, 1789, 1791, and 1795; St. Bartholomew's Parish, 1783–87 and 1798; St. Helena's Parish, 1798; St. James Goose Creek, 1796; St. John's Berkeley Parish, 1793; St. Luke's Parish, 1798–99; St. Paul's Parish, 1783, 1785–96, and 1798–99; Ninety-Six District, 1787; Orangeburgh District, 1787; Lancaster County in Camden District, 1797; and Lexington County in Orangeburgh District, 1788. Many of these tax lists are incomplete. They are located at the South Carolina Department of Archives and History.

Most districts/counties have some tax records dating from 1800 to the present, with the majority of tax records dating from 1865. A fairly complete series from 1824, mostly of the Low Country districts, is available at the South Carolina Department of Archives and History and is indexed in the Combined Alphabetical Index (see Background Sources). The South Carolina Department of Archives and History has originals of most extant tax lists, and microfilmed copies of county tax records are available at the South Carolina Department of Archives and History and the FHL.

The best available substitutes for colonial tax lists are jury lists. The jury lists include men eligible to serve on juries and were compiled from tax lists. See Mary Bondurant Warren, comp., *South Carolina Jury Lists, 1718–1783* (Danielsville, Ga.: Heritage Papers, 1977). Ge Lee Corley Hendrix and Morn McKoy Lindsay, comps., *The Jury Lists of South Carolina, 1778–1779* (1975; reprint, Baltimore, Md.: Genealogical Publishing Co., 1980), is accepted as proof of service for Revolutionary War patriots.

Voter registration lists, 1867, 1868, and 1898 are another valuable substitute for tax records. The lists from 1867 and 1868 are particularly useful for Black American research because the newly freed slaves registered to vote; many blacks make their first appearance in the voter registration lists. Although voter registration was conducted by counties, the originals of the 1867, 1868, and 1898 lists are at the South Carolina Department of Archives and History; counties maintained copies for their records.

Directories for the city of Charleston date from 1782. These directories may help locate a Charleston ancestor who does not appear in other records. They are housed at the Charleston Library Society (see Archives, Libraries, and Societies).

Church Records

In the absence of early marriage and vital records, South Carolina church records play an important role in genealogical research. The Church of England (known later as the Protestant Episcopal church) was established as the official state-supported church of South Carolina in 1706, with responsibility for recording births, christenings, marriages, and burials. Between 1706 and 1778, twenty-five parishes were established, including two for the Huguenots, who were allowed to use a French version of the Book of Common Prayer. All of the extant parish registers have been published; most have appeared in *The South Carolina Historical and Genealogical Magazine* or in book form. Extant records of the Protestant Episcopal Church may also be found in the Dalcho Historical Society, Episcopal Diocese of

South Carolina, 1020 King Street, Charleston, South Carolina 29403.

Quakers settled in South Carolina early; the first group was joined by emigrants from Ireland in the 1750s and by Quakers from Pennsylvania, North Carolina, New Jersey, New York, and Virginia after 1760. See William F. Medlin, *Quaker Families of South Carolina and Georgia* (Ben Franklin Press, 1982). South Carolina Quaker records are included in William Wade Hinshaw, ed., *Encyclopedia of American Quaker Genealogy*, vol. 1 (1936; reprint, Baltimore, Md.: Genealogical Publishing Co., 1969).

French Huguenots began to settle permanently in South Carolina in 1685 when land grants were issued along the shoreline. While most of the group's early records have been lost, some publications speak of early members and their families. See *Transactions of the Huguenot Society of South Carolina* (1888–present), the publication of the Huguenot Society of South Carolina, 25 Chalmers Street, Charleston, South Carolina 29401.

Presbyterians established their denomination in South Carolina during the early eighteenth century and later became associated with the Reformed Presbyterian Church. See *Inventory of the Church Archives of South Carolina Presbyterian Churches: 1969 Arrangement with Indexes* (South Carolina Historical Records Survey, WPA, 1969). Write to the Historical Foundation of the Presbyterian and Reformed Churches, P.O. Box 847, Montreat, North Carolina 29757, or Presbyterian College Library, Due West, South Carolina 29325.

Lutherans also established themselves in South Carolina during the eighteenth century with the arrival of German and Swiss settlers. Early Evangelical Lutheran records are excellent genealogical resources. Write to Lutheran Theological Seminary Library, Columbia, South Carolina 29203.

The first Roman Catholic parish was established at Charleston in 1789. Known for keeping excellent records of christenings, marriages, and burials, the church has preserved its registers at the Charleston Diocesan Archives, Chancery Office, 119 Broad Street, P.O. Box 818, Charleston, South Carolina 29402.

The Baptist church is contemporary South Carolina's largest religious group, despite the fact that it was not established there until 1783. Write to South Carolina Baptist Historical Collection, James B. Duke Library, Poinsett Highway, Furman University, Greenville, South Carolina 29613. A list of the church records available at the James B. Duke Library is found in the *Journal of the South Carolina Baptist Historical Society* 3 (1977): 32–43.

Methodists arrived in South Carolina about 1783. Methodist records include conference records, membership lists, and historical and biographical information. Write to South Carolina Methodist Conference Archives, Sandor Teszler Library, Wofford College, Spartanburg, South Carolina 29301.

Some of South Carolina's church records have been microfilmed. Copies are available at the South Carolina Department of Archives and History and the FHL.

Cemetery Records

The WPA and the DAR have compiled major collections of South Carolina tombstone inscriptions. Cote, *Local and Family History*, cited in Background Sources, provides a listing of major published collections. Most South Carolina counties have historical or genealogical societies that have compiled cemetery records. Schweitzer has addresses for local historical and genealogical societies. Cemetery records are frequently published in the major genealogical periodicals of South Carolina (see Periodicals).

Military Records

Colonial Wars. South Carolina's military history began in 1670 when the Spanish attacked "Old Town." Frequent battles with the Spanish, French, and Indian tribes continued throughout the colonial period. Unfortunately, few records have survived to tell of the participants and the nature of their involvement. Leonardo Andrea compiled a list of soldiers who served in various military capacities between 1715 and 1772 in *South Carolina Colonial Soldiers and Patriots* (Columbia, S.C., 1952). See also Murtie June Clark, *Colonial Soldiers of the South, 1732–1774* (Baltimore, Md.: Genealogical Publishing Co., 1986). Mention of South Carolina soldiers may be found in works dealing with specific wars of a national or regional scope.

Revolutionary War. South Carolinians were heavily involved in the Revolutionary War on both sides. Although some records were destroyed, the Revolutionary War resources for South Carolina are quite rich.

Patriots who served in the Continental Line may be found by examining the National Archives microfilm publications (see page 7) which are available at the South Carolina Department of Archives and History and the FHL. Original pension records are available at the National Archives, but a published index is widely available.

South Carolina militia units that participated in the Revolutionary War are not included in the service records listed above. A recent compilation of Patriot records, including militia records, is Bobby Gilmer Moss, comp., *Roster of South Carolina Patriots in the American Revolution* (Baltimore, Md.: Genealogical Publishing Co., 1983). See also Alexander S. Salley, Jr., comp., *South Carolina Provincial Troops in Papers of the First Council of Safety, 1775* (1900–02; reprint, Baltimore, Md.: Genealogical Publishing Co., 1977).

Loyalists may be found in Murtie June Clark, *Loyalists in the Southern Campaign of the Revolutionary War*, 3 vols. (Baltimore, Md.: Genealogical Publishing Co., 1981). See also *South Carolina Royalist Troops, Muster Rolls, 1777–1783*, on two microfilm reels at the South Caroliniana Library in Columbia (see Archives, Libraries, and Societies).

Many South Carolinians can be found in the *Accounts Audited of Claims Growing Out of the Revolution* at the South Carolina Department of Archives and History. The

Accounts Audited are indexed in the Combined Alphabetical Index (see Background Sources).

Stub Indents are another important resource. When South Carolina paid claims for goods, services, or damages from the Revolutionary War, they were paid with certificates called indents. Rather like stub checkbooks, the certificates were in two parts: one part was issued to the claimant as compensation; the other part was a stub on which pertinent information, such as the claimant's name, the nature of the claim, and the amount paid was recorded. The state retained the stub of the indents, and they are found at the South Carolina Department of Archives and History in Office of the Commissioners of the Treasury, *Stub Indents and Indexes, 1779–1791,* 22 vols. See also Alexander S. Salley, Jr., ed., *Stub Entries to Indents Issued in Payment of Claims Against South Carolina Growing Out of the Revolution,* 12 vols. (Columbia, S.C.: University of South Carolina Press, 1910–27). Irregularly issued reprints may be available.

War of 1812. The National Archives has service records, pension files, and indexes to the War of 1812 service and pension records (see page 7). See also Virgil D. White, comp., *Index to War of 1812 Pension Files,* 3 vols. (Waynesboro, Tenn.: National Historical Publishing Co., 1989). Extensive manuscript and microfilmed records of South Carolina units and soldiers of the War of 1812 are at the South Caroliniana Library in Columbia (see Archives, Libraries, and Societies).

Civil War. The military personnel records of the Confederate States of America, along with other confederate records captured by the Union Army, were taken to Washington and preserved by the War Department. Consequently, service records for South Carolina Confederate soldiers can be found in the National Archives. See the National Archives microfilm publications: *Compiled Service Records of Confederate Soldiers Who Served in Organizations from the State of South Carolina; Index to the Compiled Service Records of Confederate Soldiers Who Served in Organizations from the State of South Carolina;* and *(Service) Records Relating to Confederate Naval and Marine Personnel.* These three series are available at the National Archives and the South Carolina Department of Archives and History. See also Alexander S. Salley, Jr., comp., *South Carolina Troops in Confederate Service,* 3 vols. (Columbia, S.C.: R. L. Bryan, 1913–14, 1930). References to South Carolina regimental histories are found in C. E. Dornbusch, comp., *Military Bibliography of the Civil War,* vol. 2 (New York, N.Y.: New York Public Library, 1967), pp. 84–90.

South Carolina enacted a pension law for indigent Confederate veterans in 1888. Subsequent revisions in 1895, 1896, 1900, 1903, and 1910 added widows of veterans and all veterans who gave service in any Confederate state. A complete revision in 1919 established the Confederate Pension Department and County Pension Boards. Virtually all veterans and their widows qualified for pensions, but everyone receiving or wishing to receive a pension had to reapply. The reapplications are at the South Carolina Department of Archives and History and are indexed in the "Card File Index of 1919–1926 South Carolina Confederate Pension Applications" at the Department.

Periodicals, Newspapers, and Manuscript Collections

Periodicals

South Carolina historical and genealogical organizations publish excellent periodicals including *South Carolina Historical Magazine* (Charleston, S.C.: South Carolina Historical Society, 1900–present), *Carolina Herald* (Greenville, S.C.: Carolina Genealogical Society, 1974–present), and *Transactions of the Huguenot Society of South Carolina* (Charleston, S.C.: Huguenot Society of South Carolina, 1888–present). Two important private publications are *The South Carolina Magazine of Ancestral Research* (Columbia, S.C.: Brent Howard Holcomb, 1973–present) and *Carolina Genealogist* (Danielsville, Ga.: Mary B. Warren, 1969–present). The South Carolina Department of Archives and History and the FHL have these and other periodicals pertaining to South Carolina genealogy.

Newspapers

South Carolina's newspaper history began with the publication of the first issue of the *South Carolina Gazette* in 1732. The largest collection of South Carolina newspapers is found at the South Caroliniana Library; the Charleston Library Society and the South Carolina Department of Archives and History have slightly smaller collections (see Archives, Libraries, and Societies for addresses).

Newspapers are an important source of South Carolina vital records because marriage and death notices appeared in most newspapers. Newspaper extracts have been regularly published in *The South Carolina Magazine of Ancestral Research* and *South Carolina Historical Magazine* (see Periodicals). Dozens of published books of newspaper extracts are available. A bibliography is found in George K. Schweitzer, *South Carolina Genealogical Research* (Knoxville, Tenn.: the author, 1985), pp. 114–19.

Manuscripts

There are two major manuscript collections of South Carolina genealogical material. Leonardo Andrea compiled a vast collection of research notes tracing families during their residence in South Carolina as well as tracking them back to earlier residences and forward as they migrated south and west. The Leonardo Andrea Collection is available on microfilm at the FHL. Motte Alston Read collected information on colonial South Carolina families from court records, deeds, church records, newspapers, and other sources. The Motte Alston Read Collection is housed at the South Carolina Historical Society and is available on microfilm at the FHL.

The largest collection of South Carolina manuscripts is housed at the South Caroliniana Library of the University of South Carolina in Columbia. The Manuscript Division holds over 1.3 million manuscripts, including church records, letters, Bible records, and numerous other public and private records. See Allen H. Stokes, Jr., comp., *A Guide to the Manuscript Collection of the South Caroliniana Library* (Columbia, S.C.: South Caroliniana Library, 1982).

Archives, Libraries, and Societies

South Carolina Department of Archives and History
1430 Senate Street
P.O. Box 11669, Capitol Station
Columbia, SC 29211-1669

Publishes *The New South Carolina State Gazette.* The South Carolina Department of Archives and History has South Carolina county and district records, colonial and state records, federal census records and indexes, colonial land records indexes, military records, and a large microfilm collection of genealogical and historical information. Most pre-1865 records are housed at the South Carolina Department of Archives and History, but some local records are found only in county courthouses. The Department of Archives and History also produces the Combined Alphabetical Index (see Background Sources). The holdings of the South Carolina Department of Archives and History are detailed in *A Guide to Local Government Records in the South Carolina Archives* (Columbia, S.C.: University of South Carolina Press, 1988).

South Carolina Genealogical Society
P.O. Box 16355
Greenville, SC 29606

Publishes *Carolina Herald.*

South Carolina Historical Society
100 Meeting Street
Charleston, SC 29401

Publishes *South Carolina Historical Magazine.* The South Carolina Historical Society maintains a library with a large collection of genealogical and historical records and publications. See David Moltke-Hansen and Sallie Dosser, comps., *South Carolina Historical Society Manuscript Guide* (Charleston, S.C.: South Carolina Historical Society, 1979), and supplements published in the *South Carolina Historical Magazine.*

South Caroliniana Library
University of South Carolina
Columbia, SC 29208

The library has a Book Division with over 65,000 volumes in book or microform and a Manuscript Division with over 1.3 million manuscripts (see Manuscripts). The library also has a major collection of newspapers.

Charleston Library Society
164 King Street
Charleston, SC 29401

The Society was founded in 1748 and collected books, magazines, and pamphlets by subscription. Although virtually destroyed in 1778, the collection was rebuilt. The Society has an important collection of eighteenth century newspapers and also houses a collection of Charleston City Directories dating from 1782.

Special Focus Categories

Immigration

Passenger lists for the Port of Charleston are at the National Archives (see page 10): NARA microfilm publication series M575 includes arrivals, 1820–28; NARA microfilm publication series M334 is an index.

Black American

Blacks arrived with the first ships in 1670 and were the majority of South Carolina's population, as slaves, from about 1708 to the eve of the Revolutionary War. When the 1820 U.S. Census was conducted, blacks were again in the majority, a position they retained until the 1920s. They brought many important skills with them to South Carolina and made a significant contribution to the planter society of the state.

Researchers cannot afford to overlook the Voter Registration Lists of 1867 and 1868. Blacks in South Carolina gained temporary control of the state through their voting majority; many recently freed slaves made their first appearance in the Voter Registration Lists.

Lists of free persons of color, slave lists, plantation records, personal and family records, bills of sale, account books, indentures, and a variety of similar records attest to blacks in South Carolina. The South Carolina Department of Archives and History, College of Charleston, South Carolina Historical Society, University of South Carolina, and Winthrop College have important collections of these types of records and manuscripts. Not every South Carolina district or county created or preserved each type of record listed above. In fact, the number of local records attesting to a specific slave is small when compared with those available for people who were not enslaved. The best sources of information about slaves are district (county) estate and property records. See also James Rose and Alice Eichholz, *Black Genesis* (cited on page 10).

County Resources

District/Counties, 1800–present. In 1800 the nine circuit court districts and thirty-seven counties were abolished and replaced by twenty-five districts. Some of the new districts were identical with counties in districts established 1785–99; other districts were new polities entirely. As the highest level of local government, all twenty-five districts had equal status and record-keeping functions. The original districts expanded and divided between 1800 and 1867 to become thirty districts. Under the new constitution adopted in 1868, districts were renamed counties.

The forty-six present-day counties in South Carolina trace their lineage to the formation of districts in 1800. Although many can trace their geographical lineage to 1785, and some can trace their records lineage to 1785, any listing of counties that provides a formation date pre-1800 misses the essential point that the pre-1800 counties were not the highest level of local government. Before 1800, all counties were counties in circuit court districts; residents could conduct their business in either the county or the circuit court district, and researchers must check the records of both. See County Resources—Districts/Counties, for a complete listing of the counties of South Carolina and their records.

The listing of Districts/Counties includes all districts and counties in existence from 1800 to the present and refers to the county, or county and circuit court district from which the district was formed. Some counties functioned before 1800, and the date those counties began functioning is recorded. The beginning dates for land, probate, and court records are the first indicated for the type of record specified in each county's courthouse and may include records of an earlier polity. Many records were destroyed, particularly near the end of the Civil War, and many other records are fragmentary; dates given for the first record do not imply that all records from that date are extant. Residents of the Up-Country counties often kept records when they acquired local government, so some of the records pre-date the formation of local governments.

Counties in Districts, 1785–1800. In 1785 the seven circuit court districts were subdivided into thirty-three counties. Inferior courts were established in some of the counties, and record-keeping began at the local level. However, the circuit court districts continued to function, and many local actions were conducted at the district seat instead of the county seat. Three districts—Beaufort, Charleston, and Georgetown—were allowed to postpone the formation of county governments, and their counties never functioned. The residents of Orangeburgh District also preferred district government to county government, and three of the four counties in that district were disused from 1791 through 1799.

While many present-day counties were established geographically between 1785 and 1799, the counties created during that period did not keep records or function as local governments equally. The county did not become the highest level of local government throughout South Carolina until 1800.

The listing of counties in circuit court districts includes every county formed between 1785 and 1800. Counties abolished in 1800 are identified, and the location of their extant records is detailed.

Circuit Court Districts, 1769–1800. Circuit court districts were established in 1769 and began holding court by about 1772. Originally there were seven districts: Beaufort, Camden, Charleston, Cheraws, Georgetown, Ninety-Six, and Orangeburgh. Pinckney and Washington circuit court districts were added in 1791 (see Court Records). The listing of circuit court districts details the extant records of the nine circuit court districts where the extant records are located. The counties formed in each district are identified.

Townships. One of the early and genealogically important actions of the provincial (royal) government was the Township Act of 1731; additional townships were authorized in 1761. The act authorized eleven townships containing 20,000 acres each, and agents were sent to Europe to recruit families as settlers. The families were offered inducements such as free transportation to South Carolina, free provisions for one year, and free land. The townships neither created nor kept records; their functions were solely geographical. Townships, like parishes, were used for some tax districts and appeared as locators in grants and conveyances. The townships are included in the listing of Townships and Parishes.

Parishes. In 1706 the Province of South Carolina established the Church of England as the official state-supported church. The twenty-five parishes established from 1706 through 1778 recorded vital records and became districts for the proportioning and election of representatives in 1716; parishes were also used as tax districts. They functioned as geographic locators in grants and conveyances, but did not necessarily replace the proprietary counties in that function; some grants and conveyances mention the parish, some the proprietary county, and some give both. The parishes are included in the listing of Townships and Parishes.

Proprietary Counties, 1682–1785. The first division of South Carolina into local polities occurred in 1682 when Berkeley, Colleton, and Craven proprietary counties were established; Carteret was added in 1685 and renamed Granville in 1708. These counties neither created nor kept records; their function was geographical. The proprietary counties served as districts for the assignment and election of representatives until 1716, militia duty, and general reference in land grants and conveyances (deeds). The proprietary counties were superceded by circuit court districts in 1769, but continued to be used as geographical references until the formation of counties within the circuit court districts in 1785. The forty-six current counties in South Carolina are listed with their proprietary counties in the listing of Proprietary Counties.

Successful research in South Carolina requires an understanding of the unique and complex development of its local government and jurisdictions. Unlike the other twelve British colonies, South Carolina did not form counties or towns during the colonial period. The South Carolina Department of Archives and History publishes a free pamphlet, "The Formation of Counties in South Carolina," which traces the evolution of political subdivisions in the state. The department also publishes a set of ten guide maps illustrating the development of parishes, districts, and counties. Information in the following tables is quoted from South Carolina Department of Archives and History, *A Guide to Local Government Records in the South Carolina Archives* and the guides by Schweitzer (1985) and Holcomb (1964), all listed under Background Sources, and Thorndale and Dollarhide, *Map Guide* (see page 11).

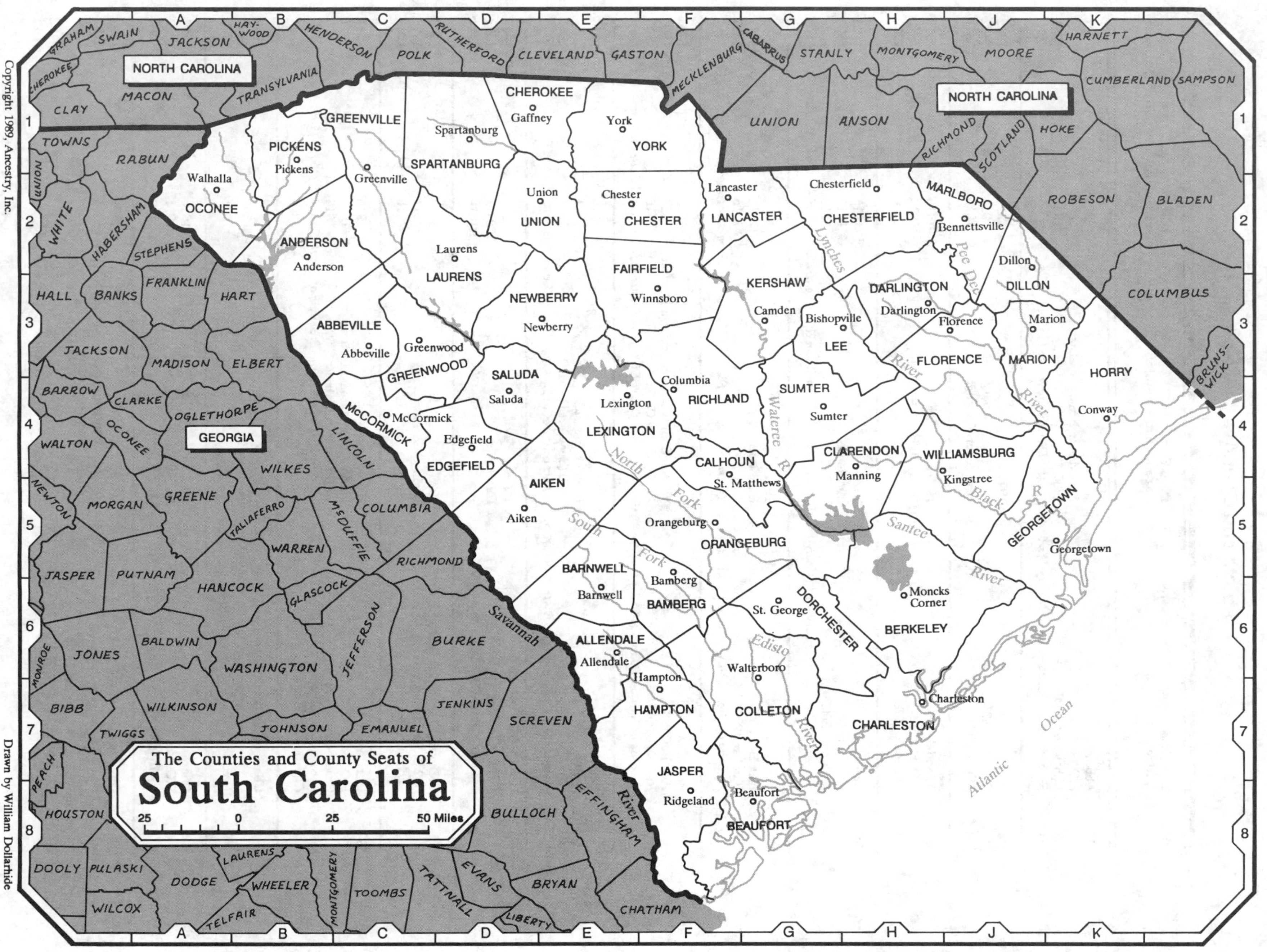

Copyright 1989, Ancestry, Inc.

Drawn by William Dollarhide

Districts and Counties, 1800–present

Map	District/County (1800–present) Address	Date Formed Parent District Functioned From	Birth Marriage Death	Land Probate Court
C3	Abbeville P.O. Box 99 Abbeville 29620	1800 Abbeville in Ninety-Six District 1785	1916 1911 1911	1791 1772 1791
	Record loss, 1873. Records of Ninety-Six Circuit Court District are housed in Abbeville County.			
D5	Aiken P.O. Box 583 Aiken 29801	1871 Edgefield/Barnwell/ Orangeburg/Lexington	1915 1911 1915	1872 1872 1871
E6	Allendale P.O. Box 126 Allendale 29810	1919 Barnwell/Hampton	1919 1919 1919	1919 1919 1919
B2	Anderson P.O. Box 1656 Anderson 29620	1826 Pendleton	1915 1911 1915	1826 1826 1826
	Records of Pendleton County and Ninety-Six, Washington, and Pendleton districts are housed in Anderson County.			
F6	Bamberg P.O. Box 150 Bamberg 29003	1897 Barnwell	1915 1911 1915	1897 1897 1897
	Records of Orangeburgh Circuit Court District, Court of Common Pleas, are housed in Bamberg County.			
E6	Barnwell P.O. Box 723 Barnwell 29812	1800 Winton County in Orangeburgh District 1785 (Winton County)	1915 1911 1915	1800 1800 1800
	Records of Winton County (1785–91) in Orangeburgh Circuit Court District are housed in Barnwell County.			
G8	Beaufort Beaufort 29901	1800 Beaufort District 1772 (Beaufort District)	1915 1911 1915	1863 1865 1865
	Record loss, 1865. Beaufort District absorbed the four counties in Beaufort Circuit Court District.			
H6	Berkeley 223 N. Live Oak Drive Moncks Corner 29461	1882 Charleston	1915 1911 1915	1883 1883 1881
F4	Calhoun 302 S. Railroad Avenue St. Matthews 29135	1908 Lexington/Orangeburg	1915 1911 1915	1908 1908 1908
H7	Charleston P.O. Box 293 Charleston 29402	1800 Marion/Washington counties in Charleston District; 1680	1915 1911 1915	1671 1671 1700
	Records of Charleston Circuit Court and Equity Circuit Districts and the Province of South Carolina (1671–1785) are housed in Charleston County.			
	Charleston (City) *Records are in Charleston County.*		1871 1871 1821	1858 1790 1774
D1	Cherokee P.O. Box 866 Gaffney 26342	1897 Union/York/Spartanburg	1915 1911 1915	1897 1897 1897
E2	Chester P.O. Box 580 Chester 29706	1800 Chester County in Pinckney District 1785 (in Camden District)	1915 1911 1915	1785 1787 1785

Map	District/County (1800–present) Address	Date Formed Parent District Functioned From	Birth Marriage Death	Land Probate Court
H2	Chesterfield P.O. Box 529 Chesterfield 29709 *Record loss, 1865. Records fragmented.*	1800 Chesterfield County in Cheraws District 1785	1915 1911 1915	1861 1865 1823
G5	Clarendon P.O. Box E Manning 29102 *Record loss, 1911. Records of old Clarendon County in Camden Circuit Court District lost, 1801.*	1855 Sumter 1785–1800	1915 1911 1915	1856 1856 1856
G7	Colleton P.O. Box 620 Walterboro 29488 *Record losses, 1805, 1865. Records fragmented.*	1800 Colleton/Bartholomew/Berkeley counties in Charleston District	1915 1911 1915	1802 1865 1807
H3	Darlington Darlington 29532 *Record loss, 1806.*	1800 Darlington County in Cheraws District 1785	1915 1911 1915	1803 1783 1801
J3	Dillon P.O. Box 1220 Dillon 29536	1910 Marion	1915 1911 1915	1910 1910 1910
G6	Dorchester 101 Ridge Street St. George 29477	1897 Berkeley/Colleton	1915 1911 1915	1897 1897 1897
D4	Edgefield 215 Jeter Street Edgefield 29824	1800 Edgefield County in Ninety-Six District 1785	1915 1911 1915	1786 1785 1785
F3	Fairfield P.O. Box 236 Winnsboro 29180	1800 Fairfield County in Camden District 1785	1915 1911 1915	1784 1787 1785
J3	Florence 180 N. Irby Street Florence 29501	1888 Marion/Darlington/ Clarendon/Williamsburg	1915 1911 1915	1889 1889 1889
J5	Georgetown 715 Prince Street Georgetown 29440 *Record loss, 1865. Records fragmented.*	1800 Kingston/Winyah/Williamburg counties in Georgetown District 1772 (Georgetown District)	1915 1911 1915	1862 1862 1783
C1	Greenville Greenville 29601	1800 Greenville County in Ninety-Six District 1786	1915 1911 1915	1784 1787 1786
C3	Greenwood 528 Monument Greenwood 29646	1897 Abbeville/Edgefield	1915 1911 1915	1897 1897 1897
F7	Hampton P.O. Box 7 Hampton 29924	1878 Beaufort	1915 1911 1915	1878 1878 1878
K4	Horry P.O. Box 677 Conway 29526 *Formed from the territory of Kingston County (non-functioning) in Georgetown Circuit Court District.*	1801 Georgetown	1915 1911 1915	1803 1799 1803
F8	Jasper P.O. Box 248 Ridgeland 29936	1912 Beaufort/Hampton	1915 1912 1915	1912 1912 1912

Map	District/County (1800–present) Address	Date Formed Parent District Functioned From	Birth Marriage Death	Land Probate Court
G3	Kershaw Camden 29020	1800 Kershaw County in Camden District 1791	1915 1911 1915	1787 1782 1783
	Records of Camden Circuit Court and Equity Circuit districts are housed in Camden County.			
G2	Lancaster P.O. Box 1809 Lancaster 29720	1800 Lancaster County in Camden District 1785	1915 1911 1915	1762 1820 1800
	Record loss, 1865. Records fragmented. Some Camden Circuit Court District conveyance records are included.			
D2	Laurens P.O. Box 287 Laurens 29360	1800 Laurens County in Ninety-Six District 1785	1915 1911 1915	1774 1766 1789
G3	Lee Bishopville 29010	1902 Darlington/Kershaw/Sumter	1915 1911 1915	1902 1902 1902
E4	Lexington Lexington 29072 *Record losses, 1839, 1865. Records fragmented.*	1804 Orangeburgh	1915 1911 1915	1839 1809 1800
	Formed from territory of Lexington County (non-functioning) in Orangeburgh District.			
J3	Marion P.O. Box 295 Marion 29571	1800 Liberty County in Georgetown District 1800	1915 1800 1915	1800 1790 1800
	Marriage records: 1800–59 (incomplete), 1911–present.			
J2	Marlboro P.O. Box 996 Bennettsville 29512	1800 Marlboro County in Cheraws District 1785	1915 1788 1915	1786 1787 1785
	Marriage records: 1788–1819 (incomplete), 1911–present.			
C4	McCormick P.O. Box 86 McCormick 29835	1916 Abbeville/Greenwood	1916 1916 1916	1916 1916 1916
E3	Newberry P.O. Box 278 Newberry 29108	1800 Newberry County in Ninety-Six District 1785	1915 1911 1915	1776 1776 1776
A2	Oconee P.O. Box 158 Walhalla 29691	1868 Pickens	1915 1911 1915	1868 1868 1868
F5	Orangeburg P.O. Box 100 Orangeburg 29116 *Record loss, 1865. Records fragmented.*	1800 Lewisburg/Lexington/Orange counties in Orangeburgh District 1772 (Orangeburgh District)	1915 1911 1915	1824 1864 1824
	Pendleton	1800 Pendleton County in Washington District 1789 (in Ninety-Six District)	— — —	1790 1790 1790
	Abolished when divided into Anderson and Pickens districts, 1826. Records transferred to Anderson District, now Anderson County.			
B1	Pickens P.O. Box 215 Pickens 29671	1826 Pendleton	1915 1911 1915	1828 1828 1823
F3	Richland 1701 Main Street Columbia 29201	1800 Richland County in Camden District 1785	1915 1911 1915	1865 1787 1793
	Record loss, 1865. Records fragmented. Records of Columbia Equity Circuit District are housed in Richland County.			

Map	District/County (1800–present) Address	Date Formed Parent District Functioned From	Birth Marriage Death	Land Probate Court
D4	Saluda Saluda 29138	1896 Edgefield	1915 1911 1915	1896 1896 1896
D1	Spartanburg 180 Magnolia Street Spartanburg 29301	1800 Spartanburg County in Pinckney District 1785 (in Ninety-Six District)	1915 1911 1915	1784 1787 1785
G4	Sumter 141 N. Main Street Sumter 29150	1800 Clarendon/Claremont/Salem Counties in Camden District 1785 (Clarendon/Claremont Counties in Camden District)	1915 1911 1915	1801 1774 1795
	Record loss, 1801; destroyed records of Clarendon and Old Claremont counties. Records fragmented.			
D2	Union P.O. Box G Union 29379	1800 Union County in Pinckney District 1785 (in Ninety-Six District)	1915 1911 1915	1778 1777 1785
	Records of Western and Pinckney Equity Circuit districts are housed in Union County.			
J5	Williamsburg P.O. Box 86 Kingstree 29556	1804 Georgetown	1915 1911 1915	1806 1802 1806
	Formed from territory of Williamsburg County (non-functioning) in Georgetown Circuit Court District.			
E1	York P.O. Box 649 York 29745	1800 York County in Pinckney District 1785 (in Camden District)	1915 1911 1915	1786 1786 1786
	Records of Pinckney Circuit Court District are housed in York County.			

Counties in Districts, 1785–1800

County (1785–1800)	Circuit Court Districts	Date Formed Parent County/ies
Abbeville *Functioned from 1785.*	Ninety-Six	1785 original
Bartholomew *Non-functioning county. Area absorbed by Colleton District, 1800.*	Charleston	1785 original
Berkeley *Non-functioning county. Area absorbed by Colleton District, 1800.*	Charleston	1785 original
Chester *Functioned 1785–91. Area absorbed by Pinckney District, 1791.*	Camden	1785 original
Chester *Functioned from 1791.*	Pinckney	1791 removed from Camden District
Chesterfield *Functioned from 1785.*	Cheraws	1785 original
Claremont *Functioned 1785–1800. Area absorbed by Sumter District, 1801.*	Camden	1785 original
Clarendon *Functioned from 1785. Area absorbed by Sumter District, 1801.*	Camden	1785 original

County (1785–1800)	Circuit Court Districts	Date Formed Parent County/ies
Colleton *Non-functioning county. Area absorbed by Colleton District, 1800.*	Charleston	1785 original
Darlington *Functioned from 1785.*	Cheraws	1785 original
Edgefield *Functioned from 1785.*	Ninety-Six	1785 original
Fairfield *Functioned from 1785.*	Camden	1785 original
Granville *Non-functioning county.*	Beaufort	1785 original
Greenville *Functioned 1786–95. Area absorbed by Washington District, 1795.*	Ninety-Six	1786 Indian lands
Greenville *Functioned from 1795.*	Washington	1795 removed from Ninety-Six District
Hilton *Non-functioning. Area absorbed by Beaufort District, 1800.*	Beaufort	1785 original
Kershaw *Functioned from 1791.*	Camden	1791 Fairfield/Lancaster/Richland counties in Camden District
Kingston *Non-functioning county. Area absorbed by Georgetown District, 1800, and reformed as Horry District, 1801.*	Georgetown	1785 original
Lancaster *Functioned from 1785.*	Camden	1785 original
Laurens *Functioned from 1785.*	Ninety-Six	1785 original
Lewisburg *Functioned from 1785. Area absorbed by Orangeburg District, 1800.*	Orangeburgh	1785 original
Lexington *Functioned from 1785. Area absorbed by Orangeburg District, 1800, and reformed as Lexington District, 1804.*	Orangeburgh	1785 original
Liberty *Non-functioning county. Renamed Marion District, 1800.*	Georgetown	1785 original
Lincoln *Non-functioning county. Area absorbed by Beaufort District, 1800.*	Beaufort	1785 original
Marion *Non-functioning county. Area absorbed by Charleston District, 1800.*	Charleston	1785 original
Marlboro *Functioned from 1785.*	Cheraws	1785 original
Newberry *Functioned from 1785.*	Ninety-Six	1785 original
Orange *Non-functioning county. Area absorbed by Orangeburg District, 1800.*	Orangeburgh	1785 original
Pendleton *Functioned 1789–95. Area absorbed by Washington District, 1795.*	Ninety-Six	1789 original

County (1785–1800)	Circuit Court Districts	Date Formed Parent County/ies
Pendleton *Functioned from 1795.*	Washington	1795 removed from Ninety-Six District
Richland *Functioned from 1785.*	Camden	1785 original
Salem *Functioned 1792–1800. Area absorbed by Sumter District, 1800.*	Camden	1792 Clarendon/Claremont counties in Camden District
Shrewsbury *Non-functioning county. Area absorbed by Beaufort District, 1800.*	Beaufort	1785 original
Spartanburg *Functioned 1785–91. Area absorbed by Pinckney District, 1791.*	Ninety-Six	1785 original
Spartanburg	Pinckney *Functioned from 1791.*	1791 removed from Ninety-Six District
Union *Functioned 1785–91. Area absorbed by Pinckney District, 1791.*	Ninety-Six	1785 original
Union *Functioned from 1791.*	Pinckney	1791 removed from Ninety-Six District
Washington *Functioned 1785–91. Area absorbed by Charleston District, 1800.*	Charleston	1785 original
Williamsburg *Non-functioning county. Area absorbed by Georgetown District, 1800, and reformed as Williamsburg District, 1804.*	Georgetown	1785 original
Winton *Functioned 1785–1800. Remaining records, 1785–91, in Barnwell County. Renamed Barnwell District, 1800.*	Orangeburgh	1785 original
Winyah *Non-functioning county. Area absorbed by Georgetown District, 1800.*	Georgetown	1785 original
York *Functioned 1785–91. Area absorbed by Pinckney District, 1791.*	Camden	1785 original
York *Functioned from 1791.*	Pinckney	1791 removed from Camden District

Circuit Court Districts, 1769–1800

Circuit Court District (1769–1800) Records Repository (Counties in District)	Date Formed Parent District	Land Probate Court 1790 Census District(s)
Beaufort (Granville, Hilton, Lincoln, Shrewsbury)	1769 original	— — — District
Camden Kershaw/Lancaster (Chester, Clarendon, Claremont, Fairfield, Lancaster, Richland, York)	1769 original	1784 1781 1782 by county

Circuit Court District (1769–1800) Records Repository (Counties in District)	Date Formed Parent District	Land Probate Court 1790 Census District(s)
Charleston Charleston (Bartholomew, Berkeley, Colleton, Marion, Washington)	1769 original	1671 1671 1671 Parishes
Cheraws (Chesterfield, Darlington, Marlboro)	1769 original	— — — Counties
Georgetown Georgetown (Kingston, Liberty, Williamsburg, Winyah)	1769 original	— — 1783 Parishes
Ninety-Six Abbeville (Abbeville, Edgefield, Greenville, Laurens, Newberry, Pendleton, Spartanburg, Union)	1769 original	1784 1782 1777 Counties
Orangeburgh (Lewisburg, Lexington, Orange, Winton)	1769 original	— — 1787 North and South
Pinckney York (Chester, Spartanburg, Union, York) *Counties enumerated in Camden and Ninety-Six districts in 1790.*	1791 Ninety-Six	— — —
Washington (Greenville, Pendleton) *Counties enumerated in Ninety-Six District in 1790.*	1791 Ninety-Six functioned from 1795	— — —

Townships and Parishes

Parish/Township	Established	Location	Proprietary County/District
All Saints Parish	1778	near Georgetown	Georgetown District
Amelia Township	1731	Congaree and Santee rivers	Orangeburgh District
Belfast Township	1761	Stevens and Long Cane creeks	Edgefield and Abbeville districts
Boonesborough Township	1761	Long Cane Creek, Saluda and Little rivers	Abbeville District
Christ Church Parish	1706	Wando River	Berkeley
Fredericksburgh Township	1731	Wateree River	Sumter and Kershaw districts
Hillsborough Township	1761	Long Cane Creek	Abbeville District
Kingston (King's Town) Township	1731	Waccamaw River	Horry District
Londonborough Township	1761	Stevens Creek of Savannah River	Edgefield District

Parish/Township	Established	Location	Proprietary County/District
New Windsor Township	1731	Savannah River	Barnwell and Edgefield districts
Orange Parish	1778	St. Matthew's	Orangeburgh District
Orangeburgh Township	1731	South Edisto or Pon Pon River	Orangeburgh District
Prince Frederick's Parish	1734	upper Prince George's	Craven
Prince George's Parish	1721	between Santee and Pee Dee rivers	Craven
Prince William's Parish	1745	upper St. Helena's	Granville
Purrysburgh	1731	Savannah River	Beaufort District
Queensborough Township	1731	Pee Dee River and Lynch's Creek	Georgetown and Marion districts
Saxegotha (Saxe-Gotha) Township	1731	Congaree River	Lexington District
St. Andrew's Parish	1706	Ashley River	Berkeley
St. Bartholomew's Parish	1706	near St. Helena	Colleton
St. David's Parish	1768	St. Mark's and Prince Frederick's	Craven
St. Denis' (French) Parish	1706	adjoining St. Thomas'	Berkeley
St. George's Dorchester Parish	1717	upper St. Andrew's	Berkeley
St. Helena's Parish	1712	St. Helena/Port Royal	Granville
St. James Goose Creek Parish	1706	Goose Creek	Berkeley
St. James Santee (French) Parish	1706	James Town	Craven
St. John's Colleton Parish	1734	Edisto and adjacent islands	Colleton
St. John's Parish	1706	Cooper River	Berkeley
St. Luke's Parish	1767	Euhaws	Granville
St. Mark's Parish	1757	Prince Frederick's	Craven
St. Matthew's Parish	1768	Orangeburgh Township	Berkeley
St. Michael's Parish	1751	St. Philip's Charles Town	Berkeley
St. Paul's Parish	1706	Stono and Edisto rivers	Colleton
St. Peter's Parish	1746	Purrysburgh	Granville
St. Philip's Parish	1706	Charles Town	Berkeley
St. Stephen's Parish	1754	upper St. James' Santee	Craven
St. Thomas' (French) Parish	1706	Wando River	Berkeley
Welch Tract (Welch Neck)	1731	Pee Dee River and Jeffry's Creek	Marion District

Parish/Township	Established	Location	Proprietary County/District
Williamsburgh Township	1731	Black River	Williamsburgh District

Proprietary Counties

Map	Current County	Proprietary County/ies (1682–1785)
C3	Abbeville	Carteret (Granville)/Colleton
D5	Aiken	Berkeley/Colleton
E6	Allendale	Carteret (Granville)
B2	Anderson	Carteret (Granville)/Colleton
F6	Bamburg	Carteret (Granville)/Colleton
E6	Barnwell	Berkeley/Carteret (Granville)
G8	Beaufort	Carteret (Granville)
H6	Berkeley	Berkeley/Colleton
F4	Calhoun	Berkeley/Colleton
H7	Charleston	Colleton
D1	Cherokee	Craven
E2	Chester	Craven
H2	Chesterfield	Craven
G5	Clarendon	Berkeley/Craven
G7	Colleton	Carteret (Granville)/Colleton
H3	Darlington	Craven
J3	Dillon	Craven
G6	Dorchester	Berkeley/Colleton
D4	Edgefield	Carteret (Granville)/Colleton
F3	Fairfield	Berkeley/Craven
J3	Florence	Craven
J5	Georgetown	Craven
C1	Greenville	Berkeley/Colleton
C3	Greenwood	Colleton

Map	Current County	Proprietary County/ies (1682–1785)
F7	Hampton	Carteret (Granville)
K4	Horry	Craven
F8	Jasper	Carteret (Granville)
G3	Kershaw	Berkeley/Craven
G2	Lancaster	Craven
D2	Laurens	Berkeley/Colleton
G3	Lee	Craven
E4	Lexington	Berkeley/Colleton
J3	Marion	Craven
J2	Marlboro	Craven
C4	McCormick	Carteret (Granville)/Colleton
E3	Newberry	Berkeley/Colleton
A2	Oconee	Carteret (Granville)/Colleton
F5	Orangeburg	Berkeley/Colleton
B1	Pickens	Colleton
F3	Richland	Berkeley
D4	Saluda	Colleton
D1	Spartanburg	Berkeley/Craven
G4	Sumter	Berkeley/Craven
D2	Union	Berkeley
J5	Williamsburg	Craven
E1	York	Craven

SOUTH DAKOTA

Laura Hall Heuermann and Marsha Hoffman Rising, C.G., C.G.L.

French explorers are known to have made their way to what is now South Dakota as early as 1743. Creating a topographical transition between the prairies of the midwest and the Rocky Mountains to the west, South Dakota's eastern glacial drift river region and western Black Hills remained the home of the Arikara and the Sioux until 1825 when tribal conflict drove the Arikara farther west. Sioux remained in the state and still comprise most of South Dakota's Native American population.

The Spanish held dominion over the land for the last part of the eighteenth century, but South Dakota was sold to the United States as part of the Louisiana Purchase in 1803. Early nineteenth century trappers and traders established headquarters in the area, transporting furs down the Missouri from Ft. Pierre, then part of Missouri Territory. It was not until the 1850s that any permanent U.S. settlements began. Land east of the Missouri River fell under the successive jurisdictions of the Michigan, Wisconsin, and Iowa territories before finally settling in Minnesota Territory in 1849. The portion west of the Missouri River became part of the vast, unsettled, northern Nebraska Territory in 1854.

In the winter of 1856–57, the Dakota Land Company from Minnesota received a charter to establish a settlement in Medary, now the town of Brookings. At about the same time, Western Town Company from Iowa received a charter to establish settlements in the area along the Sioux River. A sawmill, store, and houses were built in what is now Sioux Falls.

By 1860 settlements could be found in the southeastern part of the state and along the Missouri, Big Sioux, Vermillion, James, and Red rivers. A bill signed 2 March 1861 by the U. S. Congress created Dakota Territory, then consisting of what would become North and South Dakota, separating it from Nebraska Territory and the recently created state of Minnesota. By the fall of that year, there were eleven post offices in the territory, among them Yankton, Vermillion, and Sioux Falls. Territorial counties were established by the legislature in April, 1862—Lincoln, Minnehaha, Brookings, and Deuel. A request to have a military fort for the protection of the settlers led to the creation of Ft. Dakota located in the Sioux Falls area.

During the next two decades significant changes led to a massive influx of population. The Homestead Act of 1862 encouraged settlers to stake claims. Although economic depression, drought, and grasshoppers plagued expansion, the development of land offices, railroad expansion, and changing crop conditions contributed to the economic growth. Gold was discovered in the Black Hills in 1874, a lode that today is still the largest in the Western hemisphere. The discovery pressured western migration into that portion of the state previously closed to settlers by agreement with the Sioux. The state's reservation system began with the Yankton in the southern part of Douglas County in 1858. In 1863 the Winnebago and Santee Sioux were moved from Minnesota to a small reservation near Ft. Thompson, which later became the Crow Creek Reservation. The Battle of the Little Big Horn in Montana led to the legal opening of South Dakota's mining region and its adjacent grazing land.

With the peak of expansion in 1885, Sioux Falls became an area where people from the east could come for a short period of time and obtain a divorce. Easterners brought a demand for culture with them—operas, plays, concerts, and hotels. Rapidly growing eastern river region settlements and prosperity in the mines created pressure for statehood below the 46th parallel for the southern part of the territory. The U.S. Congress approved the division of the territory creating the states of North Dakota and South Dakota in 1889.

Throughout the push toward statehood, relations between the Sioux and the settlers remained difficult, climaxing in the warfare at Wounded Knee in 1890. At the time, nearly one third of the white population was foreign-born, coming primarily from eastern Europe and Scandinavia.

Life for the pioneer farmers in the Dakotas was a hard one, immortalized by the words and experiences of such authors as Laura Ingalls Wilder and Ole Rölvaag. It was not an easy task to develop a home and farm from the raw, pathless prairie. Remote from neighbors, the prairie dweller led a lonely life. Only through perseverance and determination was a home carved out of what had heretofore been the great plains. Today, the state can still be considered a frontier state, its economy dependent on livestock, food, lumber and undeveloped products and, to a lesser extent, its mining production.

Vital Records

Statewide vital record registration for births, deaths, and marriages began in South Dakota in July 1905. Copies of later vital records may be obtained from the State Department of Health, Health Statistics Program, Joe Foss Building, Pierre, South Dakota 57501. The current fee is $5. Some earlier marriage records may be found in the office of the register of deeds of a particular county. Published records of marriages exist for Minnehaha and Pennington counties. Divorce records were recorded statewide after 1905, but earlier ones may be at the clerk of the court in the appropriate county.

Census Records

Federal

Population Schedules.

- Indexed—1860, 1870 (both as Dakota Territory), 1890 (fragment)
- Soundex—1880 (Dakota Territory), 1900, 1920
- Unindexed—1910

Agriculture.

- 1870, 1880

Mortality Schedules.

- 1860, 1870, 1880 (all as Dakota Territory)

Union Veterans Schedules.

- 1890

Although the Dakotas fell under Minnesota Territory for the 1850 federal census, the only whites enumerated actually lived in that territory's Pembina County, now North Dakota. Only the schedule for Jefferson Township of Union County remains of the 1890 population census. Microfilmed copies of all federal censuses listed above are available in the South Dakota State Historical Society (see Archives, Libraries, and Societies) and are available from them on interlibrary loan. The 1880 and 1900 Soundex indexes do not circulate.

The mortality schedules are available on microfilm and also have been indexed by AISI. These are available at the South Dakota State Historical Society in Pierre as well as various other repositories.

The Sioux Falls Public Library, 201 North Main Avenue, Sioux Falls, South Dakota 57102, has microfilm copies of the 1860, 1870, 1880 federal population schedules for the territory.

Territorial and State

Numerous state-generated censuses for Dakota Territory and the state of South Dakota were compiled and are available for research at the South Dakota State Historical Society. The Dakota Territory Special Federal 1885 census was taken under federal guidelines just before statehood; enumerations for only some present-day South Dakota counties were completed: Beadle, Butte, Charles Mix, Edmunds, Fall River, Faulk, Hand, Hanson, Hutchinson, Hyde, Lake, Lincoln, Marshall, McPherson, Moody, Roberts, Sanborn, Spink, Stanley, and Turner. When it was determined enough people existed in the territory to create two states, no further schedules were completed. The 1885 census also contains a veterans and mortality schedule. These listings may be borrowed on interlibrary loan.

State censuses include the 1895 census, available with ledger-style indexes for Beadle, Brule, Pratt (now Jones), Presho (now Lyman), Campbell, and Charles Mix counties only. The census can be borrowed on microfilm from the South Dakota State Historical Society. The censuses taken in 1905, 1915, 1925, 1935, and 1945, are also located there but are not on microfilm. Card file indexes exist for the 1905–45 censuses. The 1905 census is especially valuable for the genealogist as a land description is given, which can then be used to locate federal land records. Additional information in the 1905 enumeration gives the length of time the individual was in South Dakota, and, if the individual was foreign-born, the time of residence in the United States.

Many early censuses of the state's Indian Reservations have been microfilmed and are available at the South Dakota State Historical Society where they are available on interlibrary loan and from the FHL.

Background Sources

The South Dakota State Historical Society published an extensive collection of historical material in forty-one volumes between 1902–82 entitled *South Dakota Historical Collections*. An index, published in 1989, is available from the society. Volumes circulate from the state library, and a few are still in print and available for sale at the society.

There are many histories of counties and towns found in town or county libraries in the state. The Sioux Valley Genealogical Society (see Archives, Libraries, and Societies), for example, has county histories for Minnehaha County as well as histories for Brookings, Brown, Clay, Faulk, Grant, Hamlin, Hand, Hanson, Jones, Jerauld, Lincoln, McCook, Moody, Potter, Turner, and Yankton.

The following provide additional background understanding of South Dakota's history and its people, particularly nineteenth century immigrants:

Dvorak, Joseph A. *Memorial Book: History of the Czechs in the State of South Dakota.* Tabor, S.Dak.: Czech Heritage Preservation Society, 1980. Topics here include church history, Czech history and immigration, and county histories for Brule, Tripp, Gregory, Charles Mix, Bon Homme, and Yankton counties.

Fanebust, Wayne. *Where the Sioux River Bends.* Sioux Falls, S.Dak.: Minnehaha County Historical Society, 1985.

Historical Records Survey. *South Dakota Place Names.* Vermillion, S.Dak.: University of South Dakota, 1940.

Karolevitz, Robert F. *Challenge: The South Dakota Story.* Brevet Press, 1975.

Kingsbury, George Washington and George Martin Smith. *History of Dakota Territory and South Dakota: Its History and Its People.* 5 vols. Chicago, Ill.: S. J. Clarke, 1915. Volumes 4 and 5 contain biographical sketches.

Laubersheimer, Sue. *South Dakota: Changing, Changeless, 1889–1989: A Selected Annotated Bibliography.* N.p.: South Dakota Library Association, 1985. Two supplements consisting of subject index were published in Pierre by the South Dakota Library Association in 1986.

Phillips, George H. *The Post Offices of South Dakota 1861–1930.* Crete, Nebr.: J-B Publishing, 1975.

Rath, George. *The Black Sea Germans in the Dakotas.* Freeman, S.Dak.: Pine Hill Press, 1977.

Schell, Herbert S. *History of South Dakota.* 3d rev. Lincoln, Nebr.: University of Nebraska, 1975. A standard historical account with descriptive maps.

Sittig, Emily Brende, and Clara Brende Christenson, trans. *Norwegian Pioneer History of Minnehaha County, 1866–1896.* Freeman, S.Dak.: Pine Hill Press, 1976.

Sneve, Virginia Driving Hawk. *South Dakota Geographic Names.* Brevet Press, 1973. Inventories old names used for counties, towns, villages, lakes, mines, and many other landmarks.

Turchen, Lesta Van Der West and James D. McLaird. *County and Community: A Bibliography of South Dakota Local Histories.* Mitchell, S.Dak.: the author, 1979.

Watson, Parker. "A Black Hills Bibliography," *South Dakota Historical Collections* 35 (1970): 169–301.

Maps

R. L. Polk and Company, *Northwestern Gazetteer: Minnesota, North and South Dakota and Montana—Gazetteer and Business Directory* (St. Paul, Minn.: R. L. Polk, 1914), is of great benefit to the Dakota researcher. Another good gazetteer containing much local history is *Black Hills Ghost Towns* by Watson Parker and H. K. Lambert (Chicago, Ill.: Swallow Press, 1974).

A number of county atlases have been filmed and are available on interlibrary loan from the South Dakota State Historical Society. Those accessible to the researcher include the counties of Aurora (1909), Beadle (1906 and 1913), Bon Homme (1912), Brookings (1909), Brown (1905 and 1911), Brule (1911), Campbell (1911), Charles Mix (1906 and 1912), Clark (1929), Clay (1901 and 1924), Codington (1929), Davison (1901 and 1929), Day (1909 and 1929), Deuel (1909), Douglas (1901 and 1910), Edmunds (1905), Faulk (1910), Grant (1910 and 1929), Gregory (1912), Hand (1912), Hanson (1902 and 1910), Hughes (1916), Hutchinson (1910), Hyde (1911), Jerauld (1909), Kingsbury (1909 and 1929), Lake (1911), Lincoln (1910), Lyman (1911), Marshall (1910 and 1924), McCook (1911), McPherson (1911), Miner (1917), Minnehaha (1903), Moody (1909), Potter (1911), Roberts (1910), Sanborn (1912), Spink (1909), Sully (1916), Tripp (1915), Turner (1893 and 1902), Union (1924), Walworth (1941), and Yankton (1910).

Other atlases on microfilm include Andreas's 1884 *Historical Atlas of Dakota* and Peterson's 1904 *Historical Atlas of South Dakota.* The Sanborn fire insurance maps (see page 4) are located at the South Dakota State Historical Society.

Land Records

Public-Domain State

The original patents and copies of tract books and township plats are at the BLM, 222 North 32nd Street, Box 30157, Billings, Montana 59107. The United States GLO unapproved homestead files, 1905–20, are housed at the South Dakota State Historical Society as are tract books for land claims 1864–1915. Once granted by the federal government, later land transactions were filed with the county register of deeds.

Probate Records

Wills and intestate proceedings originate at the county in which the deceased lived, usually at the county clerk of the court's office. Some have been transferred to the state archives at the Cultural Heritage Center and cataloged under Unified Judicial System—Circuit Courts—Division of [County name] County (see Court Records below).

Many probate records for Indian agencies have been microfilmed and are available through the FHL. Those that have not been microfilmed will be available through the National Archives (see Special Focus Categories—Native American).

Court Records

The county court had original jurisdiction over all matters of probate, guardianship, and settlement of estate, as well as civil and criminal jurisdiction conferred by law. The circuit courts held some case files, judgments, and depositions related to civil and criminal actions, naturalization records, and juror lists. In November 1972, the state's constitution covering the Judicial Department was amended to create a unified judicial system. All judges then became either circuit court judges or supreme court judges. This eliminated former county or district courts. Many of the counties simply left their old files with the clerk of the courts in the county; however, the state archives in Pierre has notified all counties that they can transfer their old files to the archives. A few South Dakota counties have turned over some of their court records to the state archives, which also holds criminal dockets for Huron, Beadle County (1919–23); Jones County (1919–39); Mellette County (1912–57); and Minnehaha County (1890–96, 1923–73) with police dockets (1884–1909).

Tax Records

Most tax lists which have survived are housed at the county seat in the auditor's office. A few early tax records have been microfilmed and remain at the South Dakota State Historical Society, including those of "Old Stanley County," comprised of present-day Stanley, Haakon, and Jackson counties. The microfilms for tax records are not always easy to read but can include county commissions work in selecting juries, docket books, and real and personal property taxes. Other microfilm at the archives includes Huron in Beadle County (1883–1902); Edmunds (1887–1924); Roberts (1884–1929); Stanley (1891–1930); Union (1870–1901); and delinquent tax lists from Walworth (before 1899).

Cemetery Records

In 1940 the WPA compiled a "grave registration" that attempted to document the cemeteries of South Dakota. Although incomplete, this survey included either actual cemetery records or surveys of what cemeteries were available in each county. The survey can be searched at the state historical society and is available through the FHL. Volume one of the periodical *South Dakota Genealogical Society Quarterly* began a publication that listed these cemeteries, their location, and whether the transcriptions had been published.

As part of the WPA grave registration project, records of burials of Civil War veterans were completed for the following counties: Aurora, Beadle, Bennett, Bon Homme, Brookings, Brule, Butte, Charles Mix, Clay, Codington, Custer, Davison, Douglas, Fall River, Faulk, Gregory, Haakon, Hand, Hanson, Harding, Hughes, Hutchinson, Hyde, Jackson, Jerauld, Jones, Kingsbury, Lake, Lincoln, Lyman, McCook, Meade, Mellette, Miner, Minnehaha, Moody, Pennington, Potter, Sanborn, Shannon, Stanley, Sully, Todd, Tripp, Turner, Union, Washabaugh, and Yankton.

The Sioux Valley Genealogical Society (see Archives, Libraries, and Societies) has received a number of monetary grants from the Mary Chilton Chapter of the DAR, which have been used to microfilm Minnehaha County cemeteries and those in some neighboring counties. The microfilm, also available through the FHL, includes records of funeral homes in the county.

The Rapid City Society for Genealogical Research published four volumes of *Some Black Hills Area Cemeteries* in an ongoing publication effort begun in 1973. Other genealogical societies have been working diligently to transcribe cemetery records in their areas and publish them in the *South Dakota Genealogical Society Quarterly* or other local genealogical publications.

There is one national cemetery in South Dakota: Black Hills National Cemetery, P.O. Box 640, Sturgis, South Dakota 57785.

Church Records

Most church records remain in private hands. Two helpful publications are *Guide to the Archives of the Episcopal Church in South Dakota* (1981), by Alan Schwartz, Archivist, housed at Center for Western Studies, Mikkelsen Library, Augustana College, Sioux Falls, South Dakota 57102; and *Early Churches and Towns in South Dakota* by Donald D. Parker (Brookings, S.Dak.: the author, ca. 1964). Other publications include Ralph Tingley and Kathleen Tingley, *Mission in Sioux Falls: First Baptist Church 1875–1975* (O'Connor Productions, 1975), *Pioneer Church: The History of the South Dakota District of the Evangelical Lutheran Church, 1860–1960* (Evangelical Lutheran Church, 1961), and *That They May Have Life; The Episcopal Church in South Dakota, 1850–1976,* by Virginia Driving Hawk Sneve (New York, N.Y.: The Seabury Press, 1977).

The Sioux Valley Genealogical Society has been microfilming church records in Minnehaha county as part of a DAR grant.

Military Records

Microfilmed copies of records of Union volunteers from the Dakota territories during the Civil War are available from the National Archives and other interlibrary loan resources. They also may be searched at the South Dakota State Historical Society.

A publication that may be useful to the genealogist with early pioneer ancestors is *Memorandum and Official Records Concerning Dakota Militia, Organized in 1862 for the Protection of the Frontier Settlements from the Hostile Sioux Indians,* compiled by R. E. McDowell in connection with Senate Bill No. 5353, Doc. 241, 58th Cong., 2d sess., Washington, D.C., 1904.

A roster of soldiers from the First Infantry Regiment, South Dakota Volunteers in the Spanish-American War, has been published in Doane Robinson, *History of South Dakota,* 2 vols. (Chicago, Ill.: B. F. Bowen & Co., 1904).

South Dakota World War II History Commission records may be used at the archives, and although there are some restrictions, World War II service records from South Dakota may also be researched there.

Some soldiers' discharge papers may be found in the register of deeds office.

The South Dakota State Archives holds a few military records and military benefit records of interest to the genealogist. These include mother's pension records for Deuel (1913–40), Hughes (1923–40), Kingsbury (1922–40), Lawrence (1918–40), McCook (1917–31), Mellette (1914–40), Minnehaha (1913–40), Union (1922–40), and Walworth (1926–40) counties. These records have restricted access. They also hold militia lists for Edmunds (1918–19) and McCook (1889–1920).

Manuscripts

Manuscript sources include both governmental archival material and personal papers held by repositories. The largest collection in the state is at the South Dakota State Historical Society, although the published guide is out-of-date. The following may be of interest to genealogists: records of the State Railroad Division of the Milwaukee Railroad, railroad tract maps, Rapid City flood records, secretary of state papers, teacher certification records, and some supreme court case files.

A number of school records can be found in the archives at the South Dakota State Historical Society. These consist of teachers' term reports, school censuses, and student records. The records for the specific counties are Aurora (1912–18), Brown (1891–1942), Butte (1918–70), Day (1891–1969), Edmunds (1905–73), Jackson (1918–81), Jones (1916–71), Lyman (1923–69), McCook (1904–11), Perkins (1916–70), Roberts (1944–59), Forestburg District, Sanborn County (1914–81), Spink (few records, 1887–1904), Tripp (1911–73), Turner (1902–69), and Walworth (1906–72). The *Handy Guide to Non-current South Dakota School Records* (1983) is available from the society.

Other records in the South Dakota archives which should be considered by genealogists include coroners' inquests for Deuel (1889–1952), Edmunds (1887–1912), Hand (1921–69), Hughes (1885–1968), Jones (1922–49), Lawrence (1880–1917), and Minnehaha (1883–1929). They also hold insanity records for Deuel (1906–20), Hughes (1881–1956), Lawrence (1879–1976), and Walworth (1891–95). They hold estray records for Edmunds (1897–1912), marks and brands for Union (1865–1900), and records of the Tuberculosis Sanatorium of Deuel (1906–39) and Lawrence (1923–62).

Periodicals, Newspapers, and Manuscript Collections

Periodicals

Two periodicals with statewide exposure are *South Dakota History,* published by the South Dakota State Historical Society, and *South Dakota Genealogical Society Quarterly,* published by the South Dakota Genealogical Society. Other local societies publish periodicals in their areas.

Newspapers

Approximately 150 weekly and twelve daily South Dakota newspapers are currently being microfilmed as part of the nearly 1,000 titles of South Dakota newspapers located at the South Dakota State Historical Society. Many can be borrowed on interlibrary loan. No current, reliable published guide exists because the cataloging is continuously updated.

Archives, Libraries, and Societies

South Dakota State Historical Society
Cultural Heritage Center
900 Governors Drive
Pierre, SD 57501-2294

Under state reorganization, this society is now administratively responsible for the state's archives and library of printed and microfilmed material. Within this society is the research collection, as well as separate museums, the Agricultural Heritage Center in Brookings, the Historical Preservation Center in Vermillion, and the Archaeological Research Center. Its holdings increase annually.

South Dakota Genealogical Society
P.O. Box 490
Winner, SD 57580

Since the society has no permanent address, the above is the mailing address for the society's secretary. Local genealogical societies are scattered throughout the state.

The Center for Western Studies
Box 727, Augustana College
Sioux Falls, SD 57197

This constitutes a fine collection on Native Americans and Scandinavian pioneers in particular.

Sioux Valley Genealogical Society
Old Courthouse Museum
200 West Sixth Street
Sioux Falls, SD 57102

A good microfilmed collection of cemetery and old church records, South Dakota histories, and family records, including a surname file with obituaries and other vital records is located here.

Special Focus Categories

Naturalization

Naturalization records, including declarations of intent, petitions, and final papers, have been deposited in the South Dakota State Historical Society for the following counties: Beadle (unprocessed), Bon Homme (1871–1942), Brookings (1873–1955), Clark (1881–1945), Codington (1880–1930), Davison (1878–1954), Douglas (1882–1943), Edmunds (1884–1952), Faulk (1884–1945), Hand (1882–1940), Harding (1909–44), Hughes (1881–1956), Hutchinson (1876–1944), Jones (1903–59), Kingsbury (1883–1945), Lawrence (1879–1954), Mellette (1912–46), Minnehaha (1868–1954), Stanley (1892–1927), Union (1872–1946), Walworth (1883–1954), and Yankton (1874–1955).

Native American

The account of its native peoples is the bedrock of South Dakota history. The three major local history collections in the state for Native American research are the South Dakota State Historical Society (reservation censuses, school reports, photos, maps, manuscripts); Sinta Gleska College in Rosebud, Rosebud Indian Reservation, South Dakota; and Oglala Lakota College, Pine Ridge Indian Reservation, Kyle, South Dakota.

Records for several agencies are available on microfilm both at the South Dakota State Historical Society and the FHL. Among them are the Cheyenne River Agency (1886–1951); Crow Creek Agency (1895–1976); Pine Ridge Agency (1874–1932); Rosebud Agency (1886–1942); and Standing Rock Agency (1876–1939). Types of records vary, but many include census and vital statistics. Both the National Archives-Central Plains Region and the National Archives-Rocky Mountain Region hold materials generated by the Bureau of Indian Affairs (see page 11).

County Resources

The South Dakota State Historical Society began a project in 1990 to survey the existing records at the county level. This information will be available at a central location in the future. At present, there are some county records housed at the state archives, but many remain at the local level.

Inventories of county archives were made by the WPA, but were only published for the counties of Bennett, Buffalo, Clark, Faulk, Haakon, Jackson, Mellette, Miner, and Washabaugh. Unpublished materials were deposited at the University of South Dakota in Vermillion.

The register of deeds holds land records, births (except for those adopted), death and marriage records; clerk of the courts keeps probate records, divorce records, and civil and criminal court cases. Some of the records held by the state archives, such as adoption records, insanity records, and mother's pension records, have restricted access. Dates with a question mark (?) have not been verified by the state, but are assumed, based on the best information presently available. Dates without questions are verified by publications or the county staff.

For some counties on the chart, there are two years listed for "Date Formed." The first is the year the county was created; the second is the year it was fully organized if it differs from the creation year. Under the heading "Parent County/ies," the term "unorganized land" denotes that it was formed from non-county lands, and counties listed with an asterisk (*) are those to which the county was at one time "attached" before it was fully organized.

There were other name changes and counties whose existence was of short duration. For clarification see Long, *Historical Atlas* (see page 11).

Drawn by William Dollarhide

Map	County Address	Date Formed Parent County/ies	Birth Marriage Death	Land Probate Court
	Armstrong (old)	1873 (abolished, 1879; became part of Hutchinson) Charles Mix/Hutchinson		
	Armstrong (present)	1883 (as Pyatt; renamed, 1895) Cheyenne/Rusk/Stanley *Lawrence		
	In 1952 Armstrong was abolished and became part of Dewey.			
	Ashmore	1873 (renamed Potter, 1875) Buffalo		
H5	Aurora P.O. Box 366 Plankinton 57368	1879 (1881) Cragin	— ? —	1882 1882 1882
	Beadle (old)	1873 (abolished, 1879; became part of Brown) Hanson		
H4	Beadle (present) P.O. Box 1358 Huron 57350	1879 (1880) Clark/Spink/Burchard/Kingsbury	— 1880 —	1879? 1882 1882
	State archives holds probate records, including inventories, appraisements, and wills (1882–1934); and justices' court records (1882–98).			
D6	Bennett P.O. Box 281 Martin 57551	1909 (1912) Pine Ridge Indian Reservation *Fall River	— 1912 —	1907 1912 1912
J7	Bon Homme P.O. Box 6 Tyndall 57066	1862 unorganized land	— 1874 —	1865 1877 1871
	Boreman	1873 (abolished, 1909; became part of Corson) unorganized land *Campbell		
	Bramble	1873 (abolished, 1879; became part of Miner) Hanson		
K4	Brookings 314 Sixth Avenue Brookings 57006	1862 (1871) unorganized land	— 1871 —	1871 1873? 1873?
H2	Brown P.O. Box 1087 Aberdeen 57401	1879 (1880) Beadle (old)/Mills/Stone	— ? —	1879? 1879? 1879?
	Bruguier	1862 (abolished, 1864; became part of Buffalo and Charles Mix) unorganized land *Charles Mix		
G5	Brule 300 S. Courtland Chamberlain 57325	1875 Charles Mix	— ? —	1875? 1875? 1875?
G5	Buffalo P.O. Box 148 Gann Valley 57341	1864 (1871) Bruguier/ Charles Mix/unorganized land *Bon Homme	— 1887	1885 1884 1890
	Parts of the original Buffalo County became counties in North Dakota.			
	Burchard	1873 (abolished, 1879; bacame part of Beadle and Hand) Hanson		

Map	County Address	Date Formed Parent County/ies	Birth Marriage Death	Land Probate Court
A3	Butte P.O. Box 237 Belle Fourche 57717	1883 Lawrence/ Mandan	— ? —	1883? 1883? 1883?
F1	Campbell P.O. Box 146 Mound City 57646	1873 (1884) Buffalo	— ? —	1873? 1873? 1873?
H6	Charles Mix P.O. Box 602 Lake Andes 57356	1862 (1879) unorganized land	— ? —	1875? 1875? 1875?
	Charles Mix was fully organized in 1862 but was dissolved in 1864 and attached to Bon Homme. It was fully reorganized in 1879.			
	Cheyenne	1875 (abolished, 1883; became part of Jackson, Nowlin, Pyatt, and Sterling) Pratt/Rusk/Stanley/unorganized land		
	Choteau	1883 (abolished, 1898; became part of Butte and Meade) Martin *Lawrence		
J3	Clark P.O. Box 275 Clark 57225	1873 (1881) Hanson	— 1883 —	1881 1882 1885
K7	Clay P.O. Box 377 Vermillion 57069	1862 unorganized land	— ? —	1862? 1862? 1862?
J3	Codington P.O. Box 1054 Watertown 57201	1877 (1878) Clark/Grant/Gamlin/unorganized land	— ? —	1877? 1877? 1877?
	Cole	1862 (renamed Union, 1864) unorganized land		
D2	Corson P.O. Box 175 McIntosh 57641	1909 Boreman/DeweySchnasse/ unorganized land	— ? —	1909? 1909? 1909?
	Cragin	1873 (abolished, 1879; became part of Aurora) Hanson		
A5	Custer 420 Mount Rushmore Road Custer 57730	1875 (1877) unorganized land	— 1891 —	1875? 1875? 1875?
H5	Davison P.O. Box 927 Mitchell 57301	1873 (1874) Hanson	— ? —	1873? 1873? 1873?
	State archives holds inventory and appraisement books (1915–45); and circuit court journals (1882–1930).			
J2	Day 710 W. First Street Webster 57274	1879 (1882) Greeley/Stone	— ? —	1879? 1879? 1879?
	Delano	1875 (abolished, 1898; became part of Meade) unorganized land *Lawrence		
K3	Deuel P.O. Box 125 Clear Lake 57226	1862 (1878) unorganized land	— ? —	1862? 1862? 1862?
	State archives holds circuit court judgment dockets (1879–1931).			

Map	County Address	Date Formed Parent County/ies	Birth Marriage Death	Land Probate Court
E3	Dewey P.O. Box 96 Timber Lake 57656	1873 (as Rusk; renamed, 1883) (1910) unorganized land	— ? —	1883? 1883? 1883?
H6	Douglas P.O. Box 36 Armour 57313	1873 (1882) Charles Mix	— ? —	1873? 1873? 1873?
	Edmunds P.O. Box 384 Ipswich 57451	1873 (1883) Buffalo	— ? —	1873? 1873? 1873?
	State archives has marriage records (1884–1917); miscellaneous probate records (1893–1958); wills (1884–1919); and circuit court records (1890–1902).			
	Ewing	1883 (abolished, 1894; became part of Harding) Harding *Butte		
A6	Fall River 906 N. River Hot Springs 57747	1883 Custer	— ? —	1883? 1883? 1883?
G3	Faulk P.O. Box 357 Faulkton 57438	1873 (1883) Buffalo	— 1885 —	1883 1884 1883
	State archives has records of the clerk of the circuit court (1883–1958).			
	Forsythe	1875 (abolished, 1881; became part of Custer) unorganized land		
K2	Grant P.O. Box 509 Milbank 57252	1873 (1878) Deuel/Hanson	— — —	1878 1878 1878
	Courthouse fire destroyed deed books 17–18 and mortgage books 10a, 18, 26, 28 and 29.			
	Greeley	1873 (abolished, 1879; became part of Day) Hanson		
G6	Gregory P.O. Box 430 Burke 57523	1862 (1898) unorganized land *Todd/*Charles Mix	— ? —	1862 1862 1862
D4	Haakon P.O. Box 70 Philip 57567	1914 (1915) Stanley	— 1915 —	1893 1915 1915
J3	Hamlin P.O. Box 256 Hayti 57241	1873 (1878) Deuel/Hanson	— ? —	1873? 1873? 1873?
G4	Hand P.O. Box 122 Miller 57362	1873 (1882) Buffalo	— ? —	1873 1873 1873
J5	Hanson P.O. Box 127 Alexandria 57311	1871 (1873) Brookings/Buffalo/Charles Mix/Deuel/ Hutchinson/Jayne/Minnehaha/ unorganized land	— ? —	1871? 1871? 1871?
A2	Harding P.O. Box 534 Buffalo 57720	1881 (1911) unorganized land	— ? —	1881? 1881? 1881?
	State archives has Territorial Registers of Action (1881–90); probate and circuit court records (1881–1957). In 1890 Harding was attached to Butte, and in 1898 it was abolished and became part of Butte. In 1908 Harding was re-created from Butte and was fully organized in 1911.			

Map	County Address	Date Formed Parent County/ies	Birth Marriage Death	Land Probate Court
F4	Hughes P.O. Box 1112 Pierre 57501	1873 (1880) Buffalo	— ? —	1873? 1873? 1873?
	State archives has divorce records (1905–34); probate records (1881–1948); district court records (1882–1928); and circuit court records (1881–1957).			
J6	Hutchinson P.O. Box 7 Olivet 57052	1862 (1871) unorganized land	— ? —	1862? 1862? 1862?
G4	Hyde P.O. Box 306 Highmore 57345	1873 (1883) Buffalo	— ? —	1873? 1873? 1873?
D5	Jackson P.O. Box 128 Kadoka 57543	1883 (1915) Cheyenne/Lugenbeel/White River *Pennington	— 1915 —	1901 1915 1915
	In 1909 Jackson was abolished and became part of Mellette and Washabaugh. Jackson was re-created from Stanley in 1914, becoming fully organized in 1915.			
	Jayne	1862 (abolished, 1871; became part of Hanson, Hutchinson, and Turner) unorganized land *Yankton		
H5	Jerauld P.O. Box 435 Wessington Springs 57382	1883 Aurora/Buffalo	— ? —	1883? 1883? 1883?
E5	Jones 310 S. Main Murdo 57559	1916 (1917) Lyman	— ? —	1917? 1917? 1917?
	State archives has probate records and circuit court judgments (1917–78).			
J4	Kingsbury P.O. Box 176 De Smet 57231	1873 (1880) Hanson	— ? —	1873? 1873? 1873?
	State archives has probate bonds (1882–1964); probate records (1885–1942); and wills (1911–69).			
K5	Lake P.O. Box 447 Madison 57042	1873 Brookings/Hanson/Minnehaha	— ? —	1873? 1873? 1873?
A4	Lawrence P.O. Box 626 Deadwood 57732	1875 (1877) unorganized land	— ? —	1875? 1875? 1875?
	State archives has probate records and wills (1877–1935); guardianship and adoption records (1910–58); marriage records (1879–1956); and circuit court journals (1891–1930).			
K6	Lincoln 100 E. Fifth Street Canton 57013	1862 (1867) unorganized land	— ? —	1862? 1862? 1862?
	Lugenbeel	1875 (abolished, 1909; became part of Bennett and Todd) Meyer/Pratt/unorganized land		
F5	Lyman P.O. Box 235 Kennebec 57544	1873 (1893) Gregory/unorganized land	— ? —	1873? 1873? 1873?
	Mandan	1875 (abolished, 1887; became part of Lawrence) unorganized land		
J1	Marshall P.O. Box 130 Britton 57430	1885 Day	— ? —	1885? 1885? 1885?

Map	County Address	Date Formed Parent County/ies	Birth Marriage Death	Land Probate Court
	Martin	1881 (abolished, 1898; became part of Butte) unorganized land *Lawrence		
J5	McCook P.O. Box 504 Salem 57058	1873 (1878) Hanson	— ? —	1873? 1873? 1873?
G1	McPherson P.O. Box 248 Leola 57456	1873 (1884) Buffalo	— ? —	1873? 1873? 1873?
B4	Meade P.O. Box 939 Sturgis 57785	1889 Lawrence	— ? —	1889? 1889? 1889?
E6	Mellette P.O. Box 257 White River 57579 *State archives holds probate cases (1913–42).*	1909 (1911) Jackson/Meyer/Washabaugh/ unorganized land	— 1911 —	1907 1912 1912
	Meyer	1873 (abolished, 1909; became part of Mellette and Todd) unorganized land		
J5	Miner P.O. Box 265 Howard 57349	1873 (1880) Hanson	— 1882 —	1881 1883 1881
K5	Minnehaha 415 N. Dakota Avenue Sioux Falls 57102	1862 (1868) unorganized land *Union	1905 1890 1905	1870 1873 1862
K5	Moody P.O. Box 226 Flandreau 57028	1873 Brookings/Minnehaha	— ? —	1873? 1873? 1873?
A5	Pennington P.O. Box 230 Rapid City 57709	1875 (1877) unorganized land	— 1887 —	1875? 1875? 1875?
C2	Perkins P.O. Box 27 Bison 57620	1908 (1909) Butte	— ? —	1909? 1909? 1909?
F3	Potter 201 S. Exene Gettysburg 57442	1873 (as Ashmore; renamed, 1875) (1883) Buffalo	— ? —	1875? 1875? 1875?
	Pyatt	1883 (renamed Armstrong, 1895) Cheyenne/Rusk/Stanley *Lawrence		
K1	Roberts 411 Second Avenue E. Sisseton 57262	1883 Grant/Sisseton- Wahpeteon Indian Reserve	— ? —	1883? 1883? 1883?
	Rusk	1873 (renamed Dewey, 1883) unorganized land		
H5	Sanborn P.O. Box 56 Woonsocket 57385	1883 Miner	— ? —	1883? 1883? 1883?

Map	County Address	Date Formed Parent County/ies	Birth Marriage Death	Land Probate Court
	Schnasse	1883 (abolished, 1911; became part of Ziebach) Boreman/unorganized land		
B6	Shannon 906 N. River Street Hot Springs 57747 *Shannon is still attached to Fall River.*	1875 unorganized land *Fall River	— ? —	1883? 1883? 1883?
H3	Spink 210 E. Seventh Avenue Redfield 57469	1873 (1879) Hanson	— ? —	1873? 1873? 1873?
E4	Stanley P.O. Box 97 Ft. Pierre 57532	1873 (1890) unorganized land	— ? —	1873? 1873? 1873?
	Sterling	1883 (abolished, 1911; became part of Ziebach) Cheyenne *Lawrence		
	Stone	1873 (abolished, 1879; became part of Brown and Day) Hanson		
F3	Sully P.O. Box 188 Onida 57564	1873 (1883) Buffalo	— ? —	1873? 1873? 1873?
	Todd (old) *In 1890 Todd deorganized and became attached to Charles Mix.*	1862 (abolished, 1897; became part of Gregory) unorganized land		
E6	Todd (present) Mission 57555 *State archives has birth register. Todd is still attached to Tripp; write Tripp County for records.*	1909 Meyer/Lugenbeel/Washabaugh/ unorganized land *Lyman/*Tripp		1909? 1909? 1909?
F6	Tripp 200 E. Third Street Winner 57580	1873 (1909) unorganized land/Gregory/Todd (old)	— ? —	1873? 1873? 1873?
K6	Turner P.O. Box 446 Parker 57053	1871 Lincoln/Jayne	— ? —	1871? 1871? 1871?
K7	Union P.O. Box 757 Elk Point 57025 *State archives has court records including land transactions (1860–1929); marriages (1919–23); wills (1870–1910); probate records (1869–1962); justice dockets (1868–1903); and bonds and court judgment books (1876–1948).*	1862 (as Cole; renamed, 1864) unorganized land	— ? —	1862? 1862? 1862?
F2	Walworth P.O. Box 328 Selby 57472 *State archives holds circuit court judgment records (1884–1932).*	1873 (1883) Buffalo	— ? —	1873? 1873? 1873?
	Washabaugh Kadoka 57543	1883 Lugenbeel *Custer/*Jackson	— ? —	1883? 1883? 1883?
	Washington *Included land now in Meyer and Pratt.*	1883 (abolished, 1943; became part of Shannon) Lugenbeel/Shannon *Custer		

Map	County Address	Date Formed Parent County/ies	Birth Marriage Death	Land Probate Court
	Wetmore	1873 (abolished, 1879; became part of Aurora and Miner) Hanson		
	White River	1875 (abolished, 1883; became part of Jackson) Pratt/unorganized land		
J7	Yankton P.O. Box 155 Yankton 57078	1862 unorganized land	— ? —	1862? 1862? 1862?
	State archives has probate records (1877–1909); wills (1870–1909); notary records (1877–1909); and judgment books (1898–1907).			
	Ziebach (old)	1877 (abolished, 1898; became part of Pennington) Pennington		
D3	Ziebach (present) P.O. Box 306 Dupree 57623	1911 Schnasse/Sterling/Armstrong (Cheyenne River Reservation)	— ? —	1911? 1911? 1911?

TENNESSEE

Wendy L. Elliott, C.G., C.G.L.

At the time of Tennessee's first exploration by Europeans, Cherokee inhabited the area of present-day Tennessee, residing in the region east of the Tennessee River after eradicating the Uchee. The area of today's state was used by neighboring Native American tribes as a hunting ground. Cherokee claimed east Tennessee, while Choctaw asserted rights to middle Tennessee and the upper Cumberland River area. Shawnee claimed the lower Cumberland area, and Chickasaw used and claimed the territory between the Tennessee and Mississippi rivers, in west Tennessee.

The British organized Ft. Loudon in east Tennessee in 1756, and the 1763 Treaty of Hard Labour opened the region for settlement by North Carolinians and Virginians. The Watauga Association, formed about 1771, organized the first government for what is now Tennessee. North Carolina claimed the region, along with portions of what became middle and western Tennessee, based on its colonial charter granting land from sea to sea. A settlement, made by former Wataugans at French Lick in 1779 in present-day central Tennessee, was organized as the Cumberland Compact.

During the Revolutionary War, small groups of hunters and trappers, some with their families, trekked across the Blue Ridge to nestle in the deep river valleys in east Tennessee marking the first permanent settlements. Claims to Tennessee's western lands were ceded to the United States government after a difficult and complicated series of events beginning with the first cession act of 1784 that was repealed that same year. Frustrated over proceedings and lack of representation in the North Carolina legislature, settlers on the frontier of present-day East Tennessee formed the independent State of Franklin in 1784. Lasting only four years, it failed in 1788. North Carolina ceded the area of Tennessee to the U.S. government in 1790, reserving some sections, and Congress created the "Territory South of the River Ohio." North Carolina granted Revolutionary soldiers land in the reserved area in middle Tennessee. In 1796, Tennessee separated from North Carolina and became the sixteenth state.

Frontier settlers from North Carolina, South Carolina, and Virginia migrated to Tennessee. Many were Scots-Irish who had traveled through the Shenandoah Valley down the Great Wagon Road to reach the territory. Germans from Pennsylvania and Virginia settled in the region west of Chattanooga. Others followed Robertson's Road into middle Tennessee.

Tennessee's history, following statehood, was partially linked with that of Andrew Jackson's military career and campaigns in the Battle of New Orleans and the Indian Wars. As part of the U.S. government policy toward Native Americans, West Tennessee was purchased from the Chickasaw who were removed, along with the Cherokee and other native tribes, to what is now Oklahoma.

Strong sentiments existed for the Union, particularly in east Tennessee. Opposing sentiments were advocated by those whose plantation economy depended on the institution of slavery. Black slaves were an important part of the state's farm economy. During the Civil War, Tennessee was an active battleground, with over 400 battles fought within its borders. Tennessee voted to withdraw from the Union but was the first to be readmitted.

Several epidemics swept through the populace following the war. Most of the state's railroads had to be rebuilt during the Reconstruction as Tennessee attempted to reclaim its previous importance in agriculture and commerce. In the beginning of the twentieth century a project to control floods and capture the Tennessee River's power with the building of Wilson Dam over the state's border in Muscle Shoals, Alabama, culminated in the Tennessee River Valley Authority in 1933. The energy production from the TVA created new industry and jobs in time to serve production needs during World War II.

Vital Records

Several early attempts were made to record births and deaths statewide, but the attempts were not effective until the twentieth century. The best reference for this information is *Guide to Public Vital Statistics in Tennessee* (Nashville, Tenn.: Tennessee Historical Records Survey, 1941). Only one type of vital record was maintained consistently throughout the history of the state and territory, and that was the marriage record. Some marriage records were recorded as early as 1778, but a law requiring registration did not pass until 1815. A subsequent law in 1838 required marriages to be registered in "well-bound" books. Many county vital records began in that same year.

A 1914 state law required statewide registration of births, marriages, and deaths, but general compliance was not complete until the late 1920s. Birth and death records between 1 July 1908 and 30 June 1912 and from 1 January 1914 to the present are available from the Vital Records Office, State Department of Public Health, Cordell Hull Building, Nashville, Tennessee 37219. When requesting copies, first write for the form, then complete the required information on it, including relationship and purpose.

There are indexes for 1908–12 available at the Tennessee State Library and Archives (see Archives, Libraries, and Societies). Statewide death records are available there from 1936, as is an index to death notices from Nashville newspapers.

Beginning in 1881 some counties maintained birth and death records. A few continued for a longer period. These original records are housed in the county courthouses with many microfilm copies at the Tennessee State Library and Archives and the FHL.

Birth records for Nashville from June 1881, Knoxville from July 1881, and Chattanooga from January 1882 are available at the Division of Vital Records in Nashville, although these records are incomplete. Records for Memphis are extant from 1 April 1874 through December 1887 and from 1 November 1898 to 1 January 1914. These are available from the Memphis-Shelby County Health Department, Division of Vital Statistics, 814 Jefferson Street, Memphis, Tennessee 38105.

Some deaths were recorded for Nashville as early as July 1874, Knoxville from 1 July 1887, and Chattanooga from 6 March 1872. These are maintained in the Vital Records Office in Nashville. Records for Memphis are extant from 1874–86 and from 1898 to 1 January 1914. Some Memphis death records are extant from 1 May 1848. These can be obtained from the Memphis-Shelby County Health Department (address above).

Beginning 1 July 1945, marriage records for Tennessee are available from the Division of Vital Records in Nashville. Prior to 1945, records of marriage can be found at the county clerk's office in the county where the license was obtained. Some marriages were recorded as early as 1783, and most counties maintained marriage records from the time of county organization.

Some marriage records for Tennessee have been compiled and published. See Silas E. Lucas and Ella L. Sheffield, *35,000 Tennessee Marriage Records and Bonds, 1783–1870*, 3 vols. (Easley, S.C.: Southern Historical Press, 1981); Byron Sistler and Barbara Sistler, *Early East Tennessee Marriages* (Nashville, Tenn.: Byron Sistler and Associates, 1987); Byron Sistler and Barbara Sistler, *Early Middle Tennessee Marriages* (Nashville, Tenn.: Byron Sistler and Associates, 1988); Silas Emmet Lucas, Jr., ed., *Marriages From Early Tennessee Newspapers, 1794–1851* (Easley, S.C.: Southern Historical Press, 1978); and Pollyanna Creekmore, ed., *Tennessee Marriage Records*, 3 vols. (Knoxville, Tenn.: the author, 1958–68). Edythe Rucker Whitley compiled separate marriage records for twenty-two counties, and these are published. Examples include:

Whitley, Edythe Rucker, comp. *Marriages of Blount County, Tennessee, 1795–1859*. Baltimore, Md.: Genealogical Publishing Co., 1982.

———. *Marriages of Claiborne County, Tennessee, 1838–1850, and Campbell County, Tennessee, 1838–1853*. Baltimore, Md.: Genealogical Publishing Co., 1983.

The WPA copied many early Tennessee marriage records; these are available in some counties, the Tennessee State Library and Archives, the Allen County Public Library (Ft. Wayne, Indiana), and the FHL. These transcripts contain numerous errors; originals should always be checked. The Tennessee State Library and Archives has microfilm copies available on interlibrary loan. An early Tennessee marriage index and an index to marriage notices published by Nashville newspapers are both available at the Tennessee State Library and Archives.

Prior to 1834, divorces could only be granted by an act of the general assembly; therefore, these records are among the legislative papers. The state constitution of 1834 took the power to grant divorces from the legislature and authorized courts to grant them. Divorce records are normally maintained by the respective county's circuit court. Statewide registration of divorces began on 1 July 1945. Early divorce records are compiled in Gale W. Bamman and Debbie W. Spero, *Tennessee Divorces, 1797–1858* (Nashville, Tenn.: G. Bamman, 1985), which abstracts 750 divorce records statewide.

Census Records

Federal

Population Schedules.

- Indexed—1810 (part), 1820 (part), 1830, 1840, 1850, 1860, 1870, 1880 (part)
- Soundex—1880, 1900, 1910, 1920

Industry and Agriculture Schedules.

- 1850, 1860, 1870, 1880

Mortality Schedules.

- 1850, 1860, 1870, 1880

Slave Schedules.

- 1850, 1860

Union Veterans Schedules.

- 1890

Federal census records for Tennessee are lost for 1790, 1800, and 1890. Only U. S. censuses for Grainger and Rutherford counties for 1810 are extant. Only twenty-six counties have federal census records for 1820. These middle and west Tennessee counties are Bedford, Davidson, Dickson, Franklin, Giles, Hardin, Hickman, Humphreys, Jackson, Lawrence, Lincoln, Maury, Montgomery, Overton, Perry, Robertson, Rutherford, Shelby, Smith, Stewart, Sumner, Warren, Wayne, White, Williamson, and Wilson. Except for Grainger, no early east Tennessee county censuses are available until 1830.

The Tennessee State Library and Archives (see Archives, Libraries, and Societies) has microfilm copies of all of Tennessee's censuses. In addition to the statewide AISI indexes, some county Federal population censuses have been indexed individually for 1870, 1880, 1900, and 1910. A study of land tenure, slavery, and agricultural economy during the late antebellum period was conducted under the direction of Frank L. Owsley, Professor of History, Vanderbilt University. Data was charted from agricultural census schedules for twenty-two Tennessee counties from the 1850 and 1860 enumerations. These compilations contain a wealth of information, including the amount of improved and unimproved land of each farmer or tenant farmer, types and value of crops produced, value of livestock, value of manufactures, and other related data. Charts were created for the following Tennessee counties: Davidson, DeKalb, Dickson, Dyer, Fayette, Fentress, Franklin, Gibson, Grainger, Greene, Hardin, Hawkins, Haywood, Henry, Johnson, Lincoln, Maury, Montgomery, Robertson, Stewart, Sumner, and Wilson. Entitled "Owsley Charts: Master Charts Compiled From the Unpublished Census, 1850–1860," this compilation was microfilmed and is available at the Tennessee State Library and Archives, Vanderbilt University, and the FHL. Originals of industry and agriculture schedules are at Duke University, Chapel Hill, North Carolina.

The 1870 Mortality Schedules were lost. Others have been published by Byron Sistler and Barbara Sistler: *Tennessee Mortality Schedules, 1850, 1860, 1880* (Nashville, Tenn., 1984).

Compilations of early Tennessee tax records assist in replacing the lost U. S. censuses. Among these are Byron Sistler and Barbara Sistler, *Index to Early Tennessee Tax Lists* (Evanston, Ill.: Byron Sistler and Assoc., 1977); Pollyanna Creekmore, comp., *Early East Tennessee Taxpayers* (Easley, S.C.: Southern Historical Press, 1980); Mary Barnett Curtis, *Early East Tennessee Tax Lists* (Ft. Worth, Tex.: Arrow Printing Co., 1964); and Richard Carlton Fulcher, comp., *1770–1790 Census of the Cumberland Settlements: Davidson, Sumner, Tennessee Counties (In What is Now Tennessee)* (Baltimore, Md.: Genealogical Publishing Co., 1987).

Background Sources

In the late 1880s, Goodspeed Publishing Company produced eighteen volumes of Tennessee county history, arranged regionally. Many volumes have been reprinted by Southern Historical Press, P.O. Box 738, Easley, South Carolina 29640. Two are *The Goodspeed History of Tennessee: Dyer, Gibson, Lake, Obion and Weakley Counties* (1887; reprint, Easley, S.C.: Southern Historical Press, 1978) and *History of Tennessee: From the Earliest Time to the Present; Together with an Historical and a Biographical Sketch of Maury, Williamson, Rutherford, Wilson, Bedford & Marshall Counties . . .* (1886; reprint, Easley, S.C.: Southern Historical Press, 1988).

Other volumes for the following counties are also available: Hamilton, Knox, and Shelby; Fayette and Hardeman; Lawrence, Wayne, Perry, Hickman, and Lewis; Madison; Sumner, Smith, Macon, and Trousdale; Montgomery, Robertson, Humphreys, Stewart, Dickson, Cheatham, and Houston; White, Warren, DeKalb, Coffee, and Cannon.

Other published sources include the following:

Caldwell, Mary French. *Tennessee, The Dangerous Example: Watauga to 1849.* Nashville, Tenn.: Aurora Publishers, 1974.

Carter, Clarence Edwin, comp. and ed. *The Territorial Papers of the United States: The Territory South of the River Ohio, 1790–1796.* Vol. 4. Washington, D.C.: Government Printing Office, 1953.

Corlew, R. E. *Tennessee: A Short History.* Knoxville, Tenn.: University of Tennessee Press, 1981. This is a condensed version of the standard, larger work which follows.

Folmsbee, Stanley John, Robert E. Corlew, and Enoch L. Mitchell. *History of Tennessee.* 4 vols. New York, N.Y.: Lewis Historical Publishing Co., 1960. Volume 2 includes a good bibliography, and volumes 3 and 4 contain family history.

Miller, Charles A. *The Official and Political Manual of the State of Tennessee.* 1890. Reprint. Easley, S.C.: Southern Historical Press, 1974. This volume was compiled by the secretary of state in 1890. It includes a chronological table from 1540 through 1888, briefly mentioning factors in Tennessee's history, and the constitutions of 1790, 1834, and 1870.

Schweitzer, George K. *Tennessee Genealogical Research.* Knoxville, Tenn.: the author, 1983. This valuable volume provides historical information as well as listing the most helpful source material. It details library collections and county records with dates.

Smith, Sam B. *Tennessee History: A Bibliography.* Knoxville, Tenn.: University of Tennessee Press, 1974. A comprehensive compilation of works pertaining to the state's history.

Williams, Samuel Cole. *Beginnings of West Tennessee in the Land of the Chickasaws, 1541–1841.* 1930. Reprint. Nashville, Tenn.: Blue and Gray Press, 1971.

———. *History of the Lost State of Franklin.* Johnson City, Tenn.: Watauga Press, 1924. Includes early maps and well-documented history.

Maps

Understanding history and the use of maps and gazetteers are essential for tracing early Tennessee families. The Tennessee State Library and Archives has a fine collection of maps, including early surveyors' maps and civil district maps. Helpful publications include:

Fullerton, Ralph O. *Place Names of Tennessee.* Bulletin No. 73. Nashville, Tenn.: State of Tennessee, Department of Conservation, Division of Geology, 1974. Arranged alphabetically by counties and, within the counties, alphabetically by place-name. Depicts county outline with geological survey overview.

McBride, Robert M., and Owen Meredith, eds. *Eastin Morris' Tennessee Gazetteer, 1834, Matthew Rhea's Map of the State of Tennessee, 1832.* Nashville, Tenn.: Gazetteer Press, 1971. A valuable guide to Tennessee's early history.

Tennessee maps can be purchased from the State of Tennessee, Department of Conservation, Division of Geology, Nashville, Tennessee 37203. General Highway Maps for Tennessee counties are available from the Tennessee Department of Transportation, Bureau of Planning and Development, Planning Division, Nashville, Tennessee 37219, and from respective counties.

The McClung Collection at the East Tennessee Historical Center (see Archives, Libraries, and Societies) includes a set of maps for the state dating from 1777. This series, drawn by Rene Jordan, depicts the development of east Tennessee over twenty years of county organization and jurisdictional changes (see Manuscripts).

The Tennessee State Library and Archives holdings include historical and current maps, including the U. S. Geological Survey topographical maps (see page 4). It maintains maps of some Mountain District grants and Ocoee District plat books.

Land Records

State-Land State

Only a small portion of the land granted in Tennessee was free land, and that was granted to those who provided some form of service to North Carolina. Earliest land records, including early grants issued by North Carolina and Tennessee, are microfilmed with a card index available in the Public Services Section of the Tennessee State Library and Archives. Other holdings include land warrants, survey certificates, and records from county register of deeds offices.

The earliest land grants are now maintained and available on microfilm at the Tennessee State Library and Archives. Official copies of all Tennessee land grants are bound and filed in the archives. All known grants are indexed in the master index, which is included on these microfilm reels. These consist of the following:

- North Carolina grants in Tennessee, 1783–1800, including North Carolina state grants. These land grants are also in the North Carolina State Archives (see North Carolina).
- Tennessee general grants date from 1806 to 1927.
- Grants were issued by district land offices from 1807 through 1838: East Tennessee District grants, from 1807; Hiwassee District grants, from November 1820; Middle Tennessee District, from 1824; West Tennessee District, beginning in 1826; Mountain District, opening in 1828; Ocoee District, starting in 1838. A pamphlet entitled "Land Grants in the Tennessee State Library and Archives," explains the holdings and is available from the repository.

The North Carolina Military Reservation was established in 1783 in the northern section of what was then west Tennessee (present-day middle Tennessee). It encompassed all the area surrounding the loop of the Cumberland River north to the Kentucky/Tennessee state line. A Congressional Reservation was organized on 18 April 1806 in the southwest section of middle Tennessee. The Congressional Reservation's northern border was the North Carolina Military Reservation's southern boundary. The western border for both was that portion of the Tennessee River that flows north. Several published volumes relate to North Carolina Revolutionary service land grants in middle Tennessee.

Land grants for the area south of Walker's Line (in Tennessee) are microfilmed and available through the FHL. Originals are indexed and housed in the Kentucky Land Office, Frankfort. Williard Rouse Jillson's work (see Kentucky) covers these grants. A printed source to North Carolina land grants is Betty G. C. Cartwright and L. J. Gardiner, *North Carolina Land Grants in Tennessee,*

1778–1791 (1958; rev. ed., Easley, S.C.: Southern Historical Press, 1981).

Beginning with county organization, land records are available from the register of deeds at the respective county courthouse. Land and property records include transfer of real estate or personal property, mortgages, leases, surveys, and entries. The Tennessee State Library and Archives has microfilmed county deed records that can be ordered by providing name, date, county, and type of record in the request.

Probate Records

The county court maintains jurisdiction over probate cases. Wills, administrations, and all other records pertaining to probate are recorded in the respective county clerk's office. If the will or administration was contested, the records of these actions may be filed in the circuit court or chancery court. Shelby and Davidson counties have separate probate courts.

Many early court records and lists of wills were transcribed by the WPA. Copies of these are usually in the county clerk's office and in the Tennessee State Library and Archives. Most records have been microfilmed and are available through the FHL.

Projects to preserve and microfilm probate files, or loose papers, were started in Franklin County in 1979 and in Shelby County in 1981. Microfilm copies are at the Tennessee State Library and Archives. Other counties are following this fine example of record preservation.

County courts also hear guardianship and minor civil and criminal cases. Court records date from the organization of the county except in cases where records have been destroyed. See Annie W. Burns, *Major Index to Wills and Inventories of Tennessee at the D.A.R. Library,* 6 vols. (Washington, D.C.: n.p., 1962–65), which covers Bedford through Meigs counties alphabetically.

Court Records

Court records for Tennessee can be difficult to use. Indexes are seldom, if ever, complete. Names may be indexed under various letters of the alphabet, but not necessarily by the individual's name. *A* for adoptions or *I* for "in regards to" are examples. Mortgaged estates may be indexed under the name of the bank holding the lien or mortgage, such as *B* for Bank of Commerce. Records may be indexed by other than surname, for example, *C* for commissioners/commission, *J* for jury, and *W* for will. In cases where property is sold by the sheriff, records can be found under *S* for sheriff, who was ordered by the court to sell the property to settle the estate or for back taxes. *S* for state may indicate records in which the state was a party, such as state land grants recorded in court records.

Tennessee court records can be complicated to use because there were various courts in which activities could be recorded. Some larger counties have superior courts of law and equity that hear minor civil and equity cases. Probate records normally were under the jurisdiction of the county court, but if the case was contested, then it could be filed in chancery or circuit court. Chancery courts have jurisdiction over property disputes, and circuit courts oversee criminal cases, divorces, and adoptions. Early courts included courts of common pleas and quarter sessions.

Original court records, including minute and order books, boxes of loose papers, case files, and folders, are maintained by the county. Each source should be thoroughly examined for pertinent entries. Many of these were microfilmed and are available at the Tennessee State Library and Archives and through the FHL. Marjorie Hood Fischer, comp., *Tennessee Tidbits, 1778–1914,* 4 vols. (vol. 1, Easley, S.C.: Southern Historical Press, 1986; vol. 2, Vista, Calif.: RAM Press, 1988), is a continuing series which contains abstracts of minutes from county courts, circuit courts, and chancery courts. Volume 1 includes abstracts from Blount, Davidson, Dickson, Fayette, Giles, Greene, Hardin, Haywood, Hickman, Humphreys, Lincoln, Putnam, Rutherford, Washington, and Williamson. Volume 2 covers Bedford, Claiborne, Dyer, Fentress, Jackson, Madison, McMinn, Obion, Roane, Robertson, Sevier, Stewart, Washington, and Wilson.

Under the WPA, approximately 1,000 typed volumes of county records were transcribed for most counties in Tennessee. These are microfilmed and available on interlibrary loan from the Tennessee State Library and Archives. There is a card index inventory to this compilation arranged by county. Court records included in this collection are wills; county, chancery, and circuit court minutes; and estate settlements. Because these WPA transcripts contain numerous transcription and typographical errors, the original records should always be reviewed.

Tax Records

The 1796 Constitution levied taxes on "every freeman of the age of twenty-one years and upward possessing a freehold in the county wherein he may vote, and being an inhabitant of this State, and every freeman being an inhabitant of any one county in the State six months immediately preceding the day of the election, shall be entitled to vote . . . ."

Many early surviving tax records were published in an effort to replace the missing federal censuses (see Census Records). Original extant tax records are preserved in the respective county courthouse as well as in the Tennessee State Library and Archives, where a card index exists for tax records in its collection pre-dating 1835, arranged by county, date, and district. Some early original tax lists are available in the McClung Historical Collection at the Lawson McGhee Library (see Archives, Libraries, and Societies), including those for Washington County, 1778 and 1787;

Greene County, 1783; Carter and Sullivan counties, 1796; and Grainger County, 1799.

Original tax schedules for most Tennessee counties for 1836 through 1839 are available at the Tennessee State Library and Archives. In addition, the Indiana State Library, the FHL, and the Allen County Public Library (see Indiana) have microfilmed copies of early Tennessee tax records.

The 1891 tax lists of male inhabitant voters in each county were recently found. Available on microfilm at the Tennessee State Library and Archives, these nine reels are arranged alphabetically within each district in each county. Tax records from trustees office in counties are available on microfilm as well.

Cemetery Records

A large collection of transcripts of Tennessee cemetery records has been compiled by members of chapters of the DAR (see page 6). Other compilations of cemetery records are those in the Calvin M. McClung Historical Collection in the Lawson McGhee Library and in the Tennessee Miscellaneous Family and Cemetery Records collection available at the Tennessee State Library and Archives and through the FHL. The state library and archives has notebooks containing listings of cemetery records.

County genealogical and historical societies and local citizens have collected, compiled, and published numerous volumes of cemetery records. Other notable sources include:

Acklen, Jeannette T., et al. *Tennessee Records.* 2 vols. 1933. Reprint. Baltimore, Md.: Genealogical Publishing Co., 1974. Vol. 1 contains tombstone inscriptions.

Hunkins, Lillian. *Tombstone Inscriptions and Marriages of Middle Tennessee.* Houston, Tex.: the author, 1965.

Church Records

Although few histories for Tennessee churches have been published, there are church records for almost every county in the state. Baptist, Presbyterian, and Methodist were the principal religions of early settlers in the state, and documents from these groups make up the largest number of records available. Other representative religions include Lutheran, Church of Christ, Episcopal, Roman Catholic, and Jewish. Most early Tennessee churches only kept minutes and membership records.

Church records could, however, include records of baptism, marriage, burial, membership, or removal, but it is rare to find all or several of these categories maintained by one church. Some Presbyterian churches kept registers with some genealogical information in the session minutes or in a separate register. Each Baptist congregation is usually self-governing, and there is no set procedure for recording data for its members. Methodist ministers were charged with maintenance of permanent records of marriages, baptisms, and dismissals. The Episcopal and Roman Catholic churches maintain registers that contain genealogical data for all members.

A published guide is Historical Records Survey, *Guide to Church Vital Statistics in Tennessee* (Nashville, Tenn.: War Services Section, Service Division, WPA, 1943). Thirty-nine counties compose this historical records survey of Tennessee church records. This reference details records for certain churches, varying from three to 349 per county. Beverly West Hathaway, *Genealogy Research Sources in Tennessee* (West Jordon, Utah: Allstates Research Co., 1972), contains a denominationally arranged guide to church records in Tennessee. This data includes dates and places of numerous churches as well as names of organizers.

As with cemetery records, the DAR has collected church records for Tennessee, available at the DAR Library in Washington, D.C., and through the FHL. Many compilations of church records have been compiled and/or published for the state. The Tennessee State Library and Archives has records of over one hundred churches that pre-date 1900. Byron Sistler and Barbara Sistler compiled an index to these records in *Vital Statistics from 19th Century Tennessee Church Records,* 2 vols. (Nashville, Tenn.: Byron Sistler and Assoc., 1979), which contains births, baptisms, marriages, deaths, and burials from 104 churches and/or church associations in Tennessee.

Microfilmed records and manuscripts of several churches in the state are described in the card catalog and published by the Tennessee State Library and Archives' *Guide to the Microfilm Holdings* (see Manuscripts).

The McClung Collection of the Lawson McGhee Library in Knoxville holds microfilm of Methodist, Baptist, and Presbyterian church records. The Burrow Library in Memphis also has Presbyterian church records. The Historical Commission of the Southern Baptist Convention, Disciples of Christ Historical Society, Catholic Diocese of Nashville Archives, and Archives of the Jewish Federation of Nashville and Middle Tennessee, all located in Nashville, hold representative collections.

Military Records

Tennessee began granting pensions for military service to resident Confederate veterans in 1891 and to veterans' widows in 1905. The Tennessee State Library and Archives has the applications and many additional records relating to military and naval service during the War Between the States on microfilm. Indexes for Revolutionary War pensioners; muster rolls for soldiers of the War of 1812, Indian wars of 1818 and 1836, Mexican War, Civil War, and Spanish-American War; and service records for Tennesseans who served during the Mexican War and Civil War (both Confederate and Union) are among the archives' collections.

Considerable material exists in the manuscript collection at the state archives. Their Register Number 10 includes an index and list of some holdings for Confederate and Union soldiers. A valuable source is the Confederate and Union veterans questionnaires sent by the Tennessee Historical Committee. Containing details about military and personal data, these have been published without index in five volumes in Gustavus W. Dyer and John Trotwood Moore, *Tennessee Civil War Questionnaires* (Easley, S.C.: Southern Historical Press, 1985). An unpublished index is available at the state archives.

A card index to the *Confederate Veteran* magazine and a card index to Lindsay, *Military Annals of Tennessee (Confederate)*, are maintained in the state archives, as are National Archives indexes for service in the Revolutionary War, War of 1812, Mexican War, and hundreds of monographs concerning the War Between the States.

Printed sources abound in the state for military service and pension records. A few are the following:

Allen, Penelope Johnson. *Tennessee Soldiers in the Revolution: A Roster of Soldiers During the Revolutionary War in the Counties of Washington and Sullivan, Taken from the Revolutionary Army Accounts of North Carolina.* 1935. Reprint. Baltimore, Md.: Genealogical Publishing Co., 1967.

Armstrong, Zella. *Some Tennessee Heroes of the Revolution.* 3 parts. Chattanooga, Tenn.: n.p., 1933–35.

———. *Twenty-four Hundred Tennessee Pensioners—Revolution, War of 1812.* Chattanooga, Tenn.: n.p., 1937.

———. *Tennessee Soldiers in the War of 1812: Regiments of Col. Allcorn and Col. Allison.* Chattanooga, Tenn.: Tennessee Society U. S. Daughters of 1812, 1947. Taken from the Tennessee State Archives photostats of original records in Washington D.C.

Lindsley, John B. *The Military Annals of Tennessee.* 1886. Reprint. Spartanburg, S.C.: Reprint Co., 1974.

McCown, Mary Hardin, and Inez E. Burns. *Soldiers of the War of 1812 Buried in Tennessee.* Johnson City, Tenn.: Tennessee Society U. S. Daughters of the War of 1812. 1959. Reprint. Johnson City, Tenn.: Overmountain Press, 1977. A standard published source on the subject of Tennessee soldiers.

Mills, Gary. *Civil War Claims in the South: An Index of Civil War Damage Claims Filed Before the Southern Claims Commission, 1871–1880.* Laguna Hills, Calif.: Aegean Park Press, 1980.

Sistler, Byron, and Barbara Sistler. *1890 Civil War Veterans Census—Tennessee.* Nashville, Tenn.: Byron Sistler and Assoc., 1978.

Tennessee Civil War Centennial Commission. *Tennesseans in the Civil War, A Military History of Confederate and Union Units with Available Rosters of Personnel.* 2 vols. 1964–65. Reprint. Nashville, Tenn.: Civil War Centennial Commission, 1981–84.

Tennessee State Library and Archives. *Index to Tennessee Confederate Pension Applications.* Nashville, Tenn.: State Library, 1964.

Wright, Marcus J. *Tennessee in the War, 1861–65. Lists of Military Organizations and Officers from Tennessee in Both the Union and Confederate Armies . . .* New York, 1908.

Periodicals, Newspapers, and Manuscript Collections

Periodicals

Major periodicals for Tennessee that publish source material from most categories include these:

Ansearchin' News (1954–present). A publication of the Tennessee Genealogical Society, P.O. Box 12124, Dept. AN, Memphis, Tennessee 38112.

Bulletin (1972–present). A publication of the Watauga Association of Genealogists, Johnson City, Tennessee 37605.

Chattanews. Published by the Chattanooga Area Historical Association, Chattanooga, Tennessee 37402.

East Tennessee Roots. Published by Tennessee Valley Publications, Paula Gammell, ed., 1345 Oak Ridge Turnpike #318, Oak Ridge, Tennessee 37830.

Echoes (1955–1984). The East Tennessee Historical Society ceased its publication but replaced it with *Tennessee Ancestors* (see below).

Family Findings (1969–present). A publication of the Midwest Tennessee Genealogical Society, P.O. Box 3343, Jackson, Tennessee 38303.

Pellissippian (1980–present). A publication of the Pellissippian Genealogical and Historical Society, 118 Hicks, Clinton, Tennessee 38303.

The River Counties Quarterly (1972–present). Published by Jill Garrett, 610 Terrace, Columbia, Tennessee 38401.

Tennessee Ancestors (1985–present). This publication replaced *Echoes* for the East Tennessee Historical Society, 500 West Church Avenue, Knoxville, Tennessee 37902-2505.

The Tennessee Historical Quarterly (1942–present). Published by the Tennessee Historical Commission, Nashville, Tennessee 37203.

Newspapers

The Tennessee State Library and Archives has a large collection of newspapers and an incomplete card index to marriage and death notices published in Nashville newspapers. The Draper Manuscript Collection, housed at the State Historical Society of Wisconsin, includes early Tennessee newspapers (see Wisconsin— Manuscripts). One published compilation of data extracted from eight Tennessee newspapers is Sherida K. Eddlemon, comp.,

Genealogical Abstracts from Tennessee Newspapers, 1791–1808 (Bowie, Md.: Heritage Books, 1988).

A guide to newspaper collections is:

Tennessee Newspapers: A Cumulative List of Microfilmed Tennessee Newspapers in the Tennessee State Library, 1978 Progress Report. Nashville, Tenn.: Tennessee State Library and Archives, 1978.

Manuscripts

The largest collections of manuscripts pertaining to Tennessee are in the Tennessee State Library and Archives. Published guides to this collection are available, including *Guide to the Microfilmed Manuscript Holdings of the Tennessee State Library and Archives,* 3d ed. (Nashville, Tenn.: Tennessee State Library, 1983). Acklen's two volume work (see Cemetery Records) includes references to manuscripts.

In addition to the card indexes cited under land and military records, an interesting index at the state archives is for Tennessee century farms (histories compiled of families whose farms have remained in use by the family for over 100 years).

During the 1930s the WPA collected a series of verbatim transcripts of the records of some Tennessee counties. This includes a considerable number of early county records. The only complete set of abstracts are in the Tennessee State Library and Archives. Nearly 1,500 volumes are available on ninety-three reels of microfilm.

Archives, Libraries, and Societies

Tennessee State Library and Archives
403 Seventh Avenue, North
Nashville, TN 37243-0312

Its holdings include state agency records, executive branch papers, territorial records, records for courts of appeal and supreme court. Many of the abundant holdings for this repository have already been discussed. As a bicentennial project, the library sponsored an extensive program of microfilming county records, concentrating on the records that were not in the WPA series. Inventories of most Tennessee county records, as well as microfilms of most early county records, are located here. The inventory has been printed and can be purchased from the repository for a nominal fee.

Vertical family files and the genealogical exchange card file are additional sources. The library and archives also maintains territorial and state records as well as county records, providing correspondence service except during the summer months; expect a response time of several weeks. Each request should include name, date of interest or state a period of ten years or less, county, and type of record requested. Only one search per request. There is a minimum photocopy charge.

Tennessee Historical Society
War Memorial Building
300 Capital Boulevard
Nashville, TN 37243

Harriet C. Owsley, *Guide to the Processed Manuscripts of the Tennessee Historical Society* (Nashville, Tenn.: Tennessee State Library, 1963), describes and serves as a finding aid to the manuscript section of the archives for the holdings of the Tennessee Historical Society that were processed prior to 1963. The collection is arranged alphabetically, and the entire volume is indexed for ready reference.

East Tennessee Historical Center
at the Lawson McGehee Library
of the Knox County Public Library System-
Mailing Address:
314 West Clinch Avenue
Knoxville, TN 37802-2203
Street Address:
500 West Clinch Avenue
Knoxville, TN 37902-2505

Three distinct entities operate out of this center: The McClung Historical Collection (which is the local history and genealogy department of the Lawson McGhee Library); the Knox County Archives; and the East Tennessee Historical Society.

The McClung Historical Collection contains over 500 manuscript collections, most pertaining to east Tennessee. These holdings must be accessed personally. The McClung Collection maintains a genealogy file that consists of data submitted by various patrons. The staff will try to answer basic genealogical queries from indexed published sources. A self-addressed stamped envelope is necessary.

The collection contains a large body of published works, many of which are rare. Some may no longer be photocopied because of deterioration, but supervised access is allowed. A set of microfilmed records of the surviving service records of Tennessee soldiers for the War of 1812 is found in the collection, which has extensive holdings of the records of the Tennessee WPA and other assorted manuscripts.

The East Tennessee Historical Society promotes the development of the library holdings.

The Knox County Archives provides access to the county government records dated from 1792 to present. Among its holdings are marriage records, 1792–1974; tax records, 1806–1974; court records, 1792–1979; chancery court records, 1832–; circuit court records, 1810–; Knoxville birth and death records, 1881–1911.

Williamson County Historical Society
P.O. Box 72
Franklin, TN 37064

This library houses information pertaining to middle Tennessee. See J. B. Howell *Special Collections in Libraries of the Southeast* (Jackson, Miss.: Southeastern Library Association, 1978) for more information on the holdings in this and other libraries.

Williamson County Public Library
611 West Main Street
Franklin, TN 37064

This library holds the Whitley collection of marriage and county records from over twenty-two counties, collected by a local genealogist.

Tennessee Genealogical Society
P.O. Box 12124
Memphis, TN 38112
Publication: *Ansearchin' News*

Publication includes materials for the entire state. Articles include abstracted wills, marriage records, probate records, church records, newspaper notices, and more.

Other historical record repositories for Tennessee include:

Chattanooga-Hamilton County Bicentennial Library
1001 Broad Street
Chattanooga, TN 37402

Mississippi Valley Historical Collection
Brister Library
Memphis State University
Memphis, TN 38152

Special Collection, Vanderbilt University
419 21st Avenue South
Nashville, TN 37240-0007

Metro Davidson County Archives
1113 Elm Hill Pike
Nashville, TN 37210

Holdings include chancery court records, 1846–1961; circuit court records, 1943–55; county clerk papers and records, 1783–1971; register of deeds, 1785–1951; and various other records. A detailed, itemized description is available upon request from the repository.

Special Focus Categories

Black American

The National Archives (see page 8) and the DAR Library (see page 9) have the original and microfilm slave-owner census schedules for the 1850 and 1860 U. S. censuses. The Tennessee State Library and Archives has some records of blacks who served in the Civil War.

Native American

Most records for Native American families from Tennessee will be located in Oklahoma. The main repository is the Bureau of Indian Affairs, Department of Interior, Muskogee, Oklahoma 74401, although another source is the Oklahoma Historical Society (see Oklahoma).

Chickasaw ceded their territory in present-day west Tennessee on 19 October 1818. The Cherokee claimed land in the southeastern section of the state until December 1835, when their final exodus began. Even though all land had been ceded, some Native Americans remained in Tennessee after that date.

Data on Native American endeavors and actions was published in *The American State Papers, Class II, Indian Affairs.* This volume is in the Tennessee State Library and Archives in closed stacks. A collection of records pertaining to Cherokees (Register Number 11) and the Cherokee Census of 1835 is available to the public. J. J. Hill prepared an index to Emmett Stark's two volume, *Cherokee Families.* Both are available in the Metro Davidson County Archives in Nashville (see Archives, Libraries, and Societies).

County Resources

Tennessee deeds are recorded at the register of deed's office. The county court maintains jurisdiction over the probate and court records, except for Shelby and Davidson counties where the county court handles probates, and circuit court handles civil matters. Dates given are for the first known records in each category at the county seat. It does not imply that all records are extant from that date. County formation is from information supplied by the Tennessee State Library and Archives. See resources below for further assistance.

Richard Carlton Fulcher, comp., *Guide to County Records and Genealogical Resources in Tennessee.* Baltimore, Md.: Genealogical Publishing Co., 1987. This is a county-by-county guide to published, WPA typescript and microfilmed records.

Historical Records Survey. *Survey of Tennessee County Court Records, Prior to 1860 in the Second, Third, and Fourth Districts.* Nashville, Tenn.: Historical Records Survey, 1943.

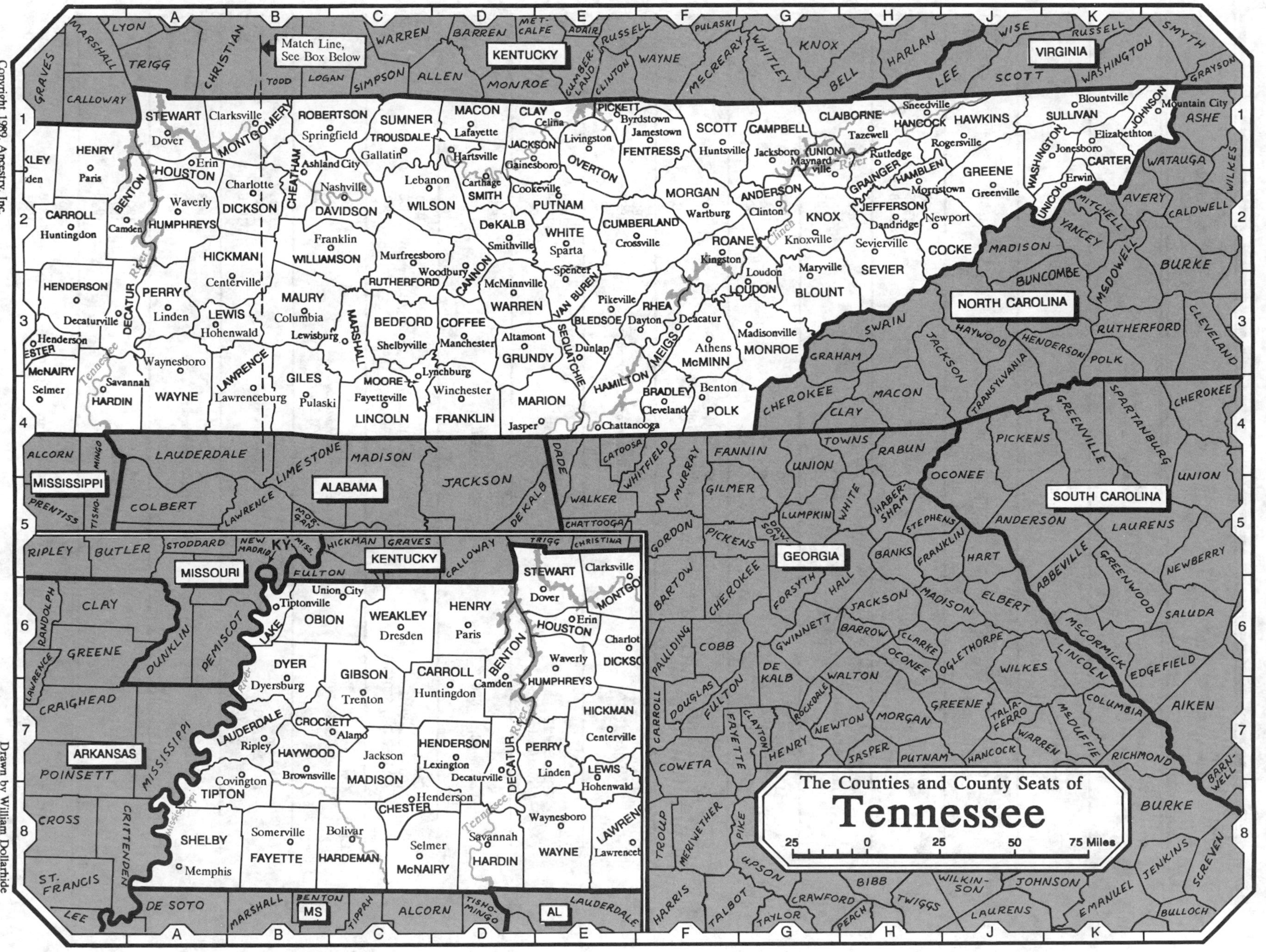

Copyright 1989, Ancestry, Inc.

Drawn by William Dollarhide

Map	County Address	Date Formed Parent County/ies	Birth Marriage Death	Land Probate Court
G2	Anderson Clinton 37716	1801 Knox/Grainger	1881 1838 1891	1801 1830 1801
C3	Bedford Shelbyville 37160	1807 Rutherford/Indian lands	1908 1861 1908	1808 1852 1830
D7, A2	Benton P.O. Box 8 Camden 38320	1835 Humphreys	1881 1837 1881	1836 1858 1836
E3	Bledsoe Pikeville 37367	1807 Roane/Indian lands	1908 1905 1908	1896 1884 1810
G3	Blount Maryville 37803	1795 Knox	1881 1795 1881	1795 1795 1795
F4	Bradley P.O. Box 46 Cleveland 37364	1836 Cherokee land	1908 1864 1908	1839 1859 1836
G1	Campbell P.O. Box 13 Jacksboro 37757	1806 Anderson/Claiborne	1914 1838 1914	1806 1807 1813
D3	Cannon Woodbury 37190	1836 Rutherford/Smith/Warren	1881 1838 1881	1836 1836 1836
A2, D7	Carroll P.O. Box 110 Huntingdon 38344	1821 Western District	1908 1838 1908	1822 1852 1821
K1	Carter Elizabethton 37643	1796 Washington	1881 1790 1881	1796 1794 1804
B2	Cheatham 100 Public Square Ashland City 37015	1856 Davidson/Dickson/Montgomery/Robertson	1881 1856 1881	1856 1856 1856
C8	Chester Henderson 38340	1879 Hardman/Madison/ Henderson/McNairy	1908 1891 1908	1891 1891 1882
H1	Claiborne P.O. Box 173 Tazewell 37879	1801 Grainger/Hawkins	1908 1838 1908	1801 1837 1801
D1	Clay P.O. Box 218 Celina 38551	1870 Jackson/Overton	1908 1908 1908	1871 1871 1871
J2	Cocke Newport 37821	1797 Jefferson	1908 1877 1908	1865 1876 1877
D3	Coffee 300 Hillsboro Boulevard Manchester 37355	1836 Franklin/Warren/Bedford	1881 1853 1881	1836 1836 1836

Map	County Address	Date Formed Parent County/ies	Birth Marriage Death	Land Probate Court
B7	Crockett Alamo 38001	1871 Madison/Dyer/Gibson/Haywood	1909 1872 1909	1871 1872 1872
F2	Cumberland Main Street Crossville 38555	1855 Bledsoe/Morgan/Rhea/Fentress/ Putnam	1914 1905 1914	1854 1904 1897
C2	Davidson Nashville 37201	1783 Washington, N.C.	1881 1789 1881	1784 1784 1783
A3, D8	Decatur P.O. Box 488 Decaturville 38329	1845 Perry	1881 1869 1908	1846 1869 1868
D2	DeKalb Smithville 37166	1837 Cannon/Warren/White	1914 1848 1914	1838 1838 1837
D6	Dickson Charlotte 37036	1803 Montgomery/Robertson	1908 1817 1908	1804 1803 1804
B6	Dyer P.O. Box 1360 Dyersburg 38025	1823 Western District	1909 1860 1881	1823 1853 1848
B8	Fayette P.O. Box 218 Somerville 38068	1824 Shelby/Hardeman	1914 1838 1914	1825 1836 1824
F1	Fentress P.O. Box C Jamestown 38556	1823 Morgan/Overton/White	1914 1905 1914	1823 1905 1842
D4	Franklin Winchester 37398	1807 Bedford/Warren	1881 1838 1881	1807 1808 1832
C7	Gibson Trenton 38382	1823 Western District	1881 1824 1881	1823 1824 1824
B4	Giles P.O. Box 678 Pulaski 38478	1809 Maury	1908 1818 1908	1830 1830 1810
H2	Grainger Rutledge 37861	1796 Hawkins	1908 1796 1908	1796 1796 1796
J2	Greene Greeneville 37743	1783 Washington, N.C.	1881 1783 1881	1785 1802 1783
D3	Grundy Altamont 37301	1844 Franklin/Warren	1908 1908 1908	1852 1844 1844
H2	Hamblen 511 W. Second N Street Morristown 37814	1870 Grainger/Greene/Jefferson	1908 1870 1908	1870 1870 1870

Map	County Address	Date Formed Parent County/ies	Birth Marriage Death	Land Probate Court
E4	Hamilton 105 Courthouse Chattanooga 37402	1819 Rhea	1908 1857 1908	1819 1864 1858
H1	Hancock Main Street Sneedville 37869	1844 Claiborne/Hawkins	1914 1930 1914	1879 1929 1929
C8	Hardeman 100 N. Main Bolivar 38008	1823 Hardin/Western District	1881 1823 1881	1823 1823 1810
A4, D8	Hardin Main Street Savannah 38372	1819 Western District	1881 1861 1881	1835 1836 1820
J1	Hawkins 150 Washington Street Rogersville 37857	1785 (as Spencer; renamed, 1786) Sullivan	1914 1786 1914	1787 1786 1810
B8	Haywood 100 N. Washington Brownsville 38012	1823 Western District	1881 1859 1908	1820 1824 1823
A3, D7	Henderson Lexington 38351	1821 Western District	1908 1893 1908	1856 1893 1860
A1, D6	Henry P.O. Box 24 Paris 38242	1821 Western District	1881 1838 1881	1822 1822 1822
A3, E7	Hickman Public Square Centerville 37033	1807 Dickson	1914 1868 1914	1808 1844 1840
E6	Houston P.O. Box 388 Erin 37061	1871 Dickson/Stewart/Humphreys/Montgovery	1881 1871 1914	1871 1871 1871
A2, E7	Humphreys Waverly 37185	1809 Stewart	1908 1864 1908	1810 1837 1840
D1	Jackson P.O. Box 346 Gainesboro 38562	1801 Smith/Indian lands	1881 1870 1881	1872 1872 1839
	James *County seat was Ooltewah. Records in Chattanooga, Hamilton County.*	1870 (abolished; became part of Hamilton, 1919) Hamilton/Bradley		
H2	Jefferson P.O. Box 726 Dandridge 37725	1792 Greene/Hawkins	1908 1792 1908	1792 1805 1792
K1	Johnson 222 Main Street Mountain City 37683	1836 Carter	1908 1838 1908	1836 1839 1836
G2	Knox P.O. Box 1566 Knoxville 37901	1792 Greene/Hawkins	1881 1792 1881	1791 1792 1792

Map	County Address	Date Formed Parent County/ies	Birth Marriage Death	Land Probate Court
B6	Lake Church Street Tiptonville 38079	1870 Obion	1914 1883 1914	1870 1871 1870
B7	Lauderdale Ripley 38063	1835 Dyer/Tipton/Haywood	1881 1838 1881	1835 1849 1836
B4, E8	Lawrence P.O. Box NBU #2 Lawrenceburg 38464	1817 Hickman/Indian lands	1881 1818 1881	1819 1829 1818
E8	Lewis Hohenwald 38462	1843 Hickman/Maury/Wayne/Lawrence	1908 1844 1908	1844 1846 1844
C4	Lincoln P.O. Box 577 Fayetteville 37334	1809 Bedford	1881 1823 1881	1810 1809 1810
G3	Loudon Loudon 37774	1870 Blount/Monroe/Roane/McMinn	1908 1870 1908	1870 1870 1870
D1	Macon Lafayette 37083	1842 Smith/Sumer	1909 1901 1913	1901 1901 1901
C8	Madison Jackson 38301	1821 Western District	1908 1838 1908	1821 1822 1821
D4	Marion Courthouse Square Jasper 37347	1817 Cherokee land	1881 1881 1881	1819 1875 1842
C3	Marshall Public Square Lewisburg 37091	1836 Bedford/Lincoln/Maury	1914 1836 1914	1836 1836 1835
B3	Maury Public Square Columbia 38401	1807 Williamson/Indian lands	1908 1807 1908	1807 1807 1807
F3	McMinn Athens 37303	1819 Cherokee land	1908 1820 1908	1820 1820 1819
C8	McNairy Selmer 38375	1823 Hardin	1881 1861 1908	1823 1861 1856
F3	Meigs P.O. Box 218 Decatur 37322	1836 Rhea	1908 1838 1908	1840 1836 1836
G3	Monroe College Street Madisonville 37354	1819 Indian lands	1881 1838 1881	1820 1825 1820
B1, E6	Montgomery Clarksville 37042	1796 Tennessee	1908 1881 1881	1786 1805 1805

Map	County Address	Date Formed Parent County/ies	Birth Marriage Death	Land Probate Court
C4	Moore Lynchburg 37352	1871 Bedford/Franklin/Coffee/Lincoln	1881 1872 1881	1872 1872 1872
F2	Morgan Main Street Wartburg 37887	1817 Roane/Anderson	1908 1862 1908	1818 1866 1824
B6	Obion Union City 38261	1823 Western District	1881 1824 1881	1824 1824 1824
E1	Overton Livingston 38570	1806 Jackson/Indian lands	1914 1867 1914	1806 1870 1815
A3, E7	Perry P.O. Box 16 Linden 37096	1819 Hickman/Humphreys	1908 1881 1881	1820 1826 1826
E1	Pickett P.O. Box 5 Byrdstown 38549	1879 Fentress/Overton	1934 1934 1934	1934 1934 1934
F4	Polk Benton 37307	1839 Bradley/McMinn	1908 1894 1908	1840 1890 1840
E2	Putnam Cookeville 38501	1854 White/Jackson/Overton/Smith/Fentress	1908 1879 1879	1854 1874 1874
F3	Rhea Dayton 37321	1807 Roane	1908 1808 1908	1808 1808 1815
F2	Roane P.O. Box 546 Kingston 37763	1801 Knox/Indian lands	1881 1801 1881	1801 1802 1801
B1	Robertson Springfield 37172	1796 Tennessee/Sumner	1908 1839 1908	1796 1796 1796
C2	Rutherford Public Square Murfreesboro 37130	1803 Davidson/Williamson/Wilson	1881 1804 1881	1804 1804 1804
F1	Scott P.O. Box 87 Huntsville 37756	1849 Fentress/Morgan/Anderson/Campbell	 1854 1914	1850 1929 1850
E3	Sequatchie Dunlap 37327	1857 Hamilton/Marion/Warren	1880 1858 1880	1858 1858 1858
H3	Sevier Sevierville 37862	1794 Jefferson	1914 1856 1881	1842 1849 1854
A8	Shelby 140 Adams Memphis 38103	1819 Indian lands	1881 1819 1881	1821 1824 1828

Map	County Address	Date Formed Parent County/ies	Birth Marriage Death	Land Probate Court
D2	Smith Carthage 37030	1799 Sumner/Indian lands	1881 1838 1881	1801 1805 1799
	Spencer	1785 (renamed Hawkins, 1786) Sullivan		
A1, E6	Stewart P.O. Box 67 Dover 37058	1803 Montgomery	1881 1838 1881	1803 1883 1804
K1	Sullivan Blountville 37617	1779 Washington, N.C.	1881 1861 1881	1775 1861 1787
C1	Sumner Gallatin 37066	1786 Davidson	1881 1787 1881	1787 1788 1785
	Tennessee *County seat was Clarkesville. Records in Robertson County.*	1788 (abolished; divided into Montgomery and Robertson) Davidson		
A8	Tipton P.O. Box 528 Covington 38019	1823 Western District	1914 1840 1914	1824 1824 1823
D1	Trousdale Hartsville 37074	1870 Macon/Smith/Wilson	1909 1905 1909	1905 1905 1903
K2	Unicoi P.O. Box 340 Erwin 37650	1875 Carter/Washington	1908 1876 1908	1876 1876 1875
G2	Union P.O. Box 395 Maynardville 37807	1850 Anderson/Campbell/Knox/Claiborne/ Grainger	1881 1864 1881	1856 1856 1854
E3	Van Buren P.O. Box 126 Spencer 38585	1840 Warren/White	1908 1840 1908	1840 1840 1840
D3	Warren McMinnville 37110	1807 White/Jackson/Smith	1881 1852 1881	1808 1827 1842
K1	Washington Jonesboro 37659	1777 Act of North Carolina	1908 1787 1908	1779 1778 1778
A4, E8	Wayne Waynesboro 38485 *An earlier, but separate, "Wayne County" is included in today's Carter County and part of Johnson County. It was established in 1785 under the state of Franklin but was abolished in 1788.*	1819 Hickman	1881 1851 1881	1820 1848 1837
C6	Weakley Dresden 38225	1823 Western District	1908 1842 1908	1823 1866 1826
E2	White Sparta 38583	1806 Jackson/Smith	1881 1809 1881	1806 1833 1806

Map	County Address	Date Formed Parent County/ies	Birth Marriage Death	Land Probate Court
B2	Williamson Franklin 37064	1799 Davidson	1881 1800 1881	1799 1819 1800
C2	Wilson Lebanon 37087 **Wills 1802.*	1799 Sumner	1881 1802 1881	1799 1858* 1802

TEXAS

Wendy L. Elliott, C.G., C.G.L.

Native American tribes resided in the area when present-day Texas was settled in 1682 by the Spanish at Isleta, near present-day El Paso. Between 1685 and 1700, Franciscan missions and Spanish military outposts (or presidios) were established in east Texas at Nacogdoches, Goliad, and San Antonio. In 1718 San Antonio, with its military post and mission, became the administrative headquarters of the region under Spanish jurisdiction. The province of Texas was established in 1727 with vaguely defined boundaries. Groups of colonists supplemented the population of soldiers and priests, particularly in San Antonio but in smaller numbers elsewhere. Early municipalities were organized in Texas under the Spanish and Mexican governments. Between 1731 and 1836 twenty-nine political subdivisions were founded completely or partially in Texas.

As a result of the Louisiana Purchase in 1803, a boundary dispute erupted with Spain over the Louisiana-Texas border. Spain claimed land east to the Red River, while the United States contended its territory extended west to the Sabine River. The dispute reached a temporary compromise when a region of neutral ground was established in 1806. Because neither country had jurisdiction over this area, it became a haven for outlaws.

Louisiana Catholics were encouraged to emigrate and settle in Texas, and Spanish officials loosened traditional barriers against alien immigration. The Sabine River was accepted as the western boundary of Louisiana in 1819, although border problems continued. The next year Arkansas Territory organized Miller County, partially inside Texas.

Mexico gained its independence from Spain in 1821, and claimed the area of today's Texas. The new Mexican government, while insisting that only immigrants of Roman Catholic faith were desired, did permit American settlers to enter under the auspices of certain grantees (impresarios).

Beginning about 1809, Quapaw, Osage, and Oto tribes were transported to the region. Large groups from Tennessee and Arkansas migrated into Texas beginning in the 1820s. Others from Pennsylvania, Ohio, and Kentucky followed. The municipality of Refugio was created in 1825, followed by Austin in 1827, Goliad about 1828, and Nacogdoches and Liberty in 1831.

Stephen F. Austin, the first American impresario, inherited his father's grant and established a colony in Texas that was part of the new nation of Mexico. His colonists were among the first Anglo-Americans to settle in present-day Texas. Boundaries were undefined and colonists spread from the coast to the old San Antonio road and between the Lavaca and the San Jacinto rivers. Austin's colony was the stimulus for others to follow.

Contracts from the Mexican government continued to be issued for settlement through 1832. Duplication of granted land and undefined boundaries complicated land titles. The number of early municipalities, organized in the eighteenth century under Spanish and Mexican governments, increased in the 1830s. A comparison of the names of the early and later municipalities reflects the great influx of Americans into present-day Texas.

Families from South Carolina and Georgia migrated overland to Texas; others left Alabama and Mississippi for Texas. Some traveled by ship and along major water courses, and some left from the port at New Orleans for Galveston and Indianola.

General Antonio Lopez de Santa Anna led his Mexican troops against American forces in 1836. The ensuing military conflict included the Battle of the Alamo. Four days before the decisive victory at San Jacinto, the Republic of Texas was established on 2 March 1836.

By 1836 American citizens residing in the state were actively promoting statehood for Texas. To encourage immigration, the Republic of Texas offered colonization contracts beginning in 1841. After some boundaries were defined and settled, Congress accepted the Republic of Texas into the Union in 1845 as the twenty-eighth state.

Texas's entry into the union incited the Mexicans and led to the Mexican War, 1846–48, which was fought over and on Texas soil. The Mexican government hoped to retain Texas and other territory in the southwest, including California, which both countries claimed. The United States Army seized control of the Rio Grande Valley in 1847–48. In 1848 Mexico ceded its claim to these territories to the United States, and Congress fixed the Rio Grande as the boundary in the treaty ending the Mexican War. The United States was victorious and made good its claims to the southwest. To make the area suitable for extending settlements, the federal government built a number of fortifications to protect settlers from Native Americans. Conflict with Native Americans continued intermittently through the early decades of statehood.

Prior to 1850, over 30,000 Germans had settled in Texas. Sympathies were divided among Texans over the slavery and states' rights issues that preceded the hostilities between the North and the South. Over the objections of Gov. Samuel Houston and the German settlers, Texas seceded from the Union and joined the Confederacy, supplying many soldiers to the Confederate army. Texas was readmitted in 1866.

Expansion of cotton, livestock, wheat, and oil production provided great stimuli for growth. Several groups of European immigrants settled in Texas, including Czechs, Poles, Germans, Swedes, Norwegians, and Irish. During the Depression, the Post Cereal Company offered inexpensive land in west Texas for those who would contract to grow grain for the company's products. The state continues to be a destination point for its Mexican neighbors seeking employment in farm and industry.

Vital Records

Between 1873–76 some births were recorded by county district clerks. Many of these were included in *Early Texas Birth Records, 1838–1878* (1969; 1971; reprint, Easley, S.C.: Southern Historical Press, 1982), by Alice Duggan Gracy, Jane Sumner, and Emma Gene Seale Gentry. Beginning in 1903 county clerks began to register all births and deaths, although compliance was not universal at first. Large cities with vital record offices and city secretaries maintained separate series of birth and death records. Justices of the peace also recorded births.

Beginning in 1903, with mandatory recording of births and deaths, copies of county records are maintained at the Bureau of Vital Statistics, Texas Department of Health, 1100 West 49th Street, Austin, Texas 78756. Statewide indexes were microfilmed by the Texas State Library (see Archives, Libraries, and Societies), and copies are additionally available at several genealogical libraries. The birth index covers 1903–76 and is alphabetized by year. The death index is alphabetical within broader periods of time: 1903–40; 1940–45; 1946–55; then annually for 1956–73. The Genealogy Section of the Texas State Library provides limited correspondence service by checking indexes for a particular name for a small fee. If a birth or death record is not found at the state level, it is prudent to check the proper municipal or county office.

Probated or delayed birth registrations were sometimes submitted to the respective county court. These were then forwarded to the State Bureau of Vital Statistics. Microfilm indexes to delayed birth records include Texas residents born elsewhere, many of whom were seeking Social Security registration. The bureau ended delayed birth registration in 1959.

Marriage records prior to 1836, if extant, may be in custody of the Roman Catholic church. Beginning with the date of organization, most counties maintain marriage records. These are presently in the jurisdiction of the respective county clerk where the license was issued. Statewide recording of marriages began in January 1966, but certified copies are not available through the state office. Marriages of blacks were frequently recorded in separate volumes.

Members of the Daughters of the American Revolution have compiled many marriage records for Texas. These are available in the DAR Library in Washington, D.C., and on microfilm through the FHL.

Consult the County Resources section in this chapter and the WPA, *Guide to Public Vital Statistics Records in Texas* (N.p.: Historical Records Survey, 1941), to determine availability of vital records in municipal and county offices.

Divorce records have been maintained statewide by the Bureau of Vital Statistics since January 1968, but certified copies are not available from this facility. Divorce records are maintained under the jurisdiction of the clerk of the respective district court. During the first years of the Republic of Texas, divorces were granted by special acts of Congress, but in 1841 district courts took over this responsibility, with some exceptions. After statehood, district courts had full jurisdiction over divorces.

Published works containing Texas marriage records include:

Dodd, Jordan R. *Texas Marriages, Early to 1850, a Research Tool.* Bountiful, Utah: Precision Indexing, 1990.

Grammer, Norma Rutledge. *Marriage Records of Early Texas, 1824–46.* Fort Worth, Tex.: Fort Worth Genealogical Society, 1971.

Smith, Bennett L. *Marriage by Bond in Colonial Texas.* Fort Worth, Tex.: the author, 1972.

Swenson, Helen Smothers. *8800 Texas Marriages 1824–1850.* Round Rock, Tex.: n.p., 1981.

Census Records

Federal

Population Schedules.

- Indexed—1850, 1860, 1870, 1880, 1890 (partial)
- Soundex—1880, 1900, 1910, 1920

Industry and Agriculture Schedules.

- 1850, 1860, 1870, 1880

Mortality Schedules.

- 1850, 1860, 1870, 1880

Slave Schedules.

- 1850, 1860

Union Veterans Schedules.

- 1890

The Texas State Library holds microfilm editions for all of Texas' federal censuses. Although the 1850, 1860, and part of the 1870 mortality schedules have been published, all the original mortality schedules are at the Texas State Library and on microfilm. Published indexes of federal population schedules are available.

The 1830 territorial census of Miller County, Arkansas, enumerates an area that is in today's Texas boundaries.

Vera Carpenter, *The State of Texas Federal Population Schedules, Seventh Census of the United States, 1850,* 5 vols. (Huntsville, Ark.: Century Enterprises, 1969), a published version of this census, is available in a number of large research facilities.

The surviving 1890 population schedules which exist for Texas include Ellis County (Justice Precinct 6, Mountain Peak, and Ovilla Precinct); Hood County (Precinct 5); Rusk County (Justice Precinct No. 6 and Justice Precinct No. 7); Trinity County (town of Trinity and Justice Precinct 2); and Kaufman County (town of Kaufman). Although Greer County in present-day Oklahoma functioned as part of Texas between 1886 and 1896, the 1890 census for this county was enumerated under Oklahoma Territory.

Colonial and Republic

Various censuses were enumerated under Spanish and Mexican governments, but these seldom covered all settlements in Texas for any given year. Mission rolls, reports of foreigners, and statistical reviews were recorded between 1783 and 1796. Some *rancho* censuses are extant for the years between 1797 and 1826. An 1828 *Padron* (census) lists name, age, occupation, marital status, religion, as well as family members. This is available at the Texas State Library as part of the records group contained in the Nacogdoches Archives section for 1753–1836 on microfilm. Translated mission censuses have been microfilmed and can be reviewed at the Institute of Texas Cultures, University of Texas, San Antonio.

No censuses were taken under the Republic of Texas (1836–45), although tax records provide a substitute census for 1840. See printed sources that follow and Tax Records (below) for examples of such tax records.

Some published census records for this period include:

Connor, Seymour V. *Kentucky Colonization in Texas.* Baltimore, Md.: Genealogical Publishing Co., 1983. Includes separate lists of colonists noting name, age, occupation, birthplace, number of children, removal, and county and date of settlement. The first list enumerates those who received land. Others list "colonists who moved away before receiving land," "persons issued county court certificates . . . probable colonists," "persons issued county court certificates . . . doubtful colonists," and "persons issued county court certificates who did not receive land." Most dates are between 1844 and 1848.

Mullins, Marion Day. *The First Census of Texas, 1829–1836: To Which Are Added Texas Citizenship Lists, 1821–1845 and Other Early Records of the Republic of Texas.* National Genealogical Society Special Publication No. 22. Reprinted from the *National Genealogical Society Quarterly.* Washington, D.C.: National Genealogical Society, 1959. Lists Texans from enumerations of citizens and other early records.

Osburn, Mary McMillian, ed. *The Atascosito Census of 1826.* 1963. Reprint from *Texana* 1 (Fall 1963): 299–321. N.p., n.d. A publication for the Liberty County Historical Survey Committee.

Residents of Texas 1782–1836. 3 vols. San Antonio, Tex.: University of Texas, Institute of Texas Cultures, 1984.

White, Gifford Elmore, comp., *1830 Citizens of Texas.* Austin, Tex.: Eakin Press, 1983. Taken from records in the GLO.

———. *The 1840 Census of the Republic of Texas.* Austin, Tex.: Pemberton Press, 1966.

———. *1840 Citizens of Texas.* 2 vols. Austin, Tex.: the author, 1983.

State

No state censuses were taken for Texas, although some counties enumerated children between the ages of six and sixteen years old, in school between 1854–55. These usually contain names of parents or guardians and students' names. The Archives Division of the Texas State Library houses the originals, although name indexes are kept in their Search Room. County lists for those counties beginning with letters "A" through "D" are missing. Mail or phone requests may be made for index entries. Microfilm copies of some are in the FHL.

Background Sources

Regional as well as county histories are available for Texas. John Holmes Jenkins, *Cracker Barrel Chronicles: A Bibliography of Texas Town and County Histories* (Austin, Tex.:

Pemberton Press, 1965), is a good bibliographic source. Two publications by Tom Munnerlyn: *Texas Local History: A Source Book for Available Town and County Local Histories, Local Memoirs and Genealogical Records* (Austin, Tex.: Eakin Press, 1983) and *Texas Counties, a Catalog of In-print and Out-of-print Books, Pamphlets, Maps, Memoirs, etc. Relating to Texas Towns and Counties* (Austin, Tex.: State House Books, 1985) add essential bibliographic sources.

Biographical articles in published local histories are indexed in the six volumes of *Biographical Gazetteer of Texas: Publication of the Biographical Sketch File of the Texas Collection at Baylor University, an Ongoing Project Supervised by Virginia and William L. Ming* (Austin, Tex.: Morrison Books, 1985–87), with 70,000 entries.

An important collection of manuscript and printed materials relating to Texas is available in the Barker Texas History Center at the University of Texas. A guide, published by this center, *Catalog of the Texas Collection in the Barker Texas History Center of the University of Texas at Austin,* 14 vols. (Boston, Mass.: G. K. Hall, 1979), describes the collection.

Taylor Publishing Company in Dallas has published many county and local histories for Texas during the last decade. Historical and genealogical societies publish a variety of records, including histories of the counties and towns or cities. To obtain a list of available publications, contact the genealogical or historical society in the area in which research is being conducted.

One of the finest volumes of detailed information for genealogists working in Texas records is Imogene Kinard Kennedy and J. Leon Kennedy, *Genealogical Records in Texas* (Baltimore, Md.: Genealogical Publishing Co., 1987). This volume contains historical background, land district maps, and a county-by-county listing that gives name, pronunciation, parent counties, dates of creation and organization, county seat and zip code, county organization maps where needed for boundary explanation, details of dates available and location of pertinent records, and beginning dates of records available in the county. Some minor errors appear, but as a reference tool this volume remains valuable.

Other sources include:

Ericson, Carolyn Reeves, and Frances Terry Ingmire. *First Settlers of the Republic of Texas: Headright Land Grants Which Were Reported as Genuine and Legal by the Traveling Commissioners, January, 1840.* Nacogdoches, Tex.: Carolyn R. Ericson, 1982. Taken from records in the Texas State Archives. Counties covered are Austin, Bastrop, Bexar, Brazoria, Colorado, Fannin, Fayette, Fort Bend, Galveston, Goliad, Gonzales, Harris, Harrison, Houston, Jackson, and Jasper.

Ingmire, Frances, and Carolyn R. Ericson. *First Settlers of the Republic of Texas.* Vol. 2. Utica, Ky.: McDowell Publications, 1986. Includes names from the counties of Jefferson, Liberty, Matagorda, Milam, Montgomery, Nacogdoches, Red River, Refugio, Robertson, Sabine, San Augustine, Shelby, Victoria, and Washington.

McComb, David G. *Texas: A Modern History.* Austin, Tex.: University of Texas Press, 1989.

McLean, Professor Malcolm D., comp. *Papers Concerning Robertson's Colony in Texas.* 15 vols. Arlington, Tex.: University of Texas at Arlington Press, 1974–present. This valuable material is published from the collection at the University of Texas at Arlington. Volume 12 contains lists of early colonists.

Williams, Villamae, ed. *Stephen F. Austin's Register of Families.* St. Louis, Mo.: Ingmire Publishing, 1984. Data taken from original documents in the GLO for families who arrived prior to 1845.

Maps

The GLO (see Land Records) houses original plat maps for the state. The Archives Division, Texas State Library, maintains an excellent collection of Texas maps. Original, photocopies, and compiled maps include general state, county survey, road and highway, United States Geological Survey, coastal and nautical, street, town plats, and birdseye maps with a card index to the collection, arranged by date or location. James M. Day's *Maps of Texas, 1527–1900: The Map Collection of the Texas State Archives* (Austin, Tex.: Pemberton Press, 1964) describes maps in the collection acquired prior to 1965. Other printed sources include:

Frantz, Joe Bertram. *Lure of the Land, Texas County Maps and the History of Settlement.* College Station, Tex.: Texas A & M University Press, 1988.

Gannett, Henry. *A Gazetteer of Texas.* Washington, D.C.: Government Printing Office, 1904.

Martin, James C., and Robert S. Martin. *Maps of Texas and the Southwest, 1513–1900.* Albuquerque, N.Mex.: University of New Mexico Press, 1984. Brief historical sketches accompany the maps in this atlas.

Pool, William C. *A Historical Atlas of Texas.* Austin, Tex.: Encino Press, 1975. Maps of the state depict the frontier and various historical periods as well as Indian territories.

Tarpley, Fred. *1001 Texas Place Names.* Austin, Tex.: University of Texas Press, 1980.

Texas State Gazetteer and Business Directory. R. L. Polk and Co., 1882–83, 1884–85, 1890–91. These directories provide a means of identifying business owners in Texas towns as well as locating communities which have disappeared.

Webb, Walter Prescott, and Eldon Stephen Branda, eds. *The Handbook of Texas.* 3 vols. Austin, Tex.: Texas State Historical Association, 1952–76.

Wheat, James L. *Postmasters and Post Offices in Texas, 1846–1930.* N.p., 1973. Provides most complete list of communities.

Other map collections are housed in the libraries of the University of Texas at Austin and El Paso and Southern Methodist University Library in Dallas.

Land Records

State-Land State

Texas land records were created under various governmental jurisdictions including Spain, Mexico, and both the Republic of Texas and State of Texas. Eleven land districts, each encompassing a number of counties, were established in 1836 under the Republic of Texas, and a central GLO was organized at Austin. The first district office was located near the Red River. The others were at San Augustine, Liberty, Nacogdoches, Matagorda, Washington-on-the Brazos, Cameron, Bastrop, Gonzales, San Antonio, and Victoria. The system of land districts continued when Texas became a state with previous grants being acknowledged. Nearly 150,000,000 acres of state-owned land in Texas were granted after 1836.

The GLO of Texas continues to maintain its own archives and records division housing all early land grants, including those dated in the 1700s and original grants issued by both republic and state governments. State grants are also usually recorded in county deed records; some may be filed separately as patent records. Indexes to the original land records are maintained by the GLO, Stephen F. Austin State Office Building, Room 800, 1700 North Congress Avenue, Austin, Texas 78701-1495. Requests for index entries for an individual name are provided for a minimum fee. Normal response time is about two weeks. Among the various types of original grants were:

Headright grants. These were issued to encourage immigration but were not awarded to black or Native Americans. Organized in several classes, these headright grants were issued between 1836 and 1842 to individuals and families who settled in Texas. Class 1 are Spanish or Mexican grants issued to settlers whose arrival was before 2 March 1836. Land allotted was measured as one league and one labor (4,605.5 acres) per family, or one-third league (1,476 acres) for unmarried men, twenty-one years and older. Second-class headright grants were awarded to those who arrived after 2 March 1836 and before 1 October 1837. They received 1,280 acres per family, or half that for unmarried men, with a requirement of three years residence. Third-class headright grants for those who settled between 2 October 1837 and 1 January 1840 were issued for half the acreage allotments but with the same residency requirements as second-class headrights. Fourth-class headright grants were issued between 1 January 1840 and 1 January 1842; acreage given was equal to that of the third-class headrights. Those awarded the equivalent to third-class headrights included colonists in Peters, Mercer, Castro, and Fisher-Miller colonies.

Pre-emption (squatter) grants. These were issued between 22 January 1845 and 1854 for no more than 320 acres. The minimum requirement was residence on a particular parcel for three consecutive years after 22 January 1845. After 1854 a limit of 160 acres was established for married men, and after 1870 a limit of 80 acres was established for single men. The last pre-emption grant was issued in 1898.

Bounty grants. These were issued from 1837 through 1888 for various acreage in payment for military service to the Republic. The number of acres granted varies as several legislatures modified requirements. Participants in any battle qualified. Later donation lands were awarded to widows and surviving veterans (as of 1881). Eligibility was limited to one grant. Scrip, a means of awarding or selling public land, was granted to disabled Confederate veterans; railroad, canal, and road companies; and owners of mills and factories.

Contracted grants. Both the republic and state of Texas contracted with various individuals to establish colonies in Texas and receive payment in land. Large grants were made directly to contractors, although individual grants were also given. Heads of families received 640 acres, and single men received 320 acres.

Miller's work, cited below, gives a complete account of the acquisition and disposition of public land in Texas to 1970. Fraudulent claims and legislation enacted to address these problems are discussed in Miller's volume.

Gifford E. White compiled a series of volumes, *The First Settlers in* [County], *Texas,* copied from originals in the GLO; these often include maps. Most were published by Ingmire Publications, St. Louis, Missouri, between 1981–84. A few were published elsewhere. The state land office has microfilmed copies of federal land sales to individuals up through the 1900s. In addition to the Ingmire and Ericson volumes cited in Background Sources, see:

Abstract of Land Claims, Compiled From the Records of the General Land Office. Galveston, Tex.: Civilian Book Office, published under the superintendence of the comptroller, 1852. Arranged alphabetically in districts; lists grants from Spain, Mexico, the Republic of Texas, and the state.

Abstracts of Land Titles of Texas Comprising the Titled, Patented, and Located Lands in the State. 1878. Reprint. San Augustine, Tex.: S. Malone, ca. 1985. Arranged by county for the period 1833 to 1877.

An Abstract of the Original Titles of Records in the General Land Office. 1838. Reprint. Austin, Tex.: Pemberton Press, 1964. There is no author cited for this work, but Mary Lewis Ulmer wrote the introduction. Covers headright grants for 1791 to 1836.

Bascom, Giles. *Abstract of All Original Texas Land Titles Comprising Grants and Locations to August 31, 1941.* 8 vols. *Supplements A–H.* 8 vols. Austin, Tex.: GLO, 1945–80. This set is somewhat difficult to locate. The GLO does sell out-of-print volumes on microfiche. The first volume has been reprinted as *Texas Land Title Abstracts Volume 1-A* (reprint, Paris, Tex.: Wright Press, 1984).

———. *History and Disposition of Texas Public Domain.* Austin, Tex.: GLO, 1945.

Bowden, J. J. *Spanish and Mexican Land Grants in the Chihuahuan Acquisition.* Austin, Tex.: University of Texas Press, 1971. Covers the counties of El Paso, Hudspeth, Culberson, Reeves, Jeff Davis, Pecos, Presidio, and Brewer in Texas plus six more in adjacent New Mexico.

Burlage, John and J. B. Hollingsworth. *Abstract of Valid Land Claims Compiled from the Records of the General Land Office and Court of Claims, of the State of Texas.* Austin, Tex.: J. Marshall, 1859.

Ericson, Carolyn Reeves. *Nacogdoches Headrights: A Record of the Disposition of Land in East Texas and in Other Parts of that State, 1838–1848.* New Orleans, La.: Polyanthos, 1977.

Miller, Thomas Lloyd. *Bounty and Donation Land Grants of Texas, 1835–1888.* Austin, Tex.: University of Texas Press, 1967.

———. *The Public Lands of Texas 1519–1970.* Norman, Okla.: Oklahoma University Press, 1971. Excellent source describing land records and land history in Texas.

———. *Texas Confederate Scrip Grantees, C.S.A.* N.p., 1985.

Purl, Benjamin F. *Republic of Texas Second Class Headrights, March 2, 1836—October 1, 1837.* Houston, Tex.: A. N. W. Barnes, 1974.

Sadler, Jerry. *History of Texas Land.* Austin, Tex.: GLO, 1964.

Scott, Florence Johnson. *Royal Land Grants North of the Rio Grande, 1777–1821: Early History of the Large Grants Made by Spain to Families of Jurisdiction of Reynosa Which Became a Part of Texas After the Treaty of Guadalupe Hidalgo, 1848.* Rio Grande City, Tex.: Texian Press, ca. 1969. Concerns suits recorded in deed books containing the chain of title and lines of descent and heirship for the counties of Hidalgo, Cameron, Willacy, Kenedy, Brooks, Kleberg, and Nueces.

Taylor, Virginia H. *Spanish Archives of the General Land Office of Texas.* Austin, Tex.: Lone Star Press, 1955.

Texas Family Land Heritage Registry. 10 vols. Austin, Tex.: Texas Department of Agriculture, 1974–85. These are accounts of farms that have been in agricultural production for a century or more in the same family (not limited to agnate descents) and as such are rich in genealogical detail.

Todd, William N. *Guide to Spanish and Mexican Land Grants in South Texas.* Austin, Tex.: Texas GLO, 1988.

White, Gifford. *Character Certificates in the General Land Office of Texas.* 1985. Reprint. Baltimore, Md.: Genealogical Publishing Co., 1989.

Williams, Villamae. *Stephen F. Austin's Register of Families from the Originals in the General Land Office, Austin, Texas.* Baltimore, Md.: Genealogical Publishing Co., 1989).

Once land was initially granted, all succeeding land transactions fell under the jurisdiction of the county in which the land was located at the time each record was created. County boundaries have changed over time as have county names. By law, all deeds are indexed by grantor and by grantee. Transcribed deeds from parent counties may be maintained in separate volumes. County land transactions, including deeds and mortgages, are located at the respective county clerk's office.

Century farm records for those families who worked the same land for one hundred years or more are available on microfilm at the Department of Agriculture, "Century of Agriculture Program," P. O. Box 12847, Austin, Texas 78711.

Probate Records

Probate proceedings in Texas are under the jurisdiction of the respective county court clerk except in heavily populated counties where probate courts may fill that function instead. Wills, court orders, letters of administration, inventories, sales, accounts, guardianship, and final accounts are all found in the probate records and/or minutes, although each type of record may be filed separately. Probate appeals from either the county or probate court are heard by district courts (see Court Records). Between 1869–76, when the office of county clerk was temporarily abolished, some probate records were filed in District Court Civil Minutes or District Court Minutes.

The WPA published a series of indexes to probate cases for some of the Texas counties. During the 1980s, the set was reprinted as WPA, *Index to Probate Cases of Texas* (N.p., n.d.), and included the following counties: Atascosa, Bowie, Brazoria, Brazos, Brown, Camp, Chambers, Coleman, Delta, Franklin, Gregg, Guadalupe, Hardin, Hays, Liberty, Marion, Morris, Newton, Nolan, Orange, Robertson, Runnels, Rusk, San Saba, Shelby, Titus, Trinity, Waller, Williamson, and Wood.

Court Records

Court names and jurisdictions in Texas changed over time. The history of Texas court records with dates and jurisdictions is more thoroughly outlined in Kennedy and Kennedy, *Genealogical Records in Texas* (see Background Sources). Although English common law is the basis for the court system in Texas, modifications are allowed as dictated by situations. These were usually changed based upon Spanish law, which proved beneficial to settlers.

From 1836 through 1891 the highest court, the state's supreme court, heard only appellate cases and functioned as a circuit court, holding hearings in Austin, Galveston, and Tyler for three-month sessions, annually. Supreme court records from 1838 to 1940, including litigants' records in appellate civil and criminal cases, are housed in the Archives Division of Texas State Library.

In 1891 the court of criminal appeals was established to hear criminal cases, thereby reducing the case load of the supreme court to hear only appeals of civil disputes. The Supreme Court Record Group, held in the Archives Division of the Texas State Library, contains approximately 4,500 cases. Unfortunately, a large number of files for 1840–53 are lost. Records available include case files, dockets, minute books, and opinions. Published opinions are available for all years except 1844–45. It is best to check the published records available at the archives division covering the periods 1840–44 and 1846–1963 with the direct (plaintiff) and reverse (defendant) card index to the case file numbers for the period 1836–93. For telephone or correspondence requests, the archives' staff will check the card index and case file if the case file number is referenced in the card index or can be furnished. Some original records are too delicate to be copied.

The county commissioners court conducts the daily business for each county, among other duties, setting tax rates and county budgets for such categories as schools, roads, and the poor. The county clerk serves as recorder and clerk to the commissioners court and the county court. A large number of records about the daily lives of county residents are kept, as a result, by the county clerk. In counties with less than 8,000 population, one recorder/clerk may serve both county and district courts.

County courts operated from 1836 but were abolished, temporarily, in 1869. Their jurisdiction was transferred to district courts until 1876 when county courts were reinstated. County courts hear most misdemeanor, civil, probate, and guardianship cases, all recorded by the county clerk, along with other instruments such as cattle brands, deeds, and marriage licenses. Naturalization records are found, prior to 1906, in county court records (see Special Focus Categories—Naturalizations).

District courts, one for each county, are the principal trial courts in Texas and serve as the court of appeal in probate matters (from county court) and for the commissioners court. District courts have original jurisdiction in felonies, divorce, land title, name changes, and after 1931—adoption. In the 1890s separate divorce minutes appeared. After 1906 the district court continued to handle naturalization matters (see Special Focus Categories—Naturalizations).

Justice of the peace courts, often called "poor man's court," were established in 1845. They handle civil and criminal matters under $200 and issue warrants and writs. In towns of 2,500 or less, these courts act as the registrar of vital statistics.

As a result of the destruction of records in the adjutant general's office when it burned in 1855, a court of claims was established from 1856 to 1861 to hear cases against the republic and state for claims of money or land. Approximately two-thirds of the applicants' cases were denied. The old and new "dockets" list applicants. Court approved records relating to nearly 4,500 headright certificates, over 2,000 bounty warrants, more than 650 donation certificates, almost 500 scrip certificates, and rejected claims are deposited in the GLO (see Land Records).

Tax Records

Texas tax records constitute one of the most complete sets of available records generated at the county level and maintained by the office of the county tax assessor-collector. Tax records through 1980 are filed with the state comptroller of public accounts. These lists may only include approximately 60 percent of eligible males over the age of twenty-one. Persons exempted from taxes included Native Americans and those exempted because of age. This last category of exemptions varied over time. Years without an older age exemption were 1840 and 1862–70. Between 1841–44, exemptions were allowed for those who were forty-five years; in 1845 and from 1850–61, the upward age was set at fifty years. In 1837, 1848, and 1849, the limit was established as fifty-five, in 1846–47, and 1871, the upward limit was set at sixty years.

Texas Ad Valorem (poll, personal, and real property) tax records for 1836 through 1976 are available on microfilm at the Texas State Library from the date of respective county organization; these are arranged by county and date and are somewhat alphabetized within each division. Microfilm copies are housed in the Genealogy Section. Tax lists for the various counties from creation to 1901 may be borrowed through interlibrary loan. Tax records through 1901–47 are readily accessible but not on interlibrary loan. Those for 1948 through 1976 can be obtained upon request.

Lists for various counties have been published. Multicounty compilations, in addition to White's Vol. II (see Census Records), include the following:

Dorman, Beth, and Emily Dorman. *Taxpayers of the Republic of Texas Covering 30 Counties and the District of Panola.* The authors, 1988.

Mullins, Marion Day. *Republic of Texas: Poll Lists for 1846.* 1974. Reprint. Baltimore, Md.: Genealogical Publishing Co., 1982.

Cemetery Records

Many cemetery records have been collected and transcribed. The largest is a multivolume compilation by the DAR (see page 6). A two-volume work is available for Peters' Colonists and descendants. The DAR collection, also microfilmed, is available at the Texas State Library and through the FHL.

Some Texas county historical and genealogical societies have published local cemetery and funeral home records.

These are normally available for purchase through the respective society. Two references can help determine which cemeteries have been recorded: Kim Parsons, *A Reference to Texas Cemetery Records* (Humble, Tex.: the author, 1988), arranged by county, and Sharry Crofford-Gould, *Texas Cemetery Inscriptions: A Source Index* (San Antonio, Tex.: Limited Editions, 1977).

Church Records

During Texas's colonization period, Roman Catholics were the most numerous, but early citizens also represented other religious faiths such as Baptist, Methodist, Presbyterian, and Christian or Disciples of Christ.

Many Roman Catholic records are in the Catholic Archives of Texas, North Congress and West 16th, Capitol Station P.O. Box 13327, Austin, Texas 78711. Others are deposited in the various archdiocese archives. The San Antonio archdiocese records begin in 1703.

Two sources for Baptist records in the state are Baylor University's Texas Collection, Baylor University Library, Box 6396, Waco, Texas 76706, and Southwestern Baptist Theological Seminary, A. Webb Roberts Library, Box 22, Fort Worth, Texas 76122. A collection of Baptist records maintained outside the state is at Samford University Library, 800 Lakeshore Drive, Birmingham, Alabama 35229. The collection includes books, church and association minutes, church and association histories, and nineteenth-century Southern Baptist newspapers, many of which are indexed.

Bridwell Theology Library, Southern Methodist University, Dallas, Texas 75275-0476, houses records of Methodists.

Military Records

The largest collection of military and related records pertaining to Texans is housed in the Texas State Archives, Adjutant General Record Group. Since 1919 military discharge records are filed at the local county courthouse. An extensive array of military records, too numerous to list, has been published. The list includes Revolutionary War and War of 1812 veterans who died in Texas, as well as World War I and II veterans.

Earliest Texas military records begin in 1835. Texas Revolutionary War veterans or widows or heirs were eligible for bounty and donation land grants and pensions from the Texas government. Published lists are available of soldiers and sailors of the Republic of Texas, participants in battles of the Alamo and San Jacinto, and men in the Texas Rangers, minutemen, and home guard units. Lists of those who served in the Indian Wars have been published.

A large collection of Confederate pension applications is available at the Texas State Library and Archives in Austin. These are arranged in numerical order and are indexed. Both indigent veterans and widows of veterans were allowed pensions. The applications contain some genealogical information. Copies can be obtained through correspondence once the assigned number is known. Confederate scrip was awarded veterans who were permanently disabled or to heirs of those who were killed, entitling the veteran or his widow to 1,280 acres.

In addition to the National Archives military records (see page 7), other military records are housed in the Texas State Archives and Library; these include Confederate claims, 1861–65; Confederate home records, 1886–1954; Confederate indigent families list, 1863–65; general service records, 1836–1902; muster rolls, 1836–1917; and payment records, 1836–46. Under the Adjutant General Record Group in the state archives are many additional records, including various muster rolls from 1836–1911 and service records 1836–1902. Records may be as little as one small piece of paper or as large as a complete file.

Among the numerous printed sources extant for Texas veterans are the following:

Fay, Mary Smith. *War of 1812 Veterans in Texas.* New Orleans, La.: Polyanthos, 1979. From notes compiled by Mae Wynne McFarland, this is a compilation of names, places, and dates associated with veterans of the War of 1812. Original material is in the library of the Sam Houston State University in Huntsville, arranged alphabetically.

Ingmire, Frances Terry. *Texas Frontiersman, 1839–1860: Minute Men, Militia, Home Guard, Indian Fighter.* St. Louis, Mo.: the author, ca. 1982. Contains officers index and alphabetically arranged entries taken from military records.

———. *Texas Ranger Service Records, 1830–1846.* St. Louis, Mo.: Ingmire Publications, 1982. Includes index of officers.

———, comp. *Texas Rangers: Frontier Battalion, Minute Men, Commanding Officers, 1847–1900.* 6 vols. St. Louis, Mo.: Ingmire Publications, 1982. Each volume is separately indexed.

Kinney, John M. *Index to Applications for Texas Confederate Pensions.* Rev. ed. Austin, Tex.: Archives Division, Texas State Library, 1977.

Manarin, Louis H., ed. *Cumulative Index: The Confederate Veteran Magazine, 1893–1932.* 3 vols. Wilmington, N.C.: Broadfoot Publishing Co., 1986. Every-name index to the *Confederate Veteran.* Includes a comprehensive list of Confederate military organizations, arranged by local designations.

Periodicals, Newspapers, and Manuscript Collections

Periodicals

Genealogical periodicals are numerous for Texas, with some counties having three or more societies that publish periodicals. Some representative titles are:

The Dallas Quarterly. Dallas Genealogical Society, 1955–present.

Footprints. Fort Worth Genealogical Society, 1968–present.

Genealogical Record. Houston Genealogical Forum, 1958–present.

Heart of Texas Records. Formerly *Central Texas Genealogical Society Bulletin*. Central Texas Genealogical Society, 1958–present.

The Herald. Montgomery County Genealogical and Historical Society, 1978–present.

Naše Dejiny: The Magazine of Czech Genealogy. 1982–present. Hallettsvile, Tex.: Old Homestead Publishing Co., 1982–present. Devoted to Czechs who settled in Texas.

Newsletter. German Texas Heritage Society, 1979–present.

Northeast Texas Genealogy and History. Genealogical Society of Northeast Texas, 1965–present.

Oak Leaves. Matagorda County Genealogical Society 1982–present.

Our Heritage. San Antonio Genealogical and Historical Society, 1959–present.

PGST News. Formerly HPGS News. Polish Genealogical Society of Texas, 1985–present.

The Roadrunner. Chaparral Genealogical Society, 1974–present.

Stalkin' Kin. San Angelo Genealogical and Historical Society, 1973–present.

Stirpes. Texas State Genealogical Society, 1961–present.

The Thorny Trail. Midland Genealogical Society, 1973–present.

Yellowed Pages. Southeast Texas Genealogical and Historical Society, 1971–present.

Newspapers

The Name Index to Early Texas Newspapers serves as a significant finding tool for names in newspapers between 1830 and 1885. The original card-file index is at the University of Texas Library in Austin, with a forty-three-reel set on microfilm and available in libraries throughout Texas. The card data includes the name, date, and title as well as other identifying information. Other works include:

Lu, Helen Mason. *Texas Methodist Newspaper Abstracts (17 April 1850—17 Sept. 1881)*. 4 vols. Dallas, Tex.: the author, 1987. Also in microfiche.

Kelsey, Michael. *Genealogical Abstracts from Central Texas Newspapers, 1885–1899*. Temple, Tex.: the author, ca. 1987.

———. *Genealogical Abstracts from the* Austin Texas State Gazette *1849–1859*. Temple, Tex.: the author, 1988.

———. *Miscellaneous Texas Newspaper Abstracts, 1856–1870*. Temple, Tex.: the author, ca. 1988.

Swensen, Helen S. *Early Texas News 1831–1848, Abstracts from Early Texas Newspapers*. St. Louis, Mo.: F. T. Ingmire, 1984.

Manuscript

Manuscripts containing historical and genealogical data frequently are available in university, historical society, and state and local public libraries throughout the state. Brief examples follow:

The manuscript collections maintained by the Texas State Archives are described in Jean Carefoot, *A Guide to Genealogical Resources in the Texas State Archives* (Austin, Tex.: Texas State Library, Archives Division, 1984).

The Eugene C. Baker Texas History Center at the University of Texas at Austin announced in 1986 the acquisition of the Natchez Trace Collection, an important archive of materials documenting much of the life of the Old South between 1780 and 1900. It measures over 450 linear feet and is a collection of collections, still to be cataloged.

See also:

Benavides, Adan. *The Bexar Archives 1717–1836, A Name Guide*. Austin, Tex.: University of Texas Press, 1989.

Kielman, Chester Valls. *Guide to the Microfilm Edition of the Bexar Archives, 1717–1836*. 3 vols. Austin, Tex.: University of Texas, 1969–71. This work gives a reel by reel description of the contents of the 172-reel micropublication.

McLean, Malcolm Dallas, comp. *Papers Concerning Robertson's Colony in Texas*. 15 vols. to date. Arlington, Tex.: University of Texas at Arlington Press, 1974–present.

Archives, Libraries, and Societies

Of paramount importance to the genealogical researcher working with Texas records are the holdings of the Texas State Library and Archives. Most other libraries, including public libraries, have valuable material with genealogical information, such as published histories, newspapers, telephone books, city directories, manuscripts, and oral history.

Texas State Library
State Archives and Library Building
Capitol Station
P. O. Box 12927
Austin, TX 78711-2927

Holdings under the auspices of the Texas State Library are divided. Most important for genealogical research are the Texas State Archives with its Local Records Department, the Records Management Division, and the Information Services Division, which includes a Genealogy Section and a Reference Department.

Many of its extensive holdings have been described in the sections of this chapter (see also Carefoot, *A Guide*, cited under Manuscripts).

The Genealogy Section maintains vertical files that contain notes, clippings, pamphlets, and correspondence on Texas families. These files may be accessed in person, by phone (512-463-5463, forty-five minute limit), or through correspondence.

Because so many records pertaining to Texas are available in microform, much genealogical and historical material is accessible at the following:

Dallas Public Library
1515 Young Street
Dallas, TX 75201

Houston Public Library
500 McKinney Street
Houston, TX 77002

In addition to the Texas State Library, these two libraries have the most extensive holdings. Twenty-five public and university libraries in Texas provide additional storage facilities of local records. These are identified in Heskett's work (see County Resources).

In addition to the Kennedy and Kennedy book (see Background Sources), the following guides to Texas resources are also valuable:

Keilman, Chester Valls. *Guide to the Microfilm Edition of the Texas Archives.* 3 vols. Austin, Tex.: University of Texas, 1967–71.

———. *The University of Texas Archives, A Guide to the Historical Manuscripts Collections in the University of Texas Library.* Austin, Tex.: University of Texas Press, 1967.

Texas State Library Circulating Genealogy Duplicates List. Austin, Tex.: Texas State Library, 1985. Lists books and materials available on interlibrary loan in Texas and elsewhere.

Special Focus Categories

Immigration

Both New Orleans and Galveston served as ports of entry for those who immigrated and settled in Texas. Some early immigrants entered at New Orleans. The National Archives-Southwest Region in Fort Worth is the regional location for the archives' extensive microfilm collection of immigration lists (see page 8). The FHL has microfilm copies of passenger lists for New Orleans from 1820–1921 and indexes to 1952; also, the FHL has copies for Galveston, 1846–71, 1893, and 1896–1921, with indexes grouped from 1896–1906 and 1906–51. Prior to 1852 there is no separate index to passengers.

Printed sources include the following:

Baca, Leo. *Czech Immigration Passenger Lists.* 3 vols. Hallestville, Tex.: Old Homestead Publishing Co., 1980–83. While not limited to Texas, a great many of the lists do pertain to Texas and are based on records no longer extant in Texas port of arrival records.

Biesele, Rudolph L. *The History of the German Settlements in Texas, 1831–1931.* Austin, Tex.: Von Boeckman-Jones Co., 1931.

Blaha, Albert J. *Passenger Lists for Galveston, 1850–1855.* Houston, Tex.: the author, 1985. Based on European sources. Galveston and Indianola passenger arrivals are included.

Brown, John Henry. *Indian Wars and Pioneers of Texas.* St. Louis, Mo.: L. E. Daniels Publishers, 1890.

Brozek, Andrzej and Henryk Borek, *Pierwsi Slazacy w Ameryce* (First Silesians in America). Opole, Poland, 1967.

Chabot, Fred Charles. *With the Makers of San Antonio.* San Antonio, Tex.: Ars Graphica, 1937.

Dworaczyk, Rev. Edward J. *The First Polish Colonies in America in Texas.* San Antonio, Tex.: Naylor Co., 1936.

Galveston County Genealogical Society. *Ships Passenger Lists, Port of Galveston, Texas, 1846–1871.* Easley, S.C.: Southern Historical Press, 1984. Lists surviving fragments of records.

Geue, Chester, and Ethel H. Geue. *A New Land Beckoned, German Immigration to Texas, 1844–1847.* Waco, Tex.: Texian Press, 1972. These records provide coverage for the period when the Republic of Texas kept no records of immigrants arriving at its ports and complements the fragmentary records for the port of Galveston maintained by the United States.

Geue, Ethel H. *New Homes in a New Land, German Immigration to Texas, 1847–1861.* Waco, Tex.: Texian Press, 1972. These lists are based on records in the Archives of the General Land Office. While there may be some duplication with records maintained by the federal authorities at New Orleans and Galveston, these lists are generally unique.

Haiman, Miecislaus. *The Poles in the Early History of Texas.* Chicago, Ill.: P.R.C.U. of A. Archives, 1936.

———. *Polish Past in America.* Chicago, Ill.: P.R.C.U. of A. Archives, 1939.

Hudson, Estelle, and Henry Maresh. *Czech Pioneers of the Southwest.* Dallas, Tex.: Southwest Press, 1934.

Przygoda, Jacek. *Texas Pioneers from Poland: A Study in the Ethnic History.* Waco, Tex.: Texian Press, ca. 1971.

Naturalization

The Republic of Texas had no naturalization requirement. Consequently no such records exist before 1846. After statehood and prior to 1906, naturalization records in Texas are found in both the county and district courts in the respective county. The records may be found in county court minutes, county court civil minutes, probate minutes, commissioners court minutes, or in separately maintained volumes. The Act of Congress of 1906 limited naturalization to state courts without original jurisdiction, and Texas county district courts met that requirement. Declarations, affidavits, orders of admission, and other documents are maintained by those courts and the U.S. Federal District Courts.

Native American

The most significant tribes represented in the state include Comanche, Kiowa, Arapaho, Crow, Wichita, Ute, and Creek. Other tribes in Texas include Arkokosa, Attacapa, Caddo, Coahuiltecan, Karankawa, Nacogdoches, Nasoni, Neche, and Tonkawa. Most of those remaining in Texas in 1859 were forcibly removed to Indian Territory. During 1875 the surviving Comanche surrendered to federal forces. The Alabama-Coushatta Indian Reservation remains in the state.

Records for Native Americans in Texas after 1845 are on file in the United States Bureau of Indian Affairs and in Bureau records in the National Archives. Those records in the Texas State Archives pertaining to Native Americans are usually insignificant for genealogical purposes. A better collection is housed by the Oklahoma Historical Society, Indian Archives Division, Historical Building, Oklahoma City, Oklahoma 73105.

Brown, John Henry. *Indian Wars and Pioneers of Texas.* 1978. Reprint. Easley, S.C.: Southern Historical Press, 1988.

Sowell, Andrew J. *Early Settlers and Indian Fighters of Southwest Texas: Facts Gathered from Survivors of Frontier Days.* New York, N.Y.: Argosy, ca. 1964.

Wilbarger, J. W. *Indian Depredations in Texas.* Austin, Tex.: Eakin Press, 1985.

Republic of Texas Settlers

The Republic of Texas ceased to exist when President Anson Jones handed over the reins of government to the United States of America on 19 February 1846. Descent from one of Austin's Old Three Hundred or other residents of Texas prior to that date has always been a genealogical asset. The following list of publications offers much assistance in investigation of claims to descent:

Jennett, Elizabeth LeNoir. *Biographical Directory of the Texas Conventions and Congresses, 1832–1845.* 1941. Reprint. New York, N.Y.: Antiquarian Press, 1959.

Compiled Index to Elected and Appointed Officials of the Republic of Texas: 1835–1846. Austin, Tex.: State Archives Division, Texas State Library, 1981.

Daughters of the Republic of Texas. *Founders and Patriots of the Republic of Texas, the Lineages of the Members of the Daughters of the Republic of Texas.* 3 vols. Dallas, Tex.: Huggins Press, 1963–85.

Ericson, Carolyn R. *Nacogdoches—Gateway to Texas, a Biographical Directory, 1773–1849.* 2 vols. Ft. Worth, Tex.: Arrow/Curtis Printing, 1974–87.

Kemp, Louis W. *The Signers of the Texas Declaration of Independence.* Salado, Tex.: Anson Jones Press, 1959.

Morris, Mrs. Harry Joseph. *Citizens of the Republic of Texas.* Dallas, Tex.: Texas State Genealogical Society, 1977.

Sons of the Republic of Texas. *Lineages of Members.* Microfilm, 37 reels.

Black Americans

Although most histories of Texas refer to blacks only secondarily, their presence in the state has been long and continuous. In an 1809 census of Nacogdoches there were thirty-three slave owners. Slavery in Texas increased with Anglo-American colonists in the 1820s. Under Mexican jurisdiction, slavery was opposed. A slave code was instituted in Austin's colony in 1824. Under an 1827 constitution of Coahuila and Texas, babies born of slave mothers were free at birth, and a law passed in 1832 limited bondsmen's contracts to ten years. Both laws were frequently overlooked by slave owners in Texas who held and imported slaves. By 1837 slavery was recognized and legalized in Texas.

Many immigrants to antebellum Texas came from southern states, and some brought slaves to Texas. During the 1850s less than one-third of the state's population owned slaves. Most free blacks and slaves lived in rural areas in the eastern half of the state at that time.

Tracing slave ancestors who lived prior to 1865, in most cases, must be accomplished through the records of the slave owners. Owners' wills and estate inventories often list slaves by name—sometimes including an approximate age or other description. Some estate records indicate slave families or state relationship of mother and children. Deeds and bills of sale may also identify slaves showing transfer of ownership. Court records infrequently include mention of slaves and owners. After 1865, records for blacks are maintained and filed along with others for local and state jurisdictions.

An overview of blacks in Texas may be obtained through a study of the following:

Barr, Alwyn. *Black Texans: A History of Negroes in Texas, 1528–1921.* Austin, Tex.: Pemberton Press, 1971.

Bugbee, Lester E. "Slavery in Early Texas," *Political Science Quarterly* 13 (1898): 389–412, 648–88.

Campbell, Randolph B. *An Empire for Slavery: The Peculiar Institution in Texas, 1821–1865.* Baton Rouge, La.: Louisiana State University Press, ca. 1989.

Rice, Lawrence D. *The Negro in Texas, 1874–1900.* Baton Rouge, La.: Louisiana State University Press, ca. 1971.

Smallwood, James M. *Time of Hope, Time of Despair: Black Texans During Reconstruction.* Port Washington, N.Y.: Kennikat Press, 1981.

Woolfork, George Ruble. *The Free Negro in Texas, 1800–1860: A Study in Cultural Compromise.* Published for *The Journal of Mexican American History.* Ann Arbor, Mich.: University Microfilms International, 1976.

Latinos

There were two distinct Spanish colonies in present-day Texas during the early stage of the area's settlement. Although discouraged by Apache and Comanche, the Tejas colony was founded with a mission in 1690; it was located along the Nueces River and then north and east, near present-day Crockett. The other colony was that of Nuevo Santander in the Rio Grande Valley. Twenty-four settlements were established between 1749 and 1755.

Mexican population increased slowly in the state. In the early 1800s the Tejas population was less than 5,000, concentrated near San Antonio, Goliad, and Nacogdoches. In 1835, the population of the Nuevo Santander settlements had increased to 15,000. After statehood Latinos in Texas faced difficulties such as property rights, justice in the American court system, and differences in religion, language, and custom. The 1850 federal census shows that Latinos represented only 5 percent of the state's population.

During the Civil War, approximately 3,000 Tejanos enlisted in the Confederate Army, but many deserted. Other Tejanos joined the Union Army. The state's constitutional convention of 1868 authorized bounty-land grants for Union service: eight acres for six months service and 320 acres for service of one year or longer. Many Latinos who served for the Union became U.S. citizens during Reconstruction.

During the 1920s there were waves of migration from Mexico into Texas and other southwestern states. In 1960 Latinos numbered 1,448,900 in Texas, the highest concentrations in three counties: Hidalgo, Bexar, and El Paso. In recent history there has been an urban trend, with large numbers leaving rural occupations and moving into cities.

Suggested background references include the following:

Barker, Eugene, "Land Speculation as a Cause of the Texas Revolution," *Texas Historical Association Quarterly* (1906): 76–95.

Barrera, Mario. *Race and Class in the Southwest: A Theory of Racial Inequality.* Notre Dame, Ind.: University of Notre Dame Press, 1979.

Briggs, Vernon, Walter Fogel, and Fred Schmidt. *A Statistical Profile of the Spanish-Surname Population of Texas.* Austin, Tex.: University of Texas, Bureau of Business Research, 1964.

Cardenas, Gilberto. "Mexican Migration." Paper presented at Conference on Demographic Study of the Mexican American Population. Austin, Tex.: University of Texas, 17–19 May 1973.

Connell, Earl. *The Mexican Population of Austin, Texas.* San Francisco, Calif.: R & E Research Association, 1971. Reprint of a thesis, University of Texas, 1925.

Hardman, Max. "The Mexican Immigrant in Texas," *Southwestern Political and Social Science Quarterly* (June 1926): 33–41.

Hufford, Charles. *The Social and Economic Effects of the Mexican Migration into Texas.* San Francisco, Calif.: R & E Research Association, 1971. Reprint of a thesis, 1929.

Kibbe, Pauline. *Latin Americans in Texas.* Albuquerque, N.Mex.: University of New Mexico Press, 1946.

Kielman, Chester V. *Guide to the Microfilm Edition of the Bexar Archives, 1717–1803.* Austin, Tex.: University of Texas Archives Microfilm Division, 1967.

Menefee, Selden. *Mexican Migratory Workers of Southern Texas.* Washington, D.C.: Government Printing Office, 1941.

Moquin, Wayne, and Charles Van Doren, eds. *A Documentary History of the Mexican Americans.* New York, N.Y.: Praeger Publishers, 1971.

Nance, Joseph. *After San Jacinto: The Texas-Mexican Frontier, 1936–1841.* Austin, Tex.: University of Texas Press, 1963.

O'Rourke, Thomas P. *The Franciscan Missions in Texas, 1690–1793.* Washington, D.C.: Catholic University of America, 1927.

Perrigo, Lynn. *Texas and Our Spanish Southwest.* Dallas, Tex.: Banks Upshaw, 1960.

Rosenbaum, Robert J. *Mexicano Resistance in the Southwest: "The Sacred Right of Self-Preservation."* Austin, Tex.: University of Texas Press, ca. 1981.

Thompson, Jerry. *Vaqueros in Blue and Gray.* Austin, Tex.: Presidial Press, 1976.

Weber, David J. *The Mexican Frontier, 1821–1846: The American Southwest Under Mexico.* Albuquerque, N.Mex.: University of New Mexico Press, 1982.

County Resources

In 1972 the legislature established a uniform statewide system for preservation of records in regional historical resources depositories. Under this act, the Local Records Division of the Texas State Library collects and maintains city, county, and local government records; these are available to the public. Michael Heskett, *Texas County Records: A Guide to the Holdings of the Local Records Division of the Texas State Library of County Records on Microfilm* (1978; 2d ed., Austin, Tex.: Texas State Library, 1990), is a valuable guide.

County records, such as land and property records, probate records and wills, marriage records, naturalization papers, and district court minutes, are microfilmed and kept in a depository designated for the county's respective area. Thus there is no one state depository with a complete set of records.

Each of the twenty-six depositories has some original records and manuscripts concerning that particular region. In some instances microfilming of county records has not been done. Inventories of the records available in nearly eighty of the 254 county courthouses have been made. For further information see:

Holley, Edward G., and Donald D. Hendricks. *Resources of Texas Libraries*. Austin, Tex.: Texas State Library, 1968.

Texas State Library. *Inventory of County Records*. Austin, Tex.: Texas State Library, 1973.

Many Texas counties have suffered a loss of records due to courthouse fires, floods, and theft. This is reflected in the earliest dates for record availability.

The first date in the county chart that follows is the creation date. It is sometimes followed by a second date indicating the date of organization, the date from which a researcher can expect to find vital, land, probate, and court records for each county. Some counties were organized twice. Although twenty-seven additional counties were created by the legislature, none were organized. Of these only Buchel, Encinal, and Foley counties had records. Buchel and Foley were incorporated into Brewster County, while Encinal was included in Webb County. As discussed in the appropriate sections above, deeds are located through the county clerk, probates at the county clerk's or the probate clerk's office in larger counties, and court records through the county or district court clerk. Letters should be addressed to the appropriate clerk. Kennedy and Kennedy, *Genealogical Records in Texas* (see Background Sources), and Heskett, *Texas County Records*... (cited above), are the sources for the following data. In cases of conflicting data, information contained in the latest publication is given.

Drawn by William Dollarhide

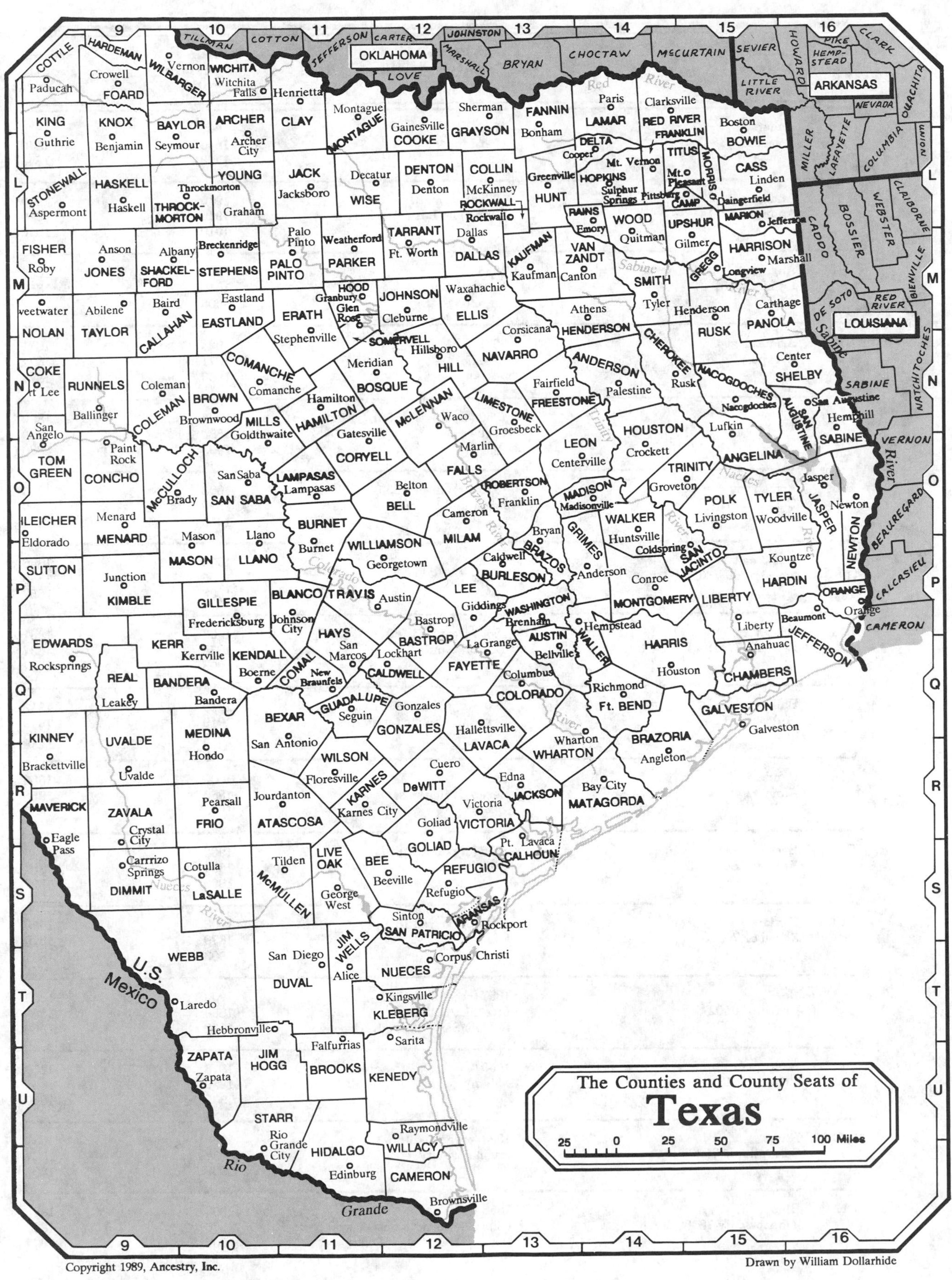

Drawn by William Dollarhide

Map	County Address	Date Formed Parent County/ies	Birth Marriage Death	Land Probate Court
N14	Anderson Palestine 75801	1846 Houston	1903 1846 1903	1846 1846 1846
F5	Andrews Andrews 79714	1876 (organized 1910) Young and Bexar territories	1910 1910 1910	1910 1910 1910
O15	Angelina Lufkin 75901	1846 Nacogdoches	1903 1846 1903	1846 1850 1847
S12	Aransas Rockport 78382	1871 Refugio	1903 1871 1903	1871 1872 1871
L10	Archer Archer City 76351	1858 (organized 1880) Cooke	1903 1881 1903	1880 1880 1880
B6	Armstrong Claude 79019	1876 (organized 1890) Bexar and Young territories	1903 1890 1903	1890 1890 1890
R11	Atascosa Jourdanton 78026	1856 Bexar	1903 1856 1903	1856 1873 1857
P13	Austin Bellville 77418	1836 (organized 1837) original county	1903 1838 1903	1837 1837 1837
C5	Bailey Muleshoe 79347	1876 (organized 1919) Bexar and Young territories	1919 1919 1919	1919 1919 1919
Q10	Bandera Bandera 78003	1856 Bexar/Uvalde	1903 1856 1903	1856 1856 1857
P12	Bastrop Bastrop 78602	1836 (organized 1837) original county	1903 1851 1903	1837 1837 1837
L10	Baylor Seymour 76380	1858 (organized 1879) Fannin	1903 1879 1903	1879 1879 1881
S12	Bee Beeville 78102	1857 (organized 1858) Live Oak/Goliad/ Refugio/San Patricio/Karnes	1903 1860 1903	1858 1859 1858
O12	Bell Belton 76513	1850 Milam	1873 1850 1903	1850 1850 1850
Q10	Bexar San Antonio 78205	1836 (organized 1837) original county	1903 1837 1903	1837 1837 1837
P11	Blanco Johnson City 78636	1858 Gillespie/Burnet/Comal/Hays	1903 1876 1903	1875 1876 1877

Map	County Address	Date Formed Parent County/ies	Birth Marriage Death	Land Probate Court
E6	Borden Gail 79738	1876 (organized 1891) Bexar Territory	1903 1891 1903	1891 1891 1891
N12	Bosque Meridian 76665	1854 McLennan/Milam	1903 1860 1903	1850 1855 1856
L15	Bowie New Boston 75570	1840 (organized 1841) Red River	1903 1889 1903	1889 1889 1889
R14	Brazoria Angleton 77511	1836 (organized 1837) original county	1903 1829 1903	1837 1837 1867
013	Brazos Bryan 77803 *Created as Navasota County.*	1841 (organized 1843) Washington/Robertson	1903 1844 1903	1841 1844 1841
J4	Brewster Alpine 79831	1887 Presidio	1903 1887 1903	1887 1887 1887
C6	Briscoe Silverton 79257	1876 (organized 1892) Bexar and Young territories	1903 1892 1903	1892 1892 1892
U11	Brooks Falfurrias 78355	1911 (organized 1912) Starr/Hildalgo/Live Oak/Zapata	1911 1911 1911	1911 1911 1911
N10	Brown Brownwood 76801	1856 (organized 1857) Travis/Comanche	1903 1880 1903	1880 1880 1884
P13	Burleson Caldwell 77836	1846 Milam/Washington	1903 1846 1903	1846 1847 1880
P11	Burnet Burnet 78611	1852 (organized 1854) Bell/Williamson/Travis	1873 1852 1903	1852 1853 1854
Q12	Caldwell Lockhart 78644	1848 Gonzales	1903 1848 1903	1846 1849 1848
S13	Calhoun Port Lavaca 77979	1846 Jackson/Victoria	1903 1846 1903	1846 1846 1847
M10	Callahan Baird 79504	1858 (organized 1877) Travis/Bexar/Bosque	1903 1878 1903	1878 1879 1879
U12	Cameron Brownsville 78520	1848 Nueces	1903 1848 1930	1848 1848 1849
L15	Camp Pittsburg 75686	1874 Upshur	1903 1874 1929	1874 1874 1874

Map	County Address	Date Formed Parent County/ies	Birth Marriage Death	Land Probate Court
B6	Carson Panhandle 79068	1876 (organized 1888) Bexar and Young territories	1903 1888 1903	1888 1888 1888
L15	Cass Linden 75563	1846 (known as Davis, December 1861–May 1871) Bowie	1873 1847 1903	1846 1846 1846
C5	Castro Dimmitt 79027	1876 (organized 1891) Bexar and Young territories	1903 1891 1903	1891 1891 1892
Q15	Chambers Anahuac 77514	1858 Liberty/Jefferson	1903 1876 1903	1875 1876 1876
N14	Cherokee Rusk 75785	1846 Nacogdoches	1903 1846 1903	1846 1839 1846
C8	Childress Childress 79201	1857 (organized 1887) Young Territory	1903 1887 1903	1887 1888 1887
	Cibilo	(see Wilson)		
L11	Clay Henrietta 76365	1857 (organized 1861; disorganized 1862; reorganized 1873) Cooke	1874 1874 1903	1873 1873 1874
D5	Cochran Morton 79346	1876 (organized 1824) Bexar and Young territories	1924 1924 1924	1924 1924 1925
N9	Coke Robert Lee 76945	1889 Tom Green	1903 1890 1903	1891 1891 1891
N9	Coleman Coleman 76834	1858 (organized 1867) Brown/Travis	1903 1876 1903	1876 1876 1876
L13	Collin McKinney 75069	1846 Fannin	1903 1846 1903	1846 1846 1846
B8	Collingsworth Wellington 79095	1876 (organized 1890) Clay/Bexar and Young territories	1903 1890 1903	1890 1890 1891
Q13	Colorado Columbus 78934	1836 (organized 1837) original county	1903 1837 1903	1836 1837 1837
Q11	Comal New Braunfels 78130	1846 Bexar/Travis/Gonzales	1903 1846 1903	1846 1846 1846
N10	Comanche Comanche 76442	1856 Coryell/Bosque	1903 1856 1903	1856 1856 1858

Map	County Address	Date Formed Parent County/ies	Birth Marriage Death	Land Probate Court
O9	Concho Paint Rock 76866	1858 (organized 1879) Bexar Territory	1903 1879 1903	1879 1879 1880
L12	Cooke Gainesville 76240	1848 (organized 1849) Fannin	1873 1848 1903	1850 1849 1849
O11	Coryell Gatesville 76528	1854 Bell/McLennan	1903 1854 1903	1854 1854 1856
C8	Cottle Paducah 79248	1876 (organized 1892) Fannin	1903 1892 1903	1892 1892 1892
G5	Crane Crane 79731	1887 (organized 1927) Tom Green	1927 1927 1927	1927 1927 1927
H6	Crockett Ozona 76943	1875 (organized 1891) Bexar Territory	1903 1892 1903	1891 1891 1892
D6	Crosby Crosbyton 79322	1876 (organized 1886) Bexar and Young territories	1903 1886 1903	1887 1887 1887
G3	Culberson Van Horn 79855	1911 (organized 1912) El Paso/Bexar and Young territories	1912 1912 1912	1912 1912 1912
A5	Dallam Dalhart 79022	1876 (organized 1891) Bexar and Young territories	1903 1891 1903	1891 1891 1892
M13	Dallas Dallas 75202	1846 Nacogdoches/Robertson	1903 1846 1911	1846 1846 1846
	Davis	(see Cass)		
E6	Dawson Lamesa 79331	1876 (organized 1905) Bexar and Young territories	1905 1905 1905	1905 1905 1905
B5	Deaf Smith Hereford 79045	1876 (organized 1890) Bexar and Young territories	1903 1890 1903	1890 1890 1890
L14	Delta Cooper 75432	1870 (organized 1870) Lamar/Hopkins	1903 1871 1903	1871 1872 1872
L12	Denton Denton 76201	1846 Fannin	1903 1875 1903	1854 1876 1877
R12	DeWitt Cuero 77954	1846 Gonzales/Goliad/Victoria	1903 1847 1903	1846 1846 1852

Map	County Address	Date Formed Parent County/ies	Birth Marriage Death	Land Probate Court
D7	Dickens Dickens 79229	1876 (organized 1891) Bexar and Young territories	1903 1891 1903	1891 1891 1891
K8	Dimmit Carrizo Springs 78834	1858 (organized 1880) Bexar/Maverick	1903 1881 1903	1880 1881 1881
B7	Donley Clarendon 79226	1876 (organized 1882) Bexar and Young territories	1903 1882 1903	1882 1882 1882
T11	Duval San Diego 78384	1858 (organized 1876) Nueces/Live Oak/Hildalgo/Starr	1903 1877 1903	1877 1877 1879
N10	Eastland Eastland 76448	1858 (organized 1873) Bosque/Coryell/Travis	1903 1873 1903	1874 1874 1874
F5	Ector Odessa 79761	1881 (organized 1891) Tom Green	1903 1891 1903	1891 1891 1891
J7	Edwards Rocksprings 78880	1858 (organized 1883) Bexar Territory	1903 1888 1903	1888 1888 1888
M13	El Paso El Paso 79901	1850 (organized 1856; reorganized 1871) Bexar Territory	1903 1866 1903	1856 1866 1861
F1	Ellis Waxahachie 75165	1849 (organized 1850) Navarro	1903 1850 1903	1845 1850 1850
	Encinal	1856 (never organized; abolished 1899— area incorporated into Webb County)		
N11	Erath Stephenville 76401	1856 (organized 1856) Bosque/Coryell	1903 1869 1903	1867 1866 1866
O12	Falls Marlin 76661	1850 Milam/Limestone	1903 1854 1903	1850 1851 1851
L13	Fannin Bonham 75418	1837 (organized 1838) Red River	1903 1852 1903	1838 1838 1838
Q12	Fayette La Grange 78945	1837 (organized 1838) Colorado/Bastrop	1903 1838 1903	1838 1838 1838
E7	Fisher Roby 79543	1876 (organized 1886) Bexar and Young territories	1903 1886 1903	1886 1886 1886
C6	Floyd Floydada 79235	1876 (organized 1890) Bexar and Young territories	1903 1890 1890	1890 1890 1890

Map	County Address	Date Formed Parent County/ies	Birth Marriage Death	Land Probate Court
C8	Foard Crowell 79227	1891 Knox/Hardeman/Cottle/King	1903 1891 1903	1891 1891 1891
Q14	Fort Bend Richmond 77469	1837 (organized 1838) Austin/Harris/Brazoria	1903 1838 1903	1838 1838 1838
L14	Franklin Mount Vernon 75457	1875 Titus	1903 1875 1903	1875 1875 1875
N13	Freestone Fairfield 75840	1850 (organized 1851) Limestone	1903 1851 1903	1838 1851 1851
R10	Frio Pearsall 78061	1858 (organized 1871) Uvalde/Bexar/Atascosa	1903 1871 1903	1871 1873 1873
E5	Gaines Seminole 79360	1876 (organized 1905) Bexar and Young territories	1905 1905 1905	1905 1905 1906
Q15	Galveston Galveston 77550	1838 (organized 1839) Brazoria/Liberty	1903 1838 1903	1838 1836 1839
E6	Garza Post 79356	1876 (organized 1907) Bexar and Young territories	1903 1907 1903	1907 1907 1907
P10	Gillespie Fredericksburg 78624	1848 Bexar/Travis	1903 1850 1903	1850 1850 1849
F6	Glasscock Garden City 79739	1887 (organized 1893) Tom Green	1903 1893 1903	1893 1893 1893
S12	Goliad Goliad 77963	1836 (organized 1837) original county	1903 1876 1903	1852 1871 1855
Q12	Gonzales Gonzales 78629	1836 (organized 1837) original county	1903 1829 1903	1837 1838 1838
A7	Gray Pampa 79065	1876 (organized 1902) Bexar and Young territories	1903 1902 1903	1902 1902 1903
L12	Grayson Sherman 75090	1846 Fannin	1903 1846 1903	1846 1846 1836
	Greer (now in Oklahoma) Mangum, OK 73554	1860 (organized 1886) Young	1901 1901 ?	? 1901 ?
M15	Gregg Longview 75606	1873 Upshur/Rusk	1873 1873 1903	1873 1876 1873

Map	County Address	Date Formed Parent County/ies	Birth Marriage Death	Land Probate Court
P13	Grimes Anderson 77830	1846 Montgomery	1903 1849 1903	1848 1838 1844
Q11	Guadalupe Seguin 78155	1846 Gonzales/Bexar	1903 1846 1903	1846 1846 1846
C6	Hale Plainview 79072	1876 (organized 1888) Bexar and Young territories	1903 1888 1903	1888 1888 1888
C7	Hall Memphis 79245	1876 (organized 1890) Bexar and Young territories	1903 1890 1903	1890 1890 1890
N11	Hamilton Hamilton 76531	1858 Comanche/Bosque/Lampasas	1903 1886 1903	1866 1870 1871
A6	Hansford Spearman 79081	1876 (organized 1889) Bexar and Young territories	1903 1889 1903	1889 1889 1889
C8	Hardeman Quanah 79252	1858 (organized 1884) Fannin	1903 1885 1903	1884 1885 1885
P15	Hardin Kountze 77625	1858 Liberty/Jefferson	1903 1862 1903	1858 1886 1871
Q14	Harris Houston 77002 *Known as Harrisburg County until 1840.*	1836 (organized 1837) original county	1903 1837 1903	1837 1837 1837
M15	Harrison Marshall 75670	1839 (organized 1842) Shelby	1903 1838 1903	1840 1840 1840
A5	Hartley Channing 79018	1876 (organized 1891) Bexar and Young territories	1903 1891 1903	1891 1891 1891
L9	Haskell Haskell 79521	1858 (organized 1885) Fannin/Milam	1903 1885 1903	1885 1885 1885
Q11	Hays San Marcos 78666	1848 Travis	1873 1848 1903	1848 1848 1850
A7	Hemphill Canadian 79014	1876 (organized 1887) Clay/Bexar and Young territories	1903 1887 1903	1887 1887 1887
M13	Henderson Athens 75751	1846 Houston/Nacogdoches	1873 1847 1903	1847 1846 1847
U11	Hildalgo Edinburg 78539	1852 Cameron	1903 1852 1903	1852 1852 1852

Map	County Address	Date Formed Parent County/ies	Birth Marriage Death	Land Probate Court
N12	Hill Hillsboro 76645	1853 Navarro	1903 1873 1903	1857 1853 1867
D5	Hockley Levelland 79336	1874 (organized 1876) Bexar and Young territories	1921 1921 1921	1921 1921 1921
M11	Hood Granbury 76048	1866 Johnson	1903 1875 1903	1875 1873 1873
L14	Hopkins Sulphur Springs 75482	1846 Lamar/Nacogdoches	1903 1846 1903	1846 1846 1846
O14	Houston Crockett 75835	1837 Nacogdoches	1903 1882 1903	1865 1859 1878
F6	Howard Big Spring 79720	1876 (organized 1882) Bexar and Young territories	1903 1882 1903	1882 1882 1882
G2	Hudspeth Sierra Blanca 79851	1917 El Paso	1917 1917 1917	1917 1917 1917
L13	Hunt Greenville 75401	1846 Fannin/Nacogdoches	1903 1858 1903	1846 1847 1851
A6	Hutchinson Stinnett 79083	1876 (organized 1901) Bexar and Young territories	1903 1901 1903	1901 1901 1901
G7	Irion Mertzon 76941	1889 Tom Green	1903 1889 1903	1889 1889 1889
L11	Jack Jacksboro 76056	1856 (organized 1857) Cooke	1903 1858 1910	1858 1858 1858
R13	Jackson Edna 77957	1836 (organized 1837) original county	1903 1837 1903	1837 1837 1838
O15	Jasper Jasper 75951	1836 (organized 1837) original county	1903 1849 1903	1849 1849 1850
H3	Jeff Davis Fort Davis 79734	1887 Presidio	1903 1931 1931	1887 1887 1887
P15	Jefferson Beaumont 77701	1836 (organized 1837) original county	1903 1837 1903	1834 1837 1838
U11	Jim Hogg Hebbronville 78361	1913 Brooks/Duval	1913 1913 1913	1913 1913 1913

Map	County Address	Date Formed Parent County/ies	Birth Marriage Death	Land Probate Court
T11	Jim Wells Alice 78332	1911 (organized 1912) Nueces	1912 1912 1912	1912 1912 1912
M12	Johnson Cleburne 76031	1854 Navarro/McLennan	1885 1860 1884	1853 1854 1852
E8	Jones Anson 79501	1858 (organized 1881) Bexar/Bosque	1903 1881 1903	1881 1881 1881
R12	Karnes Karnes City 78118	1854 Bexar/San Patricio/Goliad/Dewitt	1903 1865 1903	1855 1865 1858
M13	Kaufman Kaufman 75142	1848 Henderson	1873 1849 1903	1849 1849 1848
Q10	Kendall Boerne 78006	1862 Kerr/Blanco	1903 1870 1903	1862 1862 1862
U12	Kenedy Sarita 78385 *Created as Willacy County in 1911.*	1921 Cameron/Hidalgo/Willacy	1911 1911 1911	1911 1911 1911
E7	Kent Jayton 79528	1876 (organized 1892) Bexar and Young territories	1903 1892 1903	1892 1892 1892
J8	Kerr Kerrville 78028	1856 Bexar	1903 1856 1903	1856 1856 1856
H8	Kimble Junction 76849	1858 (organized 1876) Bexar Territory	1903 1884 1903	1884 1884 1884
D8	King Guthrie 79236	1876 (organized 1891) Bexar and Young territories	1903 1914 1903	1914 1914 1914
K7	Kinney Brackettville 78832	1850 (organized 1872) Bexar	1903 1872 1903	1872 1874 1873
T12	Kleberg Kingsville 78363	1913 Nueces	1913 1913 1913	1913 1913 1914
D8	Knox Benjamin 79505	1858 (organized 1886) Cooke	1905 1886 1909	1886 1886 1886
L14	Lamar Paris 75460	1840 (organized 1841) Red River	1903 1841 1903	1841 1841 1841
C5	Lamb Littlefield 79339	1876 (organized 1908) Bexar and Young territories	1908 1909 1908	1908 1909 1909

Map	County Address	Date Formed Parent County/ies	Birth Marriage Death	Land Probate Court
O11	Lampasas Lampasas 76550	1856 Travis/Bell	1903 1873 1903	1872 1876 1873
S10	LaSalle Cotulla 78014	1858 (organized 1880) Bexar/Webb	1903 1880 1903	1880 1881 1881
R12	Lavaca Halletsville 77964	1846 Colorado/Gonzales/Jackson/Victoria	1903 1847 1903	1846 1846 1847
P12	Lee Giddings 78942	1874 Burleson/Washington/Bastrop/Fayette	1873 1874 1903	1874 1874 1874
N13	Leon Centerville 75833	1846 Robertson	1903 1885 1903	1846 1846 1846
P15	Liberty Liberty 77575	1836 (organized 1837) original county	1903 1875 1903	1875 1873 1874
O13	Limestone Groesbeck 76642	1846 Robertson	1903 1873 1903	1873 1876 1873
A8	Lipscomb Lipscomb 79056	1876 (organized 1887) Bexar and Young territories	1903 1887 1903	1887 1887 1887
S11	Live Oak George West 78022	1856 San Patricio/Nueces	1903 1857 1903	1856 1860 1856
P10	Llano Llano 78643	1856 Bexar/Gillespie	1903 1880 1903	1875 1881 1882
F4	Loving Mentone 79754	1887 (organized 1893; disorganized 1897; reorganized 1931) Tom Green	1931 1931 1931	1931 1931 1931
D6	Lubbock Lubbock 79401	1876 (organized 1891) Bexar and Young territories	1903 1891 1903	1881 1891 1891
E6	Lynn Tahoka 79373	1876 (organized 1903) Bexar and Young territories	1903 1903 1903	1903 1903 1903
013	Madison Madisonville 77864	1853 (organized 1854) Grimes/Walker/Leon	1903 1874 1903	1873 1873 1873
L15	Marion Jefferson 75657	1860 Cass/Titus	1873 1860 1903	1860 1860 1860
F6	Martin Stanton 79782	1876 (organized 1884) Bexar and Young territories	1903 1885 1903	1885 1885 1885

Map	County Address	Date Formed Parent County/ies	Birth Marriage Death	Land Probate Court
P10	Mason Mason 76856	1858 Bexar	1903 1877 1903	1877 1877 1877
R13	Matagorda Bay City 77414	1836 (organized 1837) original county	1903 1837 1859	1837 1837 1837
K8	Maverick Eagle Pass 78852	1856 (organized 1871) Kinney	1903 1871 1903	1871 1876 1871
O10	McCulloch Brady 76825	1856 (organized 1862; reorganized 1876) Bexar Territory	1903 1876 1903	1876 1876 1876
O12	McLennan Waco 76701	1850 Milam/Navarro/Limestone	1903 1850 1903	1850 1853 1850
S10	McMullen Tilden 78072	1858 (organized 1862; reorganized 1877) Bexar/Atascosa/Live Oak	1903 1877 1903	1871 1877 1879
R10	Medina Hondo 78861	1848 Bexar	1903 1848 1903	1848 1848 1848
H8	Menard Menard 76859	1858 (organized 1866; reorganized 1871) Bexar	1903 1871 1903	1871 1871 1871
F6	Midland Midland 79701	1885 Tom Green	1903 1885 1910	1885 1885 1886
O12	Milam Cameron 76520	1836 (organized 1837) original county	1873 1874 1903	1874 1874 1872
	Miller	1820 (in Arkansas Territory; renamed Red River, 1836)		
O10	Mills Goldthwaite 76844	1887 Brown/Lampasas/Hamilton/Comanche	1903 1887 1903	1887 1887 1887
F7	Mitchell Colorado City 79512	1876 (organized 1881) Bexar and Young territories	1903 1881 1903	1881 1881 1881
L11	Montague Montague 76251	1857 (organized 1858) Cooke	1873 1873 1903	1873 1873 1873
P14	Montgomery Conroe 77301	1837 Washington	1903 1838 1903	1838 1838 1839
A6	Moore Dumas 79029	1876 (organized 1892) Bexar and Young territories	1903 1892 1903	1882 1892 1892

Map	County Address	Date Formed Parent County/ies	Birth Marriage Death	Land Probate Court
L15	Morris Daingerfield 75638	1875 Titus	1903 1875 1903	1875 1876 1875
D7	Motley Matador 79224	1876 (organized 1891) Bexar and Young territories	1903 1891 1903	1891 1891 1891
N15	Nacogdoches Nacogdoches 75961	1836 (organized 1837) original county	1903 1837 1903	1835 1838 1837
M13	Navarro Corsicana 75110	1846 Robertson	1873 1846 1903	1846 1847 1855
O16	Newton Newton 75966	1846 Jasper	1903 1846 1903	1846 1846 1846
F7	Nolan Sweetwarer 79556	1876 (organized 1881) Bexar and Young territories	1903 1881 1903	1881 1881 1881
T12	Nueces Corpus Christi 78401	1846 San Patricio	1903 1846 1903	1847 1846 1850
A7	Ochiltree Perryton 79070	1876 (organized 1889) Bexar and Young territories	1903 1889 1903	1889 1889 1889
A5	Oldham Vega 79092	1876 (organized 1881) Bexar and Young territories	1903 1881 1903	1881 1881 1881
P16	Orange Orange 77630	1852 Jefferson	1903 1852 1903	1852 1852 1852
M11	Palo Pinto Palo Pinto 76072	1856 (organized 1857) Bosque/Navarro	1903 1858 1903	1858 1858 1858
M15	Panola Carthage 75633	1846 Harrison/Shelby	1903 1846 1857	1846 1846 1846
M11	Parker Weatherford 76086	1855 (organized 1856) Bosque/Navarro	1903 1874 1903	1874 1860 1874
C5	Parmer Farwell 79325	1876 (organized 1907) Bexar and Young territories	1903 1907 1907	1907 1907 1907
H5	Pecos Fort Stockton 79735	1871 (organized 1875) Presidio	1903 1875 1903	1875 1875 1875
O15	Polk Livingston 77351	1846 Liberty	1903 1846 1903	1846 1840 1848

Map	County Address	Date Formed Parent County/ies	Birth Marriage Death	Land Probate Court
B6	Potter Amarillo 79101	1876 (organized 1887) Bexar and Young territories	1903 1887 1903	1887 1887 1889
J3	Presidio Marfa 79843	1850 (organized 1869; reorganized 1875) Bexar	1903 1875 1903	1876 1875 1875
L13	Rains Emory 75440	1870 Wood/Hopkins/Hunt	1903 1879 1903	1870 1880 1880
B6	Randall Canyon 79015	1876 (organized 1889) Bexar and Young territories	1903 1889 1903	1889 1889 1889
G6	Reagan Big Lake 76932	1903 Tom Green	1903 1903 1903	1903 1903 1903
J8	Real Leakey 78873	1913 Edwards/Kerr/Bandera	1913 1913 1913	1913 1913 1913
L14	Red River Clarksville 75426	1836 (organized 1837) original county	1903 1846 1903	1838 1838 1840
G4	Reeves Pecos 79772	1883 (organized 1884) Pecos	1903 1884 1903	1884 1884 1885
S12	Refugio Refugio 78377	1836 (organized 1837) original county	1903 1851 1903	1839 1840 1841
A7	Roberts Miami 79059	1876 (organized 1889) Bexar and Young territories	1903 1889 1903	1889 1889 1889
O13	Robertson Franklin 77856	1837 (organized 1838) Milam	1903 1838 1903	1838 1838 1843
L13	Rockwall Rockwall 75087	1873 Kaufman	1903 1875 1903	1873 1877 1875
F8	Runnels Ballinger 76821	1858 (organized 1880) Bexar/Travis	1903 1880 1903	1880 1880 1881
M15	Rusk Henderson 75652	1843 Nacogdoches	1873 1843 1903	1843 1847 1847
N16	Sabine Hemphill 75948	1836 (organized 1837) original county	1903 1880 1903	1876 1879 1876
N15	San Augustine San Augustine 75972	1836 (organized 1837) original county	1903 1837 1903	1833 1837 1837

Map	County Address	Date Formed Parent County/ies	Birth Marriage Death	Land Probate Court
O14	San Jacinto Coldspring 77331	1869 (re-created 1870) Polk/Liberty/Montgomery/Walker	1903 1870 1903	1870 1876 1871
S12	San Patricio Sinton 78387	1836 (organized 1837; reorganized 1847) original county	1903 1858 1903	1846 1847 1848
O10	San Saba San Saba 76877	1856 Bexar Territory	1903 1857 1903	1857 1868 1868
H7	Schleicher Eldorado 76936	1887 (organized 1901) Crockett	1903 1901 1903	1901 1901 1901
E7	Scurry Snyder 79549	1876 (organized 1884) Bexar and Young territories	1903 1884 1903	1884 1884 1885
M10	Shackelford Albany 76430	1858 (organized 1874) Bosque	1903 1903 1903	1874 1874 1875
N15	Shelby Center 75935	1836 (organized 1837) original county	1903 1882 1903	1838 1881 1882
A6	Sherman Stratford, 79084	1876 (organized 1889) Bexar and Young territories	1903 1889 1903	1889 1889 1889
M14	Smith Tyler 75702	1846 Nacogdoches	1903 1846 1903	1846 1846 1846
M11	Somervell Glen Rose 76043	1875 Hood	1873 1885 1903	1875 1875 1875
U10	Starr Rio Grande City 78582	1848 Nueces	1903 1858 1903	1848 1848 1848
M10	Stephens Breckenridge 76024	1858 (as Buchanan; organized 1876) Bosque	1903 1876 1903	1876 1876 1879
F7	Sterling Sterling City 76951	1891 Tom Green	1903 1891 1903	1891 1891 1891
L9	Stonewall Aspermont 79502	1876 (organized 1888) Fannin	1903 1888 1903	1887 1888 1889
H7	Sutton Sonora 76950	1887 (organized 1890) Crockett	1903 1890 1903	1890 1890 1891
C6	Swisher Tulia 79088	1876 (organized 1890) Bexar and Young territories	1903 1890 1903	1890 1890 1890

Map	County Address	Date Formed Parent County/ies	Birth Marriage Death	Land Probate Court
M12	Tarrant Fort Worth 76196	1849 (organized 1850) Navarro	1903 1876 1903	1850 1856 1876
F8	Taylor Abilene 79600	1858 (organized 1878) Bexar/Travis	1903 1878 1903	1878 1878 1879
J6	Terrell Sanderson 79848	1905 Pecos	1905 1905 1905	1906 1905 1905
D5	Terry Brownfield 79316	1875 (organized 1904) Bexar and Young territories	1904 1904 1904	1904 1904 1905
L10	Throckmorton Throckmorton 76083	1858 (organized 1879) Bosque/Fannin	1903 1879 1903	1879 1879 1879
L15	Titus Mt. Pleasant 75455	1846 Bowie/Red River	1903 1895 1903	1846 1895 1895
G7	Tom Green San Angelo 76903	1874 (organized 1875) Bexar Territory	1903 1875 1903	1875 1875 1875
P11	Travis Austin 78767	1840 Bastrop	1903 1840 1903	1840 1840 1876
O14	Trinity Groveton 75845	1850 Houston	1903 1876 1903	1873 1876 1884
015	Tyler Woodville 75979	1846 Liberty	1903 1849 1903	1846 1847 1847
M15	Upshur Gilmer 75644	1846 Harrison/Nacogdoches	1903 1846 1903	1846 1846 1846
G6	Upton Rankin 79778	1887 (organized 1910) Tom Green	1910 1910 1910	1910 1910 1910
K8	Uvalde Uvalde 78801	1850 (organized 1856) Bexar	1903 1856 1903	1856 1857 1857
J7	Val Verde Del Rio 78840	1885 Kinney/Pecos/Crockett	1903 1885 1903	1885 1885 1885
M14	Van Zandt Canton 75103	1848 Henderson	1872 1848 1903	1848 1848 1848
R13	Victoria Victoria 77901	1836 (organized 1837) original county	1903 1838 1903	1838 1837 1838

Map	County Address	Date Formed Parent County/ies	Birth Marriage Death	Land Probate Court
O14	Walker Huntsville 77340	1846 Montgomery	1903 1846 1903	1846 1846 1847
P14	Waller Hempstead 77445	1873 Austin/Grimes	1903 1873 1903	1873 1873 1873
G4	Ward Monahans 79756	1887 (organized 1892) Tom Green	1903 1893 1903	1893 1893 1893
P13	Washington Brenham 77833	1836 (organized 1837) original county	1903 1837 1903	1834 1837 1837
T10	Webb Laredo 78040	1848 Bexar/Nueces	1903 1852 1903	1848 1851 1851
R13	Wharton Wharton 77488	1846 Colorado/Jackson/Matagorda/Brazoria	1903 1847 1903	1837 1846 1848
A8	Wheeler Wheeler 79096	1876 (organized 1879) Bexar and Young territories	1903 1879 1903	1881 1879 1879
L10	Wichita Wichita Falls 76301	1858 (organized 1882) Bexar	1903 1882 1903	1873 1882 1900
L10	Wilbarger Vernon 76384	1858 (organized 1881) Cooke	1903 1882 1903	1881 1882 1882
U12	Willacy Raymondville 78580	1911 (organized 1911; re-created 1921; reorganized 1921) Hidalgo/Cameron	1921 1921 1921	1921 1921 1921
P12	Williamson Georgetown 78626	1848 Milam	1873 1848 1903	1848 1848 1848
R11	Wilson Floresville 78114 *Between 1869 and 1874 Wilson was called Cibilo.*	1860 Bexar/Karnes	1903 1860 1903	1860 1862 1893
F4	Winkler Kermit 79745	1887 (organized 1910) Tom Green	1910 1910 1910	1911 1910 1910
L11	Wise Decatur 76234	1856 Cooke	1903 1881 1903	1856 1882 1894
M14	Wood Quitman 75783	1850 Van Zandt	1903 1879 1903	1878 1878 1860
E5	Yoakum Plains 79355	1876 (organized 1907) Bexar and Young territories	1907 1907 1907	1907 1907 1907

Map	County Address	Date Formed Parent County/ies	Birth Marriage Death	Land Probate Court
L10	Young Graham 76046	1856 (organized 1858; reorganized 1874) Cooke	1903 1858 1903	1858 1858 1858
U10	Zapata Zapata 78076	1858 Starr/Webb	1903 1873 1903	1868 1886 1874
K8	Zavala Crystal City 78839	1858 (organized 1884) Uvalde/Maverick	1903 1884 *1903*	1884 1884 *1885*

UTAH

Patricia Lyn Scott and Gary Topping

Utah culture is considerably enriched by evidence of prehistoric inhabitants dating as far back as 10,000 B.C. When Spaniards, the first Europeans, arrived in the area in the eighteenth century, members of the Gosiute, Southern Paiute, Ute, Shoshoni, and Navajo cultures were already here to greet them. Two expeditions led by Juan Maria de Rivera entered southeastern Utah in 1765, and the Franciscans, Dominguez and Escalante, reached Utah Lake before turning back to Santa Fe in 1776.

Lured by the reports of John C. Fremont, Lansford W. Hastings, and others, immigrants to the Pacific left wheel tracks across Utah during the 1840s. The Bidwell-Bartleson party of 1841 was the first, and the Bryant-Russell, Harlan-Young, and Donner-Reed groups added their tracks, followed by the Gold Rushers of the early 1850s. Records of all of these parties are available, mostly in published form.

Utah's first permanent Anglo inhabitants were fur trappers who came west from St. Louis and north from Taos in search of beaver. Osborne Russell's diary records that he wintered in the Weber Valley in 1843 with a party of French-Canadian trappers, and Miles Goodyear started a trading post near present-day Ogden in 1846 to do business with emigrants on the Oregon Trail.

Before Goodyear actually opened his doors, however, he was bought out by Capt. James Brown, who represented the Church of Jesus Christ of Latter-day Saints, which began settling in the Salt Lake Valley in 1847. Since then, the Mormons, as they are popularly known, have written a large share of Utah history, virtually all aspects of which are well documented by their famous and fortunate penchant for record keeping.

Mormonism has a strong communitarian emphasis that served its adherents well in settling Utah's harsh environment. The resources of the community were pooled through tithing, and Mormon settlement was accomplished by sending out well-planned colonies, rather than individuals. Mormon colonies included men, women, and children, and representatives of every necessary trade and profession: doctors, blacksmiths, carpenters, and especially musicians for the ubiquitous Mormon dances that kept spirits up in the face of daunting material circumstances.

Under the leadership of the sagacious but controversial Brigham Young, Mormon colonies were established during the latter nineteenth century from the Salmon River country of Idaho and the Big Horn Basin of northern Wyoming all through Utah, into northern New Mexico and Arizona, and as far west as Carson City, Nevada, and San Bernardino, California. Hopes for admission of this immense "State of Deseret" to the United States were dashed by the Compromise of 1850, which created a Territory of Utah with dimensions much smaller than Deseret, though larger than the present state of Utah. Fillmore served as the territorial capital from 1851–56, after which Salt Lake City became, and remains, the capital.

Utah's remarkably cosmopolitan population today is a result of two primary factors: the Mormon missionary program that drew extraordinary numbers of converts from the Eastern United States, the British Isles, Scandinavia, and the South Pacific; and the development of mines, especially in Carbon, Juab, and Salt Lake counties that lured non-Mormon European immigrants, particularly Slavs, Italians, and Greeks. Railroad construction through Utah and other economic opportunities lured Japanese, Chinese, and blacks. The massive immigration of European converts to Mormonism began soon after the arrival of the first Mormons in Salt Lake Valley. Records of mining and of the experience of non-Mormon and non-Anglo-Saxon Utahns have been preserved and histories written.

A good deal of nineteenth century Utah history concerns the relationship between Utah Territory, created out of the Mexican Cession of 1848, and the federal government, as federal governors and judges, regarded as "carpetbaggers" by Utah Mormons, sought to dismantle or emasculate the Mormon hierarchy. The tension reached a crisis in 1857 when federal troops under Albert Sidney Johnston were dispatched to restore order in Utah. The military presence, first at Camp Floyd west of Utah Lake, then at Fort Douglas east of Salt Lake City, provided ongoing friction between the Mormons and the United States.

That friction was exacerbated by the Mormon practice of plural marriage, in which men were encouraged to have more than one wife. Federal laws against polygamy in the 1880s led to imprisonment of many Mormon men. Issuance of the "Manifesto" of Mormon President Wilford Woodruff in 1890 officially ended the practice of plural marriage. Other uniquely Mormon practices and institutions, like the one-party political system, were ended during the 1890s, a process known as the "Americanization" of Utah, and the reward was statehood in 1896.

The "Americanization" of Utah was actually a very complex process in which the abandonment of plural marriage was only one aspect. Perhaps equally important was Utah's emerging demographic diversity and abandonment of the Mormon ideal of self-sufficiency that began with the Gold Rush of 1849 and was completed by the arrival of the transcontinental railroad in 1869 and the opening of Utah's rich mineral resources—primarily a non-Mormon enterprise—in the 1870s.

The pendulum swing from dissent to conformity achieved its apogee during the early twentieth century, as Utah politics assumed a characteristically conservative quality. Reliance on federal programs became a Utah characteristic during the 1930s as the Great Depression devastated the state not unlike many other states. The WPA and Civilian Conservation Corps programs of the New Deal were especially important in Utah's economic recovery. During World War II, Utah's abundant supply of skilled labor led to the establishment of war industries and military bases that have been a prominent part of the state's economy since then.

Nevertheless, the "Americanization" of Utah has not taken place without dissent. The opening of the Uintah Indian Reservation to white settlement in 1905 created a land rush that outraged the Utes and resulted in deep resentment at what they regarded as a betrayal of their interests and cultural integrity. Shortly thereafter, in 1923, the Paiutes of San Juan County resisted white encroachment in the "Posey War," the most recent major Indian war in the United States. During the 1970s, Utah Governor Scott Matheson assumed leadership of the "Sagebrush Rebellion" to transmit Utah's federally administered lands—a majority of state land—to state control.

During the late twentieth century, Utah cultural life has dramatically matured with the emergence of organizations like the Pioneer Theater Company, the Utah Symphony, and Ballet West. The state's major economic resources are tourism, based on the ski industry in the winter, and the scenic attractions of the national parks in the southern part of the state in the summer, and the state's abundant and well-educated labor force that attracts corporate headquarters.

Vital Records

In Utah, the civil registration of births, deaths, and marriages developed slowly, culminating with a statewide system of recording births and deaths beginning in 1905. Certificates for births and deaths from 1905 until the present can be obtained from the Bureau of Vital Statistics and Health Statistics, Utah State Department of Health, 288 North 460 West, P.O. Box 16700, Salt Lake City, Utah 84116. According to Utah state law, birth and death certificates are restricted for seventy-five years.

In 1860 the Utah legislature empowered (but did not require) Salt Lake City and Ogden to maintain a register of births and deaths within their respective cities, a practice already begun by Salt Lake City in 1847. In 1880 the power to register was extended to all incorporated cities, but not all cities undertook the responsibility, nor were most births registered for areas that did register births. In 1898 the state legislature provided for a central holding of county records, requiring county clerks to keep separate birth and death registers. Most of these records do not have indexes, although the Professional Chapter of the Utah Genealogical Association (see Archives, Libraries, and Societies) is currently preparing indexes to the 1898–1905 birth and death records. Those for Salt Lake City, which date back to 1847, are being indexed separately.

Nearly all of the early county birth and death register books have been microfilmed and are accessible through the FHL. Some of the original books are still at the county seat, while others have been transferred to the Utah State Archives and Records Service (see Archives, Libraries, and Societies). For dates of availability by county, see County Resources.

Since marriage was seen as a religious sacrament, the civil registration of marriages was not required in Utah until 1887. The Edmunds-Tucker Act, which outlawed polygamy, required that everyone married in any Territory of the United States "shall be certified by a certificate stating the fact and nature of such a ceremony." In 1889 the territorial legislature accepted the general structure of the act and required the person solemnizing the marriage to return the license and certificate within thirty days of the ceremony.

A few marriage records were created before 1887 and may be found in the county justice of peace or probate court records. Early marriage records were usually interfiled with other court matters, but others may have been recorded in land records, as is the case with some early Beaver County marriage records. Marriage for the pre-1887 time period may have been performed by an LDS bishop or a clergyman of a non-Mormon denomination. From 1889 to the present, a marriage application is completed in order to obtain a license which is issued by the county clerk. County-issued licenses for some time periods are available on microfilm through the FHL, even though some original books have since been transferred to the Utah State Archives and Records Service.

The practice of both open and secret polygamy has a great impact on genealogical research in Utah. For a thorough discussion of marriage practices in the state, see Lyman D. Platt's "The History of Marriage in Utah, 1847–1905," *Genealogical Journal* 12 (Spring 1983): 28–41.

In addition to government produced vital records, there is a variety of records, not recorded in original registers, such as midwives' and physicians' records, which contain vital records. Many have been microfilmed and are accessible through the FHL under the heading of Utah/[County]/Vital Records. The LDS church also maintains an extensive array of vital statistics in its own church records. For a comprehensive discussion of various types of records, see Laureen Richardson Jaussi and Gloria Duncan Chaston's *Genealogical Records in Utah* (Salt Lake City, Utah: Deseret Book Co., 1974), described in Background Sources.

Court jurisdiction for divorces in Utah changed back and forth between probate and district courts in the county. By 1877, the district court gained sole jurisdiction. Pre-statehood divorce records may be found in either county probate court records, federal (territorial) district courts, or LDS church records. From 1896 to the present, all divorces are filed through the county's district court and are held in the court clerk's office.

Census Records

Federal

Population Schedules.

- Indexed—1850 (1851), 1860, 1870, 1880
- Soundex—1880, 1900, 1920
- Unindexed—1910

Mortality Schedules.

- 1860, 1870, 1880

Union Veterans Schedules.

- 1890

The 1850 census for Utah Territory was taken in 1851. It has been reproduced alphabetically within each county in Annie Walker Burns, *First Families of Utah, As Taken From the 1850 Census of Utah* (Washington, D.C.: the author, 1949). This volume's index is to the transcription of the census records and not the original. A second index, The Genealogical Society of Utah's *Index to Utah 1851 Census* (Salt Lake City, Utah: the society, 1950), refers to the original entry in the federal returns and is indexed by surname. Mortality schedules are available on microfilm through the FHL.

In addition to these and the AISI (see page 2) indexes for Utah, which includes the 1880 enumeration, there is a collapsed index covering the first three federal censuses for the territory:

Kearl, J. R., Clayne L. Pope, and Larry T. Wimmer. *Index to the 1850, 1860, and 1870 Censuses of Utah.* Baltimore, Md.: Genealogical Publishing Co., 1981.

Territorial

There are fragments of what could be construed as territorial or state censuses from 1852, 1856, 1872, and 1896 with enumerations derived from tax lists. The 1852 Bishops Reports, listing LDS heads of households in each LDS ward, are available on microfilm with an index through the FHL.

Only the 1856 list, originally developed in an attempt to apply for statehood, has been indexed and published by AISI and Bryan Lee Dilts, *1856 Utah Census Index* (Salt Lake City, Utah: Index Publishing, 1983). The accuracy of the original enumeration has been questioned, however, since it appears to contain names of deceased persons or members of the LDS Church who were not yet in the territory.

Background Sources

The story of the exodus of the Mormons is not the only aspect of Utah immigration, although it is a large part. Two-thirds of those early immigrants arriving in the Salt Lake basin in 1847 and in later years were largely from states north of the Ohio River. Approximately 60 percent were from New York, Pennsylvania, Illinois, and Ohio, with forebears from New England. People from Missouri, Tennessee, and Kentucky comprised the bulk of the remaining U.S. born emigrants. Foreign-born Mormons originated mostly in the British Isles, with the second largest group coming from the Scandinavian countries. Mormons have written and preserved the history of their ancestors better than most of their contemporaries. Emigration of other parties and the establishment of mining districts, particularly the Tintic district and mines around Price, Utah, constitute other major settlement groups, all with good printed sources regarding their history.

For background reading in Utah history see:

Arrington, Leonard J. *Great Basin Kingdom: Economic History of the Latter-day Saints, 1830–1900.* Cambridge, Mass.: Harvard University Press, 1958.

Arrington, Leonard J. and Davis Bitton. *The Mormon Experience: A History of the Latter-day Saints.* New York, N.Y.: Alfred A. Knopf, 1980.

Papanikolas, Helen Zeese, ed. *The Peoples of Utah.* Salt Lake City, Utah: State Historical Society, 1976. The diversity of population in Utah is covered.

Poll, Richard D., Thomas G. Alexander, Eugene E. Campbell, and David E. Miller, eds. *Utah's History.* Provo, Utah: Brigham Young University, 1978. A collection of chapters written by the editors and others, covers various aspects of Mormon and non-Mormon Utah history. A bibliographic essay covering Utah's history is included.

One unusual, highly informative set of publications is that by Kate B. Carter, *Heart Throbs of the West* (13 vols., 1939–51), *Treasures of Pioneer History* (6 vols., 1952–57), and *Our Pioneer Heritage* (18 vols., 1959–75), all published in Salt Lake City, Utah, by the Daughters of Utah Pioneers. Many personal accounts of settlers as well as invaluable source materials are included.

For genealogical research, Laureen R. Jaussi and Gloria D. Chaston, *Genealogical Records of Utah* (see Vital Records), is an essential guide, detailing church and government related documents and sources as well as discussing the genealogical uses and limitations of records and sources.

Maps

Division of Community Relations, Department of Transportation, 4501 South 2700 West, Salt Lake City, Utah 84119, provides modern county maps that include locations of residences, cemeteries, and land grid, range, and township divisions. The U.S. Geological Survey maps (see page 4) supplement the county maps with additional geographic details.

For historical maps see:

Greer, Deon C., Klaus C. Gurgel, Wayne L. Wahlquist, Howard A. Christy, and Gary B. Peterson. *Atlas of Utah.* Provo, Utah: Brigham Young University Press, 1981.

Miller, David E. *Utah History Atlas.* Salt Lake City, Utah: the author, 1964.

Moffat, Riley Moore. *Printed Maps of Utah to 1900.* Santa Cruz, Calif.: Western Association of Map Libraries, 1981.

The collection of the FHL provides a large group of early maps. See Utah/Maps in the card catalog.

Land Records

Public-Domain State

The arrival of the 1847 migration of the Mormons marked the first settlement of nonnatives in Utah. Following the war with Mexico, Utah came under United States jurisdiction in 1848, but from March 1849 until it was declared an official U.S. territory in 1850, it was known as part of the Provisional State of Deseret. The Homestead Act did not affect Utah until the first federal district land office was opened in Salt Lake City in 1869. Both Mormon landholding practices and federal distribution of land played important roles in land transactions for the state. Jaussi and Chaston's and Arrington's publications, described under Background Sources, and Lawrence L. Linford's "Establishing and Maintaining Land Ownership in Utah Prior to 1869," *Utah Historical Quarterly* 42 (1974): 126–43 provide an excellent context for researching Utah's land records.

Before the Homestead Act became effective in the territory, land was distributed by the elders of the Mormon church in lots that could easily be maintained by a family. With the creation of a Federal Land Office in Salt Lake in 1869, legal titles were granted to land that had been previously held. Since it was a federal land state, division of property was based on a rectangular survey emanating from either the Salt Lake Meridian or a smaller meridian in the Uintah Basin. For Utah there is a master card index for the cash entry files of U.S. lands sold by the Salt Lake Land Office, accessible at the National Archives-Rocky Mountain Region (see page 8) or the National Records Center in Suitland, Maryland (see page 9).

Although the office was created earlier, the county recorder's deed books did not become the predictable location for land transactions until after 1874. Earlier land records can be found among many classes of documents in the county seat, including county court and probate records. But after that date, separate books for land transactions have been continuously kept. All counties will have indexes for their land holdings, usually referred to as grantee and grantor indexes, although they may not encompass all time periods.

Probate Records

Probate functions (testate and intestate proceedings; guardianships for males under twenty-one and females under eighteen, and those incompetent to handle their legal affairs) were shared by county probate courts and territorial district courts between 1852–96. Records for these are generally at the county seat, though some probate records have been microfilmed and are accessible through the FHL. Microfilm coverage varies between counties. For example, Garfield, Sanpete, Cache (registers, not cases), Rich, Morgan, Grand, Iron, and Beaver all have records that contain large gaps, but what remains is on microfilm.

After 1896, jurisdiction for probate matters became the sole responsibility of the district court that operated for the county. There are now eight judicial districts encompassing twenty-nine counties. To determine exactly which district a county belonged to at a particular time, there are two finding aids. One is available at the Utah State Archives, and the other is a guide that can be obtained by writing the Utah Judicial Council, Administrative Office of the Courts, 23 South 500 East, Suite 300, Salt Lake City, Utah 84102. Since 1 January 1989, all Utah courts were placed under the administration of this office. In trying to determine the county seat that was functioning as the probate court during a particular time period, this office will be the most efficient source.

Currently District 1 includes Box Elder, Cache, and Rich counties; District 2—Davis, Morgan, and Weber; District 3—Salt Lake, Summit, and Tooele; District 4—Juab, Millard, Utah, and Wasatch; District 5—Beaver, Iron, and Washington; District 6—Garfield, Kane, Piute, Sanpete, Sevier, and Wayne; District 7—Carbon, Emery, Grand, and San Juan; and District 8—Daggett, Duchesne, and Uintah.

Court Records

In the first years of settlement, an LDS Bishops Court system operated within the LDS church structure maintaining jurisdiction over criminal and civil cases for those residents in a particular ward of the church. Edwin B. Firmage and Richard C. Mangrum, *Zion in the Courts: A Legal History of the Church of Jesus Christ of Latter-day Saints, 1830–1900* (Urbana, Ill.: University of Illinois Press, 1988), expertly covers the time period when church and civil courts overlapped. County courts were created in 1849, overseeing civil and criminal cases involving more than $100, until Utah became a territory in 1851 and that court was replaced by the county probate court. Justice of the peace courts where established at the same time (1849) for cases involving less than $100 (changed to $300 in 1874), and continue to operate today. When county probate court jurisdiction was restricted in 1874, civil, criminal, and probate matters were transferred to the federally operated territorial district court which had held concurrent jurisdiction with the county probate court since 1852. Concurrent jurisdiction was a result of conflicts between the federal government and local citizens as to who should have legal jurisdiction. For a discussion of court records in Utah, see Jaussi and Chaston, described in Background Sources, and James B. Allen, "The Unusual Jurisdiction of County Probate Courts in the Territory of Utah," *Utah Historical Quarterly* 36 (Spring 1968): 132–42. See also an information brochure on court records available from the Utah State Archvies for a compressed history of court records.

With statehood in 1896, a uniform statewide district court system (see Probate Records) took over civil and criminal matters as well as probate matters. There are voluminous court records available, some indexed, on microfilm at the Utah State Archives. Included in their holdings are quite a few records of miners' courts, which frequently served the function of a county clerk in registering and transferring claims. Other historical materials on mining camps can be found at the Utah State Historical Society (see Archives, Libraries, and Societies).

Tax Records

Some early tax records have been published as part of a state census (see Census Records), but microfilm copies of manuscript transcripts of crop records, school assessments, and property assessment are available for many counties on microfilm through the Utah State Archives and the FHL.

Cemetery Records

Good, although by no means complete, sources for cemetery records can be found at the Utah State Archives and the FHL. In the FHL catalog, check: Utah/[County]/[Town]/Cemetery listings first, then individual counties. Salt Lake City Cemetery (not including Mt. Olivet or Fort Douglas cemeteries) is on a computer database at the FHL but is not published. Although it is not yet complete, the Utah Genealogical Association is continuing to conduct the transcription project. Jaussi and Chaston (see Background Sources) also list a number of sources for death records from funeral homes and cemetery sexton's records at the FHL.

Church Records

The Mormon church is predominant in Utah, but other denominations are represented. Among these is the Catholic church, whose presence was announced by the diocesan seat and the Cathedral of the Madeleine, founded in 1890. Their archives is maintained by the Catholic Diocese of Salt Lake City, 27 "C" Street, Salt Lake City, Utah 84103. The Episcopal Diocese of Utah maintains an archive collection at the University of Utah, although it is not processed and consequently inaccessible; however, most parish registers remain with the local church.

Extensive material is available for those with Mormon heritage, whether from Utah or outside the state. The Church Historical Department and the FHL (see Archives, Libraries, and Societies) have extensive collections too numerous to discuss here. For an excellent discussion of the holdings, Jaussi and Chaston's work discussed under Background Sources provides a good overview of what is available and how to locate it both at the FHL and in the Historical Department of the church.

Military Records

On 19 July 1846, five hundred volunteers of the Mormon Battalion left Council Bluffs, Iowa, heading southwestward at the request of President James K. Polk. They joined other federal troops at Fort Leavenworth, Kansas, proceeded west to Santa Fe and then to San Diego, California, arriving on 29 January 1847. After a year of duty, the battalion left eighty-one officers and enlisted men in San Diego, while the main group walked north to Sutter's Fort, where half of the contingent remained for a while. Eventually, the entire group was reunited with their fellow Mormons at Salt Lake City.

A Mormon unit of 13,000 troops, known as the Nauvoo Legion, a territorial militia that included both Mormon and non-Mormon military-aged males, engaged in military activities from its earliest inception to the end of the Black Hawk War in the late 1860s. The original records for 1849–

70 are at the Utah State Archives, along with an extensive collection of other state militia, service, and veterans records compiled by the archives. Many are additionally available on microfilm through the National Archives (see page 7) and the FHL.

Volunteers from Utah served during the Civil War, and a unit of 500 engaged in the Spanish-American War in 1898. A total of 21,000 soldiers were supplied during World War I, and many more during World War II. Utah servicemen are included in the 1890 special census of the Union veterans and widows of the Civil War, as are those who served elsewhere but were living in Utah by 1890. Some Army troops served on the frontier in Utah and remained after discharge to take advantage of mining or commercial ventures.

Printed sources for military history and records include:

Carter, Kate B. *The Mormon Battalion.* Salt Lake City, Utah: Utah Printing, 1956.

Long, E. B. *The Saints and the Union: Utah Territory in the Civil War.* Urbana, Ill.: University of Illinois Press, 1981.

Powell, Alan Kent, ed., *Utah Remembers World War II.* Logan, Utah: Utah State University, 1991.

Prentiss, A. *The History of the Utah Volunteers in the Spanish-American War and in the Philippine Islands.* Salt Lake City, Utah, W. F. Ford, 1900.

Warrum, Noble. *Utah in the World War.* Salt Lake City, Utah, Arrow Press, 1924.

For veterans of all wars buried under the jurisdiction of the federal burial program since 1861, write to Cemetery Service, National Cemetery System, Veterans Administration, 810 Vermont Avenue, Washington, D.C. 20420. Headstone applications taken from 1879 to 1924 were filed by applicant, state, county, and cemetery.

Periodicals, Newspapers, and Manuscript Collections

Periodicals

Utah Historical Quarterly. Published from 1928 onward by the Utah State Historical Society. Providing good historical context of Utah research, the publication also evaluates source material for genealogical and local history research.

Genealogical Journal. Published by the Utah Genealogical Association. Not restricted to articles on Utah genealogy, the publication is of national interest, including methodology and source material from all over the world.

Utah Genealogical and Historical Magazine. Published by the Genealogical Society of Utah. Published between 1910–40, its articles were not limited to Utah or Mormon genealogy.

Newspapers

The first newspaper in Utah was the *Deseret News* which began publication in Salt Lake in 1850. Other nineteenth-century newspapers and their first date of publication include:

Ogden Standard-Examiner. Odgen, 1870.

The Daily Herald. Provo, 1873.

The Salt Lake Tribune. Salt Lake City, 1875.

The Washington County News. St. George, 1896.

Robert P. Holley, Jr., *Utah's Newspapers—Traces of Her Past* (Salt Lake City, Utah: University of Utah, 1984), contains a valuable "Checklist of Utah Newspapers" beyond those mentioned here. The University's library holds many obscure Utah newspapers on microfilm in addition to the major ones.

An Obituary Card Index of those listings found in runs of twelve Salt Lake City newspapers from the beginning of their publication, is microfilmed and available through FHL. The earliest newspaper covered is for 1850 with more recent ones running through to 1970.

Manuscripts

The Utah State Historical Society, the Church Historical Department, and each of Utah's major universities maintain large manuscript collections focusing on Utah history and containing material useful to the genealogist. While some of the institutions offer printed guides to some aspects of their holdings, the best guide to Utah manuscripts is RLIN, an online national database maintained by the Research Libraries Group and accessible at any member library. The holdings of all major Utah manuscript repositories, except the Church Historical Department and several smaller repositories as well, are exhaustively cataloged in RLIN and constantly updated. RLIN terminals are available in Utah at the Utah State Archives, the Utah State Historical Society, and Brigham Young University.

A less current but more convenient version of the RLIN entries for Utah repositories is available for a very nominal fee on IBM-compatible floppy disks from Max J. Evans, Utah State Historical Society, 300 Rio Grande, Salt Lake City, Utah 84101. The software and easily understood instructions for running it are contained on the disks.

Finally, all major Utah repositories maintain skilled reference staffs who are able to answer questions about their holdings and to do limited amounts of research in response to specific questions submitted by telephone or mail.

Archives, Libraries, and Societies

Family History Library
Genealogical Society of Utah
35 North West Temple
Salt Lake City, UT 84150

Every researcher should know of the Family History Library (FHL) operated under the auspices of the Church of Jesus Christ of Latter-day Saints and situated in Salt Lake City. The collection, owned and maintained by the Genealogical Society of Utah, is of unparalleled importance in the field of family history and is one of the foremost accumulations of records, books, microfilm, microfiche, maps, manuscript, biographies, etc., in the world. For anyone doing genealogical research, a trip to Salt Lake City can be extremely productive since so much is available in one place. If this is not feasible, there are numerous Family History Center branch libraries operated by local LDS entities in towns and cities all over the world (see page 9).

LDS Church Historical Department
Church Office Building
50 East North Temple
Salt Lake City, UT 84150

In addition to the church's library, there is a large church archives department containing many records not at the FHL. Among them are diaries of early Utah settlers and an extensive collection of official church records.

Utah State Archives and Records Service
Archives Building, State Capitol
Salt Lake City, UT 84114

The Utah State Archives permanently preserves and provides access to the records of enduring value created by Utah state, county, and municipal governments. Microfilming of county records is an ongoing process with new materials added monthly to the collection. The Records Analysis section reviews, appraises, and evaluates the retention of records. The Records Center stores records of temporary value while those of permanent value become part of the preservation process and are stored in the Utah State Archives. Public records and documents may be used at the Research Center. Finding aids, a catalog, inventories, and indexes assist researchers. There is no fee for the reference service; however, photocopying and mailing costs are charged. Researchers need to contact the Research Center to determine availability of materials since archives storage is off site.

Utah State Historical Society
300 Rio Grande
Salt Lake City, Utah 84101

The society publishes the *Utah Historical Quarterly* and *Beehive History* and maintains an extensive, well-managed collection. Because of the focus of the collection at the FHL, the historical society concentrates on printed and state history and maintains an extensive manuscript collection. Two articles in Utah Genealogical Association's *Newsletter* (4th Quarter, 1988) discuss the usefulness of this collection for genealogists: Max J. Evans, "Genealogy and History," and Standford J. Layton, "Introducing the Utah State Historical Society."

Utah Genealogical Association
Box 1144
Salt Lake City, UT 84110

This organization, often confused with the Genealogical Society of Utah, which is a department of the LDS Church, meets on a regular basis and publishes the *Genealogical Journal* and a quarterly *Newsletter* giving information about new acquisitions at the FHL and articles of local interest. The association is divided into several chapters, each with particular ongoing projects such as indexing birth and death records (see Vital Records).

Association of Professional Genealogists
P.O. Box 11601
Salt Lake City, UT 84147

Established in 1979 as an independent, international organization with a mailing address and headquarters in Salt Lake City, membership is open to anyone interested in professional development in research, writing, publishing, and librarianship. It publishes the *Association of Professional Genealogists Quarterly,* with articles written by working genealogists who give valuable information regarding methods and sources. A membership directory stating researcher's areas of interest is available for sale from the headquarters office.

University of Utah
Marriott Library
Salt Lake City, UT 84112

Both the Special Collections departments of Manuscripts and Western Americana have useful material for the genealogist.

Special Focus Categories

Naturalization

Naturalization records begin, in general, with the date the county was organized and may have been kept in one of several courts holding concurrent jurisdiction. Naturalizations that commenced between statehood (1896) and the federal changes in the naturalization process (1906) are easy to locate since the district court was the only court in the state where naturalization could be initiated, and each one kept records individually by county in the district court office. Many of these may be found at the Utah State Archives, and some are on microfilm at the FHL listed under Utah/[County]/Emigration and Immigration. The Utah State Archives has an excellent descriptive flyer for use at the facility in locating holdings of naturalizations. After 1906, an applicant could apply at the state district court for the county, the state supreme court, or the federal courts.

Since a large number of Mormons were brought to Utah from foreign countries, the number of naturalizations is rather large for a land-locked state. Passenger lists of those Mormon immigrants from foreign-country missions in Scandinavia (1872–94) and Europe (1840–1925) are on microfilm through the FHL. Jaussi and Chaston describe a full collection of emigration records in their work (see Vital Records).

Native American

The Utah State Historical Society has a collection of materials on native culture and history. For additional information, contact Paiute Tribal Council, 660 North 100 East, Cedar City, Utah 84720; Uintah and Ouray Tribal Business Council, Fort Duchesne, Utah 84026; and the Ute Tribal Museum Library, Ute Tribe, P.O. Box 190, Fort Duchesne, Utah 84026. An excellent article for background on early tribal cultures is Jesse D. Jennings, "Early Man in Utah," *Utah Historical Quarterly* 28 (1960): 3–27.

County Resources

The chart that follows is based on information from the Utah State Archives as verified by the *Atlas of Utah* (Provo, Utah: BYU Press, 1981) and John W. van Cott, *Utah Place Names* (Salt Lake City, Utah: University of Utah Press, 1990). County recorders maintain land records of transactions filed in their counties. Many original birth and death records before statewide recording have been transferred to the Utah State Archives. Since this is an ongoing process, it is best to contact the archives first regarding a specific county's records in their holdings. Those county record books before 1905 that have not been transferred are at the county clerk's office.

Courts were divided into districts with different county seats functioning as the seat of record at different times. Some of the original records that are extant for a county may not be in the county seat but may have been transferred to the Utah State Archives (see Probate Records and Court Records). Those at the county seat reside with the clerk of the court.

The listing of the dates below were verified by the Utah State Archives and checked against the FHL catalog, the State Archives' Series Catalog, and Microfilm Accession list, the WPA *Guide to Public Vital Statistics of Utah* (Salt Lake City, Utah: Utah Historical Records Survey, 1941), and individual county holdings.

Drawn by William Dollarhide

Map	County Address	Date Formed Parent County/ies	Birth Marriage Death	Land Probate Court
G2	Beaver 105 E. Center Beaver 84713	1856 Iron	1898–1905 1887 1900–05	1867 1856 1856
A2	Box Elder 01 S. Main Street Brigham City 84302	1856 Green River/Weber	1898–1905 1888 1898–1905	1856 1856 1856
A4	Cache 170 N. Main Street Logan 84321	1856 Green River	1898–1905 1887 1898–1905	1857 1960 1960
E6	Carbon 120 E. Main Street Price 84501	1894 Emery	1898–1918 1894 1898–1905	1894 1894 1894
	Carson	1854 (became part of Nevada Territory in 1861)		
	Cedar	1856 (became part of Utah County in 1862)		
B7	Daggett 95 North First West Manila 84046 ** See Uintah County*	1917 Uintah	* 1918 *	1918 1918 1918
B4	Davis State and Main Streets Farmington 84025	1850 original	1898–1905 1887 1898–1905	1870 1853 1852
	Deseret	1856 (became part of Nevada Territory in 1861)		
C6	Duchesne 50 East 100 South Duchesne 84021 ** See Uintah County*	1914 Wasatch	* 1915 *	1915 1915 1915
F6	Emery 95 E. Main Castle Dale 84513	1880 Sanpete/Sevier	1898–1905 1887 1898–1905	1881 1887 1887
H5	Garfield 55 S. Main Panguitch 84759	1882 Iron/Kane/Washington	1898–1905 1887 —	1882 1883 1882
F7	Grand 125 East Center Moab 84532	1890 Emery/Uintah	1898–1905 1890 1898–1905	1890 1890 1890
	Greasewood	1856 (discontinued in 1862; now part of Box Elder)		
	Green River	1852 (became part of Nebraska Territory in 1861; became part of Wyoming in 1868)		
	Humboldt	1856 (became part of Nevada Territory in 1861)		
H2	Iron 68 South 100 East Parowan 84761	1850 (as Little Salt Lake) original	1898–1905 1888 1898–1905	1851 1870 1851
E2	Juab 160 N. Main Street Nephi 84648	1852 original	1898–1905 1888 1898–1905	1859 1859 1859

Map	County Address	Date Formed Parent County/ies	Birth Marriage Death	Land Probate Court
J4	Kane 76 N. Main Street Kanab 84741	1864 Washington	1900–05 1887 1900–05	1872 1878 1878
	Malad	1856 (discontinued in 1862; now part of Box Elder)		
F2	Millard 60 S. Main Street Fillmore 84631	1852 Iron	— 1887 —	1852 1852 1852
B4	Morgan 48 West Young Street Morgan 84050	1862 Summit/Weber/Cache	1898–1905 1869 1898–1905	1869 1869 1869
G4	Piute P.O. Box 99 Junction 84740	1865 Sevier	1898–1900 1872 —	1868 1869 1869
A5	Rich 20 S. Main Street Randolph 84064	1864 original	1898–1912 1888 1898–1912	1872 1872 1872
	Rio Virgin	1869 (became part of Nevada state in 1870)		
	St. Mary's	1856 (became part of Nevada Territory in 1861)		
C4	Salt Lake 2001 S. State Street Salt Lake City 84190-1015	1850 original	1898–1905 1887 1897–1905	1852 1852 1851
J7	San Juan 117 S. Main Street Monticello 84535	1880 Iron/Kane/Piute	1898–1917 1888 1897–1917	1883 1888 1898
E4	Sanpete 160 N. Main Street Manti 84642	1850 original	1898–1905 1888 1898–1905	1855 1852 1852
F4	Sevier 250 N. Main Street Richfield 84701	1865 Sanpete	1898–1905 1887 1898–1905	1885 1865 1865
	Shambip	1856 (became part of Tooele County in 1862)		
B5	Summit 60 N. Main Street Coalville 84017	1854 Green River/Salt Lake	1898–1905 1887 1898–1905	1862 1866 1866
C2	Tooele 47 S. Main Street Tooele 84074	1850 original	1898–1905 1887 1898–1905	1852 1870 1859
D7	Uintah 152 E. 100 North Vernal 84078	1880 Summit/Wasatch/Sanpete	1896–1905 1888 1896–1905	1880 1880 1880
D4	Utah 100 E. Center Street Provo 84601	1850 original	1898–1905 1887 1898–1905	1851 1859 1852

Map	County Address	Date Formed Parent County/ies	Birth Marriage Death	Land Probate Court
C5	Wasatch 25 N. Main Street Heber City 84031	1862 Green River/Davis	1898–1905 1887 1898–1905	1862 1883 1862
J2	Washington 197 E. Tabernacle St. George 84770	1852 original	1898–1905 1885 1898–1905	1856 1873 1856
G5	Wayne 18 S. Main Street Loa 84747	1892 Piute	1898–1905 1892 1899–1905	1892 1892 1892
B4	Weber 2549 Washington Boulevard Ogden 84401	1850 original	1898–1905 1887 1898–1905	1850 1852 1852

VERMONT

Scott A. Bartley and Alice Eichholz, Ph.D., C.G.,

Vermont had its beginnings in a land controversy. Near the middle of the eighteenth century, both Benning Wentworth, the colonial governor of New Hampshire, and Lt. Governor Cadwallader Colden, representing the colonial government of New York, claimed territory in what is now Vermont. Massachusetts claimed a small part along Vermont's southern border. Each government petitioned the king to validate their boundaries to include the disputed Vermont land. However, the process of petitioning did not stop either New Hampshire or New York from issuing grants for the same land to their own proprietors and the proprietors in turn selling the land to settlers.

Settlers from lower New England and New York began to arrive in "The Grants," as they were called, in the 1760s. Previous residents of the land included a few French settlements in the northern part of the state, the remainder of the Native American population in the region after the French and Indian Wars, and some early New England settlers around Fort Dummer on the Connecticut River. By 1760, most of these settlers, with the exception of the remaining Abenaki tribe, had moved back to more populated areas in New England and Canada. Life for those settling "The Grants" consisted of clearing rock-laden forests. The settlers were also faced with the uncertainty as to whether the land they were homesteading was really theirs or belonged to someone else who also thought they had a legitimate claim.

The Vermont land controversy between New York and New Hampshire about the grants was complicated by different types of land ownership practiced by the two colonial governments. Those who received grants from New York were generally from the upper classes and leased their land on a rental basis to others who farmed it for them. New Hampshire grants were generally given to middle class farmers and civic leaders, who in turn sold the land outright to those who settled it and farmed it. England settled the controversy in favor of New York in 1764—a decision unpopular with most Vermonters.

This land controversy, the French and Indian War in the early 1750s, and the onset of the American Revolution kept the number of actual settlers coming into Vermont low. Vermont declared itself independent in 1777, not answerable to England or the governors of New York or New Hampshire. Vermont recognized the land grants made by New Hampshire only and began issuing grants of its own for land previously not claimed. Settlement began in earnest once the Revolution was concluded in 1783. At the same time, Vermont attempted, with a good deal of ambivalence according to some historians, to become part of the union, eventually achieving statehood in 1791.

Initially, after statehood, population soared. Geography played a critical role in the state's settlement. The Green Mountains run north-south through the center of the state, leaving the rivers as the major east-west conduits for travel and dividing the state into mountainous areas and river valleys, flood plains, and rock-laden terrain. Lake Champlain, running along most of the state's western border provided means of western migration to New York and beyond.

Today's roads generally follow the same migration trails as were cut during the settlement period. Small farms, nestled among the valleys and in the Lake Champlain region, and small industries using Vermont's forest resources constituted the major economic life of the state. Merino sheep and Morgan horses have also played their part in the attempt to create a reliable economy.

Following the War of 1812 a series of economic and meteorologic calamities occurred, including the "Year of No Summer" (1816). A major migration of those leaving the state was the result. An influx of new settlers—French-Canadians, Italians, and Irish among them—during the mid-nineteenth century changed, somewhat, the populations' ethnic constitution. Vermont contributed more per capita from its treasury and from its population of young men in the Civil War than any other state in the Union. Between the 1860s and the 1970s there was little population growth. In the twentieth century, a devastating flood in the central part of the state in 1927 and the national depression in the 1930s made it difficult for Vermont to recover economically. Tourism became a strong draw in the late twentieth century, with recreational industry and a desire to retreat from urban and suburban living as part of the impetus for new settlement today.

Vital Records

The first settlers of Vermont carried on the early New England tradition of recording events at the town level. The vital records are incomplete before mandatory registration began in 1857. It is not uncommon to find an entire family recorded as a family group before 1820. In some cases, although the event was recorded in a particular town, it may have actually occurred in another town or state where the family previously resided. Not all the births were recorded, even for families that did report some. Marriages and deaths in the pre-1857 period were less likely to be recorded.

What was recorded, with some exceptions, has been extracted from the originals in the towns and indexed in a central file held by the Vermont Public Records Division. All events indexed before 1980 can be found at the division's new facility on Route 2, Middlesex, Vermont (Exit 9 on Interstate 89). The mailing address is State Administration Building, 133 State Street, Montpelier, Vermont 05633-7601.

No thorough survey has ever been taken to determine whether some towns' early vital records were inadvertently missed in the statewide index. It is known that Holland, Sheffield, Maidstone, and Troy vital records were not included, and some vital records from Burlington in the 1870s seem to be missing entirely.

Anyone can search the microfilm at the Public Records Division, or a search can be requested by mail for a charge of $5 per event. This includes a certified copy of the microfilmed index card, if found, containing a reference for locating the original record in the individual town records. The microfilmed card index is broken down into four time periods: 1760–1870; 1871–1908; 1909–41; 1942–54. The years 1955–80. Separate cards for births, marriages (both bride and groom), death, and cemetery records are in the index. Cemetery cards, however, appear only in the 1760–1870 microfilm grouping. The statewide index was created about 1919, and in the process, the state surveyed all the cemeteries in Vermont to record deaths before 1857, the year mandatory recording began. Generally, only those gravestones that were still standing in 1919 and mentioned deaths before 1857 were included in the survey.

Microfilm copies of the first two time periods (1760–1870, 1871–1908) are additionally available at the New England Historic Genealogical Society (see page 9) and through the FHL.

After 1857, many births were recorded before a child was named. Unnamed infants are listed in reverse chronological order in the front of that surname's listing in the card index. The index is filed in strict alphabetical order. Variants in spellings must be checked thoroughly.

While the state issues a certified copy of the microfilmed index card as its "official" record, the original record in the town clerk's office, often recorded with other family vital records, may provide additional information helpful in research. Once the index card has been located with the reference for the original record, it is often important to obtain a copy of the event as it appears in its original form. The reference on the index card will indicate where to locate the event in the town's original records. Since a large majority of the town's original records are also on microfilm in the Public Records Division, microfilm copies of the originals can be researched there. Vermont's town records before 1850 are also on microfilm through the FHL, although the holdings are not as complete as at the Public Records Division.

Vital records after 1980 are found at the Vital Records Office, 60 Main Street, P.O. Box 70, Burlington, Vermont 05841. Files are open to the public but accessed by a clerk. The cost, either in person or by mail, is presently $5 per event.

At the Public Records Division, a separate statewide microfilm index to divorce decrees covers 1861–1968. The decree books themselves are also microfilmed and available there. Summary divorce papers from 1968–1979 are arranged alphabetically by surname in one group at the division.

Census Records

Federal

Population Schedules.

- Indexed—1790 (1791), 1800, 1810, 1820, 1830, 1840, 1850, 1860
- Soundex—1880, 1900, 1920
- Unindexed— 1870, 1910

Industry and Agriculture Schedules.

- 1850, 1860, 1870, 1880

Mortality Schedules.

- 1850, 1860, 1870, 1880 (all indexed)

Union Veterans Schedules.

- 1890 (indexed)

Because Vermont joined the union as the fourteenth state in 1791, it missed the first federal census by one year. Although labeled 1790, the census was actually taken one year later. Families in other states may be listed on that state's 1790 census and again in Vermont's a year later, having migrated in the interim. The Vermont Historical Society published the full 1800 census, which was reissued in a reprint edition in 1972 by Genealogical Publishing Company. Countywide 1870 census heads-of-household indexes for Windham and Windsor were privately published by Joan M. Morris in seperate volumes (1977, 1980).

The 1810 and 1820 censuses for some Vermont towns include a tally of such things as the number of yards of material made on the premises and the amount of lumber milled. When using the census records, care should be taken to consider alternate spelling, especially for French-Canadians, Italian, and Greek names of new immigrants after 1850.

Original and microfilm copies of the 1850, 1860, 1870, and 1880 population, industry, and agriculture schedules and microfilm of the mortality schedules are located at Vermont Department of Libraries, State Office Building, 109 State Street, Montpelier, Vermont 05609-0601, although originals are restricted for general research purposes.

The so-called *1771 Census* by Jay Mack Holbrook (Oxford, Mass.: Holbrook Research, 1982) is not an "official" census. It is a collection of names associated with Vermont in 1771 drawn from several sources in New York, New Hampshire, and Connecticut as well as Vermont. Many of the names listed were granted land but never lived in Vermont. Checking the appearance of the name in the original source should help clarify this.

Background Sources

Bassett, T. D. Seymour, ed. *Vermont: A Bibliography of Its History.* 1981. Reprint. Hanover, N.H.: University Press of New England, 1983. This comprehensive bibliography includes numerous local, state, and town histories, and commemorative publications.

Eichholz, Alice. *Collecting Vermont Ancestors.* Montpelier, Vt.: New Trails!, 1986. A genealogical handbook focusing specifically on the availability of the extensive original records in Vermont. A listing of available lot maps for towns (see Maps) is included.

Hemenway, Abby Maria. *Vermont Historical Gazetteer.* 5 vols. Burlington, Vt., and others, 1867–91. Hemenway enlisted the assistance of at least one knowledgeable resident of each town to research and write the histories included in these volumes. Since those people tended to know the individuals about whom they wrote, the information is reasonably good oral history. An index covering all towns except those in Windsor County was published in 1923 by Tuttle Company, in Rutland, Vermont, and indicates town as well as volume and page number for person named.

Jones, Matt Bushnell. *Vermont in the Making.* Cambridge, Mass.: Harvard University Press, 1939. This is probably the most detailed and easy to read account of the Vermont land controversy and its role in the Revolution and formation of the United States.

Lindberg, Marcia Wiswall. *Genealogist's Handbook for New England Research.* Boston, Mass.: New England Historic Genealogical Society, 1985. An essential guide for planning a research trip in Vermont, but because of its date of publication, call ahead to confirm hours, location, and record availability.

O'Callaghan, E. B. *Documentary History of the State of New York.* 4 vols. Albany, N.Y.: Weed, Parson & Co., 1849–51. This work contains much history regarding the land controversy between New York and Vermont. Volume 4 contains a large number of Vermont-related document transcriptions. Vermonters are included in Holbrook, *1771 Census* (see Census Records).

Stilwell, Lewis Dayton. *Migration from Vermont.* Montpelier, Vt.: Vermont Historical Society, 1948. This is a superbly documented description, generally using secondary sources, of migration in and emigration from Vermont as it related to social and economic problems encountered by Vermonters through 1860.

Swift, Esther Munroe. *Vermont Place-Names: Footprints of History.* Brattleboro, Vt.: Stephen Greene Press, 1977. Swift adeptly portrays the complicated history of Vermont's changing jurisdictions during the land controversy and gives fine descriptive accounts of thousands of place-names in Vermont, including Native American sources and surnames.

Maps

Excellent maps exist for use in solving genealogical problems in Vermont. Because it is still a sparsely settled state, it is possible literally to retrace many an ancestor's steps, or at least residences.

For research and traveling, one superb atlas details town divisions, geographical details, road surface types, routes of transportation, locations of buildings (including those no longer occupied), and cemeteries. It is *The Vermont Atlas and Gazetteer* (Freeport, Maine: DeLorme Mapping, 1987), published in updated versions. A smaller alternative publication is *The Vermont Road Atlas and Guide* (Burlington, Vt.: Northern Cartographic, 1985), which includes the names of all roads but does not provide details of buildings.

The *Beers Atlas,* detailing the structures and owners in the late nineteenth century in every county, has been reissued in the original county editions by Tuttle Publishing, Box 541, Rutland, Vermont 05701. Only Bennington, Chittenden, and Windsor maps still remain in print, but the entire series is available at the Vermont Historical Society and other research libraries. Originally published by F. W. Beers between 1869 and 1873, these atlases provide a valuable portrait of communities. The same details exist in a set of maps ten years earlier, but the Wallings Map Series from 1858 is only available for reference in large, wall-sized versions at the Vermont Historical Society and other research libraries.

For solving early genealogical problems in Vermont, the most important maps are the town lotting maps (see Land Records). When each town was granted, the land was divided into lots and numbered. Either the lot's number or the original proprietor are so often used in land descriptions that they are essential for locating a family in relationship to neighbors and the broader community. Lot maps may be found in town offices, the Vermont Historical Society, the Vermont Public Records Division, or other state agencies (see Background Sources—Eichholz's *Collecting Vermont Ancestors*, for location of lot maps).

Land Records

State-Land State

Much land in the state was originally granted by either Vermont, New Hampshire, or New York; some were in competing claims. When Vermont declared itself independent in 1777, all land came under its jurisdiction. Consequently, there was no other way to obtain an initial grant of land except through the auspices of the legislature, which first granted the town to a group of individuals called proprietors. The proprietors then met, although not necessarily in the town or even in Vermont, devised a plan for dividing up the land, and drew lots to determine who owned which lots. From then on, that piece of land was identified in deeds (if the descriptions are detailed enough) as the "original right" of that proprietor.

"Original right" is a term found often in deeds, often delineated as being the first, second, third, fourth, or sometimes fifth division right of the proprietor since not all of a town was divided up at one time. A division usually contained lots of equal acreage. For example, first division lots might be 100 acres, second division lots 50 acres. Some lots were set aside for the ministry, schools, and the governor to use at their discretion, though most of that was later sold in tax sales or leased by the town selectmen.

Occasionally, towns were divided up in a grid of ranges and lots and would be identified, for example, as "Lot #5 in 6th range." Once the general plan for numbering the lot—whether by divisions or ranges—was made, land tended to be sold as portions of the lot such as "south half of Lot #5." Metes and bounds descriptions were added later when land divisions did not fall neatly into portions of the original lot. Such metes and bounds descriptions often indicated names of roads, streams, or neighbors. The town is the primary legal jurisdiction for land records in Vermont. Consequently, original copies of land records are at the town clerk's office (see Town Resources). Each town has separate indexes for the grantees and grantors. Very few women owned land in their own right. They occasionally witnessed deeds but sometimes were asked to release their dower's right. A few land records were recorded by counties and are available at the county courthouse (see County [Probate] Resources), although they are primarily for those towns as noted in the Town Resources that have no formal organization.

With no statewide master index or abstract of land records in the 251 towns, this valuable genealogical information has to be searched out town by town, but it can be done centrally with microfilm copies. Land records for towns whose records were extant in the 1940s had those deed books and indexes microfilmed from inception through 1850. They are available and at the Vermont Public Records Division, Route 2, Middlesex, Vermont (mailing address: State Administration Building, 133 State Street, Montpelier, Vermont 05633-7601) and through the FHL. Only a few towns had lost their land records in fires or floods by that time. The Vermont Public Records Division is always expanding its microfilm holdings of town records beyond those done in the 1940s, and its collection now includes many town records from 1850 to the present. These are not necessarily in the FHL microfilm collection.

Probate Records

Probate Records were filed by probate district and not town, and probate districts do not strictly follow county lines. For Vermont's fourteen counties (see County [Probate] Resources), there have been twenty probate districts. One of those districts, New Haven, disbanded in 1962. By percentage, few Vermonters who died in the state have probate records filed. Many people disposed of their holdings to one or more children in land transactions before death.

Probate records are only indexed by district. Neither a statewide index nor district-wide abstracts exist. District offices have indexes filed by decedent only. Microfilm indexes are available at Vermont Public Records Division (see Land Records) and the FHL. Unlike the land records, the Vermont Public Records Division has not extensively continued the microfilming program of probate records. With some exceptions, only the official probate proceedings books were microfilmed to about 1850. Much more information exists in the original probate files that are held in the district itself, along with the probate records after 1850.

A complete probate search involves using all the files that are available in addition to the record books. Insolvent estates are not uncommon.

Court Records

Historically, the major purpose of the county system in Vermont was the operation of the county courts, which recorded deeds for unorganized towns, levied county taxes, heard civil and criminal matters, and granted divorces and naturalizations.

Before Vermont became independent (1777), New York and New Hampshire both claimed some county jurisdiction over Vermont land. For this reason, New York and New Hampshire records must be consulted even up to 1791.

Beginning in 1777, each county had one county court which heard both civil and criminal matters. The state supreme court served an appellate function. In 1967 district courts were added, covering territorial units within the counties. District court jurisdiction is not exclusively over criminal cases; it may also hear some civil cases. In 1974, the county courts were renamed superior courts, with countywide jurisdiction over all matters previously entertained by the county courts and not covered by district courts. Beginning in 1990, the superior court functions involving family matters (divorce, child custody, etc.) were transferred to one statewide family court with divisions of that court operating in each of the counties.

The Vermont Public Records Division now has microfilms of county court records for Bennington, Chittenden, and Windsor counties before 1825, with the only index available typed alphabetically by plaintiff for each book. The Division is continuing the microfilming of all the county court records and has completed Addison and Washington counties, although no comparable index exists for these. All of the originals will still be found in the county court offices, although using them is tedious work. Debts are the major subject of litigation in the courts.

Tax Records

Grand lists are the annual assessment for town tax purposes, and they were taken every year for every town in Vermont. They are the only taxes organized enough to be of genealogical use. Many of them are extant, but they are not easy to find. Sometimes they appear as part of the proprietor or town meeting records (which may be in the town records microfilms at Vermont Public Records Division or the FHL) or sometimes in separate books (which might be in town clerks' offices or vaults). The assessment might be for a poll (twenty-one year old male or eligible voter—"Freeman" in Vermont), acreage, buildings, cattle, yards of material produced, and clapboards milled. People taxed were not necessarily landowners.

Cemetery Records

Town, church, family, and private cemeteries all exist in Vermont. The cemetery cards in the vital records microfilm of the Vermont Public Records Division constitutes the only statewide cemetery index (see Vital Records for limitations). There is a Grand Army of the Republic card index of all veterans' graves through World War II at the Vermont Historical Society Library. Since 1982 there have been a number of projects undertaken to publish some Vermont cemetery records. The Vermont Historical Society has the most extensive collection, but some town offices are known to have good indexes of their own cemeteries.

Burial Grounds of Vermont (Bradford, Vt.: Vermont Old Cemetery Association, 1991), by Arthur L. Hyde and Frances P. Hyde, lists nearly 1,900 cemeteries, indexed by town. Each town entry has a road map with cemetery location and an inventory listing number of graves, condition of cemetery, and whether gravestone inscriptions have been published and where. The publication is available from the Vermont Old Cemetery Association, c/o Arthur Hyde, RR 1, Box 10, Bradford, Vermont 05033.

Church Records

Church records are under utilized in Vermont research, but they do contain good sources for genealogical research. Lists of members (sometimes the only place where wives' names are mentioned in any records), baptisms, removals, exclusions, and the intricacies of community life are obvious in many church records. The only easy way to access them is through the WPA inventory located at the Vermont Public Records Office (see Land Records). The inventory is divided into Protestant Episcopal (published), Congregational, and miscellaneous denominations (only typescript copies), and then by town. The inventory, taken in the 1940s, can be used as a guide for tracking down the whereabouts of many church records that may have been held in private homes of church members, or the town clerk's office, for safe keeping. However, both the Special Collections at University of Vermont's Bailey-Howe Library (see Manuscripts) and the Vermont Historical Society have become repositories for many records if they are not at the local church or in the town clerk's office. In some cases, the records were removed to centralized religious repositories both in and out of state.

Military Records

Original service records for Vermont before 1920 were destroyed in a fire. Printed lists of Vermonters who served in wars from the Revolution through the Korean conflict were published by the Vermont Adjutant General's Office. If you cannot find a copy in a library near you, the office at 118 State Street, Montpelier, Vermont 05602, will answer inquiries. A few records of Vermont militia for the 1820–30s can be found in some town meeting records.

Muster rolls in the Walter Sheldon papers of the Stevens Collection at the Vermont State Archives (See Archives, Libraries, and Societies) contains information on some who fought in the War of 1812.

Periodicals, Newspapers, and Manuscript Collections

Periodicals

Vermont History is published quarterly by the Vermont Historical Society (see Archives, Libraries, and Societies) and has excellent articles on Vermont history, rarely genealogy. It is indexed annually.

Branches and Twigs is published quarterly by the Genealogical Society of Vermont (see Archives, Libraries, and Societies). It is not indexed and not easy to use but is filled with bits and details on Vermont ancestors.

Across the Border, P.O. Box 31010, Bloomington, Minnesota 55431, covers northern Vermont and Quebec's eastern townships.

(See also Rhode Island—Periodicals—*The American Genealogist;* and Massachusetts—Periodicals—*The New England Historical and Genealogical Register.*)

Newspapers

There is an excellent newspaper collection for Vermont beginning with the first publication in 1781, microfilmed and available at the Vermont Department of Libraries, State Office Building, 109 State Street, Montpelier, Vermont 05609. Under "Newspapers," the card catalog lists the location of publications and all issues available. Vital records are occasionally included—births rarely. Obituaries are not prominent until well into the twentieth century.

An index to the *Burlington Free Press* in typescript form covering the years 1848–70 is in the "Vermont Room" at the state library. As a subject index, it still is essential for genealogical research since accidents and deaths, for example, can be located by topic with the names of people involved listed alphabetically.

The University of Vermont Bailey-Howe Library also has a good newspaper collection with copies of the typescript to the index, *Burlington Free Press* (1848–70).

Copies of the *Boston Evening Transcript* genealogy column (See—Massachusetts—Newspapers) for some years are held at the Vermont Historical Society in scrapbook form.

Manuscripts

The Vermont Historical Society Library, Special Collections at the Bailey-Howe Library of the University of Vermont, and the Vermont State Archives (See Archives, Libraries, and Societies) all have excellent, well-cataloged manuscript collections. The Brigham Index at the Vermont Historical Society is a thorough subject and topic index including letters to and from individuals in the collections. Bailey-Howe's collection is thoroughly cataloged and includes church records, an extensive map collection, and business and shipping records for the Lake Champlain region.

Part of Vermont State Archives' collection is every-name indexed for early documents (see Archives, Libraries, and Societies) before ca. 1830.

In addition, they publish a revised booklet entitled "A Guide to Vermont Repositories," indicating the location of many of Vermont's excellent collections of manuscript materials at such places as the Bennington, Shelburne, and Sheldon museums, and local libraries and historical societies.

Archives, Libraries, and Societies

Vermont Historical Society Library and Museum
State Office Building
109 State Street
Montpelier, VT 05609-0901

Call ahead regarding hours: (802) 828-2291. They have the single largest collection of printed Vermont and New England genealogical and historical research material in the state. Their excellent manuscript collection is extensively indexed. Membership is not required to use open stacks and collections. A very limited research service is available, but a list of independent researchers can be supplied.

Vermont State Archives
Redstone Building
26 Terrace Street
Montpelier, VT
Mailing Address:
State Office Building,
109 State Street
Montpelier, VT 05609-1101

Officially called the Office of Vermont Secretary of State, State Papers Division, it has a large collection of materials regarding all aspects of state government from the beginning (1777). It is the department of record for all Vermont State Government. Petitions, executive papers, confiscations, business patents, lotting plans, and estate sales for state use are all every-name indexed for easy access for the period before 1830. Mail and in-person inquiries are welcome.

While this office is the official archives, it does not hold records from towns. It technically shares the responsibility with the Public Records Division (See Vital Records for location), which holds the vital records and microfilm collections of town, land, probate, court, naturalization and some church records.

Bailey-Howe Library
Special Collections
University of Vermont
Burlington, VT 05401

In addition to the church manuscript and newspaper collections, the library has a small collection of printed genealogies and town histories, a fine map collection of the Lake Champlain Region, and an extensive manuscript collection of account books and diaries.

Genealogical Society of Vermont
P.O. Box 422
Pittsford, VT 05763

The society has semi-annual meetings and primarily publishes *Branches and Twigs* (see Periodicals). The library is available by appointment in the treasurer's home in Pittsford, and there are no research services.

(See also, Massachusetts—Archives, Libraries and Societies—New England Historic Genealogical Society.)

Special Focus Categories

Immigration

The "Saint Albans Passenger Arrival Records," so called, were maintained by the Immigration and Naturalization Service at St. Albans, Vermont, and span the years 1895–1954. This immigration district technically covered the entire U.S. Canadian border and documented people traveling by boat or train to the United States, entering through Canada. The original records, soundexed with three supplements, are at the National Archives and Records Administration in Washington, D.C. A complete set of microfilms are at the National Archives-New England Region (see page 8).

Naturalizations

Naturalizations might have been applied for or obtained through either the county court or U.S. District Courts. The Public Records Division (See Land Records) holds microfilm copies of some naturalizations from 1836 to 1972. A complete WPA index, which includes Vermont, along with the rest of New England for 1790–1906, is held at the National Archives-New England Region (see Massachusetts—New England).

Native American

Members and descendants of the Abenaki tribe in Vermont are active in genealogical research. Contact the Vermont Historical Society for the address of the organizers of their activities. See also:

Calloway, Colin G. *The Western Abenakis of Vermont, 1600–1800: War, Migration, and the Survival of an Indian People.* Norman, Okla.: University of Oklahoma Press, 1990.

Haviland, William A., and Marjory W. Power. *The Original Vermonters: Native Inhabitants, Past and Present.* Burlington, Vt.: University of Vermont, 1981.

Other Ethnic Groups

No special services or collections exist in Vermont for the large number of French-Canadians who migrated across the border as early as the late eighteenth century (see Periodicals; New Hampshire—American-Canadian Genealogical Society; and Massachusetts—New England Historic Genealogical Society collections).

Migration in the nineteenth century through the turn of this century included Irish, Russians, Italians, Poles, Greeks, Spanish, as well as numerous other groups, mostly employed in the quarries, iron industry, and manufacturing towns. No special collections of materials exist for research; however, the following is an excellent example of what can be found throughout Vermont's research materials:

Beavin, Daniel, et al. *Barre, Vermont: An Annotated Bibliography.* Barre, Vt.: Aldrich Public Library, 1979. An itemized list of over 500 documents and groups of materials focusing on the local history of a town heavily influenced by immigration.

County (Probate) Resources

Between 1772 and 1777, four counties existed in what is now Vermont—Albany, Charlotte, Gloucester, and Cumberland. All were politically New York counties even though they encompassed a sizeable number of New Hampshire granted towns. Some court records remain from these and have been published, while others are yet to be located. In 1777 two Vermont counties were erected—Bennington for the west part of the state and Cumberland for the east. However, the name Cumberland was abandoned in 1781 when four new counties were created—three replacing Cumberland, namely Windham, Windsor, and Orange; Bennington County was subdivided to form Rutland County.

Even though the political division of county has little meaning in Vermont, there are some county land records (see chart), primarily for unorganized towns, and county court records located at the appropriate county office. In addition, county designation is necessary for census research. For nine of Vermont's counties, the probate district follows the county's political boundaries. For six counties—Addison, Bennington, Orange, Rutland, Windham and Windsor—there are, or have been, two probate districts within the county's boundaries. The following listing delineates the county address, parent county and date of formation; what land and other records in addition to those recorded in towns are available that were recorded by entire county; the name and address of the probate district; and the dates probate district records are extant.

Map	County Address Parent County/ies	Land Records	Probate Address	Probate Records
D3	Addison Courthouse Middlebury 05753 1785 from Rutland	1774–1926 (county only)	Addison (same)	See below
	Presently includes all the towns in Addison County. The town of Orwell became part of Addison District in 1847 from Fair Haven District. Between 1824 and 1962 the northern part of the county constituted the New Haven District (see below). Those records were filed separately but are now located at Addison County Courthouse as well as an index to them and to all remaining records from Addison after 1852. On 25 February 1852 a fire in the courthouse burned the probate records for Addison district (not New Haven). What remains for Addison Probate District records before 1852 are fragments. The fragments are available on microfilm in Montpelier, in chronological order, but are extremely difficult to use.			
	Addison (same)		New Haven (same)	1824–1962
	New Haven District was set off from Addison District in 1824 and then reabsorbed in 1962.			
H3	Bennington 207 South Street, Box 157 Bennington 05201 1777 from Albany and Washington counties, N.Y.	1782–1832 (county only)	Bennington (same)	1778–present
	Bennington Probate District includes towns in the south part of the county—see Town Resources.			
	Bennington (same)		Manchester Route 7 Box 446 Manchester 05254	1778–present
	Manchester Probate District includes towns in the north part of the county—see Town Resources.			
B6	Caledonia 27 Main Street, Box 404 St. Johnsbury 05819 1796 from Orange	Land Records 1797–1896 (county only)	Caledonia (same)	1796–present
B3	Chittenden 175 Main Street P.O. Box 187 Burlington 05402 1791 from Addison		Chittenden P.O. Box 511 Burlington 05402	1795–present
	Cumberland *Originally a New York county, it went out of existence as a New York entity in 1777 when Vermont became independent. Land that had been in Cumberland and Gloucester counties, N.Y., then fell under Cumberland County, Vermont, jurisdiction. Cumberland County, Vermont, was abolished in 1781 when Windham, Windsor, and Orange counties were formed.*			
A7	Essex Guildhall 05905 1796 from Orange	Land Records 1793–1971 (county only)	Essex Main Street Island Pond 05846	1791–present
	Probate Office does not have early volumes. They are kept at county courthouse in Guildhall.			
A3	Franklin P.O. Box 808, Church Street St. Albans 05478 1796 from Chittenden	Land Records 1797–1883 (county only)	Franklin (same)	1796–present
A2	Grand Isle P.O. Box 7, North Hero 05474 1801–02 from Chittenden/Franklin		Grand Isle (same)	1796–present
	Jefferson *Formed in 1810; renamed Washington, 1814.*			
B4	Lamoille P.O. Box 303, Main Street Hyde Park 05655 1835 from Washington/ Orleans/Franklin	none	Lamoille (same)	1837–present

Map	County Address Parent County/ies	Land Records	Probate Address	Probate Records
D5	Orange County Courthouse, P.O. Box 95 Chelsea 05038 1781 from Cumberland and Gloucester counties, N.Y.; later Cumberland County VT	Land Records 1771–1952 Tax 1789–1847 Misc. 1770–81 (county only)	Randolph (same)	1792–present
	Randolph Probate District covers towns in western part of Orange County—see Town Resources.			
	Orange		Bradford P.O. Box 327 Fairlee 05045	1781–present
	Probate district covers towns in eastern part of Orange County—see Town Resources.			
A5	Orleans P.O. Box 787 Newport 05855 1796 from Orange/Chittenden	Land Records 1799–1849 (county only)	Orleans (same)	1796–present
G3	Rutland 83 Center Street P.O. Box 339 Rutland 05701 1781 from Bennington	Land Records 1763–1822 (county only)	Rutland (same)	1784–present
	Rutland Probate District covers towns in eastern part of Rutland County—see Town Resources.			
	Rutland (same)		Fair Haven Fair Haven 05743	1797–present
	Fair Haven Probate District covers towns in western part of Rutland County—see Town Resources.			
C4	Washington Courthouse Box 426 Montpelier 05602 1811 (as Jefferson) from Orange/Chittenden/ Addison/Caledonia	None	Washington P.O. Box 15 Montpelier 05602	1811–present
J4	Windham P.O. Box 207 Newfane 05345 1781 from Cumberland County, Vt.	Cumberland County Deeds 1766–74; 1772–77	Marlboro West River Rd. P.O. Box 523 Brattleboro 05301	1781–present
	Marlboro Probate District covers the towns in southern part of Windham County—see Town Resources.			
	Windham		Westminster 39 Square, P.O. Box 47 Bellows Falls 05101	1781–present
	Westminster Probate District covers the towns in northern part of Windham County—see Town Resources.			
F4	Windsor 12 The Green Woodstock 05091 1781–82 from Cumberland County, Vt.	Land Records 1784–94 (see also Windham County)	Windsor 2 Main Street, Box 4787 North Springfield 05150	1787–present
	Windsor Probate District covers towns in southern part of Windsor County—see Town Resources. First book of guardianships is missing, as are some pages in the recorded probates. Probate files for 1781–1850 were burned.			
	Windsor		Hartford Woodstock Green Woodstock 05091	1783–present
	Hartford Probate District covers towns in northern part of Windsor County—see Town Resources.			

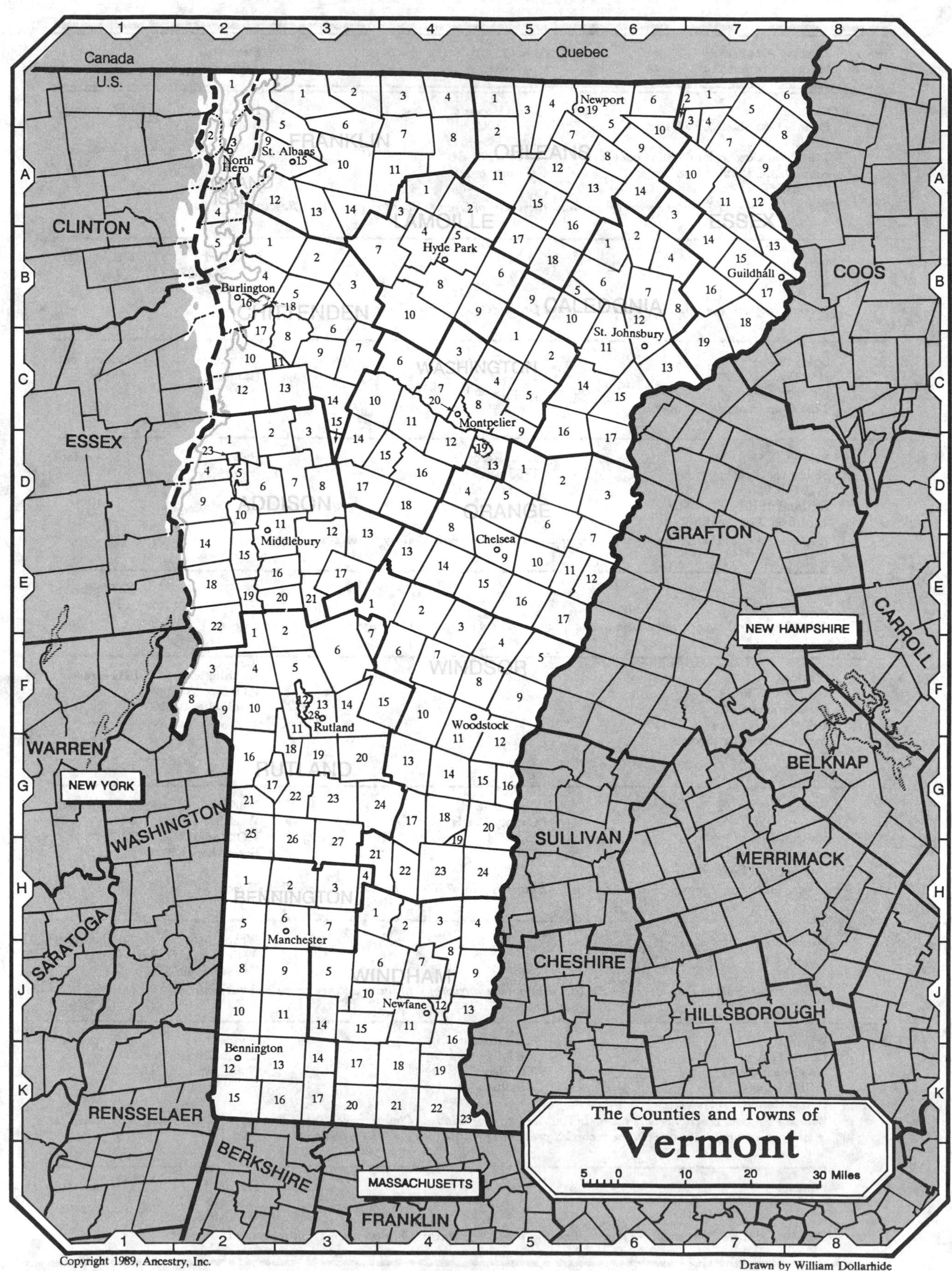

Drawn by William Dollarhide

Town Resources

Town records are extremely important in Vermont research. Each town clerk's office holds the original deed, vital, tax, and town meeting records. Included in town or proprietor's meeting records are such valuable sources as lists of freemen (new voters in town), annual election of officers, school records, hog or cattle marks, warnings out to those for whom the town will not assume legal responsibility, militia, and accounts of various town officials. Many of Vermont's town meeting records have been microfilmed and can be located at either the Public Records Division (see Land Records) or through the FHL. Town clerks rarely have time to do more than a cursory search of the deed or vital records indexes, however each office is open to the public for research purposes.

On the chart below, the town clerk's address (1990 Secretary of State listing) is given in the first column. The date that it was granted and the colony that first claimed it are given in the next column. The source here is Swift's *Vermont Place Names* (see Local History). Town-specific competing claims as illustrated by Swift are listed underneath. In some cases competing claims covered more than what is now one town; those are not listed here. For more specific information, see the maps and outlines in Swift. "Other Names" indicates the names used in early town records or the town it was part of before creation. Not all "other names" are given here, only those that are noted specifically by Swift or by the listing at the Public Records Division (see Land Records). The present county, with the Vermont parent county underneath, is listed in the next column. For county formation before 1781, see County (Probate) Resources. Since town formation often pre-dates Vermont county formation, the county designation may be helpful in identifying earlier land descriptions and locating towns in census records. The number in parentheses following the present county corresponds to that town's number in that county on the state map.

The source for parent county outlines is Steven Farrow's University of Vermont Master's thesis, "Vermont Place-Name Changes: Counties, Towns, Gores and the Evolving Map of the State," available at the Vermont State Archives and UVM Bailey-Howe Library (See Archives, Libraries, and Societies). Parent counties will be particularly helpful for census search in Washington and Lamoille County towns since those counties were formed after the 1800 census. Probate district and court district are listed in the last two columns. Use the town address for correspondence with the clerk regarding vital records and land records; use the probate and court addresses in the County (Probate) Resources for those records. Only a few towns have lost records.

Town Address	Date Formed Claims/Other Names	County (Map) Parent County	Probate District Court District
Addison RD 1 Vergennes 05491	1761 N.H.	Addison (9) Rutland	Addison Addison
Albany P.O. Box 284, Albany 05820	1782 Vt. Luterloh	Orleans (15) Chittenden	Orleans Orleans
Alburg P.O. Box 346, Alburg 05440	1781 Vt. Allenburg	Grand Isle (1) Franklin	Grand Isle Grand Isle
Andover Rt. 1, Chester 05143	1761 N.H.	Windsor (22)	Windsor Windsor
Arlington P.O. Box 304 Arlington 05250	1761 N.H.	Bennington (8)	Manchester Bennington
Athens RD 3, Box 151, Chester 05143	1780 Vt.	Windham (8)	Westminster Windham
Averill (unorganized)	1762 N.H.	Essex (5) Orange	Essex Essex
Avery's Gore	1791–96 Vt.	Essex (4) Orange	Essex
Bakersfield P.O. Box 203, Bakersfield 05441	1791 Vt. Knoulton's Gore	Franklin (11) Chittenden	Franklin Franklin

Town Address	Date Formed Claims/Other Names	County (Map) Parent County	Probate District Court District
Baltimore RR 4, Box 365 Chester 05143	1793 Vt. part of Cavendish	Windsor (19)	Windsor Windsor
Barnard P.O. Box 274, Barnard 05031	1761 N.H.	Windsor (7)	Hartford Windsor
Barnet P.O. Box 15, Barnet 05821	1763 N.H.	Caledonia (15) Orange	Caledonia Caledonia
Barre City 12 N. Main Street Box 418, Barre 05641	1894 Vt. Barre Town	Washington (19) Orange	Washington Washington
Barre Town Municipal Building, P.O. Box 124 Websterville 05678	1781 Vt. Wildersburgh	Washington (13) Orange	Washington Washington
Barton P.O. Box R Barton 05822	1789 Vt. Providence	Orleans (13) Orange	Orleans Orleans
Belvidere RR 1, Box 1062 Belvidere Center 05442	1791 Vt.	Lamoille (1) Franklin	Lamoille Lamoille
Bennington 205 South Street Bennington 05201	1749 N.H. N.Y. 1768/N.Y. 1762 Hoosick/Mapleton	Bennington (12)	Bennington Bennington
Benson P.O. Box 163, Benson 05731	1780 Vt.	Rutland (3) Bennington	Fair Haven Rutland
Berkshire RFD 1, Box 2560 Enosburg Falls 05450	1781 Vt.	Franklin (3) Chittenden	Franklin Franklin
Berlin RD 4, Box 2375 Montpelier 05602	1763 N.H.	Washington (12) Orange	Washington Washington
Bethel RD 2, Box 85 Bethel 05032	1779 Vt.	Windsor (2)	Hartford Windsor
Bloomfield RFD 1, Box 302 Guildhall 05905	1762 N.H. Minehead	Essex (9) Orange	Essex Essex
Bolton RD 1, Box 445 Waterbury 05676	1763 N.H.	Chittenden (7) Addison	Chittenden Chittenden
Bradford P.O. Box 339 Bradford 05033	1770 N.Y. Mooretown	Orange (7)	Bradford Orange
Braintree RD 1, Box 316A Randolph 05060	1781 Vt.	Orange (13) Rutland	Randolph Orange
Brandon 44 Center Street Brandon 05733	1761 N.H. Neshobe	Rutland (2) Bennington	Rutland Rutland

Town Address	Date Formed Claims/Other Names	County (Map) Parent County	Probate District Court District
Brattleboro 230 Main Street Brattleboro 05301	1753 N.H. N.Y. 1766	Windham (19)	Marlboro Windham
Bridgewater Box 14 Bridgewater 05034	1761 N.H.	Windsor (10)	Hartford Windsor
Bridport P.O. Box 27, Bridport 05734	1761 N.H.	Addison (14) Rutland	Addison Addison
Brighton P.O. Box 377, Main Street Island Pond 05846	1781 Vt. Random	Essex (10) Orange	Essex Essex
Bristol P.O. Box 247 Bristol 05443	1762 N.H. Pocock	Addison (7) Rutland	Addison Addison
Brookfield P.O. Box 463 Brookfield 05036	1781 Vt.	Orange (8) Rutland	Randolph Orange
Brookline RR 1, Box 615 Brookline 05345	1794 Vt.	Windham (12)	Westminster Windham
Brownington RFD 2, Orleans 05860	1790 Vt.	Orleans (8) Orange	Orleans Orleans
Brunswick RFD 1, Box 540 Guildhall 05905	1761 N.H.	Essex (12) Orange	Essex Essex
Buel's Gore	1780 Vt. Huntington Gore	Chittenden (15) Addison	Chittenden Chittenden
Burke RR 2, Box 24, West Burke 05871	1782 Vt.	Caledonia (4) Orange	Caledonia Caledonia
Burlington Room #20 City Hall Burlington 05401	1763 N.H. incorporated 1864	Chittenden (16) Orange	Chittenden Chittenden
Cabot P.O. Box 36, Cabot 05647	1780 Vt.	Washington (2) Caledonia/Orange	Washington Washington
Calais RR 1, P.O. Box 35, Calais 05648	1781 Vt. N.Y. 1772 Truro	Washington (4) Caledonia	Washington Washington
Cambridge P.O. Box 127, Jeffersonville 05464	1781 Vt.	Lamoille (7) Franklin	Lamoille Lamoille
Canaan P.O. Box 159 Canaan 05903	1782 Vt. Thirming	Essex (6) Orange	Essex Essex
Castleton P.O. Box 115 Castleton 05735	1761 N.H.	Rutland (10) Bennington	Fair Haven Rutland
Cavendish P.O. Box 126, Cavendish 05142	1761 N.H. N.Y. 1772	Windsor (18)	Windsor Windsor

Town Address	Date Formed Claims/Other Names	County (Map) Parent County	Probate District Court District
Charleston HCR 61, Box 26 West Charleston 05872	1789 Vt. Navy	Orleans (9) Orange	Orleans Orleans
Charlotte RR 1, Box 1549 Charlotte 05445	1762 N.H. Charlotta	Chittenden (12) Addison	Chittenden Chittenden
Chelsea P.O. Box 266 Chelsea 05038	1781 Vt. Turnersburgh	Orange (9)	Randolph Orange
Chester P.O. Box 370 Chester Depot 05144	1754 N.H. N.Y. 1766 Flamstead	Windsor (23)	Windsor Windsor
Chittenden Holden Road, Chittenden 05737	1780 Vt. Philadelphia	Rutland (6) Bennington	Rutland Rutland
Clarendon P.O. Box 30 North Clarendon 05759	1761 N.H.	Rutland (19) Bennington	Rutland Rutland
Colchester Blakely Road, P.O. Box 55 Colchester 05446	1763 N.H.	Chittenden (4) Addison	Chittenden Chittenden
Concord Main Street, P.O. Box 316 Concord 05824	1781 Vt.	Essex (19) Orange	Essex Essex
Cornith P.O. Box 161 Corinth 05039	1764 N.H. N.Y. 1772	Orange (6)	Bradford Orange
Cornwall RD 2, Box 795 Middlebury 05753	1761 N.H.	Addison (15) Rutland	Addison Addison
Coventry P.O. Box 158, Coventry 05825	1780 Vt.	Orleans (7) Chittenden	Orleans Orleans
Craftsbury P.O. Box 55, Craftsbury 05826	1781 Vt. Minden	Orleans (17) Chittenden	Orleans Orleans
Danby P.O. Box 231, School Street Danby 05739	1761 N.H.	Rutland (26) Bennington	Rutland Rutland
Danville P.O. Box 183, Danville 05828	1786 Vt. N.Y. 1770	Caledonia (11) Orange	Caledonia Caledonia
Derby P.O. Box 25, Main Street, Derby 05829	1779 Vt.	Orleans (5) Orange	Orleans Orleans
Dorset Mad Tom Road East Dorset 05253	1761 N.H.	Bennington (2)	Manchester Bennington
Dover P.O. Box 527 West Dover 05356	1810 Vt. from Wardsboro	Windham (15)	Marlboro Windham

Town Address	Date Formed Claims/Other Names	County (Map) Parent County	Probate District Court District
Dummerston RD 2, Box 995, Putney 05346	1753 N.H.	Windham (16)	Marlboro Windham
Duxbury RD 2, Box 1260 Waterbury 05676	1763 N.H.	Washington (10) Chittenden	Washington Washington
East Haven P.O. Box 10 East Haven 05837	1790 Vt.	Essex (14) Orange	Essex Essex
East Montpelier P.O. Box 157 East Montpelier 05651	1848 Vt. from Montpelier	Washington (8) Caledonia	Washington Washington
Eden P.O. Box 11, Eden Mills 05653	1781 Vt.	Lamoille (2) Orleans	Lamoille Lamoille
Elmore P.O. Box 123,Lake Elmore 05657	1781 Vt.	Lamoille (9) Washington	Lamoille Lamoille
Enosburg P.O. Box 465 Enosburg Falls 05450	1780 Vt.	Franklin (7) Chittenden	Franklin Franklin
Essex 2 Lincoln Street Essex Junction 05452	1763 N.H.	Chittenden (5) Addison	Chittenden Chittenden
Fair Haven 3 N. Park Place Fair Haven 05743	1779 Vt. N.Y. 1771 Skenesborough	Rutland (9) Bennington	Fair Haven Rutland
Fairfax P.O. Box 27, Hunt Street Fairfax 05454	1763 N.H.	Franklin (13) Chittenden	Franklin Franklin
Fairfield P.O. Box 203 Fairfield 05455	1763 N.H. N.Y. 1773 Meath	Franklin (10) Chittenden	Franklin Franklin
Fairlee P.O. Box 95, Main Street Fairlee 05045	1761 N.H.	Orange (12)	Bradford Orange
Fayston RD 1, Box 1594 Moretown 05660	1782 Vt.	Washington (14) Chittenden	Washington Washington
Ferdinand (unorganized)	1761 N.H.	Essex (11) Orange	Essex Essex
Ferrisburgh Main Street, P.O. Box 6 Ferrisburgh 05456	1762 N.H.	Addison (1) Rutland	Addison Addison
Fletcher RR 1, Box 1550 Cambridge 05444	1781 Vt.	Franklin (14) Chittenden	Franklin Franklin
Franklin P.O. Box 80 Franklin 05457	1789 Vt. Huntsburgh	Franklin (2) Chittenden	Franklin Franklin

Town Address	Date Formed Claims/Other Names	County (Map) Parent County	Probate District Court District
Georgia RD 2, Box 325 St. Albans 05478	1763 N.H.	Franklin (12) Chittenden	Franklin Franklin
Glastenbury (unorganized)	1761 N.H. Glossenbury	Bennington (11)	Bennington Bennington
Glover P.O. Box 226 Glover 05839	1783 Vt.	Orleans (16) Orange	Orleans Orleans
Goshen RR 3, Box 3384, Brandon 05733	1792 Vt.	Addison (21) Rutland	Addison Addison
Grafton P.O. Box 180 Grafton 05146	1754 N.H. Tomlinson	Windham (3)	Westminster Windham
Granby P.O. Box 126, Granby 05840	1761 N.H.	Essex (15) Orange	Essex Essex
Grand Isle 9 Hyde Road Grand Isle 05458	1769 N.Y. Vt. 1779 Two Heros/Middle Hero	Grand Isle (4) Chittenden	Grand Isle Grand Isle
Granville P.O. Box 66, Route 100 Granville 05747	1781 Vt. Kingston	Addison (13) Rutland	Addison Addison
Greensboro P.O. Box 115 Greensboro 05841	1781 Vt.	Orleans (18) Orange	Orleans Orleans
Groton RFD 2, Box 3, Groton 05046	1789 Vt. N.Y. 1772 Penryn	Caledonia (16) Orange	Caledonia Caledonia
Guildhall P.O. Box 27 Guildhall 05905	1761 N.H.	Essex (17) Orange	Essex Essex
Guilford RR 3, Box 255 Brattleboro 05301	1754 N.H.	Windham (22)	Marlboro Windham
Hailfax P.O. Box 45, West Halifax 05358	1750 N.H.	Windham (21)	Marlboro Windham
Hancock P.O. Box 132, Hancock 05748	1781 Vt.	Addison (17) Rutland	Addison Addison
Hardwick P.O. Box 523 Hardwick 05843	1781 Vt.	Caledonia (9) Orange	Caledonia Caledonia
Hartford 15 Bridge Street White River Junction 05001	1761 N.H.	Windsor (9)	Hartford Windsor
Hartland P.O. Box 349 Hartland 05048	1761 N.H. N.Y. 1766 Hereford	Windsor (12)	Hartford Windsor

Town Address	Date Formed Claims/Other Names	County (Map) Parent County	Probate District Court District
Highgate Box 67 Highgate Center 05459	1762 N.H.	Franklin (1) Chittenden	Franklin Franklin
Hinesburg P.O. Box 133 Hinesburg 05461	1762 N.H.	Chittenden (13) Addison	Chittenden Chittenden
Holland RFD 1, Box 37 Holland, Derby Line 05830	1779 Vt.	Orleans (6) Orange	Orleans Orleans
Hubbardton RR 1, Box 2828 Fair Haven 05743	1764 N.H.	Rutland (4) Bennington	Fair Haven Rutland
Huntington RD 1, Box 771 Huntington 05462	1763 N.H. New Huntington	Chittenden (14) Addison	Chittenden Chittenden
Hyde Park P.O. Box 98 Hyde Park 05655	1781 Vt.	Lamoille (5) Orleans	Lamoille Lamoille
Ira RFD 1 West Rutland 05777	1780 Vt.	Rutland (18) Bennington	Rutland Rutland
Irasburg P.O. Box 51 Irasburg 05845	1781 Vt.	Orleans (12) Chittenden	Orleans Orleans
Isle La Motte P.O. Box 135 Isle La Motte 05463	1779 Vt. N.Y. 1786	Grand Isle (2) Franklin	Grand Isle Grand Isle
Jamaica P.O. Box 173 Jamaica 05343	1780 Vt.	Windham (6)	Westminster Windham
Jay RFD 2, Box 136, Jay 05859	1792 Vt.	Orleans (1) Chittenden	Orleans Orleans
Jericho P.O. Box 67 Jericho 05465	1763 N.H.	Chittenden (6) Addison	Chittenden Chittenden
Johnson P.O. Box 383 Johnson 05656	1792 Vt.	Lamoille (4) Franklin	Lamoille Lamoille
Kirby RR 2 Lyndonville 05851	1807 Vt.	Caledonia (8) Orange	Caledonia Caledonia
Landgrove RR 1, Landgrove 05148	1780 Vt.	Bennington (4)	Manchester Bennington
Leicester RR 2, Box 2117-1, Brandon 05733	1761 N.H.	Addison (20) Rutland	Addison Addison
Lemington RR 1, Box 195, Canaan 05903	1762 N.H. Limington	Essex (8) Orange	Essex Essex

Town Address	Date Formed Claims/Other Names	County (Map) Parent County	Probate District Court District
Lewis (unorganized)	1762 N.H.	Essex (7) Orange	Essex Essex
Lincoln RD 1, Bristol 05443	1780 Vt.	Addison (8) Rutland	Addison Addison
Londonderry P.O. Box 118 South Londonderry 05155	1780 Vt. N.Y. 1770 Kent	Windham (1)	Westminster Windham
Lowell P.O. Box 7, Lowell 05847	1791 Vt. Kellyvale	Orleans (11) Chittenden	Orleans Orleans
Ludlow Depot Street, Ludlow 05149	1761 N.H.	Windsor (17)	Windsor Windsor
Lunenberg P.O. Box 54, Lunenberg 05906	1763 N.H.	Essex (18) Orange	Essex Essex
Lyndon 24 Main, P.O. Box 167 Lyndonville 05851	1780 Vt.	Caledonia (7) Orange	Caledonia Caledonia
Maidstone RR 1, Box 101 Guildhall 05905	1761 N.H.	Essex (13) Orange	Essex Essex
Manchester P.O. Box 909 Manchester Center 05255	1761 N.H. N.Y. 1765	Bennington (6)	Manchester Bennington
Marlboro P.O. Box E, Marlboro 05344	1751 N.H.	Windham (18)	Marlboro Windham
Marshfield P.O. Box 98,Marshfield 05658	1782/1790 Vt.	Washington (5) Caledonia	Washington Washington
Mendon RR 2, Box 8780 Rutland 05701	1781 Vt. Medway	Rutland (14) Bennington	Rutland Rutland
Middlebury Municipal Building Middlebury 05753	1761 N.H.	Addison (11) Rutland	Addison Addison
Middlesex RR 3, Box 4600 Montpelier 05602	1763 N.H.	Washington (7) Chittenden	Washington Washington
Middletown Springs P.O. Box 1147, Middletown Springs 05757	1784 Vt.	Rutland (17) Bennington	Rutland Rutland
Milton P.O. Box 18, Milton 05468	1763 N.H.	Chittenden (1) Addison	Chittenden Chittenden
Monkton RR 1,Box 2015 North Ferrisburg 05473	1762 N.H.	Addison (2) Rutland	Addison Addison
Montgomery P.O. Box 356 Montgomery Center 05471	1789 Vt.	Franklin (8) Chittenden	Franklin Franklin

Town Address	Date Formed Claims/Other Names	County (Map) Parent County	Probate District Court District
Montpelier City Hall, Main Street Montpelier 05602	1781 Vt. incorporated 1895	Washington (20) Caledonia	Washington Washington
Moretown P.O. Box 533, Moretown 05660	1763 N.H.	Washington (11) Chittenden	Washington Washington
Morgan P.O. Box 45, Morgan 05853	1780 Vt. Caldersburg	Orleans (10) Orange	Orleans Orleans
Morristown P.O. Box 748 Morrisville 05661	1781 Vt.	Lamoille (8) Orleans	Lamoille Lamoille
Mount Holly P.O. Box 10 Mount Holly 05758	1792 Vt.	Rutland (24) Bennington	Rutland Rutland
Mount Tabor P.O. Box 245 Danby 05739	1761 N.H. Harwich	Rutland (27) Bennington	Rutland Rutland
New Haven RD 1, Box 4, New Haven 05472	1761 N.H.	Addison (6) Rutland	Addison Addison
Newark RFD 1, Box 50A West Burke 05871	1781 Vt.	Caledonia (3) Essex	Caledonia Caledonia
Newbury P.O. Box 126, Newbury 05051	1763 N.H. N.Y. 1772	Orange (3)	Bradford Orange
Newfane P.O. Box 36, Newfane 05345	1753 N.H. N.Y. 1772	Windham (11)	Marlboro Windham
Newport City 74 Main, P.O. Box 405 Newport 05855	1917 Vt. Newport Town	Orleans (19) Chittenden	Orleans Orleans
Newport Town P.O. Box 85 Newport Center 05857	1802 Vt. Duncansborough	Orleans (4) Chittenden	Orleans Orleans
North Hero P.O. Box 38 North Hero 05474	1779 Vt. Two Heros	Grand Isle (3) Franklin	Grand Isle Grand Isle
Northfield 26 S. Main Northfield 05663	1781 Vt. N.Y. 1770 Leyden	Washington (16) Orange	Washington Washington
Norton Norton 05907	1779 Vt.	Essex (1) Orange	Essex Essex
Norwich P.O. Box 376, Norwich 05055	1761 N.H.	Windsor (5)	Hartford Windsor
Orange P.O. Box 233 East Barre 05649	1781 Vt.	Orange (1)	Randolph Orange
Orwell P.O. Box 32, Orwell 05760	1763 N.H.	Addison (22) Rutland	Addison Addison

Town Address	Date Formed Claims/Other Names	County (Map) Parent County	Probate District Court District
Panton RD 3, Box 32, Vergennes 05491	1761 N.H.	Addison (4) Rutland	Addison Addison
Pawlet P.O. Box 128, Pawlet 05761	1761 N.H.	Rutland (25) Bennington	Fair Haven Rutland
Peacham P.O. Box 80 Peacham 05862	1763 N.H.	Caledonia (14) Orange	Caledonia Caledonia
Peru P.O. Box 127, Peru 05152	1761 N.H. Brumley	Bennington (3)	Manchester Bennington
Pittsfield P.O. Box 556 Pittsfield 05762	1781 Vt.	Rutland (7) Bennington	Rutland Rutland
Pittsford Plains Road, Pittsford 05763	1761 N.H.	Rutland (5) Bennington	Rutland Rutland
Plainfield RR 2, Box 100 Plainfield 05667	1788 Vt. N.Y. 1772 Whitelaw, Savage, and Coit Grant	Washington (9) Caledonia	Washington Washington
Plymouth P.O. Box 39 Plymouth 05056	1761 N.H. N.Y. 1772 Saltash	Windsor (13)	Windsor Windsor
Pomfret P.O. Box 286, North Pomfret 05053	1761 N.H.	Windsor (8)	Hartford Windsor
Poultney 86-88 Main Street Poultney 05764	1761 N.H.	Rutland (16) Bennington	Fair Haven Rutland
Pownal RD 1, Box 41 Pownal 05261	1760 N.H.	Bennington (15)	Bennington Bennington
Proctor 45 Main Street Proctor 05765	1886 Vt. Rutland/Pittsford	Rutland (12) Bennington	Rutland Rutland
Putney P.O. Box 233, Putney 05346	1753 N.H. N.Y. 1776	Windham (13)	Westminster Windham
Randolph Drawer B Randolph 05060	1781 Vt. N.Y. 1770	Orange (14)	Randolph Orange
Reading P.O. Box 72, Reading 05062	1761 N.H. N.Y. 1772	Windsor (14)	Windsor Windsor
Readsboro P.O. Box 246, Readsboro 05350	1764 N.H. N.Y. 1770	Bennington (17)	Bennington Bennington
Richford P.O. Box 236, Richford 05476	1780 Vt.	Franklin (4) Chittenden	Franklin Franklin
Richmond P.O. Box 285, Richmond 05477	1794 Vt.	Chittenden (9) Addison	Chittenden Chittenden
Ripton P.O. Box 10, Ripton 05766	1781 Vt. Riptown	Addison (12) Rutland	Addison Addison

Town Address	Date Formed Claims/Other Names	County (Map) Parent County	Probate District Court District
Rochester P.O. Box 238 Rochester 05767	1781 Vt.	Windsor (1)	Hartford Windsor
Rockingham P.O. Box 339 Bellows Falls 05101	1752 N.H.	Windham (4)	Westminster Windham
Roxbury P.O. Box 53, Roxbury 05669	1781 Vt.	Washington (18) Orange	Washington Washington
Royalton P.O. Box 680 South Royalton 05068	1769 N.Y.	Windsor (3)	Hartford Windsor
Rupert Mill Road, P.O. Box 140 West Rupert 05776	1761 N.H.	Bennington (1)	Manchester Bennington
Rutland City City Hall, P.O. Box 969 Rutland 05701	1892 Vt. Rutland Town	Rutland (28) Bennington	Rutland Rutland
Rutland Town P.O. Box 225 Center Rutland 05736	1761 N.H.	Rutland (13) Bennington	Rutland Rutland
Ryegate P.O. Box 32, Ryegate 05042	1763 N.H. N.Y. 1775	Caledonia (17) Orange	Caledonia Caledonia
St. Albans City P.O. Box 867 St. Albans 05478	1902 Vt. St. Albans Town	Franklin (15) Chittenden	Franklin Franklin
St. Albans Town P.O. Box 37 St. Albans Bay 05481	1763 N.H.	Franklin (9) Chittenden	Franklin Franklin
St. George RD 2, Box 455 Williston 05495	1763 N.H.	Chittenden (11) Addison	Chittenden Chittenden
St. Johnsbury 34 Main Street St. Johnsbury 05819	1786 Vt.	Caledonia (12) Orange	Caledonia Caledonia
Salisbury P.O. Box 66, Salisbury 05769	1761 N.H.	Addison (16) Rutland	Addison Addison
Sandgate RR 1, Sandgate Road, Arlington 05250	1761 N.H.	Bennington (5)	Manchester Bennington
Searsburg Route 9, Searsburg 05363	1781 Vt.	Bennington (14)	Bennington Bennington
Shaftsbury P.O. Box 409 Shaftsbury 056262	1761 N.H.	Bennington (10)	Bennington Bennington
Sharon P.O. Box 8, Sharon 05065	1761 N.H.	Windsor (4)	Hartford Windsor
Sheffield P.O. Box 165, Sheffield 05866	1793 Vt.	Caledonia (1) Orange	Caledonia Caledonia

Town Address	Date Formed Claims/Other Names	County (Map) Parent County	Probate District Court District
Shelburne P.O. Box 88, Shelburne 05482	1763 N.H.	Chittenden (10) Addison	Chittenden Chittenden
Sheldon P.O. Box 66 Sheldon 05483	1763 N.H. Hungerford	Franklin (6) Chittenden	Franklin Franklin
Sherburne P.O. Box 129 Killington 05751	1761 N.H. Killington	Rutland (15) Bennington	Rutland Rutland
Shoreham P.O. Box 11, Shoreham 05770	1761 N.H.	Addison (18) Rutland	Addison Addison
Shrewsbury RR 1, Box 658 Cuttingsville 05738	1761 N.H.	Rutland (20) Bennington	Rutland Rutland
Somerset (unorganized)	1761 N.H.	Windham (14)	Marlboro Windham
South Burlington 575 Dorset Street South Burlington 05403	1864 Vt. incorporated from Burlington 1971	Chittenden (17) Addison	Chittenden Chittenden
South Hero P.O. Box 175, South Hero 05486	1779 Vt. N.Y. 1769	Grand Isle (5) Chittenden	Grand Isle Grand Isle
Springfield 96 Main Street Springfield 05156	1761 N.H. N.Y. 1772	Windsor (24)	Windsor Windsor
Stamford RR 1, Box 718 Stamford 05352	1753/1761 N.H. 1764 N.H. as New Stamford	Bennington (16)	Bennington Bennington
Stannard P.O. Box 94, Greensboro Bend 05842	1798/1867 Vt. Goshen Gore No.1	Caledonia (5) Orange	Caledonia Caledonia
Starksboro P.O. Box 91, Starksboro 05487	1780 Vt.	Addison (3) Rutland	Addison Addison
Stockbridge P.O. Box 39 Stockbridge 05772	1761 N.H.	Windsor (6)	Hartford Windsor
Stowe P.O. Box 248, Stowe 05672	1763 N.H. annexed Mansfield	Lamoille (10) Washington	Lamoille Lamoille
Strafford P.O. Box 27, Strafford 05072	1761 N.H.	Orange (16)	Bradford Orange
Stratton P.O. Box 166 West Wardsboro 05360	1761 N.H. N.Y. 1775	Windham (5)	Marlboro Windham
Sudbury RD 1, Box 1238, Sudbury 05733	1763 N.H.	Rutland (1) Bennington	Fair Haven Rutland
Sunderland P.O. Box 176 East Arlington 05252	1761 N.H.	Bennington (9)	Manchester Bennington

Town Address	Date Formed Claims/Other Names	County (Map) Parent County	Probate District Court District
Sutton P.O. Box 106, Sutton 05867	1782 Vt. Billymead	Caledonia (2) Orange	Caledonia Caledonia
Swanton P.O. Box 711, Swanton 05488	1763 N.H.	Franklin (5) Chittenden	Franklin Franklin
Thetford P.O. Box 126 Thetford Center 05075	1761 N.H.	Orange (17)	Bradford Orange
Tinmouth RR 1, Box 551 Wallingford 05773	1761 N.H.	Rutland (22) Bennington	Rutland Rutland
Topsham West Topsham 05086	1763 N.H. N.Y. 1776	Orange (2)	Bradford Orange
Townshend P.O. Box 223, Townshend 05353	1753 N.H.	Windham (7)	Westminster Windham
Troy P.O. Box 80, North Troy 05869	1801 Vt.	Orleans (3) Chittenden	Orleans Orleans
Tunbridge P.O. Box 6, Tunbridge 05077	1761 N.H.	Orange (15)	Randolph Orange
Underhill P.O. Box 98 Underhill Center 05490	1763 N.H. N.Y. 1775	Chittenden (3) Addison	Chittenden Chittenden
Vergennes City Hall, P.O. Box 35, Vergennes 05491	1788 Vt.	Addison (23) Rutland	Addison Addison
Vernon P.O. Box 116 Vernon 05354	1672 Northfield Ma. Hinsdale, N.H. 1753	Windham (23)	Marlboro Windham
Vershire RR 1, Box 66-C Vershire 05079	1781 Vt.	Orange (10)	Bradford Orange
Victory HCR, Box 511 North Concord 05858	1781 Vt.	Essex (16) Orange	Essex Essex
Waitsfield RD, Box 390 Waitsfield 05673	1782 Vt.	Washington (15) Chittenden	Washington Washington
Walden RD 1, Box 57 West Danville 05873	1781 Vt.	Caledonia (10) Orange	Caledonia Caledonia
Wallingford P.O. Box 327 Wallingford 05773	1761 N.H.	Rutland (23) Bennington	Rutland Rutland
Waltham RD 2, Box 278, Vergennes 05491	1796 Vt.	Addison (5) Rutland	Addison Addison
Wardsboro P.O. Box 48, Wardsboro 05355	1780 Vt. 1764 N.H.	Windham (10)	Marlboro Windham

Town Address	Date Formed Claims/Other Names	County (Map) Parent County	Probate District Court District
Warner's Grant	1791 Vt.	Essex (2) Orange	Essex Orange
Warren P.O. Box 337, Warren 05674	1789 Vt.	Washington (17) Addison	Washington Washington
Warren's Gore	1789 Vt.	Essex (3) Orange	Essex Orange
Washington RD 1, Box 22 Washington 05675	1781 Vt. N.Y. 1770 Kingsland	Orange (5)	Randolph Orange
Waterbury 51 S. Main Waterbury 05676	1763 N.H.	Washington (6) Chittenden	Washington Washington
Waterford P.O. Box 56,Lower Waterford 05848	1780 Vt. Littleton	Caledonia (13) Orange	Caledonia Caledonia
Waterville P.O. Box 355 Waterville 05492	1824 Vt.	Lamoille (3) Franklin	Lamoille Lamoille
Weathersfield Drawer E, Ascutney 05030	1761 N.H. N.Y. 1772	Windsor (20)	Windsor Windsor
Wells P.O. Box 585, Wells 05774	1761 N.H.	Rutland (21) Bennington	Fair Haven Rutland
West Fairlee P.O. Box 615, West Fairlee 05083	1797 Vt.	Orange (11)	Bradford Orange
West Haven West Haven Center 05743	1792 Vt.	Rutland (8) Bennington	Fair Haven Rutland
West Rutland P.O. Box 115 West Rutland 05777	1886 Vt. Rutland	Rutland (11) Bennington	Rutland Rutland
West Windsor P.O. Box 6, Brownsville 05037	1848 Vt. from Windsor	Windsor (15)	Windsor Windsor
Westfield P.O. Box 77, Westfield 05874	1780 Vt.	Orleans (2) Chittenden	Orleans Orleans
Westford P.O. Box 79, Westford 05494	1763 N.H.	Chittenden (2) Addison	Chittenden Chittenden
Westminster P.O. Box 271, Westminster 05158	1752 N.H.	Windham (9)	Westminster Windham
Westmore RFD 2, Box 854, Orleans 05860	1781 Vt. Westford	Orleans (14) Orange	Orleans Orleans
Weston P.O. Box 98 Weston 05161	1799 Vt. from Andover	Windsor (21)	Windsor Windsor
Weybridge RD 1, Middlebury 05753	1761 N.H.	Addison (10) Rutland	Addison Addison

Town Address	Date Formed Claims/Other Names	County (Map) Parent County	Probate District Court District
Wheelock P.O. Box 428 Lyndonville 05851	1785 Vt. N.Y. 1774 Bamf	Caledonia (6) Orange	Caledonia Caledonia
Whiting RR 1, Box 24 Whiting 05778	1763 N.H.	Addison (19) Rutland	Addison Addison
Whitingham P.O. Box 36 Whitingham 05361	1770 N.Y.	Windham (20)	Marlboro Windham
Williamstown P.O. Box, 399, Williamstown 05679	1781 Vt.	Orange (4)	Randolph Orange
Williston P.O. Box 137 Williston 05495	1763 N.H.	Chittenden (8) Addison	Chittenden Chittenden
Wilmington P.O. Box 217, Main Street Wilmington 05363	1751 N.H. and again in 1763 N.H. as Draper	Windham (17)	Marlboro Windham
Windham RR 1, Box 109, West Townshend 05359	1795 Vt.	Windham (2)	Westminster Windham
Windsor 147 Main, P.O. Box 47, Windsor 05089	1761 N.H. N.Y. 1772	Windsor (16)	Windsor Windsor
Winhall Box 19A, Bondville 05340	1761 N.H.	Bennington (7)	Manchester Bennington
Winooski 27 W. Allen Street Winooski 05404	1921 Vt. Colchester	Chittenden (18) Addison	Chittenden Chittenden
Wolcott P.O. Box 100, Wolcott 05680	1781 Vt.	Lamoille (6) Orleans	Lamoille Lamoille
Woodbury P.O. Box 123, Woodbury 05681	1781 Vt.	Washington (1) Caledonia	Washington Washington
Woodford HCR 65, Box 600 Bennington 05201	1753 N.H. renewed 1762 N.H.	Bennington (13)	Bennington Bennington
Woodstock 31 The Green Woodstock 05091	1761 N.H. N.Y. 1772	Windsor (11)	Hartford Windsor
Worcester RD, Box 352 Worcester 05682	1763 N.H. Worster	Washington (3) Chittenden	Washington Washington

VIRGINIA

Johni Cerny and Gareth L. Mark, A.G.

Virginia was established as an economic venture that got off to a very shaky start. In 1584 Queen Elizabeth I of England gave Sir Walter Ralegh (commonly misspelled Raleigh) permission to establish colonies in the New World. Gallantly, Ralegh named the area for the Virgin Queen, but undersupplied his colonies, which disappeared between one supply ship's arrival and the next.

The second attempt began twenty years later. English entrepreneurs were looking for a financial opportunity that would return their investment on the fabulous scale of the six-year-old British East India Company. The endless lands of the new world appeared to contain such a golden promise.

In 1606 King James I chartered the Virginia Company of London (often called the London Company). In April 1607 the *Susan Constant*, the *Godspeed*, and the *Discovery*, commanded by Capt. Christopher Newport, made landfall at Point Comfort. Sealed orders appointing seven men to the Council were opened, and the Council elected Edward Maria Wingfield president. Under his direction, "gentlemen," craftsmen, and laborers founded the first permanent English settlement on James Isle. Long on expectations but short on experience, they were struck with disaster.

The struggle and hardships that decimated and discouraged the colonists are well known. So few of those who arrived on the first three ships survived that not many Americans living today can trace their ancestry to an original Jamestown settler. The Colony was nearly abandoned in 1610 and might not have survived but for one man—John Rolfe.

In 1612 John Rolfe began experiments in growing and processing tobacco. His export of tobacco to a London merchant in 1614 began a trade that made Virginia viable economically. Then he married Pocahontas, daughter of the great werowance, or sub-chief, Powhatan, which helped assure a few years of peaceful coexistence with the native tribes of Virginia.

The London Company was reorganized under the Great Charter of 1618, and by the end of 1619, several events occurred that had far-reaching impact. Free settlers were granted land, establishing property ownership. The House of Burgesses, America's first representative assembly, was organized, setting an example for representative democracy. A program encouraging emigration of "Maides to make Wives" began in England, ensuring that the population of Virginia would be self-sustaining. Unexpectedly, a Dutch trader from the West Indies arrived in August 1619 with a cargo of black colonists who were sold into indentured servitude (slavery did not yet exist in Virginia). This event helped foreshadow slavery and the Civil War.

On Friday, 22 March 1622, disaster struck. The natives, led by Powhatan's successor, Opechancanough, attacked the English settlements, massacred a quarter of the population, and nearly succeeded in driving the English out. However, disaster then struck the natives, for the English established policies that eventually led to the near-total extermination of the Indian people and forceful removal of the survivors to reservations.

In 1624 James I revoked the charter and made Virginia a royal colony, henceforth under the direction—not always peaceable—of crown-appointed governors. Between 1652 and 1660, while Oliver Cromwell was ruling in England, Virginia experimented with what amounted to self-government and was not pleased to relinquish that control again to a royal governor.

The colony had an urgent need of merchants, skilled artisans, woodsmen, and a large labor force to cultivate the tobacco crops. Luring laborers to insect-ridden and swampy regions was a challenge. The English law of primogeniture preserved the estates of the landed gentry by transmitting the titles and property intact from eldest son to eldest son. Many younger sons saw Virginia as a prime opportunity. The London Company lured these people to Virginia with land.

The Company agreed to give anyone who paid his way to Virginia fifty acres "for his owne personal adventure." Another fifty acres was offered for each person the adventurer transported "at his owne cost." When Virginia became a royal colony, the headright system continued. Over the next century, thousands of settlers came because of Virginia's headright system.

As the young colony expanded, it experienced growing pains. The difficulty of providing a labor force led to the formal establishment of slavery (1660), disagreements with crown-appointed governors led to Bacon's Rebellion (1676), and a precipitous decline in tobacco prices resulted in the Plant-Cutting Revolt (1682). The end of the century was marked by the removal of the colony's capital to Williamsburg in 1699.

Ironically, the eighteenth century saw both the establishment of the infamous Slave Code of 1705 and the headlong rush toward the American Revolution; each embodied different views of human rights. Even as the slaves' plight grew worse, George Mason penned the Virginia Declaration of Rights. Adopted by the revolutionary convention on 12 June 1776, the Declaration was a model for the United States Bill of Rights.

It is perhaps appropriate that the first President of the United States was a native son of the first permanent English colony in North America. George Washington epitomized the upper-class Virginians of his time: a tobacco farmer, an ardent lover of freedom, and a slaveholder.

The eighteenth century also saw explosive expansion. The Shenandoah Valley and the lands west of the Appalachian Mountains were opened, and settlers poured down the Great Wagon Road from Pennsylvania. In the second half of the century, the Cumberland Gap was discovered and settlers began filling what would become Kentucky and West Virginia. Both were initially part of Virginia; Kentucky became a separate state in 1792, and West Virginia in 1863.

Many of Virginia's records have been lost to fire, war, and time. Jamestown, the original capital, was destroyed three times, and some counties lost records during the Revolutionary War. However, the greatest destruction of Virginia's records occurred during the Civil War. Many courthouses were destroyed, but the most significant loss of records resulted from the burning of Richmond in 1865. Even with the loss of records, research in most Virginia counties remains richly rewarding.

Vital Records

Virginia was one of the first states outside New England to require its counties to record births and deaths. Registration on the county level began in 1853 and continued until 1896. Many counties abandoned registration during the Civil War, or at best recorded only a small percentage of births and deaths. Except in some independent cities, records were not kept between 1896 and 14 June 1912, when statewide registration of vital statistics began. Early records, 1853–96, have been microfilmed and are available at the Virginia State Library and the FHL.

Certified copies of records from 1 January 1853 are available for a fee from the Virginia Department of Health, Division of Vital Records, James Madison Building, P. O. Box 1000, Richmond, Virginia 23208-1000.

The first laws of Virginia were called the *Lawes Divine, Morall and Martiall,* and were enacted by Sir Thomas Dale in 1610. Dale's Code required colonial Virginia ministers to record all christenings, marriages, and burials in registers, in much the same way those events were recorded in England. Most of the registers compiled in response to the law have not survived. In 1619 ministers were required to present the register to the Secretary of the Colony, and in 1642 the parish clerks were required to submit a monthly list of vital records to the "commander of every monethly court." Few, if any, of the monthly lists were recorded.

The House of Burgesses strengthened the law regarding vital records in March 1660. Act XX, *An Act to record all Marriages, Births and Burials,* decreed, "That every parish shall well, truly and plainly record and sett downe in a booke provided for that purpose, all marriages, deaths and births that shall happen within the precincts of the parish, and in the month of March in every yeare, the person appointed by the parish so to do, shall make true certificate into the clerke of every county to the intent the same may there remaine on record for ever." If the county clerks recorded the certificates, they are unfortunately lost.

Marriage in early Virginia was by publication of banns. In 1631 the House of Burgesses directed that marriage licenses were to be granted by the Governor, although couples could have banns read instead and pay less for their marriage. Consent, either written or verbal, was required for anyone under twenty-one and for all servants. Marriages were not to be performed "at any unreasonable tymes but only betweene the howers of eight and twelve in the forenoone."

Marriage bonds were first required as part of the licensing procedure in 1661. The couple wishing a license gave bond to the county clerk that there was no lawful impediment to their marriage; the clerk then issued a license. Every September, the clerk forwarded to the Secretary of the Colony a list of licenses issued. These records were burned in the various fires at Jamestown, Williamsburg, and Richmond.

The existing marriage laws were superseded by an 1853 state law requiring county and independent city clerks to issue marriage licenses and keep marriage registers. Before a license was issued, the parties to be married had to offer the following information: full names, ages, places of birth and residence, proposed marriage date and place, marital status (widowed or single), parents' names, groom's occupation, and minister's name. After the marriage ceremony, the minister returned the information to the clerk who recorded it in a marriage register. Many counties have the original form on file at the courthouse.

The majority of pre-1853 Virginia marriage records have been published. The Virginia State Library (see Archives, Libraries, and Societies) and the FHL have the most complete collections of published Virginia marriage records; however, state and genealogical libraries nationwide also have excellent collections. For reference to these, see either John Vogt and T. William Kethley, Jr., *Marriage Records in the Virginia State Library: A Researcher's Guide,* 2d ed. (Athens, Ga.: Iberian Publishing Co., 1988), or *Virginia Marriage Records from the Virginia Magazine of History and Biography, The William and Mary Quarterly, and Tyler's Quarterly* (Baltimore, Md.: Genealogical Publishing Co., 1982). A detailed explanation of marriage records is found in Arlene Eakle and Johni Cerny, eds., *The Source: A Guidebook of American Genealogy* (Salt Lake City, Utah: Ancestry, 1984).

Write to the Virginia Department of Health, Division of Vital Records (see address above), for certified copies of original marriage records dating from 1 January 1853, or write to the clerk of the county or independent city for copies of certificates, licenses, and register entries.

Virginia divorce records from 1 January 1853 to the present are only obtainable from the Division of Vital Records (see address above). Earlier records are filed with the clerk of the circuit court or the Virginia General Assembly.

The Virginia State Library and Archives has a large collection of Virginia Bible records that can provide vital records information. See Lyndon H. Hart, *A Guide to Bible Records in the Archives Branch, Virginia State Library* (Richmond, Va.: Virginia State Library, 1985). See also "Using Vital Statistics Records in the Archives," Research Notes No. 2, free from the archives.

Census Records

Federal

Population Schedules.

- Indexed—1810 (part), 1820, 1830, 1840, 1850, 1860, 1870
- Soundex—1880, 1900, 1910 (Miracode), 1920

Industry and Agriculture Schedules.

- 1850, 1860, 1870, 1880

Mortality Schedules.

- 1850 (indexed), 1860, 1870, 1880

Slave Schedules.

- 1850, 1860

Union Veterans Schedules.

- 1890

The first federal census was taken in 1790, but neither the first enumeration nor that of 1800 has survived, except for the 1800 census of Accomack County (microfilm) and Louisa County (in print). Only part of the 1810 census exists. Virginia Tax lists from 1782 through 1785 (see Tax Records) were used as a substitute for the 1790 census, reportedly lost when the British burned the city of Washington during the War of 1812. Nettie Schreiner-Yantis and Florence Speakman Love, comps., *The 1787 Census of Virginia: An Accounting of the Names of Every White Male Tithable Over 21 Years . . . ,* 3 vols. (Springfield, Va.: Genealogical Books in Print, 1987), is the best substitute available for the 1790 census. Compiled from Virginia's 1787 tax lists, this source offers both more and less information than the original census. The 1790 census listed only heads-of-household but enumerated their families, including women. In contrast, tax commissioners in 1787 were required to list all free males subject to taxation, not just heads-of-household; women were only included if they owned personal property subject to taxation or were widows with sons aged sixteen to twenty-one. In cases where 1787 tax lists have not survived, Schreiner-Yantis and Love substituted other extant records.

Beginning in 1820 and continuing every ten years through 1910 (except for the 1890 census, which was also destroyed by fire), Virginia's federal census records are available on microfilm at the Virginia State Library and Archives.

Colonial

Two early censuses of Virginia have survived intact; only statistical abstracts remain of other censuses conducted. The first census is dated 16 February 1624 and is a list of the names of persons living in Virginia and the names of those who died since April 1623. The colony conducted a second census in January and February 1625. The *Musters of the Inhabitants of Virginia* were taken by household and include ages, relationships, dates of arrival in Virginia, the name of the ship each person arrived in, and enumerations of weapons, buildings, foodstuffs, and boats. The information actually included varies from household to household and from plantation (or town) to plantation. Another census was conducted in 1634, but is apparently lost. The best transcription of the 1625 *Musters* is in Virginia F. Meyer and John Frederick Dorman, *Adventurers of Purse and Person, Virginia, 1607–1625,* 3d ed. (Richmond, Va.: Order of First Families of Virginia, 1987).

Other lists of Virginia inhabitants include militia musters (see Military Records), tithables lists, and quitrent rolls (see Tax Records). These lists cover a single county or precinct rather than the entire colony.

Background Sources

The most important local history resource, and perhaps the single most important Virginia resource, is Earl Gregg Swem, *Virginia Historical Index*, 2 vols. in 4 (1934–36; reprint, Gloucester, Mass.: Peter Smith, 1965). This should be the first resource examined in any Virginia research project.

Virginia's public records are an important source for understanding its settlers in the context of their history. The Virginia Company of London created the colony's first records during its period of governance from 1607 to 1624. Susan Myra Kingsbury transcribed and edited *The Records of the Virginia Company of London*, 4 vols. (Washington, D.C.: Government Printing Office, 1906–35). These volumes include the court book, the company's correspondence and business journals, and miscellaneous material.

The next group of public records are those of colonial Virginia's council and general court, which served both as a court and a legislative body. The Virginia State Library has most of the original records and has published transcriptions of all extant records in H. R. McIlwaine, ed., *Minutes of the Council and General Court of Colonial Virginia*, 2d ed. (Richmond, Va.: Virginia State Library, 1979), and H. R. McIlwaine, ed., *Legislative Journals of the Council of Colonial Virginia*, 2d ed. in 1 vol. (Richmond, Va.: Virginia State Library, 1979). Other records are found in H. R. McIlwaine, Wilmer L. Hall, and Benjamin J. Hillman, eds., *Executive Journals of the Council of Colonial Virginia*, 6 vols. (Richmond, Va.: Virginia State Library, 1945–78). These volumes include records from 1622 through 1775, although there are many gaps in the early records.

Virginia researchers cannot afford to overlook William Waller Hening, *The Statutes at Large: Being a Collection of all the Laws of Virginia . . .* , 13 vols. (1819–23; reprint, Charlottesville, Va.: University Press of Virginia, 1969), which is a transcription of most of the acts of the Virginia General Assembly from 1619 to 1792. Additional acts are found in Waverly K. Winfree, comp., *The Laws of Virginia: Being a Supplement to Hening's "The Statutes at Large," 1700–1750* (Richmond, Va.: Virginia State Library, 1971), and Samuel Shepherd, *The Statutes at Large of Virginia . . .* (1835; reprint, in 3 vols., New York, N.Y.: A. M. S. Press, 1970), covering 1792 through 1806. Personal names in Hening and Shepherd are indexed by Joseph J. Casey, *Personal Names in Hening's Statutes at Large of Virginia and Shepherd's Continuation* (1896; reprint, Baltimore, Md.: Genealogical Publishing Co., 1967). Hening's *Statutes* is fully indexed in Swem.

William P. Palmer, ed., *Calendar of Virginia State Papers and Other Manuscripts*, 11 vols. (Richmond, Va., 1875–93), covers records of land patents, state papers, correspondence, petitions, licenses, and other activities involving the council and general assembly from 1651 to 1869. The *Calendar* is indexed in Swem.

Swem's *Virginia Historical Index* also indexed *The Virginia Magazine of History and Biography* through 1930; *The William and Mary Quarterly*, Series 1 and Series 2 through 1930; *Tyler's Quarterly* through 1929 (see Periodicals for a discussion of these); *The Lower Norfolk County Virginia Antiquary*, 1895–1906; and the *Virginia Historical Register and Literary Advertiser*, 1848–53.

"A Guide to the Counties of Virginia," published serially in volumes 3–25 of *The Virginia Genealogist* (see Periodicals), describes county record holdings and lists published records and county histories. Additionally, there are some helpful guides for the whole state:

Clay, Robert Young. *Virginia Genealogical Resources.* Detroit, Mich.: Detroit Society of Genealogical Research, 1980.

Hart, Lyndon H. *A Guide to Genealogical Notes and Charts in the Archives Branch, Virginia State Library and Archives.* Richmond, Va.: Virginia State Library and Archives, 1983.

Jester, Annie Lash. *Some Peculiarities of Genealogical Research in Virginia: Colonial.* Salt Lake City, Utah: Genealogical Society of the Church of Jesus Christ of Latter-day Saints, 1969.

Livingston, Virginia Pope. *Some Peculiarities of Genealogical Research in Virginia: Post-Revolutionary.* Salt Lake City, Utah: Genealogical Society of the Church of Jesus Christ of Latter-day Saints, 1969.

Schweitzer, George K. *Virginia Genealogical Research.* Knoxville, Tenn.: the author, 1982.

Wardell, Patrick G. *Timesaving Aid to Virginia-West Virginia Ancestors.* 4 vols. in 1. Athens, Ga.: Iberian Publishing Co., 1991. Well over three hundred sources are indexed in this publication.

Maps

The cartographic history of Virginia begins in the early sixteenth century, and maps, atlases, and gazetteers of the area have been produced ever since. Eugene Michael Sanchez-Saavedra, *A Description of the Country: Virginia's Cartographers and Their Maps, 1607–1881* (Richmond, Va.: Virginia State Library, 1975), offers a brief history of Virginia's cartographic trends and early maps. James W. Sames III, comp., *Index of Kentucky and Virginia Maps 1562 to 1900* (Frankfort, Ky.: Kentucky Historical Society, 1976), indexes the maps on file at the Virginia State Library and the Virginia Historical Society.

The map collection of the Virginia State Library and Archives is described in Earl Gregg Swem, comp., *Maps Relating to Virginia in the Virginia State Library and other Departments of the Commonwealth . . .* (Reprint, Richmond, Va.: Virginia State Library, 1989). This volume also cites maps in other repositories.

The changing boundaries of Virginia's counties are illustrated in Michael F. Doran, *Atlas of County Boundary Changes in Virginia, 1634–1895* (Athens, Ga.: Iberian Publishing Co., 1987). This atlas is a must for Virginia research. See also John S. Hale, *A Historical Atlas of*

Colonial Virginia (Staunton, Va.: Old Dominion Publication, 1978).

Maps showing watercourses are necessary for locating land grants and property described in deeds. See *County Road Map Atlas: Commonwealth of Virginia* (Richmond, Va.: Department of Transportation, 1987), which can be ordered by individual county, free of charge, from the Department of Transportation, 1401 East Broad Street, Richmond, Virginia 23219. Detailed topographical maps of Virginia are published in *Virginia Atlas & Gazetteer* (Freeport, Maine: DeLorme Mapping Co., 1989).

The list of readily available maps of Virginia is quite long. Some important maps are:

A Map of Virginia and Maryland. 1676. Reprint. Ithaca, N.Y.: Historic Urban Plans, n.d.

Fry, Josue, and Pierre Jefferson. *Carte de la Virginie et Maryland, 1755.* Reprint. Ithaca, N.Y.: Historic Urban Plans, n.d.

McCrary, Ben C. *John Smith's Map of Virginia With a Brief Account of Its History.* Charlottesville, Va.: University Press of Virginia, 1981.

Wright, Louis B. *The John Henry County Map of Virginia, 1770.* Charlottesville, Va.: University Press of Virginia, 1977.

Identifying no-longer-used place-names also challenges researchers. Earl Gregg Swem, *Virginia Historical Index* (see Background Sources) includes place-names. A number of excellent gazetteers and place-name guides are available, including:

Gannett, Henry. *A Gazetteer of Virginia.* U.S. Geological Survey. Washington, D.C.: Government Printing Office, 1904. Reprinted as *A Gazetteer of Virginia and West Virginia.* Baltimore, Md.: Genealogical Publishing Co., 1975.

Hall, Virginius Cornick, Jr., ed. "Virginia Post Offices, 1798–1859." *Virginia Magazine of History and Biography* 81 (1973): 49–97.

Hanson, Raus McDill. *Virginia Place Names: Derivations, Historical Uses.* Verona, Va.: McClure Press, 1969.

Hummel, Ray O., Jr., ed. *A List of Places Included in 19th Century Virginia Directories.* 1960. Reprint. Richmond, Va.: Virginia State Library, 1981.

Martin, Joseph. *A New and Comprehensive Gazetteer of Virginia and the District of Columbia.* Charlottesville, Va.: the author, 1835.

Land Records

State-Land State

The original Virginia Charter, granted to the Virginia Company of London in 1606, included provisions for granting land to settlers, called planters, and investors, called adventurers. The revised Charter of 1609 specified that planters were to receive fifty acres and adventurers a hundred acres per share, but that all lands were to be held in common for another seven years. About 1614, Sir Thomas Dale began rewarding industrious planters with three acre plots. John Rolfe's successful experiments with tobacco led many planters to plant their "gardens" with tobacco. Grants of land by the London Company began about 1616; the earliest surviving grant is to Simon Codrington in March 1615/6. The Great Charter of 1618 divided Virginia into four boroughs and set aside land within each borough for public use. The governor and Council were given the authority to allot land to individuals within the boroughs. Two copies of each patent were made; one was given to the grantee as proof of title, and the other was retained for company records.

Virginia became a royal colony in 1624. In 1627 Sir George Yeardley determined that, as governor, he had the power to issue patents for settlers who met the old company definition of a planter. In 1654 the Privy Council finally agreed, and millions of acres were granted to individuals claiming headrights during the seventeenth century.

The headright was the "right" to claim fifty acres for every "head" arriving in the colony; most headrights were claimed by the person who paid the passage. Headrights of indentured servants may have been claimed more than once: by the master of the transporting ship, by the merchant who sold the indenture, by the person who bought the indenture, and/or by the servant. Headrights could be bought and sold; many people who paid their own transportation sold their headrights for money to establish themselves in the colony.

The patenting process required several steps, and most of those steps generated a record. The prospective patentee first petitioned the county court for a "certificate of importation." The certificate, often recorded in county court minute books, was considered proof of the number of headrights claimed. The patentee then carried the certificate of importation to the Secretary of the Colony, who issued a "right" of fifty acres per headright. Once he had a "right," the patentee took it to the county surveyor, who surveyed the chosen land and created a plat. The patentee returned all of these papers to the Secretary, who made two copies of the patent. One was signed by the governor, sealed, and delivered to the patentee. The other copy was retained in the Secretary's office and was supposed to be recorded.

Once the patent was issued, the patentee had three years to seat and plant the land. "Seating" required payment of the quitrent (see Tax Records), an annual payment to the crown of one shilling for every fifty acres. "Planting" required either cultivating one acre or building a house and keeping livestock. Orphans had three years after their majority to seat and plant land. Widows could get extensions of the three years by petitioning the county court.

By the end of the seventeenth century, population growth in the colony of Virginia no longer depended on immigration. Native Virginians wanted new land for tobacco, and the crown wanted to expand the colony, so the treasury right was created. Anyone who wanted new land could receive a "right" to fifty acres for a payment of five shillings. After about 1715, most land was patented by treasury right instead of by headright.

Virginia grants and deeds are readily available to researchers, including original patents and land grants from 1619 to 1921; survey plats from 1779 to 1878; Northern Neck (the area between the Rappahannock and Potomac rivers) land grants from 1690 to 1862; Northern Neck surveys from 1722 to 1781 and 1786 to 1874; land warrants from 1779 to 1926; and miscellaneous land records from 1779 to 1923. Original land office records are housed at the Virginia State Library. See Daphne S. Gentry, comp., *Virginia Land Office Inventory*, 3d ed., revised and enlarged by John S. Salmon (Richmond, Va.: Virginia State Library and Archives, 1981).

Many patents have been abstracted and published. They are included in Nell Marion Nugent, *Cavaliers and Pioneers, Abstracts of Virginia Land Patents and Grants*, 3 vols. (1934; reprint, Baltimore, Md.: Genealogical Publishing Co., 1983). Volume 1 covers 1623–66; Volume 2, 1666–95; and Volume 3, 1695–1732. The Virginia Genealogical Society sponsors a continuation of *Cavaliers and Pioneers*, with abstracts of land patents and grants published regularly in *The Magazine of Virginia Genealogy*. Northern Neck land grants are abstracted and published in Nell Marion Nugent, *Supplement, Northern Neck Grants No. 1, 1690–1692* (Richmond, Va.: Virginia State Library and Archives, 1980), and Gertrude E. Gray, comp., *Virginia Northern Neck Land Grants*, Volume I, 1694–1742 and Volume II, 1742–1775 (Baltimore, Md.: Genealogical Publishing Co., 1987, 1988). In addition, Peggy Shomo Joiner, 5008 Dogwood Trail, Portsmouth, Virginia 23703, has privately published abstracts for Northern Neck warrants and surveys.

When land was sold, the transaction was recorded in county, town, or independent city deed books. Rentals and leases were rarely recorded in deed books, excluding many people from land records. Most deed books are indexed individually, and most Virginia cities and counties have general indexes to grantees and grantors to facilitate research. Copies of deeds can be obtained from county clerks, but most pre-1865 county records in Virginia have been microfilmed and are available at the Virginia State Library and the FHL.

Probate Records

In Virginia, estate records are produced by civil courts on the county level—in the county and circuit courts—except in independent cities where probate matters are the responsibility of the circuit court. Wills, administrations, guardianships, inventories, appraisals, and settlements are some of the records related to a person's estate or probate record.

The Common Law of England applied in the colony, as did the written laws of England. Two important principles were primogeniture and the right of dower. Primogeniture is the device by which estates, particularly land, were kept whole. Basically, the eldest son, by right of birth, inherited all real estate. The right of dower is an old Common Law principle. Women acquired a dower right in all of their husbands' real estate at marriage. At his death, the widow had the right to a portion of the real estate for the remainder of her natural life; the dower was generally one-third. Widows also had a dower right to their late husbands' personal property; once again, the dower was generally one-third but might be an equal division with all of the surviving children. In 1673 the House of Burgesses confirmed the right of dower. The widow received one-third of her late husband's personal property if there were one or two children; if there were three or more, she inherited equally with the children. She also inherited one-third of her late husband's real estate for life and could not be disinherited.

Probates and administrations could be granted in three different places. English law specified that the Prerogative Court of Canterbury had probate jurisdiction in Virginia; Virginia law required probates and administrations to be granted in the quarter or general court; and after 1645, certificates of probate or administration could be granted in the county court. Wills, inventories, and appraisals were supposed to be recorded in both the county and the office of the Secretary of the Colony.

If the probate or administration was granted in England, it has probably been abstracted and published in Peter Wilson Coldham, comp., *American Wills & Administrations in the Prerogative Court of Canterbury, 1610–1857* (Baltimore, Md.: Genealogical Publishing Co., 1989). A series of articles in *The Virginia Magazine of History and Biography* was excerpted and reprinted as Lothrop Withington, *Virginia Gleanings in England: Abstracts of 17th and 18th-Century English Wills and Administrations Relating to Virginia and Virginians* (Baltimore, Md.: Genealogical Publishing Co., 1980).

The earliest records of probates and administrations are found in Susan Myra Kingsbury, ed., *The Records of the Virginia Company of London* (cited in Background Sources). Other records of probates and administrations are found in H. R. McIlwaine, ed., *Minutes of the Council and General Court of Colonial Virginia*, 2d ed. (Richmond, Va.: Virginia State Library, 1979).

The greatest source of probate records is the county. Most colonial wills, inventories, and appraisements are indexed in Clayton Torrence, comp., *Virginia Wills and Administrations, 1632–1800* (1930; reprint, Baltimore, Md.: Genealogical Publishing Co., 1990).

All aspects of probate proceedings were generally recorded in "will books." Original will books are available at the county clerk's office or the Virginia State Library; moreover, most extant will books prior to 1865 have been microfilmed and are available at the Virginia State Library and the FHL. See John Vogt and T. William Kethley, Jr., *Will and Estate Records in the Virginia State Library: A Researcher's Guide* (Athens, Ga.: Iberian Publishing Co., 1987).

Many Virginia counties have "loose papers" or "chancery court records" on file in metal boxes at the clerk's office. These often contain additional information such as affidavits, powers of attorney, letters from individuals living outside the county, and receipts submitted to the court in the process of probating an estate. These records are filed chronologically, have not been filmed, and, in many instances, are in poor condition, but can be searched at the clerk's office.

In addition to printed indexes, many early Virginia will books have been abstracted and published. The Virginia State Library and the FHL have large collections of these works, and many other libraries nationwide have some printed will abstracts.

Court Records

Most courts in America are courts of record, that is, they are required by law to keep a record of their proceedings. Virginia courts are no exception. Understanding Virginia's court system is challenging; taken a step at a time, it can be unraveled. See Suzanne Smith Ray, Lyndon H. Hart III, and J. Christian Kolbe, comps., *A Preliminary Guide to Pre-1904 County Records in the Archives Branch, Virginia State Library and Archives* (Richmond, Va.: Virginia State Library and Archives, 1987), for a more detailed explanation of state courts.

County Court (1619–1902). County courts were the court of record used by most Virginians. In 1904 county courts ceased to exist, and their functions were taken over by the circuit courts.

County courts were established as the **monthly court** in the Great Charter of 1618. The monthly court was held in different precincts and heard petty civil and criminal cases. It served two primary functions: (1) it relieved the president and council of part of their duties as justices, and (2) it brought justice closer to all Virginians. When the eight original shires were formed in 1634, the monthly court was redesignated the **court of shire,** and by 1642 was called the **county court.** The county court was required to meet at least six times per year.

The justices, first known as commissioners, were appointed by the governor; in 1662 they were called justices of the peace. The court generally included eight to ten justices, with four justices appointed to the **quorum.** One member of the quorum in company with three other justices was sufficient to make up a valid court.

The county court also sat in special terms. These were well-publicized meetings of the court for specific functions. The **orphans' court,** begun in 1642, reviewed annual accounts of orphans' estates and ensured that guardians did not waste the estates or mistreat the orphans. Apprentices could appeal to the orphans' court in cases of mistreatment or failure of masters to live up to their contracts. The **court of claim** was a special session for the county's citizens to present monetary claims against the county before the levy was laid (see Tax Records). Beginning in 1645, the county court also sat as a **court of probate,** granting certificates of probate and administration, ordering inventories and appraisements, and settling estates.

President and Council (1607–19). Until 1619, the president and members of the council heard and decided all civil and criminal cases in Virginia. Unfortunately, record of their proceedings has not survived. Once monthly courts were established in 1619, the president and council began to hear appeals of criminal and civil decisions made by those courts.

Quarter Court (1619–61). Starting in 1619, the president and council, and later the governor and council, sat as a quarter court in March, June, September, and December to handle major civil cases, chancery, and appellate matters. When they met in other months, they met as the Council. The quarter court was designated the **general court** in 1661.

General Court (1661–1851). This court had the responsibility of hearing county court appeals, major civil cases, capital crimes, and probate matters until 1851. Two other courts were established during the general court's existence: (1) the high court of Chancery and (2) district courts. The high court of chancery took over appellate functions in county court chancery cases in 1777, and district courts took over appellate functions in county court common law cases in 1789.

The judges of the general court also sat on the district courts. They spent much of their time in the lower court until 1814 when the general court was made the supreme criminal tribunal in Virginia. The general court was abolished by the 1851 state constitution, and its functions were transferred to the supreme court of appeals.

Supreme Court of Appeals (1779–present). Since the supreme court of appeals was created in 1779, it has had final jurisdiction in all civil cases. It has been the state's only court of final appeals since the general court was abolished in 1851.

High Court of Chancery (1777–1802). At its creation in 1777, the high court of chancery assumed jurisdiction over all chancery cases in the state. It was abolished in 1802 and replaced by the superior courts of chancery.

Superior Courts of Chancery (1802–31). Originally, there were three chancery districts, with superior courts of chancery in Staunton, Richmond, and Williamsburg. Additional districts were added including Wythe County, Winchester, and Clarksburg in 1812, and Greenbrier County and Lynchburg in 1814. The superior courts of chancery were abolished in 1831 and replaced by the nearest county's circuit superior court of law and chancery.

District Courts (1789–1808). In 1789 Virginia was divided into eighteen districts, each including several counties. Courts were held twice each year, always in the same location. District courts were replaced by the superior courts of law in 1808.

The eighteen district courts were held at the courthouses in Charlottesville, Fredericksburg, Richmond,

Wiliamsburg, Suffolk, Winchester, Staunton, Dumfries, Petersburg, and possibly others.

Superior Courts of Law (1808–31). Created in 1808, these courts met twice a year in each county and took over the functions of the district courts. They were sometimes called circuit courts because a general court judge rode a circuit throughout his district to hold these courts. They were replaced in 1831 by the circuit superior courts of law and chancery.

Circuit Superior Courts of Law and Chancery (1831–51). These courts were organized like the superior courts of law; sessions were held twice a year by a general court judge who rode a circuit. They assumed the functions of the superior courts of law and the superior courts of chancery. The state constitution of 1851 abolished these courts and replaced them with circuit courts.

Circuit Courts (1852–present). Courts were held twice a year in each county, and records were filed with the county. Originally, there were twenty-one judges who rode circuits to hold these courts.

The state constitution of 1902 did not include provisions for continuing county courts, and circuit courts took over their functions. The circuit courts are now the only court of record in Virginia's counties.

Original court records are housed at the Virginia State Library; pre-1865 records are available on microfilm there and at the FHL. Abstracts of early court records are being printed so rapidly that it is difficult to keep current. While it is always best to rely upon original documents for research, the condition of original court records varies considerably: some are still firmly bound and easy to read, some are faded and crumbling, some are torn or have missing pages, some have been restored through lamination, and many have been destroyed or lost. Because of these circumstances, printed transcripts can prove invaluable to the researcher who knows their limitations and uses them wisely.

The Virginia State Library and the FHL have most published transcripts, while other libraries have fewer volumes. The best individual collection, published between 1937 and 1949, is Beverly Fleet's thirty-four-volume series of *Virginia Colonial Abstracts* (1937–49; reprinted in 3 vols., Baltimore, Md.: Genealogical Publishing Co., 1988). This work brings together a wealth of data from the records of the Tidewater region of Virginia—birth, marriage, and death records, tax lists, court orders, militia lists, wills, and deeds. The result of extensive research in county courthouses, municipal and state archives, and private collections, most of the abstracts were based on the earliest records known to exist. The reprinted collection has been rearranged and consolidated in three volumes, each with its own master index.

A similar compilation for the land west of the mountains can be found in Lyman Chalkley, *Chronicles of the Scotch-Irish Settlement in Virginia*, 3 vols. (1912; reprint, Baltimore, Md.: Genealogical Publishing Co., 1989). Each volume is indexed separately.

Tax Records

Virginia's tax records are a rich—and largely untapped—resource. During the Colonial period, there were three basic forms of taxation: the quitrent, the parish levy, and the poll tax.

The quitrent was a land tax that had its roots in English manorial society where "the land obligations due the manor, such as plowing and haying the lord's land, were commuted to an annual money payment. Upon payment, the obligations were 'quit' for the year." See Arlene Eakle and Johni Cerny, eds., *The Source: A Guidebook of American Genealogy* (Salt Lake City, Utah: Ancestry, 1984). Those living south of the Rappahannock River paid a quitrent to the Crown. An original, incomplete list of land owners for the region in 1704 is in the Public Record Office in London and has been published several times, not always reliably. Residents of the Northern Neck, between the Rappahannock and Potomac rivers, paid quitrents to the agents of Lord Fairfax. Many original rent rolls of the Fairfax proprietary are housed at the Huntington Library in San Marino, California. Extant original rent rolls and facsimiles for Virginia are available at the Virginia State Library. "Using Land Tax Records," Research Notes No. 1, is available from them at no charge.

The parish levy was an annual tax paid by all tithables (see below) for support of their ministers, maintenance of the parishes' glebe lands (the parsonage and lands producing income for the parish), and support of the poor of the parish.

The poll tax, except for a brief period from 1645 to 1648, was the main source of revenue for the colony of Virginia. The annual poll tax was computed by dividing the total expenses of the colony and individual counties by the total number of tithables. The result was levied on each tithable.

Tithables were variously defined during the colonial period. The first definition, in 1624, was "every male head above sixteen years of age." All agricultural workers were added in 1629. In 1643 all males and black females aged sixteen or over were tithables. Imported male servants of any age were added in 1649.

The definition of "tithable" was rewritten in 1658. Tithables included free males aged sixteen or over, imported blacks of either sex, imported white male servants, and Indian servants of either sex; white women employed in agriculture were added in 1662. Complaints from planters with large numbers of indentured servants and slaves led to a revision in 1680 that declared Virginia-born male slaves taxable at age twelve and imported male servants taxable at age fourteen; nonwhite women and free males remained taxable at age sixteen.

The laws of Virginia were revised in 1705. From then until 1782, all males and nonwhite females aged sixteen or over were tithables. Wives of free nonwhite males were added in 1723.

While there is no comprehensive list or collection of early tax lists, many fragments have been printed in Virginia genealogical literature. See also *Virginia Tax Records: From the* Virginia Magazine of History and Biography, The William and Mary College Quarterly, *and* Tyler's Quarterly (Baltimore, Md.: Genealogical Publishing Co., 1983). Tax lists frequently appear in Virginia periodicals (see Periodicals). Original lists and facsimiles are at the Virginia State Library, and the FHL has microfilmed copies of many lists.

Virginia's tax system changed after the Revolutionary War to include taxing land and personal property in 1782, with further revision in 1787. The bulk of those tax lists prior to 1850 survive and are available on microfilm at the Virginia State Library. The 1787 tax lists are in Schreiner-Yantis and Love, *The 1787 Census of Virginia . . .* (see Census Records).

Cemetery Records

The list of published tombstone inscriptions for Virginia, if a comprehensive list existed, would be lengthy. The DAR has compiled an extensive collection of Virginia tombstone inscriptions. The collection, along with other cemetery record publications, can be found at the DAR Library in Washington, D.C., the Virginia State Library, the Virginia Historical Society, and the FHL. See also *The William and Mary Quarterly, The Virginia Magazine of History and Genealogy, Tyler's Quarterly, The Magazine of Virginia Genealogy,* and *The Virginia Genealogist,* since all these periodicals often include cemetery inscriptions in their volumes. Anna M. Hogg and Dennis A. Tosh, *Virginia Cemeteries: A Guide for Resources* (Charlottesville, Va.: University Press of Virginia, 1986), is recommended by the Virginia State Library.

Church Records

Unlike New England, colonial Virginia left few early church records. The first Virginians were members of the Church of England, or Anglican church, which became the Episcopal Church in 1786. Early parish registers are incomplete and challenging to use. Parish boundaries changed rapidly and are hard to pinpoint without Charles Francis Cocke, *Parish Lines, Diocese of Virginia* (1967; reprint, Richmond, Va.: Virginia State Library, 1978). This volume begins with a fine introduction to the Church of England's beginnings in the colony. Companion volumes by Cocke include *Parish Lines, Diocese of Southwestern Virginia* (1960; reprint, Richmond, Va.: Virginia State Library, 1980) and *Parish Lines, Diocese of Southern Virginia* (1964; reprint, Richmond, Va.: Virginia State Library, 1979).

Since colonial times, many religious groups have established congregations in Virginia, including Baptist, Catholic, Jewish, Lutheran, Presbyterian, and Quaker or Friends, to name a few. Except for the Quakers, few of these groups kept records containing such genealogical information as birth, marriage, and death dates. A number of church vestry books and registers have been published and are available at the Virginia State Library and the FHL. See Jewell T. Clark and Elizabeth Terry Long, comp., *A Guide to Church Records in the Archives Branch, Virginia State Library and Archives* (Richmond, Va.: Virginia State Library, 1981), for a complete inventory of church records at the Virginia State Library. See also Edith F. Axelson, *A Guide to Episcopal Church Records in Virginia* (Athens, Ga.: Iberian Publishing Co., 1988), for a county-by-county listing of all known records of the denomination.

Military Records

Colonial Wars. American military history in Virginia began with the establishment of the colonial militia early in the seventeenth century, primarily to fight against attacks from native inhabitants. Service records of Virginia soldiers in the colonial wars (1622–1763) offer more historical than genealogical information and usually provide only the name of the soldier and the unit in which he served. The records consist primarily of rosters, rolls, and lists that survived the wars and several fires and are helpful in placing someone in a particular place at a given time. Most of these rosters and rolls have been published and can be found in genealogical libraries throughout the nation.

A recent publication is Lloyd DeWitt Bockstruck's *Virginia's Colonial Soldiers* (Baltimore, Md.: Genealogical Publishing Co., 1988), compiled from county court minutes and orders, bounty-land applications and warrants, records of courts martial, county militia rosters, Hening's *Statutes at Large,* the Draper manuscripts (see Wisconsin—Manuscripts), and manuscripts of the Public Record Office in London. It supplements William A. Crozier, *Virginia Colonial Militia, 1651–1776* (1905; reprint, Baltimore, Md.: Genealogical Publishing Co., 1982), and H. J. Eckenrode, *List of the Colonial Soldiers of Virginia* (1917; reprint, Baltimore, Md.: Genealogical Publishing Co., 1988).

Another valuable publication is *Virginia Military Records: From the* Virginia Magazine of History and Biography, The William and Mary Quarterly, *and* Tyler's Quarterly (Baltimore, Md.: Genealogical Publishing Co., 1983), a reprint of articles published in those periodicals that deal with military records during the colonial and Revolutionary War eras. See also Murtie June Clark, *Colonial Soldiers of the South, 1732–1774* (Baltimore, Md.: Genealogical Publishing Co., 1983).

Revolutionary War. Some of the original service records for the Revolutionary War were destroyed by fire. Those remaining are on file at the National Archives, compiled primarily from rosters and rolls of soldiers serving in Virginia's militia units, with additions from correspondence and field reports of military officers. However, there is no comprehensive list of Virginia veterans of this war. Some published indexes exist, such as John Hastings Gwathmey, *Historical Register of Virginians in the Revolution, Soldiers, Sailors, Marines, 1775–1783* (Richmond, Va.: Dietz Press, 1938). A card index of Virginia soldiers is available only at the National Archives and is not on microfilm.

John Frederick Dorman continues to compile abstracts of files of Virginia soldiers who received pensions or bounty land in *Virginia Revolutionary Pension Applications,* 44 vols. (Washington, D.C., 1958–). The last volume carries the series through the surname "Goens." Another abstract of information from pension files of soldiers who received pensions from the state of Virginia is *Virginia Revolutionary War Pensions* (1980; reprint, Easley, S.C.: Southern Historical Press, 1982). Virginia Land Office records of Revolutionary War soldiers are found in Louis A. Burgess, comp., *Virginia Soldiers of 1776,* 3 vols. (1927–29; reprint, Baltimore, Md.: Genealogical Publishing Co., 1973).

Bounty-land warrants were issued to Virginia soldiers for their war service. After the war, soldiers who served in the Virginia State Line or Continental Line applied for a warrant and, when approved, received a certificate to be exchanged for a warrant. The land to be issued was located in Kentucky and the Virginia Military District of Ohio. See Gaius Marcus Brumbaugh, *Revolutionary War Records: Volume I, Virginia* (1936; reprint, Baltimore, Md.: Genealogical Publishing Co., 1967), for an index of soldiers who received warrants for Ohio. See also Willard Rouse Jillson, *The Kentucky Land Grants: A Systematic Index to All of the Land Grants Recorded in the State Land Office at Frankfort, Kentucky, 1782–1924* (1925; reprint, Baltimore, Md.: Genealogical Publishing Co., 1971). In the case of deceased soldiers, their heirs made application. Kentucky land was occupied first, then land was granted in Ohio after 1792.

The Virginia State Library and the FHL have microfilmed copies of applications for Virginia bounty-land warrants. See "Revolutionary War Bounty Warrants and Index" or Hamilton J. Eckenrode, comp., *Virginia Soldiers of the American Revolution,* 2 vols. (1912–13; reprint, Richmond, Va.: State Library and Archives, 1989). Rejected applications are filmed under *Revolutionary War Rejected Claims and Index of Soldiers from Virginia, 1811–51.* See also *Military Land Certificates, 1782–1876,* at the Virginia State Library and the FHL (see also Kentucky and Ohio).

War of 1812. Information included in service records for the War of 1812 is similar to that in the same records of soldiers in the colonial wars and the Revolutionary War. Muster rolls, pay rolls, and an index of the Virginia militia in the War of 1812 are included in a card index at the Virginia State Library (also on microfilm at the FHL). Only the National Archives has copies of original pension and bounty-land warrant applications for the War of 1812. Researchers can use microfilmed indexes at the National Archives or the FHL. See also Stuart Lee Butler, *A Guide to Virginia Militia Units in the War of 1812* (Athens, Ga.: Iberian Publishing Co., 1988), for unit histories and commanding officers, and Virgil D. White, comp., *Index to War of 1812 Pension Files,* (Waynesboro, Tenn.: National Historical Publishing Co., 1989).

Civil War. When the Confederate government evacuated Richmond in April 1865, the adjutant and inspector general, Samuel Cooper, took the centralized military personnel records of the Confederate Army to Charlotte, North Carolina. When the Confederate civil authorities left Charlotte after agreeing to an armistice between the armies in North Carolina, President Jefferson Davis instructed Cooper to turn the records over, if necessary, to "the enemy, as essential to the history of the struggle." After the armistice, when Union Gen. Joseph E. Johnston learned that the records were at Charlotte, he turned them over to the Union commander in North Carolina.

These military personnel records were taken to Washington along with other Confederate records captured by the Union Army and were preserved by the War Department. Between 1878 and 1901, the War Department employed a former Confederate general, Marcus J. Wright, to locate missing Confederate records and borrow them for copying if the possessors did not wish to donate them to the War Department. In 1903 Secretary of War Elihu Root persuaded the governors of most of the southern states to lend to the War Department all Confederate military personnel records still in their possession for copying.

The material gathered became the source for the *Compiled Service Records of Confederate Soldiers Who Served in Organizations From the State of Virginia* (similar records are available for all Confederate and border states). The records are indexed in *Index to Compiled Service Records of Confederated Soldiers Who Served in Organizations From the State of Virginia.* These National Archives' microfilm series are available at the Virginia State Library and the FHL. Visitors to the Virginia State Library and Archives should also consult the notebook entitled "Military Records Guide," found at the reference desk.

Virginia offered pensions to her Confederate veterans in 1888; further pension acts passed in 1900 and 1902. The applications have been microfilmed and may be examined at the Virginia State Library in the near future. A "Confederate Pension Index" was microfilmed and is available in the microfilm area of the Archives Branch, Virginia State Library.

Periodicals, Newspapers, and Manuscript Collections

Periodicals

Virginia has excellent genealogical and historical periodicals beginning with a trio of early publications: *The William and Mary Quarterly,* 1892–present in three series (Institute of Early American History and Culture); *Tyler's Quarterly Historical and Genealogical Magazine,* 1919–52; and *The Virginia Magazine of History and Biography,* 1893–present (Virginia Historical Society). They are filled with valuable genealogical or historical information about early Virginians. Issues through 1930 (*Tyler's Quarterly* through 1929) are indexed in Swem's *Virginia Historical Index* (cited in Background Sources). Reprints of family history articles in these periodicals appear in an encyclopedic work entitled *Genealogies of Virginia Families* (Baltimore, Md.: Genealogical Publishing Co., 1980–82), divided into three series. The first, in five volumes, consists of articles reprinted from *The Virginia Magazine of History and Biography*. The second series of four volumes is composed of articles excerpted from *Tyler's Quarterly*. The last series, derived from the *William and Mary Quarterly*, completes the work in five volumes.

Other major Virginia periodicals include *The Virginia Genealogist*, 1957–present (independently published, John Frederick Dorman, editor, P.O. Box 5860, Falmouth, Virginia 22403-5860), a quarterly with source material, genealogies of early Virginia and West Virginia families, and a query section (a cumulative index for volumes 1–20 was produced in 1981), and *The Magazine of Virginia Genealogy* (formerly: *Virginia Genealogical Society Quarterly Bulletin*), 1963–present, the quarterly of the Virginia Genealogical Society.

Newspapers

The most extensive collections of Virginia newspapers are housed at the Virginia State Library and the Virginia Historical Society, as are several indexes to newspaper articles. See Lester J. Cappon, *Virginia Newspapers, 1821–1935; A Bibliography with Historical Introduction and Notes* (New York, N.Y.: University of Virginia Institute for Research in the Social Sciences, 1936).

The Virginia Gazette, Virginia's first newspaper, includes personal notices. It is indexed in Lester J. Cappon and Stella F. Duff, *Virginia Gazette Index, 1736–1780*, 2 vols. (Williamsburg, Va.: Institute of Early American History and Culture, 1950).

Manuscripts

The Virginia State Library and Archives has produced many inexpensive guides to its manuscript collections.

Many repositories in the state hold manuscript collections of value to genealogical research. In addition to the sources listed under Manuscripts in the Introduction of this book, several important repositories are listed under Archives, Libraries, and Societies.

An important manuscript collection located outside the state dealing with Virginians is in Wisconsin (see Wisconsin—Manuscripts). The Draper Manuscripts cover a large number of events and people associated with the migration from Virginia to Kentucky, Tennessee, and the Midwest. Microfilm copies of the material are in several research libraries throughout the country and are available on interlibrary loan.

Archives, Libraries, and Societies

Virginia State Library and Archives
11th Street at Capitol Square
Richmond, VA 23219-3491

The Virginia State Library consists of the General Library Division, where printed materials are housed, and the Archives and Records Division, where historical and governmental documents, including records of genealogical interest, are kept. The Virginia State Library offers *Genealogical Research at the Virginia State Library and Archives*, an informational pamphlet, free of charge. This pamphlet offers a brief description of record holdings. A complete list of the library's publications is available upon request from the Publications Branch at the address above.

Virginia Genealogical Society
P.O. Box 7469
Richmond, VA 23221

The Virginia Genealogical Society publishes *The Magazine of Virginia Genealogy*.

Virginia Historical Society
428 North Boulevard
P.O. Box 7311
Richmond, VA 23221

The Virginia Historical Society maintains a large collection of Virginiana and publishes *Virginia Magazine of History and Biography*.

Alderman Library
University of Virginia
Charlottesville, VA 22903

A guide to the collection is found in *Virginia Genealogy, A Guide to Resources in the University of Virginia Library* (Charlottesville, Va.: University Press of Virginia, 1983).

Earl Gregg Swem Library
College of William and Mary
Williamsburg, VA 23186

Colonial Williamsburg Foundation, Inc.
Department of the Library
P.O. Box C
415 North Boundary Street
Williamsburg, VA 23187

The Colonial Williamsburg Foundation's research library focuses on the eighteenth century, but the collection covers all periods and aspects of Virginia's history.

Congregation Beth Ahabah
Museum and Archives Trust
1109 West Franklin Street
Richmond, VA 23220

Archives includes records and history of one of the oldest Jewish congregations in the colonies.

Union Theological Seminary
3401 Brook Road
Richmond, VA 23227

The Union Theological Seminary maintains Presbyterian church records.

Virginia Baptist Historical Society
P.O. Box 34
Richmond, VA 23173

The Virginia Baptist Historical Society maintains Baptists church records.

Jones Memorial Library
434 Rivermont Avenue
Lynchburg, VA 24504

This small library has an excellent collection of books and microfilms for Virginia research, including a good collection of family histories and general reference works.

Special Focus Categories

Immigration

The best compilations of early Virginia settlers are found in Peter Wilson Coldham, *The Complete Book of Emigrants, 1607–1660, The Complete Book of Emigrants in Bondage, 1614–1775,* and *The Complete Book of Emigrants, 1661–1699* (Baltimore, Md.: Genealogical Publishing Co., 1987, 1988, and 1990). Meyer and Dorman, *Adventurers of Purse and Person* (cited under Census Records) includes detailed studies of the families of Ancient Planters.

NARA microfilm publication M575, "Copies of Lists of Passengers Arriving at Miscellaneous Ports on the Atlantic and Gulf Coasts and at Ports on the Great Lakes, 1820–1875," includes arrivals at Alexandria, East River, Hampton, Norfolk, Petersburg, Portsmouth, and Richmond.

Black American

While county and city estate and property records remain the best sources for identifying slaves and their families, other records, such as lists of free persons of color, marriages, slave lists, apprenticeship bonds, trial dockets, lists of slave owners, church records, family and plantation records, account books, bills of sale, and other miscellaneous records can be found at the Virginia State Library, the University of Virginia, the College of William and Mary, the Institute of Early American History and Culture in Williamsburg, and the Virginia Historical Society.

Keep in mind that not every location in Virginia created or preserved each type of record listed above. In fact, the number of local records attesting to a specific slave is minuscule when compared to those available for people who were not enslaved. See Michael Plunkett, *Afro-American Sources in Virginia: A Guide to Manuscripts* (Charlottesville, Va.: University Press of Virginia, 1990). T. H. Breen and Stephen Innes, *"Myne Owne Ground:" Race and Freedom on Virginia's Eastern Shore, 1640–1676,* (New York, N.Y.: Oxford University Press, 1980), is an interesting study of free blacks on Virginia's Eastern Shore that offers insight into both culture and records.

For a case study approach to using slave records in Virginia, see Johni Cerny, "From Maria to Bill Cosby: A Case Study in Tracing Black Slave Ancestry," *National Genealogical Society Quarterly* 75 (March 1987): 5–14.

County Resources

Most pre-Civil War county records are now housed at the Virginia State Library and Archives, with copies maintained in the county and independent city courthouses. Many early records have been microfilmed, with copies available at the Virginia State Library and the FHL.

Research in the Virginia county collection can be done at a local library as well. The Virginia State Library and Archives participates in the American Library Association Interlibrary Loan program and will loan up to five reels of their extensive collection for a period of four weeks. Each reel of microfilm must be ordered by its number, but first order Microfilm Reel #461, which catalogs the entire collection.

County records are detailed first. Beginning dates for record categories are quoted from information provided by the county and from Ray, et al. (1987), cited under Court Records. County formation information is quoted from Doran (1987), cited under Maps. Record loss information is quoted from Clay (1980), cited under Background Sources, and *The Virginia Genealogist,* volumes 3 through 25.

Independent city records are detailed second. Virginia is the only state with independent cities; they are independent of the county or counties in which they are geographically located. Towns, however, remain a part of their counties. As of 1987, there were forty-one independent cities in Virginia; since population determines city status, more than half were incorporated after 1904. See Lyndon H. Hart III and J. Christian Kolbe, comps., *A Preliminary Guide to Pre-1904 Municipal Records in the Archives Branch, Virginia State Library and Archives* (Richmond, Va.: Virginia State Library and Archives, 1987), and Emily J. Salmon, ed., *A Hornbook of Virginia History,* 3d ed. (Richmond, Va.: Virginia State Library, 1983). Many Virginia counties have been absorbed by independent cities. To the extent possible, the records of the county are detailed separately from those of the independent city.

Previously lost records are still turning up; some are returned by descendants of Union soldiers who took souvenirs. As new information surfaces from the counties and independent cities, and "new" records are discovered, the beginning dates of record categories may change.

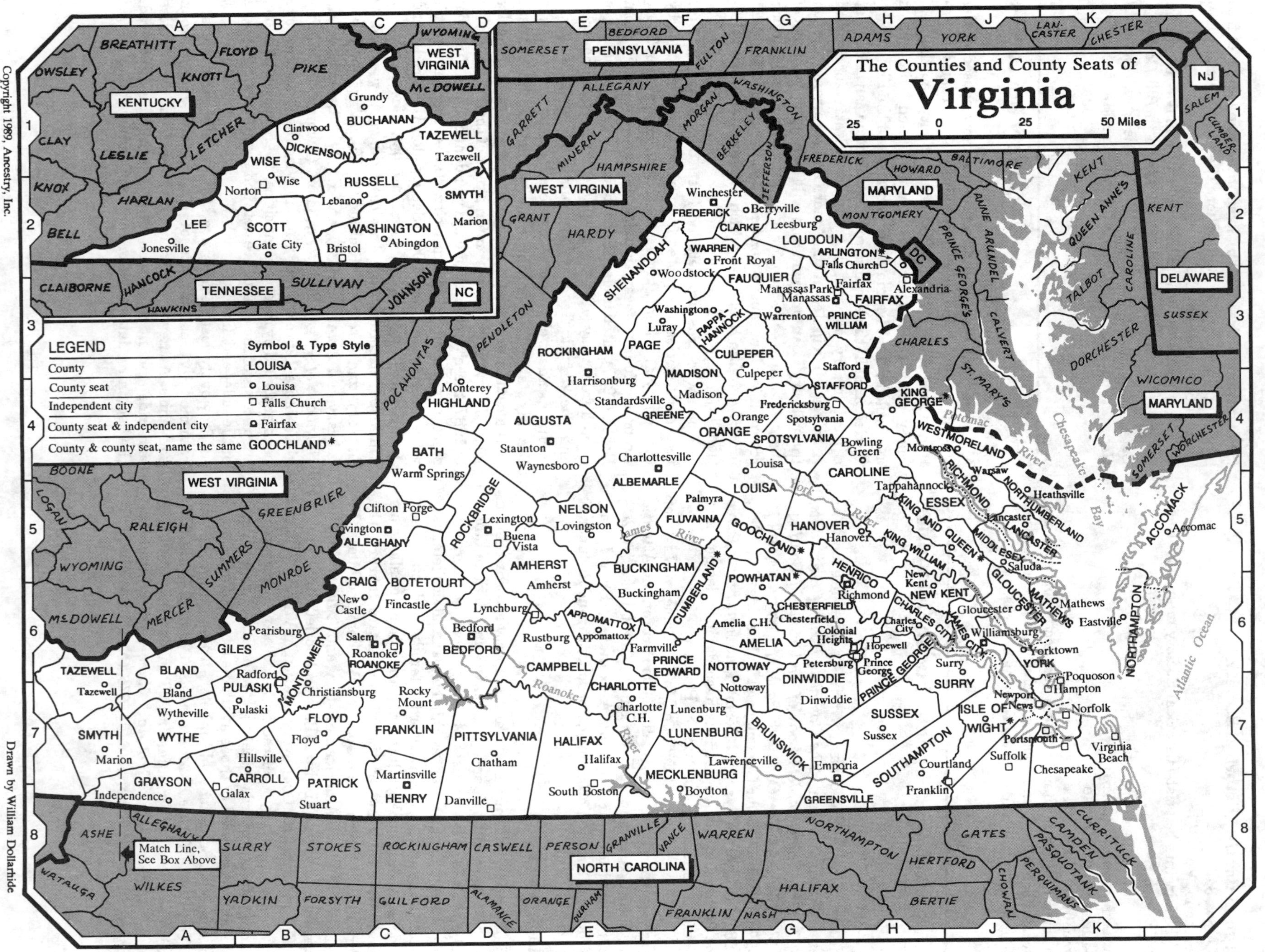

Drawn by William Dollarhide

Map	County Address	Date Formed Parent County/ies	Birth Marriage Death	Land Probate Court
	Accawmack *Records transferred.*	1634 (renamed Northampton, 1642/3) original		
A5	Accomack Accomac 23301 *Temporarily abolished, 1670, restored 1673.*	1663 Northampton	1854 1774 1853	1663 1695 1663
F4	Albemarle 401 McIntire Road Charlottesville 22901	1744 Goochland (part of Louisa added, 1761)	1853 1780 1853	1744 1744 1744
	Alexandria *Transferred to District of Columbia, 1801, returned to Virginia, 1846.*	1789 (renamed Arlington, 1920) Fairfax	1853 1801 1853	1669 1778 1772
C5	Alleghany Main Street Covington 24426	1822 Bath/Botetourt/Monroe	— 1822 —	1822 1822 1822
G6	Amelia Amelia 23002 *Records fragmented.*	1735 Prince George/Brunswick	1853 1735 1853	1734 1734 1734
E5	Amherst 100 E Street Amherst 24521	1761 Albemarle	— 1763 —	1761 1761 1761
E6	Appomattox P.O. Box 672 Appomattox 24522 *Record loss, 1892.*	1845 Buckingham/Campbell/ Prince Edward/Charlotte	— 1892 —	1892 1892 1892
H2	Arlington 1400 N. Courthouse Road Arlington 22201 *Pre-1920 records belong to Alexandria and Fairfax Counties and the District of Columbia.*	1789 (as Alexandria; renamed, 1920) Alexandria	1853 1801 1853	1669 1778 1772
E4	Augusta 6 E. Johnson Street Staunton 24401 *Authorized in 1738, but the government was not formed until 1745. See also Montgomery County.*	1745 Orange	1853 1785 1853	1745 1745 1745
	Barbour	1843 (see West Virginia) Harrison/Lewis/Randolph		
D4	Bath P.O. Box 180 Warm Springs 24484	1791 Augusta/Botetourt/Greenbrier	1853 1791 1853	1791 1791 1791
D6	Bedford Bedford 24523	1754 Lunenberg	1853 1755 1853	1754 1754 1754
	Berkeley	1772 (see West Virginia) Frederick		
A6	Bland P.O. Box 295 Bland 24315 *Record loss, 1885.*	1861 Giles/Wythe/Tazewell	1861 1861 1861	1861 1861 1861

Map	County Address	Date Formed Parent County/ies	Birth Marriage Death	Land Probate Court
	Boone	1847 (see West Virginia) Kanawha/Cabell/Logan		
C6	Botetourt Fincastle 24090	1770 Augusta	1853 1770 1853	1770 1770 1770
	Bourbon	1786 (see Kentucky) Fayette		
	Braxton	1836 (see West Virginia) Lewis/Kanawha/Nicholas		
	Brooke	1797 (see West Virginia) Ohio		
G7	Brunswick P.O. Box 399 Lawrenceville 23868 *Authorized in 1720, but the government was not formed until 1732.*	1732 Prince George/Surry/Isle of Wight	1853 1750 1853	1732 1732 1732
C1	Buchanan P.O. Box 950 Grundy 24614 *Record losses, 1885, 1977.*	1858 Tazewell/Russell	— 1885 —	1885 1885 1880
F5	Buckingham P.O. Box 252 Buckingham 23921 *Record loss, 1869.*	1761 Albemarle	1869 1784 1869	1762 1869 1868
	Cabell	1809 (see West Virginia) Kanawha		
	Calhoun	1856 (see West Virginia) Gilmer		
E6	Campbell P.O. Box 7 Rustburg 24588	1782 Bedford	1853 1782 1853	1782 1782 1782
H4	Caroline Bowling Green 22427 *Pre-Civil War records fragmented, pre-1728 records from parent counties.*	1728 Essex/King and Queen/King William	1864 1787 1865	1728 1732 1665
B7	Carroll P.O. Box 515 Hillsville 24343	1842 Grayson	1853 1842 1853	1842 1842 1842
H6	Charles City P.O. Box 128 Charles City 23030 *Pre-Civil War records fragmented.*	1634 original	1865 1762 1865	1655 1655 1650
	Charles River *Renamed York, 1642/3. Records transferred.*	1634 (renamed York, 1642/3) original		
E7	Charlotte Charlotte 23923	1765 Lunenberg	— 1765 —	1765 1765 1763

Map	County Address	Date Formed Parent County/ies	Birth Marriage Death	Land Probate Court
G6	Chesterfield P.O. Box 40 Chesterfield 23832	1749 Henrico	— 1770 1855	1749 1740 1746
F2	Clarke P.O. Box 189 Berryville 22611	1836 Frederick	— 1836 —	1836 1836 1836
	Clay	1858 (see West Virginia) Braxton/Nicholas		
C6	Craig New Castle 24127	1851 Botetourt/Giles/Roanoke/Monroe	1864 1865 1864	1851 1851 1851
G3	Culpeper Culpeper 22701	1749 Orange	1864 1781 1864	1749 1749 1749
F6	Cumberland P.O. Box 77 Cumberland 23040 *Records fragmented.*	1749 Goochland	1853 1749 1853	1749 1749 1749
B1	Dickenson P.O. Box 190 Clintwood 24228	1880 Russell/Wise/Buchanan	1880 1880 1880	1880 1880 1880
G7	Dinwiddie Dinwiddie 23841 *Record loss, 1864. Records fragmented.*	1752 Prince George	1865 1850 1865	1755 1704 1789
	Doddridge	1845 (see West Virginia) Harrison/Tyler/Ritchie/Lewis		
	Dunmore *Records transferred.*	1772 (renamed Shenandoah, 1778) Frederick		
	Elizabeth City *Records fragmented. Records transferred to City of Hampton.*	1634 original (merged with City of Hampton, 1952)	— 1865 —	1684 1684 1689
H5	Essex P.O. Box 445 Tappahannock 22560 *Records of Rappahannock County (old) are housed in Essex County.*	1692 Rappahannock (old)	1853 1804 1853	1692 1692 1692
H3	Fairfax 4110 Chain Bridge Fairfax 22030	1742 Prince William	1853 1853 1853	1742 1742 1731
G3	Fauquier 40 Culpeper Street Warrenton 22186	1759 Prince William	1853 1759 1853	1759 1759 1759
	Fayette	1780 (see Kentucky) Kentucky		
	Fayette	1831 (see West Virginia) Logan/Nicholas/Greenbrier/Kanawha		

Map	County Address	Date Formed Parent County/ies	Birth Marriage Death	Land Probate Court
	Fincastle *Records transferred to Montgomery County.*	1772 (abolished 1777) Botetourt		
B7	Floyd Floyd 24091	1831 Montgomery	1853 1831 1853	1831 1831 1831
F5	Fluvanna Palmyra 22963	1777 Albemarle	1853 1777 1853	1777 1777 1777
C7	Franklin Rocky Mount 24151	1785/6 Bedford/Henry	1853 1785 1853	1786 1785 1786
F2	Frederick 9 Court Square Winchester 22601 *Authorized in 1738, but the government was not formed until 1743.*	1743 Orange	1853 1771 1853	1743 1743 1743
B6	Giles 120 N. Main Street Pearisburg 24134	1806 Tazewell/Monroe/Montgomery	1853 1806 1853	1806 1806 1806
	Gilmer	1845 (see West Virginia) Kanawha/Lewis		
J6	Gloucester P.O. Box 329 Gloucester 23061 *Record losses, 1821, 1865. Early records fragmented.*	1651 York	1863 1853 1865	1733 1862 1820
G5	Goochland P.O. Box 10 Goochland 23063	1728 Henrico	1853 1730 1853	1728 1728 1728
	Grant	1866 (see West Virginia) Hardy		
A8	Grayson 129 Davis Street Independence 24348	1793 Wythe	1853 1793 1853	1793 1793 1793
	Greenbrier	1777 (see West Virginia) Montgomery		
F4	Greene P.O. Box 386 Standardsville 22973 *Pre-Civil War records fragmented.*	1838 Orange	1853 1838 1853	1838 1838 1838
G7	Greensville 337 S. Main Street Emporia 23847 *Some records fragmented.*	1781 Brunswick	1853 1781 1853	1781 1781 1781
E7	Halifax P.O. Box 786 Halifax 24558	1752 Lunenberg	1853 1753 1853	1746 1752 1752
	Hampshire	1754 (see West Virginia) Augusta/Frederick		

Map	County Address	Date Formed Parent County/ies	Birth Marriage Death	Land Probate Court
	Hancock	1848 (see West Virginia) Brooke		
G5	Hanover Hanover 23069 *Record loss, 1865. Records fragmented.*	1721 New Kent	1853 1863 1853	1733 1733 1733
	Hardy	1786 (see West Virginia) Hampshire		
	Harrison	1784 (see West Virginia) Monongalia		
H6	Henrico P.O. Box 27032 Richmond 23273 *Pre-Revolutionary War records fragmented.*	1634 original	1853 1781 1853	1650 1650 1650
C8	Henry Martinsville 24114	1777 Pittsylvania	1853 1777 1853	1777 1777 1777
D4	Highland Monterey 24465 *Record loss, 1947.*	1847 Pendleton/Bath	1853 1847 1853	1847 1847 1847
	Illinois	1778 Augusta (ceded to the U.S. and became part of Ohio, 1784)		
J7	Isle of Wight Isle of Wight 23397 *Records fragmented.*	1634 (as Warrosquyoake; renamed, 1637) Warrosquyoake	1853 1771 1853	1636 1636 1746
	Jackson	1831 (see West Virginia) Mason/Wood/Kanawha		
J6	James City 114 Stanley Drive Williamsburg 23185 *Record loss, 1865 (Tax Records, 1768–69, preserved).*	1634 original	1865 1865 1864	1854 1865 1865
	Jefferson	1780 (see Kentucky) Kentucky		
	Jefferson	1801 (see West Virginia) Berkeley		
	Kanawha	1789 (see West Virginia) Greenbrier/Montgomery		
	Kentucky	1777 (abolished, 1780) Fincastle		
H5	King and Queen King and Queen 23085 *Record losses, 1825, 1865. Records fragmented.*	1691 New Kent	1865 1864 1865	1719 1864 1831

Map	County Address	Date Formed Parent County/ies	Birth Marriage Death	Land Probate Court
H4	King George King George 22485 *Records fragmented.*	1721 Richmond	1871 1786 1871	1721 1721 1721
H5	King William P.O. Box 215 King William 23086 *Record loss, 1885. Records fragmented.*	1701/2 King and Queen	1885 1786 1885	1701 1701 1701
J5	Lancaster Lancaster 22503	1651 York/Northumberland	1853 1701 1853	1652 1651 1652
A2	Lee Jonesville 24263	1793 Russell	1853 1830 1853	1793 1793 1808
	Lewis	1816 (see West Virginia) Harrison		
	Lincoln	1780 (see Kentucky) Kentucky		
	Lincoln	1867 (see West Virginia) Boone/Cabell/Kanawha/Putnam		
	Logan	1824 (see West Virginia) Giles/Cabell/Tazewell/Kanawha		
G2	Loudon P.O. Box 550 Leesburg 22075	1757 Fairfax	1853 1757 1853	1757 1757 1757
G5	Louisa P.O. Box 160 Louisa 23093	1742 Hanover	1864 1763 1864	1742 1742 1742
	Lower Norfolk *Records are housed in the City of Chesapeake.*	1637 New Norfolk (abolished, 1691)	— — —	1637 1646 1637
F7	Lunenberg Lunenberg 23952	1745/6 Brunswick	1853 1746 1853	1743 1746 1745
	Madison	1786 (see Kentucky) Lincoln		
F4	Madison Main Street Madison 22727	1793 Culpeper	1853 1793 1853	1792 1793 1793
	Marion	1842 (see West Virginia) Monongalia/Harrison		
	Marshall	1835 (see West Virginia) Ohio		
	Mason	1789 (see Kentucky) Bourbon		

Map	County Address	Date Formed Parent County/ies	Birth Marriage Death	Land Probate Court
	Mason	1804 (see West Virginia) Kanawha		
K6	Mathews Mathews 23109	1791 Gloucester	1865 1827 1865	1817 1795 1795
	Record loss, 1865. Records fragmented.			
	McDowell	1858 (see West Virginia) Tazewell		
F7	Mecklenburg P.O. Box 307 Boydton 23917	1764/5 Lunenberg	1853 1765 1853	1765 1764 1764
	Mercer	1786 (see Kentucky) Lincoln		
	Mercer	1837 (see West Virginia) Giles/Tazewell		
J5	Middlesex Saluda 23149	1669 Lancaster	1853 1740 1853	1673 1673 1673
	Monongalia	1776 (see West Virginia) Augusta		
	Monroe	1799 (see West Virginia) Greenbrier		
B6	Montgomery Christiansburg 24073	1777 Fincastle	1853 1773 1853	1750 1773 1753
	Includes records of Augusta (1750–72) and Fincastle (1772–76).			
	Morgan	1820 (see West Virginia) Berkeley/Hampshire		
	Nansemond	1637 (as Upper Norfolk; renamed, 1642/3) Upper Norfolk	— 1866 —	1734 1866 1774
	Incorporated as the City of Nansemond, 1972, merged with the City of Suffolk, 1974. Record loss, 1866. Records transferred to the City of Suffolk.			
	Nelson	1785 (see Kentucky) Jefferson		
E5	Nelson Lovingston 22949	1808 Amherst	1853 1808 1853	1808 1808 1808
H6	New Kent P.O. Box 98 New Kent 23124	1654 York	1865 1850 1865	1674 1827 1820
	Record losses, 1787, 1865. Records fragmented.			
	New Norfolk	1636 (abolished, 1637) Elizabeth City (see Lower Norfolk and Upper Norfolk)		
	Nicholas	1818 (see West Virginia) Greenbrier/Kanawha/Randolph		

Map	County Address	Date Formed Parent County/ies	Birth Marriage Death	Land Probate Court
	Norfolk	1691 Lower Norfolk (merged with the City of Chesapeake, 1963)	1853 1706 1853	1691 1691 1723
	Records transferred to the City of Chesapeake. Records fragmented. Some records may also be in the City of Portsmouth.			
K6	Northampton Eastville 23347	1634 (as Accawmack; renamed, 1642/3) Accawmack	1853 1706 1853	1632 1632 1632
	Includes records of Accawmack.			
J5	Northumberland Heathsville 22473	about 1645 original (formed from Chickacoan Indian District)	— 1735 —	1650 1652 1650
	Although not authorized until 1648, Northumberland was in use by about 1645. *Record loss, 1710. Records fragmented. Birth and death records, 1650–1810, are in the St. Stephen's Parish records.*			
F6	Nottoway Nottoway 23955	1789 Amelia	— 1784 —	1789 1789 1789
	Ohio	1776 (see West Virginia) Augusta		
F4	Orange P.O. Box 111 Orange 22960	1734 Spotsylvania	1866 1747 —	1734 1734 1734
F3	Page 101 S. Court Street Luray 22835	1831 Rockingham/Shenandoah	1865 1831 1864	1831 1831 1831
B8	Patrick P.O. Box 148 Stuart 24171	1791 Henry	1853 1791 1853	1791 1791 1791
	Pendleton	1788 (see West Virginia) Augusta/Hardy/Rockingham		
D7	Pittsylvania P.O. Box 31 Chatham 24531	1767 Halifax	1853 1767 1853	1737 1767 1765
	Pleasants	1851 (see West Virginia) Wood/Tyler/Ritchie		
	Pocahontas	1821 (see West Virginia) Bath/Pendleton/Randolph		
G6	Powhatan 3834 Old Buckingham Road Powhatan 23139	1777 Cumberland	1853 1777 1853	1777 1777 1777
	Preston	1818 (see West Virginia) Monongalia		
F6	Prince Edward P.O. Box 304 Farmville 23901	1754 Amelia	1853 1754 1853	1754 1754 1754
H6	Prince George P.O. Box 68 Prince George 23875 *Pre-Civil War records fragmented.*	1702 Charles City	1865 1865 1865	1710 1713 1714

Map	County Address	Date Formed Parent County/ies	Birth Marriage Death	Land Probate Court
G3	Prince William 1 Complex Court Prince William 22192 *Pre-Civil War records fragmented.*	1731 Stafford/King George	1864 1859 1864	1731 1734 1731
	Princess Anne *Records transferred to the City of Virginia Beach.*	1691 Lower Norfolk (merged with the City of Virginia Beach, 1963)	1853 1724 1853	1691 1691 1691
B7	Pulaski Third Street Pulaski 24301 *Marriage bonds, 1844–57, also in Montgomery.*	1839 Montgomery/Wythe	1853 1839 1853	1839 1839 1839
	Putnam	1848 (see West Virginia) Cabell/Kanawha/Mason		
	Raleigh	1850 (see West Virginia) Fayette		
	Randolph	1787 (see West Virginia) Harrison		
	Rappahannock (old) *Records transferred to Essex.*	1656 Lancaster (abolished, 1692)	— — —	1656 1656 1665
F3	Rappahannock (present) P.O. Box 116 Washington 22747	1833 Culpeper	1853 1833 1853	1833 1833 1833
J5	Richmond Warsaw 22572	1692 Rappahannock (old)	1853 1853	1692 1692
	Ritchie	1843 (see West Virginia) Harrison/Lewis/Wood		
	Roane	1856 (see West Virginia) Gilmer/Kanawha/Jackson		
C6	Roanoke P.O. Box 1126 Salem 24153	1838 Botetourt	1853 1838 1853	1838 1838 1838
D5	Rockbridge Lexington 24450	1778 Augusta/Botetourt	1853 1778 1853	1778 1778 1778
E3	Rockingham Circuit Courthouse Square Harrisonburg 22801 *Record loss, 1864.*	1778 Augusta	1862 1778 1862	1778 1778 1778
C2	Russell P.O. Box 435 Lebanon 24266 *Record loss, 1853.*	1786 Washington	1853 1853 1853	1768 1803 1786
B2	Scott P.O. Box 665 Gate City 24251	1814 Lee/Russell/Washington	1853 1815 1853	1815 1815 1815

Map	County Address	Date Formed Parent County/ies	Birth Marriage Death	Land Probate Court
E3	Shenandoah P.O. Box 406 Woodstock 22644 *Includes records of Dunmore (1772–78).*	1772 (as Dunmore; renamed, 1778) Dunmore	1853 1772 1853	1772 1772 1772
D2, A7	Smyth P.O. Box 1025 Marion 24354 *Some records fragmented.*	1832 Wythe/Washington	1857 1832 1857	1832 1832 1832
H7	Southampton Courtland 23837	1749 Isle of Wight	1853 1750 1853	1749 1749 1749
G4	Spotsylvania P.O. Box 99 Spotsylvania 22553	1721 Essex/King and Queen/King William	— 1795 —	1720 1722 1724
G4	Stafford P.O. Box 339 Stafford 22554 *Pre-Civil War records fragmented.*	1664 Westmoreland	1853 1854 1853	1686 1664 1664
J7	Surry P.O. Box 65 Surry 23883	1652 James City	1853 1768 1853	1645 1652 1645
H7	Sussex P.O. Box 1337 Sussex 23884	1754 Surry	1853 1754 1853	1754 1754 1754
D1, A7	Tazewell P.O. Box 958 Tazewell 24651	1800 Wythe/Russell	1853 1800 1853	1800 1800 1800
	Taylor	1844 (see West Virginia) Harrison/Barbour/Marion		
	Tucker	1856 (see West Virginia) Randolph		
	Tyler	1814 (see West Virginia) Ohio		
	Upper Norfolk *Records transferred.*	1637 (renamed Nansemond, 1642/3) New Norfolk		
	Upshur	1851 (see West Virginia) Randolph/Lewis/Barbour		
F2	Warren Front Royal 22630	1836 Shenandoah/Frederick	1853 1836 1853	1836 1836 1836
	Warrosquyoake *Records transferred.*	1634 (renamed Isle of Wight, 1637) original		
	Warwick *Pre-Civil War records fragmented. Incorporated as City of Warwick, 1952, and merged with the City of Newport News, 1958. Records transferred.*	1634 (as Warwick River; renamed, 1642/3) Warwick River	— — —	1662 1648 1646

Map	County Address	Date Formed Parent County/ies	Birth Marriage Death	Land Probate Court
	Warwick River	1634 (renamed Warwick, 1642/3) original		
C2	Washington Court Street Abingdon 24210	1777 Fincastle	1853 1782 1853	1778 1777 1777
	Wayne	1842 (see West Virginia) Cabell		
	Webster	1860 (see West Virginia) Braxton/Nicholas/Randolph		
J4	Westmoreland P.O. Box 467 Montross 22520	1653 Northumberland	1858 1772 1857	1653 1653 1653
	Wetzel	1846 (see West Virginia) Tyler		
	Wirt	1848 (see West Virginia) Jackson/Wood		
B2	Wise P.O. Box 570 Wise 24293	1856 Lee/Russell/Scott	1856 1856 1856	1856 1856 1856
	Wood	1798 (see West Virginia) Harrison		
	Woodford	1789 (see Kentucky) Fayette		
	Wyoming	1850 (see West Virginia) Logan		
A7	Wythe P.O. Box 440 Wytheville 24382	1790 Montgomery	1853 1790 1853	1790 1790 1790
	Yohogania	1776 (ceded to Pennsylvania 1786) Augusta		
J6	York P.O. Box 532 Yorktown 23690 *Includes records of Charles River.*	1634 (as Charles River; renamed, 1642/3) Charles River	1854 1772 1853	1633 1633 1633

City Resources

Map	Independent City City Hall Address	Established (Parent County/ies) Town Incorporated City Incorporated	Birth Marriage Death	Land Probate Court
H3	Alexandria 301 King Street Alexandria 22314 *First named Hunting Creek, then Belhaven. Declared an independent municipality in 1801.*	1749 (Fairfax) 1779 1852	— 1870 —	1783 1786 1780
D6	Bedford P.O. Box 807 Bedford 24523 *Originally named Liberty; renamed, 1890.*	— (Bedford) 1839 1969		
C2	Bristol 497 Cumberland Bristol 24201 *Originally named Goodson; renamed, 1890.*	1850 (Washington) 1856 1890	— 1890 —	1890 1890 1890
D5	Buena Vista 2039 Sycamore Avenue Buena Vista 24416	1889 (Rockbridge) 1890 1892	— 1892 —	1892 1892 1892
F4	Charlottesville P.O. Box 911 Charlottesville 22902	1762 (Albemarle) 1801 1888	— — —	1871 — 1888
K7	Chesapeake P.O. Box 15225 Chesapeake 23320 *Created in 1963 by merger of the City of South Norfolk and Norfolk County.*	1963 1963		
C5	Clifton Forge P.O. Box 631 Clifton Forge *Established as Williamson's Station; renamed, 1884.*	1861 (Alleghany) 1884 1906	— 1906 —	1906 1906 1906
H6	Colonial Heights 1507 Boulevard Colonial Heights 23834	1910 (Chesterfield) 1926 1961	— 1961 —	1961 1961 1961
C5	Covington 158 N. Court Avenue Covington 24426	1818 (Alleghany) 1833 1953		
D8	Danville City Courthouse Danville 24543	1793 (Pittsylvania) 1830 1890	1874 1841 —	1841 1857 1859
G8	Emporia Emporia 23847	1887 (Greensville) 1887, 1892 1967		
H3	Fairfax 10455 Armstrong Street Fairfax 22030 *Originally Providence; renamed, 1859.*	1805 (Fairfax) 1874 1961		
H2	Falls Church 300 Park Falls Church 22046	1850 (Fairfax) 1875 1948		
J8	Franklin 207 W. 2nd Avenue Franklin 23851	1830–40 (Southampton) 1876 1961		
G4	Fredericksburg P.O. Box 7447 Fredericksburg 22404	1728 (Spotsylvania) 1782 1879	1853 1781 1853	1782 1782 1782

Map	Independent City City Hall Address	Established (Parent County/ies) Town Incorporated City Incorporated	Birth Marriage Death	Land Probate Court
A8	Galax	(Carroll/Grayson)		
	123 N. Main Street	1906		
	Galax 24333	1954		
	Originally named Bonaparte.			
K7	Hampton	1680 (Elizabeth City)		
	22 Lincoln Street	1849, 1852, 1887		
	Hampton 23669	1908		
	Extant from 1610. Consolidated with Elizabeth City County, 1952.			
E4	Harrisonburg	1780 (Rockingham)	1862	1778
	Rockingham Courthouse	1849	1778	1803
	Harrisonburg 22801	1916	1862	1778
H6	Hopewell	about 1915 (Prince George)	—	1916
	300 N. Main	—	1916	1916
	Hopewell 23860	1916	—	—
	Founded as Charles City Point, 1613; renamed Hopewell about 1913. City Point annexed in 1923.			
D5	Lexington	1778 (Rockbridge)		
	300 E. Washington Street	1874		
	Lexington 24450	1965		
D6	Lynchburg	1786 (Campbell)	1853	1805
	P.O. Box 60	1805	1805	1805
	Lynchburg 24505	1852	1853	1787
G3	Manassas	1852 (Prince William)	—	—
	9311 Lee Avenue	1874	—	—
	Manassas 22110	1975	—	1873
G3	Manassas Park	1955 (Prince William)		
	103 Manassas Drive	1957		
	Manassas Park 22111	1975		
	Manchester	—		
		1874		
	Annexed by the City of Richmond, 1910.			
C8	Martinsville	1791 (Henry)	—	1942
	City Courthouse	1873	1942	1942
	Martinsville 24112	1928	—	1942
	Nansemond	1972		
	Created from Nansemond County in 1972, it merged with the City of Suffolk in 1974.			
J7	Newport News	1880 (Warwick)	—	1866
	2400 Walsh Avenue	—	—	—
	Newport News 23607	1896	—	1866
	Extant from 1619. Consolidated with the City of Warwick, 1958.			
K7	Norfolk	1680 (Norfolk)	1792	1784
	100 St. Paul Boulevard	1736	1797	1784
	Norfolk 23501	1845	1853	1761
	Some records were destroyed during the Revolutionary War.			
B2	Norton	about 1787 (Wise)		
	P.O. Box 618	1894		
	Norton 24273	1954		
	Originally named Prince's Flats; renamed about 1891.			
H6	Petersburg	1748 (Dinwiddie/Chesterfield/Prince George)	1853	1784
	Union and Tabb Streets	1784	1780	1784
	Petersburg 23803	1850	1853	1774
	Extant by 1645 as Fort Henry; renamed Peter's Point. Pre-1784 records fragmented.			

Map	Independent City City Hall Address	Established (Parent County/ies) Town Incorporated City Incorporated	Birth Marriage Death	Land Probate Court
K7	Poquoson	1885–88 (York)		
	830 Poquoson Avenue	1952		
	Poquoson 23704	1976		
K7	Portsmouth	1752 (Norfolk)	1853	1776
	801 Crawford Street	1836	1782	1755
	Portsmouth 23704	1858	1853	1743
	Some pre-1858 records may be of Norfolk County.			
B6	Radford	1885 (Montgomery)	—	1892
	319 Second Street	1887	1892	1892
	Radford 24141	1892	—	1892
	Formerly named Lovely Mount, English or Ingle's Ferry, Central Depot, and Central City, it was renamed in 1890.			
H6	Richmond	1742 (Henrico)	1853	1782
	900 E. Broad Street	1782	1780	1810
	Richmond 23219	1842	1853	1782
C6	Roanoke	1852 (Roanoke)	1884	1884
	215 Church Avenue, S.W.	1874	1884	1884
	Roanoke 24011	1884	—	1884
	Originally named Big Lick. Renamed Roanoke in 1882.			
C6	Salem	1806 (Roanoke)		
	P.O. Box 869	1836		
	Salem 24153	1968		
E8	South Boston	1796 (Halifax)		
	P.O. Box 417	1884		
	South Boston 24592	1960		
	Originally named Boyd's Ferry.			
	South Norfolk	— (Norfolk)		
		1919		
		1921		
	Merged with Norfolk County, 1963, and renamed the City of Chesapeake. Records transferred.			
E4	Staunton	1761 (Augusta)	1854	1802
	P.O. Box 58	1801	1802	1802
	Staunton 22401	1871	1853	1796
J7	Suffolk	1742 (Nansemond)	—	1866
	441 Market Street	1808	1866	1734
	Suffolk 23434	1910	—	1774
	Record loss, 1866. Records fragmented. Merged with the City of Nansemond in 1974.			
K7	Virginia Beach	— (Princess Anne)	—	1906
	Municipal Center County	1906	1906	1906
	Virginia Beach 23456	1952	—	1906
	Absorbed Princess Anne County (and its records), 1963.			
	Warwick	1952 (Warwick)		
	Warwick county was incorporated as the City of Warwick in 1952, and merged with the City of Newport News in 1958.			
E4	Waynesboro	1801 (Augusta)	—	1948
	P.O. Box 1028	1834	1948	1948
	Waynesboro 22980	1948	—	1948
J6	Williamsburg	1633 (James City/York)	—	1865
	412 N. Boundary	1722	1854	1858
	Williamsburg 23185	1884	—	1865
	Originally Middle Plantation; renamed, 1699, and declared a city in 1722. Record loss, 1865.			
F2	Winchester	1752 (Frederick)	1853	1789
	5 N. Kent Street	1779	1790	1794
	Winchester 22601	1874	1865	1786
	Originally Opequon; renamed Frederick's Town and then Winchester in 1852. Early records fragmented.			

WASHINGTON

Dwight A. Radford

In 1844 a wagon train of settlers arrived in the western district of what was to become Washington. Among them was George W. Bush, a wealthy black man. He, and the wagon train he was traveling with, were refused settlement in Oregon Territory south of the Columbia River. Because of Bush's kindness and help to members of the wagon train during their journey, they all decided to stay together and settle north of the Columbia River. This settlement was the start of Tumwater and marked the beginning of serious settlement by Americans north of the Columbia River. Soon afterwards, the California gold rush, beginning in 1849, provided a market for lumber products needed to build the mushrooming San Francisco area. This industry brought settlers and prosperity to the Puget Sound area.

The 1850 U.S. census showed that Oregon Territory north of the Columbia River had more than 1,000 persons; most were Americans from Illinois, Indiana, Iowa, Kentucky, Missouri, Ohio, and Tennessee. A few claims were platted on the site of present-day city of Seattle in 1850. By 1855, Seattle reported a population of 500.

The reason for the separation of Washington Territory from Oregon was primarily geographic. The settlements around the Puget Sound were a great distance from the territorial capital in Salem, Oregon Territory. Settlers north of the Columbia River felt that because of the sparse population north of the river, the politicians in Salem would neglect their interests. Washington became a territory on 2 March 1853.

The Mullen Road, built from Fort Benton, Montana, to Walla Walla, Washington, was used as a highway for migration to the Columbia River area. It proved to be unsuccessful as a highway for eastern Washington settlement. Most immigrants branched off the Oregon Trail at Hermiston, Oregon, forded the Columbia River, and took up donation land claims where water was available. The rush of population into the "Inland Empire" area started in 1858 with the opening of the country east of the Cascades. In 1860 gold was first discovered in the Clearwater River region. The route to the mines lay up the Columbia River to Walla Walla and then by trail to the mining areas. During the decade of the 1860s, the population of Washington Territory doubled.

The decade of the 1880s also saw an increase in population in Washington Territory. One hundred thousand people are estimated to have arrived between 1887 and 1890, most by railroad. Washington was admitted to the Union on 11 November 1889. Washington entered the twentieth century with a population of 518,000.

Vital Records

Prior to 1891, Washington had no legislative provision for the recording of births and deaths. However, some counties and cities did record births and deaths prior to 1891. These records have been microfilmed, and copies are available at the Washington State Archives (see Archives, Libraries, and Societies). Between 1891 and 1907, birth and death registers were kept on the county level. The state legislature in 1891 made it the duty of all coroners, physicians, and midwives to report all births and deaths under their supervision. The filing of marriages with county officials has been required by law since the creation of Washington Territory in 1853. Divorces were granted beginning in 1854 by the district courts of the territory, and these records were kept from 1854 to 1889 by the clerk of the district court. Post-1907 vital records in the state office of Vital Records in Olympia are not open to the public for research.

Although not indexed, many birth and death records from 1891 through 1907 have been microfilmed by the Washington State Archives. Given the county of occurrence, the archives staff will search the records for a fee.

The mandatory recording of births and deaths on a state level began 1 July 1907 and marriage and divorce records on 1 January 1968. Prior to 1968, marriages were recorded by the county auditor. Marriage records such as applications, certificates, and returns usually begin with the date of county formation or shortly thereafter. Divorces were recorded by the county clerk at the county seat.

To obtain post-1907 vital records, specific information is required to initiate a search. For birth records, the following is needed: (1) name at time of birth or adoption, (2) date and place of birth, (3) father's full name, and (4) mother's full maiden name. For death records, the following is needed: (1) name at time of death, (2) spouse of the deceased, and (3) date and place of death. For marriage and divorce records, the following is needed: (1) name of groom/husband, (2) maiden name of bride/wife, (3) date of marriage or divorce, and (4) county where the marriage or divorce was filed.

The cost for obtaining post-1907 vital records from the Vital Records Department is $11. A certified copy of the record will be sent within three weeks from when the request is received. State records can be obtained by writing Vital Records, P.O. Box 9709, ET-11, Olympia, Washington 98504-9709.

Census Records

Federal

Population Schedules.

- Indexed—1850 (as Oregon Territory), 1860, 1870
- Soundex—1880, 1900, 1920
- Unindexed—1910

Industry and Agriculture Schedules.

- 1860, 1870, 1880

Mortality Schedules.

- 1850, 1860, 1870, 1880

Union Veterans Schedules.

- 1890 (indexed)

The 1860 enumeration included what was later to become Idaho Territory and parts of Montana and Wyoming.

Microfilm copies of federal population schedules and/or the AISI indexes for Washington are available in research repositories in the state including the National Archives-Pacific Northwest region (see page 9). The agricultural and industrial censuses are on microfilm at the Washington State Archives (see Archives, Libraries, and Societies).

Territorial and State

Several territorial censuses were recorded for Washington. These schedules were required periodically by the federal government and excluded all Native Americans. The surviving schedules are available on microfilm through the Washington State Archives or its regional branches. The University of Washington, Suzzalo Library (see Archives, Libraries, and Societies), has a two volume set of territorial censuses which have been microfilmed and are available through interlibrary loan from the Washington State Library (see Archives, Libraries, and Societies). This particular collection has been marked with an asterisk (*) in the listing below.

State and territorial censuses are available for the following counties and years:

County and Years Available

- **Adams:** 1885, 1887, 1889
- **Asotin:** 1885, 1887, 1889
- **Chehalis:** 1858, 1859*, 1860, 1861*, 1871, 1885
- **Clallam:** 1857, 1860*, 1871, 1883, 1885, 1887
- **Clark:** 1857, 1858*, 1859*, 1860, 1871, 1883, 1885, 1887
- **Columbia:** 1883, 1885, 1887, 1889
- **Cowlitz:** 1859*, 1860*, 1861*, 1871, 1883, 1885, 1887
- **Douglas:** 1885, 1892
- **Franklin:** 1885, 1887
- **Garfield:** 1883, 1885, 1887, 1889, 1892, 1898
- **Island:** 1857, 1859*, 1860, 1871, 1883, 1885, 1887
- **Jefferson:** 1860, 1861*, 1871, 1874, 1877, 1878, 1879, 1880, 1881, 1883, 1885, 1887, 1889, 1891
- **King:** 1856, 1859*, 1860*, 1861*, 1871, 1879, 1880, 1881, 1883, 1885, 1887, 1889, 1892
- **Kitsap:** 1857, 1858*, 1859*, 1860, 1861*, 1871, 1883, 1885, 1887, 1889
- **Kittitas:** 1885, 1887, 1889
- **Klickitat:** 1871, 1883, 1885, 1887, 1889, 1892
- **Lewis:** 1857, 1860*, 1871, 1883, 1885, 1887
- **Lincoln:** 1885, 1887, 1889
- **Mason:** 1857, 1859*, 1861*, 1871, 1879, 1883, 1885, 1887, 1889, 1892
- **Pacific:** 1883, 1885, 1887
- **Pierce:** 1854, 1857, 1858*, 1859*, 1871, 1878, 1879, 1883, 1885, 1887, 1889, 1892
- **San Juan:** 1885, 1887, 1889
- **Skagit:** 1885, 1887
- **Skamania:** 1860, 1871, 1885, 1887
- **Snohomish:** 1883, 1885, 1887, 1889
- **Spokane:** 1885, 1887
- **Stevens:** 1871, 1878, 1885, 1887, 1892
- **Thurston:** 1871, 1873, 1875, 1877, 1878, 1879, 1880, 1881, 1883, 1885, 1887, 1889, 1892
- **Wahkiakim:** 1857, 1860*, 1885, 1887
- **Walla Walla:** 1860*, 1885, 1887, 1892

- **Whatcom:** 1858*, 1859*, 1860, 1861*, 1871, 1885, 1887, 1889
- **Whitman:** 1883, 1885, 1887, 1889
- **Yakima:** 1871, 1883, 1885, 1887

Background Sources

Andrews, Mildred Tanner. *Washington Women as Path Breakers.* Dubuque, Iowa: Kendall/Hunt Publishers, 1989. This book with narrative and archival photographs portrays the contributions made by women in Washington.

Bancroft, Hubert Howe. *History of Washington, Idaho, and Montana.* San Francisco, Calif.: History Co., 1890. Each of the three states is considered separately in this early, but essential volume dealing with settlement, native-European relations, frontier mining, railroads, politics, and general economic development.

Brewster, David, and David M. Buerge, eds. *Washingtonians: A Biographical Portrait of the State.* Seattle, Wash.: Sasquatch Books. This celebrates legendary and ordinary men and women who helped shape the first 100 years of Washington's history.

Ficken, Robert E., and Charles P. LeWarne. *Washington: A Centennial History.* Seattle, Wash.: University of Washington Press, 1988. A colorful and comprehensive account is presented of the beginnings and potential of the state and of the people who made it what it is today.

Genealogical Resources in Washington State: A Guide to Genealogical Records held at Repositories, Government Agencies, and Archives. Olympia, Wash.: Secretary of State, Division of Archives and Records Management, 1983. This guide includes records on the state, county, and city level. Many church records are also listed.

Johansen, Dorothy., and Charles M. Gates. *Empire of the Columbia: A History of the Pacific Northwest.* 2d ed. New York, N.Y.: Harper & Row, 1967. Although now outdated, this volume was the most popular regional history for general readers and for classroom use.

Kirk, Ruth, and Carmela Alexander. *Exploring Washington's Past: A Road Guide to History.* Seattle, Wash.: University of Washington Press, 1989. A detailed guide to the state's various regions, it introduces travelers to historic and present-day places of interest.

LeWarne, Charles P. *Washington State.* Seattle, Wash.: University of Washington Press, 1986. This book was intended for high school classroom use.

Ruby, Robert H., and John A. Brown. *A Guide to the Indian Tribes of the Pacific Northwest.* Norman, Okla.: University of Oklahoma Press, 1986. This reference work, in a convenient alphabetical format, describes the histories and cultures of the various Native American groups.

White, Sid, ed. *Peoples of Washington, Perspectives on Cultural Diversity.* Pullman, Wash.: Washington State University, 1989. The book commemorates and reflects on the rich ethnic legacy Washington has inherited.

Maps

Topographical maps of Washington are available from the U.S. Geological Survey (see page 4). Ask for the following two publications: "Washington, Index to Topographical and Other Map Coverage" and "Washington, Catalog of Topographic and Other Published Maps." The latter states the current cost for each topographical map and provides a listing of over-the-counter map sellers in the state of Washington.

Major libraries in Washington have been designated by the U.S. Geological Survey as map depository libraries. They include the Public Library in Bellevue; Western Washington State University at Bellingham; Eastern Washington University at Cheney; Central Washington University in Ellensburg; Washington State Library in Olympia; Washington State University in Pullman; Public Library and the University of Washington in Seattle; Public Library in Spokane; Pacific Lutheran University, Public Library, and the University of Puget Sound in Tacoma; and Whitman College in Walla Walla.

Several publications dealing with historical and reference maps of Washington are available to the public. Among these are James R. Scott's *Washington: A Centennial Atlas.* (Bellingham, Wash.: Western Washington University, 1989); James W. Scott and Roland L. DeLorme's *Historical Atlas of Washington.* (Norman, Okla.: University of Oklahoma Press, 1988); and Ralph N. Preston's *Early Washington: Overland Stage Routes, Old Military Roads, Indian Battle Grounds, Old Forts, Old Gold Mines* (Corvallis, Oreg.: Western Guide Publishers, ca. 1974).

Land Records

Public-Domain State

Washington was settled through the donation and other land grant acts used by the federal government to attract settlers to sparsely populated regions and to distribute the land fairly to the settlers.

The federal government donated 320 acres of free land to each single man and 640 acres to each married couple who settled in Oregon Territory (including present-day Washington) by 1 December 1850. The terms of the donation stipulated that the settler would homestead for four years. In 1853 the residency was reduced to two years. In 1854

Congress passed another act providing the same donation land grants in Washington Territory.

Donation entry files for Oregon and Washington are on file separately at the National Archives-Pacific Northwest Region in Seattle (see page 9) from 1851 to 1903. A large portion of the donation land claim files have been indexed or abstracted, and these indexes are on file at either the National Archives or the FHL under the title *Abstracts of Washington Donation Land Claims, 1855–1902* (National Archives, 1951). The Seattle Genealogical Society (see Archives, Libraries, and Societies) has indexed and published the Washington Donation Land Records. The major Washington libraries have microfilm copies of the Washington Donation Land Records.

Donation land grants can be of great genealogical value because they not only provide a description of the property, but also the name of the person entering the land, place of residence at the time of notification, citizenship, the date and place of birth, marital status, wife's maiden name (where appropriate), and the place and date of marriage.

Other land entries in Washington were based on either cash payment for the land (cash entries), or on conditions of settlement (homesteads). To be eligible for these entries an individual had to be at least twenty-one years of age (or the head of a household, including widows) and a U.S. citizen (or have filed intentions to become a citizen). Cash entries could purchase any available tract up to 160 acres. After the Homestead Act was passed in 1862, anyone meeting the eligibility requirements could purchase up to 160 acres by living on the land for five years, raising crops, and making improvements. These records were kept by the local GLO, which is the modern day BLM. The land office's records were kept in tract books which recorded land transactions by section and township. These records are now at the BLM, 825 N.E. Multnomah Street, Portland, Oregon 97208.

Land entry case files are important for genealogists because they provide the name, date of birth, date and place of marriage, citizenship information, record of migration, and other data for those who obtained land. Copies of the complete Homestead file can be obtained from the National Archives, Washington, D.C.. (see page 8). To request the complete Homestead file, the homesteader's name, state, county, and legal description of the land must be included.

Water rights in Washington are as important as land rights. Water rights applications, permits, and certificates are issued by the State Department of Ecology and are usually recorded by the county auditor. State-issued water rights records began in 1917 and may be filed either at the Department of Ecology or at the state archives. Information provided in water rights records is similar to that provided in land records.

If an ancestor was a miner, the Washington State Archives publication, "Index to Mining Surveys, 1883–1964," would be valuable. This publication provides an index to the sixty-six volumes of the Surveyor General's surveys of mining claims in the territory and state of Washington. These are arranged alphabetically by mine name, mining district, volume, and page number. The mining surveys themselves are available on microfilm at the state archives.

Once land was transferred from the government to private persons, it could be sold again, lost by foreclosure of a mortgage, or distributed through death or divorce. Transactions were recorded by the county auditor in the form of a deed or mortgage and can be obtained by contacting the local county courthouse or regional branch of the Washington State Archives.

Probate Records

In Washington, probate courts had original jurisdiction on matters relating to the probate of wills and administration of estates. These courts were empowered to appoint guardians of minors and insane persons and to conduct adoption and insanity hearings. The probate courts continued to exist independently until 1891, when its functions were assumed by the state superior court system (see Court Records). Records generated by the probate courts before 1891 were transferred to the custody of the county clerk.

Court Records

Territorial

The Organic Act of 1853, which created Washington Territory, also established a judicial system. Judicial power was vested in the supreme court, district court, probate court (see above), and justice court.

An excellent guide and index to territorial court records is *Frontier Justice: Abstracts and Indexes to the Records of the Territorial District Courts, 1853–1889* (Olympia, Wash.: Secretary of State, Division of Archives and Records Management, 1987).

Washington Territory was divided into three judicial districts: eastern Washington was assigned to the First Judicial District, southwestern Washington to the second, and northwestern Washington to the third. In 1886 the Fourth Judicial District was created for the central Washington area.

The three district court justices (four after 1886) sat as the supreme court for Washington Territory. The supreme court met annually in Olympia at a time set by the territorial legislature and heard all appeals from the district court. Cases from the supreme court could be appealed to the U.S. Supreme Court.

The Washington State Archives has published a guide to territorial supreme court records entitled *Guide to the Records of the Washington Territorial Supreme Court, 1853–1889* (Olympia, Wash.: Secretary of State, Division of Archives and Records Management, n.d.). This publication lists all cases considered by the territorial supreme court, including an index to the names of plaintiffs and defendants.

The district court had original jurisdiction in all cases arising under the U.S. Constitution and the laws of

Washington Territory. This court heard cases in chancery (equity) and admiralty. Admiralty cases related to offenses committed on the seas and disputes relating to maritime matters. The district court heard divorce cases until 1864 when the territorial legislature could grant legislative divorces as well. Documents filed with the district court include naturalizations, admission to the bar, and appointments and bonds of officials. The district court had appellate jurisdiction over probate (see Probate Records) and justice courts.

The justice court set up new counties and provided for the establishment of probate and justice courts. The justice court heard petty criminal and civil cases where less than $100 in debt or damages was involved. Justices of the peace often heard the original complaint in a case and then, due to lack of jurisdiction, referred the case to the district court.

Researchers should first contact the state archives in Olympia or a regional branch to locate territorial court records. Many have been microfilmed.

State

Washington's court system is divided into the supreme court, superior courts, and district courts.

The supreme court at Olympia exercises statewide geographic jurisdiction. The supreme court has final appellate jurisdiction by review of cases from the superior courts. The court determines cases involving constitutional matters, matters of public interest, and those challenging the rule of law.

The twenty-eight superior courts are the only trial courts of record in the state. They have unlimited jurisdiction. These courts have original jurisdiction over such matters as criminal cases, which includes felonies, misdemeanors, all juvenile matters, and appellate jurisdiction in cases from courts of limited jurisdiction. Superior court cases may be appealed to the supreme court. Jury trials are available in all cases. Many superior court records are available on microfilm at the Washington State Archives.

Probate records are under the jurisdiction of the superior court, and many are available at the appropriate county courthouses, the state archives, or one of the branch archives.

The sixty-two district courts have limited jurisdiction in criminal cases concurrent with the superior courts regarding all misdemeanors and preliminary hearings for felony cases. Jury trials are available in both civil and criminal cases. Appeals are to the superior courts. The present district courts are not courts of record, and few archival records are held.

Tax Records

Washington has never had a state income tax. The only tax records are for real and personal property, which were both levied at the county level. The records are held by the county assessors and the county treasurers. In some cases, the Washington State Archives' regional branches have acquired older records. These branches are excellent places to begin searching for county tax records. Not all county tax records have survived. Inheritance tax records are on microfilm at the Washington State Archives from 1901 until the tax was discontinued in 1981.

Cemetery Records

The Washington State Genealogical Society (see Archives, Libraries, and Societies) as well as the State Cemetery Board have published statewide inventories of cemeteries in Washington. The former includes details on published cemetery inscriptions. Several local genealogical societies have published sexton's records as well as tombstone data for their areas.

Church Records

The WPA, under the sponsorship of the State College of Washington (Washington State University), inventoried church records in Washington and produced the valuable inventory, *Guide to Church Vital Statistics Records in Washington* (Washington, D.C.: Washington Historical Records Survey, 1942). Although this volume does not provide complete coverage of every church in the state at the time, it is a useful, although dated, guide.

The inventory is arranged alphabetically by the county in which the survey occurred, as well as by the denomination. It lists the date of establishment or existence of the congregation, and whether it is now defunct. Of all the congregations surveyed, only those with records that could be used to establish birth dates were added to the survey. Various church surveys similar to the WPA inventory have also been compiled for Everett, Seattle, Spokane, Wenatchee, and Yakima. Most church records are still deposited at the local congregation where they were created. Some collected registers and histories have been published or microfilmed.

The Presbyterian faith arrived in what was then Oregon Territory in 1838. The Presbyterian Church in the United States of America, Synod of Washington, collected history is in *History of the Synod of Washington of the Presbyterian Church in the U.S.A., 1835–1909* and *Local Presbyterian Church Histories of Washington Associations that Comprise the Olympia Presbyterial, 1890–1972.* A major Presbyterian archive repository is the San Francisco Theological Seminary in San Anselmo, California.

The Methodist Episcopal Church was the first Protestant group to organize a local church east of the Cascades. Methodism arrived in Vancouver in 1848 and in Olympia and Seattle in 1853. The United Methodist Church has a repository of records at the University of Puget Sound, Tacoma, Washington 98406.

Leona M. Nichols, *The Mantle of Elias, the Story of Fathers Blanchel and Demers in Early Oregon* (Portland, Oreg.: Binfords and Mort, ca. 1941), has extracts of early Catholic records from 1838 to 1869. Major Catholic record repositories are St. Thomas the Apostle Seminary, Kenmore, Washington 98023; The Catholic Diocese of Spokane, West 1023 Riverside Avenue, Spokane, Washington 99201; Diocese of Olympia, 1551 Tenth Avenue East, Seattle, Washington 98202; and Diocese of Spokane, 245 East 13th Street, Spokane, Washington 99202. Some of these libraries are open only to clergymen or church members, and it is wise to contact the repository to obtain their current regulations governing research.

Although Mormon missionaries were sent to the Pacific Northwest as early as 1850, the population did not welcome their message and religion. Although pockets of Mormons continued to meet in secret, missionary efforts did not begin seriously again until the 1880s and 1890s. For a more detailed account of the early Mormons in the Northwest, see J. Arthur Horne's, *Latter-Day Saints in the Great Northwest* (Seattle, Wash.: Graphic Art Press, n.d.). Early ward/branch and mission records have been microfilmed and are deposited at the FHL.

Seventh-day Adventists arrived in Washington Territory in the 1860s. Loma Linda University in Loma Linda, California, has major historical church collections for the west coast.

The Episcopal church arrived in Washington in 1851 at Cathlamet as a mission outreach from Portland. The major Episcopal repositories in Washington are at the Diocese of Olympia, 1551 Tenth Avenue East, Seattle, Washington 98102, and the Diocese of Spokane, 245 East 13th Street, Spokane, Washington 99202.

The Lutheran faith arrived in Washington as the result of migration by Scandinavians to the Puget Sound area. The Pacific Lutheran University Archives, Park Avenue South and South 121st Street, Tacoma, Washington 98447, has many oral histories and historical research papers in their archives concerning the Lutheran faith in western Washington.

Military Records

A series of guides on the Washington State and Territorial Militia is Virgil R. Field, *Washington National Guard Pamphlet* (Tacoma, Wash.: Washington State Military Department, Office of the Adjutant General, 1960). This seven-volume work is an overview history of the Washington National Guard during the territorial period, Indian Wars, Civil War, Philippine Insurrection, World War I, World War II, and the post-World War II era. It is an excellent introduction to the Washington State or Territorial Militia.

The Washington State Archives has early service records for the Indian Wars that include muster rolls, correspondence and financial records, as well as records of residents of the State Soldiers Home and State Veterans Home up to the mid-1930s.

Washington veterans of World War I, World War II, Korea, and Vietnam could apply for a state bonus. These applications and supporting papers were originally filed with the state auditor and are now deposited at the Washington State Archives. Information listed in these files includes residence of the veteran, occupation, relationships, birthplace, and military information. Also housed in the state archives are the National Guard statements of service cards for those guardsmen who participated in World War I and World War II, as well as National Guard special orders and circular letters.

Periodicals, Newspapers, and Manuscript Collections

Periodicals

Periodicals for the state of Washington can be of great genealogical value as they not only contain historical articles but often index cemeteries, church records, and censuses. Otherwise unknown Bible records and letters are additionally included in such periodicals. Quarterlies published in the state include those by the Eastern Washington Genealogical Society, Spokane Public Library, West 906 Main Avenue, P.O. Box 1826, Spokane, Washington 99210; Tri-City Genealogical Society, P.O. Box 1410, Richland, Washington 99352; Yakima Valley Genealogical Society, Box 445, Yakima, Washington 98907; Tacoma/Pierce Genealogical Society, P.O. Box 1952, Tacoma, Washington 98401; and the Seattle Genealogical Society, 1405 Fifth Avenue, P.O. Box 1708, Seattle, Washington 98111.

The Pacific Northwest Quarterly, a primarily scholarly publication of the University of Washington in Seattle, is not genealogical in focus but provides background material on the region.

Newspapers

All extant Washington newspapers are on microfilm at the Washington State Library in Olympia. These are available through interlibrary loan. Finding aids for Washington newspapers, such as Glenda Pearson, Lea Ehrlich, and Cynthia Flugate's *Pacific Northwest Newspapers on Microfilm at the University of Washington Libraries* (University of Washington, 1983), are helpful. Two guides have also been published by the Washington State Library entitled "Newspapers on Microfilm in the Washington State Library" and "Washington Newspapers and Historical Material on Microfilm in the Washington State Library."

Manuscripts

Several major historical and genealogical collections are held by repositories throughout the state. The University of Washington has a large holding of manuscript collections that deal with such subjects as Washington politics and government, economic history, forestry, railroads, coal mines and mining, frontier life of Washington Territory, ethnic history, and labor history. These manuscript collections are open to outside use by permission. An inventory of the manuscript collections has been compiled by name and subject.

The University of Washington's "Northwest Collection" holds material on such regional topics as northwest Native Americans, anthropology, history, and economic and social conditions of the Pacific Northwest. Special collections include diaries of eighteenth- and nineteenth-century explorers of the region and various western states documents. The Northwest Collection also includes periodicals, maps, pamphlets, and scrapbooks. Some of these can be obtained through a limited interlibrary loan. A subject index to regional periodicals and newspapers is available.

Washington State University Library Manuscript Division in Pullman houses a large collection of manuscripts relating to eastern Washington and the Palouse Country, including papers of early business and farming pioneers. The Eastern Washington Historical Society, located in Spokane, has collections relating to eastern Washington and the Inland Empire, including the founding of Spokane and other communities, mining, agriculture, and hydrology. Gonzaga University in Spokane holds records relating to Jesuit missionary activity in the northwest and papers of local pioneers. The Whitman College Library in Walla Walla has papers of local pioneers with an emphasis on missionaries connected with the American Board of Commissioners for Foreign Missions.

A listing of repositories of manuscripts and archives, with descriptions of their holdings, is found in *Historical Records of Washington State, A Guide to Records and Papers held in Repositories,* (Olympia, Wash.: Washington State Historical Records Advisory Board, 1981).

Several genealogical collections are available through the FHL. These include a large collection of DAR compiled family Bibles, family records of pioneers, and the collection entitled "Family Records and Reminiscences of Washington Pioneers prior to 1891" by the DAR.

Archives, Libraries, and Societies

Washington State Archives
P.O. Box 9000
12th and Washington Streets
Olympia, WA 98111

The holdings of the Washington State Archives are centrally located in Olympia and collected throughout the state in one of five local branches of the archives. Holdings for each branch depend on the counties they serve as follows:

Eastern Branch—Washington State Archives
J. F. K. Library
Eastern Washington University
Pullman, WA 99004
Covers Adams, Asotin, Columbia, Ferry, Garfield, Lincoln, Pend, Spokane, Stevens, Walla Walla, and Whitman.

Central Branch—Washington State Archives
c/o History Department
Central Washington University
Ellensburg, WA 98926
Covers Benton, Chelan, Douglas, Grant, Kittitas, Klickitat, Okanogan, and Yakima.

Puget Sound Regional Branch—
Washington State Archives
1809 South 140th
Seattle, WA 98168
Covers King, Kitsap, and Pierce.

Northwest Regional Branch—
Washington State Archives
Western Washington University
Bellingham, WA 98225
Covers Clallam, Island, Jefferson, San Juan, Skagit, and Snohomish.

Southwest Regional Branch—
Washington State Archives
12th and Washington, EA-11
Olympia, WA 98504-0418
Covers Clark, Cowlitz, Grays Harbor, Lewis, Mason, Pacific, Skamania, and Thurston.

Washington State Library
Capital Campus
State Library Building
Washington/Northwest Room
Olympia, WA 98504

University of Washington
Archives and Records
Suzzallo Library
Seattle, WA 98195

Washington State University Archives
Library Systems
Washington State University
Pullman, WA 98164-7310

Seattle Public Library
Genealogical Division
1000 4th Avenue
Seattle, WA 98104

Both the Seattle and Tacoma (below) public libraries have extensive collections of gazetteers and Washington city directories.

Tacoma Public Library
Northwest Room
1102 Tacoma, WA 98402

Washington State Historical Society
315 North Stadium Way
Tacoma, WA 98403

Washington State Genealogical Society
P.O. Box 549
Seattle, WA 98111

More than fifty local genealogical and historical societies exist in Washington. For a listing of the holdings of the various Washington State Genealogical Societies, see *Genealogical Research in Washington State,* published by the Washington State Archives.

Special Focus Categories

Immigration

Immigrants to the state of Washington came through the following ports: Aberdeen, Anacortes, Bellingham, Everett, Friday Harbor, Grey's Harbor, Olympia, Port Angeles, Port Bernard, Port Wells, Princeton, Raymond, Seattle, South Bend, and Tacoma. Points of entry from Canada to Washington were Blaine, Curlew, Marcus, Oroville, and Sumas. These records are filed with the Seattle passenger and ship arrival lists and cover the period from 1890 to 1957. Customs passenger lists of vessels arriving at Port Townsend and Tacoma from 1894 to 1909 and passenger lists of vessels arriving at Seattle from Insular Possessions (1908–17), along with the Seattle passengers lists (1890–1957), are at the National Archives-Pacific Northwest Region, as well as the FHL. These records provide a wealth of genealogical information and should not be overlooked when searching for an immigrant ancestor between 1890 and 1957.

Native American

The history of Washington's Native American population—Nez Perce, Yakima, and other tribes—is one of conflict with European settlers. However, Washington's native population suffered less from wars with the European settlers than from European diseases. The destruction of the native population was the greatest in the Columbia Valley; within a few years after settlers arrived, the native population of the lower valley was practically wiped out.

Agencies were organized by the U.S. government to administer the affairs of Washington's Native American population. These records include genealogically significant materials such as land ownership, school records, correspondence, ledgers, and tribal council records. They are on file at the National Archives-Pacific Northwest Region, and microfilm copies of selected records are available at the FHL. The agency and the tribes they cover are described below. (For a more detailed explanation of this topic see Oregon—Native American.)

Colville Agency, Nespellem, Washington (1874–1964), was established in 1872 for the Colville Reservation and later the Spokane and Coeur d'Alene reservations.

Puyallup Agency, Tacoma, Washington (1885–1920), was actually established in 1888 by a merger of the Nisqualli and Skokomish Agency and the Quinault Agency. It was responsible for the Quinaielt, Puyallup, Chehalis, Nisqualli, Squaxin Island, Clallam or Skalallam, and other tribes.

Spokane Agency, Spokane, Washington (1885–1950), was established in 1912 for the Spokane on the Spokane Reservation. The agency was responsible for the Kutenai, Kalispell, Wenatchi, and other tribes.

Taholah Agency, Taholah, Washington (1878–1950), was created in 1914 to administer the affairs of tribes west of the Puget Sound. From 1933 to 1950, the Taholah Agency administrated the affairs of the Chehalis, Hoh, Makah, Nisqualli, Ozette, Quileute, Quinaielt, Shoalwater, Skokomish, and Squaxon Island reservations. This agency includes the Neah Bay Agency.

Tulalip Agency, Tulalip, Washington (1854–1950), administered the Tulalip, Lummi, Port Madison, Swinomish, and Mukleshoot reservations. In 1922 the Puyallup Agency, including the Cushman Indian School, passed under the control of the Tulalip Agency.

Yakima Agency, Toppenish, Washington (1859–1964), Western Washington Agency (1950–64), was established in 1859 and administered the affairs of the Bannock, Nez Perce, Paiute, and Yakima tribes.

Other important Native American sources include school records and special compiled collections. The Chemawa School in Chemawa, Oregon, and the Fort Shaw School in Cascade County, Montana, enrolled students from all parts of the Northwest. The collection entitled "Major James McLaughlin Papers" is an important research tool as is the Pacific Northwest Tribes Missions Collection of the Oregon Province Archives of the Society of Jesus, 1853–1960. For additional details about these collections, See Montana—Native American.

George Gibbs' *Indian Tribes of Washington Territory* (Fairfield, Wash.: Ye Galleon Press, 1978) is an excellent first-hand historical account of the tribes and bands of natives in the territory, written in 1855. Another indispensable aid is Charles E. McChesney's *Rolls of Certain Indian Tribes in Washington and Oregon* (Fairfield, Wash.: Ye Galleon Press, 1969). Supervisor McChesney was commissioned by the Department of the Interior in 1906 to proceed to the reservations of Washington and Oregon to confer with Indian Agents and tribe members. Native American genealogical and historical data are found in this book.

The most extensive work ever published on the state's native peoples and their cultural traditions is Robin K. Wright, *A Time of Gathering: Native Heritage in Washington State,* (Seattle, Wash.: University of Washington Press and The Burke Museum, 1989).

Other Ethnic Groups

The pattern of immigration changed throughout western America with the development of the railroad in the 1870s and 1880s. Railroads were advertising all over the United States and Europe that "free" land was available. This brought many immigrants to Washington. By 1920, there were 250,055 foreign born whites in Washington, the majority of which came from Canada, Sweden, Norway, England, and Ireland.

A group of Dutch families who had originally settled in the Dakotas came to the Washington coast in 1894. The Dutch who came in the 1890s and 1900s went to Whidbey Island and other parts of the Puget Sound. Lynden (in Whatcom County) became the largest Dutch community in Washington, and other Dutch communities grew in Moxee City, Prosser, and Zillah.

Finns and Italians came to the urban centers of Washington to work as laborers. These two groups quickly merged into the American mainstream.

The Japanese community of Washington was largely employed in truck farming on the coast. The heaviest concentrations were on the outskirts of Seattle and Tacoma. By 1920, only 939 out of 17,387 lived east of the Cascades—mainly working on farms in Yakima County and Spokane.

During World War II, the Japanese minority was singled out and evacuated from the Pacific Coast to relocation centers for the duration of the war. A total of 14,559 Japanese were removed from Washington and sent to Minidoka Center in southern Idaho. About 200 went to Tule Lake Center in northern California. Both areas were suited to truck farming, and many Japanese chose to stay in southern Idaho after the war. The University of Washington Library Archives Manuscript Division has records of Seattle's Buddhist Church from 1938 to 1942, which predates the relocations.

Although black Americans participated in the westward movement in the mid-1800s, it was during World War II that many came to Washington coastal cities to work in the industrial plants. When agricultural workers became scarce during the war, ranchers arranged to bring in groups of Mexicans as transient labor.

The Chinese came to Washington to build the railroads and work in the mining industry, and by 1885 there were 3,000 Chinese in the territory, most of whom were living in the Puget Sound region. Anti-Chinese riots in the territory were set off by the news that a mob in Rock Springs, Wyoming, had driven out 700 Chinese miners on 4 September 1885. This led to violence towards the Chinese community employed in the mines and orchards of Washington. On 3 November 1885, several hundred Chinese were forcibly removed from their homes in Tacoma, and the city's Chinatown was destroyed. As a result, several hundred Chinese persons voluntarily left the city for British Columbia or San Francisco.

After the Seattle fire of 1889 many Chinese returned to the city to establish themselves as permanent residents. Chinese organizations, which became part of the community, included the Chinese Benevolent Society, founded in Seattle in 1929; Chinese Baptist Church, founded in Seattle in 1896; Freemason Hall; and several Chinese family organizations centered in Seattle. A study of the Chinese population of the Northwest, especially around Seattle, is found in Karen C. Wong, *Chinese History in the Pacific Northwest* (N.p., ca. 1972).

National Archives-Pacific Northwest Region has many sources for researching Chinese immigration including the following: a register of Chinese applicants for admission to ports in Washington (1896–1903); many records from the Immigration and Naturalization Service in Portland, Oregon; and a separate passengers list for Chinese arriving in Seattle from 1892 to 1916.

The Wing Luke Memorial Museum, 414 Eighth Avenue South, Seattle, Washington 98104, has materials relating to the Chinese in the Pacific Northwest and principally the Seattle area. The East Asia Library, at the University of Washington in Seattle, has holdings consisting of materials from the Chinese Empire Reform Association, a Chinese-American organization with chapters throughout the western United States.

A large community of Germans from Russia settled in Whitman County, Washington. Before the turn of the twentieth century, the center of their immigration was Endicott, and many were farming in the St. John and Colfax area.

In 1887 most of the Endicott colonists identified themselves with the Evangelical Lutheran Synod in Columbus, Ohio. Due to the strict doctrinal interpretation of the Ohio Synod, many colonists changed churches. Seventh-day Adventists came to Endicott in 1893, and by 1912 they had built a church. The Adventists as well as most of the Endicott churches of the period held services in German. By World War II, the Endicott area German-Russian population had almost totally been absorbed into the American mainstream. Books detailing the history of this German-Russian colony are Richard D. Scheurman, *The Historical Development of Whitman County's German-Russians* (Seattle, Wash.: University of Washington, 1971), and Richard D. Scheurman and Clifford E. Trafzer, *The Volga Germans: Pioneers of the Northwest* (Moscow, Idaho: University of Idaho, 1980).

Major Scandinavian groups settled in Ballard, Bellingham, Everett, Seattle, Skagit Valley, Stanwood, Stillaguamish Valley, and Tacoma. In Parkland, south of Tacoma, the Pacific Lutheran University was founded and was operated under the Norwegian Lutheran Synod.

County Resources

Although originally held in the county seat, many county land, probate, court records have been transferred to the state archives regional branches. Researchers should first consult the pamphlet, "Guide to Records in State Archives and its Regional Depositories," accessed through the state archives, to determine what has been transferred from the counties. An automated system for the guide makes it possible to search by a number of parameters, although not surname, to facilitate research. Otherwise, contact the appropriate regional depository to evaluate what records have been transferred since 1980.

The beginning dates for territorial court and probate records have been taken from the volume *Frontier Justice: Guide to the Court Records of Washington Territory 1853–1889*. For judicial purposes, many of the counties were attached to other counties. Therefore, this volume is extremely important as it will direct researchers to the correct county where older records are filed.

Drawn by William Dollarhide

Map	County Address	Date Formed Parent County/ies	Birth Marriage Death	Deeds Probate Court
H5	Adams 210 W. Broadway Ritzville 99169	1883 Whitman	1891 1891 1891	1879 1885 1890
K6	Asotin 135 Second Street Asotin 99402	1883 Garfield	1891 1891 1891	1893 1885 1886
G6	Benton Dudley Avenue Prosser 99350	1905 Klickitat/Yakima	1905 1905 1915	1905 1905 1905
	Chehalis	1854 (renamed Grays Harbor, 1915) Thurston		
E3	Chelan P.O. Box 3025 Wenatchee 98801	1899 Kittitas/Okanogan	1900 1900 1900	1900 1903 1900
A2	Clallam 223 E. Fourth Port Angeles 98362	1854 Jefferson	1891 1891 1891	1859 1862 1889
C7	Clark 1200 Franklin Street Vancouver 98660	1844 (as Vancouver District; renamed, 1849)	1891 1891 1891	1850 1890 1890
J6	Columbia 341 E. Main Dayton 99328	1875 Walla Walla	1891 1876 1891	1864 1878 1874
B6	Cowlitz 312 S.W. First Street Kelso 98626	1854 Lewis	1891 1854 1891	1854 1860 1872
F3	Douglas County Courthouse Waterville 98858	1883 Lincoln	1891 1887	1884 1884
H2	Ferry 350 E. Delaware Republic 99166	1889 Stevens	1898 1898 1889	1898 1899 1899
G6	Franklin 1016 N. Fourth Avenue Pasco 99301	1883 Whitman	1891 1892 1891	1880 1884 1890
J6	Garfield P.O. Box 915 Pomeroy 99347	1881 Columbia	1891 1892 1891	1892 1882 1883
G4	Grant C Street N.W. Ephrata 98823	1909 Douglas	1909 1909 1909	1909 1909 1909
A4	Grays Harbor 100 W. Broadway Montesano 98563	1854 (as Chehalis; renamed, 1915) Thurston	1891 1852 1891	1855 1857 1884
B2	Island Seventh and Main Coupeville 98239	1853 original	1891 1853 1891	1853 1853 1891

Map	County Address	Date Formed Parent County/ies	Birth Marriage Death	Deeds Probate Court
A3	Jefferson 1820 Jefferson Street Port Townsend 98368	1852 original	1891 1853 1891	1855 1853 1854
D4	King 516 Third Avenue * Seattle 98104	1852 Thurston	1891 1861 1891	1853 1854 1864
	** This is the address for the county courthouse, which houses probate and court records. For marriage and land records, contact the King County Administration Building, 500 Fourth Avenue, Seattle 98104. For birth and death records, contact the King County Public Safety Building, 610 Third Avenue, Seattle 98104.*			
B3	Kitsap 205 W. Fifth Avenue Port Orchard 98366	1857 (as Slaughter; renamed, 1857) King/Jefferson	1891 1860 1891	1857 1861 1888
E4	Kittitas 205 W. Fifth Avenue Ellensburg 98926	1883 Yakima	1892 1884 1891	1882 1884 1884
E7	Klickitat 205 S. Columbus Goldendale 98620	1859 Walla Walla	1891 1867 1891	1867 1882 1880
B5	Lewis 344 W. Main Chehalis 98532	1845 original	1891 1847 1891	1855 1855 1847
H4	Lincoln 450 Logan Street Davenport 99122	1883 Spokane	1883 1884 1891	1883 1884 1886
B4	Mason Fourth and Adler Shelton 98584	1854 (as Sawamish; renamed, 1864) Thurston	1891 1892 1891	1856 1871 1889
G2	Okanogan 149 Third N. Okanogan 98840	1888 Stevens	1891 1891 1891	1874 1888 1888
A5	Pacific 300 Memorial Avenue South Bend 98586	1851 original	1891 1868 1891	1851 1851 1878
K2	Pend Oreille 625 W. Fourth Newport 99156	1911 Stevens	— 1911 1911	1911 1911 1911
C5	Pierce 930 Tacoma Avenue S.* Tacoma 98402	1852 Thurston	1891 1859 1891	1858 1855 1855
	** This is the address for the County/City Building, which houses court records. For marriage, voting, and land records, contact the County Auditor in the Pierce County Annex, 2401 South 35th Street, Tacoma, Washington 98409. For tax records, contact the County Assessor also in the Pierce County Annex. For birth and death records, contact the Pierce County Health Department, Vital Statistics, 3701 Pacific Avenue, Tacoma 98408.*			
	Sawamish	1854 (renamed Mason, 1864) Thurston		
B2	San Juan 350 Court Street Friday Harbor 98250	1873 Whatcom	1892 1874 1891	1877 1874 1889

Map	County Address	Date Formed Parent County/ies	Birth Marriage Death	Deeds Probate Court
C2	Skagit 205 Kincaid Street Mount Vernon 98273	1883 Whatcom	1891 1891 1891	1872 1884 1878
C7	Skamania Second Street Stevenson 98648	1854 Clark	1893 1892 1891	1854 1854 1854
D2	Snohomish 300 Rockefeller Avenue Everett 98201	1861 Island	1881 1867 1891	1862 1866 1876
	Spokane (old)	1858 (abolished; became part of Stevens, 1864) Walla Walla		
	Old Spokane was created from Walla Walla County in 1858. It became part of Stevens in 1864, and in 1879 part of this county was set off as modern Spokane County.			
K4	Spokane (present) W. 1116 Broadway Avenue Spokane 99201	1879 Stevens	1891 1880 1891	1890 1880 1878
J2	Stevens 215 S. Oak Street Colville 99114	1863 Walla Walla	1891 1861 1891	1883 1887 1882
B5	Thurston 2000 Lakeridge Street S.W. Olympia 98502	1852 original	1891 1877 1891	1852 1853 1852
A6	Wahkiakum 64 Main Street Cathlamet 98612	1854 Lewis	1891 1868 1891	1877 1852 1890
H6	Walla Walla 315 W. Main Street Walla Walla 99362	1854 Clark/Skamania	1883 1862 1884	1859 1859 1860
C1	Whatcom 311 Grand Avenue Bellingham 98225	1854 Island	1891 1854 1891	1854 1872 1883
J5	Whitman Main and Island Colfax WA 99111	1871 Stevens	1891 1872 1891	1874 1878 1861
E6	Yakima 129 N. Second Street Yakima 98901	1865 Walla Walla	1891 1877 1891	1882 1874 1882

West Virginia

Johni Cerny

That part of Virginia which later became West Virginia was unknown to the adventurers who settled Jamestown in 1607. With the exception of a few scattered frontier outposts and even fewer permanent settlements, the area remained Native American hunting and battlegrounds until well into the 1700s. Virginia's Governor William Berkeley encouraged exploration and trade as early as 1660, but extensive settlement was discouraged by mountain barriers, resistance from original inhabitants, disputed land titles, conflicting English and French claims, and a royal proclamation of 1763 prohibiting settlement beyond the ridge line of the Blue Ridge Mountains. Settlement began in earnest by the 1730s when Morgan Morgan established a settlement in Berkeley County, Virginia.

While eastern tidewater counties of Virginia were settled by English aristocrats and their descendants, pioneers in western Virginia were generally perceived as a ragtag group from Pennsylvania, Maryland, and other parts of Virginia. The 1790 census lists more than 55,000 residents, of whom about 15,000 were of German descent. English immigrants and their descendants settled in Greenbrier, New, Kanawha, and Monongahela valleys, while Scots-Irish settlers made their homes in less accessible areas. West Virginia's mountainous terrain limited agricultural development and reduced the need for slavery. Less than one percent of the population in 1790 was enslaved. After the Civil War, blacks from southern states moved into West Virginia seeking work in the railroads, mines, and industry.

Vital Records

Since all but five of West Virginia's counties were formed before 20 June 1863 when Congress officially admitted it as a sovereign state, counties in existence prior to statehood were governed by the same laws as other Virginia counties, including the requirement to register births and marriages in 1853. While Virginia counties stopped recording births and deaths in 1896, West Virginia continued to do so until about 1900. Some county records extend beyond 1900. Statewide registration began 1 January 1917, although fire destroyed many 1917–21 records.

Early records, 1853 to 1900, have been microfilmed and are available at the Archives and History Library in Charleston (see Archives, Libraries, and Societies), the Virginia State Library (see Virginia), and the FHL. Certified copies of records from 1 January 1917 are available for a fee from West Virginia State Health Department, Division of Vital Statistics, Charleston, West Virginia 25305. The office accepts Visa or MasterCard charges as payment for requests made by phone. There is an additional fee including postal costs for this service. The Archives and History Library in Charleston has death certificates for 1917 to 1951 and delayed birth records from the 1880s to 1916.

Early Virginia law required church officials to record all marriages in registers. Most of the registers compiled in response to that law have not survived. Ministers were not required to forward a copy of the marriage entry to civil authorities until 1780. That requirement ended in 1853 when state law required county clerks to issue marriage licenses and keep marriage registers. Before a license was issued, the parties to be married had to fill out a form with the following information: full names, ages, places of birth and residence, proposed marriage date and place, marital status (widowed or single), parents' names, groom's occupation, and minister's name. After the marriage was performed, the minister returned the information to the clerk who recorded it in a marriage register with the date of the ceremony.

The FHL has filmed all early West Virginia county marriage records. Some early marriage records have been published and may be found in genealogical and local libraries with substantial genealogy collections. The West Virginia Division of Vital Statistics has marriage records from 1 January 1964, but a centralized index dates back to 1921. Send requests and fees to the address listed above.

County circuit court divorce records can be obtained from the clerk of the court at the county seat.

Census Records

Federal

Population Schedules.

- Indexed—(1810, 1820, 1830, 1840, 1850, 1860 [see Virginia]), 1870
- Soundex—1880, 1900, 1910 (Miracode), 1920

Industry and Agriculture Schedules.

- (1850, 1860 [see Virginia]), 1870, 1880

Mortality Schedules.

- (1850, 1860 [see Virginia]), 1870, 1880

Slave Schedules.

- (1850, 1860 [see Virginia])

Union Veterans Schedules.

- 1890

Since West Virginia was part of Virginia prior to 1863, see Virginia Census Records for all census records before that date. The agricultural and industrial returns for West Virginia after separation from Virginia, as well as the earlier ones for 1850 and 1860, are at the Archives and History Library in Charleston.

Transcripts of the 1870 census have been published for Barbour, Boone, Braxton, Calhoun, Doddridge, Gilmer, Lewis, Lincoln, McDowell, Mason, Monongalia, Pleasants, Ritchie, Roane, Tyler, Upshur, Wetzel, Wirt, and Wood counties. Indexes, by county, for *all* individuals listed in the 1880 census have been published for forty-three counties by William A. Marsh in an ongoing project. *Genealogical and Local History Books in Print* (see page 4) has further information.

Background Sources

The following publications are either guides for conducting research in West Virginia or publications including hundreds of biographical sketches about early West Virginia families. Many of those sketches contain ancestral lines and family migration patterns.

Brown, Stuart E., Jr. *Virginia Genealogical Resources.* Detroit, Mich.: Detroit Society for Genealogical Research, 1980.

Good, Rebecca H., and Rebecca A. Ebert. *Finding Your People in the Shenandoah Valley of Virginia.* Alexandria, Va.: Hearthside Press, 1988. A guide covering Berkeley, Hampshire, Jefferson, and Morgan counties in now West Virginia and Augusta, Clarke, Frederick, Pay, Rockingham, Shenandoah, and Warren counties in Virginia.

McGinnis, Carol. *West Virginia Genealogy Sources and Resources.* Baltimore, Md.: Genealogical Publishing Co., 1988. This recent guide provides a county-by-county breakdown of original source material and a thorough list of microfilms available in the state's repositories (see Archives, Libraries, and Societies).

Stewart, Robert Armistead. *Index to Printed Virginia Genealogies . . . 1930.* Reprint. Baltimore, Md.: Genealogical Publishing Co., 1970.

Stinson, Helen S. *A Handbook for Genealogical Research in West Virginia.* South Charleston, W.Va.: Kanawha Valley Genealogical Society, 1981.

Stinson, Helen S. *Fatalities in West Virginia Coal Mines, 1883–1925.* South Charleston, W.Va.: Stinson, 1985.

Swem, Earl Gregg. *Virginia Historical Index.* 1934–36. Reprint. (2 vols. in 4). Gloucester, Mass.: Peter Smith, 1965.

Wardell, P. G. *Timesaving Aid to Virginia-West Virginia Ancestors: A Genealogical Index of Surnames from Published Sources.* 3 vols. Athens, Ga.: Iberian Publishing Co., 1985.

West Virginia Heritage Encyclopedia. 25 vols. Richwood, W.Va.: Jim Comstock, 1976.

West Virginia Heritage Encyclopedia: Supplemental Series. 25 vols. Richwood, W.Va.: Jim Comstock, 1976.

Maps

Early Virginia maps are crucial to tracing colonial families on the Virginia/West Virginia frontier. See Virginia—Maps for a selected bibliography of early map sources. See also *New Descriptive Atlas of West Virginia* (Clarksburg, W.Va.: Clarksburg Publishing Co., 1933).

Present-day county road maps are available from West Virginia Department of Highways, Map Sales, 1900

Washington Street East, Charleston, West Virginia 25305, which include many cemetery locations.

The West Virginia and Regional History Collection (see Archives, Libraries, and Societies) and the FHL have substantial collections of West Virginia maps, including nineteenth century land ownership maps. See Edgar Barr Sims, *Making a State: Formation of West Virginia . . .* (Charleston, W. Va.: E. B. Sims, 1956).

Land Records

State-Land State

Much of western Virginia was settled by land speculators who formed land companies after 1744. Companies were awarded 1,000 acres of land for each family they moved into the area. A survey was made of each parcel of land, and then a survey was sold to individuals who received title to the land by patent from the secretary of the colony. After 1779 the Virginia Land Office issued the patents. Edgar Barr Sims, *Index to Land Grants in West Virginia* (Charleston, W. Va.: E. B. Sims, 1952), lists the names of grantees by county. See also *Making a State: Formation of West Virginia,* cited above for supplement to this index, and Gertrude E. Gray, *Virginia Northern Neck Land Grants,* 2 vols. (Baltimore, Md.: Genealogical Publishing Co., 1987, 1988), particularly Volume II that abstracts grants from 1742 to 1775, encompassing what are now Hampshire and Berkeley counties in West Virginia.

Some western Virginia lands were issued in redemption of military bounty-land warrants from Revolutionary War soldiers. While some soldiers settled the land they were granted, many sold their warrants to individuals or speculators.

Original state land grants, sales, and surveys for West Virginia are housed at the Office of State Auditor, Capitol Building, West Wing 231, Charleston, West Virginia 25305. Records on file at the Virginia State Library are also valuable for the colonial period.

When originally patented land was sold, the transaction was recorded in county deed books. Usually, deed books are indexed individually, and most West Virginia counties have general indexes to grantees and grantors to facilitate research. Copies of deeds can be obtained from county clerks or clerks of the circuit court; however, most county records in West Virginia have been microfilmed and are available at the Archives and History Library in Charleston and the FHL. County clerks are not always receptive to written inquiries, but records are open for research in person.

Probate Records

When western Virginia was a part of the Commonwealth of Virginia, estate records were produced by civil courts on the county level, such as county and circuit courts. Wills, administrations, guardianships, appraisals, and settlements are some of the records related to a person's estate or probate record. West Virginia continued in the same tradition by recording probate matters in the county courts. Most probate/estate matters were recorded in "will books." Original will books are available at the county clerk's office; however, most will books prior to 1968 have been microfilmed and are available at the Archives and History Library, West Virginia and Regional History Collection in Morgantown and the FHL. See Ross B. Johnston, *West Virginia Estate Settlements, 1753–1850* (Fort Worth, Tex.: American Reference Publishers, 1969), and Clayton Torrence, *Virginia Wills and Administrations, 1632–1800* (1930; reprint, Baltimore, Md.: Genealogical Publishing Co., 1965). Both of these works are useful to pinpoint the counties where a surname appeared during the early period.

A number of early Virginia and later West Virginia will books have been abstracted and published. The Archives and History Library in Charleston, West Virginia and Regional History Collection in Morgantown, and the FHL have collections of these works, and many other libraries nationwide have some printed will abstracts (see McGinnis in Background Sources).

Court Records

Since West Virginia was a part of Virginia until 1863, its court system matches that of the parent state (see Virginia—Court Records). The Historical Records Survey Collection on microfilm at the West Virginia and Regional History Collection and the FHL includes court minutes and order books (see McGinnis in Background Sources). Usually intermingled in court records, particularly those for the county's circuit court, are naturalizations, emancipation records for blacks, school commissioners' reports, and cattle brands.

Tax Records

While people were taxed in Virginia prior to 1782, not many tax lists for that early period have survived, and the originals that have survived are at the Virginia State Library. Colonial period taxes were imposed on the personal property of males who were twenty-one and older, and called "tithables." While there is no comprehensive list or collection of early tax lists, many fragments are printed throughout Virginia genealogical literature (see Virginia—Tax Records).

West Virginia has one of the most complete sets of old tax records in existence. Land tax records dating from 1782 to 1936 for all counties, with some through 1959, are available at the Archives and History Library in Charleston. Most county clerks have duplicate copies in their offices. As noted in the section on Virginia, the Virginia State Library has the original unindexed personal property tax records from 1782 to 1863.

Cemetery Records

The most extensive collection of West Virginia tombstone inscriptions was compiled by the Historical Records Survey. Available at the West Virginia and Regional History Collection and on microfilm at the FHL, the collection includes inscriptions through 1939–40. The DAR and others have published volumes of cemetery records (see page 6).

Church Records

With the arrival of English and Scots-Irish settlers came West Virginia's early dominant religions. Many families of English origin were Quakers and the Scots-Irish were Presbyterians. Both religions were well established by 1740, and they were followed by Baptists who settled in Berkeley County in 1743 and a Methodist circuit in Berkeley and Jefferson counties in 1778. For a complete discussion of early church records, see Virginia—Church Records.

Since colonial times dozens of religious groups have established congregations in West Virginia including the following: Baptist, West Virginia Baptist Historical Society, P.O. Box 1019, Parkersburg, West Virginia 26101; Methodist, Methodist Historical Society, West Virginia Wesleyan College, Annie M. Pfeiffer Library, College Avenue, Buckhannon, West Virginia 26201; Roman Catholic, Diocese of Wheeling/Charleston, P.O. Box 230, Wheeling, West Virginia 26003; and United Brethren, Historical Library, Church of the Brethren, 1451 Dundee Avenue, Elgin, Illinois 60120, denominations.

Many religious groups have deposited their records at the West Virginia and Regional History Collection. Church record inventories compiled as part of the Historical Records Survey are available there and at the FHL.

Military Records

Virginia's early military history is also West Virginia's (see Virginia—Military Records). Virgil A. Lewis, *The Soldiery of West Virginia* (1911; reprint, Baltimore, Md.: Genealogical Publishing Co., 1978), contains rosters of soldiers from West Virginia who served in the French and Indian War, Indian Wars, Lord Dunmore's War, Revolutionary War, Whiskey Rebellion of 1794, War of 1812, Mexican War, and the Civil War. A companion edition, Paul Berckefeldt, ed., *Index to the Soldiery of West Virginia* (Pueblo, Colo.: Pathfinders Books, 1985), is available. Ross B. Johnson, *West Virginians in the American Revolution* (Baltimore, Md.: Genealogical Publishing Co., 1977), is considered a most complete list. Anne Waller Reddy, *West Virginia Revolutionary Ancestors* (Baltimore, Md.: Genealogical Publishing Co., 1973), indexes claims reviewed by the "court of claims" for nonmilitary service.

West Virginia's military divergence came during the Civil War. At the Virginia secession convention in 1861, a majority of the state's western delegates opposed secession. In subsequent meetings at Wheeling, dominated by the western delegates, the ordinance of secession was declared an illegal attempt to overthrow the federal government. The second Wheeling convention pronounced the Richmond government void, established a restored government of Virginia, and provided for the election of new state officers. The restored governor secured federal recognition and maintained civil jurisdiction over the region until Congress admitted West Virginia to the Union on 20 June 1863 on the condition that slaves in the region were emancipated.

Although nearly 10,000 West Virginians fought for the Confederacy, most of the state's Civil War soldiers served in the Union Army. For Confederate soldiers, see Consolidated Index to Confederate Service Records microfilmed by the National Archives and available at the FHL. Compiled service records are also available in those places.

The Archives and History Library and the West Virginia and Regional History Collection have collections of published military records and indexes.

Over 200 West Virginia soldiers made claims of damage for the Civil War from the Southern Claims Commission. Those found in Gary B. Mills, *Civil War Claims in the South: an Index of Civil War Damage Claims Filed Before the Southern Claims Commission, 1871–1880* (Laguna Hills, Calif.: Aegean Park Press, 1980), are listed in McGinnis (see Background Sources).

Periodicals, Newspapers, and Manuscript Collections

Periodicals

Most West Virginia counties have organized genealogical or historical societies, some of which publish excellent quarterly periodicals (see McGinnis under Background Sources). For the pre-statehood period, see the section on Virginia for bibliographical citations of the most valuable and widely used genealogical periodicals and their appropriate indexes.

Newspapers

West Virginia newspaper collections are at the Archives and History Library and the West Virginia and Regional History Collection. See Barbara Mertin, *Newspapers in the West Virginia University Library* (Morgantown, W.Va.: West Virginia University Library, 1973). Most newspapers have been microfilmed and a large collection is available at the FHL as well.

Manuscripts

West Virginia has extensive published genealogies and manuscript collections. Three examples include the following:

Smith-Riffe Collection of New River Genealogy and Local History. This collection pertains to Boone, Fayette, Greenbrier, Mercer, Monroe, Raleigh, and Wyoming counties and is located at the Archives and History Library in Charleston and on microfilm through the FHL.

Elisha B. Iams Collection. This card index of 6,500 entries consists of more than seventy volumes of extracted records from sixteen counties in southwest Pennsylvania, West Virginia, and Ohio. It can be searched at Citizen's Library, 55 South College Street, Washington, Pennsylvania 15301.

Willis Guy Tetrick Collection. The Tetrick Collection consists primarily of family group records compiled by family members living in central West Virginia. Some records contain extensive genealogical information, and although others are less complete, they offer excellent clues to follow. While cataloged under Harrison County in the FHL, this collection has information about residents of surrounding counties. The original collection is at the West Virginia and Regional History Collection and also available on microfilm. Since many ancestors mentioned in Tetrick's collection came from counties outside the immediate Harrison County area, it is a good idea to check this source.

Archives, Libraries, and Societies

Archives and History Library
Division of Culture and History
Cultural Center, Capitol Complex
Charleston, WV 25305

Publication: *West Virginia History*. This facility consists of the library, archives, and a museum containing materials from 1760 to present.

West Virginia Historical Society
Division of Culture and History
Cultural Center, Capitol Complex
Charleston, WV 25305

The society does not maintain historical or genealogical collections. Write to the Archives and History Library above for information.

West Virginia and Regional History Collection
West Virginia University Library
Colson Hall
Morgantown, WV 26506

This extensive collection, outlined in above categories, includes the Historical Records Survey for West Virginia on microfilm along with the largest collection of West Virginia newspapers and many unpublished family papers. A *Guide to Manuscripts and Archives in the West Virginia Collection*, available from the library, catalogs the holdings.

West Virginia Genealogical Society
P.O. Box 172
Elkview, WV 25071

Special Focus Categories

Black American

West Virginia entered the Union as a separate state under the condition that slaves would be freed. Since West Virginia was a part of Virginia during the slavery era, see Virginia—Black American.

Coal Mining

Woven into West Virginia's history is that of the coal miner. Regarding coal mine accidents, the following may be helpful:

Dillon, Lacy A. *They Died in the Darkness*. Parsons, W.Va.: McClain Printing Co., 1976.

———. *They Died for King Coal*. Winona, Minn.: Apollo Books, 1985.

Stinson, Helen S. *Fatalities in West Virginia Coal Mines, 1883–1925*. N.p.: the author, 1985.

County Resources

The bulk of counties that would later comprise West Virginia were formed within the 130 years before statehood as Virginia counties. The county resources are good with much material being available in the courthouse and the two major repositories at Morgantown and Charleston. In the chart that follows, the address of the courthouse is given. Some counties will answer mail inquiries, some charge a fee, and some request research in person. Much of the microfilm available in both of the above repositories can be viewed through the FHL loan service (see page 9).

Land, probate, and vital records are all located at the county clerk's office at the county seat. Court records, including those naturalizations and divorces that were recorded there, are at the circuit court clerk's office at the county seat.

In addition to the sources listed on page 11, the following have been used for this state:

West Virginia County Formations and Boundary Changes. Charleston, W.Va.: Historical Records Survey, 1939.

Sims, Edgar Barr. *Making a State: Formation of West Virginia . . .* Charleston, W.Va.: E. B. Sims, 1956.

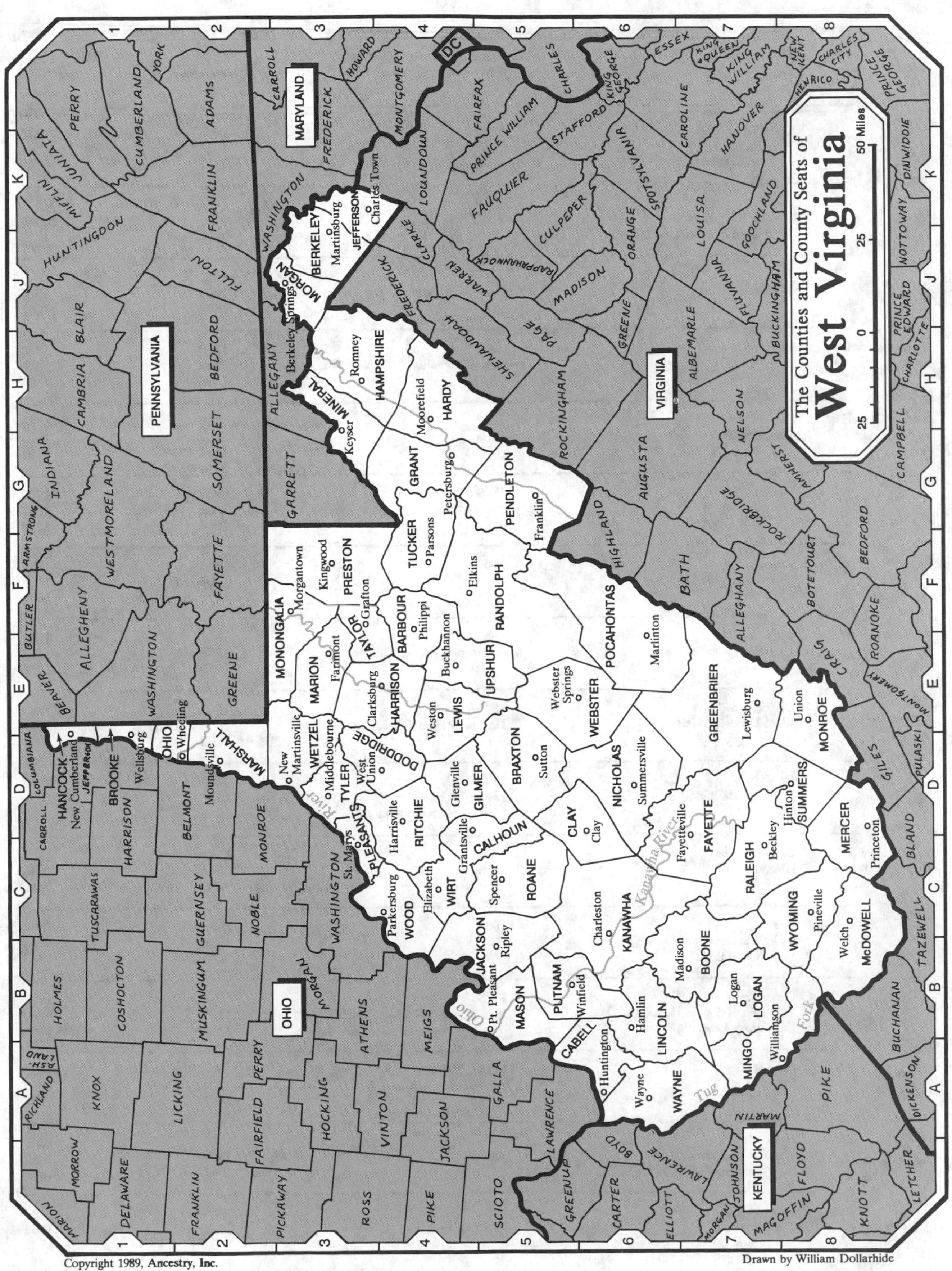

Drawn by William Dollarhide

Map	County Address	Date Formed Parent County/ies	Birth Marriage Death	Land Probate Court
F4	Barbour P.O. Box 301 Philippi 26416	1843 Harrison/Lewis/Randolph	1853 1843 1853	1843 1843 1843
J3	Berkeley 100 W. King Street Martinsburg 25401	1772 Frederick, Va.	1865 1781 1865	1772 1772 1772
B7	Boone Madison 25130	1847 Kanawha/Cabell/Logan	1865 1865 1865	1847 1865 1865
D5	Braxton P.O. Box 486 Sutton 26601	1836 Lewis/Nicholas	1858 1836 1858	1836 1836 1836
E1	Brooke P.O. Box 272 Wellsburg 26070	1797 Ohio	1853 1797 1853	1797 1797 1797
A6	Cabell Huntington 25701	1809 Kanawha	1853 1809 1853	1808 1809 1809
D5	Calhoun Grantsville 26147	1856 Gilmer	1856 1856 1856	1856 1856 1856
C6	Clay Clay 25043	1858 Braxton/Nicholas/Kanawha	1858 1858 1858	1858 1858 1858
D3	Doddridge West Union 26456	1845 Harrison/Tyler/Ritchie/Lewis	1853 1845 1862	1845 1849 1845
D7	Fayette Fayetteville 25840	1831 Logan/Nicholas/ Greenbrier/Kanawha	1866 1831 1831	1831 1832 1831
D4	Gilmer Glenville 26351	1845 Lewis/Kanawha	1853 1845 1853	1845 1845 1845
G4	Grant 5 Highland Avenue Petersburg 26847	1866 Hardy	1866 1866 1866	1866 1866 1866
E7	Greenbrier P.O. Box 506 Lewisburg 24901	1778 Montgomery, Va./Botetourt, Va.	1853 1781 1853	1780 1780 1780
H3	Hampshire Romney 26757	1754 Frederick, Va./Augusta, Va.	1865 1824 1865	1757 1756 1736
E1	Hancock 102 N. Court Street New Cumberland 26047	1848 Brooke	1853 1854 1853	1848 1848 1848
H4	Hardy P.O. Box 540 Moorefield 26836	1786 Hampshire	1853 1795 1853	1786 1786 1786

Map	County Address	Date Formed Parent County/ies	Birth Marriage Death	Land Probate Court
E4	Harrison 301 W. Main Clarksburg 26301	1784 Monongalia	1853 1784 1853	1786 1788 1784
B5	Jackson Ripley 25271	1831 Mason/Wood/Kanawha	1853 1831 1853	1831 1831 1831
K3	Jefferson Charles Town 25414	1801 Berkeley	1853 1801 1853	1801 1801 1801
C6	Kanawha P.O. Box 3226 Charleston 25332	1788 Greenbrier/Montgomery	1853 1792 1853	1790 1789 1773
E4	Lewis P.O. Box 87 Weston 26452	1816 Harrison	1853 1816 1853	1817 1816 1817
B6	Lincoln Hamlin 25523	1867–69 Boone/Cabell/Logan/ Kanawha/Wayne	1909 1909 1909	1909 1909 1909
B7	Logan Logan 25601	1824 Giles, Va./Cabell/ Tazewell, Va./Kanawha	1872 1872 1872	1824 1873 1824
E3	Marion Fairmont 26554	1842 Monongalia/Harrison	1860 1842 1842	1842 1842 1842
D2	Marshall P.O. Box 459 Moundsville 26041	1835 Ohio	1853 1835 1853	1835 1835 1835
B5	Mason Point Pleasant 25550	1804 Kanawha	1853 1806 1853	1803 1805 1805
B8	McDowell P.O. Box 967 Welch 24801	1858 Tazewell, Va.	1872 1859 1894	1868 1893 1859
D8	Mercer Princeton 24740	1837 Giles, Va./Tazewell, Va.	1853 1853 1853	1837 1837 1837
H3	Mineral P.O. Box 250 Keyser 26726	1866 Hampshire	1866 1866 1866	1866 1866 1866
A7	Mingo P.O. Box 1197 Williamson 25661	1895 Logan	1895 1895 1895	1895 1895 1895
E3	Monongalia Morgantown 26505	1776 District of West Augusta, Va.	1853 1796 1853	1776 (index) 1774 1774
E8	Monroe Union 24983	1799 Greenbrier	1853 1799 1853	1799 1799 1799

Map	County Address	Date Formed Parent County/ies	Birth Marriage Death	Land Probate Court
J3	Morgan Fairfax Street Berkeley Springs 25411	1820 Berkeley/Hampshire	1865 1820 1865	1820 1820 1820
D6	Nicholas Summersville 26651	1818 Greenbrier/Kanawha/Randolph	1853 1817 1853	1818 1820 1818
D2	Ohio City County Building Wheeling 26003	1776 District of West Augusta, Va.	1853 1793 1853	1778 1776 1777
G5	Pendleton Franklin 26807	1788 Augusta, Va./Hardy/ Rockingham, Va.	1853 1800 1853	1789 1789 1789
C3	Pleasants St. Marys 26170	1851 Wood/Tyler/Ritchie	1853 1853 1853	1851 1852 1851
E6	Pocahontas 900 C 10th Avenue Marlinton 24954	1821 Bath, Va./Randolph/Pendleton	1853 1822 1853	1822 1822 1822
F3	Preston 101 W. Main Kingwood 26537	1818 Monongalia	1868 1869 1868	1818 1869 1881
B5	Putnam P.O. Box 508 Winfield 25213	1848 Kanawha/Cabell/Mason	1854 1848 1853	1848 1848 1848
C7	Raleigh Beckley 25801	1850 Fayette	1853 1850 1853	1850 1850 1850
F5	Randolph Elkins 26241	1787 Harrison	1856 1787 1853	1787 1787 1787
D4	Ritchie Harrisville 26362	1842 Harrison/Lewis/Wood	1853 1843 1853	1844 1843 1844
C5	Roane Spencer 25276	1856 Kanawha/Calhoun/Jackson	1856 1856 1856	1856 1856 1856
D8	Summers P.O. Box 97 Hinton 25951	1871 Fayette/Mercer/Greenbrier/Monroe	1871 1871 1871	1871 1871 1871
E3	Taylor Grafton 26354	1844 Harrison/Barbour/Marion	1853 1853 1853	1844 1844 1844
F4	Tucker Parsons 26287	1856 Randolph	1856 1856 1856	1856 1856 1856
D3	Tyler P.O. Box 66 Middlebourne 26149	1814 Ohio	1853 1815 1853	1813 1815 1815

Map	County Address	Date Formed Parent County/ies	Birth Marriage Death	Land Probate Court
E5	Upshur Buckhannon 26201	1851 Randolph/Lewis/Barbour	1853 1853 1853	1851 1852 1851
A6	Wayne Wayne 25570	1842 Cabell	1853 1853 1853	1842 1843 1842
E5	Webster Webster Springs 26268	1860 Nicholas/Braxton/Randolph	1887 1887 1887	1887 1887 1887
D3	Wetzel P.O. Box 156 New Martinsville 26155	1846 Tyler	1854 1845 (index) 1854	1846 1847 1846
C4	Wirt P.O. Box 53 Elizabeth 26143	1848 Wood/Jackson	1870 1854 1870	1848 1848 1848
C4	Wood Parkersburg 26101	1798 Harrison	1853 1800 1853	1798 1800 1798
C8	Wyoming P.O. Box 309 Pineville 24874	1850 Logan	1853 1855 1853	1850 1850 1850

WISCONSIN

Carol L. Maki

Called the "fairest portion of the Great West," Wisconsin was first observed by Europeans in 1634. Late that summer a young but seasoned voyageur, Jean Nicolet, sent by New France, arrived at Red Banks on the Green Bay of Lake Michigan. He explored the area and returned to Canada to explain to Samuel de Champlain that he had not found the passage to China. In the spring and summer of 1673, Louis Joliet, a cartographer and explorer, Father Jacques Marquette, and five others made a journey that would greatly expand the French knowledge of this territory. The course of their canoes was guided by two Miami-nation guides down the Fox, Wisconsin, and Mississippi rivers. They traversed the Mississippi south to a Quapaw village near the present boundary of Arkansas and Louisiana.

Nicolas Perrot, born in France about 1644, and Toussaint Baudry, one of his partners in a trading company in New France (Canada), visited Green Bay in 1668 by invitation of the Potawatomi they had met in an earlier visit at Chequamegon Bay. Perrot, known as an expert in tribal diplomacy, visited many natives, creating valuable alliances with them. His influence with the Wisconsin tribes continued at least through 1698.

Jesuit Father Claude Allouez opened a mission in 1669 in what is now Brown County. It became a major point in the French fur-trading empire until it was closed in 1728. Fort Francis, built on the Fox River in 1717, was rebuilt by the British as Fort Edward Augustus, establishing their presence in the area in 1763. Charles de Langlade and his family arrived at Green Bay in 1765, establishing the first permanent white settlement in Wisconsin.

The Treaty of Paris in 1783 theoretically put Wisconsin under U.S. control, although in reality the British were in command of the area. Four years later Wisconsin was included in the newly organized Northwest Territory and in 1800 was included in Indiana Territory. When Michigan Territory was created in 1805, it left Wisconsin in Indiana Territory. On 3 February 1809, Wisconsin, except for the Door County Peninsula, became part of Illinois Territory. Nine years later Illinois became a state, and Wisconsin was redefined as Michigan Territory. Wisconsin became a territory in 1836 and a state in 1848.

Two years after statehood, the population of Wisconsin was over 300,000. The ratio of American-born to foreign-born was two to one, with immigrants' birthplaces being Canada, England, Switzerland, Germany, Ireland, Wales, the Netherlands, and Norway. Approximately one-fifth of the American-born were Wisconsin-born, and most were children. The migrants came from Ohio, Indiana, Illinois, Michigan, New England, New York, the mid-Atlantic, and the South. New Yorkers numbered about 68,600 in Wisconsin in 1850 (see Smith in Background Sources).

A few generalizations are important in researching immigrant or migrant Wisconsin ancestors. Most of them traveled directly from their home state or their port of debarkation. Some Germans and some Dutch stayed temporarily in the east for financial reasons, and the Irish often took years to work their way west from the east coast or Canada. Those from New York, Pennsylvania, and New England traditionally made the journey in stages, as indicated by birth records for their children which may be found from the Northeast through Ohio, Indiana, and Illinois.

Vital Records

Wisconsin issued marriage applications as early as the 1820s in some counties, although most jurisdictions began maintaining them with county organization. The state directed the counties, in 1852, to record births and deaths, a mandate generally ignored. In 1878 a similar law received more attention and adherence. A separate volume was kept for recording births which had occurred prior to 1852. The earliest delayed birth record dates to 1746.

However, it was 1907 before the State Bureau of Vital Statistics was established. Researchers may apply to this office for records (certified, for descendants) of births, deaths, and marriages. The nonrefundable charges are presently $10 for births and $7 for deaths and marriages. A self-addressed stamped envelope is required. The address is State of Wisconsin Department of Health and Social Services, Division of Health, 1 West Wilson Street, P.O. Box 309, Madison, Wisconsin 53701-0309.

On-site searching in the state vital records is possible with advance appointments at particular hours and on particular days, for one-hour time blocks. Contact the office for complete information on this procedure before traveling to Madison. Some records are not accessible.

Vital records at the county level are held by the register of deeds at each county government center. Indexes and original records may be searched within established guidelines. Photocopies or certificates of county records can be obtained at the same rate schedule as the state's.

Of great value to the genealogist in Wisconsin is the statewide microfiche index to the births, deaths, and marriages recorded in the state prior to October 1907. The State Historical Society of Wisconsin, all Area Research Centers (see Archives, Libraries, and Societies), and the FHL hold copies of this index that has to be searched in person. The State Historical Society of Wisconsin Library at Madison has microfilmed copies of all the actual records referred to in the index, and each Area Research Center has those microfilmed records for the counties covered by that center. There will be some records at the county level not included in the statewide index. Some specific counties are not indexed for specific types of vital events. In the marriage records index, for example, the entries for Racine County are incomplete, and counties following Racine alphabetically are not included. It is necessary to go directly to the microfilm records for those counties to locate marriage records. However, the index is a tool that should certainly be used in Wisconsin research.

Divorce records are usually found in the county government centers and most often in the civil court records. Post-1907 divorce decrees, although they actually contain very little genealogical information, can be located at the State Bureau of Vital Statistics. From 1836 through 1848, the territorial legislature granted the divorces listed in the *Wisconsin State Genealogical Society Newsletter* (April, 1980).

The "Wisconsin Necrology" at the State Historical Society of Wisconsin is a collection of several thousand selected obituaries of Wisconsin citizens (1890–1945). The obituaries are in scrapbooks that are indexed in the library's subject and printed card catalogs. The scrapbooks have been microfilmed and are available on interlibrary loan.

Other obituary indexes can be located in numerous local libraries and in some Area Research Centers. Some early vital records have been extracted and published in state and county genealogical periodicals.

Census Records

Federal

Population Schedules.

- Indexed—1820 and 1830 (as Michigan Territory), 1840, 1850, 1860, 1870
- Soundex—1880, 1900, 1920
- Unindexed—1910

Industry and Agriculture Schedules.

- 1850, 1860, 1870, 1880

Mortality Schedules.

- 1850, 1860, 1870, 1880

Union Veterans Schedules.

- 1890

All federal census schedules, for all states, are at the State Historical Society of Wisconsin. The society also has original *state* copy manuscripts of the 1850, 1860, and 1870 federal census for Wisconsin. Every-name indexes to the state copies of the 1850, 1860 and 1870 censuses, on microfilm, are available on interlibrary loan from that repository. There may be variations between the state and federal copies of the federal population censuses. Mortality schedules are indexed and available on interlibrary loan, except for the 1880, which is microfilmed, not indexed, and noncirculating. The 1820–70 censuses for Wisconsin were indexed by the WPA, listing each individual within the state in a given census year.

Territorial and State

When the territorial government of Wisconsin was established on 20 April 1836, it provided that an enumeration of the inhabitants of the several counties in the territory be taken by the sheriffs and sent to the governor before the election. This first Wisconsin census did not have preprinted forms. The sheriffs wrote the names of heads of white families with number of persons in each family divided by sex and age in four groups. The sheriff of Crawford County regrouped his constituents who were deaf and dumb, or blind, and included tables of aliens and "slaves and coloured." Some heads of households on this census appear to have unusually large families. It appears, for example, that in Brown County, Daniel Whitney's "family" of forty-nine included his workmen in sawmills, lumber camps, and at the Helena shot-tower.

Wisconsin territorial and state census original schedules, with a few exceptions, are in the State Archives at the State Historical Society of Wisconsin. Microfilm copies are available in the microforms reading room, on interlibrary loan, and for purchase. They include the following:

1836 (AISI index): Names only head of household, plus numeric listing of household; published in *Wisconsin Historical Collections* 13 (1895): 247–70.

1838 (AISI index): Includes name of master, mistress, steward, overseer, or other principal person; name of head of family and numeric listing of household; extant only for certain counties.

1842 (AISI index): Similar to 1838.

1846: Includes name of head of family; numeric listing of household by sex and color; some counties missing.

1847: Same as 1846; some counties missing.

1855 (AISI index): Similar to 1847, plus number of deaf and dumb, blind, or insane; includes number of individuals in each household of foreign birth; Kewaunee County not included.

1865: Listing same as 1855; schedules apparently destroyed at an unknown date; some schedules survived at the county level (Dunn, Green, Jackson, Kewaunee, Ozaukee, and Sheboygan).

1875: Listing similar to 1865.

1885: Listing similar to 1865, plus some additional information on number of foreign-born persons and a special enumeration of "Soldiers and Sailors of the Late War."

1895: Same as 1885, including veterans' schedules.

1905: Includes name of each individual, relationship to head of household, color or race, sex, age at last birthday, marital status, place of birth, place of birth of parents, occupation, number of months employed, whether home or farm is owned or rented; also includes veterans' enumeration; indexed, by county, on microfilm.

A very complete listing of Wisconsin Territorial and State Censuses is in James P. Danky, *Genealogical Research: An Introduction to the Resources of the State Historical Society of Wisconsin* (Madison, Wis.: State Historical Society of Wisconsin, 1986).

Local census enumerations were taken between 1848 and 1959, ordered for qualification as a municipality by the state. Copies were required to be kept by the county register of deeds and the village or city clerk. Some of these censuses have been found in circuit court files.

Evidence of migration to Wisconsin through the upper Great Lakes may be found in Donna Valley Russell, *Michigan Censuses 1710–1830 Under the French, British and Americans* (Detroit, Mich.: Detroit Society for Genealogical Research, 1982). Canadian voyageurs may be found in the same author's *Michigan Voyageurs, From the Notary Book of Samuel Abbott, Mackinac Island 1807–1817* (Detroit, Mich.: Detroit Society for Genealogical Research, 1982).

City directories for urban areas may help fill the gaps where census records are nonexistent. The State Historical Society of Wisconsin has an extensive collection that includes directories for Milwaukee as early as 1846 and several cities for the 1850s. Local libraries, historical societies, and the Area Research Centers network may have directories for their specific locales.

Background Sources

Initial or advanced genealogical research in Wisconsin should include the Wisconsin chapter by James L. Hansen in volume two of *Genealogical Research: Methods and Sources,* edited by Kenn Stryker-Rodda (Washington, D.C.: American Society of Genealogists, 1983).

There is an abundance of county histories for the state of Wisconsin. Some are written for individual or several counties and others for sections of the state, such as John G. Gregory, *Southwestern Wisconsin: A History of Old Crawford County,* 4 vols. (Chicago, Ill.: S. J. Clark Pub. Co., 1932). Wisconsin State Genealogical Society (see Archives, Libraries, and Societies) has published every-name indexes to a large number of these county and regional histories. Most, if not all, of the older histories are microfilmed and included in *County Histories of the Old Northwest Series 1: Wisconsin* (New Haven, Conn.: Research Publications, n.d.). This microfilm is available on interlibrary loan through the State Historical Society of Wisconsin. The films also include county directories, atlases, plat books, city histories, and biographical compendiums.

For territorial and early state history, the twenty volumes of Lyman Copeland Draper and Reuben Gold Thwaites, eds., *Collections of the State Historical Society of Wisconsin* (Madison, Wis.: the society, n.d.), are outstanding. The scope of the volumes covers every aspect of Wisconsin's creation, from official documents, census enumerations, and the very earliest baptism and marriage records at Mackinac. Augustin Grignon's "Seventy-two Years' Recollections" (volume 3) and James H. Lockwood's "Early Times and Events in Wisconsin" (volume 2) are personal and detailed accounts of early Wisconsin, including many notations on early settlers. Each volume of the *Collections* is indexed. Volume 21 is an all-volume index. Major research libraries should have the complete set.

Highly recommended is the *History of Wisconsin* series published by the State Historical Society of Wisconsin between 1973–90 as follows (volume 4 has yet to be published):

Smith, Alice E. *From Exploration to Statehood* (volume 1).

Current, Richard N. *The Civil War Era, 1848–1873* (volume 2).

Nesbit, Robert C. *Urbanization and Industrialization, 1873–1893* (volume 3).

Glad, Paul W. *War, a New Era and Depression, 1914–1940* (volume 5).

Thompson, William F. *Continuity and Change, 1940–1965* (volume 6).

For a concise one volume history, see Robert C. Nesbit, *Wisconsin: A History,* 2d ed. (Madison, Wis.: State Historical Society of Wisconsin, University of Wisconsin Press, 1989).

Maps

The State Historical Society of Wisconsin has microfilm copies of Wisconsin county plat books, ca. 1870–1900, which are accessible on interlibrary loan. Earlier county plat maps are not microfilmed but can be photocopied on request. State atlases were published for Wisconsin in 1876, 1878, and 1881, and include county maps. They show post offices, schools, churches, and road systems, all valuable information in locating an ancestral family in Wisconsin.

Michael Fox's *Maps and Atlases Showing Land Ownership in Wisconsin* (Madison, Wis., 1978) is very important in determining precisely what maps are available at the State Historical Society of Wisconsin.

Aerial photographs of Wisconsin are in the collection of the Arthur Robinson Map Library, Science Hall, University of Wisconsin, Madison. The first topographical map of Wisconsin, of the Stoughton quadrangle, is dated 1889. Bird's-eye view maps are significant for Wisconsin research, inasmuch as they cover the period from 1867 to the end of World War I. There are over 200 for Wisconsin towns and villages. Most are listed in Elizabeth Maule, *Bird's Eye View of Wisconsin Communities* (Madison, Wis., 1977), and available at the State Historical Society of Wisconsin. The maps were drawn with great attention to the buildings existing at the time.

The Golda Meir Library at the University of Wisconsin, Milwaukee, holds the map collection of the American Geographical and Statistical Society. The worldwide collection includes thousands of bound books, maps, gazetteers, and photographs. A unique cataloging program at this repository references maps that appear in books. Queries by mail or phone are answered, most material can be photocopied, and some holdings may be borrowed on interlibrary loan. The library is located at 2311 E. Hartford Avenue, Milwaukee; the mailing address is the American Geographical Society Collection, University of Wisconsin, Milwaukee Library, P.O. Box 399, Milwaukee, Wisconsin 53201.

Robert E. Grad and L. G. Sorden, *The Romance of Wisconsin Place Names* (1968. Reprint. Minocqua, Wis.: Heartland Press, 1988), has an alphabetical list of towns and cities, county in which they are located, and a brief history.

The earliest Sanborn map (see page 4) for Wisconsin is 1883.

Land Records

Public-Domain State

Being a public-domain state, Wisconsin was divided into a grid of 1,554 townships by the GLO survey crews. The earliest land office was at Mineral Point, opening on 10 November 1834. Land that is presently Grant County, with the exception of mineral land, was available at that time. The local records of the nine GLO district offices are at the Commissioner of Public Lands, 127 West Washington Avenue, Madison, Wisconsin 53703. Many records of the Commissioners of Public Lands are in the State Archives, State Historical Society of Wisconsin. These include, for example, copies of original federal survey plat books, 1834–58. The State Archives, State Historical Society of Wisconsin, holds copies of all Wisconsin Local Land Office Tract Books, showing original owners or recipients of most land in Wisconsin. The BLM Eastern States Land Office in Alexandria, Virginia (see page 5), has patents, copies of tract books, and township plats. The National Archives has land-entry case files. See Alexander F. Pratt, "Reminiscences of Wisconsin," in *Collections of the State Historical Society of Wisconsin*, Vol. 1, Lyman Copeland Draper, ed. (1855; reprint, Madison, Wis.: State Historical Society of Wisconsin, 1855), page 137, in regard to claims associations near Milwaukee in the late 1830s.

Subsequent land transactions after initial ownership are recorded in the county's register of deeds. Most counties have grantor/grantee indexes to their land records.

Additional information is available in Paul W. Gates, "Frontier Land Business in Wisconsin," *Wisconsin Magazine of History* 52 (1962): 306–27; and Frederick N. Trowbridge, "Confirming Land Titles in Early Wisconsin," *Wisconsin Magazine of History* 26 (1942): 314–22.

Probate Records

Probate records in Wisconsin include wills, guardianship, administrator or executor bonds, and inventories. They are the responsibility of the register of probate for the county. Records were usually established with the formation of the county. The FHL has microfilmed some Wisconsin probate files.

Court Records

The Northwest Ordinance provided a flexible framework of government that operated in the region until Wisconsin Territory was formed in 1836. Government control over the area of Wisconsin was, however, minimal during the territorial periods. Civil law at the wilderness outposts of Prairie du Chien and Green Bay was difficult, if not impossible. Travel was dangerous, literate citizens were few and far between, and the upper Mississippi fur-trading frontier seemed somewhat capable of governing itself.

Beginning in the 1820s justices of the peace were appointed. Early records from Green Bay's justices of the peace can be found in the Grignon, Lawe, and Porlier Papers, 1712–1884, at the State Historical Society of Wisconsin.

Lewis Cass, who had been appointed governor of Michigan Territory in 1813, began making county divisions and announcing civil offices in 1818. The justice courts dealt with minor civil cases of $20 or less. County courts covered civil cases not to exceed $1,000 and noncapital criminal cases. The supreme court, meeting annually in Detroit, had jurisdiction for larger civil cases, appeals from lower courts, and capital criminal cases. In the winter of 1822–23, a separate circuit court was established for the three western counties of Michigan Territory. The new court was, in effect, a supreme court. It was not given a title, however, and was generally called an "additional court." Native Americans accused of crimes were not included in the jurisdiction of the court unless a white person was involved.

When Wisconsin Territory was created in 1836 the judicial system included a supreme court, district courts, probate courts, and justice of the peace courts, which were retained when statehood was attained in 1848. There were territorial courts in Green Bay, Prairie du Chien, and Mineral Point.

County Government in Wisconsin, Vol. 2 (Madison, Wis.: Wisconsin Historical Records Survey, 1942), explains the creation, structure, and function of courts in Wisconsin. Probate and related files can be found in the county courts, while criminal and civil cases are in the circuit courts. Old court records are generally still located in the county's courthouse.

Tax Records

The earliest tax records in Wisconsin appear to be for real estate. Brown County has an extant tax roll for 1824. Tax rolls are kept by the county treasurer for each county. Many of these records have been transferred to the appropriate Area Research Centers.

Cemetery Records

Numerous cemeteries have been read and transcribed by local genealogical societies in Wisconsin. The transcriptions are frequently deposited with an Area Research Center, a local library, or the State Historical Society of Wisconsin. A considerable number have been printed in the Wisconsin State Genealogical Society *Newsletter*. Some have been privately published.

The Wisconsin State Old Cemetery Society, 3325 S. 26th Street, #18, Milwaukee, Wisconsin 53215, publishes a newsletter and maintains an archive of tombstone inscriptions from around the state. Contact the society for membership information.

Church Records

Religion of the European in Wisconsin began with the French when Father René Ménard, born in Paris in 1605 and the first Jesuit sent from Canada to Wisconsin, offered the first mass in the state in 1661. Beginning in 1687, the missions became almost nonexistent in Wisconsin because of problems with the natives and the British government in control.

Father Bonduel wrote of Green Bay, "The Catholics of this little French colony lived sometimes ten, twenty, and thirty years without seeing a priest." Marriages and baptisms in the state were often officiated by missionary priests, resulting in large numbers of Catholic records in Wisconsin either being lost or sometimes located in repositories in Quebec Province, Canada. Tracing Catholic families in Wisconsin could require searching French-Canadian records. Some of the oldest Catholic marriage and baptism records for Wisconsin are in the "Mackinac Register" in *Collections of the State Historical Society of Wisconsin* (see Background Sources).

When the American flag first flew over eastern Wisconsin in 1816, the Catholic religion again took a firm hold among the French settlers in the state. European immigration and American migration brought other religious affiliations, but the heavy German and Irish settlement in the state provided for continued numbers in the Roman Catholic denomination.

Missionary clergy for other denominations in the state frequently took their records with them as they traveled from place to place. Therefore, although searching for church records in Wisconsin should begin with the local church, denominational archives and headquarters might have helpful material.

The most widely represented Protestants in Wisconsin were the Lutherans, the first faithful of that group coming from Germany and Scandinavia. Despite divisions, dissensions, and reorganizations within the Lutherans, they remain a religious force in the upper Midwest.

Smaller numbers of Methodists, Episcopalians, and Congregationalists also settled in Wisconsin. In 1834 the first Baptist church was established in the state by Brotherton Indians on the east shore of Lake Winnebago.

The Wisconsin Historical Records Survey Project of Madison published the *Directory of Churches and Religious Organizations in Wisconsin* in 1941 and *Guide to Church Vital Statistics Records in Wisconsin* in 1942. There are also numerous publications by the project for specific denominations. Extensive microfilm collections of church records in Wisconsin are available through the FHL. The State Historical Society of Wisconsin and Area Research Centers have a variety of church records including microfilm and original records.

Military Records

The State Historical Society of Wisconsin has very few records of Wisconsin residents involved in military action prior to the Civil War. When beginning a search for a Wisconsin Civil War veteran consult:

Wisconsin. Adjutant General's Office. *Wisconsin Volunteers, War of the Rebellion, 1861–1865.* Madison, Wis.: Democrat Printing Co., 1914. An alphabetical index (also available on microfiche) to the *Roster of Wisconsin Volunteers, War of the Rebellion, 1861–1865,* 2 vols. (Madison, Wis.: Democrat Printing Co., 1886).

Other helpful sources include:

Love, William DeLoss. *Wisconsin in the War of Rebellion: A History of all Regiments and Batteries.* Chicago, Ill.: Church and Goodman, 1866.

Paul, William G. *Wisconsin's Civil War Archives.* Madison, Wis.: State Historical Society of Wisconsin, 1965.

Quiner, E. B. *The Military History of Wisconsin: A Record of the Civil and Military Patriotism of the State, in the War for the Union.* Chicago, Ill.: Clarke & Co., 1866.

For re-creating the background of a Civil War ancestor in Wisconsin see Carolyn J. Mattern, *Soldiers When They Go—The Story of Camp Randall, 1861–1865* (Madison, Wis.: State Historical Society of Wisconsin for the Department of History, University of Wisconsin, 1981), and Ethel Alice Hurn, *Wisconsin Women in the War Between the States* (Madison, Wis.: Democrat Printing Co. for the Wisconsin History Commission, 1911).

A certificate of service for Civil War service can be obtained from the State Historical Society of Wisconsin. The certificate will usually show name, physical description, occupation, rank, when and where enlisted, by whom enlisted, for how long, when and where mustered into service, and date of termination of service. Birthplace is frequently given, although if foreign it will only state the country. With this certificate, the society will include a brief history of the respective regiment.

No pension records, outside of those available through the National Archives (see page 7) exist for Wisconsin. The State Archives of the State Historical Society of Wisconsin is the repository for other numerous miscellaneous records pertaining to Wisconsin residents and units in the Civil War. These include records of the quartermaster general and various regiments. Of special importance to the genealogist are county draft books, lists of persons eligible for military service, regimental muster rolls, hospital reports, certificates of service, duty rosters, and records of the disposition of personal effects. Not all types of records exist for all regiments. Records are originals, with some indexes, and need to be searched at the archives. Staff assistance is available. The archives has a manuscript index for the Spanish-American War; staff will check the index and their records and provide a summary upon request. There are no records in the archives for veterans of World Wars I and II, the Korean, or Vietnam conflicts. Information from the index of graves registrations for veterans buried in Wisconsin through 1970 is available through the Wisconsin Department of Veterans Affairs, Records Section, P.O. Box 7843, Madison, Wisconsin 53707. In requests include full name of veteran, date of birth, approximate date of death, and county or city of residence at time of death, if known.

Periodicals, Newspapers, and Manuscript Collections

Periodicals

The *Wisconsin Magazine of History,* published in Madison by the State Historical Society of Wisconsin, is a quarterly publication with historical articles, book reviews, and listings of acquisitions of historical and genealogical material. There are published indexes to this periodical.

The Wisconsin State Genealogical Society *Newsletter,* originally titled *Wisconsin Families* from 1940–41, is available quarterly through membership or at subscribing libraries (see Archives, Libraries, and Societies for address). The periodical contains pertinent state activities, queries, and recent publications acquired by the group. The majority of material is the publication of records from Wisconsin counties, including cemetery readings, church records, vital records, newspaper extractions, and other genealogically important items.

Various local and county genealogical and historical societies publish excellent newsletters helpful in research.

Newspapers

Newspaper publishing began in Wisconsin in 1833 with the printing of the *Green Bay Intelligencer.* First issued on 11 December of that year, it contained four twelve-by-eighteen-inch pages, and was printed semi-monthly for $2 a year. A good finding guide to the early papers of that area is Barry C. Noonan, *Index to Green Bay Newspapers 1833–1840* (Monroe, Wis.: Wisconsin State Genealogical Society, n.d.). The index includes the name of the newspaper, date, page, column, and brief description of the subject matter.

Included in the outstanding newspaper collection of the State Historical Society of Wisconsin (second only to the Library of Congress in the United States) are over 1,600 titles of Wisconsin's newspapers, almost three-fourths of all the newspaper issues ever published in the state. James L. Hansen, *Wisconsin Newspapers, 1833–1850: An Analytical Bibliography* (Madison, Wis.: State Historical Society of Wisconsin, 1979), contains information on the very earliest Wisconsin newspapers. An excellent index to this collection, although no longer inclusive, is Donald E. Oehlerts, *Guide to Wisconsin Newspapers, 1833–1957* (Madison, Wis.: State Historical Society of Wisconsin, 1958). This volume lists the papers (organized by county and town), dates of publication, availability for research, and the respective repository. James P. Danky, ed., *Periodicals and Newspapers Acquired by the State Historical Society of Wisconsin July 1974–December 1983* (Madison, Wis.: State Historical Society of Wisconsin, 1984), is a more recent update.

All Wisconsin newspapers held by the state historical society on microfilm are available on interlibrary loan. The newspaper collection also is important in the areas of blacks, ethnic groups, and Native Americans. Specialized bibliographies on some of these collections have been published by the society.

The *Milwaukee Sentinel*, which covered statewide local news, has a two part index (1837–79; 1880–90). Originals are at the Milwaukee Public Library, 814 W. Wisconsin Avenue, Milwaukee, Wisconsin 53233, with microfilm copies at the State Historical Society of Wisconsin.

Manuscript

Manuscript collections at the State Historical Society of Wisconsin are extensive. The following are a few representative, important examples:

A manuscript collection with some of the oldest Wisconsin records is the Grignon, Lawe, and Porlier Papers, 1712–1884. The sixty-five volumes contain the business, personal, and official papers and correspondence of three early Green Bay families that were involved in the fur-trading industry. Included in the papers are allusions to native Americans in connection with the fur trade, to treaties, and to annuity payments. Related collections can be consulted for early fur trade documentation. An excellent index to all fur trade manuscripts is Bruce M. White, *The Fur Trade in Minnesota: An Introductory Guide to Manuscript Sources* (St. Paul, Minn.: Minnesota Historical Society, 1977).

Betty Patterson, ed., *Some Pioneer Families of Wisconsin, An Index*, Vol. 1 (Wisconsin State Genealogical Society, 1977), and Vol. 2 (1987) are indexes of applications for pioneer or century certificates. The indexes include the following, if available: name of ancestor, birth date and place, death date, name of spouse, county of residence, and name of applicant. The supporting documentation is deposited in the State Archives at the State Historical Society of Wisconsin and is accessible to researchers.

Manuscript collections at this excellent repository are extremely diverse in character and content. Genealogists researching in the state must be diligent and imaginative in using these sources. Many collections not considered genealogical in nature may very well contain valuable information. The society is currently processing several Wisconsin business collections, including the Island Woolen Company of Baraboo (including payroll books) and the Connor Forest Industries (including records related to the "company towns" of Laona and Wakefield).

The most noted and widely used are the Draper Manuscripts, collected in the nineteenth century by Lyman Copeland Draper. The variety of the collection includes correspondence, interview notes, extracts from newspapers and other published sources, muster rolls, transcripts of official documents and research notes for the western Carolinas and Virginia, Kentucky, Tennessee, the entire Ohio River valley, and parts of the Mississippi River valley. There is a mass of genealogical and historical information in the microfilmed copies (134 reels), which have been deposited in numerous libraries across the nation. Before attempting to use the collection, consult Josephine L. Harper, *Guide to Draper Manuscripts* (Madison, Wis.: State Historical Society of Wisconsin, 1983).

Archives, Libraries, and Societies

State Historical Society of Wisconsin
816 State Street
Madison, WI 53706-1488

Nearly one-fifth of the entire State Historical Society of Wisconsin Library collection, now more than one million items, deals with family or local history, making it one of the largest genealogical collections in the country. It is not, however, limited to Wisconsin history. The library attempts to acquire all U.S. and Canadian historical and genealogical materials. Vital records prior to 1907 are on microfilm for the entire state (see Vital Records). Census holdings include all federal censuses for all states. The society has all federal census indexes for Wisconsin and is acquiring some indexes for other states. There is an extensive collection of passenger lists and one of the nation's largest newspaper collections, national in scope, but predominantly concerning Wisconsin (see Newspapers, Manuscripts, and Map sections). Books, except for rare editions and pamphlet-size, are on open shelves.

The State Archives, housed in the Historical Society Building, holds manuscript copies of early state censuses (see Census Records), sets of land, probate, court and tax records from many Wisconsin counties and municipalities.

The society reports data on its holdings to Research Libraries Information Network. As of July 1990, information on all state government records, local and court records, and portions of manuscripts were included.

For more detail on the society, see James P. Danky, ed., *Genealogical Research: An Introduction to the Resources of the State Historical Society of Wisconsin* (Madison, Wis.: State Historical Society of Wisconsin, 1986). Hours at the library include some evenings, but are also affected by university calendars since the building is on the campus of the University of Wisconsin. Call (608) 262-9590 or write for schedules.

Wisconsin State Genealogical Society
2109 Twentieth Avenue
Monroe, WI 53566

This society serves as the parent body for eleven local chapters. It holds two all-day meetings each year, featuring state or national speakers. Their quarterly newsletter includes material extracted from original sources. The society also publishes numerous indexes to Wisconsin county histories (see Background Sources). The Wisconsin State Genealogical Society purchased the microfilm copies of the pre-1907 vital indexes and records (see Vital Records), which are held by the State Historical Society of Wisconsin.

Wisconsin Genealogical Council
c/o Carolyn Habelman
Route 3, Box 253
Black River Falls, WI 54615

Established in 1986 to promote open communication, education, and exchange of information among Wisconsin counties, libraries, organizations, businesses, and individuals, the group publishes a quarterly newsletter, sponsors an annual Gene-A-Rama, and maintains a file of family names being researched by members.

Wisconsin Area Research Center Network

Thirteen area research centers in Wisconsin hold public records transferred by counties, towns, cities, and other local governments and collections of papers and records from private individuals and organizations. The goal of each center is to build comprehensive collections documenting the history of its region. The collections include photographs, newspapers, maps, and family histories. Many of the centers are enhanced by the contributions and volunteer hours of local genealogy groups. Newspaper indexes to vital records, cemetery readings, and original local church records can be located in some of the centers. Centers vary considerably in their collections and, therefore, in their value to genealogists. Archival collections usually located at the State Historical Society of Wisconsin or at one of the centers may be transferred temporarily within the network to accommodate local researchers. All archive and manuscript materials at the centers are cataloged centrally at the State Historical Society of Wisconsin. Write or call the appropriate center *before* visiting since hours vary by center, the calendar, staffing, and university schedules. The State Historical Society of Wisconsin serves Columbia, Dane, and Sauk counties. The other Area Research Centers and the counties they serve are:

Dexter Library
Northland College
1411 Ellis Avenue
Ashland, WI 54806
Phone: (715) 682-1311
Serves Ashland, Bayfield, and Iron counties.

William D. McIntyre Library
University of Wisconsin-Eau Claire
Eau Claire, WI 54701
Phone: (715) 836-2739
Serves Buffalo, Chippewa, Clark, Eau Claire, Price, Rusk, Sawyer, and Taylor counties.

Library-Learning Center
University of Wisconsin-Green Bay
2420 Nicolet Drive
Green Bay, WI 54302
Phone: (414) 465-2539
Serves Brown, Calumet, Door, Florence, Kewaunee, Manitowoc, Marinette, Menominee, Oconto, Outagamie, and Shawano counties.

Eugene W. Murphy Library
University of Wisconsin-La Crosse
1631 West Pine Street
La Crosse, WI 54601
Phone: (608) 785-8511
Serves Jackson, La Crosse, Monroe, Trempeleau, and Vernon counties.

Golda Meir Library
University of Wisconsin-Milwaukee
2311 East Hartford Avenue
Milwaukee, WI 53201
Phone: (414) 229-5402
Serves Milwaukee, Sheboygan, Ozaukee, Washington, and Waukesha counties.

Forrest R. Polk Library
University of Wisconsin-Oshkosh
800 Algoma Boulevard
Oshkosh, WI 54901
Phone: (414) 424-3347
Serves Dodge, Fond du Lac, Green Lake, Marquette, and Winnebago counties.

Wyllie Library/Learning Center
University of Wisconsin-Parkside
Box 2000
Kenosha, WI 53141
Phone: (414) 553-2411
Serves Kenosha and Racine counties.

Elton E. Karrmann Library
University of Wisconsin-Platteville
725 West Main Street
Platteville, WI 53818
Phone: (608) 342-1688
Serves Crawford, Grant, Green, Iowa, Lafayette, and Richland counties.

Chalmer Davee Library
University of Wisconsin-River Falls
120 East Cascade Avenue
River Falls, WI 54022
Phone: (715) 425-3567
Serves Burnett, Pierce, Polk, St. Croix, and Washburn counties.

Learning Resources Center
University of Wisconsin-Stevens Point
Stevens Point, WI 54481
Phone: (715) 346-2586
Serves Adams, Forest, Juneau, Langlade, Lincoln, Marathon, Marquette, Oneida, Portage, Vilas, Waupaca, Waushara, and Wood counties.

Library-Learning Center
University of Wisconsin-Stout
Menomonie, WI 54751
Phone: (715) 232-2300
Serves Barron, Dunn, and Pepin counties.

Jim Dan Hill Library
University of Wisconsin-Superior
18th and Grand Avenues
Superior, WI 54880
Phone: (715) 392-8512
Serves Douglas County.

Harold W. Anderson Library
University of Wisconsin-Whitewater
800 West Main Street
Whitewater, WI 53190
Phone: (414) 472-5520
Serves Jefferson, Rock, and Walworth counties.

Special Focus Categories

Naturalization

Naturalization records for Wisconsin have historically been kept in the county courthouses. However, they are now generally being transferred to the respective Area Research Center. As of 1989, it is estimated that three-fourths of counties have transferred these records. Two significant exceptions to this policy are Milwaukee and Waukesha counties, where the papers are deposited with the respective county historical society. Some naturalizations for La Crosse and all those applied for in federal courts are at the National Archives-Great Lakes Region (see page 8).

Black American

Records indicate, according to Zachary Cooper in *Black Settlers in Rural Wisconsin* (Madison, Wis.: State Historical Society of Wisconsin, 1977), that blacks were in Wisconsin as early as the 1700s serving as trappers, guides, boatmen, and interpreters to the French voyageurs and fur traders. Southerners from Kentucky, Virginia, and North Carolina who migrated to Wisconsin during the territorial period settled in the lead-mining, southwestern counties of Grant and Iowa, some bringing their black slaves. Blacks also came as slaves to military personnel, immigrated as freemen or runaway slaves. In 1840 Wisconsin Territory counted 185 free blacks and eleven slaves. Ten years later the there were 635 free blacks and no slaves counted.

The numbers from that 1840 census exemplify the state's position on slavery. The first abolition society was formed in Racine County in 1840, followed by the publication of the anti-slavery newspaper, *Wisconsin Aegis,* in 1843. Blacks from the South were assisted in the 1850s through the "underground railroad" of Wisconsin to freedom in Canada. In 1857 the legislature passed a "personal liberty law."

The Wisconsin Black History Museum, 4508 North 39th Street, Milwaukee, Wisconsin 53209, is collecting museum artifacts, photographs, papers, and books related to Wisconsin's black population, especially from rural areas.

For additional information see:

Bryl, Susan, and Erwin K. Welsch, comps. *Black Periodicals and Newspapers: A Union List of Holdings in Libraries of the University of Wisconsin and the Library of the State Historical Society of Wisconsin.* Madison, Wis.: Memorial Library, University of Wisconsin-Madison, 1975.

Clark, James I. "Wisconsin Defies the Fugitive Slave Law: The Case of Sherman M. Booth." *Chronicles of Wisconsin.* Vol. 5. Madison, Wis.: State Historical Society of Wisconsin, 1955.

Davidson, John Nelson. *Negro Slavery in Wisconsin and the Underground Railroad.* No. 18. Milwaukee, Wis.: Parkman Club Publications, 1897.

Gilson, Norman Shepard, Papers, 1860–1901. State Historical Society of Wisconsin. These papers include muster rolls for the 58th Infantry Regiment of U.S. Colored Troops from Wisconsin, MS 62-2651 at State Historical Society of Wisconsin.

Native American

When Jean Nicolet landed at the Red Banks of Lake Michigan in 1634, he would have been met by the Winnebago tribe which lived in large numbers in the Green Bay region. The Native Americans in the seventeenth century included the Sioux, Potawatomi, Sauk, Fox, Mascouten, Miami, Kickapoo, Huron, and Ottawa. In the early nineteenth century, the removal and containment of the natives began its deceptive chronicle. In some cases, land vacated by one tribe was occupied by another, resulting in two treaties on one parcel of land, sometimes requiring the repurchase of that same land.

There were eleven treaties between 1829 and 1848 with the Native Americans of Wisconsin. The Kickapoo, Winnebago, and Potawatomi migrated to Nebraska, Kansas, Oklahoma, and Mexico after surrendering all their land except for their reservations. The Menominee nation remained in Wisconsin, as did a few Potawatomi and many Chippewa.

In 1984 there were six Chippewa reservations in northern Wisconsin, a group of Potawatomi on federal trust tribal land in Forest County, and a Menominee reservation in Menominee County. The Stockbridge-Munsee reservation is in Shawano County, and the Brotherton tribe has been assimilated into this group. The Oneida reservation lies in Brown and Outagamie counties. The Wisconsin Winnebago, versus those removed to a reservation in Nebraska, live in tribal settlements and scattered tracts of land across the state. For further information refer to Stewart Rafert, "American-Indian Genealogical Research in the Midwest: Resources and Perspectives," *National Genealogical Society Quarterly* 76 (September 1988): 212–24. This excellent and informative article identifies pertinent local and county level records, extensive federal documentation, and miscellaneous resources.

A search of the county court records could be useful. Many Native Americans tried to sue those settlers who they believed had unjustly acquired their Indian land allotments. Probate files may contain guardianship records. National Archives collections of treaties and annuity rolls are of utmost importance (see page 11).

Also see Philip C. Bantin, *Guide to Catholic Indian Mission and School Records in Midwest Repositories* (Milwaukee, Wis.: Marquette University Libraries, Department of Special Collections and University Archives, 1984); Nancy Oestreich Lurie, *Wisconsin Indians* (Madison, Wis.: State Historical Society of Wisconsin, 1980); and William C. Sturtevant, ed., *Handbook of North American Indians.* Vol 15, "The Northeast" (Washington, D.C.: Smithsonian Institution, 1978).

The State Historical Society of Wisconsin has the largest collection in the United States of Native American newspapers and periodicals. Refer to James P. Danky, *Native American Periodicals and Newspapers, 1828–1982: Bibliography, Publishing Record and Holdings* (Westport, Conn.: Greenwood Press, 1984).

Other Ethnic Groups

French-Canadians were the earliest European immigrants in Wisconsin. They had crossed the border as fur traders and military personnel, settling in Prairie du Chien, Green Bay, and points west, marrying into the native families. Later French-Canadian immigrants came to the state with the lumber industry, and many migrated from previous homes in New York state. There were also numerous Canadian immigrants who were neither of French descent nor from Quebec. Many came from Ontario and the Atlantic provinces.

In 1850 there were over 21,000 Irish living in Wisconsin. The Irish were the largest English-speaking foreign-born group in the state. Their population was spread across the southern counties, with the largest number in Milwaukee County and a sizeable number in the lead-mining county of Lafayette. The English also settled in the southern counties, coming to the lead region as early as 1827. Colonies of English settlers were established in Racine, Columbia, and Dane counties. The Scots settled, although not in great numbers, in the southern and eastern sections of the state; the Welsh immigrated to Wisconsin basically in the 1840s and 1850s. The German influx began in the late 1830s, the first German colony of 800 (possibly an exaggerated number) landing in Milwaukee in 1839. By 1850 first-generation Germans constituted about 12 percent of the state population. The government had actively sought German immigrants, beginning in the 1840s, by distributing leaflets in Germany's coastal areas. Later they established, via an 1852 law, a commissioner of immigration to live in New York and promote Wisconsin's advantages. In 1854 a branch office was established in Quebec, although German immigration through that port was small. It was, however, letters sent from Wisconsin to Germany by the first settlers that actually stimulated the continued immigration to Wisconsin. Many of the letters, telling of good available land and the freedom to prosper, were published in Germany.

Although there were not large numbers of Norwegians in Wisconsin compared to Germans, two-thirds of all Norwegians in the United States in 1850 resided in Wisconsin. Most of the Dutch that had immigrated early to Wisconsin, lived in Sheboygan, Brown, and Milwaukee counties. A few Swiss were in the state as early as 1834 but came in larger numbers in the 1840s. The village of New Glarus in Green County still maintains the Swiss heritage of the original settlers in 1845. Danish immigrants to Wisconsin settled in Winnebago, Racine, and Dane counties prior to 1870. Icelanders settled on Washington Island in Door County in the early 1870s. From 1870 through 1920 there was immigration from Poland to Wisconsin, and by the 1890s Russians made their way to this midwest state. Finns and Italians arrived after 1900 as did Russian Jews who relocated in Milwaukee in 1910 and 1911.

Sources for ethnic study in Wisconsin include the following centers and publications:

The Vesterheim Genealogical Center, University of Wisconsin Madison, Library, 728 State Street, Madison, Wisconsin 53706, is a division of the Norwegian-American Museum of Decorah, Iowa. The collection holds 2,000 Norwegian local histories, church records, immigrant lists, passport records, and more. Some records are available on microfilm on interlibrary loan. The center acts as a clearinghouse for Norwegian-American research. Genealogical inquiries should be sent to Prof. Gerhard B. Naeseth, 4909 Sherwood Road, Madison, Wisconsin 53711.

The State Historical Society of Wisconsin holds the Rasmus B. Anderson papers, 1841–1931, fifty-five boxes of family and personal papers.

The University of Wisconsin Memorial Library at Madison has extensive material on Norwegian local history and United Kingdom research.

See also:

Rippley, La Vern J. *The Immigrant Experience in Wisconsin.* Boston, Mass.: G.K. Hall, 1985.

County Resources

In mailing requests to any Wisconsin county office, use the name of the county and "County Courthouse," with the address listed below. Records at the county level are the responsibility of the following offices: birth, marriage, death, and land—register of deeds; court—clerk of courts; probate—county probate court.

The setting up of a county with a fully functional government was usually done in three stages: "establishment," legally defining a specific area as a county; "organization for county purposes," which involved setting up a governing body or board, land registry office, and fiscal structure; and "organization for judicial purposes" which involved setting up a county court and law enforcement. In some counties the three stages were accomplished more or less simultaneously. In others they were done separately over many years. When a county was established, but not fully organized, it was typically "attached" to another county, often, but not always, a parent county. Since these levels of organization and questions of attachment affect the creation and location of records, they can be quite important to the researcher.

For example, when Ashland County was attached for judicial purposes to Bayfield County in 1866, the courthouse in Ashland County did not close. The county board still met, land transactions and marriages were still recorded by the register of deeds, and taxes were still collected in and for Ashland County. Only the courts and law enforcement were affected, and for those records between 1866 and 1873, the researcher would have to check in Bayfield County.

The year given in the county charts for "Date Formed" is the year passage of the law created the county. With that date is the name of the parent county or counties. Additional lines identify the purposes (c-county purposes; j-judicial purposes), the county or counties to which it was attached, and the dates of that attachment.

The date listed for each category of record is usually the earliest registration filed. The earliest date does not indicate that there are numerous records for that year and does not mean that all such events were actually registered. It has been estimated that less than 50 percent of the vital records, for example, were prepared and submitted for permanent filing prior to 1907. Land deeds, probate, and court records generally begin in Wisconsin with the organization of the county. Prior to that date, check the "Parent County." Some counties formed from other counties transcribed their portion of property deeds to be kept with the new county deed records.

The county information has been provided by James L. Hansen, Reference Librarian, State Historical Society of Wisconsin.

 Drawn by William Dollarhide

Map	County Address	Date Formed—Parent County/ies Jurisdictional Purposes	Birth Marriage Death	Land Probate Court
G5	Adams 402 Main Friendship 53934	1848 Portage (c/j-Sauk, 1848–53)	1857 1854 1876	1853 1855 1854
C4	Ashland 201 Second Street W. Ashland 54806	1860 La Pointe (j-Bayfield, 1866–73)	1876 1871 1877	1856 1878 1873
	Bad Ax	1851 Crawford Renamed Vernon, 1862		
D2	Barron 330 E. LaSalle Avenue Barron 54812	1859 (as Dallas) Polk (c/j-Polk, 1859–60; Dunn, 1860–68; j-Dunn, 1868–74) Renamed Barron, 1869	1877 1868 1877	1870 1880 1874
B3	Bayfield 117 E. Fifth Street Washburn 54891	1845 (as La Pointe) St. Croix (j-Crowford, 1845; St. Croix, 1849–50) Renamed, 1866	1879 1869 1870	1850 1857 1859
F7	Brown 111 N. Jefferson Green Bay 54301	1818 unorganized territory	1814 1823 1834	1820 1824 1823
F2	Buffalo 407 Second Street Alma 54610	1853 Jackson	1855 1856 1873	1854 1854 1853
C1	Burnett 7410 County Road K Siren 54872	1856 Polk (j-Polk, 1856–59; c/j-Polk, 1859–64; j-Polk, 1866–71)	1853? 1869? 1846?	1866 1868 1870
G7	Calumet 206 Court Street Chilton 53014	1836 Brown (c/j-Brown, 1836–42; j-Brown, 1842–44 Fond du Lac, 1844–50)	1858 1850 1856	1840 1850 1850
E3	Chippewa 711 N. Bridge Street Chippewa Falls 54729	1845 Crawford (c/j-Crawford, 1845–51; La Crosse, 1851–53)	1858 1854 1855	1854 1856 1856
F4	Clark 517 Court Street Neillsville 54456	1853 Jackson (c/j-Jackson, 1853; j-Jackson, 1854–56)	1869 1857 1877	1855 1870 1857
H5	Columbia 400 DeWitt Street Portage 53901	1846 Portage	1860 1849 1877	1826 1847 1851
J3	Crawford 220 N. Beaumont Road Prairie du Chien 53821	1818 unorganized territory	1858 1816 1876	1820 1819 1824
	Dallas	1859 Polk Renamed Barron, 1869		
J5	Dane 210 Martin Luther King, Jr., Boulevard Madison 53709	1836 Crawford/Iowa/Milwaukee (c/j-Iowa, 1836–39)	1860 1839 1876	1835 1847 1841
H6	Dodge 127 E. Oak Street Juneau 53039	1836 Brown/Milwaukee (c/j-Milwaukee, 1836–40)	1870 1843 1852	1877 1844 1844

Map	County Address	Date Formed—Parent County/ies Jurisdictional Purposes	Birth Marriage Death	Land Probate Court
E8	Door 138 S. Fourth Avenue Sturgeon Bay 54235	1851 Brown (j-Manitowoc, 1851–55; Brown, 1855–60)	1852 1856 1856	1857 1861 1861
B2	Douglas 1313 Belknap Superior 54880	1854 La Pointe	1861 1854 1877	1854 1856 1855
E2	Dunn 800 Wilson Avenue Menomonie 54751	1854 Chippewa (j-Chippewa, 1854–56)	1861 1858 1869	1877 1858 1859
F3	Eau Claire 721 Oxford Avenue Eau Claire 54701	1856 Chippewa	1870 1857 1876	1856 1858 1854
C7	Florence 501 Lake Avenue Florence 54121	1882 Marinette/Oconto	1882 1882 1882	1882 1882 1882
H7	Fond du Lac 160 S. Macy Street Fond du Lac 54935	1836 Brown (c/j-Brown, 1836–39; j-Brown, 1839–44)	1852 1844 1854	1836 1839 1844
D6	Forest Crandon 54520	1885 Langlade	1891 1886 1871	1865 1887 1885
	Gates	1901 Chippewa Renamed Rusk, 1905	—	
J3	Grant 130 W. Maple Lancaster 53813	1836 Iowa	1870 1842 1876	1837 1836 1836
K5	Green 17th Avenue and 10th Street Monroe 53566	1836 Iowa (c/j-Iowa, 1836–38)	1862 1838 1874	1836 1850 1838
H6	Green Lake 492 Hill Street Green Lake 54541	1858 Marquette	1864 1858 1877	1843 1853 1858
J4	Iowa 222 N. Iowa Street Dodgeville 53533	1829 Crawford	1876 1836 1871	1832 1837 1834
B4	Iron 300 Taconite Street Hurley 54534	1893 Ashland	1886 1893 1887	1886 1893 1893
G3	Jackson 307 Main Street Black River Falls 54615	1853 La Crosse	1861 1853 1872	1854 1869 1854
J6	Jefferson 320 S. Main Street Jefferson 53549	1836 Milwaukee (c/j-Milwaukee, 1836–39)	1852 1844 1856	1838 1846 1842
G4	Juneau 220 E. State Street Mauston 53948	1856 Adams	1877 1857 1876	1857 1860 1857

Map	County Address	Date Formed—Parent County/ies Jurisdictional Purposes	Birth Marriage Death	Land Probate Court
K7	Kenosha 912 56th Street Kenosha 53140	1850 Racine	1876 1850 1876	1838 1850 1852
F8	Kewaunee 613 Dodge Street Kewaunee 54216	1852 Door (j-Manitowoc, 1852–55; Brown, 1855–58)	1861 1859 1872	1856 1859 1858
G3	La Crosse 400 N. Fourth Street La Crosse 54601	1851 Crawford	1866 1851 1876	1851 1851 1850
K4	Lafayette 626 Main Street Darlington 53530	1846 Iowa (c/j-Iowa, 1846–47	1854 1847 1877	1836 1847 1847
E6	Langlade 800 Clermont Street Antigo 54409	1879 (as New) Oconto (c/j-Shawano, 1879–81) Renamed, 1881	1882 1881 1882	1858 1881 1881
	La Pointe	1845 St. Croix Renamed Bayfield, 1866		
E5	Lincoln 1110 E. Main Street Merrill 54452	1874 Marathon (j-Marathon, 1874–75)	1875 1875 1871	1867 1883 1885
G7	Manitowoc 1010 S. Eighth Street Manitowoc 54220	1836 Brown (c/j-Brown, 1836–38; j-Brown, 1839–48)	1858 1849 1864	1835 1850 1848
E5	Marathon 500 Forest Street Wausau 54401	1850 Portage	1870 1861 1868	1841 1851 1849
D7	Marinette 1926 Hall Avenue Marinette 54143	1879 Oconto	1874 1878 1868	1879 1879 1849
H5	Marquette 77 Park Street Montello 53949	1836 Brown (c/j-Brown, 1836–44; j-Fond du Lac, 1844–48)	1864 1848 1876	1836 1860 1849
E6	Menominee 800 Wilson Avenue Keshena 54135 **In Shawano County, except for Native Americans.*	1961 Oconto/Shawano Attached for judicial and some county purposes to Shawano	1961 1961 1961	1961 1961* 1961
K7	Milwaukee Room 101 901 N. Ninth Street Milwaukee 53233	1834 Brown (j-Brown, 1834–35)	1835 1836 1872	1836 1838 1837
G3	Monroe 112 S. Court Street Sparta 54656	1854 La Crosse	1854 1854 1867	1851 1855 1854
	New	1879 Oconto Renamed Langlade, 1881		
E7	Oconto 300 Washington Street Oconto 54153	1851 Brown (c/j-Brown, 1851–52; j-Brown, 1852–54, 1855–57)	1876 1859 1872	1838 1857 1857

Map	County Address	Date Formed—Parent County/ies Jurisdictional Purposes	Birth Marriage Death	Land Probate Court
D5	Oneida P.O. Box 400 Oneida Avenue Rhinelander 54501	1885 Lincoln (c/j-Lincoln, 1885–86)	1887 1887 1888	1887 1887 1887
F7	Outagamie 410 S. Walnut Street Appleton 54911	1851 Brown/Winnebago (j-Brown, 1851–52)	1856 1852 1869	1851 1853 1852
H7	Ozaukee 121 W. Main Street Port Washington 53074	1853 Washington	1852 1855 1849	1835 1849 1853
F2	Pepin 740 Seventh Avenue W. Durand 54736	1858 Dunn	1863 1858 1857	1855 1856 1858
F1	Pierce 414 W. Main Street Ellsworth 54011	1853 St. Croix	1870 1851 1876	1855 1875 1854
D1	Polk 5 Courthouse Avenue Balsam Lake 54810	1853 St. Croix	1867 1855 1865	1853 1855 1859
F5	Portage 1516 Church Street Stevens Point 54481	1836 Brown/Crawford/Iowa/ Milwaukee (c/j-Brown, 1836–41; j-Dane, 1841–44)	1866 1848 1876	1841 1837 1844
D4	Price 126 Cherry Street Phillips 54555	1879 Chippewa/Lincoln (j-Taylor, 1879–82)	1880 1880 1879	1882 1881 1892?
K7	Racine 730 Wisconsin Avenue Racine 53403	1836 Milwaukee	1877 1839 1880	1837 1849 1837
H4	Richland Seminary Street Richland Center 53581	1842 Crawford/Sauk (c/j-Iowa, 1842–50)	1875 1850 1876	1850 1839? 1861
K6	Rock 51 S. Main Street Janesville 53545	1836 Milwaukee (c/j-Racine, 1836–39)	1856 1840 1860	1839 1850 1840
D3	Rusk 311 E. Miner Avenue Ladysmith 54848	1901 (as Gates) Chippewa Renamed, 1905	1900 1901 1901	1872 1901 1901
E1	St. Croix 911 Fourth Street Hudson 54016 *Some records. 1840–49 at Washington County Historical Society, Stillwater, Minnesota.*	1840 Crawford (j-Crawford, 1843–49)	1858 1852 1876	1849 1849 1850
H4	Sauk 515 Oak Street Baraboo 53913	1840 Crawford/Dane/Portage (c/j-Dane, 1840–44)	1864 1844 1876	1844 1847 1844
C3	Sawyer 406 Iowa Avenue Hayward 54843	1883 Ashland/Chippewa (j-Ashland, 1883–85)	1869 1883 1883	1883 1900? 1883

Map	County Address	Date Formed—Parent County/ies Jurisdictional Purposes	Birth Marriage Death	Land Probate Court
F6	Shawano 311 N. Main Street Shawano 54166	1853 Oconto/Waupaca/Winnebago (j-Outagamie, 1853–59)	1854 1848 1860	1854 1861 1861
H7	Sheboygan 615 N. Sixth Street Sheboygan 53081	1836 Brown (c/j-Brown, 1836–39; j-Brown, 1839–46)	1848 1852 1854	1835 1860 1851
E4	Taylor 224 S. Second Street Medford 54451	1875 Chippewa/Clark/Lincoln/ Marathon	1877 1875 1877	1875 1876 1875
G2	Trempealeau 1720 Main Street Whitehall 54773	1854 Buffalo/Chippewa/ Jackson/La Crosse (j-La Crosse, 1854)	1845 1856 1847	1855 1855 1855
H3	Vernon W. Decker Street Viroqua 54665	1851 (as Bad Ax) Crawford Renamed, 1862	1863 1855 1878	1851 1850 1853
C5	Vilas Court and Main P.O. Box 369 Eagle River 54521	1893 Oneida	1889 1893 1889	1893? 1900? 1900?
K7	Walworth Courthouse Square Elkhorn 53121	1836 Milwaukee (c/j-Racine, 1836–38)	1872 1839 1872	1839 1839 1840
C2	Washburn 110 Fourth Avenue W. Shell Lake 54871	1883 Burnett	1883 1883 1883	1883 1883 1878
J7	Washington 432 E. Washington Street West Bend 53095	1836 Brown/Milwaukee (c/j-Milwaukee, 1836–40; j-Milwaukee, 1840–45)	1859 1846 1873	1835 1845 1855
J7	Waukesha 515 W. Moreland Boulevard Waukesha 53188	1846 Milwaukee	1860 1846 1872	1841 1847 1847
F6	Waupaca 811 Harding Street Waupaca 54981	1851 Brown/Winnebago (j-Winnebago, 1851–53)	1858 1852 1848	1851 1860 1853
G5	Waushara 209 St. Marie Street Wautoma 54982	1851 Marquette (j-Marquette, 1851–52)	1859 1852 1876	1852 1854 1868
G6	Winnebago 415 Jackson Street Oshkosh 54901	1840 Brown/Calumet/Fond du Lac/ Marquette (c/j-Brown, 1840–42; j-Brown, 1842–44; Fond du Lac, 1844–47)	1876 1848 1863	1837 1838 1848
F4	Wood 400 Market Street Wisconsin Rapids 54494	1856 Portage	1871 1867 1872	1836 1858 1872?

WYOMING

Dwight A. Radford

Wyoming Territory was created on 25 July 1868 mostly from Dakota Territory. Forts, fur trading, and the Oregon Trail had been a part of its early history. From 1867 to 1869, the coming of the Union Pacific Railroad through Wyoming left a string of towns—Cheyenne, Laramie, Rawlins, Rock Springs, Green River, and Evanston—along the railroad line. Much of the business history of present-day Wyoming is connected to the Union Pacific Railroad. The construction of the railroad brought a number of Chinese laborers to Wyoming.

The mining influx during the late 1860s and 1870s brought settlers into Sweetwater country. As mining broadened out to encompass several additional industries, towns such as Atlantic City, Miner's Delight, Red Canyon, South Pass City, and others were formed.

Statehood was achieved 10 July 1890. One-fourth of Wyoming's population at that time was foreign born, originating from England, Germany, Ireland, Scotland, Sweden, Canada, Russia, Denmark, Wales, China, Norway, Italy, Austria, and France.

In January of 1890, two-hundred blacks, mostly from Harrison County, Ohio, were brought to Dana (near Hanna) to work the coal mines, but most did not stay long. A small German-Russian colony from Chicago arrived in the Big Horn Basin in 1896.

Although land opened up for settlement in 1890, very little was filed or patented from 1890 to 1897. In 1909 dry-farming was tried in Wyoming, and the enlarged homestead acts brought more dry farmers to the state. Congress changed the homestead residence requirement in 1912 from five years to three years and permitted the homesteaders to absent the property for five months each year. These concessions gave renewed emphasis to dry farming and settlement.

The great era of public land entries in Wyoming was in the twentieth century, with the peak years being 1920–21.

Vital Records

Wyoming began recording births and deaths in 1909. Very few birth and death records were kept at the county level prior to that time. Most of the early births filed at the state office are delayed birth registrations. When specifics are not known, the officials at the State Vital Records Services can check the alphabetical index for a desired entry, but an hourly fee will be charged.

Certified copies of birth, marriage, and death certificates for the period after statewide recording are available from the Vital Records Services, Division of Health and Medical Services, State Office Building West, Cheyenne, Wyoming 82002.

Wyoming has been recording marriages and divorces statewide since 1941. Earlier marriages where recorded by the county clerk in the county were the license was issued. All Wyoming marriage records from 1869 to 1970 are available from the Wyoming State Archives and Historical Department (see Archives, Libraries, and Societies) for all Wyoming counties. Early divorce records were kept by the clerk of the district court where the divorce took place.

Census Records

Federal

Population Schedules.

- Indexed—1850 (as part of Utah Territory) 1860 (as part of Nebraska Territory), 1870, 1880, 1910
- Soundex—1880, 1900, 1920

Industry and Agriculture Schedules.

- 1880

Mortality Schedules.

- 1870, 1880 (indexed)

Union Veterans Schedules.

- 1890 (indexed)

The 1850 U.S. census schedule recorded residents of Fort Bridger in 1851 as part of the Green River Precinct, Weber County, Utah Territory. Green River County was never organized and was discontinued in 1868 when Wyoming Territory was created. People residing at Fort Laramie were enumerated as part of the unorganized portion of Nebraska Territory. The census of 1870 was the first federal schedule of Wyoming Territory.

In 1880, Wyoming Territory included seven counties as well as Yellowstone National Park. All counties are extant in the 1880 census. Mammoth Hot Springs of Yellowstone National Park was enumerated with Uinta County, and this census has been both soundexed and indexed.

The 1900 U.S. census for Wyoming is soundexed, but the 1910 enumeration is not. All counties are extant for these two censuses. The 1910 U.S. census for Wyoming has been indexed and published.

Territorial

A relatively unknown source is the First Wyoming Territorial Census, which was enumerated soon after formation in 1869. This comprehensive census includes names, lengths of residency, and place of origin. This census is available on microfilm at the Wyoming State Archives and the FHL.

Background Sources

Bartlett, Ichabod S. *History of Wyoming.* Chicago, Ill.: S. J. Clark Publishing Co., 1918. This is a three-volume set. Volume one is a history of the state, and volumes two and three contain valuable biographies.

Beach, Cora May Brown. *Women of Wyoming.* Casper, Wyo.: S. E. Boyer, 1927. Considering the early equality status of women in Wyoming, this two-volume set of biographies is especially valuable. The photographs of the women in the biographical sketch and the genealogical information is noteworthy.

Beard, Frances Birkhead, ed. *Wyoming from Territorial Days to the Present.* Chicago, Ill.: American Historical Society, 1935. Volume one is a history, and volumes two and three provide valuable biographical sketches which include church leaders, political figures, ranchers, etc.

Erwin, Marie. *Wyoming Blue Book.* Cheyenne, Wyo.: Wyoming State Archives and Historical Department, 1974. Reprint. This original three volume work is currently being updated and republished in four volumes. It should not be overlooked because it is an excellent historical reference for Wyoming, including details on county formation; territorial, county, and state government; and holdings in the archives.

Hendrickson, Gordon Olaf, ed. *Peopling the High Plains, Wyoming's European Heritage.* Cheyenne, Wyo.: Wyoming State Archives and Historical Department, 1977. This volume examines six of Wyoming's ethnic European groups which contributed to the settlement and development of the state, namely British, German, Italian, Basque, Eastern European miners, and Greeks. It is a welcome contribution to the study of ethnic Wyoming.

Gallagher, John S., and Alan H. Patera. *Wyoming Post Offices: 1850–1980.* Burtonsville, Md.: Depot, 1980. An excellent genealogical tool for identifying defunct as well as continuous towns throughout Wyoming, this book is divided by county with an accompanying map of each county showing the location of the post offices.

Larson, Taft Alfred. *History of Wyoming.* Lincoln, Nebr.: University of Nebraska Press, 1965. The self proclaimed purpose of this book is to provide a critical history of Wyoming for adults. It is an excellent history of the territorial and statehood periods of Wyoming. Only minor mention is made of the pre-territorial period.

Murray, Robert A. *Military Posts of Wyoming.* Fort Collins, Colo.: Old Army Press, 1974. This book provides history, drawings, and photographs for each of Wyoming's old military posts scattered throughout the state.

Peterson, C. S. *Men of Wyoming.* Denver, Colo.: n.pub., 1915. Contains photographs and biographies for over 300 men who were residents of Wyoming in 1915.

Rollins, George W. "The Struggle of the Cattleman, Sheepman, and Settler For Control of Lands in Wyoming: 1867–1910." Master's thesis, University of Utah, 1951. Outlines the struggles of competing groups on the semi-arid land of Wyoming.

Spiros, Joyce V. Hawley. *Genealogical Guide to Wyoming.* Gallup, N.Mex.: Verlene Publishing, 1982. No research in Wyoming county sources should begin without examining this book first.

Triggs, J. H. *History of Cheyenne and Northern Wyoming.* Laramie, Wyo.: Powder River Publishers and

Booksellers, 1876. This early volume consists of a history of the town of Cheyenne and many portions of Wyoming Territory, including the gold fields of the Black Hills, Powder River, and Big Horn counties.

Urbanek, Mae. *Wyoming Place Names*. 1967. Reprint. Missoula, Mont.: Mountain Press Publishing Co., 1988. This publication lists geographic places and town names.

Welch, Charles A. *History of the Big Horn Basin*. Salt Lake City, Utah: Deseret News Press, 1940. The history of the basin with emphasis on the Mormon colonies in the area is detailed in this useful resource.

Wheeler, Denice. *The Feminine Frontier: Wyoming Women . . . 1850–1900*. N.p., 1987. This work informs readers about the lives and accomplishments of Wyoming's pioneer women. The study is based on local and national historical studies.

Maps

The United States Geological Survey publishes catalogs of topographical maps (see page 4) covering the state of Wyoming: "Wyoming Catalog of Topographic and other Published Maps" and "Wyoming Index to Topographic and other Map Coverage." The catalogs list over-the-counter dealers of U.S. Geological maps in Wyoming.

The U.S. Geological Survey has designated certain libraries in Wyoming as map depositories. These include Casper College and Natrona County Public Library in Casper; Wyoming State Library in Cheyenne; Campbell County Public Library in Gillette; University of Wyoming, Coe Library, and Geology Library in Laramie; Central Wyoming College in Riverton; Western Wyoming Community College in Rock Springs; and Sheridan College in Sheridan.

Land Records

Public-Domain State

Land records in Wyoming begin as early as 1841. Several land offices were opened in Wyoming, the first having opened at Cheyenne in 1870. As additional land opened up for settlement, other land offices opened at Evanston (1877), Buffalo (1888), Douglas (1890), Lander (1890), and Sundance (1890). Records generated through these offices include cash entries, homestead certificates, canceled homestead entries, timber-culture final certificates, canceled timber-culture entries, desert-land final certificates, canceled desert-land entries, and timber and stone lands.

An inventory of all BLM records on file at the National Archives-Rocky Mountain Region (see page 8) can be found in Eileen Bolger, *Preliminary Inventory of the Records of the Bureau of Land Management—Wyoming* (Denver, Colo.: Federal Archives and Records Center, 1983). BLM records consist of the records of the six land offices and include land patents, rights, and claims. The BLM Wyoming State Office, 2515 Warren Avenue, P.O. Box 1828, Cheyenne, Wyoming 82003, has records of the grantees of the original land patents.

Most county land records begin after 1869. All county land transactions are available at the Wyoming State Archives from 1869 to 1970, as well as all unpatented homestead records. Later county records can be found in the county's courthouse.

Probate Records

Probate records in Wyoming are kept by the clerk of the district court in each county. During the territorial period, probate records were kept by the territorial probate court and include appraisements, bills of sale, claims against estates, final accounts, guardian bonds, guardian annual reports, inheritance tax records, inventories, letters of testamentary or of administration, oaths and bonds for executors and administrators, petitions, probate journals, and wills. Most county probate records are on file at the Wyoming State Archives.

Court Records

The judicial system in Wyoming was set up in 1868 with a supreme court that performed the duties of an appellate court. It could hold trials in one of the three judicial districts of the territory. In 1869 women in Wyoming Territory were given the right to vote and, therefore, could become jurists. With statehood, the court system developed into three major courts: justice of the peace courts, district courts, and the supreme court. The justice of the peace courts are countywide courts with jurisdiction over minor actions and misdemeanors. District courts are countywide courts with jurisdiction over civil cases including criminal cases, divorces, probate matters, and some appeals. The supreme court continues to be the statewide appellate court.

Most Wyoming court records are on file either at the Wyoming State Archives or at the local courthouse.

Tax Records

The Wyoming State Archives does not have all of the county tax and assessment records. The county assessor and treasurer use their own discretion as to whether their records are sent to the archives. In order to check the records on file at the Wyoming State Archives, the researcher must know the county (or general area) and the years that the ancestor resided in Wyoming. If tax records are not at the archives, they are likely still at the local courthouses.

Wyoming county tax records may be arranged chronologically and then alphabetically by school district. These records include assessment rolls and appraisement of personal and real property for tax purposes. The total amount of tax is then apportioned under the various county and state taxes. Tables list name and address, legal description of the real property, value of real and personal property, amount owed for specific taxes, and date paid.

Cemetery Records

All Wyoming burials, including pioneer graves, are currently being compiled into a statewide resource. Some are available at the Wyoming State Archives.

Church Records

A guide to church inventories was completed in 1939 by the WPA and entitled *A Directory of Churches and Religious Organizations In the State of Wyoming* (Cheyenne, Wyo.: Historical Records Survey, 1939). This directory listed 470 congregations, institutions, and organizations in Wyoming in the late 1930s. It is not a complete listing for the period but is useful in locating congregations by county and city.

A few Idaho Mormons settled in Star Valley in the 1870s, and many more arrived in the 1880s. Star Valley has a large Mormon population as a result of this colonization. There were Mormon colonists in the Big Horn Basin by 1895, but the main body of Latter-day Saint settlers came there as an organized group from Utah and Idaho in 1900. All ward, branch, and mission records are on microfilm at the Family History Library in Salt Lake City, Utah.

An inventory of many Presbyterian congregations was undertaken by the WPA in 1936, entitled "Inventory of the Church Archives in Wyoming: Presbyterian Churches." Although an incomplete inventory, it is on file at the Wyoming State Archives, was photocopied and indexed by the Presbyterian Historical Society in Philadelphia, Pennsylvania. It consists of nineteen out of the forty-two congregations associated with the Presbyterian Church in the U.S.A. and one congregation affiliated with the United Presbyterian Church of North America. These inventories were in the form of questionnaires asking what record sources were available and what years were covered. Histories of each congregation are included in this collection. It is indexed, has been microfilmed, and is at the FHL.

The Catholic faith came to Wyoming through the migration of many Irish immigrant laborers. The Irish impact on Wyoming Catholicism is reflected in the fact that three out of the first four bishops of the Diocese of Cheyenne were from Ireland. The Diocese of Cheyenne was formed in 1887 and covers the entire state of Wyoming and Yellowstone Park. Requests concerning their record collection should be directed to the Diocese of Cheyenne, 2105 Capitol Avenue, Cheyenne, Wyoming 82001. The diocesan cemetery is Olivet Cemetery in Cheyenne.

The Greek Orthodox churches in Cheyenne and Rock Springs were the only two in the state until 1964. Orthodox members from many Eastern European countries became part of the Rock Springs church.

There are records of Methodists in Wyoming before the area was organized into Wyoming Territory. Churches were built in Laramie in 1867 and in Cheyenne in 1870. Black members withdrew from the Cheyenne church in 1875 to form the African Methodist Episcopal Church. For a detailed history of Methodism in Wyoming, see Doris Whithorn, *Bicentennial Tapestry of the Yellowstone Conference* (Livingston, Mont.: Livingston Enterprise, 1984).

Wyoming has had a small Jewish community since territorial days. Also, Cheyenne and Rock Springs both have Jewish communities.

Military Records

The Wyoming State Archives has records of those killed during World War I and the records of National Guardsmen from the state.

The archives also has military discharge records. Since soldiers were not required to file their discharge records at the county clerk's office, they may not be complete. Most of the discharge records begin in the early twentieth century, and in order to check these records the researcher needs to know the county in which the ancestor filed for discharge. Most of the county discharge records are indexed.

The State Adjutant General's Office also has military records. For more information, contact the Adjutant General's Office, 5500 Bishop Boulevard, Cheyenne, Wyoming 82002.

Periodicals, Newspapers, and Manuscript Collections

Periodicals

Two periodicals on Wyoming history are valuable to the genealogist. *Bits and Pieces* is a magazine of western history with special interest in Wyoming, the Black Hills area, and surrounding states. It is published monthly from Newcastle, Wyoming, and contains a wide variety of articles. The second periodical is *Annals of Wyoming*, published biennially by the Wyoming State Archives.

Newspapers

The first newspaper established in Wyoming was the *Cheyenne Leader*, which began in 1867. The first permanent newspaper in Laramie was founded in 1869 and was named the *Laramie Daily Sentinel*.

Lola Homsher has compiled an inventory of all known Wyoming newspapers entitled *Guide To Wyoming Newspapers, 1867–1967* (Cheyenne, Wyo.: Wyoming State Library, 1971). The Wyoming State Archives began collecting and microfilming the state's newspapers in 1953 and maintains the most complete collection in the state.

Manuscripts

The Wyoming State Archives has many collections, as well as county records, which are valuable to the researcher. Other holdings include the "European Heritage Study Collection," which contains administrative records for the Wyoming European Ethnic Project. The collection includes research collected by individual teams on Basque, British, Eastern Europeans, German-speaking Europeans, Greeks, and Italians. It has been subsequently published in *Peopling the High Plains: Wyoming's European Heritage,* described in Other Ethnic Groups.

Another widely used collection is the "Carter Collection," which consists of the papers of William Alexander Carter, who was a sutler and post trader at Fort Bridger, Wyoming, from 1857 until his death in 1881. A sutler was a civilian merchant in charge of the general store at a military site. After 1867, sutlers were called post traders. His business dealings touched every phase of economic development of the Rocky Mountains, Great Basin, Missouri River, and the Pacific. His papers were microfilmed in 1959 from the originals which are deposited at the Western Americana Division, Yale University Library, New Haven, Connecticut. They consist of twelve reels of microfilm and include correspondence, forty-five journals, ledgers, cashbooks, and other papers relating to Carter's business activities at Fort Bridger; diaries, genealogy, papers relating to Lot Smith's Company of Utah (Mormon) Militia, and Camps Floyd and Scott (Utah Territory); and legal documents from Carter's term as probate judge of Green River County, Utah.

Archives, Libraries, and Societies

Wyoming State Archives and Historical Department
Barrett Building
Cheyenne, WY 82002

This repository is the prime resource for state and county records. Most county records in Wyoming have been microfilmed and are available at the archives.

Fremont County Genealogical Society
Riverton Branch Library
1330 West Park
Riverton, WY 82501

A survey of Wyoming genealogical societies was compiled by the Fremont County Genealogical Society in 1986. A detailed listing of each society's collections can be found as part of the survey. Contact the society for the publication, which is entitled *Wyoming Genealogical Society Survey* (Riverton, Wyo.: Fremont County Genealogical Society, 1986).

Special Focus Categories

Native American

According to the 1900 U.S. census, members of the following tribes were residing in Wyoming: Arapaho, Cheyenne, Cree, Gros Ventre, Menominee, Sioux, Ute, and Ute Southern.

The Wind River Agency was established in 1870 for the Shoshone and Bannock tribes. In 1878 a number of northern Arapaho and a few Cheyenne from the Red Cloud Agency settled on the Wind River Agency. The agency records cover 1873 to 1952 and include letters received and sent, decimal files, school records, photographs of Indians, land records, and censuses. These records are available at the National Archives-Rocky Mountain Region in Denver (see page 8) and at the FHL.

Two major school record collections may be helpful when researching Native American ancestry in Wyoming. The Fort Shaw School in Cascade County, Montana, and the Chemawa Indian School in Chemawa, Oregon, enrolled students from many states. For more details, see Montana and Oregon—Native American.

An important collection for Native American history and genealogy is entitled the "Major James McLaughlin Papers." This valuable collection has information on Wyoming's territorial period. For a more detailed discussion of these papers, see Montana—Native American.

Other Ethnic Groups

In 1976 the Wyoming State Archives conducted a study of six of the major European ethnic groups in the state. This study broke ground in a previously ignored area of Wyoming history. The findings were edited by Gordon Olaf Hendrickson in *Peopling the High Plains: Wyoming's European Heritage* (Cheyenne, Wyo.: Wyoming State Archives and Historical Department, 1977). The six groups represented in this volume are the British, Germans, Italians, Basques, Eastern Europeans, and Greeks.

In 1870 immigrants from the British Isles represented one-fifth of the Wyoming territorial population and over one-half of the foreign born population. British converts to the Church of Jesus Christ of Latter-day Saints traveled to Salt Lake City through Wyoming. Many of these same converts colonized the western and north central section of the state a few years later.

Soon after the Mormon migration through Wyoming, the Irish came as laborers on the Union Pacific Railroad. Others served as soldiers. Between 1865 and 1874, half of the Regular Army consisted of recruits from foreign countries, 20 percent were Irish.

British Isles immigrants came to Wyoming as miners, saloon keepers, bankers, and missionaries. Many Irish were Roman Catholic, Scots were Presbyterian, and the English were Episcopalians, Methodists, or Congregationalists. In Wyoming, British companies had considerable land holdings and controlled numerous cattle and horse ranches.

Two groups of Germans came to Wyoming—native Germans and Russian-Germans. These two groups began their migrations westward in the late nineteenth and early twentieth centuries. They usually settled in other states before arriving in Wyoming. The cattle industry and the railroad provided incentive for many Germans to become permanent residents of the state.

A large number of Russian-German people moved into Worland and Lovell about 1915 to 1916, reflecting the beginnings of the sugar beet industry in that part of Wyoming. The largest settlement of Russian-Germans was in Goshen County where Volga Germans from the Scottsbluff, Nebraska, region settled.

Among the early German immigrants to Wyoming was a group of German Jews. Enough Jewish people came to Wyoming that by 1888 Temple Emmanuel was founded in Cheyenne. Other German Jews were part of Jewish farming communities such as Huntley, Wyoming, founded in 1906. Most of Huntley's Jewish community was from Romania. The community was dissolved in the 1920s.

Wyoming had a visible Italian population at one time. Immigrants came in the late nineteenth and early twentieth centuries, and most worked in Wyoming's mining industry. The bulk of Italian immigration to Wyoming was between 1890 and 1910. The Italian immigrants originated from the northern provinces of Lombardy, Tuscany, and Piedmont. Many settled in Laramie, Sweetwater, and Uinta counties.

The Basque in Wyoming were instrumental in the development of the sheep industry in the state. By 1902 Basque had settled in Buffalo, Johnson County. The founding Basque families in Wyoming were influential in Johnson and Sweetwater counties.

The ancestry of Eastern European immigrants to Wyoming were mainly from Czechoslovakia, Hungary, Poland, and Yugoslavia. While still in Europe or upon their arrival in America, they learned that jobs were available in Wyoming mines. Many Eastern European Jews first settled in eastern America and then moved to Wyoming. Some who homesteaded near the coal mines in Sheridan County realized considerable profit from their real estate.

The mining communities near Rock Springs, Lander, Riverton, and Sheridan attracted the majority of Eastern Europeans to Wyoming, the largest immigration occurring between 1910 and 1920. Most of the immigrants were either Roman Catholic or Orthodox, and almost every mining community had a Roman Catholic church even if it did not have a regular priest. The Orthodox did not always have available churches in the mining communities.

The first permanent Greek residents arrived in Cheyenne near the turn of the twentieth century. Many worked on the railroad as laborers; others moved into business. The Greek Orthodox Church of Saints Constantine and Helen in Cheyenne, established in 1922, is the center of the Greek community in the area. The other Greek Orthodox church in Cheyenne was Holy Trinity.

Some Greeks came to Wyoming to work in the mines near Hartville-Sunrise and Rock Springs. The Orthodox church in Rock Springs was founded not only to serve the needs of the Greek community, but also Russian, Serbian, Montenegrin, Slavic, Bulgarian, Romanian, and Dalmatian Orthodox members. Greeks in Casper were ministered to for many years by the priest from the Church of Saints Constantine and Helen in Cheyenne.

From the construction of the Union Pacific Railroad, a number of Chinese laborers resided in Wyoming. They first appeared in Rock Springs in 1875 to work on the railroad or to work for the railroad's coal contractors. In 1885 a wave of anti-Chinese violence broke out in Wyoming that had repercussions throughout the northwestern United States. On 2 September 1885, the coal miner's union massacred twenty-eight Chinese and wounded fifteen. The mobs destroyed Rock Springs's Chinatown and drove several hundred from the city. This event led to more anti-Chinese violence throughout Washington, Oregon, and Montana. The Chinese returned to Rock Springs under federal troop escort, but they gradually left Wyoming. The Wyoming State Archives has many collected articles and old newspaper clippings concerning Wyoming's Chinese community and the 1885 massacre. These should not be overlooked when researching this ethnic group.

County Resources

An important research consideration for Wyoming is that its counties, as they exist today, went through many changes in a relatively short period of time. When organized, it included four counties from Dakota Territory—Albany, Carbon, Carter, and Laramie—and Green River Precinct from Utah Territory. Green River was never organized into a county and ceased to exist upon creation of Wyoming Territory in 1868. When the territory was organized on 19 May 1869, Uinta County was created from unorganized portions of Utah and Idaho. At that time, Carter County was renamed Sweetwater. By 1923, Wyoming had been subdivided into its present twenty-three counties.

In addition to the territorial and homestead land records held by the Wyoming State Archives, the county clerk holds land records filed by county after the date of formation. District clerks are to be addressed for court and probate records, though most will also be found at the Wyoming State Archives. No county birth or death records exist before mandatory statewide recording, but most counties hold marriage records. Some even date before incorporation.

The archives suggests that a researcher contact them prior to conducting extensive research on the county level. By doing so, the researcher can determine which county records have been deposited at the Wyoming State Archives and which are on a county level.

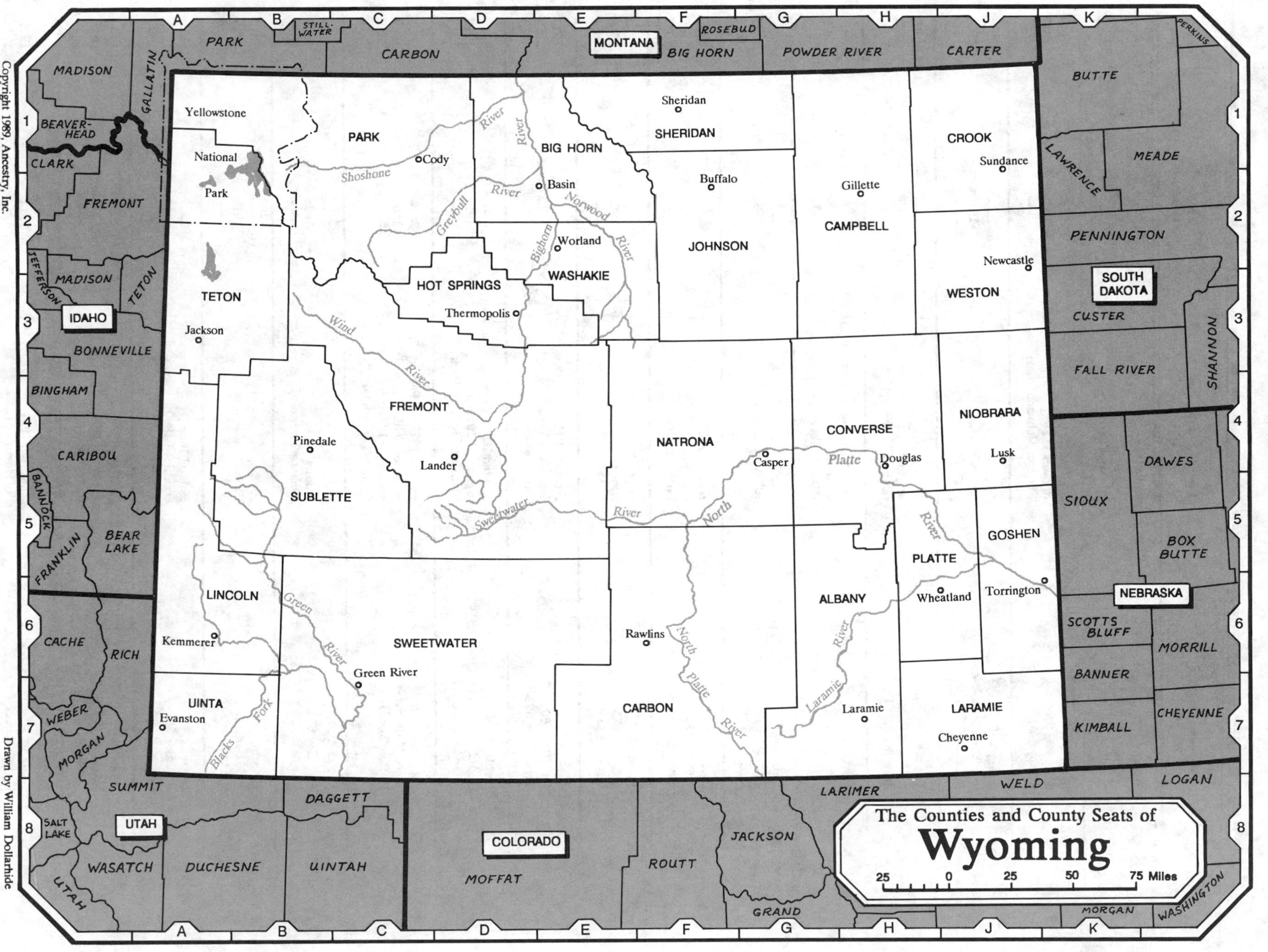

Drawn by William Dollarhide

Map	County Address	Date Formed Parent County/ies	Birth Marriage Death	Deeds Probate Court
G6	Albany County Courthouse Laramie 82070	1868 original (Dakota Territory)	— 1868 —	1869 1869 1869
D1	Big Horn P.O. Box 31 Basin 82410	created 1890 organized 1897 Fremont/Johnson/Sheridan	— 1897 —	1897 1897 1897
H2	Campbell 500 S. Gillette Avenue Gillette 82716	1911 Crook/Weston	— 1913 —	1913 1913 1913
F6	Carbon P.O. Box 6 Rawlins 82301	1868 original (Dakota Territory)	— 1870 —	1871 1871 ?
	Carter	1867 (renamed Sweetwater, 1869) original (Dakota Territory)		
H4	Converse P.O. Drawer 990 Douglas 82633	1888 Albany/Laramie	— 1888 —	1888 1888 1888
J1	Crook P.O. Box 37 Sundance 82729	created 1875 organized 1877 Laramie/Albany	— 1885 —	1885 1890 1885
D4	Fremont P.O. Box CC Lander 82520	1884 Sweetwater	— 1884 —	1884 1900 1884
J6	Goshen P.O. Box 160 Torrington 82240	created 1911 organized 1913 Laramie	— 1913 —	1913 1913 1913
D3	Hot Springs County Courthouse Thermopolis 82443	created 1911 organized 1913 Fremont/Big Horn/Park	— 1913 —	1917 1913 1913
F2	Johnson 76 N. Main Street Buffalo 82834	created 1875 (as Pease; renamed Johnson, 1879) organized 1877 Carbon/Sweetwater	— 1881 —	1883 1882 1882
J7	Laramie P.O. Box 608 Cheyenne 82003	1867 original (Dakota Territory)	— 1868 —	1868 1898 1898
A5	Lincoln P.O. Box 670 Kemmerer 83101	1913 Uinta	— 1913 —	1913 1915 1915
F4	Natrona P.O. Box 863 Casper 82602	created 1888 organized 1890 Carbon	— 1890 —	1890 1892 1890
J4	Niobrara P.O. Box 420 Lusk 82225	created 1911 organized 1913 Converse	— 1913 —	1890 1913 1913
C1	Park P.O. Box 160 Cody 83414	created 1909 organized 1911 Big Horn	— 1911 —	1911 1911 1911

Map	County Address	Date Formed Parent County/ies	Birth Marriage Death	Deeds Probate Court
	Pease	1875 (renamed Johnson, 1879) Carbon/Sweetwater		
H6	Platte P.O. Drawer 728 Wheatland 82201	1913 Laramie	— 1913 —	1873 1913 1913
F1	Sheridan 224 S. Main Suite B17 Sheridan 82801	1888 Johnson	— 1888 —	1898 1895 1888
B4	Sublette P.O. Box 250 Pinedale 82941	created 1921 organized 1923 Fremont/Lincoln	— 1923 —	1923 1923 1923
C6	Sweetwater P.O. Box 730 Green River 82935	1867 (as Carter; renamed, 1869) original (Dakota Territory)	— 1864 —	1869 1869 1869
A3	Teton P.O. Box 1727 Jackson 83001	created 1921 organized 1922 Lincoln	— 1923 —	1902 1923 1923
A7	Uinta P.O. Box 810 Evanston 82930	1869 original (Utah and Idaho Territories)	— 1872 —	1870 1891 1872
	Washakie P.O. Box 260 Worland 82401	created 1911 organized 1913 Big Horn	— 1913 —	1897 1913 1913
J3	Weston 1 W. Main Newcastle 82701	1890 Crook	— 1890 —	1886 1896 1889

Contributors

SCOTT A. BARTLEY is manuscript curator for the New England Historic Genealogical Society and coordinator for the bicentennial project of Genealogical Society of Vermont.

BETH BAUMAN is director of the Bismarck Family History Center and is a member of Bismarck-Mandan Historical and Genealogical Society where she is a volunteer in responding to queries on North Dakota research.

SHARON SHOLARS BROWN, C.G., is a genealogical researcher and lecturer specializing in southern states and Louisiana/Texas Spanish era borderlands research.

JOHNI CERNY is president and founder of Lineages, Inc., and is a nationally known lecturer and researcher specializing in black slave, colonial Virginia, and immigrant ancestry. She is editor of many major genealogical resource publications.

ROBERT SCOTT DAVIS, JR., is a professor of history and is a genealogical researcher and author of more than twenty books on Georgia.

ALICE EICHHOLZ, C.G., PH.D., is a professor of psychology and family history at Norwich University and a professional genealogical researcher specializing in Vermont and northern New England. Dr. Eichholz is the author of numerous publications.

WENDY L. ELLIOTT, C.G., C.G.L., is a nationally recognized lecturer and seminar instructor and is a professional genealogical researcher specializing in the South and Midwest. She is an editor of major genealogical resource publications.

LAURA HALL HEUERMANN, J.D., is a practicing attorney with a long-term interest in genealogical problem solving in South Dakota.

KATHLEEN HUTCHISON is a professional librarian, administrator, and genealogical researcher in Hazelhurst, Mississippi.

ROGER D. JOSLYN, C.G., F.A.S.G., is a professional genealogical researcher specializing in Mid-Atlantic and New England states. He is past president of the Association of Professional Genealogists and is author of numerous articles in genealogical journals.

CAROL MAKI is a professional genealogical researcher in Stillwater, Minnesota, offering services to both national and international clients.

GARETH MARK, A.G., is a professional genealogist specializing in research of colonial Virginia, Tennessee, and several other southern states.

BRIAN E. MICHAELS is a professor of English and is a member of the Florida State Historical Records Advisory Board. He is a nationally recognized lecturer on genealogical research and records.

MARY BESS KIRKSEY PALUZZI is a professional librarian and genealogical lecturer specializing in Alabama research.

DWIGHT A. RADFORD is a professional genealogist practicing in Salt Lake City. He specializes southern United States, British Canada, and Ireland research.

MARSHA HOFFMAN RISING, C.G., C.G.L., is a professional genealogical researcher specializing in all aspects of research in Missouri and is a lecturer on genealogical problem solving. She is president of the Federation of Genealogical Societies.

GEORGE F. SANBORN, JR., is director of technical services for the New England Historic Genealogical Society. He is president of the New Hampshire Society of Genealogists and is editor of its periodical.

THELMA BERKEY WALSMITH is a professional genealogical researcher and is chaplain and lineage research chairperson of the Captain Henry Sweetser chapter of the DAR—Santa Maria, California.

MARGARET WINDHAM is president and publication chairperson of the New Mexico Genealogical Society.

NELL SACHSE WOODARD is a professional genealogical researcher and lecturer specializing in teaching genealogy to local groups in the West.

INDEX

A

B

C

D

M

N

W

Y

Z